BLUE GUIDE

NORTHERN ITALY

Paul Blanchard

Somerset Books • London
WW Norton • New York

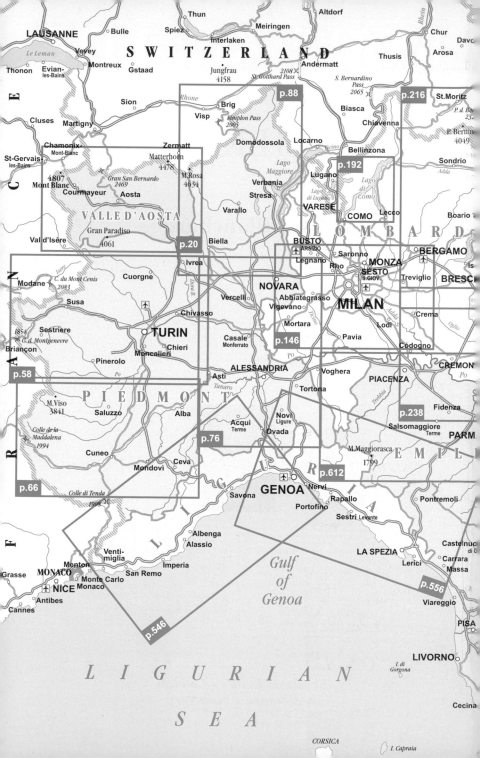

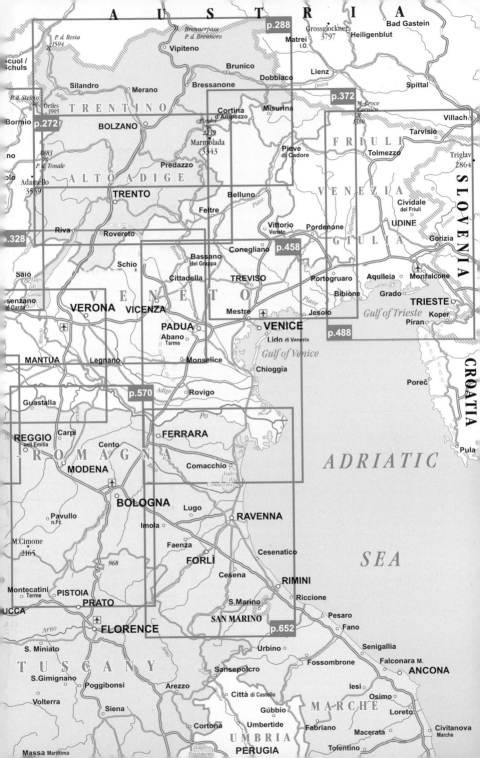

Twelfth edition 2005

Published by Blue Guides Limited, a Somerset Books Company
49–51 Causton St, London SW1P 4AT
www.blueguides.com
'Blue Guide' is a registered trademark

ISBN 1–905131–01–1

A CIP catalogue record of this book is available from the British Library.

Published in the United States of America by
WW Norton and Company, Inc
500 Fifth Avenue, New York, NY 10110
USA ISBN 0–393–32730–2

The first Blue Guide—*London and its Environs*—was published in 1918 by two Scottish brothers,
James and Findlay Muirhead. The first edition of Blue Guide Northern Italy was compiled by them
in 1924. Subsequent editions were revised, compiled or written by the Muirhead brothers (1927,
1937); Stuart Rossiter (1971); Alta Macadam (1978, 1984, 1991, 1997) and Paul Blanchard (2001).

Cover photographs: View of Manarola, Liguria. © The Travel Library
Raphael: *The Ecstasy of St Cecilia* (1514), Pinacoteca Nazionale, Bologna
Title page: Stefano da Verona: *Madonna del Roseto* (c. 1425),
Museo Civico d'Arte (Castelvecchio), Verona

All other acknowledgements, photo credits and copyright information are given on p. 736.

CONTENTS

MAPS & PLANS

About the author

Paul Blanchard was born in Amsterdam, New York. He studied art history in Florence and has lived in Italy since 1975. He has taught at the Italian study centres of several American universities, has shown his own artwork (which includes a large body of landscape photographs) in Europe and the US, and has lectured on college campuses throughout the US. He has published widely in North America, Great Britain, France and Italy, and has contributed to European and American art magazines.

HIGHLIGHTS
OF THE REGION

Valle d'Aosta

Aosta itself has some important Roman remains, and the valley is guarded by numerous medieval castles. The Parco Nazionale del Gran Paradiso has fine mountain scenery.

Piedmont

Turin has a 17th–18th-century aspect and some very fine museums (including an important Egyptian collection), and grand Savoy residences on the outskirts. On the picturesque Lago d'Orta is the lovely village of Orta San Giulio. The Langhe and Roero districts are famed for their vineyards and their excellent restaurants.

Lombardy

The capital of Lombardy is Milan, with its splendid Gothic cathedral, the Brera Gallery containing a superb collection of paintings, Leonardo da Vinci's famous fresco of the *Last Supper*, and La Scala opera house. Lago Maggiore and Lago di Como have been drawing visitors for centuries for their beautiful scenery. Mantua is a lovely old town, famous for the Mantegna frescoes in its huge Palazzo Ducale, and for the architecture of Giulio Romano. Bergamo's upper town is particularly well-preserved with some important art treasures, and Cremona is renowned for its violin-making. The small towns of Castiglione Olona, with its Renaissance works, and Sabbioneta, laid out in the 16th century, are of the greatest interest. There are important prehistoric rock carvings in the Val Camonica.

Trentino-Alto Adige

Trento, Bolzano and Bressanone are the principal towns of this high alpine region. The mountain valleys and the area's many large nature reserves offer stunning scenery.

Veneto

Apart from Venice, the Veneto includes Verona, a particularly beautiful city with a celebrated Roman amphitheatre. The university town of Padua has important frescoes by Giotto; Vicenza was laid out by the great 16th-century architect Palladio. All over the Veneto are splendid country villas, some by Palladio, others by 17th- and 18th-century architects. Veneto is also home to perhaps the most beautiful of the Italian lakes: Lago di Garda, with the spectacular Roman villa at Sirmione.

Friuli-Venezia Giulia

The 18th-century city of Trieste has a distinctive atmosphere, still redolent of the old Austro-Hungarian empire. Udine possesses fine frescoes by Tiepolo, and the little town of Cividale has beautiful Lombard works. Aquileia is an important Roman site, and it also has superb early-Christian mosaics.

Liguria

Genoa is a historic maritime city with fine palaces and magnificent art collections. The peninsula of Portofino is particularly beautiful, as are the unspoiled Cinque Terre, a series of remote villages in spectacular coastal scenery.

Emilia Romagna

Bologna is one of northern Italy's secret gems, full of medieval atmosphere and with some superb architecture. Ravenna has the most important Byzantine mosaics in western Europe, and in Rimini there are Roman monuments and the famous Renaissance Tempio Malatestiano. Parma is known for its many masterpieces by Correggio (as well as for its cheese and ham). Faenza is famous for its ceramics.

HISTORICAL
INTRODUCTION

by Charles Freeman

In September 1786 the German poet Goethe entered northern Italy for the first time, over the Brenner Pass. The impact of the transition from northern Europe, down across an Alpine pass and into an ancient cradle of civilization, was profound. At Verona he saw his first Roman building, the Arena, the great amphitheatre in the Piazza Brà. At Vicenza he admired the works of Palladio. In Padua it was the 'astonishing' Mantegnas in the church of the Eremitani (tragically the victim of American bombs in World War Two) which enthralled him. Finally, in the late afternoon of the 28th September, Goethe had his first sight of Venice—a gondola coming out to meet him as his boat crossed the lagoon.

The modern traveller's entry to northern Italy is usually more abrupt, with the Alps some thousands of feet below; but the ranges have never been impassable. In fact the first human settlers probably came into Italy across the Alps, while the discovery of the body of Ötzi, 'the iceman' (*see p. 290*) suggests they were being crossed with ease some 5,000 years ago. The Romans used 17 of the 23 passes on a regular basis. Rather, the Alps' importance as a barrier is largely symbolic. When Jean-Louis David painted Napoleon at the top of the St Bernard Pass on his way to invade Italy in 1800, he engraved on the rocks the names of previous invaders: Hannibal (218 BC) and Charlemagne (AD 773). For centuries Italy, whether as the focus for invaders, the core of a great empire, the home of civic liberty or the cradle of artistic genius, has been etched into the European imagination as a culture profoundly different from those in the north. It needs a transition such as a passage through the Alps to make the point.

Those coming down into Italy from the Alps soon reached the peninsula's largest and most fertile plain, centred on the river Po, a river which, as the elder Pliny put it in the first century AD, 'deposits its soil and bestows bounteous fertility'. When the plain was settled and peaceful it provided, then as now, an underlying prosperity for the region; but the real fount of northern Italy's commercial and cultural wealth was the Mediterranean, to which it had full access through its ports and rivers. It was this same prosperity that made the area a lure for outsiders. The history of northern Italy alternates between periods of strong outside control (the Roman period, for instance) and virtual independence when, as in the Middle Ages, the larger cities struggled between themselves for land and trade routes. What follows is a simplification of a very complicated story.

Etruscans, Celts and Romans

The early history of Italy is being continually rewritten as new sites emerge and interpretations develop. If one starts, however, with the Bronze Age (2200–1000 BC), its culture seems to have been remarkably homogenous—but there is a break about 900

BC (with the coming of the Iron Age) when the indigenous peoples of northern Italy develop distinct cultures. There were the Veneti in the foothills of the Alps in the northeast, the Golasecca culture around the central lakes, and the Ligures in the northwest. South of the Appenines the Villanovan cultures were stimulated by their contacts with Greek traders in search of iron ores, and developed into the Etruscans. By the 6th and 5th centuries BC the Etruscans themselves had expanded northwards to colonise the remaining Villanovan village communities in the Po valley. Mantua and Bologna were Etruscan foundations, while at Spina on the Adriatic coast Etruscans and Greeks appear to have lived together in a prosperous trading community.

While the Etruscans moved up from the south there were Celtic groups expanding across the Alps from the north. The earliest migrations led to settlement around the lakes, but a much more determined migration of Celts, probably impelled by the breakdown of societies to the north and population increase, took place in the late 5th century. It was not peaceful. A stele from Bologna shows Celts and Etruscans in battle, and the Etruscan site of Marzabotto near Bologna has a layer of destruction. By the early 4th century Celtic warbands were raiding further south, reaching Rome in 390 BC.

Roman retaliation was inevitable. The exuberant but ill-disciplined Celtic warbands were no match for a Roman legion, and after Celtic tribes had helped the Carthaginian Hannibal in his invasion of Italy in 218, total subjection of northern Italy followed. Roman citizens, many of them former soldiers, were settled on the land in what were called *coloniae* (among them the modern Piacenza, Parma and Aquileia). Originally the sites were chosen for strategic reasons, but many *coloniae* prospered in their own right. Aquileia had a sheltered river port at the end of a trade route which brought amber down from the Baltic and it soon developed its own industries. It was to become one of the largest cities of Italy. In contrast to the *coloniae* were the *municipia*. These were earlier urban settlements which were Romanised. Bologna passes from Etruscan to Celtic to Roman. Genoa, always important as a port, was originally a Ligurian settlement which was rebuilt by the Romans after being sacked by the Carthaginians. Padua and Verona appear to have been founded by the Veneti. Como was a Celtic foundation as was Milan. Many *municipia* flourished as a result of their position on roads or rivers. Major roads such as the Via Emilia, which ran from Rimini along the base of the Appenines though Milan and then through Aosta over the St Bernard Pass into Gaul, and the Via Postumia which linked Aquileia with Genoa were impressive engineering achievements. Just as important, however, was the prosperity of the plain now that the Romans had brought peace. Land was drained and vast quantities of grain were produced. The foothills provided excellent grazing for sheep. The landed elite enjoyed a lavish lifestyle. The younger Pliny (at his wealthiest in the early second century AD) had no less than three major villas on his ancestral estates around Como.

The coming of Christianity

Northern Italy played an important part in the Christianisation of the empire. It was from Milan in 313 that Constantine issued his famous Edict of Toleration which initiated imperial patronage of the hitherto persecuted Christian communities. Just how quickly they took advantage of it can be seen at Aquileia, where the basilica (*see p. 519*) was largely finished by 319. It was here in 381 that St Ambrose (then bishop of Milan) browbeat a council of bishops into accepting Nicene orthodoxy (what is now known as Catholicism). In Milan itself Ambrose constructed a series of major church-es around the city walls, thereby establishing the Church as a dominant physical pres-ence. Vast resources were sucked into the construction and decoration of these early basilicas. It has been estimated that the earliest cathedral in Milan would have held a congregation of some three thousand.

One reason for the prosperity of Milan was that it had become a capital from which the emperors conducted the defence of the empire. By the late 4th century the empire had come under pressure from Germanic tribes, some of whom had already settled inside its borders. Urban life was in decay—Ambrose described the once prosperous cities along the Via Emilia as 'corpses'. In 401 the emperor Honorius abandoned Milan for Ravenna, which was then protected by marshes, leaving the fighting to his generals. In 410, after failed negotiations with an army of Goths who were rampaging through Italy, Rome was sacked for the first time since 390 BC.

From the fall of Rome to the Holy Roman Empire

The collapse of Roman civilization was, however, gradual. 476 traditionally marks the end of the western empire, but there was no abrupt transition. Many of the 'barbar-ians' had by now become Romanised, and in any case they were a small minority in a Roman population. When the Ostrogoth Theodoric became ruler of much of Italy in 493, it is estimated that his followers numbered 100,000 in a native population of four million. He ruled through Roman bureaucrats and was sympathetic enough to Roman culture to restore buildings in Rome. He too made Ravenna his capital, and Gothic and Roman quarters of the city, with their respective churches, existed along-side each other.

The first abrupt break with the Roman past came with the invasion of northern Italy by the Lombards in 568. The Lombards were a mix of peoples from northern Europe, forged by their king Alboin into a military force who would cooperate when attacked by the Byzantine troops from the south or the Franks from the north. Their capital was at Pavia but their dukes set up courts at other cities, among them Turin, Brescia and Trento. One reason for the Lombards' continuing success was a succession of charismatic kings who kept the allegiance of these dukes and through them sustained what remained of urban life. Some cities, such as Pavia and Brescia, saw significant building. By the 8th century most Lombards had become Catholics, using Roman law alongside their own.

In 751 the Lombards took Ravenna, which until then had been under Byzantine rule, though Byzantine power in Italy had long been in decline, and the Popes had gradually exerted their independence of the east. It was Pope Stephen II (752-70) who finally steered the west on a new course. He called on the king of the Franks, the most powerful Christian nation in the west, to come to his aid against the Lombards. In 753 or 754 King Pepin the Short came over the Alps. The Lombards had finally met their match and their kingdom collapsed. In 773, Pepin's successor, Charlemagne, received the iron crown of Lombardy in Pavia. In 800 he was crowned 'Roman emperor' by Pope Leo III in Rome. The Holy Roman Empire, which passed from the Franks to German kings in the 10th century, was to survive until dissolved by Napoleon in 1806.

The rise of the city states

The problem for northern Italy was that the relative roles of pope and emperor within the empire were never clearly defined. The Church remained strong on the ground; the emperors claimed overall responsibility as successors of the Lombards. This, however, was also northern Italy's opportunity. Many cities, though greatly diminished from the days of the Roman empire, had remained relatively intact, while in a sheltered lagoon in the northern Adriatic tenacious settlements of refugees from the Lombard invasions were being forged into a trading community. These refugees, the Venetians, were nominally part of the Byzantine empire (their first patron saint, Theodore, was a soldier martyr from Asia Minor), but they were determined to achieve independent control of their destiny. Contemporary documents from the 8th century show trading links between Venice and Constantinople, Sicily, the whole of north Africa, Syria and France. Trading prosperity on the mainland was supplemented by the rise of a landowning class (made up, it appears, of both Frankish and Lombard aristocrats) on the plains. The rivers opened again to trade, and it was only now that cities such as Ferrara, well placed on the Po, became important.

Politically the most remarkable development was the rise of communal government. In the 11th century the weakening of imperial rule led to revolts by many northern cities (Milan, Parma, Cremona and Pavia), a sign of a vibrant local identity. There was also increasing irritation with the power of the Church, and bishops were expelled from a number of cities. Communal government can be seen as the political structure which filled a vacuum, with different social groups all interested in a share of power: local landowners anxious for a foothold in the local city, a rising merchant class, administrators whose knowledge of Roman law was instrumental in defining the checks and balances of communal government.

The most common form of communal government consisted of 'consuls' (an echo of Roman times), who took responsibility for internal order and foreign relations with an assembly of 'the people' who could check the misuse of power. The assemblies ratified major decisions such as the making of peace and war, the approval of alliances and the acceptance of new laws. It was the ability to create and sustain a legal structure of government which was especially important and which provided the impetus for cities to set up their own institutions for the study of the arts and law (notably Roman law). So were born the first universities, Bologna in the 12th century and—one of the most successful of all—Padua, in 1222. These universities themselves were organised on communal lines as if the teachers were the consuls and the students the citizens. Communal activities also spread to trade, and fraternities of citizens were formed for charitable purposes, such as the *scuole* of Venice which gave a continuing role to Venetian citizens after government was restricted to the nobility in 1297. In 1300 there were an estimated 150 guilds or trade associations in Milan, 142 in Venice, 48 in Verona and 38 in Padua.

The wealth of these cities was boosted by trade. The Italians were pioneers in every aspect of commerce from banking to the design of ships. They dominated the Mediterranean trade routes, their tentacles penetrating deep into the Islamic world. Islamic motifs are to be found in the architecture of both Genoa and Venice, and both cities competed for trading concessions from the Byzantine emperors. The Venetians won a great coup when they manipulated the Fourth Crusade of 1204 to their advantage, ending up not in the Holy Land as intended but in Constantinople, which they sacked, on the grounds that the Greeks were heretics. Not only did they bring rich treasures back home (the famous horses of St Mark's among them), they also awarded themselves strategic trading posts throughout the east. The returns for these cities were fantastic. The revenue of Genoa for 1293 has been estimated at some ten times the annual receipts of the French royal treasury. The money was ploughed back into trade and building. 'While the burghers and barons of the north were building their dark streets and grisly castles of oak and sandstone, the merchants of Venice were covering their palaces with porphyry and gold', wrote John Ruskin in *The Stones of Venice*. In Padua, the vast Palazzo della Ragione, built first in the early 1200s and then rebuilt a hundred years later, acted as law court and assembly hall, with shops for merchants on the ground floor. Its size was also a symbol of the city's wealth and status. The ambiguous attitude to wealth creation in a Christian society is beautifully illustrated in Padua. Giotto's frescoes in the Arena chapel were commissioned by a wealthy merchant, Enrico Scrovegni, who sought, by his piety, to distance himself from the usury of his father, who had been named by Dante amongst the denizens of Hell.

From commune to seigniory

Despite its successes, northern Italy always remained vulnerable to invasion from its nominal overlord, the Holy Roman Emperor. Frederick Barbarossa, elected in 1152, waged five campaigns over 30 years, although at last he was forced to accept the independence of the communes. (The battle of Legnano in 1176, in which the Lombard League defeated him, has been idealised as the triumph of Italy over foreign tyranny.) Barbarossa's grandson Frederick II launched further campaigns between 1225 and 1250, but again was unsuccessful. The invasions placed immense burdens on the communes, with factions in the cities supporting either the emperors (the Ghibellines) or the papacy (the Guelphs). These factions were often a mask for local ambitions and the combination of marauding imperial armies and social tensions was devastating. 'O servile Italy, breeding ground of misery, ship without a pilot in a mighty tempest' wrote Dante, himself a Guelph. After his exile from Florence in 1302, Dante's wanderings around the courts and universities of northern Italy—he sheltered in Verona, taught at Padua, ended his days in Ravenna—are symbolic of a troubled age. He yearned for the return of a strong emperor who would rule under the auspices of the papacy.

The communes were idealised by later generations but, as Dante's experience suggests, their history was also filled with factional in-fighting and popular unrest. One pragmatic response was to elect, often from outside the city, a *podestà*, an official given wide powers for a fixed period of time. In the lower Po valley this was a particularly popular solution and it proved the forerunner of the next development in northern Italy: the emergence of the seigniories, governments based on one man, with power then being passed on to the next generation of his family. As with communal government it is difficult to generalise: sometimes the lord enjoyed popular support, in other cases he emerged from aristocratic in-fighting, and the path to power was invariably tortuous. Milan provides a good example. Matteo Visconti, a member of one of the ancient noble families of the area, used his aristocratic position to achieve prominence in the city in the 1280s, which he then strengthened by being elected *capitano del popolo* in 1288. He further consolidated his position with marriage alliances with other seigniorial families, and placed members of his own family as lords of neighbouring cities. His son Galeazzo Visconti, originally subject to his father as lord of Piacenza, incorporated Cremona, Como, Bergamo, Piacenza and Brescia into Milanese territory. This dominance over Lombardy was extended to Bologna (1350), Genoa (1353), and into the Veneto. The power and wealth of the family was shown off in the massive Gothic cathedral provided for Milan by Gian Galeazzo Visconti (ruled 1385–1402). Yet even the Visconti respected the sovereignty of the emperors, and Gian Galeazzo paid 100,000 florins to the emperor in 1395 to be granted the formal title Duke of Milan.

The stories of individual seigniorial families are too varied to be followed here, but many cities of northern Italy have monuments of their rule. The lives of the *signori* were often precarious, with the result that their residences were as much fortresses as palaces. Good examples are the Castelvecchio of the Scaligeri in Verona (1350s), the Castello Estense of the Este in Ferrara (1380s), which still retains its moat and drawbridges, and the 15th century additions to the vast Palazzo Ducale in Mantua, built by the Gonzaga.

In their time the *signori* attracted both praise and blame. For those who retained the ideal of *libertas*, the ancient rallying cry of republican Rome, revived by the communes, they were tyrants, 'a breed of cruel destruction', as one opponent of the lords of Milan put it. Others stressed that strong rule brought an end to factional squabbles and that the *signori* were often effective patrons. Not that seigniorial rule was universal. Savoy and Piedmont, at the head of the Po valley, seemed to belong to an earlier feudal age (as well as being as much French as Italian). Ravenna, Aquileia and Trento remained under the control of the Church. The most important example of a city which maintained its republicanism is Venice. Although political participation was restricted to the nobility, a variety of councils and a doge led to a balanced government which survived intact for centuries.

The rise of France and Spain

A new period of vulnerability for northern Italy began in 1494, with a sequence of invasions from French, Spanish and imperial troops. The cities were no match for these well organised states, although they tried to play one off against another. It was

Venice who encouraged the French to attack Milan, their main rival on the mainland, in 1499, with the result that Lombardy fell under French control. However, Venice had its come-uppance when an alliance under the Pope defeated its forces at Agnadello near Milan in 1509. The French in their turn were defeated at Pavia in 1525 by the new Holy Roman Emperor Charles V. Charles, whose territories already extended across Europe from Spain to Austria, now stamped his rule on northern Italy. Venice and Genoa were allowed to survive as republics (and Venice regained much of its mainland) but Milan became a capital of a province of the Holy Roman Empire. Savoy was prised from the French and made into an hereditary dukedom, as were Ferrara, Mantua, Modena and Parma. The whole arrangement was later confirmed by the Treaty of Cateau-Cambrésis in 1559. The predominant influence on the region for the next two hundred years was Spanish.

The 16th century saw a shift in perspective with the opening up of trade routes round the Cape to the Far East and across the Atlantic. Mediterranean trade was in decline but the Italians focused their ingenuity on agricultural innovation and new industries such as silk. A hundred silk workshops in Bologna made it the most highly mechanised city in Europe. Great banking families of Genoa such as the Doria and Grimaldi financed the transatlantic fleets of Spain. However, by the end of the 16th century a sustained decline began as wealth creation shifted to the more lively and untrammelled (by guilds) economies of England and Holland. The prosperous merchant families began to transform themselves into an aristocracy living on the land, and villas and palaces replaced the warehouses of earlier centuries. The cultural interests of these patricians were broad, as can be seen from their patronage of Palladio in Vicenza. The Palladian villa was designed to exploit the aesthetic appeal of the landscape without losing touch with the labour on the land which was required to sustain the ideal.

The universities of northern Italy had long had an international clientele. (Teaching was, of course, in Latin, still the universal language of scholarship.) The Palazzo del Bo, the 16th-century core of the university of Padua, is filled with the insignia of students from all over Europe. The area was now also attractive to collectors, prominent among them Thomas Howard, second Earl of Arundel, who in a seminal trip to Italy in 1613 was enthused by Italian art and architecture. Among his retinue was the architect Inigo Jones, who had already encountered Palladio's work in England through the latter's *I Quattro Libri dell' Architettura* (1570); Arundel's purchase of several chests full of Palladio's drawings proved the catalyst by which Britain became the first country outside Italy to adopt Palladianism. In the same period, Charles I bought up many of the treasures of the now bankrupt Gonzaga. Italy was being redrawn as a place to go for cultural improvement, the Grand Tour providing the 'gap year' experience for the European aristocracy.

The emergence of Savoy

In the 18th century came the War of the Spanish Succession, fought between the Bourbon French and the Austrian and Spanish Habsburgs. Once again northern Italy became a playground for imperial ambitions. In 1707 the Austrians acquired Milan and later Mantua, so replacing Spain as the dominant power in Lombardy, although there was a continual reshuffling of control of the smaller cities until the Treaty of Aix-la-Chapelle in 1748 brought a lasting settlement. This was the Age of Enlightenment, and there was some response in Italy. Reforming rulers and intellectuals tried to confront the nobility and the Church, but as these two groups controlled 70 per cent of the land in the north, sustained programmes of reform were difficult. Reform was further hampered by the mass of small semi-independent cities and duchies, each with its own legal systems and weights and measures. Venice survived as an independent republic, but its territories in the east had long succumbed to the Ottoman empire and its façade of opulence was now sustained by outsiders buying their way into the nobility. (The Ca' Rezzonico on the Grand Canal is an excellent example of a grand 18th-century palace completed by a wealthy Lombard family.) Abroad the city was no longer taken seriously. 'The English use their powder for their cannon, the French for their mortars. In Venice it is usually damp, and, if it is dry, they use it for fireworks', as one observer recorded. The antics of its aristocratic revellers in their villas on the mainland are brilliantly evoked by the comedies of Carlo Goldoni.

There was one exception to this picture of relative stagnation. In 1563, the Dukes of Savoy had moved their capital to Turin, an ancient Roman city beautifully situated in the foothills of the Alps. Its new prestige stimulated a flowering of Baroque architecture. In the wars of the 18th century the dukes exploited their position between France and Austria to expand their territory (also acquiring Sardinia), after which they were acknowledged as kings. Now they launched one of the most effective programmes of reform in the peninsula. They broke down the power of the Church and of feudal landlords, reorganised the law and made the education system relevant to economic needs. Though the kings maintained an absolutist regime with no concessions to popular feeling, they nevertheless gave Piedmont, as the mainland kingdom was now known, an authority and respect which was to prove crucial to Italy in the next century.

The Napoleonic Wars

The outbreak of the French Revolution in 1789 was greeted in Italy with a mixture of fear and enthusiasm. The momentous significance of the event hit Italy in 1796, when one of the revolution's generals, Napoleon Bonaparte, arrived over the Alps. His first lightning campaign saw the defeat of Piedmont, the destruction of Austrian rule in Lombardy and, in 1797, the bullying of the Venetian Republic into an ignominious dissolution. By 1800 Napoleon had completely subjugated the north. Piedmont and Liguria were annexed to France and the rest of northern Italy was incorporated into the Kingdom of Italy, with Napoleon as its monarch (he had himself crowned at Milan). Napoleonic rule was a powerful experience: the emperor broke down the intricate network of legal and administrative boundaries and replaced them with a centralised state. Some Italians responded to the siren song of reform and of new opportunities in government, but primarily the kingdom, like all Napoleon's fiefdoms, existed to be milked for taxes and men. By 1812 Italians were fighting Napoleon's battles all over Europe, and suffering heavy casualties. Few regretted the collapse of his empire in 1814.

Unification: the Kingdom of Italy

In the settlement which followed at the Congress of Vienna (1814–15), Piedmont recovered its independence and Austria was given control of the rest of the north, including Venice. The Austrians were not particularly brutal rulers, but the Italians had a growing sense of national consciousness, partly a reaction to Napoleonic rule, but also given inspiration through the impassioned writings of an ebullient native of Genoa, Giuseppe Mazzini (1805–72), the founder of the revolutionary movement 'Young Italy'. This was the period known as the Risorgimento, literally the 'resurgence', denoting an awakening of Italian nationalist feeling. The sophistication of Italian intellectuals can be seen from the meeting rooms of the Caffè Pedrocchi in Padua (opened in 1831, *see p. 466*), which were dedicated to the great civilizations of the past. Such people needed to be treated sensitively but the inept response of Metternich's Austria to the economic tensions of the 1840s ensured that Italy was at the forefront of the revolutions of 1848. The Austrians were thrown out of Milan and a Piedmontese army came to support the rebels. From then on, Piedmont remained the focus of nationalist hopes. By now a constitutional monarchy, it enjoyed a relatively prosperous economy and had, in Camillo Cavour (1810–61), an able and pragmatic statesman. In 1859 Cavour engineered the support of Napoleon III in a war against Austria which led to the absorption of Lombardy and later central Italy into a new Kingdom of Italy under the Piedmontese monarch Vittorio Emanuele II. After the killing fields of Magenta and Solferino, Napoleon III began to question the wisdom of what he had set in motion. Bismarck had no such qualms. His Prussian armies conclusively defeated Austria in 1866, after which Venice itself was joined to the new kingdom of Italy.

This historical introduction has covered the background to the major historical monuments a visitor is likely to encounter from the rich past of northern Italy. Themes of invasion (the appalling fighting in the northeast of the First World War), centralised rule (the Fascist era), desires for independence (the Northern League of the 1980s and 1990s), and an underlying prosperity have persisted through the 20th century. The north has, like the rest of Italy, deep-rooted social and political problems which the visitor often passes by. However, the cities of the region are alive and immensely proud of their heritage. Restoration work is effective and expert. There are happy signs of a post-industrial society which will sustain ancient traditions. The 'Slow Food' movement in a region where good food and wine has always been linked to courteous hospitality offers much hope, while the former Fiat complex in Turin now houses the outstanding art collection of the Agnellis. It is even possible that Venice will not sink beneath the weight of its tourists.

VALLE D'AOSTA

The Mont Blanc and Great St Bernard tunnels are two of the most important transalpine entrances into Italy. The Valle d'Aosta begins in this region of high Alpine peaks (Mont Blanc, the Matterhorn and Monte Rosa). It has always been a place of transit for travellers and armies entering Italy. A stretch of the Roman road from Milan to Gaul (which went over the St Bernard Pass) can still be seen, including three Roman bridges. Imposing medieval castles that once defended the valley still stand on the steep slopes above the Dora Baltea river. Tourists first discovered the valley in the early 19th century, when British alpinists and excursionists came to explore and admire the mountain scenery. Murray's guide of 1838 was the first guide to the region in any language, and many alpinists who made ascents in the mountains published illustrated descriptions of their travels. Today the region is known for its ski resorts, Courmayeur and Breuil Cervinia being the most famous. Just south of Aosta itself, is the Parco Nazionale del Gran Paradiso, Italy's first national park (created in 1922).

Although never for long under French dominion, the valley had a long tradition of bilingualism under the Savoy kings. Though French was prohibited under the Fascist regime, it is now once again an official language of the region, though Italian is the language most heard, and is the language common to all. Patois, a French-Italian dialect, is spoken in the villages. An interesting relic of the colonisation of the valley from the Swiss Valais remains in the German dialect that survives at Gressoney.

The most important industry in the valley from the Second World War up to the 1960s was steel, though the magnetite mines in the mountains above Cogne were closed down in 1974. Agriculture is subsidised by the regional government, and the brown-and-white cows (with loud bells) are taken up to high pasture from May to the end of September. The valley is noted for its *fontina* cheese, some of which is still made in the old farm buildings raised on stone bases and wooden stilts, with slate roofs. The slopes of the valley are covered with trellised vineyards. These yield some excellent wines. Reds include Aymavilles (Torrette) and Donnas, and whites are Chambave, Nus and Morgex.

Unfortunately there is a lot of undistinguished new building throughout the valley, and the motorway (still being completed) detracts from the otherwise impressive natural beauty. The Valle d'Aosta is also now visited for its casino at St-Vincent, the second most important in Europe after Monte Carlo.

AOSTA

Aosta is a pleasant small town surrounded by snow-capped mountains. Once the chief town of the Gallic Salassi, it was captured by Terentius Varro in 24 BC and renamed Augusta Praetoria. You can still see the Roman influence in its regular, grid-like street plan—a characteristic evolved from the Roman battle camp. The character of the later city, however, is southern French rather than Italian. The architecture is essentially Burgundian, and the people speak a French dialect. Throughout the later Middle Ages, town and valley owed allegiance to the great house of Challant, viscounts of Aosta. It was they who built the most important of the valley's castles, in the 14th and 15th centuries. Later the dukedom was a prized apanage of the house of Savoy. The most famous native of Aosta is the Benedictine monk St Anselm (1033–1109), who became Archbishop of Canterbury in 1093, and strove with all his might against King William Rufus' habit of using religion for political ends.

Aosta's town centre, less than 2km square, is still enclosed by Roman walls and contains many Roman monuments. Sant'Orso and the cathedral are both interesting medieval buildings with remarkable 11th-century paintings, and the cathedral museum has numerous works of art.

Around the cathedral

Piazza Emile Chanoux is the centre of the town, site of the hôtel de ville, the grand town hall of 1837. There is an attractive old-fashioned café here, the Nazionale. The square is named after local hero Emile Chanoux (1906–44), founder of the Jeune Vallée d'Aoste, a movement in defence of local language and culture at a time when Fascism was working hard to Italianise the region. Conscripted in 1943, he escaped to France, returning to Aosta after the Armistice of 8 September to fight with the Partito d'Azione and other partisan groups. The Nazis captured his wife and daughters in May 1944; Chanoux surrendered on the condition that they be released, was tortured and executed.

Via Hotel des Etats leads north to Via Monsignor De Sales, where remains of Roman baths dating from the 1st century AD have been excavated. To the left is the **cathedral**, founded in the early Christian age but rebuilt in the Romanesque and Gothic styles and given a sculptured west portal in 1526, now framed by a Neoclassical façade of 1848. Inside you can see remains of the early Christian baptistery and traces of the original 3rd–4th-century church. The stained glass dates from the late 14th and early 15th centuries. 16th-century frescoes and a 16th-century painted lunette illustrating the legend of St Grato adorn the south side. St Grato, a local saint, was a 5th-century bishop of Aosta. His protection is invoked against locusts, caterpillars and other farm pests.

The **treasury** is beautifully arranged in the deambulatory (*open in summer, daily 10–12 & 3–5; in winter, Sun and holidays 3–6.30*). It contains precious objects from the cathedral and from churches in the valley. The 15th-century tombs include that of Count François de Challant (c. 1430). The bishop's missal, illuminated around 1420 by Giacomo Jaquerio (the foremost Savoy artist of the first half of the 14th century), is also displayed. There is also the wood-and-silver tomb of St Grato, exquisitely decorated between 1415 and 1458. Nearby is a crucifix of 1499, removed from below the Arch of Augustus (*see p. 25*).

In the **choir** are interesting mosaic pavements dating from the 12th and 14th centuries, one with the *Labours of the Months*, the other depicting lively animals and the

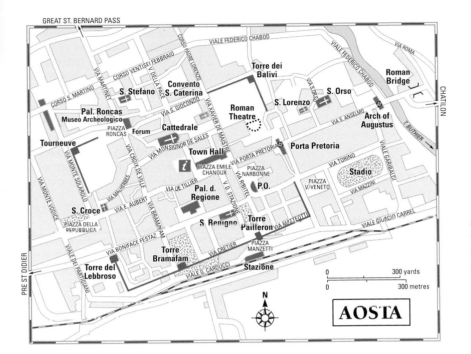

Tigris and Euphrates; 15th-century stalls and a crucifix dating from 1397. The crypt has a miscellany of Roman and medieval columns. The Ottonian **frescoes** in the roof, discovered in 1979, have been meticulously restored. Illustrating the story of St Eustachio and biblical scenes, they are the upper band of a fresco cycle that once decorated the nave and was covered when the 15th-century vault of the church was constructed. They date from 1030 or 1040, and are rare survivals in Italy of mural paintings of this date.

From the Roman forum to the medieval market

In a sunken garden beside the cathedral façade are some remains of the Roman forum, with the base of a temple now part of the foundations of a house. From here you can enter a splendid underground Roman **cryptoporticus** (*open daily March–June 9–7; July–Aug 9–8; Oct–Feb 10–5, Sun & holidays 10–6; if closed enquire at the Museo Archeologico*).

Via Forum and Via San Bernardo lead northwest to Piazza Roncas, where a 17th-century palace houses the **Museo Archeologico Regionale** (*open daily 9–7*). The first two rooms illustrate the history of the city from the 4th century BC onwards. The best exhibit is an exquisite bronze of the 2nd century AD, once part of a horse's bridle, showing a battle scene between Romans and barbarians. Stairs lead down to the excavations of one of the four Roman gates of the city and part of the walls.

Across the courtyard is a room (unlocked on request) with the remarkable **numismatic collection** of Andrea Pautasso (1911–85), particularly notable for its Celtic coins found in northern Italy (many of them, in gold, silver and bronze, in imitation of Greek coins). There are also examples from the Roman, Byzantine and medieval periods, as well as the 19th century.

Via Martinet leads to the church of **St Etienne** (or Santo Stefano), which has an elaborate high altar and a little museum of liturgical objects. There is a striking 15th-century wood statue of St Christopher.

Via Croix de Ville, on the line of the cardo maximus of the Roman town, leads south to the medieval market place and a cross set up in 1541 to commemorate the expulsion of the Calvinists from the town. Via Tillier leads back to Piazza Chanoux past the 15th-century chapel of San Grato, with frescoes.

Roman remains

Via Porta Pretoria leaves Piazza Emile Chanoux on the east side. Under an archway on the left, an alley leads to a terrace overlooking the Roman theatre (*described below*), near excavated houses with pebble pavements on a Roman road once lined with a portico. At no. 41 is the house of Philippe-Maurice de Challant (1724–1804), the last descendant of the family who built numerous castles in the valley.

The **Porta Praetoria**, a massive, well-preserved double Roman gateway of three arches, stands at the end of the street. This was the main gate of the city. The two fortified gates, built in pudding-stone, are separated by a small square defended by two towers. The side facing away from the city was originally faced in marble. The side arches were used by pedestrians and the central one by carriages. The level of the Roman road was 2.6m below the present pavement. The gate was incorporated in a medieval fortress until the 18th century, and the main arches and those on the right were blocked up. This explains why the axis of Via Porta Pretoria is not aligned with the gate.

Beside the gate is the entrance to the **Roman theatre** (*open March–Sept 9–8; Oct–May 9.30–6.30*). The most conspicuous part of the monument is the tall façade, 22m high, decorated with arched windows. Behind it are remains of the seats in the cavea and the foundations of the scena.

Via Sant'Anselmo continues east from the Porta Praetoria to Via Sant'Orso, which you follow left. Here are the priory and collegiate church of **Sant'Orso**, or St-Ours (*open Apr–Sept 9–7; Oct–March 10–5*), founded by St Anselm. The church has a campanile finished in 1131 and a late-Gothic façade, 16th-century stalls and an 11th-century crypt with 12 plain Roman columns. In the roof vaulting are remarkable Ottonian frescoes, dating from 1030 or 1040, and thought to be by the same hand as those in the cathedral. A custodian shows them at close range from a system of platforms and walkways. Two of the scenes represent the *Miracles on Lake Gennesaret* and the *Marriage at Cana*; they were damaged in the 15th century by the construction of the nave vault. These frescoes, together with those found beneath the cathedral roof (*described above*), are among the very few mural paintings of this date to have survived in Italy.

To the right of the church façade is the cloister (*open as the church*), with fascinating Romanesque capitals, carved in white marble but covered at a later date with a dark patina. Placed at the top of unusually low columns, they date from c. 1132. They illustrate biblical scenes (*Story of Jacob, Childhood of Christ, Raising of Lazarus, Noli Me Tangere, Stoning of St Stephen*), fantastic and stylised animals, a fable of Aesop (*The Wolf and the Stork*) and prophets. This and the cloister of Monreale in Sicily are the only surviving examples in Italy of large Romanesque cloisters with representations of historical and legendary scenes.

A passage opposite Sant'Orso leads round the deconsecrated church of San Lorenzo to a **5th-century chapel** excavated beneath the church's east end (*open March–June daily 9–7; July–Aug 9–8; Oct–Feb, Mon–Sat 10–5, Sun and holidays 10–6*). The Latin-cross chapel, with apses at the end of each arm, was the burial place of the first bishops of Aosta. It was destroyed in the Carolingian era.

Via Sant'Anselmo continues to the **Arch of Augustus**, a triumphal arch erected in 24 BC to commemorate the defeat of the Gallic Salassi. Decorated with ten Corinthian columns, the arch was drawn and engraved many times in the 19th century, and before that by Sir Roger Newdigate, who gave his drawing to Piranesi when he reached Rome. The roof was added in 1716. Further on, beyond the modern bridge over the Buthier, is a remarkable single-arched Roman bridge, still in use, over a dried-up channel.

The **Roman walls**, forming a rectangle 724m long and 572m wide, are best preserved on the southern and western sides of the town. Standing across the west wall is the medieval Torre del Lebbroso, now used for exhibitions. Near the Torre Bramafan, an 11th-century relic of the lords of Challant, remains of the Roman Porta Principalis Dextera have been unearthed. The Torre del Pailleron, with Roman masonry, stands in a garden near the station.

On the northern outskirts of the town lies the **Villa della Consolata**, a Roman villa that has been excavated and can be visited by appointment (*T: 0125 300222*).

THE VALLE D'AOSTA

This section follows the Valle d'Aosta downstream from its beginning, at the foot of the 4000m peak of Mont Blanc, to its end on the Piedmont Plateau. It also explores the four main side valleys—the Great St Bernard Valley, Val di Cogne, Valtournenche and Val di Gressoney, renowned for their immaculate farms, stony little villages and majestic alpine vistas.

West towards France

Beyond Aosta stands the 13th-century castle of **Sarre**, rebuilt in 1710 (*open Jan–Feb Tues–Sat 10–12 & 1.30–4.30, Sun & holidays 10–12 & 1.30–5.30; March–June daily 9–6.30; July–Aug 9–7.30; Sept 9–6.30*). It is notable for its hall decorated with thousands of hunting trophies, including numerous ibex shot by Vittorio Emanuele II in the Gran Paradiso park. The castle of **St-Pierre** was first built in the 12th century but transformed in the 19th, when the four cylindrical towers and castellations were added. In a splendid position on an isolated rock, above the church and bell tower of St-Pierre, it has a good view of the snow-capped mountain of La Grivola. It is owned by the city of St-Pierre and houses the Museo Regionale di Scienze Naturali (*open Apr–Sept 9–7*). A display of minerals, mostly from Mont Blanc, occupies the stable block; other rooms have exhibits illustrating the geology, flora and fauna of the area, including 290 ibex antlers.

Low down on the river is the castle of **Sarriod de la Tour**, dating in part from the 14th century (*open daily 9–6.30*). **Morgex** is the principal village in the Valdigne, the upper valley of the Dora. The church, founded in the 6th century, has an unusual onion-shaped steeple and contains early 16th-century frescoes.

On Italy's highest mountains

The great ones, the giants of Alps, stood about us here and there in a cloudless sky, a burning serenity. Their immobility never seems to me static; it has a vitality that seems to us repose, like that of a humming top at rest on its axis, spinning along its orbit in space.

Freya Stark, Traveller's Prelude, 1950

Courmayeur (1228m) is a famous ski resort in a deep vale at the southern foot of Mont Blanc. It has a much milder climate than Chamonix, on the other side of the mountain in Savoy. A museum illustrates the history of alpinism in the area. La Palud is the starting point of the cable railway to Chamonix, which crosses over Mont Blanc in c. 1hr 30mins. It runs every hour (weather permitting) and provides a magnificent panorama of the Graian Alps and the south side of the Pennine Alps. It crosses the French frontier at an altitude of 3462m.

Mont Blanc (4807m) is the highest mountain in western Europe. It was first climbed from Chamonix in 1786 by Jacques Balmat and Michel Paccard. The Col de la Seigne (2512m), on the French frontier, is the watershed between the basins of the Po and the Rhône. The Mont Blanc Tunnel, built through the mountains in 1958–65, is 11.6km long. The road descends over 100m from the Italian to the French side.

The passes

The Valle del Gran San Bernardo extends north from Aosta to the Swiss frontier on the Passo del Gran San Bernardo. The busy tunnel (approached by a stretch of motorway) was built in 1958–64 (toll).

The road over the **Great St Bernard Pass** (Passo del Gran San Bernardo) is usually closed Nov–June. It was known and used by Celts and Romans. The latter called it Mons Jovis (Mont Joux) after a temple of Jupiter Paeninus that once stood on the Plan de Jupiter, near the saddle. It acquired its present name in the 12th century. The pass was much used by pilgrims and clerics bound to or from Rome, and between 774 and 1414 it was crossed 20 times by medieval emperors, including Frederick Barbarossa in 1162. Coaches that entered Italy here in the 18th century had to be dismantled and carried piece by piece over the pass on the backs of local mountaineers. Both French and Austrian soldiers crossed the pass in the campaigns of 1798–1800. The most famous passage was made by Napoleon, who on May 14–20 1800, led 40,000 troops by this route into Italy and a month later defeated the Austrians at the Battle of Marengo. Numerous engravings were made of the pass both immediately after this event and throughout the 19th century. A proper road was constructed only in 1905.

Just beyond the Swiss frontier is the **Hospice du Grand-St-Bernard** (2469m), a massive stone building on the summit of the pass, exposed to storms from the northeast and southwest. On the northwest it is sheltered by the peak of Chenalette (2889m), on the southeast by Mont Mort (2867m). The hospice was supposedly founded in the 11th century by Bernard of Menthon, archdeacon of Aosta, a native of Savoy (*see below*); by 1215 it was kept by Austin canons from Martigny. Since 1925 the hospice has been managed by 10 or 12 canons and a number of lay brothers called *aumoniers*. In their rescue of snow-bound travellers the canons are assisted by the famous St Bernard dogs, a breed said to be a cross between the Pyrenean sheepdog and the Newfoundland.

The **Passo del Piccolo San Bernardo** (2188m) is just over the French frontier, on the watershed between the Dora Baltea and the Isère. Nearby is the Colonne de Joux, probably a Roman monument of *cipollino* marble, with a statue of St Bernard added in 1886. A little below it is an Iron Age stone circle just over 73m in diameter, in which Gaulish and Roman coins have been discovered. The trail across the pass was transformed into a road for carriages in 1871. The ruined Hospice du Petit-St-Bernard (2152m), founded c. 1000, used to offer free hospitality to poor travellers. The botanical garden established here in 1897 is being reconstructed and is open to the public.

ST BERNARD OF AOSTA

The St Bernard passes are named after Bernard of Menthon (d. 1081), vicar of the diocese of Aosta where he founded schools and churches, and built guest-houses for mountain travellers. The twin perils of snowdrifts and brigands made traversing the Alps extremely hazardous. St Bernard's guest-houses tended victims of exhaustion or assault, and the specially trained dogs which bear his name helped track down wayfarers lost in the snow. The dogs were also put to work in the hospice kitchens, where a specially constructed running wheel also turned the roasting spit. Pope Pius XI, a keen mountain-climber, made Bernard patron saint of mountaineers in 1923.

The Val di Cogne

The upper reaches of this pretty valley border the Gran Paradiso national park. The road from Aosta passes the unusual castle of **Aymavilles**, altered in the 18th century when the turrets were added and it was surrounded by a park. Just off the road, a by-road (signposted) descends right to the tiny isolated hamlet of **Pondel**, with a remarkable Roman bridge that once also served as an aqueduct. As the inscription states, it was built privately by two Paduans in the 3rd century BC; 50m long and 50m high, it crosses the ravine made by the Grand'Eyvia torrent. A splendid covered passageway, still passable, runs beneath the aqueduct channel. It is extremely well preserved. The valley on the other side of the bridge is well known for its butterflies (you can take lovely walks in the area along marked trails). There is a good view from here of the peak of the Grivola mountain (3969m) at the top of the valley. The pretty little resort of Ozein (1300m), with a few hotels and a fine view of the peak of the Grivola, stands above the main road.

The valley opens out into a wide basin at **Cogne** (1533m), just outside the limits of the national park. It has a large common (where you can often see ibex in May), across which rises the snow-capped Gran Paradiso. Cogne was developed as a resort after the magnetite mines were closed down in 1974. You can see remains of the mines, at an altitude of some 2000m on the hillside (the miners were transported by lift). Next to the church are a small museum of lace-making, for which Cogne is famous, and the modest hunting lodge of Vittorio Emanuele III. A by-road ends at **Lillaz** (also reached by a path along the river from Cogne), where most of the houses preserve their typical slate roofs, and a path leads past a number of waterfalls.

THE PARCO NAZIONALE DEL GRAN PARADISO

The whole of the Gran Paradiso Massif (4061m) lies within the Parco Nazionale del Gran Paradiso, an area of some 70,000 hectares and the oldest national park in Italy (established in 1922). The park was created in 1856 as a hunting reserve for King Vittorio Emanuele II, and presented to the state by Vittorio Emanuele III in 1919. Many of the bridlepaths made by Vittorio Emanuele II are still in use. This is the only part of the Alps in which the ibex (*stambecco*) has survived in its natural state (some 5,000 live here). The chamois and Alpine marmot are also common. The flowers are at their best in May and June. There are three entrances from the Valle d'Aosta: at Valnontey, Valsavarenche and Val di Rhêmes (the rest of the park lies within Piedmont).

The road into the park from Cogne takes you to Valnontey, an attractive group of houses with a few simple hotels, the starting point of numerous nice walks. The Paradisia alpine garden (1700m), founded here in 1955, is open July–September. *To find out about climbs and walks, contact the Comunità Montana Gran Paradiso, Villeneuve, Località Champagne 18, (T: 0165 95055), or the information office in Cogne.*

Châtillon and the Valtournenche

Châtillon is built on the Marmore torrent, with 19th-century foundries, mills and forges on its banks. On high ground across the valley stands the castle of Ussel (1351). **Chambave**, beneath the ruined castle of Cly, is noted for its Moscato wine.

The castle of **Fénis** (*open Mon–Sat 10–5, Sun and holidays 10–6; visitors admitted every 30mins; audio guide available*) is the most famous medieval fortress in the Valle d'Aosta and former seat of the Challant family. With numerous towers, it is enclosed by double walls (the outer circuit was reconstructed in 1936). An older fortress, possibly dating from Roman times, was rebuilt c. 1340 by Aimone de Challant and heavily restored at the end of the 19th century. The charming courtyard, with wooden balconies and a lovely semicircular staircase, has remarkable frescoes in a refined International Gothic style by Giacomo Jaquerio and his school (15th century), including *St George and the Dragon* and a frieze of philosophers and prophets holding scrolls with proverbs in Old French. The rooms of the castle have interesting local furniture, although not all of it is authentic. The furnished guardroom contains a model of the castle.

The Valtournenche, extending north from Châtillon to the base of the Matterhorn along the Marmore valley, has numerous resorts, including **Valtournenche** (1528m). **Breuil-Cervinia** (2004m) has become one of the most popular ski resorts in Italy, with numerous cableways ascending the main ridge of the Alps, dominated by the Matterhorn (Monte Cervino in Italian; 4478m) and Breithorn (4171m) on either side of the Theodule pass on the Swiss frontier. Most of the early attempts to scale the Matterhorn were started from Breuil, but the summit was not reached directly from this side until 1867.

St-Vincent

This is the second most important town in the valley after Aosta, and is famous for its casino. The approach road passes the remains of a Roman bridge that collapsed in the 19th century. Beside the Art Nouveau Hotel Billia (1910), and a congress hall built in 1983, is the **Casinò** (*open 3pm–2am*), which was opened in the 1950s and renovated in the 1970s. The Region of Valle d'Aosta has a majority holding in the casino, which is closed to residents of the valley. It is the most important gambling house in Italy (and considered the second in Europe after Monte Carlo). It is frequented mostly by Italians, and there are direct train and bus services from Turin to St-Vincent in the afternoon.

The old church, built on a prehistoric and Roman site, has a 14th-century fresco in a niche outside the apse. The interior, with Romanesque columns, has 15th- and 16th-century frescoes and a little museum. The frescoes in the window jambs are attributed to the school of Jaquerio.

St-Vincent has been known since 1770 as a health resort, and the spa (*open May–Oct*) is reached by a funicular railway from the centre of the town in 3 minutes. The Palazzo delle Fonti was built in 1960 above the source of the mineral spring (*fons salutis*).

Descending to Pont-St-Martin

The Parco Regionale di Mont Avic is a protected area surrounding the pointed mountain of Avic (3006m). Marked trails lead up through the park's pine and larch woods to crystalline alpine lakes. The castle of **Verrès** (*open July–Aug 9–8; March–June and Sept 9–7; Oct–Feb 10–12.30 & 1.30–5; Sun & holidays 1.30–6*) commands the mouth of the Val d'Ayas. A road leads up to the car park (or a path ascends in 15 minutes from Piazza Chanoux in Verrès village), from where a steep path continues up the hill, taking you to the entrance in 5–10 minutes. This four-square castle, with sheer walls 30m high, was founded by the Challant family in 1390 and strengthened by them in 1536 (it was acquired by the state in 1894). Never a residence, it was used purely for defensive purposes, and its bare interior has huge fireplaces, an old kitchen built into the rock, and an imposing staircase. Just below the castle is the abbey of St Gilles, founded c. 1050 (now a school).

The **Val d'Ayas** leaves the main valley at Verrès and follows the River Evançon. The ruined 13th-century castle of Graines stands on a prehistoric site in an attractive landscape with cherry trees. The valley has pine forests and massive wooden chalets. Antagnod (1710m) has a fine church. Champoluc (1570m), surrounded by splendid forests, is an important ski resort for Monte Rosa.

Back at the main road, on the other side of the river, is the castle of **Issogne**, rebuilt by Georges de Challant in 1497–98. This is a splendid example of a late medieval residence (*open as the castle of Verrès, T: 0125 929373*). It retains some of its original furnishings and lovely Gothic double doors carved in wood. It was donated to the state in 1907. Notice the 16th-century frescoed lunettes beneath the arches in the courtyard illustrating scenes of everyday life, including a guardhouse with a game of backgammon in progress and various shops. The unusual wrought-iron fountain, in the form of a pomegranate tree, was made in the 16th century. The little walled garden has box hedges. Next to the dining room is the kitchen, with three fireplaces. The chapel has a lovely late 16th-century altarpiece and an unusual lunette fresco of the *Dormition of the Virgin*. Stairs continue up to the loggia on the top floor. Off the main staircase is the bedroom of Georges de Challant, which has a pretty wood ceiling and a little oratory with a *Crucifixion* and the kneeling figure of Challant. Another room has views of the two castles of Verrès and Arnad. A small room used as a schoolroom has sums scratched on the walls. The *sala baroniale* has delightful painted walls depicting the *Judgement of Paris*, and lovely landscapes with birds behind painted crystal columns.

The church of **Arnad**, founded in the 11th century and restored in the early 15th century, is one of the older churches in the valley. The exterior frescoes in late-Gothic style are part of the 15th-century restoration.

The interesting castle of **Bard**, an 11th-century foundation, was largely reconstructed in the 19th century. At present only the courtyard can be visited, but there are plans to open the whole castle. In 1800 Napoleon's progress was halted here for a week by the defenders of the castle, but in the end he managed to pass unnoticed with his army during the night; they went through the narrow gorge in silence, having muffled the wheels of the gun carriages with straw. As an over-liberal young officer, Camillo Cavour (*see p. 19*) was despatched to this remote garrison by Carlo Felice of Savoy, King of Sardinia and Piedmont, in 1830–31.

Just before Donnas you can see the valley's best surviving stretch of the Roman road to Gaul above the modern road on the left. It was built just above the level of the river, to avoid flooding, and ran mostly along the left bank, where the warmth of the sun (stronger here than on the other side) helped to melt the snow in winter. A conspicuous arch cut into the rock by the Romans survives here—a demonstration of the skill required by the stoneworkers, who in places had to construct the road out of the sheer rockface. A round column serves as a milestone (56km from Aosta). The road was in use up to the 19th century, and if you look closely you can see the ruts made by cart-wheels.

Pont-St-Martin lies on the southernmost border of the Valle d'Aosta. It has a well-preserved single-arch Roman bridge (1st century BC) over the Lys, which can be crossed on foot (the bridge downstream was built in 1876). Above are the ruins of a 12th-century castle.

The Val di Gressoney

The tributaries of the Dora Baltea rush and tumble through steep, wooded alpine valleys that are every bit as interesting as the main Valle d'Aosta and often more dramatic in their natural beauty. The Val di Gressoney, which leads north towards Monte Rosa, is ascended by road from Pont-St-Martin. It contains the largest and oldest of the German-speaking colonies formed by settlers who crossed over from Valais in the Middle Ages. The people of this valley, known as the Walsers, are mentioned as early as 1218. They were subjects of the Bishop of Sion and have kept their language and customs distinct from their Italian neighbours. The attractive chalets (*rascards*) in the lower valley, the farmhouses (*stadel*) in the upper valley, and the costume of the women (which is brightly coloured in red and black, with a remarkable headdress adorned with hand-made gold lace) all suggest a northern origin.

Fontainemore has a lovely medieval single-arched bridge across the Lys. **Issime** (939m) has an interesting German Walser dialect, known as *titsch*, and the signs here are written in all three languages. The church, rebuilt after 1567, has a fresco of the *Last Judgement* on the façade, opposite which is a pretty porch with niches, painted in 1752. Inside is a little museum. The elaborate high altar, in gold and turquoise, is decorated with numerous statues (1690–1710). At the west end is an interesting judge's chair, with a chain collar for those found guilty: it was used up to 1770 in the piazza.

Gaby, where the fiercely anti-sentimental, republican poet Giosuè Carducci (1835–1907) used to stay at the end of the 19th century, is a French-speaking village (1032m), but the German dialect is used again at Gressoney-St-Jean (1385m), the principal village in the valley and a summer and winter resort. You can still see some old houses (*stadel*) here, and there is a fine view of snow-covered Monte Rosa

Queen Margherita of Savoy, who loved the alpine scenery of the Valle d'Aosta.

(4637m) at the head of the valley. The town hall occupies Villa Margherita, a remarkable Art Nouveau building built for Queen Margherita of Savoy (1851-1926), the wife of Umberto I, noted for her piety and good works. It is said that the Pizza Margherita was created in her honour.

Across the river in fir and larch woods is the turreted Gothic-revival castle of **Gressoney** (or Castel Savoia; *open March 9.30–12.30 & 1.30–4.30; Apr 10–12 & 1.30–5.30, Sun & holidays to 6.30; July–Aug 9–7.30; Oct–Feb 10–12 & 1.30–4.30, Sun & holidays 10–12 & 1.30–5.30, closed Thur*), built in 1899–1904 by Emilio Stramucci for Queen Margherita, who spent every summer here up to 1925. The veranda enjoys a splendid view of Monte Rosa. The kitchen was in a separate building, connected to the castle by a miniature railway.

The pretty little village is German in atmosphere. The church has a bust of Queen Margherita on the façade and a Baroque interior with charming wooden altars and a small museum. A statue of Umberto I graces the adjoining piazza.

The sister village of **Gressoney-la-Trinité** (1628m), is a ski resort for Monte Rosa, with a view of the grand line of snow peaks from Monte Rosa to the Gran Paradiso.

PRACTICAL INFORMATION

GETTING AROUND

• **By road:** On the Autostrada A5 between Aosta and Turin, traffic is thick on Fri and Sun evenings with escaping/returning *torinesi*. There are bus services from Turin and Milan to Aosta (*see below*) with some international services through the tunnels. Car parking (free) in Aosta in Piazza Plouves.
• **By bus:** Buses run all year from Aosta (opposite the train station) to centres of the Valle d'Aosta to Turin and Milan; via the Great St Bernard Tunnel to Martigny, and via Courmayeur and the Mont Blanc Tunnel to Chamonix. For the side valleys a change is usually necessary at the town at the beginning of

the valley.
• **By rail:** Slow Diretti and Regionali link Aosta with Turin and Milan via Chivasso (a change is sometimes necessary). The 100km run, on a single track after Chivasso, is made in 2hrs–2hrs 15mins. A pretty line built between the two World Wars continues from Aosta to Pré-St-Didier, a few kilometres south of Courmayeur, in c. 50mins.

INFORMATION OFFICES

Aosta Piazza Chanoux 1, T: 0165 236627, www.regione.vda.it/turismo. For hiking and alpine or cross-country ski trails: Club Alpino Italiano, Piazza Chanoux 8, T: 0165 40194.

Breuil-Cervinia Via Carrel 29, T:
0166 949136, www.montecervino.it
Champoluc Via Varasch, T: 0125
307113.
Cogne Piazza Chanoux 36, T: 0165
74040, www.cogne.org
Courmayeur Piazzale Monte Bianco
13, T: 0165 842060,
www.aostashop.com/apt.htm
Gressoney-St-Jean Villa Deslex,
Lyskamm Waeg 8, T: 0125 355185,
www.aiatmonterosawalser.it
Pont-Saint-Martin Via
Circonvallazione 30, T: 0125 804843,
laportadellavallee@libero.it

HOTELS

Aosta

€€ **Europe**. Elegant and friendly, in the
city centre. Piazza Narbonne 8, T: 0165
236363, www.ethotels.com
€€ **Milleluci**. A beautiful, rustic family-run establishment on a sunny hillside
just 1km from the centre of town.
Località Porossan Roppoz, T: 0165
235278, www.hotelmilleluci.com
€ **Roma**. Calm and comfortable, near
the Roman theatre; closed Jan. Via
Torino 7, T: 0165 40133,
hroma@libero.it

Breuil-Cervinia

€€€ **Hermitage**. A warm, atmospheric
château steeped in tradition, with stunning views over the Matterhorn and
Grandes Murailles. Open July–Sept and
Dec–April. Strada Cristallo, T: 0166
948 998, F: 0166 949032,
www.relaischateaux.com
€€ **Bucaneve**. Calm, restful and centrally located, with good views of the
Matterhorn and Grandes Murailles.
Open Dec–May and July–Aug. Piazza

Jumeaux 10, T: 0166 949119,
www.hotel-bucaneve.it
€€ **Hostellerie des Guides**. Simple
but rich in atmosphere, with antique
furniture and ample documentation of
alpinists in the Valtournenche. Open
Nov–Apr and July–Aug. Via Carrel 32,
T: 0166 949473, F: 0166 948 824.

Champoluc

€€ **Villa Anna Maria**. Set amid pines
and wildflowers, with warm, woody
interiors and friendly staff. Via Croues
5, T: 0125 307128, www.hotelvilla
annamaria.com

Cogne

€€€ **Bellevue**. Lovely building, locally crafted antiques, staff in traditional
dress and a small collection of arts and
crafts from the valley. Open Jan–Sept.
Via Gran Paradiso 22, T: 0165 74825,
F: 0165 749192,
www.relaischateaux.com
€€ **Miramonti**. A restful family-managed place rich in atmosphere, with
views of the Gran Paradiso. Viale
Cavagnet 31, T: 0165 74030, F: 0165
749378, www.miramonticogne.com
€€ **Sant'Orso**. A tranquil place, with
pleasant garden and good views of the
Gran Paradiso. Closed May and Nov.
Via Bourgeois 2, T: 0165 74821, F:
0165 74822.

Courmayeur

€€ **Dolonne**, at Dolonne (across the
Dora from Courmayeur). In a 17th-cen-
tury farmhouse with good views over
the valley and mountains. T: 0165
846674, F: 0165 846671, www.
hoteldolonne.com
€€ **Palace Bron**, at Plan Gorret.
Beautifully located in the woods above
Courmayeur, with stunning views.
Open Dec–Apr and July–Sept. T: 0165

846742, F: 0165 844015,
hotelpb@tin.it
Gressoney-Saint-Jean
€€ **Gran Baita.** Just 12 rooms in an
18th-century lodge with stupendous
views of Monte Rosa. Open Dec–Apr
and July–Sept. Strada Castello Savoia
26, at Gresmatten, T: 0125 356441, F:
0125 356441, www.hotelgranbaita.it
Saint-Vincent
€€€ **Grand Hotel Billia.** Large, luxurious hotel in a lovely park, with direct
underground access to the casino. Viale
Piemonte 72, T: 0166 5231, F: 0166
523799, www.grandhotelbillia.com
€ **Elena.** Calm and efficient. Closed
Nov–Dec. Piazza Monte Zerbion, T:
0166 512140, F: 0166 537459,
www.logis.it/elena.htm

RESTAURANTS

Aosta
€€ **Le Foyer.** One of the finest restaurants in town, with traditional local
dishes. Closed Mon evening, Tues, Jan
and July. Corso Ivrea 146, T: 0165
32136.
€ **Degli Artisti**. This little trattoria
lives up to its name: creative cuisine,
good ambience, and prices even a starv-
ing artist could afford. Closed Sun,
mid-day Mon and two weeks in July.
Via Maillet 5–7, T: 0165 40960.
€ **Taverna da Nando.** A family-run
restaurant serving excellent regional
specialities. Closed Mon and June–July.
Pass. Folliez 4, T: 0165 44455.
Allein (27km north of Aosta)
€ **Lo Ratelé.** Good farm lunches in a
former stable; open by reservation only.
Arnad (Machaby)
€ **Lo Dzerby.** Farmhouse serving hot

meals by reservation. Open Sat and
Sun, May–Oct. Località Machaby, T:
0125 966067.
Châtillon
€€€ **Privé Parisien.** Traditional
restaurant, with rooms. Closed midday
(except Sat, Sun & holidays), Thur and
July. Regione Panorama 1, T: 0166
537053.
Cogne
€€ **Lou Ressignon.** Rustic *osteria*,
with game and other mountain dishes.
Closed Tues (and Mon evening in low
season), June, Sept and Nov. Rue des
Mines de Cogne 23, T: 0165 74034.
€€ **Lou Tchappè.** Traditional restau-
rant in a mountain cabin. Closed Mon
(except July–Aug), June and Nov.
Località Lillaz 126, T: 0165 74379.
€ **Les Pertzes.** Wine bar and brasserie
offering good, simple fare. Closed Tues
and mid-day Wed, Nov and May–June.
Via Grappein 93, T: 0165 749227.
Courmayeur
€€ **Gallia Gran Baita.** Hotel restau-
rant offering innovative interpretations
of traditional recipes. Closed May and
Nov. Strada Larzey, T: 0165 844040.
€€ **Grill Royal e Golf.** Refined
regional cuisine, in the Royal e Golf
hotel. Open Dec–March and July–Aug,
closed mid-day and Mon (except Aug
and 25 Dec). Via Roma 87, T: 0165
846787.
Gignod
€ **Locanda La Clusaz.** Trattoria (with
rooms) offering delicious local fare.
Closed Tues, May–June and Oct–Nov.
Località La Clusaz 32, T: 0165 56075.
Gressan (Aosta)
€€ **Hostellerie de la Pomme
Couronée.** An old farmhouse with
good regional dishes, especially recipes

with apples. Closed Tues. Località Resselin 3, T: 0165 251191.

Morgex

€€ **Café Quinson Vieux Bistrot**. Wine bar and café. Closed Tues, June and Oct. Piazza Principe Tommaso 9, T: 0165 809499.

Nus

€ **Maison Rosset**. Farmhouse in the village, offering rustic dinners by a roaring fire. Open evenings only (midday on Sun & holidays), closed Mon. Via Risorgimento 39, T: 0165 767176.

Saint-Christophe (Aosta)

€€ **Sanson**. Traditional restaurant in a panoramic position above the city. Closed Wed and July. Regione Chabloz, T: 0165 541410.

Saint-Pierre (Homené-Sainte-Marguerite)

€ **Les Ecureuils**. Farmhouse (with rooms) in a village at 1500m, famous for its seasonal cuisine. Open evenings, by reservation, Nov–June (summer for guests only); closed Jan–Feb. Località Homené Dessus, T: 0165 903831.

Saint-Rhemy en Bosses

€€ **Suisse**. Restaurant (with rooms) known for its delicious regional cuisine and interesting 18th-century ambience. Open Dec–Apr and June–Sept. Via Roma 21, T: 0165 780 906, F: 0165 780 007.

Saint-Vincent

€€€ **Batezar**. Traditional restaurant serving delicious regional delicacies. Closed mid-day (except Sat, Sun & holidays), Wed, Nov and June. Via Marconi 1, T: 0166 513164.

€€ **Le Grenier**. Good traditional fare, in an old granary. Closed Tues, midday Wed, Jan and July. Piazza Monte Zerbion 1, T: 0166 512224.

Sarre

€ **Mille Miglia**. A family-run place serving good local dishes. Closed Mon and Nov. Località Saint Maurice 15, T: 0165 257227.

Valgrisenche (Bonne)

€ **Perret**. Trattoria (with rooms) offering strictly local fare. Closed June and Nov. Località Bonne 2, T: 0165 97107.

Verrès

€€ **Chez Pierre**. Restaurant (with rooms), offering excellent regional delicacies and summer seating outside. Closed Tues. Via Martorey 73, T. 0125 929376.

CAFÉS & REGIONAL SPECIALITIES

Aosta The best café is the **Nazionale** (Piazza Chanoux 9). For fresh pastries, go to **Pasticceria Boch**, Via De Tillier 2. **Enoteca la Cave**, Via Festaz 53, has fine wine from the valley; you can get cheese to go with it at **Latteria Gerard Lale**, Via De Sales 14.

Allein In the village, at Località Ville 2, **Enoteca La Croix Blanche** has a wide selection of wines from the region. 8km down the road at Etroubles, **Luca Tamone**, Rue des Verges 13, grows all sorts of berries.

Cogne **Pasticceria Elda Perret**, at Via Bourgeois 57, makes delicious pastries, notably the local Christmas cake called *meculin*.

FESTIVALS & MARKETS

Market day in Aosta is Tues, in Piazza Cavalieri di Vittorio Veneto. The Fair of St Orso is held on 30 and 31 Jan, with local artisans' products.

At Cogne, the *Veillà*, a local artisans'

fair, is held on a Sat in mid-July and in mid-Aug. The *Battaglia delle Regine*, a contest between horned cattle, is held in various heats throughout the valley (the finals in late Oct usually take place in a field outside the castle of Fénis). Carnival is celebrated with a traditional *festa* on Shrove Tues at Pont-Saint-Martin when the devil is 'hung' from the Roman bridge, followed by a party in the castle of Verrès. From Fontainemore there is a procession every 3 or 4 years in summer across the mountains to the sanctuary of Oropa in Piedmont. At Gressoney-St-Jean a procession in local costume is held on 24 June and 15 Aug. On the last Sun of May there is a music festival in the park of the castle of Aymavilles.

PIEDMONT

The ancient principality of Piedmont, the cradle of the Italian nation, occupies the upper basin of the Po—mainly *al piè dei monti*, 'at the foot of the mountains' which encircle it: the Pennine, Graian, Cottian, and Maritime Alps. The cultural relations between Piedmont and France have always been very close, and the French language was long used at the court and parliament of Turin. Its influence survives in the Piedmontese dialects.

Historically Piedmont combines the territories of the old marquisates of Ivrea and Monferrato and the county of Turin. The territory of Turin came into the hands of the House of Savoy in 1045, following the marriage of Adelaide of Susa to Otho, son of Humbert, Count of Savoy. The Piedmontese kingdom, like all other Italian states, was obliterated by the Napoleonic conquests; but the Congress of Vienna (1814) reinstated the Savoy kings at Turin and also gave them suzerainty over Liguria.

The decades following the Napoleonic interlude witnessed the emergence of Piedmont as the principal agent of Italian nationhood. Vittorio Emanuele II—thanks to the astuteness of his minister Cavour—won the goodwill of France and England by taking part in the Crimean War, then turned this privilege to his advantage by calling Napoleon III to his aid when the second War of Italian Independence broke out in 1859. The war was fought against Austria, whose empire encompassed northern Italy from Milan to Trieste. The Austrian army was crushed in a succession of defeats, and Lombardy was annexed to Piedmont in the first year of the war. The Piedmontese dominions west of the Alps (Savoy and Nice) were ceded to France, and the remaining Italian provinces (except the areas north and east of Venice, acquired after the First and Second World Wars, respectively) were added one by one to Vittorio Emanuele's kingdom. In 1865 he transferred his capital from Turin to Florence, and the history of Piedmont became merged in the history of Italy.

TURIN

My arrival at Turin was the first and only moment of intoxication I have found in Italy. It is a city of palaces.
William Hazlitt, Notes of a Journey through France and Italy, 1826

Turin, in Italian *Torino*, is the most important city in Piedmont. The regular Roman street plan of its ancient core, consciously developed when the city was enlarged in the 17th–18th centuries, gives it the air of a French rather than an Italian town. In its 18th-century heyday Turin must have been a very striking place indeed. The English writer Horace Walpole, who passed through on his 1739 tour of Italy, wrote of it as 'by far one of the prettiest cities [in Italy], clean and compact, very new and very regular'. His travelling companion Thomas Gray called it 'a place of many beauties', expressing particular regard for the 'streets all laid out by the line, regular uniform buildings, fine walks that surround the whole, and in general a good lively, clean appearance'. The centre of the city, with some splendid palaces and churches built in a late Baroque style by Guarino Guarini and Filippo Juvarra (*see p. 48*), is remarkably homogeneous, still retaining the orderly, rational aspect that Walpole and Gray found so appealing.

Long a centre of metalworking, Turin has been famous since 1899 as the home of the Fiat motor company. Today there is an ongoing effort to restore the city to its past splendour, particularly in view of the 2006 winter Olympics.

HISTORY OF TURIN

No one knows who established Turin, but it is fairly clear that the city began as a Celtic or Ligurian settlement. It was Romanised as Julia Augusta Taurinorum in the 1st century BC, and the Goths, Lombards and Franks held sway in the Middle Ages. The marriage in 1045 of Countess Adelaide, heiress of a line of French counts of Savoy, to Oddone (Otho), son of Humbert 'the White-Handed', united the Cisalpine and Transalpine possessions of the House of Savoy, with Turin as their capital. After a period of semi-independence in the 12th–13th centuries, the city consistently followed the fortunes of the princely house of Savoy. It was occupied by the French in 1506–62, but was awarded to Duke Emanuele Filiberto 'the Iron-Headed' by the Treaty of Cateau-Cambrésis (1559). It was besieged in 1639–40, and again in 1706, when it was saved from the French by the heroic action of Pietro Micca (*see p. 49*).

From 1720 Turin was capital of the kingdom of Sardinia, and after the Napoleonic occupation (1798–1814) it became a centre of Italian nationalism and the headquarters of Camillo Cavour (1810–61), a native of the town and the prime mover of Italian liberty (*see p. 19*). Prince Carlo Alberto, who succeeded to the Savoy throne in 1831, had a profound influence on the appearance of the city, and most of its important art collections date from his time. In 1861–65 Turin was the capital of Vittorio Emanuele II (1820–78) as king of Italy. Allied air raids caused heavy damage during the Second World War. After the war new suburbs grew up to accommodate the huge number of immigrants from the south of Italy who came here to find work. The novelist Primo Levi (1919–87), and Carlo Levi (1902–75), writer and painter, are among the famous modern natives of Turin.

EXPLORING TURIN

Piazza Castello and Palazzo Madama

The huge, rectangular **Piazza Castello** (Map 6–7) is the centre of the city. The square was laid out by Ascanio Vittozzi in 1584 around the castle, now called Palazzo Madama, and is surrounded by uniform monumental buildings with porticoes. Beneath the porticoes on the corner nearest Via Accademia delle Scienze are two elegant cafés (Mulassano and Baratti, with elaborate decorations by Edoardo Rubino), on either side of the Galleria dell'Industria Subalpina (Map 6), a delightful shopping arcade built in 1873–74.

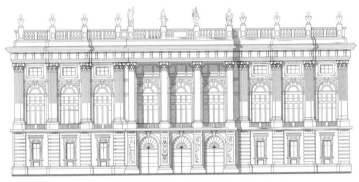

PALAZZO MADAMA

Palazzo Madama (Map 6–7), is the most imposing of the old buildings of Turin, a four-square castle of the 15th century, one side of which has been replaced by a wing and façade of 1718–21 by Filippo Juvarra. A castle was begun here after 1276 by William VII of Monferrato on the site of the Roman Porta Praetoria, the east gate of the ancient city. The palace takes its present name from the two regents, Maria Cristina, widow of Vittorio Amedeo I, and Giovanna Battista, widow of Carlo Emanuele II; both were entitled Madama Reale, and both resided here and remodelled the old castle. The palazzo was the seat of the Subalpine Senate in 1848–60 and of the Italian Senate in 1861–65.

Since 1935 the palace has housed the **Museo Civico di Arte Antica** (*closed at time of writing*). Here you can see Romanesque, Gothic and Renaissance sculpture, including works by Tino da Camaino and Bambaia. The precious collection of codexes includes the illuminated 14th-century statutes of the city of Turin and the celebrated *Hours of Milan*, attributed to Jan van Eyck. The paintings include a *Portrait of a Man* by Antonello da Messina (whom Vasari wrongly claims to have been a pupil of van Eyck's), signed and dated 1476, one of his best and last works. On the first floor, beyond the central hall, seat of the senate, are the royal apartments. Some of the furniture here dates from the time of Carlo Emanuele II (d. 1675), but the fittings are mainly in early-18th century style.

At no. 191 is the entrance to the **Armeria Reale** (Map 7; *open Tues, Thur, Sat and Sun 1.30–7.30, Wed and Fri 8.30–2*), housed in a wing of the Palazzo Reale (the palace as a whole is described below). The royal armoury, one of the more important in Europe, includes some remarkable pieces by the great Bavarian and Austrian armourers and gunsmiths. It was transferred here by Prince Carlo Alberto and opened to the public in 1837. The monumental staircase, designed by Filippo Juvarra and built by Benedetto Alfieri (who succeeded Juvarra as court architect), leads up to the 18th- and 19th-century galleries. These provide a magnificent setting for the collection. The rotonda was decorated in 1841–45 by Pelagio Pelagi (chief architect to Carlo Alberto). The collections of the last princes of the House of Savoy and arms and ensigns of the Risorgimento period are displayed here. The splendid Galleria Beaumont, designed by Filippo Juvarra in 1733, is named after Claudio Francesco Beaumont who painted the vault in 1738–64, and contains a superb display of about 30 complete suits of armour (12 equestrian), some of which were made for the Martinengo family of Brescia. Oriental arms are displayed in the Medagliere.

The Biblioteca Reale has miniatures and drawings collected by Carlo Alberto, including a self-portrait of Leonardo da Vinci and works by Dürer, Rembrandt and Raphael.

Palazzo Reale, the cathedral and Turin Shroud

Palazzo Reale (Map 7; *open Tues–Sun 8.30–7; T: 011 436 1455*) is a former royal residence, built for Madama Reale Maria Cristina. The Cappella della Sacra Sindone (*see below*), built in 1694 to contain the Holy Shroud, is in the west wing of the palace, adjoining the apse of the cathedral. You have a good view of its spiral dome by Guarino Guarini from here.

The state apartments, on the first floor (shown on conducted tours), were lavishly decorated from the mid-17th to the mid-19th centuries, with some good ceilings and floors; they contain porcelain, tapestries and furniture (some by local cabinet maker and master of inlay work Pietro Piffetti). The Gabinetto Cinese is a delightful work by Filippo Juvarra, who also built the ingenious Scala degli Forbici staircase (1720). The feat of creating a monumental staircase in a confined space is one of Juvarra's great achievements.

The **Giardino Reale**, approached through the palace (*and normally open May–Oct daily 9am–dusk*), was enlarged

Dome of the Cappella della Sacra Sindone.

by André Le Nôtre in 1697 for Carlo Emanuele II but has since been altered.

In Piazza Castello is the church of **San Lorenzo** (Map 7), formerly the royal chapel, a superb Baroque work by Guarino Guarini, with a delightful cupola and lantern. It has a complex, beautifully lit interior of 1667.

The **cathedral** (Map 7) was built in 1491–98 for Archbishop Domenico della Rovere by Meo del Caprino and other Tuscans, after three churches had been demolished to make way for it. It has a Renaissance façade and a campanile (1468–70) completed by Juvarra in 1720.

Inside are 15th-century tombs and a polyptych, in a fine Gothic frame, attributed to Giovanni Martino Spanzotti, with delightful little pictures of the life of Sts Crispin and Crispinian, including scenes of mercantile life. Behind the apse is the **Cappella della Sacra Sindone** (*open daily 9–12 & 3–7*), the chapel of the Holy Shroud, built by Guarino Guarini in 1668–94 and restored after a fire of 1997. It has dark marble walls and family monuments erected in 1842 by Prince Carlo Alberto. The urn that traditionally held the Holy Shroud—in which the body of Christ is believed to have been wrapped after his descent from the Cross—is on the altar. The Shroud itself is periodically displayed in a special case.

THE STORY OF THE HOLY SHROUD

This greatly revered sacred relic was said to have been taken from Jerusalem to Cyprus, and from there to France in the 15th century, and to have been brought to Turin by Emanuele Filiberto in 1578. The shroud is a piece of linen measuring 4.36 x 1.10m, on which is imprinted the negative image of a crucified man. In 1988 the Archbishop of Turin announced that scientific research using carbon 14 dating had proved that this icon must have been made between 1260 and 1390, but discussion still continues about its origins, particularly as another, still fainter image, was detected on the reverse side of the shroud in 2002, following the removal of a piece of cloth stitched onto it in the 16th century. Today the shroud is kept in a silver casket inside an iron box enclosed in a marble case. It is rarely on display, and has in fact only been shown five times in the last century. Its next public outing is scheduled for 2025.

Beside the campanile are pretty railings in front of a wing of Palazzo Reale, built in 1900. Here are the ruins of a Roman theatre of the 1st century AD. On the left, in an unattractive setting, is a stretch of Roman and medieval wall beside the impressive **Porta Palatina** (Map 7), an exceptionally well-preserved two-arched Roman gate flanked by two 16-sided towers. This was the Porta Principalis Sinistra in the wall of the Roman colony of Augusta Taurinorum.

A garden house of Palazzo Reale (entrance at Corso Regina Margherita 105) holds the **Museo di Antichità** (*open Tues–Sun 8.30–7.30*), with archaeological material dis-

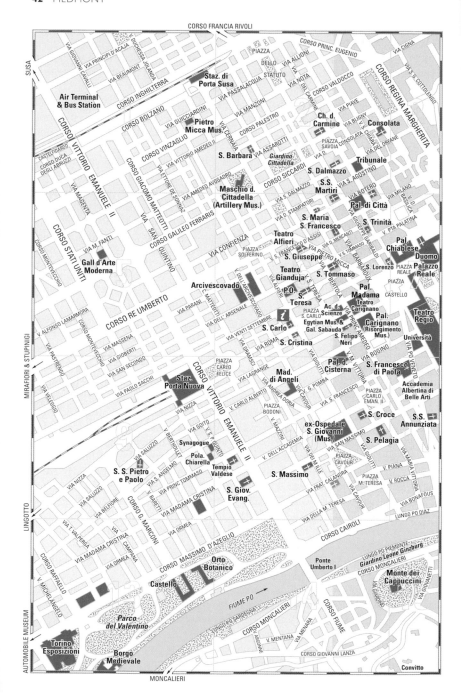

TURIN

covered mainly in Piedmont and Liguria and dating from the Stone Age to the barbarian invasions. Roman finds include the Marengo treasure, discovered in 1928, with
a silver bust of Emperor Lucius Verus (reigned 161–69).

The Museo Egizio and Galleria Sabauda

The centre of Turin is roughly bisected by the fashionable Via Roma (Map 6), halfway
along which is the arcaded **Piazza San Carlo**, a handsome monumental square begun
in 1640. Here are the twin churches of **San Carlo** and **Santa Cristina**, the latter with
a façade (1715–18) by Filippo Juvarra and 18th-century stucco decoration in the interior. The monument to Duke Emanuele Filiberto, whose equestrian figure (*El caval
d'brôns*, in dialect) is shown sheathing his sword after defeating the French at St
Quentin (1557), is considered the masterpiece of the sculptor Carlo Marochetti
(1838). The two long yellow-and-grey palazzi have wide porticoes, beneath which are
several cafés, including, on the corner of Via San Teresa, the well-known Caffè San
Carlo. On the opposite side of the piazza, Palazzo Solaro del Borgo (no. 183), partly
reconstructed by Benedetto Alfieri in 1753, is the seat of the Accademia Filarmonica
and the Circolo del Whist, an exclusive club with delightful 18th-century premises.

At the end of the piazza (right; entrance on Via Accademia delle Scienze) is the
Palazzo dell'Accademia delle Scienze, with a fine exterior, built for the Jesuits by
Guarino Guarini (1678). The building also houses the Museo Egizio (ground and first
floors) and the Galleria Sabauda (second floor).

Museo Egizio

Map 6. *Open Tues–Sun 8.30–7.30; T: 011 561 8391.*
The collection here is extremely fine, comparable to those of Cairo and London. The
real founder of this remarkable museum was Carlo Felice, who in 1824 bought the
collections of Bernardo Drovetti, the trusted counsellor of Mohammed Ali. Later
important acquisitions came from the expeditions of Schiaparelli (1903–20) and
Farina (1930–37), notably in the Theban region, at Ghebelein (Aphroditopolis), Qau
el-Kebir (Antaepolis, near Assiut) and Heliopolis. The museum played a leading part
in the rescue digs in Nubia before the completion of the Aswan high dam and was
rewarded with the rock temple of Ellesiya, which was transported by sea in sections
via Genoa in 1967 and then reconstructed.

Ground Floor: Highlights include objects dating back to the prehistoric period and to the first three dynasties, 2920–2575 BC; findings dating back to the Old Kingdom (2575–2134 BC), with the reconstruction of the Tomb of Iteti as it was discovered by Schiaparelli in 1903. There are also several documents crucial to the reconstruction of the history of this period: the *Royal Canon*, also called the *Papyrus of the Kings*; a copy of the Rosetta Stone (the original is in the British Museum, London) and a copy of the Palermo Stone. Also on this floor are a diorite statue of Rameses II (1299–33 BC), statues of Amenhotep II and Thuthmosis I; Horemheb and his wife; figures of Sekhmet and Ptah.

There is a seated figure of Thuthmosis III (1496–1422 BC) and a statue of Tutankhamon, with the god Amon-Ra. The statue is popularly believed to be cursed, and is held responsible for a number of accidents that tend to occur wherever it is displayed. Another room contains the reconstructed rock temple of Ellesiya (15th century BC), with its bas-relief frieze showing Thuthmosis III. In some underground rooms (where you can see parts of the Roman wall of Turin) are finds from the excavations of Schiaparelli and Farina, including a fragment of painted linen from about 3500 BC.

First floor: The room at the entrance contains mummies and mummy-cases, scarabs, amulets, canopic vases, ushabti figures, etc. The next room shows the findings from Schiaparelli's excavations at Deir el-Medina, the village where the Pharaoh's workmen lived in the New Kingdom (1500–1050 BC). The reconstructed tomb of Kha, director of the works at the Necropolis of Thebes, and his wife Merit (18th Dynasty) preserves intact its furniture, food, cooking utensils, etc. The following room contains textiles. The next room contains administrative and literary papyri with architectural plans and plans of gold mines; a love poem; the *Papyrus of the Palace Conspiracy* (20th Dynasty); writing materials, rolls of papyrus, etc. The other rooms of the first floor were closed for rearrangement at the time of writing.

Galleria Sabauda

Map 6. *Open Tues, Fri, Sat, Sun 8.30–2, Wed 2–7.30, Thur 10–7.30; T: 011 564 1755.* The nucleus of the exhibit are the collections of paintings made by the princes of the House of Savoy, from the 16th century onwards. The gallery was first opened to the public in 1832 by Prince Carlo Alberto. Remarkably rich in Flemish and Dutch works acquired in 1741 through Eugene of Savoy, it is interesting also for its paintings by Venetian and Piedmontese masters, some of them hardly represented elsewhere. The works are arranged in two distinct groupings: the Savoy family collections, and the acquisitions made after 1832. Rearrangement has been in progress since 1987. The collections are displayed in five broad sections.

First section: Illustrates the birth of the collection with items acquired c. 1550–1630. Works by Roger van der Weyden, Gaudenzio Ferrari, Mantegna (*Madonna*), Veronese, court painters (including Moncalvo), Orazio Gentileschi (*Annunciation*, painted in 1623 for Carlo Emanuele I), Guercino, Morazzone, Giulio Cesare Procaccini, Cerano and Rubens.

Second section: Traces the history of the collection from the time of Vittorio Amedeo I to Vittorio Amedeo II (1630–1730), through works by François Duquesnoy, Francesco Albani, Francesco Cairo (1598–1674), and Guercino. The *Children of Charles I* (1635) by van Dyck was presented by Henrietta Maria, Charles' queen, to her sister Cristina of Savoy.

Third section: Works reflecting the artistic taste of the Savoy court from 1730 to 1830. These include two views of Turin commissioned from Bernardo

Bellotto by Carlo Emanuele III in 1745, and works by Carle van Loo, Sebastiano Conca, Pompeo Batoni, Anton Raphael Mengs and Elisabeth Vigée-Lebrun. The copies on porcelain of famous works owned by the Tuscan grand-dukes and acquired by Carlo Alberto in 1826 are by Abraham Constantin.

Fourth section: Dedicated to works collected by Prince Eugene in 1737–41, including Poussin and Guido Reni (*St John the Baptist*). The superb Flemish and Dutch collection includes works by Jan van Eyck, Petrus Christus, Rembrandt (*Old Man Asleep*, perhaps the artist's father), Jacob van Ruisdael, Hans Memling (*Passion of Christ*), David Teniers the Younger, Jan van Huysum, Jan Brueghel, Holbein the Younger and van Dyck (*Madonna and Child*).

Fifth section: Works acquired by the gallery from 1832 onwards. The Piedmontese school is well represented (Gaudenzio Ferrari, Bernardino Lanino, Defendente Ferrari, Giovanni Martino Spanzotti). Among the Tuscan works are a *Madonna* (c. 1433) by Fra Angelico, *Tobias and the Archangel Raphael* by Piero and Antonio Pollaiolo, *Tobias and the Three Archangels* by Filippino Lippi, and a *Madonna and Saints* by Sodoma. The schools of Lombardy (Bergognone, Moretto, Giovan Gerolamo Savoldo) and Venice (Giovanni Bellini, Veronese, Tintoretto and Francesco Bassano) are also represented.

The Gualino Collection, donated to the museum in 1928, contains Italian paintings (including a *Madonna* attributed to Duccio di Buoninsegna, and works by Taddeo di Bartolo, Veronese, and Jacopo Sansovino), German paintings, ancient sculpture, Roman and medieval ivories, goldsmiths' work, Chinese works, medieval furniture and lace.

The modern collection has works by Italian painters between the two World Wars.

Around Piazza Carignano

Opposite the palace, on the corner of Via Accademia delle Scienze, is the large church of **San Filippo Neri** (Map 6), rebuilt by Filippo Juvarra (c. 1714), with a Corinthian pronaos from 1823. The fine Baroque interior (with, unexpectedly, a parquet floor) has an altarpiece by the great Roman artist Carlo Maratta (1625–1713).

Just beyond, in Piazza Carignano, is **Palazzo Carignano** (Map 6), the residence of the princes of Savoy until 1831. It has an interesting Baroque front, faced with brick, by Guarino Guarini (1679), and an oval vestibule with a pretty double staircase. The east façade, facing Piazza Carlo Alberto, dates from 1864–71. The palace was the birthplace of Carlo Alberto (1798) and of Vittorio Emanuele II (1820). It was used for the meetings of the lower house of the Subalpine Parliament (1848–61) and of the first Italian Parliament (1861–65). On the piano nobile (first floor) is the **Museo Nazionale del Risorgimento** (*open Tues–Sun 9–7*), founded in 1878 and one of the more important museums of this crucial period in Italian history (*see p. 19*). The fine hall of the Subalpine Parliament is also shown.

Piazza Carlo Alberto has a bronze equestrian statue of Carlo Alberto by Marochetti (1861). The **Biblioteca Nazionale** here has over 850,000 volumes and some 5,000 manuscripts, mainly from religious institutions in Piedmont. The 17th-century Palazzo Graneri della Roccia, at Via Bogino 9, is the seat of the Circolo degli Artisti, founded in 1855 and closed to women until 1987.

Via Garibaldi

The handsome Via Garibaldi (Map 6–2), a street about 1km long, closed to traffic and lined with characteristic 18th-century balconied palaces, leads west from Piazza Castello. One block along, on the north side of the street, is the church of the **Trinità** (1590–1606), by Ascanio Vittozzi, with a marble interior by Filippo Juvarra (1718). It contains fine carved confessionals.

In Via Porta Palatina to the right is the church of **Corpus Domini** (1607–71), also by Vittozzi, with a lavishly decorated interior by Benedetto Alfieri. Jean-Jacques Rousseau abjured the Protestant faith in this church in 1728. A few paces further on is Piazza di Palazzo di Città, laid out in 1756 by Benedetto Alfieri, with a bronze monument by Pelagio Pelagi (1853) to the 'Green Count' (so named because of the colour of his ensign) Amedeo VI (d. 1383), famed for his feats of arms and for his defeat of the Turks in Greece. Here is **Palazzo di Città** (Map 6), the town hall, begun in 1659 and modified a century later by Benedetto Alfieri. The nearby church of **San Domenico** (Map 2) dates from 1354; its belfry, from 1451. It has a painting by Guercino and a chapel with 14th-century frescoes.

Back on Via Garibaldi is the church of the **Santi Martiri** (Map 6). Begun in 1577, probably by Pellegrino Tibaldi. It has an 18th-century cupola by Bernardino Quadri and a Baroque interior. The high altar is by Filippo Juvarra. Next door, at no. 25, is the **Cappella dei Banchieri e Mercanti** (Map 2–6. *Open Sat 3.30–6, or by appointment, T: 011 562 7226*). A delightful Baroque chapel dating from the late 17th century, with paintings by Andrea Pozzo, Stefano Maria Legnani, Carlo Carlone and others, in huge black frames decorated in gold. The vault is frescoed by Legnano. The high altar is by Filippo Juvarra. The benches and lanterns survive intact, and the organ dates from 1748–50. In the sacristy is an ingenious mechanical calendar constructed by Antonio Plana in 1831. Northwest of here is the **Consolata** (Map 2), a popular place of worship made by joining two churches by Guarino Guarini (1679), one oval, the other hexagonal.

Around the Mole Antonelliana

Turin's **University** (Map 7) has a chequered history dating back to the early 15th century. Erasmus took a degree in theology here in 1506. A short way to the east is the **Mole Antonelliana** (Via Montebello, Map 11), the symbol of Turin. Begun in 1863 as a synagogue, it is the most famous work of the Piedmontese architect Alessandro Antonelli. Its extraordinary shape and enormous height make it an amazing feat of engineering skill. It was finished by the municipality in 1897 as a monument of Italian Unity (the Risorgimento Museum, now in Palazzo Carignano, was first opened here). It was much admired by Nietzsche. The terrace (86m; view) is reached by a lift (*open Tues–Fri 10–4, Sat–Sun and holidays 9–7; closed Mon*); the granite spire, 167m high, was rebuilt in aluminium after it lost its upper 47m in a gale in 1953. The interior has been restored to house the Cinema Museum (*open Tues–Sun 9–8, Sat 9–11*) which has an absorbing collection founded in the 1950s. The collection illustrates the history of photography and cinema in Italy and abroad, and incorporates an important film library. Close by is the **Accademia Albertina di Belle Arti** (Via dell'Accademia Albertina, Map 11). An academy of fine arts founded in 1678. The Pinacoteca dell'Accademia Albertina (*open Tues–Sun 9–1 & 3–7*), in the same building, is interesting mainly for its 60 drawings by Gaudenzio Ferrari, the eminent Piedmontese painter (*see p. 90*), and his workshop. There are also paintings by Filippo Lippi, Bernardino Lanino, and Piedmontese masters.

TWO IMPORTANT TURIN ARCHITECTS

Filippo Juvarra (1678–1736)
Juvarra was an architect, draughtsman and urban planner. He was born the son of a silversmith and entered the priesthood as a young man. He trained as an architect under Carlo Fontana in Rome (1703–14) and was hired as a stage designer by a number of illustrious patrons, including the queen of Poland and the emperor Joseph I of Austria. In 1714 he was appointed architect to the King of Sicily (who resided in Piedmont) and given the commission to rebuild and enlarge Turin. Here and in the environs of the city he left many important works, including two masterpieces: the royal hunting lodge at Stupinigi (1729) and the basilica of Stuperga (1731). His style, highly decorative, light and gracious, typifies the transition between the Baroque and the Rococo.

Guarino Guarini (1624–83)
As a schoolboy Guarini excelled at mathematics, and chose architecture as a career. He became famous for his domes: an excellent example is that of the Sacra Sindone, the chapel to house the Holy Shroud, which plays with optical illusion. Guarini was also known for his genius at geometry, and in the Sacra Sindone he makes repeated play on the number three, symbol of the Trinity, using equilateral triangles, and having three pendentives instead of four.

Beside the Po

The **Parco del Valentino** (Map 14–13) contains a fine botanic garden (*open Mon–Fri 2–5, Sun 2–7*), founded in 1729, with a museum and library. The latter contains the remarkable Iconographia Taurinensis, a collection of 7,500 botanical drawings dated 1752–1868. The **Castello del Valentino**, now used by the university, was built in 1630–60 by Maria Cristina in the style of a French château. The **Borgo e Rocca Medievali**, reproductions of a medieval Piedmontese village and of a castle in the Valle d'Aosta (*open Tues–Sun 9–7 or 8*), were erected for the Turin exhibition of 1884.

Nearby is the fine equestrian monument of Prince Amedeo, the masterpiece of Davide Calandra (1902). At the southwest end of the park is an exhibition ground with various buildings erected between 1938 and 1950, notably **Palazzo Torino-Esposizioni**, whose spectacular vaulted ceiling was designed by architect and engineer Pier Luigi Nervi. It was built in 1948 for the first Turin Motor Show. Further out (just beyond the map) is the **Museo dell'Automobile** (Corso Unità d'Italia 40. *Open Tues–Sat 10–6.30, Sun 10–8.30*), with an international collection of vehicles, admirably displayed and technically documented. Further on, overlooking the river, is the huge **Palazzo del Lavoro**, designed by Pier Luigi Nervi for the 1961 exhibition. The **Lingotto Fiat factory** is in Via Nizza (Map 9). The factory started production in 1923 and closed down in 1983. Its interesting building, which has played an important part in the history of the industrialisation of the city, has a test circuit on the roof. In 1991 part of the factory was demolished and part-converted by Renzo Piano into an exhibition and congress centre (also used for concerts). The Turin Motor Show is now appropriately held here (biennially in Apr–May). The **Mirafiori Fiat factory**, built in 1935–38 and extended 1958–70, where the Fiat motorworks now operate, is to the west, across Corso Unione Sovietica and Corso Giovanni Agnelli. **Villa della Regina** (Map 15; *closed for restoration at the time of writing*) is a Baroque residence built for Cardinal Maurizio of Savoy to a design probably by Ascanio Vittozzi, and executed by Amedeo di Castellamonte in 1620. It was altered in the 18th century by Filippo Juvarra. The villa is named after Marie-Anne d'Orléans, queen of Vittorio Amedeo II, who resided here. It has a beautiful park and garden laid out in terraces on the hillside in the style of a Roman villa. Back towards the river is the church of the **Gran Madre di Dio** (Map 15), whose chill white façade dominates the east end of the Ponte Vittorio Emanuele I. This Neoclassical church was built in 1818–31, in imitation of the Pantheon at Rome, to celebrate the return from exile of Vittorio Emanuele I (1814). A monument to the king stands in front of the porch. On the banks of the river here are pleasant public gardens.

Elsewhere in town

The Museo Civico Pietro Micca (entrance at Via Guicciardini 7, Map 1; *open Tues–Sun 9–7*), is dedicated to the French siege of 1706. The museum is named after the Piedmontese sapper who exploded a mine on this site and saved the city from the French at the cost of his own life. From the museum you can visit part of the remarkable underground defence works, which extend for several kilometres beneath the city. Further south is the **Galleria Civica d'Arte Moderna e Contemporanea** (Map 5. *Open Tues–Sun 9–7*). Founded in 1863 and reopened in 1993, the gallery houses one of the more important collections of 19th- and 20th-century painting in Italy. Highlights include 19th-century Italian works by Francesco Hayez, Antonio Canova, Massimo d'Azeglio, Vincenzo Vela and Giuseppe Pellizza da Volpedo; the Macchiaioli group of post-Impressionist realist painters (Telemaco Signorini, Silvestro Lega, Giovanni Fattori), and works by French artists (Renoir, Courbet), on the second floor; and paintings by Umberto Boccioni, Giacomo Balla, Giorgio de Chirico, Giorgio

Morandi, Carlo Carrà, Filippo de Pisis and the artists known as the Gruppo dei Sei (influential in Turin from about 1928 until 1935), on the first floor. Another wing has an extensive collection of works from the 1950s and 1960s. Contemporary works are displayed on the ground floor. **Piazza della Repubblica** (Map 3), known locally as Porta Palazzo, is the scene of a popular general market (and, on Saturday and the second Sunday of the month, of the Balôn antiques market). Two noted charitable institutions of Piedmontese origin lie in Via Cottolengo to the north: the Cottolengo, founded for the aged infirm in 1828 by St Joseph Benedict Cottolengo (1786–1842), and the Istituto Salesiano, established in 1846 by Don Bosco (1815–88, *see overleaf*) for the education of poor boys.

ENVIRONS OF TURIN

The most interesting monument in the immediate environs of Turin is the basilica of **Superga** (*open daily 9–12 & 3–5 or 6*), splendidly situated on a wooded hilltop on the right bank of the Po (*map p. 58*). The church was built in 1717–31 by Vittorio Amedeo II in fulfilment of a thanksgiving vow for the deliverance of Turin from the French in 1706. It is considered Filippo Juvarra's finest work. It has an impressive exterior, with a columned portico, a dome, and two *campanili*; and a fine interior with the tombs of the kings of Sardinia, from Vittorio Amedeo II (d. 1732) to Carlo Alberto (d. 1849), in the crypt. Superga is reached by a cog railway.

Moncalieri, also on the right bank of the Po, lies 8km from the centre of Turin and can be reached by train and bus. It is an industrial town with a castle (*open Mon, Tues, Wed, Fri 8.30–7.30*) reconstructed in the 15th century and enlarged in the 17th–18th centuries. It was the favourite residence of Vittorio Emanuele II; Vittorio Amedeo II (1732) and Vittorio Emanuele I (1824) died here. The apartment of the Savoy princess Letizia Bonaparte, and the 19th-century royal apartments can be visited.

At **Stupinigi**, 10km southwest of the centre (*map p. 58*; bus 41), is the magnificent Palazzina di Caccia, a royal hunting lodge built for Vittorio Amedeo II in 1729–30 by Filippo Juvarra to an ingenious and complex plan. Surrounded by a fine park, it is now the property of the Mauritian Order. The palace has been undergoing restoration since 1988, but it is open (*summer Tues–Sun 9-6; winter 10–5*) and contains a museum of furniture, arranged in some 40 rooms. The queen's apartment has ceiling paintings by Carle van Loo and Giovanni Battista Crosato, and the splendid central hall is frescoed by Giuseppe and Domenico Valeriani (1732). The apartments of Carlo Felice and Carlo Alberto are also shown. The original 18th-century bronze stag, which used to crown the roof of the elliptical central hall, is now displayed inside the palace. A stable block is used for exhibitions.

Rivoli, 13km west of the city centre (bus 36), was once a favourite residence of the Counts of Savoy. The so-called Casa del Conte Verde is a typical early 15th-century patrician house. The huge, square castle was left unfinished by Filippo Juvarra in 1715. It was restored and modernised in 1984 to house the splendid **Museo d'Arte Contemporanea** (*open Tues–Thur 10–5, Fri, Sat, Sun & holidays 10–10; T: 011 956*

5220). Here you can see an outstanding selection of international contemporary art displayed in rooms that merit a trip in themselves.

The **Castello della Venaria Reale**, 9km north of central Turin, is a royal hunting lodge built for Carlo Emanuele II in 1660 by Amedeo di Castellamonte and destroyed by French troops in 1693. It was reconstructed by Juvarra in 1714–28 and is now open (*Tues, Thur, Sat, Sun & holidays 9–11.30 & 2.30–5.30*) as a museum. A long avenue of plane trees leads to the Castello della Mandria, built for Vittorio Amedeo II in 1713 by Filippo Juvarra, in a large park (*open daily*) that was once a hunting reserve.

South of Turin near the Po, is **Carignano**, an ancient lordship long associated with the royal house of Savoy. The cathedral (1757–67) is the masterpiece of Juvarra's successor as court architect Benedetto Alfieri. To the east of Turin is the pleasant little industrial town of Chieri. The cathedral has a 13th-century baptistery and a small crypt incorporating Roman work. The 14th-century church of San Domenico and remains of the Commandery of the Templars are also worth seeing.

From Chieri a road leads eastwards to the hill-village of **Castelnuovo Don Bosco**, birthplace of the saint and founder of the Salesian Order. Giovanni Melchior Bosco was born in 1815, in a mountain hut at Becchi, near Castelnuovo. He worked as a shepherd before training for the priesthood. Shocked by what he saw of the brutal and loveless existence endured by child prisoners in the gaols of Turin, he set up a seminary in 1841 to care for street urchins and teach them the Bible. In 1859 he founded the Salesian Society, aimed at caring for boys from poor backgrounds, and training them for a trade or for the priesthood. The society took its name from St Francis de Sales, by whose example Don Bosco was inspired. After only a few years the original 17 members has swelled to 400. Don Bosco would take them on Sunday excursions in the hills outside Turin, where he would celebrate Mass in the open air, light a camp fire, and treat the boys to a picnic lunch. Don Bosco died in 1888, and was canonised in 1934.

North of here is **Albugnano** with the Benedictine Abbey of Vezzolano (*open Tues–Sun 9–12 or 12.30 & 2–6.30*), the finest group of Romanesque buildings in Piedmont, with remarkable sculptures, especially on the façade and the unusual rood-screen. The complex dates from 1095–1189.

PRACTICAL INFORMATION

GETTING AROUND

• **By rail:** The main train station in Turin is Porta Nuova (Map 9), though Milan-bound trains often stop also at Porta Susa (Map 1) and Genoa-bound trains at Lingotto (beyond Map 9). There are also slow, local connections to places throughout Piedmont and western Liguria. Information from Trenitalia, T: 8488 88088, 166 105 050, www.trenitalia.it

• **By car:** The centre of Turin is closed to motor traffic. You can walk across central Turin in about 40 minutes.

• **By bus:** Country buses depart from the bus station, 3 Corso Inghilterra (Map 1), to Sestriere, Milan, Valle d'Aosta etc., and from Corso Marconi (corner of Via Nizza; Map 9) to Cuneo, Saluzzo, Alba, etc.

• **Alternative transport:** Bicycles may be rented from Risciò, Viale Virgilio, T: 011 605 1241 (*daily 10–7*). Electrically assisted bicycles and motor scooters can be hired at the Palagiustizia (*Mon–Fri 9–6*) and Fontanesi (*Mon–Fri 9–1*) car parks; information from ATM, T: 011 167 019 152, www.comune.torino.it/atm/avvisi/ruoto.htm

• **Public transport:**
Trams
4 Via Venti Settembre (near the main railway station) to the duomo.
1 Stazione Porta Nuova—Corso Vittorio Emanuele II—Stazione Porta Susa.
15 Stazione Porta Nuova (Corso Vittorio Emanuele)—Via XX Settembre—Piazza Castello—Via Po—Piazza Vittorio Veneto—Via Napione—Corso Regina Margherita—Corso Belgio—Corso Casale—Sassi (for the Superga railway).
13 Stazione Porta Susa—Via Cernaia—Via Micca—Piazza Castello—Via Po Piazza Vittorio Veneto—Piazza Gran Madre di Dio (at the foot of Monte dei Cappuccini).
16 Piazza Repubblica—Corso Regina Margherita—Via Rossini—Corso San Maurizio—Via Bava—Piazza Vittorio Veneto—Corso Cairoli—Corso Vittorio Emanuele II—Corso Massimo d'Azeglio (Parco del Valentino).
Buses
67 Largo Marconi—Corso Marconi—Corso Massimo d'Azeglio—Piazza Zara Corso Moncalieri—Moncalieri.
35 Stazione Porta Nuova—Lingotto.
Suburban buses
41 Corso Vittorio—Stupinigi.
36 Corso Francia—Rivoli.
Taxis
T: 011 5737, 011 5730, 011 3399.

SIGHTSEEING TOURS

Tours of the city centre and the royal residences (Palazzina di Caccia di Stupinigi, Castello di Rivoli, Reggia di Venaria Reale) depart daily at 2.30 from Piazza Castello; a historic cog railway runs from Torino Sassi to the Basilica of Superga (660m); and boat trips on the Po, lasting c. 1hr 30mins, depart from the Murazzi (quays) and Borgo Medioevale. For information and reservations T: 011 576 4590.

Valid for 48 or 72 hours, the Torino Card gives free access on the TurismoBus Torino sightseeing bus, all urban public transport and free entrance to 120 museums, monuments, castles, fortresses and royal residences in Turin and in Piedmont. It also gives free access to the panoramic lift in the Mole Antonelliana, to boats on the Po and to the Sassi-Superga cog railway. It offers reductions of up to 50% on theatre and musical shows, guided visits, etc. The Torino Card can be bought at €15 (48 hours) or €17 (72 hours) at Turismo Torino information points, hotels, Ventrina per Torino, Automobile Club Torino, Basilica di Superga, and other points.

INFORMATION OFFICES

Piazza Castello 161, T: 011 535181, www.turismotorino.org
Information point at Porta Nuova Station, T: 011 531327.
Informagiovani: Via Assarotti 2, T: 800 998 500 (free), 011 442 4977, www.comune.torino.it/infogio/welcome.htm

HOTELS

€€€ **Grand Hotel Sitea**. Central and classy, with a famous restaurant. Via Carlo Alberto 35, T: 011 517 0171, www.thi.it
€€€ **Le Meridien Lingotto**. A super-chic luxury hotel in the historic Fiat factory of Lingotto, recently converted by Renzo Piano; also with a famous restaurant (Torpedo). Closed Aug. Via Nizza 262, T: 011 664 2000.
€€€ **Relais Villa Sassi**. An 18th-century villa in a lovely park, with an excellent restaurant. Closed Aug. Strada al Traforo di Pino 47 (at the base of the hill of Superga), T: 011 898 0556, www.villasassi.com

€€€ **Turin Palace**. An older, more traditional establishment, next to Porta Nuova Station. Via Sacchi 8, T: 011 562 5511, www.thi.it
€€ **Boston**. In the heart of an elegant residential area, 800m east of Porta Nuova Station. Via Massena 70, T: 011 500 359, www.hotelres.it
€€ **Stazione e Genova**. A thoroughly comfortable establishment in a recently renovated building in the historic city centre. Via Sacchi 14b, T: 011 562 9400, www.hotelres.it
€€ **Piemontese**. Small and comfortable, in a quiet street of the city centre. Via Berthollet 21, T: 011 669 8101, www.hotelpiemontese.it
€€ **Victoria**. An elegant boutique hotel in the heart of town. Via Nino Costa 4, T: 011 561 1909, www.hotelvictoria-torino.com

YOUTH HOSTEL

€ **Torino**, Via Alby 1, T: 011 6602939, hostelto@tin.it

RESTAURANTS

€€€ **Balbo**. Restaurant renowned for its delicious regional dishes. Closed Mon and July–Aug. Via Andrea Doria 11, T: 011 839 5775.
€€€ **Dai Saletta**. Good trattoria near the Parco del Valentino and Torino Esposizioni. Closed Sun and Aug. Via Belfiore 37, T: 011 668 7867.
€€€ **Del Cambio**. Restaurant famous for its 19th-century décor. Piazza Carignano 2, T: 011 543760.
€€ **Al Gatto Nero**. Restaurant famous for its grill. Closed Sun and Aug. Corso Turati 14, T: 011 590414.

€€ **Antiche Sere**. An excellent traditional *osteria* in the working-class quarter of Borgo San Paolo. Open evenings only, closed Sun, Aug and Dec–Jan. Via Cenischia 9, T: 011 385 4347.

€€ **Caval'd Brôns**. Well-known traditional restaurant. Closed midday Sat and Sun. Piazza San Carlo 157, T: 011 543 610.

€€ **C'Era una Volta**. Restaurant famous for its large portions of traditional regional fare. Open evenings only, closed Sun and Aug, Corso Vittorio Emanuele 41, T: 011 655 498.

€€ **Da Benito**. Restaurant famous for its seafood. Closed Mon and Aug. Corso Siracusa 142, T: 011 309 0353.

€€ **Ij Brandé**. Restaurant serving Barolo braised beef and other regional specialities. Closed Sun, midday Mon and Aug. Via Massena 5, T: 011 537 279.

€€ **Torricelli**. Restaurant serving traditional dishes with an innovative twist. Closed Sun, Aug and Jan. Via Torricelli 51, T: 011 599 814.

€€ **Tre Galline**. Traditional restaurant, in the same spot for three centuries. Closed Sun, midday Mon and Aug. Via Bellezia 37, T: 011 436 6553.

€ **L'Agrifoglio**. Small, friendly and delicious restaurant in the heart of town. Closed Sun, midday Mon and July–Aug. Via Accademia Albertina 38, T: 011 837 064.

€ **L'Osto dël Borgh Vej**. Tiny place offering good regional cuisine, near the duomo and Palazzo di Città; closed Sun and Aug. Via Torquato Tasso 7, T: 011 436 4843.

€ **Locanda Mongreno**. *Osteria* serving creative variations of traditional recipes, in the hills outside the city centre. Open evenings only, closed Mon, Aug and Jan. Strada Mongreno 50, T: 011 898 0417.

€ **Ostu**. Popular *osteria* and wine bar. Closed Sun and July–Aug. Via Cristoforo Colombo 63, T: 011 596 789.

€ **Porta di Savona**. The traditional place to go for honest, wholesome regional cuisine, in a warm friendly setting (crowded in the evening). Closed Mon, mid-day Tues and Aug. Piazza Vittorio Veneto 2, T: 011 817 3500.

CAFÉS & CONFECTIONERS

San Carlo, **Torino** and **Stratta**, all in Piazza San Carlo, are the city's top venues for pastries and confectionery. **Mulassano** and **Baratti**, both in Piazza Castello, are well-known cafés.

Al Bicerin, in Piazza della Consolata, takes its name from a drink combining coffee, chocolate, cream—even if you're not hungry or thirsty, go there to see the décor.

Fiorio, at Via Po 8, and **Platti**, at Corso Vittorio Emanuele II 72, also have good coffee, cakes and candies.

Caffetteria Viennese, at Corso Re Umberto 19g, has delicious hot chocolate.

Gertosio, at Via Lagrange 34, and **Giordano**, at Via San Domenico 21, are good for chocolates and pastries.

SPECIALITY FOOD SHOPS

The things for which Turin is most famous are chocolate, wine and breads (especially breadsticks, *grissini*). The best chocolate is at **Baratti & Milano**, Piazza Castello 29; **Confetteria Giordano**, Piazza Carlo Felice 69; **Peyrano**

Pfatisch, Corso Vittorio Emanuele II 76; **Laboratorio Artigianale del Giandujotto**, Via Cagliari 19b; **Peyrano**, Corso Moncalieri 47; **Pfatisch,** Via Sacchi 42; and **Stratta**, Piazza San Carlo 191. The most characteristic form of chocolate is the *giandujotto*, the famous long, triangular ingot that comes in a gold or silver wrapper; the chocolate is mixed with toasted, chopped hazelnuts. **Avvignano** and **T.R.**, in Piazza Carlo Felice, have *giandujotti* and other local confectionery.

The outstanding wines are Barolo (produced in the hills between Alba and Cuneo), Barbaresco (also made from the Nebbiolo grape), Dolcetto (from vineyards around Dogliani, Alba, Asti, Acqui and Ovada) and Barbera (the object of a historic rivalry between Alba and Asti). **Il Vinaio**, at Via Cibrario 38, has collector wines, especially Barolo. Other good places for wines are **Il Bottigliere**, Via San Francesco da Paola 43 (with snacks; open until midnight); and **La Petite Cave**, Via De Gasperi 2.

For *grissini*, try **Marta Bera**, Via San Tommaso 12; **Guala**, Piazza Statuto 13; **Panaté**, Via Palazzo di Città 6; and **Panificio Serra**, Via Palazzo di Città, Chieri. **Delicatesse**, at Via Madama Cristina 62, is an excellent choice for picnic supplies. For *agnolotti* and other fresh pastas, try **Giulio Gallo**, at Corso Sebastopoli 161.

CINEMA

There are some truly majestic cinemas in the city centre, successors to the first halls that helped make the history of film. The Lux in Galleria San Federico is a rare example of Art Deco interior design; the Rationalist Ideal was once the biggest cinema in Italy, whereas the Massimo in Via Montebello is a municipal multi-cinema that stages the events of the Museo Nazionale del Cinema and screens interesting retrospectives or thematic film series.

SHOPPING & MARKETS

The main shopping streets in central Turin are Via Roma, Via Lagrange, Via Carlo Alberto, Via Mazzini, Via Cavour, Via Maria Vittoria, Via Santa Teresa, Via Pietro Micca, Via Monte di Pietà, Via Garibaldi, Via Barbaroux, Via dei Mercanti, Via Santi Agostino and Via San Tommaso. Here you'll find mainly designer clothing, furniture and housewares. Via Po and the streets around the Mole Antonelliana are for lovers of antiques and antiquarian and secondhand books.

Turin also has many markets, notably the Gran Balôn in Borgo Dora, where you can find period magazines, toys, antiques and more. Every morning the market at Porta Palazzo (Piazza della Repubblica) overflows with thousands of stalls selling fruit, vegetables, flowers, clothing; there is also a periodic antiques market (second Sun of the month).

FESTIVALS & EVENTS: TURIN

Festa di San Giovanni Battista (patron saint, 24 June), celebrated with music, food, fireworks on the Po River and a famous bonfire in Piazza San Carlo; *Ad Ovest di Paperino*, cabaret festival, June–July; *Colonia Sonora*, music festival, July; *Settembre Musica*, chamber music series, with an accent on contemporary composers, Sept; *Torino Danza*, biennial contemporary dance festival, even years; Torino Film Festival, Nov; Torino International Jazz Festival, July.

FESTIVALS & EVENTS: REGIONAL

Agliè *Sagra del Torcetto*, festival centred on a small curved biscuit made of butter, mid-April.

Carmagnola *Sagra del Peperone* or pepper festival, late Aug early Sept.

Chieri *Nel Borgo di Landolfo*, pageant in 14th-century costume, late May; *Sagra della bagna caôda*, dedicated to the famous peasant dish and to the cuisine of the area, second Sunday in Nov.

Grugliasco *Palio della Gru* evoking the plague and St Roch's miraculous cure of 1599: the seven districts of the town compete in sport and folk competitions.

Marentino Honey fair offering rare tastes of dandelion honey or cherry honey, last Sun in Sept.

Moncalieri *Il Beato Bernardo* (patron saint), pageant in medieval costume, second Sat in July; *Fera dij Subiét*, whistle and flute fair, and *Orti e Fiori in Piazza*, garden fair, October (the latter ends with a record-breaking pot of tripe: 1,500 kilos cooked over a wood fire for more than six hours); *Bue Grasso* festival (second Sunday in December).

Pecetto Torinese *Sagra della ciliegia* or cherry festival, second Sunday in June.

Piossasco *Piossasco nei secoli* celebrating the 13th-century reconciliation between the lords of Piossasco and the bishop of Turin.

Poirino Festival of the tench, a delicate fresh-water fish, May.

Rivoli *C'era una Volta un Re*. Historic re-enactment of the abdication of Vittorio Amedeo II in favour of his son Carlo Emanuele III (at Rivoli, 1730) second week in Sept.

CARNIVAL

This period is particularly important in Turin. Around Chieri, where rural folk traditions still survive, you can watch goats fighting, donkeys racing and a procession of allegorical floats. The most distinctive aspect of the festival is the exhibition of farmer-poets, who publicly challenge each other at the end of the procession of carnival floats in ironic verse spoken in dialect. Rivoli, too, celebrates carnival with a historic parade in which 40 masked groups take part: the Sunday before Ash Wednesday, dozens of floats parade along Corso Francia accompanied by bands and majorettes. The most coveted mask is that of Amedeo VI of Savoy, called the *Conte Verde*.

THE NORTHWEST

The northwest of Piedmont is a land of great natural beauty. It is also a place of historical significance, the theatre of religious struggles whose violence and duration made 'Piedmont' sound in the 17th century as 'Ulster' sounded in the 20th.

THE VALLI VALDESI

The Valle del Chisone and the Valle del Pellice, also known as the Valli Valdesi, have been inhabited for centuries by the Protestant Waldensians or Vaudois. **Torre Pellice** their main centre, and has a Waldensian church and college, and a museum illustrating the history of the religious community. It originated in the south of France about 1170, under the inspiration of Peter Waldo, a Lyons merchant who abjured commerce and started preaching the gospel. His adherents were formally condemned by the Lateran Council in 1184, and persecution drove them to take refuge in these remote valleys. About 1532 the Vaudois became absorbed in the Swiss Reformation. When renewed persecution broke out in 1655 under Carlo Emanuele II, assisted by the troops of Louis XIV, a strong protest was raised by Cromwell in England, and Milton wrote his famous sonnet (*see below*). Further persecution followed the revocation of the Edict of Nantes (1685), but the remnant of the Vaudois, about 2,600 in number, were allowed to retreat to Geneva. In 1698 Henri Arnaud led a band of 800 to the reconquest of their valleys, and a rupture between Louis XIV and Vittorio Amedeo of Savoy was followed by their recognition as subjects of Savoy.

On the Valdesi

Avenge, O Lord, thy slaughter'd saints, whose bones
Lie scatter'd on the Alpine mountains cold,
Ev'n them who kept thy truth so pure of old,
When all our fathers worshipp'd stocks and stones;
Forget not: in thy book record their groanes
Who were thy sheep and in their ancient fold
Slain by the bloody Piemontese that roll'd
Mother with infant down the rocks. Their moans
The vales redoubl'd to the hills, and they
To Heav'n. Their martyr'd blood and ashes sow
O'er all th' Italian fields where still doth sway
The triple tyrant; that from these may grow
A hundred-fold, who having learnt thy way
Early may fly the Babylonian woe.

John Milton, Sonnet XVIII—On the Late Massacre in Piedmont, 1655

EXPLORING THE VALLI VALDESI

Around Pinerolo

Pinerolo, the historic capital of the Princes of Acaia, ancestors of the Savoy kings, is in a beautiful position at the foot of the hills where the Chisone and Lemina valleys merge into the Piedmontese plain. The fortress of Pignerol was under French control from 1630 to 1706 and, because of its remoteness from Paris, was used as a state prison.

The hub of life in Pinerolo is the large Piazza Vittorio Veneto, with the adjacent Piazza Cavour, beyond which are the public gardens and the Waldensian church (1860). In the old military school, founded in 1849 and closed down in 1943, is a museum of the history of Italian cavalry regiments. The restored Gothic cathedral stands at the centre of the old town. Via Trento and Via Principi d'Acaia, with ancient houses, ascend to the early 14th-century palace of the Princes of Acaia and the church of San Maurizio (also early 14th century, though reconstructed in 1470), where eight princes are buried. South of Pinerolo is **Cavour**, ancestral home of the great statesman's family. Giovanni Giolitti, five times prime minister of Italy, died here in 1928.

The **Valle del Chisone** is remarkable for the fortifications built in 1727 by Vittorio Amedeo II and his son Carlo Emanuele III to defend **Fenestrelle** (1154m), now a summer resort surrounded by forests between the peaks of the Orsiera (2878m) and the Albergian (3043m). The fortifications climb up the hillside from the Chisone to Pra Catinat, with numerous forts, barracks and bridges, and a five-storey palace used also as a prison, connected to a church by a splendid covered ramp with 4,000 steps, about 1km long. The buildings are now abandoned, but can be visited by appointment (*T: 0121 83600*). **Pragelato** is noted for its alpine flowers and for the honey they produce. The famous ski resort of Sestriere is described below.

THE VALLE DI SUSA

The Valle di Susa in the western corner of Piedmont has been crossed by travellers and armies on their way across the Alps for many centuries. Before it was transferred to Turin in 1713, it belonged to the Dauphiny (the carved symbol of the dolphin can still be seen in some places). In the lower valley is the medieval abbey church of **Sant'Antonio di Ranverso**, one of the most interesting medieval buildings in Piedmont. Founded in 1188, it was extended in the 13th–14th centuries, and the apse and unusual façade were added in the 15th century. The interior (ring for the custodian except Fri and Mon) has 15th-century frescoes and a polyptych of the *Nativity* by native Piedmontese artist Defendente Ferrari (1531) on the high altar. This is his only documented work, though much else has been attributed to him. The presbytery and sacristy contain frescoes by Giacomo Jaquerio The tower and the little cloister are Romanesque.

Avigliana, an ancient little town with many fine 15th-century mansions, is dominated by a ruined castle of the Counts of Savoy. The church of San Giovanni contains two paintings by Defendente Ferrari. Above the valley, with a fine view of the Alps, is the Sacra di San Michele (*open daily 9.30–12.30 & 3–5.30*), an important abbey founded c. 1000, enlarged in the 12th century, and suppressed in 1622.

Susa, on the Dora Riparia, is on the main roads from France through the Mont Cenis tunnel and over the passes of Mont Cenis and Montgenèvre (Monginevro). It preserves some interesting buildings of Roman Segusium, the seat of the Gaulish chief Cottius, who received the dignity of prefect from Augustus Caesar and gave his name to the surrounding Cottian Alps (Alpi Cozie). The town was burned in 1173 by Barbarossa in revenge for its rebellion against him in 1168. **San Giusto**, a cathedral since 1772, is an interesting 11th-century church with a massive tower. It has 14th-century stalls; an incomplete polyptych attributed to Bergognone, and the *Triptych of Rocciamelone*; and a Flemish brass of 1358 (shown on 5 August). Via Archi ascends from the 4th-century Porta Savoia past the Parco d'Augusto to the **Arco di Augusto**, an arch erected in 8 BC by Cottius in honour of Augustus, decorated with processional reliefs. Higher up is a double Roman arch, with remains of an aqueduct and Roman baths. Piazza della Torre, with the best of the town's medieval mansions (13th century), lies below an 11th-century tower of the castle of Countess Adelaide, the heiress whose marriage in 1045 to Duke Otho united the Savoy holdings on either side of the Alps. Southwest of the town is the 13th-century church of San Francesco, with ruined 15th-century frescoes, near a small Roman amphitheatre (2nd century AD).

North of Susa is the **Mont Cenis Pass** (Col du Mont Cenis; 2083m), one of the historic passes over the Alps, crossed by the King of the Franks, Pepin the Short, in 755, and by his son Charlemagne in 774. Many other sovereigns and their armies followed in their footsteps. **Novalesa** has remains of a Benedictine abbey founded in 726, a famous centre of learning in the Middle Ages (Charlemagne stayed here in 773). It was suppressed under Napoleon, but the Benedictines returned here in 1973, and now run a centre for book restoration. The main church was rebuilt in 1712, but several 11th-century chapels survive, one of them dedicated to St Heldrad (died 842), abbot here for 30 years. In the parish church of Novalesa are some paintings donated by Napoleon in 1805 to the abbot of the hospice of Mont Cenis, including a good copy of Caravaggio's *Crucifixion of St Peter*. The hospice was built at St Heldrad's request in c. 815, by Louis I of France. It now lies submerged under the huge lake of Moncenisio (1974m), beyond the French border.

That's progress

Before the carriage road was constructed by Napoleon in 1803–13 the old road to Italy terminated here, and travellers continued on mule-back or were carried over the pass in a wicker chair. Edward Gibbon, on his way from Lausanne to Rome in 1764, chose the latter means of transport and praised the 'dexterous and intrepid Chairmen of the Alps'.

In the upper Valle di Susa is the fort of **Exilles** (strengthened by the great French military engineer Marshal Vauban in 1799), on the site of many previous impregnable fortifications that defended the frontier with the Dauphiny. **Salbertrand** was the site of a famous defeat of the French by the Waldensians in 1689. It has a fine parish church (1506–36). The lovely woods on the left bank of the Dora Riparia are now in a protected area. **Sauze d'Oulx** (1510m) is a well-known ski resort.

Bardonecchia is another ski resort (1312m) in a wide basin at the junction of several valleys. It is at the end of the busy Mont Cenis road tunnel (Traforo del Frejus), the second longest road tunnel in Europe. The railway tunnel across the frontier was begun in 1857 and finished in 1871 to the plans of the engineers Sommeiller, Grandis, and Grattoni. The first great Transalpine tunnel, it reaches a summit level of 1295m. It had an immediate effect on world communications, speeding the transmission of mail from the East to northern Europe by several days, with Brindisi replacing Marseilles as the transit port. Originally 12.2km long, the tunnel was realigned in 1881 and again after the Second World War, and is now 12.8km long. Cars were carried by train through the tunnel from 1935 until the opening of the road tunnel in 1980.

Southwest of Oulx is **Cesana Torinese**, where the painter Paul Cézanne spent much time: his family originally came from here, though they had moved to France in the 18th century, and Cézanne himself was born in Aix-en-Provence. The **Col du Montgenèvre** (1860m), the frontier before 1947, is one of the older, as well as one of the lower passes over the main chain of the Alps. It was crossed by the Roman imperial armies of Marius, Augustus and Theodosius, by the Holy Roman Emperor Charlemagne, and again in 1494 by Charles VIII of France and his army, dragging with them 600 cannon. The present road was constructed by Napoleon in 1802–07. French armies used it to enter Italy by in 1818 and 1859; and in 1917–18 French reinforcements were sent to the Italian armies over this pass. The road descends to Briançon.

Sestriere (2030m), the most fashionable ski resort in Piedmont, has become one of the better-known resorts in Europe since it was first developed in 1928–32. Unfortunately, this has led to a lot of new building.

IVREA & THE CANAVESE

The pleasant old town of **Ivrea** was the Roman Eporedia, a bulwark in the 1st century BC against the Salassian Gauls of the Upper Dora. In the Middle Ages its marquises rose to power, and Arduino of Ivrea was crowned King of Italy in 1002. The town has expanded as an industrial centre since the Olivetti typewriter factories were founded here in 1908.

The Ponte Vecchio, or old bridge, was built across the Dora Baltea in 1716 on older foundations. In the upper part of the town, approached by steep lanes, is the cathedral, of which two apsidal towers and the crypt date from the 11th century. Look in the raised ambulatory for a row of columns taken from older buildings. The sacristy contains two paintings by the 16th-century Piedmontese painter Defendente Ferrari.

The castle was built by Aymon de Challant (1358) for Amedeo VI, with four tall angle towers, one of which was partially destroyed by an explosion in 1676. It was used as a prison from 1700 to 1970 and has since been restored. The bishop's palace has Roman and medieval fragments in its loggia, and a small diocesan museum occupies San Nicola da Tolentino. The municipal museum, in the Neoclassical Piazza Ottinetti (1843), has Oriental and archaeological collections.

In the public park by the river, below the Dora bridges, is the Romanesque bell tower (1041) of Santo Stefano. The extensive Olivetti works, built between 1898 and 1971, extend beyond the railway station. They incorporate the late Gothic convent of San Bernardino with an interesting fresco cycle by Giovanni Martino Spanzotti (late 15th century).

The **Castello di Masino**, one of the best preserved castles in Piedmont, stands on an isolated wooded hill south of Ivrea, surrounded by a *borgo* (*open Feb–Dec Tues–Sun 10–12 & 2–5; guided visits every hour*). It occupies the site of an 11th-century castle, but was rebuilt in the following centuries. Its present appearance dates largely from the 18th century, when it was the residence of Carlo Francesco II, viceroy of Sardinia, and his brother Tommaso Valperga, abbot of Caluso. At this time the double ramp up to the entrance was constructed, and many of the rooms were furnished. These include the print room with French etchings, the library, the Spanish ambassador's bedroom, and a gallery lined with family portraits. Tommaso Valperga, a friend of the poet Vittorio Alfieri, designed the decoration in the poets' gallery.

The medieval northeast tower was adapted in 1730 as a ballroom. The rectangular keep has a lower room, frescoed in the 1690s with coats of arms, and an upper hall, with numerous 18th-century portraits of the royal house of Savoy. The remains of King Arduino (brought here in the 18th century from the castle of Agliè) are preserved in the little family chapel. The stable block has a collection of carriages, open at weekends. The castle is surrounded by an attractive formal garden, the design of which survives in part from the 17th and 18th centuries, and a large park (*open Feb–Dec Tues–Sun 10–5 or 6*), laid out in 1840.

The Valle dell'Orco is the chief valley of the **Canavese**, a subalpine district extending to the foot of the Gran Paradiso. The valley extends southeast of Ivrea. **Valperga**, in the upper part of the valley near Cuorgnè, has a restored castle and a charming little 15th-century church (frescoes). Above rises the **Santuario di Belmonte**, founded by King Arduino of Ivrea, but rebuilt in the 14th century. The 12th-century Castello Ducale at **Agliè** (*open for guided visits: summer, Thur–Sun 10–12.30 & 2–6.30; winter, 10–12.30 & 2–5.30*) was rebuilt as a ducal palace in 1646, reconstructed by the Savoy in 1763—when the park was laid out—and again by Carlo Felice in 1825. The interior has 19th-century decorations and Roman sculptures.

At **Chivasso**, where the Orco meets the Po, the 15th-century church contains a painting by Defendente Ferrari (1470–1535), who was born in the town. San Benigno has remains of the **abbey of Fruttuaria**, where King Arduino died, a monk, in 1013.

PRACTICAL INFORMATION

GETTING AROUND

• **By rail:** The main line between Turin and Chambery (France) traverses the Val di Susa. Slow Regionali reach Bussoleno (where there are connections for Susa, just 5mins away) in 45mins and Oulx-Claviere-Sestriere in 1hr 15mins. Fast Eurocity trains rush non-stop to Oulx-Claviere-Sestriere in 50mins. Ivrea is c. 1hr from Turin on the Aosta line; a change is sometimes necessary at Chivasso. Minor lines run from Turin Porta Nuova Station to Pinerolo (40mins), where there are connections to Torre Pellice (25mins more); and from Turin Porta Susa or Dora Station to Lanzo Torinese (65mins), with some trains continuing to Ceres (20mins more).

INFORMATION OFFICES

Ivrea Corso Vercelli 1, T: 0125 618 131, www.eponet.it/turismo/apt
Pinerolo Viale Giolitti, 7/9, T: 0121 795 589, www.montagnedoc.it
Sauze d'Oulx Piazza Assietta 18, T: 0122 858 009.
Val di Susa Piazza Garambois 5, Oulx, T: 0122 831 596.

HOTELS

Chiaverano
€€ **Castello San Giuseppe**. A magnificently restored and converted former Carmelite convent, on a hilltop with a garden and fine views. Previous house-guests have included Eleonora Duse and Ginger Rogers. Località San Giuseppe, T: 0125 424 370, www.castellosangiuseppe.it

Ivrea
€€ **Sirio**. A family-managed place with a popular restaurant, on Lake Sirio. Via Lago di Sirio 85, T: 0125 424 247, www.hotelsirio.it

Quincinetto
€ **Mini Hotel Praile**. Small, friendly and inexpensive. Via Umberto I 5, T: 0125 757 188.

Sauze d'Oulx
€€ **Il Capricorno**. A cordial, family-run place with just 7 rooms, in the forest at 1800m. Open June–Sept and Dec–March. Via Case Sparse 21, Le Clotes, T: 0122 850 273, www. chaletilcapricorno.it

Sestriere
€€€ **Grand Hotel Principi di Piemonte**. *The* place to stay in *the* resort in Piedmont, set in a beautiful larch grove somewhat outside the town. Open Dec–Apr and July–Aug. Via Sauze 3, T: 0122 7941, F: 0122 755 411, www.framonhotels.com

RESTAURANTS

Bardonecchia
€ **La Ciaburna**. Rustic restaurant with good food and excellent wines. Località Melezet 48, T: 0122 999849.

Cavour
€ **La Posta**. Restaurant (with rooms) in a historic building, renowned for its delicious regional cuisine. Closed Fri and July–Aug, Via dei Fossi 4, T: 0121 69989.

Ivrea
€ **La Trattoria**. Unpretentious trattoria

strong on local tradition. Closed Sun
and July.

Lessolo
€ **La Miniera**. Good country cooking
in an old mine. Closed Mon–Wed and
Jan. Via delle Miniere 9, Località
Valcava, T: 0125 58618.

Pinerolo
€€ **Locanda della Capreria Occitana**.
Famous cheese makers, also serving
country meals. Open Fri–Sat evenings,
all day Sun. Via Nazionale 370r,
Abbadia Alpina.

Quincinetto
€€ **Da Giovanni**. Good views, great
food. Closed Tues evening and Wed. Via
Fontana Riola 3, Montellina, T: 0125
757447.

San Giorgio Canavese
€ **Trattoria della Luna**. Good, simple
lunches. Closed evenings, Mon and
July–Aug. Piazza Ippolito San Giorgio
12, T: 0124 32184.

Sant'Antonio di Susa
€€ **Il Sentiero dei Franchi**.
Traditional trattoria in a clifftop hamlet
above Sant'Antonio. Closed Tues and
June. Borgata Cresto 16, T: 011
9631747.

Scarmagno
€€ **La Pergola**. Good traditional

restaurant, 5km south of Ivrea. Closed
Mon and Jan. Via Montalenghe 59,
Masero. T: 0125 712747.

Torre Pellice
€€ **Flipot**. Excellent regional cooking,
in an old farmhouse. Closed Mon and
Tues (except June–Sept). Corso Gramsci
17, T: 0121 91236.

Usseaux
€€ **Lago del Laux** (with rooms).
Small and delicious, on the lakeside
1km south of the town. Closed Wed
and Nov–March; reservations required.
Via al Lago 7, T: 0121 83944, F: 0121
83944.

FESTIVALS & MARKETS

Chivasso *Assedio di Chivasso*. Re-enactment of a siege of 1705, last weekend
in Sept. Carnival is also important here,
with a three-hour-long procession of
folk groups and musical bands from all
over Europe.
Ivrea Carnival celebrations have been
held at Ivrea for some 200 years. The
most important events take place from
the Thursday before Ash Wednesday
(with a famous battle of oranges).

CUNEO & THE LANGHE

The province of Cuneo lies in the southwest corner of Piedmont, between the Alps, the source of the river Po and its plain, and the low hills known as the Langhe. The main towns are Saluzzo, below the splendid mountain peak of Monviso, and at the head of the Po Valley, Cuneo with its Alpine valleys, Alba and Bra in the Langhe and Roero districts, and Mondovì. The area is famed for its cuisine—considered by many to be the best in Italy. There are grounds for arguing that the restaurants (of which there are thousands) could form the sole substance of a tour of the region, not just because they are unusually good (which they are), but because each valley and each village has its own, peculiar culinary tradition. This is also the home of the Nebbiolo grape, the variety that produces two of Italy's most famous wines: Barolo and Barbaresco.

CUNEO & ENVIRONS

Cuneo, approached by a monumental viaduct over the Stura, is a pleasant provincial capital deriving its name from the wedge (*cuneo*) of land at the confluence of the Gesso and the Stura. The huge arcaded piazza, the cathedral, and the public buildings were mostly rebuilt after a destructive siege in 1744, when Spain, trying to regain the Italian territory she had lost after the War of the Spanish Succession, was defeated here by Austria. Via Roma, with heavy arcades, is the main street of the old town. **San Francesco**, a deconsecrated church of 1227, with a good portal (1481), houses a small museum. Magnificent boulevards have replaced the former ramparts. Cuneo is the gateway to the southern Cottian Alps (Alpi Cozie), approached by the Val Maira and the Val Varaita.

In the valley of the Gesso are the **Terme di Valdieri** (975m)—rebuilt in 1952–53—with hot sulphur springs. Monte Matto (3088m) and Cima di Argentera (3297m), the highest peak of the Maritime Alps, lie within the **Parco Regionale Alpi Marittime**, a protected area once part of the royal hunting reserve of Valdieri-Entracque. The Col du Clapier on the ridge here is thought by some scholars to have been Hannibal's route across the Alps.

At the head of the wooded Valle Stura, with hot sulphur springs at Terme di Vinadio (1274m), is the **Colle della Maddalena** (1991m), an easy pass with meadows noted for their flowers, and free from snow between mid-May and mid-October. Francis I passed this way on his invasion of Italy in 1515, and Napoleon decreed that 'the imperial road from Spain to Italy' should be carried over the pass.

The Palanfrè park in the upper Val Vermenagna has remarkable beechwoods and interesting wildlife. **Limone Piemonte** (998m) is a large village among open pastures, one of the older ski resorts in Italy, with a 12th–14th-century church. The French frontier is quite nearby, on the Colle di Tenda. The districts of Tende and La Brigue, although parts of the County of Nice, were given to Italy in the Franco-Italian treaty of 1860, by courtesy of Napoleon III, because a great part of the territory was a favourite hunting-ground of Vittorio Emanuele II. In 1947 they were returned to France, an act which enjoyed majority local support.

Mondovì, east of Cuneo, grew up in the Middle Ages and by the 16th century probably had more inhabitants than any other city in Piedmont. The architect Francesco Gallo (1672–1750), a native, designed numerous buildings in the town. It was the birthplace of Giovanni Giolitti (1842–1928), who was five times prime minister of Italy from 1892 to 1921 and who introduced universal suffrage. In the upper town of Mondovì Piazza, with an attractive large square, is the elaborate Chiesa della Missione (1678), with a trompe-l'oeil vault-painting by the great Jesuit architect Andrea Pozzo. The cathedral was built by Gallo in 1743–63. From the garden of the Belvedere there is a fine view.

THE LANGHE

The Langhe and the neighbouring district of Roero, in the northeast corner of the province, are crossed by the River Tanaro. The low rolling hills are famous for their vineyards, which produce excellent wines (*see box*). The territory includes numerous chestnut, pine and oak woods, particularly beautiful in the autumn. The main towns are Alba and Bra, and there are good restaurants in the area, many of them specialising in truffles (found locally).

Bra and Alba

Bra is a pleasant town with a small archaeological museum in the 15th-century Palazzo Traversa, containing finds from the Roman Pollentia (now Pollenzo, south of Bra). Also south of Bra is **Cherasco**, again of Roman origin, which has a Visconti castle of 1348, a 13th-century church and 17th-century palaces. At **Alba**, further east, the historic centre has preserved its polygonal plan from Roman days, and some tall medieval brick tower-houses and decorated house-fronts survive. The duomo, over-restored in the 19th century, contains fine carved and inlaid stalls by Bernardino da Fossato (1512). In the town hall is a painting of the *Madonna and Child*, a good work by the local 16th-century artist Macrino d'Alba, and a *Concert* attributed to Mattia Preti (17th century). The deconsecrated church of the Maddalena (rebuilt in 1749) contains the **Museo Federico Eusebio** (*open Oct–May Tues–Fri 3–6, Sat & Sun 9.30–12.30 & 3–6; June–Sept Tues–Fri 4–7, Sat & Sun 9.30–12.30 & 4–7*), with local Neolithic finds, Roman material, and natural history and ethnographic sections. **San Giovanni** contains a *Madonna* by Barnaba da Modena (1377) and two more paintings by Macrino. San Domenico has 14th- and 15th-century frescoes. Alba is also the truffle capital of Italy, as the many signs around town (*tartuffi*) announce. Among the best-known truffle vendors are Martino, at Corso Cortemila 43; Morra, at Piazza Pertinace 2; and Ponzio, at Via Vittorio Emanuele 26. In autumn (Oct–Dec) there is a Saturday-morning truffle market at the Maddalena, on Via Vittorio Emanuele.

BAROLO & BARBARESCO

The Nebbiolo grape, which grows on the hillsides of the Langhe, produces what is without doubt the most prestigious and aristocratic of all Italian wines. Nebbiolo is grown only in the triangle formed between Treiso, Neive and Barbaresco, and is native to the village of Barolo. The wines Barolo and Barbaresco are its two greatest expressions. These are real terroir wines, and the best growths are indicated on the label, with *sorì* and *bricco* the rough equivalents of a French *cru*. The parallels with France are not accidental: it was a French winemaker, Louis Oudart, who first showed the Piedmontese how to make dry red wine from Nebbiolo. Before

that it had been used to make sweet whites. One of the greatest Barbaresco producers today is Angelo Gaja. His family settled in Piedmont over 300 years ago; by the 1960s they were a world name. He caused a sensation when he opted out of the DOC system, in order to avoid rules and produce the kind of wine he wanted. Superb wines like Sorì Tildin and Costa Russi are not traded as Barbaresco, but are labelled Langhe Nebbiolo.

Barolo is the *ne plus ultra* of Italian wine. Like Barbaresco, it takes its name from the name of a village: Barolo, which lies to the southwest of Alba. Much Barolo comes from the La Morra region: perfectly positioned and with its own special microclimate. Its limey soils produce wines with excellent fruity aromas. The sandstone terroir of Castiglione Falleto to the east and Monforte d'Alba to the north yield denser, more robust wines. The basis of viticulture here is the family winery. The best known are Bruno Giacosa, Giacomo Conterno, Elio Altare, Domenico Clerico, Angelo Gaja and Costa di Bussia, which cleverly blends tradition with modern technology.

SALUZZO & ENVIRONS

Saluzzo, north of Cuneo, is the historic seat of a line of marquises famous in the 15th and 16th centuries; the upper town is particularly attractive. The large cathedral was built in 1481–1511, and the ancient streets lead up to the castle (turned into a prison in 1821). Just below it is the church of San Giovanni, erected in 1330, with a choir extension of 1480 containing finely crafted stalls and the tomb of Marquess Lodovico II (d. 1503). On the north side are the cloister and chapter house, the latter with a monument of 1528 to Galeazzo Cavassa. Galeazzo's former residence is further along

Small chapel in the fertile Piedmont landscape.

Via San Giovanni: the charming 15th–16th-century Casa Cavassa (*open Wed–Sun 9–12 & 2–5.15*). Restored in 1883, it is interesting for its architecture and furniture; the marble portal was added in the early 16th century by Matteo Sanmicheli. Since 1891 it has housed the municipal museum, illustrating the history of the marquisate. There is also a section devoted to Silvio Pellico (1789–1854), the patriot author born in the town.

The Castello della Manta (*open Feb–Sept Tues–Sun 10–1 & 2–6, park 10–6; Oct–Dec Tues–Sun 10–1 & 2–5, park 10–5*), to the south, is a medieval castle rebuilt by the Saluzzo della Manta family at the beginning of the 15th century, later modified and 'reconstructed' in 1860. The church contains early-15th-century frescoes and the late-16th-century funerary chapel of Michelantonio di Saluzzo. In the Palazzo di Michelantonio, with a Mannerist staircase, one of the rooms (1563) has a ceiling decorated with painted grotesques and stuccoes. The Castello di Valerano has remarkable frescoes (c. 1420; restored 1989), in the International Gothic style, attributed to the Maestro della Manta. The frescoes show 18 historical heroes and heroines in contemporary costume, and allegorical scenes of the *Fountain of Eternal Youth*. They form one of the more interesting secular fresco cycles of this period.

A short distance southwest of Saluzzo is **Castellar**, where the 14th-century castle (reconstructed in the 19th century and after the last war) contains the Museo Aliberti (*open Oct–Dec Sun 2–6*), devoted to the uniforms of the Italian army from the Unification to the Second World War.

West of Saluzzo is **Revello** where, next to the town hall, the Cappella Marchionale, with 15th–16th-century frescoes, is all that remains of the summer palace built by Marquess Lodovico II.

Savigliano, east of Saluzzo, is the birthplace of the astronomer Giovanni Schiaparelli (1835–1910). Schiaparelli's observation of striated patterns on the surface of Mars led to a flood of investigation, with scientists hoping to find life on the planet. Near the central Piazza Santarosa are the Museo Civico and a *gipsoteca* with works by the sculptor Davide Calandra (1856–1915).

At **Racconigi**, north of Savigliano, is a castle (*open Tues–Sun 9–1 & 2–5*), built by the Savoy kings. The front overlooking the park (1676) is by Guarino Guarini (*see p. 48*). Umberto of Savoy was born here in 1904 (the ex-king died in exile in 1983). The large park can be visited in summer (*open Sun 2–7 or by appointment*).

North of Saluzzo near the Po is **Staffarda**, with a fine Cistercian abbey founded in 1135 and well restored. Since 1750 the abbey has been owned by the Order of Santi Maurizio e Lazzaro. It contains a polyptych by Oddone Pascale (1531) and an altar by Agostino Nigra (1525).

The French frontier

The source of the Po is at **Piano del Re** (2050m), in an area interesting for its flora. The first 235km of the banks of the Po are now protected as a park by the Region of Piedmont.

The splendid mountain of **Monviso** (3841m) was climbed by Quintino Sella, founder of the Club Alpino Italiano, in 1863. Beneath the Colle delle Traversette (2950m) is a tunnel built by Marquis Lodovico II in 1480 for the use of merchants trading with Dauphiny. It leads into the French valley of the Guil and Abriès. This pass is one of several thought by scholars to have been Hannibal's route over the Alps.

In the Valle Varaita, on the southern slopes of Monviso, is **Casteldelfino** (1295m), a village named from a castle founded in 1336, once the centre of the Dauphins' Cisalpine territory. The **Colle dell'Agnello** (2699m) pass on the French frontier was often used by invading armies: it was crossed by the French hero Bayard in 1515 and by Philip, Duke of Parma, in 1743.

PRACTICAL INFORMATION

GETTING AROUND

• **By road:** Buses run several times daily from Turin to Cuneo via Saluzzo in c. 2hrs 30mins; also from Cuneo to Limone.
• **By rail:** The main rail line serving Cuneo and its province is the Turin–Savona; slow local Regionali, Interregionali and Diretti make the run from Turin to Cuneo in c. 1hr 15mins. The trip from Savona to Cuneo takes about the same time (Genoa–Savona is c. 20mins more). Branch lines connect Cuneo to Saluzzo, Mondovì and Ventimiglia. Alba is served by another branch line, between Asti, Bra and Cavallermaggiore, where you can change for Cuneo.

INFORMATION OFFICES

Alba Piazza Medford, T: 0173 35833, www.langheroero.it
Cuneo Via Vittorio Amedeo II 13, T: 0171 690 217, www.cuneoholiday.com
Mondovì Viale Vittorio Veneto 17, T: 0174 40389.
Saluzzo Via Griselda 6, T: 0175 46710.

HOTELS

Alba
€€ **I Castelli**. A large, modern establishment recently built just outside the city centre. Corso Torino 14, T: 0173 361 978, www.hotel-icastelli.com
€€ **Villa la Meridiana-Cascina Reine**. Seven rooms and two suites on a beautiful estate in the hills above the town.

Località Altavilla 9, T: 0173 440 112, www.guestinitaly.com/countryside/n001_3.htm
€ **Savona**. A friendly, family-run place with its own in-house *pasticceria*. Via Roma 1, T: 0173 440 440, www.hotelsavona.com

Bra
€ **Elizabeth**. Central, comfortable and inexpensive. Piazza Giolitti 8, T: 0172 422486, hotel.elizabeth@libero.it
€ **Giardini**. In a renovated townhouse. Piazza XX Settembre 28, T: 0172 412866, albergogiardini@libero.it

Cuneo
€€ **Principe**. Distinguished and well located, in the heart of town. Piazza Galimberti 5, T: 0171 693 355, www.hotel-principe.it
€ **Royal Superga**. Comfortable family-run establishment. Via Pascal 3, T: 0171 693223.

La Morra
€ **Villa Carita**. Five rooms and one suite on a lovely country estate among the vineyards. Open March–Dec. Via Roma 105, T: 0173 509 633, www.villacarita.it

Limone Piemonte
€€ **Grand Palais Excelsior**. A grand old hotel brought back nicely as an informal, family place. Open June–Sept and Dec–Apr. Largo Roma 9, T: 0171 929 002, www.grandexcelsior.com
€€ **Le Ginestre**. Modern with a lovely garden and good views of the valley. Open Dec–Easter and July–Sept. Via Nizza 68 (1km south), T: 0171 927 596.

Mondovì
€ **Park**. Quietly elegant and reasonably

priced, in a park. Via Delvecchio 2, T: 0174 46666, www.parkhotel.cn.it

Monforte d'Alba
€€ **Villa Beccaris**. 17th-century villa in a park amid hills and vineyards. Open Feb–Nov. Via Bava Beccaris 1, T: 0173 78158, www.villabeccaris.it

Saluzzo
€ **Astor**, Piazza Garibaldi 39. Centrally located and recently renovated. T: 0175 45506.
€€ **Griselda**. Modern and comfortable. Corso XXVII Aprile 13, T: 0175 47484, F: 0175 47489.

Santa Vittoria d'Alba
€€ **Castello di Santa Vittoria**. A particularly tranquil place, in a former castle, with good restaurant. Open March–Dec. T: 0172 478 198.

Verduno
€€ **Real Castello**. A quiet old castle, a Savoy residence dating from the 18th century. Open March–Nov. Via Umberto I 9, T: 0172 470 125, www.castellodiverduno.com

YOUTH HOSTEL

Pietraporzio (Cuneo)
€ **Al Tenibres**, Via Nazionale 8, T: 0171 96602.

RESTAURANTS

Alba
€€ **Il Vicoletto**. Excellent renditions of traditional local dishes. Closed Mon and July–Aug. Via Bertero 6, T: 0173 363 196.
€ **Lalibera**. Traditional *osteria*. Closed Sun and midday Mon, Jan and Feb. Via Pertinace 24a, T: 0173 293 155.
€ **Osteria dell'Arco**. Restaurant

renowned for its warm friendly atmosphere and excellent regional cuisine. Closed Sun, midday Mon, July and Jan. Piazza Savona 5, T: 0173 363 974.
€ **Osteria Italia**. Traditional *osteria* 5km outside Alba. Closed Wed (except in Oct) and Jan–Feb. Frazione San Rocco Seno d'Elvio, T: 0173 441 547.

Barbaresco
€€ **Antica Torre**. Good traditional restaurant. Closed Sun evening, Mon and Aug Via Torino 8, T: 0173 635 170.

Barolo
€€ **La Cantinella**. Traditional *osteria-trattoria*. Closed Mon evening, Tues (except in autumn) and Aug. Via Acquagelata 4a, T: 0173 56267.
€€ **Locanda nel Borgo Antico**. Family *osteria* serving good local fare. Closed Wed, Feb and July–Aug Piazza del Municipio 2, T: 0173 56355.

Boves
€€€ **Al Rododendro**. Restaurant serving outstanding creative and traditional dishes using local ingredients. Closed Sun evening, Mon and June. Frazione San Giacomo, T: 0171 380 372.
€€ **Trattoria della Pace**. Renowned for its original twists on old recipes. Closed Sun evening, Mon and Jan. Via Santuario 97, T: 0171 380 398.

Bra
€€ **Battaglino**. Trattoria serving mainly traditional dishes. Closed Mon and Aug Piazza Roma 18, T: 0172 412 509.
€ **Boccondivino**. Excellent traditional *osteria*. Closed Sun, mid-day Mon and July–Aug. Via Mendicità Istruita 14, T: 0172 425 674.

Briaglia
€€ **Marsupino**. Traditional trattoria known for its fine food and excellent wines. Closed Wed, Jan and Sept. Via

Roma 20, T: 0174 563 888.

Carrù

€€ **Moderno**. Very traditional restaurant, with a remarkable wine list. Closed Mon evening, Tues and Aug. Via Misericordia 12, T: 0173 75493.

Cervere

€€ **Antica Corona Reale - da Renzo**. Great trattoria offering local delicacies such as frogs and snails. Closed Tues evening, Wed, March and Sept. Via Fossano 13, T: 0172 474 132.

Cherasco

€ **Osteria della Rosa Rossa**. Warm, friendly trattoria serving excellent food and wines. Closed Tues and Wed, Jan and Aug. Via San Pietro 31, T: 0172 488 133.

Cissone

€€ **Locanda dell'Arco**. Delicious traditional fare and excellent wines in a warm, quiet restaurant. Closed Tues and Jan. Piazza dell'Olmo 1, T: 0173 748 200.

Cravanzana

€€ **Da Maurizio - Trattoria del Mercato**. Excellent trattoria (with rooms) specialising in regional food and wines. Closed Wed, Jan and June. Via San Rocco 16, T: 0173 855 019.

Cuneo

€€ **Le Plat d'Etain**. Restaurant specialising in French cuisine. Closed Sun Corso Giolitti 18, T: 0171 681 918.

€€ **Ligure**. Restaurant (with rooms) known for its traditional cooking; closed Sun evening and Jan. Via Savigliano 11, T: 0174 681 942.

€ **Osteria della Chiocciola**. Excellent restaurant and wine bar offering creative and traditional dishes using local ingredients. Closed Sun and Aug Via Fossano 1, T: 0171 66277.

Grinzane Cavour

€ **Nonna Genia**. Good trattoria in an old house in the hills. Closed Wed, Jan and July. Località Borzone, T: 0173 262 410.

La Morra

€ **Fratelli Revello**. Wine estate offering delicious country meals. Closed Jan-Feb. Frazione Annunziata 103, T: 0173 50276.

Limone Piemonte

€€ **Lu Taz di Matlas**. Restaurant specialising in local mountain dishes. Closed Mon, June and Oct. Via San Maurizio 13, T: 0171 929 061.

Mondovì

€€ **Croce d'Oro**. Trattoria just outside the town, serving delicious local fare with a personal touch. Closed Mon, Jan and July–Aug. Via Sant'Anna Avagnina 83, T: 0174 681 464.

€€ **Mezzavia**. Restaurant offering good regional cuisine. Closed Wed and July Via Villanova 38, T: 0174 40363.

Monforte d'Alba

€€€ **Giardino-da Felicin**. Restaurant (with rooms) serving outstanding traditional dishes, on a panoramic terrace in summer. Closed evenings Mon–Fri, Jan–Feb and July. Via Vallada 18, T: 0173 78225.

Piobesi d'Alba

€€ **Locanda le Clivie**. Restaurant (with rooms) renowned for its carefully prepared local dishes. Closed Sun evening (except Oct) and Mon. Via Canoreto 1, T: 0173 619 261.

Robilante

€ **Leon d'Oro**. Old-fashioned trattoria offering dishes from Piedmont and its former dominion, Sardinia. Closed Wed and Jan–Feb. Piazza Olivero 10, T: 0171 78679.

Saluzzo

€€ **La Gargotta del Pellico**. Traditional restaurant. Closed Tues and midday Wed. Piazzetta Mondagli 5, T: 0175 46833.

€€ **La Taverna di Porti Scür**. Trattoria known for its creative interpretations of traditional recipes. Closed Mon and midday Tues. Via Volta 14, T: 0175 41961.

€€ **L'Ostü dij Baloss**. Excellent traditional restaurant in a beautiful 17th-century setting. Closed Sun and midday Mon, Jan and July–Aug Via Gualtieri 38, T: 0175 248 618.

Stroppo

€€ **L'Ortica**. *Osteria* with good local cooking and wines. Closed Tues and Oct–June weekdays. Frazione Bassura di Stroppo 58, T: 0171 999 202.

€€ **Lou Sarvanot**. Excellent country restaurant (with rooms). Closed Mon (and Tues in winter), midday weekdays (except Aug), Jan–Feb and Sept. Frazione Bassura di Stroppo 64, T: 0171 999159.

Treiso

€€ **La Ciau del Tornavento**. Restaurant specialising in traditional local cuisine with a personal twist. Closed Wed, midday Thur and Jan. Piazza Baracco 7, T: 0173 638 333.

€€ **Osteria dell'Unione**. *Osteria* offering delicious seasonal menus; closed Sun evening, Mon and Aug. Via Alba 1, T: 0173 638303.

Verzuolo

€€ **San Bernardo**. Old-fashioned trattoria with garden seating in summer and no written menu. Closed Tues, midday Wed and Jan. Via San Bernardo 63, T: 0175 85882.

WINE & SPECIALITY FOODS

Alba

Non Solo Vino, at Corso Vittorio Emanuele 31, is a good wine shop with a bar serving snacks. **Umberto** has Alba's best cakes and coffee; you can find all sorts of sweets (including chocolate *torrone*) at **Io, Tu e i Dolci**, at Piazza Savona 12. For wines of the Langhe, try **Enoteca Fracchia**, at Via Vernazza 9; **Grandi Vini**, at Via Vittorio Emanuele 1a; and '**L Crotin**, at Via Cuneo 3.

Carrù

Carrù is famous for its smoked ox, *bue di Carrù*, available at most grocers' shops.

Saluzzo

For a selection of fine cheeses, try **La Casa del Parmigiano**, Corso Italia 112; or the factory outlet at **Caseificio San Martino**, Corso Piemonte 129.

CENTRAL PIEDMONT

On sunny days the landscape of this part of Piedmont can be very striking—especially in spring, when the meadows come alive with wild flowers, or in autumn, when the vine-leaves turn bright red. The wines of this region are justly famous—particularly the whites of Canelli, near Asti, and the Monferrato reds.

ASTI & ENVIRONS

Asti, an old Piedmontese city and provincial capital, was founded by the Romans. The Torre San Secondo, a Romanesque tower on a Roman base, serves as bell tower for the church of Santa Caterina (1773). The main street, extending the whole length of the town, is the long Corso Vittorio Alfieri. The early 18th century Palazzo Alfieri, birthplace of Vittorio Alfieri (1749–1803), has collections devoted to his work. Alfieri is Italy's finest tragic poet. His main theme is the overthrow of tyranny, and his literary works helped awaken the national spirit of Italy which culminated in the Risorgimento. He lived a life of unmarried bliss with the Countess of Albany, widow of the pretender to the English throne Charles Edward Stuart (Bonnie Prince Charlie) and is buried in Santa Croce, Florence, with a monument by Canova.

Asti's **cathedral** is a Gothic building of 1309–54, with a bell tower of 1266 and a florid south porch of c. 1470; the east end was extended in 1764–69. It contains stoups and a font with Roman elements, 18th-century stalls, and frescoes by Carlo Carlone and Francesco Fabbrica. Near the cloister is the small church of San Giovanni, covering a 7th- or 8th-century crypt, perhaps the original baptistery.

The 18th-century Palazzo Mazzetti houses a small picture gallery, closed for restoration at the time of writing. In Piazza Medici is the **Torre Troya**, the finest medieval tower in the city. The large Gothic church of **San Secondo** contains a fine polyptych by Gaudenzio Ferrari. At the extreme east end of the Corso is the church and cloister of San Pietro in Consavia (1467), which now contains the small **Museo Archeologico e Paleontologico** (*open Nov–March Tues–Sun 10–1 & 3–6; Apr–Oct Tues–Sun 10–1 & 4–7*).

ALESSANDRIA & ITS PROVINCE

Alessandria is a cheerful town and capital of an interesting province. It was founded by seven castellans of the duchy of Monferrato who rebelled against Frederick Barbarossa in 1168 and named their new city after Pope Alexander III. Most of its buildings date from the 18th and 19th centuries. The **Palazzo della Prefettura** (1733), by Benedetto Alfieri (a relative of the poet; *see above*), in the central Piazza della Libertà, is the best of the city's mansions. The 14th–15th-century church of Santa Maria di Castello incorporates remains of an earlier 6th-century church.

To the south of Alessandria is the battlefield of **Marengo**, where Napoleon defeated the Austrians on 14 June 1800, in a battle that he regarded as the most brilliant of his career. There is a small museum in the villa. The remarkable church of Santa Croce at **Bosco Marengo** was erected in 1567 by Pius V (d. 1572), a native of the village, as his mausoleum. His splendid tomb remains empty, however, as he is buried in Rome. The paintings include works by Giorgio Vasari.

The remains of the Roman town of Libarna, with traces of its decumanus maximus, amphitheatre and theatre, lie near Serravalle Scrivia. The communal cemetery at Arquata Scrivia contains 94 Second World War graves of British soldiers.

Acqui Terme, southwest of Alessandria, is the Roman Aquae Statiellae, well known for its sulphurous waters and mud baths. The thermal waters (75°C) bubble up beneath a little pavilion in the middle of the town, known as La Bollente (1870), designed by the local architect Giovanni Ceruti. The Romanesque cathedral, with a fine portal beneath a 17th-century loggia, still has its triple apse of the 11th century, a campanile completed in the 13th century, and a 15th-century Catalan triptych. In the public gardens are remains of the Paleologi family castle, with an archaeological museum (*open Wed–Sat 9.30–12.30 & 3.30–6.30, Sun & holidays 9.30–12.30*). The church of San Pietro has a fine 11th-century apse and octagonal campanile. On the other side of the River Bormida are four arches of a Roman aqueduct.

Nearby **Ovada** was the birthplace of St Paul of the Cross (Paolo Danei; 1694–1775), founder of the Passionist Order.

THE WINES OF ASTI

The wines of Asti—Barbera, Dolcetto, Freisa, Favorita—are known only by their grape variety. If the name of a village or region is added (for example, Barbera d'Asti), you can be sure you are getting a wine from one of the better vineyards. Say Asti to people, though, and what first comes into their minds is the sweet, bubbly Moscato d'Asti. For generations this was the traditonal style of wine in Piedmont, and its origins go back to the 13th century. It is made exclusively from Moscato Bianco grapes, and is produced only in the environs of Asti, Alessandria and Cuneo.

The Monferrato

Casale Monferrato lies north of Alessandria, on the south bank of the Po. It is the chief town of the old duchy of Monferrato, whose princes of the Paleologi family held a famous court here from 1319 to 1533. In 1873 the first Italian Portland cement was made here, and the town was noted for its production of cement and artificial stone up to the Second World War. Excellent wines are produced in the vineyards of the Monferrato, including the red Barbera and Grignolino.

The cathedral, consecrated in 1107, was over-restored in the 19th century, though it preserves a remarkable narthex. Inside is a Romanesque sculpted crucifix. San

Vineyards in the rolling countryside around Asti.

Domenico is a late-Gothic church with a fine Renaissance portal of 1505. Via Mameli has a number of fine buildings, including Palazzo Treville by Giovanni Battista Scapitta (1725; Rococo atrium and courtyard), the 18th-century Palazzo Sannazzaro, Palazzo Gozani di San Giorgio (now the town hall, built in 1775 and still with its late 18th-century furnishings) and the church of San Paolo (1586). In Via Cavour the cloister of Santa Croce houses the municipal museum, with sculptures by Leonardo Bistolfi and late 16th-century paintings by Matteo da Verona, Moncalvo and others.

The synagogue (1595) contains an important Museo Ebraico (*open Sun & holidays 10–12 & 3–5, otherwise by appointment; T: 014 271 807*). The huge Piazza Castello to the west, on the Po, surrounds the 14th-century castle (radically remodelled in the 19th century); the church of Santa Caterina here is by Scapitta (c. 1725). The Teatro Municipale is a very fine building dating from 1791.

To the west of Casale Monferrato, in a protected park, is the **Santuario di Crea**, founded in 1590 on the site of the refuge of St Eusebius, Bishop of Vercelli (340–70). The church (13th century, altered 1608–12) has frescoes by Macrino d' Alba (1503) and a triptych of 1474. The 23 chapels of the Sacro Monte host paintings by Moncalvo and late-15th-century sculptures by the Flemish artist Jean Wespin (known as 'Il Tabacchetti'; his chief works in Italy are polychrome terracotta statues for this sanctuary and for the Sacro Monte of Varallo, *see p. 89*). The highest chapel, restored in 1995, contains frescoes attributed to Giorgio Albertini and remarkable statues by Tabacchetti hanging from the ceiling. It has a good view over the Monferrato.

VERCELLI

Vercelli is the largest rice producer in Europe. It began as a Roman *municipium*, founded in 49 BC. In the 16th century it was noted for its school of painters, chief of whom were Giovanni Martino Spanzotti, Sodoma, Gaudenzio Ferrari and Bernardino Lanino.

Piazza Cavour is the old market square, with attractive arcades and the battlemented Torre dell'Angelo rising above the roofs. In Via Gioberti is the tall, square Torre di Città, dating from the 13th century. Corso Libertà is the main street of the old town. Palazzo Centoris (no. 204) has a delightful interior courtyard with frescoes and arcades in three tiers (1496). In Via Cagna is **San Cristoforo**, with crowded scenes frescoed in 1529–34 by Gaudenzio Ferrari, and the *Madonna of the Pomegranate* (1529), considered his masterpiece. The church of San Paolo (begun c. 1260) has a *Madonna* by Bernardino Lanino.

The **Civico Museo Borgogna** (*open Tues–Fri 3–5.30, Sat 10–12.30, Sun 2–6*) preserves the most important collection of paintings in Piedmont after the Galleria Sabauda in Turin. It is especially representative of the Piedmontese schools. Highlights include the founder Antonio Borgogna's original Borgogna collection (works by Antonio da Viterbo, Francesco Francia, Marco Palmezzano, Bergognone and Bernardino Luini); a *Deposition*, a replica by Titian of his painting in the Louvre; early-16th-century altarpieces by Defendente Ferrari and Lanino; 18th- and 19th-century works by Angelica Kauffmann, Girolamo Induno, Filippo Palizzi and others; Flemish paintings, notably a 16th-century *Madonna and Child* by Hans Baldung Grien and works by Jan Brueghel the Elder, a *Holy Family* attributed to Andrea del Sarto and a collection of Meissen, Doccia and Ginori porcelain.

The **Museo Leone** (*open Tues, Thur, Sat 3–5.30, Sun & holidays 10–12 & 3–6*) is an unusual museum housing the collection of Camillo Leone (1830–1907). The entrance is through the lovely courtyard of the 15th-century Casa degli Alciati, which has early-16th-century frescoes and wood ceilings. Rooms built in 1939 to connect the house with the Baroque Palazzo Langosco have a display illustrating the history of Vercelli, interesting for a museographical arrangement which dates from the Fascist period. The 18th-century Palazzo Langosco, once the residence of Leone, retains part of its original decoration. There are also some mementoes of the Risorgimento.

In front of the station is the basilica of **Sant'Andrea** (1219–27), a largely Romanesque church showing Cistercian Gothic elements at a very early date for Italy. It was founded by Cardinal Guala Bicchieri with the revenues of the Abbey of St Andrew at Chesterton (Cambridgeshire) bestowed on him by his young ward, Henry III of England. The fine façade is flanked by two tall towers connected by a double arcade, and the cupola is topped by a third tower. The two lunettes hold sculptures by the school of Antelami. The detached campanile dates from 1407. Inside, the pointed arcades are carried on slender clustered piers, with shafts carried up unbroken to the springing of the vaults. The crossing and cupola are particularly fine. At the east end are intarsia stalls of 1514. The remains of the Cistercian abbey include a lovely cloister and chapterhouse.

Via Bicheri leads to the huge cathedral, begun in 1572 to a design of Pellegrino Tibaldi, but preserving the Romanesque campanile of an older church. The octagonal chapel—built in 1698 and decorated in 1759—of the Blessed Amedeo IX of Savoy (who died in the castle 1472) contains his tomb and that of his successor Charles I (d. 1490). The chapter library includes the 4th-century *Evangelistary of St Eusebius* (in a 12th-century binding); some Anglo-Saxon poems (11th century); the *Laws of the Lombards* (8th century); and other early manuscripts, perhaps relics of the Studium, or early university, which flourished here from 1228 for about a century.

NOVARA

Novara, a Roman town, was occupied in 569 by the Lombards and became a free city-state in 1116. Important battles were fought here throughout the town's history. Lodovico il Moro, Duke of Milan, was taken prisoner by the French after one of them, in 1500. The last famous battle, in 1849, resulted in the defeat of the Piedmontese by the Austrians under the 82-year-old Field Marshal Radetzky. That same evening Carlo Alberto of Savoy abdicated in favour of his son, Vittorio Emanuele II, marking the beginning of the Risorgimento movement in Italy.

Today Novara is an extremely pleasant and well-kept provincial capital. Its streets are paved in granite and porphyry, quarried locally, and it has particularly good 19th-century architecture.

In the arcaded Via Fratelli Rosselli is the **duomo**, rebuilt by Alessandro Antonelli in 1865–69 with a Neoclassical colonnade. Six Brussels tapestries (1565) by Jan de Buck hang in the gloomy interior. Behind the huge orange stucco columns, on the south side, are a 14th-century carved wooden crucifix, an altarpiece by Gaudenzio Ferrari (c. 1525–30), and works by his pupil Bernardino Lanino. The chapel of San Siro, which survives from the earlier church, contains damaged late 12th-century frescoes; the *Crucifixion* dates from the 14th century. The adjoining 18th-century room contains frescoes by Bernardino Lanino (1546–53) from the old cathedral, and paintings by Gaudenzio Ferrari and Callisto Piazza.

Remarkable black-and-white mosaic panels from the original cathedral, dating from the 12th century, with symbols of the Evangelists, Adam and Eve, and other biblical subjects, are displayed in the sacristy. The Neoclassical high altar is by Antonelli and Thorvaldsen. On the north side are a reliquary bust (1424) of St Bernard of Aosta (after whom the St Bernard dog is named, *see p. 27*).

The **baptistery** is a centrally planned octagonal building of the late 4th century, with 1st-century Classical columns and an 11th-century cupola. High up above the windows are very worn 11th-century frescoes of the *Apocalypse*, one of them covered with a 15th-century *Last Judgement*. The funerary monument of Umbrena Polla (1st century AD) was once used as a font.

Opposite the duomo is the entrance to the finely paved courtyard of the Broletto, a medley of buildings dating from the 13th and 15th centuries with terracotta windows and remains of frescoes above Gothic arches. The third side dates from the 18th century. Here is the entrance to the **Museo Novarese di Arte e Storia** (*open Oct–Apr Tues–Sun 9–12 & 3–6; May–Sept 10–1 & 4–7*). Inside are terracotta statuettes, 17th–18th-century paintings, an archaeological collection including finds dating from the Golasecca culture (9th–8th centuries BC) and the Roman period, and medieval ceramics and sculpture.

Via Fratelli Rosselli, with porticoes, leads east to the arcaded Piazza delle Erbe, the old centre of the town. In the other direction, Classical colonnades continue past a statue of Carlo Emanuele III to Piazza Martiri della Libertà, with an equestrian statue of Vittorio Emanule II by Ambrogio Borghi (1881). Here are the handsome Neoclassical buildings of the huge Teatro Coccia (1888) and Palazzo del Mercato (1817–44). You can see some remains of the Sforza castle on the south side of the piazza. In Via Dominioni is the yellow building of the former Collegio Gallarini (restored as a music conservatory), with remarkable late-19th-century terracotta decoration and a coloured roof. There are also stretches of Roman walls here, in a little park

Leave the courtyard of the Broletto by Corso Italia. Via San Gaudenzio, on your left, continues north to the church of **San Gaudenzio**, built 1577–1690 from a design by Pellegrino Tibaldi. The church has a fine brick exterior. The cupola, crowned by an elaborate spire 121m high, is by Alessandro Antonelli (1844–80). The campanile (92m) is another exceptionally original work by Benedetto Alfieri (1753–86). Within, on the south side, are works by Morazzone, Fiammenghino and Gaudenzio Ferrari. The Baroque chapel of San Gaudenzio opens off the south transept. On the north side are works by Ferrari (a polyptych of 1514 in a beautiful frame), Paolo Camillo Landriani, Tanzio da Varallo and Giacinto Brandi.

In the nearby Via Ferrari, Palazzo Faraggiana has been restored as the seat of the natural history, ethnographical and music museums. The Museo Etnografico Ugo Ferrandi (*closed at the time of writing*) features items brought back from Somalia and Eritrea by explorer Ugo Ferrandi, plus other material from Africa, Oceania and the Americas.

Via Fratelli Rosselli is continued east by Via Canobio, in which are two fine old palaces—Palazzo Natta-Isola, attributed to Pellegrino Tibaldi, and the Casa dei Medici by Seregni.

PRACTICAL INFORMATION

GETTING AROUND

• **By road:** Several companies offer country bus services between the main towns. For information, contact ARFEA (T: 0131 225810), Franchini SATA (T: 0141 593673), ATAV Vigo (T: 011 854853) or SATTI (T: 011 57641). Car parking in marked areas in most towns. In Alessandria, on Piazza Garibaldi and Piazza Libertà, there is a minibus service to the city centre.

• **By rail:** Asti and Alessandria are served by the main Turin–Genoa rail line, and fast Eurostar and Intercity trains stop in both cities. From Turin to Asti in c. 30mins, to Alessandria in c. 50mins (the line continues via Piacenza to Bologna); from Genoa to Asti in c. 1hr 10mins, to Alessandria in c. 50mins. You can get from Asti to Alessandria by train in c. 20mins. Branch lines run from Asti to Acqui Terme, and via Alba and Bra to Cavallermaggiore, where there are connections to Cuneo. Novara and Vercelli are on the main Milan–Turin line; from Milan to Novara in 30mins; to Vercelli in 45mins. From Turin to Vercelli in 40mins; to Novara in 50mins. Slower commuter services between Milan and Novara are operated by the Ferrovia Nord Milano (station at Corso Vittorio 15).

INFORMATION OFFICES

Asti Piazza Alfieri 33, T: 0141 530 357, www.terredasti.it
Informagiovani: Piazza Alfieri 33, T: 0141 433 315.

Alessandria Piazza Santa Maria di Castello 14, T: 0131 220 056, www.alexala.it
Novara Baluardo Sella 40, T: 0321 394 059.

HOTELS

Asti
€€ **Aleramo**. Modern and central. Via Emanuele Filiberto 13, T: 0141 595661, F: 0141 30039.
€€ **Reale**. A traditional place with a history of eminent guests. Piazza Alfieri 6, T: 0141 530240, F: 0141 34357.
Alessandria
€ **Alli Due Buoi Rossi**. A fine, family-run establishment with a good restaurant. Closed Aug. Via Cavour 32, T: 0131 445252, F: 0131 445255.
€ **Europa**. Modern and comfortable. Via Palestro 1, T: 0131 236226, F: 0131 252498.
Agliano
€ **San Giacomo**. A small, cosy place with just six rooms. Closed Jan, Feb and Aug. Via Arullani 4, T: 0141 954178.
€ **Fons Salutis**. Calm and quiet, with a nice garden and its own spa. Via alle Fonti 125, T: 0141 954018.
Canelli
€€ **La Casa in Collina**. Just six rooms in a tastefully restored farmhouse surrounded by vineyards producing excellent wines. Località Sant'Antonio 30, T: 0141 822 82, www.casaincollina.com
Cioccaro di Penango
€€ **Locanda del Sant'Uffizio**. A country house with park and pool. Closed Jan and Aug. T: 0141 916 292.

Isola d'Asti
€€ **Castello di Villa**. Fourteen rooms in a 17th-century patrician villa. Open March–Nov. Località Villa, Via Bausola 2, T: 0141 958 006, www.castellodivilla.it

Montegrosso d'Asti
€€ **Locanda del Boscogrande**. A lovely renovated farmhouse with just seven rooms and an excellent restaurant. Open Feb–Dec. Via Boscogrande 47, T: 0141 956 390, www.locandaboscogrande.com

Novara
€€ **Italia**. Modern and comfortable, if a bit austere. Via Solaroli 10, T: 0321 399 316, F: 0321 399 310, italia@panciolihotels.it
€ **Croce di Malta**. Small and conveniently located, a short walk from the castle and cathedral. Closed Aug. Via Biglieri 2a, T: 0321 32032, F: 0321 623 475, hcrocemalta@iol.it
€ **Garden**, Quiet and convenient, across from the train station. Corso Garibaldi 25, T: 0321 625 094, F: 0321 613 320.

Novi Ligure
€€ **Relais Villa Pomela**. A stately villa with park 2km ouside the town. Via Serravalle 69, T: 0143 329 910, www.pomela.it

RESTAURANTS

Asti
€€€ **Gener Neuv**. Excellent restaurant devoted to local tradition. Closed Sun evening (all day Sun in summer), Mon, Aug, Dec or Jan. Lungo Tanaro 4, T: 0141 557 270.
€€ **Da Aldo**. Friendly family-run restaurant with good local cooking.

Closed Wed and Jan. Frazione Castiglione 22 (8km east), T: 0141 206 008.
€ **Barolo & Co**. Old-fashioned restaurant with good wholesome food and down-home style. Closed Sun evening, Mon and Aug. Via Cesare Battisti 14, T: 0141 592 059.

Alessandria
€ **Cappelverde**. Warm, friendly trattoria. Open evenings only, closed Tues. Via San Pio V at Via Plana, T: 0131 251 265.

Acqui Terme
€ **Da Bigât**. Traditional *osteria*. Closed Wed, Via Mazzini 30–32, T: 0144 324 283.
€ **San Guido**. Old-fashioned *osteria*. Closed Sat and Aug. Piazza San Guido 5, T: 0144 320 420.

Calamandrana
€€ **Violetta**. Traditional restaurant in an old farmhouse. Closed Sun evening, Wed and Jan. Viale San Giovanni 1 (2km north), T: 0141 75151.
€ **Osteria dei Puciu**. *Osteria* in an old farmhouse near Canelli. Closed Tues and Jan. Regione Quartino, Casina Lacqua, T: 0141 75122.

Camagna
€€ **Taverna di Campagna dal 1997**. A rustic farmhouse with good country cooking. Open midday weekdays, all day at weekends; closed Mon and Jan. Vicolo Gallina 20, T: 0142 925 645.

Canelli
€€ **Al Grappolo d'Oro**. Restaurant (with rooms) known for its good local dishes. Closed Mon. Via Risorgimento 59–61, T: 0141 823 812.
€€ **San Marco**. Restaurant famous for its great regional delicacies and fabulous wines. Closed Tues evening, Wed and

July–Aug. Via Alba 36, T: 0141 823 544.

€ **Piccolo San Remo dal Baròn**. Trattoria specialising in regional cuisine. Closed Sun evening and Mon, Aug and Jan. Via Alba 179, T: 0141 823944.

Casale Monferrato

€€ **La Torre**. Traditional restaurant with garden and views. Closed Wed, Dec–Jan and Aug. Via Garoglio 3, T: 0142 70295.

Castellazo Bormida

€ **Lo Spiedo**. Traditional trattoria serving strictly local fare. Open evenings Tues–Fri, all day Sun & holidays, closed Aug. Via Acqui 25, T: 0131 278 184.

Castelnuovo Calcea

€ **Il Boschetto di Vignole**. Well-known traditional trattoria. Closed Mon evening, Tues and July. Via Marconi 16, T: 0141 957 434.

Castiglione Tinella

€€ **Da Palmira**. Trattoria offering excellent regional dishes. Closed Mon evening, Tues, and July–Aug. Piazza XX Settembre 18, T: 0141 855 176.

Cavatore

€ **Cascina Camolin**. Farm serving excellent lunches using fresh, home-grown and home-made ingredients. Open evenings and mid-day Sun. Via Valle Prati 17, T: 0144 322 673.

Cossano Belbo

€€ **Universo**. Trattoria with simple but delicious regional food. Closed Mon, Tues, Wed and June–July. Via Caduti 6, T: 0141 88167.

Costigliole d'Asti

€€€ **Da Guido**. Outstanding local and regional cuisine and wines. Closed mid-day, Sun & holidays, late Dec–early Jan and three weeks in Aug. Piazza Umberto I 27, T: 0141 966 012.

Gavi

€€ **Cantine del Gavi**. Excellent traditional restaurant, in a historic building. Closed Mon, Jan and July. Via Mameli 69, T: 0143 642 458.

Masio

€€ **Losanna**. An old post stage in the countryside now a trattoria serving regional fare. Closed Mon and Aug. Via San Rocco 36, T: 0131 799 525.

Montaldo Scarampi

€€ **Il Campagnin**. Trattoria combining tradition and imagination in delicious lunches. Closed evenings, Sun and Tues. Via Binello 77, T: 0141 953 676.

Montechiaro d'Asti

€€ **Tre Colli**. Warm, friendly trattoria with a good wine list. Closed Mon, Jan and July–Aug. Piazza del Mercato 5, T: 0141 901 027.

€€ **Da Elvira**. Farm serving delicious country meals (try the warm vegetable tarts). Closed Sun evening, Mon and Aug. Via Santo Stefano 75, T: 0141 956 138.

Nizza Monferrato

€€ **Le Due Lanterne**. Restaurant offering classic Piedmontese food and good wines. Closed Mon evening, Tues and Aug. Piazza Garibaldi 52, T: 0141 702 480.

Novara

€€ **La Famiglia**. Trattoria (with rooms) offering creative interpretations of traditional recipes. Closed Fri and Aug. Via Solaroli 8, T: 0321 399 316.

€€ **Monte Ariolo**. Restaurant serving traditional regional cuisine. Closed mid-day Sat, Sun and Aug. Vicolo Monte Ariolo 2a, T: 0321 623 394.

Pasturana

€€ **Locanda San Martin**. Restaurant

renowned for its creative interpretations of traditional recipes. Closed Mon evening, Tues and Jan. Via Roma 26, T: 0143 58444.

Quattordio
€ **Castello di Lajone**. Restaurant with rooms, in a lovely old fortress. Via Castello 1, Località Piepasso, T: 0131 773 692.

Roccaverano
€€ **Aurora**. Old-fashioned restaurant (with rooms) serving good country meals. Closed Dec–March. Via Bruno 1, T: 0144 93023.

San Marzano Oliveto
€€ **Del Belbo da Bardon**. Restaurant serving excellent food and wine of the region. Closed Wed evening, Thur and Dec–Jan. Via Valle Asinari 25, T: 0141 831 340.
€ **La Viranda**. Delicious country meals on a farm set amid orchards and vineyards. Closed Mon, Jan and Aug. Regione Corte 69, T: 0141 856 671.

San Marzanotto (Asti)
€ **Fratelli Rovero**. Wine estate (Barbera and Grignolino) offering great farm lunches. Closed Sun evening and Mon, Dec–Jan, July and Aug. Località Valdonata, T: 0141 530 102.

Santo Stefano Belbo
€ **Club di Bacco**. Refined regional cuisine in the house where writer Cesare Pavese was born. Closed Mon, midday Tues–Fri and Jan. Via Cesare Pavese 18, T: 0141 843 379.

Tigliole d'Asti (*see map p. 58*)
€€ **Vittoria**. Restaurant offering great food and fine views. Closed Sun evening, Mon, Jan and Aug. Via Roma 14, T: 0141 667 123.

Valle San Bartolomeo (Alessandria)
€ **Da Pietro**. Old-fashioned trattoria popular with locals. Closed Wed and Aug. Piazza Dossena 1, T: 0131 59124.

Vercelli
€ **Il Giardinetto**. Restaurant (with rooms) known for its good regional cooking. Closed Mon and Aug. Via Sereno 3, T: 0161 257230, F: 0161 259 311.

Vignale Monferrato
€€ **Gabriella Trisoglio**. Farm serving country meals, with a strong local following. Closed Mon and Tues. Ca' Ravino, San Lorenzo, T: 0142 933 378.

Villa San Secondo
€ **Per Bacco**. Wine-bar and *osteria* especially popular at weekends. Open evenings only, closed Tues. Via Montechiaro 26, T: 0141 905525.

FESTIVALS & EVENTS

Asti The ancient *Palio d'Asti*, a pageant and horse race similar to that of Siena, takes place in early Sept, when there is also a wine fair.
Canelli The *Assedio di Canelli* (Siege of Canelli) is re-enacted annually in June, with mock skirmishes, tableaux of daily life in 1613, and a huge public dinner.
Novara Annual festival of San Gaudenzio, 22 Jan.

THE NORTHEAST

Northeastern Piedmont includes the renowned ski areas of Monte Rosa and Monte Cervino (the Matterhorn), as well the romantic summer resorts of Lago d'Orta and Lago Maggiore. Economic life revolves around the textile trade (centred in Biella) and around large-scale farming, the chief product being the famous *arboreo* rice from which risotto is made.

BIELLA & THE VALSESIA

Biella, on the River Cervo, is the capital of a small province. A funicular railway connects the lower town, site of a 10th-century baptistery and the Renaissance church of San Sebastiano, with the upper town and its 15th–16th century mansions. At Via Serralunga 27, in a renovated Industrial building, is Cittadellarte, a centre for contemporary art (*open Tues–Fri 4–7.30, Sat & Sun 11–7.30*) offering a permanent collection devoted to Arte Povera, a movement defined in 1967 as exploring the relationship between art and life, the natural and the artificial. The Villa Sella (*open by appointment, T: 015 23778*) was the home of the photographer, alpinist, and explorer Vittorio Sella (1859–1943). The Istituto Nazionale di Fotografia Alpina Vittorio Sella conserves his remarkable collection of negatives made during mountain expeditions in Europe, Asia, Africa and Alaska, as well as his photographic equipment.

Northwest of Biella is **Pollone** with the Parco della Burcina, noted especially for its rhododendrons, in flower May–June. Beyond is the sanctuary of **Oropa** (1181m), the most popular pilgrimage resort in Piedmont, said to have been founded by St Eusebius of Vercelli in 369. Eusebius (d. 371) is thought to be the author of the Athanasian Creed. The sanctuary consists of a large hospice of three quadrangles that can house hundreds of visitors, a modest church by Filippo Juvarra, and a grander church, with a large dome, begun in 1885 to an earlier design by Ignazio Galletti and completed in 1960.

South of Biella is **Gaglianico**, which has a splendid castle, mainly 16th century, with a well-decorated courtyard. **Candelo**, further east, has a remarkable *ricetto*, or communal fortress and storehouse, built in the 14th century as a refuge for the townsfolk.

The Valsesia

Northeast of Biella is the Valsesia, a lovely valley famous for its lace. East of the Sesia river is **Valduggia**, the birthplace of Gaudenzio Ferrari (1471–1546, *see overleaf*). The church of San Giorgio has a *Nativity* by him, and a *Madonna* by Bernardino Luini. **Varallo**, the capital of the upper Valsesia, is famous for its Sacro Monte, the ascent to which begins at the church of Madonna delle Grazie, with frescoed scenes of the *Life of Christ* by Ferrari (1513). The sanctuary (608m; reached on foot in 20mins or by cable railway or road), was founded c. 1486 by the Blessed Bernardino Caimi, a Franciscan friar. The 45 chapels, completed in the late 17th century, recall various holy sites in Jerusalem and are decorated by local artists—Ferrari, Giovanni Tabacchetti, Giovanni d'Errico and Morazzone. Tabacchetti's best chapels are the Temptation (no. 38; with a *Crucifixion* by Ferrari) and *Adam and Eve* (no. 1); d'Errico's is the *Vision of St Joseph* (no. 5). The Basilica dell'Assunta, dating from 1641–49, has a façade of 1896.

Winding northwest from Varallo the Valsesia is known as Valgrande. **Alagna Valsesia** (1183m) is a fashionable summer and winter resort. The Museo Walser occupies a characteristic wooden house here. The Funivia di Monte Rosa, a cableway in three stages, rises to Punta Indren (3260m), another resort. The Regina Margherita CAI Refuge Observatory (4559m), on the site of a hut built here in 1893 and inaugurated by Queen Margherita, is the highest refuge in Europe.

Gaudenzio Ferrari (c. 1470–1546)

Ferrari, the greatest artist of the Piedmontese school, is barely known outside his native Piedmont, perhaps because he never left it throughout his long life (with the exception of one possible visit to the Rhineland). He was born in Valduggia, and probably trained in Milan, under old-fashioned masters who preserved their old archaic styles against the encroaching rationalist spirit of the Renaissance. Ferrari had no aristocratic patrons: he painted exclusively for churches and convents. There is always something rather homespun about his art, but it is neither naive nor foolish. His religious beliefs seem to have been sincere, and his art is suffused with an intense lyricism. His greatest works are on the Sacro Monte at Varallo (*see above*), his *Madonna of the Pomegranate* in the church of San Cristoforo in Vercelli (*see p. 80*), and his *Madonna in Paradise* at Saronno (*see p. 148*).

LAGO D'ORTA

Lago d'Orta is a beautiful little lake 13km long and about 1km wide, surrounded by mountains, and lying just west of the much more famous Lago Maggiore. Also called Cusio (from the Roman Cusius), the lake has been admired by numerous travellers over the centuries, including Balzac and Nietzsche. Its only outlet is the little River Nigoglia, which flows northwards from Omegna (all the other subalpine Italian lakes have southern outflows).

Orta San Giulio, with its elegant buildings and peaceful atmosphere, is the most beautiful place on the lake. Its picturesque narrow old streets and cobbled lanes lead down to the water, from where there is a splendid view of the Isola San Giulio just offshore.

In Piazza Motta, which opens onto the lake, is the lovely little Palazzo della Comunità, the former town hall, built in 1582. Nearby, a wide thoroughfare with steps, known as La Motta, leads up past a number of handsome palaces to the parish church, with a decorative façade (1941) and an 11th-century doorway. The Baroque interior has interesting frescoes and works by Carlo Beretta, Giulio Cesare Procaccini, Morazzone and Fermo Stella.

A lane to the right of the church (Via Gemelli) continues uphill for 20 minutes past the cemetery (with an 18th-century wrought-iron gate) to an avenue (left) that ends at the monumental gateway of the **Sacro Monte** (you can also get there by car from the Via Panoramica). On this low wooded hill (396m), now a park with some rare plants (including palm trees), are 20 pretty little chapels dedicated to St Francis of Assisi.

A path beyond the gateway (*usually open 9.30–4; otherwise enquire at the Capuchin monastery at the top of the hill*) continues straight uphill, with good views over the lake, and then leads through the woods past the chapels. Most of them were built between 1592 and 1670, and most of them were designed by Padre Cleto (1556–1619). Each chapel has a different ground plan, usually with a pretty loggia or porch. They contain remarkable groups of life-size terracotta figures illustrating scenes from the life of the saint, as well as frescoes. There are notices in each chapel describing the works of art. Carved wooden or wrought-iron screens protect the sculptures; the best are the earliest (1607–17) by Cristoforo Prestinari (chapels I–VI, XI and XV). The 17th-century frescoes include works by Antonio Maria Crespi and Morazzone.

A gravel lane at the northern end of the town, beyond the Hotel San Rocco, leads past a few villas and ends at the wrought-iron gate in front of the pink **Villa Motta**, built in the late 19th century in Venetian style and surrounded by a pretty garden (*open by appointment March–Dec, T: 02 4802 2501*). First laid out in 1880, it has camellias, rhododendrons and azaleas, and some fine trees. A delightful path, called the Passeggiata del Movero, continues to the left round the headland, following the water's edge past more villas with their boathouses (including an eccentric Art Nouveau villa) and lawns.

Outside the town, on the Via Panoramica, is Villa Crespi (now a hotel), a remarkable building in the Arab style.

Isola San Giulio

Isola San Giulio, a picturesque little island, is especially beautiful from a distance (the best view, which changes constantly according to the light, is from Orta San Giulio). With a perimeter of just 650m, it has no cars and hardly any shops. There is only one lane, which circles the island past a few villas. The huge former seminary building, with an overgrown garden, is now a Benedictine convent. The 30 nuns (closed order) run a restoration centre here and offer hospitality for retreats.

Boats dock in front of the **basilica of San Giulio**, traditionally thought to have been founded by St Julius. This saint is supposed to have purged the island of serpents and other dangerous beasts in 390—though the first written document testifying to his cult dates from 590 (Paolo Diacono). The interior of the church is Baroque, though there are 14th–16th-century frescoes. The pulpit, in dark Oira marble, dates from the 11th–12th centuries, and the sombre carvings show German influence. A white mar-

Isola San Giulio.

ble sarcophagus with Roman carvings now serves as an alms-box. Some of the chapels are decorated with 15th-century Lombard frescoes, one of which is attributed to Gaudenzio Ferrari.

In 962 the island was defended by Willa, wife of Berengar II of Lombardy, against the incursions of the Emperor Otho the Great: the charter of Otho giving thanks for his eventual capture of the island is preserved in the sacristy. The whale's vertebra here is supposed to be a bone of one of the serpents destroyed by St Julius. Fragments of exquisite marble intarsia panels of the 4th–5th centuries, from the cenotaph of the saint (formerly in the apse, destroyed in 1697), are displayed in a room off the crypt. The body of St Julius, and a Greek marble panel incised with the palm, peacock and Cross (6th–7th centuries), are also preserved here.

Other towns on the lake

Vacciago lies between Orta San Giulio and Gozzano, to the south. A handsome collection of modern art (*open mid-May–mid-Oct Tues–Sun 10–12 & 3–6*) is displayed in the former home of the painter Antonio Calderara (1903–78), a 17th-century villa built in Renaissance-revival style. At the southern end of the lake is a hill crowned by the tall (24m) Torre di Buccione, a Lombard watch-tower. On the other side of the lake is **Pella**, with a little port. The terraced hills above the town hold some small villages and the sanctuary of the Madonna del Sasso, built in 1748 on a granite spur overlooking the lake (panoramic view).

Omegna, a small manufacturing town at the north end of the lake, retains a few old houses, a medieval bridge, and an ancient town gate. It lies at the foot of the Valstrona, a narrow winding glen that descends from the Laghetto di Capezzone (2104m), a lovely tarn beneath the Cima di Capezzone (2420m).

A by-road leads from Omegna to **Quarna Sotto**, where wind instruments have been made since the early 19th century. The Forni manufactory was succeeded here by the Rampone company at the end of the century. A small museum (*open July–Aug 4–7*) illustrates the history of the craft and preserves a collection of clarinets, oboes, saxophones, flutes and brasses. Another section is devoted to farm life in the valley.

THE VAL D'OSSOLA

This Alpine district in the northernmost corner of Piedmont is bordered on three sides by Switzerland. The main town is Domodossola, at the entrance to Italy from the Simplon Pass and railway tunnel.

Domodossola

Of Roman origin, the town became important as a halting place for travellers after the opening of the road over the Simplon Pass by Napoleon in 1805, and again after the construction of the railway tunnel through the Alps in 1906. It is still an important rail junction and preserves its grand station, built in 1906.

Corso Ferraris leads from the station to the old part of the town. Beyond Piazza Cinque Vie is the pretty arcaded Piazza Mercato, with 15th–16th-century houses, some with balconies and loggias. A market is held here on Saturday. Just off the Piazza is the handsome grey-and-white Teatro Municipale Galletti.

Via Paletta leads from Piazza Mercato to Piazza della Chiesa and the church of **Santi Gervaso e Protasio**, which has a façade rebuilt in 1953 but retains an old porch with 15th-century frescoes. Palazzo Silva is a handsome building, begun in 1519 and enlarged in 1640, with a frieze, pretty windows and a spiral staircase. It houses the **Museo Galletti** (*open for guided visits, Wed 3–6, Sat–Sun 10–12 & 3–6*), which includes a room illustrating the construction of the Simplon tunnel, and material relating to the flight of Georges Chavez, a Peruvian airman who was killed in a fall near Domodossola after having made the first flight over the Alps, on 29 September 1910). Via Carina is an attractive old street with wooden balconies and water channelled beneath the paving stones. To the north, on Via Monte Grappa, is an old medieval tower.

To the west of the town in a protected park is an interesting **Via Crucis**, with a view from the top. The 14 chapels, built from the 17th–19th centuries, each to a different design, contain life-size sculptures of the *Passion of Christ* by Dionigio Bussola, Giuseppe Rusnati and others, as well as frescoes.

TWO WAYS ACROSS THE ALPS

Whether you travel by rail or by car, Domodossola is the traditional gateway between Piedmont and Switzerland.

The Simplon Railway Tunnel is the longest rail tunnel in the world (19.8km); its first gallery was constructed in 1898–1905. It is also the lowest of the great Alpine tunnels, with a maximum elevation of only 705m—which means there are 2134m of mountain overhead where the main ridge is pierced.

The Simplon Pass (2009m; Passo del Sempione) is wholly on Swiss soil. It became important when Napoleon chose it, after the battle of Marengo, as the route for the Simplon road connecting the Rhône valley with the northern Italian plain (182km from Geneva to Sesto Calende). It was begun on the Italian side in 1800, on the Swiss side a year later, and was completed in 1805. About 1km below the summit on the south side is the Simplon Hospice (2001m), built by Napoleon as a barracks in 1811 and acquired by the monks of St Bernard in 1825.

The Upper Val d'Ossola and the side valleys

The **Val Vigezzo**, running east from Domodossola, followed by a spectacular railway line to Locarno opened in 1923, has been visited by artists since the 19th century. Santa Maria Maggiore has a little museum illustrating the work of chimneysweeps.

The **Val Divedro**, northwest of Domodossola, leads to the Simplon Pass. The Parco Naturale di Alpe Veglia (1753m), below Monte Leone (3552m), has beautiful scenery, with meadows and larch woods laced with hiking trails (information from the tourist office in Varzo). Excavations here in 1990 uncovered a Mesolithic site.

The **Upper Val d'Ossola**, with spectacular scenery, vineyards, fig trees, and chestnut woods, extends north to Switzerland. The Alpe Devero (1640m) is in the centre of a park with fine scenery and Alpine lakes. The beautiful **Val Formazza** is an interesting region colonised in the Middle Ages by German-speaking families from the Valais. The Cascata della Frua (1675m) is one of the great waterfalls of the Alps (viewable on Sun June–Sept).

South of Domodossola, in the **Valle d'Antrona**, is the beautiful little Lago d'Antrona (1083m), formed by a landslip in 1642.

The **Valle Anzasca** also has spectacular mountain scenery, beneath Monte Rosa (Dufourspitze, 4638m); Macugnaga (1326m) is its most important resort.

PRACTICAL INFORMATION

GETTING AROUND

• **By rail:** The main rail line from Milan to Geneva, Bern and Basel passes through Domodossola and the Val d'Ossola; fast Cisalpina, Eurocity and Intercity trains make the run from Milan to Domodossola with just one stop (at Stresa) in 1hr 10mins. Secondary lines link Domodossola with Novara (90km in 2hrs 10mins). Along the line is Orta-Masino Station, which has buses to the lakeside.

• **By boat:** Lago d'Orta boat services run from Easter to Oct to the Isola San Giulio (5mins) and Pella (20mins). A less frequent service runs from Orta via the Isola San Giulio and Pettenasco to Omegna (in 1hr 15mins). Information from Navigazione Lago d'Orta, T: 0322 844862. There is also a regular cheap motorboat service (c. every 20mins) throughout the year from Piazza Motta to the Isola San Giulio.

INFORMATION OFFICES

Biella Piazza Vittorio Veneto 3, T: 015 351 128, www.atl.biella.it
Domodossola Via Romita 13b, T: 0324 46391, www.cmvo.net
Orta San Giulio Via Olina 9–11, T: 0322 905 614. In summer there is another information office open on the approach road (Via Panoramica).
Stresa (For information about the lakes) Via Principe Tomaso 70/72, T: 0323 30416, www.distrettolaghi.it
Varallo (For the Valsesia) Corso Roma 35, T: 0163 51280.

Varzo (Parco Naturale Alpe Veglia) Piazza Castelli 2, T: 0324 72572.

WHERE TO STAY

Biella
€€ **Astoria**. Elegant and efficient. Closed Aug. Via Roma 9, T: 015 402750, www.astoriabiella.com
€€ **Augustus**. Central and quiet. Via Orfanotrofio 6, T: 015 27554, www.augustus.it
€€ **Michelangelo**. A small place, with courteous staff. Piazza Adua 5, T: 015 849 2362, www.hotelmichelangelo.com
Domodossola
€ **Corona**. Small, quiet and comfortable, in the heart of the town. Via Maroni 8, T: 0324 242 114, www.coronahotel.net
Formazza
€ **Pernice Bianca - Schneehendli**. Small (six rooms) and cosy, at 1700m with views of the mountains and cascades. Piano Cascata del Toce (5km north), T: 0324 63200.
Macugnaga (Valle Anzasca)
€ **Alpi**. A small, seasonal inn. Open Dec–Apr and June–Sept. Frazione Borca, T: 0324 65135.
€ **Girasole**. A small, cosy Alpine inn. Località Staffa, Via Monte Rosa 72, T: 0324 65052, hotel.girasole@tiscalinet.it
Oropa
€€ **Croce Bianca**. In the guest house of the sanctuary, with a good restaurant. Via Santuario di Oropa 480, T: 015 245 5923, F: 015 245 5963.
Orta San Giulio
€€€ **San Rocco**. Elegant and quiet, in a former convent with a lakefront ter-

race and pool. Via Gippini 11, T: 0322 911 977.

€€ **Leon d'Oro**. In a fine old building with good views of Isola San Giulio. Open Apr–Oct. Piazza Motta 1, T: 0322 90253.

Varallo (Valsesia)

€ **Sacro Monte**, at Sacro Monte (4km north). Quiet and comfortable. Open March–Dec. T: 0163 54254.

RESTAURANTS

Biella

€€ **Orso Poeta**. Restaurant offering great local atmosphere and cuisine. Closed midday, Wed and Jan. Via Orfanotrofio 7, T: 015 21252.

€€ **Prinz Grill**. Friendly restaurant offering good local dishes; closed Sun, Jan and Aug. Via Torino 14, T: 015 53876.

Borgomanero

€€€ **Pinocchio**. Restaurant renowned for its delicious personal interpretations of traditional recipes. Closed Mon, Aug and Dec. Via Matteotti 147, T: 0322 82273.

Domodossola

€ **Sciolla**. Trattoria with good local dishes. Closed Wed, Jan and Aug–Sept. Piazza Convenzione 5, T: 0324 242 633.

Orta San Giulio

€€ **Taverna Antico Agnello**. Traditional *osteria*. Closed Tues (except in Aug), Nov and Jan–Feb. Via Olina 18, T: 0322 90259.

€€ **Villa Crespi**. Excellent traditional restaurant (with rooms) in a Moorish folly with park on the outskirts of the town. Closed Jan. Via Fava 18 (1km east), T: 0322 911 902, F: 0322 911 919.

Piode (Valsesia)

€€ **Giardini**. Small, refined restaurant with good wines. Closed Mon and Sep. Via Umberto I 9, T: 0163 71135.

Romagnano Sesia (Valsesia)

€€ **Alla Torre**. Restaurant in the old village watch-tower, offering traditional dishes with a creative twist. Closed Mon. Via I Maggio 75, T: 0163 826 411.

Soriso

€€€ **Al Soriso**. Restaurant (with rooms) offering truly memorable, creative cuisine. Closed Mon, midday Tues, Jan and Aug. Via Roma 18, T: 0322 983 228.

LOCAL SPECIALITIES

Good coffee and pastries in **Biella** can be found at Caffè Ferrua, Via San Filippo 1. *Toma* and other local cheeses from Caseificio Alta Val Sesia, Via Varallo 5, in **Piode**. In **Romagnano Sesia**, try Gelateria Corradini, Via Grassi 8, for ice-cream; and Pasticceria Costantino, Via dei Martiri 9 for pralines, biscuits and the delicious signature cake, Torta Costantino.

FESTIVALS & EVENTS

Lago d'Orta Annual festival of early music in June on the Isola San Giulio. The steps up to the parish church in Orta San Giulio are covered with flowers in April and May.

LOMBARDY

L ombardy, with Milan as its capital, has played an important part in the making of Italy. The region includes areas of remarkable diversity, extending as it does from the summits of the central Alps to the low-lying fertile plain of the Po.

The association of Lombardy with Transalpine powers dates from the time of Charlemagne (742–814): though actually under the control of the Bishops of Milan, Lombardy remained nominally a part of the Germanic Empire until the 12th century. At this time the major Lombard cities formed the Lombard League, which defeated the Holy Roman Emperor Frederick Barbarossa at Legnano in 1176. In the following two centuries power was in the hands of local dynasties: these included the Torriani, Visconti and Sforza at Milan, Pavia, Cremona, and Bergamo; the Suardi and Colleoni at Bergamo; the Pallavicini, Torriani, Scaligeri and Visconti at Brescia; and the Bonacolsi and Gonzaga at Mantua. Many of these families became important patrons of the arts within their dominions.

The Venetian Republic encroached on the eastern part of the region after the fall of the powerful Visconti rulers at the beginning of the 15th century. Lombard territory was invaded by the kings of France in the 16th century, and in 1535 the Duchy of Milan became a dependency of the Spanish Habsburgs, though Ticino and the Valtellina in the north were incorporated into the Swiss Confederation. With the extinction of the Habsburg line in Spain (1700), Lombardy was transferred to Austrian dominion and, with the brief interlude of the Napoleonic Cisalpine Republic and the French kingdoms of Lombardy and of Italy (1797–1814), it remained a subject-province of Austria, the Valtellina being detached from Switzerland in 1797. National aspirations were repressed by the Austrian military governors of the 19th century until the victory of the allied French and Piedmontese brought Lombardy beneath the Italian flag in 1859.

THE LOMBARDS

The Lombards (or Langobards, so named for their long beards) were a Germanic tribe who arrived in Italy in the 6th century. Though initially they occupied much of the peninsula, they were driven back by the Frankish kings Pepin the Short and Charlemagne, eventually consolidating their power base in the northern area now known as Lombardy. Over the centuries the Lombards adopted both the Latin language and Roman Catholic religion, though their relationship with Rome was never easy, and they were constantly at odds with the Pope: Lombardy was under the control of the bishops of Milan. In 774 Charlemagne defeated the Lombards and had himself crowned with the famous iron crown. That crown (now kept at Monza, *see p. 147*) was also used for the coronation of Otto I, the first Holy Roman Emperor.

Lombardy and the poets

Lombardy has always been celebrated for its beauty and fertility. In Shakespeare's *Taming of the Shrew* Lucentio speaks of 'fruitfull Lumbardie, The pleasant garden of great Italy'. The Bard's judgement was soon seconded by others—for example the 17th-century traveller Thomas Coryate, who wrote:
> 'Surely such is the fertility of this country, that I thinke no Region or Province under the Sunne may compare with it. For it is passing plentifully furnished with all things, tending both to pleasure and profit, being the very Paradise and Canaan of Christendome. For if Italy is the garden of the world, so is Lombardy the garden of Italy.'

From the Euganean Hills Shelley observed, in 1818:
> 'Beneath is spread like a green sea
> The waveless plain of Lombardy,
> Bounded by the vaporous air,
> Islanded by cities fair'.

His metaphor of Lombard cities as islands in a sea of green was reworked and re-employed by countless other writers.

MILAN

Milan is the second largest city in Italy and the principal commercial and industrial centre of the country. At the same time it is a place of great historical and artistic interest, with magnificent art collections (notably the Brera Gallery), the renowned La Scala opera house, a remarkable Gothic cathedral and many important churches, including Santa Maria delle Grazie, home to Leonardo da Vinci's famous fresco of the *Last Supper*. Many of the large palaces of Milan have handsome courtyards; some of the best are to be found on Via Borgonuovo and Via Brera (most of them are marked with yellow signs). Huge 19th-century residential blocks with numerous apartments arranged around pretty interior courtyards are characteristic of the city. The northern skyline is punctuated by skyscrapers, and Milan is a good place to study 19th- and 20th-century Italian architecture.

Milanese history

Milan has long been an important place. The city's ancient predecessor, Mediolanum (middle of the plain), was a Celtic settlement which came under Roman control in 222 BC. Occupying a key position on trade routes between Rome and northern Europe, by the 4th century AD it had a population of nearly 100,000 and rivalled Rome in importance. It was by an edict made here, in 313, that Constantine the Great officially recognised the Christian religion, and in the years that followed the city became a major centre of Christianity. Among the more influential Church fathers who lived and worked here was the great bishop of Milan, St Ambrose (340–397), the friend and mentor of St Augustine.

Though devastated by the barbarian invasions, Milan survived to become a typical Italian city-state, governed by an assembly of free citizens who cast off their feudal obligations and advanced one of Europe's early claims to self-determination. In an attempt to crush Milan's independent spirit, Holy Roman Emperor Frederick Barbarossa sacked Milan in 1158 and 1162, but was beaten at Legnano in 1176 by the survivors and their allies, who came together to form the *Lega Lombarda* (Lombard League). In recent years the name and example of this medieval alliance have been taken up by a separatist movement whose declared goal is to free Lombardy once again—this time from lawmakers in Rome.

In the late Middle Ages Milan was ruled by a succession of powerful families, including the Torriani, who took control of the city around 1260. They were overthrown in 1277 by the Visconti, who held power until 1447. The city had a period of particular splendour under Gian Galeazzo Visconti (1385–1402), who founded what is still the city's most impressive monument, the cathedral (duomo), in 1386. After a republican interlude of three years, Francesco Sforza, the famous mercenary general and defender of Milan against Venice, who had married Bianca, daughter of the last Visconti, proclaimed himself duke. He was succeeded by his son Galeazzo Maria, and then by his infant grandson Gian Galeazzo, under the regency of his mother. The infant duke's power was usurped by his uncle Lodovico il Moro, who, despite his low opinion of rule by law, was a great patron of the arts, and under whose rule the city flourished.

A succession of invasions, which would bring Milan under foreign rule for nearly four centuries, began in 1494 with the expedition of Charles VIII of France. Between 1499 and 1535 the dukedom was contested by the French and the Spanish, and under the Spanish emperor Charles V Milan became capital of a province of the Holy Roman Empire. In 1713 the city passed to Austria under the Treaty of Utrecht, which marked the end of the War of the Spanish Succession. In 1796 it was seized by Napoleon, who three years later made it capital of his Cisalpine Republic, and, after a brief occupation by the Austrians and Russians, capital of the Italian Republic (1802) and of the Kingdom of Italy (1805). After the fall of Napoleon (1814) the Austrians returned, but the Milanese tenaciously opposed this renewed imposition of foreign rule. After three decades of passive resistance the populace rose up in the rebellion known as the *Cinque Giornate* (18–22 March 1848). When the troops of Vittorio Emanuele II and Napoleon III defeated the Austrian forces at the battle of Magenta in 1859, the city declared its allegiance to the nascent Kingdom of Italy.

Milanese art and architecture

Milan is primarily an architect's city, where ideas are transposed with singular grace and skill from the two-dimensional surface of the drawing table to the three-dimensional volume of real space. Here you can trace the history of Italian architecture from antiquity right up to the present day. And although all periods are represented, the very old and the very new are those that draw the greatest attention.

Romanesque to Art Nouveau

In the early Middle Ages Milan's church builders gave rise to a style now known as the Lombard Romanesque. Its distinctive characteristic is the mixture of Roman architectural devices such as round arches and cylindrical columns with elements inherited from the Byzantine tradition, such as the extended forecourt or narthex. The most important example is the magnificent basilica of Sant'Ambrogio (*see p. 120*).

Milan's duomo is one of the most striking Gothic buildings in the world. Its flamboyant tracery rivals the best examples of the genre in France and northern Europe.

The wealthy and cultured court of the Sforzas attracted many great Renaissance artists, including the architects Filarete, Michelozzo and Bramante, the sculptor Amadeo, and the painters Foppa and Bergognone. Bergognone (active 1480–1522) is an important exponent of the native Milanese style, a style he clung to despite the artistic revolution that took place around him. For Milanese art was completely transformed by the arrival from Tuscany in 1483 of Leonardo da Vinci. This great artist and the city he adopted were the centre of an artistic and humanistic flowering that continued until the fall of Lodovico il Moro in 1499. Leonardo's pupils Luini and Gaudenzio Ferrari formed schools of their own. The sculptors Bambaia and Cristoforo Solari also felt his influence.

Towards the end of the 16th century Camillo and Giulio Procaccini introduced a new, Baroque style of painting from Bologna, and Galeazzo Alessi imported Baroque ideas from Rome into architecture. Milan's most important Baroque architect is Francesco Maria Richini (*see p. 129*). The Neoclassical buildings of Luigi Cagnola and Luigi Canonica (both born in 1762) reflect the tastes of the Napoleonic period. At the turn of the 20th century a number of districts were built in a distinctive Art Nouveau style, called Liberty after the London shop that played so large a part in the style's dissemination.

Twentieth-century trends

In the early 20th century, bustling, industrial Milan was one of the centres of Futurism, Italy's great contribution to the Modern movement, which hailed the new world of mechanical forces and denounced all attachment to the past. 'A roaring motorcar, its hood adorned with pipes like serpents with explosive breath ... is more beautiful than the *Winged Victory of Samothrace*', declared Futurist theorist Filippo Tommaso Marinetti. The original members of the movement were the painters Umberto Boccioni, Carlo Carrà, Luigi Russolo, Giacomo Balla and Gino Severini, and the architect Antonio Sant'Elia. They were later joined by many others. The Futurists aspired to bring art into closer contact with life, which they conceived as force and movement. Like the French Cubists, they held that movement and light destroy the static materiality of objects. The Futurist doctrine of simultaneity, by which movement was to be rendered by simultaneous presentation of successive aspects of form in motion, was similar to the Cubist notion of the simultaneous presentation of multiple views of a single object; but the Futurist idea differed from the more exclusively visual simultaneity put forward by Apollinaire in his theory of Cubism in 1911, in that the Futurists spoke of simultaneity of plastic states of the soul in artistic creation. The Futurists were also the first to advocate a new conception of picture space whereby the observer would be situated at the centre of the picture.

The most important artistic event of the 1920s in Italy was the formation, in Milan, of the group that exhibited together in 1924 under the name Novecento. The name, coined by the theoretician of the movement, Margherita Sarfatti, means 'nine hundred', a reference to the new century. Its leading figure, the former Futurist painter Carrà, called for a return to a quieter figurative style based on traditional values. But to find a common denominator for all the artists associated with Novecento is difficult. Even Sarfatti was vague in describing the goals of her artists: she cited 'clarity of form and dignity of

Fountain at Milan's main railway station.

conception, nothing magical, nothing eccentric, an increasing closure toward the arbitrary and the obscure'. Thus one finds in Novecento such painters as Mario Sironi, who captured the movement of modernity with expressionistic force, as well as subtly melancholy artists such as Pietro Marussig. The movement was much loved by the Fascists because of its emphasis on tradition and national identity.

The architecture of the 1920s developed in two distinct directions. The Modernist movement gave rise to the functionalist trend known as Rationalism, which made an appeal to ideals of logic and order but claimed also a definitive break with the past. Though initially apolitical, the movement later won the support of the Fascist regime, by this time in full power and needful of a cultural trademark. The protagonists of the movement were Giuseppe Terragni and Giuseppe Pagano, but many other architects—including Giò Ponti, Sartoris, and Gardella in Milan—expressed Rationalist ideals in their buildings and objects.

In reaction to this, conservative architects of the period proposed yet another return to Classical models. A new traditionalist orientation, called Novecento to underscore its bonds with the conservative trend in painting, developed throughout Italy and particularly in Milan, where growth was most rapid and where the Neoclassical tradition of the early 19th century offered inspiration and continuity with the past. The leading figure of this movement was Marcello Piacentini, promoter of a supposedly balanced and dignified, spiritual and expressive Classicism.

After the Second World War Milan became the undisputed centre of contemporary culture in Italy, asserting its primacy in painting, sculpture and architecture as well as in industrial design and fashion. Lucio Fontana, the painter, and Piero Manzoni, the precursor of Conceptual Art, both lived and worked here.

The first clearly identifiable architectural style of the postwar period was Neorealism. This trend, like Neorealism in Italian cinema, arose in reaction to Fascist triumphalism, to which it opposed simpler, more organic forms. It clearly reflected the desire, of a generation of architects compromised by association with the regime, to atone for past sins; but it was also brought about by the arrival in Italy of ideas originating in the United States and northern Europe and expressed in the work of figures such as Frank Lloyd Wright and Alvar Aalto.

By the early 50s Italy was well on the way to attaining the status of a modern industrial democracy. Here, as elsewhere in Europe and in North America, the dominant architectural trend became the International Style, a functionalist rereading of the teachings of the great masters of the Modern movement that advocated the adoption of common standards in all buildings, regardless of location. Giò Ponti and Pier Luigi Nervi's Pirelli Building is a good example of the International Style. In more recent times this trend has been followed, in Milan as elsewhere, by a Post-Modern reaction, embodied in a new eclecticism combining Classical elements (such as arches and columns) with forms derived from vernacular architecture. This is reflected in many Milanese interiors—shops, cafés, hotels and restaurants.

The 1950s marked the beginning of Italy's economic miracle: the standard of living increased enormously, creating demand for high-quality consumer goods. Industry responded by increasing production and by involving some of the country's great creative talents in product design, giving rise to that distinctive look for which Italian products are famous. Today the creations of Milanese designers grace homes and workplaces throughout the developed world.

THE DUOMO & ENVIRONS

The duomo

Map p. 107; 11

Milan's magnificent late-Gothic duomo is the second largest church in Italy, after St Peter's in Rome. The impressive exterior, with its numerous flying buttresses, is decorated with some 2,000 sculptures. It has a superb tower over the crossing and a remarkable 16th-century façade, which blends elements of the Classical and Gothic. It was particularly admired in the Romantic age.

The cathedral was begun in 1386 under Gian Galeazzo Visconti, who presented it with a marble quarry at Candoglia which still belongs to the cathedral chapter. The

MILAN: THE DUOMO

design is attributed to the Lombard masters Simone da Orsenigo and Giovanni Grassi, who were assisted by French, German, and Flemish craftsmen. Filippino degli Organi was appointed master mason in 1400, and he was succeeded by Giovanni Solari and his son Guiniforte, and Giovanni Antonio Amadeo. In 1567 St Charles Borromeo (then bishop of Milan) appointed Pellegrino Tibaldi as architect, and under him the church was dedicated. The statue of the Virgin was placed on its summit in 1774. The façade, begun in the 16th century, was completed in 1805, just in time for Napoleon to crown himself King of Italy here. The façade was in fact completed to Napoleon's orders.

Some celebrated reactions

How glorious that Cathedral is! worthy almost of standing face to face with the snow Alps; and itself a sort of snow dream by an artist architect, taken asleep in a glacier!

Elizabeth Barrett Browning, letter, 1851

The cathedral is an awful failure. Outside the design is monstrous and inartistic. The over-elaborated details stuck high up where no one can see them; everything is vile in it; it is, however, imposing and gigantic as a failure, through its great size and elaborate execution.

Oscar Wilde, letter to his mother, 25 June 1875

… the beautiful city with its dominant frost-crystalline duomo…

John Ruskin, Praeterita, 1885–89

The interior

The huge cruciform interior, with double-aisled nave, single-aisled transepts and a pentagonal apse, has a forest of 52 tall columns, most of which bear circles of figures in canopied niches instead of capitals. The splendid effect is heightened by the stained glass of the windows. The Classical pavement is by Tibaldi.

The visit starts in the **south aisle**. Above the plain granite sarcophagus of Archbishop Aribert (d. 1045) is a stained-glass window by Cristoforo de' Mottis (1473–77). The red-marble sarcophagus on pillars is of Archbishop Ottone Visconti (d. 1295). The tomb of Marco Carelli is by Filippino degli Organi (1406). Beyond a relief with a design for the façade by Giuseppe Brentano (1886) is the small monument of Canon Giovanni Vimercati (d. 1548), with two fine portraits and a damaged *Pietà* by Bambaia. The stained glass (1470–75) shows the influence of Vincenzo Foppa. The glass above the sixth altar is by Nicolò da Varallo (1480–89).

In the south transept is the monument of Gian Giacomo Medici, with bronze statues, by Leone Leoni (1560–63). The stained glass in the two transept windows is by Corrado de' Mocchis (1554–64). In the transept apse is the monumental altar of San Giovanni Bono (1763). On the altar with a marble relief by Bambaia, is a statue (right) of *St Catherine*, by Cristoforo Lombardo. The statue of St Bartholomew flayed and carrying his skin is by Marco d'Agrate (1562).

On the impressive *tiburio*, or **tower over the crossing**, are medallions (on the pendentives) with 15th-century busts of the Doctors of the Church, and some 60 statues (on the arches). The four piers had to be reinforced in 1984 in order to consolidate the structure of the building. The presbytery (usually open to worshippers only) was designed by Pellegrino Tibaldi (1567). It contains two pulpits (supported by bronze figures by Francesco Brambilla), and a large bronze ciborium, also by Tibaldi. High above the altar hangs a paschal candlestick by Lorenzo da Civate (1447).

The **treasury** (*open Mon–Sat 9–12 & 2.30–6, Sun 2.30–6*) contains a silver reliquary box of the late 4th century; a 13th-century dove with Limoges enamels; three ivory diptychs (5th–11th century); an ivory bucket of 979–80; the pax of Pio IV, attributed to Leone Leoni; the evangelistary cover of Archbishop Aribert (11th century) decorated with enamels; and church vestments. The **crypt**, decorated with stucco reliefs by Galeazzo Alessi and Tibaldi, contains the richly-robed body of St Charles Borromeo, the leading spirit of the Counter-Reformation, made Cardinal Archbishop of Milan in 1560 and canonised in 1610.

The **ambulatory** is separated from the choir by a beautiful marble screen designed by Pellegrino Tibaldi (1567). The sacristy doorways date from the late 14th century. The **sacristy** contains a statue of Christ at the Column by Cristoforo Solari. Beyond (high up) is a statue of Martin V, the pope who consecrated the high altar in 1418, by Jacopino da Tradate (1424), and the black marble tomb of Cardinal Caracciolo (d. 1538), by Bambaia. The large embroidered standard dates from the late 16th century.

In the middle of the **north transept** is the Trivulzio candelabrum, a seven-branched bronze candlestick nearly 5m high, of French or German workmanship (13th or 14th century). The stained-glass window above the sculptured altarpiece of the Crucifix

(1605) is by Nicolò da Varallo (1479). The altar in the transept apse dates from 1768. The Gothic altar of St Catherine has two statues attributed to Cristoforo Solari.

In the **north aisle**, the eighth altarpiece is by Federico Barocci. The next four stained-glass windows date from the 16th century. On the sixth altar is the crucifix carried by St Charles Borromeo during the plague of 1576; at the third altar, the tomb of three archbishops of the Arcimboldi family, attributed to Galeazzo Alessi; in the second bay, late-12th-century marble reliefs of apostles. Opposite is the font, a porphyry urn thought to date from Roman times, covered with a canopy by Tibaldi.

The **excavations** beneath the church (*open Tues–Sun 9–12 & 2.30–6*) are entered from the west end. Here you can see the 4th-century octagonal baptistery where St Ambrose baptised St Augustine in 387; remains of the basilica of Santa Tecla (begun in the 4th century); and Roman baths of the 1st century BC.

An interesting series of 52 paintings illustrating the **life and miracles of St Charles Borromeo** are hung in a double row between the nave and transept pillars between 1 November and 6 January every year. Known as the *Quadroni di San Carlo*, they were commissioned in 1602 by Cardinal Federico Borromeo to honour the memory of his cousin Charles. Above are hung the scenes from his life (1602–04) and below the scenes of his miracles (1609–10): the best ones are by Il Cerano and Giulio Cesare Procaccini (others are by Morazzone, Carlo Buzzi, Duchino, Fiammenghino, and Domenico Pellegrini). The last eight were painted in 1660–1740 to complete the series, which survives intact.

The roof
The entrance to the roof (*open 9–5.45; winter 9–4.15; also lift, entered from outside the north or south transept*) is a small door in the corner of the transept, near the Medici tomb. The ascent (up 158 steps) provides a superb view of the sculptural detail of the exterior and is highly recommended. From the walkways across the roof you can examine the details of the carving, and beyond are magnificent views of the city. The Carelli spire, the oldest pinnacle, is at the angle facing the corso. From above the west front it is possible to walk along the spine of the nave roof to the base of the crossing, by Amadeo (1490–1500), who also planned the four turrets but finished only the one at the northeast angle. Stairs lead up from the southwest turret to the platform of the crossing. From here another staircase, in the northeast turret, ascends to the topmost gallery at the base of the central spire, surmounted by the **Madonnina** (108m from the ground), a statue of gilded copper, nearly 4m high. From this height there is a magnificent view of the city, the Lombard plain, the Alps from Monte Viso to the Ortles (with the prominent peaks of the Matterhorn, Monte Rosa, the two Grigne, and Monte Resegone), and the Apennines.

The Museo del Duomo
Map p. 107, 11
The former Palazzo Reale stands to the south of the cathedral, on the site of the 13th-century town hall. It was rebuilt in Neoclassical style in 1772–78 for the Austrian

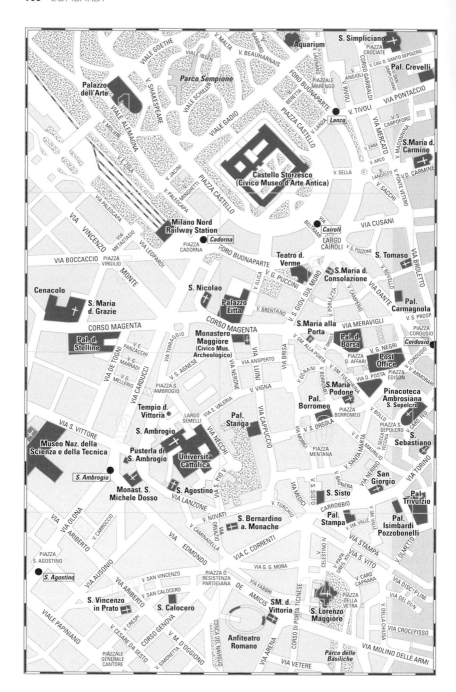

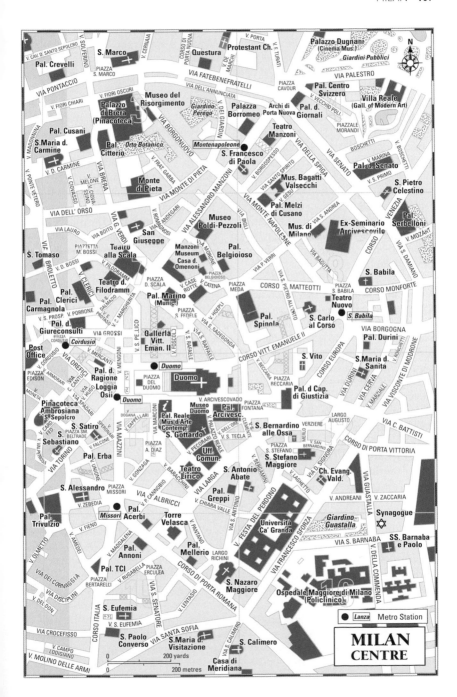

MILAN
CENTRE

grand dukes by Giuseppe Piermarini (and altered again in the 19th century, and restored after bomb damage in 1943). It now belongs to the municipality, and there are long-term plans to restore it and open it to the public. At present important exhibitions are held here.

Opposite the south transept of the cathedral is the entrance to the **Museo del Duomo** (*open daily 10–1.15 & 3–6*). Highlights are Room 3, an 18th-century Neoclassical vaulted hall by Piermarini, with a fine display of sculpture from the Visconti period from the exterior of the cathedral, and 14th–15th-century stained glass; Room 9, containing sculptures attributed to Giovanni Antonio Amadeo and Andrea Fusina, and a 15th-century Flemish tapestry of the Passion; Room 10, with an altar frontal of St Charles Borromeo (1610) and drawings by Il Cerano; Room 11, with tapestries made in Ferrara c. 1540, probably on cartoons by Giulio Romano, and the *Infant Christ among the Doctors*, an early work by Jacopo Tintoretto. The gallery (room 15) displays plans illustrating the history of the duomo, and Room 16 contains a splendid wooden model of the duomo constructed by Bernardino Zenale da Treviglio in 1519, and later models.

The second floor of Palazzo Reale (entered through the main courtyard) hosts the **Civico Museo d'Arte Contemporanea**, known as CIMAC (*closed at the time of writing; T: 02 8646 3054*). This fairly representative collection of 20th-century Italian art, in a stark temporary arrangement, is divided into two parts: works up to 1950 in the rooms on the left, later works and the Jucker collection in the right-hand rooms. The rooms on the left (1–23) contain paintings by the Futurists Umberto Boccioni, Giacomo Balla and Gino Severini; by Novecento artists Pietro Marussig, Carlo Carrà and Mario Sironi; and by Modern masters such as Amedeo Modigliani, Giorgio de Chirico, Arturo Martini, Giorgio Morandi, Felice Casorati, Massimo Campigli, Filippo de Pisis and Pablo Picasso. The rooms on the right of the entrance include the Jucker Collection, with works by Balla, Severini, Sironi, de Pisis, Carrà, Morandi, Braque, Matisse and Picasso.

Around the cathedral square

The **Arengario**, on Via Marconi, is an interesting modern building (1939–56) designed by Giovanni Muzio, with reliefs by Arturo Martini. It is now the headquarters of the tourist board.

The church of **San Gottardo** (Map p. 107, 11), formerly the palace chapel, lies beyond the courtyard of the Palazzo Reale. It is entered from Via Pecorari. The exterior and beautiful campanile are attributed to Francesco Pecorari (1330–36), and the Neoclassical interior has stuccoes by Giocondo Albertolli. It contains a very damaged 14th-century fresco of the *Crucifixion* showing the influence of Giotto, who is known to have been in the city in 1335. The monument to Azzone Visconti is by Giovanni di Balduccio.

The archbishops' palace (marked Pal. Arcivesc. on the map) is mainly the work of Tibaldi (after 1570), with a façade by Giuseppe Piermarini (1784–1801) on Piazza Fontana. This square is associated with a disquieting episode in recent Italian history: a terrorist bomb killed 16 people here (and wounded 88) in 1969.

The north side of Piazza del Duomo is connected with Piazza della Scala by the colossal **Galleria Vittorio Emanuele II** (Map p. 107, 7). This huge glass-roofed shopping arcade, with cafés and restaurants, was designed in 1865 by Giuseppe Mengoni, who fell from the top and was killed a few days before the inauguration ceremony in 1878. Mengoni's design combines a severely Classical style with a remarkable sensitivity for new materials such as iron. The gallery was part of a grandiose project to renovate Piazza del Duomo, and its success led to the construction of numerous imitations in other Italian cities, notably the Galleria Mazzini in Genoa, the Galleria Principe in Naples and the Galleria Sciarra in Rome.

On the west side of Piazza del Duomo, Via Mercanti leads past Palazzo dei Giureconsulti (1560–64), used for exhibitions. The fine Palazzo della Ragione (Map p. 107, 11), erected in 1228–33, has an upper storey added in 1771, and remains of 13th-century frescoes inside. A remarkable equestrian relief of 1233 adorns its rear wall in the peaceful Piazza Mercanti. In this old square are the Gothic Loggia degli Osii (1316) and the Baroque Palazzo delle Scuole Palatine (1645).

La Scala

Map p. 107, 7

Piazza della Scala, reached from Piazza del Duomo by the Galleria Vittorio Emanuele, has a monument to Leonardo da Vinci (by Pietro Magni, 1872), surrounded by figures of his pupils, Boltraffio, Salaino, Cesare da Sesto and Marco d'Oggiono. The square takes its name from the Teatro alla Scala, Italy's most famous opera house. It was built for Empress Maria Theresa of Austria, in 1776, by Giuseppe Piermarini on the site of the church of Santa Maria della Scala after the destruction by fire of the Regio Ducale Teatro. It opened in 1778 with *Europa Riconosciuta* by Antonio Salieri and Mattia Verazi. Works by Rossini, Donizetti, Bellini, Verdi and Puccini were first acclaimed here. From the beginning of the 20th century its reputation was upheld by the legendary figure of Toscanini (who led the orchestra again in 1946 when the building was reopened after serious war damage). *NB: At the time of writing La Scala was being renovated, and performances are held in the new Teatro degli Arcimboldi, built by the City of Milan in conjunction with Pirelli.*

Palazzo Marino, the town hall, stands opposite La Scala. It has a fine façade on Piazza San Fedele by Galeazzo Alessi (1558), who also designed the splendid Mannerist courtyard. The façade on Piazza Scala was completed by Luca Beltrami (1892). Behind the Palazzo, in Piazza San Fedele, are a statue of Alessandro Manzoni (*see below*) and the church of **San Fedele**, begun by Tibaldi (1569) for St Charles Borromeo and completed by Martino Bassi and Francesco Maria Richini. It has an elaborate pulpit. The elegant Baroque church of **San Giuseppe** is held to be Richini's masterpiece. From here, Via Romagnosi leads into Via Alessandro Manzoni, named after Italy's most famous novelist (1785–1873). At Via Morone 1 is the **Museo Manzoniano** (*open daily except Sat, Mon and holidays 9.30–12 & 2–4*), containing memorabilia. Manzoni lived here from 1814 until his death, and met Balzac here in 1837.

Museo Poldi-Pezzoli

Map p. 107, 7. *Open Tues–Sun 10–6.*

Back on the busy and fashionable Via Manzoni, at no. 12, is the entrance to the **Museo Poldi-Pezzoli**, once the private residence of Gian Giacomo Poldi-Pezzoli. It was bequeathed by him, with his art collection, to the city in 1879, and opened to the public in 1881. It is a delightful museum, considered a little-known jewel by the Milanese.

The entrance hall contains a portrait of Poldi-Pezzoli by Italy's foremost Romantic painter, Francesco Hayez. A fine elliptical staircase with a Baroque fountain and landscapes by Alessandro Magnasco ascends to the main gallery. To the left are the three little Salette dei Lombardi, with *Madonnas* by Foppa and Bergognone; *The Rest on the Flight* by Andrea Solario; a *Madonna* by Boltraffio; and works by Luini and the Lombard school. The Salone Dorato has the masterpieces of the collection: a *Madonna and Child* and *Portrait of a Man* by Mantegna; a *Pietà* and *Madonna* by Botticelli; *St Nicholas of Tolentino* by Piero della Francesca; and a famous *Portrait of a Lady* by Andonio Pollaiolo or his brother Piero. Other highlights include the Bruno Falck donation of antique clocks and scientific instruments; a beautiful painting of Artemesia by the 'Maestro di Griselda' (recently attributed also to Luca Signorelli); and paintings by Guardi (*Gondolas on the Venetian Lagoon*), Rosalba Carriera and Tiepolo. There are also portraits by Cranach (including one of Martin Luther) and, on the ground floor, a splendid Persian carpet with hunting scenes, signed and dated 1542-43.

Pinacoteca di Brera

Map p. 107, 3; *open Tues–Sun 8.30–7, www.brera.beniculturali.it*

Brera is traditionally the artists' quarter of Milan and its great pinacoteca is one of the most famous art galleries in Italy. It contains the finest existing collection of Northern Italian painting from the 13th to the 20th centuries, and is a centre of the arts and sciences in Lombardy. The gallery was founded in the 18th century by the Accademia di Belle Arti, and was enlarged through acquisitions and paintings from Lombard and Venetian churches before it was officially inaugurated in 1809. The collection is never shown in its entirety. Some rooms are closed when there is a shortage of custodians; scholars can sometimes ask for special permission to see them. The collection is extremely well displayed: the arrangement proceeds chronologically and by schools.

The building was begun by Francesco Maria Richini in 1651 on the site of the medieval church of Santa Maria di Brera, the nave of which survives. The main portal (1780) is by Giuseppe Piermarini, architect of La Scala. In the monumental courtyard is a heroic statue in bronze of Napoleon I by Antonio Canova (1809; the marble version of the statue is in Apsley House, London).

I: Beyond a small room with a self-portrait by the Romantic artist Francesco Hayez, the long gallery temporarily displays early 20th-century works (particularly the Futurists) from the Jesi collection: Umberto Boccioni, Mario Sironi, Giacomo Balla, Gino Severini, Carlo Carrà, Giorgio Morandi, Filippo de Pisis, Medardo Rosso and Arturo Martini. New acquisitions are also hung

Bernardino Luini: *Madonna del Roseto* (1508–10).

here. In a little room off the gallery, the Mocchirolo chapel, frescoed by a close follower of Giovanni da Milano, has been reconstructed.

II–V: The chronological display begins here. 13th-century Italian paintings include works by Giovanni da Milano, Ambrogio Lorenzetti (*Madonna and Child*), and Bernardo Daddi. There is a fine polyptych by Gentile da Fabriano, and works of the 15th- and 16th-century Venetian school.

VI: Works by 15th-century painters from Padua and the Veneto, including some masterpieces by Mantegna: his famous *Dead Christ*, with remarkable foreshortening, and a polyptych representing *St Luke the Evangelist with Saints* (1453). Also three exquisite works by Giovanni Bellini: a *Pietà, Madonna Greca* (one of his most beautiful paintings), and a *Madonna and Child* in a landscape (1510). Vittore Carpaccio is also well represented, with scenes from the life of the Virgin, two works from the Scuola degli Albanesi in Venice, and *St Stephen Disputing with the Doctors* (1514). *St Peter Martyr with Saints*, and *Madonna and Child Enthroned* are two works by

Cima da Conegliano.

VII: 16th-century Venetian portraits by Titian, Lorenzo Lotto, Torbido, and Tintoretto.

VIII: The highlight is *St Mark Preaching in Alexandria*, a splendid large painting commissioned from Gentile and Giovanni Bellini by the Scuola Grande di San Marco in Venice.

IX: 16th-century Venetian paintings. Works by Jacopo Bassano; Veronese (*Agony in the Garden, St Anthony Abbot with Saints, Supper in the House of Simon, Baptism* and *Temptation of Christ, Last Supper*); Tintoretto (*Deposition, Saints*

PINACOTECA DI BRERA

Numbers on the floorplan correspond to the numbering in the text and in the gallery itself.

Beneath the Cross, Finding of the Body of St Mark at Alexandria); Titian (*St Jerome*); Lorenzo Lotto (*Pietà*).

X–XIII: Works by Bonifacio Bembo, Luini, Bramante and Bergognone.

XIV: The 16th-century Venetian school: Palma Vecchio; Paris Bordone (*Baptism of Christ*), Giovanni Battista Moroni and Giovanni Gerolamo Savoldo.

XV: 15th–16th-century Lombard paintings and frescoes: Marco d'Oggiono and Bergognone. The Pala Sforzesca (*Madonna enthroned with Doctors of the Church and the Family of Lodovico il Moro*) is by an unknown Lombard painter (c. 1490–1520), known from this painting as the Maestro della Pala Sforzesca. Also here are works by Vincenzo Foppa, Bramantino, and Gaudenzio Ferrari.

XVI: The highlight is Sofonisba Anguissola's *Portrait of Minerva Anguissola* (after 1560).

XVIII: 16th-century Lombard paintings by Callisto Piazza, Giulio, Antonio and Bernardino Campi and Boccaccino.

XIX: Followers of Leonardo da Vinci: Giovanni Ambrogio de Predis, Andrea Solario, and Giovanni Antonio Boltraffio (*Gerolamo Casio*). Works by Bergognone, and Bernardino Luini's celebrated (*Madonna del Roseto*).

XX: The 15th-century Ferrarese and Emilian schools: Francesco del Cossa (*St John the Baptist, St Peter*); works by Lorenzo Costa, Gian Francesco Maineri, Marco Palmezzano, Francesco Zaganelli, and Filippo Mazzola.

XXI: Polyptychs by 15th-century painters from the Marche, and a delightful group of works by Carlo Crivelli: *Crucifixion*, *Madonna della Candeletta*, *Coronation of the Virgin* and *Pietà* (1483).

XXII–XXIII: 15th–16th-century Ferrarese and Emilian schools, including Ercole de' Roberti, and two works by Correggio.

XXIV: Contains the two most famous works in the collection, Raphael's *Marriage of the Virgin* and Piero della Francesca's *Montefeltro Altarpiece* (*see overleaf*). There is also a processional standard, an early work by Luca Signorelli. *Christ at the Column* is the Bramante's only known panel painting.

XXIX: Works by Caravaggio (*Supper at Emmaus*), Mattia Preti, Jusepe de Ribera, Giovanni Battista Caracciolo, and Orazio Gentileschi (*Three Martyrs*).

XXX: The 17th-century Lombard school. Giulio Cesare Procaccini, Daniele Crespi, Giovanni Battista Crespi, Morazzone and Tanzio.

XXXII: 16th- and 17th-century Flemish and Dutch paintings. There is also a *St Francis* by El Greco.

XXXIII: Portraits by Rembrandt (of his sister) and van Dyck, and works by Brueghel the Elder.

XXXIV–XXXVI: 17th- and 18th-century works by Pierre Subleyras, Giuseppe Maria Crespi (*Crucifixion*), Sebastiano Ricci, Luca Giordano (*Ecce Homo*), and Giovanni Battista Tiepolo. Portraits by Sir Joshua Reynolds and Anton Raphael Mengs. Venetian works by Tiepolo, Guardi, Bernardo Bellotto, Canaletto, Piazzetta and Rosalba Carriera.

XXXVII, XXXVIII: 19th-century works by Silvestro Lega (the *Pergolato*), Prud'hon, Francesco Hayez, Andrea Appiani and Sir Thomas Lawrence. A version of Giuseppe Pellizza da Volpedo's famous *Quarto Stato* and Boccioni's *Self-Portrait* are displayed just before the exit.

TWO MASTERPIECES AT THE BRERA

Raphael's *Marriage of the Virgin* (Room XXIV).
Perugino, Pinturicchio and Raphael form the 'Umbrian School' of Renaissance painting. But long before they were an art-historical category, these three artists were close friends, Pinturicchio and Raphael having been Perugino's most distinguished students. This is Raphael's first major painting, and both its composition and its palette recall Perugino's *Giving of the Keys to St Peter* (1481) in the Sistine Chapel in Rome—which also features a dense group of foreground figures and an idealized architectural setting rendered in clear, simple colours. But everything appears more natural in Raphael, the figures are freer and more animated, the setting less rigid and formal. Giorgio Vasari, the 16th-century biographer of Renaissance artists, put his finger on what, in modern marketing language, we might call call the Raphael Difference. 'The liberality with which Heaven now and again unites in one person the inexhaustible riches of its treasures and all those graces and rare gifts which are usually shared among many over a long period, is seen in Raphael', Varsari suggests. 'Those who possess such gifts as |he| are not mere men, but rather mortal gods'.

Piero della Francesca's *Montefeltro Altarpiece* (Room XXIV).
This beautiful painting by the masterful and influential Central Italian painter was originally made for San Bernardino degli Zoccolanti, a little country church near Urbino. The donor is the armoured gentleman praying in the foreground—Federico da Montefeltro, a famed mercenary general who eventually became one of the most powerful political and cultural figures of the Renaissance. The painting may have been a memorial to Battista Sforza, his wife, who died in childbirth. It has been dated between 1472 and 1474, and its clear, crisp presentation of forms in space was widely imitated in monumental devotional paintings in northern Italian and Venetian art. Scholars have spilled rivers of ink trying to explain the 'egg' hanging from the ceiling. Some suggest that it isn't an egg at all: Marian literature is replete with images of Mary as an oyster and Jesus as her pearl. Nevertheless, there is a convention of the egg as symbol of the Virgin Birth. The belief that ostriches left their eggs to be hatched by the sun led to comparisons with the sun and the Son. As the great medieval philosopher and theologian Albertus Magnus (guide and mentor of Thomas Aquinas) wrote: 'If the sun can hatch the eggs of the ostrich, why cannot a virgin conceive with the aid of the true Sun?'

Piero della Francesca: *Montefeltro Altarpiece* (1472–74).

THE CASTELLO SFORZESCO & ITS MUSEUMS

This part of the city can be reached easily from Piazza del Duomo on the underground (Line 1) in two stops (Cairoli station), or from Piazza della Scala by Tram 1.

During the Middle Ages Milan's northern quarters grew up around the basilica of **San Simpliciano**. This, the northernmost of Milan's early Christian basilicas, is dedicated to the successor of St Ambrose in the episcopal chair. It was probably founded by St Ambrose himself in the 4th century and, despite the alterations of the 12th century, stands largely in its original form. The interior contains the *Coronation of the Virgin*, a fine fresco by Bergognone, in the restored Romanesque apse. Although San Simpliciano remains the area's oldest monument, it has long ceased to be the most conspicuous. Today northern Milan is dominated by the huge fortified complex of the Castello Sforzesco and the shady green Parco Sempione, behind it.

The Castello Sforzesco
Map p. 106, 2.

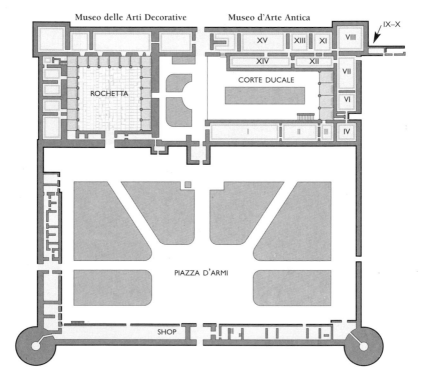

The spacious Foro Buonaparte, Largo Cairoli and Piazza Castello were all designed in a huge hemicycle in 1884 in front of the Castello Sforzesco. This was the stronghold built for Francesco Sforza in 1451–66 on the site of a 14th-century castle of the Visconti. After a long period of use as barracks, it was restored by Luca Beltrami (1893–1904). Badly damaged by bombing in 1943, when two-thirds of the archives and many other treasures were lost, it was again carefully restored. It now contains important art collections and cultural institutions.

The fortress is square in plan; on the façade are three towers, of which the central one is the **Filarete tower**, destroyed by an explosion of powder in 1521 and rebuilt by Beltrami following the supposed design of the original. The entrance to the castle from Largo Cairoli is beneath the tower that gives access to the huge Piazza d'Armi, the main courtyard. Almost in the centre of the far side is the 15th-century Torre di Bona di Savoia, beyond which to the left is the **Rocchetta**, with a courtyard, which served as a keep. On the right is the Corte Ducale, the residential part of the castle, with a charming courtyard, where you will find the entrance to the **Museo d'Arte Antica** and the **Pinacoteca**. The large collections of sculpture, paintings, furniture, musical instruments, and decorative arts are beautifully arranged and well labelled: only a few of the works are mentioned here.

Corte Ducale
Museo d'Arte Antica
Open Tues–Sun 9–5.30.

I–IV: Early Christian and Gothic art. Highlights include fragments from ancient churches and other Byzantine and Romanesque remains, including a 6th-century marble portrait head supposedly of the Empress Theodora; Visconti tombs by Bonino da Campione (1363); remains of the façade of Santa Maria di Brera and statues from the east gate of the city, by Giovanni di Balduccio of Pisa; a 14th-century pavement tomb with an effigy thought to be that of Bona di Savoia; and a sepulchral monument of the Rusca family by a late 14th-century Lombard master. The vault of room IV is frescoed with the arms of Philip II of Spain and Mary Tudor.

VI–VII: Beyond a small chapel with 14th-century Venetian sculpture are works from the communal and Spanish periods. Room VI contains 12th-century reliefs from the old Porta Romana, showing the triumph of the Milanese over Barbarossa (1176). Room VII, with frescoed escutcheons of the Dukes of Milan, is hung with 17th-century Brussels tapestries. Here is displayed the Gonfalon of Milan, designed by Giuseppe Meda (1566), and a statue of Adam by Stoldo Lorenzi.

VIII: The Sala delle Asse, with remarkable frescoed decoration in the vault, was designed in 1498 by Leonardo da Vinci, but repainted. The ilex branches and leaves are used in a complicated architectural structure in which the form of the octagon recurs. On the far wall are two fascinating fragments of monchrome tempera decoration by the hand of Leonardo (1498), depicting tree trunks with branches and roots growing out of cracks in stratified rock formations. Off the Sala delle Asse are two small rooms over the moat.

IX–X: Sforza portraits attributed to Bernardino Luini and his circle, and reliefs by Bambaia. Room X has an oval low relief carved on both faces by Pierino da Vinci.

XI: The Sala dei Ducali is decorated with coats of arms showing the ancestry of Galeazzo Maria Sforza. It contains a relief by Agostino di Duccio from the Tempio Malatestiano at Rimini, and 15th-century sculptures.

XII: The former chapel, with frescoes (restored) by Bonifacio Bembo and Stefano de' Fedeli and assistants (1466–76). The seated statue of the Madonna and Child is a Lombard work of the late 15th century, and the standing Madonna is by Pietro Solari. Outside you can see the Renaissance 'Portico of the Elephant', named after a faded fresco.

XIII: The Sala delle Colombine, with red-and-gold fresco decorations with the arms of Bona di Savoia (wife of Galeazzo Maria Sforza), and sculpture by Amadeo and Cristoforo Mantegazza.

XIV: The Sala Verde, divided by Renaissance doorways salvaged from Milanese palaces: that from the Banco Mediceo (1455) is by Michelozzo. Displayed here are tombs, armorial sculptures, and a fine collection of armour.

XV: The Sala degli Scarlioni, containing the effigy of Gaston de Foix and reliefs from his tomb (1525), masterpieces by Bambaia. In the second part of the room, on a lower level, uncomfortably placed on a Roman altar, is the *Rondanini Pietà*, the unfinished last work of Michelangelo, named after the palace in Rome where it used to be displayed. The sculptor worked at intervals on this moving, but pathetic, statue during the last nine years of his life, and up to six days before his death. According to Vasari, he reused a block of marble in which he had already roughed out a Pietà to a different design and on a smaller scale. A fine bronze head of Michelangelo by Daniele da Volterra (1564) is also displayed here.

The First Floor and Pinacoteca

Rooms XVI–XIX have a splendid collection of furniture, arranged to give a chronological picture of 15th–18th-century Lombard interiors, and the Belgioioso collection of 17th-century Flemish and Dutch paintings.

The Pinacoteca displays Italian painting from the 13th century to the 18th. Highlights are given below.

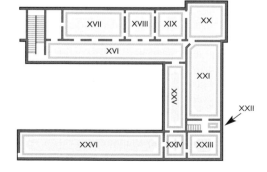

XX: Late Gothic and Quattrocento painting from Lombardy, Tuscany and the Veneto. Includes *St Benedict* by Antonello da Messina; the *Pala Trivulzio* by Mantegna (1497); a polyptych signed and dated 1462 by Benedetto Bembo; a superb *Madonna and Child* by Giovanni Bellini; and a very unusual work (the *Madonna of Humility*) by Filippo Lippi.

XXI: Lombard Renaissance works by Vincenzo Foppa, Bergognone and Bramantino; works by followers of Leonardo, including Boltraffio and Cesare da Sesto; and paintings by Sodoma and Correggio.

XXII: Mannerist works including a small *Crucifixion* attributed to Marcello Venusti.

XXIII. Lombard works by Nuvolone, Cerano and Morazzone.

XXIV: Late-16th- and early-17th-century northern Italian schools (including Moncalvo).

XXV: Contains a magnificent display of portraits by Giovanni Bellini, Correggio, Giovanni Antonio Boltraffio (*Lady in Red*), Baldassare d'Este, Lorenzo Lotto (*Boy Holding a Book*), Bronzino, Giovanni Battista Moroni, Tintoretto and Titian. A fine portrait of *Henrietta Maria of France* by van Dyck hangs at the end of the room on the right wall.

XXVI: 17th- and 18th-century Lombard, Neapolitan, and Venetian works (Daniele Crespi, Cerano, Morazzone, Giacomo Ceruti, Bernardino Strozzi, Jusepe Ribera, Alessandro Magnasco, Sebastiano Ricci, Giovanni Battista Tiepolo, Francesco Guardi and Canaletto).

Three sections of the **Civiche Raccolte Archeologiche e Numismatiche** (*see also p. 124*) are displayed in the castle (*open Tues–Sun 9–5*). From the Corte Ducale you descend to a basement room with the epigraphic section. This includes 101 Roman inscriptions from Milan arranged in four series: those concerning public life; religious inscriptions; community affairs (merchants, artisans and tradesmen); and private family life.

The Rocchetta

Museo delle Arti Decorative e Strumenti Musicali
Open Tues–Sun 9–5.30.
The Museum of Decorative Arts and Musical Instruments occupies two floors of the Rochetta tower. Highlights include a geometric compass designed by Galileo in 1606 (Room XXXII) and a spinet played by the 14-year-old Mozart (Room XXXVI). The aisled ball court (Room XXXVII) is hung with tapestries of the Months from designs by Bramantino (c. 1503). The tapestries were commissioned after the expulsion of the Sforza, by the French marshal Gian Giacomo Trivulzio, and were woven in Vigevano by Benedetto da Milano between 1504 and 1509.

In the arcaded courtyard of the Rocchetta, in the design of which both Filarete and Bramante had a hand, is the entrance to the **Egyptian section**, also arranged in the basement. It contains a small collection of objects dating from the Old Kingdom to the age of Ptolemy, illustrating the funerary cult of ancient Egypt, with sarcophagi, mummies and books of the dead (papyri), and household and personal objects, canopic vases, jewellery, funerary masks, stelae, etc.

Also off the courtyard is the entrance to the **prehistoric section**, which includes a room containing material from Lombardy dating from the late Bronze Age to the Roman period, with the Golasecca culture (9th–5th centuries BC) particularly well represented. Elsewhere in the castle (admission to scholars) are the Archivio Storico Civico, the Biblioteca Trivulziana (with an Oriental art centre), a medal collection, and the Bertarelli collection of prints and maps.

Parco Sempione
Map p. 106, 1.
The Parco Sempione, a large park of 47 hectares laid out by Emilio Alemagna in 1893 on the site of a 15th-century ducal park, begins on the far side of the castle. It contains a fountain by Giorgio de Chirico. The **Palazzo dell'Arte**, built in 1931–33 by Giovanni Muzio, has been restored as an important exhibition centre. The **Aquarium**, in a fine Art Nouveau building of 1906 (*open Tues–Sun 9–5.30*), with delightful 'aquatic' decorations on the exterior, has marine and freshwater fish, and important study collections.

The **arena** (Map p. 130, 6) was first built by Luigi Canonica in 1806–07. The high tower (110m), made of aluminium, was erected in 1933 by Giò Ponti and Cesare Chiodi. The fine equestrian monument to Napoleon III is by Francesco Barzaghi (1881). At the far end of the park is the **Arco della Pace**, a triumphal arch modelled on the Arch of Severus in Rome, built by Luigi Cagnola in 1807–38. It was begun in honour of Napoleon, but was dedicated to Peace by Ferdinand I of Austria on its completion. It marks the beginning of the **Corso Sempione**, part of the 182km-long historic Simplon Road, constructed by order of Napoleon from Geneva to Sesto Calende across the Simplon Pass (1800–05).

SANT'AMBROGIO & THE WEST

This area is probably the most expensive residential neighbourhood in Italy. The stately old flats, many in period-revival buildings, overlook shady boulevards and wide, elegant streets.
The district can be reached from central Milan (Via Mazzini) by bus 54. Sant'Ambrogio station is on Metro Line 1.

The church of Sant'Ambrogio
Map p. 106, 9. *Closed 12–2.30.*
This, the most interesting church in Milan, was the prototype of the Lombard basilica, built in 379–86, beside a Christian cemetery, enlarged in the 9th century and again after 1080. It was founded by St Ambrose, Bishop of Milan, the friend and mentor of St Augustine, whom he converted to Christianity. The present building is the result of numerous careful restorations, and the dating of the various parts of the building is

still uncertain. After a radical restoration in the 19th century, it had to be repaired again after serious war damage in 1943.

The splendid atrium in front of the church, on an early Christian plan, was probably built in 1088–99, but was reconstructed in 1150. The austere façade consists of a five-bayed narthex below, with five arches above, graduated to fit the gable with decorative arcading. The south, or monks', campanile dates from the 9th century; the higher canons' campanile to the north is a fine Lombard tower of 1128–44, crowned with a loggia of 1889. The great doorway has wood imposts made up of fragments from the 8th and 10th centuries (heavily restored in the 18th century); the bronze doors date from the 11th–12th centuries.

The interior

The beautiful interior has a low rib-vaulted nave divided from the side aisles by wide arcades supported by massive pillars beneath a matroneum. There are no transepts, and beyond the tower over the crossing, with its magnificent ciborium, are three deep apses, the central one raised above the crypt.

On the right is a statue of Pius IX (1880). On the left, beyond a column with a bronze serpent of the 10th century, is the pulpit, reconstituted from fragments of the 11th and early 12th centuries, saved after the vault collapsed in 1196 and one of the most remarkable Romanesque monuments known. Beneath it is a Roman palaeo-Christian sarcophagus (4th century).

In the **south aisle**, the first chapel has a fresco attributed to Gaudenzio Ferrari and Giovanni Battista della Cerva. The second chapel has an altarpiece by Gaudenzio Ferrari, and two detached frescoes by Tiepolo. In the sixth chapel is a *Legend of St George* by Bernardino Lanino. To the left, beyond a fine 18th-century wrought-iron screen, is another 18th-century chapel with frescoes by Ferdinando Porta. At the end is the Sacello di San Vittore in Ciel d'Oro, a sepulchral chapel built in a Christian cemetery in the 4th century and altered later. Its name refers to the splendid 5th-century mosaics, with a golden dome and six panels representing saints (including St Ambrose) on the walls. At the end of the south aisle is a 6th-century sarcophagus.

The **north aisle** (first chapel) has a fresco of the *Redeemer* (with very unusual iconography) by Bergognone, and (in the third chapel) a tondo attributed to Bernardino Luini. In the **sanctuary**, under the dome (which was rebuilt in the 13th century and restored in the 19th), is the great ciborium, thought to date from the 9th century. The shafts of the columns, however, are probably of the time of St Ambrose. The four sides of the baldacchino are decorated with reliefs in coloured stucco in the Byzantine style (mid-10th century). The altar has a magnificent and justly celebrated casing presented in 835 by Archbishop Angilberto II, made of gold and silver plates sculptured in relief, with enamel and gems, the work of Volvinius, and representing scenes from the *Lives of Christ and St Ambrose*. In the apse are mosaics of the 4th or 8th century reset in the 18th and restored after the Second World War, and the 9th-century bishop's throne in marble. The crypt contains the bodies of Sts Ambrose, Gervase and Protasius in a shrine of 1897.

From the east end of the north aisle a door admits you to the **Portico della Canonica**, with columns carved in imitation of tree trunks, which was left unfinished by Bramante in 1499 (and reconstructed after the Second World War). A second side was added in 1955. The upper part houses the **Museo di Sant'Ambrogio** (*open daily 10–12 & 3–5*). This contains textiles, including the Dalmatic of St Ambrose (protected by a curtain); early Christian mosaic fragments; 4th- and 9th-century wood fragments from the old doors of the basilica; medieval capitals; a triptych by Bernardino Zenale; frescoes by Bergognone and Bernardino Luini; a 15th-century embroidered altar frontal; and two 17th-century Flemish tapestries. The church treasury includes a 12th-century Cross and the early-15th-century Reliquary of the Innocents. Most of the frescoes of the 15th-century Oratorio della Passione by the school of Bernardino Luini were detached in 1869 and sold to the Victoria and Albert Museum in London.

The Museo Nazionale di Scienza e Tecnica

Map p. 106, 9. *Open Tues–Fri 9–4.50, Sat–Sun and holidays 9.30–6.30.*
The museum is housed in the old Olivetan convent (1507), which still contains a collection of frescoes by Bernardino Luini. The vestibule contains frescoes of the 15th-century Lombard school. To the right in the first cloister are displayed ancient carriages and velocipedes. The collection is described below.

First floor: On the right is the Sala della Bifora (kept locked) with the Mauro collection of goldsmiths' work and precious stones. The gallery is devoted to cinematography. Rooms to the right demonstrate the evolution of the graphic arts (printing, typewriters, etc.). At the end of the gallery, to the right, is the long Leonardo Gallery, which extends the entire length of the first and second cloisters. Here are exhibited models of machines and apparatus invented by Leonardo da Vinci, of the greatest interest.

The rooms (right) which border the first cloister are devoted to time measurement and sound, including musical instruments and the reproduction of a lute-maker's shop. In the middle of the Leonardo Gallery are detached frescoes, and (right), the Sala delle Colonne, formerly the conventual library, used for exhibitions. Three galleries round the second cloister illustrate the science of physics, including electricity, acoustics and nuclear reaction. Beyond the astronomy gallery are rooms devoted to optics and to radio and telecommunications (with mementoes of Marconi).

Lower floor: The exhibit here is devoted to metallurgy, to the petrochemical industries and to transport, with a fine gallery of early motor cars. An external pavilion, in the form of a 19th-century railway station, contains railway locomotives and rolling stock. Another huge external pavilion illustrates air and sea transport, with a splendid display of airplanes, along with relics of aeronautical history, and ships, including a naval training ship.

Ground floor: Civico Museo Navale Didattico, founded in 1922, with navigational instruments and models of ships.

Santa Maria delle Grazie and the Cenacolo

Map p. 106, 5. *Cenacolo open Tues–Sun 8.15–6.45; reservations required. T: 02 498 7588, 199 199100.*

A church of brick and terracotta with a very beautiful exterior, Santa Maria delle Grazie was erected in 1466–90 to the design of Guiniforte Solari. In 1492 Lodovico il Moro ordered the striking new choir and unusual domed crossing, and this has for long been attributed to Bramante, although it is now uncertain how much he was directly involved. The fine west portal is also usually attributed to Bramante.

Inside, the nave vault and aisles have fine frescoed decoration of c. 1482–85 (restored in 1937). In the aisles, between the chapels, are frescoes of Dominican saints attributed to Bernardino Butinone. The first chapel in the south aisle has a fine tomb of the della Torre family; in the third chapel are lunette frescoes attributed to Aurelio and Gian Pietro Luini. The fourth chapel has frescoes by Gaudenzio Ferrari (1542), and in the fifth are stucco bas-reliefs (late 16th century) of angels. The seventh has an altarpiece by Leonardo's pupil Marco d'Oggiono.

The lovely light *tribuna*, or domed crossing, designed by Bramante, has very unusual bright graffiti decoration. The choir also has graffiti decoration and fine stalls of carved and inlaid wood. A door leads out to the *chiostrino*, also traditionally attributed to Bramante, with a delightful little garden. Off it is the old sacristy (only open for concerts), which marked a significant step in the development of Renaissance architecture.

At the end of the north aisle is the elaborate entrance (with 17th-century stuccoes and a lunette painting by Il Cerano) to the **chapel of the Madonna delle Grazie**, containing a highly venerated 15th-century painting of the *Madonna* beneath a vault with restored 15th-century frescoes. The sixth chapel has a small *Holy Family* by Paris Bordone, and the second chapel has a funerary monument with sculptures attributed to Bambaia. The first chapel has frescoes by Giovanni Donato Montorfano.

In the **cenacolo**, or refectory, of the adjoining Dominican convent is the world-famous *Last Supper* by Leonardo da Vinci, painted in 1494–97. In order to protect the painting from dust and lessen the effects of pollution, visitors (only 15 or 20 at a time) go through a series of glass 'cubicles', equipped with air-filtering systems, from which there is a good view of the main cloister and exterior of Santa Maria delle Grazie. The vault and right wall of the refectory were rebuilt after they were destroyed by a bomb in 1943.

This extraordinary painting, which was to have a lasting effect on generations of painters, depicts the moment when Christ announces Judas's betrayal at the Last Supper. The monumental Classical figures of the Apostles are shown in perfect perspective in a stark room, an extension of the refectory itself. The light enters through the real windows on the left and the painted windows in the background which look out over a landscape, and the wonderful colours culminate in the blue and red robe of Christ. On the side walls Leonardo painted tapestries decorated with bunches of flowers. Fascinating details of the objects on the table have recently been revealed, including the colour of the Apostles' robes reflected in the pewter plates and the transparent glass carafes. Above are lunettes with garlands of fruit and flowers around the coats of arms of the Sforza family. There is no evidence that Leonardo made use of a cartoon while working on this masterpiece.

At the bottom of the fresco, at either side, are the kneeling figures, now nearly effaced, of Lodovico il Moro and his wife Beatrice d'Este and their two children, added by Leonardo before 1498.

NOTES ON LEONARDO'S TECHNIQUE

The *Last Supper* is painted with a technique peculiar to Leonardo, in tempera with the addition of later oil varnishes, on a prepared surface in two layers on the plastered wall. It is therefore not a fresco. In fresco-painting pigments are dissolved in water and then painted onto a surface primed with fresh lime plaster. If the climate is dry, true frescoes will retain their brightness for an exceptionally long time. In Leonardo's work, errors in the preparation of the plaster, together with the dampness of the wall, have caused great damage to the painted surface, which had already considerably deteriorated by the beginning of the 16th century. On the wall opposite the *Last Supper* is a large *Crucifixion* by Giovanni Donato Montorfano (1495), the fine preservation of which is a vindication of the lasting quality of true fresco-painting. The *Last Supper* has been restored repeatedly, and was twice repainted (in oils) in the 18th century. Careful work (begun in 1978 and completed in 1999) has been carried out to eliminate the false restorations of the past and to expose the original work of Leonardo as far as possible.

Monastero Maggiore; Civice Raccolte Archeologiche e Numismatiche

Map p. 106, 6. *Open Tues–Sun 9.30–5.30.*

The former monastery church of San Maurizio was begun in 1503, perhaps by Gian Giacomo Dolcebuono. It has a façade of 1574–81. The harmonious interior is divided by a wall into two parts. The western portion, originally for lay worshippers, has small chapels below and a graceful loggia above and contains numerous frescoes by Bernardino Luini and his sons Aurelio and Gian Pietro (1522–29), and other members of his school. A long and careful restoration project has been in progress here since 1980. In the loggia are frescoed medallions by Boltraffio (1505–10).

The cloisters now form the entrance to the Civice Raccolte Archeologiche e Numismatiche, with Greek, Etruscan and Roman material relating to the history of Milan. In the cloisters are Roman sculpture and a large incised stone from the Valle Camonica dating from the late Bronze Age.

The highlight of the ground floor exhibits is the famous **Coppa Trivulzio**. Dating from the early 4th century AD, it is an intricately worked double coloured glass drinking cup—white on the inside, blue on the outside—with the inscription '*bibe vivas* *multis annis'* (drink and live for many years). It was found in a sarcophagus near Novara in 1675 and was acquired by Abbot Carlo Trivulzio in 1777. The silver Parabiago Patera, with Attis and Cybele and other fine figures in relief, a Roman work of the late 4th century AD, is also displayed here. Other exhibits include a fine collection of antique vases; Roman sculpture (including a colossal torso of Hercules); mosaics found in the city; portrait busts (1st century BC–4th century AD); finds from Caesarea in the Holy Land and 6th–7th-century jewellery from Nocera Umbra and Milan.

In the basement are (left) Etruscan material (bucchero vases, etc.) and (right) Indian Gandhara sculpture (2nd–3rd centuries AD). The hall beyond has a fine display (chronological and topographical) of Greek ceramics (including Attic red- and black-figure vases). At the end of the room you can see the base of a stretch of Roman wall, part of the city walls. There is also a section devoted to barbarian invaders of Lombardy, with Gothic, Germanic and Lombard gold, arms and armour.

The garden contains the **Torre di Ansperto**, an octagonal tower of Roman origin, with interesting traces of 13th-century frescoes, and a Roman sarcophagus of the 3rd century AD.

THE PINACOTECA AMBROSIANA & ITS DISTRICT

The Pinacoteca Ambrosiana

Map p. 106, 10. *Open Tues–Sun 10–5.30.*

The Palazzo dell'Ambrosiana contains the famous library and Pinacoteca founded by Cardinal Federico Borromeo at the beginning of the 17th century. The palace was begun for the Cardinal by Lelio Buzzi in 1603–09 and later enlarged. The Pinacoteca Ambrosiana, entered from the left side of the courtyard, contains a superb collection of paintings.

The core of the collection is a donation that was assembled by the cardinal and donated to an art academy founded here in 1621 under the direction of Giovanni Battista Crespi, known as Il Cerano. The original donation included 250 paintings, including originals and about 30 copies. Now there are more than 1,500 works on panel, canvas and other supports.

The Pinacoteca is arranged in 24 rooms on the first and second floors. The collection is arranged chronologically, though an effort has been made to distinguish Federico Borromeo's original collection, reassembled in the first rooms.

The Borromeo Collection

Borromeo Collection I: At the entrance to the Pinacoteca and along the stairs are arranged 16th-century plaster casts from Trajan's Column, the *Laocoön* and Michelangelo's Vatican *Pietà*, made by the sculptor Leone Leoni and later used in the Accademia del Disegno. The same teaching role was assigned to the many copies of paintings commissioned by the Cardinal, such as the copy by Vespino of Leonardo's *Last Supper*. At the top of the stairs one immediately comes to the heart of Federico Borromeo's collection, Bernardino Luini's *Holy Family with St Anne and the young St John*, from a cartoon by Leonardo, and Titian's *Adoration of the Magi* (painted, with assistants, for Henri II and Diane de Poitiers in 1560, and still in its original frame); also by Titian is a portrait of an old man in armour, thought to be the artist's father (Gregorio Vecellio, captain of the Centuria di Pieve). The *Profile of a Young Lady* by Giovanni Ambrogio de Predis, was long believed to be a work of Leonardo. The subject may be Beatrice d'Este, great patroness of the arts and wife of Lodovico il Moro.

15th–16th-century Italian and Lombard paintings: In the two rooms that host Italian Renaissance paintings not part of the collection of Federico Borromeo are several outstanding masterpieces: Leonardo's *Musician* (thought to be Franchino Gaffurio, *maestro di cappella* of Milan cathedral), of unprecedented psychological insight; Botticelli's light-filled tondo of the *Madonna and Child*; two beautifully painted *Saints* by Bernardo Zenale and Bergognone's great *Sacra Conversazione* (representative of Lombard painting of the Quattrocento). Among the Leonardo-like paintings are three intriguing works by Bramantino: the symbol-laden *Adoration of the Child*, the fresco for the church of San Sepolcro showing *Cristo in Pietà* (witnessed by an extraordinarily expressive St John), and the disquieting altarpiece with the *Madonna Enthroned between Saints Michael and Ambrose*, with the bodies of an Arian and a toad, symbols of the devil, at their feet.

Borromeo Collection II: A darkened chamber provides a fit setting for Raphael's cartoon for the *School of Athens*, the only remaining cartoon of the fresco cycle in the Vatican, purchased by Cardinal Borromeo in 1626. This is the largest known Renaissance drawing (285 x 804 cm). The figure of Heraclitus is missing from the cartoon: the Greek philosopher was in fact added by Raphael in the final fresco, using Michelangelo's features. The copy of Leonardo's *Last Supper* was made in 1612–16 by order of Cardinal Borromeo by Andrea Bianchi (Il Vespino).

Other cartoons, by Pellegrino Tibaldi for the stained-glass windows of the duomo and by Giulio Romano for the fresco of the *Battle of Constantine* (also in the Vatican), attest the educational as well as the artistic merit that artists' preparatory drawings held for Borromeo and his academy.

Leaving the Raphael room it's easy to miss Caravaggio's *Basket of Fruit*. That Cardinal Borromeo was aware of the value of this extraordinary still life is clear from his complaint that there was no other work beautiful enough to place beside it.

Borromeo Collection III: Only two of the four allegories of the elements painted by Jan Brueghel for the Cardinal and removed by Napoleon in 1796 remain to be seen at the Ambrosiana. These are *Water* and the enigmatic *Fire*, a rather fiendish forge full of tiny pieces of goldsmith's work. Brueghel also made the life-sized vase of flowers with jewel, coins and shells, one of the finer examples of this kind of still life, and the little painting on copper of a *Mouse with Roses*.

The other Flemish painter whose work Cardinal Borromeo supported is Paul Brill, here represented by a number of meticulously detailed religious landscapes. The German printmaker Luca di Leida made the grisly monochrome painting on glass of the *Triumph of David*, with Goliath's colossal head carried on his sword.

The Galbiati Wing

Paintings and objets d'art of the 14th–16th centuries: The Sala della Medusa and Sala delle Colonne are among the rooms acquired by the Ambrosiana in 1928, together with the Basilica of San Sepolcro, and redecorated by Giovanni Galbiati. Here are the important collection of objets d'art, including a curious profane reliquary with a lock of Lucrezia Borgia's hair. Byron famously obtained a few strands of it when he visited Milan, and enclosed them in a letter to Augusta Leigh. Here also is the Sinigallia collection of miniature portraits on porcelain, ivory and copper (a genre in vogue amongst the aristocracy in the 18th and early 19th centuries). There are also 15th- and 16th-century Lombard paintings, including works by Leonardo's followers Giampietrino and Antonio Solario.

16th-century Italian paintings: The Venetian, Northern Italian and Tuscan painters represented in these rooms include Girolamo Mazzola Bedoli (*Annunciation*), a follower of Parmigianino; Bonifacio Veronese and Jacopo Bassano (*Rest on the Flight into Egypt*). In the Sala dell'Esedra, decorated in 1930 with a mosaic reproducing the miniature made by Simone Martini for Petrarch's personal copy of Virgil (preserved in the library), are works by painters from Bergamo and Brescia. Moretto's dramatic *Martyrdom of St Peter of Verona*, in which the martyr writes on the ground, in his own blood, *credo* ('I believe'), and Giovanni Battista Moroni's remarkable full-length portrait of *Michel de l'Hopital*, French ambassador to the Council of Trent, are perhaps the most striking.

16th- and 17th-century Italian and Flemish paintings: Stairs lead up from the Sala dell'Esedra to the first-floor Sala Nicolò da Bologna, named after the 14th-century miniaturist from whom the reliefs of *Sciences* and *Virtue* in the lunettes were drawn. Here and in the next room are 16th-century Flemish and 17th-century Italian paintings, including Guido Reni's *Penitent Magdalene*, represented kneeling holding a skull; one of Evaristo Baschenis' celebrated still lifes of musical instruments; and Giuseppe Vermiglio's beautiful *Judith with the Head of Holofernes*. Plenty of room is given to the Lombard Seicento, represented mainly by religious paintings by Giulio Cesare Procaccini, Morazzone, Francesco Cairo, Nuvolone and Daniele Crespi. Among the paintings that mark the passage from the 17th to the 18th century in the various Italian schools are the

Francesco Hayez: La *Maddalena* (1831).

small gilt bronzes of the 19th century; and the marble self-portraits of the Neoclassical sculptors Antonio Canova and Bertel Thorvaldsen.

19th- and 20th-century Italian paintings: The last room on the second floor holds a selection from the Ambrosiana's 200-odd 19th-century paintings. Highlights are Andrea Appiani's *Portrait of Napoleon* (c. 1805) and Francesco Hayez's highly naturalistic portraits for the Morosini family. There

Portrait of a Young Man seemingly caught by surprise by Fra Galgario and the stiff official *Portrait of Leopold II of Habsburg Lorraine* by Anton Raphael Mengs. The pastoral genre is represented by *Rebecca Going to the Well* by Giovan Francesco Castiglione (the son of Grechetto), and by eight of the museum's 35 sketches by Francesco Londonio of goats, cows, lambs, shepherds and farmers.

A recently opened room holds a selection of works from the De Pecis collection, given to the Ambrosiana in 1827 and including several 19th-century miniatures on ivory by Giambattista Gigola depicting historic and literary scenes; the beautiful portrait of the French dancer *Carolina Pitrot Angiolini* painted by Andrea Appiani; numerous

is also an important group of 16th-century Flemish and German paintings and sculpture (partly from the De Pecis collection). The works range from Roman and Lombard fragments to reliefs by Bambaia for the unfinished tomb of Gaston de Foix (other pieces of the tomb are in the Museo d'Arte Antica, Castello Sforzesco, *see p. 118*). The installation ends with more sculptures by Bambaia, and Lombard frescoes of Dominican saints from the 15th-century church of Santa Maria della Rosa, which was acquired by the Ambrosiana in 1829 and demolished to build the library. There are plans to install here the 17th-century 'Wunderkammer' of scientist Manfredo Settala with curiosities of nature, scientific instruments, objets d'art, etc.

San Satiro

Map p. 107, 11.

This beautiful church succeeds a much earlier building whose 11th-century campanile still survives. Bramante designed the church and its façade in 1478, though work on the latter lasted until 1871. The T-shaped interior, by a clever perspective device and the skilful use of stucco, is given the appearance of a Greek cross; the rear wall is actually almost flat. On the high altar is a 13th-century votive fresco. The Cappella della Pietà, dating from the time of Archbishop Ansperto (868–81), was altered during the Renaissance with an attractive plan and large capitals. The terracotta *Pietà* is by Agostino de Fondutis. The eight-sided baptistery is a beautiful Renaissance work, with terracottas by Fondutis to a design by Bramante.

Sant'Alessandro and Palazzo Trivulzio

Map p. 107, 11.

The best Baroque church in the city has elaborate marquetry and inlaid confessionals, as well as a striking Rococo high altar of *pietre dure*, inlaid gems and gilt bronze. The adjacent Palazzo Trivulzio (1707–13) is attributed to Giovanni Ruggeri and contains, in its courtyard, a doorway from a destroyed house attributed to Bramante.

TWO IMPORTANT MILAN ARCHITECTS

Donato Bramante (1444–1514)

Though Bramante began his career as a painter, it is as an architect that he made his name, after he came to Milan in 1479, in the service of Lodovico Sforza. Through the influence of Leonardo, he turned his attention to church architecture, and in the church of San Satiro (*see above*) built the first coffered dome since ancient times, and introduced sophisticated tricks of perspective to give an illusion of depth to the shallow chancel. When the Sforzas fell from power, Bramante went to Rome. Under the patronage of Pope Julius II he produced buildings which secured his reputation as an architect of comparable genius to those of Classical times.

Francesco Maria Richini (1584–1658)

The influence of this important Baroque architect, deservingly hailed as the greatest architect of the Milanese Settecento, was not confined to his native city: all across Central Europe there are churches inspired by his designs. His most successful surviving buildings in Milan are the courtyard of the Brera, and the church of San Giuseppe (1607–30), where a showy aediculed façade with lateral volutes disguises an interior of pleasantly unexpected grace and simplicity. Richini also built the crypt in the duomo (1606), which house the remains of St Charles Borromeo.

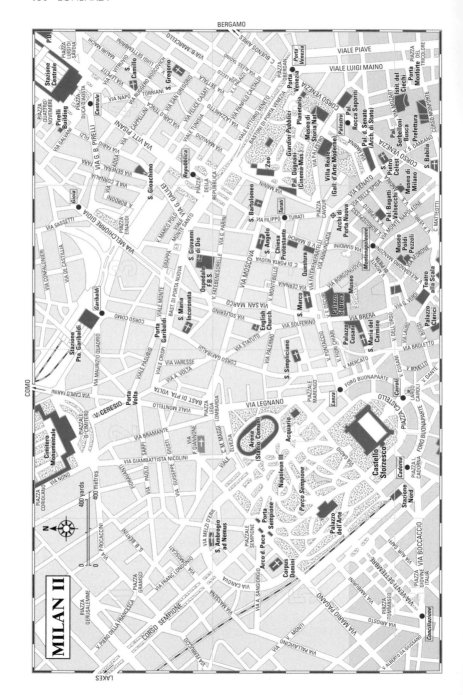

MILAN II

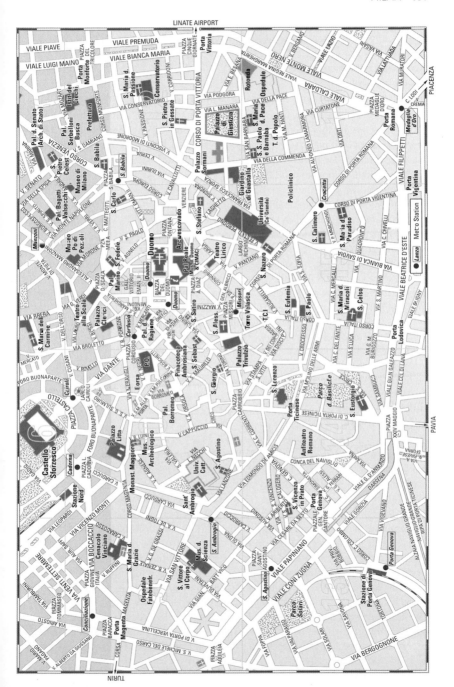

SAN LORENZO & THE SOUTH

San Lorenzo Maggiore

Map p. 131, 14.

Behind a striking colonnade of 16 Corinthian columns, the remains of a 4th-century Roman portico, rises the basilica of **San Lorenzo Maggiore**, founded in the 4th century. It was rebuilt after the collapse of the vault in 1103, and again in 1574–88 by Martino Bassi (who preserved the original octagonal form and much of the original masonry) and has four heavy square towers. The façade dates from 1894.

The spacious domed interior, built of grey stone, is of great architectural interest; it is surrounded by an ambulatory beneath a gallery. The Chapel of Sant'Aquilino was built in the 4th century, probably as an imperial mausoleum. In the vestibule (light on right) are fragments of 5th-century mosaics and early-14th-century frescoes. The door jambs (1st–3rd century AD) were brought from a Roman building. The octagonal hall (light on right), a remarkable Roman room, contains an early Christian sarcophagus and two lunettes with 5th-century mosaics. Beyond is a 17th-century silver urn with the relics of St Aquilino, beneath a little vault frescoed by Carlo Urbini. Steps behind it (light on the stairs) lead down to an undercroft with Roman masonry of the imperial period, probably once part of an amphitheatre.

Corso di Porta Ticinese continues south from San Lorenzo, passing through the arches of the medieval Porta Ticinese (c. 1330; with a tabernacle by the workshop of Balduccio) at Via Mulino delle Armi. The street is paralleled to the east by the quiet, green Parco delle Basiliche, which links San Lorenzo with the area's other great medieval church, Sant'Eustorgio.

Sant'Eustorgio

Map p. 131, 14.

This church is also of ancient foundation. The 11th-century church was rebuilt, except for the apse, in the 12th–13th centuries, and the façade was reconstructed in 1863–65. The three 15th-century chapels on the south side, the apse, the slender campanile (1297–1309), and the graceful Portinari chapel are easy to see from the outside. To the left of the façade is a 16th-century open-air pulpit.

The long, low interior, with aisles and apse, is typical of the Lombard basilicas, but an important series of chapels was added on the south side from the 13th to the 16th centuries. The first chapel (light on right) dates from 1484, and has good sculptural detail. It contains the tomb of Giovanni Brivio by Tommaso Cazzaniga and Benedetto Briosco (1486), and an altarpiece by Bergognone. In the fourth chapel the tomb of Stefano Visconti (d. 1327), probably by Giovanni di Balduccio, and a 14th-century painted crucifix. In the sixth chapel is the tomb of Uberto Visconti (14th century). In the south transept is the chapel of the Magi, where the relics of the Magi were preserved until their transfer to Cologne in 1164 (some were returned to Milan in 1903). It contains a huge Roman sarcophagus that held the relics, and on the altar are reliefs of 1347. On the high altar is a finely carved 14th-century dossal.

Cross the *confessio*, with nine slender monolithic columns (above early Christian foundations), beneath the raised apse, to reach the Cappella Portinari (1462–68), a beautiful Renaissance chapel built for Pigello Portinari and dedicated to St Peter Martyr. A graceful choir of angels with festoons, in coloured stucco, plays over the drum of the dome. The frescoed scenes of the *Life of St Peter Martyr*, by Vincenzo Foppa (1466–68), comprise the most important Renaissance fresco cycle in the city (unfortunately, they are in very poor condition). In the centre is the tomb, borne by eight Virtues, of St Peter Martyr, Dominican friar and fierce inquisitor of heretics, being a converted Cathar himself. He was ambushed and murdered by brigands on his way from Como to Milan in 1252. The tomb (1339) is by Giovanni Balduccio.

The sacristy shows the early Christian cemetery beneath the nave, with tombs dating from the 1st–4th century AD and some inscriptions, and the old sacristy where the church treasury and vestments are carefully preserved in 16th-century cupboards.

The Museo Diocesano in Sant'Eustorgio
Open Tues–Sun 10–6, Thur 10–8.
Occupying the second cloister of the basilica of Sant'Eustorgio, the museum documents the importance of Christianity locally from the time of St Ambrose (334–397), to the present. The permanent collection is arranged in ten sections.

I. Sant'Ambrogio: The visit begins with works brought here from Museum of the Basilica di Sant'Ambrogio. Most interesting, for historical as well as aesthetic reasons, are the large 10th-century stucco tondo with the bust of St Ambrose and the fragments of the wooden main door of the basilica of Sant'Ambrogio, which date from the 4th or 5th century.

II. Works from the diocese: In this section paintings from the various parishes of the Diocese of Milan (an area that includes the present provinces of Milan, Varese and Lecco, and part of the province of Como) are gathered in a chronological arrangement that begins with the 14th century and ends with the 19th. Highlights are Anovelo da Imbonate's *Crucifixion*, Alessandro Magnasco's *Il furto sacrilego*, and Bergognone's *St Catherine of Alexandria*.

The *Ancona della Passione*, made in Antwerp in the 16th century, is also noteworthy.

III. Liturgical objects: Lombard goldsmiths' work, particularly that of the Diocese of Milan, has always been much admired: Milanese craftsmen have set the standard of excellence from the time of the Visconti until the 20th century. The display of sacred objects from the 6th to the 20th centuries occupies the great undergound halls of the third side of the cloister. Highlights include a 16th–17th-century amphora by W. Jamnitzer, a chalice (1866) by Giovanni Bellezza, and the 18th-century Ambrosian monstrance by an anonymous Milanese artist.

IV. Salone dell'Arciconfraternità del Santissimo Sacramento: A large hall hosts the cycle of paintings commissioned by the Arciconfraternità del Santissimo Sacramento, dedicated to miracles of the Eucharist, and to St Catherine, the lay brotherhood's patron. The large canvases were commissioned in the late 17th century, from the most important painters in Milan, to be hung in the aisles of the cathedral, where the Arciconfraternità was headquartered, during the feast of Corpus Domini. The recovery of these valuable works, finally restored and made visible after decades of neglect, introduces the visitor to the theme of the confraternities—which played an important religious and social role in the Milanese diocese. Highlights: Carlo Preda, *Boy Extracted Unharmed from a Kiln for Having Received Communion*; Filippo Abbiati, *Miracle of the Mula*; *St Peter Martyr Unmasks a False Madonna*.

V. Gold-ground paintings: Gold-ground painting is one of the fundamental categories of medieval Italian religious art (*see p. 352*). The 41 panels in this gathering were executed in the 14th and 15th centuries, mainly in Tuscany and Umbria. Among the principal artists are Gerardo di Jacopo, 'Il Starnina' (*Madonna and Child with angels*) and the Florentine Bernardo Daddi (*St Cecilia*).

VI. Monti collection: The 172 paintings and drawings that made up the private collection of Cardinal Cesare Monti (1593–1650) constitute the first core of the Milanese archbishops' collections. They adorned the archbishop's palace until 1811, when Andrea Appiani transferred a selection to the Pinacoteca di Brera. The cardinal's

tastes, perfectly aligned with the spirit of the Counter Reformation, are oriented toward the 16th-century Venetian school, the early 17th-century Lombard painters and the Emilian school. Among the best works that Monti left to the diocese are Bernardino Lanino's *Salvator Mundi*; Cerano's *Fall of St Paul*; Tintoretto's *Christ and the Adultress* and Simone Peterzano's *Christ in the garden*.

VII. Pozzobonelli collection: The paintings in this collection, left to the diocese by Cardinal Giuseppe Pozzobonelli (1696–1783), point to the culture of Arcadia that spread through Milan in the 18th century. All depict Arcadian subjects—mainly landscapes, with and without figures. The paintings are by Roman, Venetian, Lombard, and to a lesser degree, Tuscan, Neapolitan and Flemish painters; they range in date from the end of the 17th century to the third quarter of the 18th.

VIII. Visconti collection: The collection of Federico Visconti (1617–93), here represented by three works, including Cerano's little panel painting of *St Charles in Glory*, is made up of roughly 40 paintings and drawings, almost all by 17th-century artists. This is a complex collection, put together at different times; it shows the increasing interest in Lombard art that Federico Visconti developed as his intention to give it to the bishops of Milan became clearer.

IX. Odescalchi collection: Benedetto Erba Odescalchi (1679–1740), appointed Archbishop of Milan in 1712, gave the diocese this series of 41 portraits of

Milanese bishop-saints in 1737. Highlights are two works by an anonymous 18th-century Lombard painter: *St Barnabas* and *St Castriziano*.

X. Gaetano Previati's *Stations of the Cross*: Previati is best known for his painting of the rural working class, *The Third Estate*. His frescoes of the *Stations* of the Cross from the cemetery of Castano Primo, are a work of his early period (1882–88), and show a firm adherence to the Symbolist movement that had developed north of the Alps. The third station (Christ falls for the first time), and the fourth station (Jesus encounters his Mother), are particularly moving.

Porta Ticinese and the Navigli

Map p. 131, 13-14.

Just south of Sant'Eustorgio is the huge Piazza XXIV Maggio, with the handsome Neoclassical Porta Ticinese, an Ionic gateway by Luigi Cagnola (1801–14), in the centre. To the west is the **Darsena**, once the port of Milan. It was connected to an extensive system of rivers and canals, and was particularly busy in the 19th and early 20th centuries. The **Naviglio Grande**, the most important of Milan's canals, once linked the Darsena to the River Ticino, 50km away. It was begun in the 12th century and was navigable as far as Milan by the 13th. It used to carry commodities to and from the city, and there was a regular passenger navigation service along it from the beginning of the 19th century. The nearby **Naviglio Pavese** was begun as an irrigation canal from Milan to Pavia by Gian Galeazzo Visconti in the 14th century. In this area, known as the Navigli, once a neglected part of the city, many of the characteristic houses and courtyards have recently been restored. Now you'll find numerous architects' and designers' studios as well as a selection of fine restaurants. The neighbourhood is particularly lively at night, and there is a festival here in June when restaurants are opened on boats.

San Nazaro Maggiore

Map p. 131, 15.

The easternmost of the four churches founded by St Ambrose outside the walls, **San Nazaro Maggiore**, was consecrated in 386. It was reconstructed after a fire of 1075, altered c. 1578, and restored in the 20th century after war damage.

The entrance on Corso di Porta Romana is preceded by the hexagonal Trivulzio Chapel, begun in 1512 by Bramantino and continued by Cristoforo Lombardo. It has an elegant plain interior with uniform family tombs in niches high up on the walls.

The interior of the church preserves in part the plan of the early Christian church (and some of its masonry). In the nave are paintings by Camillo Procaccini and Daniele Crespi. The architecture of the crossing is particularly fine. In the south transept is a *Last Supper* by Bernardino Lanino. In the sanctuary is the reconstructed dedication stone (with two original fragments), and off the south side the little 10th-century Chapel of St Lino (restored in 1948). In the north transept you can see a

16th-century carved-wood Gothic tabernacle with the *Nativity* (light on right), very well preserved; a reconstructed funerary epitaph (435); and a painting by Bernardino Luini, who also frescoed the Chapel of St Catherine.

Other sights in the neighbourhood

The former **Ospedale Maggiore** or Ca'Granda (Map p. 107, 16) has been the head-quarters of the University of Milan since 1958. The hospital was founded by Francesco Sforza in 1456. One of the larger buildings in the city, it was designed by Filarete with two matching wings, one for men and one for women, each laid out around four courtyards which were separated by a larger central courtyard, off which was the church. Filarete completed only the right wing (towards the church of San Nazaro). The work was continued by Guiniforte Solari after 1465, and taken up again by Francesco Maria Richini and others in the 17th century.

The curiously medieval-looking skyscraper known as the **Torre Velasca** (Map p. 107, 15) was designed by Studio BBPR (Banfi, Belgiojoso, Peressuti and Rogers). One of the more important Modern buildings in the city, it was built in 1956–58.

Santa Maria dei Miracoli or Santa Maria presso San Celso (Map p. 131, 15) stands next to a pretty little garden in front of San Celso (with a façade reconstructed in 1851–54 and a graceful campanile). Santa Maria was begun by Gian Giacomo Dolcebuono in 1490 with a façade by Galeazzo Alessi and Martino Bassi (1572). The fine atrium is by Cesare Cesariano. The pictures in the dark interior are difficult to see. At the end of the south aisle is a *Holy Family* by Paris Bordone; statues by Annibale Fontana and Stoldo Lorenzi adorn the dome piers. The inlaid choir stalls are by Galeazzo Alessi, and the ambulatory has altarpieces by Gaudenzio Ferrari and Moretto. In the north aisle is an altarpiece by Bergognone. The Romanesque church of San Celso (normally kept closed), entered from the south aisle, dates from the 10th century. It has a well-restored interior with fine capitals and a 14th-century fresco.

NORTHEAST OF THE DUOMO

Museo Bagatti Valsecchi

Map p. 107, 4. *Open Sept–July, Tues–Sun 1–5.30.*

At Via Gesù 5 is the entrance to the **Museo Bagatti Valsecchi**. The palace was built by the brothers Fausto and Giuseppe Bagatti Valsecchi in 1876–87 in the style of the Lombard Renaissance and furnished by them with 16th-century works of art or excellent 19th-century imitations by Lombard craftsmen. It was the family home until 1974, when the Bagatti Valsecchi established a foundation and sold the palace to the regional government of Lombardy. Its main façade is in Via Santo Spirito (opposite another fine palace in red brick, also built by the brothers in 1895 in 15th-century style). The palace and its contents represent an extremely interesting and well-preserved example of the eclectic taste of 19th-century collectors. It was opened to the public in 1994 as a delightful private museum, carefully looked after by volunteer custodians. All the works are well labelled, also in English.

The two brothers lived in separate apartments in the palace on either side of the drawing room, gallery of arms, and dining room, which they shared. The rooms are richly decorated with carved ceilings, fireplaces, doorways, floors and wall hangings, and filled with a miscellany of furniture and works of art, some of it Renaissance and some exquisitely made 19th-century imitations commissioned by the brothers to fit the rooms.

The main staircase leads up to a vestibule, beyond which a marble portal carved in 1884 in Renaissance style gives access to the Sala dell'Affresco, with a fresco by Antonio Boselli (1496). The Sala Bevilacqua takes its name from a painting by Ambrogio Bevilacqua. Beyond the panelled library, with a collection of 17th-century sundials, is Fausto's bedroom with an intricately carved 16th-century bed and two paintings by Giampietrino. Beyond the dressing room and bathroom, with ingenious plumbing masked by Renaissance carvings, is the Galleria della Cupola, interesting for its architecture and containing a collection of ceramics.

The three rooms of Giuseppe's apartment have a magnificent old stove, a late-15th-century Venetian painting of the *Blessed Lorenzo Giustiniani*, a painting attributed to Giovanni Bellini, and an early 17th-century Sicilian bed. The largest room in the house is the drawing room, with a 19th-century fireplace (made up of 16th-century fragments) and red wall hangings. The long Galleria delle Armi was created to display the collection of 16th- and 17th-century armour. The dining room has a pair of sideboards, one 16th century and the other a 19th-century copy. The walls are covered with 16th-century tapestries. The cupboards contain 16th-century Murano glass and Faenza ceramics. Beyond the study a staircase leads down to the Via Santo Spirito entrance.

Porta Nuova and the Giardini Pubblici

Map Milan p. 130, 7–8.

At the end of Via Manzoni are the Archi di Porta Nuova, a gate reconstructed in 1171, with sculptures by a follower of Giovanni di Balduccio (14th century). On Piazza Cavour, outside the gate, by a monument to Cavour, stands the Palazzo dei Giornali, by Giovanni Muzio (1937–42), with external reliefs by Mario Sironi and a mosaic by him inside. On the north side of the piazza is the entrance to the Giardini Pubblici, notable for fine trees. The gardens contain monuments to distinguished citizens. **Palazzo Dugnani**, on Via Manin, has frescoes by Giovanni Battista Tiepolo (1731) and a Museo del Cinema (*open Fri, Sat, Sun 3–6.30*). The Neoclassical **Planetarium**, by Piero Portalupi, stands on the farther side of the gardens (entered from Corso Venezia 57). Nearby, facing Corso Venezia, is the **Museo di Storia Naturale** (*open Tues–Fri 9.30–6, Sat–Sun and holidays 9.30–6.30*), founded in 1838 and the most important collection of its kind in Italy. The museum building was erected in 1893, but was badly damaged in the Second World War. The mineral collection includes the largest sulphur crystal in the world and a topaz weighing 40kg. The extensive zoological section contains reptiles, giant dinosaurs, etc. There are also a good library and study collections.

The Galleria d'Arte Moderna

Map p. 107, 4. *Closed at the time of writing; T: 02 7600 2819.*

On the other side of Via Palestro, which borders the southern side of the park, is the **Villa Belgioioso** or Villa Reale, built by Leopold Pollack for the influential Belgioioso family in 1790. It was once occupied by the Regent Eugène Beauharnais and by Field Marshal Radetzky, who died here in 1858. Its attractive garden *all'inglese* was laid out in 1790 (open as a public park). The villa now contains the **Galleria d'Arte Moderna**. Highlights include works by Antonio Canova, and good portraits by Italy's most celebrated Romantic painter, Francesco Hayez. The Carlo Grassi bequest of 19th-century French and Italian works includes paintings by Corot, and especially good works by Giuseppe de Nittis. French painting is represented by Eugène Boudin, Alfred Sisley, Gauguin, Manet and van Gogh. There are also graphic works by Corot and Toulouse-Lautrec. In the last group of rooms are Italian paintings of the late 19th century and early 20th century by Armando Spadini, Giovanni Segantini, Antonio Mancini, Umberto Boccioni, Giacomo Balla, Giorgio Morandi, Renato Guttuso, and Filippo de Pisis. On the first floor (on the other side of the stairs) is a section dedicated to Marino Marini, with drawings and sculptures.

Next door, the **Padiglione d'Arte Contemporanea** (PAC), which was added to the museum in 1955 to display contemporary works, has recently reopened (for exhibitions only) after extensive renovation.

Around Piazza della Repubblica

Map p. 130, 3–7.

This huge square has skyscrapers, including the first to be built in the city (1936, by Mario Baciocchi) at no. 27, and more houses (nos 7–9) by Giovanni Muzio. In Via Turati the Montecatini office buildings, built in 1926–36 by Giò Ponti and others, face the Novecento-style apartment house known as **Ca' Brutta** (1923) by Giovanni Muzio.

The regularly-built Via Pisani leads up to the monumental **Stazione Centrale**, the largest in Italy, designed in an eclectic Art Nouveau style by Ulisse Stacchini and built in 1925–31. In the piazza is the **Pirelli Building**, built in reinforced concrete in 1955–59 by Giò Ponti and Pier Luigi Nervi (127m), one of the best modern buildings in the city. Built on the site of the first Pirelli factory, it is now the seat of the Lombard regional government. The area to the west around Via Galvani, known as the Centro Direzionale, has numerous skyscrapers built in the 1960s.

THE EASTERN DISTRICTS

Around San Babila

Map p. 131, 12.

From behind the duomo, **Corso Vittorio Emanuele**, a pedestrian street with numerous shops and shopping arcades as well as theatres and hotels, leads through a modern area. On the left is the classic portico of the round church of **San Carlo al Corso** (1839–47), modelled on the Pantheon, and on the right, at the beginning of Corso Venezia, is **San**

Babila, a 12th-century church over-restored at the end of the 19th century. The 17th-century column outside bears the Lion of St Mark. At Corso Venezia 11 is the monumental gateway of the former seminary (1564), with huge caryatids; opposite is **Casa Fontana**, now Silvestri (no. 10), with interesting terracotta work of c. 1475. The corso is lined with fine mansions of the 18th–19th centuries, including the Neoclassical Palazzo Serbelloni (no. 16) by Simone Cantoni (1793), Palazzo Castiglioni (no. 47; 1900–04), a famous Art Nouveau palace, and Palazzo Saporiti (no. 40), built in 1812.

A little to the east, at Via Mozart 12, is the **Collezione Alighiero de' Micheli** (*open by appointment on the first Sat of the month, except July–Aug, 10.30–5, T: 02 4815556*). It contains 18th-century furniture and works of art.

At Via Andrea 6, the 18th-century Palazzo Morando houses, on the upper floor, the **Museo di Milano** (*closed at the time of writing; T: 02 7600 6245*), with an interesting collection of paintings, drawings, prints etc., depicting the changing face of Milan from the mid-16th century onwards. On the ground floor is the **Museo di Storia Contemporanea**, with material related to the two World Wars.

Santa Maria della Passione

Map p. 131, 12.

This huge church, founded c. 1485, has an octagonal dome by Cristoforo Lombardi (1530–50), and a façade by Giuseppe Rusnati (1692). Inside, in the nave are hung a fine series of portraits of popes and monks (in matching frames), some by Daniele Crespi. The vault is frescoed by Martino Bassi. The chapels in the south aisle have Lombard frescoes and altarpieces of the 16th–17th centuries. In the crossing, beneath the fine dome, is another series of paintings (in their original frames) of the *Passion*, one by Daniele Crespi. Crespi's most famous work is his *St Charles Borromeo at Supper* (1628), a perfect example of how his work reflected the devotional world of the Counter Reformation. It has none of the sumptuous, stagey sensuality of the Baroque; instead it is notable for an austere—but sympathetic—naturalism, showing the saint as a middle-aged balding cleric, eating alone in a sparsely furnished room, his repast mere bread and water, his only companion a Bible and a Crucifix, emblem of the Passion. The organ on the left (1613) has doors also painted by Crespi. The right-hand organ (1558) has doors painted by Carlo Urbini. Beneath it is the funerary monument of the founder of the church, Archbishop Daniele Birago, by Andrea Fusina (1495). The beautiful choir stalls are attributed to Cristoforo Solari.

In the south and north transepts are altarpieces by Bernardino Luini, Gaudenzio Ferrari and Giulio Campi. The chapels in the north aisle have more 16th–17th-century works, including one by Daniele Crespi.

Various rooms of the former convent and the museum can usually be visited on request. Beyond the old sacristy is the chapter house, decorated c. 1510 by Bergognone, including nine paintings of *Christ and the Apostles* opposite frescoes of *Saints and Doctors of the Church*. Beyond is a gallery with 17th-century Lombard paintings, and a room with the church treasury in 17th-century cupboards, vestments, and a large painting, *Daniel in the Lions' Den*, by Giuseppe Vermiglio.

San Pietro in Gessate

Map p. 131, 12.

This Gothic church, built c. 1475, is entered from Via Chiossetto. In the last chapel in the south aisle is a very damaged detached fresco of the *Funeral of St Martin* by Bergognone. The Cappella Grifo has interesting remains of frescoes depicting the *Life of St Ambrose* by Bernardino Butinone and Bernardino Zenale (1490–93), the best-preserved part of which is the vault with delightful angels. The tomb effigy of Ambrogio Grifo (with two portrait medallions) was carved by Benedetto Briosco c. 1490. In the south transept is an unusual painting of the *Madonna and Child* by a follower of Leonardo. In chapels in the north aisle are works by Giovanni Donato Montorfano.

PRACTICAL INFORMATION

GETTING AROUND

• To and from the airport

Milan is served by two airports: Malpensa, 45km northwest, for most international and domestic flights, and Linate, 7km east, for a few international and domestic flights and the shuttle to Rome (schedules and information at www.sea-aeroportimilano.it). Bus 73 runs to Linate from Piazza San Babila (*map p. 131, 12*) every 10mins. There are also airport express buses from the central station (Piazza Luigi di Savoia; *Map p. 130, 4*) to both airports every 20–30mins. There is a long-term plan to move all traffic except the Milan–Rome shuttle from Linate to Malpensa. For information on both airports, T: 02 7485 2200.

• **By rail:** Milan has several railway stations. The most important by far is Centrale (*map p. 130, 4*), Piazzale Duca d'Aosta, northeast of the centre, for all main services of the FS (T: 02 675001). Some international expresses stop only at Lambrate (on the east side of the city, *beyond map p. 130, 4*). Nord (*map p.*

130, 6–10) handles services of the Ferrovie Nord Milano (for Como, Novara, etc., schedules and info at www.ferrovienord.it). Porta Genova (*map p. 131, 13*) has trains for Alessandria (with connections to Genoa). Subsidiary stations include Porta Vittoria (*beyond map p. 130, 3*). FS Lost Property Office, 108 Via Sammartini (T: 02 67712667).

• **By car:** There are free car parks by the underground stations of Pagano (on Line 1) and Lambrate (Line 2), and fee-paying car parks at Rogoredo (Line 3) and Romolo (Line 2). Car Pound, Piazza Beccaria (city police station, T: 02 77271).

• **By public transport:** The underground lines, buses and trams run by ATM are very efficient. Information offices (with a map of the system) in the underground station of Piazza Duomo and at the central railway station (T: 02 89010797). Tickets (which can be used on buses, trams or the underground) are valid for 1hr 15mins (flat rate fare). They are sold at ATM offices, automatic machines at bus stops, and newsstands and tobacconists, and must be stamped on board. Tickets valid for 24 or 48 hours can also be purchased at ATM offices or newsstands.

Trams

1 Milano Centrale railway station—Piazza Cavour—Piazza Scala—Largo Cairoli (for the Castello Sforzesco)—Milano Nord railway station—Corso Sempione.

4 Piazza Repubblica—Via Manzoni—Piazza Scala—Via Legnano—Via Farini.

24 Via Mazzini—Corso Magenta (Santa Maria delle Grazie, for the Last Supper).

19 Corso Sempione—Milano Nord railway station—Via Broletto—Via Orefici (for the duomo)—Via Torino.

Buses

50/54 Largo Augusto (duomo)—Corso Magenta—Via Carducci (for Sant'Ambrogio)—Via San Vittore.

61 Corso Matteotti—Piazza Scala—Via Brera—Via Solferino (for San Marco).

65 Milano Centrale railway station—Via San Gregorio—Corso Buenos Aires—Corso Venezia—Piazza Fontana—Via Larga—Corso Italia—Porta Lodovico.

Metro

1 (red) from Sesto railway station to Bisceglie and Molino Dorino. The central section runs from Loreto Via Lima, Porta Venezia, Palestro, San Babila, duomo, Cordusio, Cairoli (for Castello Sforzesco) to Cadorna (for Milan Nord station);

2 (green) from Gessate and Cologno Nord to Famagosta in its central section links the railway stations of Lambrate, Centrale, Garibaldi, Milano Nord (Cadorna) and (by way of Sant'Ambrogio) Porta Genova;

3 (yellow) from Sondrio to San Donato links the central station Via Repubblica, Turati and Monte Napoleone with the duomo and continues along Corso di Porta Romana to southern Milan.

Taxis

Various companies run taxi services, and as in the rest of Italy there are no cruising taxis. T: 02 5353; 02 6767; 02 8585.

INFORMATION OFFICES

Via Marconi 1 (Piazza Duomo; *Map p. 107, 11*), T. 02 723241, www.milanoinfotourist.it, www.inlombardia.it; Stazione Centrale (*Map p. 130, 4*), T: 02 7252 4360; Piazza Diaz 5, T: 02 8646 1251.

HOTELS

There are nearly 400 hotels in Milan, but very few nice ones (and most of those are at the high end). A brief selection follows. Bear in mind that it is difficult to find accommodation when big international trade fairs are in progress (Feb–March and Sept–Nov).

€€€ **Brunelleschi**. An elegant Post-Modern creation in the heart of the historic centre. 12 Via Baracchini, T: 02 8843, F: 02 870144.

€€€ **Carlton Baglioni**. Modern and comfortable, on the edge of the historic city centre. Via Senato 5, T: 02 77077, F: 02 78330.

€€€ **De la Ville**. Comfortable and strategically located between the cathedral, La Scala and the shopping district. Via Hoepli 6, T: 02 867651, F: 02 866609.

€€€ **Four Seasons**. The usual high standard of luxury offered by this inter-

national group, in a beautifully restored convent in the shopping district. Via Gesù 8, T: 02 77088, F: 02 7708 5000.
€€€ **Grand Hotel et de Milan**. Milan's finest for over 130 years, in a centrally located, tastefully renovated patrician palace. Via Manzoni 29, T: 02 723141, F: 02 8646 086, www.grandhoteletdemilan.it
€€€ **Manin**. Central, quiet and comfortable, overlooking the public gardens. Via Manin 7, T: 02 659 6511, F: 02 655 2160, www.hotelmanin.it
€€€ **Pierre Milano**. Quiet and atmospheric, in the historic city centre. Via De Amicis 32, T: 02 7200 0581, F: 02 805 2157, www.hotelpierremilano.it
€€€ **Principe di Savoia**. A luxury hotel popular with Americans, in a shady square midway between the Stazione Centrale and the historic city centre. Piazza della Repubblica 17, T: 02 62301, F: 02 909 0888.
€€€ **Sir Edward**. A refined establishment with 38 rooms, on the edge of the shopping district. Via Mazzini 4, T: 02 877877, F: 02 877844.
€€ **Gran Duca di York**. A comfortable hotel in a carefully restored early 19th-century townhouse. Via Moneta 1a, T: 02 874863, F: 02 869 0344.
€€ **Manzoni**. Quiet, comfortable and popular, in the heart of the shopping district. Book in advance. Via Santo Spirito 20, T: 02 7600 5700, F: 02 784212, www.hotelmanzoni.com
€ **Antica Locanda Solferino**. In the heart of the Brera district, Milan's 'left bank', with a wide following of return clients. Book well in advance. Via Castelfidardo 2, T: 02 657 0129, F: 02 657 1361, www.anticalocandasolferino.it

YOUTH HOSTEL

€ **Piero Rotta**, Via Martino Bassi 2, T: 02 39267095, F: 02 33000191, ostellomilano@aiglombardia.it

RESTAURANTS

€€€ **Aimo e Nadia**. Generally considered to be Milan's finest restaurant, offering traditional and innovative cuisine. Closed midday Sat and Sun, Aug and Jan. Via Montecuccoli 6, T: 02 416886.
€€€ **Alfredo Gran San Bernardo**. Restaurant known especially for its *risotti*. Closed Sun, Aug and Dec–Jan. Via Borgese 14, T: 02 331 9000.
€€€ **Bice**. Restaurant serving traditional Milanese cuisine. Closed Mon, midday Tues and Aug. Via Borgospesso 12, off Via Monte Napoleone, T: 02 7600 2572.
€€€ **Bottiglieria da Pino**. Cosy place open for lunch only; closed Sun and Aug. Via Cerva 14, T: 02 7600 0532.
€€€ **Don Carlos**. Restaurant of the Grand Hotel et de Milan, specialising in fish. Open evenings only. Via Manzoni 29, T: 02 7231 4640.
€€€ **L'Ami Berton**. Restaurant serving creative fish dishes. Closed midday Sat, Sun, Aug and Jan. Via Nullo 14 at Via Goldoni, T: 02 7012 3476.
€€€ **Savini**. Traditional restaurant in a historic setting. Closed midday Sat, Sun, Aug and Jan. Galleria Vittorio Emanuele II, T: 02 7200 3433.
€€ **Al Pont de Ferr**. Traditional *osteria* overlooking the iron bridge on the Naviglio. Closed Sun, Aug and Dec–Jan. Ripa di Porta Ticinese 55, T: 02 8940 6277.
€€ **Da Francesca**. Small, cosy trattoria serving traditional Lombard fare. Closed

Sun and Aug. Viale Argonne 32, T: 02 730608.

€€ Grand Hotel. *Osteria* serving northern Italian cuisine in an informal atmosphere. Open evenings only, closed Mon and Aug. Via Ascanio Sforza 75, T: 02 8951 1586.

€€ Joia. Restaurant known for its fine vegetarian cuisine. Closed midday Sat, Sun, Easter, Aug and Dec–Jan. Via Panfilo Castaldi 18, T: 02 2952 2124.

€€ La Brisa. Traditional trattoria with a pleasant garden. Closed Sat, midday Sun, Aug and Dec Jan. Via Brisa 15, T: 02 8645 0521.

€€ La Piola. Trattoria serving traditional Lombard dishes. Closed Sun, Aug and Dec–Jan. Viale Abruzzi 23, T: 02 2953 1271.

€€ L'Osteria del Treno. Still the railway workers' favourite lunch spot, with Liberty-style dining room. Closed Sat, midday Sun and two weeks in Aug. Via San Gregorio 46 48, T: 02 670 0179.

€€€ Olivia. Restaurant with a vegetarian bias. Closed midday Sat and Sun, Aug and Dec–Jan. Viale D'Annunzio 7–9, T: 02 8940 6052.

€€ Trattoria all'Antica. Simple trattoria in the Porta Genova-Navigli area. Closed Sat and midday Sun, Aug and Dec–Jan. Via Montevideo 4, T: 02 837 2849, 02 5810 4860.

€€ Trattoria del Pescatore. Excellent, popular trattoria specialising in fish (reserve in advance). Closed Sun, Aug and Dec–Jan. Via Vannucci 5, T: 02 5832 0452.

€€ Trattoria Milanese. Trattoria run by the same family since 1913, serving classic Milanese fare. Closed Tues, Aug and Dec–Jan. Via Santa Marta 11, T: 02 8645 1991.

€ Da Abele. Trattoria known for its *risotti*, open evenings only. Closed Mon and mid-July–mid-Sept. Via Temeranza 5, T: 02 261 3855.

€ L'Osteria. Wine bar on the Naviglio Grande. Open for lunch and dinner, year round except 25 Dec and 1 Jan. Alzaia Naviglio Grande 46, T: 02 837 3426.

€ New Bar Pascone. Trattoria (despite the name) known for its fresh, homemade pasta. Closed Sun and two weeks in Aug. Viale Montenero 57, T: 02 551 0259.

€ Tagiura. Friendly, informal *osteria*. Open midday and evenings by reservation, closed Sun and Aug. Via Tagiura 5, T: 02 4895 0613.

€ Taverna Visconti. Wine bar in a quiet central sidestreet, with restaurant in the former cellar. Closed Sun. Via Marziale 11, T: 02 795821.

CAFÉS & CONFECTIONERS

No Italian city has contributed so much to the culture of the *aperitivo* as Milan, the home of Campari, Zucca and Fernet Branca. For over a century animated discussions of social, cultural and political issues have enlivened the pre-dinner hour in the city's cafés, especially on Sunday, when the Milanese take their traditional downtown stroll; and the *trani*, or wine bars of the working-class neighbourhoods, have been a Milanese institution for as long as anyone can remember.

Cafés, of course, come and go as their popularity rises and falls. Today the most fashionable include **Bar Metro**, Via dei Martinitt 3. Open 7am–9pm, closed Sun and Aug; **Bee Tee's**, Via Santa Croce 21.

Open 10am–1am, closed Mon and Aug; **Bell'Aurore**, Via Castelmorrone at Via Abamonti. Open 8am–2am, closed Sun and Aug; **Cantina Isola**, Via Sarpi 30. Open 9.30–9.30; closed Mon, except in summer, and Aug; **Jamaica**, Via Brera 32. Open 9am–2am. Closed Sun; **La Cantina di Manuela**, Via Cadore 30. Open 7.30am–1am, closed Sun and Aug; **Le Terre di Marengo**, Viale Gorizia 34. Open 7am–8.30pm, closed Sat afternoon and Sun; **Luca's**, Corso di Porta Ticinese 51b, at San Lorenzo. Open 7am–1am, closed Sun and Aug; **Lucky Bar**, Via Tito Livio 2, at Viale Umbria. Open 8am–2am, closed Sun and Aug; **Tango**, Via Casale 7. Open 6pm–2am, closed Mon, except in summer, and Jan.

Milan's best pastries are to be found at **Marchesi**, Corso Magenta 13; **Panarello**, Via Speronari 3 (Corso di Porta Romana); **Ranieri**, Via della Moscova. **San Carlo**, Via Bandello 1 (near Santa Maria delle Grazie); **Supino**, Via Cesare de Sesto; **Taveggia**, Via Visconti di Modrone 2 (with Liberty-style interior).

For ice-creams, try **Buonarroti**, Via Buonarroti 9. **Marghera**, Via Marghera 33l. For unusual flavours (sesame-honey, date), **Gelateria Ecologica Artigiana**, Corso Porta Ticinese 40.

SPECIALITY FOOD SHOPS

Casa del Formaggio, Via Speronari 3, features cheeses from all parts of Italy and Europe; **Casa del Fungo e del Tartufo**, Via Anfossi 14, offers a vast assortment of fresh and preserved mushrooms and truffles; **Cremeria D'Angelo**, Via Galiani 4, also has fine cheeses and dairy products; **Enoteca Ronchi**, Via San Vincenzo 12, stocks great wines and liqueurs; **Focaccerie Genovesi**, Via Plinio 5, makes focaccia bread with olives, cheese, onions, etc; **Friggitoria Vomero**, Via Cimarosa 44, excellent *arancini*, potato croquettes, pizzas and pasties; **Guida**, Via dei Mille 46, delicious sandwiches, cheeses, cold meats, roasts, ice cream, etc; **Il Girasole**, Via Vincenzo Monti 32, is the place to go for organic foods; **La Fungheria di Angelo Bernardi**, Viale Abruzzi 93, for fresh, dried and canned porcini mushrooms and truffles; **L'Altro Vino**, Via Piave 9, has over 900 Italian and foreign wines, liqueurs, jams, patés, etc; **La Baita del Formaggio**, Via Foppa 5, has the best of Lombard cheeses; **Peck**, Via Spadari 9, is probably the city's most famous delicatessen, with a wide selection of cheeses, cold meats, and a well-stocked wine collection. If you're in the shopping district, try Milan's other spectacular deli, **Il Salumaio**, Via Montenapoleone 12; the same people have a fine pastry shop at Via San Gregorio 1.

OPERA, THEATRE & CONCERTS

Information on theatre performances and concerts is carried in *Milano Mese*, published free every month. It is available at most hotels, or from the tourist information offices.

The opera season at **La Scala** opens on 7 Dec; ballet and concerts run Sept–Nov. Theatres, offering avant-garde and traditional performances, include the **Piccolo Teatro**, Largo Greppi; **Teatro Manzoni**, Via Manzoni 42; **Lirico**, Via Larga 14; **Nuovo**, Piazza San Babila; **Nazionale**, Piazzale Piemonte 12;

Carcano, Corso di Porta Romana 66.
Tickets can be purchased at the theatres
or at various agencies, including La
Biglietteria, 81 Corso Garibaldi (T: 02 ·
6590188).

Musica e Poesia a San Maurizio, with
classical music concerts in Milanese
churches, runs throughout the year; T:
02 7600 5500.

SHOPPING

The area north of the duomo, around
Via Montenapoleone, is Milan's famous
Fashion Triangle. The great designers
have their showrooms on Via S. Andrea,
Via della Spiga, Via Gesù, Via
Borgospesso, Via Santo Spirito, Via Verri
and, of course, Via Montenapoleone.
Important jewellery shops, and design
and furnishing showrooms, can also be
found here. This district is one of the
most elegant parts of the city from the
architectural standpoint, as it has preserved the fascination of 19th-century
Milan, with its Neoclassical townhouses.

Via Manzoni is another historic street,
with its famous jewellers, antique shops
and banks. East of the duomo, Corso
Vittorio Emanuele is Milan's high street:
now a pedestrian precinct, it is a popular
meeting place for residents as well as visitors, with cafés and open-air tables.

The area around Porta Venezia is less
chic than the Fashion Triangle, but good
if you're on a limited budget. The area
south of the duomo and around the
Navigli hosts Milan's trendiest shops.

LOCAL SPECIALITIES

Milan's famous Christmas cake, the tall,
dome-like *panettone* (made with bread
dough, eggs, sugar, nuts and candied
fruit), is available in bakeries throughout
the city.

A very different kind of shopping is
offered by Milan's many markets. The
Fiera di Senigallia, a large flea market, is
held on Sat morning in Viale
d'Annunzio. Antiques are sold along the
Naviglio on Sun morning (except
July–Aug). Open-air markets are held in
Viale Papiniano (Tues and Sat), Piazza
Mirabello (Mon and Thur), and Largo
Quinto Alpini (Fri).

FESTIVALS & EVENTS

Available at most hotels is the tourist
board's free booklet on Milan, *Milano
Mese*, with a map of the city and a summary of current events. Some of the
main ones are:
Festival of St Ambrose (patron saint of
Milan) 7 and 8 Dec; *Oh Bei Oh Bei* street
fair near Sant'Ambrogio. *Corteo dei Re
Magi*, a procession with elaborate costumes, animals, bands and majorettes, 6
Jan. *Stramilano*, a marathon race in
which some 50,000 people take part,
April. An open-air art exhibition is held
in Via Bagutta in April and Oct. The
Associazione Dimore Storiche Italiane (T:
02 9547311) organises the opening of
some historic courtyards in the city
(*Cortili Aperti*) for a week in May. On
June evenings the *Festa del Naviglio* takes
place around the Naviglio Grande (street
fairs, musical events, restaurants on
boats, etc.).

AROUND MILAN:
MONZA, LODI & PAVIA

Situated so close to Milan that it is now a suburb, Monza is the most important town in the province and the third largest town in Lombardy. It is a wealthy industrial city, known chiefly now for its Formula 1 racetrack, though it was important under the Lombard Queen Theodolinda in the 7th century, and has a cathedral of great interest, a 13th–14th-century building on the site of a church founded by Theodolinda around 595, after Gregory the Great had converted her and her people to Christianity. The fine parti-coloured marble façade by Matteo da Campione (1370–96; restored) is flanked by a brick campanile of 1606 by Pellegrino Tibaldi.

The interior contains more work by Matteo da Campione, including the organ gallery in the nave and the relief of an imperial coronation. The chapel of Queen Theodolinda contains her tomb and is decorated with frescoes by the Zavattari family (1444). Enclosed in the altar is the famous iron crown of Lombardy (*shown with the contents of the treasury, see below*), used at the coronation of the Holy Roman Emperors since 1311 and containing a strip of iron said to have been hammered from one of the nails used at the Crucifixion. The last Holy Roman Emperor to be crowned with it was Charles V (1519). Napoleon had himself crowned with it at Milan in 1805.

The Museo del Duomo houses the rich treasury (*open Tues–Sun 9–11.30 & 3–5.30*). Here are the personal relics of Theodolinda, including her silver-gilt hen and chickens, supposed to represent Lombardy and its seven provinces (possibly made in the 4th century and adapted for the queen in the 7th century), her votive cross and crown, and a book cover with a dedicatory inscription. Also here are three ivory diptychs (4th–9th centuries). Sixteen phials from Palestine, illustrated with biblical scenes, are rare works dating from the 6th century. The silk embroideries date from the 6th–7th centuries. The processional cross was given to Theodolinda by St Gregory (altered in the 15th and 17th centuries). There is also a collection of 26 glass phials from Rome (5th–6th centuries), and 16th-century tapestries made in Milan.

Outside Monza

Just to the north of the old city is the huge decaying **Villa Reale**, a Neoclassical masterpiece by Giuseppe Piermarini (1777–80), built as a residence for Archduke Ferdinand Habsburg, governor of Lombardy and Duke of Modena, the brother of Marie Antoinette. This remarkable palace is in urgent need of restoration, and sadly the state rooms and royal apartments are all closed indefinitely, though there are long-term plans to open a Neoclassical museum here. In the garden is a rotunda with delightful frescoes (1789) by Andrea Appiani (whose portrait of Napoleon hangs in the Pinacoteca Ambrosiana in Milan).

The huge park with fine trees, traversed by the Lambro river, was created in 1805–10 by Luigi Canonica and Luigi Villoresi. It now contains the famous *autodromo*, a motor-racing circuit built in 1922 (plans to extend it have so far been suppressed) and an 18-hole golf course. From behind the villa an avenue leads to the expiatory chapel, by Giuseppe Sacconi, erected by Vittorio Emanuele III on the spot where his father Umberto I was assassinated on 29 July 1900 by the anarchist Gaetano Bresci.

North of Monza is **Agliate**, with a remarkable 10th–11th-century church and baptistery traditionally thought to have been founded in 881 by Ansperto, Bishop of Milan. Restored by Luca Beltrami in 1895, they contain remains of 10th-century frescoes. Southeast of Monza is **Gorgonzola**, from which the famous cheese takes its name. Gorgonzola is still produced in the district, as is Bel Paese.

Saronno

North of Milan is Saronno, an industrial town noted for its macaroons, the famous *amaretti*. The sanctuary of the **Madonna dei Miracoli** here was begun in 1498 perhaps by Giovanni Antonio Amadeo, who designed the cupola in 1505. It was enlarged after 1556 by Vincenzo Seregni. The façade is by Pellegrino Tibaldi (1596). It contains beautiful, brightly coloured frescoes by Bernardino Luini (1525 and 1531), including the *Presentation in the Temple* and *Adoration of the Magi*, admired by Stendhal in his diary. The large fresco in the cupola of the *Virgin in Paradise*, with a concert of angels, was painted after Luini's death by Gaudenzio Ferrari (*see p. 90*), and is usually considered his masterpiece. The remarkable group of lifesize polychrome wood figures representing the *Last Supper* by Andrea da Milano (c. 1548–52) have recently been restored. They are apparently a copy of Leonardo's famous painting in Milan. Saronno also has an interesting **Collezione di Ceramiche e Maioliche** (Via Carcano 9, *open Tues, Thur and Sat 3–6 or 7*), featuring Asian and Meissen porcelain and Italian and European majolica.

LODI

Lodi, 31km southeast of Milan, is an important provincial capital and a centre for dairy produce on the right bank of the Adda, in the fertile and well-irrigated district known as the Lodigiano.

HISTORY OF LODI

An ancient town, Lodi was refounded in 1158 by Frederick Barbarossa, after the destruction of Lodi Vecchio by the Milanese. The Piazza family of painters were born here in the 16th century, and works by Callisto, Albertino and Scipione Piazza are preserved in churches in the town and province. Lodi was known for its ceramics in the 17th and 18th centuries (and several small ceramics factories still operate here, including Franchi in Via Sant'Angelo). At the famous Battle of Lodi in 1796, on the bridge over the river, Napoleon defeated the Austrians.

EXPLORING LODI

Around the duomo

In the centre of the town is the large arcaded Piazza della Vittoria. Here is the 18th-century façade of the Broletto (town hall), and the **duomo**, with a 12th-century façade including a fine portal bearing the carved figures of Adam and Eve on the door jambs, attributed to sculptors from Piacenza. The interior was well restored in the 1960s in the Romanesque style. In the first south chapel (lights) is a triptych of the *Crowning of the Virgin* by Alberto Piazza, and a polyptych with the *Massacre of the Innocents* by Callisto Piazza, both in their original frames. In the nave is a 13th-century gilt statue of San Bassiano. The choir has intarsia panels set into modern stalls, exquisite works by Fra Giovanni da Verona (1523). By the entrance to the crypt is a Romanesque relief of the *Last Supper* above fresco fragments. In the crypt, where the body of St Bassiano is preserved, is a wooden Deposition group by a local 16th-century sculptor.

Piazza Broletto, on the north side of the duomo, has remains of the 13th-century part of the Broletto and the Romanesque cathedral font, used as a fountain. From here a passageway leads into Piazza Mercato (markets on Tues, Thur, Sat and Sun).

Via dell'Incoronata leads from Piazza della Vittoria to the inconspicuous entrance to the **church of the Incoronata**, built in 1488–94 by Giovanni Battagio and Gian Giacomo Dolcebuono (who may also have designed the great portal of the Certosa di Pavia, *see p. 156*). The octagonal interior is totally covered with 16th-century paintings, frescoes, and gilded decoration, to a design by Callisto Piazza. In the first chapel on the right, the altarpiece of the *Conversion of St Paul*, a late work (1580) by Callisto, is flanked by four exquisite panels by Bergognone. The chapels on either side of the main altar also have altarpieces by Callisto, with the intervention of his son Fulvio, and his brother Scipione. In the last chapel is a polyptych of 1519 by Albertino Piazza in its original frame, and four small paintings by Scipione. The original 16th-century organ survives. The charming frescoed decoration on the pilasters, etc., is also by Scipione Piazza. A gonfalon, painted on silk by Albertino Piazza, and Rococo carved stalls can be seen behind the high altar. The 18th-century sacristy preserves its cupboards and pretty vault. A small museum with 15th–16th-century church silver and vestments is usually kept closed.

Corso Umberto leads out of Piazza della Vittoria to the **Museo Civico** (*open June–Sept Sat–Sun 9.30–12.30; Oct–May Sat 9.30–12.30 & 3.30–6.30*), with a fine collection of local ceramics on the ground floor, including works with floral decorations in the 'Vecchia Lodi' style produced by the Ferretti family in the late 18th century. The museum also houses an *Adoration of the Magi*, the only signed and dated work by Scipione Piazza (1562). There is also an archaeological section, a collection of paintings and a museum dedicated to the Risorgimento.

From the other side of Piazza della Vittoria, Via Marsala leads to Sant'Agnese (left), a 15th-century church with terracotta decoration on the façade, and a polyptych by Albertino Piazza. From here Via XX Settembre, with the fine 15th-century Palazzo Mozzanica (no. 51; now Varesi), with a good portal and terracotta friezes, leads east to

San Francesco (1289), a church with an unusual façade. The interior has numerous 14th–15th-century frescoes, the most interesting on the nave pillars, in the third chapel on the south, and in the aisles and south transept. The hospital in the piazza has a charming little 15th-century cloister with a double loggia decorated with terracotta.

THE LODIGIANO

The Lodigiano, or territory of Lodi, was an unhealthy, marshy area before the local monastic communities constructed canals, many of which still survive. In the well-irrigated countryside there are numerous dairy farms producing mascarpone and a cheese known locally as *raspadura*, a type of unmatured Parmesan served as an hors d'oeuvre which you eat with your fingers. Near the River Adda, which borders the eastern side of the province, there are good cycling routes (information from the tourist office in Lodi).

Lodi Vecchio

Lodi Vecchio is 5km west of Lodi. The Roman Laus Pompeia was a constant rival of Milan until its total destruction in 1158. Only the church of **San Bassiano** was left standing, and it is now in an isolated position outside the village. Of ancient foundation, it was rebuilt in Gothic style in the early 14th century, with a fine exterior. High up on the façade is a ceramic statue of the 4th-century bishop St Bassiano.

The interior is interesting for its early-14th-century frescoed decoration (restored in the early 1960s) in the nave vaults and apse, with colourful geometric designs and flowers, and including one bay with very unusual rustic scenes of four carts drawn by oxen (the frescoes were financed by a local farming corporation in 1323), and Christ Pantocrator in the apse. Votive frescoes include a scene of St Eligius blessing a horse. At the end of the north aisle (high up) is a relief with bulls and a man on a horse dated 1323. The 11th-century capitals are also interesting, and in the south aisle is a series of 17th-century paintings. The site of the Roman city was identified in 1987 by aerial photography, and excavations are in progress near the village.

Elsewhere around Lodi

Sant'Angelo Lodigiano to the southwest (on the Pavia road), has a restored 14th-century **Visconti Castle** (*open Sun and holidays, March–July, Sept–Oct, 2.30–5*). **Codogno**, south of Lodi, is an agricultural centre. In the 16th-century church of San Biagio are an *Assumption* by Callisto Piazza, *Madonna and Child between St Francis and Charles Borromeo* by Daniele Crespi, and 16th-century works by Cesare Magni.

At **Ospedaletto Lodigiano**, west of Codogno, is an abbey founded in 1433, with a 16th-century church containing paintings (formerly part of a triptych) by Giampietrino. Part of the 16th-century cloister survives.

East of Lodi is **Abbadia Cerreto**, where there is a Cistercian Lombard church built in the 12th century, with a fine exterior and an altarpiece by Callisto Piazza.

PAVIA & ITS PROVINCE

Pavia is an old provincial capital of Roman origin on the River Ticino. On 24 February 1525 the famous Battle of Pavia was fought here, in which the French king Francis I was defeated by Habsburg Emperor Charles V, who deployed a new weapon—the cannon—against the old-fashioned crossbow. The beginning of Habsburg power and influence in Italy dates from this battle. King Francis was imprisoned in the castle of Belgioioso, east of Pavia, and at Pizzighettone, an old town on the Adda towards Cremona. He was ultimately taken to Madrid, and surrendered French claims to Italy the following year.

Although virtually nothing remains of the Roman city, Pavia itself has a number of fine medieval churches and palaces in its cobbled streets, and interesting art collections in the Castello Visconteo. There are some exceptionally fine sights in the province of Pavia, chief of which is the beautiful 15th–16th-century Certosa di Pavia, a few kilometres north of the town.

HISTORY OF PAVIA

The Roman Ticinum was founded on this site about 220 BC. In the 6th century the town became the capital of the Lombards, who called it Papia. It was here that the Lombards crowned their sovereigns: the church of San Michele hosted the coronations of Charlemagne (774), Berengar, the first king of Italy (888), Berengar II (950) and Frederick Barbarossa (1155).

The commune of Pavia took the Ghibelline side against Milan and Lodi, afterwards passed to the Counts of Monferrato and, from 1359 onwards, to the Visconti. After the failure of the French to win control of Pavia from the Spaniards in the decisive battle fought here in 1525, Francis I wrote to his mother: '*Madame, tout est perdu hors l'honneur*' (All is lost save honour). The ramparts which still surround part of the city were built by the Spanish in the 17th century. Pavia was the birthplace of Lanfranc (1005–89), the first Norman archbishop of Canterbury. The name of the Piazza Petrarca recalls Petrarch's visits to his son-in-law here.

The town centre

Pavia's two main streets, the Strada Nuova and Corso Cavour-Corso Mazzini, intersect in the centre of the town in true Roman style near the huge arcaded Piazza Vittoria, its market now relegated below ground. At the southern end of the piazza rises the Broletto (12th century; restored in the 19th century), with a double loggia of 1563.

Next to the town hall is the **duomo**, a modification by Bramante (with, possibly, also the intervention of Leonardo da Vinci) of an older building begun in 1488. The immense cupola, the third largest in Italy, was not added until 1884–85, and the

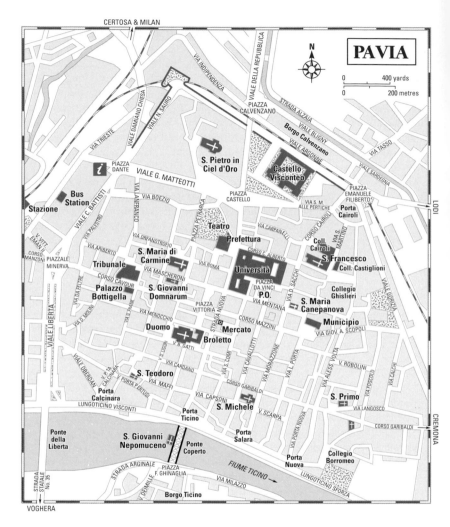

façade was completed in 1933. The rest of the exterior remains unfinished. The impressive, centrally-planned interior has a very pronounced cornice above the capitals. On the west wall are paintings by Cerano, Daniele Crespi and Moncalvo. In the transepts are altarpieces by Carlo Sacchi and Bernardino Gatti, and the 17th-century *Madonna di Piazza Grande*.

Several palaces with porticoes, including the handsome Palazzo Vescovile (1577), line the piazza. The equestrian statue by Francesco Messina (1937) recalls the gilded bronze Roman statue that stood here from the 11th century until its destruction in 1796. Next to the duomo are the neglected ruins of the **Torre Civica**, the campanile of two demolished Romanesque churches, with a bell-chamber by Pellegrino Tibaldi (1583) that collapsed without warning in 1989, killing four people and wounding 15. Discussions continue about whether it should be reconstructed.

Via dei Liguri leads downhill out of the piazza and Via Maffi continues right to the 12th-century church of **San Teodoro**, with its octagonal cupola-tower and 16th-century lantern. Inside, the remarkable 15th–16th-century frescoes include a view of Pavia with its numerous towers (west wall) in 1522, by Bernardino Lanzani, and the *Lives of St Theodore* (north transept) and *St Agnes* (south transept), attributed to Lanzani. The short, broad crypt lies beneath the sanctuary.

Below the church, Via Porta Pertusi continues to the picturesque **Ponte Coperto**, a covered bridge across the Ticino, still used by cars. The original bridge, built in 1351–54 on Roman foundations and roofed in 1583, collapsed in 1947 after bomb damage. The present one, a few metres further east, is to a different design, as is the chapel replacing the 18th-century bridge-chapel. In the suburb across the bridge is the 12th-century church of Santa Maria in Betlemme, which has a façade decorated with faience plaques and a plain Romanesque interior.

The Strada Nuova leads uphill from the bridge back towards the centre of the town. Via Capsoni leads right to **San Michele**, the finest church in Pavia, consecrated in 1155, with an octagonal cupola. The elaborately ornamented front has profusely decorated triple portals and sculptured friezes, but the sandstone in which they are carved has been almost totally worn away, despite restoration in 1967. The portals of the transept and the galleried apse also have interesting carving. The lower part of the campanile, decorated with terracotta tiles, dates from c. 1000. The interior is similar to that of San Pietro in Ciel d'Oro (*see below*), whereas the gallery above the nave recalls that of Sant'Ambrogio in Milan. There is fine sculptural detail in many parts of the interior, particularly on the capitals. The rood above the crossing is 15th century. In the crypt is the tomb of Martino Salimbeni (d. 1463), by the school of Amadeo.

Opposite the church, behind a railing and surrounded by a garden, is Palazzo Corti (or Arnaboldi), an 18th-century building altered in 1875 by Ercole Balossi.

The university quarter

Via San Michele and Via Cavalotti lead uphill to the north. Across Corso Mazzini, Via Galliano continues past the post office to Piazza Leonardo da Vinci, where three ancient tower-houses survive, built by the noble families of Pavia (the town was once called the 'city of a hundred towers', and some 80 of them survived up to the 19th century). Under cover are remains of the 12th-century crypt of Sant'Eusebio (*open by appointment at the Castello Visconteo*), with restored early-13th-century frescoes.

Here is the **University of Pavia**—one of the oldest in Europe—the successor to a famous school of law, the ancient Studio, where Lanfranc is said to have studied. The school was made a university in 1361 by Galeazzo II Visconti, and is now particularly renowned for its faculties of law and medicine. The buildings of 1533 were extended by Giuseppe Piermarini in 1771–79, and by Leopold Pollack in 1783–95. The Aula Magna was begun in 1827.

Off Corso Carlo Alberto and the Strada Nuova are numerous attractive courtyards, all of which are open to the public. From the one with a war memorial you enter the **Museo per la Storia dell'Università di Pavia** (*open Mon 3.30–5, Fri 9.30–12, or by appointment; T: 0382 29724*), with interesting collections relating to the history of medicine and physics in an old-fashioned arrangement (the display-cases survive from the 18th century). The collections include mementoes of the most distinguished alumni, including Alessandro Volta (*see p. 186*), whose statue is in the central courtyard. The Teatro Fisico and the anatomical theatre were both designed by Leopold Pollack (1787). The anatomical theatre is named after Antonio Scarpa. Scarpa (1752–1832), was a brilliant but famously irascible surgeon, founder of the School of Anatomy at Pavia. As the father of orthopaedic science, he has bequeathed his name to no less than ten medical terms, including Scarpa's Shoe, a device for correcting club foot. He was much admired by Napoleon, who made him a present of silver instruments with ivory handles. He was less beloved by students and colleagues. After his death, in fact, his body was decapitated in a revenge attack by one of his housemen.

Via Roma leads left from the Strada Nuova to the large red brick church of **Santa Maria del Carmine**, begun in 1373. It has an attractive façade adorned with terracotta statues and an elaborate rose window. On some of the nave pillars and in the transept are frescoes by local 15th-century painters. The charming lavabo in the sacristy (south transept) is by Giovanni Antonio Amadeo.

Strada Nuova continues north past the Teatro Fraschini, built in 1771–73 by Antonio Galli, to the **Castello Visconteo**, surrounded by public gardens. The great fortress was built in 1360–65 by Galeazzo II Visconti, who housed his important collections of literature and art here. A huge park (with a perimeter wall of some 22km) extended north from the ducal residence as far as the Certosa di Pavia. The famous Battle of Pavia (*see p. 151*) took place in this park in 1525; two years later, in revenge for their defeat in battle, the French destroyed the northern wing of the castle and two of its corner turrets. The restored interior (entrance on the west side; *open March–June and Sept–Nov Tues–Fri 9–1, Sat–Sun 10–7; July–Aug and Dec–Feb Tues–Sat 9–1.30, Sun 9–1*) with a splendid courtyard, now houses the civic collections of art and antiquities. Highlights include exhibits from the Lombard period when Pavia was capital of the Lombard court, and a collection of Lombard jewellery. The painting of *Christ Carrying the Cross* by Bergognone shows a procession of Carthusian monks in front of the Certosa di Pavia (*see overleaf*) with the façade still under construction, c. 1494.

The north and east

Via Liutprando leads northwest from Piazza Castello to the quiet square in front of the Lombard church of **San Pietro in Ciel d'Oro**, consecrated in 1132. The church's name comes from its former gilded vault. The church is mentioned by Dante in his *Paradiso* (X, 128) as the place where the mortal remains of Boethius (who was executed here, *see below*) find eternal peace. The passage is quoted on the façade. The single portal is asymmetrically placed, and the buttress on the right is made broader than that on the left in order to contain a stairway.

The fine Romanesque interior, restored in 1875–99, has 'bestiary' capitals. The altar-piece is the Arca di Sant'Agostino, a masterpiece of Italian sculpture. It was executed c. 1362 by Campionese masters (from Campione d'Italia on Lago di Lugano), whom scholars say were influenced by the Pisan Giovanni di Balduccio. It has a galaxy of stat-uettes, and bas-reliefs illustrating the story of the saint (the details are difficult to see from a distance). It is supposed to contain the **relics of St Augustine** (d. 430), removed from Carthage during the Arian persecutions. The large crypt contains the **remains of Boethius** (476–524), the Roman poet and statesman clubbed to death in Pavia by order of the Ostrogothic king Theodoric, on charges of treason. He wrote *The Consolation of Philosophy* while in prison awaiting execution.

In the eastern part of the city is the church of San Francesco d'Assisi, a late-Romanesque edifice (1238–98) with a restored Gothic façade. Also on Corso Cairoli is a Renaissance building readapted to its original purpose when the Collegio Cairoli was founded in 1948. Further east, in Via San Martino (no. 18), is the Collegio Castiglione Brugnatelli (for women), which occupies a 15th-century building. The college chapel (shown on request) has restored 15th-century frescoes by the school of Bonifacio Bembo. A bronze statue of Pope Pius V by Francesco Nuvolone (1692) faces the Collegio Ghislieri, which the Pope founded in 1567. The square is closed by the façade of San Francesco di Paola, beyond which are the Botanical Gardens.

Via Scopoli returns towards the centre of the town past Santa Maria delle Cacce, rebuilt in 1629, with frescoes of the life of St Theodoric—not to be confused with Theodoric the nemesis of Boethius. St Theodoric was a French monk (known in France as St Thierry), who earned his fame in Pavia by curing King Theodoric of an eye com-plaint. The church of Santa Maria Canepanova, at the corner of Via Sacchi and Via Negri, is a graceful octagonal building begun by Giovanni Antonio Amadeo in 1507, probably to a design by Bramante; it has a pretty little cloister.

The south and west

In the southern part of the town, near Corso Garibaldi, is the much altered Lombard church of San Primo. Further south, reached by Via San Giovanni, is the Collegio Borromeo, founded by St Charles Borromeo in 1561 and built in 1564–92 largely by Pellegrino Tibaldi; Leopold Pollack's river façade was added in 1808–20.

In the western part of the town, off Corso Cavour, is the 11th-century Lombard cam-panile of San Giovanni Domnarum. The crypt and its frescoes go back to the 11th cen-tury. Corso Cavour is distinguished by a 15th-century tower (at no. 17) and the Bramantesque Palazzo Bottigella (no. 30), with fine brick decorations. Corso Manzoni prolongs Corso Cavour to the railway, beyond which (5mins) is the church of San Salvatore, reconstructed in 1467–1511 with frescoes by Bernardino Lanzoni. A further 10-minute walk brings you to **San Lanfranco**, a 13th-century building containing the fine cenotaph (by Amadeo; 1498) of the beatified Lanfranc—actually buried at Canterbury—and traces of 13th-century frescoes on the right wall of the nave, includ-ing one showing the murder of St Thomas Becket at Canterbury. One of the cloisters retains some terracotta decoration, also by Amadeo.

THE PROVINCE OF PAVIA

The province of Pavia abounds in interesting sights, but in all seasons except summer the roads are subject to heavy fog, so cautious driving is necessary.

The Certosa di Pavia

Open 9–11.30 & 2.30–4.30, 5, 5.30 or 6 (closed Mon and major national holidays).
The Certosa is difficult to reach by public transport. Buses run every 30 minutes from the bus station in Pavia, but from the bus stop it is an unpleasant walk of at least 20 minutes along a busy road; from the train station, on the other side of the Certosa, the walk is even longer. If you come by car or taxi, glance out of the window from time to time: you will notice the Milan road from Pavia is skirted by the Naviglio di Pavia, an irrigation and transportation canal begun by Galeazzo Visconti, lined with abandoned locks and lock-houses.

The Certosa di Pavia, a Carthusian monastery, was founded by Gian Galeazzo Visconti in 1396 as a family mausoleum. Its construction was entrusted to the Lombard masons of Milan cathedral and the builders of the castle of Pavia. The monastery proper was finished in 1452 and the church in 1472, under the Sforzas. The façade was completed in the 16th century. Today just ten Cistercian monks occupy the Certosa.

From the entrance, facing west, a vestibule with frescoed saints by Bernardino Luini leads through to the great garden-court in front of the church. On the left are the old pharmacy and food and wine stores; on the right the prior's quarters and the so-called Palazzo Ducale, rebuilt by Francesco Maria Richini (1620–25) to house distinguished visitors and now containing a museum (*described below*).

The sculptural and polychrome marble decoration of the west front of the church, of almost superabundant richness, marks the height of the artistic achievement of the Quattrocento in Lombardy; it was begun in 1473 and worked on up to 1499 by Cristoforo and Antonio Mantegazza and Giovanni Antonio Amadeo. In the 16th century, Cristoforo Lombardo continued the upper part in simplified form, but it was never completed. The attribution of the various parts is still under discussion. On the lowest order of the façade are medallions of Roman emperors; above, statues and reliefs of prophets, apostles and saints by the Mantegazza; and scenes from the *Life of Christ* by Amadeo. The great portal was probably designed by Gian Cristoforo Romano (also attributed to Gian Giacomo Dolcebuono and Amadeo) and executed by Benedetto Briosco, the sculptor also of the bas-reliefs of the *Life of the Virgin* and of four large reliefs: the *Foundation of the Carthusian Order, 1084*; *Laying the First Stone of the Certosa, 27 August 1396*; *Translation to the Certosa of the Body of Gian Galeazzo, 1 March 1474*; *Consecration of the Church, 3 May 1497*. On each side are two very rich windows by Amadeo. The upper part, by Cristoforo Lombardo (1540–60), is decorated with 70 statues of the 16th century by Lombard masters. The rest of the exterior is best seen from the northeast.

The interior

The interior is purely Gothic in plan, but Renaissance decorative motifs were introduced towards the east end; the chapels opening off the aisle were expensively redecorated and provided with handsome Baroque grilles in the 17th–18th centuries, and only traces remain of their original frescoes and glass. As the grilles are kept locked, the works of art in the chapels are extremely difficult to see.

In the south aisle, the first chapel is a Baroque work by Camillo Procaccini with a lavabo by the Mantegazza. The altarpiece of the second chapel incorporates panels by Macrino d'Alba and Bergognone. In the fourth chapel is a *Crucifixion* by Bergognone, and in the fifth chapel an altarpiece of St Syrus, first bishop of Pavia, by Bergognone, and unrestored ceiling frescoes by Jacopo de' Mottis (1491).

In the north aisle, the first chapel has a lavabo by the Mantegazza (c. 1470). The altarpiece in the second chapel is made up from a painting representing *God the Father* by Perugino, flanked by *Doctors of the Church* by Bergognone, and below—17th-century copies of panels by Perugino (1499), now in the National Gallery, London. In the fourth chapel, the *Massacre of the Innocents* by Dionigi Bussola is the best of the Baroque altar reliefs. The altarpiece in the sixth chapel, of *St Ambrose and Saints*, is by Bergognone (1492).

In the centre of the north transept are tomb statues of Lodovico il Moro and Beatrice d'Este by Cristoforo Solari (1497), brought from Santa Maria delle Grazie in Milan in 1564. The frescoes include *Ecce Homo* (over the small west door) and the *Crowning of the Virgin*, with the kneeling figures of Francesco Sforza and Lodovico il Moro (north apse), both by Bergognone. The two angels on either side of the window above are attributed to Bramante. The two candelabra are by Annibale Fontana.

The south transept holds the tomb of Gian Galeazzo Visconti by Gian Cristoforo Romano (1493–97; the *Madonna* is by Benedetto Briosco, the sarcophagus by Galeazzo Alessi, the figures of Fame and Victory by Bernardino da Novate). The lunette fresco in the south apse by Bergognone depicts Gian Galeazzo, with his children, presenting a model of the church to the Virgin; higher up are two angels attributed to Bramante. Over the altar is a *Madonna Enthroned with St Charles and St Bruno*, by Cerano. The fresco over the small west door depicting the *Madonna* is by Bergognone.

Off the south transept, a pretty door by Amadeo, with profile-portraits of the Duchesses of Milan, leads into the lavatorium, which contains a finely-carved lavabo by Alberto Maffiolo of Carrara, and, on the left, a charming fresco of the *Madonna* by Bernardino Luini. A matching doorway by Amadeo, with medallions of the Dukes of Milan, in the north transept, leads into the old sacristy, with a good vault. It contains fine 17th-century presses. The remarkable ivory altarpiece, with nearly 100 statuettes, attributed to Baldassare degli Embriachi, was made in the early 15th century.

The choir contains carved and inlaid stalls (1498), frescoes by Daniele Crespi (1629), and a sumptuous late-16th-century altar.

From the south transept a doorway by the Mantegazza leads into the small cloister, with a garden, and embellished by terracotta decorations in the Cremonese style by

Rinaldo de Stauris (1465), and a terracotta lavabo. The beautiful little doorway into the church, with a *Madonna*, is by Amadeo (1466). There is a good view of the southern flank of the church. Off this cloister is the new sacristy (*only open for services*), with an altarpiece of the *Assumption* by Andrea Solari (completed by Bernardino Campi) and 16th-century illuminated choirbooks. The refectory has ceiling frescoes by Ambrogio and Bernardo Bergognone, a reader's pulpit, and a little fresco of the *Madonna* by the Zavattari or Bergognone (1450).

A passage leads from the small cloister into the great cloister, with 122 arches and more terracotta decoration by de Stauris (1478). Above the porticoes on three sides you can make out 24 identical monks' cells, each with its chimney. Entered by a decorative doorway, they have two rooms, with a little garden below, and a bedroom and loggia above.

The **museum** in the Palazzo Ducale, on the garden-court in front of the church, has two frescoed rooms by Fiammenghino and Giovanni Battista Pozzo (attributed). The paintings include works by Bartolomeo Montagna, Bergognone, Bernardino Luini, Giuseppe Vermiglio, and Vicenzo and Bernardino Campi. The portrait of Pope Paul V is a copy by Gerolamo Ciocca of a work by Caravaggio. There are also sculptures by Bambaia, Mantegazza and Cristoforo Solari. A gallery of plaster casts occupies the ground floor, where the arms from the tomb of Gian Galeazzo Visconti are also preserved.

Vigevano and the west

The western part of Pavia province, between the Ticino, Sesia and Po rivers, is known as the Lomellina. Rice has been grown here since the 16th century. The ancient capital of the region is **Lomello** (*see map on p. 76*) interesting for its medieval monuments, including Santa Maria Maggiore (11th century) and its baptistery (5th century; upper part rebuilt in the 8th century). The chief town of the Lomellina today is **Mortara**. A local speciality is salami made from goose meat. Nearby is **Cilavegna**, known for its asparagus.

Northeast of Mortara near the Ticino is **Vigevano**, an ancient town which grew to prominence in the 14th century under the Visconti. Lodovico il Moro and Francesco II Sforza were born here. It has been famous for the manufacture of shoes since the end of the 19th century, and the modern city expanded rapidly in the 1950s. Its chief beauty, though, is its lovely main square, the Piazza Ducale, one of the great achievements of Italian Renaissance town planning. In 1492–94 buildings were demolished to create space for the square by order of Lodovico il Moro. It is surrounded on three sides by uniform graceful arcades, and its classical design may owe something to Bramante (or even Leonardo da Vinci). The other end was closed in 1680 when the unusual curved façade of the duomo was added to give the cathedral prominence. The cathedral interior (1532–1612) is interesting for its paintings by the 16th-century Lombard school. A museum (*open Sun and holidays 3–6; closed Aug and mid-Dec–mid-Jan*) houses the rich treasury, which includes Flemish and local tapestries, illuminated codexes, and goldsmiths' work.

A tall Lombard tower (probably redesigned by Bramante; open on request) belongs to the huge castle (*open Tues–Sun 8.30–1.30, Sat and holidays guided visits at 2.30 and 6.30; closed mid-Dec–mid-Jan*), begun by Lucchino Visconti in the mid-14th century. On a raised site, this was connected to the piazza by a monumental entrance (destroyed) beneath the tower. The castle was transformed by Lodovico il Moro (with the help of Bramante) into a very grand ducal palace. It has remarkable stables and a beautiful loggia. The raised covered way built by Lucchino Visconti to connect the castle with the Rocca Vecchia survives.

Palazzo Crespi, in Corso Cavour on the outskirts of the old town, houses a museum illustrating the history of footwear, including a collection of shoes (some dating from the 15th century), and the Museo Civico (*closed at the time of writing*), with an archaeological collection and picture gallery.

Southeast of Vigevano is the large Sforzesca, a model farm designed by Guglielmo da Camino for Lodovico il Moro in 1486.

The Oltrepò Pavese

NB: This area is covered by the maps on pp. 76 and 612.
The southern part of the province of Pavia, beyond the Po, is known as the Oltrepò Pavese. It is well known for its wines (particularly Pinot Nero). Here is **Voghera**, (*map on p. 76*) an important industrial centre and railway junction, with a 12th-century church (Santi Flavio e Giorgio, a cavalry memorial chapel), a Visconti castle, and a museum of fossils.

A road ascends the Val di Staffora to the southeast passing Salice Terme, a little spa with iodine waters (season May–Oct). The **Abbazia di Sant'Alberto di Butrio** (*map on p. 612*) was founded in the 11th century. Three Romanesque churches here have 15th-century frescoes. The road continues through **Varzi**, noted for its salami, and up over the Passo del Penice (1149m). Here you can visit the Giardino Alpino di Pietra Corva (950m; *open May–Sept, Tues–Sun 9–12 & 3–7*), a little botanical garden planted in 1967.

East of Voghera is **Montebello della Battaglia** (*map on p. 612*), where a monument marks the site of two important battles: a victory of the French over the Austrians in 1800, and the Franco-Italian success of 1859, the first battle of the second Italian War of Independence. Nearby is **Casteggio**, where the 18th-century Palazzo della Certosa contains the Museo Storico Archeologico dell'Oltrepò Pavese (*open by appointment; T: 0383 83941*), with material from the Roman Clastidium.

PRACTICAL INFORMATION

GETTING AROUND

• **By car:** Traffic is limited in the centre of Pavia. You can park free on Piazza Petrarca and Piazzale Libertà, and there are pay car parks on Viale Matteotti, Viale II Febbraio and Piazzale Cairoli. Bus 3 runs from the railway station to the centre of the town along Corso Cavour and Corso Mazzini.

• **By bus:** A comprehensive network of country buses run by the Trasporti Regione Lombardia serves western Milan and the province of Varese, southern Milan and the province of Pavia, and the Brianza in the north. Pavia's bus station, with buses to places in the province, is on Via Trieste.

• **By rail:** There are trains linking Milan (Stazione Centrale) and Lodi roughly hourly throughout the day (more frequent at rush hours). Travel time is c. 45mins. A frequent train service links Milan (Porta Garibaldi station) and Monza in 10–15mins. Pavia is on the main Milan–Genoa line. Fast Intercity trains make the run from Milan in c. 30mins; from Genoa in c. 70mins. There is also a slow local service from Codogno (on the Milan–Piacenza line).

INFORMATION OFFICES

Lodi Piazza Broletto 4, T: 0371 421391, www.apt.lodi.it
Monza Palazzo Comunale, T: 039 323222.
Pavia Via Fabio Filzi 2, T: 0382 22156, www.apt.pv.it
Certosa di Pavia At the entrance to the monastery (closed in winter).

Vigevano Corso Vittorio Emanuele 29, T: 0381 299282.

HOTELS

Lodi
€ **Europa**. Classic small-town hotel, simple but comfortable. Closed Aug and Dec–Jan. Viale Pavia 5, Lodi, T: 0371 35215, www.hoteleuropa-lodi.it
Monza
€€€ **De la Ville**. A fine old place (renovated) near the Villa Reale. Closed Aug and Dec–Jan. Viale Regina Margherita 15, T: 039 38258, www.hoteldelaville.com
€€ **Della Regione**. Modern and business-like. Via Elvezia 4, T: 039 387205, www.hoteldellaregione.com
Pavia
€€ **Moderno**. Modest but comfortable, a stone's throw from the train station. Closed Dec–Jan.Viale Vittorio Emanuele 41, T: 0382 303401, www.hotelmoderno.it
Cervesina
€€ **Castello di San Gaudenzio**. 14th-century castle with a lovely park and an excellent restaurant. Via Mulino 1, T: 0383 3331.
Salice Terme
€€ **President Terme**. A large, modern spa. Closed Dec–Jan. Via Enrico Fermi 5, T: 0383 91941, www.president-hotel.it.
€ **Roby**. A small, pleasant place. Open Apr–Oct only. Via Cesare Battisti 15, T/F: 0383 91323.
Vigevano
€€ **Europa**. Modern and friendly. Closed Dec–Jan. Via Trivulzio 8, T: 0381 9085, www.heuropa.it

RESTAURANTS

Lodi
€ **La Quinta**. Restaurant, closed Sun evening, Mon and Aug. Piazza della Vittoria 20, T: 0371 424232.

Monza
€€ **La Riserva**. Restaurant serving Piedmontese specialities, closed Fri, midday Sat, Aug and Dec–Jan. Via Borgazzi 12, T: 039 386612.

Pavia
€€€ **Locanda Vecchia Pavia**. Restaurant featuring seasonal dishes based on fresh ingredients. Closed Mon, midday Wed, Jan and Aug. Via Cardinal Riboldi 2, T: 0382 304132.

€€ **Osteria della Madonna de Peo**. Traditional *osteria* popular with the locals. Closed Sun and Aug. Via dei Liguri 28, T: 0382 302833.

€ **Antica Osteria del Previ**. Traditional trattoria on the banks of the Ticino. Closed Wed and midday in summer. Via Milazzo 65, T: 0382 26203.

€ **Osteria del Naviglio**. Wine bar, good for *bruschette*, cheese and salads. Open evenings only, closed Mon and July. Via Alzaia 39, T: 0382 460392.

Casaletto Ceredano
€€ **Antica Locanda del Ponte**, Via al Porto 19, Ca' de Vagni, T: 0373 262474. Simple trattoria serving local dishes. Closed Tues evening, Wed and Aug.

Certosa di Pavia
€ **Vecchio Mulino**. Restaurant offering excellent regional cuisine. Closed Sun evening, Mon and Jan. Viale Monumento 5, T: 0382 925894.

€€ **Chalet della Certosa**. Restaurant in a pleasant garden, serving good country cuisine. Closed Mon and Jan. Viale Monumento 1, T: 0382 934935.

Mortara
€€ **La Gambarina**. Farm serving country lunches made from home-grown ingredients. Closed Mon–Wed, except holidays. Strada Milanese 2260, T: 0384 98399.

Salice Terme
€€ **Ca' Vegia**. Restaurant specialising in fish, with garden seating in summer. Closed Mon. Via Diviani 23, T: 0383 93248.

Vigevano
€€ **I Castagni**. Restaurant with excellent regional cuisine. Closed Sun evening, Mon, Aug and Jan. Via Ottobiano 8/20 (2km south), T: 0381 42860.

€€ **Da Maria**. A fine regional restaurant. Closed Wed, Aug and Dec–Jan. Via Bellaria 5, T: 0381 347429.

CAFÉS & PASTRY SHOPS

Vignoni, at Strada Nuova 110, Pavia, is the pastry shop where the city's signature cake, *torta paradiso*, was invented. **Demetrio**, also in Pavia (Via Guidi 33), has excellent cakes.

REGIONAL SPECIALITIES & MARKETS

Pavia has an antiques market (first Sun of the month, except Jan and Aug). Elsewhere, there are antiques markets at **Vigevano** (third Sat), **Voghera** (fourth Sun; *map on p. 76*), **Belgioioso** (week before Easter; *map on p. 146*). Presentation and sale of new wine, **Canneto Pavese** (first and second weekends in Mar; *map on p. 612*), **Rovescala** (all Mar weekends; *map on p. 612*). Plants and flowers (plus farm machinery and more), **Belgioioso** (Easter weekend; *map* *on p. 146)*; other events at Belgioioso include a book fair (late April); *Officinalia*, natural food and medicine fair (early May); *Amicolibro*, children's book fair (last weekend in Oct). *Festa dell'Uva*, vintage feast and wine fair, **Broni** (third Sun in Sept; *map on p. 612*). Black truffle fair, **Menconico** (third Sun in Sept; *map on p. 612*). Forest fair, with truffles, mushrooms, honey and other forest products, **Casteggio** (late Oct; *map on p. 612*).

FESTIVALS & EVENTS

Lodi Festival of San Bassiano (patron saint), 19 Jan. *Palio dei Rioni* on 1 Oct;

fair and market around 13 Dec (Santa Lucia).

Any occasion is good for a *festa* in most villages. Highlights of the year's events include colourful Carnival celebrations at Menconico and Varzi. *Scarpe d'Oro* amateur footrace at Vigevano (Easter Mon); extemporaneous painting competitions at Salice Terme (second Sun); horse show, Salice Terme (Sept); historic procession, Vigevano (first Sun in Oct); *Festa di San Martino*, with roasted chestnuts and vin brulé, *Canneto* (second sun in Oct); *Capodanno Anticipato*, New Year's Eve for those who can't wait, Borgo Priolo (29 Dec).

LAGO MAGGIORE

Surrounded by picturesque snow-capped mountains, Lago Maggiore is the second largest lake in Italy (the largest is Lake Garda). Its 121 sq km divide Piedmont to the west from Lombardy to the east. The north end (about one-fifth of its area), including Locarno, is in Swiss territory.

Lago Maggiore became well known at the beginning of the 19th century as a European resort, visited for its romantic scenery and good climate. The lake is often called Verbano, from the Latin Lacus Verbanus, a name derived from the vervain (verbena) which grows abundantly on its shores. The central part of the lake, around Stresa, is particularly interesting. Since the 15th century the Italian family of Borromeo have held important possessions on the lake, notably the Isole Borromee and the castle of Angera.

NB. Towns and sights in this chapter are marked on the map on pp. 170–71.

THE WEST SIDE OF THE LAKE

The Simplon road from Geneva to Milan, constructed by Napoleon in 1800–05, skirts the lake's southwest shore from Sesto Calende at the southern tip. **Arona** is an ancient town looking across the lake to Angera. The Palazzo Podestà dates from the 15th century. In the upper town, the church of Santa Maria contains an altarpiece by Gaudenzio Ferrari (1511) in its Borromeo chapel. The lunette over the main door has a charming 15th-century relief of the *Holy Family*. The nearby church of the Santi Martiri has an altarpiece by Bergognone. The church of the Madonna di Piazza (1592) is attributed to Pellegrino Tibaldi. To the north, above the road, stands San Carlone, a colossal copper statue of St Charles Borromeo (1538–84), Archbishop of Milan and an important figure of the Counter-Reformation. He was born in the castle that now lies in ruins above the town. The statue, 23m high, standing on a pedestal 12m high, was commissioned from Giovanni Battista Crespi (Il Cerano) by a relative of the saint and finished in 1697. It can be climbed by steps and an internal stair.

Stresa

The most important place on the west side of the lake is **Stresa**, nestled in a charming position on the south shore of the gulf of Pallanza. It became fashionable as a European resort in the mid-19th century, but is now somewhat in decline. On the lake front, with pleasant gardens, is the orange-and-grey Villa Ducale, an 18th-century edifice that once belonged to the philosopher Antonio Rosmini (1797–1855). It is now a study centre devoted to Rosmini, who founded an order of charity in 1852 (the Rosminian college is above the town). Beyond the Regina Palace Hotel, opened in 1908, at the bend of the road, is the huge monumental Hotel des Iles Borromées, which has had many famous guests since it opened in 1863. Frederick Henry in

Hemingway's *Farewell to Arms* also stayed here. South of the pier is the Villa Pallavicino, built in 1855 with a small formal garden at the front of the house. It is surrounded by a fine wooded park (*open March–Oct 9–6*) planted with palms, magnolias and cedars, with a zoological garden.

Above Stresa is Monte Mottarone (1491m), reached by a cableway (which replaces a funicular inaugurated in 1911), or by road. The local industry of umbrella-making at Gignese is recorded in the umbrella museum here, founded in 1939, which has a collection of umbrellas and parasols dating from 1840 to 1940. At Alpino is the **Giardino Alpinia** (605m), a botanical garden founded in 1933, with some 544 species of Alpine plants (*open Apr–mid-Oct Tues–Sun 9–6*). Here a private tollroad, owned by the Borromeo since 1623 (9km; *always open*), continues through the meadows and woods of the **Parco del Mottarone** on the slopes of Monte Mottarone, with a view of the whole chain of the Alps from Monte Viso in the west to the Ortles and Adamello in the east, and the Monte Rosa group especially conspicuous to the northwest. Below, on a clear day you can make out seven lakes and the wide Po Valley.

Lago Maggiore at the turn of the 20th century

The Italian lakes have that in them and their air which removes them from common living. Their beauty is not the beauty which each of us sees for himself in the world; it is rather the beauty of a special creation; the expression of some mind ... I am sure there is something unnatural in this beauty of theirs ... Have you not read in books how men when they see even divine visions are terrified? So as I looked at Lake Major in its halo I also was afraid, and I was glad to cross the ridge and crest of the hill and to shut out that picture framed all round with glory.

Hilaire Belloc, 1902

The Isole Borromee

This group of beautiful little islands is named after the Italian Borromeo family, who still own the Isola Madre, Isola Bella and Isola San Giovanni. There are regular daily boat services for Isola Bella, Isola dei Pescatori and Isola Madre from Stresa, Baveno, Pallanza and Intra.

Isola Bella

This is the most famous of the islands, once just a barren rock with a small church and a few cottages, until it was almost totally occupied by a huge palace with terraced gardens built in 1631–71 by Angelo Crivelli for Count Carlo III Borromeo, in honour of his wife, from whom it takes its name. The island measures just 320 x 180m, and there is a tiny hamlet by the pier outside the garden gates, with tourist shops and a few restaurants and cafés. (*The palace and gardens—combined ticket—are open late March–late Oct daily 9–5.30.*)

To the left of the pier is the vast grey **palace**, entered from an open courtyard behind four palm trees. On the right of the courtyard (seen through a grille) is the chapel, which contains three family tombs with elaborate carvings by Giovanni Antonio Amadeo and Bambaia, brought from demolished churches in Milan. On the left of the courtyard is the entrance to the palace. Twenty-five rooms on the piano nobile, decorated with Murano chandeliers and Venetian mosaic floors, can be visited (the three floors above are the private apartments of the Borromeo family). The English historian Edward Gibbon stayed here as a guest of the Borromeo in 1764.

The octagonal blue-and-white Sala dei Concerti was built in 1948–51 in Baroque style following the original plans. There is a view of the Isola dei Pescatori and (right) the Isola Madre. The Sala di Musica has musical instruments, two Florentine cabinets in ebony and semi-precious stones (17th–18th century), and paintings by Jacopo Bassano and Tempesta. In 1935 a conference took place here between Mussolini and the French and British governments in an attempt to guarantee the peace of Europe. Napoleon stayed in the next room in 1797. The library preserves, besides its books, some paintings by Carlevalis. Another room has paintings by Luca Giordano, and beyond a room with views of the Borromeo properties, by Zuccarelli, is the ballroom.

Stairs lead down to the grottoes built on the lake in the 18th century. Beyond a room with 18th–20th-century puppets (once used in puppet shows held in the 'amphitheatre' in the garden) are six grottoes encrusted with shells, pebbles, marble, etc. Displayed here are statues by Gaetano Matteo Monti and remains of an ancient boat found in the lake off Angera. A spiral staircase in an old tower that pre-dates the palace leads up to a short corridor of mirrors and from there to the *anticamera*, with a ceiling tondo attributed to Giovanni Battista Tiepolo and two paintings by Daniele Crespi. Beyond the chapel of St Charles Borromeo is the gallery of tapestries, with a splendid collection of 16th-century Flemish tapestries commissioned by St Charles Borromeo. The painting of *St Jerome* is by Moretto.

A door leads out to the famous **gardens**, inhabited by white peacocks. The terraces are built out into the lake, and soil for the plants had to be brought from the mainland. A double staircase leads up onto a terrace with a huge camphor tree, camellias, bamboos, breadfruit, sugar cane, tapioca and tea and coffee plants. Beyond is the 'amphitheatre', an elaborate Baroque construction with statues, niches, pinnacles and stairs, crowned by a unicorn (the family crest). The terrace at the top looks straight to Stresa, and below is the Italianate garden with box hedges and yew, and ten terraces planted with roses, oleanders and pomegranates descending to the lake. Other parts of the garden are laid out in the 'English style', with beds of tulips and forget-me-nots in spring and geraniums in summer. Below the terraces are rhododendrons and orange trees (protected in winter). The azaleas are at their best during April and May. The second exit leads out of the gardens through the delightful old-fashioned greenhouse.

Near Isola Bella are a tiny islet inhabited by cormorants in winter and the **Isola dei Pescatori**, or Isola Superiore, not owned by the Borromeo. It is occupied by a pretty little fishing village, and has a hotel and restaurant.

Isola Madre

The Isola Madre is nearer to Pallanza than to Stresa. It is entirely occupied by a Borromeo villa and botanical garden (*open late March–end Oct daily 9–5.30*), and inhabited only by a custodian. It has one restaurant. The landscaped gardens, at their best in April, are laid out in the English manner and were replanted in the 1950s by the botanist Henry Cocker. The particularly mild climate allows a great number of exotic and tropical plants to flourish here. Viale Africa, with the warmest exposure, is lined with a variety of plants, including citrus fruits. The camellia terrace has numerous species of camellia and mimosa. Beyond a wisteria-covered arboured walk is the Mediterranean garden and a rock garden. The cylindrical tower was once used as an ice house; beyond it are ferns. From the little port with its boat house (and an 18th-century boat suspended from the roof) is a view of Pallanza. Nearby is the oldest camellia on the island (thought to be some 150 years old). On a lawn is a group of taxodium trees, with their roots sticking up out of the ground—an odd sight—and beyond are banks of azaleas, rhododendrons, camphor trees and ancient magnolias. Beside steps up to the villa, by a remarkable Kashmir cypress—said to be 200 years old—is an aviary with parrots that nest in the cedar of Lebanon here. Near the villa are ornamental banana trees and the Art Nouveau family chapel. The terrace near the villa is planted with tall palm trees, including a majestic Chilean palm, planted in 1858, which bears miniature edible coconuts. The steps nearby are covered with a trellis of kiwi fruit.

The 18th-century villa is also open to the public. It contains 17th- and 18th-century furnishings from Borromeo properties and servants' livery, as well as a collection of porcelain, puppets and dolls (19th-century French and German), and paintings by Pitocchetto. The little theatre dates from 1778.

The Isola San Giovanni is not open to the public. The villa on the island was once the summer home of Toscanini.

Baveno and Verbania

Baveno, northwest of Stresa, is in a fine position on the south shore of the gulf of Pallanza opposite the Isole Borromee. Quieter than Stresa, it preserves a pleasant little square with a Renaissance baptistery (frescoes) and a church with an early façade and campanile. The landing stage is a pretty Art Nouveau building, and the delightful shore road to Stresa, with a good view of the islands, is flanked by villas and hotels built in the 19th century when the town was well known as a resort. Among these is the Castello Branca (formerly Villa Clara), built in 1844, where Queen Victoria spent the spring of 1879. To the northwest of Baveno rises Monte Camoscio (890m), with quarries of pink granite for which Baveno is famous.

Across the lake from Baveno is **Verbania**, which includes the towns of Pallanza and Intra on either side of the promontory of the Punta della Castagnola. In a charming position in full view of the Isole Borromee and below Monte Rossa (618m), it has a mild climate which makes the flora particularly luxuriant; the lake front is planted with magnolias. The Hotel Majestic was opened here in 1870. Near the pier is the mausoleum, by Marcello Piacentini, of Marshal Cadorna (1850–1928), Italian Chief of Staff during the first 30 months of the First World War and a native of Pallanza; and just inland is the market-place, with the town hall and the church of San Leonardo (16th century; modernised in the 19th century), the tall tower of which was completed by Pellegrino Tibaldi in 1589. In the Baroque Palazzo Dugnani is a small local museum (*open Tues–Sun 10–12 & 3.30–6.30*), founded in 1914 and containing 19th-century landscapes of the lake, as well as sculptures by Paolo Troubetzkoy and Arturo Martini. The Villa Kursaal (1882), surrounded by gardens, is open to the public.

The narrow Via Cavour leads north from the market-place. Some way beyond is the fine domed church of the Madonna di Campagna, which was begun in 1519 and contains contemporary decorations (notably works attributed to Carlo Urbini, Aurelio Luini and Gerolamo Lanino).

On the Punta della Castagnola, a promontory on the lake, is the **Villa San Remigio**, built in 1903 (now the seat of the administrative offices of the regional government, *open only by appointment, T: 0323 504401*). The formal gardens, when they were laid out in 1905 by Sophie Browne, an Irish painter, and her husband, the marquess Silvio della Valle di Casanova, were among the best in northern Italy, with topiary terraces, fountains, and statues by Orazio Marinali, who produced much of the statuary for the Palladian villas near Vicenza. The plants include yellow and white banksia roses, wisteria, camellias, myrtle, conifers and palm trees.

Next to Villa San Remigio on the slopes of the Punta della Castagnola is the 19th-century **Villa Taranto**, with famous botanical gardens (*open Apr–Oct 8.30–7.30, last entry 6.30*)—the villa has a landing stage served by regular boat services. The huge estate was bought by Captain Neil McEacharn (1884–1964) in 1930. Together with Henry Cocker, he created a garden with an outstanding collection of exotic plants from all over the world, which he later donated to the Italian state. The plants include magnolias (at their best at the beginning of April), superb camellias (which flower in April), rhododendrons (which flower May–June), azaleas and paulownias (best in May). The herbaceous borders and dahlias (over 300 varieties) are at their best in July and August. Birches, maples and conifers distinguish the woodlands. The statues include a bronze fisher-boy by Vincenzo Gemito.

Above Verbania is the Parco Nazionale della Val Grande, a protected mountainous area with fine walks.

Intra is the most important commercial centre on Lago Maggiore, with a car ferry (every 20mins) across the lake to Laveno on the opposite shore. To the north, close to the lake, are the beautiful private gardens of the Villa Poss and Villa Ada. Roads lead up to Miazzina (719m) at the foot of Monte Zeda (2188m), and Premeno (802m), a winter and summer resort.

Ghiffa and Cannobio

The road skirts the lake to **Ghiffa**, a scattered village, with the castle of Frino. The lake reaches its greatest depth (372m) just off this point. The little 13th-century church of Novaglio, above the road, is built in a mixture of Lombard and Gothic styles. Above Oggebbio, in chestnut groves, is the little oratory of Cadessino, with 15th–16th-century frescoes. Ahead, across the lake, Luino comes into view, as, beneath **Oggiogno** high up on its rock, the road passes the villa of the statesman Massimo d'Azeglio (1798–1866), who effectively launched Camillo Cavour on his career, but fell out with him shortly afterwards. He retired from public office as a result, and spent his latter years writing his memoirs here. **Cannero Riviera** is a resort lying in a sheltered and sunny position at the foot of Monte Carza (1118m). Off the coast are two rocky islets on which stood the castles of Malpaga, demolished by the Visconti in 1414. One island is now occupied by the picturesque ruins of a castle built by Ludovico Borromeo in 1519–21. On the hill above the town is the 14th–15th-century church of Carmine Superiore, built on the summit of a precipice. It has some ceiling paintings and a triptych of the 14th-century Lombard school. The road rounds Punta d'Amore opposite Maccagno.

Cannobio has ancient origins and preserves some medieval buildings. Near the pier is the Santuario della Pietà (reconstructed in 1583–1601), with a fine altarpiece by Gaudenzio Ferrari. The town hall, called Il Parrasio, is a 13th-century building with 17th-century alterations.

Inland, in the Val Cannobina is the Orrido di Sant'Anna, a romantic gorge with a waterfall. Just beyond Cannobio is the frontier with Switzerland. The road goes on via Brissago to Ascona and Locarno, which are famous for their climate and views.

THE EAST SIDE OF THE LAKE

Luino and Laveno

Luino is the most important centre on the Lombard side of the lake. A small industrial town, it lies a little north of the junction of the Tresa and Margorabbia, which unite to flow into the lake at Germignaga. Near the landing stage is a statue of Garibaldi, commemorating his attempt, on 14 August 1848, to renew the struggle against Austria with only 1,500 men, after the armistice which followed the defeat of Custozza. The town hall occupies an 18th-century palazzo by Felice Soave. An *Adoration of the Magi*, attributed to Bernardino Luini, who was probably born here, decorates the cemetery church of San Pietro, and the Madonna del Carmine has frescoes by his pupils (1540). The little Museo Civico Archeologico Paleontologico (*open by appointment; T: 0332 532057*) has local antiquities, minerals and fossils, and a small painting collection. A market has been held in the town on Wednesdays since 1541. On the landward side of the town is the railway station where the Swiss line from Bellinzona meets the Italian line from Novara and Milan. This was an important frontier station (with custom-house) on the St Gotthard line.

Laveno, now part of the municipality of Mombello, is in a fine position on the lake, with good views of the Punta della Castagnola and the Isola Madre in the distance. Its small port serves the car ferry to Intra. The old-fashioned railway station of the Milano-Nord line for Varese and Milan (one of two stations in Laveno) adjoins the ferry station. The town was once noted for its ceramics, and there is a ceramics museum (*open Tues–Thur 2.30–5.30, Fri–Sun also 10–12*) in the adjacent village of **Cerro**. A monument in the piazza by the waterside commemorates the *garibaldini* who fell in an attempt to capture the town from the Austrians in 1859 (the Austrian fort was on the Punta di San Michele).

Towards Angera and Sesto Calende

The road follows the shore of the lake past the ceramics museum at Cerro (*see above*) and Leggiuno, where the Oratory of Santi Primo e Feliciano (9th century) has Roman foundations. The solitary convent of **Santa Caterina del Sasso** (reached in 10 minutes by a steep path which descends from the main road, or by boat from Laveno or Stresa in summer) was founded in the 13th century and reinhabited by Dominicans in 1986. (*Open daily 9.30–12 & 2–5 or 3–6.*) It is built into a sheer rock-face directly above the lake (there is an 18m drop to the water). The picturesque Romanesque buildings, particularly attractive when seen from the water, were restored in 1624 and have a good view of the gulf of Pallanza and the Isole Borromee. They contain 15th- and 16th-century frescoes and a 17th-century *Last Supper*.

Ispra is the seat of Euratom, the first centre in Italy for nuclear studies. **Angera** has a pleasant spacious waterfront planted with horse chestnuts. A road (signposted) leads up to the Rocca Borromeo (*open Mar–Oct 9–5.30 or 6*). Formerly a castle of the Visconti, it passed to the Borromeo in 1449 and is still owned by them. It was extensively restored in the 16th–17th centuries. The fine gateway leads into a charming courtyard with a pergola open to the south end of the lake. Off the second courtyard is a wine press dating from 1745. The Sala di Giustizia has interesting 14th-century Gothic frescoes commissioned by Giovanni Visconti, Bishop of Milan, with signs of the zodiac and episodes from the battles of Archbishop Ottone Visconti. In other rooms are displayed paintings, Roman altars, and detached frescoes from Palazzo Borromeo in Milan. It also has a doll museum, and you can climb the 13th-century Torre Castellana. In Via Mazzini, for grappa lovers, is a distillery dating from 1850. At nearby **Ranco** is an interesting transport museum (*open Tues–Sun 10–12 & 2–4.30*), mostly displayed in the open air. It illustrates the history of transport from horse-drawn carriages to steam engines, electric tramways, funicular railways, etc. There are quite a few original vehicles and reconstructions of several stations.

Sesto Calende is the southernmost town on the east bank of the lake. It is said to derive its name from its market day in Roman times—the sixth day before the Calends. A small Museo Civico (*open Mon–Thur 9–12 & 2.30–4.30, Sun 3–6; July–Aug, Mon, Wed, Fri 9–1, Tues, Thur 9–12 & 2.30–5, Sun 10–12*) houses archaeological finds from tombs of the local Golasecca culture (800–450 BC).

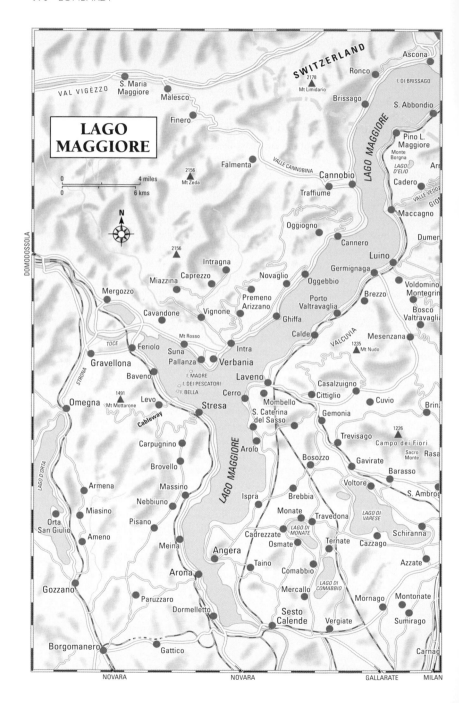

LAGO MAGGIORE

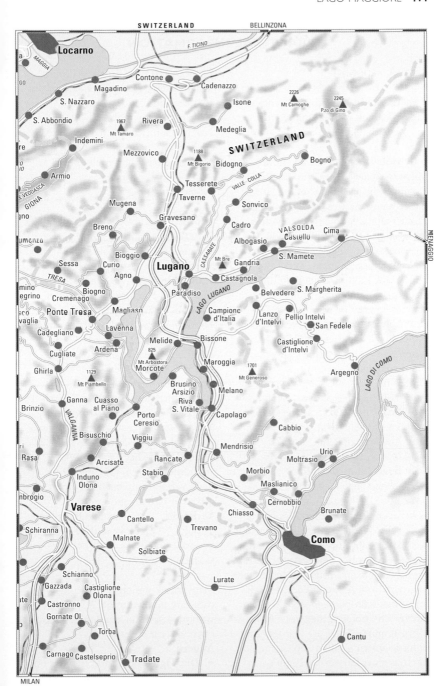

PRACTICAL INFORMATION

GETTING AROUND

• **By road:** On Fri and Sun evenings the A8 is thick with escaping/returning Milanese; the 33 offers a viable alternative.

• **By rail:** The main rail line from Milan to Geneva, Bern and Basel via Domodossola and the Simplon Tunnel, passes along the west shore of the lake. Fast Cisalpina, Eurocity and Intercity trains stop at Arona and/or Stresa (both c. 50mins from Milan). The stations of Baveno, Stresa, Belgirate, Lesa, Meina, and Arona, built by Luigi Boffi, date from the the beginning of the 20th century, when the line was opened. The east shore of the lake is served by a minor line from Milan to Bellinzona via Luino (c. 90mins), with a change of trains sometimes necessary at Gallarate. Laveno has a second station serving the Nord railway for Varese and Milan.

• **By bus:** There are local bus services between the main towns; information from Autoservizi Nerini, T: 0323 401526.

• **By boat:** Information from Navigazione Lago Maggiore, Arona, T: 0322 46651. There are frequent services between Stresa and Intra, calling at Isola Bella, Isola dei Pescatori, Baveno, Isola Madre, Pallanza and Villa Taranto. There is also a frequent service between Arona, Angera and Belgirate. In summer the route from Arona to Locarno, calling at the main ports, is served once a day by a hydrofoil (2hrs) and a boat (3hrs 30mins). There are also services linking Cannero, Luino and Cannobio. There is a car ferry every 20mins

between Intra and Laveno (10mins). The timetable changes for each of the four seasons.

• **By cable car:** Cableways connect Laveno, San Domenico di Varzo, Stresa, Alagna Valsesia (Bonda) and Neggio Magliasco with sites in the hills.

INFORMATION OFFICES

Arona Piazzale Duca d'Aosta, T: 0322 243601, www.distrettolaghi.it
Baveno Corso Garibaldi 16, T: 0323 924632, www.distrettolaghi.it
Cannobio Viale Vittorio Veneto 4, T: 0323 71212, www.distrettolaghi.it
Laveno Palazzo Municipale, T: 0332 666666, www.distrettolaghi.it
Luino Via Piero Chiara 1, T: 0332 530019; Piazza Crivelli 1, T: 0332 532542, www.distrettolaghi.it
Stresa (for the west—Piedmontese—side of the lake) Piazza Marconi 16, T: 0323 31308, www.distrettolaghi.it
Varese (for the east—Lombard—side of the lake) Via Carrobio 2, T: 0332 283604, www.hcs.it/varese; Viale Ippodromo 9, T: 0332 284624, www.varesottoturismo.com; branch offices at Laveno and Luino.
Verbania Corso Zanitello 8, Pallanza, T: 0323 503249, www.distrettolaghi.it

HOTELS

Many hotels are open only Easter–Oct; these are marked in the text. Those without a specific mention of season are open all year round.
Angera
€ **Dei Tigli**. Simple and friendly, on

the lake. Via Paletta 20, T: 0331 930836, www.hoteldeitigli.com

Ascona

€€€ **Castello del Sole**. A fine garden hotel. Via Muraccio 142 (1km north-east), T: 091 7910202.

€€€ **Eden Roc**. Grand hotel in a lakeside garden. Open Apr–Dec. Via Albarelle 16, T: 091 785 7171, www.edenroc.ch

€€€€ **Europe au Lac**. A big lakefront establishment. Open Apr–Oct. Via Albarelle 10, T: 0917912881.

€€ **Ascona**. A pleasant place with garden and views. Via Collina, T: 091 785 1515, www.hotel-ascona.ch

Baveno

€€€ **Grand Hotel Dino**. Large, modern hotel in a beautiful park with views of the Isole Boromee. Via Garibaldi 20, T: 0323 922201.

€€ **Lido Palace Baveno**. A large 19th-century establishment with luxuriant gardens, overlooking the Isole Boromee. Via Sempione 30, T: 0323 924444.

€ **Rigoli**. Simple, family-run establishment on the lake, with views of the Isole Boromee. Open Apr–Oct. Via Piave 48, T: 0323 924756, www.hotelrigoli.com

Belgirate

€€ **Villa Carlotta**. On the lake with a beautiful park and fine restaurant. Via Sempione 121/125, T: 0322 76461.

Cannobio

€€ **Pironi**. Small and intimate, in a 15th-century convent with frescoed rooms. Open Mar–Nov. Via Marconi 35, T: 0323 70624, www.pironihotel.it

€€ **Villa Belvedere**. Lovely small villa and annexe in a verdant park on the western edge of the village; excellent restaurant. Closed Nov–Feb. Via Casali

Cuserina 2, T: 0323 70159, www.villabelvederehotel.it

€ **Antica Stallera**. An old stage-halt, with a pleasant garden. Open Mar–Dec. Via Zaccheo 3, T: 0323 71595, www.anticastallera.com

Ghiffa

€€ **Park Hotel Paradiso**. Small (15 rooms) and quiet, in a Liberty-style villa with garden. Via Marconi 20, T: 0323 59548.

Isole Boromee

€€ **Verbano**. On the charming Isola dei Pescatori. Closed Jan–Feb. Via Ugo Ara 2, T: 0323 30408, www.hotelverbano.it

Ispra

€€ **Europa**. A cordial, family-run place in a lovely park. Via Verbano 19, T: 0332 780184

Locarno

€€ **Grand Hotel Locarno**. Calm and quiet, in a verdant garden. Via Sempione 17, T: 093 330282, www.grand-hotel-locarno.ch

€€ **Orselina**. Likewise restful, in a tropical garden with views over the lake and mountains. Open March–Nov. Località Orselina (2km north), T: 091 7357350, www.orselina.com

Luino

€€ **Camin Luino**. Warm and comfortable, a 19th-century villa in a lakefront park, with Liberty furniture and 13 rooms. Open March–Dec. Viale Dante 35, T: 0332 530118, www.caminhotelluino.com

Sesto Calende

€ **David**. An old townhouse, with garden, in the historic centre. Closed Dec–Jan. Via Roma 56, T: 0331 920182, www.hotel-david.com

€ **Tre Re**. An old *locanda*, simple but

comfortable. Open March–Nov. Piazza Garibaldi 25, T: 0331 924229, www.hotel3re.it

Stresa

€€€ **Des Iles Borromées**. A fine luxury hotel with a lovely park and views of the Isole Boromee. Lungolago Umberto I 67, T: 0323 938938.

€€€ **Villa Aminta**. Recently renovated luxury hotel with verdant gardens, heated pool and frescoed rooms with lake views. Closed Nov–Feb. Strada Statale del Sempione 123, T: 0323 933818, www.villa-aminta.it

€€ **Du Parc**. Hotel with a shady garden. Open Easter–Oct. Via Gignous 1, T: 0323 30335, www.duparc.it

€ **Ariston**. A small (11 rooms), friendly place. Open March–Nov. Corso Italia 60, T: 0323 31195.

Verbania

€ **Majestic**. Elegant 19th-century establishment on the lakefront. Open Easter–Oct. Via Vittorio Veneto 32, T: 0323 504305, www.granhotelmajestic.it

€ **San Gottardo**. Recently renovated early-20th-century villa on the lakefront. Open March–Oct. Viale delle Magnolie 4, T: 0323 504465.

€ **Villa Azalea**. Small and simple, in a Liberty-style villa. Open Easter–Oct. Salita San Remigio 4, T: 0323 556692, www.albergovillaazalea.com

YOUTH HOSTEL

Verbania Verbania, T: 0323 501648, ostello_verbania@libero.it

RESTAURANTS

Arona

€€€ **Taverna del Pittore**. Restaurant widely known for its salt- and freshwater fish dishes. Closed Mon, June and Nov. Piazza del Popolo 39, T: 0322 243366.

€€ **Campania**. Trattoria serving creative and traditional dishes using local ingredients. Closed Mon evening (in winter), Tues, July and Nov. Via Vergante 12, T: 0322 57294.

Ascona

€€ **Da Ivo**. Traditional restaurant with garden. Closed Mon, Tues and Jan–March. Via Collegio 7, T: 093 351031.

€€ **Giardino**. Excellent restaurant of the Hotel Giardino, on the northeastern outskirts of the city. Open March–Nov, closed midday Mon and Tues, T: 093 350101.

Cannobio

€€€ **Del Lago**. Restaurant offering innovative variations on old regional recipes. Closed Tues, midday Wed, Feb and Nov. Località Carmine, on the Swiss border, Via Nazionale 2, T: 0323 70595.

Laveno

€€ **Il Porticciolo** (with rooms). Restaurant specialising in fresh- and saltwater fish. Closed Tues (midday only in July–Aug) and Jan–Feb. Via Fortino 40, T: 0332 667257.

Lesa

€€€ **L'Antico Maniero**. Restaurant in a 19th-century villa with park (reservations necessary). Open evenings only (except Sun), closed Mon, Nov and Jan. Via alla Campagna 1, T: 0322 7411.

Locarno

€€€ **Centenario Perriard**. Fine international cuisine. Closed Sun, Mon, Feb and July. Lungolago Motta 17, T: 093 338222.

Ranco

€€€ **Il Sole di Ranco**. Restaurant (with rooms) famous for its lake fish and seafood. Closed Mon evening (except May–Sept), Tues and Dec–Jan. Piazza Venezia 5, T: 0331 976507.

Sesto Calende

€€ **Da Mosè**. Restaurant serving traditional dishes with a special flair. Open evenings only (except weekends and holidays), closed Mon, Tues and Jan–Feb. Via Ponzello 14, T: 0331 977240.

€ **San Pietro**. Trattoria serving traditional local dishes. Closed Wed and Jan. Località Lisanza, Via Crocera 38, T: 0331 977197.

Stresa

€€ **Il Piemontese**. Restaurant in a 17th-century building with private garden, known for its fine regional cuisine. Closed Mon and Dec–Jan. Via Mazzini 25, T: 0323 30235.

€€€ **L'Emiliano**. Restaurant serving innovative fish dishes, wide selection of local cheeses. Closed Tues, midday Wed and Nov–Dec. Corso Italia 50, T: 0323 31396.

Verbania

€ **Osteria dell'Angolo**. Restaurant known for its lake fish and other local specialities. Closed Mon. Piazza Garibaldi 35, T: 0323 556362.

REGIONAL SPECIALITIES

Sweets are the main things to buy, especially *Margheritine di Stresa* and *Baci di Stresa*. Traditional markets at Baveno, Mon; Arona, Tues; Luino, Wed; Stresa and Pallanza, Fri; Intra, Sat; Cannobio, Sun.

FESTIVALS & EVENTS

Food, music and pageantry accompany patron-saints' days in most towns. In addition, several interesting fairs and events are held annually at Stresa; among the more important are the Camellia Show, Apr; Piedmont Wine Show, June; *Settimane Musicali*, international music festival, Aug–Sept.

VARESE & ENVIRONS

The town of Varese has only a few monuments worth visiting, but there are various places of interest nearby, notably Castiglione Olona with its Renaissance works of art and frescoes by Masolino. The Sacro Monte above Varese has beautiful 17th-century chapels, and Castelseprio, south of the town, is one of the most important Lombard sites in Italy. There are many villas in the province with particularly beautiful gardens open to the public. These include the Villa Porta Bozzolo at Casalzuigno, Villa Cicogna Mozzoni at Bisuschio, and the Palazzo Estense in Varese.

NB: *Towns and sights in this chapter are marked on the map on pp. 170–71.*

VARESE

A flourishing industrial town of 91,000 inhabitants, Varese still has a few attractive streets of old houses with fine courtyards. After the opening of the State and Nord Milano railway lines to Milan (only 50km away) in 1865 and 1886, many Milanese built their summer homes in the environs, and some Art Nouveau villas also survive.

The city centre

The attractive, arcaded Corso Matteotti leads to Piazza del Podestà, separated from the church square by a war memorial arcade. **San Vittore** was built in 1580–1625, probably to designs by Pellegrino Tibaldi. It has a Neoclassical façade by Vienna-born architect Leopold Pollack. In the interior are some good paintings by Il Cerano and Morazzone, and magnificent 17th-century carved wooden pulpits and choir galleries. The baptistery behind (unlocked on request) dates from the 12th century. It has an interesting plan and 14th-century Lombard frescoes on the right wall. The unfinished 13th-century font has been raised to reveal the earlier 8th-century font.

At the southern end of Corso Matteotti is Piazza Monte Grappa, laid out in 1927–35 and brimming with Fascist architectural rhetoric. Via Marcobi and Via Sacco lead to the huge, monumental **Palazzo Estense** (now the town hall), built by Francesco III d'Este, Duke of Modena, in 1766–72 as the seat of his imperial court. Called by Stendhal the Versailles of Milan, it is one of the best palaces of its period in Italy. The attractive garden façade overlooks the spacious gardens (*open daily*), laid out in imitation of the imperial gardens of Schönbrunn in Vienna (after Duke Francesco's death, his dukedom passed to the crown of Austria). Paths lead up past a grotto to terraces with a good view of the Alps, and a little children's playground in a wood.

On the hill is the eccentric 18th–19th-century **Villa Mirabello** with a tall tower, surrounded by a garden in the English style. The villa houses the Musei Civici (*open Tues–Fri 9.30–12.30 & 2–5, Sat, Sun and holidays 9.30–12.30 & 2–5.30*), with prehistoric Roman and medieval material, and the mummy of a boy dating from 1645. Another room has a display of butterflies and birds.

North of the centre

On a low hill is the residential district of Biumo Superiore. Here is the 18th-century **Villa Litta**, which was donated to the FAI (Fondo per l'Ambiente Italiano) in 1996 by Giuseppe Panza, together with 133 works from his collection of 20th-century American art (most of which was sold, and partially donated, to the Museum of Contemporary Art in Los Angeles and the Guggenheim Museum of New York). The villa (*open Tues-Sun 10–6*) also contains furniture and African and pre-Columbian sculpture, and is surrounded by a park. Also in this district is the Villa Andrea Ponti, a vast 19th-century pile, with a park, adjoining another 19th-century Villa Ponti.

On the western outskirts of Varese is the **Castello di Masnago** (*open Tues–Sun 10.30–12.30 & 2.30–6.30*), a 15th-century building which incorporates a 12th-century tower. It is adorned with frescoes of court life, dating from 1450. The painting collection contains works by Jacopo Bassano and Camillo Procaccini. The 19th-century works include paintings by Futurist artist Giacomo Balla. There is also a small museum of contemporary art. The park is open to the public daily.

The Sacro Monte

Varese's 'Holy Mountain' rises on the northern outskirts of the town. It is one of numerous shrines in Piedmont and Lombardy bearing the same name: all were erected during the Counter-Reformation (in the 17th century) in honour of the Madonna, and consist of a series of chapels illustrating the Mysteries of the Rosary, subjects of meditation following the life of the Virgin Mary. In this Varese version, the 14 pretty chapels, lining a broad winding path some 2km long up the steep incline, were designed to be seen by pilgrims on their way up the hill (a walk of about an hour). The first chapel can be reached from the centre of Varese by car or bus along Via Veratti and Viale Aguggiari. The road climbs up through the residential district of Sant'Ambrogio with numerous Art Nouveau villas and their gardens, to end at an archway near the first chapel. (A less strenuous way of visiting the chapels is to continue up a by-road from the first chapel under the old stone arches of a former funicular railway with a view of the hill of Campo dei Fiori.) The chapels, each of different design, are all works by the local architect Giuseppe Bernasconi from 1604 onwards. They are all kept locked but you can see the interiors (push-button lights) through the windows. They contain lifesize terracotta groups representing the Mysteries of the Rosary. Outside the chapel of the Nativity is a 20th-century fresco by the Socialist Realist artist and virulent anti-Fascist Renato Guttuso (1912–87), depicting the *Flight into Egypt*. From the hillside there are views of Como to the left and of Lago di Varese on the right.

At the top of the Sacro Monte is a small village (880m) with a few Art Nouveau houses huddled around the sanctuary church of **Santa Maria del Monte**. The view (on a clear day) takes in Como with the mountains beyond and the plain towards Milan, and in the opposite direction the Lago di Varese. The bronze monument to Pope Paul VI dates from 1984. The church dates mostly from 1472. On the high altar (1662) is a venerated 14th-century image of the Madonna. Outside the west door is a terrace with a view of five lakes: Lago di Varese in the foreground, Comabbio and Biandronno on the left, and Monate beyond. On the right you can just make out the tip of Lago Maggiore. The hill of Campo dei Fiori is prominent on the right with a huge abandoned Art Nouveau hotel.

From the terrace a cobbled passageway leads down to the broad cobbled path that descends past a statue of Moses and the Museo Pogliaghi (*closed at the time of writing; T: 0332 226040*), surrounded by a garden, in the villa that belonged to the sculptor Lodovico Pogliaghi (1857–1950). It contains his eclectic collection of works of art, archaeological material, and some of his own sculptures, including the model for the bronze doors of the duomo of Milan.

A road continues up from the Sacro Monte to Monte delle Tre Croci (1033m), which has a wonderful view (and an observatory). The road deteriorates into a track to cross the Campo dei Fiori (1227m), a protected area with an even wider panorama. Here in 1908–12 Giuseppe Sommaruga built a huge hotel, restaurant and funicular station, all fine Art Nouveau buildings that have been abandoned since 1953.

CASTIGLIONE OLONA & ENVIRONS

Castiglione Olona lies off the road to Saronno (poorly signposted). It was practically rebuilt by Cardinal Branda Castiglione (1350–1443) when he returned from a stay in Florence, bringing with him Masolino da Panicale, who collaborated with Masaccio for much of his career, and whose superb frescoes of the *Life of John the Baptist* adorn the baptistery here (*see below*). The works of art that the cardinal commissioned to adorn the little town take their inspiration from the Florentine Renaissance. There are now a number of antiquarian bookshops in the town, and an antiques and bric-à-brac fair is held in the streets on the first Sunday of the month.

Palazzo Branda Castiglione (*open Tues–Sat 9–12 & 3–6, Sun and holidays 10.30–12.30 & 3–6*) is where the cardinal was born and died. The little courtyard has an interesting exterior, and the chapel has frescoes attributed to the great Sienese artist Vecchietta. Stairs lead up to a loggia (enclosed in the 19th century) with a wooden coffered ceiling and traces of frescoes. Low down on the wall is a frescoed still life with jars, attributed to Paolo Schiavo. The main hall has a Renaissance fireplace with Baroque stucco decoration on the upper part and family portraits on the walls. The bedroom has very unusual allegorical frescoes; dated 1423, showing ten trees and white putti. In the study are frescoes attributed to Masolino: the strange, rocky landscapes are those of the Hungarian city of Veszprém, where Castiglione served as bishop in 1412–24.

Opposite the palace, preceded by a courtyard, is the **Chiesa di Villa**, with an unusual dome, built and decorated in 1431–44 by local masons and sculptors in the style of Brunelleschi. It has a handsome exterior, and two colossal carved saints flank the fine portal. In the lovely, simple interior, with a dome and apse, are six stone and terracotta statues (including a polychrome *Annunciatory Angel* and *Madonna* that have been attributed to Vecchietta) high up on corbels. In the apse are a small fresco of the

Resurrection of Christ and a delightful frescoed frieze of red-and-white flowers below. Beneath the altar is a 15th-century stone statue of the *Dead Christ*.

The road continues uphill past the 19th-century town hall, which incorporates a school building founded by the cardinal in 1423 to teach grammar and music. Above the door is a bust of the cardinal dating from 1503, and on the left is a fresco from the early 15th century. The courtyard dates from the 18th century.

A cobbled lane leads up to the top of the hill where the **Collegiata** was built in 1422–25, replacing the Castiglione family's feudal castle. Above the portal is a lunette of the *Madonna with Saints and the Cardinal*, dating from 1428. The church is entered through a side door off the garden (*open Apr–Sept Tues–Sun 9.30–12 & 3–6.30; Oct–March 10–12 & 2.30–5.30*). The well-proportioned and luminous interior has Gothic Revival decoration in the side aisles. In the sanctuary is the funerary monument (1443) of the cardinal with his effigy supported by four statues of the Virtues. On the vault are six frescoed scenes from the *Life of the Virgin* signed by Masolino. In the lunettes below and above the windows are scenes from the *Lives of St Stephen and St Lawrence* by Paolo Schiavo and Vecchietta. The 15th-century bronze candelabrum showing St George and the Dragon was made in Flanders.

Across the garden, in a former tower of the castle, is the entrance to the family chapel, later used as a baptistery and museum. The **baptistery** is a beautiful little building dating from 1435. The frescoes of the *Life of St John the Baptist* are Masolino's masterpiece, executed on his return to the town in 1435. On the right wall is the *Banquet of Herod* with a long loggia, and in the sanctuary, the *Baptism of Christ*, with a splendid group of nude figures on the right and the river disappearing into the distance. In the vault are the symbols of the Evangelists, and in the vault of the sanctuary, *God the Father* with *Angels and Doctors of the Church* on the arch. The other frescoes (including a view of Rome on the entrance wall) are very damaged. The font is a 15th-century Venetian work.

Opposite the baptistery a small room serves as a museum with a miscellany of objects that have survived from the rich treasury (pillaged over the centuries) that the cardinal donated to the church. They include reliquaries, and a small painting of the *Annunciation* by Paolo Schiavo and frescoes of the same subject by Masolino.

Castelseprio

South of Castiglione, on a plateau in a wood above the Olona valley, is an extensive archaeological area (*open Tues–Sun 8.30–dusk*). On the site of a late Bronze Age settlement, it includes the ruins of the late Roman castrum of Sibrium, occupied throughout the Lombard period (AD 568–771). A fortified *borgo* grew up around the camp, but this was destroyed by Milan in 1287. The site is well labelled and includes the remains of two churches, an octagonal baptistery, defensive walls, towers, medieval houses, and cisterns and wells. A custodian accompanies you to unlock the most important church, **Santa Maria Foris Portas**, a short distance away from the castrum, which has a remarkable plan with lateral apses and windows in the corners of the nave. The building dates from somewhere between the 7th and 9th centuries; it was restored and partly reconstructed in the 1940s, when the frescoes were discovered, and remains of its black-and-white marble floor survive. In the apse are extraordinary mural paintings with scenes from the apocryphal Gospels illustrating the infancy of Christ, including the *Nativity* with the reclining figure of the Madonna, and the *Journey to Bethlehem* (with a graceful donkey). They are in an Oriental (Alexandrian) style and are thought to date from the 8th century.

Part of the camp of Sibrium extended across the Olona to the site later occupied by the **Monastero di Torba** (*open Tues–Sun 10–1 & 2–5; Feb–Sept 10–6*), which is reached by a path down through woods (c. 200m, but temporarily impassable) or—much longer—by a (signposted) road from Gornate Olona. Part of the ruined defensive walls have been exposed, and the massive corner tower survives, both dating from the 5th century. A Benedictine nunnery was established here in the late Lombard period (8th century), and the monastic buildings were occupied up until 1480. In a pretty position at the foot of a wooded hill, they were donated to the FAI (Fondo per l'Ambiente Italiano) in 1976 and have been beautifully maintained since their restoration in 1986. The early medieval church has an 8th-century crypt and a 13th-century apse. Opposite is a 15th-century farmhouse built above the ancient defensive walls, which incorporates the refectory, a splendid old room with a fireplace. The corner tower, on 5th–6th-century foundations, was also occupied by the nuns in the 8th century. Steps lead up past an oven, which may date from the 12th century, to the first floor and a room used as a burial place (with an 8th-century fresco of a nun named Aliberga). The room above functioned as an oratory, and it contains fascinating Carolingian (late 8th century) frescoes of female saints and nuns (uncovered in the 20th century).

Lago di Varese

West of Varese is the **Lago di Varese**, 8.5km long, a lake admired for its scenery by the English painter and nonsense poet Edward Lear. It used to have an abundance of fish, but is now polluted. **Voltorre**, on the shore of the lake, has an old monastery with an interesting Romanesque brick cloister where concerts are held in June. From Biandronno (yellow signposts), boats can be hired for the little **Isolino Virginia**, an island on which is the Museo Preistorico di Villa Ponti (*open Sat, Sun and holidays 2–6*), which contains objects found in Neolithic to Bronze-Age lake dwellings here. In May–Oct guided visits to the island are organised by the Musei Civici of Varese (*T: 0331 281590*). At **Gavirate**, at the north end of the lake, is a pipe museum (*open on request*), with some 20,000 pipes from all over the world and of all periods.

Northwards to Switzerland

A road leads north from Varese through the Valganna, the narrow valley of the Olona. At the beginning of the valley, near Induno Olona, is the Moretti (now Tuborg) brewery, in a remarkable Art Nouveau factory building. The road passes the little Laghetto di Ganna, and the **Abbey of San Gemolo**, founded in 1095 and Benedictine until 1556. It has a 12th-century church and a five-sided cloister. The Lago di Ghirla (used for swimming in summer) has a nice Art Nouveau tram station. At Ghirla the Lugano road branches right and descends to Ponte Tresa on the frontier with Switzerland. This consists of an Italian and a Swiss village separated by the River Tresa, which here marks the frontier, entering a little landlocked bay of the Lago di Lugano. Beyond Ghirla is **Cunardo**, known since Roman times for the production of ceramics. The interesting old 18th-century pottery of Ibis, with its conspicuous tall furnace, is still in use and family run. It produces traditional 18th-century blue-and-white ware, and visitors are welcome.

From Cunardo a road leads west into the Valcuvia, with hills of chestnut woods and an open landscape extending towards Lago Maggiore. Here is **Casalzuigno**, a hamlet, with the splendid Villa di Porta-Bozzolo, formerly Ca' Porta (*open Tues–Sun Oct–Dec villa 10–1 & 2–5; park 10–5; Feb-Sept villa 10–1 & 2–6; park 10–6*). The villa dates from the 16th century, when it was in the centre of a huge estate purchased by the Porta family, and silkworms were bred in the farm buildings. Additions were made to the house in the 17th century, and the splendid garden was laid out in the French style on the hillside at the beginning of the 18th century by Gian Angelo III Porta. Beyond the parterre are four stone terraces with balustrades and statues on either side of steps, up to a green lawn surrounded by cypresses and in front of a fountain. A cypress avenue climbs the wooded hillside behind. There is another little garden to the right of the parterre on a line with the façade of the villa, approached by a gate with statues of the Four Seasons and with an avenue of oak trees leading to a little Rococo frescoed garden house. The villa preserves elaborate frescoes by Pietro Antonio Magatti (1687–1768).

Above the villa a narrow road winds up to Arcumeggia, a tiny hamlet in the hills. Since 1956 the exteriors of many of the houses have been frescoed by contemporary artists, including Aligi Sassù.

To Lago di Como via Lugano

Another road (the 344) leads northeast from Varese to Porto Ceresio on **Lago di Lugano**. It passes **Bisuschio**, where the 16th-century Villa Cicogna Mozzoni, frescoed by the school of the Campi brothers and with 17th- and 18th-century furnishings, stands surrounded by a classical Renaissance garden and fine park. The greenhouses protect a good collection of orchids. (*Villa and gardens open Apr–Oct Sun and holidays 9.30–12 & 2.30–7*).

Porto Ceresio is situated at the foot of high mountains on a wide bend in Lago di Lugano (270m, 52 sq km), a little more than half of which belongs to Switzerland; only the northeast arm, the southwest shore between Ponte Tresa and Porto Ceresio, and the enclave of Campione, nearly opposite Lugano, belong to Italy. The scenery of the shores, except for the bay of Lugano, is far wilder than on the greater lakes. There are regular boat services between all the main places along the shore.

Lugano, the main place on the lake, and the largest town in the Swiss canton of Ticino, is Italian in character. On the east shore of the lake is the small Italian enclave of **Campione d'Italia**, in the province of Como, which uses Swiss money and postal services. It has long been noted for its sculptors and architects; in the 13th and 14th centuries, sculptors and masons such as Anselmo da Campione and Bonino da Campione, followers of Wiligelmus and Lanfranco (whose greatest work was carried out in Modena), made a name for themselves and for their home town. Campionese is the generic term used to describe such artists from the Lugano, Como and Swiss border area. The chapel of St Peter (1327) here is a good example of their work. In the parish church are some 15th-century reliefs, and here is kept the key to the cemetery chapel of Santa Maria dei Ghirli, with frescoes outside (*Last Judgement*, 1400) and in the interior (14th century). Today the village is famous for its casino.

At the head of the northeast arm of the lake, also in the province of Como, is **Porlezza**, where the church of San Vittorio contains beautiful 18th-century stuccowork. In the Valsolda, above the northern shore of the lake, is the picturesque village of **San Mamete**, with a 12th-century campanile. On the road which descends to Lake Como is the attractive Lago del Piano (279m).

PRACTICAL INFORMATION

GETTING AROUND

• **By road:** This is Milan's industrial hinterland, and traffic can be quite intense on local roads. Lorries are a special problem. The 233 from Milan, the shortest route in terms of distance, is the longest in terms of time, due to heavy local traffic: it's better to take the A8.
• **By rail:** There is a frequent commuter service from Milan to Varese in just over 1hr. The two train stations (one for the state railways and one for the Nord–Milano line) are only a few metres apart.
• **By bus:** Bus C goes every 15mins from Varese to Sacro Monte and Campo dei Fiori; Bus A to Biumo Superiore. Country buses to towns in the province, Lago Maggiore, Lago di Lugano, Como.

INFORMATION OFFICES

Varese Via Carrobio 2, T: 0332 283604, www.hcs.it/varese. Viale Ippodromo 9, T:

0332 284624, www.varesottoturismo.com, for the east (Lombard) side of the lake; branch offices at Laveno and Luino.
Castiglione Olona Via Roma 23, T; 0331 850084.
Luino Via Piero Chiara 1, T: 0332 530019, www.apt.varese.it

HOTELS

Varese
€€ **Crystal**. Modern and functional. Via Speroni 10, T: 0332 231145.
€€ **Palace**. A villa with garden. Via Manara 11, at Colle Campigli, T: 0332 327100, www.palacevarese.it
€ **Bologna**. Small (14 rooms) and friendly. Closed Aug. Via Broggi 7, T: 0332 234362, www.albergobologna.it
Azzate
€€ **Locanda dei Mai Intees**. Small (7 rooms) and intimate, in a 15th-century building, with a good restaurant. Closed Jan. Via Nobile Claudio Riva 2, T: 0332

457233, www.mai-intees.com

Cantello

€€ **Madonnina**. A small place, with 12 lovely rooms in a patrician villa and an excellent restaurant. Largo Lanfranco 1, Località Ligurno, T: 0332 417731.

Ganna

€ **Villa Cesarina**. Just six rooms in a cosy belle-époque villa in a garden by little Lake Ghirla. Via degli Alpini 7, T: 0332 719721, www.villacesarina.it

Induno Olona

€€ **Villa Castiglioni**. 19th-century villa set in a beautiful garden, also with a good restaurant. Via Castiglioni 1, T: 0332 200201, F: 0332 201269, www.hotelvillacastiglioni.it

Lanzo d'Intelvi

€€ **Belvedere**. An extremely friendly and comfortable family-run establishment in a charming village. Closed Nov–Dec. Via Poletti 27, T: 031 840122.

€€ **Rondanino**. Alpine atmosphere in a verdant park, with outside restaurant service in summer. Via Rondanino 1, T: 031 839858, rondanino@libero.it

Sacro Monte

€€ **Colonne**. Cosy (8 rooms), with great views of the valley and a restaurant with summer seating outside. Via Fincarà 37, T: 0332 244633, F: 0332 821593, www.hotelcolonne.com

RESTAURANTS

Varese

€€€ **Lago Maggiore**. Restaurant serving traditional regional dishes prepared with great care; reservations required. Closed Sun, midday Mon and July. Via Carrobbio 19, T: 0332 231183.

€€ **Da Annetta**. Restaurant representing the best of local tradition. Closed Tues evening, Wed and Aug. Via Fè 25 at Capolago, T: 0332 490230.

Campione d'Italia

€€ **Da Candida**. Excellent creative cuisine inspired by French models. Closed Sun, Mon, Feb and July. Via Marco 4, T: 91 649 7541.

Olgiate-Olona

€€€ **Ma.Ri.Na.** Restaurant specialising in fish. Open evenings only (except Sun and holidays), closed Wed and Aug. Piazza San Gregorio 11, T: 0331 640483.

Ternate

€€ **Locanda del Lago**. Restaurant specialising in lake fish. Closed Mon. Via Motta, T: 0332 960864.

Travedona Monate

€ **Ristorante del Torchio**. Restaurant serving traditional Lombard dishes, notably game and lake fish. Closed Mon, Feb and Aug. Via Cavour 1, T: 0332 977436.

FESTIVALS & MARKETS

Falò di Sant'Antonio, patron saint's feast in Varese, 16 Jan; *Estate Varesina*, open-air cinema, theatre and music, summer. Antiques markets in Varese, first Sun of the month; Castiglione Olona, first Sun; Sesto Calende second Sat.

Varenna.

LAGO DI COMO

Lago di Como lies below the alpine foothills, surrounded by wooded slopes. Virgil called it Lacus Larius, and it is still often known as Lario. Many of the small towns on its shores, originally fishing villages, became resorts in the 19th century. The lake was visited by the English Romantic poets, including Shelley and Byron, and Wordsworth lived here in 1790. Numerous villas surrounded by lovely gardens were built on its steep banks in the 18th and 19th centuries. The most beautiful part of the lake is in the centre, at Bellagio, from where three long, narrow arms radiate out: one stretching southwest to Como, another southeast to Lecco, the third north to Colico. The lake is subject to frequent floods (last in 1997, when Como was inundated), and is swept regularly by two winds, the *tivano* (north to south), and the *breva* (south to north) in the afternoon.

COMO

The town of Como lies in a fine position on the southern lakeshore. It has preserved its Roman plan, within high walls, to a marked degree. The city has a particularly attractive old centre with long, straight, narrow streets, many of their houses with pretty courtyards. The cathedral is a splendid Gothic building with remarkable sculptures inside and out. A delightful path, shaded by huge old trees, skirts the lake as far as the public gardens of Villa Olmo, passing charming villas with gardens and boathouses on the waterfront. The traditional local industry of silk-weaving survives here in several large factories (and silk products can be purchased all over the town).

HISTORY OF COMO

Originally a town of the Insubrian Gauls—the same people who founded Milan—Como was captured and colonised by the Romans in the 2nd century BC. The town was a city-state by the 11th century, but in 1127 it was destroyed by the Milanese. Frederick Barbarossa rebuilt it in 1155, and Como secured its future independence by the Peace of Constance (1183). In the power struggles between the Torriani and the Visconti families, Como fell to the latter in 1335 and became a fief of Milan. From then on it followed the vicissitudes of the Lombard capital, coming under Austrian rule in 1714. In March 1848 a popular uprising compelled the surrender of the Austrian garrison, and the city was liberated by Garibaldi on 27 May 1859.

Among famous natives are two Roman authors, the Elder and the Younger Pliny (AD 23–79 and AD 62–120), uncle and nephew. The Younger Pliny often mentions Como and its surroundings in his *Letters*.

EXPLORING COMO

Piazza Cavour and the lakefront

The centre of the life of Como is **Piazza Cavour**, on the lakefront adjoining the quay. It was created in 1887 by filling in the old harbour. The piazza has a splendid view: on the right bank you can see Villa Geno and the line of the funicular up to Brunate; on the left is the Neoclassical rotunda of the Tempio Voltiano and beyond it the large Villa Olmo; straight ahead amidst trees is the Villa Fiori, and in the distance the town of Cernobbio climbs the hillside above the lake. To get to the Tempio Voltiano follow the avenue of lime trees that skirts the lake, leading to the Giardino Pubblico. The **Tempio Voltiano** (*closed at the time of writing; T: 031 574705*) was erected in 1927 as a memorial to the physicist Alessandro Volta (1745–1827). In 1799 Volta developed the 'voltaic pile', the precursor of the electric battery. Napoleon created him a count in 1801. Today he is a household name: the volt is named after him. The museum contains his scientific instruments, charmingly displayed in old-fashioned show cases. The conspicuous war memorial beyond it was designed by the Futurist architect Antonio Sant'Elia, a native of Como, himself killed in 1916. It is his only constructed work.

Beyond the war memorial, Via Puecher leads past a naval club and a hangar for sea planes, beyond which a very pleasant lakeside path (marked by a broken line on the map) continues past a number of lovely private villas with their gardens and boat-houses and decorative gazebos. Beyond Villa Pallavicino, with statues on the façade and stuccoes inside by Piermarini (architect of Milan's La Scala) and his collaborator Giocondo Albertolli, is the Villa Resta Pallavicini (called 'La Rotonda') with a semicircular Neoclassical rotunda in the centre of its façade. The path ends at **Villa Olmo**, built for the Odescalchi family (1782–95; altered in 1883). It is preceded by an attractive formal garden (*open daily*) with topiary, statues and a charming fountain, and behind are remains of its large park. The villa is used for exhibitions.

The city centre

From Piazza Cavour the short Via Plinio leads away from the lake to Piazza del Duomo, with the Broletto (1215; the old town hall), built in alternate courses of black and white marble, with a few red patches, and the Torre del Comune of the same period, used as a campanile since the addition of the top storey in 1435 (partly rebuilt in 1927).

The **cathedral** (Santa Maria Maggiore), built entirely of marble, dates mainly from the late 14th century, when it replaced an 11th-century basilica. Its appearance, a union of Renaissance and Gothic architectural motifs, is remarkably homogenous. The rebuilding, financed mainly by public subscription, was entrusted first to Lorenzo degli Spazzi who, like his many successors, worked under the patronage of the Milanese court. Many of the works of art were restored in 1988–92.

The west front (1460–90) is a good example of the transition from Gothic to Renaissance. The fine rose window belongs to the Gothic tradition, whereas the three

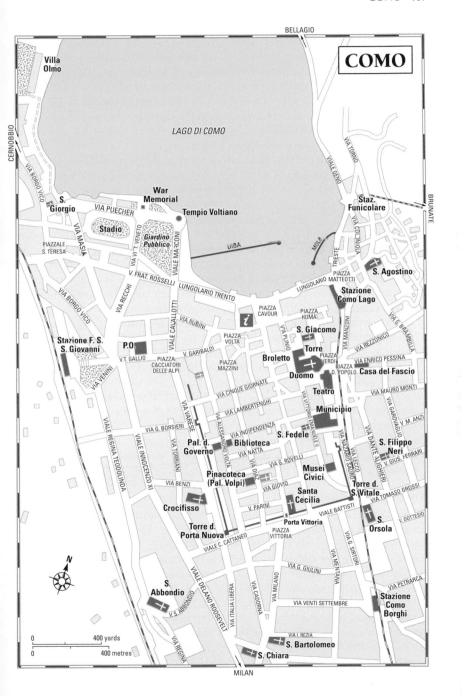

COMO

BELLAGIO

CERNOBBIO

BRUNATE

MILAN

Villa Olmo

LAGO DI COMO

VIA I. TORNO

VIALE GENO

War Memorial

Tempio Voltiano

S. Giorgio

VIA PUECHER

Stadio

Giardino Pubblico

DIGA

MOLO

Staz. Funicolare

VIA COLDNIOLA

VIA BORGO VICO

VIA MASIA

VIA VIT. VENETO

VIALE MARCONI

V. FRAT. ROSSELLI

PIAZZALE S. TERESA

VIA RECCHI

LUNGOLARIO TRENTO

LUNGOLARIO MATTEOTTI

PIAZZA MATTEOTTI

S. Agostino

TRIESTE

Stazione Como Lago

VIA MANZONI

VIA G. BRAMBILLA

VIA BORGO VICO

VIALE CAVALLOTTI

VIA RUBINI

PIAZZA CAVOUR

PIAZZA ROMA

S. Giacomo

VIA REZZONICO

VIA PUNIO

PIAZZA VOLTA

Torre

PIAZZA VERDI

VIA ENRICO PESSINA

Stazione F. S. S. Giovanni

P.O.

V.T. GALLIO

V. GARIBALDI

Broletto

PIAZZA CACCIATORI DELLE ALPI

PIAZZA MAZZINI

Duomo

PIAZZA D. POPOLO

Casa del Fascio

VIA VENINI

VIA CINQUE GIORNATE

Teatro

VIA MAURO MONTI

VIALE REGINA TEODOLINDA

VIA LAMBERTENGHI

Municipio

VIA GARVAGLIO

V. M. ANZI

VIA G. BORSIERI

VIA VARESE

VIA ALESSANDRO VOLTA

VIA INDIPENDENZA

S. Fedele

VIA VITTORIO EMANUELE II

VIA DANTE ALIGHIERI

S. Filippo Neri

VIA INNOCENZO XI

VIA TORRIANI

Pal. d. Governo

Biblioteca

VIA NATTA

VIA DIAZ

VIA G. ROVELLI

VIA NAZARIO SAURO

VIA LECCO

V. GIUS. FERRARI

VIA BENZI

Pinacoteca (Pal. Volpi)

Musei Civici

Torre d. S. Vitale

VIA TOMASO GROSSI

VIA GIOVIO

Santa Cecilia

Crocifisso

V. PARINI

VIALE BATTISTI

V. DOTTESIO

Torre d. Porta Nuova

Porta Vittoria

S. Orsola

PIAZZA VITTORIA

VIALE C. CATTANEO

VIA G. SIRTORI

VIA MENTANA

VIA G. GIULINI

VIA PETRARCA

VIALE DELANO ROOSEVELT

N

S. Abbondio

V. S. ABBONDIO

VIA ITALIA LIBERA

VIA CADORNA

VIA MILANO

VIA VENTI SETTEMBRE

Stazione Como Borghi

0   400 yards
0   400 metres

VIA REGINA

VIA I. REZIA

S. Bartolomeo

S. Chiara

doorways with their round arches owe more to the Renaissance. The twenty 15th-century statues framing the two large windows between the central doorway and the rose window are Gothic in conception; the numerous other reliefs and statues from the workshop of Tommaso and Jacopo Rodari (local sculptors from Maroggia), dating from c. 1500, are more Renaissance in style. The two lateral doorways, also decorated by the Rodari, are wonderful examples of detailed carving. The work of rebuilding continued through the 16th century (choir) and 17th century (transepts), and ended with completion of the dome in 1770 by Filippo Juvarra.

Inside, the aisled nave of five bays is covered with a groin vault and hung with tapestries (1598). On the west wall are brightly coloured stained-glass windows by Giuseppe Bertini (1850). The two stoups supported by lions are survivals from the ancient basilica. A graceful little rotunda (1590) serves as a baptistery.

In the south aisle the first altar has a wooden ancona dating from 1482. Beyond a Neoclassical funerary monument by Agliati is another ancona by Tommaso Rodari (1492). Past the south door (also well carved) is the tomb of Bishop Bonifacio da Modena (1347). The altar of Sant'Abbondio (coin-operated light) is finely decorated with gilded woodcarving (1514), and three marble panels below. The *Virgin and Child*, with four saints and the donor, Canon Raimondi, and a beautiful angel-musician in front, is a masterpiece of Bernardino Luini. Sant'Abbondio (St Abundius) was Bishop of Como and papal legate to the Council of Chalcedon (AD 451), convened to quell the monophysite heresy, which held that Christ's human and divine natures were inseparable.

The Gothic high altar dates from 1317. On the fourth altar of the north aisle is a carved *Deposition* group by Tommaso Rodari (1498) and opposite, hanging in the nave, a painted and embroidered standard of the Confraternity of Sant'Abbondio by Morazzone (1608–10). On either side of the third Neoclassical altar are paintings by Bernardino Luini and Gaudenzio Ferrari. By the side door is the sarcophagus of Giovanni degli Avogadri (d. 1293), with primitive carvings. On the second altar, between busts of Innocent XI and Bishop Rovelli, is a lovely carved ancona by Tommaso Rodari.

North of the duomo

To the north of the cathedral are the yellow bishop's palace and the church of San Giacomo, with its unusual yellow-and-red façade. The church has Romanesque elements (columns, brickwork in the aisles, apse and dome).

Behind the fine east end of the cathedral is the ruined Palazzo Pantera, the Teatro Sociale (1811) and—across the Nord–Milano railway line—the white **Casa del Fascio** (now a police station), built in 1932–36 to a design by Giuseppe Terragni and an important example of the architecture of this period. Terragni was active in CIAM, the main forum for propagating the ideas of International Modernism. A committed Rationalist and dedicated Fascist, he built a number of other important buildings in Como, including the façade of the Metropole Suisse (1927) in Piazza Cavour, and the Albergo Posta (1931) on Via Garibaldi.

The Musei Civici and the Pinacoteca

Via Vittorio Emanuele II leads south from the cathedral to the 17th-century town hall (Municipio), opposite which is the five-sided apse of **San Fedele**, a 12th-century church that at one time served as the cathedral. The angular northeast doorway, with remarkable bas-reliefs, shows Byzantine influences. The church is entered from the delightful piazza behind. The interior, partly under restoration, has an unusual plan. It contains a fresco signed by G.A. Magistris (1504), and a little painted and stuccoed 17th-century vault.

In the piazza and on Via Natta are several old houses with wooden eaves and brickwork. Further along Via Vittorio Emanuele two palaces house the **Musei Civici** (*open Tues–Sat 9.30–12.30 & 2–5, Sun and holidays 10–1*). The archaeological section includes Neolithic, Bronze Age and Iron Age finds, a stele of the 5th century BC, Roman finds and medieval fragments. There are also 19th-century American artefacts, a natural history section, an Egyptian collection, a good Risorgimento museum and material relating to the First and Second World Wars. There is also a local ethnographic collection with 18th-century costumes.

Three blocks west, at Via Diaz 84, is the **Pinacoteca** (*open as above*) housed in the modernised Palazzo Volpi (1610–30), which is also used for exhibitions. On the ground floor, beyond an 11th-century arch salvaged from a monastery in the town, are sculptural fragments, including capitals, from the Carolingian and Romanesque periods; and frescoes, including charming scenes from the lives of Sts Liberata and Faustina. Upstairs are 16th–17th-century paintings and a *Madonna Annunciate* attributed to the 15th-century Sicilian artist Antonello da Messina (not exhibited at the time of writing). Antonello is credited with having introduced oil painting into Italy (*see p. 413*).

The south and west

Southeast of the Pinacoteca is the church of Santa Cecilia, the front of which incorporates some Roman columns. It has a Baroque interior. Next door was the school where Volta once taught; there is a fragment of Roman wall in the courtyard. The Porta Vittoria is surmounted by a tower of 1192 with many windows. It is named in memory of a victory during the struggle for independence: in 1848 the Austrian garrison in the barracks immediately opposite surrendered to the Italians. The Garibaldi monument in Piazza Vittoria was erected in 1889.

Outside the gate, beyond a busy road and 500m to the southwest, is the fine Romanesque basilica of **Sant'Abbondio**, isolated amid industrial buildings near the railway. On the site of an early Christian building, the present church dates from the 11th century and is dedicated to St Abundius, bishop of Como (*see above*). The exterior has two graceful campanili and a finely decorated apse. The interior has five tall aisles, despite its comparatively small size, and a deep presbytery. The apse is entirely frescoed with scenes from the life of Christ by mid-14th-century Lombard artists. The statue of St Abondius is attributed to Cristoforo Solari (1490).

On Viale Varese, which skirts the walls and gardens, is the sanctuary of the

Crocifisso, a huge 16th-century building with a façade of 1864 by Luigi Fontana and Baroque decorations inside. In Via Alessandro Volta, inside the walls, is the house where the scientist lived and died (plaque).

An interesting Museo Didattico della Seta (*open Tues–Fri 9–12 & 3–6*), documenting Como's main industry, has been set up on the outskirts of the town, at Via Valleggio 3 (beyond the map).

A WALK ABOVE THE LAKE

There is a good circular excursion from Como, through the woodlands on the mountainside along the lake's eastern shore. The ascent from Como is made by the Brunate funicular; you then walk along the contour of the mountain before descending, by the 1,200 steps of an old mule path, to Torno. From this quiet little village there are frequent boats back to Como. The walk is easy, except for the final descent of c. 400m.

From the funicular station at Brunate, walk left on cobblestones and then right on tarmac, toward San Maurizio. After 100m the road forks; follow the blue-and-white marked trail left (Via Niorino). After 5 minutes the road forks again. Go downhill left to the end of the pavement, at the football field, then follow the blue-and-white trail downhill right, into the forest. Twenty minutes later you reach a wooden cross and switchback; proceed straight. After 25 minutes more you come to a farm; follow the arrow for Montepiatto (straight, not downhill). After just 5 minutes you come to Montepiatto, a village that can only be reached on foot. Go right at the fork (yellow tourist sign). After 25 minutes a group of houses on a hill comes into sight and the trail intersects a stepped path. Proceed downhill left. Twenty minutes (and c. 1,000 steps) later, you come upon a tabernacle with the Christ Child and the Archangel Gabriel (?). Turn downhill left. Ten minutes later you come to the first houses of Torno, a delightful little village of terraced walkways, on the water. Continue straight downhill, then left (follow the red arrow). Cross the highway and continue down the steps to the waterfront. The landing with the boat back to Como is on your right.

Environs of Como

From Piazza Cavour, Lungo Lario Trieste leads past several large hotels, the old-fashioned station of the Nord–Milano line, and a small port, to the funicular station for **Brunate** (713m; services every 15mins, taking 7mins). Brunate can also be reached from Via Grossi by road or by path. In a fine position overlooking the lake, it became a resort at the end of the 19th century. The funicular climbs steeply up the hillside through a tunnel and then traverses woods and the gardens of some fine villas. From the upper station a 10-minute walk (signposted 'panoramic view') leads gently uphill past huge, elaborate 19th- and 20th-century villas and their gardens, beneath an archway to emerge high above the lake and the Breggia river. The fine view takes in the boatyard of the Villa Lariana on the left, and to the right is Cernobbio with the huge Villa d'Este on the lakeside (*see below*).

At the highest point of the village, near the funicular station (the mechanism of which you can see in the engine room), is the church of **Sant'Andrea**. It has 19th- and 20th-century frescoes inside, as well as a charming 15th-century fresco of a certain St Guglielma, thought to have been an English princess who married a King of Hungary in the 8th century. Her cult has been known in Brunate since before the 15th century, and her feast day is celebrated here on the fourth Sunday in April. Steps lead down the other side of the hill, away from the lake to the centre of the village (pedestrians only). At San Maurizio (871m), 2km higher, is the Faro Voltiano, a monument to Alessandro Volta (1927).

FROM COMO TO COLICO BY WATER

Frequent boats connect Como with Colico all year round, and offer a calm, convenient way of touring the lake. After leaving Como the boats cross to the west shore and the red Villa Lariana, surrounded by poplars on the delightful Breggia river. Beyond is a modern congress centre in the gardens of the Villa Erba. **Cernobbio** is a resort at the foot of Monte Bisbino (1325m). It has a pleasant waterfront with boats pulled up on the quay and an attractive Liberty-style landing stage. Beyond is the huge white Villa d'Este hotel, which occupies a villa built in 1568 by Cardinal Tolomeo Gallio (1527–1607), a native of Cernobbio. It was here, in 1816–17, that Caroline of

The Villa d'Este at Cernobbio.

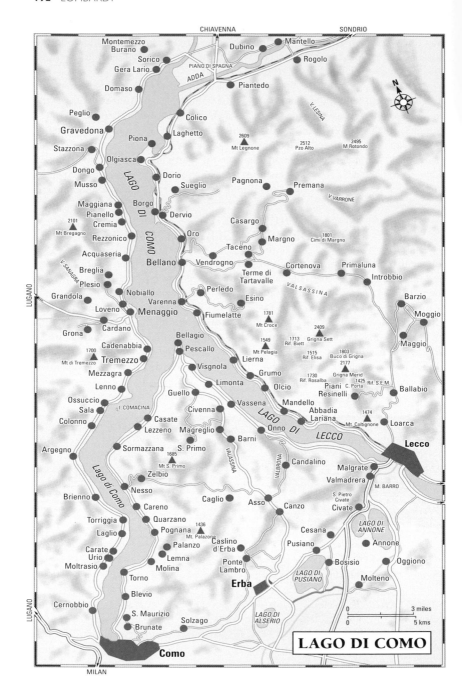

CHIAVENNA   SONDRIO

Montemezzo
Burano
Sorico
Gera Lario
Domaso
PIANO DI SPAGNA
ADDA

Dubino   Mantello
Rogolo
Piantedo

Peglio
Gravedona
Stazzona
Olgiasca
Dongo
Musso
Maggiana
Pianello
Cremia
Rezzonico
Acquaseria
Breglia
Plesio
Grandola
Loveno
Grona
Cardano
Cadenabbia
Tremezzo
Mezzagra
Lenno
Ossuccio
Sala
Colonno
Argegno
Brienno
Torriggia
Laglio
Carate
Urio
Moltrasio
Cernobbio

Piona
Laghetto
Colico
Dorio
Sueglio
Borgo
Dervio
Oro
Bellano
Nobiallo
Varenna
Menaggio
Fiumelatte
Bellagio
Pescallo
Visgnola
Limonta
Guello
Civenna
Casate
Lezzeno
Magreglio
Sormazzana
S. Primo
Zelbio
Nesso
Careno
Quarzano
Pognana
Palanzo
Lemna
Molina
Torno
Blevio
S. Maurizio
Brunate
Solzago

LAGO DI COMO

Lago di Como

Pagnona   Premana
Casargo   Margno
Taceno
Vendrogno
Terme di Tartavalle
Cortenova   Primaluna
Introbbio
Esino   Barzio
Moggio
Maggio
Grumo   Ballabio
Olcio
Mandello
Vassena
Abbadia   Loarca
Lariana
Onno   LECCO   Lecco
Barni
Candalino
Malgrate
Valmadrera   M. BARRO
S. Pietro   Civate
Caglio   Asso   Canzo   LAGO DI ANNONE
Cesana   Annone
Pusiano   Bosisio   Oggiono
Caslino d'Erba   Molteno
Ponte Lambro
Erba   LAGO DI PUSIANO

2609 Mt Legnone
2512 Pzo Alto
2495 M Rotondo

V. LESINA
V. VARRONE
V. SANAGRA
VALSASSINA
I. COMACINA
VALSASSINA
VALBRONA

2101 Mt Bregagno
1781 Mt Croce
2409 Grigna Sett
1549 Mt Pelagia
1713 Rif. Biett
1515 Rif. Elisa
1803 Buco di Grigna
2177 Grigna Merid
1730 Rif. Rosalba
1425 Rif. S.E.M.
C. Porta
Piani Resinelli
1474 Mt Coltignone
1700 Mt di Tremezzo
1801 Cimi di Margno

1685 Mt S. Primo
1436 Mt. Palazone

LAGO DI ALSERIO

0   3 miles
0   5 kms

LAGO DI COMO

LUGANO
LUGANO
MILAN
Como

Brunswick, Princess of Wales, lived in exile after her estrangement from the Prince Regent. She had the park landscaped in the English style, and turned the villa into a house of pleasure. Her lewd dress sense and licentious behaviour shocked an entire continent: when George was finally crowned George IV in 1820, Caroline was debarred from the ceremony.

On the headland amidst trees is the **Villa Il Pizzo** (*open for guided visits April–Oct, except Aug, Fri 8.30–12.30 & 2–5*), with cypresses in its park and a garden gazebo, and low down on the waterfront is the yellow Villa Fontanella. **Villa Erba** is also open to visitors (*May–Oct Sat 2–6, Sun 10–6; closed during fairs and conventions*).

Moltrasio, with a Romanesque church, is less pretty. Here at the Villa Salterio in 1831 Bellini composed the opera *Norma* in 1831. On the bay on the east bank beyond Torno is the **Villa Pliniana** (1570). In the garden is the famous intermittent spring described in detail by the Younger Pliny in his *Letters*, and also studied by Leonardo da Vinci. The abundant flow of water is channelled from a grotto down the cliff into the lake. Ugo Foscolo, Shelley, Stendhal and Rossini (who composed *Tancredi* here in 1813) were among the illustrious 19th-century visitors to the villa. The 18th-century **Villa Passalacqua** has an Italianate garden. Bellini composed *La Sonnambula* here.

On the west bank beyond Moltrasio are the yellow Villa Angelina, behind cypresses and a garden, and the double village of Carate Urio; Urio has a tall Lombard campanile, but a lot of unattractive new building spoils Carate. Laglio, beyond, has another tall church tower. A mountain torrent enters the lake in a waterfall between two hills near the green and white Villa Annetta. At the narrowest reach of the lake is **Torriggia**, with the small Villa Pia and its garden on the point. Beyond the churches of Sant'Anna and Brienno is **Argegno**, where the high mountain ranges northeast of the lake come into view. Argegno lies at the foot of the beautiful, fertile Val d'Intelvi, also reached by a road to Lanzo d'Intelvi above Lago di Lugano (*see p. 181*).

From Isola Comacina to Cadenabbia

Opposite Sala Comacina (marked Sala on the map), is the **Isola Comacina**, a pretty little wooded island with a trattoria (*open March to October*) but no permanent residents. The regular boat services call here, and a ferry service operates from Sala Comacina.

The island was used as a hiding place by political refugees during the disturbed medieval history of Lombardy, and it was captured and raided by Como in 1169. In 1917 it passed by inheritance to Albert, King of the Belgians, but was later given to the Accademia delle Belle Arti of Milan, who built three houses here as artists' retreats. Paths lead along the shore of the lake and over the top of the island through wild vegetation past the ruins of its six medieval churches.

The boats skirt the wooded headland called the Punta del Balbianello with an excellent view of the **Villa del Balbianello**, the garden and loggia of which can be visited April–Oct (*open Mon, Thur, Fri 10–1 & 2–6; Sat–Sun and holidays 8–6*). It can only be reached by water (regular boat service every 30 minutes from Sala Comacina to coincide with the opening hours) or on foot (only April–Oct, on the last Sunday of the month) by a signposted path of roughly 800m, which starts from the church square in Lenno. The villa is surrounded by plane trees, magnolias, ilexes and cypresses. It was left to the FAI (Fondo per l'Ambiente Italiano) in 1988 by the explorer Guido Monzino, who was the first Italian to climb Everest (in 1973), and who reached the North Pole in 1971.

A steep flight of steps lead up from the dock to the villa, built by Cardinal Angelo Maria Durini in 1787 and incorporating the scant remains of a Franciscan convent (the façade of the church and its twin *campanili* survive). In the small formal garden above the villa, with laurel and box hedges, wisteria, azaleas and rhododendrons, is a delightful garden loggia with fine views. It incorporates a library and map room with Monzino's collections relating to the polar regions and mountaineering. The villa contains more of Monzino's collections from his explorations, and 18th- and 19th-century English and French furniture.

At Lenno the shore is flatter at the mouth of the Acquafredda, at the south end of the Tremezzina (*see below*). The parish church has an 11th–12th-century crypt and an 11th-century octagonal baptistery adjoining. Here on the shore was the **site of Pliny's villa 'Comedia'** (his other villa, called 'Tragedia', was at Bellagio, at the tip of the inlet between the two forks, *see below*). Mussolini and his mistress, Claretta Petacci, were shot by partisans at nearby Giulino on April 28, 1945 while attempting to escape via the Valtellina to Austria. Beyond Lenno the boats follow the attractive Tremezzina, the fertile green shore dotted with villas and gardens, which extends along the foot of Monte di Tremezzo to just north of Cadenabbia.

Tremezzo and Cadenabbia are both elegant resorts with numerous hotels and some fine villas. On the busy road between them is the prominent **Villa Carlotta** (*open Apr–Sept 9–6; Mar and Oct 9–11.30 & 2–4.30; T: 0344 41011*), built at the beginning of the 18th century by Marchese Giorgio Clerici. The interior was altered after 1795 by the Marchese Giambattista Sommariva, and the opening scenes of *La Chartreuse de Parme* (1839) recall Stendhal's stay here as Sommariva's guest in 1818. The villa was bought in 1843 by Princess Albrecht of Prussia, who gave it to her daughter Carlotta on her marriage to the Crown Prince of Saxe-Meiningen. The magnificent wooded park was laid out by Princess Carlotta in the Romantic style. It has always been much admired by the English, and has beautiful camellias, rhododendrons and azaleas in spring.

You enter by the Neoclassical funerary chapel of the Sommariva. The villa is interesting for its early 19th-century decorations, including Neoclassical works and Empire-style French furniture, and for its lovely painted ceilings dating from the 18th century. In the main room is Thorvaldsen's frieze of the *Triumphal Entry of Alexander into Babylon*, cast in plaster for Napoleon in 1811–12 and intended for the throne-room at the Quirinal. Also here are works by Canova (*Cupid and Psyche*, *The Repentant Magdalen*, and *Palamedes*), and *Mars and Venus* by Luigi Acquisti. In other rooms on the ground floor are three Gobelin tapestries (1767–73), fine frescoes by Andrea Appiani, paintings by Francesco Hayez and Giovanni Battista Wicar, and plaster models by Canova and Acquisti.

The upper floor has good views of the gardens, fine painted-wood 18th-century ceilings and Empire-style French furniture. The view from the terrace extends across the lake to San Giovanni with its church, just to the left of which is Villa Melzi, and further left on the hill the Villa Serbelloni, with Bellagio and its church below. Beyond Bellagio the Lecco arm of the lake can just be seen.

In front of the house is a formal Italianate garden reached by a theatrical flight of steps that descend to the entrance gate on the lake. The park is of great botanical interest, and is very well cared-for. A path leads past rhododendrons and tropical plants to a hillside planted with azaleas. Beyond a rock garden is a plantation of palms and cacti. A valley watered by a stream has a splendid variety of tree ferns. Beyond, a straight path leads past banks of azaleas, and higher up the hillside are conifers, camphor trees and beech trees. Behind the villa is a hedge of azaleas, and a bridge leads across a stream to a smaller garden on the other side of the villa, with tropical plants, plane trees, monkey-puzzle trees, Japanese maples and palms.

At the Villa Margherita on the shore just north of Cadenabbia, while staying with his publisher Ricordi, Verdi composed Act II of *La Traviata* in 1853.

The Centro Lago

The Centro Lago, where the Como and Lecco arms meet, is the most beautiful part of the lake. In a lovely, quiet position on a headland at the division of the lake is the famous resort of **Bellagio**, which retains much of the picturesque aspect of an old Lombard town. It has local industries of silk-weaving and olive-wood carving. To the left of the car ferry station is an attractive arcaded piazza with the boat and hydrofoil pier. Stepped streets lead up to the church of San Giacomo, with a 12th-century apse. It contains a reconstructed primitive pulpit with symbols of the Evangelists, a painted triptych by the late-15th-century Lombard school, a 19th-century copy of a *Deposition* by Perugino, and a 16th-century wooden *Dead Christ* (a Spanish work). In the apse is a gilded tabernacle (16th- and 18th centuries).

In the old tower opposite is the Tourist Information Office and, on the floor above, the ticket office for the **Villa Serbelloni** (*the park is shown April–Oct at 11am & 4pm to a maximum of 30 people on a guided tour of about an hour and a half, except Mon and when raining*). The entrance gate is behind San Giacomo. The villa and grounds were left to the Rockefeller Foundation of New York in 1959 by Ella Walker Della Torre Tasso to be used as a study centre for students (who come here on scholarships for one month) from all over the world. The younger Pliny's villa 'Tragedia' is thought to have occupied this site. Stendhal stayed here in 1825.

The magnificent park on the spectacular high promontory overlooking the lake was laid out at the end of the 18th century by Alessandro Serbelloni. A gravel road leads up past a delightful little pavilion used as a student's study, and just before the villa there is a good view of Cadenabbia. In front of the villa, which incorporates a Romanesque tower, is a formal garden with topiary and olive, cypress and fruit trees. From here there is a view of the Lecco branch of the lake, with the little fishing village of Pescallo and a 17th-century monastery. On the hill in front is the Villa

Belmonte, below which you can see a Gothic-Revival building that was once the English church and is now a private villa. A path continues through the park past artificial grottoes created in the 19th century up to the highest point on the promontory with remains of a ruined castle and an 11th-century chapel. The splendid view takes in Varenna with the Villa Cipressi and the Villa Monastero (separated by a prominent square boathouse), and to the north are the high mountains beyond Colico. Another path returns to the villa, from which steps continue down to the town.

From the car ferry station it is a 5–10-minute walk along the road to Loppia to **Villa Melzi** (*grounds open March–Oct 9–6.30*), standing in a fine park with an interesting garden. The villa, chapel and greenhouse were built in 1808–10 by Giocondo Albertolli as a summer residence for Francesco Melzi d'Eril. Franz Liszt, the composer and pianist, stayed here (his daughter Cosima was born at the Casa Lillia in Bellagio in 1837). From the entrance a path leads past a little Japanese garden and a circular pavilion on the lake to an avenue of plane trees which leads to the villa. On the left is the former orangery, which contains a small museum. The two statues in front of the villa of Meleager and Apollo are 16th-century works by Guglielmo della Porta. The park contains beautiful rhododendrons and azaleas. Beyond the villa at the end of the gardens is the chapel with particularly fine Neoclassical family tombs.

The road continues to Loppia with a half-ruined church in a romantic site beside a great grove of cypresses. At **San Giovanni** the church contains an altarpiece by Gaudenzio Ferrari.

A road leads south from Bellagio to Asso via Civenna, with a fine panorama of the lake. Beyond Guello a road on the right ascends to the foot of Monte San Primo (1686m). At the edge of the town of Civenna by the cemetery is a small park with spectacular views of the lake from Gravedona in the north to Lecco in the south. From the small church of Madonna del Ghisallo (754m; with votive offerings from champion cyclists), the highest point of the road, there is a view of the lake (left) with the two Grigne beyond, and of Bellagio behind. The road descends the steep Vallassina to Asso with remains of a medieval castle. Here the graceful 17th-century **church of San Giovanni Battista** has an elaborate gilded-wood Baroque altar and an *Annunciation* by Giulio Campi. Almost continuous with Asso is Canzo, the centre of valley life. Another road from Bellagio, with magnificent views, goes along the west bank of the Lecco arm of the lake, via Limonta, Vassena and Onno, and ascends the Valbrona to Asso.

The upper lake

The next place of importance on the west bank of the lake is **Menaggio**, a pleasant little town. Beyond the pier and the Grand Hotel, the busy main road can be followed on foot for a few minutes to the pretty piazza on the waterfront. Roads lead uphill behind the church to the narrow cobbled lanes which traverse the area of the castle, with some fine large villas and a 17th-century wall fountain. Beyond the Sangra river is Loveno; the Villa Calabi was the home of Massimo d'Azeglio (1798–1865), patriot and writer (*see p. 168*). There are several fine walks in the area beneath the beautiful

Monte Bregagno (2107m). Acquaseria lies at the foot of the Cima la Grona; to the south rises the Sasso Rancio. Further north is Rezzonico, with a castle, the home of the powerful family which bore its name and numbered Pope Clement XIII among its famous members. The old church of San Vito has a fine *Madonna and Angels* attributed to Bergognone.

From Menaggio the boat crosses to the eastern shore of the lake, offering spectacular views of both southern stretches with Bellagio on its headland in the middle.

Lago di Como and the Romantics

This lake exceeds any thing I ever beheld in beauty, with the exception of the arbutus islands of Killarney. It is long and narrow, and has the appearance of a mighty river, winding among the mountains and the forests...

This shore of the lake is one continued village, and the Milanese nobility have their villas here. The union of culture and the untameable profusion and loveliness of nature is here so close, that the line where they are divided can hardly be discovered.

Percy Bysshe Shelley, letter to Thomas Love Peacock, 20 April 1818

As I sit writing in the garden under a magnolia I look across to Varenna in the sun ... and the grand jagged line of mountains that bound the lake towards Colico, almost snowless in August, stand glittering now like the Oberland range. You never saw anything so calculated to make you drunk.

Matthew Arnold, letter to Walter Arnold, 5 May 1873

Varenna is a delightful little town whose port can be reached only on foot, by narrow stepped streets. It has a good view across the lake of the promontory of Bellagio with the park of Villa Serbelloni. On the main road are the piazza with plane trees, the Royal Victoria Hotel and four churches. San Giorgio has a 14th-century fresco on its façade. It contains a pavement and altar made of the local black marble and a 15th-century polyptych by the local artist Pietro Brentani. The 11th-century church of San Giovanni has a fine apse and remains of frescoes. The spring of Fiumelatte, active from May to October, can be reached from the piazza by a pretty path (c. 1km) via the cemetery. Like the spring at the Villa Pliniana (*see p. 193*), its flow is intermittent, and though it has been studied by numerous experts (including Leonardo da Vinci), it is still not known why.

Just out of the piazza, on the main road to Lecco is the entrance to Villa Cipressi (*garden open daily April–Oct*), an annexe of the Royal Victoria, with a 19th–20th-century interior. The villa takes its name from its numerous cypresses, 60 of which had to be felled after a tornado in 1967. The well-maintained garden, with a venerable wisteria, descends in steep terraces down to the lakeside. It has a good view of Villa Monastero, which it adjoins, beyond an attractive little boathouse and private dock.

A few metres further along the main road towards Lecco is the entrance to the Villa Monastero (*open as Villa Cipressi*). The monastery here founded in 1208 was closed down in the 16th century by St Charles Borromeo, and the villa is now owned by a science research centre. The garden is laid out on a long, narrow terrace on the lakeside with 19th-century statuary, fine cypresses, palms, roses and cineraria, and one huge old magnolia tree. The enormous greenhouse protects orange and lime trees. The gloomy villa, with elaborately carved furniture, yellow and black marble, and Art Nouveau decorations, is in urgent need of repair.

The old stepped streets of Varenna lead down from the piazza to the picturesque little port, with an arcaded street on the waterfront where the workers who prepared the black marble and green *lumachella,* or shell-marble, from the neighbouring quarries for shipping used to have their workshops. A walkway built in 1982 continues above the lake (with wonderful sunsets across the water in October) round to the car ferry pier. There is an ornithological museum in the upper town.

Back on the lake shore, **Bellano** is a town with silk and cotton mills at the mouth of the Pioverna. The deep Pioverna Gorge can be viewed from stairs and walkways (*Easter–Sept Thur–Tues 9.30–12.30 & 1.30–5.30*). The restored church of Santi Nazaro e Celso is a good example of the 14th-century Lombard style. From Bellano a road runs to Premana (with a local ethnographic museum). Dervio has a ruined castle and an old campanile at the foot of Monte Legnone (2601m). Just beyond Dorio a cobbled road (signposted for Piona) diverges left and traverses woods for c. 2km to end at the Benedictine Abbey of Piona in a peaceful spot on the lake. The simple church has two large stoups borne by Romanesque lions, and behind it is the ruined apse of an earlier church. The irregular cloister has a variety of 12th-century capitals. There is a ferry station here open in summer. The boat crosses back to the west shore. The village of Pianello del Lario has a 12th-century church and a small museum of lake boats (*open July–Sept, or by appointment; T: 0344 87235*). **Musso** is overlooked by the almost impregnable Rocca di Musso, the stronghold in 1525–32 of the piratical Gian Giacomo Medici, who levied tribute from the traders of the lake and the neighbouring valleys.

Dongo, with Gravedona and Sorico, formed the independent Republic of the Three Parishes (Tre Pievi), which survived until the Spanish occupation of Lombardy. Mussolini was captured by partisans at Dongo in the spring of 1945. The 12th-century church of Santa Maria in the adjacent hamlet of Martinico preserves an interesting doorway. Gravedona is the principal village of the upper lake. The foursquare, turreted Villa Gallio at the north end of the village was built c. 1586 by Pellegrino Tibaldi for Cardinal Tolomeo Gallio. Surrounded by a garden where there is a giant rhododendron, it is now used for exhibitions. Nearer the boat station are the very scant remains of the ivy-covered castle with its clock tower. Beyond Domaso, at the mouth of the Livo, at the extreme north end of the lake where the Mera flows in, are the villages of Gera and Sorico. The boat continues to Colico, an uninteresting town on a plain near the mouth of the Adda at the junction of the routes over the Splügen and Stelvio passes.

THE LECCO REACH OF THE LAKE

Boats ply several times daily from Bellagio to Lecco, May to October, in just over an hour. From Colico an old road with fine views skirts the water.

Lecco itself is an unattractive town. Its old metalworks have been demolished and numerous ugly new buildings have taken their place. It is, however, in a fine position. Above it rise high mountains—the Grigna group to the north with San Martino on the lake, and the Resegone to the south. The town is well known in Italy for its associations with the novelist Alessandro Manzoni (1785–1873), who lived here as a boy and whose famous novel I Promessi Sposi (The Betrothed) is set in and around Lecco.

Beyond the railway is **Villa Manzoni** (open Tues–Sun 9.30–5.30), a gloomy, austere house, bought by Manzoni's ancestors before 1621, where Manzoni lived as a boy. It contains a small museum of memorabilia and a collection of local paintings.

In the southern suburbs, beyond the railway bridge, is **Pescarenico**, a fishermen's hamlet also associated with Manzoni, with narrow streets and an attractive little piazza on the waterfront (paved in the 17th century). Here you can sometimes see the flat-bottomed covered lucie, characteristic fishing boats once used all over the lake (and named after Lucia in I Promessi Sposi). Across the main road is the church, interesting for its eccentric triangular campanile of 1472 and a 16th-century ancona with little polychrome scenes in papier mâché and wax. In front of the church is a tabernacle with friars' skulls, a reminder of the plague.

Around Lecco

The river Adda is crossed by four bridges, including the Ponte Vecchio, built by Azzone Visconti in 1336–38 and later altered and enlarged. This, the 'old bridge', was the only road bridge before 1956. The most interesting town on this reach of the lake is on the west shore, reached from Lecco by the Ponte Nuovo. This is Malgrate, a pleasant little lakeside resort with good views of Lecco backed by mountains. The huge old red silk mill on the waterfront has been restored as a conference centre.

A road leads northeast from Lecco through Ballabio, a rock-climbing centre, past a by-road for the ski resort of Piani Resinelli (1276m), with the wooded Parco Valentino (waymarked trails and a museum dedicated to the Grigne group) overlooking the lake. At the Colle di Balisio the road divides: the right-hand branch leads to the resorts of Moggio and Barzio (with skiing), and the left-hand branch traverses the Valsassina. Its principal village, Introbbio, is known for its cheeses.

Southwest of Malgrate is the Lago d'Annone. From Civate a footpath leads in just over an hour to the sanctuary of **San Pietro al Monte**, with the partly ruined church of San Pietro dating from the 10th century; it has lateral apses, 11th–12th-century mural paintings, and a remarkable baldachin above the main altar. The triapsidal oratory of San Benedetto was also built in the 10th century. Further west is the Lago di Pusiano with its poplar-grown islet.

PRACTICAL INFORMATION

GETTING AROUND

• **Airport bus:** There is a bus service linking Como to Milan Malpensa.

• **By rail:** Como and Lecco are easily reached by frequent train services from Milan, and there is a railway line that skirts the eastern shore of the lake from Lecco to Colico. From Milan to Como by the main St-Gotthard line, 35–55mins; fast Cisalpina and Intercity trains depart from the Stazione Centrale; slower trains from Porta Garibaldi station. Beyond Como the international trains go on to the frontier at Chiasso, for Lugano and the north. When planning your journey bear in mind that Como has two train stations: San Giovanni for the State Railway line to Milan, Lecco, and to Lugano and the rest of Switzerland; and Como–Lago (on the lakeside; the more convenient station for visitors) for trains on the Nord–Milano line to Milan via Saronno. From Milan to Lecco, 50–65mins; to Varenna 1hr 15mins; to Colico 1hr 40mins. Trains continue on to Sondrio and Tirano in the Valtellina (*see p. 232*).

• **By bus:** There are bus services between all the main centres around the lake, run by Trasporti Regione Lombardia (information offices in Lecco, T: 0341 367244; Como, T: 031 247111). Buses leave from Piazza Matteotti for towns on the lake, and in the province.

• **By boat and hydrofoil:** An efficient service is maintained throughout the year between Como and Colico, calling at numerous places of interest on the way (information from Como, Via per Cernobbio 18, T: 031 579211, www.navigazionelaghi.it). Tickets valid for 24hrs or for several days can be purchased. The timetable changes according to season. Most of the boats run between Como and Bellano (boats in c. 2hrs 30mins, hydrofoils in c. 1hr), while most of the hydrofoils continue to Colico (Como to Colico in c. 1hr 30mins). There is a less frequent service between Bellagio and Lecco in summer (only on holidays for the rest of the year). In the central part of the lake a service runs between Bellano (or Varenna) and Lenno. A car ferry runs frequently between Bellagio and Varenna (in 15mins), Bellagio and Cadenabbia (in 10mins), and Cadenabbia and Varenna (in 30mins). Fewer services in winter.

Boats for hire at Bellagio, Barindelli, T: 031 950834, 0368 3677844; Gilardoni, T: 031 950201; Venini, T: 031 951376. Como, Tasell, T: 031 304084; Lezzeno, Mostes, T: 031 914621; Moltrazio, Aquilini, T: 031 376120; Sala Comacina, Boat Service, T: 031 821955, 0337 384572; Tremezzo, T: 0344 40151.

INFORMATION OFFICES

Bellagio Piazza della Chiesa 14, T: 031 950204, www.lakecomo.it
Cernobbio Via Regina 33b, T: 031 510198, www.lakecomo.it
Como Piazza Cavour 17, T: 031 269712, www.lakecomo.it; Stazione San Giovanni, T: 031 267214
Lecco Via Nazario Sauro 6, T: 0341 362360, www.aptlecco.com

HOTELS

Bellagio

€€€ **Grand Hotel Villa Serbelloni**.
Ideally situated in a former villa of the
Serbelloni family, on the headland of
Bellagio with stunning views, lakeside
pool and excellent restaurant. Lakefront
rooms are fabulous, rooms on the back
are not. Open Easter–Oct. Via Roma 1,
T: 031 950216, www.villaserbelloni.it

€€ **Florence**. On Bellagio's lakefront
square, charming and elegant with a
fabulous café and restaurant (seating on
the water in summer); some rooms
have terraces, others overlook the gardens of Villa Serbelloni. Open Apr–Nov.
Piazza Mazzini 46, T: 031 950342.

€ **Silvio**. A quiet, restful place on the
lake within walking distance of Bellagio.
Closed Dec–Jan. Località Loppia, Via
Carcano 12, T: 031 950322,
www.bellagiosilvio.com

Cernobbio

€€€ **Villa d'Este**. An historic property
on the lake, with National Landmark
park, excellent restaurant and
Lombardy's friendliest bartender; only
suites and junior suites have lake views.
Open Mar–Nov. Via Regina 40, T: 031
3481, www.villadeste.it

€€ **Centrale**. Small but comfortable,
with a shady terrace on Cernobbio's
main street. Via Regina 39, T: 031
511411, www.albergo-centrale.com

€€ **Miralago**. Facing the lake, on the
square where the boats land. Open
March–Nov. Piazza Risorgimento 1, T:
031 510125, www.hotelmiralago.it

Como

€€€ **Terminus**. In a Liberty-style
building on the water, with good views
of the lake and mountains. Lungo Lario

Trieste 14, T: 031 329111, www.hotel-
terminus-como.it

€€ **Barchetta Excelsior**. On Como's
lakefront square. Piazza Cavour 1, T:
031 3221, www.hotelbarchetta.com

€€ **Como**. On the south side of the
town, with a rooftop terrace and pool.
Via Mentana 28, T: 031 266173,
www.hcomo.it

€€ **Metropole Suisse**. On the waterfront, in a building designed by
Terragni. Open Feb–Nov. Piazza Cavour
19, T: 031 269444.

€€ **Villa Fiori**. A favourite place of
Garibaldi, on the lake just outside
Como, on the road to Cernobbio. Open
Feb–Nov. Via per Cernobbio 12, T: 031
573105, info@hotelvillafiori.it

Malgrate

€€ **Il Griso**. In a lovely garden with
good views over the lake and mountains, and an excellent restaurant.
Closed Dec–Jan. Via Provinciale 51, T:
0341 202040.

Margno (above Bellano)

€ **Baitock**. A small (15 rooms) mountain inn popular with hikers and skiers.
Via Sciatori 8, T: 034 803042.

Torno

€ **Villa Flora**. On the outskirts of the
village, by the lakeside, a bit down at
heel but quiet and comfortable with
pool, terrace restaurant and lake views
from most rooms. Closed Nov–Feb. Via
Torazza 10, T: 031 419222.

Tremezzo

€ **Rusall**. Simple, family-run establish-
ment in a quiet, panoramic location.
Closed Jan-Mar. Località Rogaro Ovest,
T: 0344 40408, rusall@tiscali.it

Varenna

€€ **Du Lac**. Small and intimate, in a
former lake house. Open Mar–Nov. T:

0341 830238, www.albergodulac.com
€€ **Royal Victoria**. In a 19th-century
villa, with garden. Piazza San Giorgio 5,
T: 034 815111, www.royalvictoria.com

YOUTH HOSTELS

Como
€ **Villa Olmo**, Via Bellinzona 2, T: 031
573800, ostellocomo@tin.it
Menaggio
€ **La Primula**, Via IV Novembre 106,
T: 0344 32356,
menaggiohostel@mclink.it

RESTAURANTS

Bellagio
€€ **La Barchetta**. Restaurant offering
innovative variations on traditional
recipes. Closed Tues (except June–Sept)
and Nov–March. Salita Mella 13, T: 031
951389.
€ **Mella**. Restaurant specialising in lake
fish, with good views over the lake. Via
Jacopo Rezia 1, at San Giovanni (just
beyond the Villa Melzi gardens), T: 031
950205.
Cernobbio
€€ **Terzo Croto**. Restaurant (with
rooms) serving outstanding interpretations of local recipes. T: 031 512304.
Como
€€€ **Navedano**. Refined, romantic
place with garden seating in summer
and fresh flowers on every table in winter. Closed Tues, Jan and Aug. Via
Pannilani-Velzi, T: 031 308080.
€€ **Croto del Lupo**. Traditional
restaurant with garden. Closed Mon
and Aug. Via Pisani Dossi 17, at
Cardina, T: 031 570881.
€€ **Terrazo Perlasca**. Old regional

dishes served with a special flair. Closed
Mon and Aug. Piazza De Gasperi 8, T:
031 303936.
Lecco
€€ **Al Porticciolo 84**. Restaurant spe-
cialising in grilled fish and meats.
Closed Mon, Jan and Aug. Via Valsecchi
5/7, T: 0341 498103.
€ **Antica Osteria Casa di Lucia**.
Osteria and wine bar with a wide selec-
tion of cheese and good local dishes;
closed midday Sat, Sun and Aug. Via
Lucia 27, T: 0341 494594.
€ **Trattoria di Montalbano**. Trattoria
just outside town, with good local
cooking and outside seating in summer.
Closed Tues (except in Aug) and
Jan–Feb. Via Montalbano 30, T: 0341
496707.
Lenno
€ **Santo Stefano**. Trattoria specialising
in fish. Closed Mon and Oct–Nov.
Piazza XI Febbraio 3, T: 0344 55434.
Lierna
€€ **La Breva**. Traditional restaurant
with lakeside seating in summer. Closed
Mon evening, Tues (except June–Sept),
Nov and Jan. Via Imbarcadero 3, T:
0341 741490.
Torno
€ **Belvedere**. Trattoria offering deli-
ciously prepared home cooking and
great lake views. At the boat landing, T:
031 419100.
Tremezzo
€ **La Fagurida**. Good local cuisine,
especially polenta. Closed Mon. Via San
Martino 17, T: 0344 40676.
Rusall. Family-managed place in the
hotel of the same name, also offering
wholesome local cuisine. Closed Wed
and Jan–March. Via San Martino 2 (at
Rogaro), T: 0344 40408.

Varenna
€ **Vecchia Varenna**. Restaurant with summer service on a terrace overlooking the port. Closed Mon, Tues (in Feb–March) and Jan. Contrada Scoscesa 10, T: 0341 830793.

LOCAL SPECIALITIES

Como The town is famous for its silk, and the major mills all have outlets in or near the town. Those in town include **Mensitieri**, Viale Cavallotti 3; **Binda**, Viale Geno 6, **Mantero**, Via Volta 68; **Martinetti**, Via Torriani 4; **Ratti**, Via per Cernobbio 19; **Ricci**, Via Scalabrini 85; gift shop of the **Museo Didattico della Seta**, Via Valleggio 3. Hours vary, but most are open Tues–Fri or Sat 10–12 & 3–6.
Bellagio Here too there is a tradition of silkmaking and several good shops.
Lecco The **Nuova Casa del Formaggio**, at Via Roma 81, and

Spaccio del Parmigiano at Via Roma 13, have delicious local cheeses.
Panificio Enoteca Negri, at Corso Matteotti 65, sells excellent focaccia bread, and wine to drink with it.
Lenno The **Oleificio Vanini**, at Via Pellico 10, has extra virgin olive oil made from olives grown on the lakeshore.

FESTIVALS & MARKETS

Como *Fiera di Pasqua*, with a flea market by the walls from Maundy Thur–Easter Mon. St Abbondio, the patron saint, is celebrated 31 Aug with a livestock fair. *Il Canto delle Pietre*, music festival, May–June. *Palio del Baradello*, historical pageant, late Aug–early Sept; *Autunno Musicale*, concert series, Sept–Dec. Street markets are held Tues and Thur mornings, and all day Sat.

BERGAMO & THE BERGAMASCO

A beautiful and interesting city, Bergamo is divided into two sharply distinguished parts. The pleasant Città Bassa, laid out on a spacious plan at the end of the 19th and the beginning of the 20th centuries, has numerous squares between wide streets, as well as nearly all the hotels and the principal shops. The Città Alta (366m), the lovely old town, has a varied and attractive skyline crowning a steep hill and peaceful narrow streets. The Città Bassa and Città Alta have been connected since 1887 by funicular railway. Bergamo stands just below the first foothills of the Alps, between the valleys of the Brembo and the Serio.

HISTORY OF BERGAMO

Bergamo has been split in two since Roman times, when the *civitas* stood on the hill, the *suburbia* on the plain below. The centre of a Lombard duchy in the early Middle Ages and seat of a bishop in the 10th century, it emerged as a free commune in the 12th century. In the 14th century the Visconti and the Torriani families disputed possession of the city, and in 1408–19 Pandolfo Malatesta was its overlord. Another period of Visconti rule ended in 1428, when Venice took the town. Bergamo remained a Venetian possession until the fall of the Venetian Republic to Napoleon in 1797. From the Congress of Vienna (1815) until 1859 it was part of the Austrian empire. The Bergamasques played a prominent part in the Risorgimento and contributed the largest contingent to Garibaldi's 'Thousand' (*see p. 543*). Bergamo's most famous citizens are Bartolomeo Colleoni, the 15th-century mercenary general, and Gaetano Donizetti (1797–1848), the composer. The painters Giovanni Battista Moroni (c. 1525–78) and Palma Vecchio (c. 1480–1528) were born in the neighbourhood. Another native, the explorer Costantino Beltrami (1779–1855), discovered the source of the Mississippi in 1823.

The lower town

The Città Bassa, or lower town, was laid out at the foot of the hill on which the old city was built, in the area between the medieval *borghi*, successors of the Roman *suburbia*. The broad avenues and pleasant squares, which were laid out in the first decades of the 20th century, give it a remarkable air of spaciousness. The principal thoroughfare is Viale Vittorio Emanuele II, and its continuation, Viale Giovanni XXIII, which extends beyond the Porta Nuova with its two little Doric 'temples', opened in 1837 as the monumental entrance to the new city. Before Porta Nuova is the huge Piazza Matteotti, with the Municipio (town hall) to the left. In front is a

Piazza Vecchia and the Torre Civica.

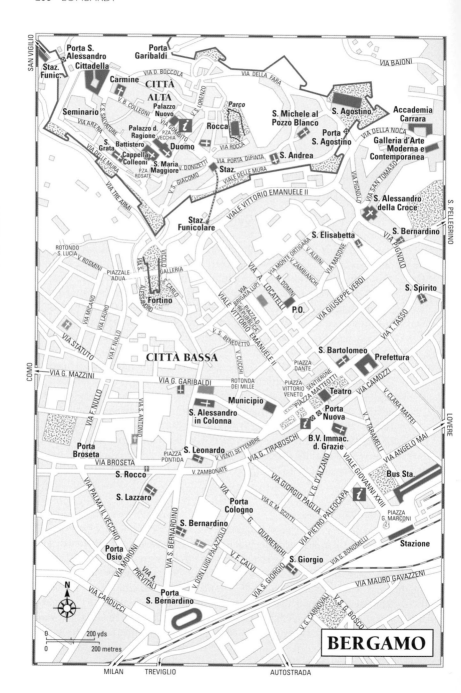

SAN VIGILIO

Porta S. Alessandro

Staz. Funic.

Cittadella

Porta Garibaldi

VIA D. BOCCOLA

Carmine

VIA DELLA FARA

VIA BAIONI

CITTÀ ALTA

Palazzo Nuovo

Seminario

V. B. COLLEONI

V. S. LORENZO

Parco

Rocca

S. Michele al Pozzo Blanco

S. Agostino

Accademia Carrara

VIA S. SALVATORE

Palazzo d. Ragione

PZA VECCHIA

Porta S. Agostino

VIA ARENA

Duomo

VIA GOMBITO

Galleria d'Arte Moderna e Contemporanea

VIA DELLA NOCA

S. Grata

Battistero

Cappella Colleoni

S. Maria Maggiore

VIA DELLE MURA

PZA ROSATE

V. DONIZETTI

VIA PORTA DIPINTA

S. Andrea

Staz.

VIA S. GIACOMO

VIALE DELLE MURA

S. Alessandro della Croce

VIA SAN TOMASO

VIA PIGNOLO

VIA TRE ARMI

Staz. Funicolare

VIALE VITTORIO EMANUELE II

S. Bernardino

VIA PIGNOLO

S. PELLEGRINO

ROTONDO S. LUCIA

V. ROSMINI

PIAZZALE ADUA

VIA S. CARLO

GALLERIA

S. CARLO

Fortino

S. Elisabetta

VIA MONTE ORTIGARA

V. ALBINI

VIA MASONE

VIA MICANO

VIA LAURO

VIA F. NULLO

S. ALESSANDRO

VIA A. LOCATELLI

VIA ZAMBIANCHI

V. M. DOMINI

P.O.

VIA GIUSEPPE VERDI

S. Spirito

VIA STATUTO

VIA BRIGATA LUPI

VIALE VITTORIO EMANUELE II

VIA BRIGATA REPUBBLICA

PIAZZA REPUBBLICA

V. S. BENEDETTO

V. CUCCHI

VIA T. TASSO

COMO

VIA G. MAZZINI

CITTÀ BASSA

VIA G. GARIBALDI

ROTONDA DEI MILLE

PIAZZA DANTE

S. Bartolomeo

Prefettura

VIA CAMOZZI

VIA F. NULLO

VIA S. ANTONIO

Municipio

PIAZZA VITTORIO VENETO

PIAZZA MATTEOTTI

SENTIERONE

Teatro

V. CLARA MAFFEI

S. Alessandro in Colonna

Porta Nuova

V. T. TARAMELLI

Porta Broseta

PIAZZA PONTIDA

S. Leonardo

V. VENTI SETTEMBRE

VIA G. TIRABOSCHI

B.V. Immac. d. Grazie

VIALE GIOVANNI XXIII

VIA ANGELO MAI

LOVERE

VIA BROSETA

V. ZAMBONATE

Bus Sta.

S. Rocco

VIA PALMA IL VECCHIO

S. Lazzaro

VIA MORONI

VIA S. BERNARDINO

Porta Cologno

VIA GIORGIO PAGLIA

VIA G. M. SCOTTI

G. QUARENGHI

VIA PIETRO PALEOCAPA

PIAZZA G. MARCONI

Stazione

Porta Osio

VIA DON LUIGI PALAZZOLO

S. Bernardino

V. F. CALVI

S. Giorgio

VIA G. BONOMELLI

VIA A. PREVITALI

N

VIA CARDUCCI

Porta S. Bernardino

VIA S. GIORGIO

V. S. G. BOSCO

VIA MAURO GAVAZZENI

V. G. CARNOVALI

0   200 yds

0   200 metres

BERGAMO

MILAN   TREVIGLIO   AUTOSTRADA

monument to the Calvi brothers (1933) with bas-reliefs by Giacomo Manzù (1908–91), sculptor of serene and fluid calm, best known for his bronze doors for St Peter's in Rome. Next to the town hall is a bank in a building of 1909 decorated by Luca Beltrami. Adjoining Piazza Matteotti to the north is the arcaded Piazza Vittorio Veneto, designed by Piacentini (1929), with the Torre dei Caduti ('Tower of the Fallen', 1924) as a war memorial. The monument to the Partisans is by Giacomo Manzù.

The wide promenade known as the *sentierone*, opened in 1762, leads (east) past the Teatro Donizetti with a façade of 1897 by Pietro Via and a late 18th-century interior, to Piazza Cavour, with gardens surrounding a monument to Donizetti himself (he was born in Bergamo in 1797). Opposite is the church of **San Bartolomeo**, with fine intarsia choir stalls and a large but poorly lit altarpiece (1516) by Lorenzo Lotto, the great Venetian painter who lived and worked in Bergamo c. 1512–26 (*see p. 213*).

Via Torquato Tasso continues past the Palazzo della Prefettura e Provincia (1870) to the church of Santo Spirito with a good interior of 1521. It contains paintings by Lorenzo Lotto, Andrea Previtali and Bergognone.

Via Pignolo, which leads left through Borgo Pignolo, is the street with the greatest number of noble houses in Bergamo, dating from the 16th–19th centuries. No. 80 once belonged to Tasso's family, and the 17th-century Palazzo Agliardi (no. 86) has a *salone* frescoed by Carlo Carlone. On the corner of Via San Giovanni is the church of San Bernardino (if closed ring at the door on the left of the façade), which contains a particularly beautiful altarpiece by Lorenzo Lotto, painted in 1521 (and restored in 1993). Further on is Sant'Alessandro della Croce with small paintings in the sacristy by Lorenzo Lotto, Andrea Previtali and Lorenzo Costa, who did his best work for noble patrons in Bologna and Mantua. Via San Tommaso continues uphill to the Accademia Carrara (*see p. 213*).

To the west of Piazza Matteotti, reached by Via Venti Settembre, a shopping street, is the old district of Borgo Sant'Alessandro (or Borgo San Leonardo). Here Piazza Pontida is still the commercial centre of the city. The interesting old Via Sant'Alessandro runs north from the piazza past the church of Sant' Alessandro in Colonna. The paintings in the interior include works by Leandro Bassano, Lorenzo Lotto and Francesco Zucco. Outside the church is a column erected in 1618 made up from Roman fragments. Via Sant'Alessandro winds northwards around an old fort before entering the upper town by a stone bridge built in 1780 through the Porta San Giacomo, a splendid 16th-century gateway in the Venetian walls.

The upper town

At the point where Viale Vittorio Emanuele II bends sharply east is the lower station of the funicular, which tunnels through the Venetian walls to the Città Alta. Here the quiet, narrow streets, attractively paved in a herringbone pattern, have many large mansions, handsome shop fronts, and some old-fashioned cafés.

The funicular brings you up to Piazza Mercato delle Scarpe, paved with small cubes of porphyry, where seven roads meet. The fountain covers a cistern built in 1486.

Upper town: the western quarter

Via Donizetti leads steeply uphill out of Piazza Mercato delle Scarpe past the **Casa dell'Arciprete** (no. 3), a Renaissance mansion of c. 1520 attributed to the local architect Pietro Isabello, with an elegant marble façade and delicate windows. It contains a small diocesan museum (*open by appointment only*).

From Via Gombito, just out of Piazza Mercato delle Scarpe, Via Solata leads to Piazza Mercato del Fieno, with two medieval towers and the former **Convent of San Francesco**, dating from the end of the 13th century, with two fine cloisters and 14th-century frescoes. Inside is a small museum of local history (*open Apr–Sept Tues–Fri 9.30–1 & 2–5.30, Sat–Sun 9–7; Oct–March Tues–Sun 9.30–1 & 2–5.30*).

The narrow old Via Gombito, with pretty old-style shop fronts, climbs up past a little piazza with a 16th-century fountain and the church of San Pancrazio, its Gothic portal decorated with 14th-century statues and a 15th-century fresco. Beyond the 12th-century Torre di Gombito (52m high) the road ends in the spacious Piazza Vecchia, the centre of the old town, with a pretty fountain (1780). On the right is Palazzo Nuovo (designed by Palladio's follower Vincenzo Scamozzi in 1611, but unfinished until the 20th century), opposite which rises Palazzo della Ragione, rebuilt in 1538–43, bearing a modern Lion of St Mark and with a meridian of 1789 beneath the portico. The massive 12th-century **Torre Civica** or Torre del Campanone (*open May–Sept 10–8 or 10; or by appointment T: 035 247116*) can be climbed (the lift is out of action). From the top, beside the three bells, the view north takes in the green fields within the walls with an old ammunition store, the hill of San Vigilio and, nearer at hand, the Cappella Colleoni, Santa Maria Maggiore and the duomo. Beyond Piazza Vecchia rises the square, medieval Torre di Gombito and the Rocca on its hill.

Beyond the arcades of Palazzo della Ragione lies the small Piazza del Duomo, crowded with fine buildings. The **cathedral**, altered in 1689, has a 19th-century west front. The St Benedict altarpiece on the first south altar is by Andrea Previtali (1524). In the south transept are an altar by Filippo Juvarra and a painting by Sebastiano Ricci. Opposite is a painting by Giovanni Battista Cignaroli. The 18th-century paintings in the apse include one by Giovanni Battista Tiepolo. The carved panels in the north transept are by Andrea Fantoni. On the second north altar is a statue of St Charles Borromeo by Giacomo Manzù. The altarpiece on the first north altar is by Giovanni Battista Moroni.

The charming little **baptistery** opposite, by Giovanni da Campione (1340), originally stood inside Santa Maria Maggiore (*described below*).

Santa Maria Maggiore and the Cappella Colleoni

Between the cathedral and the baptistery rises the church of Santa Maria Maggiore, against the south wall of which—behind a railing of 1912—is the colourful **Cappella Colleoni**. The famous mercenary general Bartolomeo Colleoni (d. 1476), having ordered the demolition of the sacristy, commissioned Giovanni Antonio Amadeo to erect his funerary chapel on this site in 1472. It is one of the finest High Renaissance works in Lombardy, although the over-lavish decorations are unconnected with the architectural forms. The elaborate carving celebrates the brilliant captain-general (who served both the Visconti and the Venetian Republic, *see p. 436*) by means of complicated allegories combining classical and biblical allusions. The charming exterior details include copies of cannon shafts (which Colleoni used for the first time in pitched battle) in the eccentric windows. The 12 statues are to be replaced by copies. The interior contains the tomb of Colleoni and that of his young daughter Medea (d. 1470), both by Giovanni Antonio Amadeo. The equestrian statue in gilded wood is by Leon and Sisto Siry (c. 1493). The tomb of Medea was transferred in 1842 from the country church of Basella, on the Crema road. The three altar statues are by Pietro Lombardo (1490). The remaining decoration of the chapel is 18th-century work, including some excellent marquetry seats, ceiling frescoes by Giovanni Battista Tiepolo, and a *Holy Family* by Angelica Kauffmann.

CAPPELLA COLLEONI

Santa Maria Maggiore, a Romanesque church begun by a certain Maestro Fredo in 1137, has a beautiful exterior. Next to the Cappella Colleoni is its north porch (1353) by Giovanni da Campione. Above the delightful arch, borne by two red marble lions, is a tabernacle with three statues of saints, including an equestrian statue of St Alexander. Above is another tabernacle with the *Madonna and Child and Saints* sculpted by Andreolo de' Bianchi (1398). The door itself is surrounded by more carving. To the left you can see the exterior of the apses, the Gothic sacristy door (northeast), also by Campione, and the exterior of the polygonal new sacristy (1485–91). Steps lead up beside the fine apse and campanile (1436) and a lane goes round to the south porch, again by Campione (1360), above which is a little tabernacle with statues by Hans von Fernach (1401).

The centrally-planned interior is decorated with splendid 16th-century stuccoes, and late-16th- and 17th-century frescoes and paintings in the vault. At the west, north and south ends are three large paintings in elaborate frames, and on the walls are fine tapestries, most of them Florentine works dating from 1583–86 to designs by Alessandro Allori. At the west end the well-preserved Flemish tapestry of the *Crucifixion* dates from 1696–98. Above it is a painting by Luca Giordano. The monument to Donizetti is by the great realist sculptor Vincenzo Vela (1820–91). The funerary monument of Cardinal Longhi is attributed to Ugo da Campione (1330).

In the south transept is a fresco of the *Tree of Life* dating from 1347, a large painting of the *Flood* by Pietro Liberi, and an altarpiece of the *Last Supper* by Francesco Bassano; and in the north transept are interesting 14th-century frescoes (including a scene in a smithy and a *Last Supper*). The two side cantorials are decorated with paintings by the local painters Il Talpino and Gian Paolo Cavagna (1595 and 1593). In the chapel to the right of the choir is an altarpiece by Antonio Boselli (1514).

At the entrance to the sanctuary are six 16th-century bronze candelabra and two 16th-century pulpits with fine bronze railings. A wooden crucifix hangs above. The choir screen has four splendid large intarsia panels (kept covered except on holidays, but shown on request) designed by Lorenzo Lotto, showing the *Crossing of the Red Sea*, the *Flood*, *Judith and Holofernes* and *David and Goliath*. There are also beautiful intarsia choir stalls in the sanctuary, and in the apse is a large curving painting of the *Assumption* by Camillo Procaccini.

Just behind the cathedral and Santa Maria Maggiore is a building dating from 1769, which was adapted in the early 19th century as the seat of an academy known as the Ateneo (it is now in very poor repair).

From the Cappella Colleoni to Piazza della Citadella

Between the Cappella Colleoni and the baptistery, steps lead up to a passageway through the ground floor of the Curia Vescovile. It has a fine arch and frescoes of the 13th–14th centuries. Beyond is the centrally-planned **Tempietto di Santa Croce** (probably dating from the 11th century, but altered in the 16th century). Steps lead down to the south porch of Santa Maria Maggiore. On the right is the pretty, cobbled Via Arena, which leads uphill past the interesting monastery wall of Santa Grata (with traces of frescoes) and an eccentric portal opposite the Istituto Musicale Donizetti (no. 9). Here is a **Donizetti Museum** (*open Sat–Sun 9.30–1 & 2.30–5.30; summer Tues–Sun 9.30–1 & 2–5.30*), founded in 1903. In a large room, decorated at the beginning of the 19th century, are manuscripts, documents, wind instruments, portraits, mementoes, etc. Also here is the piano at which the composer worked. Via Arena ends at the huge seminary building (1965); Via Salvecchio leads right to Via Salvatore (left), which continues downhill past high walls and gardens into Piazza della Cittadella (*see below*).

From Piazza Vecchia (*see above*) Via Colleoni, with attractive shops and cafés, is a continuation of Via Gombito. It passes (left) the Teatro Sociale, designed by Leopold Pollack (1803–07), and (right; no. 9) the **Luogo Pio Colleoni** (*open by appointment, T: 035 210061*), beside a little garden bequeathed by the *condottiere* to a charitable institution founded by him in 1466. On the ground floor are 15th-century detached frescoes (two of them depicting Colleoni), and a pretty vault dating from the late 15th century. Upstairs a room contains a few mementoes and a portrait of Colleoni by Giovanni Battista Moroni.

Via Colleoni next passes the church of the Carmine, rebuilt in the 15th century and again in 1730. It contains a painting by Andrea Previtali, and a finely carved 15th-century Venetian wooden ancona. The road ends in Piazza della Cittadella, with a

View over the Città Alta.

14th-century portico and two museums. The **Museo di Scienze Naturali Enrico Caffi** (open *Apr–Sept Tues–Fri 9–12.30 & 2.30–6, Sat, Sun and holidays 9–7; Oct–March Tues–Sun 9–12.30 & 2.30–5.30*) contains a well arranged collection, including a section devoted to the explorer Costantino Beltrami. The **Museo Archeologico** (*open Apr–Sept Tues–Fri 9–12.30 & 2.30–6, Sat, Sun and holidays 9–7; Oct–March Tues–Sun 9–12.30 & 2.30–6*), which originated in a collection formed by the town council in 1561, is also well arranged and has locally found material from prehistoric times to the early Christian and Lombard era. The Roman section includes epigraphs, funerary monuments, statues, mosaics, and frescoes from a house in Via Arena.

San Vigilio

Beyond the courtyard is the Torre di Adalberto, a tower probably dating from the 12th century, beside a little walled public garden. Outside the gateway is Colle Aperto, usually busy with cars and buses, with an esplanade overlooking fields that stretch to the northwest corner of the walled city (the powder store was built in the 16th century by the Venetians). Here is the well-preserved Porta Sant' Alessandro.

Just outside the gate is the station of the funicular railway (*open 10–8, every 15 minutes, taking 3 minutes; longer hours in summer*) to San Vigilio (461m). Opened in 1912, closed in 1976, but rebuilt in 1991, it runs along the walls of the Forte di San Marco. San Vigilio is a quiet little resort with several restaurants and a hotel. On the right of the upper station a cobbled lane (with a view of the Città Alta) leads uphill: by an Art Nouveau house, steps continue up left to a little public garden on the site of the castle (*open 9 or 10–dusk*) with remains of a 16th–17th-century Venetian fortress on a mound with views on every side. A number of pleasant walks can be taken in the surrounding hills (Monte Bastia and San Sebastiano); or the Città Alta can be reached on foot by descending, from the church of San Vigilio, the stepped Via dello Scorlazzone and (left) Via Sudorno.

Also outside Porta Sant'Alessandro, on the hillside at Via Borgo Canale 14, is **Donizetti's birthplace** (*open by appointment only, T: 035 244483*).

Upper town: the east

From Piazza Mercato delle Scarpe (*see above*) a road is signposted uphill for the Rocca (*open Tues–Sat 9, 9.30 or 10–dusk*), the remains of a **castle** built by the Visconti in 1331 and reinforced by the Venetians in the 15th century (restored in 1925). It contains a Risorgimento museum (*Tues–Fri 9.30–1 & 2–5.30, Sat–Sun 9–5.30*) and incorporates the little church of Sant'Eufemia, documented from 1006. Outside the walls is a public park, with conifers, cypresses and a few palm trees, laid out as a war memorial with weaponry used in the First World War. There is a path right round the castle and the fine view takes in Santa Caterina and the lower town and a hillside with the orchard and terraced gardens of Palazzo Moroni, while to the west there is a splendid panorama of the upper city, with its towers and domes.

Via Porta Dipinta (for centuries the main approach to the town) descends from Piazza Mercato delle Scarpe. At no. 12 is the 17th-century **Palazzo Moroni**, still owned by the family (*usually open at weekends mid-April to mid-July; enquire at the information office*) with good windows and a handsome portal and a grotto in the courtyard. It has a very large garden behind, which covers about a twelfth of the entire area of the Città Alta. The interior has 17th-century frescoes by Gian Giacomo Barbelli on the staircase and on the ceilings of the piano nobile. The furnished rooms have 15th–19th-century paintings, including three by Giovanni Battista Moroni, and works by Previtali, Fra Galgario and Hayez. Opposite the palace is a little garden with a view of the lower town. The Neoclassical church of **Sant'Andrea** (*open Sun morning*) has an *Enthroned Madonna* by Moretto, pupil of Titian and master of Moroni. Further on is **San Michele al Pozzo Bianco** with a fine interior, with 12th–14th-century frescoes in the nave and, in the chapel on the left of the sanctuary, a fresco cycle of the *Life of the Virgin* by Lorenzo Lotto.

The road now skirts the Prato della Fara, a pleasant green with an attractive row of houses. At the end is the former church of Sant'Agostino (which has been undergoing restoration for years) with a Gothic façade. It has a green-and-red vault dating from the 15th century and numerous interesting fresco fragments.

From the church, Viale della Fara leads above the northern stretch of walls, overlooking open country, in which you can see defence banks. Via San Lorenzo leads away from the walls to the church of San Lorenzo, next to which is the **Fontana del Lantro** (*opened by a group of volunteers who restored it in 1992; enquire at the information office*). This 16th-century cistern, fed by two springs, was built at the same time as the city walls. The water source was already known by the year 928, and the name is thought to come from *atrium* or from *later*, referring to the milky colour of the water as it gushes out of the spring. There is a walkway with a view of the cistern with its 16th-century vault pierced by holes through which buckets were drawn up. A second cistern dates from the 17th century.

Beside the church of Sant'Agostino is the Porta Sant'Agostino near a little public garden. There is a good view of the Venetian walls (begun 1561–88), which still encircle the upper town. Off Via Vittorio Emanuele is the entrance to the **Cannoniera di San Michele** (*open on special occasions and by appointment, T: 035 251233*). One of about 27 such defences in the walls, this protected the Porta Sant'Agostino. A tunnel leads down to a hall, used by the soldiers, which still contains cannon balls. You can see the two holes (now blocked) used for positioning the cannon, as well as a passageway—high enough for a horse—which leads outside the walls. The limestone has formed into stalactites.

LORENZO LOTTO IN BERGAMO

Lorenzo Lotto (1480–1556) is a late Renaissance painter known for his perceptive portraits and mystical paintings of religious subjects. In the earlier years of his life he lived at Treviso, and, although biographer Giorgio Vasari says he trained with Giorgione and Titian in the Venetian workshop of Giovanni Bellini, he always remained somewhat apart from the main Venetian tradition. In 1509 he was called to Rome by Pope Julius II; afterwards he lived in Bergamo, where he worked until 1525. After that date he travelled to Venice, Treviso and Bergamo again before retiring to the monastery of Loreto, in the Marche, where he died. Though now considered one of the most individual painters of the Renaissance, his personal records suggest that he enjoyed little material success. You can see his works in churches throughout Bergamo (San Bartolomeo, Santo Spirito, San Bernardino, Sant'Alessandro della Croce, Sant'Alessandro in Colonna, Santa Maria Maggiore, San Michele al Pozzo Bianco), and in the Galleria dell'Accademia Carrara.

The Galleria dell'Accademia Carrara

Open Tues–Sun 10–1 & 3–6.45; T: 035 39964.
The building was purchased by Count Giacomo Carrara for his gallery and academy, both founded in 1780. The Venetian school is particularly well represented. There are long-term plans to re-hang the works by collections rather than chronologically. In the courtyard is a sculpture by Giacomo Manzù. The fine collection of prints and drawings, especially important for the Lombard and Venetian schools, is open to scholars by special request. The seven rooms on the first floor (*usually closed, but opened with special permission*) contain 15th–17th-century paintings (Lombard and Veneto masters). The main collection is exhibited on the second floor.

Room 1: Works by Bonifacio Bembo, Antonio Vivarini and Jacopo Bellini (*Madonna and Child*).

Room 2: Works by Alesso Baldovinetti (a self-portrait in fresco), Sandro Botticelli (including a *Portrait of Giuliano de' Medici*, one of several versions of this subject), Donatello (a relief), Francesco Botticini, Francesco Pesellino, Benedetto da Maiano, Fra'Angelico (and his school), Pisanello (*Portrait of Lionello d'Este*) and Lorenzo Monaco.

Room 3: Works by Jacobello di Antonello (a copy of 1480 of a lost painting by the father of Antonello da Messina), Bartolomeo Vivarini, Pietro de Saliba, Giovanni Bellini (*Pietà, Madonna Lochis, Madonna di Alzano, Portrait of a Young Man*), Marco Basaiti, Andrea Mantegna (*Madonna and Child*), Vincenzo Catena, Lorenzo Lotto, Carlo Crivelli (*Madonna and Child*), and small works by Gentile Bellini and Lazzaro Bastiani.

Room 4: Lorenzo Costa, Gian Francesco Bembo and Bergognone.

Room 5: Andrea Previtali and Marco Basaiti.

Room 6: Lorenzo Lotto (*Mystic Marriage of St Catherine, Holy Family with St Catherine*, 1533), Giovanni Cariani (*Portrait of Giovanni Benedetto Caravaggi*), Palma Vecchio and Titian.

Room 7: El Greco (attributed), Jacopo Bassano, and Gaudenzio Ferrari.

Room 8: Portraits by the Florentine school, Marco Basaiti and Pier Francesco Foschi.

Room 9: Contains a fine series of portraits by Giovanni Battista Moroni, including *Old Man with a Book*.

Room 10: Dürer, Master of the St Ursula Legend, Jean Clouet (portrait of *Louis of Clèves*).

Room 11: Portraits by the local painter Carlo Ceresa and works by Guercino and Sassoferrato.

Room 12: Portraits by the local painter Fra'Galgario, and beyond this three small rooms with 19th-century works by Il Piccio, Giuseppe Pelliza da Volpedo (*Allegorical Portrait of a Woman*) and Francesco Hayez.

Room 13: Flemish and Dutch paintings, including one by Rubens, and a portrait by Velázquez.

Room 14: Francesco Zuccarelli, Piero Longhi and Piazzetta.

Room 15: The Venetian school, including Francesco Guardi, Giovanni Battista Tiepolo and Canaletto.

Across the road, a 14th-century monastery which was transformed into the Camozzi barracks has been partially restored by Vittorio Gregotti as an exhibition centre. Another part of the building is to be used to display the permanent collection of 20th-century works.

The nearby **Galleria d'Arte Moderna e Contemporanea**, with its entrance at Via San Tommaso 53, (*open Apr–Sept Tues–Sun 10–1 & 3–6.45; Oct–March Tues–Sun 9.30–1 & 2.30–5.45; during special exhibitions, Tues–Sun 10–7, Thur 10–10*) hosts a small but beautiful collection of modern Italian art and temporary exhibitions of 19th- and 20th-century art.

THE BERGAMASCO

The Bergamasco, the traditional territory of Bergamo, consists of two main valleys, the Valle Brembana and the Valle Seriana, in the mountains north of Bergamo (*see map overleaf*). The lower reaches of the valleys are industrial, but the higher regions are prettier with small ski resorts. The interesting churches in these two valleys, and the castle of Malpaga on the plain south of Bergamo, are best reached in a day from Bergamo—preferably by car, as they are not well served by bus.

The Valle Brembana

The lower part of this verdant valley north of Bergamo runs through part of the Parco Regionale dei Colli di Bergamo. Here the village of **Ponteranica** has a fine parish church containing a polyptych by Lorenzo Lotto. Valcalepio wine is produced in the hills of the Valle Imagna, which branches west.

 Almenno San Bartolomeo and **Almenno San Salvatore** are two neighbouring municipalities. In the former is the **Museo del Falegname**, a private museum dedicated to the work of carpenters, with a collection of tools (from the 17th century), reconstructed artisans' workshops, bicycles and puppets. In the latter is the Pieve di San Salvatore (or Madonna del Castello), marked by a tall campanile, above the River Brembo (in which you can see a few remains of a large Roman bridge destroyed in a flood). This is the oldest church in Almenno and is thought to have been founded c. 755. The interior (key at the priest's house next door), altered in the 12th century, has a fine 12th-century pulpit in sandstone with the symbols of the Evangelists. The sanctuary has Ionic capitals and frescoes (c. 1150). The ancient columns in the crypt date from before the 11th century. The church adjoins the 16th century Santuario della Madonna del Castello, which has a delightful early-16th-century ciborium over the high altar, with paintings of sibyls attributed to Andrea Previtali, and an altarpiece by Gian Paolo Cavagna.

 Close by (5-minute walk) is the large 12th-century Basilica di San Giorgio, with a good exterior. The whale bone hanging in the nave, dating from the Pliocene era, was found nearby. The most interesting frescoes are those high up—and difficult to see—on the inside of the nave arches (on the right): they date from the late 13th or early 14th century.

 Also outside Almenno San Salvatore is the **church of San Nicola** (or Santa Maria della Consolazione), next to the former convent of the Agostiniani, founded in 1486. It has an attractive interior, with stone vaulting supporting a painted wood roof, and side chapels beneath a matroneum. It contains 16th-century frescoes by Antonio Boselli, and an altarpiece of the *Trinity* by Andrea Previtali.

 Outside Almenno San Bartolomeo is the little circular church of **San Tomé**, one of the best Romanesque buildings in Lombardy (*usually open at weekends spring–Oct; otherwise the key is kept at a house nearby—no. 21*). Excavations in the area have revealed remains of tombs dating from the 1st and the 9th centuries, but the date of the church is still under discussion. It is now generally thought to be an 11th-century building,

although the apse and presbytery may have been added later. The nun's door connected the church to a fortified convent. It was restored in 1892. The beautiful interior has an ambulatory and above it a matroneum (which can be reached by stairs) beneath a delightful cupola and lantern lit by four windows. The capitals are decorated with sirens, eagles, etc.

San Pellegrino Terme has famous mineral water springs. It is an elegant spa town, laid out at the beginning of the 20th century: the grand Art Nouveau buildings include the Palazzo della Fonte and the former Casinò Municipale.

The Val Taleggio, branching west, is noted for its cheese. In the main valley is the remarkable medieval village of **Cornello**, which was the 14th-century home of the Tasso family, who are supposed to have run a European postal service from here. Piazza Brembana is a summer resort and a base for climbs in the mountains. **Serina**, northeast of San Pellegrino, was the birthplace of Palma Vecchio (*see below*), a polyptych by whom is in the sacristy of the church.

The Valle Seriana

This is the principal valley in the Bergamesque Alps, and is mainly industrial, with silk and cotton mills and cement works, but the upper reaches are unspoilt. The churches have some fine works by the Fantoni family of sculptors and carvers, who lived and worked in the valley in the 15th–19th centuries (Andrea Fantoni made the elaborate confessional in Santa Maria Maggiore in Bergamo).

Alzano Lombardo is noted for its wool workers. The basilica of San Martino was rebuilt in 1670 and has a splendid interior designed by Girolomo Quadrio, with coupled marble columns and stuccoes by Angelo Sala. It has a pulpit by Andrea Fantoni and a painting by Andrea Appiani. The three sacristies have superb carvings and intarsia work, beautifully restored in 1992. The first sacristy has Baroque walnut cupboards carved by Grazioso Fantoni (1679–80), while the second sacristy (1691–93) has even better carving in walnut and boxwood by his son Andrea Fantoni and his three brothers. Above are statuettes showing the martyrdom of saints and apostles, and in the ovals the story of Moses and scenes from the New Testament. The seated statues represent the Virtues; the prie-dieu has a *Deposition*, also by Fantoni; and the stuccoes are by Girolamo Sala. The intarsia (1700–17) in the third sacristy is partly by Giovanni Battista Caniana; the barrel vault has more stuccoes by Sala.

At **Olera** the parish church contains a polyptych by Cima da Conegliano. **Albino**, an industrial village, has a *Crucifixion* by Giovanni Battista Moroni (born nearby at Bondo Petello) in the church of San Giuliano.

Vertova has a prominent 17th-century parish church surrounded by a portico. On the wooded hillside above you can see the sanctuary of San Patrizio, a 16th-century building with an earlier crypt.

The valley now becomes distinctly pretty. **Gandino**, an ancient little town noted for its carpets, was the birthplace of the sculptor Bartolomeo Bon the Elder. The basilica of Santa Maria Assunta was rebuilt in 1623–30 and has a very fine interior on an interesting central plan. The dome was finished in 1640 and the trompe l'oeil fresco was added in 1680. The bronze balustrade dates from 1590. Giacomo Ceruti painted the spandrels above the arches, and the organ was built by Adeodato Bossi in 1868 (in an earlier case by Andrea Fantoni). Outside the church a little baptistery was erected in 1967, and beside it is the Museo della Basilica, first opened in 1928 (*now open by appointment, T: 035 745567*). It contains two series of Flemish tapestries (1580), a silver altar (begun in 1609 and finished in the 19th century) and an organ made by Perolini in 1755. On the first floor are vestments, church silver, a 16th-century German sculpture of Christ on the Cross (with movable arms) and ancient textiles.

TWO LOCAL ARTISTS

Giovanni Battista Moroni (c. 1525–78)
Moroni is known above all for his quiet, dignified portraits. These very particular works—he was one of the few Italian Renaissance artists to make portraiture his speciality—combine the realism of German painters like Holbein with a Venetian sense of light, like that in the portraits of Titian, who personally commended Moroni's work. The strength of Moroni's style lies in the unforced poses of his sitters, the strong sense of composition, and a restrained treatment of texture and colour. Moroni's portraits are mostly of the petty aristocracy and merchant middle class of Bergamo. There are works in the city's churches and museums, of course, but also in the major public collections of Europe and North America. One of his best-known works is *The Tailor* (c. 1571), now in the National Gallery, London. Milan's Pinacoteca Ambrosiana holds another exceptional portrait (*see p. 127*).

Palma il Vecchio (Jacopo Negretti, c. 1480–1528)
This High Renaissance painter is noted for the craftsmanship of his religious and mythological works. Born near Bergamo, when the city and its territory belonged to the Republic of Venice, he naturally gravitated to the capital. He may have studied under Giovanni Bellini, the originator of the Venetian High Renaissance style, and he was influenced by Titian, Giorgione and Lotto. Palma specialised in the type of contemplative religious picture known as the *sacra conversazione* (a group of historically unrelated sacred personages grouped together). His masterpiece is the *St Barbara and Four Saints* in Santa Maria Formosa, Venice, but he too is well represented in major European and American museums.

Clusone is a small resort in the Valle Seriana. The medieval town hall has a remarkable astronomical clock made by Pietro Fanzago in 1583, and numerous remains of frescoes. Above is the grand basilica of Santa Maria Assunta, built in 1688–1716 by Giovanni Battista Quadrio, preceded by an impressive terrace with statues added at the end of the 19th century. The high altar has sculptures by Andrea Fantoni (who also designed the pulpit) and an *Assumption* by Sebastiano Ricci. To the left is the

Oratorio dei Disciplini with a remarkable fresco on the exterior depicting the *Dance and Triumph of Death* (1485), fascinating for its iconography. Inside (unlocked by the sacristan) are well-preserved frescoes showing small, colourful scenes of the *Passion*, dating from 1480. Over the choir arch is a fresco of the *Crucifixion* (1471). The life-size polychrome wood group of the *Deposition* is attributed to the school of Fantoni. Further downhill are the grand Palazzo Fogaccia, built in the early 18th century by Giovanni Battista Quadrio, with a garden; and the church of Sant'Anna, with 15th- and 16th-century frescoes inside and out and a fine altarpiece by Domenico Carpinoni, in a lovely frame.

Just outside Clusone is **Rovetta**, where the house and workshop of the Fantoni family of sculptors, who were born here, is now a little museum, and the church has an early altarpiece by Giovanni Battista Tiepolo.

On the plain

East of Bergamo is **Trescore Balneario**, a small spa with sulphur and mud baths. A chapel (shown on request) in the park of the Suardi villa at Novale contains frescoes by Lorenzo Lotto (1524). At **Credaro** the church of San Giorgio has another chapel, with more frescoes carried out a year later by Lotto.

South of Bergamo, the castle at **Malpaga** (*open for guided tours on holidays 2.30–dusk; otherwise by appointment; T: 035 840003*) is approached by a road bordered on either side by narrow canals regulated by locks connected to the Serio river. It is set in the centre of an agricultural estate, surrounded by farm buildings with double loggias. The 14th-century castle, on the extreme western limit of the land controlled by the Venetian Republic, was bought as a residence by Bartolomeo Colleoni in 1456, the year after he became captain of the Venetian army. He heightened the castle in order to protect it against firearms (you can see the castellations of the first castle in the walls) and built the pretty loggias. The castle is particularly interesting for its frescoes, carried out in Colleoni's own lifetime and in the following century. The main entrance has 16th-century frescoes of courtiers, and the courtyard has frescoes commissioned by Colleoni's grandchildren in the early 16th century to illustrate his achievements in battle: the siege of Bergamo in 1437 includes a good view of the Città Alta, and under the loggia is a scene of the great soldier's last battle in 1497 (Colleoni is shown in a red hat). The Sala dei Banchetti contains more 16th-century frescoes, here showing the visit of King Christian I of Denmark to the castle in 1474 on his way to Rome (the soldiers in white-and-red uniform are those of Colleoni). The reception room upstairs retains its original 15th-century frescoes (in poor condition), with courtly scenes in the International Gothic style. Colleoni died at the age of 80, in the bedroom that has a 15th-century *Madonna and Child with Saints* in a niche.

At **Treviglio**, an agricultural and industrial centre, the Gothic church of San Martino contains a beautiful polyptych by Bernardino Zenale and Bernardino Butinone (1485). Santa Maria delle Lacrime is a Renaissance building with another triptych by Butinone. Here in 1915, while in hospital with jaundice, Mussolini was married (probably bigamously) to Donna Rachele.

Caravaggio was the probable birthplace of the painter Michelangelo Merisi (1571–1610), known to the world as Caravaggio. An avenue leads to a large sanctuary dedicated to the Madonna, who is said to have appeared to a peasant woman here in 1432 on the site of a miraculous spring. The domed church was enlarged by Pellegrino Tibaldi in 1575 and is visited by thousands of pilgrims every year (festival on 26 May). There is a little Museo Navale (*open Sat, except Aug, 3–6*).

On the other side of the Serio river is **Romano di Lombardia**, with an interesting urban plan. The medieval Palazzo della Comunità was altered in later centuries. The church of Santa Maria Assunta, reconstructed in the 18th century by Giovanni Battista Caniana, contains a *Last Supper* by Giovanni Battista Moroni.

PRACTICAL INFORMATION

GETTING AROUND

• **By bus:** Long-distance buses leave from the bus station in front of the railway station for the Bergamasque valleys and places in the province (SAB), and for Milan (Piazza Castello). Country buses from the bus station in Piazza Marconi to Milan, Como, Cremona, Lodi and points throughout the province.
• **By rail:** Trains link Bergamo with Milan Centrale, Porta Garibaldi or Lambrate stations (journey time 1hr) via Treviglio Ovest; or 1hr 15mins via Monza and Carnate-Usmate, where a change is usually necessary. Branch lines to Lecco, 40mins; Brescia, 50mins (connecting with Intercity and Eurostar trains on the main Venice–Milan line); Cremona, c. 90mins. Railway station at Piazza Marconi in the lower town.

TRANSPORT IN BERGAMO

Funicular: Runs 7am to half past midnight every 10–15mins (in connection with bus no. 1 to and from the railway station: same ticket), used by residents as well as visitors.
Buses: From Bergamo station along Viale Papa Giovanni through Piazza Matteotti (the centre of the lower town), Viale Roma and Viale Vittorio Emanuele II to the funicular station for the upper town (same ticket). Also through the lower town to the funicular station and through the upper town to Colle Aperto.
Car parking: In the upper town (except on Sun afternoon, when the upper town is totally closed to cars) in Piazza Mercato del Fieno. In the lower town, Piazzale della Malpensata, otherwise numerous pay car parks.

INFORMATION OFFICES

Bergamo (Upper town) Vicolo Aquila Nera 3, T: 035 242226. (Lower town) Viale Vittorio Emanuele 20, T: 035 213185, www.apt.bergamo.it
Informagiovani: Via Paleocapa 2, T: 035 238187.
San Pellegrino Terme Viale Papa Giovanni XXIII 18, T: 0345 21020, www.apt.bergamo.it

HOTELS

Bergamo (Lower town)
€€€ **Excelsior San Marco**, Modern and efficient, with a roof garden. Piazzale Repubblica 6, T: 035 366111, www.hotelsanmarco.it
€€ **Arli**, Simple but comfortable. Largo Porta Nuova 12, T: 035 222014, arli@spm.it
(Upper town)
€ **Agnello d Oro**. In a historic 17th-century building. Via Gombito 22, T: 035 249883.

Clusone
€ **Erica** Small and cosy. Closed Feb–March. Viale Vittorio Emanuele II, T: 0346 21667.

San Pellegrino Terme
€ **Ruspinella**. Small, warm and friendly, on the outskirts of the town. Closed Sept. Via De' Medici 47, T: 0345 21333.
€€ **Terme**. A quiet, restful place with a large garden. Open May–Oct. Via Villa 26, T: 0345 21125.

YOUTH HOSTEL

Bergamo
€ **Nuovo Ostello di Bergamo**, Via Galileo Ferraris 1, T: 035 361724/343038, hostelbg@libero.it

RESTAURANTS

Bergamo
€€€ **Lio Pellegrini**, Restaurant offering creative cuisine. Via San Tommaso 47; T: 035 247813. Closed Mon, midday Tues, Jan and Aug.
€€ **Dell'Angelo–Taverna del Colleoni**. Restaurant in a historic build-

ing, serving regional dishes with an innovative twist. Closed Mon and Aug. Piazza Vecchia 7, T: 035 231991.
€€ **Il Pianone**. Traditional restaurant with summer seating on a panoramic terrace. Closed Wed, midday Thur and Jan–Feb. Vicolo al Pianone, T: 035 216016.
€ **Antica Hosteria del Vino Buono**. *Osteria* serving Bergamasque delicacies. Closed Mon (except in summer). Piazza Mercato delle Scarpe at Via Donizetti, T: 035 247993.
€ **Antica Trattoria della Colombina**. Traditional trattoria with Liberty-style dining room and summer seating outside. Closed Mon. Via Borgo Canale 12, T: 035 261402.
€ **Bar Donizetti**. Wine bar in the upper town serving light meals. Closed Dec–Jan. Via Gombito 17a, T: 035 242661.
€ **Da Ornella**. Trattoria serving dishes from the Valle Brembana. Closed Thur and midday Fri, July and Dec. Via Gombito 15, T: 035 232736.
€ **La Cantina**. *Osteria* offering the best of Bergamasque cuisine. Closed Sun. Via Ghislanzoni 3, T: 035 237146.
Albino (Abbazia)
€€ **Il Beccofino**. Traditional restaurant known for its vegetable terrines, stuffed quail and beef stew with Cabernet. Closed Sun evening, Mon, Aug and Jan. Via Mazzini 200, T: 035 773900.
€ **Trattoria della Civetta**. Trattoria offering outstanding mushroom dishes in season. Closed Tues. Via Lunga 89–91, T: 035 770797.
Almè
€€ **Frosio**. Excellent fish restaurant in a historic palace with garden. Closed Wed and Aug. Piazza Unità 1, T: 035

541633.

Costa di Serina (Gazzo)

€ **La Peta**. Farm serving delicious country lunches and giving a part of the revenues to charity. Closed Mon–Thur (except in summer) and Jan. Don't leave without sampling their olive oil, aromatic vinegars, honey, jams and vegetable preserves. Via Peta 3, T: 0345 97955.

Mozzo

€€ **La Caprese**. Trattoria offering excellent fish and seafood. Closed Sun evening, Mon, Dec and Aug. Via Crocette 38, T: 035 611148.

Palazzolo Sull'Oglio

€€ **Osteria della Viletta**. *Osteria* serving excellent traditional fare. Closed Mon–Tues, Aug and Jan. Via Marconi 104, T: 030 7401899.

Pontida

€ **Hosteria La Marina**. *Osteria* offering good home-made *foiade* (pasta cut in squares, usually with a mushroom sauce) and *risotti* as well as other traditional dishes. Closed Tues, Aug and Sept. Via Bonanomi 7, T: 035 795063.

Trescore Balneario

€ **Conca Verde**. Trattoria known for its cheese-and-walnut crêpes, pappardelle with rabbit sauce, potato tortelli and other fine pasta dishes. Closed midday Sat, Mon and Tues evening, Aug–Sept and Jan. Via Croce 3, T: 035 940290.

€€ **Della Torre**. Restaurant with rooms, serving regional specialities. Piazza Cavour 26, T: 035 941365.

REGIONAL SPECIALITIES

Bergamo For *taleggio*, *formmai de mut* and other local cheeses, try **Ol Forgamer** at Piazzale Oberdan 2. **Pasticceria Jean Paul**, at Via Moroni 361, has wonderful marrons glacés.

MARKETS & FESTIVALS

Bergamo Antiques market in Piazza Cittadella, third Sun of the month. *Celebrazioni di Mezza Quaresima*, Lenten festival with a bonfire, etc. Bergamo Film Meeting, March. *Immagini–Appuntamento con la Danza*, dance festival, Teatro Donizetti, Feb–April. Opera season is Sept–Oct; a Donizetti festival is held every autumn.

Clusone and neighbouring towns, *Clusone Jazz*, jazz festival, Sept.

Martinengo International Sacred Music Festival, Sept.

Trescore Trescore in Blues, blues festival, June.

Carnival celebrations in towns and villages throughout the province. *Andar per Musica*, music series in towns and villages throughout the province, June–Sept. *A Scena Aperta*, open-air theatre around the province, July–Aug. *Musiche di Natale*, Christmas concerts in Bergamo and throughout the province, Dec. *Il Canto delle Pietre*, sacred and secular medieval music festival in towns throughout the province, May–Oct. *Gli Organi Storici della Lombardia*, organ music series in churches, May–Oct.

BRESCIA, LAGO D'ISEO & THE VAL CAMONICA

Situated at the mouth of the Val Trompia, Brescia has always enjoyed an abundance of water and still today it is a city of fountains. It is also the second most important industrial town in Lombardy after Milan, and has long been known for its production of arms and cutlery.

The province of Brescia includes the Val Camonica in the north, famous for its prehistoric rock carvings, the Lago d'Iseo, the smaller Lago d'Idro, the Franciacorta winemaking district, and several mountain valleys with ski resorts.

BRESCIA

Modern Brescia extends in a haphazard manner around the historic city centre, dominated by the old castle on its little knoll. It has interesting Roman remains, important Lombard relics, a beautiful Renaissance building known as the Loggia, and numerous churches with paintings by the early 16th-century artist Moretto.

NB: This chapter is covered by the map on p. 216.

HISTORY OF BRESCIA

Just who founded Brescia is a mystery. Legend speaks—or rather, whispers—of the Ligurians; historians point to Gaulish Celts. Certainly by the 3rd century BC the city had come under Roman influence, and you can still see traces of the criss-cross Roman street plan in the old city centre. Reduced to rubble by Goths and Visigoths, the Roman colony of Brixia re-emerged into prominence under the 8th-century Lombard king Desiderius, who was born in the neighbourhood. The city was a member of the Lombard League, but in 1258 it was captured by the tyrant Ezzelino da Romano. Later it was contested by a number of powerful families: the Milanese Torriani and Visconti, the Veronese Scaligeri, and Pandolfo Malatesta; but from 1426 to 1797 it prospered under Venetian suzerainty. Between 1509 and 1516 it was twice captured by the French under Gaston de Foix. In March 1849 it held out for ten days against the notoriously ruthless Austrian general, Baron von Haynau (nicknamed the 'hyena of Brescia').

Piazza della Vittoria and the Loggia

The wide, arcaded Corso Zanardelli, together with the adjoining Corso Palestro and Via delle X Giornate, can be regarded as the centre of the town. **Piazza della Vittoria**, designed by Marcello Piacentini (1932), is built in grey marble and white stone and presents an interesting example of the kind of rhetorical Modernism that was dear to the Fascist regime. The red marble Arengario, a rostrum for public speaking, has bas-reliefs by Antonio Maraini. At the north end is the striped post office, near which, but hidden by a war memorial, is the church of Sant'Agata, built c. 1438–72. In the attractive interior is an apse fresco of the *Crucifixion* (1475; attributed to Andrea Bembo).

An archway under the Monte di Pietà (with a loggia of 1484 and an addition of 1597), behind the post office, leads to the harmonious Piazza della Loggia. On the left rises the **Loggia**, or Palazzo Pubblico, a beautiful Renaissance building with exquisite sculptural detail. The ground floor was built between 1492 and 1508, the upper storey between 1554 and 1574. The architect is unknown, although Jacopo Sansovino, Galeazzo Alessi and Andrea Palladio are all thought to have been involved. It was restored in 1914. On the right of the Loggia is a fine 16th-century portal.

Above the northeast end of the square rises the Porta Bruciata, a fragment of the oldest city wall. The arcade at the east end was the scene of a brutal political murder in 1974: eight people lost their lives and over a hundred were injured in a bomb blast. The memorial is by Carlo Scarpa.

The new and old cathedrals

Beneath the Torre dell'Orologio (c. 1547) a passageway leads right to Piazza Paolo VI, with a pretty row of buildings lining its east side. The local inhabitants gravitate here in summer when it is the coolest place in the town; for the rest of the year it remains comparatively deserted.

The **duomo nuovo** (new cathedral), begun in 1604 by the local architect Giovanni Battista Lantana on the site of the old 'summer cathedral' of San Pietro de Dom, was completed only in 1914. The elaborate white marble interior contains a wooden 15th-century crucifix, and the fine tomb (1504) of the bishop-saint Apollonius with beautiful carving attributed to Maffeo Olivieri. The Mannerist Zorzi Chapel has an altarpiece by Palma il Giovane.

The Romanesque **Rotonda or duomo vecchio** (old cathedral) is sometimes closed in winter; ask at the duomo nuovo to be let in. This is an extremely interesting building of the 11th or early 12th century, with a central rotunda supported on eight pillars (the transepts and choir, at the east end, were added in the 15th century). The church was built above the 6th-century basilica of Santa Maria Maggiore, scattered remains of which have survived.

Inside, in the south transept, is an elaborate painting by Francesco Maffei, the *Translation of the Patron Saints from the Castle to the Cathedral*. Above the altar opposite is a curious 15th-century fresco of the *Flagellation*. In the presbytery are two paintings by Moretto, and over the high altar is an *Assumption*, also by him. Three more works by Moretto decorate the north transept. The contents of the treasury here are displayed only on the last Friday in March and on 14 September. They include a Byzantine cross-reliquary (with a base by Bernardino delle Croci, 1487) and the *Croce del Campo*, a crucifix dating from the 12th century. Protected by glass in the pavement is a mosaic fragment of the apse of the 8th-century Basilica di San Filastrio, burned down in 1097 with the exception of the crypt. You can see other fragments of the mosaic pavement beneath the floor on the west side of the rotunda. In the ambulatory of the rotunda is the tomb of Bishop De Dominicis (d. 1478). The ancient stairs which led up to the campanile (destroyed in 1708) survive.

On the left of the duomo nuovo is the **Broletto**, a fine Lombard town hall of 1187–1230, now serving as the prefecture. The exterior preserves its original appearance; in the courtyard one loggia is a Baroque addition. Frescoes attributed to Gentile da Fabriano were found in the Cappella Ducale here in 1986. Beyond the sturdy, battlemented Torre del Popolo (11th century), the north part of the Broletto incorporates the little church of Sant'Agostino, the west front of which has early 15th-century terracotta ornamentation with two lion gargoyles.

Moretto da Brescia (c. 1498–1554)
Moretto was born in Brescia and mainly active in and around his native city. His master was Titian. The bulk of his output was religious; though what he is really famous for are his portraits. Moretto might have been the first Italian painter to produce full-length portaits of a single sitter—a custom that had developed in Germany, especially with Cranach, but that was untried in Italy. His most famous painting is his *Portrait of a Gentleman* (National Gallery, London). In Brescia his works can be seen in the church of San Clemente, where he is buried, and in the duomo vecchio (*see opposite*). Moroni (*see p. 218*) was his pupil. Many of Moretto's religious works were made in collaboration with Floriano Ferramola, a competent but conservative local painter.

Roman Brescia

The imposing **Capitolium**, east of the Broletto, is a Roman temple erected by Vespasian (AD 73) which stands on a high stylobate approached by steps, 15 of which are original, and which has a hexastyle pronaos of Corinthian columns with, behind, a colonnade of three columns on each side. The three cellae were probably dedicated to the Capitoline Trinity (Jupiter, Juno and Minerva). The temple was excavated in 1823–26 and reconstructed in brick in 1939–50. Beneath it is a republican sanctuary (*open only by special permission*), dating from after 89 BC, with mosaics of small uncoloured tesserae.

The temple stood at the north end of the Roman forum, of which remains of porticoes can be seen in the piazza, beside a stretch of the paved decumanus maximus. On the right of the temple are the neglected remains of a Roman amphitheatre.

The **Museo Romano** (*closed at the time of writing*), founded in 1826, is arranged in the cellae of the temple and in a building behind it. In the cellae are inscriptions and mosaics. The museum collection includes a Greek amphora (c. 510 BC), Gaulish silver horse-trappings (3rd century BC), an Italic bronze helmet and a marble head of an athlete (5th century BC), Roman terracottas and glass, Lombard arms and bronzes and,

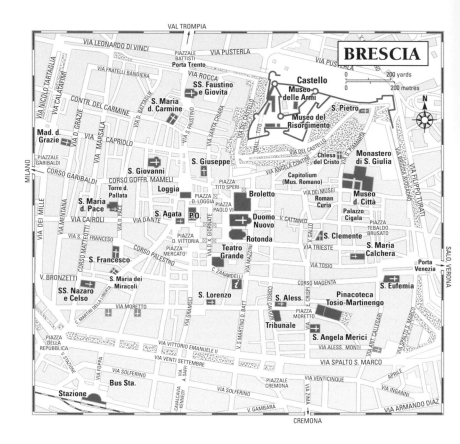

treasure of treasures, the remarkable *Winged Victory*, a splendid bronze statue nearly 2m high, probably the chief figure of a chariot group from the roof of the Capitol. It appears to be a Venus of the Augustan age (of the *Venus of Capua* type) remodelled as a Victory under Vespasian. There is also the gilded bronze statuette of a captive (2nd century AD?) and six bronze heads, all from the same group, discovered at the same time as the statue in 1826. Via Gallo leads south from here past the site (Piazza Labus 3) of the Roman curia, fragments of which can be seen below ground level and on the façade of the house.

Santa Giulia

On the corner of Via dei Musei and Via Piamarta, is the monastery of **Santa Giulia**, a huge group of buildings with three Renaissance cloisters and several churches. Formerly called San Salvatore, the monastery was founded by the Lombard king Desiderius in 753 on the site of a Roman edifice. Ermengarde, the daughter of Lothair I, and many other royal and noble ladies were sisters in the original Benedictine nunnery, which survived here until it was suppressed by Napoleon in 1798. Part of the complex houses the Museo della Città (*open Tues–Sat 10–6, Sun 10–7*), with displays covering all periods of the city's history; special exhibitions are held frequently in the church of Santa Giulia, in rooms near the entrance to the monastery, and in the lower part of Santa Maria in Solario.

Guided tours of the monastery are given every half-hour. The first area visited is a **Roman house** (seen from a walkway), with remains of rooms round a peristyle with black-and-white mosaic floors and traces of wall paintings. Beyond is the atrium of the church of San Salvatore, where Lombard sculptural fragments (8th century) are displayed. A walkway continues (above excavations of various periods from the Roman era to the 9th century) to the church proper, founded c. 753. Here you can see 13 Roman columns in the nave, all with beautiful capitals (only some of them Roman; the others date from the 8th century); chapels frescoed in the 15th century; and traces of Carolingian frescoes, above the nave arches. The southwest chapel has frescoes by Gerolamo Romanino. Below is the crypt, dating from 760–63 (enlarged in the 12th century), with 42 columns of varying origins and capitals by the school of Antelami.

The square undercroft below Santa Maria in Solario, with a cippus for a central column, is used for exhibitions. The building beyond is to exhibit the Renaissance collections. The upper church of **Santa Maria in Solario**, built in the 12th century, is covered with early-16th-century frescoes by Floriano Ferramola and his workshop. Three showcases here contain the rich treasury of San Salvatore. The so-called *Cross of Desiderius* (late 8th–early 9th century) is made of wood overlaid with silver gilt and set with over 200 gems (dating from the Roman period to the 9th century). It incorporates cameos, miniatures (9th–15th centuries), a 16th-century crucifix and, on the lower arm, a remarkable triple portrait painted on gilded glass in the 4th century. Another case has early ivories, including the Querini diptych (5th century), with Paris and Helen (?) on each leaf; the consular diptych of Boethius (5th century), and a leaf of the diptych of the Lampadii, with circus scenes (late 5th century). The last case displays an exquisite 4th-century ivory coffer with scriptural scenes in relief.

The former church of Santa Giulia (1599), which has handsome 16th-century frescoes by Floriano Ferramola, is only open for exhibitions. From Via Turati the Strada Panoramica leads up to Monte Maddalena (875m), a noted viewpoint.

The castle

The castle stands on the Cydnean hill, mentioned by Catullus. There are two ways to approach it. From the little, secluded Piazza Tito Speri, northwest of the Broletto, steep (signposted) steps lead you to the top in 15 minutes. If that sounds too strenuous, take the gentler Via Piamarta, a deserted old cobbled street between high walls, which ascends past the Chiesa del Cristo and through public gardens.

The castle was rebuilt by the Visconti in the 14th century. Its extensive walls now enclose gardens, museums and an observatory. At the highest point of the hill is the Museo delle Armi Luigi Marzoli (*open June–Sept Tues–Sun 10–5; Oct–May 9.30–1 &*

2.30–5). Beyond a drawbridge, a path leads up through a fort to the cylindrical Torre della Mirabella on a lawn with wide views. Many of the arms and firearms were made in Brescia, which was renowned for its weapons production. In one room there are remains of the steps of a Roman temple.

Downhill to the right is the Museo del Risorgimento (*open June–Sept Tues–Sun 10–5; Oct–May 9.30–1 & 2.30–5*), founded in 1887 and arranged on two floors of a large 16th-century grain store. The collection illustrates Italian history from the last years of the 18th century up to Unification.

Around Piazza Moretto

Due south of the castle is the Piazza Moretto, in which stands the **Pinacoteca Tosio-Martinengo** (*open June–Sept Tues–Sun 10–5; Oct–May 9.30–1 & 2.30–5*). It contains a large collection of paintings and frescoes in which the local schools are well represented. Highlights of the collection are works by Moretto (including his *Salome*); portraits by the circle of François Clouet, and Romanino; Raphael's *Angel and Risen Christ* (two fragments); a copy of a Raphael *Madonna* by an early-16th-century painter; a charming painting of *St George and the Dragon* by a Lombard master (c. 1460–70); works by Vincenzo Foppa, Lorenzo Lotto (*Nativity*), Giovanni Battista Moroni, Savoldo (*Nativity, Boy with a Flute*), Giulio and Antonio Campi and Luca Giordano.

Outstanding in the fine collection of drawings (shown only with special permission) is a *Deposition* by Giovanni Bellini.

Sant'Angela Merici, just to the south of the Pinacoteca, has a *Transfiguration* by Jacopo Tintoretto in the apse and works by Francesco Bassano and Giulio Cesare Procaccini, among others. The nearby church of **Sant'Alessandro** contains a beautiful painting of the *Annunciation* by Jacopo Bellini, and works by Vincenzo Civerchio and Lattanzio Gambara.

West of the centre

In the western part of town is the church of **San Francesco**, built in 1254–65, with a handsome façade. Inside, the south aisle contains an altarpiece by Moretto; a Giottesque fresco of the *Entombment* (with a scene of monks above, dating from the mid-14th century); and 14th-century frescoes including a charming frieze of angels. The high altarpiece is by Romanino. The fine cloister dates from 1394.

Santa Maria dei Miracoli preserves an elaborately carved Renaissance façade of 1488–1560. It contains *St Nicholas of Bari with his Pupils*, taken to be a copy of a work by Moretto (now in the Pinacoteca). The paintings (1590–94) in the presbytery are by the local artists Tommaso Bona, Pietro Bagnadore, Grazio Cossali and Pietro Marone.

The 18th-century church of **Santi Nazaro e Celso** (*if closed, ask for admission at Santa Maria dei Miracoli*) contains the *Averoldi Polyptych*—a superb early work by Titian (1522)—and paintings by Moretto (including the *Crowning of the Virgin*), and monuments by Maffeo Olivieri. North of this is the massive 13th-century Torre della Pallata. Nearby is San Giovanni Evangelista, which contains handsome paintings (1521) by Moretto and Romanino in the Corpus Domini chapel, and an altarpiece of the *Madonna and Saints* by Moretto. Further north Santa Maria del Carmine, a 15th-century building with a fine façade and portal, contains paintings by Vincenzo Foppa. At the west end of Via Capriolo is the Madonna delle Grazie by Lodovico Barcella (1522). The delightful Rococo interior (1617) has an exuberance of stucco reliefs and frescoes.

FRANCIACORTA & LAGO D'ISEO

The fertile, vine-clad foothills between Brescia and the Lago d'Iseo are known as the Franciacorta, a pretty region with a number of villas built by the noble families of Brescia in the 18th century. It has long been known for its excellent red and white wines (and since the 1960s for the *spumante* Franciacorta, produced with Chardonnay, Pinot Bianco and Pinot Nero grapes). Numerous cellars in the area welcome visitors, and at the Villa Evelina at Capriolo there is a private agricultural museum. At **Rodengo** is the Abbazia di San Nicola, a Cluniac foundation, inhabited by Olivetan monks since 1446. It contains three cloisters, frescoes by Romanino and Lattanzio Gambara, a painting by Moretto, and fine intarsia stalls (1480).

THE WINES OF FRANCIACORTA

Franciacorta is a tiny wine district at the tip of the Lago d'Iseo. Geography has played an important role here. Scree, silt and sand brought down from the mountains by glaciers have created ideal terrain for grape-growing. In the 13th century Franciacorta wine already enjoyed a considerable reputation. In a document dated 1570 a certain Conforto, a doctor from Brescia, makes mention of the health-promoting properties of the bright and bubbly elixir. Today the region's wines are still known for their bubbles. Franciacorta produces Italy's best *metodo classico*, some of which (for instance wines from the Ca' del Bosco winery) rivals champagne in quality. Franciacorta has some good still wines too, for example the Pinero Pinot Nero. The best and most famous cuvées come from the Bellavista winery, and from the Bredasole cellars in Paratico.

Lago d'Iseo

The pretty Lago d'Iseo, an expansion of the Oglio river, surrounded by mountains, was the Lacus Sebinus of the Romans. On its southern shore is the pleasant resort of **Iseo**. Its church tower was built by Count Giacomo Oldofredi (1325), whose tomb is built into the façade alongside. Inside is a painting of *St Michael* by Francesco Hayez. On the southern edge of the lake is a marshy area known as the Torbiere d'Iseo, a large peat bog surrounded by reeds, and an important wildlife habitat. Waterlilies grow here in abundance, and it is a sanctuary for aquatic birds. Traces of Bronze Age pile-

Lago d'Iseo, with a view of Monte Isola.

dwellings were found here. On the east bank are Sulzano, a sailing centre and port for Monte Isola, and **Sale Marasino**, another port for the island, with a conspicuous 18th-century church and the 16th-century Villa Martinengo. The wooded island of **Monte Isola**, 3.2km long, where all the lake boats call, is closed to private cars (although there is a bus service from the fishing village of Peschiera Maraglio), and it can be toured on foot in around 3 hours. The hill in the centre is covered with chestnut woods and broom.

Marone is a large village beneath Monte Guglielmo (1949m), the highest point in the mountain range between the lake and the Val Trompia. A road winds up to an area of chestnut woods, of geological interest for its erosion pyramids surmounted by granite boulders, caused by the erosion of the moraine deposits. At the northeast end of the lake is the little town of **Pisogne**, where the church of Santa Maria della Neve contains splendid frescoes of the *Passion of Christ* by Romanino (1532–34).

On the Bergamo side of the lake is **Lovere**, the principal tourist resort on its shores. To the north of the town is the church of Santa Maria in Valvendra (1473–83), which contains organ-shutters decorated outside by Ferramola and inside by Moretto (1518). To the south, on the shore of the lake, is the Galleria dell'Accademia Tadini (*open May–Oct Tues–Sat 3–7, Sun and holidays 10–12 & 3–7*), whose collection includes works by Jacopo Bellini, Magnasco and Vincenzo Civerchio, as well as porcelain, arms and bronzes. In the garden, the cenotaph of Faustino Tadini (d. 1799) is by Antonio Canova. There is a path above the town to the Altipiano di Lovere (990m), with some attractive country villas, and to Bossico, among meadows and pine woods.

A road follows the west side of the lake through **Riva di Solto**, whose quarries provided the black marble for the columns of the basilica of San Marco in Venice, with two little bays displaying unusual rock strata. On the western side of the lake, beneath the barren slopes of Monte Bronzone (1333m), is **Sarnico**, at the outflow of the Oglio, well known to motor-boat racing enthusiasts. It has a number of Art Nouveau villas built at the beginning of the 20th century by Giuseppe Sommaruga.

THE VAL CAMONICA

The lovely, fertile Val Camonica, the upper course of the Oglio, lies to the north of Pisogne and the Lago d'Iseo. It is famous for its remarkable prehistoric rock carvings, which you can see throughout the valley, especially in the two parks at Capo di Ponte and Darfo-Boario Terme, and at Cimbergo, Ossimo and Sellero. The chestnut woods were once an important source of wealth, as both nuts and timber were exported. The inhabitants of the valley (and especially of Boario) are excellent woodcarvers. Ironworks were established here in the Middle Ages, and the valley now has hydroelectric power stations. The cheeses and salt meats locally produced are of excellent quality. The extreme upper end, below the Tonale Pass, was the scene of many dramatic battles in the First World War.

Touring the Val Camonica

Regardless of whether you are travelling by road or rail, the first village of importance in the valley is **Darfo**, where the parish church has an *Entombment* attributed to Palma Giovane. **Boario Terme** is the main town in the valley and an important mineral spa. It is noted for its cabinetmakers. Over 10,000 rock carvings may be seen here in the Parco delle Luine (*open Tues–Sun 9–12 & 2–6*). Most of them date from 2200–1800 BC, but some are even earlier—the oldest found in the valley. You can see the rock known as Corni Freschi, with its rock carvings, on a country road just outside the town near the *superstrada* for Edolo.

From Boario a road ascends the Val di Scalve past Gorzone, dominated by a castle of the Federici first built in the 12th century (privately owned), through Angolo Terme, a small spa with a very fine view of the triple-peaked Pizzo della Presolana. Further on the road enters the gorge of the Dezzo, a narrow chasm with overhanging cliffs. Unfortunately, the torrent and its falls have almost been dried up by hydroelectric works.

Just north of Boario is Erbanno, unusual for its plan consisting of parallel straight streets along the hillside and a piazza on two levels. The main road continues to Esine, with the church of Santa Maria Assunta containing frescoes by Giovan Pietro da Cemmo (1491–93), from Cemmo in this valley. **Cividate Camuno** is the site of Civitas Camunnorum, the ancient Roman capital of the valley. It preserves a few ancient remains and a much more conspicuous medieval tower. Roman finds are displayed in an archaeological museum.

A winding road ascends west via Ossimo (where prehistoric statue-stele dating from 3200–2000 BC have been found) to **Borno**, a resort among pine woods in the Trobiolo valley, beneath the Corna di San Fermo (2326m). The Santuario dell'Annunciata, with a fine view of the valley, has two 15th-century cloisters.

Breno, an important town in the valley, is dominated by the ruins of its medieval castle (9th century and later). The parish church has a granite campanile and frescoes by two native artists, Giovan Pietro da Cemmo and Romanino. A mountain road leads east towards the Lago d'Idro via Bienno, a medieval village with fine 17th- and 18th-century palaces. Several old forges are still operating here, worked by channelled water. The church of Santa Maria degli Orti has frescoes by Romanino. Above Breno the dolomitic peaks of the Concarena (2549m) rise on the left and the Pizzo Badile (2435m) on the right. The villages are mostly high up on the slopes of the foothills on either side, and include Cerveno with a remarkable 18th-century Via Crucis that has nearly 200 life-size statues.

Capo di Ponte came to prominence with the discovery in the Permian sandstone of tens of thousands of rock engravings dating from Neolithic to Roman times, a span of some 8,000 years. These are the feature of the **Parco Nazionale delle Incisioni Rupestri di Naquane** (*open summer Tues–Sun 8.30–7.30; winter 8.30–4.30*), one of the best prehistoric sites in the world. So far some 180,000 engravings made by the Camuni, a remarkable Alpine civilisation, depicting hunting scenes, everyday life, religious symbols, etc., have been catalogued here. The largest rock has 900 figures carved in the Iron Age. Other prehistoric carvings have been found in the localities of Ceto, Cimbergo and Paspardo, on a secondary road to the south, and above Sellero to the north. There is a research centre (the Centro Camuno di Studi Preistorici) at Capo di Ponte. Just outside Capo di Ponte, in woods to the north, is San Salvatore, a Lombard church of the early 12th century. Across the river in Cemmo is the church of San Siro, dating from the 11th century, probably on the site of a Lombard church. The road continues to Pescarzo, a pretty little village with interesting peasant houses.

Cedegolo, with a church entirely frescoed by Antonio Cappello (17th century), stands at the foot of the lovely Val Saviore, below Monte Adamello (3555m). Edolo, surrounded by beautiful scenery, is the main place in the upper Val Camonica. Ponte di Legno (1260m) is the main resort of the region in a wide-open mountain basin, beneath the Adamello and Presanella mountains. To the north a road, one of the highest in Europe, ascends the Val di Pezzo and crosses the Passo Gavia (2652m) to Bormio. The Tonale Pass (1884m), in the Presanella foothills, is on the former Austro-Italian frontier, separating Lombardy from the Trentino.

THE VALTELLINA

The Valtellina, the upper valley of the River Adda, is famous for its ski resorts. It also produces good wines (Grumello, Sassella, etc.) from vines trained to grow on frames on the steep hillsides. The valley has had a chequered history. In the 14th century it came under the control of Milan, but in 1512 it was united to the Grisons in Switzerland. The Reformation took a firm hold here, and on 19 July 1620, at the instigation of the Spanish governor of Milan, the Catholic inhabitants of the valley ruthlessly massacred the Protestants (the 'Sacro Macello'). Twenty years of warfare followed, but in 1639 the valley was regained by the Grisons, who held it until Napoleon's partition of 1797. The area has for long been subject to disastrous landslides and flooding, particularly in the 1980s as a result of uncontrolled new building, deforestation and changes in the traditional methods of cultivation. In some places, landslides have interrupted the course of the Adda and changed the geological formation of the valley.

Exploring the region

From Edolo at the top of the Val Camonica, a road winds west to meet the Adda. Following the river upstream from here you come to **Tirano**. Its old district on the left bank of the Adda has the historic mansions of the Visconti, Pallavicini and Salis families. The late-16th-century Palazzo Salis, with a garden, is still owned by the family (*open Apr–Nov 10–12 & 2–4*). Many of the Protestant inhabitants of the town were massacred in 1620. The Bernina and Valtellina railways terminate here. To the north is the pilgrimage church of the Madonna di Tirano, begun in 1505, in the style of Bramante, with a fine doorway by Alessandro della Scala. The convent buildings house a local ethnographic museum. North of Tirano is the Swiss border: the road continues over the Bernina pass to St Moritz.

Further up the Adda valley is **Grosio**, a large village with 15th–16th-century houses, including a mansion owned by the Venosta (restored as the seat of the Museo Civico). It was the birthplace of Cipriano Valorsa (1514/17–1604), 'the Raphael of the Valtellina', whose paintings adorn nearly every church in the valley. In the chestnut woods above the road are the ruins of two Venosta castles, one dating from the 12th century with the Romanesque campanile of the church of Santi Faustino e Giovita, and the other from the 14th century with fine battlements. Here in 1966 were discovered thousands of rock carvings (including human figures) dating from the Neolithic period to the Iron Age, the most interesting of which are on the Rupe Magna. The park is shown on request (*T: 0342 847454*). Yellow signs indicate the paths through the park from near the huge electric power station (1917–22) beside the main road.

Following the Adda downstream takes you past **Teglio** (776m), once the principal place in the valley, to which it gave its name (Vallis Tellina). The road continues through the pleasant little town of Sondrio to Lake Como.

LAGO D'IDRO & MONTIRONE

The **Lago d'Idro**, the Roman Lacus Eridius, 9.5km long and 2km wide, is surrounded by steep, rugged mountains. Its waters are used for hydroelectric power, and it is renowned for its trout. On the west bank are Anfo with an old castle, founded by the

Venetians in 1486 but largely rebuilt, and Sant'Antonio, where the church has a 15th-century fresco cycle. Bagolino is a mountain village in a good position on the Caffaro (visited by skiers, and famous for its carnival). Ponte Caffaro, beyond the head of the lake, marks the old international frontier.

To the south of Brescia is **Montirone** (*shown on the map on p. 238*) where the beautiful Palazzo Lechi (1738–46), by Antonio Turbino, is very well preserved and has magnificent stables of c. 1754. It contains paintings by Carlo Carlone (his best work), and was visited by Mozart in 1773 and Napoleon in 1805.

PRACTICAL INFORMATION

GETTING AROUND

• **Airport bus**: Shuttle buses connect Brescia with its airport at Montichiari (30km from the centre).
• **By rail:** Main line trains to Turin, Venice and Trieste. Fast Intercity trains make the run to Milan in 50mins, Verona in 25mins. There are also trains to Lecco (1hr 20mins), Cremona (35–50mins), Parma (1hr 25mins) and Edolo (2hrs 2mins)—the latter plying a very scenic route through the Val Camonica. Brescia is also served by commuter trains from Milan (operated by FNME).
• **By bus:** There is a comprehensive network of country buses, with services to/from Bergamo, Milan, Lake Como, Cremona, Mantua and places of interest in the province (information, T: 035 3774237 or 030 44915). In Brescia buses arrive at or depart from the bus station (Via Solferino 6) or the railway station. City bus D runs from the station to Corso Zanardelli.

INFORMATION OFFICES

Brescia Corso Zanardelli 34–38, T: 030 43418, and Piazza Loggia 6, T: 030 240 0357, www.bresciaholiday.com. A seasonal kiosk operates at the Brescia-Centro autostrada exit.
Informagiovani: Piazza Vittoria 5a, T: 030 375 3004.
Boario Terme Piazza Einaudi 2, T: 0364 531609, www.vallecamonica.info
Idro Via Trento 46, T: 0365 83224.
Iseo Lungolago Marconi 2c, T: 030 980209, www.vallecamonica.info

HOTELS

Brescia
€€€ **Vittoria**. The only real possibility in this very business-minded city. Elegant, comfortable late Liberty-style hotel. Via X Giornate 20, T: 030 280061, www.hotelvittoria.com
€€ **Cappuccini**, (at Cologne, outside Brescia). In a former 16th-century convent, with a good restaurant. Via Cappuccini 54, T: 030 7157254.
Aprica (Valtellina)
€ **Larice Bianco**. Small and comfortable. Open Dec–Apr and June–Sept. T: 0342 746275, laricebianco@hotmail.com
Bellavista (Franciacorta)
€€€ **L'Albereta Locanda in Franciacorta**. In a beautifully restored

19th-century villa, with a renowned restaurant (closed Sun evening, Mon and Jan). Via Vittorio Emanuele 11, T: 030 7760550, www.albereta.it

Boario Terme (Val Camonica)
€€ **Rizzi**. A homelike, family-managed establishment, with a nice garden. Via Carducci 5/11, T: 0364 531617, www.hotelbenessere.it
€ **Brescia**. Small, central and comfortable. Via Zanardelli 6, T: 0364 531409, www.hotelbenessere.it

Iseo
€ **Ambra**. Warm and hospitable. Porto Rosa 2, T: 030 980130, ambrahotel@tiscali.it
€€ **I Due Roccoli**. A lovely country house amid woods and meadows, with wonderful views over the lake. Closed Jan. Via Silvio Bonomelli, T: 030 982 2977, www.idueroccoli.com

Lovere (Lago d'Iseo)
€ **Moderno**. A cordial, family-run place at the north end of the lake. Piazza 13 Martiri 21, T: 035 960607, www.albergomoderno.bg.it

Ponte di Legno (Val Camonica)
€€ **Mirella**. Modern and efficient, amid woods and meadows. Via Roma 21, T: 0364 900500, hotmirtin.it

Sondrio (Valtellina)
€€ **Della Posta**. Central, in a 19th-century building. Piazza Garibaldi 19, T: 0342 510404, www.hotelposta.so.it

Teglio (Valtellina)
€ **Combolo**. Simple but nice, with a garden terrace, in the centre of town. Via Roma 5, T: 0342 780083, www.hotelcombolo.it

Villa Dalegno (Val Camonica)
€€ **Sorriso**. A sober but elegant place with a good restaurant. Via Plaza 6, T: 0364 900488, www.hotelsorriso.com

YOUTH HOSTEL

Lovere
€ **Ostello del Porto**, Via G.Paglia 70, T: 035 983529, info@ostellodibergamo.it

RESTAURANTS

Brescia
€€€ **La Sosta**. Fine regional cuisine in a historic building with garden. Closed Sun evening, Mon, Jan and Aug. Via San Martino della Battaglia 20, T: 030 295603.
€€ **Il Ciacco**. Good traditional restaurant in a neighbourhood known locally as 'Food Valley' for its many *osterie*. Closed Mon, Jan and Aug. Via Indipendenza 23b, T: 030 361797.
€ **La Vineria**. Wine bar serving great *risotti* and other warm dishes. Closed Mon and Aug. Via X Giornate 4, T: 030 280477.

Concesio (Franciacorta)
€€€ **Miramonti l'Altro**. Delicious, refined interpretations of traditional recipes. Closed Mon and Aug. Via Crosette 34, Località Costorio, T: 030 275 1063.

Grosio (Valtellina)
€€ **Sassella**. Restaurant with rooms, serving great game and regional dishes. Closed Mon (except June–Sept). Via Roma 2, T: 0342 847272.

Iseo
€€ **Il Castello**. Traditional trattoria with garden. Via Mirolte 43, T: 030 981285.
€€ **Il Volto**. *Osteria* serving excellent regional dishes. Closed Wed, midday Thur and July. Via Mirolte 33, T: 030 981462.

€€ **La Fenice**. Simple restaurant specialising in lake fish. Closed Thur and Aug. Via Fenice 21, T: 030 981565.

Morbegno

€€ **Osteria del Crotto**. Trattoria in a *crotto*, or mountain farmhouse, with wood-panelled interiors, majolica wood stove and other rustic amenities in winter, garden seating in summer. Closed Sun and Aug–Sept. Via Pedemontana 22/24, Località Madonna, T: 0342 614800.

€€ **Vecchio Ristorante Fiume**. Trattoria in a historic building, serving excellent local fare. Closed Tues evening and Wed. Località Cima alle Case, T: 0342 610248.

Ponte in Valtellina (Valtellina)

€€ **Cerere**. Traditional restaurant, in an old historic house, serving local delicacies such as air-dried venison and *sciatt*. Closed Wed (except Aug) and July. Via Guiccardi 7, T: 0342 482294.

€ **Osteria del Sole**. Trattoria serving great game and local delicacies such as *sciatt*, wholewheat fritters made with grappa, and local cheese. Closed Tues and Sept. Via Sant'Ignazio 11, T: 0342 482298

Sondrio (Valtellina)

€ **Amici Vecchie Cantine**. *Osteria* and wine bar, the place to go for Valtellina wines and snacks (and, perhaps, a game of cards). Open 10–9, closed Sun. Via Parravicini 6, T: 0342 512590.

€ **Mossini**. Trattoria with good local food. Closed Mon and July. Località Mossini, T: 0342 514040.

Tirano (Valtellina)

€€ **Bernina**. Restaurant with rooms, specialising in local and regional cuisine. Closed Mon (except June–Nov) and Jan. Via Roma 24–28, T: 0342 701302.

Travagliato (Franciacorta)

€ **Ringo**. Simple trattoria serving outstanding fish dishes. Closed Mon, midday Tues (except holidays) and Aug. Via Brescia 41, T: 030 660680.

Pezzo (Ponte di Legno, Val Camonica)

€ **Da Giusy**. Trattoria, simple but good. Closed Tues (except July–Aug) and weekdays Oct–Nov. Via Ercavallo 39, T: 0364 92153.

Riva dei Balti (Artogne, Val Camonica)

€ **Le Fise**. A mountain cabin (with rooms) surrounded by flowers and orchards, serving delicious farm meals made with genuine home-grown ingredients. Open all year Fri–Sun. Via Pieve 2, T: 0364 598298.

CAFÉS

Brescia

Pasticceria San Carlo, on the corner of Corso Zanardelli and Via 10 Giornate.

Bar Impero, Piazza Vittoria.

Capuzzi, Via Piamarta.

REGIONAL SPECIALITIES

Brescia Try **G.A. Porteri**, an excellent delicatessen, with a warm, friendly *osteria* next door, run by the same people. (Via Trento 52; T: 030 380947. Closed Sun evening, Mon and Aug.)

Sondrio **Motta**, at Piazza Rusconi 4, is a delicatessen with good bresaola and cold meats. **Torrolina**, at Via Beccaria 4, has *bitto* and other local cheeses.

Darfo **Gatti** has a selection of local salami and cold meats ideal for picnics.

Iseo The **Cinema Teatro Eden**, a wine shop taking its name from the theatre that used to occupy the building, stocks excellent wines as well as pastas, jams, etc.

Some of Lombardy's best red wines are made in the upper reaches of the Valtellina (the others come from the Oltrepò Pavese and Garda Bresciano). The Valtellina dinner wines all share the general appellation Valtellina Superiore, which encompasses five types: Francia, Grumello, Inferno, Sassella and Valgella. The strong (15%) Sfursat della Valtellina, made from dried grapes, is drunk as a dessert wine or with game. Most of the vintners of the Valtellina sell wine directly from the estate. The best known is Nino Negri, with vineyards here and there in the valley and cellars at Chiuro (Sondrio).

Also famous are the kitchen utensils and other household objects made from the smooth local grey stone known as *pietra ollare*.

EVENTS & FESTIVALS

Brescia Arturo Benedetti Michelangeli International Piano Festival, Apr–June. Organ concerts from mid-Sept–mid-Oct

in various churches in the city. Choral music is performed in various churches Apr–June. *Teatro Grande*, opera season Sept–Nov, concerts Oct–March. In summer, music is performed in the gardens of palaces, etc (information from your concierge or the information office). The *Mille Miglia* veteran car race is held in May (the three-day course of 1,000 miles—1,600km—runs from Brescia via Ferrara to Rome and back to Brescia).
Lovere *Stagione dei Concerti*, concert season, Accademia Tadini, Apr–June.
Sarnico World Music Festival, July.
Sondrio *Omaggio al Santuario della Sassella*, concert series, June. Valtellina Jazz Festival, Aug. *Fiera Città di Sondrio*, food and wine fair, Sept. Michelangelo Abbado International Violin Competition, Sept. Sondrio Festival, international festival of documentary films on nature and parks, Oct. Classical music season at Teatro Pedretti, Nov–April.

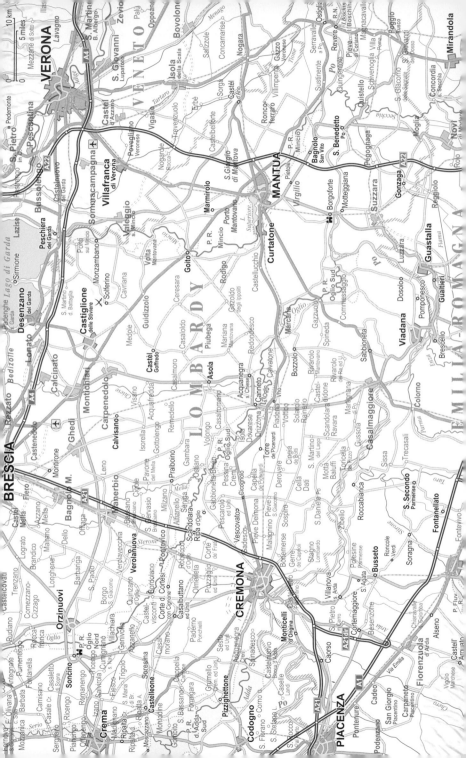

CREMONA & ITS PROVINCE

Cremona, a busy, cheerful city, has a world-wide reputation for its stringed instrument makers and restorers. In the 16th–18th centuries it was home to the most famous violin-makers of all time, including Antonio Stradivari (some of whose precious instruments are preserved here). Cremona's many ancient brick buildings are survivals of the age of the Lombard city-states, and it has a beautiful Romanesque cathedral. Its churches are particularly noteworthy for their 16th-century frescoes, many of them by the Campi brothers (*see p. 245*), a gifted Cremonese family of painters, some of whose best work you can see in San Sigismondo. Cremona is an important agricultural market for southern Lombardy.

The small province of Cremona is chiefly bordered by rivers. Its rich alluvial soil makes it ideal for farming, and in fact the area's agricultural vocation can be seen and felt everywhere. The countryside is studded with huge *cascinali*, rural building complexes in which haybarns, stables, granaries and peasant labourers' quarters rise side by side; and most of the towns and villages still bear the imprint of the country market centre, with lovely central squares often surrounded by arcaded walks.

HISTORY OF CREMONA

Founded by the Romans as a colony in 218 BC, Cremona became an important fortress and road junction on the Via Postumia. Its decline after a siege and sacking in AD 69 ended in destruction by the Lombards in 603. Cremona re-emerged as a free commune in 1098, at war with its neighbours, Milan, Brescia and Piacenza. In 1334 it was taken by Azzone Visconti of Milan, and from then on remained under Milanese domination. It enjoyed a century of patronage and prosperity after it was given in dowry to Bianca Maria Visconti on her marriage to Francesco Sforza in 1441.

EXPLORING CREMONA

The beautifully paved Piazza del Comune is the centre of the life of Cremona and has its most important buildings. The Romanesque Torrazzo (*open Tues–Sun 10–1*) is one of the highest medieval towers in Europe (112m). It was completed in 1250–67 and crowned with a Gothic lantern in 1287–1300, probably by the local sculptor Francesco Pecorari. 502 steps lead up past a room with an astronomical clock, made in 1583 by the Divizioli, still with its original mechanism (it is wound by hand every day). The double loggia that stretches across the front of the cathedral is known as the Bertazzola. The Palazzo del Comune (marked on the map) houses the Room of the Violins (*see overleaf*).

THE VIOLINS OF CREMONA

Cremona is famous for the violins and violas made here in the 16th–18th centuries by the Amati family and their pupils, the Guarneri and Antonio Stradivari. Stradivari (in Latin, Stradivarius, 1644–1737) was born and died in Cremona. Cremona is now home to the International School of Violin Making. Examples of these exquisite instruments can be seen in the **Room of the Violins** in the **Palazzo del Comune** (*open Tues–Sat 9–6, Sun and holidays 10–12.45*). Five famous Cremona violins are displayed here. The one by Andrea Amati is thought to have been commissioned by Charles IX of France in 1566; the Hammerle of 1658 is by Nicolò Amati, Andrea's grandson. The others are a violin made by Giuseppe Guarneri in 1689, the *Cremonese* made in 1715 by Antonio Stradivari, and the *Guarneri del Gesù* (1734) by Guarneri's son Giuseppe Guarneri del Gesù. A recording of the instruments is provided, but it is also possible, by appointment, to hear them being played by a violinist who comes here regularly to keep them in tune. At Via Palestro 17 is the **Stradivarius Museum** (*open Tues–Sun 9–6, Sun and holidays 10–6*). In the gallery are models made by Stradivarius in wood and paper, his tools, drawings, etc., as well as a fine collection of stringed instruments (17th–20th centuries). It was here, in the 16th century, that Andrea Amati founded the school of stringed-instrument makers that is still renowned to this day. His grandson Nicolò Amati (1596–1684) was his most famous follower.

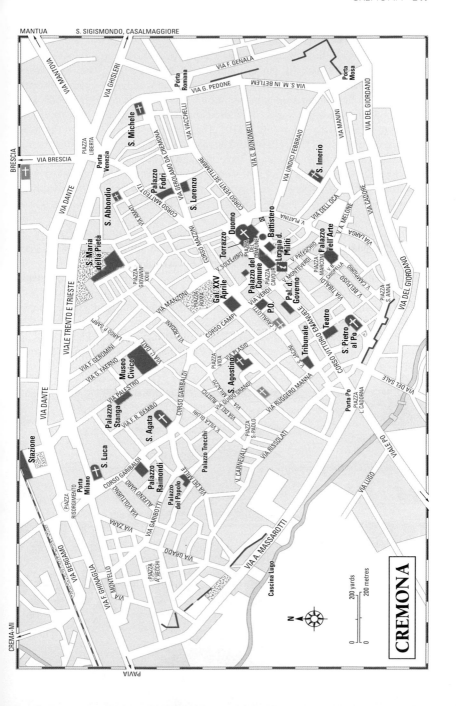

CREMONA

The duomo and baptistery

The duomo is a splendid Romanesque basilica of 1107, consecrated in 1190 and finished considerably later. It has a particularly fine exterior. The west front (1274–1606) has a rose window of 1274 and a tabernacle above the main door with three large statues of the Madonna and Child and the patron saints Imerio and Omobono. These unusual works, influenced by the French Gothic style, are now thought to be by Marco Romano (c. 1310). The lions date from 1285, and the marble frieze of the Months from 1220–30. The later transepts, which altered the basilican plan of the church to a Latin cross, have splendid brick façades: the north transept dates from 1288, with a fine porch (the *Annunciation* is attributed to Wiligelmus, who worked also in Modena—*see p. 597*—and *Christ and the Apostles* dates from the 12th century), and the south transept from 1342. The beautiful apse faces the piazza behind.

The interior is remarkable, especially for the frescoes (1514–29; extremely difficult to see without strong light) on the walls of the nave and apse, by Boccaccino, Gian Francesco Bembo, Altobello Melone, Romanino, Pordenone and Bernardino Gatti. On the west wall is a *Deposition*, beneath a *Crucifixion*, both by Pordenone. In the south aisle, the first altarpiece is by Pordenone, the second by Alessandro Arrighi (1650), and the third by Luca Cattapane. In the south transept (high up, looking back towards the nave) is a huge painting *The Triumph of Mardocheus* (1567) by Giulio Campi (*see p. 245*). The Sagrestia dei Canonici has a ceiling painted by Antonio Bibiena and an *Assumption* by Giulio Campi. The unusual funerary monument of Cardinal Sfondrati

The west front of Cremona's duomo.

is by Giovanni Battista Cambi. Outside the 17th-century Cappella del Sacramento stairs lead down to the crypt, with the beautifully carved tomb of Sts Peter and Marcellius (1506). On a nave pillar by the crypt steps is a marble triptych of 1495, and (protected by glass) a high relief by Amadeo (1482), showing the *Charity of St Imerio*.

The chapel of the Madonna del Popolo is beautifully decorated with stuccoes by Carlo Natali (1654) and paintings by Bernardino and Giulio Campi. In the north transept is an altarpiece by Giulio Campi, and a splendid silver cross, nearly 2m high, with numerous tabernacles and statuettes. The work of Ambrogio Pozzi and Agostino Sacchi, it was completed in 1478 (the base was added in 1774). Also here are a *Deposition* by Antonio Campi, four marble reliefs by Giovanni Antonio Amadeo, and high up, looking back towards the nave, a large painting by Sante Legnani (1815).

The octagonal baptistery is a plain Lombard building dating from 1167 and partially faced with marble. The Loggia dei Militi is a fine Gothic Lombard building of 1292 (with handsome three-light windows), restored as a war memorial.

East of the Piazza del Comune

Via Solferino leads out of the piazza towards Piazza Roma, a public garden. Here is a statue of Amilcare Ponchielli (1834–86), composer of the opera *La Gioconda*, with its famous 'Dance of the Hours', who was born near Cremona. The **tombstone of Stradivarius** also stands here. It was salvaged from the church of San Domenico, which stood on this site but was demolished in 1878. From Piazza Roma, Corso Mazzini leads northeast into Corso Matteotti, with many fine old mansions. Notice especially Palazzo Fodri (no. 17), dating from c. 1500, decorated with a terracotta frieze and with a lovely courtyard. A road on the other side of the corso leads to the church of Sant'Abbondio, with an interesting 16th-century interior. The vault frescoes are by Orazio Sammacchini. In the sanctuary are paintings by Malosso and Giulio Campi. The Loreto chapel dates from 1624, and there is a Renaissance cloister.

On the other side of the corso, narrow roads lead to Via Gerolamo da Cremona, which continues east to the church of **San Michele**, near remains of the walls. Lombard in origin (7th century), it is the oldest church in Cremona. It was reconstructed in the 11th and 12th centuries (the exterior of the apse dates from this time) and contains 12th-century columns in the nave with fine leafy capitals as well as noteworthy fresco fragments, including one by Benedetto Bembo. The paintings are by Bernardino Campi, Alessandro Pampurino and Antonio della Corna (attributed), among others.

The Museo Civico

Open Tues–Sun 9–6, Sun and holidays 10–6.
The museum is housed in the huge Palazzo Affaitati built in 1561 by Francesco Dattaro, with a good staircase by Antonio Arrighi (1769). The collection of Count Sigismondo Ala Ponzone, left to the city in 1842, was transferred here in 1928. The arrangement is provisional: only the highlights are described.

Pinacoteca: *Scherzo con Ortaggi*, a well-known portrait by Arcimboldo; *St Francis in Meditation* by Caravaggio. 15th-century paintings by Benedetto and Bonifacio Bembo, works by Camillo Boccaccino, Bernardino and Antonio Campi; 16th–17th-century works by the Cremonese school. Flemish paintings, including a *Madonna* by Jan Provost. 19th-century paintings including portraits by Il Piccio, and works by Luigi Sabatelli and Giuseppe Dotti. **Decorative arts collection:** 16th-century Limoges enamels, ivories, wrought-iron work. 18th–19th-century porcelain including Wedgwood, Meissen and Ginori (Doccia) ware.

Archaeological collection: Sword from the 9th century BC, Attic kraters and a good Roman section: helmets, fine geometric mosaic pavements (1st–3rd centuries AD), coins, epigraphs, portrait heads and the front of a legionary's strongbox. The cache of at least 650 amphorae was found in the centre of Cremona in 1993, in an area once probably part of the Roman port on the Po.

West of the Museo Civico

In Corso Garibaldi, which branches off to the left from Corso Campi, is the conspicuous Neoclassical façade of **Sant'Agata**, built in 1848 by Luigi Voghera. Inside, on the right, is the Trecchi tomb by Giovanni Cristoforo Romano (1502–05), with beautifully carved bas-reliefs. The painting of the *Life of St Agatha* (painted on both sides) is by a northern Italian master of the 13th century. The handsome frescoes on the sanctuary walls are by Giulio Campi (1536).

Across the Corso is the **Palazzo del Popolo** or Palazzo Cittanova (1256), with a ground-floor portico, the headquarters of the popular—or Guelph—party in the days of the free city-state of Cremona. Nearby, in Via Grandi, is the little church of **Santa Margherita** (1547), in an extremely ruinous state. The frescoes inside (now almost invisible) are the best work of Giulio Campi. Not far off, at Via Milazzo 16, is a remarkable Art Nouveau house façade with floral motifs and leaves.

On the left of Corso Garibaldi (no. 178) is the fine Palazzo Raimondi (1496; by Bernardino de Lera), with damaged frescoes on its curved cornice. It is the seat of the international **Scuola di Liuteria** (school of violin-making). Beyond on the right is the church of San Luca, with a 15th-century façade in poor repair adorned with the terracotta ornament typical of Cremona; adjoining is the little octagonal Renaissance chapel of Cristo Risorto (1503), attributed to Bernardino de Lera.

Southwest of Piazza del Comune

From Sant'Agata (*see above*), Via Trecchi and Via Guido Grandi lead southwest to **Sant'Agostino**, a 14th-century church with a handsome tower and terracotta ornamentation on the façade. In the interior are frescoes by Bonifacio Bembo, a stoup with reliefs by Bonino da Campione (1357), an *Annunciation* by Antonio Campi, and a *Madonna and Saints* by Perugino. Via Plasio leads south to the church of Santi Marcellino e Pietro, with elaborate marble and stucco decorations in the interior (1602–20; being restored). Further south is Corso Vittorio Emanuele with (right) the

Teatro Ponchielli by Luigi Canonica (1808). Behind the theatre is the monastic church of **San Pietro al Po**, sumptuously decorated with 16th-century paintings and stuccoes by Malosso, Antonio Campi, Gian Francesco Bembo, Bernardino Gatti and others. The cloister at Via Cesari 14 is by Cristoforo Solari (1509).

THE CAMPI FAMILY

Not a particularly talented painter himself, Galeazzo Campi (1475–1536) nevertheless left the world three gifted sons: Antonio (1524–87), Vicenzo (1536–91) and the most famous, Giulio (c. 1508–73). Antonio and Vicenzo are both noted for a use of chiaroscuro that foreshadows Caravaggio (Caravaggio is known to have been influenced by the Campis' works). Giulio's works can be seen in the churches of Sant'Abbondio, Sant'Agata, Santa Margherita, San Sigismondo and in the duomo. Works by Antonio hang in the Museo Civico. Both Giulio and Antonio worked for Habsburg patrons, Giulio for Charles V, and Antonio for Philip II. Bernardino Campi (1522–c. 1592) was a pupil of Giulio and the son of the goldsmith Pietro Campi.

Antonio Campi: *Visitation* (1567).

San Sigismondo

On the outskirts of the town (on the Casalmaggiore road; bus no. 2 for the hospital) is the fine Lombard Renaissance church of **San Sigismondo**, where Francesco Sforza was married to Bianca Visconti in 1441, with the town of Cremona as the bride's dowry. The present building was started in 1463 in celebration of the event. The interior contains splendid painted decoration carried out between 1535 and 1570, much of it by the local artists Camillo Boccaccino, Bernardino Gatti and the Campi family. The nave vault was decorated by Bernardino and Giulio Campi and Bernardino Gatti. In the south aisle, the first chapel contains a niche in which two glass carafes are preserved; these were found in 1963 on a brick dated 1492 at the base of the façade (they were filled with oil and wine to commemorate the beginning of its construction). The fifth chapel has a vault exquisitely decorated by Bernardino Campi and an altarpiece by Giulio Campi, and the sixth chapel has an altarpiece by Bernardino Campi. The transept vaults were painted by Giulio Campi. The dome bears a fresco of *Paradise* by

Bernardino Campi. The presbytery and apse have fine frescoes by Camillo Boccaccino, and the high altarpiece, in a beautiful contemporary wooden frame, is by Giulio Campi (1540). Behind the high altar is the foundation stone of the church. In the north aisle, the fifth chapel is entirely decorated with paintings, frescoes and stuccoes by Antonio Campi, and the third chapel has fine works by Bernardino Campi.

AROUND CREMONA

Crema and the west

Crema, on the west bank of the Serio, is the most important town in the province after Cremona. It was under Venetian rule from 1454 to 1797 and was the birthplace of the composer Francesco Cavalli (1600–76). The cathedral (1284–1341), in the Campionese style (the medieval style of stonecarvers and masons in the Campione region), has a fine tower and contains one of the last works of Guido Reni. The piazza in front of it is surrounded by Renaissance buildings, including the 16th-century Palazzo Pretorio with an archway leading to the main street.

The ex-convent of Sant'Agostino houses the library and Museo Civico (*open Mon 2.30–6.30, Tues–Fri 9.30–12 & 2.30–6.30, Sat–Sun and holidays 2.30–6.30*), which has burial armour from Lombard tombs. The refectory, restored as a concert hall, has frescoes attributed to Giovan Pietro da Cemmo (1498–1505). Santa Maria della Croce, north of the town, is a handsome, centrally-planned church (1490–1500) in the style of Bramante, by Giovanni Battagio. It contains altarpieces by the Campi brothers.

Pizzighettone is an old town divided in two by the Adda. Significant remains of its fortifications are preserved, including the circuit of walls (last strengthened in 1585), the passageways and battlements of which can be visited; and the Torrione, where Francis I was imprisoned after the Battle of Pavia (1525, *see p. 151*). The church of San Bassiano has a frescoed *Crucifixion* by Bernardino Campi.

Soncino and environs

East of Crema is **Soncino**. The castle here (*open Tues–Sat 10–12, Sun and holidays 10–12.30 & 2.30–6 or 7*) was rebuilt by Galeazzo Maria Sforza and is among the best preserved in Lombardy. It was restored in 1886 by Luca Beltrami, the *enfant terrible* of Milanese architecture at the turn of the 19th century. Ezzelino da Romano died here after his defeat in the battle of Cassano d'Adda. The splendid town walls (13th–15th century) are nearly 2km in circumference. Five watermills survive in or near the town, one of which is still in operation; the town preserves a 13th-century drainage system.

The wide main street descends from the site of the south gate past the 15th-century Palazzo Azzanelli, with terracotta decoration, to the main square with the 11th-century Torre Civica and the church of San Giacomo, which has a curious seven-sided tower (1350) and a cloister. It contains two stained-glass windows by Ambrogio da Tormoli (1490) and a late 15th-century terracotta *Pietà*. Nearby is the Casa degli Stampatori, a medieval tower house thought to be on the site of the first printing works founded in the town in 1480. The press was set up by the Jewish Nathan family, who were allowed by the Sforza (in return for cash loans) to take up residence here, having been forced to leave Germany. They adopted the name of the town for their press and, in the decade in which they lived and worked here, they printed their first book (in 1483) and the first complete Hebrew Bible (in 1488). There is a little museum, and a reproduction press is still in operation.

The pieve of **Santa Maria Assunta** was reconstructed in the 17th–19th centuries on the site of a much older church. On the outskirts of the little town is the church of Santa Maria delle Grazie (ring for admission at the convent), begun in 1492 and consecrated in 1528, splendidly decorated with terracotta friezes and frescoes, many of them by Giulio Campi (including the triumphal arch and sanctuary vault). East of Soncino is Orzinuovi, with imposing remains of Venetian ramparts. From here the road descends to **Verolanuova**, where the church contains two large paintings by Giovanni Battista Tiepolo, in excellent condition.

PRACTICAL INFORMATION

GETTING AROUND

• **By rail:** To Milan (1hr 15mins). Branch lines to Piacenza (30mins), Fidenza (30mins), Bergamo (1hr 15mins) and Brescia (30–40mins).
• **By bus:** Bus no. 1 from the station to the centre of the town. Buses from Via Dante next to the railway station for places in the province.

INFORMATION OFFICES

Cremona Piazza del Comune 5, T: 0372 23233, www.aptcremona.it
Crema Via Racchetti 8, T: 0373 81020.

HOTELS

Cremona
€€ **Continental**. Large (57 rooms), comfortable and fairly central. Piazza della Libertà 26, T: 0372 434141, www.hotelcontinentalcremona.it
Crema
€€ **Palace**. Central and comfortable.

Closed Aug. Via Cresmiero 10, T: 0373 81487 www.palacehotelcrema.com

RESTAURANTS

Cremona
€€ **Ceresole**. Restaurant offering brilliant interpretations of traditional recipes. Closed Sun evening, Mon, Jan and Aug. Via Ceresole 4, T: 0372 23322.
€€ **La Sosta**. Modern décor and old-fashioned cuisine in a 15th-century building. Closed Mon and Aug. Via Sicardo 9, T: 0372 456656.
€€ **Mellini**. Trattoria known for its fresh, home-made pasta and fine wines. Closed Sun evening, Mon and July. Via Bossolati 105, T: 0372 30535.
€ **Porta Mosa**. Simple but delicious trattoria where wine is served in the traditional bowls called *pauline*. Closed Sun, Aug–Sept and Dec–Jan. Via Santa Maria in Betlem 11, T: 0372 411803.
Calvisano
€€ **Gambero**. Restaurant featuring outstanding regional cuisine. Closed

Wed, Jan and Aug. Via Roma 11, T: 030 968009.

Casalbuttano

€ **La Granda**. *Osteria* in a traditional *cascinotta* with central courtyard. Closed Wed, Jan and Aug. Via Jacini 51, T: 0374 362406.

Pralboino

€€€ **Leon d'Oro**. Restaurant known for its *lumacche* (snails) and other regional delicacies. Closed Sun evening, Mon, Jan and Aug. Via Gambara 6, T: 030 954156.

Ripalta Cremasca

€€ **Via Vai**. Country trattoria combining excellent local cuisine with great wines. Closed Tues–Wed. Via Libertà 18, T: 0373 268232.

Scandolara Ripa d'Oglio

€€ **Al Caminetto**. Restaurant serving outstanding seasonal dishes. Closed Mon–Tues, Jan and Aug. Via Umberto I 26, T: 0372 89589.

Torre de' Picenardi

€ **Italia**. On the Mantua road, delicious creative interpretations of traditional regional dishes. Closed Sun evening, Mon, Jan, July or Aug. Via Garibaldi 1, T: 0375 94108.

Vho di Piadena

€ **Trattoria dell'Alba**. Trattoria on the road to Mantua serving great local cuisine. Closed Sat, Mon evening and Aug. Via del Popolo 31.

CAFÉS & FOOD SHOPS

Cremona is absolutely brimming with cafés and pastry shops. Just outside the station, to the right, is **Dondeo**, one of the favourite cafés of the Cremonese. The author's favourite is opposite the north flank of the cathedral: at **Pasticceria Duomo** (Via Bocaccino 6) you can sip cappuccino, sample delightful cakes and pastries and admire the finest brickwork in Lombardy, all at once.

Cremona is known also for its *mostarda* (pickled fruit), *torrone* (nougat), salami and aged cheeses. There are at least two good *salumerie* in town: **Saronni**, Corso Mazzini 38, which makes an explosive garlic salami; and **Barbieri**, on route 10 just beyond the bridge over the Po.

MARKETS

The Cremona area is known for its flea markets and antiques fairs: **Cremona**, *Mercatino d'Antiquariato*, Piazza Cavour, third Sun of the month except July–Aug; **Piadena**, *Mercatino delle Pulci*, Piazza Garibaldi, second Sat of the month except Aug; **Castelleone**, *Mostra-Mercato dell'Antiquariato e dell'Artigianato*, in the historic centre, second Sun of the month except Aug. **Pandino**, *Cose d'Altri Tempi*, Castello Visconteo, first Sun of the month except Jan, July–Aug.

FESTIVALS & EVENTS

Cremona is best known for its classical music festivals. Some of the best are: *Antiche Accademie Musicali*, chamber-music series, Mar. *Omaggio a Cremona*, stringed-instrument festival, spring. *Festival di Cremona*, classical music for strings, May–June. *Il Canto delle Pietre*, sacred music concert series, Cremona and province, June–Oct. *Oh, Che Armonico Fracasso*, opera music, Vescovato, Nov–Dec.

MANTUA & SABBIONETA

Mantua is the unofficial capital of this corner of Lombardy—a flat, fertile area possessing bucolic charm, and studded with architectural jewels like the little theatre at Sabbioneta. Mantua itself is an ancient town, famous for its associations with the Gonzaga, under whose rule it flourished as a brilliant centre of art and civilisation in the 15th and 16th centuries. In the centre of the town, with its quiet old cobbled streets and piazzas, is the huge Palazzo Ducale of the Gonzaga, celebrated for its Camera degli Sposi, frescoed by Mantegna. The dukes' summer villa, the Palazzo del Te, is the masterpiece of Giulio Romano.

Mantua is surrounded on three sides by the River Mincio, a tributary of the Po, which widens out to form a lake of three reaches, Lago Superiore, Lago di Mezzo and Lago Inferiore. The presence of so much water, which cools the air more in winter, it would seem, than in summer, gives the town its rather chill atmosphere. In winter, in fact, it can feel like one of the coldest spots on earth, due to its high relative humidity and the biting wind that blows down the river. In recent years naturalists have taken an interest in the birdlife and flora of the marshlands and lakes, where lotus flowers introduced from China in 1921 grow in abundance.

Impressions of Mantua

Over no city did there brood so profound a melancholy as over Mantua; none seemed so dead or so utterly bereft of glory .... And not in Mantua alone. For wherever the Gonzaga lived, they left behind them the same pathetic emptiness, the same pregnant desolation, the same echoes, the same ghosts of splendour.

Aldous Huxley, Along the Road, 1925

Mantua itself rises out of a morass formed by the Mincio, whose course, in most places is so choked up with reeds, as to be scarcely discernible. It requires creative imagination to discover any charms in such a prospect, and a strong prepossession not to be disgusted with the scene where Virgil was born ... I abandoned poetry and entered the city in despair.

William Beckford, Dreams, Waking Thoughts and Incidents, 1783

The Citie is marveilous strong, and walled round with faire bricke wals, wherein there are eight gates, and is thought to be foure miles in compasse: the buildings both publique and private are very sumptuous and magnificent: their streets straite and very spacious. Also I saw many stately Pallaces of a goodly height: it is most sweetly seated in respect of the marvailous sweete ayre thereof, the abundance of goodly meadows, pastures, vineyards, orchards, and gardens about it.

Thomas Coryate, Crudities, 1611

HISTORY OF MANTUA

Virgil was born on Mantuan territory about 70 BC, and some of the town's earliest recorded history is due to the poet's interest in his birthplace. Mantua became a free commune about 1126 and was afterwards dominated by the Bonacolsi and Gonzaga families. Under Gonzaga rule from 1328 the town was a famous centre of art and learning, especially in the reigns of Lodovico II (1444–78), Francesco II (1484–1519), husband of Isabella d'Este, the greatest patron of her time (who died in Mantua in 1539), and their son Federico II (1519–40).

The city was sacked by imperial troops in 1630, and many of the best Gonzaga paintings were sold to Charles I of England. The duchy was extinguished in 1708 by the Austrians, who fortified the town as the southwest corner of their 'quadrilateral'. It held out against Napoleon for eight months in 1796–97, and was retaken by the French in 1799. The town was again under Austrian rule in 1814–66.

EXPLORING MANTUA

The Palazzo Ducale

The whole of the upper side of the large, cobbled **Piazza Sordello** is occupied by the famous Palazzo Ducale, a huge fortress-palace that remains a fitting emblem of the hospitality of the Gonzaga princes.

The vast rambling palace is divided into three main parts, all connected by corridors and courtyards: the original 14th-century Bonacolsi palace, known as the Corte Vecchia, on Piazza Sordello, which was adapted by the Gonzaga rulers; the castle added by the Gonzaga in the 15th century to defend the approach to the city from the lake (and once connected to the palace by drawbridges only); and the Corte Nuova wing, mainly planned by Giulio Romano in the 16th century. Architects who worked on the palace included Luca Fancelli in the 15th century and, in the 16th and early 17th centuries, Giulio Romano and Antonio Maria Viani. The palace is now chiefly remarkable for its decorations, including the famous Camera degli Sposi in the castle (*see p. 258*). Most of the great Gonzaga art collections begun by Isabella d'Este, wife of Francesco II, and enriched in the 16th century, have been dispersed. Many of the palace rooms contain excellent Classical sculpture. The success of Monteverdi's *Orfeo* here in 1607 was the first landmark in the history of opera.

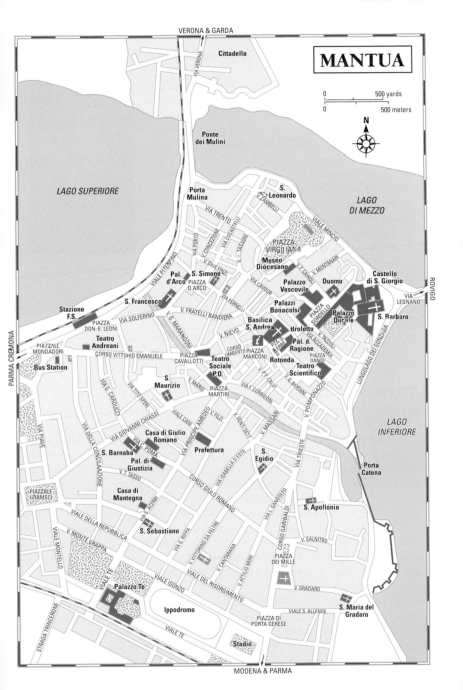

MANTUA

VERONA & GARDA

Cittadella

VIA VERONA

Ponte dei Mulini

LAGO SUPERIORE

LAGO DI MEZZO

Porta Mulina

S. Leonardo

V. ZAMBELLI

VIALE MINCIO

VIA TRENTO

VIA PORTO

VIA COCASTELLI

V. TASSONI

PIAZZA VIRGILIANA

Museo Diocesano

V.E. CAIROLI

V. MONTANARI

VIALE PITERZINO

V. CONCEZIONE

V. GIUS. FINZI

VIA CAVOUR

Pal. d'Arco

S. Simone

PIAZZA D'ARCO

Palazzo Vescovile

Duomo

Castello di S. Giorgio

ROVIGO

S. Francesco

VIA FERNELI

Palazzi Bonacolsi

VIA LEGNANO

Stazione F.S.

V. FRATELLI BANDIERA

Basilica S. Andrea

Palazzo Ducale

S. Barbara

PIAZZA DON. E. LEONI

VIA SOLFERINO

V. G. MARANGONI

V. NIEVO

Broletto

VIA ACCADEMIA

PIAZZALE MONDADORI

Teatro Andreani

CORSO VITTORIO EMANUELE

PIAZZA CAVALLOTTI

CORSO UMBERTO I

PIAZZA MARCONI

Pal. d. Ragione

PIAZZA DANTE

Bus Station

Rotonda

Teatro Scientifico

G. BERTANI

LUNGOLAGO DEI GONZAGA

S. Maurizio

VIA G. CARDUCCI

VIA TITO SPERI

V. MARIO

Teatro Sociale P.O.

PIAZZA MARTIRI

V. P. F. CALVI

VIA F. CORRIDONI

LAGO INFERIORE

VIALE CANI

V. FILZI

K. VENTI SET.

V. MASSARI

VIA TRIESTE

PARMA CREMONA

VIA PIAVE

VIA DELLA CONCILIAZIONE

VIA GIOVANNI CHIASSI

VIA C. POMA

VIA PRINCIPE AMEDEO

Casa di Giulio Romano

Prefettura

VIA ISABELLA D'ESTE

S. Egidio

Porta Catena

S. Barnaba

Pal. di Giustizia

V.T. TASSO

CORSO GIULIO ROMANO

PIAZZALE GRAMSCI

Casa di Mantegna

VIA G. ACERBI

VIA G. GANDOLFO

S. Apollonia

VIALE DELLA REPUBBLICA

V. MONTE GRAPPA

VIALE MONTELLO

S. Sebastiano

V. G. RIPPA

VIA VITTORINO DA FELTRE

V. CANTARANA

V. ATTILIO MORI

CORSO GARIBALDI

V. SALNITRO

PIAZZA DEI MILLE

VIALE TE

VIALE ISONZO

VIALE DEL RISORGIMENTO

V. GRADARO

Palazzo Te

Ippodromo

VIALE TE

PIAZZA DI PORTA CERESE

VIALE S. ALLENDE

S. Maria del Gradaro

STRADA TRINCERONE

Stadio

MODENA & PARMA

0   500 yards
0   500 meters

N

ART AT THE COURT OF THE GONZAGA

In 1490 the 16-year-old Isabella d'Este, daughter of the Duke of Ferrara and sister of the Duchess of Milan, married Francesco Gonzaga of Mantua. Together they gathered around them artists, writers and musicians to create a court of high culture and discriminating taste. Among the artists who flourished under the Gonzagas were Leon Battista Alberti, Luca Fancelli and Pisanello. Andrea Mantegna was court artist from 1460 until his death in 1506. Giulio Romano, architect and painter, was called to Mantua in 1524 by Isabella's son Federico II, and worked there until his death in 1546, leaving numerous monuments in the city (most important of all are the Palazzo del Te (*see p. 263*), and the Cortile della Cavallerizza in the Palazzo Ducale, where the

Isabella d'Este.

columns are teased into outlandish corkscrew forms. Titian often visited the city, and it was here that he first saw the works of Giulio Romano. He painted Isabella d'Este's portrait twice. Alari Bonacolsi, nicknamed 'L'Antico', was born in Mantua, and he was commissioned by the Gonzaga to make bronze copies of Classical statues, for which Isabella nurtured a particular passion.

Tour of the palace

The **Corte Vecchia**, or ducal palace proper, overlooking Piazza Sordello, consists of the low Domus Magna, founded by Guido Bonacolsi c. 1290, and the higher Palazzo del Capitano, built a few years later by the Bonacolsi at the expense of the city. The Austrians altered the windows of the façade in the Gothic style, and it was restored to its original 15th-century appearance at the beginning of this century by the Samuel Kress Foundation. After the sack of Mantua in 1630 a large part of the fabric of the palace deteriorated. Restoration, begun in 1902, was completed in 1934.

The palace consists of some 700 rooms and 15 courtyards. Some of these are never open to the public, and other parts are sometimes closed. The description below covers all the areas normally accessible: scholars may be given special permission to see any parts not shown on the tour. As the order of the visit sometimes changes, the room numbers given below refer to the plan overleaf.

NB: The palace is open Tues–Sun 8.45–9.15; T: 041 241 1897. Visitors are conducted in parties of about 30 (there is usually no more than 15mins wait at the ticket office for a group to form), although there are plans to open at least parts of the palace to visitors not on the guided tour. The most crowded periods of the year are March to May and September to October.

1: The 17th-century **Scalone delle Duchesse** by Antonio Maria Viani ascends to the first floor. Notice here the interesting painting of *Piazza Sordello* by Domenico Morone, illustrating the expulsion of the Bonacolsi in 1328. It shows the front of Palazzo Ducale (a detail of which was useful during restoration work on the building in this century) and the Gothic façade of the duomo (pulled down in 1761).

4: Corridoio del Passerino, or Corridoio del Palazzo del Capitano, has interesting late-Gothic mural decorations and numerous coats of arms. The seated figure of Virgil dates from c. 1220, and the stemma of the podestà Ginori (1494) is by the Della Robbia workshop. The mantelpiece is attributed to Luca Fancelli.

5–10: Appartamento Guastalla. These rooms contain a lapidary collection; a group of five terracotta statues attributed to the school of Mantegna; a terracotta bust of Francesco II Gonzaga by Gian Cristoforo Romano; the tomb effigy of Margherita Malatesta (wife of Francesco I) by Pier Paolo dalle Masegne; a Classical relief of *Philoctetes* attributed to Tullio Lombardo; a 16th-century sleeping cupid with two serpents; and a large ruined fresco of the *Crucifixion* attributed to the 14th–15th-century Bolognese school. In the last room (10) are displayed detached frescoes (1303) and a Byzantine *Madonna*.

11: The **Sala del Pisanello** or Sala dei Principi contains a splendid fragment of a mural painting discovered in the 1960s showing a battle tournament.

The unfinished but vivacious composition is one of the masterpieces of Pisanello. Forming a border along the top of the painting is a beautiful frieze incorporating the Lancastrian 'SS' collar entwined with marigold flowers, the emblem of the Gonzaga—it was Henry VI of England who granted the Gonzaga the concession to use the heraldic crest of the House of Lancaster. On the other wall are *sinopie* of Arthurian scenes by Pisanello.

13–14: The **Salette dell'Alcove** are not always open. They contain 18th-century works including *St Thomas with Angels* by Giuseppe Bazzani.

15: The **Galleria Nuova** (*closed at the time of writing*) displays 17th-century paintings including works by Carlo Bononi and Giuseppe Maria Crespi.

16–19: Appartamento degli Arazzi, overlooking the Cortile d'Onore, with Neoclassical decoration (1779). The Brussels tapestries here, designed after Raphael's cartoons of the *Acts of the Apostles* (now in the Victoria and Albert Museum, London), are the most important replica of the Vatican series. They were acquired by Ercole Gonzaga. Some of the other rooms have false painted 'tapestries'.

20: The **Sala dello Zodiaco** has delightful frescoes by Lorenzo Costa the Younger (1580).

21: The **Sala dei Fiumi**, decorated in 1775 by Giorgio Anselmi, with allegories of river gods, two stucco 'grottoes' and a 16th-century table of *pietre*

PALAZZO DUCALE

1	Scalone delle Duchesse
4	Corridoio del Passerino
5–10	Appartamento Guastalla
11	Sala del Pisanello
13–14	Salette dell'Alcove
15	Galleria Nuova
16–19	Appartamento degli Arazzi
20	Sala del Zodiaco
21	Sala dei Fiumi
22–24	Appartamento dell'Imperatrice
25	Sala dei Falconi
26	Saletta dei Mori
29–33	Pinacoteca
39–42	Domus Nova
44–47	Appartamento delle Metamorfosi
55	Galleria della Mostra
56	Galleria dei Mesi

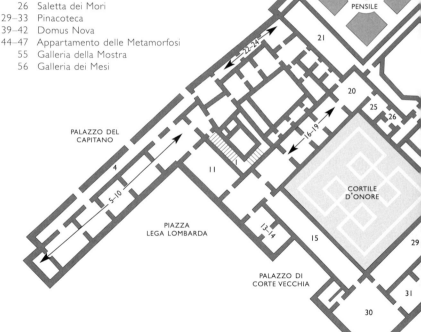

57	Sala di Troia
62	Camerino degli Ucelli
63	Sala dei Cavalli
65–66	Appartamento del Tasso
67	Stanza d'Apollo
68	Sala dei Marchesi
70	Salone di Manto
71	Scalone di Enea
72	Camera degli Sposi
73	Corridoio Bertani

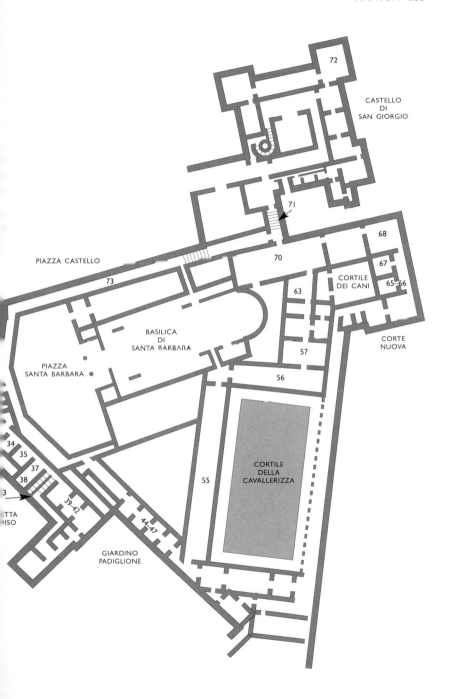

CASTELLO
DI
SAN GIORGIO

72

71

68

PIAZZA CASTELLO

70

67

65–66

CORTILE
DEI CANI

73

63

CORTE
NUOVA

BASILICA
DI
SANTA BARBARA

57

56

PIAZZA
SANTA BARBARA

34

35

37

38

55

CORTILE
DELLA
CAVALLERIZZA

39–42

3

ETTA
ISO

44–47

GIARDINO
PADIGLIONE

dure made in Florence. It overlooks the Giardino Pensile, a hanging garden off which is a 'Kaffeehaus' with ceilings decorated in the 18th century by Antonio Bibiena.

22–24: Appartamento dell' Imperatrice, with Empire-style furniture dating from the early 19th century. (*Usually closed.*)

25: Sala dei Falconi, named after a ceiling painting of hawks, attributed to Ippolito Andreasi.

26: The **Saletta dei Mori** has a fine gilded-wood ceiling and 16th- and 17th-century paintings.

39–42: In the **Domus Nova** (*closed*) are the **Appartamento di Eleonora Medici Gonzaga**, wife of Vincenzo II, designed by Viani. On a mezzanine floor, the so-called **Appartamento dei Nani** (*also closed*), once thought to have been for the Court dwarves, is in fact a miniature reproduction of the Scala Santa in Rome made by Viani for Ferdinando Gonzaga c. 1620, and used for religious functions.

44–47: The **Appartamento delle Metamorfosi**, with ceilings by Viani and his school, and Roman busts and reliefs, looks out onto the Giardino del Padiglione, with a view of the Domus Nova by Luca Fancelli.

55: The **Galleria della Mostra**, with a magnificent ceiling, was built by Viani for the display of the most important part of the ducal collection: it now contains original busts of Roman emperors. There is a view of the splendid Cortile

del Cavalerizza by Giulio Romano and Bertani, and the lake beyond.

56: Galleria dei Mesi, built as a loggia by Giulio Romano and now holding a large antique relief brought by him from Rome.

57: Sala di Troia, with frescoes of the *Trojan War* designed by Giulio Romano and executed by his pupils.

62: Camerino degli Uccelli has a pretty ceiling and contains a statuette of Aphrodite, a Roman copy of a 3rd-century BC original.

63: Sala dei Cavalli, which takes its name from paintings of horses by Giulio Romano, which formerly hung here. It has a fine wooden coffered ceiling. The classical sculpture includes two circular altars.

65–66: Appartamento del Tasso, where the Gonzaga are supposed to have received Torquato Tasso on his flight from Ferrara. In July 1586 Vincenzo Gonzaga, negotiated Tasso's release from the Arcispedale di Sant'Anna at Ferrara, where he had been confined in 1579 for mental disorders. At the Mantuan court he enjoyed a brief moment of creative fervour, completing his tragedy *Galealto*, retitled *Re Torrismondo* (1587), but then relapsed into his state of inquietude and fled from Mantua, wandering largely between Naples and Rome.

67: The **Stanza di Apollo** has beautiful decoration attributed to Francesco Primaticcio (from a previous building).

68: The **Sala dei Marchesi** has fine allegorical figures and busts in stucco by Francesco Segala. The beautiful Greek sculpture here includes the stele of a male figure and child (4th century BC), and an Attic lute player.

70: The **Salone di Manto**, with its beautiful coffered ceiling, has more Classical sculpture, including a Caryatid of the 5th century BC and the *Mantua Apollo*.

71: The **Scalone di Enea** and the spiral Scala dei Cavalli lead into the Castello di San Giorgio, a keep built in 1395–1406 (the exterior was formerly covered with frescoes). The design of the courtyard loggia, built by Luca Fancelli, is attributed to Mantegna. A spiral ramp leads up to a series of rooms beyond which is the famous **Camera degli Sposi** (72; *see overleaf*), formerly known as the Camera Picta.

73: **Corridoio Bertani**, with modern copies of the stucco portraits of the Gonzaga in the Palazzo Ducale of Sabbioneta.

The Pinacoteca

30: As well as an unusual frescoed frieze of horses behind curtains, the **Salone degli Arcieri** has some of the most important paintings in the palace. *The Gonzaga Family in Adoration of the Trinity* by Rubens was cut into pieces during the French occupation; two other fragments of it are exhibited here. Three works by Domenico Fetti include a monochrome lunette showing Viani presenting a model of the church of Sant'Orsola to Margherita Gonzaga d'Este, and a lunette with the *Miracle of the Loaves and Fishes*. There are also two paintings by Viani.

31: The **Appartamento Ducale**, arranged by Vincenzo I shortly after 1600, begins here. The first room, the **Sala di Giuditta**, has fabulous nocturnal scenes telling the *Story of Judith* by the Neapolitan painter Pietro Mango, and paintings of *Apostles and Saints* by Domenico Fetti.

32: The **Sala del Labirinto**, named after the labyrinth carved in the wood ceiling, has sculptures and paintings from the palace of the Pico at Mirandola. The episodes from the *Story of Psyche* are by Sante Peranda, and the two marble busts are portraits of Beatrice d'Este Pico (with lace) and Maria Cybo Pico (with a veil), both duchesses of Mirandola. High up on the walls are paintings by Sante Peranda and Palma Giovane.

33: The ceiling has the gold crucible motif, Vincenzo's emblem, and more Pico portraits, including *Alfonso and Giulia d'Este* by Sante Peranda.

The **Appartamento di Isabella d'Este**, off the Cortile d'Onore, is sometimes opened on request. Her *studiolo*, for which she commissioned paintings from Mantegna, Perugino, Lorenzo Costa and Correggio (all of them now in the Louvre) has a door by Gian Cristoforo Romano. Her grotto contains *intarsie* by the Della Mola brothers. Both rooms have fine gilded wood ceilings.

THE CAMERA DEGLI SPOSI

The magnificent paintings by Mantegna (1465–74) were commissioned by Lodovico, the second Marquis of Mantua, and illustrate the life of Lodovico and his wife Barbara of Brandenburg. The work was immediately recognised as a masterpiece and was of fundamental importance to later Renaissance artists. The room appears to have been used by Lodovico as a bedroom, as well as an office and as a place for receiving visiting dignitaries.

On the north wall, above the fireplace, the marquis and his wife are shown seated, surrounded by their family, courtiers and messengers. Between the husband and wife is their son Gianfrancesco with his hands on the shoulders of a younger son, Lodovico, and a daughter, Paola, shown holding an apple. Rodolfo stands behind his mother, and to the right is his pretty sister Barbara (with her nurse behind and a dwarf in front). Beneath Lodovico's chair is his old dog Rubino, who died in 1467. On the right is a group of courtiers dressed in the Gonzaga livery.

On the west wall are three scenes presumed to represent the 1462 meeting between the marquis, on his way to Milan, and his son Francesco, the first member of the Gonzaga family to be nominated cardinal, travelling back from Milan. On the left are servants in the Gonzaga livery with hounds and a horse—the Gonzaga were famous horse breeders and dog lovers. Above the door is a dedicatory inscription, supported by winged putti, signed and dated 1474, by Mantegna. In the right-hand section is the scene of the meeting: the first full figure in profile is the marquis, dressed in grey with a sword at his side, talking to Francesco, in cardinal's robes; the children are also members of the Gonzaga family. The group to the right is thought to include Holy Roman Emperor Frederick III (in profile) and, dressed in red in the background, Christian I of Denmark. The landscape in the background of all three scenes is particularly beautiful and includes Classical monuments (derived from buildings in Rome and Verona) and an imaginary city. In the frieze on the pilaster to the right of the door is Mantegna's self-portrait.

The vaulted ceiling has a trompe l'oeil oculus in the centre, one of the first examples of aerial perspective in painting. The curious, inventive scene (*pictured opposite*) shows a circular stone balustrade on which winged putti are playing; and peering over the top of it are five courtly female figures, a peacock and more putti, and balanced on the edge is a plant in a tub. The vault, with a background of painted mosaic, is divided by trompe l'oeil ribs into eight sections with medallions containing the portraits of the first Roman emperors and, below (damaged) mythological scenes. The last two walls were decorated with painted gold damask (now very damaged), and the lower part of the walls has painted marble intarsia.

Mantegna: ceiling of the Camera degli Sposi (1465–74).

Around the Duomo

On the opposite side of Piazza Sordello are two grim, battlemented **Bonacolsi palaces**, belonging to the family who ruled Mantua before the Gonzaga. Above the first rises the **Torre della Gabbia**, from which (seen from Via Cavour) an iron cage protrudes where condemned prisoners were exposed. The second, Palazzo Castiglioni, dates from the 13th century. Beyond is the Rococo Palazzo Bianchi, now the bishop's palace.

At the end of the piazza is the **duomo**. The late Gothic building burned down in 1545 (although part of the south side survives), and the unsuccessful façade was built in 1756 next to the broad brick campanile. The light interior was designed by Giulio Romano (after 1545) in imitation of an early Christian basilica. It is covered with exquisite stucco decoration. In the south aisle is a 6th-century Christian sarophagus, and the baptistery with remains of 14th- and 15th-century frescoes. The Cappella dell'Incoronata, a charming work in the style of Alberti, is reached by a corridor off the north aisle.

At the opposite end of the piazza an archway leads into **Piazza del Broletto**, where a small daily market is held. On the **Broletto** (1227), with its four corner towers, is a quaint figure of Virgil sculpted in the 13th century, showing the poet at a rostrum wearing his doctor's hat. At no. 9 is the entrance to a small museum (*open daily except*

Palazzo della Ragione in Piazza delle Erbe.

Mon and Thur 10–1 & 3.30–6.30), dedicated to Tazio Nuvolari (1892–1953), the famous motor-racing champion, who was born in Mantua. Connected to the Broletto by an archway is the **Arengario**, a little 13th-century building with a loggia. A restaurant beneath the archway occupies a Gonzaga office with an early 14th-century fresco of the city, and the arms of Gianfrancesco, the first marquis. Palazzo Andreasi, with a portico, has an interesting first floor, now used by a shop (entered from 79 Via Cavour), with handsome wood ceilings.

BASILICA OF SANT'ANDREA

On the other side of the Broletto is **Piazza delle Erbe**, a charming square with a delightful row of houses at the far end. There is a small daily market here, and a large general market on Thursdays. A long portico faces **Palazzo della Ragione**, dating partly from the early 13th century but with 14th–15th-century additions, including a conspicuous clock tower (1473) by Luca Fancelli with an astrological clock by Bartolomeo Manfredi (1473), in perfect working order. Next to it is the **Rotonda di San Lorenzo**, a small round church founded in 1082 and restored in 1908. The domed interior has two orders of columns and a matroneum. To the southwest of here, on Piazza Dante, is the **Accademia Virgiliana**, built by Piermarini in 1767. Here you can visit the Teatro Scientifico (or Teatro Bibiena) by Antonio Bibiena (*open Tues–Sun 9.30–12.30 & 3–6*), where Mozart gave the inaugural concert in 1770 at the age of 13, during his first visit to Italy. It is still sometimes used for concerts.

Sant'Andrea

The basilica of **Sant'Andrea**, facing Palazzo della Ragione across Piazza delle Erbe, is a very important Renaissance building commissioned from Leon Battista Alberti by Lodovico II Gonzaga in 1470 as a fit setting to display the precious relic of the Holy Blood. Although it was built by Luca Fancelli between 1472 and 1494, after Alberti's death, then enlarged in 1530 under the direction of Giulio Romano, and the dome was added by Filippo Juvarra in 1732, it remains the most complete architectural work by Alberti. The remarkable façade, with giant pilasters, is Classical in inspiration. In the barrel-vaulted vestibule, a beautiful marble frieze with animals and birds surrounds the west door. The brick campanile of 1413 is a survival from the 11th-century monastery on this site.

The huge interior, on a longitudinal plan, has a spacious barrel-vaulted **nave** without columns or aisles. The rectangular side chapels, also with barrel vaults, are preceded by giant paired pilasters raised on pedestals. Between them are small, lower domed chapels. The transepts, with the same proportions, are also rectangular. The nave chapels were decorated in the 16th century, partly by pupils of Giulio Romano, and the rest of the church in the 18th century.

Begin your visit in the **south aisle**. You can appreciate Alberti's architecture in the first little chapel (the baptistery), whose walls are bare. Detached frescoes by Correggio have been placed here, but they do not interfere with the overall effect. In the next chapel are 16th-century frescoes attributed to Benedetto Pagni, and the pretty little third chapel is frescoed by Rinaldo Mantovano (1534). In the fourth chapel is a 16th-century wood ancona. The sixth chapel has a fine altarpiece, a 16th-century copy of the original by Giulio Romano (now in the Louvre); the frescoes, designed by Romano, were executed by Rinaldo Mantovano.

The frescoes in the **dome and apse** are late 18th century. On the left of the high altar is a statue of Guglielmo Gonzaga at prayer (1572). Beneath the dome is an octagonal balustrade marking the crypt, which contains the precious reliquary of the Holy Blood. The crypt is opened on request.

In the **north transept** is a door that leads out to a piazza, from where you can see the exterior of the church and a walk of the Gothic cloister of the monastery that stood on this site. The transept chapel contains 16th- and 17th-century funerary monuments including that of Pietro Strozzi, an ingenious work of 1529 with four caryatids, designed by Giulio Romano. On the north side, the sixth chapel has an altarpiece of the *Crucifix* by Fermo Ghisoni, a pupil of Giulio Romano. The third chapel has an early 17th-century wooden ancona, and in the second chapel there is a beautiful altarpiece by Lorenzo Costa (1525).

The first little chapel, the Cappella del Mantegna (unlocked on request), was chosen by Mantegna in 1504 as his funerary chapel. It contains his tomb with his bust in bronze, possibly his self-portrait. The charming panel of the *Holy Family and the Family of St John the Baptist* is almost certainly by Mantegna. Above is his coat of arms. The terracotta decoration and frescoes on the walls and dome, including the symbols of the Evangelists, were designed by Mantegna and probably executed by his son Francesco. The painting of the *Baptism of Christ*, probably to a design by Mantegna, is also the work of Francesco.

From Piazza Martiri to Palazzo del Te

Beside **Piazza Martiri**, below a little park on the river, is a fish market with a rusticated portico, built by Giulio Romano in 1546. From here, Via Principe Amadeo leads down to the Palazzo del Te past two interesting houses. The first, at Via Carlo Poma 18, is the **house of Giulio Romano**: he purchased it in 1538 when it was on the outskirts of the town. He transformed it in the 1540s, and it was enlarged in the 19th century. Sadly it is not open to the public. Opposite it is the huge domed church of **San Barnaba** containing works by Lorenzo Costa the Younger (16th century) and Giuseppe Bazzani (18th century), and a fine high altar in *pietre dure*. Left of the church is the Palazzo della Giustizia, formerly the Palazzo Guerrieri, with bizarre monster caryatids attributed to Viani.

Continue down towards Palazzo del Te now, and you will come to the **Casa di Mantegna** on your right. This plain brick house (*open Mon–Fri 10–12.30 & 3–6; when used for exhibitions, Tues–Sun 10–12.30 & 3–6; T: 0376 360506*) was built to Mantegna's design in 1466–74 as a studio and private museum. It has a remarkable circular courtyard. The artist lived here until 1502 when he donated it to Francesco II Gonzaga. A painting by Titian of Mantegna (or Giulio Romano) is exhibited here.

Diagonally opposite the house is the ducal church of **San Sebastiano** (1460), designed by Alberti on a Greek-cross plan. This unusual building, with a beautiful raised vestibule, a side portico and a ground-level crypt, has been brutally altered over the centuries. The interior (*open by appointment; apply at Palazzo del Te*) now contains the sarcophagus of the 'Martyrs of Belfiore' (Italian nationalists shot by the Austrians in 1851–52), and the crypt serves as a war memorial.

Giulio Romano (?1499–1546)
The architect and painter Giulio Romano is mentioned by Shakespeare in *The Winter's Tale*: '...that rare Italian master, Julio Romano, who, had he himself eternity and could put breath into his work, would beguile Nature of her custom, so perfectly he is her ape'. Giulio Romano was a distinguished Renaissance painter and architect and one of the creators of Mannerism. Born Giulio di Pietro di Filippo de' Gianuzzi, his birth date is a matter of some dispute (1492/99), but his birthplace was definitely Rome. The chief assistant and principal heir of Raphael, he completed several of his master's unfinished works, notably the *Transfiguration* and the Vatican frescoes. In his own work he developed a highly personal, anti-Classical style of painting. In 1524, at the invitation of the Gonzaga, Giulio left Rome for Mantua, where he remained until his death, completely dominating the artistic affairs of the duchy. The most important of all his works is the Palazzo del Te, begun in 1525 or 1526 and built and decorated entirely by him and his pupils. His painting of the *Fall of the Giants* in that building is a masterpiece of illusionism.

Palazzo del Te

Open Mon 1–6, Tues–Sun 9–6; T: 037 632 3266.
On the southern edge of the old town, about 1.5km from Piazza Sordello, surrounded by a public garden is the Mannerist **Palazzo del Te** (the name is probably derived from Teieto, the name of the locality), one of the most important secular buildings in Italy. It was built as a summer villa on the site of the Gonzaga stables, and much used

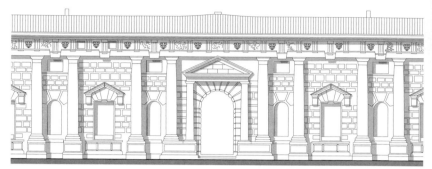

PALAZZO DEL TE, COURTYARD ELEVATION

by Federico II Gonzaga. Begun in 1525, it is built of brick and stucco with bold rustication and giant orders of pilasters giving the façades a monumental appearance. Spaciously laid out around a courtyard with symmetrical loggias, it is Giulio Romano's most famous work, inspired by the great villas of Rome. Inside the courtyard you will see how he gently subverted the rigid rules of Classical architecture, designing sections of the entablature to look as though they were slipping out of place. In the decorative design he was helped by his pupils, including Primaticcio, who executed some of the stucco work. The rooms of the palace, bare of furniture, are of interest for their painted and stuccoed decoration.

It was in this palace that Federico held his splendid entertainments and in 1530, when Emperor Charles V granted him the Dukedom of Mantua, Federico received his imperial benefactor here. The entrance is through the west loggia, beyond which you can see the beautiful Cortile d'Onore. The **Camera del Sole** has a fine ceiling with stuccoes by Primaticcio and a painting of the *Sun and Moon* by Giulio Romano. On the walls are casts of ancient reliefs put here in the Neoclassical era. Across the Loggia delle Muse is the Sala dei Cavalli, with frescoed portraits of horses from the Gonzaga stables by Rinaldo Mantovano (to a design by Giulio Romano).

The **Sala di Psiche** has splendid frescoes by Giulio Romano illustrating the *Story of Psyche* as told by Apuleius. The next room, the **Sala dei Venti**, was the studio of Federico II. It has a ceiling with signs of the zodiac and *tondi* illustrating horoscopes, together with a fine stucco frieze and fireplace. The **Camera di Fetonte** or Camera delle Aquile has a fresco of the *Fall of Phaëthon* in the centre, and stuccoes including four eagles.

The fine **Loggia di Davide** (or Loggia d'Onore), with biblical frescoes, opens onto two fishponds and the gardens beyond. The **Sala degli Stucchi** was the last work executed by Primaticcio before his departure for France (where he went on to produce his finest work). The two Classical friezes, in imitation of a Roman triumphal column, are thought to have been executed in honour of Charles V's visit. The **Sala dei Cesari** has a trompe l'oeil frieze of putti and Roman historical scenes in the vault.

The famous **Sala dei Giganti**, in which painting and architecture are united in a theatrical trompe l'oeil, is the work of Rinaldo Mantovano and others, to designs by Giulio

Romano. It represents the *Fall of the Giants*, crushed by the thunderbolts of Jupiter hurled from Mount Olympus. The pavement was originally concave and was made up of large stones in imitation of a river bed. The room has strange acoustical properties.

The three **Camerini a Grottesche** are painted with grotesques (1533–34). Beyond are three more rooms, the **Camere dell'Ala Meridionale**, with coffered ceilings and friezes of 1527–28, and Neoclassical stuccoes on the lower part of the walls.

The garden, beyond the fishponds, is closed at the end by an exedra (seated arcade), added c. 1651. The huge **Frutteria** to the right is now used for important exhibitions. On the left is the little **Casino della Grotta**, a secret apartment with more charming stuccoes by Giulio Romano and Primaticcio. There are long-term plans to reconstruct the gardens to the north of the villa.

The upper floor of the palace contains collections from the **Museo Civico**. These include an Egyptian collection; the Gonzaga collection of weights and measures; a numismatic collection; and a gallery of modern art.

The Museo Diocesano and Piazza d'Arco

The spacious **Piazza Virgiliana**, fronting the Lago di Mezzo, was laid out in the Napoleonic period, with fine trees and a grandiose monument to Virgil. At no. 55 is the **Museo Diocesano Francesco Gonzaga** (*open Apr–June and Sept–Oct Tues–Sun 9.30–12 & 2.30–5; Nov–Mar only on Sun and holidays, and July and Aug only on Thur, Sat and Sun*), which contains a large miscellany of works of art in a provisional arrangement. It is entered through a pleasant courtyard with four large lime trees.

In the corridor is a Greek marble female head dating from the 1st century AD (from the campanile of the duomo). In the large hall are paintings, including a tondo of the *Ascension* attributed to Mantegna (with its sinopia). The church silver includes processional crosses of the 14th and 15th centuries. Also here are paintings by Francesco Borgani, Girolamo Mazzola Bedoli, Giuseppe Bazzani and Domenico Fetti. The second part of the room displays a bronze crucifix by Pietro Tacca; more paintings by Bazzani; a collection of Limoges enamels (mostly 16th–19th century); a 17th-century oval relief in silver; and the missal of Barbara of Brandenburg illuminated by Belbello da Pavia, Girolamo da Cremona and others. At the end is a small room that displays ivories, a German jewel pendant that belonged to Duke Guglielmo Gonzaga, and a large reliquary chest made of rock crystal (Venetian, c. 1600). Another section of the museum displays the splendid suits of armour (some of them 15th-century) found on the life-size ex-voto statues in the sanctuary of Santa Maria delle Grazie (*see p. 269*). A marble statue by the Dalle Masegne family (1401) is also displayed here.

From the museum Via Cavour and Via Finzi lead to the **Piazza d'Arco**, with the Neoclassical **Palazzo d'Arco** (*open March– Oct Tues–Sun 10–12.30 & 2.30–6; Nov–Feb Sat–Sun and holidays 10–12.30 & 2–5*), built in 1784. A large number of rooms in the palace are on show, with their 18th- and 19th-century furniture. A room dedicated to Andreas Hofer (*see p. 294*), the Tyrolean patriot who was tried by a Napoleonic court here before being shot outside the walls in 1810, is decorated with wallpaper of 1823 painted with grisaille views of Italy. Other rooms contain a collection of musical instruments, including a spinet, and many paintings, including works by Lorenzo Lotto (attrib.), Giuseppe Bazzani, Pietro Muttoni, Sante Peranda, Fra Semplice da Verona and Alessandro Magnasco.

In the garden are the remains of a 15th-century palace, where the **Sala dello Zodiaco** has remarkable painted decoration attributed to Giovanni Maria Falconetto (c. 1520). The frieze around the top of the walls, decorated with gilded wax, illustrates Classical myths. Below are 12 lunettes with the signs of the zodiac over elaborate representations of Classical myths against landscapes with Roman or Byzantine buildings (derived from monuments in Rome, Ravenna and Verona). Below each scene is a panel in grisaille.

Nearby is the Gothic church of **San Francesco** (1304; rebuilt in 1954), which contains a chapel where the first Gonzaga were buried with their wives, with frescoes (very worn) by Tommaso da Modena.

SABBIONETA

NB: This section is covered by the map on p. 238.

Sabbioneta, southwest of Mantua, was planned in 1556 by Vespasiano Gonzaga (1531–91) as an ideal fortified city, with regular streets within hexagonal walls and some beautiful buildings, including two palaces, a gallery and a theatre, all of which reflect his admiration for the classical world of Rome. Now a quiet little village, it is extremely well preserved, with fields reaching up to its walls. Vespasiano, who received the Dukedom of Sabbioneta from the Holy Roman Emperor in 1577, was a cultivated man, as well as a *condottiere*, and he spent many years at the court of Philip II of Spain. Besides its splendid 16th-century monuments, many of them recently restored, the town—which probably had a population of some 2,000 at its height—preserves pretty streets of simple houses with a number of walled gardens.

NB: The information office at Via Vespasiano Gonzaga 27, T: 0375 52039 is open Oct–March Tues–Sun 9–12 & 2.30–5 or 6; Apr–Sept daily 9–12 & 1.30 or 2.30–6 or 7. It is necessary to book here (and purchase a ticket) for a guided tour of the monuments of the town (the theatre, the Palazzo Ducale, the church of the Incoronata, Palazzo del Giardino and the Galleria), otherwise they can only be seen from the outside. A separate ticket has to be purchased here for the tour of the synagogue.

EXPLORING SABBIONETA

At the entrance to the town is the huge **Piazza d'Armi**, on the site of the 14th-century castle (only the foundations of two towers remain) that occupied this part of the town until it was demolished at the end of the 18th century. The Corinthian Roman column, which supports a Roman statue of Athena, was set up here by Duke Vespasiano. Also here are the Palazzo del Giardino and the Galleria (*both described below*), and a monumental school building erected in 1930, as well as the tourist office.

Just off Via Vespasiano Gonzaga is the **Teatro all'Antica**, by Vincenzo Scamozzi, the last building erected for the duke (1588–90). This is the first example of a theatre built as an independent structure (not within a larger building) and provided with a foyer, separate entrances for the public and artists, dressing rooms, etc. It has a handsome exterior with an inscription dedicated to Rome, and a charming interior (which can hold 200). The peristyle has stucco statues and busts of the Greek gods, and monochrome painted figures of Roman emperors. Above is a frescoed loggia with painted spectators and musicians, by a Venetian artist. On the two side walls are large frescoes of the Campidoglio and Hadrian's mausoleum in Rome. The fixed backdrop, which represented a piazza and streets, was destroyed in the 18th century (although there are plans to reconstruct it). The ceiling, which is lower than the original ship's keel roof, also dates from the 18th century.

The **Porta Vittoria** (1567) was the main gate of the town. From outside there is a good view of the walls. The Convent of the Servi di Maria incorporates the octagonal church of the **Incoronata**, built in 1586–88 and modelled on the Incoronata of Lodi. It was beautifully decorated with frescoes in the 18th century. The late 17th-century mechanical organ has its original pipes (concerts are given here in Sept). The monument to Vespasiano, with numerous rare marbles, was erected by Giovanni Battista della Porta in 1592 and incorporates his bronze statue by Leone Leoni (1588). He is buried in the crypt below.

In the delightful Piazza Ducale is **Palazzo Ducale**, built by the duke as his official residence. On the first floor the Salone delle Aquile has frescoes with festoons of fruit, and four wooden equestrian statues representing Vespasiano, two of his ancestors, and a captain. They were made in 1589 by a Venetian sculptor and were part of a group of ten (the other six perished in a fire in the early 19th century, except for the five busts exhibited here). The Sala degli Imperatori has a panelled oak ceiling and a frieze of fruit and vegetables including peppers and maize (which Vespasiano must have seen in Spain as they were not grown in Italy in the 16th century). The Galleria degli Antenati, probably used as a studio, has reliefs in stucco of Vespasiano's ancestors by Alberto Cavalli, and a barrel-vaulted ceiling with stuccoes and paintings. Other rooms on this floor have a painted frieze of elephants, a ceiling of carved cedar, and frescoes with views of Constantinople and Genoa. On the ground floor are rooms with *grottesche*, gilded wood ceilings and a monumental fireplace.

Also in the piazza is the church of **Santa Maria Assunta** (*open for services on holidays*), built in 1582. The chapel of the Holy Sacrament was added by Antonio Bibiena in 1768 and has a delightful double perforated dome in stucco and wood and two marble reliquary 'cupboards'. The **Museo d'Arte Sacra** (*open Sun and holidays 10–12.30 & 2.30–6.30*) has two paintings by Bernardino Campi. The Teson d'Oro (Golden Fleece) was the gold medal presented to Vespasiano in 1585 by Philip II of Spain when he was made a knight of the Order; it was found in his tomb in the Incoronata.

In Piazza d'Armi is the **Palazzo del Giardino**, which was Vespasiano's summer villa, built in 1578–88, with an oak cornice on the exterior. The room adjoining the ground-floor atrium has a charming vault with birds attributed to Bernardino Campi, and a lovely fireplace. From here you can see the remains of the walled garden with three nymphaeums. The first floor has a delightful series of rooms with stuccoes and frescoes by Campi and his pupils. They depict the Circus Maximus and Circus of Flaminius in Rome; myths from Ovid; Gonzaga personal devices (*imprese*); scenes from the *Aeneid*; and exotic animals (some of them probably seen by Vespasiano on his travels in Africa). The original polychrome marble floors are preserved. Another room (once decorated with Venetian mirrors) has painted landscapes.

Beyond a little room with grotesques is the entrance to the Galleria, built in 1583–84. This remarkable gallery, 96m long, was built to display the duke's superb collection of Classical busts, statues and bas-reliefs (most of them taken to the Palazzo Ducale in Mantua in 1774). Decorated with frescoes and trompe l'oeil perspectives at either end, it has a handsome brick exterior and an open, well ventilated loggia below.

The **synagogue** (*for admission enquire at the tourist office*) is on the top floor of a house in Via Bernardino Campi. It has a fine interior by Carlo Vizioli (1824). There was a Jewish community in the town from 1436.

Outside Sabbioneta is the church of **Villa Pasquali** (*if closed, ring at no. 1*), built in 1765 by Antonio Bibiena. The second tower on the handsome brick façade was never completed. The interior is especially remarkable for the beautiful perforated double ceiling of the dome and three apses in terracotta. The various treasures of the church are carefully preserved.

SOUTHEASTERN LOMBARDY

San Benedetto Po and environs

Southeast of Mantua is **Pietole**, a village usually regarded as the birthplace of Virgil. At Bagnalo San Vito is the first Etruscan site (5th century BC) discovered north of the Po and the most ancient site in Lombardy. The road crosses the Po, and there is a good view from the bridge. On the right bank is **San Benedetto Po**, which grew up round the important Benedictine abbey of San Benedetto Polirone, founded in 1007 and protected by Countess Matilda of Canossa (1046–1115), who was buried here. United to the abbey of Cluny until the 13th century, it was suppressed by Napoleon in 1797. The extensive abbey buildings, mostly dating from the 15th century, are in the large central piazza of the little town. The fine church was rebuilt by Giulio Romano in 1540–44 and is one of his best works. Off the ambulatory is the Romanesque church of Santa Maria, with a pretty interior. The fine mosaic pavement of 1151, with figures of animals, the Cardinal Virtues, etc., is well preserved at the east end (and there is another fragment in the nave). In the sacristy, with frescoes by the school of Giulio Romano and fine wooden cupboards, is an equestrian portrait of Matilda of Canossa: her empty tomb is just outside (her remains were sold by the abbot to Pope Urban VIII in 1633 when Bernini was commissioned to provide a monument in St Peter's).

To the right of the church is the entrance to a cloister, off which a Baroque staircase by Giovanni Battista Barberini (1674) leads up to the Museo della Cultura Popolare

Padana (*open summer Mon 9–12.30, Tues–Fri 9–12.30 & 2.30–6.30, Sat–Sun 9–12.30 & 3–7; by appointment in winter; T: 037 6623036*), a large ethnographic museum of the region. Displays are arranged around the upper floor of the cloister of San Simeone, in the grand abbot's apartments and the simpler monks' cells, and in the late-18th-century library, a Neoclassical space designed by Giovanni Battista Marconi. The lower walk of the 15th-century cloister of San Simeone has 16th-century frescoes and a garden that has been replanted following its 16th-century design.

Across the piazza, on the other side of the church, is the former refectory (*open as above*) built in 1478, with a museum of sculptural fragments and ceramics, and a *Madonna* by Begarelli. The huge fresco, discovered in 1984, and attributed as an early work (1514) to Correggio, provided the architectural setting for a *Last Supper* by Girolamo Bonsignori, now in the Museo Civico of Badia Polesine and replaced here by a photograph. Two sides of the 15th-century cloister of St Benedict survive in the piazza, and the huge 16th-century infirmary behind the refectory is to be restored.

Along the Po

Further downstream is **Ostiglia**, where the marshes are now a bird sanctuary. A short distance further downriver is the Isola Boschina, its woods a rare survival of the vegetation that was once typical of the Po landscape. On the south bank of the river is **Revere**, where there is a palace of Lodovico Gonzaga with a charming courtyard and portal by Luca Fancelli, and an 18th-century parish church with paintings by Giuseppe Bazzani. Here the Museo del Po has archaeological and historical material.

South of Mantua is **Borgoforte**, with an 18th-century castle and a parish church containing works by Giuseppe Bazzani. On the south bank of the river at Motteggiana is the **Ghirardina**, a 15th-century fortified villa attributed to Luca Fancelli. Southeast of here is **Gonzaga**, a pretty little town which was the ancestral home of the famous ducal family.

West and north of Mantua

West of Mantua on the Cremona road is the unusual church of **Santa Maria delle Grazie**, founded by Francesco I Gonzaga in 1399. The nave has two tiers of lifesize statues in various materials set up as ex-votos—an astonishing sight. Some of the figures were clad in the armour now exhibited in the Museo Diocesano in Mantua. Also here is the tomb of Baldassare Castiglione (d. 1529), probably by Giulio Romano. From Rivalta, to the north, boat excursions can be taken on the Mincio.

Canneto sull'Oglio preserves a massive tower belonging to its former castle. The Museo Civico (*open Sun 10–12.30 & 2.30–6 or 3–7; March–Oct also Sat 2–6 or 3–7*) is dedicated to life on the River Oglio and also has a collection of dolls, which have been manufactured in the town since 1870. Nearby are Asola, which preserves its old walls, and Bozzolo, with its 14th-century tower and a Gonzaga palace.

In the northern part of the province is **Castiglione di Stiviere**, which was once a fief of the Gonzaga. The Museo Storico Aloisiano in the Collegio delle Nobili Vergini (*open by appointment, T: 0376 638062*) has mementoes of St Luigi Gonzaga, born here in 1568; paintings by Francesco Bassano, Federico Barocci, Giulio Carpioni and Giambettino Cignaroli; and collections of glass, ironwork and furniture. The **Museo Internazionale della Croce Rossa** (*open Apr–Sept, Tues–Sun 9–12.30 & 3–6; Oct–March 9–12 & 2–5.30*) commemorates the Red Cross, which was founded after the famous battle of Solferino, at which Napoleon III—in alliance with Vittorio Emanuele—defeated the Austrians in 1859. There is a memorial here to Jean Henri Dunant who, horrified by the sufferings of the wounded in this battle, took the first steps to found the international relief organisation. The tower of **Solferino** was erected on a hill probably by the Scaligers in 1022; it contains a Risorgimento museum.

PRACTICAL INFORMATION

GETTING AROUND

• **By road:** Mantua's feeling of isolation is emphasised by the practical difficulties of reaching it by public transport. Buses run by APAM (T: 0376 230338), from Mantua to Sabbioneta-Parma, Brescia, Sirmione (Lago di Garda), San Benedetto Po and Ostiglia; bus station at Via Mutilati e Caduti del Lavoro 4 (Piazza Mondadori).

• **By rail:** There are rail links to Milan, 2hrs–2hrs 30mins via Codogno, where a change is sometimes necessary; Verona, 35mins; Modena, 1hr 15mins; Cremona 1hr via Piadena, where the line is met by trains from Brescia and Parma. The Parma stretch also serves Castelmaggiore, from where there are buses to (5km) Sabbioneta.

• **By bicycle:** Cycles can be rented for the day from La Rigola, Lungolago Gonzaga, T: 0335 605 4958.

INFORMATION OFFICES

Mantua Piazza Mantegna 6, T: 0376 321601, www.aptmantova.it
Informagiovani: Via Chiassi 18, T: 0376 364233.

Sabbioneta Via Vespasiano Gonzaga 27, T: 0375 52039. Open Oct–March Tues–Sun 9–12 & 2.30–5 or 6; Apr–Sept daily 9–12 & 1.30 or 2.30–6 or 7. You must book here for a guided tour of the monuments of the town, otherwise they can only be seen from the outside. A separate ticket covers the synagogue.

HOTELS

Mantua
€€€ **Rechigi**. Central, with a small contemporary art collection. Via Calvi 30, T: 0376 320781.
€€€ **San Lorenzo**. Elegant and refined, with genuine antiques and a rooftop terrace with views over the city. Piazza Concordia 14, T: 0376 220500.
€ **Mantegna**. Simple but adequate, halfway between the Palazzo Ducale and Palazzo del Te. Closed Dec–Jan. Via Filzi 10, T: 0376 328019, www.hotelmantegna.it

RESTAURANTS

Mantua
€€ **Aquila Nigra**. Fine regional dishes prepared with a special touch. Closed

Mon, Sun evening in Apr–May and Sept–Oct, all day Sun at other times, and Jan. Vicolo Bonacolsi 4, T: 0376 327180.
€€ Grifone Bianco. Excellent Mantuan cuisine (especially first courses) and pleasant ambience in the heart of the old town. Closed Tues and July. Piazza Erbe 6, T: 0376 365423.
€€ Il Portichetto. *Osteria* famous for its freshwater fish dishes. Closed Sun evening, Mon and Aug. Via Portichetto 14, T: 0376 360747.
€ Due Cavallini. Trattoria serving the best traditional Mantuan cuisine. Closed Tues and July–Aug. Via Salnitro 5, T: 0376 322084.
€ L'Ochina Bianca. Warm, friendly *osteria* with a strong local following. Closed Mon, midday Tues and Jan. Via Finzi 2, T: 0376 323700.
Canneto sull'Oglio
€€€ Dal Pescatore. Restaurant famous for its highly refined renditions of traditional Mantuan dishes. Via Runate 13, T: 0376 723001.
Castel d'Ario
€ Castello. Trattoria famous for its *risotti*. Closed Wed–Thur, Aug and Dec. Via di là dell'Acqua 8 (off the Cremona road), T: 0376 660259.
€€ Nizzoli. A good traditional restaurant—try the *risotto di zucca* and the fried snails in Parmesan sauce. Closed Wed and Dec–Jan. Via Garibaldi 8, at Villastrada.
Goito
€€€ Al Bersagliere. On the Mincio. Renowned for its masterful interpretations of old Mantuan recipes. Closed Mon, midday Tues and Dec–Jan. Strada Statale Goitese 260, T: 0376 688399.

Pomponesco
€€ Il Leone. A family-run restaurant with rooms, offering good local fare. Closed Sun evening, Mon and Dec–Jan. Via 4 Martiri 2, T: 0375 86077.
€ Saltini. Traditional trattoria on the village square. Closed Mon and July–Aug. Piazza XXIII Aprile 10, T: 0375 86017.

CAFÉS

For good coffee and cakes in Mantua, try **Caffè Caravatti**, Piazza delle Erbe. If you like *tortelli di zucca* (made with pumpkin), try **Panificio Freddi**, Piazza Cavallotti 7. There are plenty of other Mantuan pastas and breads there too. You can get Mantua's famous (infamous?) garlic salami at **Salumeria Carra**, Via Tassoni 1.

REGIONAL SPECIALITIES

Mantua is famous for its *tortelli di zucca* (pumpkin tortelli), *insaccati di maiale* (pork salami) and *torta sbrisolona* (low, crisp shortbread cake).

FESTIVALS & EVENTS

Sacri Vasi (Good Friday procession) and saint's day in **Mantua** (18 March); *Invito a Corte* (Gonzaga-era costumes), *Re Gnocco* (historic carnival celebration) at **Castel Goffredo** (Feb) and *Rievocazione Storica Aloisiana* (Renaissance costume) at **Castiglione delle Stiviere** (June). At **Sabbioneta**, concerts are held in May–June in the Theatre; organ recitals take place in Sept in the Incoronata.

TRENTINO-ALTO ADIGE

Trentino-Alto Adige, the mountain territory of the upper Adige Valley and South Tyrol, incorporates the modern provinces of Bolzano and Trento. It is a semi-autonomous region with a special administrative order—much like that of the Valle d'Aosta—that reflects its multi-cultural (Germanic, Italian and pre-Italian Latin, or Ladin) make-up. Most characteristic among the mountains of this region are the fantastic pinnacles of the Dolomites, the strangely shaped mountains disposed in irregular groups between the Adige and Piave valleys.

Strictly speaking, the Dolomites are a sub-range of the Eastern Alps. But anyone who has seen them knows that they are much more than that. 'The Dolomites ... recall quaint Eastern architecture, whose daring pinnacles derive their charm from a studied defiance of the sober principles of stability,' wrote Leslie Stephen in *The Playground of Europe* (1871).

The province of Trento is almost entirely Italian-speaking. In Bolzano (the Alto Adige) the native language of Ladin has, except in the more remote valleys, been overlaid by the official language of the ruling power: German until 1918 (because the region was part of the Austro-Hungarian empire) and, since then, Italian. The two provinces represent respectively the old ecclesiastic principalities of Trento and Bressanone (or Brixen), both of which in the Middle Ages paid nominal allegiance to the Holy Roman Emperor. In the 14th and 15th centuries the prince-bishops held the balance between the rising power of Venice to the south and the Counts of Tyrol to the north, while in the 16th century, under the bishops Clesio of Trento and Madruzzo of Bressanone, the valleys were practically independent.

The decay of local powers prevailed here as elsewhere in the 17th–18th centuries, and the Trentino and southern Tyrol became more closely attached to the Holy Roman Empire. During Napoleon's campaigns the region was transferred to Bavaria; it was returned to Austria after the Congress of Vienna. Austrian misgovernment in the 19th century caused great discontent in the Trentino, and a movement for absorption into the Veneto was born. Following the collapse of the Austro-Hungarian empire after the First World War, Trentino came under Italian control, and the frontier was extended northward to the Brenner.

TRENTO & ITS TERRITORY

The gateway to the Eastern Alps is the valley of the River Adige, the southern entrance to which is guarded by Trento and its sister city, Rovereto. To the east and west lies some of the finest country in the Italian Alps, including the soaring Adamello-Brenta group with the lovely Non and Sole valleys; and the peaks known as the Pale di San Martino, with the long, beautiful Val di Fiemme and Val di Fassa. There are marvellous parks in the high-mountain areas, and numerous summer and winter resorts in the valleys.

Trento itself is a cheerful town, capital of the region. It is encircled by spectacular mountain ranges. Though it remained in Austrian hands until 1918, it is a typically northern Italian city and entirely Italian speaking. It has a number of fine palaces and churches as well as the Castello di Buonconsiglio, famous seat of the prince-bishops.

HISTORY OF TRENTO

Trento was Romanised in the course of the 1st century BC and became a *municipium* and an honorary colony (called Tridentum) in the Antonine period. During the Middle Ages Trento owed its importance to its position on the main road from Germany to Italy. It became an episcopal fief in 1027, its bishops acquiring the temporal power that they held almost without interruption until 1802. Early in the 15th century the citizens rebelled against the overwhelming power of the bishops, but local unrest came to an end with the threat of a Venetian invasion, Venice having secured control of the Val Lagarina as far up as Rovereto (1416). The Tridentines (as the inhabitants of Trento are known) asked for help from the Count of Tyrol, the Venetians were defeated in 1487, and in 1511 Austria established a protectorate over the Trentino. In the 16th century the city rose to prominence under Bishop Bernardo Clesio and Bishop Cristoforo Madruzzo, and during the episcopate of the latter the famous Council of Trent met here (1545–63, *see p. 277*). The last prince-bishop escaped from the French in 1796, and the Austrians took possession of the town in 1813, holding it until 1918 through a century of great unrest.

The duomo and its neighbourhood

Piazza del Duomo is the monumental centre of the city. It is an extraordinarily handsome square, with an 18th-century Neptune fountain standing in the shadow of the 13th-century Palazzo Pretorio and Torre Civica.

On the south side of the square extends the austere left flank of the cathedral of San Vigilio, a Romanesque-Gothic building of the 12th–13th centuries with a powerful 16th-century campanile and a Romanesque-revival dome. Faced entirely in marble, it has magnificent decorative detailing and a beautiful apse against which stands the 13th-century **Castelletto**, with mullioned windows and crenellated roof.

The interior has three tall aisles with compound piers, a small clerestory in the nave, and cross vaults. Arcaded staircases ascend the west wall, amid 16th-century tomb monuments, to the galleries. The large **Cappella del Crocifisso**, in the south aisle, preserves a 16th-century wooden crucifix before which the decrees of the Council of Trent were promulgated. In the transepts are remains of 13th- and 15th-century frescoes, and at the end of the north aisle, a 13th-century stone statue known as the *Madonna degli Annegati* (Madonna of the Drowned), at the foot of which people drowned in the Adige were identified. It used to stand in a niche outside. The baldachin over the high altar is more or less a copy of that of St Peter's in Rome.

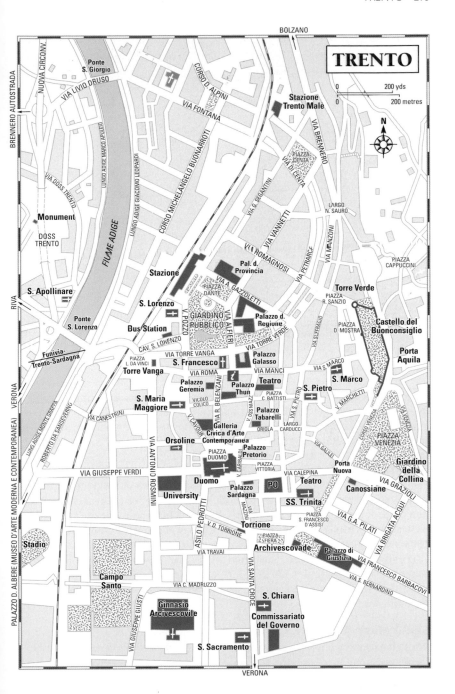

Fresco of the emperor Maximilian I on the 16th-century Palazzo Geremia.

Inside the **Castelletto**, clusters of tall columns carry the arcades, surmounted by a diminutive clerestory, and unusual arcaded staircases lead up to the galleries. It contains numerous tombs of bishops, 13th–14th-century frescoes (some attributed to Tommaso da Modena), a 13th-century statue of the Madonna, and two 13th-century marble reliefs of St Stephen.

The **Museo Diocesano** (*open Mon–Sat 9.30–12.30 & 2.30–6*) occupies the Palazzo Pretorio, once the bishops' palace. It has a wonderful and beautifully displayed collection of paintings and sculpture from local churches and the most valuable objects from the cathedral treasury. These include the 13th-century treasure of Bishop Federico Vanga, the 15th-century crosier of Bishop Giorgio Hack, and a fine series of 16th-century Flemish tapestries by Pieter van Aelst.

The 18th-century **Palazzo Sardagna** houses the Museo Tridentino di Scienze Naturali (*open Tues–Sun 9–12.30 & 2.30–6*), with interesting natural history collections. Near the Renaissance Palazzo Tabarelli is the picturesque Cantone, once the chief crossroads in the town.

Santa Maria Maggiore

Via Belenzani, the city's elegant shopping street, is flanked by Renaissance palaces showing a strong Venetian influence, some with painted façades—like the 16th-century Palazzo Geremia (no. 19), with frescoes of the early-16th century showing the Emperor Maximilian, who stayed here in 1508–09, and members of his court; and Palazzo Alberti-Colico (no. 32). Across the street stands Palazzo Thun, today the town hall, with frescoes by Brusasorci in the Sala della Giunta. West of here is **Santa Maria Maggiore**, a Renaissance church of 1520–24 with a remarkable doorway and a fine campanile. Several sessions of the Council of Trent were held here, including the last one. The great portal of the façade dates from 1535; on the south side is a 16th-century Lombardesque portal. The *Assumption* over the high altar is by Pietro Ricchi, a pupil of Guido Reni; the marble organ gallery of 1534 is a masterpiece of the Vicentine sculptors Vincenzo and Gian Gerolamo Grandi.

THE COUNCIL OF TRENT

The 19th ecumenical council of the Roman Catholic Church (1545–63) was convoked under Holy Roman Emperor Charles V in response to the spread of Protestantism across Europe. Alarmed by the number of Christians massing under Luther's banner, the emperor was concerned to put the Roman Catholic Church in order, addressing both church discipline and dogma. The council did not begin as a Counter Reformatory project to repudiate Protestants: Protestant delegates were present, and the original aim was to find a solution—this proved impossible. What the council concluded included the following: the Nicene Creed was the basis of faith; Luther, Calvin and Zwingli were all repudiated; the Catholic Church's stance on Original Sin, Transubstantiation, purgatory, indulgences, the veneration of relics and the role of the saints was defined. To the end the Council was dogged by disagreement between Pope and emperor. When Charles V died he was succeeded by his even less conciliatory brother Ferdinand, and disagreement between the Pope's prelates and those from Spain and the empire became worse than ever. In the end the papal faction prevailed. The Protestant question was not settled, but the Council's decrees formed a manual for Roman Catholicism which remained unchanged up to 1967.

The Castello del Buonconsiglio

The Castello, once the stronghold of the bishop-princes, is approached up Via San Marco, the continuation of Via Manci (no. 63 is the Baroque Palazzo Galasso, built in 1602 by Georg Fugger, banker and money-lender to popes and prelates and Holy Roman Emperors). It has two main parts. The crenellated Castelvecchio to the north was built in the 13th century and altered in 1475. The Magno Palazzo to the south is a Renaissance edifice built in 1528–36 by Bernardo Clesio, then imperial chancellor, who intended it to express the power his position had brought him. The two wings are joined by the 17th-century addition of bishop-prince Francesco Alberti Poja.

The Museo del Castello del Buonconsiglio

Open Oct–March Tues–Sun 9–12 & 2–5, Apr–Sept 10–6; T: 0461 233770.
The museum houses the municipal collections of antiquities, coins, manuscripts and incunabula, liturgical objects, paintings and ethnographic material. To reach the museum, cross the pretty garden courtyard to the open stairway, built under bishop-prince Johannes Hinderbach (1465–86), whose coat of arms (the unicorn and flames) appears together with those of the principality of Trento (the eagle) and of the religious authority of the bishop (the pastoral staff and mitre) on the capitals of the columns here.

The stairs are frescoed by Marcello Fogolino, who painted the Renaissance decorative motifs and historical portraits (Charlemagne with dignitaries and soldiers, and the early bishops of Trento) on a commission from Clesio. At the top the lovely Loggia Veneziana, with Venetian-style trilobate arches, overlooks the city in its amphitheatre of mountains. Through the former apartment of the bishop you reach the private chapel, adorned with the arms of Clesio (on the doorposts) and Hinderbach (on the ceiling) and figures of the Evangelists, Doctors of the Church (seated) and bishop-princes (standing).

The State Rooms

These are on the first floor. At the centre of the ceiling in the entrance hall is the Clesio coat of arms surrounded by a garland. The lunette frescoes of Greek mythological figures were painted in 1531–32 by Dosso Dossi and his brother Battista, and make reference to the prince's humanistic political platform. The **Cappella Clesiana** or Domus Orationis was the state chapel; it has niches in the vault containing terracotta figures (of apostles, Evangelists and four Doctors of the Church) by Zaccharia Zacchi, a painted leather altar frontal and a 16th-century Veronese *Madonna*. The lovely **Cortile dei Leoni**—named after the two stone lions, all that remain of a 16th-century fountain—follows. On its west side, a suite of magnificent rooms used by Bishop Clesio have ceilings frescoed in 1531–32 by the Dossi, Romanino and Fogolino, and plaster and terracotta decoration by Zaccaria Zacchi. In the **Camera delle Udienze** you can see Holy Roman Emperor Charles V speaking to his brother Ferdinand and, above the entrance, Clesio with his secretary—together with lunettes in which eminent Habsburgs are compared to Roman emperors (a deliberate linking of the Holy Roman Empire with the administrative might of ancient Rome). The **Stua delle Figure** has terracotta detailing by Zacchi and frescoes by Dosso and Battista Dossi, who also worked together on the rich decorative programme of the Camera del Camin Nero or 'Camara di Stucchi' (in the paintings, cardinal virtues, arms of Pope Clement VII and Emperor Charles V, the liberal arts and their ancient epitomes, and medallions of Roman emperors); the **Sala del Tribunale**, formerly Stua de la Famea, was the dining room of the bishop's 'family', or court, before coming to host a court of a different kind: it was here that Italian resistance fighter Cesare Battisti was condemned to death in 1916.

Returning to the Cortile dei Leoni, you immediately come to the monumental loggia that encloses its south side: on the ceiling is an ambitious cycle of mythological figures, allegories of night and day, and other humanistic subjects, frescoed in 1531–32 by Romanino.

The Sala Grande, bishop's apartments and library

Stairs at the west end of the loggia lead to the second floor and (straight ahead) the **Sala Grande**, where state ceremonies were held. The frieze, painted by Dosso and Battista Dossi in 1532, shows playful putti, letters of Clesio's Christian name, Berenardt (Bernardo), and elements of the Clesio arms mixed with symbols of ecclesiastic and temporal power. On the walls are the emblems of Charles V and Ferdinand I, bishop Francesco Felice Alberti d'Enno and the bishopric of Trento. The gilt coffered ceiling dates from 1531; the marble fireplace, by Vincenzo Grandi, from 1532. At the south end of the hall (left of the entrance) is the **Sala degli Specchi**, the room of mirrors, in the circular **Torion de Sora**. At the north (far) end a doorway leads into four more handsome rooms.

The first is the **Stua Grande**, where the frescoes, executed by the Dossi brothers in 1532, were destroyed and replaced in 1759 by the ones you see today, representing the Creation, the planets, the constellations, the zodiac and mythological scenes from Ovid's *Metamorphoses*. The large majolica stove, decorated with Old Testament scenes and grotesques, was part of the original 16th-century furnishings. From the Stua Grande you can visit the **Camera degli Scarlatti**, named after the scarlet tapestries that once adorned its walls (gone today, though the complementary frescoes by the Dossi survive); and the rooms of the **Giunta Altertiana**, with fabulous carved wooden ceilings.

Return through the Sala Grande and past the stairs to enter the private apartments of the bishop, consisting of the **Stua del Signor**, the bishop-prince's bedchamber (frescoed by Romanino with busts of Roman emperors and other motifs calculated to remind Clesio of his status even as he slept), the **Stua de la Libraria**, and the large, luminous library, with original wood ceiling (you recognise the arms by now) and 18th-century mural decorations. In the ceiling coffers paintings by Dosso Dossi reflect the prince's humanistic aspirations: pagan and Christian sages, orators, poets, and philosophers, all look down over a faux parapet.

The Towers

The custodian takes groups of visitors into the towers to see two more frescoed rooms and a part of the old fortifications. Be sure to make time for this, as it is the highlight of the visit to the castle. On a commission from Clesio the **Torre del Falco** was decorated after 1530 by an anonymous German painter, with a delightful series of hunting scenes; the city in the background is Salzburg, Austria. In the **Torre dell'Aquila** are the castle's most famous frescoes, commissioned probably from a Bohemian artist by bishop-prince Giorgio di Liechtenstein, c. 1400. Known as the *Cycle of the Months*, they are a perfect compendium of farming in the South Tyrol. In eleven handsome frames (March, unfortunately, has been destroyed) they show seasonal agricultural activities in the minutest detail. Harvests are plentiful and life is good—for the leisured, at least: in winter while the peasants prepare for the spring planting, the nobles frolic in the snow...

The castle complex also houses the **Museo Civico del Risorgimento e della Lotta per la Libertà** (*open as the Museo del Castello*) with memorabilia mainly of the Irredentist movement, of the First World War, and of the Resistance.

Along the river

The 14th-century church of **Sant'Apollinare**, with a doorway and rose window in Veronese red porphyry, lies on the right bank of the Adige. Behind it rises the Doss Trento, crowned by the mausoleum of anti-Austrian freedom fighter Cesare Battisti, from which there is a fine view over the city. Nearby are the remains of an early-Christian basilica and, to the south, the Museo Storico delle Truppe Alpine, tracing the history of the famous Italian Alpine Corps. Returning to the left bank and walking southwards, you come to Palazzo delle Albere, a square suburban villa encircled by a moat, built around 1535 for Bishop-Prince Cristoforo Madruzzo. Decorated with frescoes of which only traces remain today, it is home to the Trentine section of the Museo d'Arte Moderna e Contemporanea di Trento e Rovereto (*open Tues–Sun 10–6; freephone 800 397760*), with exhibitions of contemporary art.

AROUND TRENTO

Monte Bondone, cloaked in forests, overlooks the city from the southwest. It is known for its alpine flora (it produces herbs used in spa establishments) and as a ski resort. The Conca delle Viotte, set beneath the peaks of the massif (Palon, 2090m; Doss d'Abramo, 2140m; and Monte Cornetto, 2180m) hosts the **Giardino Botanico Alpino** (*open June–Sept 9–12 & 2–5 or 6*), with over 2,000 plant species from the Trentino and the principal mountains of the world.

The **Lago di Toblino**, lying amid rocky mountains in the valley of the Sarca, 16km west of the city, is overlooked by a medieval castle. The lake is joined by an isthmus to the Lago di Santa Massenza, surrounded by olive trees.

The modern Museo Aeronautico Gianni Caproni (*open Tues–Fri 9–1 & 2–5, Sat–Sun and holidays 10–1 & 2–6*), at Mattarello, near the airport, has 18 antique planes and various exhibits regarding the history of flight in Italy.

The **Castel Beseno** (*open March and Oct 9–12 & 2–5; Apr–June and Sept 9–12 & 2–5.30; July–Aug 10–6*) which controlled the valley south of Trento, is near Calliano, between Trento and Rovereto. The hill was inhabited in the Iron Age, as well as in the Roman and Lombard periods. The castle dates from the 12th century and was owned by the Castelbarco from 1303 until the 15th century, when it was given to the Trapp family, who donated it to the province in 1973. It has recently been restored and includes two large courtyards within its impressive walls. A room of the castle preserves 16th-century frescoes of the Months.

Rovereto and environs

The most important town in the environs of Trento is Rovereto, a city possibly of Roman origin, spread out at the foot of a 14th-century castle. Behind the historic façades of Corso Bettini, the main street of the old town centre, lies a superb museum combining the facilities of the **Biblioteca Civica** and the **Museo d'Arte Moderna e Contemporanea di Trento e Rovereto** (*open Tues, Wed, Thur 10–6, Fri–Sun 10–9; freephone 800 397760*). It exhibits the finest collection of Italian Modernism anywhere:

Lago di Toblino.

works by Fortunato Depero (a native of Rovereto), Filippo Tommaso Marinetti, Giacomo Balla, Enrico Prampolini, and other artists of the Futurist area, are displayed together with paintings and sculptures by artists ranging in date from the early years of the 20th century until the present day (Fontana, Burri, Merz and others) as well as significant works of European and American contemporary art. Depero's tapestries, furniture, mosaics, paintings and graphic works were all produced in Rovereto, in the artist's 'Casa d'Arte', between 1920 and 1942.

Rovereto's castle is now home to the **Museo Storico Italiano della Guerra** (*open July–Sept Tues–Sun 8.30–6.30, Oct–May 8.30–12.30 & 2–6*), with some 30 rooms devoted to the First World War. The war is commemorated also by the Sacrario (1936) and the Campana dei Caduti, the largest bell in Italy, which tolls every evening for the fallen of all nations. The front line of 1916–18 was in the valley south of the town.

The 15th-century Palazzo del Municipio has remains of façade frescoes attributed to Fogolino, and the contemporary Palazzo della Cassa di Risparmio shows Venetian influence. The **Museo Civico** (*open Tues–Sat 9–12 & 3–6; July–Oct Sun 8pm–10pm*), first opened to the public in 1855, houses the collections of the archaeologist Paolo Orsi (1849–1925), who was a native of the town, as well as a planetarium and a natural history section.

The picturesque **Castello di Sabbionara d'Avio**, the home of the counts of Castelbarco since the 14th century, lies to the south of Rovereto in a fine position on a hillside with woods and cultivated terraces above the Adige (*open Tues–Sun 10–1 & 2–5 or 6*). The Casa delle Guardie has remarkable frescoes (1345–60) of battle scenes. The well-preserved keep, which dominates the fortress, dates from the 11th–12th centuries. The Stanza d'Amore, on the fourth floor, preserves fragments of 14th-century frescoes with courtly scenes. In front of the tower is the Palazzo Baronale with remains of its chapel.

The Adamello-Brenta Mountains

The west flank of the Adige Valley, opposite Trento, is formed by the Presanella and Brenta mountain groups which, together with the east flank of Monte Adamello (3539m), constitute a protected area rich in sights of natural and historic interest. The Brenta mountains, an isolated Dolomitic group between Madonna di Campiglio and the Adige valley, are for expert climbers only, but there are many easier walks (marked by coloured signs) in their foothills. The Presanella (3556m) was first ascended by the English alpinist Douglas Freshfield (d. 1929) in 1864.

Touring the area

In the Valli Giudicarie, between Stenico and Tione, is the Gola della Scaletta, a narrow winding gorge of the Sarca. **Stenico castle** (*open Apr–Sept Tues–Sun 9–12 & 2–5.30; Oct–Mar 9–12 & 2–5*), dating from the 12th century, was a stronghold of the prince-bishops of Trento. It is now owned by the province and has been restored. Inside are frescoes including battle scenes and female allegorical figures, as well as arms, furniture and archaeological material. To the north of Stenico is the lovely, peaceful **Lago di Molveno**, 6.5km long, lying under the lee of the Brenta mountains. Spectacular walks can be taken in the area.

The beautiful **Val di Non**, above Molveno, with its woods and ruined castles, is known for its apples: the landscape is particularly beautiful in spring, when the trees are in blossom. A scenic branch railway line runs through the valley, connecting Trento to Malè. The most important place along the way is **Cles**, whose castle was the ancestral home of the famous episcopal Clesio family (*see p. 274*), rebuilt in the 16th century. Standing at the foot of Monte Peller (2319m), the northern peak of the Brenta group, it has a good Renaissance church and old houses.

To the northwest of Cles is the Val di Sole, the upper glen of the Noce (now used for canoeing and rafting). **Malè**, the main village in the valley, has a local ethnographic museum (Museo della Cività Solandra). **Madonna di Campiglio** (1522m) is a famous winter and summer resort in a wooded basin in the upper valley of the Sarca, below the Brenta mountains. It has excellent ski facilities. A path (or chair-lift) ascends Monte Spinale (2104m), from which there is a splendid circular view of the Brenta, Adamello, Presanella and Ortles mountains. To the south is the magnificent Val Brenta.

Pinzolo, another ski resort and climbing centre, is in a splendid position at the junction of the two main upper valleys of the Sarca. The church of San Vigilio has a remarkable external fresco of the *Dance of Death* by Simone Baschenis (1539). A similar painting (1519) by the same artist decorates the exterior of the church of Santo Stefano, which also contains frescoes by him inside.

The Val di Genova, the main approach to the Presanella and Adamello groups from the east, is a magnificent valley, thickly wooded in parts and with several waterfalls.

RISERVA NATURALE ADAMELLO-BRENTA

Park offices: Strembo (Val Rendena), Via Nazionale 12, T: 0465 804637.
Visitors' centre: Tuenno (Val di Non), Lago di Tovel, T: 0463 451033,
www.parks.it/parco.adamello.brenta/Eindex.html
The largest protected area in the Trentino, the Adamello-Brenta nature reserve extends from the Dolomiti di Brenta in the east to the Adamello and Presanella massifs in the west. It forms a sort of natural bridge between the limestone-like Dolomites and the granite massifs of the Central Alps, presenting visitors with majestic glaciers, secluded high-mountain lakes and a variety of flora and fauna.

As elsewhere in the Alps, thousands of years of human presence have left their mark: not only is settlement intense in the valley areas (especially on the hillsides, at a safe distance from the 'bad air' or *malaria,* which made the valley floor uninhabitable); seasonal grazing has turned many of the areas above the treeline into pasture. These high meadows have, in their turn, been colonised by innumerable species of Alpine flowers.

The reserve is the last refuge in Italy of the Alpine brown bear. As a rule the bear are too few and too secluded (they live largely on the wild northeast slopes of the Brenta) to be sighted, but chamois are quite common: there were over 6,000 at last count, nearly half the population of the Trentino.

The Val di Fiemme and Val di Fassa

Cavalese is the main village in the Val di Fiemme, northwest of Trento. Like many of the valleys of the Pyrenees, this glen has preserved something of its medieval independence, and the 'Magnifica Comunità', installed in the ancient palace of the bishops of Trento, still administers the valuable communal lands. The palace contains a museum (*closed at the time of writing; T: 0462 340365*), illustrating the history of the valley.

The Ladin-speaking Val di Fassa is in the heart of the Dolomites; following the course of the Avisio between Pozza di Fassa and Canazei it forms part of the Strada dei Dolomiti. The main village is **Vigo di Fassa** (1382m), a winter sports resort, where the Museo Ladino (being moved to new quarters at the time of writing) records the history of the fascinating Ladin cultural-linguistic minority, which inhabits the area around the Sella massif (Val di Fassa, Val Badia, Val Gardena, and parts of the Livinallongo-Ampezzano, Comelico and Canton Grison in Switzerland). The fantastic Torri del Vaiolet are typical of the Dolomitic mountains.

PARCO NATURALE PANEVEGGIO-PALE DI SAN MARTINO

Park offices: Tonadico, Via Roma 19, T: 0439 64854.
Visitors' centres: Predazzo, Statale per il Rolle, Località Paneveggio, T: 0462 576283;
Tonadico, Via Castelpietra 2, Località Val Canali, T: 0439 64854;
www.parks.it/parco.paneveggio.pale.s.martino/Eindex.html
The marvellous peaks of the Pale di San Martino and the vast national forest of
Paneveggio, to the east of Predazzo, comprise the most spectacular nature
reserve in the province of Trento. It is an area of extraordinary beauty, marred
only by the ski slopes around San Martino di Castrozza.

The great green mantle of the Foresta di Paneveggio, which occupies the upper
valley of the Travignolo, includes 2,690ha of conifers and 1,300ha of active pasture. Although it suffered extensive damage during the First World War, it
remains an example (rare in Italy) of correct forest management, where a centu-
ry-old tradition, inaugurated during the Austro-Hungarian period, has been carefully preserved. Here you'll find red and white firs, larches, cembra pines, yews
and various deciduous trees, including beeches, oaks and aspens. At higher altitudes the ground is covered with scrub pine and rhododendron, whortleberry
and heather. The best area for flowers is the Val Venegia, where you can find rare
endemisms such as *Saxifraga facchinii*, *Primula tyrolensis* and *Dactilorhiza cruenta*.

PRACTICAL INFORMATION

GETTING AROUND

• **By road:** A long but scenic route
(Road 38) connects Lombardy with
Bolzano via the Stelvio Pass, and a series
of beautiful but tiring mountain roads
links Trieste, Venice, Padua and Vicenza
with Trento and Bressanone. Frequent
bus services (operated by SAD, T: 0471
450111 or freephone 800 846047,
www.sii.bz.it; and Atesina, T: 0461
821000, www.atesina.it) connect Trento
to Rovereto, Verona, Bolzano, Bressanone
and most towns and resorts in the
Dolomites.
• **By rail:** Trento is on the main rail line
to Verona, Florence, Rome and Naples.

INFORMATION OFFICES

Malè Viale Marconi 7, T: 0463 901280,
www.valdisole.net
Trento Via Manci 2, T: 0461 983880,
www.apt.trento.it
Rovereto Corso Rosmini 6/A, T: 0464
430363, www.apt.rovereto.tn.it
Cavalese Via Fratelli Bronzetti 60, T:
0462 241111, www.valdifiemme.info
Predazzo Via Cesare Battisti 4, T: 0462
501237, www.valdifiemme.info

HOTELS

Most of the hotels in the Trentino are
open during the winter and summer hol-

iday seasons, Dec–April and June–Sept. Hotels in the city of Trento are open all year round, unless otherwise marked.

Trento

€€ **Aquila d'Oro**. Adjoining the cathedral square, closed late Dec–early Jan. Via Belenzani 76, T: 0461 986282, www.aquiladoro.it

€€ **Villa Madruzzo**. A fine hotel and restaurant in a tranquil 19th-century villa with park, situated in a panoramic position above the city. Ponte Alto 26, T: 0461 986220.

Canazei

€ **Cesa Tyrol**. Family run, good views, great cuisine. Strada de la Cascata 2, T: 0462 601156, www.hotelcesatyrol.net

€ **Stella Alpina**. Delightful small hotel (8 rooms) in a 17th-century house. Closed Nov and May. Via Antermont 6, T: 0462 601127, stella.alpina@softcom.it

Cles (Val di Non)

€ **Cles**. A cordial and comfortable family-run place. Piazza Navarrino 7, T: 0463 421300, albergocles@tin.it

Madonna di Campiglio

€€ **Oberosler**. A delightful, comfortable chalet with a good restaurant. Via Monte Spinale 27, T: 0465 441136, F: 0465 443220, www.hoteloberosler.it

€€ **Spinale Club Hotel**. Centrally located and especially child-friendly. Via Monte Spinale 39, T: 0465 441116.

€ **La Baita**. Small, cosy and centrally located. Piazza Brenta Alta 17, T: 0465 441066, F: 0465 440750, www.hotellabaita.com

Malè (Val di Sole)

€ **Henriette**. Warm and comfortable, with lots of wood; sauna and pool. Via Trento 36, T: 0463 902110, F: 0463 902114.

Molveno (Val di Non)

€ **Alexander/Cima Tosa**. Central and elegant, with good views over the mountains and lake. Piazza Scuole 7, T: 0461 586928, F: 0461 586950, www.alexandermolveno.com

€ **Dolomiti**. In a lovely lakeshore garden. Via Lungolago 8, T: 0461 586057, F: 0461 586985, www.alledolomiti.com

Moena

€€ **Catinaccio/Rosengarten**. A lovely alpine hotel looking over the town square to the mountains. Via Someda 6, T: 0462 573235, www.hotelcr.com

€€ **Post**. Central and comfortable, with a famous restaurant (Tyrol). Piazza Italia 10, T: 0462 573760, www.posthotelmoena.it

Pejo (Val di Sole)

€ **Chalet Alpenrose**. An impeccably restored 18th-century farmhouse in the hills, with just ten rooms. Via Malgamare, Località Cògolo, T: 0463 754088.

Pinzolo

€€ **Corona**. Family-run establishment with a wellness centre. Corso Trento, T: 0465 501030, F: 0465 503853, www.hotelcorona.org

€€ **Maso Doss**. Just six rooms in an ancient, 17th-century farmhouse away from the crowds. Via Brenta 72, Località Sant'Antonio di Mavignolat, T: 0465 502758, www.masodoss.com

Predazzo

€€ **Redagno/Radein Zirmerhof**. A lovely, quiet place in an old farmhouse surrounded by woods and meadows. Open Dec–Mar and May–Nov. T: 0471 887215, F: 0471 887225, www.zirmerhof.com

Rovereto

€€ **Leon d'Oro**. Quiet and warmly furnished. Closed Feb. Via Tacchi 2, T:

0464 437333, www.hotelleondoro.it

€€ **Rovereto**. A quiet, welcoming place, with a good restaurant; closed Jan. Corso Rosmini 82d, T: 0464 435454, www.hotelrovereto.it

San Martino di Castrozza

€€ **Cristallo**. Friendly and family-run, with cosy rooms and fine views. Via Passo Rolle 51, T/F: 0439 68134.

€€ **Des Alpes**. Warm and comfortable, with views of the forests and mountains. Via Passo Rolle 118, T: 0439 769 069.

€€ **Letizia**. Centrally located, with lots of wood and a good restaurant. Closed Oct–Nov and May. Via Colbricon 6, T: 0439 768615, www.hletizia.it

€€ **Regina**. A classic family-run mountain resort hotel. Closed Oct–Nov and May. Via Passo Rolle 154, T: 0439 68221, www.hregina.it

Tonadico

€ **Chalet Pierini**. A cosy chalet where the owner is an expert chef and alpine guide. Closed Oct–Nov and May. T: 0439 62348.

Vigo di Fassa

€€ **Park Hotel Corona**. A traditional old hotel, all wood and fireplaces, with an excellent *pasticceria*. Via Dolomiti 8, T: 0462 764211, www.hotelcorona.com

RESTAURANTS

Trento

€€ **Chiesa** Fine local cuisine and ambience. Closed Sun, Wed evening and Aug. Parco San Marco, T: 0461 238766.

€€ **Le Due Spade**. *Osteria* established in 1545, offering creative interpretations of traditional recipes and regional, Italian and imported wines. Closed Sun, Mon morning and Aug. Via Don Rizzi 11, T: 0461 234343.

Cavalese

€€ **Al Cantuccio**. A family-managed place offering creative interpretations of traditional recipes. Closed Mon evening, Tues (except in high season), late autumn and late spring. Via Unterberger 14, T: 0462 340140.

€ **Alla Chiusa**. A simple trattoria with fixed menu (always delicious). Closed weekdays in low season. Via Chiusa, 1 (the Cavalese-Lavazé road), Varena, T: 0462 340626.

Giustino

€ **La Trisa**, Via Manzoni 50, Giustino, T: 0465 501665. On a dairy farm, serving great cheeses and other local delicacies. Open evenings only, closed June, Oct–Nov.

Malè (Vall di Sole)

€€ **Conte Ramponi**. Excellent traditional fare and atmosphere to match, in a 16th-century building with plenty of wood and old ceramic stoves; closed Mon (except in high season), June and Nov. Piazza San Marco 38, T: 0463 901989.

€ **Mangiasa**. Characteristic local cuisine on a flower farm. Open Fri–Sun, evenings only, closed May–June. Località Mangiasa, T: 0463 902123.

Moena

€€ **Ja Navalge**. Exquisite game, mushrooms and other local delicacies. Closed Sun evening and Mon in low season, and June and Nov. Via dei Colli 4, T: 0462 573930.

€€ **Malga Panna**. Delicious country cooking, with outside seating and great views in fair weather. Closed Mon (except July–Aug) and in low season. Via Costalunga 29, T: 0462 573489.

Molveno (Val di Non)

€ **Filò**. Good country *osteria* in the heart of the village. Closed weekends in low season, and Nov. Piazza Scuole 3, T: 0461 586151.

Nogaredo,

€ **Le Stie**. A wonderful *osteria* with a good wine list, in the medieval Val Lagarina. Open evenings only, closed Mon and July–Aug. Piazza Centrale 10, T: 0464 412220.

Pergine Valsugana

€€ **Al Castello** (with rooms). An excellent restaurant and small hotel in a 10th-century castle enjoying marvellous views over the surrounding countryside. Closed some Mons and Oct–May. T: 0461 531158.

Pozza di Fassa

€€ **Da Bocol**. Good wine, great local cuisine, beautiful location. Closed Thur and Sun in low season. Via Avisio 10, T: 0462 763752.

Rovereto

€€€ **Al Borgo**. Restaurant famous for its fish dishes and its wine cellar (which you can visit). Closed Sun evening (all day Sun in summer), Dec–Jan and July–Aug. Via Garibaldi 13, T: 0464 436300.

San Martino di Castrozza

€ **Malga Ces**. An elegant and inexpensive restaurant in a magnificent position, serving traditional Tyrolean fare with regional and Italian wines. Closed May–June and Oct–Nov. Località Ces (3km west of San Martino). T: 0439 68145.

Soraga

€€ **Fuchiade**. Exquisite traditional food in an alpine hut (with rooms), accessible by foot or 4WD in summer, on skis or snowcat in winter (telephone ahead to reserve a ride). Open June–Oct and Dec–April. Località Fuchiade (Passo di San Pellegrino), T: 0462 574281.

Spiazzo

€€ **Mezzosoldo**. A hotel restaurant famous among locals for its exquisitely prepared regional dishes. Closed Thur (except in summer), Oct–Nov and Apr–June. Via Nazionale 196, Spiazzo (Mortaso), T: 0465 801067.

Vezzano

€€ **Fior di Roccia**. Has a reputation for exquisite cuisine served with flair. Closed Sun evening and Mon. Località Lon, T: 0461 864029.

REGIONAL SPECIALITIES

Trento and Rovereto The area is renowned for its wines, both red (Marzemino, Merlot, Cabernet) and white (Nosiola, Pinot Grigio, Moscato); the best growing district is the Vallagarina.

Malè At Piazza Garibaldi 5 you will find **Gelateria Roby**: try their aromatic herb and wine ice cream.

ENTERTAINMENT & EVENTS

Trento *Mostra dei Vini del Trentino*, regional wine fair, Apr; *Festival Internazionale del Film della Montagna, dell'Esplorazione e dell'Avventura*, International Festival of Mountain, Exploration, and Adventure Films, Apr–May; *Feste Vigiliane*, with the *Palio dell'Oca*, popular feast and pageant, June; *Mostra Micologica*, mushroom fair, Sept; *Autunno Trentino*, classical music, Sept–Oct.

Rovereto *Torneo Internazionale di Tiro con l'Arco*, archery tournament, Sept; *Fiera di Santa Caterina*, local folk fair with street theatre, Nov; *Rassegna Jazz*, international jazz festival, Nov.

BOLZANO & ENVIRONS

To the east of the provincial capital of Bolzano rise the pale rock towers of the Dolomites; to the west the dark-grey granite peaks of the Central Alps. The difference in atmosphere between the two areas is remarkable. The Dolomites are more picturesque while the Central Alps, the higher of the two ranges, are craggy and imposing, and covered with snow much of the year. There are magnificent nature reserves in both areas—the most accessible, the Parco Naturale dello Sciliar, is just a stone's throw from the city—and summer and winter resorts abound.

Bolzano, in German Bozen, is the largest town in the upper basin of the Adige and has been the capital of the (mainly German-speaking) province of Bolzano-Alto Adige since 1927. It has the character of a German rather than Italian town, although its population is now mainly Italian-speaking. The old town, with its low-pitched Tyrolean arcades and Gothic architecture, has a distinctly medieval appearance.

HISTORY OF BOLZANO

Mentioned for the first time (as Bauzanum) by Paulus Diaconus in his medieval history of the Lombards, Bolzano formed part of the episcopal principality of Trento in the 11th century and was joined to the Tyrol in the 16th century. The oldest part of the city grew up around the little Romanesque church of San Giovanni in Villa (12th century), but the greatest building activity was that of the Gothic period, when Bolzano became a major mercantile centre. Long a possession of the bishop-princes of Trento, it eventually passed to the Counts of Tyrol, who were succeeded by the Dukes of Carinthia and, after 1363, the Dukes of Austria. The Habsburgs held the city until 1918, except during the Napoleonic period, when it was briefly united first to Bavaria and then to the Napoleonic Kingdom of Italy. In the late 19th century the old city, having remained substantially unchanged over the centuries, grew to include the elegant suburb of Gries. In the 1930s industrial development gave rise to a number of new factories and working-class neighbourhoods towards the west and south, which also changed the city's predominantly German ethnic composition by attracting large numbers of labourers from southern Italy.

The town centre

The centre of town is the busy, spacious **Piazza Walther**. It takes its name from a monument erected in the 19th century to the medieval German composer, minnesinger and poet Walther von der Vogelweide, thought to have been a native of the region. Vogelweide's political poems staunchly supported the Holy Roman Emperor against the Pope. The **cathedral**, a Gothic church of the 14th and 15th centuries (restored after 1945) with an elegant apse, a steep tile roof and a fretwork spire, overlooks the square from the south. Fine doorways and reliefs adorn the exterior, and the three-aisled interior has frescoes of the 14th–16th centuries, a fine pulpit with reliefs, of 1514, and a fine Baroque altar.

The **Chiesa dei Domenicani**, one block west, is the old church of the Italian community in Bolzano. It too was damaged in the war and has subsequently been rebuilt. The interior preserves remains of 14th- and 15th-century frescoes. Over the last north altar is a restored altarpiece by Guercino (1655), and adjoining the apse, the Cappella di San Giovanni, with fine frescoes by followers of Giotto (c. 1340). More frescoes, dating from the 14th–16th centuries, are in the Gothic cloister (entrance at no. 19a), the Chapter House and the Cappella di Santa Caterina.

Piazza Domenicani ends on the west at the corner of Via Sernesi, where a new university building partially conceals the entrance to the **Museion-Museum für Moderne Kunst** (*open Tues–Sun 10–12 & 3–6, Thur 10–8*), with a small permanent collection of modern and contemporary art and an excellent programme of temporary exhibitions.

Returning to the church, turn left at the east end of the square to reach **Piazza Erbe**, the site of a colourful fruit-and-vegetable market. This lively square, at the crossing of two major pedestrian streets, is flanked by fine old houses and adorned, on one side, by the 18th-century Fontana del Nettuno, with a bronze statue by Georg Mayr, a local artist. To the east stretches the straight, narrow Via dei Portici, the oldest thoroughfare in the city and now also its main shopping street. It is flanked by handsome porticoed houses dating from the 15th–18th centuries, with distinctive bay windows; at no. 39 (the main façade is in Via Argentieri) is the Baroque Palazzo Mercantile (1708), by the Veronese architect Francesco Pedrotti.

From Piazza Erbe, Via dei Francescani winds northwards to the 14th-century Gothic **Chiesa dei Francescani**, with a richly carved high altar (1500) and a graceful 14th-century cloister with fragmentary frescoes. At the next corner Via Vinfler leads right to the Museo di Scienze Naturali (*open Tues–Sun 10–6, last entry 5*), devoted to the landscape and ecosystems of the upper valley of the Adige. Continuing along Via Hofer you take the first left, first right, and first left again to reach **San Giovanni in Villa**, the oldest church in Bolzano, built in the 13th century and enlarged in the early 14th. It has a powerful Romanesque-Gothic campanile and 14th-century frescoes.

From the centre to Gries

Via del Museo, with elegant shops (and cafés serving unforgettable cakes and pastries), leads west from Piazza Erbe. The **Museo Archeologico dell'Alto-Adige** (*open Tues–Sun 10–6, Thur 10–8*) displays antiquities from the Mesolithic to the Roman age. The most outstanding exhibit of the museum is **Ötzi**, the 5,000-year-old Neolithic huntsman found mummified beneath the ice of the Similaun Glacier, preserved here in a special refrigerated cell. Studies of the body have revealed that Ötzi was about 45 years of age, that he suffered from bad teeth and hardened arteries, and that he died from arrow wounds as he tried to run away from up to four assailants. Numerous well-mounted displays show his garments and tools and explain his life and times. The pictures are sufficiently clear if you don't read Italian or German, and recorded tours are available.

The Ponte Tàlvera crosses the river to the **Monumento della Vittoria**, a huge triumphal arch celebrating the victory over the Austrians in 1918, and erected to a design by the Roman architect Marcello Piacentini in 1928. The monument, seen as a provocation by ethnic Germans in the region, has been the object of several terrorist attacks and is now inaccessible. On the river banks are a park and beautiful promenades. The one on the east bank leads northwards to join the Passeggiata Sant'Osvaldo, which climbs the slopes of the Renon hill, offering splendid views back over the town and valley. At the foot of the hill the promenade passes the medieval Castel Maréccio, now a convention centre.

West of the Tàlvera, Corso Libertà leads through the **Rationalist neighbourhoods** of the early 20th-century extension of the city. These districts give architectural expression to the philosophy that views reason as the essential source of truth and knowledge. Razionalismo in Italy, like the Bauhaus in Germany or de Stijl in the Netherlands, took reason as the basic criterion of design and extended this into urban planning. These neighbourhoods, centred on Corso Libertà, were developed by Marcello Piacentini (1881–1960), possibly Italy's foremost Rationalist architect. The precise geometry of the elevations and street plans adheres closely to Mies van der Rohe's famous dictum that form follows function. Beyond these is the garden suburb of **Gries**. On the main square is the Abbazia dei Benedittini, whose late-Baroque church (1771) has frescoes and altarpieces by the Tyrolean painter Martin Knoller. A little further on is the old Gothic parish church, with a carved and painted altarpiece by Michael Pacher (1475).

Around Bolzano

One of the characteristic features of Bolzano is the number of walks you can take in the immediate environs of the city. The **Passeggiata del Guncina** winds up the hill behind the parish church in Gries to the Castel Gùncina (476m), with great views over Bolzano and the Dolomites. The path, cut out of a porphyry wall, is planted with Mediterranean flora. The **Passeggiata Sant'Osvaldo-Santa Maddalena** ascends the hill of Santa Maddalena, with a Romanesque church of Mary Magdalen in a picturesque setting amidst vineyards. It can be followed from Via Sant'Osvaldo to the Lungotàlvera and vice versa. A cableway (lower station in Via Sarentino) climbs the 1087m to **San Genesio Altesino**, a busy summer and winter resort on the Altopiano del Salto, with splendid views over the Val Sarentina and the Dolomites. Another cableway starts from Via Renon (near the station) and mounts to Soprabolzano/Oberbozen, on the Renon highland north of the city. Near **Collalbo**, the main town of the plateau and an excellent starting point for walks and climbs, are the earth-pillars of Longomoso, the most dramatic of the many examples of this curious erosion phenomenon in the area; the path continues to the Rifugio Corno di Renon (2259m, a 3hr ascent), commanding a magnificent view.

You'll need a car to reach **Castel Ròncolo/Schloss Runkelstein**, a 13th-century castle on a clifftop at the mouth of the Val Sarentina. Inside are frescoes (*shown on a guided tour March–Nov Tues–Sat 10–5*) of late-medieval court life and stories of Tristan and Isolde (in the Palazzo Occidentale, Stua da Bagno and Sala del Torneo), 16th-century scenes of chivalry (in the Casa d'Estate) and a *Martyrdom of St Catherine* (in the

13th-century chapel). On the other side of the Adige is the ruined castle of Appiano, founded in the 12th century, which retains a Romanesque chapel with murals (*open Apr–Nov*). **Terlano/Terlan**, 10km northwest on the road to Merano, is the centre of a wine-growing district. It has a Gothic parish church with a 15th-century fresco of St Christopher on the façade, and two *campanili*. **Appiano sulla Strada del Vino** has several fine 17th–18th-century houses in a Renaissance style peculiar to the district. At Caldaro, on the Lago di Caldaro, there is a wine museum.

The Val Gardena

The Val Gardena is a Ladin-speaking valley reached via Ponte Gardena/Waidbruck, north of Bolzano on the Brenner road. Wedged between the steep walls of the Val d'Isarco, **Ponte Gardena** is a rather dark place nestled around the Castel Forte Trostburg, a 12th-century castle of the Wolkenstein, with a 16th-century hall (*open Easter–Oct Tues–Sat at 10, 11, 2, 3 and 4*).

The Val Gardena road winds up and out of the Isarco Valley, through verdant forests and farmland, to **Ortisei/St Ulrich** (1234m), a small resort. The 18th-century church here contains good examples of woodcarving, for which Ortisei is noted. The Museo della Val Gardena (*open July–Aug Mon-Fri 10–12 & 2–6, Sun 2–6, Sept Mon–Fri 2–6, Thur also 10–12; Oct–June Tues–Fri 2–6, Thur 10–12 & 2–6*) has art, craft and natural history collections of local interest.

The road continues to climb, offering a series of changing views over the Sciliar and peaks of the Puez-Odle park. Selva di Val Gardena/Wolkenstein in Groden (1563m), stands at the foot of the Vallunga, which penetrates the heart of the Puez and Gardenaccia mountains to the northeast. The valley ends at the Passo Sella (2213m), which has a splendid view, perhaps the finest in all the Dolomites.

The Strada delle Dolomiti

The famous Strada delle Dolomiti (Road 241) runs from Bolzano, on the west side of the Dolomites, to **Cortina d'Ampezzo** on the east. It is one of the most beautiful roads in the Alps, as well as a magnificent feat of engineering.

From Bolzano the road enters the wild and romantic gorge of the Val d'Ega, passing the Ponte della Cascata. It then passes the resorts of Nova Levante/Welschnofen (1182m), and Carezza al Lago (1609m), dominated by the two most typical Dolomite mountain groups with their characteristic battlemented skyline, the Látemar (2842m) and the Catinaccio (2981m). The latter is especially famous for its marvellous colouring at sunrise, from which it takes the German name Rosengarten ('Rose Garden').

The road summit is reached at the **Passo di Costalunga** (1745m), with a splendid view ahead of the Val di Fassa and the Marmolada and San Martino mountains. The **Marmolada** (3342m), the largest and highest group of peaks in the Dolomites, is approached by cableways and chair-lifts. A winding descent through high pastures brings the road into the Val Cordevole, with the villages of Arabba (1601m) and Pieve di Livinallongo (1475m). A long ascent beneath the ruined castle of Andraz leads to the Passo di Falzarego (2165m), beyond which the road descends to Cortina d'Ampezzo.

THE PARCO NATURALE DELLO SCILIAR

Park offices: Provincia Autonoma di Bolzano, Via Cesare Batisti 21, T: 0471 994300,
www.parks.it/parco.sciliar/index.html

The Parco Naturale dello Sciliar combines the rocky walls, cliffs and the ledges of the Sciliar Massif with the verdant pastures of the Alpe di Siusi. Its geological history is clearly shown in its succession of rock layers. Above the dark-red quartziferous porphyry of the Adige valley are the sandstones of the Val Gardena which, because of their high iron content, colour the soil of the fields red. Higher up, covered by forests, are rocks that were formed just 65 million years ago. There follow layers of sedimentary and volcanic rock—a clear sign that the coral reefs of the ancient Mediterranean (which over time would become the pink stone of the Sciliar) were periodically submerged beneath layers of lava and ash (to which the soil of the Alpe di Siusi owes its fertility). The Sciliar accommodates an extraordinary variety of plant species: numerous saxifrages, the so-called 'strega dello Sciliar' (*Armeria alpina*), edelweiss, alpine poppies, and many more. The park is reached via Siusi/Seis am Schlern, with its pleasant square, or Castelrotto/Kastelruth, a fairytale village huddled around a massive 18th-century bell tower and taking its name from the medieval castle, set on a wooded knoll. Tires and San Cipriano are the gateways to the wild Val Ciamin and the adjacent Catinaccio/Rosengarten group, the mythical lair of the dwarf-king Laurin.

MERANO

Merano, in German Meran, is famous as a climatic resort and spa, and also a climbing centre and ski resort. Together with Maia Alta/Obermais and Maia Bassa/Untermais on the opposite bank of the torrent, it consists of monumental hotels and villas, many of them built in the last century by Austrian architects, surrounded by luxuriant gardens in a sheltered valley. Spring and autumn are the fashionable seasons for visiting Merano. The inhabitants are mainly German-speaking.

The town centre

The old main street of the medieval town is the narrow **Via dei Portici**, lined by lovely old houses painted in pastel tones. Beneath its low arcades are excellent shops and the town hall (1930). **Kunstmeranoarte**, in the Haus der Sparkasse, has changing exhibitions of international contemporary art (*open Tues–Sun 10–6*). Behind Via dei Portici is the well preserved **Castello Principesco** (*open Tues–Sat 10–5, Sun and holidays 10–1*), built by Archduke Sigismund in 1445–80 and containing contemporary furnishings. The arms of Scotland alongside those of Austria recall Sigismund's marriage to Eleanor, daughter of James I of Scotland. Also in Via Galilei is the Museo Civico (*open as the castello, cumulative ticket available*), with local collections.

At the end of Via dei Portici is the duomo, a Gothic church of the 14th–15th centuries with a curious battlemented façade, a tall tower, and 14th–16th-century tomb-reliefs. Inside are two 15th-century altarpieces by Martin Knoller. Along the River Passirio extend gardens and promenades laid out at the turn of the century. The cheerful Corso Libertà, with its fashionable shops, was laid out before the First World War. It passes the Kursaal (1914), the Neoclassical theatre, and several elaborate hotels.

THE VAL PASSIRIA & ANDREAS HOFER

In the pastoral Val Passiria, near San Leonardo, is Maso dell'Arena (Sandwirt), the birthplace of Tyrolean patriot and martyr Andreas Hofer (1767–1810). Hofer, an innkeeper and cattle-trader, was one of many Tyroleans who advocated the return of the Tyrol to Austria after it had been ceded to Bavaria in 1805, under pressure from Napoleon. With encouragement from Vienna, Hofer led a band of Tyrolese against Franco-Bavarian troops, and won several victories, only to be sacrificed on the altar of military expediency. After suffering defeat at Wagram, and knowing that Napoleon was advancing on Vienna, the Austrian emperor Franz I was persuaded to sue for peace. The conditions of the treaty were the hand of his daughter in marriage to Bonaparte, and the handing over of Tyrol. Hofer fled to a mountain hideout in his native valley. Betrayed to the French and deserted by his emperor, he was executed at Mantua on the personal order of Napoleon. His house (now a hotel) contains a little private museum.

Around Merano

Tirolo to the north is a village given over to tourism. Ezra Pound stayed in the Castel Fontana (reconstructed in 1904), which contains mementoes of the poet as well as a local ethnographic museum (*open Apr–Nov Wed–Mon 9.30–12 & 2–5*). On the opposite side of a ravine, in a superb position, is Castel Tirolo (*open March–Nov Tues–Sun 10–5*), the 12th-century castle of the counts of Tyrol which gave its name to the region. With the abdication of Margaret Maultasch, the 'ugly duchess', in 1363, the castle and province passed to the Habsburgs.

PARCO NAZIONALE DELLO STELVIO

Park offices: Bormio, Via Roma 26, T: 0342 901654.
Visitors' centres: Prato allo Stelvio, Via Croce 4/c, T: 0473 618212; Stelvio, Trafoi 57, T: 0473 612031; Cògolo di Peio, Via Roma, 28, T: 0463 754186.
Runcal game preserve: Peio, Località Peio Fonti, T: 0347 7708380, www.stelviopark.it
This immense nature reserve, straddling the boundary between the Trentino-Alto Adige and Lombardy, is the largest national park in Italy (135,000ha) and one of the oldest, established in 1935. It encompasses the magnificent mountain group of the Ortles-Cavedale, with peaks well over 3000m, and is one of the two designated wilderness areas of northern Italy (the other is the Parco Nazionale del Gran Paradiso in Piedmont, *see p. 28*). Logging, mining, farming and grazing are all discouraged, with a view to allowing the area to return as nearly as possible to a 'natural' (though by no means 'original' or 'virgin') state. At Gomagoi (1266m) a minor road ascends the Val di Solda, a lovely side valley inside the park boundaries. Its main village, Solda (1907m), is one of the most important climbing centres in the upper Adige and a holiday resort. Above rise Monte Cevedale (3769m) and the Ortles (Ortler, 3905m), a magnificent peak, defended by the Austrians throughout the First World War. Trafoi (1543m) is a summer and winter resort with a magnificent panorama of the Ortles massif. Beyond Trafoi begins the long, winding ascent to the Passo dello Stelvio/Stilfserjoch (2758m), generally open only June–October. It was the meeting-place of the frontiers of Italy, Switzerland and Austria until 1918. There is a good view from the Pizzo Garibaldi (2838m), in German called Dreisprachenspitze ('Three Languages Peak') from the meeting of the districts where Italian, Romansch and German are spoken. A minor road winds over the Giogo di Santa Maria (2502m) to Switzerland.

The Val Venosta

The Val Venosta (Vinschga) is the wide and fertile upper valley of the Adige to the west of Merano, near the Austrian and Swiss borders. It has numerous small summer and winter resorts and fine mountain scenery. Part of the valley lies in the Parco Nazionale dello Stelvio.

The summer resort of **Naturno/Naturns** has a little Romanesque church, San Procolo, with remarkable 8th-century mural paintings. From here a minor road winds northwards up the long Val Senales, dominated by the great pyramid of the Similaun (3597m), on the Austrian frontier. Ötzi (*see p. 290*) was found in the glacier on the saddle between the Val Senales and the Venter Tal in Austria.

The main place in the Val Venosta is **Silandro/Schlanders**, with the valley's highest vineyards (722m). The Val Venosta turns to the north beyond Spondigna/Spondinig, gaining in altitude as it approaches the source of the Adige. The Castel Coira/Churburg, above Sluderno, is the 13th-century castle of the bishops of Coire. It was restored in the 16th century by the Counts Trapp. **Glorenza**, to the west, is a typical old Tyrolean town with medieval and 16th-century ramparts and three gates. It is particularly well preserved and draws quite a few visitors. In the Val Monastero (Münster-Tal), to the west of Glorenza, is the **Calven Gorge**: here in 1499 the Swiss defeated the Austrians and won their practical independence of the empire.

Malles Venosta (1051m) is an old mountain town. The church of San Benedetto dates from the 9th century or earlier; it has an important Carolingian fresco cycle. Other medieval remains include the ruined Castel Fröhlich (near the parish church), the Torre Dross (near the Casa della Cultura), and the Preschgenegg (in Via Winkel), Lichtenegg (in the main square), Goldegg, Pracassan and Malsegg (in Via General Verdross) houses. The large Benedictine abbey of Monte Maria, outside the town, mainly rebuilt in the 17th–19th centuries, preserves frescoes of c. 1160.

At the north end of the Lago di Resia, below the source of the Adige, stands **Resia** (1525m), with a splendid view down the valley of the Ortles group. It was rebuilt when its original site was submerged. The Austrian frontier lies just beyond the Passo di Resia.

PRACTICAL INFORMATION

GETTING AROUND

• **By road:** A long but scenic route (Road 38) connects Lombardy with Bolzano via the Stelvio Pass, and a series of beautiful but tiring mountain roads links Trieste, Venice, Padua and Vicenza with Trento and Bressanone. Frequent bus services (operated by SAD, T: 0471 450111 or freephone 800 846047, www.sii.bz.it; and Atesina, T: 0461 821000, www.atesina.it) connect Bolzano to Trento, Rovereto, Verona, Bressanone and most towns and resorts in the Dolomites.

• **By rail:** Bolzano has rail links to Verona, Florence, Rome and Naples. Merano has a rail service to Verona, Milan, Florence and Rome. A secondary rail-and-bus line runs from Padua to Cortina d'Ampezzo via Castelfranco, Feltre and Belluno, with connections for the Val Pusteria, Bressanone and Bolzano.

INFORMATION OFFICES

There is a central information office for all the resorts in its province at Bolzano, Piazza Parrocchia 11, T: 0471 993808,

www.provincia.bz.it/turismo.htm. Hotel reservation service, T: 0471 222220, F: 0471 222221. Snow bulletin, T: 0471 200198. Walking and climbing bulletin, T: 0471 993809. Südtirol Marketing Gesellschaft, Bolzano, Pfarrplatz 11, T: 0471/99 99 99, www.altoadige.info More summer and winter sports info: Ufficio Provinciale per il Turismo dell'Alto Adige, Servizio Informazioni Alpine, Bolzano, Piazza Walther 8, T: 0471 993809.
Bolzano Piazza Walther, T: 0471/307001, www.bolzano-bozen.it
Merano Corso Libertà 45, T: 0473 272000, www.meraninfo.com
Val Gardena Ortisei/St Ulrich, Via Rezia 1, T: 0471 796328, www.valgardena.it
Val Venosta Curon Venosta, Paese 61, T: 0473 634603, www.reschenpass-suedtirol.com

HOTELS

Most of the hotels in the environs of Bolzano are open during the winter and summer holiday seasons, Dec–Apr and June–Sept. Hotels in the city are open all year round unless otherwise marked.
Bolzano
€€€ **Park Hotel Laurin**. Named after the mythical dwarf-king of the Dolomites, a great historic hotel in a lovely park a stone's throw from the train station and from Piazza Walther. Via Laurin 4, T: 0471 311000, www.laurin.it
€€ **Greif**. Established in the 16th century and managed since the early 19th century by the same family, this venerable establishment has been renovated in a beautiful contemporary Viennese style. Piazza Walther 7, T: 0471 318000, www.greif.it
€ **Magdalenerhof**. A carefully appointed place with Tyrolean ambience, set amid vineyards on the outskirts of town. Via Rencio 48a, T: 0471 978267, magdalenerhof@dnet.it
Merano
€€ **Aurora**. Quiet and elegant, in the pedestrian area. Closed Dec–Mar. Passeggiata Lungo Passirio 38, T: 0473 211800, www.hotel-aurora-meran.com
€€ **Castel Fragsburg**. A beautiful historic home, impeccably restored and expertly managed; 10 rooms. Closed Nov–March. Via Fragsburg 3, at Freiberg, T: 0473 244072, www.fragsburg.com
€€ **Kurhotel Schloss Rundegg**. Probably the most interesting place to stay in town, a 12th-century building enlarged in the 16th century, immersed in a lush garden. Closed Jan. Via Scena 2, T: 0473 234100, www.rundegg.com
€€ **Meister's Hotel Irma**. Refined atmosphere, indoor and outdoor pools, library, verdant park and great food. Via Belvedere 17, T: 0473 212000, www.hotel-irma.it
€€ **Schloss Labers**. An old (13th-century) castle, surrounded by vineyards, with garden restaurant in summer. Closed Nov–March. Via Labers 25, T: 0473 234484, www.labers.it
€ **Isabella**. Comfortable and relaxed—ask for a rooftop suite. Closed Nov–Mar. Via Piave 58, T: 0473 234700, www.hotel-isabella.com
Castelrotto/Kastelruth
€€ **Cavallino d'Oro-Goldenes Rössl**. Dating back to the 14th century and offering the most distinctive Tyrolean atmosphere, including two fine *stuben*.

Closed Nov–Dec. T: 0471 706337, www.cavallino.it

Fiè allo Sciliar

€€ **Emmy**. In a fine position surrounded by meadows, with views of the forests and mountains. Closed Nov–Mar. Via Putzes 5, T: 0471 725006, www.hotel-emmy.com

€€ **Thurm**. Once a medieval prison but now a refined, comfortable hotel with an excellent restaurant. Closed Nov–Dec. Piazza della Chiesa 9, T: 0471 25014, www.hotelturm.it

Lagundo/Algund

€€ **Pünthof**. A tastefully renovated farmhouse with fine restaurant, tavern, orchard and pond. Closed Nov–March. Via Steinagh 25, T: 0473 448553, www.charmerelax.it

€ **Ludwigshof**. Small and cosy, with a nice garden. Closed Nov–March. Breitofenweg 9a, T: 0473 220355, www.ludwigshof.com

€ **Pionerhof**. Just six rooms in a lovely little 13th-century farmhouse on the outskirts of the town. Via Peter Thalguter 11, T: 0473 448728.

Naturno/Naturns

€€ **Lindenhof**. Nice rooms, good restaurant, covered pool. Closed Nov–March. Via della Chiesa 2, T: 0473 666242, www.lindenhof.it

Ortisei/St Ulrich

€€€ **Grien**. Excellent creature comforts, and better views, over the Sella Massif and Sassolungo. Via Mureda 178, T: 0471 796340, www.hotel-grien.com

Renon

€€ **Kematen**. A particularly tranquil place in a lovely park with great views of the Dolomites and a very good restaurant; closed Nov and Jan. At Caminata, T: 0471 356356, kematen@chet.it

€€ **Lichtenstern**. Set in an immense park, with walking paths and a playground. At Costalovara/Wolfsgruben. T: 0471 354147, www. lichtenstern.it

Selva di Val Gardena

€ **Pozzamanigoni**. Restful and secluded, with great food and fabulous views. La Selva 51, T: 0471 794138.

€ **Prà Ronch**. Simple and comfortable, in a beautifully restored old farmhouse. Via La Selva 80, T/F: 0471 794064, www.val-gardena.com/room/praronch/

Siusi/Seis

€€ **Steger Dellai**. With swimming in a nearby lake; closed Oct–Nov and May Alpe di Siusi/Seiser Alm, T: 0471 727964.

€€ **Waldrast**. Simple and inexpensive. Closed Oct–Dec and late April–early May. Via Hauenstein 25, T: 0471 706117, www.hotel-waldrast.com

RESTAURANTS

Bolzano

€€ **Belle Epoque**. One of the finest restaurants in the city: traditional local dishes and a wide selection of wines; prices are surprisingly moderate, given the setting. Park Hotel Laurin, Via Laurin 4, T: 0471 311000.

€€ **Da Abramo**. Elegant interiors and skilfully prepared traditional dishes. A local favourite. Closed Sun and a few days in Aug. Piazza Gries 16, T: 0471 280141.

€ **Amadè**. Offering traditional cuisine with a personal twist. Closed Sun and Aug. Vicolo Cà dè Bezzi 8, T: 0471 971278.

€ **Cavallino Bianco/Weisses Rössl**. A favourite old-fashioned *osteria*, always crowded, with delicious local food.

Closed Sat evening and Sun. Via Bottai 6, T: 0471 973267.

€ **Da Cesare**. A friendly, centrally located establishment where fresh pasta and grilled meats are specialities. Closed Mon. Via Perathoner 15, T: 0471 976638.

€ **Rastbichler**. A well-known place with a nice garden for the warmer months, offering periodic 'gourmet weeks'. Closed Sat morning and Sun, Jan and July. Via Cadorna 1, T: 0471 261131.

Merano

€€ **Sissi**. A family restaurant offering good traditional cuisine. Closed Mon and July. Via Galilei 44, T: 0473 231062.

Castelbello Ciardes/Kastelbell Tschars

€ **Schlosswirt Juval**. A *buschenschankl*, or old farmhouse-cum-wine tavern, serving traditional Tyrolean fare and wines. Closed Wed, Dec–Easter and July. Località Juval-Stava Venosta, T: 0473 668238.

Lagundo/Algund

€ **Oberlechnerhof**. An old farmhouse with cosy *stuben*, serving local food and wines. Closed Wed and Jan.

Naturno/Naturns

€€ **Steghof**. Featuring authentic medieval ambience and delicious cuisine. Open evenings only, closed Sun, Mon and Jan–Feb. T: 0473 668224.

Renon

€€ **Patscheiderhof**. A farm, famous among *bolzanini* but unknown to outsiders, serving delicious country meals. Closed Tues and July. Località Signato/Signat 178, T: 0471 365267.

San Leonardo in Passiria/Sankt Leonard in Passeier

€ **Jägerhof**. A friendly family-run place (with rooms) offering delicacies of the Val Passiria. Closed Mon and Nov. Via Passo del Giovo 80, Vàltina/Walten.

REGIONAL SPECIALITIES

In these Alpine regions bread is often eaten with *speck*, a delicacy born of the necessity to preserve freshly slaughtered pork. Farmers realised that by hanging a ham above the hearth and then exposing it to the cool, dry air of the forest, they could preserve it for a long time. Over the years both the conservation and the flavour of the meat were improved by salting it before smoking it, and the smoking was refined by the addition of juniper branches.

Cheese is another important ingredient of Alpine cuisine. Time was when every *malga* (shepherd's hut) had its own unique cheese. Now the factories process the milk of an entire valley, and many small producers have disappeared. But there are plenty of good local cheeses left. Try *spressa*, a low-fat, flavourful cheese typical of the Val Rendena; or the famous *puzzone di Moena*, from the Val di Fassa, whose curious name ('stinker') doesn't do justice to its flavour and aroma. On the other side of the Passo Rolle, at Primiero, is the homeland of fresh *tosella*, eaten with polenta accompanied by the wild yellow mushrooms known as *finferli*. The Latteria Sociale at **Lagundo** is a dairy-farmers' co-op selling fresh and aged local cheese. (Località Velloi 7, T: 0473 222557.) Moserspeck, at Via Stein 17 in **Naturno**, has good local *speck* and salami. In **Merano**, Greiterhof, on the Stradel di Castel Verruca, near Avelengo, has home-brewed beers.

For vacationing Italians, Austrians and Germans, **Bolzano** seems to be the place in the Dolomites to shop. As a result, the shops are filled with beautiful merchandise, from clothing to Italian designer housewares. Unfortunately, high demand tends also to drive up prices. Throughout the region farms sell local products, ranging from herbal teas, grappa, honey and fruit preserves, to handmade pillows and slippers.

FESTIVALS & EVENTS

Bolzano Local crafts fair in Piazza Walther, April. *Concerto di Pasqua*, traditional music and costume at San Genesio, Easter Sunday. Flower show in Piazza Walther, May. *Internazionale di Vini*, wine fair and tasting at Castel Mareccio, May. *Musica in Piazza Walther*, outdoor concert series, April–May. *Festa dello Speck*, feast of local dishes, featuring the famous streaky bacon, May. *Bolzano Danza*, dance festival, July; *Passeggiata Gastronomica a San Genesio*, food fair, July; *Alla Corte di Re Laurino*, folk fair with local farm and craft products, food and drink, Sept. *Mercatino di Natale*, folk fair with Christmas-tree ornaments, vin brûlé, Christmas pastries and live music, Nov–Dec.

Merano International Wine Festival, Merano, Nov. *Mercatino di Natale*, market of Christmas ornaments and sweets, Merano, Nov–Dec. *Ballo di San Silvestro*, Boxing Day ball, Merano, Dec.

Val Gardena-Alpe di Siusi *Settimane Musicali Gardenesi*, classical music festival at Selva, Santa Cristina and Castel Gardena, July–Aug. *Festa del Folclore Gardenese* and *Corteo Storico*, folk festival and historic procession, Aug. *Concorso di Sculture di Neve*, snow-sculpture competition, Selva Gardena, Feb. *Matrimonio Contadino*, historic pageant, Castelrotto, Jan. *Come Sciavano i Nostri Nonni*, old-fashioned ski festival, Sciliar Plateau, March.

September is the month of grape-harvest feasts in wine districts, and the month in which the cows are brought down from the high pastures, amidst great celebration and pageantry, in mountain villages. The shepherds of the Val Senales celebrate the *transumanza*, or driving of the (3,000) sheep over the Giogo passes to their summer pastures in the Ventertal in Austria, in June and Sept. Exact dates vary, of course, with the weather.

BRESSANONE
& THE EASTERN ALPS

Bressanone, in German Brixen, stands at the meeting-point of two Alpine streams, the Isarco and the Rienza, and of two important old roads, from the Val Pusteria and the eastern Tyrol, and from Brennero and Austria. Situated in a lovely open landscape of cultivated hills between steep mountain peaks and green forests and meadows, the city preserves the mark of its history as a centre of a vast ecclesiastical principality. The power of its bishop-princes lasted 800 years, from 1027 to 1803. Its architecture, monuments and artworks, which embody the full variety of styles from the Romanesque to the Baroque, carry the singular inflexions of a site on a cultural frontier.

NB: This chapter is covered by the map on p. 288.

BRESSANONE

The **cathedral**, built in the 9th century, enlarged in the 13th century, and completely rebuilt in Baroque forms in 1745–90, dominates the shady Piazza del Duomo. The beautifully preserved interior is adorned with ceiling frescoes by the Austrian artist Paul Troger, and fine carvings. In the adjacent Romanesque cloister are 14th- and 15th-century frescoes of Old and New Testament scenes and the entrance to the 11th-century baptistery, which hosted the famous council convoked in 1080 to depose Pope Gregory VII (Hildebrand) and elect the Antipope Clement III.

The **Palazzo dei Principi Vescovi** is a fortified building, preceded by a moat, rising in the nearby Piazza del Palazzo. Built in the early 13th century by the bishop-prince Bruno de Kirchberg, it was several times enlarged and then rebuilt as a Renaissance château, after 1595, for Cardinal Andrea of Austria. Rendered in Baroque forms after 1710, it remained the residence of the bishop-princes and the administrative centre of their feudality until 1803. It has an elegant façade and an imposing courtyard with 24 life-size terracotta statues of members of the Habsburg family. The interior hosts the Museo Diocesano (*open Tues–Sun 10–5*) with one of the largest art collections in northeastern Italy. Especially noteworthy is the collection of *presepi* (Christmas crèches).

Adjoining Piazza del Duomo to the north, Piazza della Parrocchia takes its name from the 15th-century Gothic parish church of **San Michele**, with a spired campanile called the Torre Bianca. Inside are 18th-century frescoes by the Viennese painter Josef Hautzinger. To the north of the church stands the Renaissance Casa Pfaundler (1581), a medley of Nordic and Italian elements. From here Via dei Portici Maggiori, a lovely old street full of shops, leads westward, flanked by houses of the 16th and 17th centuries, many with crenellated roofs and bay windows. The old town hall at no. 14, has a painting of the *Judgement of Solomon* in the courtyard. The Museo della Farmacia at Via Ponte Aquila 4 (*open Tues–Wed 2–6, Sat 11–4*) has displays documenting 400 years of the history of pharmacy.

AROUND BRESSANONE

In an incomparable setting at 2447m above the town is the **Rifugio Città di Bressanone/Plosehütte**, an alpine shelter that be reached by cableway, or by 23km of scenic highway in the Valle d'Eores. In the latter case you drive as far as Valcroce/Kreuztal (2050m) then continue the ascent on foot (1hr 30mins) or by chairlift. The shelter is on the southern crest of the Cima della Plose, a massif frequented for its spectacular views over the Dolomites and the Alpi Aurine as well as for its skiing.

Surrounded by meadows and vineyards 3km north on the main road to Brennero and the Val Pusteria is the **Abbazia di Novacella/Neustift**, a vast complex of monastic buildings ranging in date from the 12th–18th centuries. The church (exuberantly and colourfully Baroque) and cloister are open all day, but the library and pinacoteca are only shown on guided tours at 11 and 3 (*or by appointment, T: 0472 836189*).

The Baroque church of Novacella, frescoed by Matthäus Gündter, a disciple of Tiepolo.

Three beautiful marked trails starting near the little Chiesa dell'Angelo Custode in Bressanone make walking to the abbey easy—many of the townsfolk go this way on warm, sunny Sundays. The abbey was founded in 1141–42 and now belongs to canons of the Augustinian order. Among its older structures are the circular chapel of San Michele (12th century, fortified in the 16th century); the campanile (12th–13th centuries); the cloister, rebuilt at the end of the 14th century, with frescoes of the same period; the Romanesque chapel of San Vittore, with frescoes of the early 14th century; and the monastery church (Santa Maria Assunta), a Romanesque foundation rebuilt in the Bavarian Baroque style in the 18th century and adorned with exuberant frescoes by Matthäus Gündter of Augsburg, a disciple of Tiepolo. Also noteworthy is the library by Antonio Giuseppe Sartori (1773), with stuccoes by Hans Mussack. It preserves some 75,000 volumes and 14th- and 15th-century paintings by local artists.

THE PUEZ-ODLE NATURE RESERVE

Park offices: Bolzano, Via Cesare Battisti 21, T: 0471 994300,
www.parks.it/parco.puez.odle/index.html
The Puez-Odle Nature Reserve is situated just south of Bressanone, in the western Dolomites on the watershed between the upper Val di Funes and the Val Badia. It includes the towering peaks of the Puez mountains and Sasso Putia, as well as the dramatically beautiful Vallunga and Val di Longiarù. The easiest way to reach the park is from Bressanone, via the Val di Funes to Zanser Alm, where there are refreshments and parking. The mountains of the park are classic Dolomites, dominated by craggy pinnacles. As in all the nature reserves of the Alto-Adige, traditional farming and grazing have been allowed to continue in the low-lying areas and on the high pastures, whereas the mountain slopes in between are heavily wooded. In May and June the high pastures explode with wild flowers. Deer and chamois abound, marmots whistle among the rocks in the more remote areas, and wood grouse live on the slopes of the Putia.

The upper Val d'Isarco

North of Bressanone the upper Val d'Isarco has beautiful scenery and spectacular views of the mountains. Followed by both the railway and the *autostrada*, the valley gives access via the Brenner Pass to Austria. For many centuries this has been an important route over the Alps. Imposing fortifications defend the way. The most recent is the bleak Austrian structure of Fortezza/Franzensfeste (1833–38), which is still used by the Italian Alpine Corps (and, hence closed to the public); the earliest, Castel Tasso/Reifenstein (*open Easter–Nov Sat–Thur at 9.30, 10.30, 2 and 3*), dating from the 12th–16th centuries, with late-Gothic decorations.

Vipiteno/Sterzing takes its Italian name from a Roman post established here. The town owed its importance to the mines that were worked in the side-valleys until the 18th century. The Palazzo Comunale is an attractive building of 1468–73, and around the tall Torre di Città are 15th–16th-century mansions, many with battlements, built by the old mine-owning families. The Casa dell'Ordine Teutonico, with the Museo Civico and Museo Multscher (*closed at the time of writing, T: 0472 766464*) contains maps, prints, artisans' products, and paintings by Hans Multscher (1458). The 15th-century Palazzo Jochelsthurn houses the Museo Provinciale delle Miniere (*open Apr–Oct Tues–Sat 10–12 & 2–5*), which illustrates the history of mining in the area.

North of Vipiteno the valley narrows and its higher slopes are covered with pine forests. Colle Isarco/Gossensass (1098m) is a resort at the foot of the wooded Val di Fléres, once famous for its silver mines.

Brennero/Brenner (1375m) is the last Italian village, just south of the stone pillar (1921) that marks the Austrian frontier on the Brenner Pass (Passo di Brennero; 1375m). This is the lowest of the great Alpine passes, and the flat broad saddle of the Brenner, first mentioned with the crossing of Augustus in 13 BC, was the main route of the medieval invaders of Italy.

The lower Val Pusteria

The Val Pusteria, the valley of the Rienza, is one of the loveliest districts in the South Tyrol. In the attractive, brightly coloured villages many of the churches have onion domes and contain good local woodcarvings. The breadth of the valley allows splendid views of the mountains at the head of the side-glens on either side. In the main valley German has replaced Ladin as the language of the inhabitants, but in one side-valley (the lovely Val Badia) the old language has been preserved. The Val Pusteria has good facilities for cross-country and downhill skiing. There are numerous small family-run hotels in the valley, and bed and breakfasts scattered through the countryside.

The entrance to the valley is guarded by handsome castles. **Castello di Rodengo/Schloss Rodeneck** (868m; *open May–Oct Tues–Sun at 10, 11 and 3*), a 12th-century fortress overlooking the valley of the Rienza near the ski resort of Rio di Pusteria/Mühlbach, is a well-preserved fortress dating from 1140 (but altered in the 16th century). It contains secular frescoes of c. 1200. Casteldarne/Ehrenburg has a fine 16th-century Baroque castle (*open in summer, not Sun and holidays, for guided tours*). The convent of **Castel Badia/Sonnenburg** (in part restored as a hotel), with a

12th-century chapel, can be seen on the left on the approach to San Lorenzo di Sebato, a village on the site of the larger Roman Sebatum (partly excavated: you can see the walls). The 13th-century church here contains good carvings; a covered bridge still marks the original approach to the village from the Val Pusteria road.

The Val Badia

South of San Lorenzo a winding road, built for the Austrians by Russian prisoners at the turn of the 19th century, leads through a steep, narrow gorge to the Val Badia. This Ladin-speaking valley is one of the most secluded and spectacular in the Dolomites. The most charming of its resorts is **San Vigilio di Marebbe/Sankt Vigil im Enneberg/La Plan**, a Brigadoon-like spot at the foot of the Fanes highlands. The Museo Provinciale della Cultura e Storia dei Ladini delle Dolomiti, housed in the medieval castle of **San Martino in Badia**, is a superb ethnographic museum (*open in summer, Tues–Sat 10–6, Sun 2–6; in winter Wed–Fri 2–6. Closed Nov*) San Cassiano/Sankt Kassian also has a small museum (Paese 21; *open Tues–Sun 4–7*), with collections illustrating the valley's natural history and Ladin ethnography.

PARCO NATURALE FANES-SENNES-BRAIES

Park offices: Bolzano, Via Cesare Battisti 21, T: 0471 994300,
www.parks.it/parco.fanes.sennes.braies/index.html
Situated between the Val Pusteria to the north and the Val Badia to the west, the park extends eastwards and southwards over more than 25,000ha. The central nucleus is formed by the limestone plateaux of Fanes and Sennes, separated by the deep furrow of the Val dai Tàmersc and dominated to the north by the Dolomiti di Braies, which includes the Croda Rossa (3148m), the highest peak of the park. At the foot of the Croda del Becco lies the marvellous Lago di Braies (1493m), a vividly green mountain lake surrounded by pinewoods.

Imposing stratifications of sedimentary dolomite form the geological under-pinnings of these mountains. Over these lie deposits of Jurassic limestone, often marked by dolinas, furrows, etc., caused by water erosion of the porous stone. Here surface waters vanish rapidly into the subsoil, leaving a fairly arid envi-ronment on the plateaux, where streams flow only during summer storms and spring thaw. This fact determines a marked contrast between the high central areas with sparse plant cover and the lower regions where the waters re-emerge: these are covered by dense forests of red fir, alternating at the higher altitudes with larch and cembra pine. Further up, beyond the low growths of scrub pine, rhododendron and whortleberry, the alpine meadows, rocks and rubble are populated by a rich alpine flora. The park's fauna includes roe deer, chamois and small colonies of ibex in the area of the Croda del Becco, where they were intro-duced in the 1960s.

PARCO NATURALE DELLE VEDRETTE DI RIES

*Park offices: Bolzano, Via Cesare Battisti 21, T: 0471 994300,
www.parks.it/parco.vedrette.ries.aurina/index.html*
Established in 1989, the Parco Naturale delle Vedrette di Ries extends between
the Val Pusteria and the Valle di Anterselva to the south, the Val di Tures to the
west, the Valle Aurina to the north and the Austrian border to the east. In addition to the crystalline Riesenferner Group, the park includes the southwest
slopes of the Durreck Massif. These mountains constitute a small subgroup of
the chain of the Alti Tauri (Hohe Tauern), with a dozen peaks over 3000m and
some fine glaciers on the northern slopes.

The rocks that form much of the Riesenferner group are Palaeozoic gneiss and
schist. Glaciers have deeply moulded these mountains, transforming the heads
of the valleys into glacial cirques, carving grooves in the mountain walls, accu-
mulating moraines along their path and hollowing in the rock the niches now
occupied by numerous high-mountain lakes. Lower down, the streams have
formed spectacular gorges and cascades like the Cascate di Riva, near Campo
Tures. At the head of the Valle di Anterselva is the Lago di Anterselva, formed by
the alluvial cones that descend the southern slope of the Collalto and the
Rotwand. At the entrance to the same valley, but outside the borders of the park,
is the Rasun wetland, frequented by migratory birds.

Brunico and the Alpi Aurine

Brunico/Bruneck is the picturesque capital of the Val Pusteria. It stands in a small
upland plain overlooked by the castle of Bruno, named after its founder, a 13th-cen-
tury bishop of Bressanone. Brunico is the native town of Michael Pacher (c. 1430–98),
whose sculpted wooden crucifixes can be found in the churches of the region. The
main Via di Città is lined with pretty alpine houses with bay windows and fanciful
gables; many of the shops have old (or old-fashioned) wrought-iron signs. The castle
was built in the 13th–14th centuries and altered in the 15th–16th. In the suburb of
Teodone (Dietenheim), on the Mair am Hof farm, is an interesting museum of local
agriculture and folk customs, the Museo Etnografico (*open Apr–Oct Tues–Sat
9.30–5.30, Sun and holidays 2–6; July–Aug Tues–Sat 9.30–6.30, Sun 2–7*).

North of Brunico the Val di Tures provides access to a group of thickly wooded
mountain glens lying beneath the peaks and glaciers of the Alpi Aurine on the
Austrian frontier. **Campo Tures/Sand in Taufers** is the main centre. It is dominated
by the 13th–15th-century castle (*shown on guided tours*) of the barons of Tures. In the
Valle Aurina is the **Vetta d'Italia** (2912m), the northernmost point in Italy. The Picco
dei Tre Signori (3498m) further east, marked the junction of the counties of Tyrol,
Salzburg and Gorizia.

The Val Badia and the Fanes Highlands, viewed from the Val di Funes.

The upper Val Pusteria

The Val Pusteria opens out at Rasun and the three interlocking villages of **Valdaora** (Valdaora di Sotto, di Mezzo and di Sopra), each with a church. In the lovely Val Casies are the picturesque 12th-century castle of Monguelfo, and Tesido, a pretty village on the lower, sunny slopes of the hillside with two delightful churches, one Baroque, with a pink exterior, and the other—older—with a large external fresco of *St Christopher*. **Dobbiaco/Toblach** (1256m) has a large church and a castle built in 1500 for the Emperor Maximilian I. Gustav Mahler stayed here in 1908–10. **San Candido/Innichen** (1175m) is a lovely little summer and winter resort, with a Baroque parish church. The 13th-century **Collegiata**, the most important Romanesque monument in the Alto-Adige, with interesting sculptural details, is dedicated to St Candidus and St Corbinian, who are depicted in the fresco by Michael Pacher above the south door. The 15th-century atrium protects the main portal with Romanesque carvings. In the interior is a splendid *Crucifixion* group above the high altar (c. 1200). The remarkable frescoes in the cupola date from about 1280. The crypt has handsome columns, and there is a small museum open in summer.

East of San Candido the Dolimiti di Sesto take their name from the village of **Sesto/Sexten**, a small summer and winter resort with a Baroque parish church (San Vito), frescoed houses, and a small museum with works by local painter Rudolf Stolz (1874–1960).

PARCO NATURALE DELLE DOLOMITI DI SESTO

Park offices: Bolzano, Via Cesare Battisti 21, T: 0471 994300,
www.parks.it/parco.dolomiti.sesto
Seen from the Val Pusteria, the landscape of this park is indescribably dramatic. In the foreground are the subgroups of the Baranci and the Tre Scarperi, among which open two parallel valleys (Val di Dentro and Val Fiscalina) closed at their upper ends by the spectacular vertical walls of the Tre Cime di Lavaredo (2999m), Paterno (2744m), and Cima Dodici (3094m).

The oldest rocks of this last northeastern bastion of the Dolomites are conglomerates of porphyry and sandstone, buried beneath layers of black limestone, dolomite and gray marl. During the Ice Age the region was almost completely buried beneath a gigantic glacier, which has left clear signs of its presence—particularly in the Valle del Rio Alto Fiscalina, where you can see moraines and streaked and round-backed rocks formed by the retreating ice. Today the glaciers have practically disappeared. Interesting semi-natural environments are the *prati a larice* (larch meadows) of the Val Fiscalina and Val Campo di Dentro. Fauna includes the alpine bat (*Hypsugo savii*), which is found in the forests and even above the treeline.

PRACTICAL INFORMATION

GETTING AROUND

A series of beautiful but tiring mountain roads link Trieste, Venice, Padua and Vicenza with Trento and Bressanone. Frequent bus services (operated by SAD, T: 0471 450111 or freephone 800 846047, www.sii.bz.it) connect Bressanone to towns and resorts throughout the northern Dolomites, as well as to Bolzano and Innsbruck.
• **By rail:** Bressanone is on the main rail line to Verona, Florence, Rome and Naples. A secondary rail-and-bus line runs to Padua, Cortina d'Ampezzo via Castelfranco, Feltre and Belluno, with connections for the Val Pusteria, Bressanone and Bolzano.

INFORMATION OFFICES

There is a central information office for all the resorts in the province (*see p. 296*).
Bressanone/Brixen Via Stazione 9, T: 0472 836401, www.brixen.org
Brunico/Bruneck Via Europa 24, T: 0474 555722, www.bruneck.com
Val Badia Badia, Picenin 10, T: 0471 847037, www.altabadia.org
Val d'Isarco Vipiteno/Sterzing, Piazza Città 3, T: 0472 765325, www.infosterzing.it
Val Pusteria Sesto/Sexten, Via Dolomiti 9, T: 0474 710310, www.sexten.it

HOTELS

Bressanone/Brixen This is the best place to stay if you wish to explore the peaks and valleys of the northern Dolomites without changing hotels.
€€€ **Elefante**. A 16th-century building with antique furniture, a large garden, and the city's most renowned restaurant. Closed Nov–Christmas and Jan–March. Via Rio Bianco 4, T: 0472 832750, hotelelephant@conmail.it
€€ **Dominik**. An extremely refined, comfortable place in a quiet, secluded position amid trees and lawns yet within walking distance of the cathedral; it has an excellent breakfast buffet, with table service under an arbour in warm weather. Cosed Jan–Mar. Via Terzo di Sotto 13, T: 0472 830144, www.hoteldominik.com
€€ **Goldener Adler**. Beautiful rooms and warm, cosy public spaces in an expertly restored historic building in the town centre. Via Ponte Aquila 9, T: 0472 200621, www.goldener-adler.com
€€ **Grüner Baum**. Offers a cordial, homely atmosphere in an elegant old house on the left bank of the Isarco. Closed late Nov–early Dec. Via Stufles 11, T: 0472 832732, www.gruenerbaum.it
€ **Gasser**. Situated in the oldest part of town, near the Parco Rapp; guests use the pool and other facilities of the Grüner Baum (*listed above*), which is under the same management. Closed late Nov–early Dec. Via Giardini 19, T: 0472 832732.
Braies
Croda Rossa/Hohe Gaisl. A fabulous old lodge stunningly set at 2000m, overlooking the Croda Rossa peak. Closed Apr–May and Oct–Nov. Località Prato Piazza/Plätzwiese, T: 0474 748606, www.hohegaisl.com

Brunico/Bruneck

€€ **Royal Hotel Hinterhuber**. On the Riscone highland, 3km southeast of the city, a fine old Tyrolean farm complex renovated to the highest modern standards, in truly splendid surroundings. Closed Easter–May and Oct–Dec. T: 0474 541000, www.charmerelax.it

Cleran/Klerant

€ **Fischer**. In a magnificent position overlooking Bressanone and the Valle d'Isarco. Closed Nov. T: 0472 852075, F: 0472 852060, www.hotel-fischer.it

Dobbiaco/Toblach

€ **Alpino Monte Rota-Alpen Ratsberg**. Fresh air, magnificent surroundings, and a view you won't easily forget more than compensate for the trouble of getting to this secluded establishment. Closed Apr–May and Nov–Dec. At Monte Rota/Radsberg (1650m; chair lift), 5km northwest of the village, T: 0474 972213, www.alpenhotel-ratsberg.com

La Villa

€ **La Villa**. Simple and refined, in a splendid position enjoying some of the most dramatic views in the Dolomites. Closed May and Oct–Nov. Strada Bosc da Plan 176, T: 0471 847035, www.hotel-lavilla.it

Rasun Anterselva/Rasen Antholz

€€ **Ansitz Heufler**. A renovated 16th-century castle with fairytale rooms and an outstanding restaurant. Closed Apr and Nov. T: 0474 498582, www.heufler.com

San Candido/Innichen

€€ **Park Hotel Sole Paradiso/ Sonnenparadies**. Offers warm atmosphere, good location, and a great restaurant. Closed Apr–May and Oct–Nov. T: 0474 913120, www.sole-paradiso.com

San Cassiano

€€€ **Rosa Alpina**. Very comfortable indeed, with spa facilities and an excellent restaurant. Closed May and Nov. Via Centro 31, T: 0471 841111, F: 0471 849377, www.rosalpina.it.

San Vigilio di Marebbe

€€€ **Excelsior**. Elegant and refined, in an elevated position just outside the village. Closed Apr–May and Oct–Dec. Via Vallares 44, T: 0474 501036, www.excelsior-call.com

€€ **Monte Sella**. A delightful Jugendstil villa built for an Austrian aristocrat at the turn of the 20th century and tastefully renovated; within walking distance of the ski-lifts and recently provided with a beautiful top-floor health centre. Closed Apr–May and Oct–Dec. Strada Catarina Lanz 7, T: 0474 501034, www.monte-sella.com

€ **Ücia de Fanes**. A back-country lodge on the Fanes highlands, popular with hikers and skiers; access by foot, jeep or snowcat only. Alpe di Fanes, T/F: 0474 501097, www.rifugiofanes.com

Sesto/Sexten

€€ **Dolomiti-Dolomitenhof**. A starting point for most excursions in the Val Fiscalino and Tre Cime areas of the park as well as a marvellous place to stay. Closed May and Nov. Via Val Fiscalina 33, Località Campo Fiscalino/Fischleinboden, T: 0474 713000, www.dolomitenhof.com

€€€ **Sport e Kurhotel Bad Moos**. A modern establishment incorporating 15th- and 16th-century *stuben*, in a fine location. Closed Nov–Dec and Easter–May. Via Val Fiscalina 27, Località Moso/Moos, T: 0474 713100, badmoos@sudtirol.com

Valle di Casies/Gsies

€€€ **Quelle**. Quiet luxury, with richly appointed rooms, indoor and outdoor pools and wellness centre, in one of the more verdant valleys of the Italian Alps. Closed Apr–May and Oct–Nov. Località Santa Maddalena (1398m), T: 0474 948111, www.hotel-quelle.com

Vipiteno/Sterzing

€€ **Aquila Nera/Schwarzer Adler**. The traditional place to stay (and to eat) in Vipiteno, dating back to the 16th century. Closed June–July and Nov–Dec. Piazza Città 1, T: 0472 764064, schwarzeradler@rolmail.net

€ **Kranebitt**. Friendly if secluded, 16km up a verdant valley from Vipiteno. Closed Nov–Dec and Apr–May. Kematen/Pfitsch–Caminata/Val di Vizze, T: 0472 646019, www.kranebitt.com

RESTAURANTS

Bressanone/Brixen

€€ **Fink**. A simple place established in 1896, serving local specialities, especially meats and cheeses (Zieger, Graukäse, Lista). Closed Tues evening except July–Oct, Wed and two weeks in July. Via Portici Minori 4, T: 0472 834883.

€€ **Oste Scuro/Finsterwirt**. A characteristic Tyrolean restaurant (with rooms on separate premises) established in 1879, with a lovely garden for the warm months, an innovative twist on traditional recipes, and a good selection of regional and Italian wines; closed Sun evening, Mon, and a few days in Jan and June. Vicolo del Duomo 3, T: 0472 835343.

€€ **Sunnegg**. Quintessential Tyrol—fine regional food and wines, warm atmosphere and an incomparable setting among vineyards and apple groves overlooking the Val d'Isarco. Closed Wed, midday Thur, Jan–Feb and June–July. Via Vigneti 67, T: 0472 834760.

€€ **Traubenwirt**. Good international cuisine and excellent wines, coupled with pleasant ambience; a tad pricey. Via Portici Minori, T: 0472 834731.

€ **Kutscherhof**. A traditional restaurant serving regional cuisine and the excellent beer of Kloster Andechs (Bavaria) in the former carriage-house of the bishop's palace, with a garden seating in summer. Hofgasse 6, T: 0472 802674.

€ **Grissino**. The restaurant of Bressanone's fabulous spa centre, Acquarena, Grissino serves everything from pizza to Thai food, and it's all delicious. Via Mercato Vecchio 28b, T: 0472 823670.

€ **Vinus—Peter's Weinbistro**. Outstanding wines and great light meals in a warm, refined setting in the heart of town. Altenmarktgasse 6, T: 0472 831583.

Brunico

€€ **Agnello Bianco/Weisses Lamm**. Good regional food and wines on the first floor of a historic building. Closed Sun and June. Via Stuck 5, T: 0474 411350.

€€ **Oberraut**. A *maso* or mountain farm (with rooms) above Brunico. Outstanding local fare, good wines, friendly people, fabulous views. Località Ameto/Amaten 1, T: 0474 559977.

Falzes/Pfalzen

€€€ **Schöneck**. Probably the best restaurant in the valley: delicious, straightforward dishes, excellent wines

and summer seating outside. Closed
Mon, midday Tues and Oct. Via Castello
Schöneck, Località Molini/Mühlen, T:
0474 565550

La Villa
€€ **Ciastel Colz** (with rooms). A fabulous 16th-century castle offering exquisite cuisine from the Ladin tradition and
a good selection of wines. Via Marin 80,
T: 0471 847511.

Moso/Moos
€€ **Reidere**. A fine old restaurant with
a beautiful little *stube* and traditional
menu. Closed Tues, Jan and June. Via
San Giuseppe 27, T: 0474 710304.

Rio di Pusteria/Mühlbach
€€ **Pichler**. Known for its creative
interpretations of traditional Tyrolean
specialities, as well as for its ambience
and wines. Closed Mon, midday Tues
and July. T: 0472 849458.

€€ **Strasshoff**. An 11th-century castle
entirely dedicated to the preservation of
local culinary traditions. Closed Wed,
midday Thur and Jan–Feb. Località
Spinga/Spinges 2, T: 0472 849798.

Rodengo/Rodeneck
€ **Rastnerhütte** (with rooms). A fabulous find for hikers and backcountry
skiers: great food and ambience on the
rolling Alpe di Rodengo/Rodenicker Alm
(1930m), with breathtaking views over
the Dolomites and the Central Alps. T:
0472 546422.

San Candido/Innichen
€ **Kupferdachl**. Friendly ambience and
excellent regional cuisine that appeals to
locals as well as to travellers. Closed
Thur, June and Nov. T: 0474 913711.

€ **Uhrmacher's Weinstube**. Wine bar
serving excellent regional wines and
cheeses. Closed Wed (except in summer)
and June. Via Tintori 1, T: 0474 913158.

San Cassiano/St Kassian
€€€ **St Hubertus**. Small and refined,
traditionally considered the best in the
valley. Closed Tues, midday Wed, May
and Oct, Nov. Hotel Rosa Alpina, St
Micura de Rue 20, T: 0471 849500.

San Vigilio di Marebbe
€€ **Ciasa Sorega** (with rooms). A
beautifully restored house with original
16th-century interiors. Specialises in
grilled meats and other regional delicacies. Via Plazores 22, T: 0474 501397.

Valle di Casies/Gsies
€ **Durnwald**. Offers a perfect combination of local delicacies and regional
wines. Closed Mon and June. Località
Planca di Sotto/Unterplanken, T: 0474
746920.

Vipiteno/Sterzing
€€ **Pretzhof**. Fine local food and ambience; closed Mon–Tues, Dec, Jan and
June–July. Località Tulve/Tulfer, T: 0472
764455.

REGIONAL SPECIALITIES

Brunico Speck and other delicacies at
Gastronomia Bernardi; wines at
Enoteca Schöndorf; home-made jams
at **Willy Horvat**, all in Via Centrale.
Vipiteno The **Caffè Konditorei
Prenn**, at Altstadt 17, is a café serving
truly memorable cakes and pastries.
San Candido For great Graukäse,
Bergkäse, Zieger and other Val Pusteria
cheeses, try the **Latteria Sociale di San
Candido**, at Via Castello 1.

FESTIVALS & EVENTS

Bressanone *Mercatino di Natale*, market of Christmas ornaments and sweets,
Nov–Jan. *Grande Festa di San Silvestro,*

Boxing Day folk festival, Dec.
Val d'Isarco *Corteo di San Nicolò* and
Corteo di Natale, folk processions,
Vipiteno, Dec. *Settimana della Buona
Cucina*, regional cuisine week, Alta Val
d'Isarco, March.
Val Badia Horse-drawn sleigh races,
La Villa, Jan–Feb. Hay-sledge races,
Colfosco, Jan–Mar; New Year's Eve cele-
bration with fireworks, candlelight pro-
cession and concert, Corvara, Jan.
*Festival Internazionale delle Sculture di
Neve*, international snow-sculpture
competition, San Vigilio di Marebbe,
San Candido and Sesto, Jan. *Simposio
Internazionale di Sculture in Legno*,
woodcarving competition, San Vigilio di
Marebbe, Sept.
Brunico/Bruneck *Mercatino Pasquale
Brunicense* (folk fair with local farm and
craft products, food and drink), Easter.
Aria di Jazz, jazz festival, Brunico, July.
Concerti Estivi Brunicensi, chamber
music concerts, July–Aug. *Mercatino
Natalizio Brunicense* (Christmas folk fair)
Nov–Dec.
Val Pusteria *Festival Nazionale di
Canto Corale*, chorus festival, Alta

Pusteria (Sesto, San Candido, Dobbiaco,
Villabassa, Braies), July. *Settimana
Musicale Gustav Mahler*, classical music
festival, Dobbiaco, July. *Degustazione
Estiva dei Vini*, summer tasting of Alto-
Adige wines, Valdaora, Aug. *Alpitrail*,
dog-sledge races, Sesto, Jan. *Festival
Internazionale delle Sculture di Neve*,
international snow-sculpture competition, San Candido, Sesto and San
Vigilio di Marebbe, Jan. *Gran Premio
Valle d'Anterselva*, Italian championship
dog-sledge races, Feb. *Locknfest—Festa
delle Pozze* party on the last day of the
downhill skiing season; participants
negotiate a steep run in or on beds,
bathtubs, wheelless cars, frying pans,
etc., then dive into a frozen pond while
spectators look on; prizes for most original vehicle and bathing costume; live
music and roasted *würstel*; Plan de
Corones (Valdaora), April.

September is the month for harvest
feasts, as well as the month in which
the cows are brought down from the
high pastures, amidst great celebration
and pageantry in many villages. Exact
dates depend on the weather.

THE VENETO

The Veneto has a rich and varied history. Though its name derives from Venice, its character is more than simply Venetian, including as it does the provinces of Belluno, Padua, Rovigo, Treviso, Venice, Verona and Vicenza.

In the 12th century Verona, Padua, Vicenza and Treviso formed the Veronese League in imitation of the Lombard League, as a means of containing the power of the Holy Roman Emperor. In the following century important families—such as the Scaligeri in Verona and Vicenza, and the Carraresi in Padua and Vicenza—held courts that developed a reputation throughout Europe for their generous support of the arts. When the maritime expansion of Venice in the east was checked by the rising power of the Turkish Empire and the Venetians turned their interests to the *terraferma*, Treviso, Padua and numerous other cities willingly joined the Most Serene Republic. By 1420 the whole territory, from Verona to Udine and from Belluno to Padua, was under the banner of a larger and more compact Republic of Venice. Further extensions of the doges' dominion, to Bergamo in the west, Rimini in the south, and Fiume in the east (now Rijeka, Croatia), provoked the jealousy of the powers beyond the Alps, and the League of Cambrai (1508) put an end to Venice's imperial ambitions. But the Venetian dominions in Italy remained united for 300 years.

The Napoleonic invasion of Italy saw the dismemberment of the Veneto; after the Treaty of Campo Formio in 1797, Venice itself and the area east of the Adige was ceded to Austria in return for parts of the Low Countries. Austria also took control of areas in the west in 1814. Many of those areas were lost by Austria in bloody battles against the united armies of Napoleon III and Cavour (*see p. 19*). In 1859, however, alarmed by the strength of nationalist feeling in Italy, Napoleon III concluded an armistice with Austria, and it was not until Austria was defeated by Prussia in 1866 that the Veneto was able—by plebiscite—to join the Piedmontese kingdom.

Since the Second World War the Veneto has become the centre of what Italians call the 'Miracle of the Northeast'. This is the wealthiest region of the country and its fastest-growing industrial district. But it is also the area where economic development has most successfully adapted itself to ideas of conservation. Thanks to a prevalence of small, flexible and clean industries, affluence has made a 'soft landing' in the area, whose stunning natural and artistic assets remain relatively unspoilt. As a result, the Veneto has become one of Europe's more successful 'post-industrial' experiments—a fascinating place to visit, but also a wonderful place to live.

LAGO DI GARDA

Lago di Garda is the largest and perhaps the most beautiful of the northern Italian lakes. Its mild climate permits the cultivation of olives and lemon trees, and the vegetation of its shores is characterised by numerous cypresses in thick woods. Most of its resorts were developed in the 1920s and 1930s, although some grand hotels had

Fishing on Lago di Garda.

already been built at the end of the 19th century for Austrian and German visitors who came to the mild western shore, many of them to cure respiratory disorders. Sirmione, in a spectacular position on a narrow peninsula on the south shore, was known in Roman times as a resort on Lacus Benacus (from a Celtic word meaning 'horned').

Its inspiring beauty has made it traditionally popular with writers. Goethe visited the lake at the start of his Italian journey in 1786 and saw his first olive trees here. Byron stayed at Desenzano in 1816, and Tennyson visited the lake in 1880. D.H. Lawrence lived on its shores in 1912 and 1913, and he describes the lemon gardens in *Twilight in Italy*. Winston Churchill wintered at the Grand Hotel in Gardone Riviera in 1949.

Citrus cultivation around the lake dates from at least the 16th century and reached a height in commercial production in the early 19th century. It was the northernmost locality in the world where citrus fruits could be grown commercially. A few of the characteristic monumental pavilions, with tall stone pilasters covered with wooden slats and glass in winter, where lemons and citrons were cultivated in the 19th century, still survive at Gargnano and Torri del Benaco. These shelters, unique to Garda, were designed for maximum protection from the cold. Duck and swans flourish on the lake, and fishing is still practised in a few localities (the *salmo carpio*, a kind of large trout, is found only in Garda; other fish include pike, trout and eel).

The best time to visit Lago di Garda is May to June: in August it is very crowded and can be extremely hot. The breezier upper part of the lake, where the water is deepest, is much used for sailing and windsurfing (boats can be hired), and there are regattas in summer. The predominant winds (which can swell into violent storms) are the *sover*, from the north, in the morning, and the *ora*, from the south, in the after-noon. The waters are considered the cleanest of the big Italian lakes, and swimming is permitted (the best places include the peninsula of Sirmione, the Isola dei Conigli off Moniga, the Baia del Vento between Salò and Desenzano, and the Isola San Biagio).

Sirmione

Sirmione stands at the tip of a narrow promontory 3.5km long and in places only 119m wide, in the centre of the southern shore of the lake. It was a Roman station on the Via Gallica, halfway between Brescia and Verona. Now it is a famous resort with numerous hotels and is usually crowded with tourists in the season (though deserted in winter). There are many enjoyable walks on the peninsula, and you can swim in the lake on the east side.

The picturesque 13th-century **Rocca Scaligera** (*open Tues–Sun 9–dusk, and Mon 9–12 in July–Aug*), where Dante is said to have stayed, marks the entrance to the town. Completely surrounded by water, it was a stronghold of the Scaligeri family, lords of Verona. The massive central tower, 29m high, has a good view.

Via Vittorio Emanuele (closed to cars) leads north from the castle through the sce-nic little town towards the Grotte di Catullo at the end of the peninsula. A road on the right leads to the 15th-century church of Santa Maria Maggiore, which preserves some antique columns. At the end of Via Vittorio Emanuele is a spa with a hotel that uses warm sulphur springs rising in the lake. Via Catullo continues, passing close to San Pietro in Mavino, a Romanesque church of 8th-century foundation with early frescoes. At the end of the road is the entrance to the so-called **Grotte di Catullo** (*open Tues–Sun 9–dusk*), really the romantic ruins of a large Roman villa. This is the most important example of Roman imperial domestic architecture in northern Italy. It is set amid olive groves on the end of the headland, with splendid views out over the lake and of the rocks beneath the clear shallow water. The most beautiful spot on the lake, the site is very well maintained and planted with trees. The vast ruins belong to a country house of the 1st century BC (abandoned by the 4th century) that may have belonged to the family of Valerii Catulli. Many wealthy Romans came to Sirmione for the summer, and Catullus—who is known to have had a villa here—speaks of '*Paene peninsularum, Sirmio, insularumque ocelle*' ('Sirmione, gem of all peninsulas and islands'). Though the ruins have been known for many centuries, excavations took place here only in the 19th century and the beginning of the 20th century. Near the entrance is a small antiquarium, with exquisite fragments of frescoes dating from the 1st century BC.

The most conspicuous remains are the vast substructures and vaults built to sus-tain the main buildings of the villa, which occupied an area over 150m long and 100m wide on the top of the hill: virtually nothing is left of the villa itself, as it was

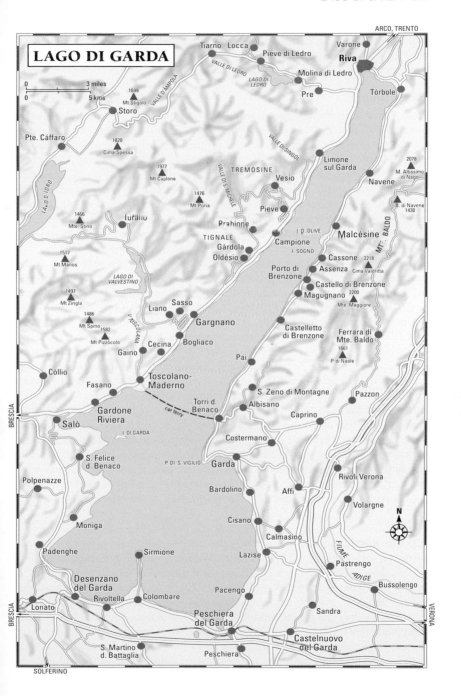

LAGO DI GARDA

ARCO, TRENTO

0 ___ 3 miles
0 ___ 5 kms

Tiarno Locca
Pieve di Ledro
Varone
Riva

VALLE DI LEDRO

LAGO DI LEDRO
Molina di Ledro

VALLE D'AMPOLA

1699 Mt Stigolo
Storo

Pre
Tòrbole

Pte. Càffaro

1820 Cima Spessa

VALLE DI SINGÒL

Limone sul Garda
2078 M. Altissimo di Nago

1977 Mt Caplone

TREMÒSINE
Vesio

Navene

VALLE DI S. MICHELE

1476 Mt Pùria
Pieve

B. di Navene 1430

1466 Mte. Stino

Turàno

Prahinne

I. D. OLIVE

MT. BALDO

Malcésine

1517 Mt Manos

TIGNALE
Gàrdola
Oldésio

Campione
I. SOGNO

Cassone 2218 Cima Valdritta

LAGO DI VALVESTINO

Porto di Brenzone
Assenza

1497 Mt Zingla

LA D'IDRO

Liano Sasso

Castello di Brenzone
Magugnano 2200 Mte. Maggiore

1486 Mt Spino 1582 Mt Pizzòcolo

V. TOSCOLANA

Gargnano

Castelletto di Brenzone
Ferrara di Mte. Baldo

Gaino Cecina Bogliaco

Pai

1661 P. di Naole

Còllio
Fasano

Toscolano-Maderno

S. Zeno di Montagne
Pazzon

Gardone Riviera
Salò

car ferry
Torri d. Benaco
Albisano

Caprino

I. DI GARDA

Costermano

S. Felice d. Benaco

P. DI S. VIGILIO
Garda

Polpenazze

Bardolino
Affi

Rivoli Verona

Moniga

Cisano

Volargne

Padenghe

Sirmione

Calmasino
Lazise

N

FIUME

Pastrengo

ADIGE

Bussolengo

Desenzano del Garda
Rivoltella Colombare

Pacengo

Lonato

Sandra

BRESCIA

VERONA

Peschiera del Garda

Castelnuovo del Garda

S. Martino d. Battaglia
Peschiera

SOLFERINO

plundered for building material over the centuries, and its site is now covered by an olive grove. You can see a number of huge cisterns, as well as thermal buildings and a long colonnaded terrace with a covered walkway below.

Desenzano

From Rivoltella, halfway between Sirmione and Desenzano, a by-road leads away from the lake up to the tower (74m high) of San Martino della Battaglia, which commemorates Vittorio Emanuele II's victory over the right flank of the Austrian army on 24 June 1859. The interior contains sculptures and paintings relating to the campaign. At **Solferino** (in the province of Mantua, *see p. 270*), Napoleon III, in alliance with Vittorio Emanuele, defeated the rest of the Austrian army on the same day. The low moraine hills south of the lake, formed by the ancient glacier of the Adige, have been the theatre of many battles: during Prince Eugene's campaign in the War of the Spanish Succession (1701–06), during Napoleon's enterprises (1796–1814), and during the Wars of Italian Independence (1848–49, 1859 and 1866).

Desenzano del Garda is a pleasant little resort, well equipped with hotels. From the quay a bridge crosses a tiny picturesque inlet used as a harbour for small boats. Behind is the main piazza, with pretty arcades and a monument to St Angela Merici (1474–1540), foundress of the Ursuline order, who was born here. Just out of the piazza is the parish church with a *Last Supper* by Giovanni Battista Tiepolo.

Nearby is the entrance to the excavations of a **Roman villa** (*open Tues–Sun 8.30–dusk*), mostly dating from the 4th century AD but on the site of an earlier edifice of the 1st century AD. The various building stages are still unclear. It is the most important late Roman villa in northern Italy, of great interest for its colourful 4th-century mosaics. The grandiose design of the reception rooms of the main villa includes an octagonal hall, a peristyle, an atrium with two apses, and a triclinium with three apses, all with mosaics. Other, less grand rooms to the south may have been baths. An antiquarium (beneath which the Roman edifice of the 1st century AD, with an underfloor heating system, was discovered) has finds from the site, including remains of wall paintings. Separate excavations to the north have revealed a residential area, with part of an apsidal hall and baths, to the east. The villa was discovered in 1921, and excavations have continued even though the site is in the centre of the town.

Salò

Salò, the Roman Salodium, is perhaps the most appealing town on the western lakeshore, with a slightly old-fashioned atmosphere. It has two gates, one surmounted by a lion, the other by a clock. It was the birthplace of Gaspare Bertolotti (also known as Gaspare da Salò, 1540–1609), generally considered to be the first maker of violins, and also gave its name to Mussolini's short-lived puppet republic (the Repubblica Sociale Italiana, or Repubblica di Salò). Mussolini returned here, in a last attempt to re-establish the Fascist government of Italy, a few months after his release from prison and his escape to Germany in 1943. Salò was an ideal place for the re-establishment of Fascist authority, as the borders of the German Reich had reached

Limone, only 20km north, with the annexation of the Trentino-Alto Adige, and the many huge hotels and villas by the lake were easily adapted as ministries. The Republic of Salò ended with the Liberation in 1945 and Mussolini's execution a few days later.

Near the waterfront is the cathedral, a fine building in a late-Gothic style built at the end of the 15th century, with a good Renaissance portal (1509). It contains paintings by Zenon Veronese and Romanino, and a carved 15th-century tabernacle. Palazzo Fantoni is the seat of the Biblioteca Ateneo, which has its origins in the Accademia degli Unanimi founded by Giovanni Maione in 1560. The library has over 25,000 volumes, many of great historical interest. There is also a small museum relating to the Republic of Salò. Villa Laurin (now a hotel), built in 1905, has a fresco by Angelo Landi (1907–96).

Gardone Riviera and Toscolano

Gardone Riviera was once famous as a winter resort. It has a sheltered position and its parks and gardens are planted with rare trees. On the left of the highway here is the **Vittoriale degli Italiani** (*open summer Tues–Sun 9–8; winter 9–12.30 & 2 or 2.30–6 or 6.30*), the famous residence of Gabriele d'Annunzio (*see overleaf*), designed for him in the last years of his life by Gian Carlo Maroni. It takes its name from the Italian victory over Austria in 1918, and is a remarkable monument to the eccentric martial poet, who had a great influence on Italian poetry of the last century.

From the gate a path leads up past the amphitheatre (used for theatre and music performances in summer), built by Maroni, to the villa itself (*shown in a 30-minute tour to a maximum of 6–10 people by appointment at the ticket office*). It has been preserved, with its elaborate and gloomy décor, as a museum. Off the dark hallway is a reception room with an inscription that d'Annunzio made Mussolini read on his visit here: 'Remember that you are made of glass and I of steel'. Other rooms are crammed with a jumble of items: Art Nouveau objets d'art, chinoiserie, mementoes, sacred objects, Indian works of art, and even an organ. The Art Deco dining room was also designed by Maroni.

The private garden in front of the villa harbours odd statuary and columns surmounted by projectiles. A path leads down through the pretty woods of the Acquapazza Valley towards the main road. Behind the villa, Viale di Aligi leads past a building that houses d'Annunzio's motorboat to his grand mausoleum at the top of the hill, where he and his architect are buried. Another path leads through woods to the prow of the ship *Puglia*, reconstructed here as a monument. D'Annunzio's private plane is also exhibited.

Downhill, on the other side of the road, are the small privately owned botanical gardens (*open March–Oct 9–6*), laid out by Arturo Hruska in 1940–71, with narrow paths through luxuriant vegetation. Nearer the lake is the conspicuous Neoclassical Villa Alba, now a conference centre with a fine large public park. Claretta Petacci, Mussolini's mistress, lived in Villa Fiordaliso (now a restaurant) during the Republic of Salò.

Gabriele d'Annunzio (1863–1938)
Gabriele d'Annunzio was born Francesco Rapagnetta, the son of a well-to-do
and politically prominent landowner. He married the daughter of a duke but
was not a model husband—among his mistresses was Eleonora Duse, for whom
he wrote a number of plays (no longer performed today). He also wrote a play
set to music by the French composer Claude Debussy; Marcel Proust was at the
opening night and said the best thing about it were the lead actress's legs.

D'Annunzio began his career as a poet: his first verses, *In Early Spring*, were
published when the author was just 16; they were closely followed by *New Song*
(1882), which established his fame. His best-known poetic work is the anthol-
ogy *In Praise of Sky, Sea, Earth and Heroes* (1899). His novels raised eyebrows
because of their self-seeking, amoral Nietzschean-superman heroes, but stylisti-
cally they were dull and academic.

Outside Italy d'Annunzio is much better known for his military exploits. In
1914-16 he called for Italy to enter the First World War on the side of Britain
and France, rather than honour the Triple Alliance, the secret agreement
between Germany, Austria-Hungary and Italy formed in 1882. He volunteered
for dangerous duty in several branches of service, notably the air corps, and lost
an eye in action. When Italy lost Istria at the Treaty of Versailles, he and a few
hundred supporters occupied the port city of Fiume and held it for 18 months,
until forced to withdraw by the Italian navy. He made peace with Mussolini, but
never held an important government position (his legions were the first to wear
the black shirt that became emblematic of the Fascists). He spent his last years
writing here on Lake Garda. He died in 1938 and was given a state funeral.

Toscolano-Maderno is another resort, with a little port. In Maderno the 12th-centu-
ry church of Sant'Andrea on the waterfront shows remains of Roman and Byzantine
architecture, especially in the decoration of the pillar capitals, doors and windows: an
older church seems to have been incorporated in the building. Across the Toscolano
River, in Toscolano, is the church of Santi Pietro e Paolo (unlocked on request at the
house on the right). It has paintings by Celesti and early-20th-century stained glass.
The Santuario della Madonna di Benaco, behind it on the lake, has a barrel vault and
numerous 15th-century frescoes. Four Roman columns stand in front of the church.
Nearby, opposite a large paper mill, is an enclosure with scant remains (under a roof)
of a Roman villa of the 1st–2nd century AD with mosaics. Toscolano, called Benacum,
was the chief Roman settlement on the west shore of the lake.

The northwest shore
Beyond Toscolano the landscape becomes prettier, with green hills and few buildings.
At Bogliaco, on the right of the road, is the huge 18th-century **Villa Bettoni** (*not
open*); its lovely garden is on the left of the road. This was the seat of the Prime

Minister of Mussolini's Republic of Salò.

Gargnano is a very attractive little port. Several large stone pavilions where lemon trees were once cultivated seem to march up the hillside in terraces. San Francesco is a 13th-century church with a cloister. An inland road from Gargnano to Limone has spectacular views: it passes the hill sanctuary of Madonna di Monte Castello, which has the finest view of the whole lake. Mussolini lived here, at Villa Feltrinelli, from 1943 until three days before his death.

Limone sul Garda takes its name from its lemon groves, said to be the first in Europe. Up until the beginning of the 20th century it was surrounded by terraced lemon and citron gardens, but now only two pavilions survive; one of them, in Via Orti, was bought by the town council in 1995 in order to preserve it. Limone was accessible only by boat before the road along the shore from Gargnano was built in 1931, and its unattractive buildings and numerous hotels date from its development as a resort in the 1950s and 1960s. In previous centuries it was a very romantic spot indeed, possibly the inspiration for one of Goethe's best-known lyrics: *Kennst du das Land, wo die Zitronen blühn* ('Do you know the land where the lemon trees blossom; where golden oranges gleam amidst dark foliage...?') Goethe had sailed down from Torbole past Limone, where he admired the lemon gardens. Unfavourable winds forced him to land for a night at Malcesine, and it was while sketching the castle there that he was almost arrested as an Austrian spy. The next day he docked at Bardolino, where he mounted a mule to cross into the Adige Valley for Verona.

Riva del Garda and the north end of the lake

Riva del Garda, the Roman Ripa, is an agreeable, lively little town and the most important place on the lake. Sheltered by Monte Rochetta to the west, it became a fashionable winter resort at the turn of the 20th century and remained in Austrian territory until 1918. The centre of the old town is Piazza III Novembre overlooking the little port. Here are the 13th-century Torre Apponale, the 14th-century Palazzo Pretorio, the 15th-century Palazzo Comunale and some medieval porticoes. The Rocca, a 14th-century castle encircled by water, has been heavily restored over the centuries. The Museo Civico here (*open Sept–June Tues-Sun 9.30–12.30 & 2.30–5.30; July–Aug daily 9–6*) has an archaeological section including finds from the lake dwellings of the Lago di Ledro; there is also a collection of armour, and locally printed works, including a Talmud of 1558. On the road to Arco is the church of the Inviolata, begun in 1603 by an unknown Portuguese architect. It has a graceful Baroque interior.

At the mouth of the Vale di Ledro, a valley of great botanical interest, is the **Lago di Ledro**, nearly 3km long, with the little resort of Pieve di Ledro. When the water is low, on the east side of the lake near Molina, you can see some of the c. 15,000 wooden stakes from lake dwellings of the early Bronze Age, discovered in 1929. There is a small museum (*open summer daily 10–1 & 2–6; winter 9–12 & 2–5*), and a Bronze Age hut has been reconstructed on the lakeside.

Torbole sul Garda, a summer resort on the northeastern tip, played a part in the war of 1439 between the Visconti and the Venetians, when fleets of warships were dragged overland by teams of oxen and launched into the lake here. Goethe stayed at Torbole in 1786.

The eastern shore

The east side of Lago di Garda is bounded by the cliff of Monte Altissimo di Nago (2079m). This is the northern peak of Monte Baldo, which lines the shore as far as Torri del Benaco. A region of great interest for its flora and fauna, part of it is a protected area. It was once known as *Hortus europae* from its remarkable vegetation, which varies from lemon trees and olives on its lower slopes to beech woods and Alpine flowers on the summit. The highest peaks are Cima Valdritta (2218m) and Punta Telegrafo (2290m). There are numerous marked hiking trails on the slopes of Monte Baldo, some of them starting from Navene and Malcesine (*information and an excellent guide from the Comunità Montana del Baldo, T: 045 724 1600*).

Malcesine is a likeable resort with a little port. It was the seat of the Veronese Captains of the Lake in the 16th–17th centuries, and their old palace is now used as the town hall. The little garden on the lake is open to the public. Narrow roads lead up to the 13th–14th-century castle of the Scaligeri, restored by Venice in the 17th century. Very well maintained (*open daily in summer 9.30–6.30, Sat–Sun in winter, 9.30–5*), it has various small museums in separate buildings, including one dedicated to Goethe, who had his run-in with the law here (*see above*), and another with finds from a Venetian galley salvaged from the lake off Lazise after 1990; it was probably used in the battle of 1439. There is a fine view from the top of the tower. Concerts are often held in the castle. A cableway runs to the top of Monte Baldo (1748m), and there are pleasant walks in the area, as well as good skiing, mountain-biking and hang-gliding (your gear can ride the cableway with you).

To the south the coast becomes less wild. At Cassone a stream only 175m long enters the lake, and at Brenzone there is another small island offshore. Further on, the road passes a cemetery and the early-12th-century church of San Zeno, and at Pai there is a magnificent view of the opposite shore of the lake. The coast here is known as the Riviera degli Olivi, from its many olive trees.

Torri del Benaco, the Roman Castrum Turrium and the chief town of the Gardesana after the 13th-century, has a pretty port. The fine castle of the Scaligeri dates from 1383 and is open daily. It contains a small museum illustrating the history of fishing on the lake and the production of olive oil. There is a also a section dedicated to the rock carvings found in the district, the oldest dating from 1500 BC. A splendid pavilion of 1760, which protects a plantation of huge old lemon trees—as well as citrons, mandarins and oranges—against its south wall, can also be visited. This is one of very few such structures to survive on the lake where once lemons were cultivated in abundance. On the other side of the castle is a tiny botanical garden illustrating the main plants which grow on the lakeshore. There are 15th-century frescoes in the church. Benaco is locally famous for its red-and-yellow marble. A car ferry crosses from here to Maderno.

The headland of **Punta di San Vigilio** (parking on the main road) is the most romantic and secluded place on the lake. A cypress avenue ends at Villa Guarienti

(1540), possibly by Sanmicheli, and a path continues downhill on the left, past a walled lemon garden, to a hotel in a lovely old building next to the church of San Vigilio, among cypresses. A stone gate leads out to a picturesque miniature port, with reeds and a few old fig trees.

The resort of **Garda** was developed after the Second World War at the head of a deep bay. It was famous in the Roman and Lombard periods, and was later a fortified town; it still retains some interesting old houses.

Bardolino

The hills become lower and the landscape duller as the broad basin at the foot of the lake opens out. Bardolino, another ancient place retaining some commercial importance, is well known for its wine: not great wine, it is true, but fresh and fruity and easy to drink. There is a private wine museum in the Cantina Guerrieri Rizzanti. A tower and two gates remain from an old castle of the Scaligeri. On the left of the main road, in a little courtyard, is the tiny Carolingian church of San Zeno, which retains its 9th century form with a tower above the crossing and ancient paving stones. It has four old capitals and fragments of frescoes. The 12th-century church of San Severo, with contemporary frescoes, is also on the road.

Lazise retains part of its medieval wall and a castle of the Scaligeri, with Venetian additions. The 16th-century Venetian customs house on the lakefront attests to its former importance. San Nicolò is a 12th-century church with 16th-century additions and 14th-century frescoes.

Peschiera del Garda, an ancient fortress and one of the four corners of the Austrian 'quadrilateral' (the other three are Verona, Mantua and Legnago), stands at the outflow of the Mincio from Lago di Garda. The impressive fortifications, begun by the Venetians in 1553, were strengthened by Napoleon and again by the Austrians.

PRACTICAL INFORMATION

GETTING AROUND

• **By rail:** The Venice–Milan line serves Peschiera del Garda, Desenzano del Garda–Sirmione and Lonato, from which there are frequent country bus services to outlying points. Regional trains connect the lake stations to Verona or Brescia in less than 30mins; fast Intercity trains stop at Desenzano–Sirmione only, making the run in c. 20mins.

• **By bus:** Bus services run several times daily by the roads on the west and east banks from Peschiera and Desenzano to Riva. Frequent service from Verona via Lazise and Garda to Riva, and from Brescia to Desenzano, Sirmione, Peschiera and Verona, and between Salò and Desenzano, and Desenzano, Salò and Riva.

• **By boat:** Boat services (including two modernised paddle-steamers built in 1902 and 1903) are run by Navigazione sul Lago di Garda, Desenzano, Piazza Matteotti, T: 030 914 9511, from around mid-March–early Nov (the timetable changes three times a year). A daily boat service runs between Desenzano and Riva in 4hrs, calling at ports on the west bank and Malcesine. Hydrofoils run twice daily in 2hrs 40mins (with fewer stops). More frequent boats between Desenzano and Maderno (in 1hr 50mins). Services also run between Peschiera, Lazise, Bardolino and Garda, and between Malcesine, Limone, Torbole and Riva. A boat or hydrofoil runs c. every hour between Desenzano and Sirmione. All year round a car ferry operates between Maderno and Torri di Benaco in 30mins (every 30mins, but less frequently in winter) and there is a summer ferry from Limone to Malcesine in 20mins (hourly). Tickets are available allowing free travel on the lake services for a day. Tours of the lake in the afternoons in summer are also organised. Ask the information offices listed below for timetables and fares.

INFORMATION OFFICES

Desenzano del Garda Via Porto Vecchio 34, T: 030 914 1510, www.bresciaholiday.com
Garda Lungolago Regina Adelaide 13, T: 045 627 0384, www.aptgardaveneto.com
Gardone Riviera Corso della Repubblica 8, T: 0365 20347, www.bresciaholiday.com
Malcesine Via Capitanato 6, T: 045 740 0044, www.aptgardaveneto.com
Peschiera Piazzale Betteloni 15, T: 045 755 1673, www.aptgardaveneto.com
Riva del Garda Giardini di Porta Orientale 35, T: 0464 554444.
Salò Lungolago Zanardelli 39, T: 0365 21423, www.bresciaholiday.com
Sirmione Viale Marconi 2, T: 030 916114, www.bresciaholiday.com
Torri del Benaco Viale Fratelli Lavanda, T: 045 722 5120, www.aptgardaveneto.com

HOTELS

Most of the places on Lago di Garda are open during the summer season only, Apr/May–October.

Garda

€€€ **Locanda San Vigilio**. Small and on the lakefront, with a good restaurant and garden. Località San Vigilio, T: 045 725 6688, www.gardalake.it/sanvigilio/gallery

€€ **Madrigale**. In the hills, with spectacular views; all rooms have balconies. Località Marciaga, T: 045 627 9001, www.madrigale.it

Gardone Riviera

€€€ **Fasano e Villa Principe**. A former hunting lodge of the emperors of Austria set in a lovely park with garden terrace overlooking the lake. Località Fasano del Garda, T: 0365 290220, www.grand-hotel-fasano.it

€€€ **Villa del Sogno**. Another villa in a romantic garden with an immense terrace on the lake. Via Zanardelli 107, T: 0365 290181, www.villadelsogno.it

Gargnano

€€€ **Villa Feltrinelli**. A magnificent villa with frescoed rooms and lots of old wood, set in a lakeside park. It was Mussolini's home during the Republic of Salò. Via Rimembranza 38/40, T: 0365 798 000, www.villafeltrinelli.com

€€ **Villa Giulia**. A lakeside villa with lovely garden. Closed Jan–March. Viale Rimembranza 20, T: 0365 71022, www.villagiulia.it

Limone sul Garda

€ **Capo Reamolo**. Park, pool, and everything from Oriental medicine to windsurfing. Via IV Novembre 92, T: 0365 954040, F: 0365 954262, www.gardaresort.it

€€ **Park Hotel Imperial**. An elegant modern establishment, in a shady park with pool. Extensive health facilities. Open Mar–Nov. Via Tamas 10b, T: 0365 954 591, www.hotelimperial.com

Malcesine

€ **Park Hotel Querceto**. Away from the crowds on a hill outside the town, small (19 rooms) and relaxed, with restaurant service outside in summer. Località Campiano 17/19, T: 045 740 0344.

Riva del Garda

€€ **Du Lac et du Parc**. A luxurious establishment in a large park, offering peace and quiet, elegance, and refinement. Viale Rovereto 44, T: 0464 551500, www.hoteldulac-riva.it

€€ **Grand Hotel di Riva**. A classic hotel with a quiet park, frequented also for its roof-garden restaurant. Piazza Garibaldi 10, T: 0464 521800, www.gardaresort.it

Salò

€€ **Duomo**. On the lakefront, with antiques in the rooms and pleasant views. Closed Jan–March and Nov–Dec. Lungolago Zanardelli 91, T: 0365 21026, hotel.duomo@tin.it

€ **Vigna**. Historic *locanda* with quiet rooms and panoramic breakfast room. Lungolago Zanardelli 62, T: 0365 520144, www.hotelvigna.it

Sirmione

€€€ **Palace Hotel Villa Cortine**. Luxury accommodation in a 19th-century villa with large park, on the lakeshore. Via Grotte 6, T: 030 990 5890, www.hotelvillacortine.com

€€ **Ideal**. One of the finest settings on the peninsula, a tranquil olive grove overlooking the lake and the Grotte di Catullo. Via Catullo 31, T: 030 990 4245.

Torbole sul Garda

€€ **Piccolo Mondo**. A modern establishment in a quiet park, with a good restaurant and well-equipped wellness

centre. Via Matteotti 7, T: 0464 505
271
Torri del Benaco
€ **Europa**. A small establishment (18
rooms) in a renovated villa with a pleasant garden, enjoying splendid views
over the lake and mountains. Closed
Nov–March. T: 045 722 5086.
Tremosine
€ **Le Balze**. On a rocky cliff above the
lake, with good views. Closed
Nov–March. Località Campi-Voltino, T:
0365 917 179, www.hotel-lebalze.it
€ **Pineta Campi**. A delightful, restful
place nestled in the hills above the lake,
with good views. Closed Nov–March.
Località Campi-Voltino, T: 0365
917158, www.pinetacampi.com
€ **Villa Selene**. A family-managed
establishment with 11 lovely rooms
and breathtaking views over the lake
and Monte Baldo. Località Pregasio, T:
0365 953036,
www.hotelvillaselene.com

RESTAURANTS

Desenzano del Garda
€€€ **Esplanade**. Fresh seasonal cui-
sine with summer seating in a garden
overlooking the lake. Closed Wed. Via
Lario 10, T: 030 9143361.
€ **Cavallino**. Good seasonal dishes
made with the freshest ingredients.
Closed Mon, Jan and midday Aug. Via
Gherla 30, T: 030 912 0217.
Gardone Riviera
€€ **Villa Fiordaliso** (with rooms). In
business since 1890, in an old villa in a
small park with summer seating on a
terrace overlooking the lake. Closed
Mon, midday Tues and Jan–Feb. T:
0365 20158.

Gargnano
€€€ **La Tortuga**. A gourmet's delight,
known for fine food and excellent selection of regional, Italian, and imported
wines. Closed Mon evening (except
June–Sept), Tues and Jan. By the har-
bour, T: 0365 71251.
Lazise
€€ **Porticciolo**. Traditional cuisine of
the lake area, especially fish. Closed
Tues and Nov. Lungolago Marconi 22,
T: 045 758 0254.
Lugana (5km southeast of Sirmione)
€€ **Vecchia Lugana**. Summer seating
on a terrace overlooking the lake and
creative interpretations of local speciali-
ties, with special attention to seasonal
dishes. Closed Mon evening, Tues and
Jan–Feb. T: 030 919 012.
Manerba del Garda
€€€ **Capriccio**. Refined restaurant in
a villa with summer seating on a terrace
overlooking the lake; cuisine of the lake
area, especially fish. Closed Tues and
Jan–Feb. Località Montinelle, Piazza San
Bernardo 6, T: 0365 551 124.
Peschiera del Garda
€ **Papa** (with rooms). Good local food
and wine. Closed Wed and Nov–Dec.
Via Bella Italia 40, T: 045 755 0476.
€ **Pescatore**. Friendly family-run trat-
toria specialising in fish. Closed Tues
evening and Nov–Feb. Località Fornaci,
T: 045 755 0281.
Riva del Garda
€€ **Villa Negri**. Good traditional cui-
sine and an exceptional location on
high ground overlooking the entire
lake, with summer seating outside. Via
Bastioni 31–35, T: 0464 555 061.
Salò
€€ **Gallo Rosso**. Excellent small
restaurant in the historic town centre.

Closed Wed and one week in Jan and June. Vicolo Tomacelli 4, T: 0365 520 757.

€ **Osteria dell'Orologio**. Wine bar with good selection of snacks and light meals downstairs and full restaurant service upstairs. Closed Wed and June–July. Via Butturini 26, T: 0365 290 158.

Serniga (Salò)

€ **Il Bagnolo**. A working farm (with rooms) in a splendid location overlooking the lake, serving its own meats and other fresh products. Open May–Sept daily; Oct–Apr Fri evening–Sun. Località Bagnolo Ovest, T: 0365 20290.

Torri del Benaco

€€€ **Gardesana** (with rooms). Fine restaurant famous for its lake-fish soup. Closed Tues (except in summer) and Nov–Feb. Piazza Calderini 20, T: 045 722 5411.

€€ **Al Caval** (with rooms). Hearty local cuisine and regional wines. Closed Mon, Jan–Feb and Nov–Dec. Via Gardesana 186, T: 045 722 5666.

€€ **Galvani**. Excellent fish dishes and home-made pasta. Closed Mon, Jan and Feb. Località Pontirola, T: 045 722 5103.

FESTIVALS & EVENTS

Riva del Garda *Intervela*, international sailing week, July; *Flicorno d'Oro*, international band competition, Aug. *Mostra Internazionale di Musica Leggera Vela d'Oro*, pop festival, Sept.

Salò Music festival, July.

Torri del Benaco *Festa dell'Oliva*, with food fair, market of local products and folk music.

VERONA & ENVIRONS

Prosperous, busy Verona is one of the most attractive towns in northern Italy. The wide pavements of its pleasant streets, made out of huge blocks of red Verona marble, give the town an air of opulence. The birthplace of Catullus and perhaps Vitruvius in the 1st century BC, Verona has impressive Roman remains including the famous Arena. Its finest church is the basilica of San Zeno, which contains works by important local artists. Shakespeare's *Romeo and Juliet* was set in Verona. The Scaligeri family who ruled the town from the late 13th century are commemorated by their sumptuous tombs and their castle, Castelvecchio. The Piazza dei Signori and the adjoining Piazza delle Erbe are two of the finest squares in Italy.

The environs of Verona are famous for their wine-making districts, Soave and Valpolicella, and for the beautiful scenery of the Alpine foothills, the Monti Lessini.

HISTORY OF VERONA

Archaeologists have found evidence of Bronze Age settlements on this site, and Goths may have entered the area as early as the 4th century BC. Contacts with Rome began in the 3rd century, and Verona became a Roman colony in 89 BC. The seat of various monarchies (Ostrogoths, Lombards and Franks), in the 11th century it became an independent commune. It reached its golden age under the Della Scala family (or Scaligeri). Mastino della Scala, the *podestà* (or elected governor), established his position as overlord of Verona in 1260, and his family held power until 1387. This was the most brilliant period of Veronese history. Dante found a refuge in the Ghibelline city under Bartolomeo (nephew of Mastino) in 1301–04, and in the reign of Cangrande I (1311–29) Verona reached its greatest period of magnificence. Scaligeri hegemony came to an end in 1387, when Gian Galeazzo Visconti took the city.

Verona chose to become part of the Venetian Republic in 1405, and remained there until 1796, when it was occupied by Napoleon. Armed protest against the invaders (the '*Pasque Veronesi*', 1797) was avenged by the destruction of much of the city, and Verona was several times exchanged between France and Austria by the treaties of the early 19th century, until Napoleon finally fell and it was awarded to Austria at the Congress of Vienna (1814). During the Italian wars of independence it formed the strongest point of the Austrian 'quadrilateral' (together with Peschiera, Mantua and Legnago), but in 1866, when Austria was defeated by Prussia, it was united with the Italian kingdom. During the Second World War the city suffered considerably from bombing, and the bridges were all blown up. In the Castelvecchio in 1944, Mussolini's puppet Republican government staged the trial of Count Galeazzo Ciano, Mussolini's son-in-law, who had been a Fascist minister but later became a leading opponent of the Duce.

EXPLORING VERONA

Piazza Brà and the Arena

Once a suburban meadow (*braida*), Piazza Brà is the undisputed centre of modern Verona. Its most remarkable monument by far is the great elliptical **Arena** (*open Tues–Sun 8.30–dusk; during the opera season, July–Aug 8–4*). This is one of the largest extant Roman amphitheatres, third in size after the Colosseum in Rome and the amphitheatre of Capua. It was built in the 1st century AD using limestone quarried in the nearby Valpolicella. It retains only four of the triple archways of its outer walls, but the second circuit of 74 double arcades is intact. The interior has a cavea of 44 tiers (restored), capable of holding 22,000 spectators. The Arena hosts a famous opera festival in July–Aug, and if you are in town at this time be sure to ask your hotel staff to obtain tickets. The performances are truly spectacular.

The south side of the square is dominated by the immense Doric façade of the **Gran Guardia**, begun in 1609 (using stones taken from the Arena) by Domenico Curtoni, the nephew and pupil of Sanmicheli. Taking two centuries to complete, it was originally built as a military parade-ground, and is now used as a venue for exhibitions. On the other side of the Portoni di Brà is the **Accademia Filarmonica**, a concert hall with a majestic Ionic porch, also designed by Curtoni (1604) in the courtyard. Here is the **Museo Lapidario Maffeiano** (*open Tues–Sun 8–2, Mon 1.30–7.30, last admission 30mins before closing*), with a collection that includes some 100 Greek inscriptions ranging in date from 5th century BC–5th century AD, as well as Etruscan, Roman, early-Christian and medieval material from sites throughout the Veneto. Steps ascend

The Arena.

to the walkway over the Portoni di Brà, a double archway (1389), which once carried a covered passage joining the Scaligeri fortress of Castelvecchio to the Visconti citadel. A pentagonal tower of the latter can still be seen to the right of the arches. On the northwest side of the square extends the lively promenade known as the Listón, lined with fashionable cafés and restaurants and backed by patrician palaces. Via Mazzini (commonly called Via Nuova), Verona's elegant shopping street, leads from the north-west corner of Piazza Brà towards Piazza delle Erbe.

JULIET'S VERONA

Turn right at the end of Via Mazzini, and you come to a Gothic townhouse with a balcony of questionable authenticity and a bronze statue of the fictional heroine (touching her breast will supposedly bring you a new lover). This is the so-called **Casa di Giulietta** (*Via Cappello 23; open Tues–Sun 8.30–7.30, Mon 1.30–7.30*). Shakespeare's *Romeo and Juliet*, set in Verona, tells the story of Juliet Capulet (the Anglicisation of Cappelletti) and Romeo Montague (Montecchi), an adaptation of a tale by the 16th-century novelist Luigi da Porto. The legend of a feud between the two families is apocryphal; in fact, it is probable that the clans were in close alliance. The house certainly failed to impress Arnold Bennett. 'I am [determined] somehow to vent my rage at being shown Juliet's house, a picturesque and untidy tenement, with balconies certainly too high for love, unless Juliet was a trapeze acrobat, accustomed to hanging downwards by her toes. This was not Juliet's house, for the sufficient reason that so far as authentic history knows, there never was any Juliet.' Although true that there is nothing here that relates concretely to Juliet, the painted walls and finely crafted ceilings of the interior merit a glance.

A Gothic house to the northeast of here (marked on the map) is said to be the home of Romeo, though on what grounds nobody seems to know. In the south-ern part of the city is the so-called Tomba di Giulietta, which was visited by Byron. 'I have been over Verone,' he wrote to Augusta Leigh, 'Of the truth of Juliet's story, they seem tenacious to a degree, insisting on the fact—giving a date (1303), and showing a tomb. It is a plain, open, and partly decayed sarcophagus, with with-ered leaves in it, in a wild and desolate conventual garden, once a cemetery, now ruined to the very graves. The situation struck me as being very appropriate to the legend, being blighted as their love. I have brought away a few pieces of the gran-ite, to give to my daughter and my nieces.'

Piazza dei Signori

The long, rectangular **Piazza delle Erbe** stands over the ancient Roman forum. Today, as in the Middle Ages, it is the site of a colourful market, in the midst of whose hustle and bustle you can see some fine medieval sculptures: the 15th-century Colonna del Mercato (with a Gothic stone lion), the 16th-century Berlina or Capitello (where the

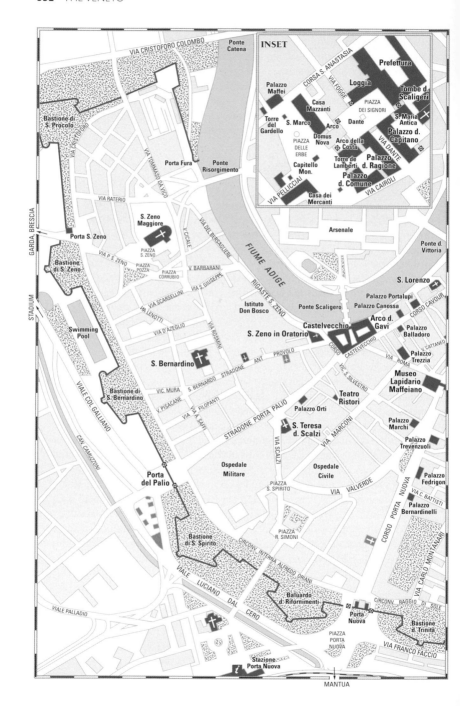

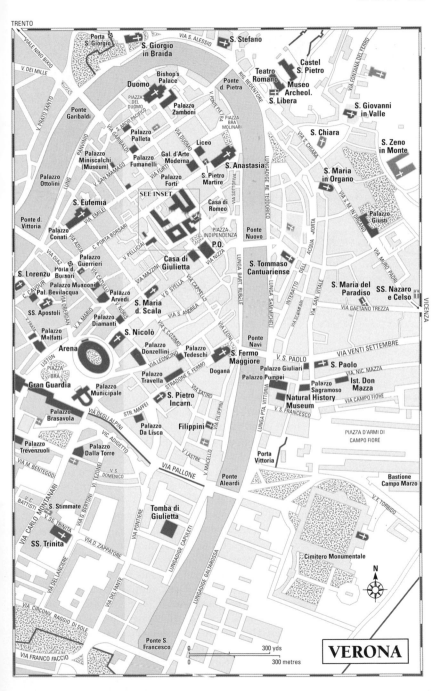

TRENTO

VIALE NINO BIXIO

V. DEI MILLE

V. PRATO SANTO

PANVINIO

Porta
S. Giorgio

S. Giorgio
in Braida

VIA S. ALESSIO

S. Stefano

Castel
S. Pietro

VIA FONTANA DEL FERRO

Bishop's
Palace

Teatro
Romano

RIG. REDENTORE

Ponte
d. Pietra

Museo
Archeol.

S. Libera

S. Giovanni
in Valle

Duomo

PIAZZA
DEL
DUOMO

Palazzo
Zamboni

VIA PIE TRA

VIA ARCO PACIFICO

Ponte
Garibaldi

VIA GARIBALDO

Palazzo
Palleta

PIAZZA
BRA
MOLINARI

S. Chiara

VIA S. CHIARA

S. Zeno
in Monte

VIA DUOMO

Liceo

VIA S. M. IN ORGANO

S. Maria
in Organo

Palazzo
Miniscalchi
(Museum)

Palazzo
Fumanelli

Gal. d'Arte
Moderna

VIA SAN MAMASO

VIA FORTI

Palazzo
Ottolini

LUNG

Palazzo
Forti

S. Pietro
Martire

S. Anastasia

S. Maria
in Organo

S. Maria
in Organo

Palazzo
Giusti

VIA MURO PADRI

VIA S. M. IN ORBANO

S. Eufemia

VIA EMILEI

SEE INSET

Casa di
Romeo

VIA SOTTORIVA

LUNGADIGE RE TEODORICO

INTERRATO DELL ACQUA MORTA

Ponte d.
Vittoria

Palazzo
Conati

VIA ADUA

C. PORTA BORSARI

PIAZZA
INDIPENDENZA

Ponte
Nuovo

V. PELLICCIAI

P.O.

Palazzo
Guerrieri

VIA DIAZ

Porta d.
Borsari

Casa di
Giulietta

VIA MAZZINI

VIA NIZZA

LUNGA BART. RUBELE

S. Tommaso
Cantuariense

LUNGA SAN MICHELI

VIA S. VITALE

S. Maria del
Paradiso

SS. Nazaro
e Celso

S. Lorenzo

C. CAVOUR

Palazzo Musoni
Pal. Bevilacqua

VIA CATULLO

Palazzo
Arvedi

V. D. S STELLA

VIA CAPPELLO

VIA GAETANO TREZZA

SS. Apostoli

VIA OBERDAN

V. A. MARIO

Palazzo
Diamanti

S. Maria
d. Scala

VIA S. ANDREA

VIA LEONI

Palazzo
Malfatti

V. FRA Z.

S. Nicolò

VIA S. COSIMO

Palazzo
Donzellini

Palazzo
Tedeschi

Ponte
Navi

VIA VENTI SETTEMBRE

Arena

LISTON

PIAZZA
BRA

VIA LEONCINO

S. Fermo
Maggiore

V. S. PAOLO

S. Paolo

VIA NIC. MAZZA

Gran Guardia

Palazzo
Municipale

STRADONE S. FERMO

Dogana

Palazzo Giuliari

Palazzo Pumpei

LUNGA PTA VITTORIA

Palazzo
Sagramoso

Ist. Don
Mazza

VIA CAMPO FIORE

Palazzo
Travella

VIA SATIRO

S. Pietro
Incarn.

VIA FILIPPINI

Natural History
Museum

V. S. FRANCESCO

Palazzo
Brasavola

VIA DEGLI ALPINI

STR. MAFFEI

Palazzo
Da Lisca

Filippini

PIAZZA D'ARMI DI
CAMPO FIORE

Palazzo
Trevenzuoli

Palazzo
Dalla Torre

VIC ADIGETTO

V. S.
DOMENICO

VIA PALLONE

V. LASTRE

V. MACELLO

Porta
Vittoria

Bastione
Campo Marzo

V.F. TORBIDO

VIA M. BENTEGODI

V. C.
BATTISTI

VIA CARLO MONTANARI

S. Stimmate

V. G. BERTONI

V. SS TRINITA

VI. TEZONE

Ponte
Aleardi

VIA D. ZAPPATORE

VIA D. FANTE

VIA PONTIERE

LUNGADIGE CAPULETI

Tomba di
Giulietta

SS. Trinita

VIA DEL LANCIERE

Cimitero Monumentale

VIA CIRCONV. RAGGIO DI SOLE

LUNGADIGE GALTAROSSA

N

VIA FRANCO FACCIO

Ponte S.
Francesco

0   300 yds

0   300 metres

VERONA

VICENZA

Frescoed façade of the Case Mazzanti on Piazza delle Erbe.

city's rulers took office), the 14th-century Fontana di Madonna Verona (incorporating a Roman statue) and the 16th-century Colonna di San Marco (with a Venetian lion).

The square is bounded on the southwest by the 14th-century **Casa dei Mercanti**, or merchants' hall, now the chamber of commerce; its mullioned windows and crenellated roof are all that remains of the original building, extensively altered in the 17th century. The monument in the small piazzetta here commemorates the victims of an Austrian bomb that fell nearby during the First World War. At the narrow northwest end of the piazza are the 14th-century Torre del Gardello (or Torre delle Ore) and the Palazzo Maffei, a Baroque building of 1668 crowned by statues. The northeast side is bounded by the frescoed **Case Mazzanti**, begun in the 14th century as a residence of the Scaligeri but radically altered in the 16th century; the Domus Nova (or Palazzo dei Giudici), a 17th-century reconstruction of the 14th-century residence of the *podestà*; and the Palazzo della Ragione and Palazzo del Comune, begun in the late 12th century but modified in the 16th century and again in the 19th century, when the Neoclassical façade on this side was added.

By the 15th-century **Arco della Costa**—which takes its name from a whale's rib hung beneath the vault, ready to fall, the legend says, on the first honest person to walk beneath it—you enter **Piazza dei Signori**, a small, handsome square with monumental buildings surrounding a central monument to Dante. This was the seat of city government in the Middle Ages. The **Palazzo della Ragione**, here seen in its earlier form, has a splendid Romanesque courtyard encircled by a portico on piers and occupied in part by a fine external Gothic-Renaissance staircase. Above it rises the symbol of civic power, the 84m **Torre dei Lamberti**, begun in 1172 and completed in the mid-15th century. Stairs and a lift go to the top (84m; *open Tues–Sun 9.30–7.30, Mon 1.45–7.30; last admission 30mins before closing*), from which there is a splendid view over the city and its surroundings.

The **Palazzo del Capitanio**, now the courthouse, stands on the other side of the narrow Via Dante. It is a 14th-century building with a crenellated tower and a doorway by Michele Sanmicheli (1531). The **Palazzo della Prefettura** (formerly Palazzo del Governo) rises at the end of the square. Built in the 14th century, it was restored to its original appearance in 1929–30; the doorway of 1533 is by Sanmicheli. Dante and Giotto stayed here as guests of the Scaligeri.

THE SCALIGERI

The Scaligeri, or della Scala family, ruled Verona during the 13th and 14th centuries. The founder of the dynasty was Mastino I, who became *podestà* (chief magistrate) after the death of the tyrant Ezzelino da Romano in 1259. He converted the position into a hereditary one, and named himself *capitano del popolo*. A faction of disaffected nobles plotted his downfall, and in 1277 he was assassinated in the Piazza dei Signori. The greatest of the Scaligeri was Mastino's grandson, Cangrande I, who inherited the title in 1311. Cangrande was the archetypal medieval Italian ruler: ruthless warrior, tyrannical overlord, and cultured patron of the arts. He supported the Ghibelline faction (the imperial party) against the Guelphs (the papal party), and harboured Dante, who had been exiled from Florence for his political views. Cangrande conquered Padua, Treviso and Vicenza. His foul-tempered nephew Mastino II brought Verona to the zenith of her power, capturing Brescia and Parma. He was also cursed with a line of cruel and murderous heirs. Their unscrupulous lust for conquest led the powerful city states of Florence and Venice to make a pact against them, and gradually much of Verona's territory was lost again. When Gian Galeazzo Visconti, Duke of Milan, made an assault on Verona, the last of the Scaligeri fled the town under cover of darkness, on 19 October 1387. The Scaligeri were never to rule in Verona again.

The adjoining **Loggia del Consiglio**, built in the late 15th century as the seat of the city council, is the first significant expression of the Veronese Renaissance. It consists of an elegant portico and an order of mullioned windows flanked by small pilasters; the coloured-marble facing and the sculptural decoration (by Alberto da Milano, 1493) give it a sense both of vivacity and of delicate harmony. An arch surmounted by a 16th-century statue joins the loggia to the Casa della Pietà, built in 1490. On the side facing Piazza delle Erbe is the ornate façade of the Domus Nova.

The passage on the right of the Palazzo della Prefettura leads into the little **Piazzaletto delle Arche**, which takes its name from the monumental *arche*, or tombs, of the Scaligeri (*open June–Sept 9.30–7.30, Mon 1.45–7.30, last admission 30mins before closing*), executed in the 14th century by Bonino da Campione and his followers. At the centre of a stone-and-iron enclosure bearing the family emblem, the ladder (in Italian, *scala*), stands the graceful Romanesque church of **Santa Maria Antica** (1185, several times restored), its doorway surmounted by the tomb of Cangrande I (d. 1329), with a copy of the equestrian statue now in the Museo del Castelvecchio (*see p. 340*). Inside the enclosure are, against the wall of the church, the simple tomb of Mastino I, the first of the dynasty, assassinated in 1277 (*see box*); on the left of the entrance, the tomb of Mastino II (d. 1351); in the opposite corner, that of Cansignorio (d. 1375); and at the rear, the tomb of Giovanni della Scala (d. 1359)—all in the form of aedicules surmounted by rich Gothic baldachins and adorned with statues. Also part of the complex are the profusely carved sarcophagi of Bartolomeo (1304), Alboino (1311), Cangrande II (1359) and Alberto (1301) della Scala.

Sant'Anastasia and environs

The polygonal apses and spired campanile of the Gothic church of Sant'Anastasia rise above the river. The largest church in Verona, it was erected by the Dominicans between 1291 and 1323 and reworked in 1423–81. The unfinished façade has a superb 14th-century doorway with coloured marbles and carvings. Inside, the 16th-century stoups, the Acquasantiere dei Gobbi, take their name from the crouching figures (*gobbi* means 'hunchbacks') in their bases. The first altar on the south side, incorporating the Fregoso tomb, was designed by Sanmicheli in 1565. The third altar on this side is surrounded by frescoes attributed to Liberale and Benaglio da Verona. Over the altar in the south transept is a painting of the *Madonna and Sts Thomas Aquinas and Augustine* by native artist Girolamo dai Libri. The first south apsidal chapel has a large fresco depicting the *Cavalli Family Presented to the Virgin*, by Altichiero (1390–95). This is the artist's only surviving work in Verona. Though locally born, his best known works are in Padua (*see p. 463*). The second south apsidal chapel has two Gothic tombs and 24 terracotta reliefs with stories from the *Life of Christ* by Michele da Firenze (1435). In the sanctuary are a large 14th-century fresco of the *Last Judgement* by a painter called the Master of the Last Judgement, and the tomb of General Cortesia Serego, attributed to the Florentine Nanni di Bartolo (1424–29). From the north transept, with an altarpiece by Francesco Morone, a Gothic doorway leads into the sacristy, with a delightful detached fresco of *St George and the Dragon* by Pisanello, the church's chief claim to fame. Here too are 15th-century stalls and stained glass, and the banner of the Millers' and Bakers' Guild.

Beyond the Gothic tomb of Guglielmo Castelbarco (d. 1320), above the former convent-gate, rises the little 14th-century church of **San Pietro Martire**, now used for exhibitions. It contains a large frescoed lunette of the *Annunciation*, a very unusual allegorical composition by Giovanni Maria Falconetto, with symbolic animals and idealised views of Verona. The two German knights who commissioned the fresco are shown kneeling. Changing exhibitions of modern and contemporary art are held in the nearby Palazzo Forti, now the **Galleria d'Arte Moderna** (*open during exhibitions,*

Tues–Sun 9.30–7; entrance at Via Forti 1). Napoleon lodged in the 13th-century palace in 1796–97; it was rebuilt in the mid-19th century, and hosted the Accademia di Belle Arti until the mid-20th century.

Impressions of Verona

Romeo: There is no world without Verona walles,
But Purgatorie, Torture, hell itselfe:
Hence banished, is banisht from the world,
And world's exile in death.

> *William Shakespeare, Romeo and Juliet, c. 1594–95*

This most faire City is built in the forme of a Lute.... It hath a pure aire, and is ennobled by the civility and auncient Nobility of the Citizens, who are inbued with a chearfull countenance, magnificent mindes, and much inclined to all good literature.

> *Fynes Moryson, An Itinerary, 1617*

Certainly this Citty deserv'd all those Elogies Scaliger has honour'd it with, for in my opinion, tis situated in one of the most delightfullst places that ever I came in, so sweetly mixed with risings, & Vallies, so Elegantly planted with Trees, on which Bacchus seems riding as it were in Triumph every Autumn, for the Vines reach from tree to tree; & here of all places I have travell'd in Italy would I fix preferable to any other, so as well has that learned Man given it the name of the very Eye of the World.

> *John Evelyn, Diary, May 1646*

The duomo and environs

Via Duomo leads northwest from Sant'Anastasia. The duomo or cathedral of Santa Maria Matricolare, dominating the secluded Piazza del Duomo, is a 12th-century Romanesque building with Gothic and Renaissance additions. The front has a monumental two-storeyed porch adorned with column-bearing lions and reliefs by Maestro Nicolò (1139); another Romanesque porch is on the south side. The campanile, Romanesque at the bottom and 16th century above, was completed in the 20th century. The overall design is by Sanmicheli. The 12th-century semicircular tufa apse, a pure expression of the Veronese Romanesque style, is adorned with pilasters and a fine Classical frieze. The entrance is by a door in the south flank, with a good porch.

The Gothic interior has broad arches on tall compound piers. The walls of the west bays are decorated with architectural frescoes by Giovanni Maria Falconetto (c. 1503). More frescoes, by Francesco Torbido after cartoons by Giulio Romano, adorn the sanctuary, which is enclosed by a fine curved choir screen by Sanmicheli, incorporating a *Crucifixion with the Virgin and St John* by Giambattista da Verona (1534). The second south chapel has a painting of the *Adoration of the Magi* by Liberale da Verona, and the first north chapel an *Assumption* by Titian, in a frame by Jacopo Sansovino. The Nichesola tomb here is also by Sansovino.

From the north side entrance is gained to the church of **San Giovanni in Fonte** (1123), the former Romanesque baptistery, a three-aisled apsidal building with fine 9th-century capitals and an octagonal baptismal font decorated with reliefs attributed to Brioloto (c. 1200). The fragmentary frescoes date from the 13th–14th centuries: on the left of the entrance is a *Baptism of Christ* by Paolo Farinati (1568). The same vestibule gives entrance to the little church of **Sant'Elena**, from the 9th century, rebuilt in the 12th century and preserving part of its early Christian structures. Excavations here have revealed 6th-century mosaic pavements and the tombs of two early bishops. The finely carved narrow stalls date from the 16th century. The altarpiece is by Brusasorci, sometimes known as 'the Titian of Verona' for his imitations of the great artist.

Opposite the south door of the cathedral, a seated 14th-century figure of St Peter surmounts the doorway of San Pietro in Archivolto. In Piazza Vescovile, where you can see the cathedral's beautiful apse, the **Bishop's Palace** has an unusual façade of 1502 with Venetian crenellations and a portal decorated with statues, including a delightful *Madonna and Child* attributed to Fra Giovanni da Verona. The attractive courtyard, with curious Romanesque capitals, is dominated by the **Torrione di Ognibene** (1172). Next to the palace is the flank of San Giovanni in Fonte (*described above*), and opposite is an ancient wall (now propped up) with a gate into a neglected garden. Nearby, the Ponte Pietra, guarded by a medieval gateway, crosses the Adige.

A passageway to the left of the façade of the duomo leads past the exterior portico of Sant'Elena and (opposite) the charming Romanesque cloister (with a double arcade on one side), also partly on the site of the 5th-century basilica, with remains in two places of a 6th-century mosaic pavement (one of which is coloured).

Stradone Arcidiacono Pacifico extends from the cathedral square past Palazzo Paletta (no. 6; with a finely carved portal) to Via Garibaldi, which you follow to the left. Turn right at the next corner and, after a few paces, look right to see the monumental Neoclassical façade of **Palazzo Miniscalchi**. The present entrance to the palace is in Via San Mamaso, where the beautiful side façade can be seen. This one-family townhouse was built in the mid-15th century by the Miniscalchi and has handsome marble windows and doorways. The painted decoration was carried out c. 1580 by Michelangelo Aliprandi and Tullio India il Vecchio. It is one the last vestiges of what was once a common tradition (numerous palaces in Verona once had painted façades). The **Museo Miniscalchi-Erizzo** (*open Tues–Sat 4–7; Sun and holidays 10.30–12.30 & 4–7*) was opened here in 1990, after the last descendant of the family had left the house and collections to a foundation in 1955. It contains a miscellany of objects, all well labelled and spaciously arranged. The ground floor is used for exhibitions of the decorative arts. The permanent collections include ivories, 16th–18th-century furniture, family portraits by Alessandro Longhi and Sebastiano Bombelli, 17th–18th-century majolica, a plate decorated in 1519 which belonged to Isabella d'Este, 16th-century ceramics from Urbino, Venetian bronzes, Murano glass, a fireplace decorated in majolica from Faenza (17th–18th century), a good collection of 16th–17th-century drawings (mostly by Venetian masters), an armoury, 17th-century wooden soldiers, and curios that belonged to Ludovico Moscardo (1611–81).

VERONESE ART & ARCHITECTURE

Verona is the richest artistic centre in northeast Italy after Venice. It was the birthplace of the great architect Michele Sanmicheli (1486–1559), whose legacy includes numerous palaces with stately, harmonious frontages, sculptural work and fortifications. His Porta del Palio (*see p. 342*) is a Mannerist masterpiece. Verona's artists were many, and include Altichiero, active in Verona in the 15th century, though his best work is in Padua; Domenico and Francesco Morone, Francesco Torbido and Gian Francesco Caroto. Most famous of all are the early masters Stefano da Zevio (Stefano da Verona) and Pisanello, medallist and painter, whose *Madonna della Quaglia* is housed in the Castelvecchio. Paolo Caliari, called 'Il Veronese' (1528–88), was born here, though active almost entirely in Venice.

From Porta dei Bórsari to the Castelvecchio

Corso Porta Bórsari follows the straight line of the Roman decumanus maximus to the 1st-century Porta dei Bórsari, which takes its name from the episcopal tax collectors, or *bursari*, whose offices were located here. Beyond the gate Corso Cavour continues along the path of the decumanus. Set back from the street to the south are the campanile and flank of the Romanesque church of the Santissimi Apostoli, from the sacristy of which you can enter the small, semi-interred church of Santi Tosca e Teuteria, which supposedly dates back to the 5th century. Across the street is the beautiful Romanesque church of **San Lorenzo** (1110), in alternating bands of tufa and brick, with a narrow façade flanked by towers. No. 19 (left) is the spectacular **Palazzo Bevilacqua**, Sanmicheli's masterpiece, with rusticated ground floor, balcony, loggia with spiral columns, and a fine cornice. Sanmicheli also designed the Palazzo Canossa (no. 44), with a splendid atrium and courtyard. At the end of the street, in a little garden on the right, is the **Arco dei Gavi**, a Roman arch erected in the 1st century AD in honour of the family of the Gavii. Demolished in 1805, it was reconstructed from the fragments in 1932.

Corso Cavour takes you down to the Castelvecchio, the main monument of medieval civil architecture in Verona. It was built by Cangrande II della Scala as his home and fortress in 1354–57, and was completed with the addition of the keep in 1375. The imposing brick fortress consists of two main blocks divided by the crenellated Ponte Scaligero, which extends to the north bank of the Adige, and the tall tower of the keep. The rectangular east block surrounds a large courtyard, formerly a parade ground; the trapezoidal west block (the original fortified residence of Cangrande) has a double circuit of walls with two courtyards and drawbridges. Inside the castle is the Museo Civico d'Arte, famous for its holdings of Veronese painting, sculpture, decorative art and arms.

The Museo Civico d'Arte in Castelvecchio
Open Tues–Sun 8.30–7.30, Mon 1.45–7.30, last admission 45mins before closing.

Sculpture collection: This is arranged in two large halls. In the first are reliefs and epigraphs from the late Medieval and Romanesque periods, notably the sarcophagus of Sts Sergius and Bacchus, dated 1179, showing two archers shooting an eagle and the two saints in profile holding palms of martyrdom on the lid, and reliefs of the saints' stories on the sides. The second hall displays statues from the first half of the 14th century, arranged to appear as players on a stage. These works, which were often part of monumental groups, are attributed to the circle of the Master of Sant'Anastasia and represent the most original period in Veronese sculpture. Carved in *pietra gallina*, a soft sandstone quarried locally, they were originally painted. The highlight of the sculpture collection is the **equestrian statue of Cangrande I**, from the Arche Scaligere, dramatically installed on an elevated platform.

Decorative arts collection: This contains some important antiquities and artefacts—notably early Christian glass, 7th-century gold, the so-called Tesoretto di Isola Razza, including 4th-century devotional spoons—fabrics and silks from the Arca di Cangrande I and miniatures by Liberale and by Girolamo dai Libri. Of particular interest is a

14th-century fibula of precious and semi-precious stones (*pietre dure*) and pearls set in gold, found in Verona in 1938. The elegant star form is decorated with alternating amethysts and emeralds arranged in a sunburst pattern surrounded by white Oriental pearls. This object was probably a gift of the Venetian Republic to Mastino II della Scala. The outstanding collection of arms and armour ranges from the Lombard period to the 18th century.

Painting collection: Here are works by the primitives Turone (*Trinity*), Altichiero, Stefano da Verona (Stefano da Zevio; *Madonna del Roseto*) and Pisanello (*Madonna della Quaglia*); the 15th-century painters Francesco Morone, Liberale da Verona, Paolo Cavazzola and Gian Francesco Caroto (*Boy with

Pisanello: *Madonna della Quaglia* (c. 1420).

Drawing); and the 16th-century masters Paolo Veronese (*Bevilacqua-Lazise Altarpiece, Deposition*) and Paolo Farinati. Among the Venetian artists are Andrea Mantegna (*Holy Family*), Jacopo Bellini (*St Jerome, Crucifix*), Giovanni Bellini (two *Madonnas*), Carlo Crivelli (*Madonna della Passione*), Bartolomeo Montagna, Alvise Vivarini (*Madonna*), Bernardo Strozzi (*Male Portrait*), Jacopo Tintoretto (*Concert of the Muses* and *Adoration of the Shepherds*) Giovanni Battista Tiepolo (*Heliodorus* and the *Treasure of the Temple*; sketch for a ceiling painting), and Francesco Guardi (two *Capricci*). Also present are Tommaso da Modena and several Flemish artists.

San Zeno Maggiore

Open Mon–Sat 8.30–6, Sun and holidays 1–6. Tickets, required for admission, are sold on the left as you enter Piazza San Zeno.

The basilica of **San Zeno Maggiore** is one of the most important Romanesque churches in northern Italy, and home to Mantegna's splendid *Madonna and Saints*.

Erected in the 5th century and rebuilt in the 9th as the church of the Benedictine monastery, of which one stout battlemented tower remains (to the north of the façade as you face the church), San Zeno was reconstructed in 1120–38 and completed in the 13th century. The polygonal apse, with Gothic ogival windows and engaged buttresses, dates from 1385–98. The warm-hued tufa façade is divided horizontally by pilaster strips and vertically by a gallery with mullioned windows, and pierced by a large rose window (representing the Wheel of Fortune) and a fine doorway of 1138. The latter, with an attached porch, carved arch, lunette, column-bearing lions and two splendid bands of reliefs representing biblical and allegorical scenes, was executed by Maestro Nicolò and his pupil Guglielmo around 1135. Equally splendid are the 12th-century doors, with bronze relief panels depicting Old and New Testament stories and the lives of St Michael and St Zeno, who was Verona's first bishop (d. 380). The south flank presents the red-and-white marble bands typical of Veronese churches. The tall, detached campanile (1045–1140) terminates in a two-tiered belfry with mullioned windows.

From the north side you enter the noble interior, with three aisles on piers and columns, a wooden ship's-keel roof and split-level east end—sanctuary above, crypt below. Fine 13th-century statues decorate the choir screen. On the west wall is a *Crucifixion* by Lorenzo Veneziano, painted around 1360; at the beginning of the south aisle, an octagonal baptistery of the late 12th century. The walls of the nave and sanctuary are decorated with fragments of Romanesque-Gothic frescoes; over the high altar is Mantegna's *Madonna and Saints* triptych (1457–59), one of the key works of Renaissance painting in Verona. The wooden choir stalls date from the 15th century. The 13th-century crypt, with antique columns, holds a modern sarcophagus containing the remains of St Zeno, and the tombs of other saints and bishops. In the north apse is a curious 13th- or 14th-century polychrome statue of St Zeno laughing. From the north aisle you go out into the fine Romanesque cloister (with small double columns of red marble, dating from the 12th–14th centuries), left over from the abbey. Beneath the portico are tombs and sepulchral monuments. A doorway on the left leads to the Oratorio di San Benedetto, a 13th-century chapel displaying columns and piers with 'recycled' capitals, some dating as far back as the 6th century.

The Porta del Palio

The Porta del Palio (1552–57) is the gate in the city walls through which the palio horse race passed. Mentioned by Dante, it is the most harmonious of the four city gates designed by Sanmicheli—the others are the Porta San Giorgio (1525); Porta Nuova (1533–46); and Porta San Zeno (1541–42). The design and construction of these gates and fortifications was probably Sanmicheli's greatest single commission. Go through the Porta del Palio and you get a splendid view of the walls from the outside. Skirting round them to the south, you soon reach the Porta Nuova, from which Corso Porta Nuova takes you to Piazza Brà and the town centre.

San Fermo

At the end of Via Cappello is the Roman Porta dei Leoni, built in the 1st century AD, with a great arch, fluted columns, pedimented windows, loggia and niches. Just outside the gate is one of Verona's great medieval monuments, **San Fermo Maggiore**, a complex of two superimposed churches, the lower one of 1065–1143, the upper of 1313–20. It has a fine façade featuring a broad Romanesque doorway with deep splay, a gallery of small arches, tall ogival windows, and a central mullioned window. On the north side is another doorway (the usual entrance) of 1363, beneath an attached porch. The interior, a single aisle covered by a ship's-keel roof of 1314, holds a number of important artworks, most precious of which is an *Annunciation* by Pisanello.

In the lunette over the entrance is a *Crucifixion* attributed to Turone; on the south side, next to the ambo with its baldachin and pointed spire, a fragment of a detached fresco of *Angels* by Stefano da Verona (Stefano da Zevio). Halfway along the north side is the Baroque Cappella della Madonna, with a *Madonna and Saints* by Gian Francesco Caroto (1528). Over the first north altar is a *St Nicholas with Saints* by Battista dal Moro and, in the corner, the Brenzoni tomb by the Florentine Nanni di Bartolo (1427–39). This is framed by a famous fresco of the *Annunciation* by Pisanello. From the right transept you can enter the old Romanesque cloister and from here descend to the lower church, with fragmentary frescoes of the 11th–13th centuries and, behind the high altar, a 14th-century wooden crucifix.

Across the river

The **Ponte Nuovo** crosses the Adige, with good views of the Roman theatre and the hill of San Pietro. On the other side of the river Via Carducci leads past the 15th-century church of **San Tommaso Cantuariense** (Thomas Becket) to the Giardini di Palazzo Giusti (*open daily, summer 9–8; winter 8–7*), a beautiful formal garden with terraces, a boxwood labyrinth and a belvedere. This green hillside oasis, laid out in the 16th cen-

Stefano da Verona: *Madonna del Roseto* (c. 1425).

Verona: view from the hill of San Pietro.

tury, was one of Goethe's favourite spots in Italy. One block northwest is **Santa Maria in Organo**, founded in the 7th century but dating in its present form from 1481. Michele Sanmicheli is probably the author of the white-marble west façade (1546). The elegant interior is entirely covered with frescoes, by Nicolò Giolfino (south side), Gian Francesco Caroto (north side), Brusasorci (north transept and sacristy) and Francesco Morone (sacristy), among others. The choir and sacristy have extraordinary inlaid woodwork executed in the late 15th century by Fra' Giovanni da Verona. In the crypt are traces of the original church (7th or 8th century) and remains of the Roman walls. A large Renaissance cloister of the Olivetan convent adjoins the church to the north.

To the northwest, in a lovely position on the hill of San Pietro, is the **Roman Theatre** (*open Tues–Sun 8.30–7.30, Mon 1.45–7.30; last admission 45mins before closing*). This extraordinary complex, of which the scena, the semicircular cavea, and the two entrances survive, was built in the early 1st century AD and later enlarged. The ruins of the cavea end on one side in the small church of **Santi Siro e Libera**, founded in the 9th century and altered in the 14th. Plays and ballet are held in the theatre in summer.

Above the theatre (lift), the Renaissance cloister of the former convent of San Girolamo houses a **Museo Archeologico** with glass, sculpture and mosaics from Roman Verona, and Greek and Etruscan material. The views from the windows and terraces over the theatre, the river and the city are themselves worth the climb. The church has a fine ceiling and frescoes by Gian Francesco Caroto and others; over the altar is a Renaissance triptych by an anonymous Veronese artist. High up on the hill is the Castel San Pietro, built by the Visconti, destroyed by the French and rebuilt by the Austrians.

ENVIRONS OF VERONA

The road from Verona to Soave passes the sanctuary of the **Madonna di Campagna**, at San Michele Extra, a round church with a peristyle, designed by Michele Sanmicheli (1484–1559), who was born in the village. **Caldiero** has hot springs (perhaps the Roman Fontes Junonis—two of the thermal pools are Roman).

Soave is a pleasant little town famous for its white wine (*see box*). A wine festival is held here in September. The impressive battlemented walls, extremely well preserved, were built by the Scaligeri before 1375. In the central Piazza Antenna (named after a mast from which the flag of St Mark was flown, after Verona voted to join the Venetian Republic) are Palazzo Cavalli, a Venetian Gothic palace of 1411, and Palazzo di Giustizia (1375). A paved path leads up from the piazza to the medieval castle (also reached by road), enlarged by the Scaligeri in 1369. The keep is defended by three courtyards, each on a different level. Privately owned (*open summer Tues–Sun 9–12 & 3–6.30; winter 9–12 & 2–4*), it was restored and partly reconstructed in 1892. The residence has an armoury on the ground floor, and above are rooms with Gothic Revival painted decorations and imitation furniture. There is a fine view from the battlements.

SOAVE

Soave is one of the best known of all Italian wines. It is grown on the fertile hillsides east of Verona, around the village that bears its name. Though a great deal of wine is produced, quality fluctuates wildly from the barely drinkable to the exquisite. The soil here is volcanic, perfect for the Garganega grape that makes up 70 per cent of all Soave. One of the best producers in Leonildo Pieropan, who has vineyards on some of the best sites in the Soave Classico zone, including Calvarino and La Rocca, where the vines cluster around an old Scaligeri castle. Monteforte d'Alpone, famous for its cherries, is also known for its Soave Classico. Though Roberto Anselmi's wines are labelled in the IGT category (*see p. 697*)—it was Anselmi's own decision to leave the DOC system—they are distinctly characterful, subtly crafted vintages, with all the soft, lemony intensity that Soave is famous for.

The Monti Lessini

To the north of Verona are the volcanic Monti Lessini, with the valleys of the *tredici comuni*, a high-lying district occupied by the descendants of Germanic settlers who migrated here in the 13th century. Their dialect has practically died out. This pleasant remote area, with cherry trees and chestnut and beechwoods, has been visited for holidays by the Veronese since the beginning of the 20th century. The flint outcrops in the limestone hills were used in the Palaeolithic era for making tools, and remarkable fossils have been found in the volcanic and sedimentary rocks. Some of the houses still have characteristic roofs made out of slabs of local stone. This stone is also sometimes used for drystone walls around fields. **Bosco Chiesanuova**, the main resort, has a museum illustrating the history of Lessinia—as the region as a whole is known. Near here the Riparo Tagliente, a shelter used by Palaeolithic hunters, has revealed numerous interesting finds. In the easternmost valley are Roncà, with a fossil museum, and Bolca, with a museum famous for its fossilised tropical fish found in the area. The neighbouring Val d'Illasi is known for its wrought-iron craftsmen. Beyond **Illasi**, with two grand 18th-century villas and a fresco by Stefano da Verona in the church, is **Cogollo**, with a wrought-iron workshop, responsible for the town's pretty, locally made street lights. At the head of the valley is Giazza, where a German dialect is still spoken. It has a local ethnographic museum.

The **Valpolicella**, in the westernmost part of Lessinia, is a hilly district near a bend in the Adige. Sant'Ambrogio has quarries of *rosso di Verona* marble. At Volargne the 15th-century Villa del Bene (*open Tues–Sun 9–12 & 3–6*) has frescoes by Brusasorci, Gian Francesco Caroto and Bernardino India. At Negrar is the 15th-century Villa Bertoldi. The valley is planted with cherry trees.

THE WINES OF VALPOLICELLA

The DOC of Valpolicella embraces 19 villages stretching from the Lago di Garda to just north of Verona. The most valuable grape grown here is Corvina, yielding wines of impressive power and density. DOC regulations permit only 70 or 80 per cent Corvina in the wine, leaving lesser varieties to make up the rest. This has led to some of the most talented and adventurous producers opting out of the DOC system—a story so familiar in Italy—and producing 100 per cent Corvina wines, some of them true classics, though not labelled Valpolicella.

There are three styles of Valpolicella. Straight Valpolicella is a youthful, easy-drinking wine, often slightly rustic. 'Valpolicella Superiore' on the label means that the alcohol content is slightly higher, and that the wine has been at least a year in the bottle. Recioto and Amarone are made from selected bunches, picked two weeks before the harvest and dried on wooden slats under a straw roof. If the wine ferments to dryness it is Amarone. If there is residual sugar, it is Recioto. It is probable that *retico*, to which—according to Suetonius—Augustus Caesar was particularly partial, was precisely the same wine, with all its smoky, fruity, marzipan flavours. The third type of Valpolicella is Ripasso, made by a second fermentation of ordinary Valpolicella on used Recioto skins. The result is a full bodied, powerful, alcoholic wine.

The best producers include Allegrini in Fumane (key wines are La Poja and La Grola); the Tedeschi family near Pedemonte; and Giuseppe Quintarelli (key wines are his Monte Ca' Paletta Recioto and his Valpolicella Classico Superiore) and the Galli family (Le Ragose estate), both in Negrar.

Elsewhere around the province

South of Verona, **Villafranca di Verona** preserves a castle of the Scaligeri (1202), now home to a Risorgimento museum (*open Sat 4–6, Sun 3–7; second Sun of every month, 10–12*). The armistice of Villafranca was concluded here on 11 July 1859 between Napoleon III and Austrian emperor Franz Joseph. Through the secret deals he had done with Cavour, Napoleon III had done much to set the independence ball rolling in Italy. When the ball began to reach full momentum after the bloody battle of Solferino, the French leader began to be wary and concluded an armistice with Austria, in effect halting Italian expansion into Austrian territory. It wasn't until the 1860s, when Prussia defeated Austria at Königgratz, that Italy's dreams of independence came nearer to fulfilment.

PRACTICAL INFORMATION

GETTING AROUND

• **Airport bus:** Buses run to Verona airport every 20 mins to/from Verona Porta Nuova railway station. Information and ticket office: APT bus terminal, Piazzale XXV Aprile, www.aptv.it
• **By rail:** Verona has direct links with Venice, Trieste, Milan, Turin and Genoa; Bologna, Florence and Rome; and Trento, Bolzano and Bressanone.
• **By bus:** Town buses connect Porta Nuova railway station with the Arena (nos 11, 12, 13, 72 and 73); with the Castelvecchio (nos 21, 22, 23 and 24); and with Piazza Erbe (nos. 72, 73). From the Castelvecchio to San Zeno take nos 31, 32 or 33. From the station to the Roman theatre, nos 72 or 73. Information from AMT, T: 045 887 111. Country buses run by APT depart from Porta Nuova station (T: 045 800 4129) for Lago di Garda and other points in the province.
  The Verona Card gives free access to AMT bus services and free admission to museums, churches and monuments; it can be purchased at museums, monuments, churches, tobacconists, and at sales points on Lake Garda.
• **Taxis:** Radiotaxi, operational 24 hours a day, T: 045 532 666. Taxi stands at Porta Nuova railway station, Piazza Brà, Piazza delle Erbe, Valerio Catullo Airport.
• **Bicycle:** Rental is available on an hourly or daily basis; stand in Piazza Brà (Apr–Sept), T: 333 536 7770.

INFORMATION OFFICES

Verona Via degli Alpini 9 (Piazza Brà), T: 045 806 8680; Piazza XXV Aprile (Stazione Porta Nuova), T: 045 800 0861; Aeroporto Valerio Catullo, T: 045 861 9163, www.tourism.verona.it
Monti Lessini Piazza della Chiesa 34, Bosco Chiesanuova, T: 045 705 0088.

HOTELS

Verona
€€€ **Due Torri Baglioni**. A 17th-century inn transformed into a luxurious hotel with rooms furnished in different styles using genuine antiques (the

restaurant, L'Aquila, is also warm and refined). Piazza Sant'Anastasia 4, T: 045 595 044, www.duetorrihotelbaglioni.com

€€€ **Gabbia d'Oro**. A small hotel (27 rooms) known for its genteel, cosy atmosphere, situated in the very centre of the old town. Corso Borsari 4a, T: 045 800 3060, www.hotelgabbiadoro.it

€€ **Grand**. Near the train station, with antique furniture, old paintings, and a small garden with a fountain. Corso Porta Nuova 105, T: 045 595 600, www.grandhotel.vr.it

€€ **Montresor Giberti**. Quiet and comfortable, outside the city walls. Via Leopardi 16, T: 045 810 1444, F: 045 810 0523, www.leopardi.vr.it

€€ **Victoria**. Occupying a tastefully restored historic building and hosting a small display of Roman archaeology (near the Ponte della Vittoria, half-way between the cathedral and the Castelvecchio). Via Adua 8, T: 045 590566, www.hotelvictoria. veronahotels.de

€ **Torcolo**. A warm, cosy hotel in a small square near the Arena but off the beaten track, with restaurant service outside during summer; closed Jan. Vicolo Listone 3, T: 045 800 7512, www.hoteltorcolo.it

Valpolicella

€€€ **Villa del Quar**. Just 18 rooms, in a splendid villa. Closed Jan–Feb. Via Quar 12, Località Pedemonte, San Pietro in Cariano, T: 045 6800681, www.hotelvilladelquar.it

€€ **Villa Quaranta**. An 18th-century villa in a lovely old park, with a renowned fitness centre. Via Brennero 65, Località Ospedaletto, Pescantina, T: 045 676 7300, www.villaquaranta.com

RESTAURANTS

Verona

€€€ **Accademia**. Elegant, classic restaurant known for its creative interpretations of traditional recipes. Closed Sun except July–Aug. Via Scala 10, T: 045 800 6072.

€€€ **Arche**. A seafood restaurant near Sant'Anastasia, in business since 1879. Closed Sun, Mon morning and Jan. Via Arche Scaligere 6, T: 045 800 7415.

€€€ **Dodici Apostoli**. An elegant restaurant located in a historic building in the heart of the city centre, serving traditional Veronese dishes since 1750. Closed Sun evening, Mon, Jan and June. Vicolo San Marco 3, T: 045 596 999.

€€ **Bottega del Vino**. A very traditional Veronese restaurant in a quiet lane off Via Mazzini. Closed Tues and Feb. Via Scudo di Francia 3, T: 045 800 4535.

€€ **Maffei**. With pavement seating in Verona's most colourful square in summer. Closed Sun, Mon in July and Aug. Piazza delle Erbe 38, T: 045 801 0015.

€ **Al Bersagliere**. Authentic Veronese cuisine and great wines in a friendly trattoria. Closed Sun. Via Dietro Pallone 1, T: 045 800 4824.

€ **Al Parigin**. Small but good trattoria amidst olives and vines in the hills just outside town. Closed Weds and in Sept. Via Trezzolano 13, T: 045 988 124.

€ **Il Busòlo**. Warm, friendly *osteria* with a good wine list. Closed Thur. Località Vago, T: 045 982146.

€ **La Taverna di Via Stella**. At Lavagno, 12km east on Road 11, a new place with good old-fashioned Veronese cooking. Closed Mon. Via Stella 5, T: 045 800 8008.

€ **Trattoria all'Isolo**. Family-run trattoria with wholesome home cooking. Closed Weds evening and in Aug. Piazza Isolo 5a, T: 045 594291.

Soave

€€ **Alpone**. Restaurant offering delicious local food and home-grown wine. Closed Sun evening, Tues, Jan and Aug. Via Pergola 51, Costalunga, Montecchia di Crosara (9km north), T: 045 617 5387.

Valpolicella

€€ **Dalla Rosa Alda**. A simple, genuine trattoria with a great wine list. Closed Sun evening (except in summer), Mon, Jan and June. Strada Garibaldi 4, Frazione San Giorgio di Valpolicella, Sant'Ambrogio di Valpolicella, T: 045 770 1018.

€€ **Enoteca della Valpolicella**. Not merely a wine bar, but a fine country restaurant in a 15th-century farm complex. Closed Mon and midday Sat. Via Osan 45, Fumane, T: 045 683 9146.

€ **Alla Ruota**. Carefully prepared local specialities, served on a large scenic terrace in summer. Closed Mon evening and Tues (except in summer). Via Proale 6, Località Mazzano, Negrar, T: 045 752 5605.

WINE BARS

Verona

€ **Brigliadoro**. *Osteria*, wine bar and wine shop all rolled into one. Closed Sun and in Aug. Via San Michele alla Porta 4, T: 045 800 4514.

€ **Enolibreria Calmierino**. In Veronetta, the quarter of Verona across the Adige; simple meals and fine wines. Closed Sun and in Aug. Via San Nazaro 27, T: 045 803 0575.

€ **Enoteca Cangrande**. Wine bar and shop established by a group of well known Veronese winemakers. Closed Mon and in Jan. Via Dietro Listone 19d, T: 045 595 022.

€ **Enoteca Segreta**. *Osteria* and wine shop with a good selection of Veronese delicacies. Closed Wed. Vicolo Samaritana 10, T: 045 801 5824.

FESTIVALS & MARKETS

Daily markets in Piazza Erbe; Tues and Fri in Piazza San Zeno; Tues in Piazza Isolo (near the Roman theatre); Wed and Fri in Piazza Santa Toscana (Porta Vescovo); Fri in Piazza degli Arditi (Volto San Luca). A market with bric-à-brac and artisans' ware is held on the third Sat of the month at San Zeno. *Settimana Cinematografica Internazionale*, film festival, April; *Benvenuti a Verona* Monday evening concert series, July–Aug. *Concerti Scaligeri* international acoustic music festival, July–Sept. *Estate Teatrale Veronese* drama at the Roman theatre, June–Sept; information T: 045 807 7500, www.estateteatraleveronese.it; tickets T: 045 806 6485; *Stagione Lirica* opera at the Arena, July–Aug; information and tickets from Fondazione Arena di Verona, Via Dietro Anfiteatro, 6b, T: 045 800 5151, www.arena.it

Annual festivals include the *Festa di Santa Lucia*, with a street market in Piazza Brà and Via Roma from around 10–12 Dec. Carnival celebrations, which have been held in the town since the 16th century, culminate on the Fri before Shrove Tuesday (*Venerdì Gnocolar*). 12 April is the festival of the patron saint, Zeno.

VICENZA & ENVIRONS

Vicenza is a thriving provincial capital at the confluence of two mountain torrents, the Retrone and the Bacchiglione, at the foot of the Colli Berici. It flourished under Venetian rule, which began in 1404, and although it did not achieve the greatness of its neighbours, Verona and Padua, it experienced a period of splendour during the 16th century that was reflected in a vast building programme. The many fine buildings by the town's favourite son, Andrea Palladio, have given the city centre a noble, Classical aspect and an unmistakable elegance.

The environs of Vicenza are studded with magnificent Renaissance villas, many of which were designed by Palladio. There are also charming towns, such as Bassano del Grappa, Marostica, Schio and Asiago, in the foothills of the Alps.

NB: This chapter is covered by the map on p. 328.

EXPLORING VICENZA

Vicenza's ancient Roman street plan is clearly recognisable, structured along the monumental Corso Palladio (the Roman *decumanus maximus*) and around Piazza dei Signori (probably the ancient forum), both of which are now distinguished by the creations of Palladio. Central Vicenza is really quite small, and can be visited comfortably in a couple of hours.

Corso Palladio and its palaces

The 11th-century **Porta Castello**, the west gate of the city, is the most conspicuous remainder of the town walls. It is adjoined by a shady garden, with a 16th-century loggia on a small canal. Just inside the gate, in Piazza Castello, stand the Palazzo Piovini (1656–58) and Palazzo Porto Breganze, begun by Vincenzo Scamozzi to a design by Palladio (c. 1600) and never finished.

Here begins the magnificent **Corso Andrea Palladio**, the main street of the city centre, lined with monumental palaces and churches dating from the 14th–18th centuries. The corner house, Palazzo Bonin Thiene (no. 13), was designed by Palladio, continued by Vincenzo Scamozzi and, like the Palazzo Porto Breganze, left incomplete; the Renaissance Palazzo Capra-Clementi (no. 45) dates from the late 15th century. Nos 47 and 67 are 15th-century Venetian Gothic houses.

The first important cross street, Corso Fogazzaro, is flanked by more fine palaces. Turn left: on the right (no. 16) stand the splendid Palazzo Valmarana-Braga (1566), a remodelling by Palladio of an earlier building; and further on on the left, the Palazzo Repeta, now the Banca d'Italia, by Francesco Muttoni (1711). The latter fronts onto Piazza San Lorenzo, which takes its name from the simple Franciscan church erected in the 13th century. The single-gabled façade has an elaborately carved doorway of 1344 set against a tall, blind arcade and flanked by monumental tombs. The three-aisled interior with polygonal apses is entirely Gothic in flavour and contains the Poiana Altar, with a delicate relief (1474), and a detached fresco of the *Beheading of St Paul* by Bartolomeo Montagna (1450–1523), famed as the greatest artist of his day, and who produced his best work in Vicenza. The cenotaph of architect Vincenzo Scamozzi (d. 1616) is also here. In the north aisle is the door to the cloister (1492), where some sculptural fragments are displayed.

Around the duomo

Dating from the 14th–16th centuries, Vicenza's cathedral has a coloured-marble façade designed in 1467 by Domenico da Venezia, a stout Romanesque campanile on a Roman foundation, a Gothic lateral doorway, another attributed to Palladio, and a large Renaissance tribune begun in 1482 and finished nearly a century later. The interior, a single broad aisle with tall lancet arches and a high, vaulted ceiling, contains a number of fine artworks, notably Lorenzo Veneziano's polyptych of the *Dormitio Virginis* (fifth south altar, 1356), a gold-ground altarpiece of considerable primitive charm showing the sleeping Virgin. 'Gold-ground' describes a medieval technique whereby a panel is first primed with a glue-and-gypsum mixture and covered with gold leaf, which then forms the backdrop to the painting. There are also an *Adoration of the Magi* by Francesco Maffei (third south altar), and a *Madonna* by Bartolomeo Montagna (fourth north altar). The adjoining Neoclassical bishop's palace has a splendid Renaissance portico, known as the Loggia Zeno, in the courtyard. On the south side of the square is the entrance to the Criptoportico Romano (*open Sat 10–11.30, or by appointment, T: 0444 321 716*), probably part of a 1st-century Roman house.

Back in Corso Palladio, the **Galleria d'Arte Municipale**, displaying canvases by local painters of the 16th and 17th centuries, occupies the restored 16th-century church of Santi Giacomo e Filippo, set back from the street. Vincenzo Scamozzi's masterpiece is no. 98, the Palazzo del Comune, originally a private palace (designed 1592, completed 1662), with a doorway flanked by Ionic columns and a large arched window at the centre of the middle floor. Four symmetrical atria lead into the solemn rectangular courtyard; within are rooms with 17th- and 18th-century decorations.

Piazza dei Signori

Piazza dei Signori is the centre of civic life. The south side of the square is occupied by the **Basilica**, or Palazzo della Ragione, Vicenza's most important monument and one of the finest buildings of the Venetian Renaissance, created by Palladio after 1549. In essence he created a transparent involucre that encircles a pre-existent Gothic construction, built in the latter half of the 15th century. A double order of porticoes and *logge*, carried by Tuscan Doric columns on the ground floor and Ionic columns on the floor above, frames rounded arches and is crowned by a balustrade with statues. The huge interior hall (*open Tues–Sat 9.30–12 & 2.15–5, Sun and holidays 9–12.30*) is covered by a ship's-keel vault and lighted by 24 ogival windows opening onto the *logge*.

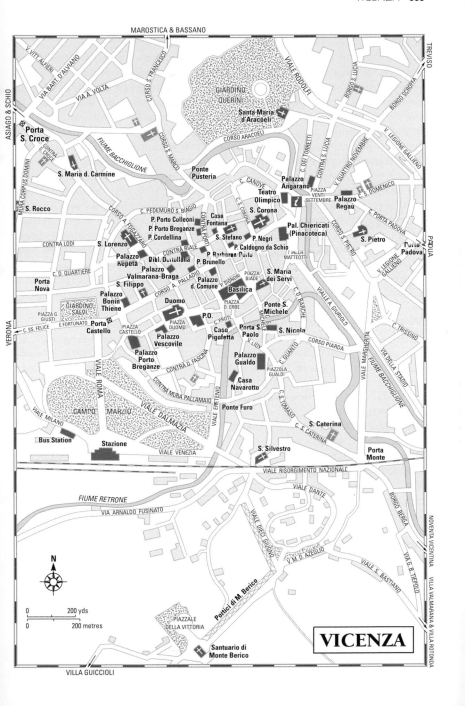

MAROSTICA & BASSANO

TREVISO

ASIAGO & SCHIO

V. VITT. ALFIERI
VIA BART. D'ALVIANO
VIA A. VOLTA
CORSO S. FRANCESCO
VIALE RODOLFI
BORGO S. LUCIA
BORGO SCROFFA

GIARDINO QUERINI

Santa Maria d'Aracoeli

Porta S. Croce

CONTRÀ S. CROCE
FIUME BACCHIGLIONE
CORSO S. MARCO
CORSO ARACOELI

V. LEGIONE GALLIENO

S. Maria d. Carmine

C. CANOVE
Palazzo Angarano
PIAZZA VENTI SETTEMBRE
CONTRÀ S. LUCIA
V. QUATTRO NOVEMBRE

MURA CORPUS DOMINI

S. Rocco

CORSO A. FOGAZZARO
C. PEDEMURO S. BIAGIO

Teatro Olimpico
S. Corona
i
C. S. DOMENICO

Palazzo Regaù
C. S. PORTA PADOVA

CONTRÀ LODI

S. Lorenzo

P. Porto Colleoni
P. Porto Breganze
P. Cordellina
Casa Fontana
C. CORONA
CONTRÀ PORTI

S. Stefano
P. Negri
Pal. Chiericati (Pinacoteca)

CORSO S. PIETRO
S. Pietro
Porta Padova

PADUA

C. D. QUARTIERE

Palazzo Repeta
Bibl. Bertoliana
CONTRÀ RIALE
P. Caldogno da Schio
PIAZZA MATTEOTTI

Palazzo Valmarana-Braga
P. Barbaran Porto
CORSO A. PALLADIO
P. Brunello
V. LEGIONE GALLIENO

Porta Nova

S. Filippo
Palazzo d. Comune
P. SIGNORI
PIAZZA BIADE
S. Maria dei Servi
C. TRISSINO

Palazzo Bonin Thiene
Duomo
Basilica
VIALE A. GIURIOLO
C. D. BARCHE
VIALE MARGHERITA

PIAZZA G. GIUSTI
GIARDINO SALVI
E FORTUNATO
C. SS. FELICE

Duomo
PIAZZA D. ERBE
Ponte S. Michele
VIALE BACCHIGLIONE
VIA DELLA STADIO

VERONA

Porta Castello
PIAZZA CASTELLO
PIAZZA DUOMO
P.O.
C. PROTI
Porta S. Paolo
S. Nicola
CORSO PIARDA

Palazzo Vescovile
Casa Pigafetta
C. GUANTO
PIAZZOLA GUALDI

Palazzo Porto Breganze
CONTRÀ D. FASCINA
V. LIOY
Palazzo Gualdo

VIALE ROMA

Casa Navarotto

VIALE DALMAZIA
CONTRÀ MURA PALLAMAIO
VIALE ERETENIO
Ponte Furo
C. S. TOMASO
S. Caterina
C. S. CATERINA

CAMPO MARZIO

Bus Station
Stazione
VIALE VENEZIA

S. Silvestro
Porta Monte

VIALE MILANO

VIALE RISORGIMENTO NAZIONALE

FIUME RETRONE
VIA ARNALDO FUSINATO
VIALE DANTE
BORGO BERGA

NOVENTA VICENTINA

N

VIALE DIECI GIUGNO
V. M. D. AZEGLIO
VIALE S. BASTIANO
VIA G. B. TIEPOLO

VILLA VALMARANA & VILLA ROTONDA

0   200 yds
0   200 metres

Portici di M. Berico

PIAZZALE DELLA VITTORIA

Santuario di Monte Berico

VILLA GUICCIOLI

VICENZA

Across the square stands the **Loggia del Capitaniato** (or Loggia Bernarda), which Palladio designed in 1571, when construction on the basilica was well underway. Once the residence of the military commander, it has immense, engaged Corinthian columns rising from the pavement to the attic level and framing the tall arches of the ground-floor portico as well as the windows and balconies of the floor above. The roofline is marked by a trabeation and balcony, behind which the discreetly low, set-back attic can be glimpsed. On the same side of the square, across the street from the Loggia, is the Renaissance **Monte di Pietà** (1499). It incorporates the church of **San Vincenzo**, which was built a century and a quarter later than the palace proper, and shows a lively Baroque face with two tiers of arcades and locally-made sculptures. The complex stands in the shadow of the **Torre di Piazza**, a slender campanile begun in the 12th century and completed in the 14th, rising 82m above the pavement and ending in a fine Gothic belfry with mullioned windows and dome. Below, two columns, surmounted by the Lion of St Mark and Christ the Redeemer, and respectively dating from 1520 and 1640, separate Piazza dei Signori from the adjoining Piazza delle Biade, where the 15th-century church of **Santa Maria dei Servi** presents a curious façade of 1710 incorporating the original Renaissance doorway. Inside is an *Enthroned Madonna* by Benedetto Montagna, son and pupil of Bartolomeo.

Away from the Corso

The square on the south side of the basilica, the narrow **Piazza delle Erbe**, is a marketplace, packed with colourful stalls and thronged with shoppers on weekday mornings. As though to ensure that the difference in symbolic value between the two squares is understood, the humble Piazza delle Erbe lies on a lower level than its grandiose counterpart. The outstanding buildings here are the medieval Torre del Girone or (del Tormento), and the late-15th-century Arco del Registro.

Continuing southwards, just before the bridge over the River Retrone you come to the birthplace (Via Pigafetta 9) of Antonio Pigafetta, the navigator who accompanied Magellan on his first trip around the world (1519–22), and whose journals may have inspired *Gulliver's Travels*. It is a graceful Gothic mansion with a small façade delicately adorned with spiral columns. On the other side of the Retrone, here little more than a creek, stands **San Nicola da Tolentino**, a 17th-century oratory with elaborate stuccoes framing canvases by Vicenza-born Francesco Maffei (who also did the *Trinity* over the altar) and painters of the Venetian school Giulio Carpioni and Antonio Zanchi. The **Ponte San Michele**, of 1623, offers a good view over the city centre.

Contrà Porti and its palaces

Contrà Porti, another street running north from Corso Palladio, is flanked by superb palaces. Here are, at no. 6–10, Palazzo Cavalloni-Thiene, a 15th-century Venetian Gothic building; and at no. 11, the majestic Palazzo Barbaran da Porto, by Palladio (1571). The **Centro Internazionale di Studi di Architettura Andrea Palladio** here (*open Tues–Sun 10–6*) hosts temporary exhibitions regarding the architect and his times. Across the street is no. 12, Palazzo Thiene, with a main façade and terracotta doorway attributed to Lorenzo da Bologna (1489), and a courtyard and rear façade (1550–58) designed by Palladio; further along the street you reach, at no. 14, the Gothic Palazzo Trissino-Sperotti (1450–60); at no. 17 the Palazzo Porto-Breganze, a Venetian Gothic building of 1481 with a fine Renaissance doorway and porticoed courtyard; at no. 16 the Renaissance Palazzo Porto-Fontana; at no. 19 the magnificent, early-14th-century Palazzo Porto-Colleoni, the oldest Venetian Gothic house on the street; and at no. 21 the unfinished Palazzo Iseppo da Porto, by Palladio (1552).

Now go around the block to the east and return by Contrà Zanella. No. 2 is the Palazzo Sesso Zen Fontana: its large, mullioned windows are unusual in Vicentine Gothic architecture. No. 1, at the corner of Piazzetta Santo Stefano, is the crenellated Palazzo Negri De Salvi, a 15th-century Renaissance mansion. Beyond the Baroque church of **Santo Stefano** (where there is a tabernacle decorated by Giandomenico Tiepolo on the high altar, and a *Madonna and Child with Saints* by Palma Vecchio in the north transept), is Palladio's rear façade of Palazzo Thiene.

Back in Corso Palladio you soon reach the Palazzo Caldogno da Schio (no. 147), also called Ca' d'Oro, a gem of Venetian Gothic architecture with fine mullioned windows and round-arched Renaissance doorway. Its design is attributed to Lorenzo da Bologna, who also worked on the Santa Corona (*see below*); in the atrium are architectural fragments and antique inscriptions. No. 165–67 is the Casa Cogollo, a house once attributed to Palladio, with a late-Renaissance façade of 1559–62, possibly by Giovanni Antonio Fasolo.

Santa Corona

The most magnificent religious building in town is the Dominican monastic church of **Santa Corona**, built in the 13th century, given a new transept and apse in the 15th, and further refined over the following centuries. The single-gabled façade has Gothic windows, including a large rose window. Inside, the sense of space is Romanesque; the verticality, Gothic; and the harmony of the easternmost areas, Renaissance. The deep, raised Renaissance sanctuary was laid out in 1489 by Lorenzo da Bologna. The crypt is entered through the Cappella Valmarana, designed by Palladio. Above, the 17th-century high altar and 15th-century choir stalls bear beautiful inlay work. Among the many altarpieces are two genuine masterpieces: Paolo Veronese's *Adoration of the Magi* (1573; third south altar) and Giovanni Bellini's magnificent *Baptism of Christ* (c. 1502; fifth north altar), the latter set in a monumental architectural frame of 1501. The third altar on this side has a *St Anthony* by Leandro Bassano; the second, a *Magdalen and Saints* by Bartolomeo Montagna. The church takes its name from a thorn of the Crown of Christ, donated by St Louis of France and shown on Good Friday.

On the other side of Contrà Santa Corona is **Palazzo Leoni Montanari** (*open Fri–Sun 10–6*), now owned by Banca Intesa, which has carefully restored it. The building was begun in the late 17th century and has interesting architectural elements (some of which were added in 1808). The interior, with 18th-century decorations (frescoes by Giuseppe Alberti and Louis Dorigny), and Neoclassical elements, includes the elaborate Baroque Galleria della Verità and a loggia profusely decorated with stuccoes. In one room are displayed seven paintings by Pietro Longhi (and seven by his school) from the 19th-century collection of Giuseppe Salom. The top floor holds a superb collection of Russian icons, ranging in date from the Middle Ages to the 19th century. This is perhaps the largest and most complete collection of its kind in Western Europe; it is beautifully displayed and well labelled in Italian and English.

Piazza Matteotti: Palladian highlights

Piazza Matteotti lies to the east of the old city nucleus, just on the banks of the Bacchiglione. On the north side of the square, in a garden surmounted by a crenellated medieval tower, stands the **Teatro Olimpico**, Palladio's last work, completed in 1584 by Scamozzi (*open Tues–Sun 9–5; summer 10–5*). It was built for the Accademia Olimpica, founded in 1555, of which Palladio was a member and which produced numerous plays. The opening play, given in 1585, was Sophocles' *Oedipus Rex*.

A corridor leads from the entrance to the Odeon, the meeting place of the Accademia degli Olimpici, realised by Scamozzi in 1608, with a magnificent wooden ceiling and walls frescoed by Francesco Maffei. The Antiodeon, also with a wooden ceiling, follows; from here you enter the theatre proper. This is made of wood and stucco, and takes up the forms of the theatres of Classical antiquity described by Vitruvius. It has a cavea of 13 semi-elliptical tiers ending in a Corinthian colonnade crowned by an attic. The Classical *frons scenae*, built in wood and stucco, its architecture derived from ancient Roman buildings, has niches with statues of academicians and reliefs of the *Labours of Hercules*. Scamozzi designed the magnificent, two-storeyed fixed backdrop, populated by statues (95 in all) and presenting spectacular architectural views of seven streets, supposedly of the ancient city of Thebes.

The majestic **Palazzo Chiericati** (now home to the Pinacoteca) was designed by Palladio in 1550–57, and stands alone on the west side of the square, without the spatial limitations of adjoining buildings—which left the architect free to design a double portico, Doric below and Ionic above, closed in the central part of the upper level by a wall with rectangular windows. The luminous, elegant solution of the façade finds an ideal complement in the spatial definition of the courtyard and of the ground-floor rooms, decorated with frescoes by Domenico Ricci (Il Brusasorci) and Giovanni Battista Zelotti (who also frescoed the Villa Foscari, *see p. 474*), and with stuccoes by Bartolomeo Ridolfi, who frequently collaborated with Palladio.

The building is home to the **Pinacoteca** (*open Tues–Sun 9–5*), displaying mainly Venetian painting of the 16th–18th centuries, by Cima da Conegliano, Bartolomeo Montagna (*Madonna and Child with Saints*), Paolo Veronese (*Madonna and Child with Saints*), Jacopo Tintoretto, Jacopo Bassano, Francesco Maffei, Sebastiano and Marco Ricci, Pietro Muttoni, Giuseppe Zais, Giovanni Battista Tiepolo (*Time Revealing Truth*) and Piazzetta. Among the artists of other schools are Memling (*Crucifixion*) and van Dyck (*The Three Ages of Man*). The museum also possesses a precious collection of drawings by Andrea Palladio, the Neri Pozza Collection of contemporary painting, and a small but valuable selection of Renaissance sculptures.

Andrea Palladio (1508–80)
Andrea di Pietro della Gondola, better known as Palladio, designed villas, palaces and churches throughout the Veneto in a Classical style that would profoundly change the face of the region and inspire numerous imitations. His *Quattro Libri*, or *Four Books on Architecture*, became a manual for later architects, especially in England and the United States. In the engraved illustrations for this treatise, Palladio noted the significant dimensions of his buildings, linking together their plan, section and elevation in a series of proportional relationships. The seemingly easy elegance that distinguishes Palladio's designs was, in fact, the result of his careful calculation of such proportional relationships. In applying these systems of numerical progression, which were often associated with contemporary musical harmonic theory, to the spatial relationships of a building, Palladio succeeded in creating the pleasing visual harmonies that characterise his architecture.

The province of Vicenza is particularly rich in villas of the famous *ville venete* type. These were built from the 15th century onwards by rich noble Venetian families who were anxious to invest in land on the *terraferma* and contribute to its fertility by the construction of canals and irrigation systems. In the early 16th century Palladio invented an architecture peculiarly fitted to these prestigious villas, which he saw both as places of repose and as working farms. He derived their design in part from the villas of the ancient Romans and used Classical features in their construction. He took particular care in the siting of his villas, sometimes on low hills or near canals, and almost always surrounded by gardens and farmland. The outbuildings, known as *barchesse*, were often porticoed.

Numerous villas by Palladio survive in the province. In the 17th and 18th centuries many more villas were constructed, some of these particularly interesting for their interiors and frescoes (including some by Tiepolo and his son Giandomenico). Architects of importance who succeeded Palladio include Vincenzo Scamozzi, Antonio Pizzocaro, Francesco Muttoni and Giorgio Massari. Orazio Marinali was responsible for the statuary in many of the gardens.

The Santuario di Monte Berico

Easily reached on foot from the centre of town, the Santuario is a popular point of pilgrimage in a panoramic position south of the city centre, to which it is connected by a long portico (Viale X Giugno) designed by the 18th-century architect Francesco Muttoni. The church (1668–1703), the work of Carlo Borella, has three symmetrical Baroque façades with 42 statues by Orazio Marinali. The stout campanile dates from the early 19th century. The Greek-cross interior (*open Mon–Sat 7–12 & 2.30–6 or 7, Sun and holidays 7–1 & 2.30 or 3.30–6 or 7*) conserves, in its eastern part, the primitive sanctuary of 1428, which legend holds was traced out by the Virgin Mary who appeared to a woman of the people. Among the votive decorations are a venerated statue of the Virgin, of 1430, and a splendid painting of the *Pietà* by Bartolomeo

Montagna. A 15th-century cloister precedes the refectory, in which is set the large painting of the *Supper of St Gregory the Great* by Veronese (1572).

Piazzale della Vittoria beside the church, built as a memorial of the First World War, commands a magnificent view of Vicenza and of the mountains that once marked the front line. Viale X Giugno continues to the Villa Guiccioli, built at the end of the 18th century, with a beautiful park (*open 1 Apr–30 Sept, Tues–Sun 9–7.30*).

Villa Valmarana and Villa Rotonda

NB: The Vicenza Card, available at most museums, gives reduced admission to museums and palaces in Vicenza and the villas on the outskirts of town.

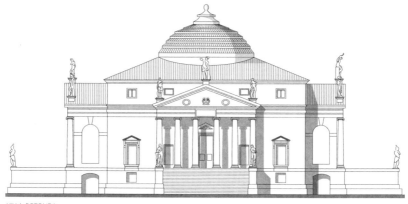

VILLA ROTONDA

Viale d'Azeglio and Via San Bastiano (*marked on the map*) wind southeast to two spectacular villas. The **Villa Valmarana ai Nani** (*open Mar–Nov Wed–Thur, Sat–Sun 10–12 and all afternoons except Mon, Mar–Apr 2.30–5.30; May–Sept 3–6; Oct–Nov 2–5*), attributed to Francesco Antonio Muttoni, has a panoramic terrace overlooking the sanctuary of Monte Berico. Five rooms of the villa are decorated with frescoes by Giovanni Battista Tiepolo (1757), inspired by classical poems (*Iliad, Aeneid, Orlando Furioso, Gerusalemme Liberata*); the guest-house is frescoed with scenes of country life by Giandomenico Tiepolo, Giovanni Battista's son.

The stony path (Stradella Valmarana) on the right beyond the villa continues downhill to the equally famous Villa Capra Valmarana, better known as **La Rotonda** (*open Mar–Nov: admission to the garden Tues–Thur 10–12 & 3–6; other days usually on request; to the interior, Wed only, 10–12 & 3–6; T: 0444 321 793*). La Rotonda was built as a belvedere for Paolo Almerico. In his *Four Books on Architecture*, Palladio writes of it thus: 'Its situation is as advantageous and delicious as can be desired, being seated on a hillock of a most easy ascent'. The villa itself has a central plan consisting of a circular core within a cube. The four Classical porticoes complete its symmetry. Crowned with a remarkable low dome, its design is reminiscent of the Pantheon in

Rome. Begun c. 1551 by Palladio, it was taken over at his death by Vincenzo Scamozzi and finished in 1606 for the Capra family. The Villa Rotonda had a profound influence on the history of architecture and was copied in numerous buildings, including Chiswick House, London. The domed central hall was frescoed at the end of the 17th century by Louis Dorigny, and the piano nobile was painted by Anselmo Canera, Bernardino India and Alessandro Maganza. The *barchessa* (service wing) was designed by Vincenzo Scamozzi.

To get back into town, follow Via Rotonda to the bottom of the hill (200m), and take bus no. 8. From Villa Valmarana, Via Giovanni Battista Tiepolo descends to the Porta Monte, just above which is a charming little arch attributed to Palladio and dated 1595. Bus no. 8 runs back along the main road into Vicenza.

VILLAS OUTSIDE VICENZA

The names of the villas change with each new owner, but they generally also carry the name of the original proprietor. They are scattered widely over the province, often in remote areas outside small towns (where available, street addresses have been given in the description below to help with their location, as signposting is generally poor). The villas are often privately owned, and many of the interiors are closed to the public (except with special permission), but the exteriors and gardens are often their most important features. Opening times change frequently and accessibility varies; it is therefore advisable to consult the information office in Vicenza (*see p. 368*) before starting a tour, or to ring the villa for confirmation of opening times. Concerts are organised in some of the villas in July. The most important villas (but by no means all of them) are listed below by geographical area: the outskirts of Vicenza; east of Vicenza; south and west of Vicenza; north of Vicenza.

The outskirts of Vicenza

Cricoli
Villa Trissino Trettenero. Designed (1531–38) by Palladio's first patron, Gian Giorgio Trissino. Palladio probably worked here as a young artist. The exterior can be viewed by appointment. *Strada Marostica 6; T: 0444 922 122.*
Bertesina
Villa Gazzotti Grimani Curti. Built by Palladio (1542–43). *Via San Cristoforo 73; T: 0444 504 674. Open by appointment daily 9–12 & 2.30–6.30.*
Villa Negri Ceroni Feriani. Built in

1709, perhaps by Carlo Borella, in Palladian style, with a park and garden. *Strada di Ospedaletto 148; T: 0444 504 136. Closed for restoration.* **Villa Marcello Curti**. *Via San Cristoforo 23; T: 0444 504 674. Open by appointment;* **Villa Ghislanzoni Curti**. Built in 1764. *Via San Cristoforo 73; T: 0444 504 674. Open by appointment.* **Villa Piovene Pigatti**. Lovely garden. *Strada di Casale 432; T: 0444 913 039. Open winter 2–5; summer 2–6 or by appointment.*

Northeast of Vicenza

Monticello Conte Otto
Villa Valmarana Bressan. Begun in
1541 by Palladio, it is an austere building with a typical Palladian entrance.
There is no evidence to suggest that this
village directly influenced Jefferson's
choice of the name Monticello for his
own home in Virginia, but Jefferson certainly owned Palladio's *Four Books on
Architecture*, and considered it his 'Bible'.
*Via Vigardoletto 31; T: 0444 596 242.
Open daily 9–12 & 2–6.*

Quinto Vicentino
Villa Thiene. Another work by Palladio
(c. 1546, left unfinished). *Via IV
Novembre 41; T: 0444 584 224. Open
Mon–Sat 9.30–12.30, Mon and Thur also
5.30–7.*

Bolzano Vicentino
Villa Valmarana Zen. Built in 1570 to a
Palladian design, with numerous statues
in the garden and a pretty little chapel.
*Via Ponte 1, Località Lisiera; T: 0444 356
920. Open by appointment.*

South and west of Vicenza

Altavilla Vicentina
Villa Valmarana-Morosini. Built by
Francesco Muttoni in 1724; restored by
the university. *Via Marconi 103; T: 0444
333 736. Gardens open Wed–Thur
2.30–5.30; interior by appointment.*

Near Monteviale
Villa Loschi Zileri Motterle. Attributed
to Francesco Muttoni and Muttonio
Massari, surrounded by a fine park with
exotic trees. The staircase and *salone*
have the earliest frescoes by Tiepolo
(1734) outside Venice. *Via Zileri 1,
Località Biront. Open by appointment; T:
0444 570 141.*

Costabissara
Villa Bissari Curti. Reconstructed in
the 19th century. It has a loggia attributed to Ottone Calderari, and a garden
with antique fragments and an
amphitheatre. *T: 0444 971 031. Closed
for restoration.*

Montecchio Maggiore
This picturesque village and legendary
stronghold of the 'Montagues' of *Romeo
and Juliet*, has two restored Scaliger castles. Just outside is the **Villa Cordellina
Lombardi**. Built by Giorgio Massari
(1735), it has very fine frescoes (1743)
by Giovanni Battista Tiepolo in the central hall (restored in 1984). *Via Lovara
36, open Apr–Oct Tues–Fri 9–1, Sat, Sun
and holidays 9–1, 3–6; T: 0444 399 111.*

Castelgomberto
Villa Piovene da Schio. Built in 1666,
probably by Antonio Pizzocaro (chapel
of 1614); it has 18th-century additions
and is surrounded by a garden with statues by the workshop of Marinali. Inside
are three early works by Giovanni
Battista Tiepolo. *Via Villa 121, T: 0445
940 052. Viewing by appointment,
Apr–Sept Sat 9–12.*

Montorso Vicentino
Villa da Porta Barbaran. Dates from
1724, with an Ionic pronaos and a pretty Ionic *barchessa*.

Sarego
Villa da Porta 'La Favorita'. Built by
Francesco Muttoni (1714–15). *Località
Monticello di Fara; T: 0444 421 202. Open
daily by appointment.*

Lonigo
Town hall in **Palazzo Pisani**, a very
grand mansion of 1557. On the outskirts stands the **Rocca**, or **Villa Pisani**
(1576), a charming work by Vincenzo
Scamozzi (recalling Palladio's Villa
Rotonda). *Via Rocca 1, T: 0444 831 625.*
Visits 1 Apr–4 Nov by appointment.
Bagnolo
Villa Pisani Ferri Bonetti. A beautiful
villa, one of Palladio's earlier creations,
built in 1542. The main entrance has
rusticated arches beneath a pediment,
and the villa is surrounded by farm
buildings. *Via Risaie 1; T: 0444 831 104
Open daily 1 Apr–4 Nov by appointment.*
Orgiano
Villa Fracanzan Piovene. Built in 1710
and attributed to Francesco Muttoni,
with an interesting garden (and *barchessa*). *Via San Francesco 2; T: 0444 874
589. Open March–Nov for guided tours on
Sun and holidays 3–7; otherwise by
appointment.*
Near Agugliaro
Villa Saraceno. Begun by Palladio
between 1545 and 1555, and surrounded by farm buildings. Acquired by the
Landmark Trust of Great Britain, it was
beautifully restored in 1988–94. *Open 1
Apr–31 Oct on Wed at 2–4; at other times
by appointment; T: 0444 891 371.* **Villa
Saraceno delle Trombe**. Designed in
1550 by Sanmicheli. *Via Finale 10; T:
0444 891 084. Open Wed 9–12 & 2–4.*
Pojana Maggiore
Villa Pojana. Built in 1555 by Palladio,
with a typical Palladian arch over the
entrance. It has contemporary frescoes
by Bernardino India and Anselmo
Canera and stuccoes by Bartolomeo
Ridolfi. The frescoes in the atrium are
attributed to Giovanni Battista Zelotti.

*Via Castello, T: 0444 898 554. Open
Apr–Sept Tues–Sun 10–12.30 & 2–7,
Oct–May 10–12.30 & 2–5.*
Mossano
Villa Pigafetta Camerini. A charming
late-17th-century building attributed to
Antonio Pizzocaro. The *barchesse* and
chapel may be by Francesco Muttoni.
*Via Montruglio 9; T: 0444 886 838. Open
May–Oct, weekdays by appointment.*
Longare
Villa Trento-Carli. Built in 1645, it is
attributed to Antonio Pizzocaro. *Via Nino
Bixio 8; T: 0444 510 499. Open Apr–Oct
Sun 3–6, or by appointment.* **Villa da
Schio**. Three buildings on a hillside sur-
rounded by a lovely garden with sculp-
tures by Orazio Marinali. The Villino
Garzadori here, built into the hillside in
1690, has frescoes by Louis Dorigny.
*Piazza Da Schio 4; T: 0444 555 099. Park
open Tues–Sun 9.30–12.30 & 3–7.*
Vancimuglio
Villa Chiericati da Porto Rigo. Built in
1554, almost certainly by Palladio (but
left unfinished), with an Ionic portico.
*Via Nazionale 1; T: 0444 387 076. Open
last Wed of every month 8–10 or by
appointment.*
Grisignano di Zocco
Villa Ferramosca-Beggiato. Designed
by Gian Domenico Scamozzi around
1568. *Via Vittorio Veneto, Località
Barbano; T: 347 775 0587. Open by
appointment.*
Montegalda
Castello Grimani Sorlini. A 12th-cen-
tury castle adapted as a villa in the 18th
century, with a fine park. *Via Castello 21;
T: 030 601 031. Open by appointment.*
Colzè
Villa Colzè Feriani. Rebuilt in the 17th
century, with a chapel containing sculp-

tures by Orazio Marinali.
Montegaldella
Villa Conti Campagnolo. Called *La*

Deliziosa (built 17th century, altered in the 19th). Its garden is decorated with statues by Orazio Marinali.

North of Vicenza

Caldogno
Villa Caldogno Nordera. Built in 1570, attributed to Palladio, with frescoes by Fasolo, Zelotti and Giulio Carpioni. *Via Pagello 2; T: 0444 905 054, 0444 585 385. Open March–Oct Fri 3–6, Sat 9–12.*
Villaverla
Villa Verlato. Built in 1576 by Vincenzo Scamozzi, with frescoes by Girolamo Pisano and Giovanni Battista Maganza. *Piazza del Popolo 1; T: 348 351 9260. Open by appointment.* **Villa Ghellini.** Built in 1664–79 by Antonio Pizzocaro. *Via Sant'Antonio 6; T: 348 351 9260. Open Mon–Sat 10–12 & 3–5 or 4–6.*
Thiene
Castello Porto Colleoni Thiene. A late-Gothic Venetian castle perhaps begun by Domenico da Venezia and completed in 1476. It has frescoes by Fasolo and Zelotti, a charming contemporary chapel, and a stable block attributed to Francesco Muttoni. *Via Garibaldi 2; T: 041 380 879. Open for guided tours March–Nov on Sun and holidays at 3, 4 and 5, or by appointment.* **Villa Beregan Cunico.** Long, low façade and portal attributed to Pizzocaro. *T: 0445 380 944. Open Wed and Sat 9–12.30 & 3–5.*
Lonedo di Lugo
Villa Godi Malinverni. One of the earlier known works by Palladio (1540–42). The piano nobile was frescoed in the 16th century by Battista dal Moro and Giovanni Battista Zelotti. A wing of the palace has a representative collection of 19th-century Italian paintings. *Via*

Palladio 44; T: 0445 860 561. Open March–May and Oct–Nov 2–6; June–Sept 3–7. **Villa Piovene Porto Godi.** A Palladian core altered in the 18th century by Francesco Muttoni. It is surrounded by a park designed by Antonio Piovene. *Via Palladio 51; T: 0445 860 613. Open daily 2.30–7.30 or by appointment.*
Breganze
Villa Diedo Basso. Built 1664–84, with additions. Breganze is known for its wines (including the justly famous Maculan Fratte, a red made from Cabernet and Merlot grapes grown on the sunny slopes to the north) which can be purchased at the beautiful modern Maculan Cellars in the village.
Dueville
Villa Da Porto Casarotto. Built by Ottone Calderari in 1770–76. *Via Da Porto 89; T: 0444 590 709. Open daily for guided tours.* **Villa Da Porto del Conte.** Built to a Palladian design but remodelled in 1855. The town hall occupies **Villa Monza**, built in 1715, probably by Francesco Muttoni. *Piazza Monza 1; T: 0444 367 324. Open Mon–Fri 9.30–1.*
Sandrigo
Villa Sesso Schiavo Nardone. Built by a follower of Palladio in 1570, with contemporary frescoes. *Via San Lorenzo 5; T: 0444 659 344. Open by appointment.*
Longa di Schiavon
Villa Chiericati Lambert. Built in 1590 (altered in the 19th century); with 16th-century frescoes attributed to Pozzoserrato.

BASSANO DEL GRAPPA

Situated where the Brenta River emerges from the hills, Bassano is a pleasant town of arcaded streets and old houses, many of which have frescoed façades. It was home to a family of well-known painters—the da Ponte, called Bassano after this, their birth-place (*see box*). The Austrians were defeated here by Napoleon in 1796, and by the Italians in 1917–18. The city suffered severe damage in the latter campaign, which was fought on nearby Monte Grappa; but this and the flourishing of small industries have done little to mar the integrity of the city centre, which is still one of the finest in the region. There is a strong tradition here in wrought iron and ceramics. Bassano is known also for its asparagus and porcini mushrooms—and of course for its grappa, the best in Italy.

THE BASSANO FAMILY

There were four main members in this prominent family of Venetian painters. Francesco da Ponte the Elder (c. 1475–1539) worked in Bassano and painted in a rustic style, using soft colours like those of the Bellini. His son Jacopo (c. 1510/18–1592) the most famous of the family, rose to prominence in late-Renaissance and early-Baroque Venice. His religious paintings, lush landscapes, and scenes of everyday life show the influence of fashionable contemporaries such as Parmigianino. A pioneer of the genre scene and one of the first painters to be interested in peasants and animals, his Biblical characters are represented as real yokels, and he often pays more loving attention to the ox and the ass than to the human characters. Jacopo had four painter sons: Francesco, Gerolamo, Giovanni Battista and Leandro. Leandro and Francesco achieved fame and some fortune in Venice. Leandro was even given a noble title by the doge. Francesco worked a lot with his father, but his life ended in tragedy: he threw himself to his death from a top floor window at the age of 44.

The town centre

The northernmost part of the historic centre, including the 15th-century cathedral (with paintings by the Bassano), stands inside the walled complex of the Castello Superiore, which dates as far back as 900–950 but was enlarged and fortified in the 13th, 14th and subsequent centuries. A tower of the old fortress serves as the base of the campanile. The area to the south of this, occupied in part by the 14th-century Castello Inferiore, developed around three adjacent squares, Piazza Garibaldi, Piazza Libertà, and Piazzetta Monte Vecchio

In Piazza Garibaldi stands the former Franciscan church of **San Francesco**, a Romanesque-Gothic building with an elegant vestibule of 1306 and a graceful cam-panile. It conserves remains of 15th-century frescoes and, in the apse, a painted wooden crucifix of the 14th century. A door on the right of the porch leads to the Museo Civico. This museum (*open Tues–Sat 9–6.30, Sun and holidays 3.30–6.30*), housed in the former Franciscan friary, in the beautiful 17th-century cloister (partly rebuilt), has a collection of Roman and medieval inscriptions and another of ceramics. The archaeological section includes protohistoric material of the Angarano culture (11th century BC); Greek, Italiot and Roman finds; and antique coins. The print and drawing cabinet (with works by Vittore Carpaccio, Lorenzo Lotto, Gian Lorenzo Bernini, Giovanni Battista Tiepolo, Francesco Guardi and Antonio Canova) is famous for the Remondini collection of 17th–19th-century popular prints.

On the first floor is the picture gallery, with paintings by Jacopo Bassano (*Flight into Egypt; Baptism of St Lucilla; St Martin and the Beggar*), Francesco and Leandro Bassano, Michele Giambono and Guariento; and numerous works from the 17th and 18th centuries by Francesco Maffei, Marco Ricci, Giovanni Battista Tiepolo, Pietro Longhi and Alessandro Magnasco. The last rooms are dedicated to Antonio Canova (casts and models); to painters of the 19th century; and to Tito Gobbi (1913–84), the great baritone, who was born in Bassano.

From Piazza Libertà to the river

Piazza Libertà, near Piazza Garibaldi, has the Loggia del Commune (1582) with a fresco of *St Christopher* ascribed to Jacopo Bassano, and two 18th-century buildings, the Palazzo del Municipio and the church of San Giovanni Battista.

Piazzetta Monte Vecchio, which was the main square of the city in the Middle Ages, is lined with fine old frescoed palaces, most notably the 15th-century Palazzetto del Monte di Pietà, with inscriptions and coats of arms on the façade. The square leads down to the **Ponte Vecchio** or Ponte degli Alpini, a famous covered wooden bridge across the picturesque River Brenta, which retains the form designed for it by Palladio in 1569. The river is subject to sudden floods, and the bridge has had to be rebuilt many times: it has been proved over the centuries that only a wooden structure (rather than stone) can survive the force of the water. There is a lovely view of the mountains upstream from the bridge, and the houses on the riverfront are well preserved. Beside the bridge is a characteristic little wine bar, with a grappa distillery of 1769 (there is a private museum in the nearby Poli distillery illustrating the production of grappa, *open daily 9–7.30*). The bridge is named after the Alpini regiment, who crossed it numerous times during the campaigns on Monte Grappa and above Asiago in the First World War. The regiment was also responsible for its reconstruction after the last war (small museum in the Taverna al Ponte, Via Angarano 2, *open Tues–Sun 8.30–8*). The best view of the bridge is from the other side, from a lane which leads left beside a little garden on the banks of the river.

Also on the river (south bank) is the lovely 18th-century Palazzo Sturm, which houses the **Museo della Ceramica**, part of the Museo Civico (*open Apr–Oct Tues–Sat 9–12.30 & 3.30–6.30, Sun and holidays 3.30–6.30; June–Sept Sun 10–12.30; Nov–March Fri 9–12.30, Sat–Sun 3.30–6.30*). The entrance is through the attractive Neoclassical courtyard overlooking the river. The entrance hall (1765) has frescoes by Giorgio

Bassano del Grappa.

Anselmi. The collection of ceramics illustrates the production of local manufactories, including Manardi ware, made here in the 17th century, and later pieces from Nove and Faenza. Beyond a belvedere (now enclosed) overlooking the river is the delightful little boudoir, which preserves its original Rococo decoration intact (after careful restoration), including very fine stuccowork.

Villas in the environs of Bassano

On the outskirts of Bassano, at Sant'Eusebio, is the **Villa Bianchi Michiel**, built in the late 17th century by Domenico Margutti, perhaps to a design by Longhena, the great Venetian Baroque architect. It has two wings with Doric porticoes (*not open*).

A road leads northeast out of Bassano to **Romano d'Ezzelino**, with the 17th-century Villa Corner, with an orangery by Vincenzo Scamozzi. Nearby is **Mussolente**, with the Villa Negri Piovene on a low hill approached by a flight of steps from the Asolo road, and flanked by two porticoes.

To the south of Bassano is the **Villa Rezzonico Borella**, reminiscent of a medieval castle, built in the early 18th century and attributed as an early work to Longhena. It has a fine park and garden (Via Ca' Rezzonico 66, *open Feb–Oct Mon 9–1, Sat 9–2*). At **Rosà** is the late-17th-century Villa Dolfin-Boldù (*visitors admitted to the park*). **Rossano Veneto** has two 18th-century villas. On the Brenta at **Cartigliano** is the eccentric, unfinished Villa Morosini Cappello (now the town hall). It was begun in 1560 probably by the engineer Francesco Zamberlan, who was a friend and collaborator of Palladio, and is best known for La Rotonda at Rovigo (*see p. 480*). The remarkable Ionic loggia which surrounds the building may have been added in the 17th century (*open Mon–Fri 9–1, Sat 9–12, Wed 4.30–6.30*). In the parish church, the Chapel of the Rosary is decorated with frescoes (1575) by Jacopo Bassano and his son Francesco, and has an altarpiece by Bartolomeo Montagna.

Marostica

Marostica, a stronghold of the Ezzelini in the 12th–13th centuries, was rebuilt in 1311–86 by the Scaligeri. It came under Venetian control in 1404 and remained faithful to the Republic from then onwards. Today it is a charming old fortified townlet preserving its medieval ramparts, which connect the lower castle on the piazza with the upper castle on the green hillside above. It has a particularly pleasant climate, and excellent cherries are grown in the surroundings. It is also known for its straw hats. Its biennial chess game with human combatants has become a famous spectacle (*see box*). The delightful Piazza Castello, with the stone chessboard on which the chess game is played, has a superb view of the ramparts climbing the green hillside to the upper castle. The battlemented Castello Inferiore (*open daily 10–12 & 2.30–6*) in the piazza was built by the Scaligeri in the early 14th century and restored in 1935. There are a beautiful well and an ancient ivy in the courtyard; stairs lead up to the loggia with a catapult reconstructed in 1923. The Sala del Consiglio was frescoed in the 17th century. Chessboards are provided for the public at the other end of the piazza, in a loggia beneath a bank building (matches are often played here at weekends).

THE PARTITA

A chess game (*Partita a Scacchi*) in which the whole town participates takes place every two years (even years) on a Friday, Saturday and Sunday evening in early September. The tradition commemorates a duel fought in 1454 between Rinaldo d'Angarano (black) and Vieri da Vallonara (white) for the hand of Lionora, daughter of Taddeo Parisio, the local Venetian governor. Vieri won the first match, and white still wins every game today, although a different game from the history of chess is chosen to be re-enacted each year. The herald who conducts the event speaks in Venetian dialect. At the end of the game the wedding takes place, with some 500 participants in 15th-century costume—flag-throwers, drummers, medieval musicians and a host of attendants. The game is held at 9pm (also at 5pm on the last day) and tickets should be bought by June. In odd years, when the 'players' are sent abroad to perform the game, an international chess festival is held in the town. *Information from the Associazione Pro Marostica, Piazza Castello 1, T: 0424 72127.*

Via Sant'Antonio leads past the church of **Sant'Antonio**, which contains an altarpiece by Jacopo Bassano and his son Francesco (1574), to the 17th-century church of the Carmine. A path leads up the green hillside to the **Castello Superiore**, also built by the Scaligeri, but ruined by the Venetians in the 16th century (it can also be reached by road).

Near Marostica, at **San Luca di Crosara**, the parish church has an early work (c. 1537) by Jacopo Bassano. South of the town is **Nove**, known for its ceramics. The Antonibon family were active here from 1727 producing majolica and porcelain, examples of which you can see in the **Museo Civico in Palazzo De Fabris** (*open Tues–Thur 4–6, winter 3–5; Fri–Sun 10–12.30 & 4–7, winter 3–6*). The collection is particularly representative of ceramics from the Veneto from the 18th century onwards. There is also a ceramics museum in the Istituto Statale d'Arte per la Ceramica (founded in 1875), with a chronological display of ceramics produced in Nove from the beginning of the 18th century to the present day.

The Altopiano dei Sette Comuni

Bassano and Marostica lie at the foot of the Altopiano dei Sette Comuni—a plateau c. 1000m above sea level that takes its name from seven townships (Asiago, Enego, Foza, Gallio, Lusiana, Roana and Rotzo), united from 1310–1807 in an autonomous federation. The inhabitants of the plateau are of Germanic origin (the Cimbri) and the area is now both a winter and summer resort.

Asiago, near the centre of the plateau, was the scene of bitter fighting in the First World War (1916–18); a monumental war cemetery (1932–38) has the remains of 33,086 Italian and 18,505 Austro-Hungarian dead. Near Asiago is an important astrophysical observatory, administered by Padua University, which includes the largest telescope in Italy (built in 1973). The pretty old railway line (closed down in 1958) from Asiago south to Cogollo can be followed on foot. Asiago is the centre of the area producing the cheese to which it gives its name.

Recoaro Terme is a spa with ferruginous springs discovered in 1689 (beneficial to liver, intestine and kidney complaints), with hotels of all categories. A cable car ascends to the ski resort of Recoaro Mille (1021m). Near Tunkelwald, in the *comune* of Roana, 1,000 inscriptions were found on a rock wall 40m long and 7m high; you can still see animal and human figures, cross-shaped and geometric forms, fertility symbols, representations of the sun, etc. The protohistoric village of Bostel is situated at **Castelletto di Rotzo** and is considered the first human settlement on the Altopiano.

On the other side of the lovely Valle del Posina is **Tonezza del Cimone**, a mountainous plateau (1000–1500m) with fine walks. **Schio** has a long industrial tradition rooted in its wool manufactories. It has a good 15th–16th-century church (San Francesco) and an ossuary-cloister on the Asiago road, with 5,000 graves of soldiers who fell in 1915–18.

PRACTICAL INFORMATION

GETTING AROUND

• **By rail:** Most trains on the main Venice–Milan line stop at Vicenza, from which there are frequent country bus services to outlying points. Intercity, Eurocity and Eurostar trains connect with Venice, Trieste, Verona, Milan, Turin and Genoa; and with Trento, Bolzano and Bressanone. There are branch railways from Vicenza to Schio, Bassano del Grappa (via Cittadella) and Treviso (via Cittadella and Castelfranco Veneto). At Castelfranco you can connect to Belluno, Pieve di Cadore and Cortina d'Ampezzo; and from Bassano del Grappa to Trento.
• **By bus:** City buses will take you to the Santuario di Monte Berico on Sun and holidays (bus no. 18) from Viale Roma, near the train station. The Villa Valmarana is reached in c. 15mins by bus no. 8 from Viale Roma (direction

Noventa Vicentina) to Borgo Berga (request stop at Via Tiepolo, 500m below the villa); it continues along the Viale Riviera Berica to another request stop at the foot of Via della Rotonda, 200m below Villa Rotonda. If you intend to visit both villas (and not the basilica) it is best to take bus no. 8 to the stop below Villa Rotonda, and from there walk back to Villa Valmarana.

Country buses run by FTV (Ferrovie e Tramvie Vicentine, T: 0444 223115) and AIM (Aziende Industriali Municipali, T: 0444 394909) for places in the province.
• **Taxis:** Radio Taxi (24 hours a day), T: 0444 920 600; taxi stand at Piazzale Stazione.

INFORMATION OFFICES

Vicenza Piazza dei Signori 8, T: 0444 544 122; Piazza Matteotti 12, T: 0444

320 854, www.vicenza.com
Asiago Via Stazione 5, T: 0424 462
221.
Bassano del Grappa Largo Corona
d'Italia 35, T: 0424 524 351.
Recoaro Terme Via Roma 25, T: 0445
75070.

HOTELS

Vicenza

€€ **Campo Marzio**. A quiet place in
the large public garden between the train
station and Corso Palladio. Viale Roma
21, T: 0444 545 700,
www.hotelcampomarzio.com
€ **Cristina**. A family-run hotel at the
edge of the city centre, just outside Porta
Giusti. Closed Dec–Jan. Corso Santi
Felice e Fortunato 32, T: 0444 323751,
www.paginegialle.it/hotelcristinavicenza

Arcugnano

€€ **Villa Michelangelo**. In the Colli
Berici, a splendid 18th-century villa and
garden. Via Sacco 35, T: 0444 550 300,
www.hotelvillamichelangelo.com

Bassano del Grappa

€€ **Ca' Sette**. An 18th-century villa
with contemporary interiors and a fine
restaurant. Via Cunizza da Romano 4, T:
0424 383 350, www.ca-sette.it

Carrè

€€ **Locanda La Corte dei Galli**. Just
seven rooms on an ancient Venetian
estate, with elegant charm, antiques and
a small indoor pool. Via Prà Secco 1a, T:
0445 893 333, lacortedeigalli@tiscali.it

Gazzo Padovano

€€ **Villa Tacchi**. Magnificent 17th-cen-
tury villa with excellent restaurant, in a
shady park. Via Dante 11, Località
Villata Ovest, T: 049 942 6111,
www.antichedimore.com

Mussolente

€€ **Villa Palma**. A lovely villa (20
rooms), with an excellent restaurant. Via
Chemin Palma 30, T: 0424 577 407,
www.villapalma.it
€ **Volpara**. Small and quiet, with good
restaurant. Via Volpara 3, T: 0423 567
766, www.volpara.com

Rosà

€ **La Dolfinella**. Seven quiet, comfortable rooms on a working farm. Via
Ronaclli 1, T: 0424 582 440, F: 0424
587 833.

Sarcedo

€€ **Relais Casa Belmonte**. Exquisite
country estate with just four tasteful
rooms, in the hills near Vicenza. Via
Belmonte 2, T: 0445 884 833,
www.casabelmonte.com

YOUTH HOSTELS

Vicenza

€ **Olimpico**, Viale Giuriolo 9, T: 0444
540 222, ostello.vicenza@tin.it

Asiago

€ **Ekar**, Via Ekar 2–5, T: 0424 455138,
ostelloechar@tiscalinet.it

RESTAURANTS

Vicenza

€€€ **Cinzia e Valerio**. Seafood restaurant generally considered the best place
in town. Closed Mon, Jan and Aug.
Piazzetta Porta Padova 65/67, T: 0444
505 213.
€€ **Antica Trattoria Trevisi**. Trattoria
in an aristocratic palace of the 15th century, serving Vicentine specialities with
regional and Italian wines; closed Sun
evening, Mon and July. Contrà Porti 6, T:
0444 324 868.

€€ **Scudo di Francia**. Just a few steps from the Basilica, offering classical Vicentine cuisine. Closed Sun evening, Mon, Dec–Jan and Aug. Contrà Piancoli 4, T: 0444 323 322.

€ **Da Remo**. A converted farmhouse with garden seating in summer, serving regional dishes. Closed Sun evening, Mon, Aug and Dec–Jan. Via Caimpenta 14, Caimpenta (2km east), T: 0444 911 007.

€ **Tinello**. A renovated train station provides the setting for a popular restaurant serving local delicacies with regional and Italian wines; closed Sun evening, Mon and Aug. Corso Padova 181, T: 0444 500 325.

Altissimo
€€ **Casin del Gamba**. Regional cuisine and wines well worth the trip. Closed Sun evening, Mon, Jan and Aug. Strada per Castelvecchio, T: 0444 687 709.

Arcugnano
€€ **Da Zamboni**. Simple but good trattoria. Closed Mon, Tues, and late July–early Aug. Via Santa Croce 14, Località Lapio, T: 0444 273 079.

Asiago
€€ **Tre Fonti**. Friendly *osteria* offering creative interpretations of traditional dishes and great wines. Closed Mon, midday Tues and in Aug. Via Rovelieri 16, T: 0424 462 601.

Bassano del Grappa
€€ **Ostario al Borgo**. One restaurant run by two chefs—who know their business. Closed Wed, midday Sat and in May and Oct. Via Margnan 7, T: 0424 522 155.

€ **Bauto**. An inexpensive place with a great deal of rustic charm, run by the same family since 1917. Closed Sun and in Aug. Via Trozzetti 27, T: 0424 34696.

Breganze
€ **La Cusinetta**. Good seasonal cuisine in a simple trattoria. Closed Mon and July. Via Pieve 19, T: 0445 873 658.

Lonigo
€€€ **La Peca**. Truly outstanding creative cooking, in a refined setting in the Vicentine hills. Closed Sun evening (also mid-day, in July), Mon, Jan and Aug. Via Principe Giovanelli 2, T: 0444 830 214.

Lusiana
€€ **Valle dei Molini**. Exceptional regional food and wines between Vicenza and Lugo Vicentina. Closed Tues and mid-day Wed, Dec–Jan and Aug. Via Valle di Sopra 11, Località Valle di Sopra, T: 0424 407 372.

Montecchia di Crosara
€€ **La Terrazza**. Astonishingly good fish restaurant considering the location (in the hills between Vicenza and Verona) with summer seating on a panoramic terrace. Closed Sun evening and Mon, Jan and Aug. Via Cesari 1, T: 045 745 0940.

Montecchio Precalcino
€€ **La Locanda di Piero**. Traditional Venetian cuisine with a delicious creative twist. Closed Sun, midday Sat and Mon, and in Mar and Nov. Via Roma 32, T: 0445 864 827.

Monticello Conte Otto
€€ **Al Giardinetto**. Simple restaurant with an outstanding wine list, in a beautiful garden. Closed Sun evening and Mon. Via Roi 71, T: 0444 595 044.

Mussolente
€ **Volpara**. Simple Venetian cooking with fresh local ingredients. Via Volpara 3, T: 0424 577 019.

Sarcedo
€ **Villa di Bodo**. Delicious innovative interpretations of traditional cuisine, on

a beautiful old farm with outside seating in summer; closed Monday. Via San Pietro 1, T: 0445 344 506.
Trissino
€€ **Ca' Masieri** (with rooms). An 18th-century manor house with excellent traditional cuisine and summer seating outdoors; closed Sun and midday Mon. Località Masieri, T: 0445 962 100, www. camasieri.com
Valdagno
€ **Hostaria a le Bele**. Good food and friendly service at a former coach stop along the road from Valdagno to Recoaro. Closed Mon, midday Tues and Jan–Feb. Via Maso 11, Località Maso, T: 0445 970 270.

WINE BARS & CAFÉS

Vicenza The best wine bar is **Bere Alto** in Contrà San Biagio, though there are numerous others. For coffee and pastries, try **Pasticceria Sorarù**, Piazza dei Signori and **Offelleria della Meneghina**, Contrà Cavour.
Bassano del Grappa A good wine bar is **Breda**, at Vicolo Iacopo da Ponte 3. For coffee try **Nardini** and **Taverna degli Alpini** at either end of the Ponte Vecchio, and **Danieli** by the Museo Civico.
Breganze For an excellent wine bar in a historic setting, go to **La Ciacola**, at Via Marconi 8. (Closed Mon.)
Marostica For wine try **Osteria alla Madonnetta** in Piazza Castello.

REGIONAL SPECIALITIES

Keep an eye open for Bassano grappa, Marostica cherries, and Colli Berici extra-virgin olive oil and DOC wines. There is also interesting jewellery, and ceramics from Bassano are locally renowned.
Vicenza Markets in Piazza dei Signori and Piazza Duomo on Thur.
Bassano del Grappa Markets Thur and Sat in the two piazzas.

FESTIVALS & EVENTS

There are carnival celebrations and patron saints' feast days with processions and festivities throughout the area. *Cantine Aperte*, weekend of wine-tastings at area estates, May. *Concerti in Villa*, classical music concerts in many of the Vicentine villas, June–July.
Vicenza *Viva il Cabaret*, cabaret festival, Apr–May. *Il Suono dell'Olimpico*, classical music at the Teatro Olimpico, May–June. *Estate Show*, open-air music, dance, theatre and cinema at sites throughout the city, June–Sept. *Festival d'Autunno*, classical theatre festival at the Teatro Olimpico, Sept. *Vicenza Danza*, dance festival with performances at various sites around the town, Oct–Dec.
Bassano del Grappa *Concerti di Pasqua*, classical music, Easter. *Minimondo*, collectables fair, May. Alpine Choral Festival, May. Organ Music Festival, Oct. *Fiera d'Autunno*, autumn fair on the weekend after the first Thur of Oct. Opera Festival, Nov–Dec.
Breganze Wine Festival, with presentation and tasting of new wines, May. *Teatro in Corte*, theatre festival, June–July.
Lonigo Horse Show, Aug.
Marostica *Umoristi a Marostica*, comic-strip and cartoon exhibition, April–May. Cherry Fair, May. *Partita a Scacchi*, early Sept.
Thiene *Thienedanza*, dance festival, April. Cabaret Festival, Nov–Feb.

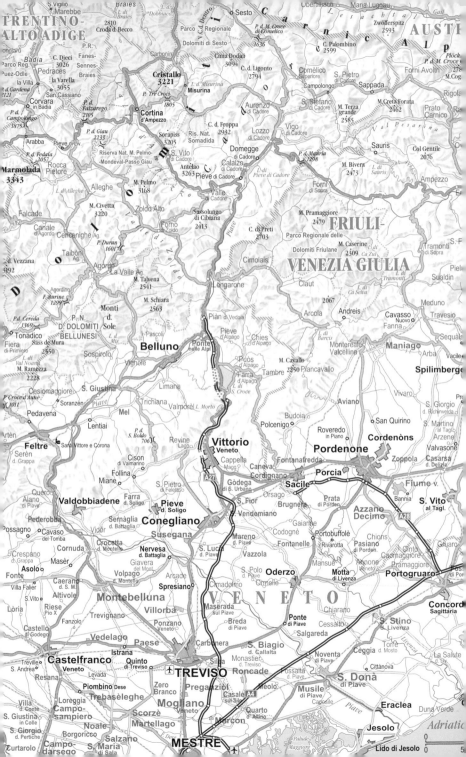

TREVISO & THE NORTHERN VENETO

North of Venice begin the Prealpi, the foothills of the Alps, sprinkled with beautiful old towns and imposing villas and castles where noble Venetians sought respite from the summer heat. The air is crisp and fragrant with mountain breezes in spring and autumn, noticeably lighter than that of Venice, even in summer. The capital of the area is Treviso, a lively town whose nearness to Venice (less than half an hour by train) causes most visitors to overlook it—a genuine shame. Further north are the lovely towns of Castelfranco and Asolo, and the alpine centres of Feltre and Belluno.

TREVISO

A city of porticoed streets and fine old houses situated at the confluence of two rivers, Treviso is known for its medieval atmosphere and for the picturesque canals that flow through and around the old centre, giving the town its nickname, 'Little Venice'.

HISTORY OF TREVISO

Although a palaeo-Venetic settlement and a Roman *municipium*, called Tarvisium, existed on more or less the same area the old city occupies today, Treviso reached its greatest prosperity in the Middle Ages. It was the centre of a Lombard duchy, then the capital of a Carolingian *marca*, or frontier buffer zone, a free commune, a seigniory and, after 1389, a part of the Venetian Republic. Old prints showing Treviso as a fortified city bear witness to the importance that Venetian military planners gave to its strategic location, on the northwestern border of their republic. The town walls were considered impenetrable, and their impression of fortitude was enhanced by the fact that they were pierced by just three gates: Porta Altinia, Porta Santi Quaranta and Porta San Tomaso. Only the 18th-century agricultural revolution and construction of patrician residences in the countryside to the north, brought expansion outside the walls.

In the Middle Ages, Treviso was well known for its hospitality to poets and artists, especially under the dominion of the da Camino family (1283–1312). Today the city has the best works of Tommaso da Modena (*see p. 376*). Unfortunately, little else remains of its medieval past: during both world wars it suffered severely from air raids, notably on Good Friday 1944, when half the city was destroyed in a few minutes.

Piazza dei Signori

This has been the political and social centre of the city since Roman times, and its graceful palaces were built in the 13th century on the site of the Roman forum. The most important is the Palazzo dei Trecento on the east side of the square, named after the 300 members of the Greater Council. It was built in 1210 and has a ground-floor loggia of 1552 on the main façade. An external staircase and another 16th-century loggia grace the flank facing Piazza Indipendenza. On the north side of the square is the **Palazzo del Podestà** (now the Prefecture), surmounted by the Torre Civica, which the Trevisans call *Il Campanon* (the Big Bell). Both were rebuilt in the 19th century in a Gothic-revival style. Next door is the Palazzo Pretorio, with a rusticated façade of the 17th century.

In a little square behind these buildings is the **Monte di Pietà** (*open Fri 9–12*), which incorporates the 16th-century Cappella dei Rettori, a small chapel with gilt-leather wall coverings of the 17th century, frescoes and canvases, and a fine ceiling. On your right as you return are Santa Lucia and San Vito, two adjoining churches of medieval origin. The more interesting is **Santa Lucia**, a 14th-century building containing frescoes by Tommaso da Modena and his school (*Madonna delle Carceri*), and 14th- and 15th-century sculptures, notably busts of saints on the balustrade. **San Vito**, built in the 11th and 12th century and rebuilt in 1568, conserves a Byzantine-Romanesque fresco of the 12th or 13th centuries depicting *Christ among the Apostles*.

The cathedral

Views of considerable charm are offered along the Via Calmaggiore, the street that links Piazza dei Signori with Piazza del Duomo. The street is lined with 15th- and 16th-century townhouses, many with porticoes and frescoed façades. Just before meeting Piazza del Duomo it passes (left) the church of **San Giovanni**, or baptistery, a Romanesque building of the late 11th and early-12th centuries with pilaster strips, small blind arches, a 14th-century relief on the gable, Roman-age friezes at the sides of the doorway and, within, some fresco fragments of the 12th–14th centuries in the apses. Behind rises the massive 11th- and 12th-century campanile, unfinished at the top.

The **cathedral of San Pietro** was founded in the late 12th or early 13th century, but its present form has little in common with the original church. The apses were rebuilt in the 15th and 16th centuries to a design by Pietro Lombardo, the central structure was altered in the 18th century, and the façade with its Ionic hexastyle porch was added in 1836.

The three-aisled interior, covered by seven lead-and-copper domes, contains an *Adoration of the Shepherds* by Paris Bordone, a statue of *St John the Baptist* by Alessandro Vittoria and a marble relief of the *Annunciation* by Lorenzo Bregno (or Antonio Lombardo). The Cappella dell'Annunziata, at the end of the south aisle, was built to a design by Martino Lombardo in 1519 for the Malchiostro family. In the vestibule are several sculptures, notably an *Adoration of the Shepherds* and *St Lawrence and Saints* by Paris Bordone and a *Madonna and Child with Saints* (the *Madonna of the Flower*) by Girolamo da Treviso il Vecchio. Titian's splendid *Annunciation* hangs over the altar, and the walls have frescoes by Giovanni Antonio Pordenone and assistants, notably the *Adoration of the Magi* (1520). In the sanctuary, designed by Pietro Lombardo and his

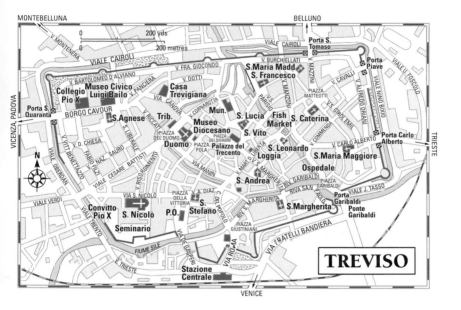

sons, are frescoes by Lodovico Seitz (1880); the tomb of Pope Alexander VIII (d. 1691), with a remarkable portrait-statue by Giovanni Bonazza; the monument to Bishop Giovanni Zanetto by Pietro, Antonio and Tullio Lombardo; and, above the altar, the Urn of Sts Teonisto, Tabra and Tabrata, with carved portraits attributed to Tullio Lombardo. In the Cappella del Santissimo Sacramento (in the north; 1513) are more Renaissance sculptures, by Pietro and Tullio Lombardo and Lorenzo Bregno. Beneath the sanctuary extends the 12th- and 13th-century Romanesque crypt, with mosaic pavement fragments and remains of frescoes. The capitals on the columns were taken from earlier buildings.

Flanking the cathedral is the Bishop's Palace, built in the 12th and 13th centuries and later altered, with a large hall frescoed by Benedetto Calieri. From Piazza Duomo, Via Canoniche leads under an arch to a circular Roman mosaic, an early-Christian work of the early 4th century AD, probably belonging to a baptistery.

Treviso museums

Museo Civico Luigi Bailo

Borgo Cavour 24. Open Tues–Sat 9–12 & 2–5, Sun and holidays 9–12.
The picture gallery contains paintings, frescoes, and statues of the 12th–20th centuries, with works by Giovanni Bellini (*Madonna*), Cima da Conegliano, Girolamo da Treviso, Girolamo da Santacroce, Titian (*Portrait of Sperone Speroni*), Lorenzo Lotto (the famous *Portrait of a Dominican*), Jacopo Bassano (*Crucifixion*), Govanni Antonio da Pordenone, Francesco Guardi (*View of the Isle of San Giorgio*), Giandomenico Tiepolo, Pietro Longhi and Rosalba Carriera (three portraits). There are also 19th-cen-

tury works by Francesco Hayez and Antonio Canova, and sculptures and drawings by the 20th-century Trevisan artist Arturo Martini. A section of the museum housed in the former Gothic church of Santa Caterina dei Servi contains a fragmentary *Madonna* by Gentile da Fabriano and an important cycle of detached frescoes by Tommaso da Modena. Tommaso (c. 1325–79) was an important follower of Giotto, and one of the leading artists of his day in northern Italy. His reputation was such that work was commissioned from him by the emperor Charles IV in Bohemia. The museum also owns the prisms with which Isaac Newton made his experiments with the refraction of light, and which passed into the hands of his disciple Count Algarotti.

Museo Diocesano di Arte Sacra
Via Canoniche 9. Open Mon–Thur 9–12; Sat 9–12 & 3–6.
Located in the restored Canoniche Vecchie, the collection includes paintings, sculpture and liturgical items. Highlights include the Arca del Beato Enrico, acquired by the commune in 1315; several marble reliefs from the cathedral (notably a 13th-century *Enthroned Christ*); a detached fresco by Tommaso da Modena, and tapestries and objects from the cathedral treasury.

Casa Trevigiana
Via Canova 38.
Occupying the Casa da Noal, a 15th-century Gothic mansion, it contains medieval and Renaissance marbles and terracottas, wood sculptures of the 15th–18th centuries, furniture, ceramics, wrought iron, weapons, and antique prints and musical instruments, shown on a rotating basis.

San Nicolò
From the Museo Bailo it is a short walk southwards to the 14th-century Dominican church of **San Nicolò**, with a fine rose window and doorway on the façade, slender windows on the flanks and three tall polygonal apses. The vast three-aisled interior, with a beautiful ship's-keel ceiling, has frescoes by Tommaso da Modena and his school on the columns and other paintings ranging from the 16th to the 18th century. In the south chapels are a finely carved altar of Lombardesque workmanship, a large fresco of *St Christopher* attributed to Antonio da Treviso (1410), and a 16th-century organ by Gaetano Callido with shutters painted by Antonio Palma. In the apse are a *Sacra Conversazione* begun by Fra' Marco Pensaben and completed by Giovan Gerolamo Savoldo (1521), a 17th-century memorial to St Benedict XI (Nicolò Bocassino, 1240–1303, born in Treviso and the founder of the church) and (left) the 16th-century tomb of Agostino Onigo, incorporating a fresco of pages attributed to Lorenzo Lotto.

Next to the church is the former convent of San Nicolò, now the Seminario Vescovile (*open 8–12.30 & 3.30–5.30 or 7*). The complex is connected by cloisters to the 14th-century chapter house, which is decorated with charmingly realistic frescoes (1352) of 40 eminent Dominicans by Tommaso da Modena. The Abbot of Cluny wears the first pictorially documented pair of eyeglasses.

The northern quarters

In Via Martiri della Libertà, leading northeast from the Corso dei Popolo, is the **Loggia dei Cavalieri**, a Romanesque building of 1195. Near San Leonardo, beyond remains of an old watermill beneath a modern building, is the picturesque fish market on an island in the Cagnan. Via San Parisio continues left to **San Francesco**, a large brick church of the 13th century. In the floor near the south door is the tomb slab of Francesca, daughter of Petrarch, who died in childbirth in 1384; in the north transept that of Pietro Alighieri (d. 1364), the son of Dante; and in the chapel to the left of the high altar is a fresco by Tommaso da Modena (1351).

The deconsecrated church of **Santa Caterina** (*open Tues–Sun 9–12.30 & 2.30–6*) stands a little to the east of the fish market. It contains fine frescoes by Tommaso da Modena, including some detached in 1882 from a church before its demolition (*Virgin Annunciate* and *Story of the Life of St Ursula*).

Via Carlo Alberto leads to **Santa Maria Maggiore**, a church of 1474 containing a tomb by Bambaia and a much-venerated *Madonna* originally frescoed by Tommaso da Modena. The lovely Riviera Garibaldi, which runs alongside the Sile—and is faintly reminiscent of Amsterdam—returns towards the centre.

ENVIRONS OF TREVISO

The Valley of the Piave

East of the city runs the Piave, a river famous as the line of Italian resistance after the retreat from Caporetto in 1917–18. At **Fossalta di Piave**, Ernest Hemingway, as a member of the US Red Cross, was wounded in 1918 at the age of 19 (the episode is described in *A Farewell to Arms*). A memorial stele was set up here in 1979.

Eraclea, a modern village on east bank of the river, has taken the name of the ancient Heraclea (named after Emperor Heraclius), the episcopal and administrative centre of the Venetian lagoon in the 7th–8th centuries after the sack of Oderzo by the Lombards. The site of the ancient city, near Cittànova, has been identified by aerial photography. It was formerly surrounded by a lagoon, and it recalls Venice in plan, with a central canal and many smaller canals. From 750 onwards the inhabitants migrated to the safer islands of Malamocco and Rialto, and a leader from Heraclea is thought to have become the first Doge of Venice. Heraclea rapidly declined as its lagoon silted up and Venice grew in importance.

Caorle is an ancient fishing village and now a seaside resort near the mouth of the Livenza. Founded by refugees from Concordia (*see p. 524*), it was a bishop's see for 12 centuries and has a cathedral of 1048 with a celebrated Venetian pala of gilded silver. To the north is a beautiful lagoon with fishing huts and interesting wildlife.

Castelfranco Veneto

Castelfranco Veneto is west of Treviso. According to a medieval chronicle, anyone who settled in this castello was freed (*affrancato*) of all fiscal obligations. The town was founded by the commune of Treviso in 1199 to defend its western frontier, and a rectangular fortification with five towers and brick walls and doorways, encircled by a moat (the castello proper), still encloses its centre. Throughout the town are small porticoed palaces, some of them frescoed. The sky, the clouds, and green fields of the environs are those of Giorgione (c. 1476–1510) who was born and began to paint here. His famous altarpiece of the *Madonna and Child with Sts Francis and Liberale* (c. 1505) is in the Palladian-style **cathedral** (San Liberale), in the south apsidal chapel. Also in the cathedral, in the sacristy, are works by Palma Giovane and Jacopo Bassano and early frescoes by Paolo Veronese (*Allegorical Figures*, 1551) brought from the destroyed Villa Soranza. The cathedral's campanile is one of the towers of the defensive walls.

Adjoining the piazza, to the east, is the 15th-century **Casa di Giorgione** (or Casa Pellizzari), where Giorgione lived and worked (he painted the chiaroscuro decorative band, with symbols of the liberal and mechanical arts, in one room). Inside are reproductions of his works.

Outside the walls are the old market square (now Piazza Giorgione), lined with 16th–18th-century townhouses, some with frescoed façades; the church of Santa Maria della Pieve (founded in the 11th century, but rebuilt 1821–25, with a Corinthian porch); and the Villa Revedin-Bolasco (built in 1607 by Vincenzo Scamozzi, but remodelled in the 19th century), surrounded by a large park with an open amphitheatre decorated with statues by Orazio Marinali.

Villas around Castelfranco

Istrana
Villa Lattes. 18th-century villa now part of the Museo Civico of Treviso. Has a collection of furniture, Oriental art, musical boxes and 19th-century dolls. *Open March–Nov, Tues and Fri 9–12, Sat–Sun and holidays 9–12 & 3–6.*

Sant'Andrea
Villa Corner (now Chiminelli). Has frescoes of the school of Veronese. *Open by appointment. T: 0424 525 103.*

Fanzolo di Vedelago
Small farm town known for the splendid **Villa Emo** (c. 1564), one of Palladio's masterpieces. The central building, preceded by a wide, stepped ramp, has a monumental porch with seven Doric columns surmounted by triangular pediments. At the sides are two long, symmetrical *barchesse* terminating in the little towers of the dovecotes. The interior is frescoed with mythological scenes by Giovanni Battista Zelotti, possibly with the help of Paolo Veronese. *Open in daylight-saving months daily 3–7, Sun and holidays also 10–12.30; in other months, Sat–Sun and holidays 2–6; T: 0423 476 334.*

Piombino Dese
Villa Cornaro. By Palladio (1560–70). *Open May–Sept Sat 3.30–6.*

Treville
Remains of the **Villa Priuli Gran Can** (1530) and **Villa Priuli San Felice**, by Vincenzo Scamozzi.

ASOLO

Called 'City of a Hundred Horizons' and 'Pearl of the Veneto', Asolo is a charming little town with numerous private villas surrounded by luxuriant gardens and picturesque old streets with miniature arcades and a number of fountains. The town was presented by Venice to Queen Caterina Cornaro in exchange for her dominions of Cyprus, and she lived in the castle here from 1489 to 1509. From the name of this town Cardinal Bembo (who frequented Queen Catherine's court) coined the term '*asolare*' (to spend time in amiable aimlessness), from which is derived *Asolando*, the name chosen by Robert Browning 'for love of the place' for his last volume of poems (1899). Browning's first visit to Asolo was in 1836, and it is the scene of *Pippa Passes*, published five years later. The actress Eleonora Duse (1850–1924), and Browning's son, Pen (1849–1912) are both buried at Asolo in the cemetery of Sant'Anna. Dame Freya Stark (1893–1993), the traveller and writer, lived here for most of her life. Other eminent visitors to Asolo include Henry James, Ernest Hemingway, Arnold Schoenberg and contemporary architect Carlo Scarpa.

Impressions of Asolo

I assure you that, even though I have knowledge of and have seen with my own eyes the most beautiful panoramas in Italy and elsewhere, I have found nothing quite like the view one can enjoy from the tower of the Queen's palace.

Robert Browning

I love Asolo because it is so beautiful and peaceful, a town full of fine lace and poetry.

Eleonora Duse

Neither San Gimignano, Siena, nor Volterra takes my breath away as does Asolo, a town that from my very first visit has ruled my emotions and made me its slave.

Gian Francesco Malipiero

Exploring the town

By the entrance gate nearest the car park is **La Mura**, a palace where Browning stayed on his second visit to the town, and where Eleonora Duse later lived. Villa Freia, where Freya Stark lived, is on the right, preceded by a little garden (the house is now owned by the province). Via Browning, with delightful little arcades along one side, continues from the gate past another house where Browning stayed (plaque) to Piazza Brugnoli, overlooked by the grandiose Villa Scotti, with its impressive terraced garden. Below the piazza is the **duomo**, rebuilt in 1747 over the remains of Roman baths. It contains a copy of Titian's *Martyrdom of St Lawrence*, a baptismal font by Francesco Graziolo donated to the church by Caterina Cornaro, two angels by Torretti (to whose nephew Canova was apprenticed), and two paintings of the *Assumption*, by Jacopo Bassano (1549) and Lorenzo Lotto (1506; with an interesting predella).

CATERINA CORNARO

Caterina Cornaro was betrothed, at the age of 14, to James II Lusignan, King of Cyprus. The Cornaro family had always been influential in Cyprus, and this match was brokered by Caterina's father and uncle. The wedding was celebrated in 1472, but James died only a year later, in 1473, leaving the kingdom to Caterina and her unborn child. When the infant James III died the following year Caterina found herself ruler of Cyprus—but not for long. A number of conspiracies weakened her hold on the kingdom until, in 1489, she ceded her dominions to the Republic of Venice. In return she was granted a large estate at Asolo, which she turned into a famous resort of artists and poets. The Renaissance cardinal and scholar Pietro Bembo wrote extensively of his life at her court, and the 19th-century composer Gaetano Donizetti has written an opera about her.

In the central **Piazza Maggiore** (officially Piazza Garibaldi) is the 15th-century **Loggia del Capitano** with a fine portico and frescoed façade of 1560. Once the seat of municipal government, today it hosts the **Museo Civico** (*open Sat and Sun 10–12 & 3–7*), with palaeontological and archaeological collections, historical memorabilia, and 15th–20th-century paintings and sculpture.

Just out of the piazza are the remains of the castle where Caterina Cornaro lived (before she moved downhill to the larger Barco at Attivole). It incorporates the Teatro Duse, which was sold to America at the beginning of the 20th century but is now being reconstructed. At present only the battlements of the castle may be visited. Part of the large garden that surrounded the castle was purchased by Browning (despite local opposition) so that he could construct here the Villa La Torricella (in Via Sottocastello) for his son Pen. Eleonora Duse's home is in the Contrada Canova (marked), near Porta Santa Caterina.

From the empty **rocca**, above the town (*open at weekends 9–dusk*), there are fine views from the ramparts. It can be reached by a pleasant path that follows the walls from Porta Colmarion (or by car from Via Rocca).

Around Asolo

The countryside around Asolo—a harmonious ensemble of handsome farms and vineyards—is enchanting, and it is dotted with fine old villas, such as the 18th-century **Villa Falier**, on the outskirts of the town, visited for its lovely park (the house is privately owned, and the interior is not on view). According to popular legend it was at this villa that Canova came to the attention of Giovanni Falier, the Venetian noble who became his first patron. Preparations for a banquet were in the final stages when news reached the kitchens that the pastrychef had spoiled the centrepiece. There was consternation all round until the 12-year-old grandson of a stone-carver, who was employed as a kitchen-boy, shyly offered to carve something from butter. The result—a figure of a lion—so impressed Falier and his guests that Falier took the boy under his wing and arranged for him to be apprenticed to a master sculptor.

In the cemetery of San Vito di Altivole, 5km southeast of the town, is Carlo Scarpa's **Brion tomb** (a cult piece among modern architects).

VILLA BARBARO

At **Maser**, in a lovely setting at the foot of the hills of Asolo, is the **Villa Barbaro** (now Villa Luling Buschetti), built by Palladio in the late 1550s for Daniele Barbaro, patriarch of Aquileia. This villa is one of the architect's finest achievements: following the traditional plan of the Venetian Renaissance farm, it has a central manor house with engaged Ionic columns and carved tympanum, and symmetrical porticoed *barchesse* (utility buildings). The interior (*open March–Oct Tues, Sat–Sun and holidays 3–6; Nov–Feb, Sat–Sun and holidays 2.30–5*) contains beautiful frescoes (1560–62) by Veronese and stuccoes by Alessandro Vittoria. In the grounds are a nymphaeum and a carriage museum. The little tempietto, a private chapel built on a centralised plan, was one of Palladio's last works (1580).

Possagno, northwest of Asolo, was the birthplace of the sculptor Antonio Canova. His house has a museum of models and plaster casts of his works (*open Tues–Sat 9–12 & 2 or 3–5 or 6, Sun 9–12 & 2–7*). Canova (1757–1822) has been hailed as the greatest Italian sculptor of the modern age. His patrons were many, and included the Habsburg court in Vienna and Napoleon Bonaparte. In 1802, at Napoleon's express request, he went to Paris to model a nude statue of the emperor, holding a Victory in his hand. That statue is now in Apsley House, London (former home of Napoleon's nemesis the Duke of Wellington). In 1815 Canova went back to Paris on a papal mission: to retrieve the treasures which Napoleon had carried out of Italy. He died in 1822 and is buried here in his native town, in the Tempio, a memorial chapel of his own design, and now the parish church. It contains two of his works: a bronze *Pietà*, and a painting, *The Descent from the Cross*.

Conegliano Veneto and Vittorio Veneto

The wine-growing town of **Conegliano Veneto**, noted also as the birthplace of the painter Giovanni Battista Cima (c. 1459–1518), has many attractive 16th–18th-century houses, especially in the central Via XX Settembre. The **Casa di Cima** (*Via Cima 24; open Aug, Sat–Sun 4.30–7.30, other times by appointment; T: 0438 21660*) has an archive dedicated to the painter. The cathedral (14th–15th-century) contains a fine altarpiece by Cima (1492); the adjacent guildhall (Scuola dei Battuti; *open Sat 10–12, Sun 3–6*) is covered with 16th-century frescoes attributed to the Flemish painter Lodewijk Toeput (known as Pozzoserrato), and inside are frescoes by Andrea Previtali, Jacopo da Montagnana, Francesco da Milano and Girolamo da Treviso.

Vittorio Veneto was created in 1866 by merging the lower (now industrial) district of Ceneda with the old walled town of Serravalle. The town is famous as the site of the final victory of the Italians over the Austrians in October 1918, and takes its name, 'Victory of the Veneto', from that battle. Ceneda has a museum relating to the battle (*open daily except Mon 9.30 or 10–12.30 & 2 or 3–6 or 7*) in the former town hall. The 14th-century cathedral, rebuilt in 1776, contains a fine altarpiece by Titian (1547).

FELTRE

The northern Veneto, where the Dolomites merge with the white limestone peaks of the eastern Alps, is renowned above all for its ski resorts, the most famous of which is Cortina d'Ampezzo. But there are also a number of places you can visit out of season, where natural beauty goes hand-in-hand with historical heritage.

Feltre was a Roman centre, probably a *municipium*, and before that it may have been a Raetian community on the Via Opitergium–Tridentum (Roman Opitergium is the modern-day village of Oderzo). In the Middle Ages Feltre was a free commune and a seigniory of various families before coming under Venice in 1404. The Venetian heads of state dated their dispatches *ex cineribus Feltri*, 'from the ashes of Feltre', after forces of the Holy Roman Empire sacked the city twice (in 1509 and 1510) during the War of the Cambrai League. The architectural uniformity of the city centre, Feltre's most distinctive asset, is a direct consequence of this double debacle and of the ambitious programme of reconstruction that followed it.

EXPLORING FELTRE

The old walled city has numerous 16th-century buildings with projecting roofs and façades bearing frescoes or graffiti. Almost all the city gates date from the Renaissance. The porticoed Via Mezzaterra begins at the 16th-century Porta Imperiale, or Castaldi, and runs uphill through the old city to the Renaissance **Piazza Maggiore**. This is laid out on several levels. On the north side stands the church of San Rocco (1599); the fine fountain is attributed to Tullio Lombardo (1520). On the west is the 19th-century Gothic-revival Palazzo Guarnieri; and on the south, the unusual Palazzo della Ragione or Palazzo del Municipio, actually two buildings meeting at the corner—the one with the rusticated arcade (1558) is the former Palazzo dei Rettori Veneti, attributed to Palladio. Inside is a small wooden theatre of 1802. Above the square rises the castello with its square keep, a Roman watchtower rebuilt in the Middle Ages.

The continuation of Via Mezzaterra, called Via Luzzo, is lined with interesting houses. The Venetian-Gothic-revival building at no. 23 is now home to the **Museo Civico** (*open Tues–Fri 10.30–12.30 & 3 or 4–6 or 7, Sat, Sun and holidays 9.30–12.30 & 3 or 4–6 or 7*), containing a small portrait by Gentile Bellini, a triptych by Cima da Conegliano, a *Resurrection of Lazarus* by Palma Giovane and four views by Marco Ricci. There are also works by the native artists Pietro Mariscalchi and Morto da Feltre. Outside the walls at the northeast end of the town is the 15th-century church of the Ognissanti, with a 9th- or 10th-century campanile, fragmentary frescoes on the outside and a *Madonna with Sts Victor and Nicholas of Bari* by Tintoretto within.

From Piazza Maggiore, Via del Paradiso leads past the elaborately decorated Monte di Pietà to the **Galleria d'Arte Moderna Carlo Rizzarda** (*Via del Paradiso 8; open as Museo Civico*), situated in the 16th-century Palazzo Cumano. This is interesting for its 19th- and 20th-century Italian paintings and sculpture by Giovanni Fattori, Francesco Paolo Michetti, Carlo Carrà and Arturo Tosi.

Outside the walls, to the south, is the cathedral of **San Pietro**. Its present appearance dates from the 16th century, notwithstanding the 14th-century Gothic apse and campanile. The three-aisled interior, with its 9th-century crypt, conserves paintings of the *Adoration of the Shepherds* and *St John the Baptist* by Pietro Mariscalchi, the tomb of Andrea Bellati by Tullio Lombardo (in the sanctuary), the 13th-century throne of Bishop Vilata (at the end of the north aisle), a fine Byzantine crucifix of 542 (in the Archivio Capitolare), and other interesting artworks. Steps behind the cathedral ascend to the baptistery of San Lorenzo, with a 15th-century apse, a 17th-century doorway on the façade and a Renaissance doorway on the side. Inside are a baptismal font of 1399 with a Baroque wooden cover, and paintings by Leandro Bassano and other artists of the 16th and 17th centuries. Remains of an early-Christian baptistery have been found nearby (*excavations open Sat, Sun and holidays 10–1 & 3.30 or 4–6.30 or 7*).

Around Feltre

A pleasant excursion can be made to the **sanctuary of Santi Vittore e Corona**, 4km southeast of Feltre. This is a Byzantine-Romanesque church of 1096–1101 with a narrow façade adorned with chiaroscuro frescoes. The three-aisled interior has 13th–15th-century frescoes (some of which are thought to be by the school of Giotto) and 11th-century sculptures. The adjoining convent of 1494 has more frescoes in the cloister. Other points of interest in the environs are the 15th-century church of Santa Maria Assunta at **Lentiai**, with coffered ceiling and paintings by Palma Vecchio; and the Villas Bovio, Martini e Moro and Mauro, dating from the 17th and 18th centuries, at **Soranzen**. **Pedavena**, north of Feltre, is noted for its beer, and is also a climbing centre. The 17th-century Villa Pasole here has an interesting little garden (*open by appointment; T: 0439 301748*).

BELLUNO

The old town of Belluno stands on a rocky eminence at the point where the River Ardo flows into the Piave—a position which protected it over the centuries both from foreign incursions and from seasonal flood waters. Here you immediately feel the nearness of the Alps (the Dolomiti Bellunesi, the most southerly of the Dolomite ranges, rise just to the west), and of the forests that have long been the city's principal asset. From Belluno, in fact, came the piles on which Venice is built; and something of the deep greens and browns of the Alpine woodlands can be seen in the paintings of Sebastiano Ricci and his nephew Marco, who were born here in 1659 and 1679, respectively. The Baroque wood-sculptor Andrea Brustolon (1660–1732) was also a native.

EXPLORING BELLUNO

The **cathedral** is a 16th-century edifice designed by Tullio Lombardo, with an unfinished façade and a detached campanile (1743) by Filippo Juvarra. The luminous interior has paintings by Jacopo Bassano (third south altar) and Palma Giovane (fourth south altar). The two small marble statuettes in the first north chapel are attributed to Tullio Lombardo. The baptistery, also called Santa Maria delle Grazie, dates from the 16th century.

On the north side of Piazza del Duomo is the 19th-century town hall and its historic predecessor, the **Palazzo dei Rettori** (now the prefecture), a Venetian Renaissance building of 1491 with porticoed façade, mullioned windows, central *logge*, and an imposing clock tower (1549) over the eastern corner. The former palace of the bishop-counts (1190), opposite, has been completely rebuilt, the Torre Civica being the only vestige of the original structure.

One block east of the cathedral, at Via Duomo 16, is the **Museo Civico** (*open April–Oct Tues–Sat 10–12 & 4–7, Sun 10.30–12.30; Nov–March Mon and Sat 10–12, Tues–Fri 3–6*), arranged in the 17th-century Palazzo dei Giuristi. Its picture gallery has works by Bartolomeo Montagna, Palma Giovane and Sebastiano and Marco Ricci.

The street continues to **Piazza Erbe** or Piazza del Mercato, on the site of the Roman forum. It has a fountain of 1410 at the centre and porticoed Renaissance buildings all around, the finest of which is the Monte di Pietà (1531), adorned with coats of arms and inscriptions.

Sebastiano Ricci: *Bacchanal in Pan's Honour* (in the Gallerie dell' Accademia, Venice).

Sebastiano Ricci (1659–1734)

Ricci is famous as much for the scandals in his private life as for his painting. He had a marked appetite for other men's wives, and often found himself having to leave town in a hurry when his liaisons were discovered. Nor was he above resorting to desperate measures to cover his traces. When he made one of his lovers pregnant in Venice, he hatched a plot to poison her. The lady in question had Ricci imprisoned instead. He escaped to Bologna, where he continued to receive commissions from enthusiastic noblemen and prelates. All this tends to obscure his value as an artist. And because he often finished his paintings in a hurry, his style is sometimes too dashing, and he has been accused of superficiality. But Ricci was a virtuoso talent. And the helter-skelter energy which compelled him to rush his works to completion translates into nervous brushwork which give them an amazing lightness of touch. Ricci has been compared to Veronese. He certainly studied Veronese, and reinterpreted him in a dazzling, colourful style which was to lift early 18th-century Venetian painting out of its doldrums and steer it on a new course, towards the later brilliance of Tiepolo. Ricci was highly sought-after in his own lifetime, and travelled widely to commissions both in and outside Italy, including Vienna (Karlskirche, Schönbrunn) and London, where he narrowly lost a competition to fresco the dome of St Paul's. Ricci's intemperate eating, drinking and womanising took its toll on his health: he suffered acutely from gallstones, and died on the operating table.

From Piazza Erbe you have a choice: continuing north along Via Rialto and, beyond the ancient Porta Doiona, Via Roma, you come to the late Gothic church of **Santo Stefano** (1468), with a large 15th-century doorway on the side. The Cappella Cesa, within, has frescoes by Jacopo da Montagna (c. 1487) and painted wood statues of Matteo, Antonio, and Francesco Cesa, by Andrea Brustolon, over the altar. To the south, Via Mezzaterra—lined with Venetian-style townhouses—and Vicolo San Pietro lead to the Gregorian church of **San Pietro**, a 14th-century edifice rebuilt in 1750, with a bare façade and, inside, paintings by Sebastiano Ricci (over the high altar) and two wooden altar panels carved by Andrea Brustolon.

PARCO NAZIONALE DELLE DOLOMITI BELLUNESI

Park offices: Feltre, Piazzale Zancanaro 1. T: 0439 3328, www.dolomitipark.it
Visitors' centre: Pedavena (Belluno), Piazza Primo Novembre. T: 0439 304400,
www.parks.it/parco.nazionale.dol.bellunesi/Ecen.html
The Parco Nazionale delle Dolomiti Bellunesi covers the southernmost ramifications of the Dolomites, including the great limestone massifs of the Talvena (2542m), the Schiara (2565m), the Monti del Sole (2240m) and the Alpi Feltrine (Sass de Mura, 2550m). These mountains join typically alpine landscapes, characterised by bold peaks and powerful vertical walls, with the grassy meadows and shady forests and valleys of the Prealpi.

The park's flora is one of its prime assets, and includes numerous native species and rarities. Magnificent beechwoods yield at higher altitudes to firs and larches. Watch out for ticks, though, which can be bothersome.

The Venetian Dolomites

The Cadore is the mountainous district surrounding the upper valley of the Piave and its western tributaries. Until 1918 only the southeastern half of the district was Italian territory, and there was heavy mountain fighting during the First World War on the old frontier line. The Cadorini still speak Ladino, a Romance language, with Ladino-Venetian dialects in the lower valleys; but German is understood everywhere from Cortina northwards.

Pieve di Cadore (878m), the chief town of the Cadore, is now a summer and winter resort beneath the southern foothills of the Marmarole. The **Palazzo della Magnifica Comunità Cadorina** (*open in summer 9–12 & 3–7*), rebuilt in 1525, contains a small archaeological museum. Outside is a statue of Titian, who was born here c. 1488. His modest birthplace has a small museum (*open in summer 9–12 & 3 or 4–7; closed Mon*). The parish church has a *Madonna with Saints* by him. The Casa di Babbo Natale on the hillside of Montericco receives mail addressed to Father Christmas.

Cortina d'Ampezzo (1210m at the church) is a summer and winter resort once frequented by the best society, though now definitely démodé. It lies in a sunny upland basin, and the view of the mountains on all sides is magnificent. The church has a wooden tabernacle by Andrea Brustolon and an altarpiece by Antonio Zanchi. The pinacoteca contains works by Filippo de Pisis (1896–1956), who often stayed in Cortina, and other modern Italian painters. Aldous Huxley wrote much of *Point Counter Point* here in 1926–27. A spectacular road across the Dolomites, built by the Austrians in 1901–09, leads west from here to Canazei and Bolzano. The **Lago di Misurina** (1737m), northeast of Cortina, is one of the most beautifully situated lakes in the Dolomites.

PRACTICAL INFORMATION

GETTING AROUND

• **By rail:** Treviso is on the main rail line from Venice to Udine and Trieste; from here secondary lines connect with Castelfranco, Bassano, Feltre and Belluno. There are also direct trains from Vicenza to Castelfranco and Treviso; from Padua to Castelfranco, Fanzolo, Feltre and Belluno (continuing on to Cortina d'Ampezzo); and from Portogruaro to Treviso.
• **By bus:** Buses run from Treviso station to Piazza Indipendenza. Country buses to Mestre and Venice, and to points throughout the province (information from Dolomitibus, T: 0437 941 167)

INFORMATION OFFICES

Asolo Piazza Garibaldi 73, T: 0423 529 046, iat.asolo@provincia.treviso.it
Belluno Piazza dei Martiri 7, T: 0437 940 083; Via Rodolfo Psaro 21, T: 0437 940 084, www.infodolomiti.it
Cortina d'Ampezzo Piazzetta San Francesco 8, T: 0436 3231; Piazza Roma 1, T: 0436 2711, www.infodolomiti.it
Treviso Piazzetta Monte di Pietà 8, T: 0422 547 632,

www.provincia.treviso.it, iat.treviso@provincia.treviso.it

HOTELS

Asolo
€€€ **Villa Cipriani**. Simply the area's oldest and finest, a 16th-century villa with gardens and incomparable views. Via Canova 298, T: 0423 523 411.
€€ **Al Sole**. A charming place right in the centre of town, yet quiet and panoramic. Via Collegio 33, T: 0423 528 111, www.albergoalsole.com
€ **Duse**. Small (12 rooms), comfortable, and centrally located. Via Robert Browning 190, T: 0423 55241.
Belluno
€€ **Delle Alpi**. A comfortable place with a good restaurant, in a house midway between the train station and the cathedral. Via Jacopo Tasso 13, T: 0437 940 545.
€€ **Villa Carpenada**. A calm, relaxing hotel in an 18th-century villa with park, 2km west of the city centre. Via Mier 158, T: 0437 948 343.
€ **Alle Dolomiti**. Modern, comfortable and centrally located. Via Carrera 46, T: 0437 941 660.
€ **Astor**. On a lovely square in the city

centre. Piazza dei Martiri 26e, T: 0437 942 094.

Campolongo

€€ **Grifone**. A beautiful new place built with environmentally-friendly methods and materials; good atmosphere, lots of light-coloured wood. Closed May and Oct–Nov. On the Campolongo Pass. T: 0436 780 034, griffone@altabadia.it

Castelfranco Veneto

€€ **Alla Torre**. In a tastefully-renovated old home conveniently located in the heart of the historic city centre. Piazzetta Trento e Trieste 7, T: 0423 498 707.

€€ **Fior**. A very comfortable place in an old patrician home with garden. Via dei Carpani 18, Località Salvarosa, T: 0423 721 212.

€ **Al Moretto**. A renovated old home, this time dating from the 17th century, managed by the same family for three generations. Via San Pio X 10, T: 0423 721 313.

Cortina d'Ampezzo

€€€€ **Park Hotel Faloria**. A warm, elegant luxury establishment in two immense chalets. Closed May and Oct–Nov. Località Zuel 46, T: 0436 2959, www.phfaloria.com

€€ **De la Poste**. The classic place to stay in Cortina, in the very heart of the town. Closed May and Oct–Nov. Piazza Roma 14, T: 0436 4271, www.hotel.cortina.it

€ **Oasi**. A wonderful small place with pleasant rooms and atmosphere, near the centre of Cortina. Closed Oct. Via Cantore 2, T: 0436 862 019, www.hoteloasi.it

Treviso

€€ **Al Foghèr**. In a nicely-renovated building with a renowned restaurant,

outside the city centre on the road to Padua. Viale della Repubblica 10, T: 0422 432 950, www.alfogher.com

€ **Campeol**. A small (14 rooms), family-run establishment with a good restaurant, a stone's throw from Piazza dei Signori. Piazza Ancilotto 11, T: 0422 56601, www.albergocampeol.it

€ **Scala**. A small hotel (20 rooms) in a patrician home next to the gardens of Villa Manfrin, along the road to Conegliano. Viale Felissent 1, T: 0422 307 600, www.hotelscala.com

RESTAURANTS

Asolo

€€ **Ca' Derton**. A good wine bar and restaurant in the very heart of the village. Closed Sun evening, Mon and late July–early Aug. Piazza D'Annunzio 11, T: 0423 529 648.

€€ **Ai Due Archi**. Wholesome, straightforward regional cuisine in a warm atmosphere with wood panelling and antique furniture. Closed Wed evening, Thur, Jan and Feb. Via Roma 55, T: 0423 952 201.

€€ **Due Mori**. Restaurant with rooms, offering delicious regional dishes on a panoramic terrace in summer. Closed Wed. Piazza D'Annunzio 5, T: 0423 952 256.

€€ **La Trave**. Traditional *osteria* in business for over 250 years, just outside Asolo. Closed Mon, Feb and Aug. Via Bernardi 15, Località Pagnano (2km west), T: 0423 952 292.

€ **Tavernetta**. An old tavern at once rustic and refined. Closed Sun and July. Via Schiavonesca 45, T: 0423 952 273.

Belluno

€ **Al Borgo**. Traditional fare and

regional, Italian and imported wines in an 18th-century villa with gardens. Closed Mon evening, Tues, Jan and July. Via Anconetta 8, T: 0437 926 755.

€ **La Taverna**. A simple trattoria with good local dishes, behind the Teatro Comunale. Closed Sun and July. Via Cipro 7, T: 0437 25192.

Castelfranco Veneto

€€ **Alle Mura**. An elegant place set against the medieval town walls and specialising in seafood. Closed Thur, Jan and Aug. Via Preti 69, T: 0423 498 098.

€€ **Barbesani**. Rustic elegance in a fine country restaurant. Closed Wed evenings and Thur, Dec–Jan and Aug. Via Montebelluna 41, Località Salvarosa, T: 0423 490 446.

€€ **Osteria ai Due Mori**. Small but excellent selection of refined, innovative dishes, especially game and mush-rooms. Closed Wed, midday Thur and Sept. Vicolo Montebelluna 24, T: 0423 497 174.

€€ **Rino Fior**. Good Venetian cooking loved by the locals. Closed Mon evening and Tues, in Jan and July–Aug. Via Montebelluna 27, T: 0423 490 462.

Cavaso del Tomba

€€ **Al Ringraziamento**. Restaurant famous for its delicious seasonal dishes. Closed Mon, Tues morning and Aug. Via San Pio X 107, T: 0423 543 271.

Cison di Valmarino

€ **Da Andreetta**. Good country restau-rant famous among locals for its panoramic terrace. Closed Wed and Aug–Sept. Via Enotria 5–7, Località Rolle, T: 0438 85761.

Conegliano

€€ **Al Salisà**. An elegant restaurant in an old building with garden. Closed Tues evening, Wed and Aug. Via XX Settembre 2, T: 0438 24288.

€€ **Tre Panoce**. Impeccably prepared regional dishes plus extraordinary ambience in an 18th-century villa with gardens. Closed Sun evening, Mon, Jan and Aug. Via Vecchia Trevigiana 50, T: 0438 60071.

Cortina d'Ampezzo

€€€ **Bar Grill Hotel de La Poste**. The in place to eat in Cortina, especially during ski season. Closed Wed, May–July and Oct–Dec. Piazza Roma 14, T: 0436 4271.

€€ **Baita Piè Tofana** (with rooms). A lodge, popular with hikers and climbers, with good traditional food and fabulous views. Closed Wed, June and Oct. Località Rumerlo, T: 0436 4258.

Miane

€€€ **Da Gigetto**. The area's finest restaurant, where regional dishes are served with an original twist, the wine list is endless, and there is summer service in the garden. Closed Mon evening, Tues, Jan and Aug. T: 0438 960 020.

€ **Al Contadin**. A simple, rustic *osteria* in a delightful little village. Closed Mon. Via Capovilla 11, Località Combai, T: 0438 960 064.

Motta di Livenza

€€ **Bertacco** (with rooms). Hotel restaurant locally renowned for its fish dishes. Closed Sun evening and Mon. T: 0422 861 400.

Nervesa della Battaglia

€€ **Roberto Miron**. Traditional restau-rant known for its wild-mushroom dishes. Closed Sun evening and Mon, in Jan and Aug. Piazza Sant'Andrea 26, T: 0422 885 185.

Pieve di Soligo
€€ **Locanda da Lino** (with rooms). The extraordinary collection of old copper pots on the walls presages the good traditional cooking for which this fine country restaurant is famous. Closed Mon and in Dec and July. Via Brandolini 31, Località Solighetto.

Ponte di Piave (Treviso)
€ **Torre Morosini**. Great wines and food in a former warehouse on the outskirts of the village. Closed Sat morning and Sun. Via Terreni 1, T: 0422 857 575.

Quinto di Treviso
€€ **Da Righetto** (with rooms). The place to go for eel (*bisata* in dialect) and other fresh-water fish, as well as a good selection of wines. Closed Mon, Jan and Aug. Via Cardi 2, T: 0422 379 101.

Sappada
€€ **Laite**. Astonishingly good creative interpretations of traditional dishes, in rooms dating from the 16th century. Closed Wed, midday Thurs, early June and late Oct. Borgata Hoffe 10, T: 0435 469 070.

Spresiano
€ **La Primizia**. Delicious wines, snacks and light meals, on the outskirts of the village along the road to Conegliano. Closed Mon and Aug. Via Mario Fiore 1a, T: 0422 928 910.

Treviso
€ **Al Bersagliere**. Offering traditional Trevisan dishes with a personal twist—the building dates from the 13th century. Closed midday Sat, Sun, Jan and Aug. Via Barberia 21, T: 0422 541 988.
€€ **Alfredo-Relais el Toulà**. An elegant restaurant in a historic building, serving regional specialities and classic Italian dishes with a wide selection of regional, Italian and imported wines. Closed Sun evening, Mon and Aug. Via Collalto 26, T: 0422 540 275.
€€ **Beccherie**. In a historic building, locally renowned for its Trevisan cuisine. Closed Sun evening and Mon. Piazza Ancillotto 10, T: 0422 540 871.
€€ **Incontro**. Nice ambience, great food, in the shadow of the old town gate. Closed Wed, Thur morning and in Aug. Largo Porta Altinia 13, T: 0422 547 717.
€€ **Toni del Spin**. Typical trattoria much loved by the *trevigiani*. Closed Sun, Mon morning and in July–Aug. Via Inferiore 7, T: 0422 543 829.

WINE BARS

Asolo
€ **Alle Ore**. Excellent wine bar serving snacks and light meals. Closed Mon and Jan. Via Browning 185, T: 0423 952 070.

Domegge di Cadore (Belluno)
€ **Casa da Deppo**. Well-stocked wine bar in a beautiful old historic house; closed Wed (except in summer). Bar Serenissima, Via Roma 38, T: 0435 728 038.

Oderzo (Treviso)
€ **Borgo San Rocco**. Wine bar counting c. 1,000 labels classified and described with the care of a librarian. Closed Mon and Tues morning. Via Postumia 15, T: 0422 712 121.

Valdobbiadene
€ **Ombrecciacole**. Wine bar with snacks and light meals. Closed Wed. Via Garibaldi 2, T: 0423 973 986.

Vittorio Veneto
€ **Enoteca**. Wine bar with snacks, by the public gardens near the station;

closed Mon and Tues morning. Viale
Trento e Trieste 6; no telephone.

REGIONAL SPECIALITIES

Especially good are local farm cheeses,
grappas (some flavoured with whortle-
berries, mugo pine, juniper or other
essences), herbal liqueurs, honey and
mushrooms. Conegliano and
Valdobbiadene, especially, are famous
for their wines. There is an antiques fair
in Belluno, June–Sept (fourth Sun of
the month). Strong local crafts are
woodcarving and wrought iron work.
Treviso is famous for its radicchio (*see p.
694*).

FESTIVALS & EVENTS

Asolo Annual Chamber Music Festival,
Sept.
Belluno Classical music at sites around
the town throughout the year. Jazz and
ethnic or ancient music, in city squares
and at Centro Giovanni XXIII,
June–Sept.
Feltre *Palio della Città*, historic pag-
eant, first weekend in Aug.
Treviso *Treviso in Fior*, flower show,
May–Sept; *Concorso Internazionale
Cantanti Lirici*, opera competition, June;
Autunno Musicale Trevigiano, classical
music, Oct–Dec; *Teatro Comunale*, clas-
sical concert season, Oct–Jan.

VENICE

A unique position, the grace of her buildings, the changing colours of the lagoon, and not least the total absence of wheeled transport make Venice the most charming and poetic city in the world. It stands on an archipelago of islets or shoals, roughly 3km from the mainland and 2km from the open sea, whose force is broken by the natural breakwater of the Lido. The buildings are supported on piles of local pine, driven beneath the water to a solid bed of compressed sand and clay, on foundations of Istrian limestone which withstand the corrosion of the sea. The official population (334,000) includes the mainland community of Mestre; that of the historic centre is now only 70,000, compared with 200,000 when the Republic was at its zenith, in the 15th and 16th centuries.

HISTORY OF VENICE

Venice was founded in the wetlands between the mouths of the Piave and the Brenta rivers by fugitives from the barbarian invasions inland, around AD 450, and its population grew as a result of the Lombard invasion of 568–69. The city was first governed by *tribuni* named by the Byzantine exarch of Ravenna, and subsequently by a duke (*doge* in Venetian) who, by playing the interests of the Eastern Empire against those of the Holy Roman Empire to the north, attained first a relative independence, and then complete sovereignty, in the 11th century. As the power of its maritime republic increased, the city grew in size, gradually extending over more than 100 islands. Later, after winning a war with Genoa for the control of the Eastern Mediterranean, it extended its dominions on the mainland.

The Turkish expansion and the development of the European powers, however, caused a gradual waning of Venice's political and economic importance—an effect that was compounded by the discovery of the New World and the establishment of alternative trade routes. Conquered by Napoleon in 1797 and annexed to Austria thereafter, it was finally joined to Italy in 1866.

Today Venice is threatened by another kind of peril: the gradual sinking of the lagoon floor, which, together with the continuous flight of its population and the pollution caused by the industries of the mainland, is posing serious problems. What the future holds, lamentably, is anyone's guess.

Venetian Topography

Getting around Venice without getting lost is notoriously difficult: the city's maze of walkways, in fact, was designed to entrap and disorientate invaders. To explore the city serenely, therefore, requires a touch of preparation. It's always a good idea to have a map, and to learn the names of the major landmarks in the area. It's also helpful to have at least some command of the Venetians' special vocabulary.

The principal neighbourhoods, San Marco, Dorsoduro, Santa Croce, San Polo, Cannaregio and Castello, are called *sestieri*. They line the banks of the Grand Canal—one of just three waterways in the city that bear the name *canale* (the others are the Canale di Cannaregio and the Canale della Giudecca). The 100 or so other waterways are called *rii* (singular, *rio*). Unlike the Grand Canal, which can be tens of metres across, the *rii* have an average breadth of just 4–5 metres. They are spanned by around 400 *ponti* (bridges), mostly of brick or stone. The streets, nearly all very narrow, are called *calli*, the more important thoroughfares are known as *calle larga*, *ruga*, or *salizzada*. Smaller alleys are called *caletta* or *ramo*. A street alongside a canal is a *fondamenta*; a *rio terà* is a street on the course of a filled-in *rio*. A *sottoportico* or *sottoportego* passes beneath buildings. The only *piazza* is that of St Mark; there are two *piazzette*, one in front of the Doges' Palace, the other the Piazzetta Giovanni XXIII. Other open spaces are called *campo* or *campiello*, according to their size (*campiello* being smaller). Houses are not numbered by street, but consecutively throughout each of the six *sestieri*. A typical Venice address reads: San Marco 2467.

Venice and the poets

She looks a sea Cybele, fresh from ocean,
Rising with her tiara of proud towers
At airy distance, with majestic motion,
A ruler of the waters and their powers:
And such she was ...

States fall, arts fade—but Nature doth not die,
Nor yet forget how Venice once was dear,
The pleasant place of all festivity,
The revel of the earth, the masque of Italy
                    Lord Byron, Childe Harold's Pilgrimage, Canto the Fourth, 1816

Mourn not for Venice; though her fall
            Be awful, as if Ocean's wave
Swept o'er her, she deserves it all,
            And Justice triumphs o'er her grave.
Thus perish ev'ry King and State,
            That run the guildy race she ran,
Strong but in ill, and only great
            By outrage against God and man
                    Thomas Moore, Rhymes of the Road, 1819

THE GRAND CANAL

The Grand Canal is the main thoroughfare of Venice. In terms of beauty and sheer dramatic impact, it rivals the boulevards of the great European capitals, most of which were constructed much later and with a clear master-plan in mind. Strictly speaking, the Grand Canal has more in common with midtown Manhattan than with the Champs-Elysées—for it was the Venetian spirit of individualism which led each patrician family to build a mansion larger and more magnificent than its neighbour, or to lavish more money on its parish church. Foreign clients would be entertained and business would be conducted in the sumptuous rooms behind these grand façades, and on Sunday clients would be ushered off to Mass in churches that were as magnificent as human imagination allowed.

A boat-trip on the Grand Canal

The Grand Canal weaves through the city from northwest to southeast, forming a reversed 'S' some 4km long, 6m deep and 40–130m wide. The best way to see its extraordinary architectural parade—indeed, the only way to see it in its entirety—is from the water. Whether you choose a gondola, water-taxi or vaporetto, make sure you have a good view to both sides. This tour begins at the Stazione Santa Lucia (*see map overleaf*).

The first building of note that comes into sight is the 18th-century church of **San Geremia**, on the left bank opposite the Riva de Biasio landing stage. An inscription on the wall announces that the church contains the relics of St Lucy, martyred in Syracuse in AD 304. Her body was stolen from Constantinople in 1204, when the Venetians sacked the imperial capital during the Fourth Crusade. The church's west façade faces the Canale di Cannaregio, the largest in the city after the Grand Canal.

On the right bank, opposite the San Marcuola landing stage, is the Veneto-Byzantine **Fondaco dei Turchi**, unfortunately somewhat carelessly restored in 1858–69. A Turkish warehouse from 1621 to 1838 and now the **Natural History Museum**, it is recognisable by the tall towers on either side of its colon-nade. Among the several sarcophagi beneath its portico is one which once held the remains of Doge Marin Falier, beheaded for treason in 1355.

Across the Rio del Megio is the plain crenellated façade of the 15th-century granaries of the Republic, flanked by the **Palazzo Belloni Battaglia**, a 17th-century palace by Baldassare Longhena with an elaborate water-gate and fine first-floor loggia. The magnificent house on the left bank here is the **Palazzo Vendramin Calergi**, begun by Mauro Codussi and completed by Pietro Lombardo and his assistants (1509). Now the winter home of Venice's Casinò, its Renaissance façade, with a delicately carved cornice and frieze, is faced with white Istrian limestone. Wagner died here in 1883.

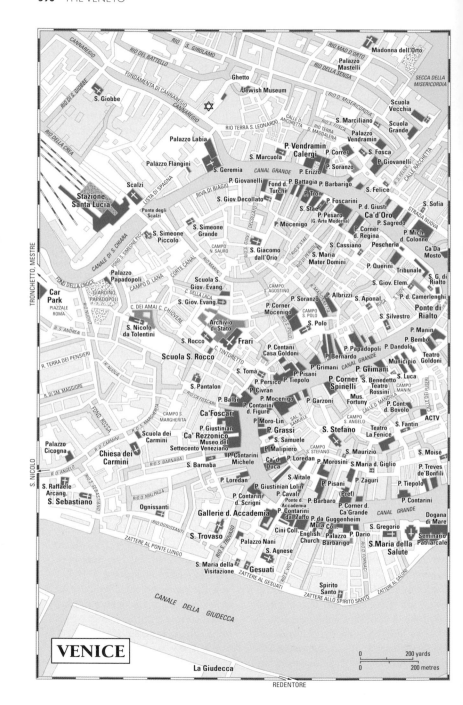

VENICE

La Giudecca

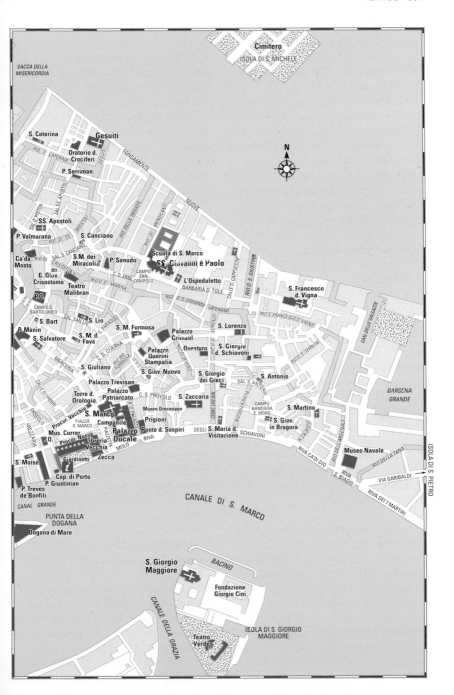

SACCA DELLA
MISERICORDIA

Cimitero
ISOLA DI S. MICHELE

N

S. Caterina
Gesuiti
Oratorio d.
Crociferi
FONDAMENTE
GESUITI
P. Serriman

NUOVE

RIO D. S. CATERINA

SS. Apostoli
P. Valmarana
S. Canciano
RIO DI SS. APOSTOLI
Ca'da
Mosto
S.M. dei
Miracoli
P. Sanudo
RIO D. S. CANCIANO
Scuola di S. Marco
RIO DELLA PANADA
RIO DI S. MENDICANTI
C. Oliv.
Crisostomo
SS. Giovanni e Paolo
CAMPO
SAN
ZANIPOLO
RIO DI S. CRISOSTOMO
Teatro
Malibran
C. D. ERBE
L'Ospedaletto
BARBARIA D. TOLE
CALLE DEI CAPPUCCINI
RIO D. S. GIUSTINA
S. Francesco
d. Vigna
P.O.
CAMPO S.
BARTOLOMEO
RIO D. S. MARINA
RIO D. S. GIOVANNI LATERANO
RIO S. FRANCESCO D. VIGNA
S. Bart
SAL SAN LIO
S. Lio
S. Lorenzo
S. M. Formosa
S. Lorenzo
P. Manin
S. Salvatore
S. M. d.
Fava
RIO D. S.
LORENZO
Palazzo
Grimani
C. D. CHERIA
RIO DI S. SEVERO
Palazzo
Querini
Stampalia
Questura
S. Giorgio
d. Schiavoni
RIO D. S. TERNITA
MERCERIA
CALLE DI FABBRI
RIO SM.
FORMOSA
S. Giuliano
S. Giov. Nuovo
S. Giorgio
dei Greci
S. Antonio
SAL S. ANTONIO
DARSENA
GRANDE
Palazzo Trevisan
Torre d.
Orologio
Palazzo
Patriarcato
C. S. PROVOLO
S. Zaccaria
RIO DELLA PIETA
CAMPO
BANDIERA
E. MORO.
S. Martino
OSSOLO G.
PIAZZA
S. MARCO
S. Marco
Museo Diocesano
S. Giov.
in Bragora
RIO DI S. MARTINO
Museo Navale
MOLO
Campanile
Prigioni
Palazzo
Ducale
Ponte d. Sospiri
DEGLI
S. Maria d.
Visitazione
SCHIAVONI
RIO DELL'ARSENALE
MERCERIA
Mus. Correr
P.O.
Procur. Nuova
Libreria
Vecchia
Procur. Vecchie
PIAZZETTA
RIVA
RIVA CA DI DIO
RIO DELLA TANA
ISOLA DI S. PIETRO
S. Moise
Giardinetti
Zecca
RIVA
RIVA S. BIAGIO
VIA GARIBALDI
Cap. di Porto
P. Giustinian
P. Treves
de'Bonfili
RIVA DEI 7 MARTIRI
CANAL GRANDE
CANALE DI S. MARCO
PUNTA DELLA
DOGANA
Dogana di Mare
S. Giorgio
Maggiore
BACINO
Fondazione
Giorgio Cini
CANALE DELLA GRAZIA
ISOLA DI S. GIORGIO
MAGGIORE
Teatro
Verde

At the next landing is the church of **San Stae**, with a Baroque façade by Domenico Rossi (1709). Rossi first came to public notice as a designer of pyrotechnical extravaganzas. He later turned to architecture, with considerable success. Left of his façade is the charming little **Scuola dei Battiloro e Tiraoro**, once the seat of the confraternity of goldsmiths. The next important building on this side of the canal is the exuberant **Ca' Pesaro**, a Baroque masterpiece begun by Baldassare Longhena in 1628 and completed by Giacomo Gaspari in 1710. The palace houses the city's Galleria d'Arte Moderna and Museo Orientale.

On the left bank, overlooking the Rio di Noale, is **Palazzo Gussoni**, a handsome 16th-century mansion attributed to the Veronese architect Michele Sanmicheli and once decorated with frescoes by Tintoretto. These were erased long ago by sun, wind and rain. **Ca' Corner della Regina**, a Classical edifice by Domenico Rossi (1724) on the right bank, belonged to the family of Caterina Cornaro, Queen of Cyprus (see p. 380), who was born on this site in 1454 (hence the name 'della Regina'). It now holds the archives of the Venice Biennale.

At the next landing stage is the superb **Ca' d'Oro**. This is not only the most beautiful Gothic mansion in Venice; it is the most lavish example of a private Gothic mansion anywhere. In the 15th century, when it was built, the carved details of the façade (the work of Giovanni and Bartolomeo Bon) were gilt and much of the remaining surface was painted deep red or bright blue. The palace now houses the Galleria Giorgio Franchetti, with a fine collection of Venetian painting and sculpture (see p. 444). Two more important houses follow: the **Palazzo Michiel dalle Colonne**, rebuilt in the late 17th century, with a ground-floor colonnade and elegant *logge*, and **Palazzo Mangilli-Valmarana**, designed by Antonio Visentini for the English consul Joseph Smith (1682–1779), patron of Canaletto.

On the right bank, on a projecting quay, is the **Pescheria**, a Gothic-revival edifice built in 1907 on the site of the 14th-century fish market. Here begin the **Rialto markets**, which include the arcaded Fabbriche Nuove, built in 1554–56 by the Florentine architect and sculptor Jacopo Sansovino, the Fabbriche Vecchie, built by Scarpagnino in 1522, and the Erberia, an open-air fruit and vegetable market.

Opposite the Fabbriche Nuove is the Veneto-Byzantine **Ca' da Mosto** (birthplace of the explorer Alvise da Mosto, 1432–88), one of the oldest houses on the Grand Canal and another fine example of the Veneto-Byzantine style. On the right is the **Palazzo dei Camerlenghi**, an elegant Renaissance building of 1528 with two storeys of arcades, now leaning conspicuously to one side (like many Venetian buildings) due the gradual subsidence of the piles on which it is built.

The boat now turns to approach the **Rialto Bridge**. On the left, just on the sharpest point of the bend, is Venice's main post office, once the **Fondaco dei Tedeschi**, the most important of the trading centres established by the

Venetians for foreign merchants. In *The Merchant of Venice* Shakespeare alludes to the business relations between Venice and the various German states in a remark made by Shylock concerning a diamond purchased in Frankfurt; the Fondaco dei Tedeschi was where these Northern European traders were obliged to live and conduct their affairs. The building was reconstructed after a fire in 1505–08 by Scarpagnino to plans by Girolamo Tedesco, and the exterior was adorned with frescoes by Giorgione and Titian (these paintings, too, have disappeared, but detached fragments are displayed in the Ca' d'Oro).

The sight of the **Rialto Bridge** invariably draws an expression of surprise and wonder from first-time visitors to Venice. What is without a doubt the most photographed bridge in the world was built in 1588–92 by Antonio da Ponte, whose design was chosen by the Venetian Senate over those of several more famous architects, including Michelangelo, Palladio and Sansovino. Its single arch, 28 metres across and 7.5 metres high, carries three parallel walkways divided by two rows of shops. The reliefs of St Mark and St Theodore are by Tiziano Aspetti; the *Annunciation* on the downstream side is by Agostino Rubini.

On the left just beyond the Rialto landing stage is the Renaissance **Palazzo Dolfin Manin**, designed by Jacopo Sansovino (1536–75). It is now the Banca d'Italia, and during office hours you can see its beautiful atrium and courtyard. Further down on the left **Palazzo Loredan** and **Ca' Farsetti**, both Veneto-Byzantine buildings of the 12th

and 13th centuries, together constitute the *municipio* (town hall). They have nearly identical *logge* and arcades. Palazzo Loredan is the more ornate of the two, with statues beneath Gothic canopies and the arms of the famous Cornaro family. Elena Cornaro Piscopia (1646–84), who lived here, was the first woman ever to receive a university degree (in philosophy, from Padua University).

The Renaissance **Palazzo Grimani**, on the left bank adjoining the Rio di San Luca, was designed by Sanmicheli shortly before his death in 1559 and built by Gian Giacomo dei Grigi. Behind its stately three-storey Renaissance façade, with broad arches on pilaster strips and columns, is the modern Court of Appeal. Opposite is **Palazzo Papadopoli**, a sumptuous 16th-century house with two broad *logge* and obelisks on the roof.

Palazzo Grimani-Marcello, also on the right bank, is an early 16th-century building in the Renaissance style called Lombardesque, after the prominent sculptor and architect Pietro Lombardo and his family, who worked extensively in and around Venice. Directly opposite is **Palazzo Corner Spinelli**, another fine Renaissance building designed by Mauro Codussi (1490–1510), with a rusticated ground floor and large mullioned windows above.

Across the canal from the Sant'Angelo landing stage are **Palazzo Pisani-Moretta**, an early 15th-century Gothic palace with two fine *logge*, and **Palazzo Giustinian-Persico**, a 16th-century Renaissance building. Further on, adjoining the San Tomà stop, is **Palazzo Marcello dei Leoni**, named after the two Romanesque lions beside the door. The **Palazzi Mocenigo**, on the left bank, appear as one building with a long, symmetrical façade. Here Byron wrote the beginning of *Don Juan* and entertained Irish poet Thomas Moore.

On the right bank, as the canal swings sharply to the left, are **Palazzo Balbi**, a large building of Classical aspect attributed to Alessandro Vittoria, and the late Gothic **Ca' Foscari** (1452), commissioned by Doge Francesco Foscari, displaying handsome columns, fine tracery and a frieze of putti bearing the Foscari arms. It is now part of the university. There follow the **Palazzi Giustinian**, elegant Gothic buildings of the late 15th century where Wagner composed the second act of *Tristan and Isolde* (1858–59); and the magnificent Baroque **Ca' Rezzonico**, designed by Longhena (1649) and completed by Massari (c. 1750), now home to the city's collection of 18th-century art (*see p. 426*). On the left bank, the large, white **Palazzo Grassi** was begun in 1748 by Giorgio Massari. It is now a venue for exhibitions. The campo and landing stage here receive their names from San Samuele, an 11th-century church rebuilt in 1685.

Further on, on the right bank, rises the 15th-century **Palazzo Loredan dell' Ambasciatore**, a late Gothic building with shield-bearing youths in niches on the façade. Just beyond the Rio San Trovaso stands **Palazzo Contarini degli Scrigni**, made up of two buildings—one late Gothic, the other designed by Vincenzo Scamozzi in 1609. On the left

bank is **Palazzo Giustinian Lolin**, a Baroque palace by Baldassare Longhena (c. 1630) with two levels of tall *logge*.

As **Gallerie dell'Accademia** (*see p. 416*), in the former convent of Santa Maria della Carità, come into sight on the right bank, you pass beneath the last of the canal's three bridges, the **Ponte dell' Accademia**, a 1986 replica of a 1930s' reconstruction, in wood, of a 19th-century iron bridge. On the left bank amid gardens, just beyond the bridge, is **Palazzo Cavalli Franchetti**, a 15th-century palace renovated and enlarged in the late 19th century. Across the narrow Rio dell'Orso are the two **Palazzi Barbaro**, of which the one on the left is 15th-century Gothic and the other, 17th century. The older one was bought in the 19th century by the Curtis family of Boston, whose guests included writers Robert Browning and Henry James (who wrote *The Aspern Papers* during his stay and described the palace in *The Wings of the Dove*), and painters John Singer Sargent, James Whistler and Claude Monet.

On the right bank is **Palazzo Contarini Dal Zaffo**, a fine example of the Lombardesque architectural style, and on the narrow Campo San Vio, **Palazzo Da Mula**, a late-Gothic building of the 15th century with three orders of quadrifoil *logge*. Past the latter, again on the right, is the **Palazzo Venier dei Leoni**, begun in 1749 but abandoned after just one storey had been built. There is a tale that the powerful Corner (Cornaro) family, fearing that their palace across the Grand Canal would be overshadowed by what promised to be a more magnificent building, drove the owners to bankrupt-cy. Peggy Guggenheim lived here from 1949 until her death in 1979; the building displays her collection of modern art (*see p. 426*).

Further on on the right is the leaning **Palazzo Dario**, built in 1487 (possibly to a design by Pietro Lombardo) and recognisable by its multi-coloured marble façade and its many chimneys. The magnificent building opposite, with a three-storey High Renaissance façade, is **Palazzo Corner della Ca' Grande**, by Jacopo Sansovino (c. 1545), now the Prefecture. Beyond the landing stage of Santa Maria del Giglio, squeezed tightly

by its neighbours, is the 15th-century **Palazzo Contarini-Fasan**, with just three windows on the piano nobile and two on the floor above; here legend places the home of Desdemona, heroine of Shakespeare's *Othello*. On the right bank, before the canal broadens into the expanse facing San Marco, is Longhena's magnificent basilica of **Santa Maria della Salute** (*see p. 429*). The right bank ends at the **Dogana di Mare**, or customs house, a Doric edifice by Giuseppe Benoni (1676–82) dramatically marking the entrance to the San Marco basin and terminating—appropriately—in a golden globe and a revolving weathervane of *Fortune*.

PIAZZA SAN MARCO & THE BASILICA

The incomparable Piazza San Marco has been the centre of Venetian public life for more than a thousand years. This immense open space, flanked on three sides by porticoed buildings, is the product of a long process of adaptation to the functional and symbolic needs of the Venetian Republic, with St Mark's Basilica and its tall, free-standing campanile at the east end. At all hours one of the world's most spectacular squares (Napoleon called it the finest drawing room in Europe), Piazza San Marco is most beautiful in the subdued light of early morning and late afternoon when the mosaics of the church come alive and the buildings take on a warm, golden glow.

The Basilica of San Marco
Open all day, but tourists are asked to visit the interior Mon–Sat 9.45–5, Sun and holidays 2–4, in order not to disturb religious services. The mosaics are lit for an hour on weekdays, 11.30–12.30, Sun and holidays 2–5.
The Basilica of San Marco is the fulcrum of religious life in the city. It was built in the 9th century to enshrine the relics of St Mark the Evangelist, stolen from Alexandria, Egypt, in 828 in a deliberately calculated raid. Venice needed important relics to give her the status (and revenue from pilgrims) that she craved. Originally the chapel of the doges (and only since 1897 the cathedral of Venice), the basilica has substantially maintained its early form and appearance despite alterations of the 11th, 14th and 16th centuries. Ruskin described it as 'a multitude of pillars and white domes, clustered into a long low pyramid of coloured light; a treasure heap'; his American contemporary Mark Twain called it 'a vast warty bug taking a meditative walk'.

The exterior

The design of San Marco is inspired by the church of the Twelve Apostles in Constantinople (no longer extant). A variant of the typical Byzantine plan, it is built in the form of a Greek cross, with a large central dome and four smaller domes over the four arms. It is adorned with marbles and mosaics combining Romanesque, Byzantine and Gothic influences. The façade has two superimposed orders of five arches and five doorways separated by groups of columns with capitals of Middle Eastern inspiration, dating from the 12th and 13th centuries. The arches springing from the balcony have imaginative Gothic aedicules, pinnacles, tracery and sculpture, added in the 14th and 15th centuries; the tabernacles at the ends contain an *Annunciation* (on one side the Archangel Gabriel, on the other the Virgin Mary) attributed to the Florentine sculptor Jacopo della Quercia. On the balcony itself are copies of the four bronze horses brought from Constantinople in 1204 and now in the cathedral museum for safekeeping (*see below*).

Above the north door **①** is a mosaic depicting *The Translation of the Body of St Mark to Venice* (1260–70). This is the oldest mosaic on the façade, and contains the earliest known image of the church. The other lunette mosaics date from the 17th to the 19th centuries. The central doorway is carved with 13th-century reliefs which, read from the inside outwards, represent allegories of the months, personifications of the virtues and Christ and the prophets.

On the south flank of the church is the door of the baptistery **②** preceded by two finely carved free-standing columns, possibly of 5th- or 6th-century Syrian workmanship, and on a corner, the outer corner of the Treasury, two 4th-century Egyptian porphyry reliefs known as the Tetrarchs, believed to represent Diocletian and his three co-rulers.

The narthex

The narthex, or vestibule leading into the nave of the church, is an ecclesiastical adaptation of the Roman triumphal arch, using columns rather than statues and mosaics rather than reliefs to animate its front. Within, the narthex has a marble mosaic pavement of the 11th and 12th centuries, and its walls, vaults and domes are covered with extraordinary gold-ground mosaics, of Veneto-Byzantine workmanship. These tell Old Testament stories. Particularly interesting are the 13th-century *Stories of Genesis* in the dome above the bronze Porta di San Clemente **③** and the 11th- and 12th-century figures of the Evangelists **④**, in the bay in front of the main door.

The interior

The opulent interior is an epitome of Byzantine decorative craftsmanship, and one of the greatest church interiors of Christendom. The 12th-century floor, the most glorious mosaic pavement in the world, has a richly decorative design of marble, porphyry and other stones, which is fully uncovered only in late July and early August: the undulating effect is due to the settling of the building over the centuries. Each arm of the cross has three aisles separated by colonnades, above which runs the matroneum—a gallery for women in the Greek Orthodox rite, here also an ingenious device for masking the buttresses that support the five great domes. The sanctuary is raised above the crypt and set off from the rest of the church by an elaborate screen. An immense Byzantine chandelier hangs at the centre of the nave.

The upper walls and ceiling vaults are completely covered with mosaics. Most are by Byzantine and Venetian artists of the 12th and 13th centuries, though some—recognisable by their greater naturalism—were reworked in the 16th and 17th centuries to designs by Titian, Tintoretto, Veronese and other Venetian painters. The mosaics celebrate the triumph of Christ and His Church.

Tour of the interior

5 The dome above the nave, above the main body of the congregation, represents *Pentecost*.

6 The arch between the west dome and the central cupola shows scenes from the *Passion of Christ*.

7 The central cupola shows the *Ascension* over figures of Virtues.

8 On the west wall, *Christ seated between the Virgin and St Mark* looks towards the high altar. Higher up are scenes from the *Apocalypse*, and the barrel vault over the narthex bears a representation of the *Last Judgement* (from a design by Tintoretto). Minor mosaics are arranged around these.

9 The baptistery (1343–54) was created by closing off a portion of the narthex. Here are a baptismal font designed by Jacopo Sansovino (1545) and the tombs of several doges—including that of Andrea Dandolo, the friend of Petrarch who commissioned the 14th-century mosaics of the life of St John the Baptist and the early life of Christ. The baptistery altar incorporates a granite slab on which Christ is said to have rested; it was brought from Tyre in the 13th century. Pius X is honoured by a statue above the altar. Before becoming Pope in 1903, he was patriarch of Venice (although traditionally known as patriarchs, bishops of Venice are not members of the Eastern Church). Reached by a door at the west end of the baptistery is the burial chapel of Cardinal Giovanni Battista Zen (d. 1501), with a bronze statue of the *Madonna* (called the *Madonna of the Shoe*) by Antonio Lombardo. The name comes from the story of a poor man who had nothing to offer the Virgin but his shoe. As soon as he offered it, it turned to gold.

10 The Treasury of San Marco, one of the richest ensembles of religious art in Italy, is reached from the end of the south transept. Here you can see a very interesting display of liturgical objects by Eastern craftsmen, many of which were looted from Constantinople when it was sacked by crusaders in 1204. All reveal the medieval preoccupation with symbolism, and many show the distinctively Byzantine concern for richness, colour and texture. Highlights include an Islamic rock-crystal ewer carved with reliefs of two seated lions; a black glass bowl decorated in enamel with nude figures and Classical busts, a work of the 11th-century Byzantine 'Renaissance'; and the so-called 'Crown

THE BASILICA OF SAN MARCO

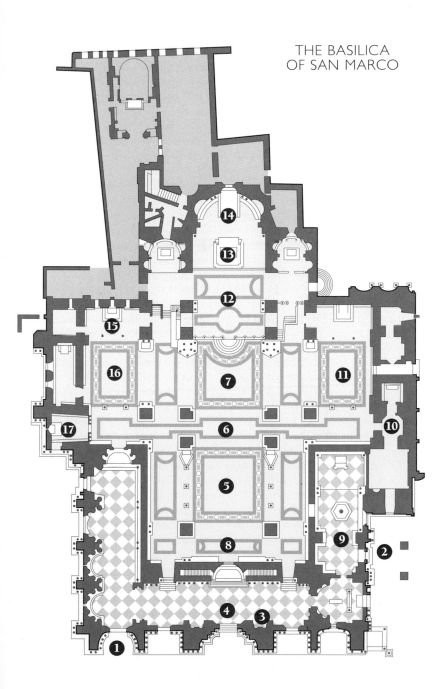

of Leo VI', decorated with enamel medallions of saints and an emperor, made in Constantinople between 886 and 912.

11 The cupola over the south transept represents action in the service of the Church: the figures represent *Sts Nicholas, Clement, Blaise* and *Leonard* and, in the squinches, *Erasmus (Elmo), Euphemia, Dorothy* and *Tecla.*

12 The highest civil and religious ceremonies of the Republic took place in the sanctuary, which is raised over the crypt and enclosed by a marble iconostasis crowned by a silver and bronze crucifix by Jacopo and Marco Bennato and statues of the *Virgin, St Mark* and the *Apostles* by Pier Paolo and Jacobello dalle Masegne (1394). Two ambones constructed in the 14th century out of earlier materials adjoin the ends of the screen: from that on the left the Epistle and the Gospel were read; from that on the right relics were displayed on feast days and newly elected doges presented themselves to the people. The cupola above the sanctuary is devoted to the Prophets, who heralded the coming of Christ.

13 The high altar, which rises over the body of St Mark, is supported by four historiated (New Testament scenes) alabaster columns with 12th-century capitals and surmounted by a ciborium decorated with six 13th-century statues. Behind it is the famous Pala d'Oro, a remarkable gold and enamel altarpiece encrusted with gems, made by Byzantine and Venetian goldsmiths between the 10th and 14th centuries. Among the precious stones that adorn the work are emeralds, rubies, amethysts, sapphires, topaz and pearls.

In the apse are an altar with six tall columns, a gilt tabernacle by Jacopo Sansovino, and statues by Lorenzo Bregno; and the bronze door of the sacristy, Sansovino's last work (1546–69). Beneath the sanctuary are the beautiful crypt and the little 15th-century church of San Teodoro, with an *Adoration of the Child* painted by Tiepolo in 1732.

14 As is customary in Byzantine iconography, *Christ Pantocrator* (the All-Powerful) is enthroned in the apse; he sits above four protectors of Venice, Sts Nicholas, Peter, Mark and Hermagoras.

15 The 12th-century Byzantine icon of the *Madonna Nicopeia*, set in a magnificent enamel frame, gives its name to the chapel at the beginning of the north transept. This is the most venerated image in the cathedral, considered the protectress of Venice. It bears the epithet *nicopeia* ('bringer of victory') because it was carried into battle by the Byzantine emperors, before being captured in Constantinople in 1204. Placed in the basilica in 1234, it has never been removed, except in 1968 when a radical cleaning removed many of the additions that had been made over the centuries and revealed the glittering, enamel-like colours of the original, restoring life to a primitive image that exudes all the mysterious fascination of the Orient but is, at the same time, intensely human.

16 The **cupola** over the north transept has scenes from the *Life of St John the Evangelist* supported by the Doctors of the Western Church in the squinches. All around are scenes from the *Life of Christ*.

17 The chapel of the Madonna dei Mascoli, which once belonged to a con-

St Peter guarding the Gates of Heaven, with the Dome of the Pentecost behind.

fraternity of laymen (*mascoli* means men in Venetian dialect). It has a *Virgin and Child between Sts Mark and James* over the altar and mosaics of the *Life of the Virgin* on the vault. The latter were carried out under the direction of Michele Giambono using cartoons attributed to Andrea del Castagno, Jacopo Bellini and Andrea Mantegna.

A narrow staircase reached from the narthex leads up to the **Museo Marciano**, arranged on the upper floor of the cathedral. Its prize exhibit are the splendid 2nd-century Roman **copper horses** brought to Venice from Constantinople in 1204, now beautifully restored to reveal their original gilding. It is thought that they originally adorned Constantinople's Hippodrome. They were looted a second time by Napoleon, who swept them off (with, among other Italian artworks, 506 paintings) to Paris for display on the Arc du Carousel. Other exhibits include the cover for the Pala d'Oro painted in 1345 by Paolo Veneziano and vestments adorned with delicate Venetian lace. The fine view of the piazza from the loggia alone justifies a visit to the museum.

Around Piazza San Marco

To the right as you come out of the basilica you will see the **Torre dell'Orologio** (1496–99) by Mauro Codussi. Codussi is one of the great architects of the transition from Gothic to Renaissance in Venice. The *orologio* in question is a handsome astronomical clock on top of which two bronze Moors (1497) strike the hours on a great bell. The event is worth waiting for, but to see it you must step back at least to the centre of the square.

Beyond the Torre dell'Orologio extend the former residence and offices of the Procurators of St Mark, known as the **Procuratie Vecchie**, with a double portico built in the 12th century and remodelled in the 16th under the direction of Jacopo Sansovino, who added the third floor after 1532. On the opposite side of the square stretches its near twin, the **Procuratie Nuove**, begun in 1582 by Palladio's follower Vincenzo Scamozzi to a plan by Sansovino and completed in 1640 by Baldassare Longhena. Napoleon made this building his royal palace and demolished the church of San Geminiano, which had stood at the western end of the piazza, to build the Neoclassical **Ala Napoleonica** (or Procuratie Nuovissime) in 1809.

Beneath the porticoes of the Procuratie Nuove, about halfway along, is the 18th-century **Caffè Florian**, the most famous in the city, with a richly decorated interior and an orchestra outside on summer evenings. During the Austrian occupation this was the watering-place of members of the Italian resistance, and its orchestra often engaged in battles to the last note with that of the philo-Austrian **Caffè Quadri**, on the other side of the square. Both are good—if expensive—places to take a break.

Opposite the southwest corner of the basilica, at the corner of the Procuratie Nuove, rises the **Campanile**, erected in the 12th century, altered in 1511 and completely rebuilt after collapsing (fortunately without claiming lives) on the morning of 14 July 1902. At the bottom is the elegant marble **Loggetta** (1537–49), with an ornate façade with three arches with sculptures and, inside, a terracotta *Madonna and Child*, all by Jacopo Sansovino. Initially a meeting place of the Venetian patricians, the Loggetta later housed the honour guard when the Great Council was in session. A lift takes you to the top (*open summer daily 9–7; winter 9–4*), nearly 100m above the square. Galileo is said to have come up here to test his telescope.

The area between the basilica and the waterfront is known as **Piazzetta San Marco**. At the far end, against the magnificent backdrop of the Island of San Giorgio, are two Syrian granite columns erected in 1180 and topped by Venice's two historic patrons: St Theodore, first patron of the Republic, who perches with his crocodile emblem, and the saint who displaced him, Mark, represented by his traditional symbol, the winged lion. Public executions took place in the area between the columns.

The Campanile di San Marco rises above the Procuratie Nuove.

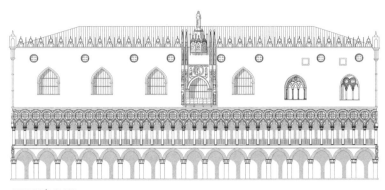

THE DOGE'S PALACE

THE DOGE'S PALACE

Open Apr–Oct daily 9–7; Nov–March 9–5. A single ticket gives admission to the palace, Museo Correr, Museo Archeologico Nazionale and Biblioteca Marciana.

Extending from the basilica to the water is the Doge's Palace (Palazzo Ducale), the residence of the doge and the seat of the highest magistrature of the Venetian Republic. Although it has stood on this site since the 9th century, its present appearance is the product of a late Gothic reconstruction (c. 1340–1420), the general design of which is attributed to the sculptor and architect Filippo Calendario. With its vast walls of white Istrian limestone and pink Verona marble, fine portico, delicate loggia, magnificent balconies (by Pier Paolo and Jacobello dalle Masegne) and crenellated roof, it is by far the highest expression of Venetian Gothic architecture. Well preserved medieval carvings (as well as some good 19th-century copies) adorn the 36 capitals of the lower colonnade, representing the months, animals and foliage. Of special note are the marble reliefs of moral exemplars high up on the corners: on the northwest (nearest the basilica), the *Judgement of Solomon* with the archangel Gabriel; on the southwest (facing the lagoon), *Adam and Eve* with the archangel Michael; and on the southeast, the *Drunkenness of Noah* with the archangel Raphael—all of uncertain 14th-century attribution.

The palace is joined to San Marco by the **Porta della Carta** (1438). The 'Paper Door' is possibly so called because placards were once displayed decreeing the Republic's ordinances. This splendid gateway, a masterpiece of Venetian Gothic architecture and sculpture, was built in 1438–42 by Giovanni and Bartolomeo Bon and their assistants. Its theme is a celebration of Justice (personified in the figure enthroned at the top) as the highest principle of government, accompanied by Temperance, Fortitude, Prudence and Charity. Doge Francesco Foscari, who commissioned the work, is shown kneeling before the lion of St Mark in the lower part. His statue is an 1885 reproduction of the original smashed by Napoleon's men in 1797.

The palazzo's magnificent courtyard is perhaps the best part of the palace interior. Here the homogenous architectural image of the exterior gives way to a medley of styles united only by a desire for impressive magnificence. The Renaissance classicism of Antonio Rizzo's east façade (1485), decorated by Pietro, Antonio and Tullio Lombardo, predominates over the Gothic west and south sides. The **Scala dei Giganti**, a monumental staircase overlooked by colossal statues of Mars and Neptune—by Sansovino, who finished them in the mid-16th century—leads up to the first-floor loggia. At its top doges were crowned after a religious service in San Marco; and from this landing they subsequently received important visitors.

The Doge's apartments
The Scala dei Censori beneath the southeast side of the portico leads up to the Gothic loggia. From here the **Scala d'Oro**—designed by Sansovino in 1554 and bearing gilt stuccoes by Alessandro Vittoria in the ceiling—ascends to a succession of 16th-century rooms, many of which have carved, gilt ceilings and fine Renaissance chimney-pieces. The best are the Robing Room or **Sala degli Scarlatti** (so called from the scarlet colour of the robes of office), decorated by Pietro Lombardo, with a marble bas-relief and blue and gold ceiling; the **Cappella Privata del Doge**, which has a *St Christopher* frescoed on the outside by Titian; the **Sala delle Quattro Porte**, named after the monumental doors decorated with statues and columns and containing Titian's *Doge Antonio Grimani Kneeling before Faith*; the **Sala dell'Anticollegio**, with Tintoretto's *Vulcan's Forge, Mercury and the Graces, Bacchus and Ariadne, Minerva and Mars*, and a *Rape of Europa* by Veronese; the **Sala del Collegio**, designed by Antonio Palladio, with canvases on the walls by Tintoretto (each showing a doge among saints) and Veronese (*Sebastiano Venier Thanking God for the Victory of Lepanto*) and a carved ceiling with more opulent paintings by Veronese; the **Sala del Consiglio dei Dieci**, with paintings by Veronese in the carved and gilt ceiling; the **Sala dell'Armamento**, with what is left of the magnificent fresco of *Paradise* by Guariento (1365–67, ruined in the fire which devastated the palace in 1577) and, in the adjoining loggia, the statues of *Adam and Eve* carved by Antonio Rizzo in 1468 for the Arco Foscari in the courtyard; and the **Sala del Maggior Consiglio**, or Great Council Chamber, a vast (53 x 24m) hall whose decoration, like that of the adjacent Sala dello Scrutinio, was executed after the 1577 fire. On the walls is the huge *Paradise* painted by Tintoretto and assistants (reputedly the largest oil painting in the world). The frieze is decorated with portraits of doges (that of Marin Falier, beheaded in 1355 for treason, has been replaced by a black curtain) and the ceiling holds Veronese's great *Apotheosis of Venice*, surrounded by paintings by Tintoretto and Palma Giovane.

The palace is connected to the 17th-century prison by the famous **Ponte dei Sospiri** (Bridge of Sighs, 1602), over which the condemned were led, often never to emerge alive. The best exterior view of the bridge is from the beautiful 15th-century Ponte della Paglia, on the quayside.

The Musei di Piazza San Marco

The piazzetta is bordered on the west by the **Libreria Sansoviniana**, a masterpiece of 16th-century Venetian architecture begun by Sansovino and completed after the architect's death by Scamozzi. This solemnly Classical building was built to house the

Biblioteca Marciana, the Library of St Mark established in 1468, but is now used as a venue for exhibitions. It is entered from the Museo Correr (*see below*). Next door is the **Palazzo della Zecca**, or Mint, likewise designed by Sansovino and built between 1537 and 1566. It is the modern home of the **Biblioteca Marciana** (*open Apr–Oct daily 9–7; Nov–March 9–5*), possessing numerous rare books and manuscripts, notably the *Breviario Grimani*, a masterpiece of 15th-century illumination. The library was designed to be entered by a monumental staircase from the piazzetta. The stairs ascend to the vestibule, the ceiling of which is frescoed with an *Allegory of Wisdom* by Titian. The present museum itinerary takes you in a back door to the magnificent main hall, with paintings of philosophers by Veronese, Tintoretto and Andrea Schiavone. The **Museo Archeologico** is housed in the Procuratie Nuove. It has an important collection of Greek and Roman sculpture. There are also marbles, inscriptions and a collection of Roman coins.

MUSEO CORRER

Open April–Oct daily 9–7; Nov–March 9–5, last admission 1hr before closing. NB: A single ticket gives admission to the Palazzo Ducale, Museo Correr, Museo Archeologico Nazionale and Biblioteca Marciana.

The Museo Correr is a beautiful and important museum of Venetian history which also contains a number of incomparable masterpieces of painting. Much of the exhibition space is the work of Carlo Scarpa, northeastern Italy's most prominent architect of the 20th century, particularly known for his exhibition spaces. The museum is well laid out and clearly labelled: what follows are some pointers to the greatest pieces.

First floor: This has important displays of work by Canova, and some fine Renaissance bronzes. Canova's popularity is as great today as it was in his own lifetime, when he was considered by many to be a sculptor of comparable greatness to Michelangelo and Bernini. Among the works displayed here are his famous *Daedalus and Icarus*, which shows his prodigious technical capabilities even at the early age of 22. Look also for his charming *Baskets of Fruit*, and for the *Orpeheus and Eurydice* carved when he was only 19 for his first Venetian patrons, the Falier family (*see p. 381*). This floor is also home to a collection of the small bronze statuettes which were so popular during the 15th and 16th centuries, when Venice and Padua emerged as the centres of bronze production, inspired by the presence of the Tuscan sculptors Donatello and Jacopo Sansovino in both cities. In addition to statuary, the bronze collections include examples of bronze household utensils.

Second floor: Displays here give a powerful sense of the history of Venice and the animating force behind the architecture and art of the city. Individual rooms are dedicated to different themes: the Doge, including his state dress and the ceremonies he had to perform (such as the famous 'marriage to the sea' in which he threw a ring into the water on Ascension Day every year, as a symbol Venice's dependence on and sovereignty over the seas); Venetian Coinage; The Arsenal, the great shipyard upon which Venice's wealth depended; The Armour of the Republic's and her enemies' soldiery; and, perhaps, finest and most nostalgic of all, memories of the great Bucintoro, the Doge's ornate ceremonial barge: here you see its magnificent red and gold banner and some of the carvings of its elaborate decoration.

The paintings: This fine collection is arranged in roughly chronological order, from the Gothic to the High Renaissance. The earliest works are interesting for the insight they give into how, at the turn of the 14th and 15th centuries, at a time when there was such a ferment of artistic experimentation in Florence, Venetian artists steadfastly remained faithful to the highly decorative, but fundamentally old-fashioned, icon-like Gothic altarpiece. A very early and beautiful example, now splendidly cleaned, is Paolo Veneziano's panel (once part of a larger polyptych) *Jesus Giving the Keys to St Peter*; and though archaic in its lineaments, its enamel-like colours show a characteristic which carries right through all Venetian painting: the unmistakable fondness for rich pigments.

A MASTERPIECE AT THE CORRER

Perhaps the most influential and important painting of the collection is Antonello da Messina's *Pietà* (Room 34). Antonello can be seen as the godfather of all subsequent Venetian painting. He came from Messina in Sicily: Giorgio Vasari says that he travelled to Flanders to study with Jan van Eyck. This is almost certainly not accurate, but what is true is that Antonello brilliantly absorbed and understood the technical revolution initiated by Flemish painting under the van Eycks, and was profoundly influenced by its subtle delicacy. In 1474/5 he came to Venice. Though he stayed only a year, he produced a number of works that changed the course of painting in Venice forever, finally wrenching it out of its rich, but backward-looking, Gothic tradition. It was Antonello—either in person or by example—who taught Bellini and his contemporaries a new technique: no longer to paint in tempera (in other words with a fast-drying and opaque mixture of egg-yolk, water and pigment), but to experiment with the new Flemish technique of painting in thin, translucent veils of pigment in an oil and varnish mixture. This allowed the brilliant white preparation of the panel to illuminate the colours from behind, giving an astonishing brilliance to both the strong and the delicate tints. Venetian painting was never to be the same again. And even though this *Pietà* has suffered terribly from overcleaning in past centuries, you can still unmistakably pick out the changing gradations of colour and the naturalism of the light.

The later works in the collection clearly show Antonello's legacy. Giovanni Bellini, for example, adopted Antonello's lesson with enthusiasm and innate understanding—but it would be wrong to assume that he was not himself already experimenting with light and atmospheric effects. His early *Pietà* (or *Dead Christ supported by Two Angels*, Room 36), dated to around the middle of the 15th century, is a prime example. Here, by mixed techniques—a combination of tempera and superimposed varnishes—the distant landscape and the foreground figures of Christ and the angels reveal a passionate interest in colour and naturalism. Cima da Conegliano's *Madonna and Child with St Nicholas and St Lawrence* (Room 37) is another superb example of the evocation of atmosphere and beautifully sculptural volumes. Room 38 is home to what Ruskin called 'the best picture in the world': Vittore Carpaccio's *Two Venetian Ladies* (c.1490). It is a fragment of a larger painting, of which the scene of *Hunting in the Lagoon* at the J. Paul Getty Museum in Los Angeles, almost certainly forms another integral part. If Carpaccio had lived in another age, he would have been an artist of strip cartoons or an illustrator of fairy tales. His eye for detail and his ability to create atmosphere are unrivalled. Here two fashionably apparelled women sit on a balcony, their hair coiffed, their bodies laced tightly into expensive gowns, but as idle and bored as two world-weary croupiers. Who are they? Affectedly insouciant aristocrats? Or high-class courtesans, as is often thought? The answer still eludes us.

The final room contains two early works by a very famous painter. Amongst a collection of Greek painters of Madonnas, from the eastern realms of Venetian influence in the Mediterranean, are two works by the young Domenicos Theotocopoulos, who left his native Crete to study painting in Venice before settling in Spain, where he went on to become one of the greatest painters in Europe, known simply as El Greco.

EXPLORING THE SESTIERI

SAN MARCO

From Piazza San Marco pass beneath the arch of the Ala Napoleonica and take the broad **Salizzada San Moisè**, which takes you past the church of the same name, a spectacular, self-indulgent building interesting above all for its façade, a stage-set where you must search determinedly for any trace of religious imagery. From here the broad Calle Larga XXIII Marzo leads westwards, running parallel to the Grand Canal amid luxury hotels and expensive shops. A few steps along, Calle del Sartor da Veste diverges right to Campo San Fantin, a picturesque old square surrounded by elegant white façades; the well-heads date from the 15th century. Here stands the famous **Teatro La Fenice**, an 18th-century phoenix that has risen twice from the ashes of disastrous fires, first in 1837 and again in 1996. It was here that Rossini gave the première performance of his

Tancredi; that Verdi delighted audiences with his *Rigoletto* and caused tongues to wag with *Traviata*. Across from the theatre is the Renaissance church of San Fantin, begun by Scarpagnino. The beautiful apse was added by Jacopo Sansovino.

Return to Calle Larga and follow it to its end. Left, right and over the bridge is the exuberant Baroque **Santa Maria del Giglio** (or Santa Maria Zobenigo, 1683). Here, too, the secular character of the design overwhelms any religious content: the sponsor stands above the door (in a position usually reserved for the patron saint), between figures of Honour and Virtue, while four relatives peer down at passers-by; detailed low reliefs of the fortresses the family commanded appear at the bottom of the façade. The interior has several fine paintings: on the south side, in the Cappella Molin, a *Madonna and Child with the Young St John*, by Peter Paul Rubens; on the third south altar, a *Visitation* by Palma Giovane; behind the high altar, an *Addolorata* by Sebastiano Ricci and *Evangelists* by Jacopo Tintoretto, who also did the painting of *Christ and Saints* over the third north altar.

The street ends in Campo Santo Stefano (or Campo Morosini), at an important crossroads. **Santo Stefano** contains valuable artworks in its sacristy: a *Crucifix* by Paolo Veneziano (c. 1348), a polyptych by Bartolomeo Vivarini, a *Holy Family* by Palma Vecchio and three large canvases (*Last Supper, Washing of the Feet* and *Agony in the Garden*) by Tintoretto. The Cappella del Battista has the funerary stele of a member of the Falier family, by Antonio Canova.

Go right as you leave Santo Stefano. Walk around the side of the church and over the bridge to **Campo Sant'Angelo** (where the composer Domenico Cimarosa lived: his house is marked by a plaque). Cross the square and descend the steps in the left-hand corner to Calle degli Avvocati, take your first right and cross another little bridge. On your right will be **Palazzo Fortuny**, a 15th-century palace whose Gothic façade overlooks the little Campo San Beneto. Here is the house-museum (*closed for restoration*) of the Catalan painter and designer Mariano Fortuny y Madrazo (1861–1949), whose fashions and textiles were the rage of fin-de-siècle Europe. Fortuny himself furnished and decorated the rooms, which now contain a number of his designs, together with curios and memorabilia.

With your back to the little church of San Beneto, walk to the end of Salizzada de la Chiesa and take Calle de la Mandorla left. You'll come out in Campo Manin. A narrow alley on the right here (marked) winds its way eventually to the **Scala del Bovolo**, in the garden court of Palazzo Contarini. This splendid late 15th-century spiralling stair (*bovolo* meals spiral in Venetian) allowed external access to the upper floors of the palace. Although you can buy a ticket and climb to the top (*open by appointment; T: 041 270 2464*), there's not much reason to do so: the best viewpoint is from the pavement just outside the garden.

Back in Campo Manin, walk diagonally across the square and bear left to reach the Grand Canal; the **Ponte di Rialto** appears quite suddenly on your right, at the end of a pleasant quay. This and the quay on the opposite bank—both of which are lined with small restaurants and cafés—are among the few places in Venice where you can actually walk along the canal. On the corner of Calle del Carbon is a commemorative plaque to Elena Lucrezia Cornaro Piscopia, born in this house in 1646. The plaque recalls that she graduated from Padua University on 25 June 1678—making her the first woman in history to receive a degree. A little further on is Sansovino's Palazzo Dolfin Manin (now the Banca d'Italia).

Just a few steps south of the Rialto Bridge, **Campo San Bartolomeo** stands at the crossroads of streets coming from Piazza San Marco and the train station. The monument at the centre commemorates playwright Carlo Goldoni (1707–93), a native. South of the square begins the lively succession of shopping streets known as the Mercerie. From its corner the white Baroque façade of the 16th-century church of **San Salvador** overlooks the campo to which it gives its name. Inside are sculptures by Sansovino and two late paintings by Titian: the *Annunciation* over an altar in the south aisle and the *Transfiguration*, over the high altar. South of the church is the former convent, with two 16th-century cloisters.

On the **Mercerie dell'Orologio** are the campo and church of **San Giuliano** (San Zulian), a very old foundation rebuilt in its present form by Jacopo Sansovino in 1553–55. Some believe Sansovino also made the bronze statue of the church's sponsor, the physician Tommaso Rangone, above the doorway. Inside are works by Paolo Veronese (*Pietà*, first south altar) and Palma Giovane (*Glory of St Julian*, on the wooden ceiling; *Assumption*, second south altar; *Resurrection*, in the arch of the chapel north of the sanctuary). From here it is a very short walk down the Mercerie and through the Torre dell'Orologio back to Piazza San Marco.

DORSODURO

Dorsoduro, the broad tongue of central Venice, bordered by the Grand Canal and the Canale della Giudecca, with the Punta della Dogana at its tip, is famous first and foremost for its three great museums: the Gallerie dell'Accademia, the Guggenheim and Ca' Rezzonico.

Gallerie dell'Accademia

Open Tues–Sun 8.15–7.15, Mon 8.15–2, www.artive.arti.beniculturali.it
As the queue can be quite long during high season (only a few visitors are admitted at a time), plan to arrive at least 20 minutes before opening time or an hour before closing.

No visit to Venice could be complete without seeing this, one of the greatest collections of painting in Europe. It gives an essential understanding of the huge influence that Venice had on European art. It is true that a crucially important revolution happened in Florence during the Renaissance; but what happened in Venice almost a century later had a direct and long-lasting influence on all subsequent Italian, French, Flemish and Spanish painting. This influence was two-fold: technical and stylistic, and it derives quite simply from the economic and geographical reality of the city of Venice. Painters use their eyes, and the light in Venice is different from anywhere else in Italy because the city is built on water: it is a diffuse, refracted, constantly shifting and reflecting light, and the focus and definition with which we see things there are modified by the humidity and haze from the lagoon. The style of Venetian painting owes much to that special light and to it effects.

The second aspect of Venice's influence is more economic: Venice dominated trade from the East, and most of the more valuable and beautiful pigments which artists craved came from the East. They were available to Venetian artists more easily than they were to artists in other areas of Europe. Venice also imported oriental textiles: you see them everywhere in Venetian paintings. But their colours and textures imbue Venetian painting at a deeper level, too. If you naturally love textiles, you will instantly feel the appeal of Venetian art, because its chromatic richness and tactile appeal are similar.

Lastly, there is a practical side to all this: Venice is built in the water, and its walls are therefore damp—a bad state of affairs for the fresco painter, who was such an important figure in Italian art generally. Fresco painting simply did not hold up in the Venetian climate. Instead, Venetian artists had the idea of stretching large areas of canvas on frames in front of the walls, above all for places where monumental paintings were required (the church of San Zaccaria is a good example, see p. 437). Added to this, the presence in the city of what must have been Europe's biggest sail-making industry at the Arsenale, meant that sail-cloth and linen canvas were in plentiful supply. Furthermore, most compatible with this flexible kind of support was the new technique of painting in oils and varnishes. With the marriage of these two—stretched canvas and oils—European painting never looked back, and tempera technique and wooden panels as supports were gone for ever. Every stage of this very important revolution will be before your eyes in the Accademia.

Francesco Guardi: *Il bacino di San Marco* (1780).

GALLERIE DELL'ACCADEMIA

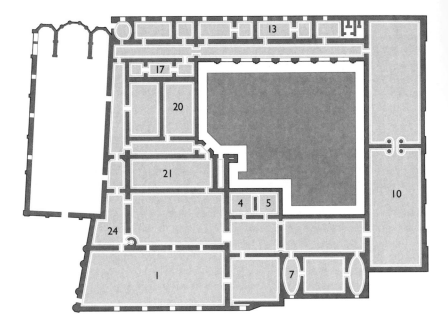

Room 1: Here it becomes immediately clear where early Venetian art comes from: the world of Byzantium. But, as you look around, you will see that much of the austere formality of the Byzantine style is lightened by the elegance of the International Gothic influence, so prevalent in France at this time, and by that innate love of brilliant colour which is the hallmark of Venetian taste. Paolo Veneziano's *Coronation of the Virgin* (mid-1300s) is a good example of this. **Paolo Veneziano** is the first great master of Venetian painting for whom we have a name, and this polyptych, from the church of Santa Chiara, is his masterpiece. The most striking feature of the work is its complexity, which suggests it was done towards the end of the artist's

career, when he was assisted by his sons Luca and Giovanni (c. 1358). Within the imposing original frame, the large central panel showing Jesus crowning his Mother is flanked by some 20 smaller panels telling stories of Christ, St Francis and St Clare, with the four Evangelists on either side. The fascination of this work is partly due to the fact that it so clearly reveals the two formal traditions on which Paolo drew—it is Byzantine in the side panels and Gothic in the large central panel, while the fine decoration of the flowing robes of Christ and the Virgin recalls the rich gold brocades that adorned Venetian garments in the 14th and 15th centuries, and the delicate tones used in portraying the angel musicians foreshadow that intense Venetian interest in colour. It is important to remember that these works were intended to be seen on altars, often in dark corners of churches, illuminated only by the flickering light of candles, and not by the bright lights of a museum gallery. Imagine them lit by a golden, wavering light and you will see their beauty and meaning more clearly.

Room 4: A complete change in scale takes place here. This room contains some of the Accademia's greatest jewels, all of them personal or devotional pieces of tiny dimensions. Look at the confident, almost archaeological, detail of Mantegna's *Saint George*. **Mantegna** married Bellini's sister, and was a considerable influence on the gentle and malleable spirit of Giovanni, teaching him

how to create figures with physical weight and assurance. But as soon as you turn to the numerous works by **Bellini** himself in these rooms, you see where his own virtues lie. He cannot paint a Pietà without deeply empathising with the feelings of the grieving mother: and the tender light and tranquil landscapes harmonise and reinforce that heartfelt empathy. The facial expressions of Mother and Child in his *Camerlenghi Madonna* give a glimpse of the artist's own moody humanity.

Room 5: Most visitors will already be familiar with the most famous painting here, Giorgione's *Tempest*. Despite the brevity of his active life (he died of plague aged 34), **Giorgione** created a lasting impact both on his own artistic

world and on that of succeeding centuries. Much ink has been spilled and many trees sacrificed for the tomes that have been written on this mysterious and fascinating work. The atmosphere of the painting is immediately comprehensible: the imminent storm makes us feel anxiety—in fact, this is one of the first 'mood' paintings in Western art. But who can explain what the young man

Giorgione: *The Tempest* (c. 1508).

with his wooden staff is doing? Or the half-naked woman breast-feeding a child? Or why the broken columns are positioned where they are, as if in centre-stage? The volunteers to explain all this are many and often unconvincing: and the matter is further complicated by the fact that X-ray examination reveals that Giorgione also changed the picture's plan and altered the dramatis personae. The key to the work may in fact be Francesco Colonna's poem *The Dream of Polyphilus*, published by the famous Venetian printer Aldus Manutius in 1499, which contains a description of Venus feeding Love while the poet-shepherd Polyphilus looks on and the sky becomes heavy with an impending storm. Whatever the correct reading—and some have argued there is no reading at all—*The Tempest* remains one of the most forceful images in the history of painting. The air of mystery in the picture is underscored by the colours—from the soft greens of the grass, to the pale glow of the nude against the white cloak and the silvery light of the towers and city walls, which seem to glow beneath the dark sky. A dramatic and visionary scene, in poetic contrast with the apparent indifference of the figures occupying it.

And realising all this, it becomes immediately clear that something very important has just happened: landscape, which was once no more than a decorative motif in the back corner of a painting, has suddenly stepped out of the shadows and become the protagonist. *The Tempest* is not figures in a landscape, it is a landscape with figures: the first modern landscape painting.

Not that Giorgione wasn't a brilliant painter of figures, too. Look at his painting of the old crone just across from *The Tempest*, a pitiful portrait of old-age. The woman's scroll reads '*Col Tempo*'—'with time'. A chilling admonition to youth-worshippers everywhere, and an utterly modern and utterly frank piece.

Room 7: Lorenzo Lotto was at times seen as the 'alternative' to Titian, though he never encouraged direct comparison. He began his career just after the encounter in Venice of the Bellini, Antonello da Messina and Albrecht Dürer, and he used this convergence of influences to good effect in his early works. Later, as a result of a long period in Rome alongside Raphael and Michelangelo, Lotto would be drawn towards Mannerism, which better suited his elegant draughtsmanship and unusual palette. His period in the Marche and in the Bergamo area (*see p. 213*) then brought him into contact with patrons whose high expectations were the result of their familiarity with the work of the Lombard and Rome schools. Though Lotto never enjoyed unbridled success—his modesty itself was against him—he was highly esteemed, particularly in the provinces, where his sophistication compared well to the less advanced styles of regional artists. The *Portrait of a Melancholic Young Man* dates from the late 1520s or early 1530s. Its 'dark' atmosphere is heightened by details that would seem to indicate a solitary existence—such as the letter and crumpled petals, which perhaps indicate some past love. An acute and sensitive psychologist, Lotto has been called the most 'modern' of 16th-century Venetian painters. Emphasis has been placed on the way his pictures would seem to suggest a very reserved character—and indeed, as he retreated further and further into himself, Lotto's work became more and more intensely religious. He died in 1556 or 1557 in the monastery of the Santa Casa di Loreto, where he had lived for years, painting his last tormented pictures.

Room 10: In April 1548 Pietro Aretino, one of the most famous and feared writers of his day, wrote a letter to **Jacopo Tintoretto** that was destined to become famous. After extensive praise, the noted critic concluded with the observation that 'blessed would be your name if you reduced the speed with which you have done by patience in doing'. The letter should be seen in the context of the debate over the relative merits of the 'rational' figurative tradition of Rome and Florence and the reckless improvisation of Venetian painters—in other words, of the fine draughtsmanship of Michelangelo and Raphael as opposed to the virtuoso brushwork of Titian and Tintoretto.

In that same year, 1548, Tintoretto completed a painting that would seem to justify Aretino's remarks—the *Miracle of St Mark Freeing the Slave*, painted in 1548 and destined for the large central hall of the Scuola di San Marco. The story concerns the slave of a landowner in Provence who left his owner's estate to journey to Venice to venerate the relics of St Mark. Recaptured, he was condemned to death, but the saint intervened to save him. In Tintoretto's then-scandalous interpretation, the crowd flees in terror, the slave's shackles break open, and the torturers' instruments fall apart in their hands. Giorgio Vasari gives an idea of contemporary public reaction

when he describes Tintoretto as 'the most terrible mind that ever dedicated itself to painting'. The work is not as shocking to modern eyes, but this is the real Tintoretto, at the height of his youthful vigour and daring inventiveness. The black-robed figure among the columns of the palace is Tintoretto himself.

Paolo Veronese (1528–88), *Mystic Marriage of St Catherine*. The original site of this painting was the church of Santa Caterina in Cannaregio—a very humble setting for one of Veronese's more sumptuous works, a symphony of gold and silver silks and brocades beneath a chorus of heavenly voices accompanied by two lutes. As if in deliberate contrast to the setting, Veronese used the whole range of his palette to create an unforgettable feast of colour. The 17th-century poet and essayist Marco Boschini wrote that the effect was one of mingled gold, pearls, rubies, emeralds and perfect diamonds. The work seems to draw on the magnificence of aristocratic life in the city: the saint's gown seems exactly like that of a Venetian noblewoman, who is tentatively approaching a ceremony she does not fully understand. As always, there is a sort of aristocratic detachment in the way Veronese follows through the ideas inspired by light and colour. 'I paint figures', he was to say to the judges of the Inquisition who, in this same period, called him before them to justify the religious coldness and decorative excess in his work. Here, once again, you can see this master of the sumptuous palette betting everything on the inevitable triumph of colour.

Room 13: In the glorious triumvirate of Venetian painting of the second half of

Gentile Bellini: *Procession in the Piazza San Marco* (1496).

the 16th-century—formed by Tintoretto, Veronese and **Jacopo Bassano**—the latter was the champion of a naturalistic poetics inspired by the world of concrete objects. Bassano had little interest in the pomp of this Golden Age and seems to have chosen his models from among humble farming folk. Painted around 1565, his *St Jerome the Hermit* appears to be a robust woodsman caught resting after a hard day's work. Around him are his customary attributes—a crucifix, a skull, an hourglass and some books—chosen to indicate his saintly vocation. Bassano was most at ease when depicting scenes of popular life—all of which are described with ingenuous faith; yet his works are painted in a manner that

reveals the artist to be capable of the most complex, refined effects.

Room 17: No city loved to glorify and to represent itself in painting as much as Venice. The further you go in this collection the more you begin to see great paintings which celebrate the pageantry and beauty and history of the city.

Bernardo Bellotto's *The Scuola di San Marco at Santi Giovanni e Paolo* and

Francesco Guardi's *Fire at San Marcuola* are examples of the work of the18th-century *vedutisti*, or 'view painters', who had a special appeal for the throngs of visitors who were passionately interested in the buildings, squares and canals of Venice. Bernardo Bellotto, like his uncle and teacher, Canaletto, belonged to the realist school of view painting, which sought accuracy in the rendering of places and events. The *Scuola di San Marco at San Giovanni e Paolo* is a sharply painted image in which the reflections of sky and architecture are rendered with meticulous care. The patches of colour are enlivened with the merest touch of paint, applied with the very point of the brush to achieve an effect of surprising naturalism. Other view painters preferred a more 'impressionistic' approach—suggesting rather than representing the scene before them. This group included the striking colourist Francesco Guardi. Whereas Bellotto represented the real world in the spirit of Enlightenment Rationalism, Guardi was much more a painter of the imagination and of individual sensibility. His works seem to anticipate Romanticism, or even Impressionism. *Fire at San Marcuola* was inspired by a real event—the fire in Venice's oil warehouses on 28 December 1789—but even here Guardi takes great liberties with his subject, creating a composition that is built around vibrant lines and dramatic atmospheric effects.

Room 20: Sometimes these often intensely accurate views can give us valuable glimpses of how the city once looked. Although a much earlier work, **Gentile Bellini**'s *Procession of the Reliquary of the True Cross in Piazza San Marco* is a fascinating glimpse of the city in 1496. The subject of the cycle is the legend of the True Cross, which was discovered in Palestine, according to tradition, by St Helen. The story was published in Venice, in Jacopo da Varagine's *Golden Legend*, in 1475. At the time, Gentile Bellini was Master Artist of the Scuola di San Giovanni Evangelista, and this painting gave him an ideal opportunity to attempt a narrative work using the theatrical techniques adopted in sacred pageants. The painter spices up his narrative by adding the anecdote of the miraculous healing of the son of Jacopo de Solis (portrayed in red, kneeling near the centre of the procession); to the left, the three figures in the red robes of the Confraternity of San Giovanni Evangelista are portraits of the artist, his father Jacopo and his brother Giovanni.

The painting is particularly interesting because of what it shows of Piazza San Marco. The Procuratie Vecchie are visible on the left; the Procuratie Nuove have yet to be built. On the façade of San Marco appear the lost lunette mosaics of the narthex and, on the loggia, the four great gilt-bronze horses flanked by the original mosaics representing scenes from the life of Christ. Some scholars see proto-Renaissance features in these mosaics which they attribute to the influence of early 15th-century Tuscan art, brought to Venice by Paolo Uccello and Andrea Castagno.

Room 21: The story **Carpaccio** chose for the cycle of paintings (*The Dream of St Ursula*) commissioned by the Loredan family for the (destroyed) Scuoletta di Sant'Orsola and painted between 1490 and 1500, was the poetic tale of a Christian princess from Brittany, whose hand is asked in marriage by the English prince Etherius, a pagan. Ursula tells the prince's ambassadors that if he truly wants her he will have to convert to Christianity and accompany her to Rome to be married by the pope. During the pilgrimage an angel appears to Ursula in a dream and tells her of her imminent martyrdom, which occurs during the return journey, at Cologne, under siege by the Huns. In the *Dream of St Ursula* the perfect perspective of the composition contributes to the creation of an atmosphere typical of Carpaccio's style—a marvellous medley of deep spirituality and meticulous attention to detail, which serves to make this supernatural event totally credible. The scene is set in the serene light of dawn, the luminescent colour veiled by particles of gold that seem to settle calmly on all the objects—especially on the bedside table and its prayerbooks, on the soft bed and on the windowsill with its potted myrtle and carnations, symbols of faith and chastity. **Room 24:** The *Presentation of the Virgin in the Temple* is a truly splendid picture, a masterpiece by **Titian**, painted for the room in which it still hangs—the *albergo* (chapter room) of the former Scuola della Carità. The composition, executed around 1539, makes ample use of details in the work of contemporary architects who were deeply influenced by Roman antiquity. The work's rigorous perspective gives it a marked theatrical quality, underscored by the stunning richness of colour in the scene and by the narrative realism of the rendering, which seem to draw the viewer into the event depicted. The theme of the Virgin's affirmation of religious faith was a reference to one of the principal functions of the Scuola della Carità, which once a year, in this room, gathered together a number of poor but virtuous girls to secure them the dowry that would enable them to marry. The widowed Titian made the painting as his own daughter Lavinia was reaching womanhood, and it may not be coincidental that there is something particularly intimate and personal about the figure of the fair-haired Mary in her blue gown, suffused by a supernatural light. At the bottom of the steps leading up to the temple Titian has portrayed a chorus of witnesses, composed of patrician ladies and gentlemen dressed in the ceremonial robes of the scuola.

The Cini Collection

Closed at the time of writing. T: 041 5210755.
The unobtrusive Palazzo Cini, between the Accademia and the Peggy Guggenheim Collection, contains the small and unusual art collection of the financier and marine businessman Vittorio Cini, made into a public foundation on his death, in memory of his son Giorgio, who died tragically in an air crash in 1949.

The first rooms contain very early masterworks by the *primitivi*: tiny devotional panels, full of the spiritual intensity of a lost world. These include an indelibly haunting *Crucifixion* by Pietro di Giovanni Ambrosi, two gracious and solid *Apostles* by Giotto, and an exquisite *Madonna and Child* by the Sienese painter Sassetta. Greatest of all, however, is the same subject of *Virgin and Child* treated with chilling intellectual detachment by Piero della Francesca.

The Peggy Guggenheim Collection

Open Wed–Mon 10–6, Sat 10–10, last admission 15mins before closing.
NB: The Guggenheim Collection is the second most visited museum after the Accademia, so in high season come a few minutes before opening or just before closing for quieter viewing.

The ivy-clad entrance of the 18th-century Palazzo Venier dei Leoni, on the Grand Canal, takes you out of one world and into another. Renaissance Venice gives way to the avant garde. Peggy Guggenheim, the spirited American heiress and patron of the arts, lived here from 1949 until her death in 1979, and her fascinating collection of modern American and European art is on display here.

In the Entrance Hall, visitors are greeted by two magnificent works by Pablo Picasso (*The Studio*, 1928, and *On the Beach*, 1937) and an Alexander Calder *Mobile* (1941). Marino Marini's *Angel of the City* (1948–50) dominates the sunny terrace overlooking the Grand Canal. The Dining Room is hung with early masterpieces of Cubism (Picasso's *The Poet*, 1911; Braque's *The Clarinet*, 1912; Marcel Duchamp's *Sad Young Man on a Train*, 1911–12). Gino Severini's *Futurist Sea = Dancer* (1914) and Kandinsky's *Landscape with Red Spots* No. 2 (1913) adorn the Kitchen. Surrealism (Dalí's *Birth of Liquid Desires*, 1931–32; Magritte's *Empire of Light*, 1953–54; Ernst's *Attirement of the Bride*; Giacometti's *Woman with her Throat Cut*, 1932) dominates the Library, and the Guest Bedroom is given over to works by Jackson Pollock, ranging from early figurative works to the signature 'drip' paintings of the Abstract Expressionist years.

A wing of the building exhibits 26 paintings on long-term loan from the collection of Gianni Mattioli (1903–77), a Milanese collector and near contemporary of Peggy Guggenheim, who became fascinated by Futurist ideas after reading Umberto Boccioni's *Pittura, Scultura Futurista*. There are intriguing parallels between Mattioli and Guggenheim as collectors: the Mattioli Collection includes legendary images of Italian Futurism by Balla, Boccioni, Carrà, Depero, Russolo and Severini; contemporary works by Sironi, Soffici and Rosai; early paintings by Morandi and a portrait by Modigliani.

Ca' Rezzonico

Open Wed–Mon 10–4; last admission 1hr before closing.

This powerful Baroque palazzo on the Grand Canal, begun in 1649 by Baldassare Longhena and completed after 1750 by Giorgio Massari, is a refined example of an 18th-century patrician home. It was the last home of Robert Browning, who died in 1889 in a small apartment (*not open*) on the first floor. Today it hosts the **Museo del Settecento Veneziano**, which, in sumptuous rooms (some with ceilings frescoed by Tiepolo and his pupils) creates a vivid image of Venetian life and culture in the 18th century, drawing on tapestries, furniture, lacquer work, costumes and paintings. Among the latter are a fine series of small canvases with scenes of family life and rustic idylls by Pietro Longhi (1701–85), who occupies a very special place among the 'realist' painters of the second half of the 18th century. His work marks the introduction into Venetian art of the 'conversation piece'—a European genre that was being popularised in France by Watteau and in England by Hogarth.

Ca' Rezzonico also has a room hung with the pastel portraits of Rosalba Carriera (1675–1752), one of Europe's first internationally acclaimed female artists. Admired and courted by many of the ruling families of Europe, she used an eminently naturalistic artistic language which made her talents respected by all. She was a significant influence on the great French pastel artists Quentin de la Tour and Chardin.

Giandomenico Tiepolo's frescoes for his own villa at Zianigo (1759–97) have been installed in another group of rooms. The top floor hosts a beautiful display of 15th–20th-century Venetian School paintings and other works from the Martini Collection (Boccaccino, Paris Bordone, Guercino, Padovanino, Sebastiano Ricci, Bernardo Strozzi, Tintoretto and others).

The Carmini and San Sebastiano

Down the little canal from Ca' Rezzonico (fruit and vegetables are sold from boats here on weekday mornings) and to the right is Campo Santa Margherita, a charming square and marketplace, surrounded by old houses. At the west end of the square, flanked by its church, stands the 17th-century **Scuola Grande dei Carmini**. This was one of Venice's six *scuole grandi*, or philanthropic confraternities (the others are the Scuola Grande dei Greci, della Misericordia, di San Giovanni Evangelista, di San Marco and di San Rocco), which engaged in charitable activities throughout the Republic. Scuole were formed by laymen involved in the same trade, who often shared a common national ancestry and were committed to a particular religious cult. These confraternities are of particular artistic interest, since their participants' annual membership fees decorated the headquarters, often supporting the more prominent Venetian artists of the day. This building's design is attributed to Baldassare Longhena.

The rooms of the interior (*open Mon–Sat 9–6, Sun 9 4*) are decorated with stuccoes, wooden benches and 17th- and 18th-century paintings. In the great upper hall, or Salone, is a fine ceiling with nine paintings by Giovanni Battista Tiepolo (1739–44) centred around a depiction of the *Virgin Presenting St Simon Stock with the Scapular of the Carmelite Order*, a work of the artist's later years. The Sala dell'Archivio has a beautiful carved wooden ceiling with paintings by Balestra, and the passage contains a *Judith and Holofernes* by Piazzetta.

The conventual church of **Santa Maria del Carmine** (or I Carmini), built in 1348, preserves a 14th-century doorway and porch on the north flank. The Renaissance façade with its arched gable was added in the early 16th century. The interior, with three aisles on monolithic columns (faced with carmine-red damask at Christmas and Easter) and a Gothic polygonal apse, has a magnificent 17th–18th-century wooden decoration in the nave incorporating statues of prophets and saints between the arches and a continuous frieze of paintings above. These illustrate the history of the Carmelite Order and are by minor artists. Over the second south altar is an *Adoration of the Shepherds* by Cima da Conegliano; the chapel to the south of the sanctuary holds a bronze relief of the *Deposition* by Francesco di Giorgio Martini and a charming little *Sacra Famiglia* by Veronese with a particularly playful young St John. Lorenzo Lotto's moody painting of *St Nicholas in Glory* hangs over the second north altar. Adjoining the church is the entrance to the former monastery (now a school), with a fine 16th-century cloister.

Upon leaving the church turn left, then left again along canals to reach **San Sebastiano**, rebuilt in 1504–48 in elegant Renaissance forms. It is famous for the impressive decorative scheme created between 1555 and 1565 by Paolo Veronese, who was buried here in 1588. The splendid complex of canvas and frescoes covers the ceiling, the walls of the nave and sanctuary, the sacristy and the nuns' choir. Particularly noteworthy are the three canvases of the nave ceiling (*Stories of Esther*); the organ shutters (*Purification of the Virgin* outside and *Pool of Bethesda* inside); the large canvases in the sanctuary (*Stories of St Sebastian*); the *Virgin in Glory with Sts Sebastian, Peter, Catherine and Francis*, over the high altar; and the ceiling compartments of the sacristy (*Coronation of the Virgin, Evangelists*), the artist's first work in Venice. Among the other works of art preserved in the church are a beautiful marble group of the *Madonna and Child with the Young St John* by Tullio Lombardo, over the second south altar; the tomb of Livio Podocattaro by Sansovino after the third south chapel; and a *St Nicholas* by Titian over the altar of the vestibule. The former convent, rebuilt in 1851, now hosts a part of the university.

Le Zattere

Le Zattere is the name of the pleasant quay along the wide Canale della Giudecca, which separates the city from the long island of the Giudecca. *Zattere* means lighters, and the fondamenta is named after the large, flat-bottomed barges that used to unload wood here. Almost 2km long, it is divided into four parts, which take their name from their most distinctive element: Zattere al Ponte Lungo, ai Gesuati, allo Spirito Santo, ai Saloni. As you cross the first little canal (Rio de San Trovaso), look left and you'll see one of Venice's last remaining *squeri*, the boatyards where gondolas are made and repaired. Further on, roughly half-way along the quay, stands the 18th-century church of the **Gesuati**, which holds works by Tiepolo (over the first south altar and ceiling fresco), Piazzetta (third south altar) and Tintoretto (third north altar).

The Punta della Dogana, the promontory separating the Grand Canal from the Canale della Giudecca, projects into the Bacino di San Marco towards the Island of San Giorgio. It receives its name from the long, low building known as the **Dogana di Mare**, the Maritime Customs House, built over an earlier edifice by Giuseppe Benoni in 1677. The spectacular construction, designed to resemble an arcaded ship's prow, terminates in a triangular piazza offering unforgettable views over the city and the lagoon. From here you can imagine what it must have been like to arrive in Venice by sea. Sailing ships moored at the Molo di San Marco, at the foot of the Doge's Palace, where foreign visitors were immediately confronted by the highest symbols of political and religious power. Above the Doric façade of the Dogana di Mare rises Bernardo Falcone's sculptural composition of atlantes carrying a golden globe, topped by a weather vane in the shape of that most fickle of influences, Fortune.

Santa Maria della Salute

Just around the point, on the Grand Canal, is Santa Maria della Salute, the masterpiece of Venetian Baroque architecture that dominates so many views of Venice. It was built to a design by Baldassare Longhena to commemorate the end of a terrible plague that swept the city in 1630, and possesses one of the most memorable silhouettes in all Italian architecture. The church is designed in the shape of a crown, possibly in reference to the invocations to the Queen of Heaven in the Venetian litany that was recited in times of plague, or to the mention in *Revelation* of 'a woman clothed with the sun, and the moon under her feet, and upon her head a crown of twelve stars'. A statue of the Virgin with these attributes stands atop the cupola. At a lower level, on huge scrolls, are statues of the Apostles—the twelve stars in Longhena's 'crown'.

The interior of the church is a spacious octagon with an ambulatory, a lofty dome and a second, smaller dome over the sanctuary. An inscription in the centre of the pavement—*unde origo inde salus* (whence the origin, thence the salvation and health)—alludes to the legend that Venice was founded under the protection of the Virgin. Around the church are a number of important artworks: the high altar, designed by Longhena with sculptures by Juste Le Court, holds a venerated Byzantine icon; on the left is the Sagrestia Grande, over the altar of which is *St Mark Enthroned between Sts Cosmas, Damian, Roch and Sebastian*, an early work of Titian painted to commemorate the plague of 1510. Titian also painted the three fine paintings on the ceiling (*Sacrifice of Abraham, David and Goliath, Cain and Abel*) originally for the church of Santo Spirito. On the wall to the south of the altar is the *Marriage at Cana*, a large painting by Tintoretto.

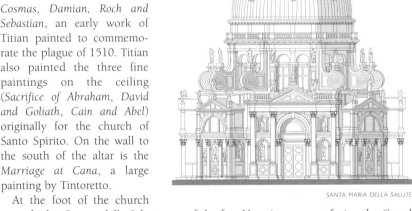

SANTA MARIA DELLA SALUTE

At the foot of the church extends the Campo della Salute, one of the few Venetian squares facing the Grand Canal. It offers a fine view over the Bacino di San Marco. West of the church, high above the steps, is the Seminario Patriarcale, a severe building by Baldassare Longhena (1671) organised around a cloister and a monumental staircase. Here is the small **Pinacoteca Manfrediniana**, with paintings by 15th–18th-century artists, notably Giorgione, Cima da Conegliano and Filippino Lippi; and sculpture, including two Renaissance reliefs by Tullio Lombardo and a terracotta bust by Antonio Canova.

SAN POLO & SANTA CROCE

Campo San Giacomo di Rialto, formerly the centre of the city's financial life and now the centre of a colourful fruit and vegetable market, lies at the foot of the Rialto Bridge on the side furthest from San Marco. Flanked by the porticoes of the Fabbriche Vecchie, it is overlooked by the 15th-century façade of **San Giacomo di Rialto** (San Giacometto), built in the 12th century and rebuilt in 1531 and 1601. From the campo, Ruga degli Orefici (Goldsmiths' Row) leads into Ruga degli Speziali (Apothecaries). Meandering along in a more or less northwesterly direction you eventually come to the 17th-century church of **San Cassiano**, on the north side of its campo. An old foundation several times altered, it has a 13th-century brick campanile and some paintings by Tintoretto.

From here you must carefully follow the signs for the Ferrovia and the Galleria d'Arte Moderna to reach **Ca' Pesaro**, one of the most magnificent Venetian palaces on the Grand Canal. Entrance to the palazzo is by a modest door on the garden side; the vast courtyard has a large well attributed to Jacopo Sansovino. On the first floor is the Galleria d'Arte Moderna (*open Tues–Sun 10–5 or 6; last admission 1hr before closing*), with a vast (though undistinguished) collection of works by the principal Italian and foreign artists of the 20th century.

On the third floor is the Museo d'Arte Orientale (*open Tues–Sun 10–6*), which has a splendid collection of Japanese paintings, sculpture and applied artworks, in addition to more modest holdings of Chinese porcelain and jades and Indonesian weapons, fabrics and shadow-theatre figures.

Leave the museum and go straight over the bridge, then down a covered portico and over another bridge. You'll come out on the Grand Canal, in front of **San Stae**, a church with a late Baroque façade by Domenico Rossi. The interior, now used for concerts and exhibitions, has 18th-century paintings by Giovanni Battista Tiepolo, Sebastiano Ricci and his contemporary Giovanni Battista Piazzetta, a gifted artist of rare chiaroscuro vision—who greatly influenced Tiepolo and was in turn influenced by him. His *Capture of St James* is a masterpiece. The Salizzada San Stae, on the south side of the church, leads past **Palazzo Mocenigo**, where there is a small museum of 18th-century frescoes, paintings, furniture and fabrics. The women's dresses and accessories are particularly interesting (*open Tues–Sun 10–5*).

Turn right in Calle del Tentor, then left at the bridge. Almost due south, in one of the few wooded spaces in the heart of the city, is **San Giacomo dell'Orto**. This is one of the older churches of Venice, built in 1225 and altered between the 14th and17th centuries; the extant elements of the original, 13th-century building are the central apse and brick campanile. The Latin-cross interior, with a 14th-century wooden ship's-keel roof, preserves several fine works of art: in the nave, a 13th-century holy-water stoup and a Lombardesque pulpit; beneath the arch of the sanctuary, a wooden crucifix by Paolo Veneziano; in the sanctuary, a *Madonna and Saints* by Lorenzo Lotto in the north transept, *Sts Jerome, Lawrence and Prosperus* by Paolo Veronese; and in the old sacristy, a cycle of paintings by Palma Giovane.

The church of the Frari

Open Mon–Sat 9–6, Sun and holidays 1–6.

From the apse of San Giacomo continue southwards via Calle del Tentor to reach Santa Maria Gloriosa dei Frari, arguably the most important church in Venice after San Marco, though Santi Giovanni e Paolo also vies for this honour (*see p. 435*). Built by the Franciscans between 1340 and 1443, the Frari is a brick edifice with a lively exterior design, magnificent apses and a slightly leaning campanile of 1361–69 (the tallest after that of San Marco). The vast façade, crowned by stone pinnacles, is pierced by a marble doorway bearing sculptures by Bartolomeo Bon and Pietro Lamberti, and by Alessandro Vittoria (who did the *Resurrected Christ* at the top).

The church is entered by the main doorway in the west façade, also faced in marble. A vast, solemn space with three aisles separated by tall pointed arches, it has numerous tombs of doges and other illustrious Venetians of the 14th to the 19th century, as well as some major works of art.

At the **centre of the nave** is the late Gothic early Renaissance monks' choir, with a marble enclosure by Pietro Lombardo and superb carved and inlaid stalls, the only stalls in Venice to retain their original position and structure. Titian's warm and vibrant *Assumption* is immediately before you as you enter, rising before the mullioned windows of the sanctuary apse. An inscription in the marble frame records that the work was commissioned in 1516 by Friar Germano, Superior of the Franciscan friary; the finished altarpiece was installed on 20 May 1518, in an elaborate public ceremony. This is probably the most famous painting of the Venetian Renaissance. At the time it was made, the painter's unorthodox approach to his subject—such a shapely Virgin and excited Apostles had never been seen before—was seen as scandalous; but the stir soon mellowed into praise, and by 1548 critic Paolo Pino could claim, 'If Titian and Michelangelo were one person; that is, if the draughtsmanship of Michelangelo went together with the colour of Titian, one could call that person the god of painting'.

In the second bay of the **south aisle** is an 1852 monument to Titian; over the third altar, a statue of St Jerome, by Alessandro Vittoria, considered one of his best sculptures. High up in the **south transept**, on the right, is Pietro Lombardo's tomb of Jacopo Marcello, with the statue of the deceased on the sarcophagus supported by three caryatids. The tomb of Beato Pacifico, on the adjoining wall, was made by 15th-century Florentine masters. Above the door to the sacristy is the tomb of Benedetto Pesaro, by Lorenzo Bregno.

In the **sacristy** are fine reliquaries displayed in an elaborate Baroque showcase; on the altar, an enchanting triptych by Giovanni Bellini showing the *Madonna and Child with Sts Nicholas, Peter, Paul and Benedict* (signed and dated 1488), commissioned for this location and still surrounded by its original gilt wood frame. The perspective effect is truly remarkable and may distract your attention from the two angel-musicians at the bottom of the throne, which are not to be missed. Paolo Veneziano's 1339 *Madonna and Child with Sts Francis and Elisabeth* has been placed at the opposite end of the sacristy. The **south apsidal chapels** hold various Gothic tombs of the 14th century. In the third (the first as you come out of the sacristy) is a *Madonna and Child* by

Bartolomeo Vivarini; in the first, Donatello's powerful wooden *St John the Baptist*, carved around 1450 but repainted in the 19th century. On the south wall here is the tomb of Doge Francesco Foscari, a late Gothic-early Renaissance monument by Antonio and Paolo Bregno. On the north wall, the marble facing with the tomb of Doge Niccolò Tron, by Antonio Rizzo and assistants, is one of the outstanding funerary monuments of the Venetian Renaissance.

The first **north apsidal chapel** contains an altarpiece by Bernardino Licinio, who also did the Franciscan martyrs on the north wall; in the third is the *St Ambrose Altarpiece* by Alvise Vivarini and Marco Basaiti; the fourth has a brilliantly colourful triptych by Bartolomeo Vivarini over the altar and a touching statue of St John by Jacopo Sansovino on the baptismal font.

Over the second altar of the **north aisle** is Titian's *Pesaro Altarpiece*, commissioned in 1519 by Bishop Jacopo Pesaro, former admiral of the Venetian fleet, who appears at the bottom left with a soldier in armour leading a Turkish prisoner. In the opposite corner of the painting is Senator Francesco Pesaro with two other brothers, Antonio and Giovanni, and Antonio's young sons Leonardo and Niccolò. St Peter and the family patron saints Francis and Anthony stand above, forming the sides of an imaginary triangle culminating in the image of the Virgin and Child. The two powerful columns, whose upper ends are lost above the top of the painting, represent the Gates of Heaven.

The lateral doorway is framed by the colossal funerary composition created by Baldassare Longhena for Doge Giovanni Pesaro (1669). The last bay on this side contains the monument to Antonio Canova, in the form of a pyramid, executed by his pupils using designs by Canova himself: he had prepared something similar for a tomb of Titian; his Vienna monument to Maria Theresa's daughter Maria Christina is largely identical. Remains of the Franciscan convent include a few rooms and the cloisters, renovated between the 16th and 18th centuries.

The Scuola Grande di San Rocco

Open daily 9–5.30.

Opposite the apse of the Frari is the **Scuola Grande di San Rocco**, built for the Confraternity of St Roch. Begun in 1516 to an initial design by Bartolomeo Bon, it was completed in 1560 under the direction of Sante Lombardo and Scarpagnino. Scarpagnino is responsible for the magnificent façade, on which High Renaissance elements (on the ground floor) are tied together with foreshadowings of the Baroque taste (above). Inside, the large halls are decorated with a magnificent cycle of large paintings executed over a period of 23 years (1564–87) by Jacopo Tintoretto.

The visit begins on the upper floor, which is reached by Scarpagnino's grand staircase. Antonio Zanchi's *Plague of 1630*, painted in 1666, lines the walls (St Roch is the patron saint of the infirm and of plague victims). Turn left at the top of the stairs and left again. In the Sala dell'Albergo (where the chapter met) is Tintoretto's vast *Crucifixion* of 1565, universally considered his masterpiece, a work so profoundly moving that it left even the eloquent Ruskin speechless ('I must leave this picture to work its will on the spectator, for it is beyond all analysis and above all praise.'). The other paintings represent scenes of the Passion (*Christ Before Pilate*, *Christ Carrying the Cross* and *Ecce Homo*). The famous—or infamous (*see box below*)—*Triumph of St Roch* shines down from the great oval in the middle of the ceiling. Set on easels are two small paintings brought here from the church of San Rocco for safekeeping: *Ecce Homo*, an early work of Titian, and *Christ Carrying the Cross*, which some ascribe to Titian and others to Giorgione.

TINTORETTO AT SAN ROCCO

The Scuola Grande di San Rocco could be described as a veritable monument to Tintoretto's art, and the adventurous (and probably true) story behind the painting here casts light on the artist's extraordinary character. Soon after the completion of the building, the Confraternity of St Roch announced a competition for the decoration of the interior, inviting four leading Venetian artists of the day (Federico Zuccari, Giuseppe Salviati, Paolo Veronese and Tintoretto) to submit proposals. The competition design had to be an oval painting of the *Triumph of St Roch*. On 31 May 1564 the committee met to judge the entries. Zuccari, Salviati and Veronese showed up with drawings and sketches; but Tintoretto—with the help of the custodian of the building—arranged for the judges to find a finished picture, whipped together with characteristic impetuosity, already installed in the oval space of the ceiling. He offered this work as a gift to the confraternity and promised to paint the rest of the ceiling at no extra cost—provided he was commissioned to do the entire decorative scheme for the scuola. Over the protests of the other artists and of a few members of the confraternity, who accused him of cheating, he won the commission.

In the large Sala Maggiore the ceiling is occupied by stories drawn from the Old Testament (*Moses Drawing Water from the Rock* in the first large frame, surrounded by *Adam and Eve*, *God Appearing to Moses*, the *Pillar of Fire* and *Jonah and the Whale*; the *Brazen Serpent*, flanked by the *Vision of Ezekiel* and *Jacob's Ladder*; and the *Gathering of Manna*, surrounded by the *Sacrifice of Isaac*, *Elijah Fed by the Angel*, *Elisha Multiplying the Loaves* and the *Passover Feast*). On the walls are *Sts Roch and Sebastian* (by the windows) and New Testament stories (*Adoration of the Shepherds*, *Baptism of Christ*, *Resurrection*, *Agony in the Garden*, *Last Supper*, *Miracle of the Loaves and Fishes*, *Resurrection of Lazarus*, *Ascension*, *Pool of Bethesda* and *Temptation*). The artist executed the cycle in just five years, between 1576 and 1581, adding the altarpiece of the *Vision of St Roch* in 1588. On the left of the altar, on easels, are Giovanni Bellini's *Ecce Homo* and an *Annunciation* by Titian; on the right, a *Visitation* and *Self Portrait* by Tintoretto and Giorgione's *Christ Carrying the Cross* surmounted by Titian's *God and Angels*. *Abraham Visited by the Angels* and *Agar Rescued by the Angels* by Giovanni Battista Tiepolo stand on easels at the other end of the hall. In the ground floor hall are eight large canvases that Tintoretto painted in 1583–87. The *Annunciation, Flight into Egypt, St Mary Magdalen* and *St Mary of Egypt* are particularly beautiful. The statue of St Roch over the altar was carved by Girolamo Campagna in 1587.

Across the way is the church of **San Rocco** (*open Mon–Sat 7.30–12.30; Sat also 2–4; Sun 8–12 & 2–4*) with an elegant façade of 1760 decorated with sculptures by Giovanni Marchiori and Giovan Maria Morlaiter. The 18th-century interior has more paintings by Tintoretto, two of which are particularly significant. The powerful handling of the nudes in *St Roch in Prison*, on the south wall, is a reminder that Tintoretto originally painted his great *Crucifixion* with naked figures, to which he later added draperies. The privileged position of *St Roch Ministering to the Plague-Stricken*—in the sanctuary—recalls that St Roch's miraculous ability to heal those afflicted with plague was intimately tied to the enormous prestige his scuola enjoyed in Venice. The church also holds paintings by Sebastiano Ricci and Giovanni Antonio da Pordenone, and (by the main door) elegant Rococo statues of David and St Cecilia by Giovanni Marchiori.

San Polo and its square

Cross back over the Rio dei Frari, go over the Rio di San Polo and follow the signs for San Marco to reach the old church of **San Polo**, a Byzantine foundation several times altered, which you enter by a large 15th-century Gothic doorway on the south flank. The interior, which still retains a marked medieval feeling, has three aisles of columns with a wooden ship's-keel roof and paintings by Tintoretto (west wall and first south altar), Tiepolo (second north altar) and Palma Giovane (on the walls). The organ dates from 1763.

The large square behind the church, where popular feasts were once held, is overlooked by several patrician palaces, all of which have their more elaborate façades on the water. Baron Corvo stayed at the Palazzo Corner Mocenigo, (no. 2128a) while writing his last book, *The Desire and Pursuit of the Whole*; nos 2169 and 2171 are Gothic palaces with finely decorated windows and balconies; next to them rises the 18th-century Palazzo Tiepolo (whose owners were no relation to the painter). Continue walking northeast, past the churches of Sant' Aponal and San Giovanni Elemosinario. In just a few minutes you'll come to the Rio degli Orefici and back to the Rialto Bridge.

CASTELLO

Looking at the crowded quay that stretches eastwards from the Palazzo Ducale to the Giardini di Castello, you'd never guess that one of the quietest and most relaxed areas of Venice lies just behind San Marco. Oddly enough, the throngs stick to the waterfront, notwithstanding the presence, just a few paces inland, of some of the most magnificent achievements of Venetian art and architecture.

From Piazza San Marco, take the Mercerie (beneath the clock tower) to the church of San Zulian, then Calle delle Bande right to **Campo Santa Maria Formosa**. Among the liveliest of Venetian *campi*, formerly used for open-air theatre, this pleasant square is surrounded by fine palaces: no. 5866, Palazzo Ruzzini, of 1580; nos 6121 and 6125–26, three Palazzi Donà—the first late 16th, the others 15th-century Gothic. At no. 5246 is Palazzo Vitturi, an unusual example of Veneto-Byzantine architecture of the 13th century.

The church of **Santa Maria Formosa**, erected according to tradition in 639 following a miraculous apparition of the Virgin Mary in the form of a beautiful (*formosa*) maiden, was rebuilt in 1482 by Mauro Codussi in Renaissance forms. In the 16th century it received its two Classical façades, and in the 17th century its Baroque campanile. The interior, whose Greek-cross plan may be a carry-over from the earlier church, combines the elegance of Renaissance ornament with the spatial values of Byzantine architecture. It preserves a *Madonna of Mercy* by Bartolomeo Vivarini, signed and dated 1473; and a polyptych with *St Barbara and Four Saints* by Palma Vecchio. St Barbara was the patron of the artillerymen who had their chapel in this church, and her valiant, resolute bearing in Palma's painting caused George Eliot to describe her as 'an almost unique presentation of a hero-woman, standing in calm preparation for martyrdom, without the slightest air of pietism, yet the expression of a mind filled with serious conviction'.

Walk all the way around the church and then south to reach Campiello Querini Stampalia, along the Rio Santa Maria Formosa. Here, in a palace of 1528, stands the **Fondazione Querini Stampalia**, with an important library and picture gallery (*open Tues, Wed, Thur and Sun 10–6, Fri and Sat 10–10*). The building was renovated in the 1960s to a design by Carlo Scarpa. The works reflect the personal taste of the founder, Count Giovanni Querini, whose interest focused on the social portraits, conversation pieces and rich furnishings of 18th-century Venice.

A PORTRAIT BY TIEPOLO

The real surprise in the Querini Stampalia collection is Giovanni Battista Tiepolo's *Portrait of the Procurator Dolfin*, painted between 1750 and 1755. Tiepolo rarely showed much interest in portraiture; his imagination was attracted more by mythological or historical subjects. The sitter has only tentatively been identified as Daniele Dolfin IV (1656–1723), a captain in the Venetian navy and Procurator of the Republic, for whose palace the young Tiepolo had painted a series of Roman generals. The cruel energy in the gloved hand and the sinisterly spectral white wig are perfectly in keeping with the prestige of such a position. The daring perspective and the theatrically billowing draperies give the painting an expressive power so strong that it verges on caricature.

Santi Giovanni e Paolo

Return to Santa Maria Formosa and walk north to reach Campo Santi Giovanni e Paolo (San Zanipolo in dialect). This, the most monumental of Venetian squares after

Piazza San Marco, opens around the imposing Dominican church of Santi Giovanni e Paolo (*open 7–12.30 & 3.30–7.30*) and the exuberant marble façade of the Scuola di San Marco (*see below*). Near the corner of the church stands the **Colleoni Monument**, a bronze equestrian statue of mercenary general Bartolommeo Colleoni, the last and grandest work of the Florentine sculptor Andrea Verrocchio, though it was not cast until after his death.

The statue comes with a story attached. Colleoni, who had commanded the land forces of the Venetian Republic, died in 1475, leaving a considerable sum of money to erect a monument in his honour. The legacy stipulated that the statue should be set up in Piazza San Marco. The authorities were prevented by constitution from erecting a monument to a single individual in the city's main public square, however, and destined the statue for a less important site, in front of the Scuola of San Marco—thus, in a sense, fulfilling the terms of the will.

In keeping with the new interests of his period, Verrocchio has abandoned the static concept of equestrian statuary expressed by Donatello in the Gattamelata monument in Padua (*see p. 468*). Gattamelata comes across as stern and dignified. The sense of impatient movement conveyed here by Verrocchio makes Colleoni appear brutal and pugilistic. The horse is strong and unruly, its veins swollen, its muscles tense. Erect in the stirrups, his torso twisted against the movement of the horse's head, the general frowns down with fierce pride, in full command of his nervous charger. Never was there a more convincing portrait of power and command than this. Ruskin considered it the most glorious work of sculpture in the world.

Santi Giovanni e Paolo is the second largest Gothic church in Venice. It was begun in the mid-14th century. The apses and transept had been completed by 1368, and the church was consecrated in 1430. The austere façade, forms a striking contrast to the extremely ornate front of the adja-

Andrea Verrocchio: Colleoni Monument.

cent Scuola di San Marco. Plain brown brick is fringed with a delicately designed roofline, and articulated by a large marble doorway by Bartolomeo Bon and assistants, flanked by tall arched niches containing sarcophagi. The vast interior is a feast of Venetian sculpture and painting. From the 15th century on, San Zanipolo was the traditional site of the doges' funerals, and splendid Gothic and Renaissance monuments to 25 of the Republic's leaders line the walls. The most impressive of these is Pietro Lombardo's 1476 monument to Pietro Mocenigo, whose family occupies the entire west wall. Two paintings are of special note: Giovanni Bellini's polyptych of *St Vincent Ferrer flanked by Sts Christopher and Sebastian* (near the Lombardo tomb, in the south aisle) and Lorenzo Lotto's *St Anthony Giving Alms*, a brilliant mix of condescension and compassion, in the south wing of the transept. Here also is the last surviving example of the large painted glass windows that were a speciality of Murano glassmakers, the *Window of Warrior Saints* (1515), based on designs by Bartolomeo Vivarini and Gerolamo Mocetto. The Cappella del Rosario, reached from the north transept, contains ceiling paintings by Paolo Veronese. Back on the south side, the Cappella di San Domenico, adjoining the south transept, has paintings by Piazzetta in the ceiling and low reliefs of St Dominic's life on the walls by Giuseppe Mazza and Giambattista Alberghetti. The Cappella della Madonna della Pace, in the south aisle, has fine paintings by Leandro Bassano, stuccoes and a Byzantine icon of rare beauty over the altar.

On the piazza's north side is the Scuola Grande di San Marco, now the city hospital. The palace, largely a work of the early Renaissance, was begun by Pietro and Tullio Lombardo, continued by Mauro Codussi and completed by Jacopo Sansovino. The splendid coloured-marble façade has sophisticated trompe-l'œil reliefs in which a marvellous sense of depth is obtained from an essentially two-dimentional surface. The roofline presents arched pediments of various size and the main doorway has a porch with lunette by Bartolomeo Bon. From the ground floor hall you can enter the former Dominican convent of Santi Giovanni e Paolo, rebuilt by Baldassare Longhena in 1660–75 to a 13th century plan around two cloisters and a courtyard.

San Zaccaria

Winding southwards towards the Riva degli Schiavoni you come to the quiet, sheltered **Campo San Zaccaria**, overlooked by the stunning façade of its church (*open 10–12 & 4–6*). **San Zaccaria** was founded in the 9th century, and there are still traces (in the crypt) of the original building, where eight of the first doges were buried. The church you see today was begun during the 15th century in Gothic forms and completed in 1480–1515 by Mauro Codussi, who gave it its multi-level white stone façade. Though it is hailed as one of the first Renaissance church façades in the city, it is in fact much more typically Venetian in its eclectic mix of vertical Gothic, classical Renaissance and undulating Romanesque forms.

The interior is tall, vaulted and three-aisled; its ambulatory with radial chapels lit by tall windows is unique in Venice. The walls are almost entirely covered with paintings, by far the most important of which is Giovanni Bellini's *Madonna and Saints* (*Sacra Conversazione*) over the second north altar, signed and dated 1505.

Giovanni Bellini (c. 1430–1516)
Bellini is the artist who can perhaps be credited with launching the Venetian Renaissance. A highly original painter, he also learned much from others, including his brother-in-law Mantegna. Acknowledged as the greatest Venetian master during his own lifetime, and appointed official painter to the Republic, he launched many younger artists on their careers, including Giorgione and Titian. Though he painted superb portraits, his main achievements are his religious works, including the monumental San Zaccaria altarpiece. Executed when the painter was in his seventies, this is considered a pivotal work in Venetian painting's progress towards the mastery of harmonious colour. The supreme expression of the Venetian attitude to painting, it seems to capture the very quintessence of the elusive Venetian light.

Off the south aisle is the late Renaissance Cappella di Sant'Atanasio, which holds paintings by Tintoretto (*Birth of the Baptist*) and Tiepolo, and inlaid choir stalls of 1455–64. From the adjoining Cappella dell'Addolorata you enter the Cappella di San Tarasio, formerly part of the apse of the church, where there are three carved and gilt Gothic polyptychs jointly painted by Antonio Vivarini, Giovanni d'Alemagna and Stefano da Sant'Agnese (1443). Perhaps the most impressive of these is the *Madonna of the Rosary, with Saints* by Vivarini, decorative panels by d'Alemagna and a *Madonna* by Sant'Agnese set in a massive wooden frame of carved niches, turrets and pinnacles. On the walls are Andrea del Castagno's *Church Fathers*, executed by the Florentine artist in 1442 with the help of Francesco da Faenza. Andrea, who had been Masaccio's first pupil, was 19 years old when he brought the Tuscan Renaissance style to Venice in these paintings.

Back in the campo, a 16th-century doorway (no. 4693) marks the entrance to the former Benedictine convent, once the wealthiest and wildest in Venice. Here the city's aristocratic families sent their surplus daughters—often against their will—to save the expense of dowries. The more rebellious naturally refused to renounce the luxury and extravagance of patrician life, with results that can easily be imagined. There is a painting by Francesco Guardi in the museum at Ca' Rezzonico (the *Parlour of the Nuns of San Zaccaria*) which shows the notoriously libertine atmosphere that prevailed in the convent, with dancing, theatre and novices making doughnuts. By a peculiar twist of fate, the convent is now a police station.

Where the Eastern merchants lived

Walk away from the church and turn right into the triangular Campo San Provolo, then follow the Fondamenta Osmarin and cross over the narrow Rio di Greci. Here, in a shady garden on the right, is **San Giorgio dei Greci**, a 16th-century church built to a design by Sante Lombardo for the Greek Orthodox community. The most important foreign church in Renaissance Venice, it has a magnificently decorated interior divided by a marble iconostasis with late Byzantine gold-ground paintings. On the north side, in the rooms of the former Scuola dei Greci (now the Istituto Ellenico), is the Museo dei Dipinti Sacri Bizantini (*open daily 9–12.30 & 1.30–4.30, Sun and holidays 10–5*), which preserves some 80 Byzantine and post-Byzantine icons and various liturgical objects. One of the highlights here is a hieratic icon of *St Anastasius* by the 16th-century painter Michele Damaskinos, who is credited with having encouraged a young artist from Crete who was in Venice at the time—Domenicos Theotocopoulos—to absorb all he could from Tintoretto's work and then move on to Spain, where he would establish a reputation under the name of El Greco.

The **Scuola di San Giorgio degli Schiavoni** (*open Tues–Sat 9.30–12.30 & 3.30–6, Sun and holidays 9.30–12.30*), one block north along the canal and to the right, was erected in the early 16th century by the Dalmatian confraternity, whose members were mainly merchants involved in trade with the East. The beautiful painting cycle on its ground-floor walls is one of the artistic jewels of Venice and should not be missed. Executed by Vittore Carpaccio, who worked in Venice between 1490 and 1523, the richly fantastic scenes portray episodes from the lives of the three protectors of Dalmatia, Sts George, Jerome and Tryphon.

Carpaccio tended to work on commissions that allowed him to indulge in his natural vocation for simple and apparently ingenuous narrative art, which in many ways recalls the *sacre rappresentazioni* that were the most widespread form of popular theatre of the time. These works, with their entrancing atmospheric power, mark the high point of his career. Most poetic of all, perhaps, is the *Study of St Augustine* (right), which depicts a scene described in the *Golden Legend*: alone in his study, the Bishop of Hippo hears the voice of his friend St Jerome (then absent in Antioch) announcing that he has died. The room is flooded with a sudden light and all movement comes to a halt (even the saint's fluffy dog is silent and still) as St Augustine interrupts his writing. The vanishing point of the perspective scheme has been shifted from the centre to the right of the painting, to coincide with the saint's pen, suspended above the page. Carpaccio never again achieved such expressive force, nor created an effect as magical as that achieved here.

Towards the Arsenale

Go down the rio, over the bridge, through a charming passageway with a tabernacle of the Madonna, then right to Salizzada San Francesco, which leads under an imposing portico to **San Francesco della Vigna**. This large 16th-century church, built to a design by Jacopo Sansovino, has a noble Classical façade by Andrea Palladio based on a complex arrangement of superimposed temple fronts. The vast Latin-cross interior contains numerous masterpieces. Over the first altar of the south transept is the one work that can be attributed with certainty to Fra' Antonio da Negroponte, a *Madonna Adoring the Child* painted in the 1450s in a curious retro style; in the sanctuary are monuments to Doge Andrea Gritti and his circle, possibly by Sansovino; in the chapel to the north of the sanctuary, an outstanding ensemble of sculptures by Pietro Lombardo and pupils (1495–1510) with a fine illusionistic floor; in the Cappella Santa, entered from the north transept, *Madonna and Child with Saints* by Giovanni

Bellini (signed and dated 1507); and in the fifth north chapel, another *Madonna and Saints*, the *Giustinian Altarpiece*, by Paolo Veronese, the earliest of his masterpieces to be seen in Venice (1551).

In Campo Bandiera e Moro, almost due south near the Riva degli Schiavoni, is the late Gothic church of **San Giovanni in Bràgora**, with a distinctive linear brick façade and a low, cosy interior. Here are more masterpieces of Gothic and Renaissance painting: a *Resurrected Christ, Madonna with Sts Andrew and John the Baptist, Praying Madonna and Child* and a small panel with the *Head of the Redeemer* by Alvise Vivarini; *Sts Andrew, Jerome and Martin* by Francesco Bissolo; *Constantine and St Helen* and *Baptism of Christ* by Cima da Conegliano; and a *Last Supper* by Paris Bordone. The stuccoed vault of the sanctuary is the work of Alessandro Vittoria.

Continuing eastwards you come to the **Arsenale**, once the greatest shipyard in the world. From here, after 1155, came the Venetian galleys, the basis of the Republic's economic and political power. From here also comes the modern European word 'arsenal'—a corruption of the Arabic *darsina'a*, workshop. Dante described this once-bustling dockyard in the *Inferno* (xxi), comparing the pitch in which he placed barterers of public offices to that boiled in the arsenal for caulking the damaged hulls of Venetian ships. The complex is usually closed to the public, except when the *corderie*—huge, long buildings originally designed for the storage of rigging—are being used for an exhibition. Part of the complex can be seen, however, from vaporetto no. 52, which runs along the canal inside. The land entrance is marked by a doorway of 1460, considered the first work of the Venetian Renaissance, surmounted by an attic with a large lion of St Mark attributed to Bartolomeo Bon. In 1692–94 the doorway was given a terraced porch adorned with Baroque allegorical statues; at the sides of this are two stone lions brought here from Greece (the one on the left comes from the harbour of Pireus). Further right are two smaller lions, one from the island of Delos.

Walk down the Rio dell'Arsenale to reach the waterfront. You'll pass two sections of the **Museo Storico Navale** (*open Mon–Fri 8.45–1.30, Sat 8.45–1*)—one with historic ships, in the Officina Remi (just outside the Arsenale); the other with a beautiful model collection of typical Adriatic galleys, Venetian gondolas and other vessels—including the famed Bucintoro, the doges' ceremonial barge—in the former Republican granary on the wharf at the end of the canal. When on display there is also an interesting model of the system of wooden piles on which Venice is built.

Riva degli Schiavoni, the broad, lively quay along the basin of San Marco, takes its name from the merchants of Schiavonia or Slavonia (modern Dalmatia), who anchored their ships and carried on their business here.

CANNAREGIO

The church of Santa Maria di Nazareth, usually known simply as **Gli Scalzi** (literally, the Barefoot) was built by Baldassare Longhena after 1654 for a community of Carmelite monks who moved here from Rome, and its design and interior décor in fact recall those of Roman Baroque churches. Giuseppe Sardi added the white marble façade in 1680. The second south and first north chapels have vault frescoes by Tiepolo, who also painted the ceiling of the nave. This painting was destroyed by Austrian bombs in 1915, and the modern replacement dates from 1934.

The Ghetto and environs

The crowded **Lista di Spagna** leads northeastwards, crossing the broad **Canale di Cannaregio** by the Ponte delle Guglie. Once across the canal you turn left then immediately right through the Sottoportico del Ghetto. The street leads past a synagogue with beautifully carved doors, and over a bridge to the Ghetto Nuovo. From 1516 to 1797 it was home to the city's Jewish population: this tiny, water-ringed neighbourhood is the oldest historically documented ghetto in the world. The site was originally occupied by a foundry—in Venetian dialect, *getto*—and this term was subsequently taken to describe the Jewish quarter in cities everywhere.

On the whole the Venetian Jews enjoyed a relatively relaxed relationship with the Republic: though they were obliged to follow certain rules that limited their social and economic activities, they maintained their religious freedom and, except for a brief period of expulsion between 1527 and 1533, they remained within the city, in this neighbourhood, until Napoleon demolished the gates of the ghetto in 1797. After this time they were allowed to live where they pleased. As the area of the ghetto was limited, the Jews were forced to build tenements that, without violating the city's height limitations, would accommodate many families. Several of the houses therefore have very low ceilings.

The **Museo della Comunità Ebraica** (*open daily 10–6, closed Sat & Jewish holidays*), in Campo Ghetto Nuovo, offers guided tours of the ghetto and of three of its synagogues, also called 'scuole' by virtue of the mixed purposes they served. The most sumptuous is the Scuola Levantina, in the Ghetto Vecchio, established in 1538 and remodelled in the 17th century, possibly to a design by Baldassare Longhena. The museum's collections include liturgical objects and other examples of Venetian Jewish art of the 17th–19th centuries, and text boards describing the plight of Venetian Jews during the Holocaust.

Madonna dell'Orto and I Gesuiti

Cross the Campo di Ghetto Nuovo to the Fondamenta degli Ormesini and turn right. This is one of the quieter parts of the city, almost untouched by tourists. Most of the alleys on the left lead eventually to the beautiful Gothic church of **Madonna dell'Orto**, founded in the 14th century and rebuilt in the 15th to hold a miraculous image of the Virgin discovered in a nearby garden (*orto* in Italian). This was the parish church of Tintoretto, who was buried in the chapel on the south side of the sanctuary in 1594. Inside are several of his works: the *Presentation of the Virgin in the Temple* at the end of the south aisle, the *Last Judgement and Worship of the Golden Calf* in the choir, and the *Vision of the Cross to St Peter* and *Beheading of St Paul* in the apse. The latter are hung around an *Annunciation* by Palma Giovane. A *St John the Baptist and Saints* by Cima da Conegliano stands over the first south altar.

It takes some fancy footwork, down the busy Rio di Noale towards the Grand Canal and up the other side almost to the Fondamenta Nuove, to reach **I Gesuiti**, the church of Venice's Jesuit community. This is an early 18th-century edifice with a lively Baroque façade based on Roman models. Like so many Jesuit churches, it has an elaborately decorated interior—in this case an extraordinary work of trompe-l'œil with green and white inlaid marbles imitating damask wall hangings, and white and gold stuccoes. Over the first north altar is Titian's *Martyrdom of St Lawrence*, and in the transept on this side is an *Assumption* by Jacopo Tintoretto. Palma Giovane decorated the nearby Oratorio dei Crociferi, founded in the 13th century and renovated in the late 16th century (*open by appointment; T: 041 270 2464*). It may seem odd that the seat of such an important order should be located so far from the mainstream of city life. In fact the Venice senate managed to keep the powerful Jesuits out of the city for a long time; when the order was finally allowed to establish itself, it was kept as far from the centres of political and economic affairs as topography would allow.

Towards the Rialto

From Campo dei Gesuiti cross the Rio Santa Caterina and follow the *calli* southwards to their end, near the church and campo of Santi Apostoli. Now turn left, cross the Rio Santi Apostoli and bear slightly left again. **Santa Maria dei Miracoli**, a lonely little church in the narrow Campo dei Miracoli, bounded by water on one side, is one of the highest achievements of the early Venetian Renaissance. Constructed between 1481 and 1489 to enshrine a miraculous image of the Virgin, it is covered with coloured marble panels whose ingeniously complex design makes the church appear larger than it really is without disturbing the overall effect of harmonious tranquillity. The church is the work of Pietro Lombardo, who was assisted here by his sons Antonio and Tullio. The interior also has exquisite Lombardesque marblework and a delightful *Madonna*, over the high altar, by Nicolò di Pietro Paradisi. The figures of *Saints* in the coffered ceiling were painted by Pier Maria Pennacchi (1528). The choir loft above the entrance bears a *Madonna and Child* by Palma Giovane.

The pleasant red and white church of **San Giovanni Crisostomo** almost fills its small campo. The last work of Mauro Codussi, it too is a masterpiece of Venetian Renaissance architecture. The Greek-cross interior preserves two important paintings—Giovanni Bellini's *St Jerome with St Christopher and St Augustine* (over the first south altar), the high altarpiece of *St John Chrysostom and Six Saints* by Sebastiano del Piombo—and an extraordinarily powerful, classically serene marble relief of the *Coronation of the Virgin* (over the second north altar) by Tullio Lombardo, who also decorated the pilasters in the chapel.

Back at Campo dei Santi Apostoli stands the plain brick church of **Santi Apostoli**, built in 1575 possibly to a design by Alessandro Vittoria. Some way down the Strada Nuova (a broad thoroughfare cut in 1871 to connect Rialto with the train station) but before the first bridge, Calle della Ca' d'Oro leads left to the land entrance of the **Ca' d'Oro**, the fine Gothic palace designed by Giovanni and Bartolomeo Bon and Matteo Raverti (1420–34), named the 'Golden House' after the splendid gilt decoration that

used to adorn the Grand Canal façade. The palace is now a museum (*open Mon 8.15–2, Tues–Sun 8.15–7.15; last admission 30mins before closing*) displaying the outstanding art collection of its former owner, Baron Giorgio Franchetti. Here you can see Italian and foreign paintings and Venetian marbles, bronzes and ceramics of the 15th–18th centuries. Highlights include Antonio Vivarini's remarkable polyptych with *Passion Scenes* (1476–84) and Andrea Mantegna's *St Sebastian*, a splendid masterpiece of the early Renaissance; a double portrait by Tullio Lombardo and fresco fragments by Giorgione and Titian from the exterior of the Fondaco dei Tedeschi. Before leaving, take a stroll outside, in the small secret garden and stunning canal-front portico.

MANTEGNA'S ST SEBASTIAN

The subject of St Sebastian seems to have held some mysterious fascination for Andrea Mantegna, who painted at least three other versions (now at the Accademia, in Paris and in Vienna); but the most powerful treatment of the theme is to be found in this Ca' d'Oro painting. The style is certainly that of the his later years (1490–1500), filled with symbolic nuance: the tortured line of the drapery accentuates the idea of Christian suffering in the name of faith, and the ample use of purple-grey 'bruise' tones emphasises the saint's human agony. The perspective rendering of anatomy (notice the foot that steps out of the frame at the bottom of the painting) is as sophisticated as that of the artist's most famous painting, the *Dead Christ* in the Brera in Milan.

AROUND THE LAGOON

The Island of San Giorgio

From Rio dell'Arsenale follow the *riva* along the waterfront past the church of the **Pietà** (where Vivaldi was choir master) to reach the landing stage of vaporetto no. 9, which plies across the San Marco basin to San Giorgio and the Giudecca. Henry James called the island of San Giorgio 'a success beyond all reason', attributing its fortune to its position, to the immense detached campanile, which seems to pin the buildings to their magnificent background.

The most striking building is Palladio's church of **San Giorgio Maggiore** (*open daily 9.30–12.30 & 2.30–6*), built between 1565 and 1580 over the remains of earlier churches dating back as far as the 8th century. On the right you can see a group of low red edifices, the convent, built by Baldassare Longhena in the 17th century. It was the colour, above all, that Henry James appreciated. 'I do not know whether it is because San Giorgio is so grandly conspicuous, with a great deal of worn, faded-looking brickwork', he wrote, 'but for many persons, the whole place has a kind of suffusion of rosiness.'

Palladio and his contemporaries were convinced that a harmony like that of music underlay the great buildings of the past, and that the secrets of that harmony could be unravelled by a careful study of mathematical proportions. You can see this belief at work on the façade of San Giorgio, where the triangle formed by extrapolating the lateral pediments reaches its apex at the base of the central pediment—an ingenious expedient that prepares the visitor, visually, for the aisled church within. Though it appears wonderfully simple, San Giorgio is Palladio's most complex church-front design. The giant order gives it monumentality. Though two-dimensional, it suggests the three-dimensionality of a Classical temple portico. It was only completed after the architect's death, in the early 17th century.

The interior of the church impresses more by virtue of its luminosity and spaciousness than for the complexity of its design, although it is the latter that gives rise to the former. Its remarkable sculptural quality is based on a sustained opposition between flat and rounded forms—walls, arches and vaults, engaged columns and giant pilasters—and decoration is almost totally eliminated. Its art treasures include two works by Tintoretto, the *Last Supper* and the *Gathering of Manna*, on the walls around the high altar (1594). The gift of manna to the Israelites in the wilderness provided the Old Testament parallel to the institution of the Eucharist, and the paintings were designed to be most effective when seen by the communicant from the altar rail. In the monks' choir are stalls carved with stories from the *Life of St Benedict*; over the altar of the winter choir is a *St George and the Dragon* by Vittore Carpaccio.

The monastery of San Giorgio Maggiore, seat of the Fondazione Giorgio Cini, is a fine complex arranged around two cloisters. Palladio designed the refectory, where there is a *Marriage of the Virgin* by Jacopo Tintoretto; and a monumental staircase by Baldassare Longhena ascends to the first floor, where the Library, also by Longhena, has 17th-century inlaid bookcases with over 100,000 books on the history of art. In the park is the Teatro Verde, for open-air theatre. The complex is open to the public only for special events. The campanile, reached by a lift, is 60m high and offers unsurpassed views of the city and the lagoon.

The Giudecca

The Giudecca is a long, narrow island delightfully off the beaten track. Originally known as Spinalonga ('long spine') because of its shape, its present name probably derives from the Jewish community that lived here in the 13th century. By the 16th century it had become a place of green quietude, abounding with lush gardens, aristocratic homes and tranquil convents. Following the decline of the Venetian aristocracy and the suppression of the convents, the island was gradually given over to barracks, prisons and factories. Today its simple houses are home to many of Venice's boatmen. The quay, along the inner, southern side of the island, takes different names as it goes along, offering splendid views of the Giudecca Canal, San Marco and the Riva degli Schiavoni. The entire section from the Rio di San Biagio canal, on the island's western tip, to the church of the Zitelle, on the east, is almost tourist-free and gives a sense of a simpler, original Venice.

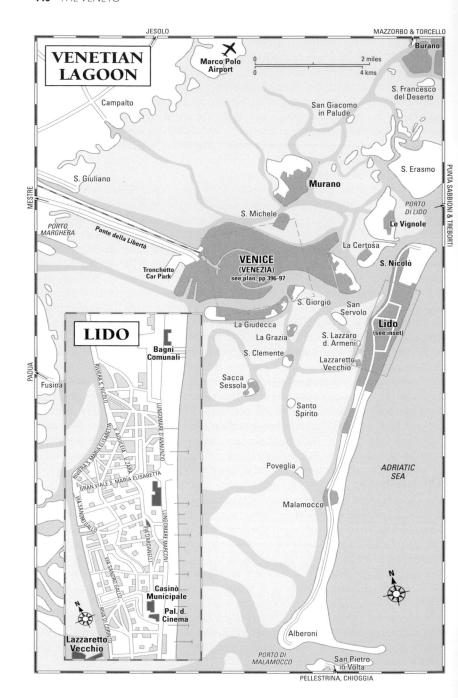

JESOLO

MAZZORBO & TORCELLO

VENETIAN LAGOON

Burano

Marco Polo Airport

0   2 miles

0   4 kms

Campalto

San Giacomo in Palude

S. Francesco del Deserto

S. Erasmo

PUNTA SABBIONI & TREPORTI

S. Giuliano

Murano

MESTRE

S. Michele

PORTO DI LIDO

Le Vignole

PORTO MARGHERA

Ponte della Libertà

La Certosa

S. Nicolò

Tronchetto Car Park

VENICE (VENEZIA) see plan, pp 396–97

S. Giorgio

San Servolo

Lido (see inset)

LIDO

La Giudecca

La Grazia

S. Lazzaro d. Armeni

PADUA

Bagni Comunali

S. Clemente

Lazzaretto Vecchio

Fusina

Sacca Sessola

Santo Spirito

RIVIERA S. NICOLO

RIVIERA S. MARIA ELISABETTA

V. AQUILEIA

V. ZARA

GRAN VIALE S. MARIA ELISABETTA

LUNGOMARE D'ANNUNZIO

VIA SANDRO GALLO

VIA D'ARDANELLI

LUNGOMARE MARCONI

Poveglia

ADRIATIC SEA

Malamocco

VIA SANDRO GALLO

Casinò Municipale

Pal. d. Cinema

RIVA DI CORINTO

Lazzaretto Vecchio

Alberoni

PORTO DI MALAMOCCO

San Pietro in Volta

PELLESTRINA, CHIOGGIA

The boat stops first at the church and convent of Santa Maria della Presentazione, usually known as **Le Zitelle** (The Virgins), where the nuns once made excellent Venetian lace. Its design is attributed to Palladio, though it was not built until after his death. From here it is a short walk to the main monument on the Giudecca, the **church of the Redentore**, designed by Palladio in 1577 and completed after the architect's death by Antonio da Ponte. This church, which was erected as a thank-offering after an outbreak of plague that killed more than one-third of the population, is another of Palladio's masterpieces. Its façade is a development of that of San Francesco della Vigna, which he had designed some ten years earlier, with pediments over the door and central bay and the end sections of a hidden pediment emerging on either side of the main block. As at San Francesco della Vigna (and again at San Giorgio Maggiore), the overall scheme is regulated by a complicated system of proportions and a superimposition of geometric shapes. In past centuries the doge paid an annual visit to this church, crossing the canal from the Zattere on a bridge of boats—and the tradition is still kept up today, with fireworks and other events on the third Saturday in July.

In the interior, Palladio appears to have paid more attention to the visual effects than he did at San Giorgio Maggiore: there is a more harmonious relationship between the various parts, and a much better climax in the semi-circular colonnade behind the high altar. From the door the church appears as a simple rectangular basilica with an apse; but as you approach the high altar, the curves of the dome and arms gradually reveal themselves, giving a sense of elation and expansion rarely achieved by purely architectural means. Over the altars are paintings by 16th- and 17th-century painters, notably, a *Nativity* by Francesco Bassano, a *Deposition* by Palma Giovane, a *Resurrection* by Francesco Bassano and an *Ascension* by Jacopo Tintoretto and assistants. Over the Baroque high altar (which Palladio certainly didn't anticipate) is a crucifix between 16th-century bronze statues of St Mark and St Francis. In the sacristy are a *Madonna and Child with Angels* by Alvise Vivarini, a *Madonna and Saints* attributed to Francesco Bissolo and a *Baptism of Christ* by Paolo Veronese.

Further west rises the church of **Sant'Eufemia**, originally of the 11th century, and at the end of the fondamenta beyond a metal bridge, the imposing Gothic-revival mass of the Mulino Stucky, presently undergoing a face-lift.

Beyond the Giudecca is the island of **San Lazzaro degli Armeni**, seat of an Armenian monastery founded in the 18th century by a group of monks who fled the Orient (*open for guided tours, daily 3.20–5*). The **Lido di Venezia** is a busy suburban neighbourhood and bathing beach on the island separating the Adriatic Sea from the lagoon. Noteworthy buildings include the Grand Hotel des Bains (1900), the setting of Thomas Mann's *Death in Venice*, and the Grand Hotel Excelsior (1898–1908), in a Moorish style.

Murano, Burano and Torcello

To see Murano, Burano and Torcello—the three inhabited islands in the lagoon between Venice and the mainland—requires a long morning or afternoon, but it is well worth the time and trouble. Murano and Burano are known for their glass and lace, respectively. Torcello, now a romantic place with a little village counting fewer than 50 souls, is famous for its great cathedral, whose sheer splendour alone justifies the journey. Take vaporetto no. 12 from Fondamenta Nuove, easily reached by the no. 52 from San Marco or on foot from the church of the Gesuiti. Remember to check schedules when you arrive on the islands, and to give yourself at least an hour to go to and from Venice.

Shortly after leaving the Fondamenta Nuove the boat passes the walled island of San Michele, the cemetery of Venice and site of the city's oldest Renaissance church— the chapel of **San Michele in Isola**, designed by Mauro Codussi in 1469. Between Murano and Burano you'll be able to spot the cypress-girt Franciscan hermitage of **San Francesco del Deserto**, on a solitary little island to the southwest. The monks do allow visits (*open daily 9–11 & 3–5; T: 041 528 6863*), and you can hire a boat from Burano to get there if you wish.

Murano

The Venetian glass factories were moved to Murano as a safety measure in 1291 (the idea was to remove the risk of fire from the city), and the town has been synonymous with exquisite craftsmanship ever since. The Venetians rediscovered this lost art in the 10th century, when merchants brought the secrets of the trade from the East, and the making of clear 'crystal' glass remained a well-kept secret until the 16th century. After a period of decline, the making of artistic glass was revived at the end of the 19th century, and today the many glass factories all welcome visitors. In the 16th century Murano became a favourite retreat of Venetian intellectuals, many of whom had splendid houses and luxuriant gardens on the island. Few of these remain, however, and it is difficult today to imagine this aspect of the island's past.

The small Grand Canal that runs between the town's shops and houses takes you to the **Museo dell'Arte Vetraria** (*Glass Museum; open daily 10–5*) located in the 17th-century Palazzo Giustinian. Here, on the ground floor, are examples of antique glass ranging in date from the 2nd century BC to the 2nd century AD, largely from the necropolis of Enona. Venetian glass of the 15th–18th centuries is displayed on the upper floor; among the earliest surviving pieces is a dark blue marriage cup of 1470–80 with portraits of the bride and groom and allegorical devices in coloured enamel, ascribed to the workshop of Angelo Barovier. There are also examples of foreign glass. Modern and contemporary glass is displayed in an annexe to the museum (one ticket gives admission to both) on Rio dei Vetrai.

Murano's main architectural monument is **Santi Maria e Donato**, a splendid example of Veneto-Byzantine church type founded in the 7th century but rebuilt in the 12th. It was originally dedicated to the Virgin Mary; St Donato's name was added when his relics were brought here from Cephalonia, in Greece, together with the bones of a dragon he supposedly slew (four of which, for sceptics, hang behind the altar). The church is known above all for its magnificent Romanesque mosaic pavement (1141), although the capitals of the columns, the Byzantine mosaic of the Virgin in the apse and the colourful wooden ancona by Paolo Veneziano in the north aisle, are also extremely beautiful.

Burano

Burano, about half an hour away from Venice, is a charming little fishing village resplendent with colour, a delightful place just to wander without any precise goal, though there are a few paintings—by Girolamo da Santacroce, Giovanni Battista Tiepolo and Giovanni Mansueti—in the **parish church**. In past centuries the island was a favourite haunt of painters, who were drawn by the maritime atmosphere of water, sky and sails, as well as by the colour of the walls and by the picturesque quality of the *merlettaie*, or lace-makers, who used to pursue their minute craft outside, in the sunlight as Canaletto shows them. Lace-making in fact has been a mainstay of the island's economy since the early 16th century, and lace is still made and sold on the island. If you plan to buy some, however, be sure to get the genuine Venetian variety, which you'll learn to recognise in the lace museum at the **Scuola di Merletti** (*open Wed–Mon 10–6*). And don't leave Burano without strolling over to its small sister-island, **Mazzorbo**, whose pretty little canal is still lined with fishing-nets spread out to dry in the sun. Here too is some of the best contemporary architecture in Venice, G. de Carlo's 1986 housing project built in full respect of local vernacular forms and colours.

Torcello

'Thirteen hundred years ago,' wrote Ruskin, 'the grey moorland looked as it does this day, and the purple mountains stood as radiantly in the deep distances of evening; but on the line of the horizon there were strange fires mixed with the light of sunset, and the lament of many human voices mixed with the fretting of the waves on their ridges of sand. The flames rose from the ruins of Altinum; the lament from the multitudes of its people, seeking, like Israel of old, a refuge from the sword in the paths of the sea'. In more prosaic terms it may be said that Torcello flourished between the 7th and the 13th centuries, when it was the insular stronghold of refugees driven from mainland Altinum by the Lombard invasions. At one time it counted as many as 20,000 inhabitants, but by the 15th century rivalry with Venice and chronic malaria had eroded its prestige and decimated its population. Now it is little more than a small group of houses in a lonely part of the lagoon, huddled in the shadow of one of the most singular and impressive churches in Venice.

The **Cathedral of Santa Maria Assunta** is a 10-minute walk from the landing stage, down a lonely canal amid fields and a few houses. This great church (*open daily 10–5*) was founded in 639, rebuilt in 864 and again in 1008. Before it are remains of the baptistery and a narthex enlarged in the 14th and 15th centuries. The tall detached campanile is a conspicuous landmark in the lagoon.

The stunningly beautiful interior is among the highest achievements of Christian architecture. Eighteen Greek marble columns with finely carved capitals separate the aisles and nave, and a superb 11th-century mosaic pavement covers the floor. Four elaborately carved screens, of Byzantine inspiration, mark the entrance to the sanctuary, surmounted by 15th-century paintings of the *Virgin and Apostles*. The relics of St Heliodorus, first bishop of Altinum, are preserved in a Roman sarcophagus beneath the 7th-century high altar. Set into the wall north of the altar is an inscription commemorating the foundation of the church (639), considered the oldest document of Venetian history.

The most striking feature of the church, however, is the important cycle of mosaics, almost certainly fully completed by the time the mosaicists set to work on San Marco in 1156. The *Virgin and Child with Apostles* in the apse represents a break with traditional iconography, which ordinarily reserves this position for Christ Pantocrator (as at San Marco; Murano is another exception to the rule). Here the exception may be justified, in part, by the inscription in the arch, which begins, 'I am God and the flesh of the Mother ...', highlighting Christ's dual nature as God and man. The work was probably executed by craftsmen from Constantinople. In the chapel to the right of the high altar is a somewhat earlier representation of *Christ between the Archangels Michael and Gabriel with Sts Nicholas, Ambrose, Augustine and Martin*, in which the workmanship is considerably coarser.

The west wall of the church holds a vast mosaic of the *Last Judgement*, thoughtlessly restored in the 19th century, when many areas were removed and replaced by copies. The most intact sections are those depicting the realm of Hell, with the Seven Deadly Sins. There are many memorable details here: the tremendous energy of the angels as they drive the Proud into hellfire; the smoky burst of flame that envelops the Lustful; the chill bodies of the Greedy depicted engulfed by darkness; the sinister pallor that throws into relief the writhing serpents emerging from the eyes of the Envious.

In front of the basilica and a little to one side is the church of **Santa Fosca**, built in the 11th century to enshrine the relics of an early Christian martyr brought to the island in 1011. This is a centrally-planned building with a projecting apse, an arcaded portico and a tiled wooden roof. It is an austere building inside and out, with little decorative detail to distract from its well proportioned forms and space. On the grass outside is a primitive stone seat known as 'Attila's chair'.

The **Palazzo del Consiglio**, across the lawn, now houses the Museo dell'Estuario di Torcello (*open Tues–Sun 10–5*), which contains an interesting and well displayed collection of objects tracing the history of the island and its environs. It includes some objects from the cathedral—fragments of 12th-century mosaics removed from the tympanum of the apse, and all that remains of the 13th-century silver-gilt altar frontal—as well as archaeological finds and a number of paintings from demolished churches in the area.

PRACTICAL INFORMATION

GETTING AROUND

• **By air:** Airport buses run to and from the terminal and the car park at Piazzale Roma, and there are regular boat connections between the airport, San Marco (Giardinetti landing stage) and the Lido. If you are carrying a lot of baggage, you might want to consider a water taxi, which will take you directly to the landing nearest your hotel.

• **By road:** Motorists have to leave their vehicles in a multi-storey garage or an open-air car park (charges according to the size of the vehicle; the rates are per day, and space is limited, especially in summer). The most convenient multi-storey garages are at Piazzale Roma, garages and huge open-air car parks also at Isola del Tronchetto. Frequent vaporetto services (*see below*) serve all of these. In summer, at Easter, and Carnival time open air car parking is usually available also at San Giuliano and Fusina (with vaporetto services).

• **By rail:** Venice's Santa Lucia station is on the Fondamenta Santa Lucia, at the west end of the Grand Canal. Trains connect with Trieste, Verona, Milan, Turin and Genoa; Bologna, Florence and Rome; and Trento, Bolzano and Bressanone. A secondary line connects to Castelfranco Veneto, Bassano del Grappa and Trento. Water-buses, motor-boat taxis, and gondolas operate from the quay outside.

VENICE TRANSPORT

There are only two ways to get around Venice—by land and by water—and neither is very fast. Walking is probably the most practical means of locomotion, though Venice's maze-like street plan makes getting from starting point to destination without making a wrong turn a challenge. If you wish to walk through Venice without carrying luggage, shopping bags, or other encumbrances, you can hire a *portabagagli* (porter), to do the work for you; details from your hotel.

• **By vaporetto:** The vaporetto (water bus) is the most convenient way of getting around town, but it is painfully slow and, in the season (May–Oct), jam-packed with passengers.

1 (accelerato): calls at all stops on the line: Piazzale Roma–Ferrovia (the train station)–Rialto–San Marco–Lido

52 (diretto): an express service calling at selected stops: Lido–San Zaccaria–Piazzale Roma–Ferrovia-Fondamenta Nuove–Murano–Fondamenta Nuove–San Zaccaria–Piazzale Roma

82 (diretto): calls at selected stops: San Marco–Rialto–Casinò–Ferrovia–Piazzale Roma–Tronchetto–Santa Marta–Saccafisola–Zattere–Giudecca–San Giorgio–San Zaccaria

6 (diretto): a fast motor boat that runs from San Marco to the Lido and back

12 & 14 serve the northern lagoon: San Zaccaria–Lido–San Nicolò–Punta Sabbioni–Treporti–Burano–Torcello–Burano–Mazzorbo–Murano–Fondamenta Nuove

Timetables are posted at most landing stages and published monthly in the tourist board's helpful booklet, *Un Ospite di Venezia* (see Information offices, below). Tickets can be bought during working hours at most landing stages and from shops displaying the municipal transport logo, ACTV, or on board after hours. There are discounts for return, 24-hour and 3-day tickets. There is also a sort of frequent-flyers card, called *Carta Venezia*, which entitles holders to substantial discounts on all lines; enquire at the ACTV offices in Corte dell'Albero (near the Sant'Angelo landing stage on the Grand Canal), or at Piazzale Roma.

• **By motoscafo:** *Motoscafi* (water taxis) are the fastest and most exclusive vehicles in Venice. Point-to-point service in town is metered, and there are fixed rates (published in *Un Ospite di Venezia*) for the most common destinations outside the city centre.

• **By taxi:** Taxi-stands on the quays in front of the Station, Piazzale Roma, Rialto, San Marco, etc. Taxis on request from:

Radio Taxi T: 041 522 2303, 041 713112.
Coop Veneziana T: 041 716124.
Coop Serenissima T: 041 522 1265, 041 522 8538.
Società Narduzzi Solemar T: 041 520 0838.
Società Marco Polo T: 041 966170.
Società Sotoriva T: 041 520 9586.
Società Serenissima T: 041 522 4281.
Venezia Taxi T: 041 723009.
At San Marco (Molo) T: 041 522 9750.

• **By gondola:** Gondolas can be hired for a leisurely tour of the city, at standard rates or on a custom-service basis. In the latter case be sure to agree upon the duration and price of your ride before setting out. Gondola stands at the station, Piazzale Roma, Calle Vallaresso (San Marco), Riva degli Schiavoni, etc.

• **By traghetto:** *Traghetti* (gondola ferries) offer a handy way of getting across the Grand Canal without walking all the way to one of the bridges. You'll see yellow signs marked *Traghetto* with a gondola here and there as you wander the city. They are extremely cheap and quite a lot of fun, for in all but the roughest weather you ride standing up. Most operate from early morning until late afternoon. Furthermore, some *vaporetti* operate as *traghetti* on short, single-stop trips: cases in which a traghetto fare applies will appear on the tariff list at the ticket booth.

INFORMATION OFFICES

Azienda Promozione Turistica, Castello 4421, T: 041 529 8711, www.turismovenezia.it
Branch offices at the train station, Piazzale Roma garage, San Marco 71f (Ascensione); Giardini di San Marco; Palazzina del Santo; Lido di Venezia (Gran Viale Santa Maria Elisabetta 6a). Ask your concierge for the valuable (free) publication, *Un Ospite di Venezia*, listing everything you need to know to get around, including current events and emergency numbers.

HOTELS

There are no street addresses in Venice. Mail is delivered by neighbourhood and number (for instance, San Marco 1243), but that's not much help if you're wandering the streets in search of a hotel. For this reason, two addresses are given for hotels and restaurants: first the postal address, then the (approximate) street location, in parentheses.

Most of Venice's luxury hotels are arranged in a neat row along the waterfront on either side of San Marco. Moderately priced hotels can be found throughout the city, but good ones are few and far between. The level of comfort and service in inexpensive hotels can be disappointing. If you're looking for an adequate place to stay but are short on cash, bear in mind that several of the city's religious communities open their convents to visitors during high season, offering very good accommodation at remarkably low prices. Details from the APT.

€€€ **Ca' Pisani**. Boutique hotel offering 14th-century architecture and Art Deco furnishings in a great location just a few paces from the Accademia bridge. Dorsoduro 979a (Rio Terà Foscarini), T: 041 240 1411, www.capisanihotel.it

€€€ **Cipriani**. Surely one of the world's finest hotels, also Venice's most exclusive, with luxuriously appointed rooms, a stunning garden and pool, and views that are hard to forget. Its position at the tip of the Giudecca, however, means that getting to the centre always involves a boat ride). Closed Nov–March. Isola della Giudecca 10, T: 041 520 7744, www.hotelcipriani.com, info@hotelcipriani.it

€€€ **Danieli**. The most famous of the city's other luxury hotels, where Marcel Proust stayed. Breakfast is served on the roof terrace overlooking the lagoon, the Island of San Giorgio and the Grand Canal, weather permitting. Castello 4196 (Riva degli Schiavoni), T: 041 522 6480, www.danieli.hotelinvenice.com

€€€ **Europa & Regina**. Difficult to find by land, but with a private dock on the Grand Canal, which it fronts. San Marco 2159 (Calle Larga 22 Marzo), T: 041 520 0477, europa&regina@westin.com

€€€ **Gritti Palace**. Rich in Venetian atmosphere, with summer dining on the Grand Canal. San Marco 2467 (Campo Santa Maria del Giglio), T: 041 794611, gritti.hotelinvenice.com

€€€ **Liassidi Palace**. Newly created from a 600-year-old palace, with soaring ceilings, Gothic windows and marble floors as well as all modern comforts and amenities. Castello 3405 (Ponte dei Greci), T: 041 520 5658, www.liassidipalacehotel.com

€€€ **Londra Palace**. Excellent waterfront location for this comfortable boutique hotel, noted for quality of service. Unusually for Venice, it was purposebuilt as a hotel (in 1860), giving wellproportioned rooms, most with lagoon views, and some with rooftop terraces. Castello 4171 (Riva degli Schiavoni), T: 041 520 0533, www.hotelondra.it, info@hotelondra.it

€€€ **Luna Baglioni**. Quieter and more secluded than the other grand hotels. San Marco 1243 (Calle Larga del 'Ascensione), T: 041 5289840, www.baglioni hotels.com, prenotazioni@baglionihotels.com

€€€ **Palazzo Sant'Angelo**. For honeymooners only: four luxurious suites in a tiny, intimate townhouse overlooking the Grand Canal, between San Marco and the Accademia bridge. San Marco 3489, T: 041 041 241 1452, www.palazzosantangelo.com

€€ **Accademia**. Near the Galleria dell'Accademia, with a shady garden. Dorsoduro 1058 (Fondamenta Bollani), T: 041 523 7846, www. pensioneaccademia.it

€€ **Ai Due Fanali**. A former religious school with ceiling frescoes by Palma Giovane, now a small, quiet place just a short walk from the station, recently renovated with all modern comforts. Santa Croce 946 (Campo San Simeon Grande), T: 041 718490, www.aiduefanali.com

€€ **Falier**. Simple but quite good (especially the top-floor rooms with private terrace). Santa Croce 130 (Salizzada San Pantalon), T: 041 710 882.

€€ **Flora**. Nicely situated between the Luna and the Gritti, with a beautiful small garden. San Marco 2283a (Calle dei Bergamaschi), T: 041 520 5844, www.hotelflora.it

€€ **La Calcina**. Where Ruskin stayed: the rooms overlooking the Giudecca are among the city's most charming. Dorsoduro 780 (Zattere), T: 041 520 6466,. www.lacalcina.com

€€ **La Fenice et des Artistes**. It really is frequented by artists (there are some original works by 20th-century masters in the lobby). San Marco 1936 (Campiello de la Fenice), T: 041 523 2333, www.fenicehotels.com

€€ **Locanda ai Santi Apostoli**. On the third floor of a 15th-century palace overlooking the Grand Canal, featuring antique beds and patterned damasks. Cannaregio 4391 (Strada Nova), T: 041 521 2612, www.locandasantiapostoli.com

€€ **Locanda al Leon**. Small, friendly, family-run hotel just off the Riva degli Schiavoni, a few minutes' walk from San Marco. Castello 4270 (Campo Santi Filippo e Giacomo), T: 041 277 0393, www.hotelalleon.com

€€ **Locanda Art Decò**. Just six delightful, luminous rooms, with Art Deco furniture. Closed Dec–Jan and Aug. San Marco 2966 (Calle delle Botteghe), T: 041 277 0558, www.locandaartdeco.com

€€ **Locanda Fiorita**. It's hard to imagine anything more charming than this refined little family-run establishment on a tiny square, with outside breakfast seating in summer. San Marco 3457a (Campiello Novo), T: 041 523 4754, www.locandafiorita.com

€€ **Metropole**. A prestigious address on the Riva degli Schiavoni, with stunning views over the water to San Giorgio and the Lido, delicious buffet breakfasts and bistrot-style restaurant. Castello 4149 (Riva degli Schiavoni), T: 041 520 5044, www.hotelmetropole.com

€€ **Quattro Fontane**. On the Lido, with a pleasant garden. Via Fontane 16, T: 041 526 0227, info@quattrofontane.com

€ **Casa Martini**. Pleasant bed & breakfast offering old-time Venetian style in air-conditioned modern comfort; breakfast is served on a sunny terrace in summer. Cannaregio 1314 (Rio Terà S. Leonardo), T: 041 717512, www.casamartini.it

YOUTH HOSTEL

€ **Venezia**. Fondamenta Zitelle (Giudecca) 86, T: 041 523 8211, vehostel@tin.it

RESTAURANTS

Restaurants in Venice can be entertaining in their own right, especially in the warmer months when most offer table service outside. Venice is traffic free, which makes eating outside and watching the boats—or crowds—go by remarkably like dinner theatre.

€€€ Harry's Bar. Draws three kinds of clientele: the people-watchers, who like to sit downstairs and watch the artists, musicians and movie stars walk in; the romantics, who prefer a table upstairs, by the window, where they can gaze out over the water; and of course the *divi*, particularly abundant during the Biennale. Founded many years ago by legendary hotelier Harry Cipriani, this is still one of Venice's finest restaurants (specialities: *risotto alle seppioline, scampi alla Thermidor* and a remarkable selection of desserts)—and one of its most expensive. Closed Mon. On the Grand Canal near San Marco, at San Marco 1323 (Calle Vallaresso), T: 041 528 5777.

€€€ La Caravella. Excellent restaurant (specialities: *antipasto Tiziano con granseola, Bigoli in salsa, filetto di branzino alle erbe*) with a distinctive maritime decor and extensive list of regional, Italian and imported wines. Closed Wed, except from June to Sept. San Marco 2397 (Calle Larga 22 Marzo), T: 041 520 8901.

€€ Ai Gondolieri. Small and refined, near the Peggy Guggenheim Collection. Closed Tues. Dorsoduro 366 (Fondamenta San Vio), T: 041 528 6396.

€€ Al Graspo de Ua. An authentic Venetian tavern. Closed Mon, Tues, late Dec–early Jan and two weeks in Aug. San Marco 5094 (Calle dei Bombaseri), T: 041 520 0150.

€€ Al Mascaron. A very well-known place, serving the best of traditional Venetian cuisine. Closed Sun and winter. Castello 5525 (Calle Lunga Santa Maria Formosa), T: 041 522 5995.

€€ Alle Testiere. A tiny (four tables), friendly place serving good Venetian dishes. Closed Aug and winter. Castello 5801 (Calle del Mondo Novo), T: 041 522 7220.

€€ Cip's. The newest addition to the Cipriani family, offering various menus from pizza up. Giudecca 10 (near the Zitelle), T: 041 240 8575.

€€ Fiaschetteria Toscana. Truly delicious cuisine (Tuscan as well as Venetian) and excellent wines, with outside seating in summer. Closed Tues and July Aug. At San Giovanni Crisostomo, T: 041 528 5281.

€€ Harry's Dolci. The same impeccable level of cuisine and service as Harry's Bar, but less formal, with tables on the water in summer. Closed Tues. Giudecca 773, T: 041 522 4844.

€€ Riviera. Simply the best fish restaurant in Venice, with outside seating on the Giudecca Canal in summer. Closed Mon. Dorsoduro 1473 (at the far end of the Zattere), T: 041 522 7621.

€€ Taverna la Fenice. Serving skilfully prepared regional specialities and great wines, with tables in the campiello in fair weather. Closed Sun, Mon morning and a few days in Jan. (Campiello de la Fenice), T: 041 522 3856.

€€ Venice Al Bacareto. *Osteria* dating back a hundred years, known for its wholesome Venetian fare, including *ombre* and *cicheti* (a glass of wine and hors d'oeuvres). Closed Sat evening, Sun and Aug. San Marco 3447 (at San Samuele), T: 041 528 9336.

€ Bentigodi da Andrea. A good place for simple food and wine. Closed Sun. Cannaregio 1423–24 (Calesele

Cannaregio), T: 041 716269.

€ **Corte Sconta**. Serving Venetian specialities, especially seafood, in a rustic interior and a pleasant garden court. Closed Sun, Mon, a few days in Jan–Feb and mid-July–mid-Aug. Castello 3886 (Calle del Pestrin), T: 041 522 7024.

€ **L'Incontro**. Traditional Sardinian cuisine, with especially good meat dishes. Closed Mon. Santa Margherita 3062a (Rio Terà Canal, Ponte dei Pugni), T: 041 522 2402.

Burano

€€ **Al Gatto Nero-da Ruggero**. Serving Venetian specialities accompanied by regional wines. Closed Mon and a few days in Feb and Nov. Fondamenta della Giudecca 88, T: 041 730 120.

€ **Antica Trattoria alla Maddalena**. The place to go for old-fashioned lagoon food—try the *selvadego de vale* (wild fowl) and *castraure* (baby artichokes). Closed Thur and Dec–Jan. Mazzorbo 7c, T: 041 730151.

Murano

€€ **Ai Frati**. A well-known seafood restaurant. Closed Thur and Feb. Fondamenta Vernier, T: 041 736694.

Torcello

€€€ **Locanda Cipriani**. Known for its black tagliatelle with clam ragout. Closed Tues and Nov–Mar. Piazza Santa Fosca 29, T: 041 730 150.

€€ **Osteria al Ponte del Diavolo**. House specialities include *polipetti caldi, filetti di sogliola in salsa di zucchine, seppioline fritte* and *crespelle alla crema della casa*. Closed Thur and all evenings except Sat, as well as Jan–Feb. Fondamenta Borgognone, T: 041 730 401.

CAFÉS & WINE BARS

Venice's best pastries, ice-cream and hot chocolate are to be had at **Rosa Salva**, in historic old rooms on Campo Santi Giovanni e Paolo. Two other cafés known for their antique décor are **Florian** and **Quadri**, located across from each other on Piazza San Marco. You can find delicious sweets (but no coffee) at **Marchini** on Calle del Spezier between Campo Santo Stefano and Campo San Maurizio.

A truly Venetian experience is to go for *ombre* and *cicheti*. An *ombra* (literally, 'shadow') is a glass of wine and *cicheti*, finger-food. Good places to *ombreggiare* and *cichetare* are: **Alla Frasca**, Cannaregio 5176 (Campiello della Carità, near the church of the Gesuiti), a time-honoured establishment in historic quarters (Titian stored his paints and canvas here) pleasantly situated in an out-of-the-way part of town; **Vino Vino**, San Marco 2007a (Calle del Cafetier), a newer and trendier place, between San Marco and the Teatro della Fenice; and **La Mascareta**, Castello 5183 (Calle Lunga Santa Maria Formosa), one of the few places in town open after midnight.

REGIONAL SPECIALITIES

The thing to buy in Venice is glass. The best value for your money is to be found on Murano, where much of the glass is made; but there are also many shops in Venice offering excellent craftsmanship at only slightly higher prices. Mass demand for Burano lace has led to a decline in quality.

FESTIVALS & EVENTS

The celebrated Venice Biennale organises biennial historical and documentary exhibitions in five areas: visual arts, cinema, theatre, music and architecture. These events, which draw immense international crowds, usually take place in odd years, between June and September. Also important are the *Mostra Internazionale del Cinema*, on the Lido (annual, Sept) and the *Premio Letterario Campiello* (Sept).

Surviving from past ages are the popular *Festa della Sensa* (late spring), culminating in a ceremony recalling the traditional marriage between the Doge and the Sea; the great gondola race known as the *Regata Storica* in the Grand Canal (first Sun in Sept); the *Festa del Redentore* (third week in Sept), with ceremonial boat processions and fireworks; and many other feasts in the towns and islands of the lagoon. Last but by no means least, *Carnevale* draws merrymakers from all parts of the world, many in fancy dress and masks.

PADUA & THE PO DELTA

Padua is a lively town. Its three central piazzas, around Palazzo della Ragione, are filled every day with busy markets. In Italy it is known as the place where St Anthony of Padua lived and carried out numerous miracles, and his tomb in the Santo is visited every year by thousands of pilgrims. Although the old town has many pretty arcaded streets, the rest of the city is unattractive. Nevertheless, Padua's cultural leadership dates back half a millennium and is closely tied to the presence in the city of one of Europe's oldest and most prestigious universities. Even after the rise of Venice, Padua remained a leading centre of humanist thought, and the best Renaissance artists were called here from Florence and elsewhere to work on important commissions for the city's enlightened patricians. Dante, Petrarch and Galileo all lived in Padua at some point in their respective lives. Here, too, is one of the key monuments of proto-Renaissance art, Giotto's magnificent fresco cycle in the Scrovegni Chapel.

Padua's environs are every bit as beautiful as the city is ugly. Between here and Venice flow the languid waters of the Brenta Canal, to whose green shores the best of Venetian society moved *en masse* in summer. The villas here and in the hills to the north attest to the tenor of life that was enjoyed during the twilight of the Republic. In the gentle southern landscape of the Euganean Hills an earlier aristocracy built its seigniories, and the religious orders constructed vast retreats. All these areas invite leisurely exploration.

HISTORY OF PADUA

According to Livy (59 BC–AD 18), the most famous native of Padua (he was born at Teolo, in the Euganean Hills), Patavium was founded by the Trojan Antenor. In reality the city was established later—not before the 8th or 7th century BC, probably by palaeo-Venetic tribes. It is known to have been an important settlement of the Euganei and Veneti, and it received full Roman franchise in 89 BC. It prospered under Byzantine and Lombard rule, and declared itself an independent republic in 1164. The foundation of the university in 1222 attracted many distinguished teachers to Padua, including Dante and Petrarch, as well as numerous students from England, and the city came to be known as *La Dotta* (The Learned). In 1237–54 Ezzelino da Romano was tyrant of Padua, then after the suzerainty of the Carraresi (1318–1405) the city was conquered by the Venetians, and remained a faithful ally of Venice until the end of the Venetian Republic.

The Scrovegni Chapel and Museo Civico agli Eremitani

Open Tues–Sun 9–6 or 7; inclusive ticket; booking necessary for the Scrovegni Chapel, T: 049 820 4550.

Padua's loveliest attraction stands north of the town centre, just within the embrace of the old city walls. The immense Museo Civico agli Eremitani occupies the former

Convento degli Eremitani on the south side of the park. From the entrance hall and gift shop you enter a lovely cloister, on the far side of which a doorway leads out to a little garden. Here are the ruined walls of the Roman amphitheatre and, on the right, the entrance (present your ticket) to the Cappella degli Scrovegni.

Also known as the Arena Chapel, it was commissioned by the merchant Enrico degli Scrovegni for his family palace (since demolished). Inside are the magnificent frescoes executed around 1305 by Giotto and his pupils—the only cycle by the master to survive intact and one of the greatest achievements of Italian painting. The frescoes tell the story of Christian redemption through the lives of Mary and Christ—an important theme for Scrovegni, whose father had been a usurer. Their monumental composition, concise representation, and intense sense of drama were revolutionary in their time.

The chapel is small, intended for a congregation of the Scrovegni family and their retainers, and the frescoes themselves are about half lifesize. They are arranged in three superimposed rows of scenes, enclosed in delicately ornamented frames that form a continuous structure, a sort of 'motion-picture' in which it is the viewer who moves from one dramatic incident to the next. The vault is painted the same bright blue as the background of the frescoes—quite naturally, as the vaults and domes of medieval churches were held to be symbolic of Heaven. This one is sprinkled with gold stars, with portraits of Christ and the four Evangelists set in circular medallions. The wall surfaces are divided into 38 scenes. The narrative begins on the top band, to the right of the chancel arch.

Top level: The frames on the south wall trace the lives of Joachim and Anna, the Virgin's parents (*Expulsion of Joachim from the Temple, Joachim among the Shepherds, Annunciation to Anna, Sacrifice of Joachim, Vision of Joachim, Meeting of Joachim and Anna*), and on the north the life of the Virgin (*Birth, Presentation in the Temple, Presentation of the Rods to Simeon, Watching of the Rods, Betrothal of the Virgin, the Virgin's Return Home*), ending with the *Annunciation* and (in a frame borrowed from the central order) *Visitation* on either side of the sanctuary and *God the Father Dispatching Gabriel* over the chancel arch.

Second level: The infancy of Christ on the south wall (*Nativity, Adoration of the Magi, Presentation in the Temple, Flight into Egypt, Massacre of the Innocents*) leads into His adult life on the north (*Dispute with the Elders, Baptism of Christ, Marriage at Cana, Raising of Lazarus, Entry into Jerusalem, Expulsion from the Temple*), ending in the *Pact of Judas* by the arch.

Bottom level: The Passion of Christ on the south (*Last Supper, Washing of the Feet, Betrayal of Christ, Christ before Caiaphas, Mocking of Christ*) is followed by His death and resurrection on the north (*Way to Calvary, Crucifixion, Deposition, Angel at the Empty Tomb and Noli me Tangere, Ascension, Pentecost*). A faux-marble dado below is punctuated by chiaroscuro images of the *Seven*

Giotto: *The Baptism of Christ*, detail (c. 1305), in the Scrovegni Chapel.

Virtues (on the south side) and the *Seven Deadly Sins* (on the north).

East and west end: The drama of human salvation reaches its climax in the *Last Judgement* on the entrance wall. The stories of Mary in the apse were executed later by followers of Giotto; Giusto de'Menabuoi frescoed the two *Madonne del Latte* in the niches at the sides of the altar, and Giovanni Pisano carved the delicate statues of the *Virgin and Angels*. Behind the altar is the tomb of Enrico degli Scrovegni, who died in 1336.

The Museo Civico

Pinacoteca: Works by Giotto (the *Arena Chapel Crucifix*), Guariento (*Madonna with Angels*), Alvise Vivarini (*Male Portrait*), Jacopo Bellini (*Christ in Limbo*), Paolo Veronese (*Last Supper, Crucifixion, Martyrdom of St Justina*), Tintoretto (*Supper in the House of Simon*), Tiepolo, Francesco Guardi, Marco and Sebastiano Ricci and others. Also small bronzes by Italian and foreign sculptors of the 14th–17th centuries; northern-Italian masters (Moderno, Antico, Riccio, Alessandro Vittoria, Tiziano Aspetti) are particularly well represented.

Bottacin Museum: Consists of the collection made between 1850 and 1875 by Nicola Bottacin (1805–76). It includes mildly interesting 19th-century paintings and sculptures, and a collection of coins and medals.

Emo Capodilista Collection: A huge collection of 15th–18th-century paintings left to the city by Leonardo Emo Capodilista in 1864. Works by Venetian and Flemish painters, notably Giorgione's *Leda and the Swan* and *Country Idyll*, and a *Portrait of a Young Senator* by Giovanni Bellini. There are also works by Titian and Luca Giordano, Jan van Scorel (*Portrait of a Man*) and Quentin Metsys (*St John the Evangelist*).

Archaeological section: Prehistoric, Roman, Egyptian, Etruscan and early Christian antiquities. Highlights are a Roman bust of Silenus (2nd century AD); an imposing aedicular tomb of the Volumnii; and two black basalt statues of the goddess Sekhmet, given to the city by Giovanni Battista Belzoni in 1819. Belzoni (1778–1823), born in Padua, was the first European to enter the tomb of Rameses II at Abu Simbel, and supplied the British Museum with many of its largest Egyptian statues. Splendid examples of Roman, Islamic and medieval European glass are displayed in vitrines throughout the museum.

The Eremitani

The adjacent church of the Eremitani, or Santi Filippo e Giacomo, was built in Romanesque-Gothic forms between 1276 and 1306 for the Augustinian order. Damaged by bombs in 1944, it was rebuilt after the war. The lower part of the façade, added in 1360, has a broad doorway and tall, deep arches that continue on the south flank. Here, beneath an attached porch, is a remarkable Renaissance doorway with carvings of the Months by the Florentine Niccolò Baroncelli. The interior, a single broad aisle with a ship's-keel roof, contains tombs and sculptures of the 14th–16th centuries and fragmentary frescoes. On the south side, the first chapel has remains of frescoes by Giusto de' Menabuoi; and the fourth chapel, a *Madonna and Child* and *Ecce Homo* by Guariento. At the end of the south aisle stands the Cappella Ovetari, once famous for its frescoes by Andrea Mantegna. Their destruction in 1944 was the greatest single loss of Italian art in the war. Of the remaining fragments, the best-preserved scenes are the *Martyrdom of St Christopher* (south wall), the *Assumption* (behind the altar) and the *Martyrdom of St James* (north wall). The terracotta altarpiece of the *Madonna and Child with Saints* was made by a follower of Donatello. There are more 14th-century frescoes in the sanctuary (*Stories of Sts Augustine, James, and Philip*, by Guariento) and in the other apsidal chapels. In the north aisle are the tombs of Marco Mantova Benavides, a law professor, by Bartolomeo Ammannati; and of Jacopo da Carrara, with Latin verses by Petrarch.

ART IN PADUA

Giotto's frescoes in the Cappella degli Scrovegni gave rise to a flourishing local school of 'Giottesque' painters (including Guariento and Giusto de' Menabuoi). The Veronese Altichiero (c. 1330–95), who was active in Padua in the 1380s, was one of the most creative interpreters of Giotto's achievements before Masaccio, filling the gap between these two great names. Though he lacks the robust individuality of Giotto, and though he is less daring with colour, he is nevertheless the most important northern Italian mural painter of the late 14th century (*see p. 470*). His love of pageant and of decorative elements marks him out as an artist in the Gothic tradition. The Renaissance came to Padua with the arrival of Donatello in 1443, to work on his equestrian statue of Gattamelata and the high altar of the Santo. He was to have a profound influence on Andrea Mantegna (1431–1506). The painter Francesco Squarcione (1397–1468) influenced a great number of followers, in particular Mantegna, who produced a superb fresco cycle in the Ovetari chapel in the church of the Eremitani between 1454 and 1457 (almost totally destroyed in the Second World War). In the late 15th century Bartolomeo Bellano (1434–96) and Andrea Briosco (Il Riccio, 1470–1532) created some of the finest small bronze sculpture of the Renaissance.

The University

Open for guided tours March–Nov Mon 3, 4, 5; Tues–Thurs and Fri 9, 10, 11, 3, 4, 5; Wed and Sat 9, 10, 11; T: 049 827 3044.

The University of Padua (founded c. 1222) is the second oldest university in Italy after Bologna. It was nicknamed 'Il Bo' (*bue*, or ox) from the sign of an inn, the most famous in the city, which used to stand on this site. Renowned as a medical school, it flourished in the 15th and 16th centuries, when it was the only university in the Venetian Republic.

The perils of academic life

The University of Padua reached the height of its fame in the 16th century, then gradually lost its international standing. Some of the reasons for its decline can be gleaned in these lines:

The scholars here in the night commit many murders against their private adversaries, and too often executed upon the strangers and innocent, and all with gun-shot or else with stilettoes.

> William Lithgow, Rare Adventures and Painfull Peregrinations, 1614–32

The University here, tho' so much supported by the Venetians, that they pay fifty Professors, yet sinks extremely: There are no Men of any great Fame now in it; and the Quarrels among the Students have driven away most of the Strangers that used to come and study here; for it is not safe to stir abroad ... after Sun-set.

> Gilbert Burnet, Some Letters..., 1687

In thine halls the lamp of learning
Padua, now no more is burning;
Like a meteor, whose wild way
Is lost over the grave of day,
It gleams betrayed, and to betray.

> Percy Bysshe Shelley, Lines Written among the Euganean Hills, 1818

The older façade dates from 1757, and the tower from 1572; the adjoining building to the right (with the entrance) was reconstructed in 1938–39. The dignified courtyard (1552) is by Andrea Moroni. In the old courtyard (where the ticket office is), at the foot of the stairs, is a statue of Elena Cornaro Piscopia (1646–84), who was the first woman to take a doctor's degree, in philosophy. The upper loggia gives entrance to a room where Galileo's wooden *cattedra* is preserved. This great teaching desk is supposed to have been made as a sign of affection by his pupils so that they could see him better: the great scientist taught physics here from 1592–1610, a period he looked back on as the best of his life.

On the other side of the courtyard a door leads into a small museum, off which is the oldest anatomical theatre in Europe (1594). It was built by the surgeon Fabricius, master of William Harvey (who discovered blood circulation), who took his degree here in 1602. Founder of the Royal College of Surgeons Thomas Linacre (1492) and the future physician to Queen Elizabeth I John Caius (1539) also qualified here as doctors, and the anatomist Vesalius (1540) and Fallopius (1561, who lends his name to the fallopian tube) were among the famous medical professors. The theatre is visited from below (where the dissecting table used to be); the wooden galleries above could accommodate (standing) some 250 students.

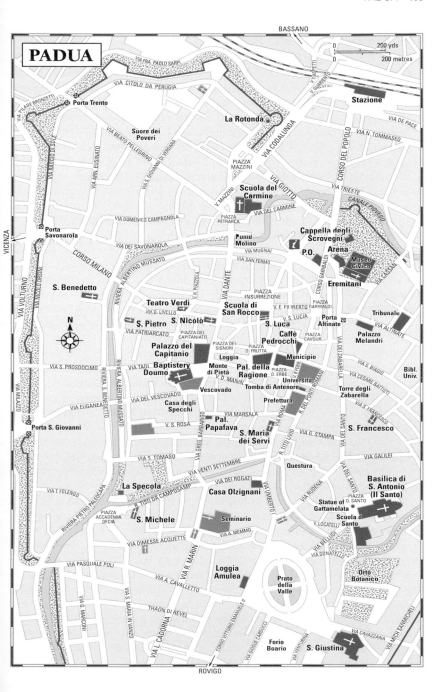

BASSANO

PADUA

0   200 yds
0   200 metres

VIA FRA. PAOLO SARPI

VIA CITOLO DA PERUGIA

VIA PILADE BRONZETTI

Porta Trento

VIA RAGGIO DI SOLE

VIA ARN. EUSINATO

VIA S. GIOVANNI DI VERDARA

VIA BEATO PELLEGRINO

Suore dei Poveri

La Rotonda

VIA CODALUNGA

VIA GIOTTO

PIAZZA MAZZINI

VICENZA

Porta Savonarola

VIA NICOLÒ ORSINI

VIA DOMENICO CAMPAGNOLA

V. MAZZINI

Scuola del Carmine

VIA DEL CARMINE

PIAZZA PETRARCA

CORSO MILANO

VIA DEI SAVONAROLA

RIVIERA ALBERTINO MUSSATO

Ponte Molino

VIA MUGNAI

VIA SAN FERMO

Stazione

VIA CASTELLI

V. GUERRO

VIA DE PACE

VIA N. TOMMASEO

CORSO DEL POPOLO

VIA TRIESTE

CANALE PIOVEGO

Cappella degli Scrovegni

P.O.

Arena

Museo Civico

Eremitani

CORSO GARIBALDI

VIA CASSAN

VIA VOLTURNO

S. Benedetto

V.R. PIAZZOLA

VIA DANTE

PIAZZA INSURREZIONE

PIAZZA GARIBALDI

V.E. FILIBERTO

Tribunale

Teatro Verdi

VIA D. LIVELLO

Scuola di San Rocco

V. S. LUCIA

S. Luca

Porta Altinate

VIA ALTINATE

Palazzo Melandri

S. Pietro

S. Nicolò

PIAZZA DEL CAPITANIATO

Caffè Pedrocchi

PIAZZA CAVOUR

VIA PATRIARCATO

VIA TADI

Palazzo del Capitanio

PIAZZA DEI SIGNORI

PIAZZA D. FRUTTA

Municipio

VIA 8 FEBB.

VIA S. BIAGIO

VIA CESARE BATTISTI

Bibl. Univ.

VIA S. PROSDOCIMO

RIVIERA ALBERTINO MUSSATO

Baptistery
Duomo

Loggia

Monte di Pietà

V.D. MANIN

Pal. della Ragione

PIAZZA D. ERBE

Università

R. DEL PONTI ROMANI

Torre degli Zabarella

VIA DEL VESCOVADO

Vescovado

Tomba di Antenore

VIA EUGANEA

Casa degli Specchi

V. S. ROSA

VIA GREG. BARBARIGO

Pal. Papafava

VIA MARSALA

Prefettura

VIA ROMA

VIA DEL SANTO

VIA S. FRANCESCO

S. Francesco

Porta S. Giovanni

VIA MILAZZO

S. Maria dei Servi

A. TITO LIVIO

VIA G. STAMPA

VIA GALILEI

VIA S. TOMASO

Questura

VIA RUDENA

VIA VENTI SETTEMBRE

VIA DEI ROGATI

Casa Olzignani

VIA UMBERTO I

Basilica di S. Antonio (Il Santo)

VIA T. FOLENGO

La Specola

Statue of Gattamelata

PIAZZA D. SANTO

RIVIERA PIETRO PALEOCAPA

VIA TISO DA CAMPOSAMP.

PIAZZA ACCADEMIA DECIA

S. Michele

Seminario

VIA A. MEMMO

Scuola di Santo

V. LOCATELLI

VIA BELLUDI

VIA DIMESSE ACQUETTE

VIA DONATELLO

VIA PASQUALE POLI

VIA R. MARIN

Orto Botanico

VIA G. MARCONI

VIA S. MARIA IN VANZO

VIA A. CAVALLETTO

Loggia Amulea

Prato della Valle

VIA L. CADORNA

THAON DI REVEL

CORSO VITTORIO EMANUELE II

VIA GIUSUE' CARDUCCI

Forio Boario

S. Giustina

VIA VENTURINA

VIA CAVAZZANA

VIA MICH. SANMICHELI

ROVIGO

The Municipio and Caffè Pedrocchi

Opposite the university, the eastern façade (1928–30) of the Municipio disguises a 16th-century building, by Andrea Moroni, that incorporates a tower of the 13th-century Palazzo del Podestà (seen from a side road). The splendid **Palazzo della Ragione** is entered from the Municipio (on Via VIII Febbraio). A broad flight of modern stairs in the courtyard of the Municipio leads to the upper-floor *salone* (*open Tues–Sun 9–6 or 7*), one of the largest and most remarkable halls in Italy. It was built by Fra Giovanni degli Eremitani in 1306–08, and is 79m long, 27m wide and 26m high, covered with a wooden ship's-keel roof. On the walls are 333 frescoes of religious and astrological subjects, divided according to the months of the year, by Nicolò Miretto and Stefano da Ferrara. These were painted shortly after a fire in 1420 that had destroyed paintings carried out by Giotto and his assistants in 1313.

It is not known how closely the frescoes follow Giotto's originals. Each month is represented by nine scenes in three tiers, representing an allegory of the month, together with its sign of the zodiac, planet and constellation. Other scenes show the labours of the month and astrological illustrations. The hall contains a block of stone that once served as a stool of repentance for debtors, and a giant wooden horse, a copy of Donatello's Gattamelata (*see p. 468*), made for a fête in 1466. From the two terraces there are delightful views of the market squares of Piazza delle Erbe and Piazza della Frutta. The ground floor of Palazzo della Ragione is also used as a market (with permanent stalls).

From here walk back to **Caffè Pedrocchi**. This huge place is one of the most celebrated cafés in Italy and was famous in the 19th century as a meeting-place for intellectuals (when it was kept open 24 hours a day). It was founded by Antonio Pedrocchi and built on a triangular site in Neoclassical style in 1831 by Giuseppe Jappelli. On the piazzetta are two protruding Doric loggias, whose four lions by Giuseppe Petrelli (copies of those at the foot of the Campidoglio in Rome) are irresistible to children. The south façade has another Doric loggia, and the little wing was added by Jappelli in Gothic-revival style in 1837. It was opened to the public in 1836 and was left to the city in 1891. The ground floor has a long white-and-yellow main room, and two smaller red-and-green drawing rooms, all prettily furnished.

The upper floor (entered from the piazzetta; *open Tues–Sun 9.30–12.30 & 3.30–6.30*) was opened in 1842. A grand staircase, with a stuccoed apse, leads up to a series of rooms decorated in styles that evoke the great civilisations of the past. First is the Etruscan room, beyond which is the octagonal Greek room with a fresco by Giovanni Demin (1842). The charming circular Roman room has four views of Rome by Ippolito Caffi (1841–42). The Herculaneum room was decorated by Pietro Paoletti. The elaborate ballroom has a stage for the orchestra. The Egyptian room was inspired by Jappelli's friend Belzoni, actor, engineer and famous Egyptologist (*see p. 462*), and it is decorated with mock porphyry and painted stucco statues attributed to Giuseppe Petrelli and Antonio Gradenigo. Off the ballroom is the little Moorish room with good wood carvings, and beyond are the Renaissance room and the Gothic room (with paintings on glass by Demin).

From Piazza dei Signori to the duomo

Piazza dei Signori is attractively enclosed by old buildings. The Loggia della Gran Guardia is a charming Lombard edifice begun by Annibale Maggi (1496) and finished in 1523. **Palazzo del Capitaniato** (1599–1605) occupies the site of the castle of the Carraresi, of which a 14th-century portico survives just off Via Accademia (at no. 11). The palace incorporates a tower, adapted in 1532 by Giovanni Maria Falconetto to accommodate an astronomical clock dating from 1344 (the oldest in Italy).

Beyond the Arco dell'Orologio lies the Corte Capitaniato, with the **Liviano**, which houses the arts faculty of the university, built in 1939 by Giò Ponti. The entrance hall was frescoed by Massimo Campigli. The building incorporates the Sala dei Giganti with frescoes of famous men by Domenico and Gualtiero Campagnolo, and Stefano dell'Arzere (1539). These were painted over earlier 14th-century frescoes, including a fragment attributed to Altichiero showing Petrarch reading in his study, possibly drawn from life (Petrarch lived in the nearby village of Arquà in 1368–74).

In Via Accademia is the beautiful **Loggia Carrarese**, seat of the Accademia Patavina di Scienze, Lettere ed Arti. The former chapel here has frescoes of Old Testament scenes by Guariento (c. 1360).

From Piazza Capitaniato, with a 16th-century loggia and ancient acacias, the Corte Valaresso (fine staircase of 1607) leads under an arch of 1632 to Piazza del Duomo, with the 13th–14th-century Monte di Pietà, remodelled with a portico by Giovanni Maria Falconetto in 1530. The **duomo** was reconstructed in 1552 by Andrea da Valle and Agostino Righetti to a much-altered design of Michelangelo. The sacristy contains works by Nicolò Semitecolo (1367), Francesco Bassano, Giorgio Schiavone (four saints), Giandomenico Tiepolo, Sassoferrato and Paris Bordone. The treasury includes 12th- and 13th-century illuminated manuscripts, a Byzantine thurible (censer) of the 11th century, a processional cross of 1228, and a large reliquary of the Cross, of silver gilt with enamels, dating from c. 1440.

The **baptistery** (*open summer daily 10–7; winter 10–6*) was built at the end of the 12th century. The interior is entirely covered with frescoes by Giusto de' Menabuoi, his best work. Executed in 1378, this is one of the most interesting medieval fresco cycles in Italy. Christ Pantocrator appears in the dome surrounded by a host of angels and the Blessed; scenes from Genesis adorn the drum; the Evangelists look down from the pendentives; and scenes from the lives of Christ and St John the Baptist cover the walls. There are scenes from the Apocalypse in the apse, and a polyptych, also by Giusto, on the altar.

To the south of the duomo is the **bishop's palace**, housing the Museo Diocesano d'Arte Sacra (*open Thur–Fri 3–7*), with a frescoed *Annunciation* by Jacopo da Montagnana. At Via del Vescovado 79 is the Casa degli Specchi, an early 16th-century Lombardesque building by Annibale Maggi with *tondi* of polished marble.

Sant'Antonio and its neighbourhood

From Via XIII Febbraio, Via San Francesco leads east from the university past the **Tomba di Antenore**, a marble sarcophagus erected in 1233 on short columns.

Allegedly it is the tomb of Antenor, reputed founder of the city. Another sarcophagus (1309) was set up here on the 2,000th anniversary of Livy's birth. The restored Torre degli Zabarella dates from the 13th century. Via Cesare Battisti to the north is a pretty road with porticoes, typical of the old town. Via San Francesco continues to the church of San Francesco, dating from 1416, which contains the monument of Pietro Roccabonella, natural philosopher, by Bartolomeo Bellano and Il Riccio (1496–97), while the narrow Via del Santo leads south to Piazza del Santo.

Piazza del Santo and Gattamelata

The famous equestrian statue of Gattamelata is a masterpiece by Donatello (1453). Gattamelata, or Erasmo da Nardo, was a celebrated Venetian *condottiere* (mercenary general) and protector of the Venetian Republic. He died in 1443 and had a state funeral in Venice: it is known that he desired to be buried in the Santo (*see below*). On the exceptionally high base are copies of the two reliefs carved by Donatello in 1447. This dignified, stately statue shows the versatile Donatello in high Roman mode. This was the very first large-scale, monumental bronze to be cast since ancient times, and Donatello closely based it on the Marcus Aurelius now in the square on the Capitoline Hill.

Sant'Antonio
Open daily 6.30–7 or 7.30.

The Franciscan basilica of Sant'Antonio, familiarly called 'Il Santo' by *padovani*, was built between 1232 and the mid-14th century to enshrine the body of St Anthony of Padua. St Anthony was born in Lisbon in 1195, but on a missionary journey to Africa he was forced in a storm to land in Italy and settled at Padua, where he preached and carried out miracles under the guidance of St Francis. He was canonised the year after his death in 1231. The church is now one of the great pilgrim shrines of Italy, for St Anthony is one of the best-loved saints in the country (it is estimated that some five million pilgrims visit the church every year).

The single-gabled façade combines motifs of Romanesque and Gothic inspiration (the tall, blind ogival arches and central rose window belong to the Gothic tradition, the round-arched doorway and the general compositional scheme, to the Romanesque). The eight-domed roof—a medley of Byzantine, Venetian and French Romanesque elements—gives the building a distinctly Eastern appearance, which is further emphasised by the small towers and the two octagonal *campanili*, seemingly drawn from the Arabian Nights.

The interior

The magnificent **nave** is separated from the lateral aisles by great piers and terminates, at the east end, in a profusely decorated ambulatory. The holy-water stoups against the first two piers bear statues of St John the Baptist (south) by Tullio Lombardo, and Christ (north) by Tiziano Aspetti. The second north pier holds the tomb of the Venetian general Alessandro Contarini (d. 1553), designed by Michele Sanmicheli and incorporating sculptures by Danese Cattaneo and Alessandro Vittoria. On the opposite side is the tomb of Cardinal Bembo (d. 1547), attributed to Palladio, with a bust by Cattaneo. The first chapel in the south aisle preserves the 15th-century tombs of Gattamelata, by Bartolomeo Bellano, and his son Giannantonio, by Pietro Lombardo. The 14th-century Capella di San Felice, in the south transept, was designed by Andriolo and Giovanni de Santi. It has frescoes representing the *Legend of St James*, the *Crucifixion* and other scenes, by Altichiero.

Behind the bronze doors of the **choir** (the custodians will unlock these on request) is the high altar, the second major commission Donatello received during his ten-year sojourn among the 'fogs and frogs' of Padua, as he put it. The altar (1443–50) is decorated with splendid bronze statues and reliefs by the master and his pupils. Their original configuration is unknown, and their present arrangement, devised by Camillo Boito in 1895, has been a matter of controversy among art historians for over a century. Above the predella, with twelve small reliefs of *Angel Musicians* and a *Pietà*, are four larger reliefs (two on the front and two on the back) of *Miracles of St Anthony*, all showing a startlingly bold treatment of architectural space that would profoundly influence Venetian Renaissance painting from Mantegna onwards. Also on this level are a small *Christ in Pietà* and, at the ends, symbols of the Evangelists. At the top of the composition are an enthroned *Madonna* in an unusual rising pose between lifesize statues of the six patron saints of Padua (Sts Louis of Anjou, Justina, Francis, Anthony, Daniel, and Prosdocimus), and a splendid bronze crucifix, probably intended to be placed elsewhere in the church. The placement of the stone *Deposition*, behind the altar, is also questionable. North of the altar stands a magnificent bronze paschal candelabrum (1507–15) by Andrea Briosco, Il Riccio. Along the sanctuary walls are twelve bronze reliefs of Old Testament stories, by Bartolomeo Bellano and Andrea Briosco.

Around the **sanctuary** are the ambulatory and its radiating chapels; the fifth chapel, known as the Cappella delle Relique or Cappella del Tesoro, built to a central plan by Filippo Parodi (who also made the statues, in 1689) holds a rich treasury, with remarkable reliquaries (including one for St Anthony's tongue), incense boats, and the wood boxes that once held the remains of the saint. At the north end of the ambulatory is the Chapel of the Madonna Mora, a vestige of the earlier (12th-century) church of Santa Maria Mater Domini.

The Cappella dell'Arca del Santo, in the **north transept**, was designed in 1499 by Tullio Lombardo and executed by his assistant, Antonio Minello. The stuccoed ceiling (1533) is the work of Falconetto. On the walls are nine large reliefs with stories of St Anthony, by 16th-century sculptors including Jacopo Sansovino (4th and 5th from the left), Tullio Lombardo (6th and 7th) and Antonio Lombardo (last). At the centre stands the magnificent altar, designed by Tiziano Aspetti (1593), behind which is St Anthony's tomb. This is still visited by hundreds of pilgrims every year, many of whom leave votive offerings. The adjacent Cappella Conti, with the tomb of the Blessed Luca Belludi, St Anthony's companion, is frescoed by Giusto de' Menabuoi.

On the wall of the north aisle of the basilica are the 17th-century tomb of General

Catrino Cornaro, by Juste le Court, and that of Antonio Roselli (d. 1466), by Pietro Lombardo.

To the south of the church are four cloisters, built between the 13th and 15th centuries. In the second, with a Romanesque doorway, a Renaissance loggia and a well of 1492, is a monument to 16th-century Franciscan preacher Cornelio Musso by Andrea Briosco. Steps climb from the fourth cloister past the original stone reliefs by Donatello from the Gattamelata monument to the Biblioteca Antoniana, with 85,000 books, manuscripts and incunabula, including a manuscript of sermons with notes in the hand of the greatest of all Franciscan preachers, St Anthony himself.

In the Chiostro del Beato Luca Belludi, with a magnificent magnolia tree, the **Museo Antoniano** preserves paintings, sculpture, and votive offerings from the basilica, notably the fresco of *Sts Anthony and Bernard Adoring the Monogram of Christ* by Andrea Mantegna, formerly in the lunette of the main doorway. In another cloister, on the north side near the church, a modest slab marks the burial-place of the entrails of Thomas Howard, Earl of Surrey and Arundel, who died in Padua in 1646. He was the patron of Inigo Jones, and together they went to Rome, where Arundel excavated some Roman statues, the seed of the collection later to be known as the Arundel Marbles (now in the Ashmolean Museum in Oxford).

The Scuola di Sant'Antonio

Open 9–12.30 & 2.30–5 or 7; inclusive ticket.
The Scuola di Sant'Antonio and the Oratory of San Giorgio adjoin the basilica on the southwest. The scuola was begun in 1427, with an upper storey added in 1504. A handsome 18th-century staircase ascends to the main hall, decorated with frescoes of the life of the saint by Venetian artists, including Bartolomeo Montagna, Domenico Campagnola, Girolamo del Santo and Titian, who painted the scenes of the *Miracle of the Irascible Son* (considered his first important independent works). The coloured terracotta *Madonna* is by Andrea Briosco. The oratory, once a chapel of the Soranzo family, is entirely covered with frescoes by Altichiero and his assistants (1379–84). The paintings represent the *Lives of Christ and Sts George, Catherine and Lucy*, and their arrangement in horizontal bands clearly calls to mind Giotto's decoration for the Scrovegni Chapel.

The Orto Botanico

Open in summer daily 9–1 & 3–6; winter daily except Sun and holidays 9–1.
The quiet Via Orto Botanico leads out of Piazza del Santo across a canal to the Orto Botanico, the oldest botanical garden in Europe, founded in 1545 and retaining its original form and structure. The circular walled space, with geometrical beds, is laid out around a pond with tropical water lilies. The various sections include medicinal and aquatic plants, rare species from northern Italy, flora from the Euganean Hills, and poisonous plants. Also here are a tamarisk tree, a ginkgo tree of 1750, a mimosa tree and an ancient magnolia dating from the mid-18th century. A palm tree, planted in 1585 and known as 'Goethe's palm' (he visited the garden in 1786), survives in a

little greenhouse. Behind this are interesting 19th-century hothouses, where succulents and carnivorous plants are kept, opposite which is a row of the plants first introduced into Italy in this garden, including the lilac, first cultivated in 1565, the sunflower in 1568, and the potato in 1590. There is also a greenhouse for orchids. Trees in the arboretum surrounding the walled garden include swamp cypresses, magnolias, Chinese palm trees, cedars, pines, a plane tree dating from 1680, and ilexes.

Prato della Valle and Santa Giustina

From Piazza del Santo, Via Beato Luca Belludi leads past an interesting Art Nouveau house (no. 3) to the pleasant **Prato della Valle**, the largest 'piazza' in Italy, surrounded by a miscellany of arcaded buildings. This huge area has been used since Roman times for public spectacles, fairs, etc. (and a large market is held here on Saturdays). In the centre is the Isola Memmia, encircled by a canal bordered by 18th-century statues of famous citizens, professors and students of the university. Four bridges lead to the centre, decorated with fountains. On the west side of the Prato is the Loggia Amulea, built in 1861 in the Venetian style with two Gothic loggias in brick and marble. The statues of Giotto and Dante are by Vincenzo Vela (1865). On the south side of the square is the monumental entrance to the former Foro Boario, now used as a car park and stadium.

Set back from the southern end of the piazza is Padua's most important 16th-century monument, the majestic brick **basilica of Santa Giustina** (1532–60), designed by Andrea Briosco and Andrea Moroni. Its plain façade and eight domes, some with metal statues of saints, recalls the exotic appearance of the church of Sant'Antonio.

The large three-aisled interior is a masterpiece of Venetian Baroque architecture, with elaborate detailing and exuberant paintings. In the south transept, the Sacello di San Prosdocimo (burial place of St Prosdocimus, the first bishop of Padua) is a remnant of the original early-Christian basilica. It contains an unusual 6th-century marble screen and an altar made from a Roman sarcophagus. The 15th-century Coro Vecchio, reached from the ninth chapel (*not always open*) has fine inlaid stalls and a statue of St Justina; in the adjoining rooms are a contemporary terracotta of the *Madonna and Child* and the lunette and lintel of a Romanesque doorway, dating from the 11th century. The sanctuary contains walnut stalls carved in 1566 by the Norman Riccardo Taurigny, with the help of Vicentine craftsmen; the large altarpiece of the *Martyrdom of St Justina* was painted by Paolo Veronese in 1575. In the north transept is the so-called Arca di San Luca, with alabaster reliefs by a Pisan sculptor (1316). The second north chapel holds a painting of *St Gregory the Great Liberating Rome from the Plague*, by Sebastiano Ricci. To the south of the church stands the Benedictine monastery, founded in the 8th century, suppressed in the 19th century, and now shared by monks and soldiers. From the Prato della Valle, Via Umberto I and Via Roma lead back to the city centre.

Part of the walls of Padua survive, built by the Venetians in 1513–44, with a circumference of some 11km. The two gates to the north, the Porta San Giovanni (1528) and the Porta Savonarola (1530) are by Giovanni Maria Falconetto, their design derived from ancient Roman architecture.

North of Padua

In the northern part of the province of Padua is **Cittadella**, built by the Paduans in 1220 as a reply to Castelfranco, fortified by Treviso some 20 years earlier (*see p. 377*). The old centre is enclosed in medieval walls, remarkably well preserved with numerous towers and gates. The two main gates, the Porta Padova and Porta Bassano, are painted with the red coat of arms of the Carraresi. The Porta Bassano and Porta Treviso can both be visited by advance appointment (made at the Municipio). The Torre Malta, built by Ezzelino III da Romano, is used for exhibitions. The moated fortifications, designed in an unusual elliptical shape, surround a simple and symmetrically planned town, which may follow the plan of a Roman town.

In the central piazza is the Neoclassical duomo (1820–28), by Giuseppe Jappelli, with works by Jacopo Bassano (including the *Supper at Emmaus* in the sacristy). In the same square is the 19th-century municipio. In Borgo Treviso is the interesting Palazzo Pretorio, with a well-carved 16th-century marble portal and 15th–16th-century frescoes. The gardens on the outside of the walls, which have a little zoo, can be entered from Porta Padova or Porta Vicenza. A weekly market is held in the town on Mondays.

To the northwest, at Santa Croce Bigolina, is the church of Santa Lucia di Brenta, frescoed by Jacopo Bassano c. 1540.

On the River Brenta north of Padua is the small town of Piazzola sul Brenta. Here is the splendid **Villa Contarini** (*open summer Tues–Sun 9–12 & 3–7; winter Tues–Sun 9–12 & 2–6; owned by a private foundation*), rebuilt in the 17th century for Marco Contarini as a summer house. It is preceded by a remarkable long avenue of magnolia trees, and a monumental semicircular portico (only half built), in Palladian style, across two canals and a fountain. The façade is 180m long. The central room is the auditorium, with remarkable acoustics (the gallery in the ceiling is for the orchestra), where concerts are held in May–June. Some of the rooms in the vast interior retain their 18th-century decorations. The carriage entrance to the villa on a lower level has a loggia decorated with shells and pebbles. There is also a small lapidarium, with Greek and Latin inscriptions.

The 45-hectare park can also be visited: it is surrounded by canals and has fishponds, and a huge lake with black and white swans. To the right of the villa is the handsome stable block. A market is held in front of the villa on Friday.

In the northeastern corner of the province is Piombino Dese, with the beautiful **Villa Cornaro** (*open May–Sept Sat 3.30–6*), built for Giorgio Cornaro by Palladio in 1552. With two storeys, it has a double portico. The rooms are frescoed by Mattia Bortoloni (1716), and have stuccoes of the same date by Bortolo Cabianca. The statues in the main room are by Camillo Mariani (c. 1592–94). Set beside the River Dese, it has a small garden.

To the northeast is **Levada** with the Villa Marcello (*privately owned; open by appointment; T: 49 935 0340*), rebuilt in the 18th century, with frescoes by Giovanni Battista Crosato. South of Piombino is **Massanzago**, where the town hall in Villa Baglioni has frescoes by Giovanni Battista Tiepolo.

THE RIVIERA DEL BRENTA

The Venetians built the canal known as the Naviglio di Brenta or Brenta Vecchia to facilitate navigation between their city and Padua, diverting the river itself to the north to reduce the amount of silt pouring into the lagoon. The magnificent villas for which the area is famous first appeared in the 16th century when, in the face of Turkish expansion in the eastern Mediterranean, Venetian patricians shifted their investments from foreign trade to real estate. The great farms that grew up here were intended both to generate income and to provide a pleasant escape from the heat and humidity of the lagoon in summer. The principal façades of the houses faced the water, like the palaces on the Grand Canal—and not by chance, for the same festive lifestyle that graced the latter in winter continued in summer in the villas of the riviera. With the approach of the 18th century, the idyllic pleasures of country life merged with a taste for the exotic, and the architecture of the noble manors became more luxurious and extravagant, with spectacular parks, gardens, aviaries, greenhouses and private zoos stocked with exotic animals. Meanwhile patricians of limited means (of whom there were quite a few), adventurers (even more) and the nouveaux riches rented lodgings in the towns, in order not to miss the great social events of the Venetian summer.

The villas of the Riviera

Those who, for one reason or another, chose not to make the trip up the canal in the family gondola took the *burchiello*, a large riverboat rowed by slaves or pulled by horses—a 'marvellous and comfortable craft', as Goldoni recalls, 'in which one glides along the Brenta sheltered from winter's cold and summer's ardour'. Today a motorised *burchiello* lazily winds its way from Padua to Venice or vice versa, for a handsome fee, stopping to visit several of the 50-odd extant villas. The trip can also be made by bicycle (there are marked cycling routes), or by car. Here the villas are listed in the order in which they appear if you depart from Padua.

Strà

The 18th-century **Villa Pisani** or Villa Nazionale (*open summer Tues–Sun 9–6; winter 9–4; T: 049 502 074*) is the largest villa on the Riviera, named after its original owner, the Venetian doge Alvise Pisani. The interior is decorated by 18th-century Venetian artists, including Tiepolo, who frescoed the *Triumph of the Pisani Family* on the ceiling of the ballroom (1762). It was purchased by Napoleon in 1807, and in 1934 was the scene of the first meeting between Mussolini and Hitler. In the vast park is the labyrinth described by Gabriele d'Annunzio in *Fire*. On the opposite bank of the canal rises the long front of the **Villa Lazara Pisani**, 'La Barbariga', with a Baroque central structure and symmetrical 18th-century wings.

Dolo

Dolo was the principal town of the Riviera in the 18th century, and still preserves its mill, a *squero* (or boatyard) and one of the old locks. The **Palazzo Faletti Mocenigo** (now a school) was designed in 1596 by Palladio's pupil Vincenzo

The Villa Pisani at Strà.

Scamozzi. In the environs are the **Villa Ferretti Angeli** (1598), also by Scamozzi; the Baroque **Villa Grimani Migliorini**, with a Doric porch; and the Villas **Andreuzzi Bon** and **Mocenigo Spiga**, both of the 18th century.

Mira

It was here that Lord Byron wrote the fourth canto of *Childe Harold* and first met Margherita Cogni, 'la bella Fornarina'. On the outskirts are the Villas **Pisani Contarini** (or dei Leoni), **Querini Stampalia** and **Valier** (or La Chitarra). A little further, at Riscossa, is the **Villa Seriman**, and at Oriago, the **Villa Widmann-Rezzonico-Foscari**, built in 1719 but remodelled in the French Rococo manner after the middle of the 18th century. The most famous of the villas of Mira, it has a two-storey façade with curved tympanum, and frescoed rooms.

La Malcontenta

On a shady bend of the river, beyond Oriago, stands the **Villa Foscari**, also known as La Malcontenta (*open May–Oct Tues and Sat 9–12 and by appointment, T: 041 547 0012*), which legend claims as the home of a Dame Foscari (the 'malcontent' of the name), exiled here for betraying her husband. It was constructed around 1555–60 for the brothers Nicola and Alvise Foscari by Andrea Palladio. The exterior is very slightly rusticated; the side towards the river is characterised by a noble seven-columned Ionic porch, which projects outward and is raised on a tall basement with lateral ramps. Within, the rooms are arranged around a large, central Greek-cross *salone* frescoed by Battista Franco and Giovanni Battista Zelotti. Further on, at Fusina, the canal enters the lagoon and you glimpse Venice, 4km away.

THE EUGANEAN HILLS

The Euganean Hills (Colli Euganei) are a volcanic formation rising unexpectedly in the midst of the Po river basin southwest of Padua. The hills have been famous since Roman times for their hot thermal springs (70°–87°C), rich in minerals, and there are four spa towns here, most notably Abano Terme. Petrarch spent the last four years of his life in a little village in the hills, and it was here that Shelley was inspired to compose his *Lines Written Among the Euganean Hills*. Protected as a regional park, the area has number of marked paths for walkers, and farms offering accommodation. A good white wine is produced here, and wild mushrooms grow in abundance.

Abano Terme and environs

Abano Terme is one of the leading spas in Europe. Known since Roman times for its hot springs, today it is famous for its mud therapy, which uses special thermophile algae and is especially helpful in the treatment of rheumatism and arthritis. Abano itself is an elegant town with a distinctive 19th-century atmosphere. Though it is virtually deserted in winter, during the season (March–Oct) it is thronged with visitors, many of whom return year after year.

The main street is the shady Viale delle Terme, where the grandest hotels are located. The most notable of these is the Neoclassical Hotel Orologio, designed in 1825 by Giuseppe Jappelli, who built the Caffè Pedrocchi in Padua (*see p. 466*). The Montirone, a knoll at the centre of the town, planted as a park and the site of Abano's warmest spring (80°C), is adorned with an early 20th-century Corinthian colonnade and a Doric column of 1825 (also by Jappelli) commemorating a visit of Emperor Franz I of Austria. The cathedral of San Lorenzo is undistinguished.

The **Santuario della Vergine** at Monteortone, 3km west of Abano Terme, was begun in 1435 on a site where a miraculous image of the Virgin Mary was reputedly found. It has a simple façade with a Baroque doorway of 1667, and a 15th-century brick campanile with pointed spire. The three-aisled interior is built in a hybrid Gothic-Renaissance style; it contains frescoes by Jacopo da Montagnana and a fine Renaissance altar in the sanctuary, and a *Crucifixion and Saints* by Palma Giovane in an adjoining chapel. The former Salesian convent, with a lovely Renaissance cloister, is now a hotel.

The **Abbazia di Praglia**, 12km further in the same direction, is approached by a beautiful, tree-lined driveway. It is a Benedictine foundation of 1080 rebuilt in the 15th and 16th centuries (*open for guided tours every 30mins, summer Tues–Sun 3.30–5.30; winter 2.30–4.30*). The church (Santa Maria Assunta) was built between 1490 and 1548, probably to a design by Tullio Lombardo; the Romanesque campanile is a remnant of the original building. The vaulted Latin-cross interior has 16th-century Venetian paintings, a 14th-century wooden crucifix over the high altar, and frescoes in the apse by Domenico Campagnola. The abbey is still active, and parts of it are closed to the public; but you can see a 15th-century *chiostro botanico* or herb-garden cloister (a reminder that the most expert pharmacists, here as elsewhere in

Europe, were once monks), a *chiostro pensile* of the late 15th century and a large refectory with ceiling paintings by Giovanni Battista Zelotti, 18th-century carved woodwork and a famous *Crucifixion* frescoed by Bartolomeo Montagna (1490–1500).

Montegrotto Terme and environs

Montegrotto Terme is another important spa, with extensive remains of Roman baths and a small Roman theatre. Above the town, a lovely park (open to the public) surrounds the Gothic-revival Villa Draghi. Nearby is the curious **Castello del Catajo** (*open Feb–Nov Tues, Sun and holidays 3–6.30*). It was built in 1570 by Andrea della Valle for Pio Enea degli Obizzi, a captain of the Venetian army. In the 19th century it became the property of the dukes of Modena. It was altered in the 17th century when part of the beautiful garden was created. The frescoes (1571–73) by Giovanni Battista Zelotti on the first floor depict the exploits of members of the Obizzi family, including one who accompanied Richard I of England on the Crusades, and another who perhaps fought for Edward III at Neville's Cross.

At **San Pelagio** the castle has a Museo dell'Aria (*open Tues–Sun 9–12.30 & 2.30–6*). The display is arranged chronologically from the experiments of Leonardo to the era of space travel. The exhibits include material relating to d'Annunzio's flight to Vienna in 1918, planned in the castle; a model of the first helicopter designed by Forlanini in 1877; and planes used in the Second World War.

Battaglia Terme is an attractive small, old-fashioned spa on the Canale della Battaglia, much less grand than the other neighbouring spa towns. A park laid out by Giuseppe Jappelli in the early 19th century surrounds the Villa Emo Selvatico (*open by appointment; T: 0444 240 380*), an unusual centrally-planned building with four corner towers and a dome dating from 1648. Just outside, on a by-road to Arquà Petrarca, is another Villa Emo, built in 1588 to a design attributed to Vincenzo Scamozzi. The garden (*open Apr–Oct Mon, Sun and holidays 10–7*) was laid out in the 1960s and has numerous rose beds.

At **Valsanzibio** is the Villa Barbarigo, built in the mid-17th century. The fine garden, probably laid out around 1699, has a maze, and numerous pools, fountains and statues. It is surrounded by a 19th-century park (*open March–Oct 9–12 & 2–dusk*).

Nearby, in a pretty position in the hills, is **Arquà Petrarca**, a delightful little medieval *borgo* with gardens. Numerous giuggiole trees grow here, producing an orange fruit in the shape of an olive (*festa* on 1 October). This is where Petrarch lived from 1370 until his death in 1374. At the top of the village is his house (*open Tues–Sun 9–12.30 & 2.30 or 3–5.30 or 7*) which contains visitors' books, one with Byron's signature. In the lower part of the village is the church, outside which is Petrarch's plain marble sarcophagus with an epitaph composed by himself. When the tomb was opened in 2003 (scientists were hoping to use his skull to recreate his features for an 'official' portrait to mark the 730th anniversary of his death), consternation ensued when the skull inside was discovered to belong to a different skeleton from the bones. The case of the missing head continues.

Further north is **Luvigliano**, above which is Villa dei Vescovi (*open March–Nov,*

Mon, Wed, Fri by appointment; T: 049 521 1118), built under the direction of Alvise Cornaro by Giovanni Maria Falconetto in 1532, and continued by Andrea della Valle in 1567. It has an unusual design with large, open loggias, contains frescoes attributed to the Netherlandish artist Lambert Sustris (1545), and is surrounded by a pretty garden. In the church is an altarpiece by Girolamo Santacroce, signed and dated 1527.

Monselice and environs

Rising on the southeast slopes of the Euganean Hills, **Monselice** was a Roman settlement, a Lombard *gastaldato*, a free commune, a seigniory, and finally a Venetian dominion. Today it is an active industrial and agricultural centre. It takes its name (literally, 'mountain of flint') from the small mound of debris dug from the quarry that twice served to pave Piazza San Marco in Venice. The castle stands at the top of the hill, the town at the bottom, the monuments along a road and walkway that wind along the slopes.

In the lower town, on the east side of Piazza Mazzini, is the medieval Torre Civica, with a fine loggia and crenellated parapet. From the square, Via del Santuario climbs past the 16th-century Monte di Pietà, with a small loggia, to the Castello Cini, a remarkable complex of buildings with an 11th- or 12th-century core, enlarged between the 13th and 16th centuries. The interior (*open for guided tours, Apr–Nov, by appointment; T: 0429 72931*) houses a collection of paintings, sculpture, weapons, Renaissance furniture, tapestries, and in the Sala del Camino Vecchio, a monumental fireplace shaped like a tower.

Continuing along Via del Santuario you soon come to the 16th- and 17th-century Villa Nani-Mocenigo, with a wall decorated with curious 18th-century statues of dwarves and a spectacular terraced staircase. Just a little further on is the Duomo Vecchio, dedicated to St Justina, a Romanesque-Gothic church of 1256 with a 12th-century campanile and a three-part façade with a rose window, smaller mullioned windows, and a 15th-century porch. Within are frescoes and altarpieces by minor 15th-century Venetian painters. At the end of the avenue stands the Villa Duodo, by Vincenzo Scamozzi (1593), enlarged in the 18th century, when the monumental staircase to the formal garden was added. It now belongs to the University of Padua. Its grounds include the cypress-shaded Santuario delle Sette Chiese, entered from the 18th-century Piazzale della Rotonda, a scenic overlook behind the Duomo Vecchio. The sanctuary comprises six chapels designed by Scamozzi after 1605, containing paintings by Palma Giovane, and the church of San Giorgio, octagonal outside and elliptical within.

In a panoramic position at the top of the hill stands the ruined rocca, built by Holy Roman Emperor Frederick II and enlarged by the Carraresi. Today little more than the keep remains, but there is a fine view. On the east slope of the hill is the old church of San Tommaso, which conserves some 13th-century frescoes. At **Valsanzibio di Galzignano**, 8km north, is the Villa Barbarigo, now Pizzoni Ardemagni, with a 17th-century formal garden and fountains.

Southeast of Monselice is **Bagnoli di Sopra**, where monastic buildings were transformed in the 17th century by Baldassare Longhena into the Villa Widmann (privately owned), with 18th-century frescoes. Carlo Goldoni stayed here with Ludovico Bagnoli in the 18th century and put on several performances of his plays. It is surrounded by a fine garden (*open Thur 3–6*) decorated with numerous statues by Antonio Bonazza (1742). Also in the piazza is the Palazzetto Widmann (owned by the town) with frescoes by Giovanni Battista Pittoni and Louis Dorigny.

Este and environs

The little town of **Este**, at the southern edge of the Colli Euganei, was a centre of the ancient Veneti before it became the Roman Ateste. Later it was the stronghold of the Este family, who afterwards became dukes of Ferrara, and from 1405 was under Venetian dominion. The huge battlemented Carraresi castle dates mainly from 1339, and its impressive walls enclose a public garden. Here in the 16th-century Palazzo Mocenigo is the **Museo Nazionale Atestino** (*open daily 9–1 & 3–7*). Many of the exhibits, arranged chronologically, come from excavations carried out near Este in the 19th century. The Roman section is on the ground floor, and includes a fine bronze head of Medusa (1st century AD). The pre-Roman section, on the first floor, has prehistoric collections that offer a glimpse of ancient Venetic civilisation, notably material of the Aeneolithic and Bronze Ages, and burial artefacts from the early Iron Age. The *Benvenuti Situla* (c. 600 BC) is decorated with bronze reliefs. A *Madonna and Child* by Cima da Conegliano is also displayed here.

Behind the castle (Via Cappuccini) are the fine parks of several villas, including the Villa Kunkler, occupied by Byron in 1817–18, where Shelley composed *Lines Written Among the Euganean Hills*.

The **cathedral of St Tecla**, a medieval church rebuilt in 1690–1708 by Antonio Francesco Gaspari, has an 18th-century campanile built on an 8th-century base. The elliptical interior abounds with sculptures and paintings, among which the large *St Tecla Freeing Este from the Plague*, by Giovanni Battista Tiepolo (1759), is certainly the most striking.

From here Via Garibaldi and Via Alessi bear southwest to the church of **Santa Maria delle Consolazioni** (or Santa Maria degli Zoccoli, 1504–10), with a campanile of 1598 and a single-aisled interior. The Cappella della Vergine contains a magnificent Roman mosaic pavement excavated nearby. The church possesses a fine *Madonna* by Cima da Conegliano, on temporary loan to the museum; and the adjoining cloister has 15th-century capitals.

On the other side of town (about 500m away) are the Romanesque church of **San Martino**, with a campanile of 1293 (leaning since 1618), 18th-century sculptures and two altarpieces by Antonio Zanchi; and the 15th-century basilica of **Santa Maria delle Grazie**, rebuilt in the 18th century, in the Latin-cross interior of which are marble altars, statues, frescoes from the earlier church and a Byzantine *Madonna* of the early 15th century, venerated as miraculous. Other interesting monuments are the 16th-century Palazzo del Principe, by Vincenzo Scamozzi, who also designed the façade of the church of San Michele; Villa Cornaro (now Benvenuti), with a 19th-century park designed by Giuseppe Japelli; the 18th-century Villa Contarini, known also as the Vigna Contarena; the Palazzo del Municipio, also dating from the 18th century; and the octagonal church of the Beata Vergine della Salute (1639), with two octagonal *campanili* flanking the apse.

Ten kilometres south of Este is the **Abbazia di Carceri**, dedicated to the Virgin Mary. Founded in the 11th century, it includes an octagonal church of 1643 with 15th–18th-century paintings, remains of a 12th-century Romanesque cloister and a 16th-century Renaissance *chiostro grande* and library.

Montagnana

Of prehistoric origin, Montagnana was a Roman *vicus* (village) and a medieval Lombard centre. The old town—with porticoed streets, a large square, and the lazy atmosphere of the quintessential Venetian farm town—lies within a well-preserved complex of turreted walls built by Ezzelino and the Carraresi between the 12th and the 14th centuries. The walls are pierced by four gates and surrounded by a moat, now a park. During the Venetian period (after 1405), hemp was grown here for use in ships' rigging.

The walls surround the entire town, enclosing an area of 24ha within a perimeter of almost 2km. The most impressive of the gates are the Rocca degli Alberi or Porta Legnano, dating from 1362, with a fortified bridge and tower with *piombatoi,* and the Porta Padova, adjoining the Castello di San Zeno, with the tall Torre Ezzelina. The **Castello di San Zeno** was built in 1242; the Venetian wing (and temporarily also the small church of San Giovanni) holds the Museo Civico, with Bronze and Iron Age finds (9th–8th centuries BC) from a local prehistoric complex, Roman burial treasures of the 1st century AD, Roman inscriptions and medieval ceramics (*open for guided tours Mon–Fri 11; Sat 10.30, 11.30, 4, 5, 6; Sun 11, 12, 4, 5, 6*).

Inside the town, on the southwest side of the central Via Carrarese, rises the Palazzo del Municipio, an austere building with rusticated portico laid out in 1538 by Michele Sanmicheli and remodelled in the 17th and 18th centuries. Within, the Sala del Consiglio has a coffered ceiling of 1555 by Marcantonio Vannini.

The **cathedral of Santa Maria,** in the large, central Piazza Vittorio Emanuele, was built in a transitional Gothic-Renaissance style between 1431 and 1502 on the site of an 11th-century structure of which a few traces remain. The brick façade, with three bell niches, has a doorway shaped like a triumphal arch, attributed to Jacopo Sansovino. Notice also the south flank and large polygonal apse of the south transept. The tall, early Renaissance interior, a single aisle with barrel vaulting, contains a Venetian School gold-ground painting of the *Annunciation*, dating from the 14th century; 15th- and 16th-century frescoes; a *Transfiguration* by Paolo Veronese over the high altar; and a large fresco of the *Assumption of the Virgin* in the apse, attributed to Giovanni Buonconsiglio, an early 16th-century painter, author also of several altarpieces. Other frescoes possibly by his hand are on the west wall of the north transept and on the inside of the façade.

Up against the wall to the south is the church of **San Francesco**, a 14th- and 15th-century edifice altered in the 17th century, with a tall campanile of 1429 or 1468. Within are a *Transfiguration* by the school of Paolo Veronese, in the sanctuary, and a *Madonna* by Palma Giovane in the apse.

Just outside the walls, across the moat from the Porta Padova, stands the **Villa Pisani Placco**, the central part of which was designed by Andrea Palladio. It was built around 1560. The two main elevations have a double central order of Ionic and Corinthian columns terminating in a pediment. Also noteworthy are the splendid frieze with bucranic metopes and the harmonious ground-floor atrium, with statues of the *Seasons* by Alessandro Vittoria (1577).

ROVIGO & THE PO DELTA

The southeastern Veneto encompasses the lower course of the River Po, a place rich in natural and human history. This is the last alluvial plain of the great river, which begins in the northwestern corner of Italy and flows toward the Adriatic bearing tons of silt from its Alpine sources and depositing it along its way, 'filling in' the sea more and more every year. The delta of the Po is Italy's most extensive wetland, a permanent home to dozens of animal species and a stopping place for migratory birds.

ROVIGO

A walled town in the 12th century, Rovigo was taken by the Venetians in 1482, and remained under their control until the fall of the Republic in 1797. Though its main street is no longer paved with water (the River Adigetto was covered over to form the Corso del Popolo in the 1930s), the town still has a Venetian atmosphere.

In the central Piazza Vittorio Emanuele II is the attractive 16th-century Palazzo del Municipio. Beside it the 18th-century Palazzo Bosi houses the **Pinacoteca dei Concordi** (*open Mon–Fri 9.30–12 & 3.30–7, Sat 9.30–12; July–Aug Mon–Sat 10–1*), whose fine collection of paintings is particularly representative of Venetian art from the 15th–18th centuries. It includes a *Madonna* by Giovanni Bellini, works by Sebastiano Mazzoni, and portraits by Alessandro Longhi and Tiepolo.

Just off the southern corner of the central Piazza Vittorio Emanuele II is **Palazzo Roncale**, a fine building by Sanmicheli (1555). To the north is Piazza Garibaldi, with an equestrian statue of the hero himself, and the Caffè Borsa. The **Camera del Commercio** encloses the well-preserved Salone del Grano, built in 1934 with a remarkable glass barrel vault.

Via Silvestri leads out of the square past the church of San Francesco (with sculptures by Tullio Lombardo) to Piazza XX Settembre, at the end of which is **La Rotonda** or Santa Maria del Soccorso, a centrally-planned octagonal church surrounded by a portico, built in 1594 by Francesco Zamberlan, who also worked on reconstructing the Doge's Palace in Venice after the fire in 1577. The campanile was designed by

Baldassare Longhena in the 17th century. The interior decoration, which survives intact from the 17th century, consists of a series of paintings celebrating Venetian offi-cials with elaborate allegories: the lower band includes five by Francesco Maffei (*see box*) and others by Pietro Liberi. Above stucco statues (1627) is another cycle of paint-ings by Antonio Zanchi, Pietro Liberi, Andrea Celesti, and others.

Francesco Maffei (1605–60)

Often overlooked as an artist, Maffei's style is usually described as being fluidly, typically Baroque, with all the opulence that that implies, tempered by the recher-ché exaggeration of Mannerism. What critics often fail to pinpoint is the nervous, haunting quality that pervades all his work. In his own day he was called a painter 'not of dwarves but of giants … whose style stupefied everyone'. Maffei worked in Vicenza for most of his career, with occasional forays to other cities, of which Rovigo is a notable example. His best works are either religious or allegorical, par-ticularly those that show the apotheosis or glorification of local dignitaries (such as his *Glorification of the Podestà Giovanni Cavalli* in La Rotonda in Rovigo). By dint of rapid, bird-like brushstrokes and an unpredictable use of colour, Maffei invests his works with a bizarre, other-worldly atmosphere. He died of plague in Padua.

THE POLESINE

This flat area west of Rovigo between the Adige and Po rivers is traversed by numer-ous canals. At **Fratta Polesine**, facing a bridge over a canal, is Villa Badoer (*open July–Oct Tues–Sun 10–12 & 4.30–7.30, or by appointment; T: 0425 21530*), built by Palladio in 1556 for the Venetian nobleman Francesco Badoer (and now owned by the province of Rovigo). It is enclosed by an attractive brick wall and preceded by a green lawn with two fountains and two 19th-century magnolia trees. The outbuildings are linked to the house by curving porticoes, and a wide flight of steps leads up to the villa with an Ionic portico and temple pediment. The empty interior is interesting for its remarkable plan (the service rooms and servants' quarters are on a lower level) and damaged contemporary frescoes by Giallo Fiorentino.

Badia Polesine has remains of the abbey of Vangadizza, founded in the 10th cen-tury and enlarged in the 11th. The attractive 12th-century campanile stands near two 12th-century tombs and the drum of the domed chapel, all that remains of the church destroyed by Napoleon. The picturesque irregular cloister is used for concerts, and the refectory is being restored. The chapel (opened on request) contains painted dec-oration attributed to Filippo Zaniberti and interesting stuccoes of the cardinal virtues. The Museo Civico Baruffaldi contains 12th–17th-century ceramics. The Teatro Sociale dates from 1813.

At **Canda**, on the Bianco canal, is the Villa Nani-Mocenigo (*no admission*), attrib-uted to Vincenzo Scamozzi (1580–84), enlarged in the 18th century.

The Po Delta

The Po is the longest river in Italy (652km). Its source is at Piano del Re (2050m) in Piedmont, on the French border, and it is joined by numerous tributaries (including the Ticino and the Adda) as it crosses northern Italy from west to east through Lombardy and the Veneto on its way to the Adriatic. In the late Middle Ages the Po was navigable, and one of the principal waterways of Europe. In 1599 the Venetian Republic carried out major works of canalisation in the delta area in order to deviate the course of the river south to prevent it silting up the Venetian lagoon. It now reaches the sea by seven different channels: the largest (which carries 60 per cent of its waters) is called the 'Po di Venezia'. The delta formed by this operation is the largest area of marshlands in Italy. Sadly, the waters of the Po are extremely polluted. Studies have shown that the river feeds hundreds of tons of arsenic into the Adriatic every year, and according to European Union regulations, none of its waters should be used for drinking, swimming or irrigation.

Despite this depressing fact, however, the flat open landscape of the delta, with wide views over the reedy marshes and numerous wetlands (known as *valli*), is remarkably beautiful, whether in typical misty weather or on clear autumnal days. Rice and sugar beet were once intensely cultivated here, and some attractive old farmhouses survive, although most of them have been abandoned.

The marshes have interesting birdlife, counting some 350 species, including cormorants, herons, egrets, grebes and blackwinged stilts. Despite opposition from naturalists, the shooting season is still open September to January. Pila and the Po della Pila have important fisheries, and all over the delta area eels, bass, carp, tench, pike and grey mullet are caught. Clams (a new clam was imported into the delta in the early 1980s from the Philippines) and mussels are also cultivated here.

Very few boats (apart from those of the fishermen) venture into the delta area, for many of the channels are only 1–2m deep. A few characteristic bridges of boats and ferries survive.

Adria, the ancient capital of the Polesine, gave its name to the Adriatic Sea (to which it is now joined only by canal). The Museo Archeologico (*open Mon–Sat 9–7, Sun and holidays 2–6*) contains proof of the city's Graeco-Etruscan origins. The earliest finds from the upper Polesine date from the 11th–9th centuries BC. There are also Greek red- and black-figure ceramics, Roman glass (1st century AD), and gold and amber objects.

Nearby is the 17th-century church of Santa Maria Assunta, which incorporates some Roman masonry. Across the Canal Bianco is the cathedral, which has a little 6th-century Coptic bas-relief and a crypt with remains of Byzantine frescoes.

A road leads east past **Loreo**, built on a canal with a parish church by Baldassare Longhena, to **Rosolina** on the Via Romea, in parts a post-war revival of the long-decayed Roman Via Popilia, which ran down the Adriatic coast from Venice to Ravenna. Following the road north you soon come to **Chioggia**, one of the main fishing ports on the Adriatic (particularly famous for mussels) and the most important town on the Venetian lagoon after Venice. It has a remarkable longitudinal urban structure with three canals and a parallel wide main street.

Porto Tolle is on the Isola della Donzella, the largest island on the delta. The island used to have *valli* with fisheries, but was reclaimed after a flood in 1966, and now has rice fields.

The southern part of the Isola della Donzella is occupied by the Sacca di Scardovari, an attractive lagoon lined with fishermen's huts and boats. Mussels and clams are cultivated here, and it is inhabited by numerous birds. On its shores is a tiny protected area illustrating the typical vegetation of the wetlands that once covered this area. The easternmost island on the delta, the Isola di Batteria, is gradually being engulfed by the sea. It is no longer inhabited and is the only oasis on the delta. At the end of the delta is a lighthouse built in 1949 on land only formed some hundred years ago.

The rest of the delta area to the south, in the province of Ferrara, is described on pp. 648–49.

PRACTICAL INFORMATION

GETTING AROUND

• **Airport buses:** Airport bus from Padua to Venice airport every 30mins Mon–Sat; hourly Sun and holidays.
• **By rail**: Padua is on the main rail lines from Milan and Rome to Venice. Fast Intercity, Eurocity and Eurostar trains connect with Verona, Milan, Turin and Genoa; and with Bologna, Florence and Rome. Secondary lines connect with Treviso, Belluno and Pieve di Cadore/Cortina; and with Cittadella and Bassano del Grappa. The Euganean Hills are served by the main rail line from Padua to Bologna and Rome (change at Monselice for Este and Montagnana). Rovigo is located on the main Bologna–Venice rail line, with fast Eurostar and Intercity trains from Venice in 55mins, Padua in 25mins and Bologna in 50mins. Branch lines connect Rovigo with Adria, Rosolina and Chioggia; and with Verona.
• **By bus:** Town buses nos 8, 12 and 18 run from the railway station to the city centre, every 5mins Mon–Fri, every 15mins Sun and holidays. Country buses run by APS (T: 049 824 1111, www.apson-line.it), and SITA (T: 049 820 6811) depart from Piazzale Boschetti for Venice (although Venice is best reached from Padua by train); to Rovigo, Monselice-Montagnana and numerous destinations in the Veneto; and to Bologna.
• **By car:** The Euganean Hills are best explored by car, but the journey can also be made by train (*see above*). The car parks in Padua at Prato della Valle, at the station and Via Fra Paolo Sarpi have a minibus service to Piazza dei Signori. There is also a large car park near the station.
• **By bicycle:** Bicycles can be hired at Taglio di Po and Ca' Tiepolo.
• **By boat:** The Burchiello motor-launch usually operates Apr–Oct from Padua along the Brenta Canal to Venice in 8hrs 30mins (on Wed, Fri and Sun) with stops at Strà, Dolo, Mira, Oriago and Malcontenta (including visits to the

villas at Strà, Mira, and Malcontenta).
At present it is operating from Strà (bus
from Piazzale Boschetti, Padua, to Strà).
Information and bookings, T: 049 876
2301, www.ilburchiello.it. Other companies now also arrange trips on the
Brenta (details from the information
office). Boat excursions on the Po Delta
are arranged by several companies,
including Marino Cacciatori (Caparin;
T: 0426 81508 or 0337 513818), starting from Ca' Tiepolo.

INFORMATION OFFICES

Padua Riviera dei Mugnai 8, T: 049
876 7911, www.turismopadova.it;
branch offices at Piazza del Santo, T:
049 875 3087; Galleria Pedrocchi, T:
049 876 7927; train station, T: 049 875
2077.
Padova Card. A combined ticket for
free entrance to the main museums and
monuments of Padua, plus free travel
on city buses, can be purchased from
the Information Office or the Museo
Civico agli Eremitani. The tourist board
also publishes the quarterly *Padova
Today* with up-to-date visitor information.
Chioggia Lungomare Adriatico 101, T:
041 554 0466, www.chioggia.tourism.it
Branch office at Museo Civico,
Fondamenta San Francesco, T: 041 550
0911.
Euganean Hills Abano Terme: Via
Pietro d'Abano 18, T: 049 866 9055,
www.turismotermeeuganee.it; Battaglia
Terme: Via Maggiore 2, T: 049 526 909;
Este: Via Negri 9, T: 0429 600 462;
Monselice: Piazza Mazzini 15, T: 0429
783 026; Montagnana, Castel San Zeno,
T: 0429 81320; Montegrotto Terme:

Viale Stazione 60, T: 049 793 384.
Riviera del Brenta Dolo: Area Servizio
Arino Sud, Autostrada Padova-Venezia,
T: 041 529 8711,
www.turismovenezia.it
Rovigo Via Dunant 10, T: 0425 361
481.

HOTELS

Padua
€€ **Donatello**. A comfortable hotel
overlooking the Santo; its Sant'Antonio
restaurant has a pleasant summer terrace. Closed Dec–Jan. Via del Santo
102, T: 049 875 0634, F: 049 875
0829.
€€ **Igea**. A warm, homely inn near the
Santo. Via Ospedale Civile 87, T: 049
875 0577, hoteligeapd@iol.it
€€ **Leon Bianco**. A small, quiet place
in the heart of the old city, next door to
the Caffè Pedrocchi. Piazzetta Pedrocchi
12, T: 049 875 0814,
majestic@toscanelli.com
€€ **Majestic Toscanelli**. An elegant,
distinctive establishment situated in a
little square near Piazza delle Erbe. Via
dell'Arco 2, T: 049 663244,
majestic@toscanelli.com
€ **Al Fagiano**. A simple establishment
just off Piazza del Santo. Via Locatelli
45, T: 049 875 3396, F: 049 875 3396.
Contarina
€ **Villa Carrer**. A 16th-century villa in
a beautiful park. Piazza Matteotti 44, T:
0426 632686, F: 0426 632676.
Euganean Hills
The best place to stay in this area is
without a doubt Abano Terme.
Hospitality is the only game in town
here, and all the hotels (open Apr–Nov
as a rule) are comfortable, modern, and

restful, though there is not one that is downright luxurious.

€€€ **Trieste e Victoria**. A well-established, elegant place with lovely gardens and thermal pool. Via Pietro d'Abano 1, T: 049 866 8333, www.gbhotels.it

€€ **Terme Columbia**. Modern and efficient, with a thermal pool. Via Augure 15, T: 049 866 9606, F: 049 866 9430.

Rosolina
€€ **Golf**. Small and elegant, with a nice garden. Closed Oct–Mar. Isola Albarella, T: 0426 367811, F: 330628.

Rovigo
€€ **Villa Regina Margherita**. In an Art-Nouveau building on a wooded boulevard. Viale Regina Margherita 6, T: 0425 361540, F: 0425 31301.

Taglio di Po
€ **Tessarin**. Simple but comfortable. Piazza Venezia 4, T: 0426 346347, F: 0426 346346.

YOUTH HOSTELS

Mira
€ **Oriago di Mira**. Casa del Sole e della Luna, Riviera Bosco Piccolo 84, T: 041 563 1799, mira@casasoleluna.it
€ **Ostello di Mira**. Via Giare 169, T: 041 567 9203, mira@casasoleluna.it

Padua
€ **Città di Padova**. The 1-star hotels Pace (Via Papafava 3) and Pavia (Via Papafava 11) are also used by students. Via Aleardi 30, T: 049 875 2219, pdyhtl@tin.it

RESTAURANTS

Padua
€€€ **San Clemente**. Probably the

city's best, located a few blocks south of the Prato della Valle, in a historic building with a lovely garden. Closed Sun evening, midday Mon, Aug and Dec. Corso Vittorio Emanule II 142, T: 049 880 3180.

€€ **Ai Porteghi**. A traditional trattoria located halfway between the Cappella Scrovegni and the Basilica del Santo, serving Paduan specialities. Closed Sun, midday Mon and Aug. Via Battisti 105, T: 049 660746.

€€ **Antico Brolo**. A small, traditional restaurant in a historic building in the city centre. Closed midday Sun, Mon and Aug. Corso Milano 22, T: 049 664555.

€€ **Belle Parti**. Situated near Piazza dei Signori, serving innovative cuisine. Closed Sun and Aug. Via Belle Parti 11, T: 049 875 1822.

€ **Cavalca**. Traditional fare accompanied by regional and Italian wines. Closed Tues evening, Wed and July. Via Manin 8, T: 049 876 0061.

€ **L'Anfora**. Wine bar and *osteria* with live jazz at lunch. Closed Sun, midday Mon and Aug. Via dei Soncin 13, T: 049 656629.

€ **Leonardi**. Wine bar serving soups and simple meals. Closed Mon, midday Tues, Feb and Aug. Via Pietro d'Abano 1, T: 049 875 0083.

Ariano Polesine
€€ **Due Leoni**. Traditional restaurant (with rooms), offering delicious local cuisine. Closed Mon and July. Corso del Popolo 21, T: 0426 372129.

Euganean Hills
€€ **Aldo Moro** (with rooms). Local specialities cooked with care, and a good selection of regional and Italian wines. Closed Mon, Jan and Aug. Via

Marconi 27, Montagnana, T: 0429 81351.

€ **Al Sasso**. Trattoria serving delicious regional dishes, not far from the Abbazia di Praglia (which also sells several varieties of honey, as well as liqueurs and herb teas). Closed Wed, Jan and Sept. Via Ronco 11, Località Castelnuovo, Teolo (12km west of Abano Terme), T: 049 992 5073.

€€ **Casa Vecia**. A great trattoria offering deliciously prepared local dishes. Closed Mon and midday Tues. Via Appia 130, Monterosso, T: 049 860 0138.

€€ **Da Mario**. Restaurant offering excellent cuisine and wines from the Veneto. Closed Tues, Feb and July. Corso Terme 4, Montegrotto Terme, T: 049 794090.

€€ **La Torre**. An inexpensive place serving traditional dishes prepared with considerable skill. Closed Sun evening, Mon, July–Aug and Dec–Jan. Piazza Mazzini 14, Monselice, T: 0429 73752.

Loreo

€€ **I Cavalli**. Restaurant (with rooms) in the heart of the Polesine, renowned for its risotto and seafood. Closed Mon. Riviera Marconi 69, T: 0426 369868.

Porto Tolle

€€ **Da Brodon**. Rustic trattoria renowned for its rice and fish dishes. Closed Mon and July. Località Ca' Dolfin, T: 0426 384240.

Riviera del Brenta

€€ **Da Conte**. Good traditional *osteria* just a few steps from the station. Closed Sun evening, Mon, Jan and Sept. Via Caltana 133, Località Marano, Mira, T: 041 479571.

€€ **Da Nalin**. A fine country restaurant established in 1914, offering Venetian specialities and grilled meat and fish. Closed Sun evening, Mon, Aug and Dec–Jan. Via Nuovissimo Argine Sinistro 29, Mira, T: 041 420083.

€€ **Margherita** (with rooms). An elegant restaurant in a garden along the Brenta offering Venetian cuisine, especially grilled meat and fish. Closed Tues evening, Wed and Jan. Via Nazionale 312, Mira, T: 041 420879.

Rosolina

€€ **SottoVento**. Excellent seafood restaurant. Closed Tues, midday Sun in summer, and Dec. Località Norge Polesine, T: 0426 340138.

Rovigo

€€ **Tavernetta Dante-Dai Trevisani**. Traditional Trevisan cooking, with outside seating in summer. Closed Sun and Aug. Corso del Popolo 212, T: 0425 26386.

Villadose

€€ **Da Nadae**. Trattoria known for its outstanding renditions of traditional local recipes. Closed Tues and Aug–Sept. Via Garibaldi 371, Località Canale, T: 0425 476082.

LOCAL SPECIALITIES

Padua Known among Italians for food and wine: *prosciutto di Montagnana*, *Vini dei Colli* DOC wines, *Dolce di Sant'Antonio*, Este ceramics, leather goods and jewellery. Daily markets open all day in Piazza delle Erbe, Piazza della Frutta and Piazza dei Signori; Sat morning clothing market at Prato della Valle; antiques at Prato della Valle the third Sun of every month). The market in Piazza delle Erbe has good-value produce, while that in Piazza della Frutta also has delicacies. A weekly market is held on Sat in the Prato della Valle.

Rovigo Upholds with honour the Venetian tradition of sipping a glass of red wine (called an *ombra*, or shadow) with finger food (*cicheti*). Good places to do this are the wine bars **Al Sole**, Via Bedendo 6; **Caffè Conti Silvestri**, Via Silvestri 6; **Caffè San Marco**, Corso del Popolo 186; and **Hosteria la Zestea**, Via X Luglio.

Po Delta Fish markets at **Donada** and **Scardovari** in the morning, and in the afternoon at **Pila**.

SPECIAL EVENTS

Padua *Festival dei Solisti Veneti*, classical music concerts in Paduan churches, May–Sept. *Villeggiando*, concerts and theatre in villas around Padua, May–Sept. *Notturni d'Arte*, music and theatre in museums, May–Sept. *Teatro Estate*, theatre festival, Aug. *Stagione Concertistica*, classical music, Oct–March. *Rassegna del Jazz Italiano*, jazz festival, Nov–Dec. Annual festival of St Anthony on 13 June, with processions, pageantry, etc. You can see more pageantry on the first Sun in Oct for the *Padova del Medioevo* celebrations.

Euganean Hills Monselice, *Giostra della Rocca*, popular feast in costume, Sept. Este, *Settembre Euganeo*, with folk and cultural events, Sept; *Mostra della Ceramica Estense*, ceramics show, Sept. Montagnana, *Palio dei 10 Comuni*, popular festival, first Sun in Sept, with a horse race outside the walls and celebrations, fairs and markets that last a week. Cittadella, *Fiera Franca*, a fair held on the third Sun in Oct since 1608.

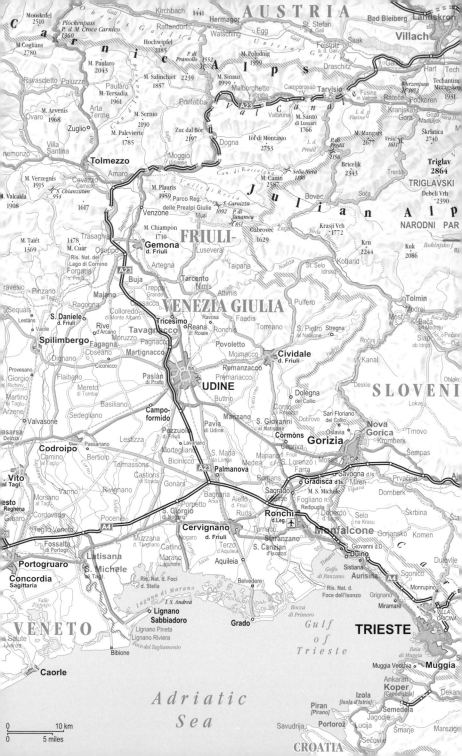

FRIULI-VENEZIA GIULIA

Friuli-Venezia Giulia lies at the northeastern corner of the Adriatic. The Friuli (the former county of Udine) was under the patriarchate of Aquileia until 1420 when, with the mountainous country of Carnia to the north and the city of Aquileia itself, it was absorbed into the Venetian Republic. Trieste, as an independent commune under her bishops, remained a rival of Venice for Adriatic trade. At certain periods Trieste held the upper hand, but on more than one occasion the Venetians captured the port.

Although the Istrian coast for the most part came under Venetian influence, the hinterland and Gorizia belonged to Austria. The Venetians made important conquests in the war against Austria in 1507–16, but outside intervention forced them to withdraw their frontier west of Aquileia. The raids of Liburnian pirates (from modern-day Croatia), nominally subject to Austria, disturbed conditions on the Istrian coast throughout the 16th century, and the power of Venice diminished.

The outcome of the Napoleonic Wars here was the short-lived Kingdom of Illyria, which extended from the Isonzo to Croatia but was shattered in 1813–14 by an Austrian army and a British fleet. From 1815 to 1918 the whole region came under Austro-Hungarian dominion. When Austria-Hungary collapsed after 1918, Italy's frontier was extended east and south to include the whole of Istria, including Fiume.

In 1945 Italian and Yugoslav claims to the territory came into conflict, and the administration of Trieste, which had been occupied by the Yugoslavs, was taken over by Allied Military Government. All territory east of the so-called 'French Line' was ceded to Yugoslavia, the ceded areas including the eastern suburbs of Gorizia and all Istria south of Cittanova. Trieste only returned to Italian rule in 1954.

TRIESTE & THE EAST

There is a curious feeling about Trieste and its environs: you really do sense you're in another country. Trieste itself is an Austrian city inhabited by Italians. 'We are the furthest limit of Latinity', one mayor of the city was quoted as saying, 'the southern extremity of Germanness'—and the city's mixed heritage may be responsible for its peculiar lack of identity, the consequence of being an 'outsider' in both cultures.

Trieste is the most important seaport of the northern Adriatic, although its commercial traffic has diminished in recent years. It lies in a gulf backed by the low, rolling hills of the Carso, across which, from the northeast, blows the *bora* wind, icy-cold in some seasons. For many centuries part of the Austrian empire, it retains something of the old-fashioned atmosphere of a middle-European city. Regular, spacious streets were laid out around the Canal Grande at the end of the 18th century, when the city flourished under the enlightened rule of the Habsburg empress Maria Theresa. Its numerous monumental Neoclassical and Art Nouveau buildings date from the 19th and early 20th centuries. Now on the borders of Slovenia, the town is increasingly looking towards Eastern Europe for commercial outlets.

EXPLORING TRIESTE

The cathedral

The old quarter of the city, commonly called the **Cittavecchia**, lies on the hill of San Giusto, at the top of which stand the cathedral and castle. The **cathedral**, dedicated to St Justus (a Christian martyr who was thrown into the sea during Diocletian's persecution), is the fruit of a 14th-century union of two earlier churches, San Giusto (to the south) and Santa Maria Assunta (to the north). The simple façade, with a single large gable, is graced by a large 14th-century rose window; the posts of the main doorway incorporate elements of a Roman tomb. Three modern busts of bishops of Trieste (including Pope Pius II) are set above the door. The campanile, also of the 14th century, resembles a defensive tower. It stands on the remains of the vestibule of a Roman temple. A Byzantine-Romanesque statue of the patron saint occupies a Gothic aedicule on the south side.

The cathedral has five asymmetrical aisles divided by columns with fine capitals. The 16th-century ship's-keel ceiling of the nave was reconstructed in 1905; also modern is the central apse, with a mosaic inspired by fragments of the original. In the south apse you can see original blind arcading, frescoes of the 13th century and, on the ceiling, a remarkable late-13th-century mosaic depicting *Christ between Sts Justus and Servulus* upon a gold ground with a beautifully decorated border. The old choir-bench and some pretty little Byzantine columns with 6th-century capitals can be seen below, between very worn early-13th-century frescoes of the *Life of St Justus*. More worn frescoes and a finely carved 9th-century pluteus (light wall) with doves are in the little side apse to the right.

In the main nave you can see fragments of the original polychrome mosaic pavement. The north apse contains a splendid 12th-century mosaic of the Veneto-Ravenna school showing the *Madonna Enthroned between two Archangels* above the Apostles, with another beautifully decorated border. In the side apse to the left is a sculptured wooden group of the *Pietà* (16th century). Next to this is the treasury, protected by a fine iron gate (1650), with remains of 15th-century frescoes. A 13th-century painting on silk of *St Justus*, a cross donated to the church in 1383, and precious reliquaries are preserved here. An inconspicuous door off the north aisle (above which is a *Madonna and Saints* by Benedetto Carpaccio, 1540) leads into the baptistery, which has a 9th-century immersion font and five frescoes detached from the south apse, illustrating the *Life of St Justus* (1350), in good condition.

The castle

Open Apr–Sept Tues–Sun 9–7; Oct–March 9–5.
At the foot of the castle (castello) stretches the area known as the Platea Romana, with remains of the basilica of the Roman forum (2nd century AD) and of the so-called Tempio Capitolino (1st century AD). The castello as it appears today was constructed between 1470 and 1630 on the site of an earlier Venetian fortress, which in its turn rose on the probable site of a prehistoric fortification. The castle contains part of the

Museo Civico (*open Tues–Sun 9–1*). A staircase, rebuilt in the 1930s, leads up to the Sala Veneta, which is the reconstruction of a 17th-century room in a private palace with its furniture and 16th-century Flemish tapestries. The wooden ceiling has a painted *Allegory of Venice* by Andrea Celesti. More stairs lead up to the (covered) battlements with a large collection of arms. The old kitchen and a loggia can also be visited here. The Lapidario Tergestino, opened in 2001 in the Bastione Lalio, has an

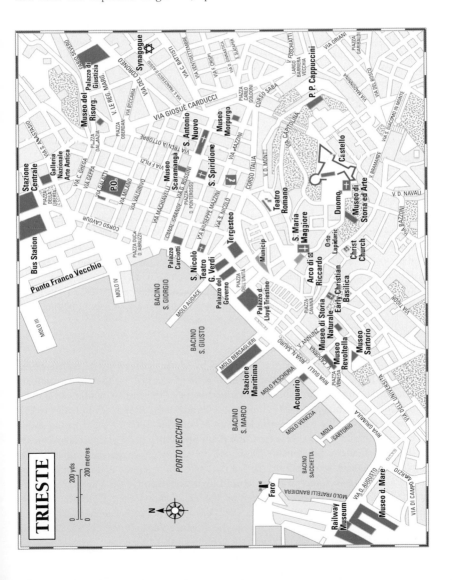

TRIESTE

interesting collection of Roman-age inscriptions, sculptures, reliefs and architectural fragments. From the courtyard near the entrance you can access the walkways above the ramparts, from which there are good views of the entire city.

The tree-lined Via della Cattedrale descends from the steps of the cathedral to the **Museo di Storia ed Arte e Orto Lapidario** (no. 15; *open Tues–Sun 9–1, Wed 9–7*), the most important museum in Trieste. Here antique and medieval sculpture and inscriptions, Egyptian antiquities, prehistoric and protohistoric material, Greek and Italic antiquities, and drawings and prints are displayed in a pleasant building and a lovely garden. Also here is the cenotaph of the archaeologist J.J. Winckelmann (1717–68), who was murdered at Trieste under the assumed name of 'Signor Giovanni' by a thief whose cupidity he had excited by displaying some ancient gold coins.

The street ends at the **Arco di Riccardo**, a vaulted Roman gate of the 1st century AD, dedicated to Augustus. Its name survives from the traditional belief that Richard I (the Lionheart) was imprisoned here after his return from the Holy Land.

LITERARY ASSOCIATIONS

Trieste was the birthplace or the chosen place of residence of several well-known modern authors. The traveller and writer Sir Richard Burton was consul here from 1872 until his death in 1890. At the Albergo Obelisco in Villa Opicina he completed the translation of the *Thousand and One Nights*. Much more famously, James Joyce lived in the city in 1904–15 and 1919–20 with his wife Nora Barnacle, and their two children were born here. They lived at Via Donato Bramante 4 (near Piazza Vico, on the far side of the hill of San Giusto), where Joyce wrote part of *Ulysses*. While here he befriended the native writer Italo Svevo (Aron Hector Schmitz; 1861–1928), widely believed to be the prototype for Leopold Bloom.

The Borgo Teresiano

The Borgo Teresiano, the quarter developed by Maria Theresa in the 18th century, extends along the waterfront. Its southern limit is marked by the large, dramatic **Piazza dell'Unità d'Italia**, which was created in the 19th century by filling in the old Roman harbour. Facing the sea is the eclectic façade of the Palazzo Comunale (1875). To the north stand the Palazzo del Governo, designed in 1904 by the Austrian architect Emil Artmann, and the historic **Caffè degli Specchi**, a good place to take a break. Coffee is particularly delicious in Trieste, which imports more than any other port in the Mediterranean. To the south, the seaward side of the square is dominated by the imposing Renaissance-revival **Palazzo del Lloyd Triestino**, by the Viennese architect Heinrich Ferstel (1880–83, architect of Vienna's famous Café Central). He also designed the two allegorical fountains. Next door stands another Renaissance-revival building, today a hotel, and next to this, the elegant Palazzo Pitteri (1785), in a style somewhere between the Baroque and the Neoclassical.

Trieste's Canal Grande.

Continuing along the waterfront takes you past the Teatro Verdi, the city's main concert hall (1801) and the church of **San Nicolò dei Greci**, built in 1784–87 by the Greek Orthodox community and with a composite Neoclassical façade with twin *campanili* by Matteo Pertsch (1819–21). Inside it boasts a magnificent silver iconostasis. Further on you come to the **Canal Grande**, constructed in 1750–56 to provide a safe harbour for merchant vessels and to allow cargo to be unloaded directly into the warehouses of the Borgo Teresiano. On the southwest corner is Matteo Pertsch's Palazzo Carciotti (1802–05; now the port authority), a Neoclassical building with a hexastyle façade and a balustrade with statues. On the opposite corner stands Palazzo Aedes, a work of the Trieste-born architect Arduino Berlam (1926–28).

From Canal Grande to Corso Italia

At its far end, the Canal Grande is spectacularly concluded by Pietro Nobile's Neoclassical church of Sant'Antonio Nuovo (1827–42). In **Piazza Ponterosso**, halfway down on the right, the house at no. 3 was the first home of James Joyce and his wife Nora, who twice lived in Trieste (*see box*). The Museo Scaramangà di Altomonte (*open Tues and Fri 10–12, or by appointment; T: 040 631 585*), across the canal at 1 Via Filzi, houses a small but important collection on the history of art in Trieste.

The area of the Borgo Teresiano between the Canal Grande and the Corso Italia, four blocks south, is a genuine goldmine of **early modern architecture**. Examples are Romeo Depaoli's Casa Smolars (1906–07), at the corner of Piazza della Repubblica and Via Dante; the Casa Fontana (Via Mazzini 5, at the corner of Via Roma); the bank at Via

Roma 9; and the Casa Bartoli (Piazza della Borsa 7b), a mansion designed in the Liberty style by Max Fabiani (1905). Along the **Corso Italia** are several buildings by major inter-war architects, notably the Casa delle Assicurazioni Generali (nos 1–3) and the Banco di Napoli (no. 5), by Marcello Piacentini (1935–39) and the *grattacielo* ('skyscraper') by Umberto Nordio (1936; in Largo Riborgo), as well as interesting remnants of Austro-Hungarian days—the Neoclassical Casa Steiner (no. 4) by Matteo Pertsch (1824), the Tuscan-revival Casa Ananian (no. 12), by Giorgio Polli (1905) and the building at no. 22 Piazza Goldoni, with a Liberty gable end, by Romeo Depaoli (1908).

At the foot of the San Giusto hill, just south of Largo Riborgo, are the remains of a 6,000-seat Roman theatre dating from the 2nd century AD; a small antiquarium displays finds from the excavations. Just one block east, on the site of the former Polish Ashkenazi synagogue, is the **Museo della Communità Ebraica** (*Via del Monte 7, open Sun 5–8, Tues 4–6, Thur 10–1*), with collections of Jewish art and culture of the Triestine community, particularly sacred vessels and vestments from the synagogue.

JEWISH TRIESTE

The Jewish community of Trieste dates back to around the year 1200. Most of those early families were money-lenders, and in exchange for the valuable service they provided, the local overlords allowed them freedom to live and worship as they chose. An enclosed ghetto was not created until the 16th century, when anti-Jewish riots made the move necessary for their own protection. The Jewish quarter of town was huddled around where the excavated Roman theatre is today. During the reign of Maria Theresa, and more especially following the Edict of Tolerance passed by her son, the emperor Joseph II, in 1781, life for Jews in the Habsburg dominions improved greatly, and in the following century the community prospered and grew, much like the Jewish communities of so many other towns and cities in the Austro-Hungarian region. Trieste's Jews made their fortunes as merchants, bankers and manufacturers; many were active in the arts and the theatre, and they became known for their avant-garde tastes in art and architecture, commissioning fine town houses in the Liberty style. In 1912 the main synagogue in Via San Francesco d'Assisi was opened. When Austria entered the Second World War as an ally of Germany, the Triestine Jewish community suffered the fate of all the other Jewish communities in the empire. Thousands went to their deaths, and Jewish life in the city was virtually extinguished.

The Risiera di San Sabba (*open Tues–Sun 9–6, Sun and holidays 9–1*) is in the industrial district south of the city on the Muggia road, at Ratto della Pileria 1. This former rice-hulling plant was the only Nazi death camp in Italy (though not the only detention centre). Some 5,000 prisoners are believed to have been murdered here between the German invasion of Italy in 1943 and the liberation of Trieste by Tito's Partisans in 1945. It is now a national monument.

A Triestine house-museum

A peculiar feature of Trieste is the unusual number of old mansions that have been turned into museums. A stately Eclectic townhouse by Giovanni Berlam (1875), just off Corso Italia at Via Imbriani 5, houses the **Museo M. Morpurgo de Nilma** (*open Tues–Sun 9–1, Wed 9–7*), with furniture, paintings, miniatures, prints, ceramics, porcelain and a library—all in a fascinating fin-de-siècle bourgeois setting. The **Civico Museo Teatrale Carlo Schmidl** (*open Tues–Sun 9–1, Wed 9–7*), with an extremely interesting collection and archive including 19th-century musical instruments and documents relating to the production of operetta, for which Trieste has been famous since the 19th century, is provisionally displayed on the first floor. The museum was founded in 1924 in the Teatro Verdi with the collection of Carlo Schmidl, and there are plans to move it to the historic Palazzo Gopcevich.

The northern districts of the city are centred around Piazza Oberdan, laid out in the 1930s. The **Museo del Risorgimento** (*open Tues–Sun 9–1*) is arranged in a fine palace by Umberto Nordio (1934), which incorporates the cell of Guglielmo Oberdan, hanged in 1882 by the Austrians in the old barracks on this site. Oberdan was a prime mover of the Irredentist movement, and had come to Trieste with bombs in his waistcoat, planning an attempt on the life of the emperor Franz Joseph, who was visiting the city.

The western districts

Riva Mandracchio leads west along the seafront from Piazza dell'Unità d'Italia. Beyond the Molo dei Bersaglieri, on another jetty, is the *pescheria* (fish market) with its spacious market hall (1913, by Giorgio Polli) open to the sea. At the side, in the Liberty-style **Pescheria Nuova**, is the entrance to the fine Civico Acquario Marino (*open daily 8.30–1*), the most popular museum in the city, with fish from the Adriatic and tropics as well as two South African penguins.

The **Museo Revoltella** (*Via Diaz 27; open Tues–Sun 9–2 & 4–7.30*) occupies a Renaissance-revival building designed by Friedrich Titzig (1852–58) for the businessman Pasquale Revoltella (1795–1869) as a museum for his art collections and as an art institute. It still has some of its interesting furnishings, handsome ceilings, inlaid wooden floors and enamelled terracotta stoves.

An allegorical fountain by Pietro Magni adorns the atrium. The ground floor exhibits include 17th- and 18th-century landscapes, a room of portraits by the local artist Giuseppe Tominz (1790–1866), the panelled library and a statue of *Napoleon as Mars* by Antonio Canova (the model for his colossal statue in Apsley House, London). On the first floor is an elaborate allegorical statuary group representing the Suez Canal by Pietro Magni (Revoltella was vice-president of the company responsible for the cutting of the canal), as well as paintings by Francesco Hayez among others.

In the adjacent building, renovated to plans by Carlo Scarpa in 1960–92, is a large collection of modern art acquired through funds set aside for this purpose by Revoltella. The artists represented include Medardo Rosso, Giuseppe de Nittis, Felice Casorati, Giorgio Morandi, Giorgio de Chirico and Lucio Fontana. The large collection of works by local artists includes paintings by Pietro Marussig. There are fine views of Trieste and the port from the sixth floor.

The **Civico Museo Sartorio** (*Largo Papa Giovanni XXIII 1; open Tues–Sun 9–1*) is located in an 18th-century mansion remodelled in 1820–38 by Nicolò Pertsch. On the ground floor are Italian and European majolica and porcelain, Triestine ceramics and rooms for temporary exhibitions. The first floor has rooms furnished in the Gothic-revival and Biedermeier styles, and paintings of the 17th–19th centuries (notably by Tiepolo and his followers).

ENVIRONS OF TRIESTE

Castello di Miramare

Open March–Oct 9–6; Nov–Feb 9–6.30; park open March–Oct 9–7; Nov–Feb 8–6.
This, the best of Trieste's house-museums, situated 8km northwest of the city, is reached by a short drive or bus ride. There are three entrances to the park. The nearest one to Trieste is on the sea (at a road fork), but from this entrance it is a good 20-minute walk to the castle. The entrance closest to the castle is on the main road before the two tunnels that precede Grignano. The third entrance is by the bus terminus at Grignano, near the Castelletto.

Surrounded by a large formal garden, and rising in a splendid position at the end of a promontory, Miramare was built to an English Renaissance-revival design by Karl Junker (1855–60) for Archduke Maximilian of Austria. Maximilian was the brother of the emperor Franz Joseph, and governor of Lombardy and Venice. In 1857 he had married Charlotte, daughter of the first king of Belgium.

In 1863 Napoleon III offered the title Emperor of Mexico to Maximilian. The beautiful, ambitious Charlotte was bored at Miramare, and urged him to accept. Maximilian did so, though not without misgivings, which were to prove well founded. Napoleon III had troops stationed in Mexico, conducting a guerilla war against Benito Juárez, whom the country's liberal faction supported as their president. Although Maximilian enjoyed the support of the conservatives at first, he alienated them by decreeing freedom of religion in his new domain. The Pope withdrew his support for Maximilian, and when the United States entered the fray on Juárez's side, Napoleon III finally withdrew his French troops. Maximilian was left friendless and unprotected. His wife went mad, seeing potential assassins around every corner. She returned to Europe to plead with both the Pope and Napoleon, but after a series of hysterical and embarrassing scenes in the Vatican, she was sent to Miramare and kept there under house arrest by Maximilian's family. Maximilian himself was captured by Juárez and sentenced to death. Despite many petitions for clemency, including one from Garibaldi, Juárez refused to relent, and Maximilian faced the firing squad on June 19 1867.

Miramare was Maximilian's home until 1864, the year in which he accepted the imperial crown of Mexico. With its furniture, paintings, porcelains, and ivories, it is a superb example of a 19th-century aristocratic residence. Notices in each room describe the contents; highlights include a painting of celebrations in Venice in honour of Maximilian and his bride. Maximilian was governor of Venice, and protocol required that his marriage be fêted, though in fact the couple were received by the Venetians with distinct froideur. The huge throne room has an elaborate Gothic-revival ceiling.

The park has some fine trees and an Italianate garden. The small Castelletto, where Maximilian lived while the castello was being built, houses the Centro di Educazione all'Ambiente Marino di Miramare, with a museum of the marine environment. The sea around the promontory is now a marine reserve. The road to Miramare passes the Faro della Vittoria (*not open*), a lighthouse and memorial to seamen who died in the First World War, designed in the 1920s by Arduino Berlam and today a popular viewpoint.

Sistiana and Duino

Sistiana, on a delightful bay known to the Romans as Sextilianum, is used as a harbour for private boats. A path (known as the 'Sentiero Rilke') follows the rocky coast from here to Duino for nearly 2km, through interesting vegetation, with fine views.

Duino is a fishing village with a ruined Castello Vecchio. The imposing Castello Nuovo, on a rocky promontory above the sea, was built in the 15th century on the ruins of a Roman tower (which has been partly reconstructed). The poet Rainer Maria Rilke stayed here as a guest of Maria von Thurn und Taxis in 1910–14, and wrote his famous *Duineser Elegien*. There is now a 'Rilke Trail' tracing his favourite walks along the coast. In a letter Rilke describes the castle as being 'piled up against the sea like a bastion of human existence, staring out through its many windows at the vast expanse of water'.

At **San Giovanni di Duino** is the mouth of the River Timavo, which emerges here from an underground course of over 38km. The six springs here have been sacred since Roman times.

The Carso

The Carso (German *Karst*, Slav *Kras*), is a curiously eroded limestone plateau, now mostly in Slovenian territory. A tramway (5km) and funicular run from Trieste (Piazza Oberdan) to Villa Opicina. In the Carsic hills between Opicina and Sistiana a good dark red wine known as *terrano* is produced. Near Opicina is the **Grotta Gigante** (*open Apr–Sept Tues–Sun 9–6; March and Oct 10–4; Nov–Feb 10–12 & 2–4*), the largest single cave yet discovered in the Carso (280m long, 107m high). It was first opened to the public in 1908 and is famous for its stalactitic formations, which are documented in the adjoining museum (*open Tues–Sun 10–12 & 2–4*).

From **Monrupino** there is a superb view of the carso. This area was the scene of the most violent struggles in the Austro-Italian campaign during the First World War. Vast trenches and veritable caverns were easily constructed by widening the existing crevasses in its surface; and although large-scale operations were made difficult by the nature of the terrain, immense concentrations of artillery were brought up by both sides for the defence of this key position. It was the Duke of Aosta's stand here with the Third Italian Army that averted complete disaster after Caporetto (October 1917).

Muggia

Muggia, across the bay south of Trieste, is a charming little fishing-port with brightly painted houses, the only Istrian town that has remained within the Italian border. For centuries a faithful ally of the Venetian Republic, it retains a remarkably Venetian atmosphere (the streets are called *calli*, like the streets in Venice). The harbour, with its fishing boats, is also used by yachts, and there are several simple fish restaurants here. The 14th-century castle rises above the harbour. Near the inner basin (or *mandracchio*) is the main piazza with the duomo, a 13th-century foundation with a 15th-century Venetian Gothic façade and an interesting treasury; the town hall; and the Palazzo dei Rettori (rebuilt after a fire in 1933), once a palace of the patriarchs of Aquileia, who controlled the town in the 10th century. An archway opposite the town hall leads into Via Dante with interesting old houses. There is a particularly pretty Venetian Gothic palace at Via Oberdan 25.

On the hillside above are the ruins of the Roman and medieval settlement of **Muggia Vecchia**, destroyed in 1356 by the Genoese for having taken the side of Venice in the battle of Chioggia. The basilica here is a 9th-century building with an ambo of the 10th century, transennae in the Byzantine style, and remains of early frescoes.

Gorizia

Gorizia stands on the Slovenian border in an expansion of the Isonzo valley, hemmed in by hills. It is a particularly pleasant and peaceful little town with numerous public gardens and pretty buildings in the Austrian style. After the fall of the independent counts of Gorizia in the 15th century, the city remained an Austrian possession almost continuously from 1509 to 1915. In the First World War it was the objective of violent Italian attacks in the Isonzo valley and was eventually captured on 9 August 1916. Lost again in the autumn of 1917, it was finally taken in November 1918. The Treaty of Paris (1947) brought the Yugoslav frontier into the streets of the town, cutting off its eastern suburbs, but in 1952, and again in 1978–79, more reasonable readjustments were made, including a 16km-wide zone in which local inhabitants may move freely.

The attractive, wide **Corso Italia**, lined with trees and some Art Nouveau villas, leads up from the railway station into the centre of the town. Via Garibaldi diverges right to the Palazzo Comunale, built by Nicolò Pacassi, court architect to Maria Theresa, in 1740, with a public garden. Via Mazzini continues to the **cathedral**, a 14th-century building much restored, with a pleasant interior including galleries and stucco decoration. It contains a pulpit of 1711, a high altarpiece by Giuseppe Tominz, and a precious treasury brought from Aquileia in 1752.

Viale Gabriele d'Annunzio leads uphill to the pleasant, peaceful **Borgo Castello** (approached on foot by steps up through the walls and past a garden). The castle was built by the Venetians in 1509; the Musei Provinciali di Borgo Castello (*open summer*

Tues–Sun 10–7; winter 10–1 & 2–7) are well arranged in two 16th-century palaces within its wards. Late-19th-century paintings by local artists, including works by Giuseppe Tominz (1790–1866), are exhibited on the ground floor. The Museo della Moda e delle Arti Applicate, on the upper floor, illustrates the history of silk production in the town from 1725 to 1915, including an 18th-century wooden twisting machine, looms, samples of silks, and costumes showing Balkan influence.

Another section of the museum has delightful reproductions of local artisans' workshops, and a street of reconstructed shops. Downstairs is the Museo della Grande Guerra (Musem of the Great War), one of the most important museums in Italy dedicated to the First World War. Excellently displayed in ten rooms, it includes the reconstruction of a trench, and material illustrating both the Italian and Austrian fronts in the Carso campaign.

The Museo di Storia e Arte next door is open for temporary exhibitions only (*summer 10–7; winter 10–1 & 2–7*). The unusual little church of **Santo Spirito**, with the copy of a 16th-century crucifix outside, dates from 1398. The **castle** (*open summer, Tues–Sun 9.30–1 & 3–7.30; winter 9.30–6*) was built by the counts of Gorizia and remodelled in 1508. Important exhibitions are held here. The rampart walk commands a good view towards Slovenia, and the interesting interior has some 17th- and 18th-century furniture and paintings. The park on the castle hill is a good place to picnic.

At the end of Via Ascoli is the little yellow **synagogue** (*open Mon, Fri, Sat 4–7, Tues, Thur 5–7 & 6–8 in summer*), first built in 1756 and restored in the 19th and 20th centuries (the façade dates from 1894). **Palazzo Attems**, beyond on the right, is a fine building by Nicolò Pacassi (1745), with a library and archive.

In Corso Giuseppe Verdi, on the corner of Via Boccaccio, is a pretty market building of 1927. Via Santa Chiara and Viale XX Settembre lead northwest from Corso Garibaldi to the late-18th-century gateway (removed from Palazzo Attems) at the entrance to **Palazzo Coronini**, left to the city by Guglielmo Coronini Cronberg in 1990. It is surrounded by a fine park laid out in the 19th century, with evergreen trees, statues by Orazio Marinali, and a sculpture of Hecate that may date from the 2nd century AD. Built in 1597 by Giulio Baldigara, the palace was purchased from Field Marshal Radetzky in 1820 by the Coronini. Charles X of France died of cholera while in exile here in 1836. The 30 rooms are preserved intact and contain 18th-century furniture, paintings and porcelain.

Environs of Gorizia

Across the Isonzo, northwest of Gorizia at **Oslavia**, a 'Gothic' castle (*open summer Tues–Sun 9–11.45 & 3–5.45; winter 8–11.45 & 2–4.45*) holds the graves of 57,000 men of the Second Army who fell in 1915–18.

To the north is the hilly area of **Collio**, famous for its excellent wine. San Floriano del Collio has a wine museum (*open by appointment; T: 0431 93217*), and the attractive little town of Cormòns, an ancient seat of the patriarchs of Aquileia, has a few hotels and good restaurants.

South of Gorizia on the Isonzo is **Gradisca**, an old Venetian fortress still preserving many of its 15th-century watchtowers and some good Baroque mansions. The 17th–18th-century Palazzo Torriani, is now the town hall; inside is a small library and local history museum. The county of Gradisca was ceded to Austria in 1511, and in 1615–17 it caused a war between Austria and Venice.

Monte San Michele was a ridge hotly contested in the Carso campaign. At Sagrado a museum (*open summer Tues–Sun 8–12 & 2–5; winter 9–3*) commemorates the battle.

Further south is **Redipuglia** with the huge war cemetery of the Third Army, containing over 100,000 graves, including that of the Duke of Aosta (1869–1931), the heroic defender of the Carso. A small museum here is dedicated to the First World War. Nearby is a war cemetery with the graves of 14,550 Austro-Hungarian soldiers. **Ronchi dei Legionari**, with the airport of Trieste, is on the edge of the Carso and the region of the battlefront of 1915–17. Guglielmo Oberdan (1858–82), the nationalist and would-be assassin, was arrested here by the Austrians in 1882, and from here in 1919 the poet and nationalist Gabriele d'Annunzio set out to occupy Fiume (*see p. 320*).

PRACTICAL INFORMATION

GETTING AROUND

• **Airport bus:** Coaches connect with the airport terminal at the Trieste railway station (journey time 50mins) and with Aquileia/Grado (50mins), Gorizia (55mins) and Udine (40mins). Airport bus in 20mins to/from Trieste's Monfalcone railway station.

• **By car:** Car parking in the centre of Trieste is particularly difficult; your best bets are on the Rive or on the hill of San Giusto. There is a multi-storey car park beside the station.

• **By bus:** Country buses depart from Trieste (Piazza Oberdan) to Miramare and Duino; and from the main bus station in Piazza della Libertà to Muggia, Sistiana and Slovenia (information from Trieste Trasporti, T: 040 7795413, freephone 800 016 675, www.triestetrasporti.it). Buses from Gorizia (Via IX Agosto) to Cormòns,

Grado, Udine and Trieste (information, APT, T: 0481 593 511, www.aptgorizia.it). There is a rack tramway from Trieste (Piazza Oberdan) to Opicina. To Miramare, bus no. 36 every 30mins from Piazza Oberdan and the station. To Muggia, bus no. 20 from the station; Muggia to Muggia Vecchia, bus no. 37 from the Porto Vecchio.

• **By rail:** There is a direct rail service from Venice to Trieste, and from Venice to Udine. Branch lines run from Trieste to Gorizia and Udine, and from Udine to Conegliano, Cividale, Palmanova and Cervignano (the latter is also on the Venice–Trieste line), from which buses shuttle passengers to Aquileia and Grado. A branch line runs from Trieste to Gorizia (in c. 25mins), continuing on to Udine (c. 45mins more)

• **By boat:** Boat services operate regularly between Trieste and Muggia, Grignano and Monfalcone (Trieste Trasporti, T:

040 7795413, freephone 800 016 675, www.triestetrasporti.it). Boat tours of the port and gulf by motor launch are organised in summer from Riva del Mandracchio.

INFORMATION OFFICES

Trieste Via San Nicolò 20, T: 040 67961, www.triestetourism.it. Branch office at Piazza Unità d'Italia 4b, T: 040 347 8312.
Gorizia Via Roma 5, T: 0481 386225.
Muggia Via Roma 20, T: 040 273259. May–Sept.
Sistiana Sistiana 56b, T: 040 299166 34015.

HOTELS

Trieste
€€€ **Grand Hotel Duchi d'Aosta.** Offering early-20th-century Austrian style and ambience, and a restaurant (Harry's Grill) among the best in town. Piazza Unità d'Italia 2, T: 040 7600011, www.grandhotelduchidaosta.com
€€ **Abbazia.** Near the train station, comfortable and practical. Via della Geppa 20, T: 040 369464.
€€ **San Giusto.** A bit out of the way (on the landward side of the hill of San Giusto) but very pleasant. Via C. Belli 3, T: 040 764824, www.hotelsangiusto.it
Gorizia
€ **Nanut.** A small, family-managed place on the outskirts of town. Via Trieste 118, T: 0481 20595/ 0481 21168.
€ **Palace.** Centrally located, modern and comfortable. Corso Italia 63, T: 0481 82166.
Muggia
€ **Sole.** Green and flowery with wiste-

ria, a stone's throw from the Slovenian border. Località Lazzaretto, T: 040 271106, www.hotelsolemuggia.it

YOUTH HOSTEL

Trieste
Tergeste, Viale Miramare 331, T: 040 224102, ostellotrieste@hotmail.com

RESTAURANTS

Trieste
€€ **Ai Fiori.** A family-run place with an innovative seafood menu. Closed Sun, Mon and July. Piazza Hortis 7, T: 040 300633.
€€ **Al Bragozzo.** A seafood restaurant with nice ambience. Closed Sun, Mon and a few days in July. Riva Nazario Sauro 22, T: 040 303001.
€€ **Al Granzo.** A good seafood restaurant, established in 1923 and offering excellent *granseola* (crab) *alla triestina*. Closed Wed. Piazza Venezia 7, T: 040 306788.
€€ **Allo Squero.** A popular trattoria drawing a strong local crowd. Closed Mon and Feb. Viale Miramare 42, T: 040 410884.
€€ **Ambasciata d'Abruzzo.** Country restaurant specialising in Abruzzo recipes. Closed Mon and July–Aug. Via Furlani 6, T: 040 395050.
€€ **Antica Trattoria Suban.** An outstanding restaurant established in 1865 and serving traditional regional cuisine. Closed Mon, Tues, Jan and Aug. Via Comici 2d, T: 040 54368, F: 040 57920.
€€ **Bagatto.** Friendly restaurant specialising in regional seafood. Closed Sun, one week for Christmas and Easter,

Aug 15. Via F. Venezian 2, T: 040 301771.

€€ **Elefante Bianco**. Situated in a historic building, this restaurant specialises in regional seafood dishes and meats. Closed Sat midday, Sun. Riva III Novembre 3, T: 040 362603.

€€ **Fiori**. Regional seafood, innovative interpretations of old recipes. Closed Sun–Mon, in July and Dec 24–Jan 1. Piazza Hortis 7, T: 040 300633.

€€ **Nastro Azzurro**. Elegant restaurant specialising in regional fish recipes. Closed Sun and Dec 25–Jan 6. Riva Nazario Sauro 12, T: 040 305789.

€€ **Savron**. Country restaurant and wine bar much loved by *triestini*. Closed Tues–Wed and Feb. Strada Devincina 25, Località Prosecco (9km northwest), T: 040 225592.

€€ **Scabar**. Family run restaurant specialising in home cooking. Closed Mon, Feb, Aug. Erta Sant'Anna 63, T: 040 810368.

€€ **Valeria**. Historic trattoria, loved by locals. Closed Thur. Località Opicina (7km from the centre of town). Strada per Vienna 52, T: 040 211204.

€ **Da Giovanni**. Simple trattoria with wholesome local food. Closed Sun and Aug. Via San Lazzaro 14, T: 040 639396.

€ **Re di Coppe**. Warm, friendly trattoria with good regional fare. Closed Sat, Sun and July–Aug. Via Geppa 11, T: 040 370330.

Cormòns
€€ **Al Giardinetto**. Restaurant (with rooms) serving outstanding dishes based on local ingredients, including Cormòns ham, and a fine wine list. Closed Mon, Tues and July. Via Matteotti 54, T: 0481 60257.

€€ **Cacciatore de la Subida**. Restaurant (with rooms) offering creative interpretations of traditional recipes. Closed Tues, Wed, Feb and July. Località Subida 22, T: 0481 60531.

Dolegna del Collio
€€€ **Aquila d'Oro**. Refined regional cuisine in a 13th-century castle with park and panoramic views (outside seating in summer). Closed Wed–Thur. Castello di Trussio, Località Rutars, T: 0481 61255.

Gorizia
€ **Alla Luna**. A place popular with townsfolk, where local traditions blend with influences from Slovenia and Austria. Closed Sun evening, Mon and Aug. Via Oberdan 13, T: 0481 530374.

€ **Rosen Bar**. Strong local ambience and cross-cultural cuisine. Closed Sun and Mon. Via Duca d'Acaia 96, T: 0481 522700.

Gradisca d'Isonzo
€ **Mulin Vecio**. Traditional *osteria* in an ancient (but working) mill, serving simple country meals. Closed Wed–Thur. Via Gorizia 2, T: 0481 99783.

Savogna d'Isonzo
€€ **Devetak**. Excellent food (especially Slovene dishes) and fabulous wines at a trattoria in the same family for nearly 200 years. Closed Mon–Tues. Località San Michele del Carso 48, T: 0481 882005.

CAFÉS & PASTRY SHOPS

Trieste imports more coffee than any other Italian city: in some areas of the town the warehouses are so numerous that the aroma of coffee lingers in the air. Naturally, where so many people are in the business you can expect some extraordinary cafés. The city's best are **San Marco**, Via Battisti 18; **Tommaseo**, Riva III Novembre 5; **Degli Specchi**, Piazza dell'Unità; and **Pirona**, Largo Barriera Vecchia 12. There are also some great pastry shops (**Penso**, Via Cadorna; **La Bomboniera**, off Via San Nicolò, where Italian, Austrian and Slovene traditions are skilfully combined).

REGIONAL SPECIALITIES

Excellent wines are made in the Collio and Isonzo districts, and there is very good locally-made honey. These items are available throughout the region. **Gorizia** holds a market on Thur in the public gardens in Corso Giuseppe Verdi; crafts market on the second Sun of the month in Via Ascoli. The Enoteca di Cormòns at **Cormòns** (Piazza XXIV Maggio 21) has good wines, light snacks and great ambience (closed Tues). The Antico Mulino Tuzzi at **Dolegna del Collio** is an old-fashioned mill known for its wholewheat and buckwheat flours and especially for its barley, used to make *fasui e vardi* (bean and barley) soup.

FESTIVALS & EVENTS

Trieste *Festival Internazionale dell'Operetta*, international operetta festival, June–Aug. Light and sound show, Castello di Miramare, July–Aug. *Mostra-Mercato dell'Antiquariato*, antiques fair, at the Stazione Marittima, late Oct–early Nov. *Barcolana*, sailing regatta, second Sun in Oct.
Cormòns *Festa dei Popoli della Mitteleuropa*, Central European folk festival, Aug; Renaissance pageant, Sept.
Gorizia Medieval Music Festival, June; National Theatre Festival, June–July; *Folkfest*, ethnic music festival, July; Amidei Film Festival, Aug. Comic Theatre Festival, Sept. Alpe Adria Puppet Festival, Sept.

UDINE & THE NORTH

The Friuli, Italy's extreme northeastern corner, is a beautiful and little known region. Most of the tourists you'll find here will be locals—Venetians drying their bones in the crisp Alpine air, or city folk from Trieste looking for a hearty country meal. The area has much to offer. Udine is a small treasure chest of Venetian art and architecture, and Cividale has some superb vestiges of Lombard art—a real rarity. And the landscape everywhere—from the verdant hills of the south and east to the white limestone peaks of the Carnic Alps in the north—is unforgettable.

NB: This section is covered by the map on p. 488.

UDINE

Udine, the historical centre of the Friuli and capital of a large province, is a delight-ful, lively town. Its attractive old streets, most of them arcaded, fan out round the cas-tle hill. A Roman station called Utina is alleged to have occupied this site. Attila the Hun is said to have stood on Udine's castle hill to watch Aquileia burn in 452. In the 13th century, the patriarch of Aquileia moved his residence here, marking the begin-ning of a period of growth of which few traces remain, but which made Udine an important regional capital. In 1420, after nine years' resistance, Udine surrendered to Venice and remained under her influence for over three and a half centuries. Some splendid examples of Tiepolo's work are preserved here. In 1797 and again in 1805, Udine was occupied by Napoleon's marshals.

Piazza della Libertà

The centre of town life is the Venetian Piazza Nuova, now called **Piazza della Libertà**. Set at the foot of the castle hill, this 16th-century square is one of the finest urban complexes in Italy. The Loggia del Lionello, on the southwest side, is the town hall. It was built in Venetian-Gothic forms in 1448–56 by Bartolomeo delle Cisterne to a design by the Udinese goldsmith Nicolò Lionello. Faced with alternating bands of white and pink stone, it has a first-floor loggia with balustrade, mullioned windows and a niche on one corner holding a 15th-century statue of the Madonna by Bartolomeo Bon (whose workshop is best known for the sculptures on Venice's Ca d'Oro and Porta della Carta).

Opposite is the Renaissance Porticato di San Giovanni (1533), and the Torre dell' Orologio (1527), by the town's most famous native artist Giovanni da Udine (*see p. 511*). The *mori* (moors) on the clock, who strike the hours, are 19th century. In the piazza are a fountain of 1542, two columns with the Lion of St Mark and Justice, and colossal statues of Hercules and Cacus (called Florean and Venturin by the *udinesi*)

Frescoed ceiling of the Villa Manin at Passariano.

from a demolished 18th-century palace. The statue of Peace (with a sarcastic inscription to the effect that freedom is a matter of choosing one's bondage) commemorates the Treaty of Campo Formio, by which Napoleon ceded Venice to Austria in 1797.

Castle hill and its museums

Beyond the Arco Bollani, a rusticated triumphal arch designed by Palladio (1556), a road lined with a delightful Gothic portico (1487) and steep steps climbs up the castle hill. The 13th-century church of Santa Maria di Castello (unlocked on request at the museum; often used for weddings at weekends) has been beautifully restored after the 1976 earthquake. The campanile dates from 1540. It has fine 13th-century frescoes and a seated wooden statue of the Madonna. Next to the church is the 15th-century Casa della Confraternità, restored in 1929. The summit of the hill has a green with two wells, from which there is a fine view stretching as far as the Alps on a clear day. The Casa della Contadinanza, with a double loggia, was reconstructed in the 20th century.

The castle, built over the ruins of the castle of the patriarchs of Aquileia, was begun in 1517 to a design by Giovanni da Udine. Today it is home to the **Civici Musei e Gallerie di Storia e Arte** (*open Tues–Sat 9.30–12.30 & 3.30–6.30, Sun and holidays 9.30–12.30, in July and Aug 3.30–7.30*), a complex of several museums and galleries.

Museo Archeologico: This presents material assembled over the past 200 years from sites in Udine and its environs, notably finds from the Mesolithic to the Iron Age from Cassacco, from Sammardenchia and from excavations in Via del Mercato Vecchio and on the castle hill in Udine; Roman-age material from excavations in town, from Aquileia and from Sevegliano; Lombard weapons; and local and imported ceramics and glass from the Middle Ages and the Renaissance. There are also extensive collections of coins (some very rare, of Roman, Byzantine, barbarian and medieval origin, including the fabulous Collezione Colloredo Mels); Roman ambers, precious stones, glass, perfume vases and gold from Aquileia; and cut gems from the Roman age and the 18th and 19th centuries.

Pinacoteca: The collection comprises Italian paintings ranging from the late Middle Ages to the 19th century, including several works by Tiepolo (*Strength and Wisdom, Consilium in Arena*). Particularly interesting are the 14th-century Friulan primitives, the 15th-century Scuola Tolmezzina, and the paintings by Vittore Carpaccio (*Christ and the Instruments of the Passion*), Giovanni Antonio da Pordenone (*Madonna della Loggia; Eternal Father*), Palma Giovane (*St Mark Placing Udine under the Protection of St Hermagoras*), Caravaggio (*St Francis Receiving the Stigmata*), Luca Carlevaris (*Plan of the City of Udine*), and Marco and Sebastiano Ricci (*Landscape*).

Galleria dei Disegni e delle Stampe: This exhibits, on a rotating basis, a selection from the enormous collection (c. 10,000 pieces) of works by Friulan and Venetian printmakers and Italian and foreign old masters.

Salone del Parlamento: This first-floor room hosts Tiepolo's *Triumph of the Christians over the Turks* and other fine paintings.

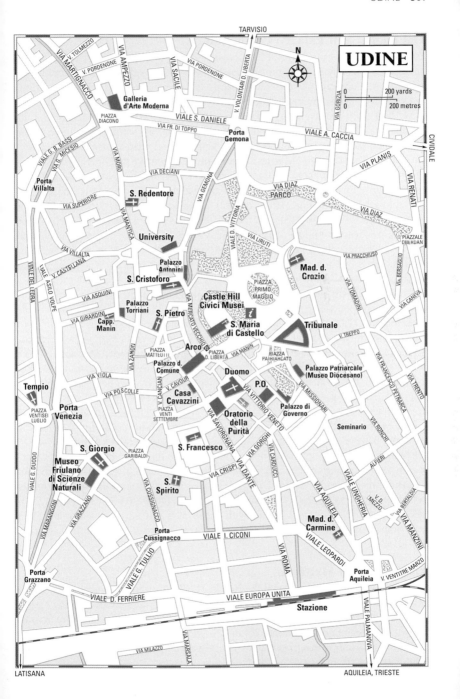

TARVISIO

UDINE

N

0   200 yards
0   200 metres

VIA V. TOLMEZZO
V. PORDENONE
VIA SACILE
VIA PORDENONE
VIA MARTIGNACCO
VIA AMPEZZO
VIA VOLONTARI D. LIBERTA
VIA GORIZIA

CIVIDALE

Galleria d'Arte Moderna

PIAZZA DIACONO

VIALE S. DANIELE
VIA FR. DI TOPPO
VIALE A. CACCIA

Porta Gemona

VIA DECIANI

VIA PLANIS
VIA RENATI

VIA G. B. BASSI
VIA G. MICESIO
VIA MORO

Porta Villalta

S. Redentore

VIA SUPERIORE
VIA MANTICA

VIA DIAZ
PARCO

VIA DIAZ

University

VIA VILLALTA
VIA D. VITTORIA
VIA LIRUTI

PIAZZALE OBERDAN

Palazzo Antonini

VIA CASTELLANA
VIALE DEL LEDRA
VIALE ASILO VOLPE

S. Cristoforo

Mad. d. Grazia

VIA PRACCHIUSO
VIA BERSAGLIO

VIA ASQUINI
VIA GEMONA
VIA MERCATO VECCHIO

PIAZZA PRIMO MAGGIO

VIA TOMADINI
VIA CANEVA

Palazzo Torriani

S. Pietro

Castle Hill Civici Musei

Capp. Manin

VIA GIRARDINI

Arco

S. Maria di Castello

Tribunale

V. TREPPO

VIA ZANOI

PIAZZA MATTEOTTI

PIAZZA D. LIBERTA VIA MANIN

PIAZZA PATRIARCATO

VIA FRANCESCO PETRARCA
VIA TRENTO

Tempio

Palazzo d. Comune

Palazzo Patriarcale (Museo Diocesano)

PIAZZA VENTISEI LUGLIO

Porta Venezia

VIA VIOLA
V. CANCIAN
VIA POSCOLLE

Casa Cavazzini

Duomo

P.O.

VIA MISSIONARI

PIAZZA VENTI SETTEMBRE

Oratorio della Purità

VIA VITTORIO VENETO

Palazzo di Governo

Seminario

VIA RONCHI
ALFIERI

S. Giorgio

PIAZZA GARIBALDI

S. Francesco

VIA SAVORGNANA
VIA GORGHI
VIA CARDUCCI

VIALE UNGHERIA

Museo Friulano di Scienze Naturali

VIA MARANGONI
VIA GRAZIANO
VIALE G. DUODO

S. Spirito

VIA CRISPI VIA DANTE

VIA AQUILEIA

V. D. MEZZO
VIA BERTALDIA
VIA MANZINI

VIA CUSSIGNACCO

Porta Cussignacco

Mad. d. Carmine

VIALE LEOPARDI

Porta Grazzano

VIALE G. TULLIO

VIALE I. CICONI

VIA ROMA

Porta Aquileia

V. VENTITRE MARZO

LATISANA

VIALE D. FERRIERE

VIALE EUROPA UNITA

Stazione

VIA MARSALA

VIA MILAZZO

VIALE PALMANOVA

AQUILEIA, TRIESTE

The duomo and Palazzo Patriarcale

The duomo preserves its original 14th-century Gothic appearance, particularly in the fine central doorway with its carved lunette, deep splays and sharp cusp, and in the other great doorway on the north flank, by the campanile (1390). A third, Renaissance doorway graces the south flank. The unfinished campanile was begun in the 15th century over an octagonal baptistery built a hundred years earlier.

The three-aisled interior has paintings by Tiepolo on the south side (*Trinità* in the first chapel; *Sts Hermagoras* and *Fortunatus* in the second; *Resurrection* and frescoes in the fourth). The stuccoed Baroque complex of the sanctuary and crossing is preceded by two organs with painted parapets; its spectacular tone is maintained by the large marble high altar with statues (1717) and, at the ends of the arms of the transept, the two colossal Manin tombs (18th century). Lodovico Manin was the last Doge of Venice (1789–97, *see p. 515*). The two side altars have dossals attributed to the Baroque woodcarver Andrea Brustolon. The vault is frescoed by Louis Dorigny, who also decorated the choir with paintings and frescoes. The 18th-century sacristy contains paintings by Giovanni Antonio da Pordenone, Franz Hals and Giovanni Battista Tiepolo.

A door on the left leads to the **Museo del Duomo**, which includes the 14th-century Cappella di San Nicolò, frescoed with episodes from the *Life of St Nicholas* by Vitale da Bologna in 1348–49; panel paintings by the Maestro dei Padiglioni, his pupil; and the old baptistery, beneath the campanile, with a beautiful vaulted ceiling and the sarcophagus of Beato Bertrando, with fine reliefs of the Lombard-Venetian school (1343).

The 18th-century **Oratorio della Purità**, across the square from the south flank of the cathedral, has an altarpiece and ceiling painting by Giovanni Battista Tiepolo and chiaroscuro mural paintings by his son, Giandomenico. The cathedral sacristan will open it for you.

East of the cathedral square is the **Palazzo Patriarcale**, decorated in 1726 by Giovanni Battista Tiepolo (*open Wed–Sun 10–5*). A pretty spiral staircase leads up to the piano nobile, with splendid frescoes which Tiepolo painted in 1726 for the patriarch Dionisio Delfino. Beyond the blue room, with ceiling frescoes by Giovanni da Udine, the red room contains Tiepolo's *Judgement of Solomon* and four Prophets in the lunettes. The gallery is entirely frescoed with Old Testament scenes (the stories of Abraham, Isaac and Jacob, with Jacob as a self-portrait of the artist) in remarkable pastel colours. On the stairs is another splendid fresco of the *Fall of the Rebel Angels*.

Around Piazza Matteotti

A good place to stop for coffee is the historic **Caffè Contarena**, with Liberty décor and furniture (1925), beneath the portico on Via Cavour, directly behind the Loggia del Lionello. The building, the monumental Palazzo degli Uffici Municipali, was designed by Raimondo d'Aronco, in an eclectic Liberty style, in 1911. One block north of Via Cavour is the elegant Via Rialto, closed to motor traffic, which runs along what was once the main axis of the medieval Villa Udin.

Turning right at the end of the street, you soon come to **Piazza Matteotti** (Piazza San Giacomo for the *udinesi*), perhaps the oldest of the city's squares, with low porticoes on columns and a fountain by Giovanni da Udine (1542). On the west side stands the 14th-century church of San Giacomo, with a lively Lombardesque façade designed by Bernardino da Morcote in the early 16th century, and 17th- and 18th-century paintings inside. One block further west (reached by a passageway next to the church) Via Zanon, flanked by one of the characteristic little canals the *udinesi* call *rogge*, is lined with fine

Vittore Carpaccio: *Christ and the Instruments of the Passion* (1496) in the Pinacoteca.

palaces mostly of the 18th century; at the corner of Via dei Torriani is the Torre di Santa Maria, a remnant of the 13th-century town wall. Behind the tower and beyond the austere façade of Palazzo Torriani (no. 4) is the 18th-century **Cappella Manin**, a gem of Baroque architecture, whose hexagonal interior has fine sculptures and high reliefs by Giuseppe Torretti, the sculptor who trained Canova.

North from Piazza Libertà

On the northwest corner of Piazza della Libertà begins the handsome **Via Mercatovecchio**, the traditional site of the evening promenade. The city's first marketplace, it is still the main shopping street. Broad and slightly curved, it is flanked by porticoed buildings, notably the monumental Monte di Pietà, today a bank, with a façade of 1690 and a chapel at the centre with fine wrought-iron work and frescoes by Giulio Quaglio (1694). Continuing north you come to the Palazzo Antonini (Via Gemona 3), today the Banca d'Italia, built after 1570 to plans by Palladio. Almost opposite, to the northwest, is the 17th-century Palazzo Antonini-Cernazai, now occupied by the University Faculty of Languages.

At the northern edge of the city centre stands the **Galleria d'Arte Moderna** (*open Tues–Sat 9.30–12.30 & 3–6, Sun and holidays 9.30–12*), where the holdings focus on Italian artists of the 20th century. On the first floor are a section devoted to modern and contemporary architecture (including some original drawings by Raimondo d'Aronco); works by the well-known Italian modernists Arturo Martini, Mario Mafai and Felice

Casorati; and a small collection of American art of the 1970s, notably by Willem de Kooning. The ground floor is mainly devoted to the Astaldi collection of modern masters, with works by Gino Severini, Giorgio de Chirico, Savinio, Mario Sironi, Giorgio Morandi, Massimo Campigli, Ottone Rosai, Fausto Pirandello and Carlo Carrà.

South from Piazza Libertà

Behind the Municipio in Piazza Libertà, Via Savorgnana leads south. At no. 5 is the **Casa Cavazzini**, bequeathed to the municipality by Dante Cavazzini, with an apartment on the first floor containing murals (1939) by Corrado Cagli and Afro. The large building is to be restored, and the Astaldi collection of modern art, at present displayed in Piazzale Diacono (*see below*), may be moved here. Further south, in Piazza Venerio, the church of San Francesco has been restored to its 13th-century appearance for use as an auditorium. To the southwest, beyond Piazza Garibaldi, in Palazzo Giacomelli in Via Grazzano, is the Museo Friulano di Scienze Naturali Moderna (*closed for renovation at the time of writing; otherwise open daily 8.30–12.30, Mon, Tues and Thur 3–6*), with an important natural history collection.

In Via Vittorio Veneto, which leads south from Piazza Libertà, is **Palazzo Tinghi** (no. 38), first built in 1392 with a wide ground-floor portico. The façade of 1532 has very faded frescoes by Pordenone.

Caravaggio: *St Francis Receiving the Stigmata* (c. 1596), in the Pinacoteca.

Giovanni da Udine (1489–1561)
Udine's most famous son, the painter Giovanni, showed an aptitude for drawing at an early age. He received his earliest training from a local Udinese master, before moving to Venice to study under Giorgione, and afterwards to Rome, where he was the pupil of Raphael. It was then that his career took off, and the debt he owes to Raphael is enormous, not only in terms of artistic inspiration, but also because it was Raphael who got him the jobs and commissions he needed, and helped him make his name. Giovanni was in Rome in the heady days of the first two decades of the 16th century, just as the great discoveries of the Baths of Titus and the Golden House of Nero were made. Seeing the Ancient Roman frescoes preserved in these hitherto undiscovered ruins changed everything for him: he stopped being merely a mediocre version of Raphael and began a great career as a decorative painter. He is best known for his *grottesche*, reworkings of the frescoes he saw in the Roman digs—swathes of grotesque figures, mythical people and animals, wonderful garlands of rich vegetation, all wound colourfully into a cursive decorative design, and called *grottesche* (plural of *grottesca*) because they came from the *grotte*, or underground vaults of the Roman remains.

CIVIDALE DEL FRIULI

This pleasant town stands on the banks of the River Natisone, on a site that once marked the meeting-point of Venetic and Celtic cultures. Founded as Forum Julii, probably by Julius Caesar, the town gave its name to the Friuli. It became a *municipium* in the Augustan age, an episcopal seat in the 5th century, and an important fortress under the Lombards. In the 8th century its name was changed to Civitas Austriae and it became the seat of the patriarch of Aquileia, a position it retained until 1031.

Piazza Diacono and Piazza del Duomo

From the station and the main road from Udine, Viale Libertà leads east to Corso Alberto, which continues south to the pleasant large **Piazza Diacono**, scene of a daily market, with an old-fashioned café and a house traditionally taken to be on the site of the birthplace of Paolo Diacono (Paul the Deacon, c. 723–799), historian of the Lombards. The fountain is surmounted by an 18th-century statue of Diana. Corso Mazzini, the main street of the town, leads past Palazzo Levrini-Stringher, with remains of 16th-century frescoes on its façade, to the cathedral square.

Piazza del Duomo stands on the site of the ancient Roman forum, enclosed on one side by the north flank of the cathedral. The church was begun in 1457 in the Venetian Gothic style to plans by Bartolomeo delle Cisterne, but it was rebuilt in the 16th century in Renaissance forms by Pietro and Tullio Lombardo, whose design is particularly evident in the interior. It has a simple stone façade with three pointed

Gothic doorways (the central one is a work of Jacopo Veneziano, 1465), and is flanked by a Baroque campanile. In the north apsidal chapel are a *Last Supper* and *Martyrdom of St Stephen* by Palma Giovane. Above the high altar is the gilt-silver altar-piece of Patriarch Pellegrino II (1195–1204), a masterpiece of medieval silver-smithing, showing the Virgin in the company of Gabriel, Michael, saints, prophets and the donor himself. The third south bay gives access to the **Museo Cristiano** (entered also from behind the bell tower on Sun; *open daily 9.30–12 & 3–6 or 7*), where exhibits include the octagonal aedicule of the 8th-century baptistery; the beautiful altar carved for Ratchis, Duke of Cividale and King of the Lombards (also from the 8th century); a marble patriarchal throne of the 11th century (the feet are 17th century); fragments of a 7th–8th-century balustrade and ciborium; and detached frescoes from the Tempietto Lombardo (*see below*).

The Museo Archeologico Nazionale
Open summer Tues–Sat 8.30–7.30, Mon 9–2.
Facing the cathedral is the 14th-century Palazzo Comunale, with the pointed arches and mullioned windows typical of Gothic public buildings. At the end of the square stands the **Palazzo dei Provveditori Veneti**, built to a design by Andrea Palladio in 1581–96, and home to the museum, which has very important collections of prehistoric, Roman and medieval archaeology, jewellery and miniatures.

Entrance Hall: A video screen greets the visitor with an excellent documentary film detailing the history of the Lombards, largely on the basis of the artefacts displayed in the building.

Ground Floor: The best displays are the Roman, Byzantine and medieval inscriptions, reliefs and architectural elements; and the fragments of Roman and early Christian mosaic pavements, including a representation of a marine deity (1st–2nd century AD).

First Floor: Extraordinary Lombard holdings, from necropoleis near Cividale and throughout the Friuli. Highlights include the material found in a knight's tomb at Cella (early 7th century) including a gold leaf disc showing a mounted knight; a sarcophagus (mid-7th century) with its contents, including a fine cross, a signet ring, an enamelled gold fibula, a glass bottle and a tiny box with polychrome enamels in the shape of a bird; the contents of a warrior's tomb, including his arms, gold and silver ornaments, and ivory chessmen; goldsmiths' work (*Pax of Duke Orso*, with a relief of the *Crucifixion* in a jewelled silver frame, and the *Croce di Invillino*, both from the 8th–9th centuries); weapons, tools and utensils. Also noteworthy are the 8th-century *Psalter of St Elisabeth of Hungary* with Saxon miniatures, and the late-13th-century *Veil of Beata Benvenuta Boiani*, embroidered with religious scenes.

Upper floor: Finds from recent excavations, including very fine glass (1st–2nd centuries AD), and a hoard of 15th-century ceramics.

Basement: Walkways provide a view of excavations showing various levels from the late-Roman period (3rd century) to the 16th.

The Tempietto Longobardo and Ipogeo Celtico

Entrance in Piazzetta San Biagio. Open Apr–Sept Mon–Sat 9.30–12.30 or 1 & 3–6.30;
Oct–March 9.30–12.30 & 2.30 or 3–5 or 6.

Via Monastero Maggiore was once the main street of the town and is attractively paved
with cobblestones. It winds through the medieval quarter, passing beneath two gates
to reach Cividale's most unusual monument, the **Tempietto Longobardo** (or Oratorio
di Santa Maria in Valle). Situated on a cliff above the Natisone and reached by a raised
walkway above the river, this is one of the most evocative early-medieval sacred buildings in Italy. Thought to date from the mid-8th century, and damaged over the centuries by earthquakes, it is in a peaceful corner of the town from which only the sound
of the river can be heard. The present entrance is through the presbytery of the little
church, with an iconostasis consisting of a marble screen and two very unusual
columns (5th–6th century) beneath three small barrel vaults, the central one of which
has 14th-century frescoes.

The little quadrangular nave preserves remarkable stucco decoration on the end
wall (formerly the entrance wall) with the monumental figures of six female saints and
beautifully carved friezes, thought to be by the hand of an artist from the east (possibly from Byzantium, though this is not certain), and contemporary with the building
(c. 760). The two side walls would have had similar decorations. Fragments of the
original frescoes also survive.

Across the square from the Tempietto is the small 15th-century church of San Biagio,
with remains of contemporaneous frescoes on its façade and inside. In a private garden
at Via Monastero Maggiore 2 is the **Ipogeo Celtico** (*key at Bar Al Ponte, Corso Aquileia,*
T: 0431 700572), a system of tunnels cut in the rock on the bank of the Natisone,
believed to have been the burial place of Celtic chieftains of the 5th–2nd centuries BC.

From the cathedral square Corso Ponte d'Aquilea leads down to the **Ponte del
Diavolo**, the devil's bridge, built to join the high rocky banks of the Natisone in the
mid-15th century and destroyed and rebuilt during the First World War. The views
are extraordinary. On the left bank a flight of steps leads down from the parapet to the
river. There is a good view of the bridge from near the church of San Martino.

From Piazza Paolo Diacono (*see above*), Via Ristori leads to **Piazza Diaz** where the
theatre, first built in 1815, is named after the tragedienne Adelaide Ristori
(1821–1906), born here, and commemorated by a monument in Foro Giulio Cesare.
In Piazzetta Terme Romane scant remains of Roman baths can be seen below the level
of the pavement. Beyond Porta San Pietro (used by the Venetians as a store) is the
church of San Pietro, with a good altarpiece by Palma Giovane.

TOWARDS THE ALPS

The area between Udine and Austria was the epicentre of earthquakes in May and
September 1976. The communes of Gemona, Tarcento, San Daniele, Maiano and
many others were devastated. Earth tremors continued for two years, and the final toll
was nearly 1,000 dead and over 70,000 homeless.

The small town of **San Daniele del Friuli**, famous for its cured ham (celebrated with a festival at the end of August), has been largely rebuilt at the foot of its hill. The former church of Sant'Antonio Abate has frescoes (1487–1522) by local artist Pellegrino da San Daniele. The duomo (1725) was designed by Domenico Rossi, architect of Venice's Ca' Cornaro on the Grand Canal.

Gemona was almost completely devastated by the earthquake. It has now been rebuilt with colourful new buildings. The fine Romanesque and Gothic cathedral has been carefully restored. Its tall 14th-century campanile had to be entirely reconstructed (the original stones were recovered and reused). The façade (redesigned in 1825) bears an inscription (above and to the left of the door) dated 1290 with the name of the architect and sculptor, Magister Johannes, in charge of work on the building and responsible for the portal. There is a gallery with niches, and statues representing the Epiphany (c. 1350) include seated statues of the weary Magi and a groom holding their three horses. The colossal statue (7m high) of St Christopher dates from 1332, and the superb rose window from 1334. In the beautiful interior the pilasters have been strengthened but left leaning out of line. The choir arch and dome over the sanctuary are particularly beautiful. The 12th-century font incorporates a Roman altar of the 1st or 2nd century AD with a delightful relief of a dolphin ridden by a putto. Beneath the sacristy is the shrine of St Michael with 14th-century frescoes. The church owns a rich treasury including a superb 15th-century monstrance made by Nicolò Lionello, the goldsmith who designed Udine's town hall.

The tiny medieval town of **Venzone** is the most spectacular example of post-earthquake reconstruction, a monument to the skill and determination of its people. Nestled on the Tagliamento and enclosed by high hills, it was first documented in 1001. It became a free commune in 1381 and part of the Venetian Republic in 1420. In 1976 it was reduced to rubble. The stones of its monuments were numbered and reused, and its *genius loci* remains. Local limestone and sandstone have been used to pave the streets. The town is surrounded in part by medieval walls. The railway station is 5 minutes' walk from Porta di Sotto (1835), on the site of the 14th-century town gate. The beautiful duomo, consecrated in 1338, was carefully reconstructed in 1988–95. Partly Romanesque and partly Gothic, it appears to have been designed by Magister Johannes, who was also responsible for the sculptural details (inscription with the date 1308 above the north door) and who also worked on the cathedral of Gemona. Above the main door is a bas-relief of the *Crucifixion*, a fine work of the mid-14th century. Between two bell towers (one never completed) at the east end is the lovely apse in the Cistercian style. In the beautiful interior is a 14th-century fresco by the school of Vitale da Bologna showing the consecration of the duomo. Only fragments now remain of the early 15th-century frescoes in the Cappella del Gonfalone.

In the pretty piazza with a 19th-century fountain is the Gothic Palazzo Comunale (also entirely reconstructed), which dates from 1410. The church of San Giovanni Battista has been left as a ruin. The Torre di Porta San Genesio is inserted in the 13th-century double walls (well seen from here, defended by a moat).

Northwest of Venzone is **Tolmezzo** is the chief centre of Carnia. To the west are summer resorts in the Carnic Alps. Nearby is the village of **Zuglio**, the ancient Iulium Carnicum, which guarded the Roman road (the Via Iulia Augusta) from Aquileia over the Monte Croce pass. A fortified settlement established here in 50 BC became a Roman colony in the following century. It was important throughout the imperial period and was the seat of a bishop up to the 8th century. Excavations were carried out here in the early 19th century and in the 1930s: the Roman forum and its basilica, as well as an early-Christian basilica with mosaics, have been exposed. An archaeological museum (*open Tues–Sun 9–12 & 3–6*) contains finds from the site. The little church of San Pietro di Carnia is the oldest in the district (possibly 14th century).

Art Park at Villa di Verzegnis hosts the Egidio Marzona collection of contemporary site-specific art, with works by Mario Merz, Bruce Nauman and other internationally known artists (*open by appointment; T: 0433 2713*).

TOWARDS THE SEA

On the main road between Udine and Pordenone is **Codroipo**, which was the Roman Quadrivium, on the Via Postumia. Nearby is Passariano with the vast **Villa Manin** (altered c. 1650, perhaps by Giuseppe Benoni, who built Venice's Dogana), and later by Domenico Rossi. It belonged to Lodovico Manin, last of the Venetian doges, who surrendered the Serene Republic to Napoleon on May 12th, 1797. When Napoleon's 4,000 soldiers marched into St Mark's Square, it was the first time in its long history that Venice had been entered by enemy troops. Today the Villa Manin is a cultural centre and the seat of a restoration school. The interior (*open Tues–Sun 9–12.30 & 3–6*) has frescoes by Louis Dorigny and Amigoni, a chapel with sculptures by Giuseppe Torretti, a carriage museum and an armoury. The fine park, the most important in the region, was first laid out in the 18th century (*open Easter–Oct Tues–Sat 9–5, Sun and holidays 9–6*). The villa was occupied by Napoleon in 1797 when he concluded the shameful treaty of Campo Formio, which forced Austria to cede all her territory west of the Rhine to France, and gave her Venice in return. The village after which that treaty is named is now called Campoformido, and is a few kilometres west of Udine.

Between Udine and Trieste is **Palmanova**, a marvellously preserved, star-shaped town built in 1593 to defend the eastern frontier of the Venetian Republic. It is one of the few brick-and-mortar examples of that order and symmetry which Renaissance culture considered a fundamental feature of the ideal city. Its centre is the hexagonal Piazza Grande, dominated by the cathedral, whose design has been attributed to Vincenzo Scamozzi, the great follower of Palladio. From this hub six streets radiate, three leading to the city's monumental gates.

PRACTICAL INFORMATION

GETTING AROUND

• **By rail:** There is a direct rail service from Venice to Udine, continuing on to Gemona; fast Intercity trains make the Venice–Udine run in c. 90mins. Branch lines run from Trieste to Udine, and from Udine to Cividale (with hourly services taking 15mins), Gorizia and Palmanova.
• **By bus:** Bus no. 1 runs from the train station to the town centre. Country buses depart from the bus station at Viale Europa Unita 31 (next to the railway station) to destinations all over the province (for information, T: 0432 50694, 0432 503004).

INFORMATION OFFICES

Udine Piazza I Maggio 7, T: 0432 295972.
Cividale Largo Bioani 4, T: 0432 731461.

HOTELS

Udine
€€ **Ambassador Palace**. Generally considered the top venue, occupying a historic building midway between the cathedral and the train station. Via Carducci 46, T: 0432 503777, www.ambassadorpalacehotel.it
€€ **Astoria Italia**. Elegant with a good restaurant, in the heart of the old town. Piazza XX Settembre 24, T: 0432 505091, www.hotelastoria.udine.it
€ **Friuli**. A comfortable place a few blocks west of the city centre. Viale Ledra 24, T: 0432 234351, www.hotelfriuli.udine.it

€ **Là di Moret**. An excellent hotel with a renowned restaurant, unfortunately somewhat distant from the city centre. Viale Tricesimo 276, T: 0432 545096.
Cividale del Friuli
€ **Locanda al Castello**. A former Jesuit convent with ten rooms, in a quiet, wooded setting. Closed Nov. Via del Castello 20, T: 0432 733242, www.alcastello.net
€ **Roma**. Centrally located, comfortable. Piazza Picco, T: 0432 731871, www.hotelroma-cividale.it
Ravosa di Povoletto
€ **Agriturismo La Faula**. Cosy, comfortable rooms in a beautifully renovated farmhouse between Udine and Cividale, with breakfast and dinner seating under a shady pergola in summer. Via Faula 5, T: 0432 666394, www.faula.com
San Daniele del Friuli
€ **Alla Torre**. Simple, pleasant and centrally located. Via del Lago 1, T: 0432 954562, www.hotelallatorre.com
Tarvisio
€ **Nevada**. Straightforward and comfortable, with good views. Via Kugy 4, T: 0428 2332, www.hotelnevadatarvisio.com

RESTAURANTS

Udine
€€ **Alla Vedova**. Established in 1887, strong points are game dishes and home-made wine. Closed Sun evening, Mon and Aug. Via Tavagnacco 9, T: 0432 470291.
€€ **Alla Colonna**. Traditional trattoria and wine bar. Closed Sun. Via Gemona 98, T: 0432 510177.

€ **Al Lepre**. Traditional *osteria*, simple but good. Closed Tues and Aug. Via Poscollo 27, T: 0432 295798.

€€ **Al Passeggio**. Good Friulan food (including fresh-baked bread), though a bit out of the way. Closed midday Sat, Sun and Aug. Viale Volontari della Libertà 49, T: 0432 46216.

€€ **Vitello d'Oro**. A popular trattoria serving local specialities, particularly seafood, around a great fireplace; closed Wed and July Via Valvason 4, T: 0432 508982.

Lavariano

€€ **Blasut**. Fine regional foods prepared with great care. Closed Sun evening, Mon, Jan and Aug. Via Aquileia 7, T: 0432 767017.

Cividale del Friuli

€€ **Alla Frasca**. A popular trattoria with garden seating in summer Closed Mon and Feb. Via de Rubeis 8a, T: 0432 731270.

€ **Al Fortino**. Traditional fare accompanied by mainly regional wines, in a setting featuring 14th-century frescoes. Closed Mon evening, Tues, Jan and Aug. Via Carlo Alberto 46, T: 0432 731217.

Il Cantiniere Romano. Wine bar with excellent restaurant, specialising in dishes from the whole country. Closed Sun–Mon evening and the last two weeks of June. Via Ristori 31, T: 0432 732033.

€ **Zorutti**. A good trattoria with cosy rooms, in an 18th-century building. Borgo di Ponte 9, T: 0432 731100.

Rive d'Arcano (Rodeano Basso)

€ **Antica Bettola-da Marisa**. Excellent trattoria with menus in Friulan dialect and summer seating outside. Closed Thur, Jan and Sept. Via Coseano 1, T: 0432 807060.

Reana del Roiale

€€ **Da Rochet**. A country restaurant in a lovely position, with garden seating in the summer. Closed Tues–Wed and July–Sept. T: 0432 851090.

San Daniele del Friuli

€€ **Da Scarpan**. Elegant restaurant that offers traditional regional dishes. Closed Tues evening–Wed and July. Via Garibaldi 41, T: 0432 943066.

€ **Ai Binars**. Crowded, lively *osteria* named after the farmhands who commuted seasonally between here and Austria. Closed Wed evening, Thur and July. Via Trento e Trieste 63, T: 0432 957322.

Sauris (Sauris di Sotto; *see map p .372*)

€€ **Alla Pace**. Traditional trattoria (with rooms) in the same family since 1804. Closed Wed (except in high season), May and June. Via Roma 38, T: 0433 86010.

€€ **Riglarhaus**. Hotel restaurant with a beautiful view of the eastern Dolomites, specialising in regional recipes. Closed Tues and 5 days in Jan. Località Lateis 3, T: 0433 86049-86013.

Stregna

€€ **Sale e Pepe**. Excellent regional cuisine using only the freshest ingredients. Open weekends, weekdays by reservation. Via Capoluogo 19, T: 0432 724118.

Tolmezzo

€€ **Roma** (with rooms). Exceptional interpretations of regional specialities. Closed Sun evening, Mon, June and Nov. Piazza XX Settembre 14, T: 0433 2081.

Tricesimo

€€ **Antica Trattoria Boschetti** (with rooms). Elegant restaurant (est. 1830), serving personal variations on local specialities. Closed Sun evening, Mon, Jan and Aug. Piazza Mazzini 10, T: 0432 851230.

WINE BARS & LOCAL SPECIALITIES

Udine Places where you can join the *udinesi* for a *tajut*, or aperitif, usually of white wine: **Ai Piombi**, Via Manin; **Ai Vecchi Parrocchiani**, Via Aquileia 66; **Al Cappello**, Via Sarpi 5; **Speziaria Pei Sani**, Via Poscolle 13. Local cheeses from **Bottega del Formaggio**, Via Poscolle 16; and **La Baita dei Formaggi**, Via delle Erbe 1b.
San Daniele is famous in Italy and beyond for its prosciutto. You can pick up some of the best at **Prosciuttificio Prolongo**, Via Trento e Trieste 115. If you'd like simply to taste some with a glass of wine, try the **Prosciutterie Dok Dall'Ava**, Via Gemona 29. Another good place is **Al Municipio**, at Via Garibaldi 21 in the centre of town. Here you'll find an excellent wine selection accompanied by the best *prosciutti*.

FESTIVALS & EVENTS

Udine *Concerto di Capodanno*, New Year's Eve concert by the Filarmonica di Udine, Teatro Nuovo Giovanni da Udine, 1 Jan. *Omaggio al Balletto*, dance festival, spring. *Udine incontri Cinema*, film festival, April. Jazz Festival, June. Friuli DOC, wine and gastronomic festival, Oct. *Festa di Santa Caterina*, with a fair and market for three days in Piazza I Maggio, 25 Nov.
Cividale del Friuli *Messa dello Spadone*, historic pageant, Jan. *Mittelfest*, festival of drama, music, dance and puppet theatre from Central Europe, July.
Palmanova Historic pageant in 16th- and 17th-century costume, July.
Tarvisio *Trofeo Alpe Adria*, international dog sledge race, Jan. *Cantine Aperte*, presentation and tasting of new wines on estates throughout the region, May. *Folkfest*, itinerant international ethnic music festival, July.

The Adriatic seaboard east of Venice is a region of broad sandy beaches and shallow waters, of lowland marshes visited by migratory birds, and of towns of great antiquity. Chief of these is Aquileia, one of the last colonies founded by the Romans as a military outpost. In time it became an important city, and its population is thought to have reached between 70,000 and 100,000 by the end of the Roman empire. It is is now a village of some 3,000 souls, in a quietly fertile plain. But it preserves magnificent and evocative remains of its great days, both under Rome and as an early medieval capital.

NB: This chapter is covered by the map on p. 488.

HISTORY OF AQUILEIA

Aquileia was founded as a Roman colony in 181 BC and quickly grew to be the fourth largest city in Italy. Small wonder, for this affluent market town was the departure point for the roads over the Alps to the Danube Basin. In 10 BC the emperor Augustus was in residence here and received Herod the Great. The 'emperor' Maximinus was murdered by his troops while besieging the city in 238 AD, and in 340 Constantine II was killed on the banks of the Aussa (a little to the west) by his brother Constans in their struggle for imperial power. The bishopric or patriarchate was founded soon after 313, but civil wars and barbarian incursions, culminating in the Lombard sack of 568, led to the transference of the see to Grado, which had become the foreport of Aquileia. There were two rival patriarchs after 606, but in 1019 the patriarch Poppo united the sees and rebuilt the basilica, and the town had a second period of splendour that lasted up to the 14th century. In the following centuries its importance declined because of malaria. Civil power passed to Venice in 1420, and in 1509 Aquileia was seized by the Holy Roman Emperor Maximilian I. The patriarchate was merged in the archbishoprics of Udine and Gorizia in 1751.

The basilica

Open daily, summer 8.30–7; winter 8.30–12.30 & 2.30–5.30.

This great church, built soon after 313 by the first patriarch Theodore, was the scene of a historic anti-Arian council in 381, attended by Sts Ambrose and Jerome. The church was extended soon afterwards, and was reconstructed in its present form by the patriarch Poppo in 1021–31. A portico, probably dating from the beginning of the 9th century, extends from the west front to the Chiesa dei Pagani (now used as a shop), a rectangular 9th-century hall for Christian converts under instruction, with remains of 13th-century frescoes, and to the much-altered remnants of the 5th-century baptistery. Beneath the font, an earlier octagonal font was discovered in 1982 above part of a Roman house. The tall leaning campanile (73m) was built by Poppo; the upper part dates from the 14th century, the bell-chamber and steeple from the 16th century. On a Roman column facing it is a figure of the Capitoline Wolf, presented by Rome in 1919.

The spacious interior is built on a Latin-cross plan. The arcades surmounting the fine Romanesque capitals date from the patriarchate of Markward (1365–81), the nave ceiling from 1526. The huge colourful mosaic pavement (700sq m), discovered at the beginning of the 20th century, dates from Theodore's original basilica. It is the largest antique mosaic pavement known. Its iconography combines Christian images (such as the Good Shepherd) with pagan symbols such as the cock fighting the tortoise, the seasons, and a winged figure of Victory holding a crown and palm branch. Other panels contain the portrait heads of donors and numerous animals and birds, including two waders catching a serpent and a frog. At the east end is one large mosaic representing the sea filled with a great variety of fish, with 12 putti fishing from boats and rocks. The story of Jonah is illustrated here in three scenes: Jonah is thrown from a boat into a sea monster's mouth (the praying figure in the boat probably represents him before his ordeal); Jonah is regurgitated safely on shore by the monster; and Jonah rests after his adventures beneath a pergola. In the centre of the sea is a circular inscription recording Theodore.

In the south aisle is the Gothic chapel of St Ambrose, built by the Torriani family in 1298, with family tombs and a polyptych by Friulan artist Pellegrino da San Daniele (1503) in a fine frame. The chapel on the right of the presbytery has a 9th–10th-century transenna, and frescoes. To the left of the chapel is the sarcophagus of the canonised Pope Mark (14th century, Venetian Gothic), and in front of the tomb is a fragment of 5th-century mosaic pavement (discovered in 1972).

In the presbytery, the central Renaissance tribune and the altar to the right of it, with a *Pietà*, are the work of Bernardino da Bissone. The high altar was carved by Sebastiano and Antonio da Osteno (1498). In Poppo's apse are faded frescoes, with a dedicatory inscription (1031), showing the patriarch (with a model of the church), Emperor Conrad II with Gisela of Swabia, and Prince Henry (later Henry III) before the Madonna and six patron saints. The bishop's throne is probably somewhat earlier. In the chapel to the left of the presbytery are interesting frescoes and (north wall) a bas-relief with *Christ between St Peter and St Thomas Becket*, sculptured soon after Becket's murder at Canterbury in 1170. Outside the chapel is a bust of Christ (1916) by Edmondo Furlan. In the north aisle is the Santo Sepolcro, an 11th-century reproduction of the Holy Sepulchre at Jerusalem.

The **Cripta degli Affreschi** (the ticket includes admission to the Cripta degli Scavi), beneath the presbytery, has frescoes of great interest, thought to date from around 1180. They depict scenes from the life of Christ (including a fine *Deposition*) and from that of the Virgin Mary, and scenes relating to Sts Hermagoras and Fortunatus.

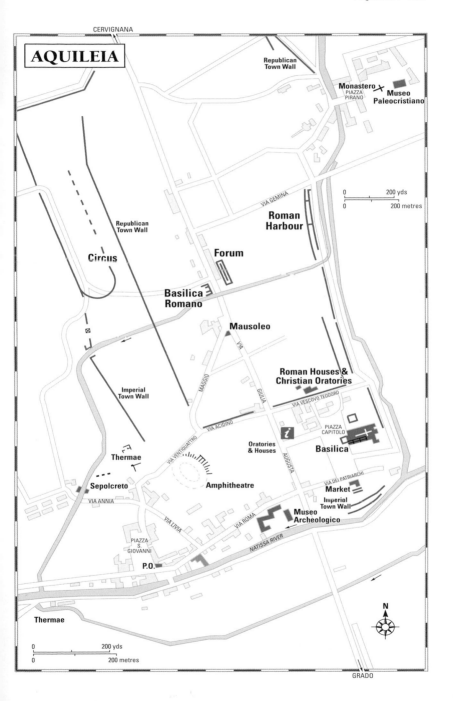

AQUILEIA

CERVIGNANA

Republican
Town Wall

Monastero ✕
PIAZZA
PIRANO   Museo
Paleocristiano

0   200 yds
0   200 metres

VIA GEMINA

Republican
Town Wall

Roman
Harbour

Circus

Forum

**Basilica
Romano**

Mausoleo

VIA MAGGIO

**Roman Houses &
Christian Oratories**

VIA GIULIA

VIA VESCOVO TEODORO

Imperial
Town Wall

PIAZZA
CAPITOLO

VIA ACIDINO

ℹ

VIA VENTIQUATTRO

Oratories
& Houses

VIA AUGUSTA

Basilica

Thermae

VIA DEI PATRIARCHI

Sepolcreto

Amphitheatre

Market

Imperial
Town Wall

VIA ANNIA

VIA LIVIA

VIA ROMA

**Museo
Archeologico**

PIAZZA
S.
GIOVANNI

NATISSA RIVER

P.O.

N

Thermae

0   200 yds
0   200 metres

GRADO

The **Cripta degli Scavi** is entered from beside the Santo Sepolcro. It is remarkable for three levels of mosaics: those of a Roman house of the Augustan period (to the left on entering); the magnificent floor of a second basilica of the time of Theodore, encircling the foundations of Poppo's campanile; and parts of the floor of the late 4th-century basilica, as well as its column-bases.

Roman and Early Christian remains

The **Museo Archeologico Nazionale** (*open Mon 8.30–2, Tues–Sat 8.30–7.30; last admission 30mins before closing*) is one of Italy's leading museums of Roman antiquities. The well-displayed collections include examples of Roman architecture, sculpture, inscriptions and mosaics; a remarkably well-conserved Roman ship; and many unique specimens of glass, amber and cut stone. Notice especially, on the first floor, the golden flies, ornaments from a lady's veil; and on the second floor, the unusual bronze relief of a head in profile, a Hellenistic work or a Roman imitation (very well preserved), and the gilded bronze head of a man dating from the 3rd century AD. In the hall with the Roman ship (2nd century AD, recovered from the sea in one of the most successful operations of underwater archaeology in recent years) is an exquisite little mosaic panel with 20 different fish from the late 1st century AD. On the south side of the quadriporticus are more Roman mosaics, including one depicting a vine branch and a ribbon tied in a bow, dating from the Augustan age.

Near the basilica, across Via dei Patriarchi, are the foundations of late Roman market halls, and, beyond, along the river, the foundations of a stretch of two circuits of the town walls. The inner walls were built c. 238 and the outer walls at the end of the 4th century. (*Excavations are open 8.15–dusk.*)

On the other side of the basilica, reached from Piazza Capitolo, are the remains of Roman houses and Christian oratories with superb mosaic pavements. A path to the east, clearly marked by a noble avenue of cypresses, follows the Natissa stream north. It is lined with architectural fragments of the 1st–4th centuries AD. The little Roman harbour has a finely wrought quay that still skirts the greatly diminished waters of the Natissa, once a navigable river as far as Grado.

Across Via Gemina a road leads past a group of modern houses to a quiet little piazza (with a fragment of Roman road) in front of the former Benedictine Monastery of Santa Maria. Here is the **Museo Paleocristiano** (*open Tues–Sun 8.30–7.30, Mon 8.30–1.45*), housed in a huge, long early Christian basilica (5th century AD). The church has a remarkable mosaic floor, with polychrome geometrical decorations and Greek and Latin inscriptions. At the west end stairs lead up to a balcony with a good collection of sarcophagi, transennae and mosaic panels. The display has been designed to show the transition of art from the Classical Roman period to the new Christian era.

Via Gemina leads right to the busy Via Giulia Augusta, which follows the course of the cardo maximus, the principal north–south thoroughfare of the ancient city. The street passes several Roman monuments on its way back towards the basilica. On the right you can see a fine stretch of Roman road, and beyond are traces of the circus.

On the left of the road, a row of fluted composite columns belongs to the forum. The sculptural fragments include a fine Gorgon's head. The west and east porticoes, as well as part of the pavement, have been uncovered, and on the other side of the road are the foundations of the Roman basilica of the forum.

At the road fork is the *grande mausoleo*, an imposing family tomb of the 1st century AD, brought here from the outskirts of Aquileia. Further on, on the right of the main road (opposite the church), is a large area—still being excavated—of Roman houses and early Christian oratories (2nd–4th centuries AD) with good pavements (especially near the vineyard). The polychrome mosaic floor, under cover, belonged to an oratory. Via Acidino leads west past (left) the scanty remains of the amphitheatre and (right) the site of the *thermae* (still being excavated) towards the *sepolcreto* (key at no. 17), a row of five family tombs of the 1st–2nd centuries.

GRADO

The road from Aquileia continues towards the sea for just over 4km to Belvedere, at the start of a causeway nearly 7km long that leads across a beautiful lagoon to the island-city of Grado. The tiny old town has been suffocated by a large seaside resort with a very popular sandy beach. An ugly raised concrete esplanade lines the seafront—only the beaches at the extreme west and east end are free.

Old Grado is a place of narrow lanes and little squares. In ancient times it was the foreport of Aquileia, and many of that city's wealthier citizens had houses on the foreshore here. It reached its greatest prosperity after the 6th century, when the patriarchate of Aquileia split in two, the second patriarch taking up residence in Grado. The rival sees were eventually reunited and moved to Venice, and by the 15th century, when the title was abolished altogether, the town was well into its decline.

In the centre of the old town is the **cathedral of Sant'Eufemia**, built in the 6th century on the site of a small 4th- or 5th-century basilica, in the style of the great churches of Ravenna. The campanile, with a distinctive pointed steeple, is crowned by a 15th-century statue of the archangel Michael. The interior, which follows the classical basilican plan, has three aisles separated by antique Roman columns with fine capitals, a large apse and a magnificent mosaic pavement dating from the 6th century. This features charming geometrical patterns and stylised waves, connected and interlinked with a knot frieze, incorporating numerous inscriptions of donors. Near the west door is a dedicatory inscription in honour of the prophet Elijah. The 11th-century ambo has reliefs with symbols of the Evangelists and an unusual Moorish dome. The sanctuary is surrounded by a 6th-century pluteus (light wall); on the high altar is a silver altarpiece of 1372, and in the apse 15th-century fresco and panel paintings.

Off the right side of the basilica is a rectangular room with another fine mosaic pavement (and inscription of Elijah). Here has been placed the cast of the bishop's throne donated to Grado by Emperor Heraclius in 630 (the original was taken to Venice after 1451, and is still there, in the treasury of the Basilica of San Marco). The lapidarium has Roman sepulchral inscriptions (1st–3rd centuries AD), 4th–5th-century early-Christian fragments, sarcophagi of the 2nd–3rd centuries AD, architectural fragments (1st–6th centuries), liturgical fragments (8th–9th centuries), and Carolingian reliefs. The **treasury** (*open in summer*) contains some splendid works, many of them made by local craftsmen, including little silver reliquary boxes (6th and 7th centuries), a 12th-century Byzantine evangelistary cover, and the silver reliquary urn of Sts Hermagoras and Fortunatus, an early 14th-century Venetian work.

North of the basilica is the 6th-century baptistery, an octagonal building with another mosaic pavement, a pretty wooden roof and a hexagonal font; and further north, the small basilica of **Santa Maria delle Grazie**, a 4th- or 5th-century church reworked in the 6th century, with a mosaic pavement and a carved transenna of the same period. In the presbytery is a marble intarsia pavement, and excavations have revealed some good 6th-century floor mosaics (seen below the level of the floor on the right side).

In the small garden of **Piazza della Vittoria** you can see traces of foundations and remains of the mosaic pavement of another 4th- or 5th-century Christian basilica; nearby are sarcophagi of the same period. On the modern esplanade on the seafront a former school building is being restored as the seat of a Museum of Underwater Archaeology, where the *Julia Felix*, a Roman wreck discovered in the sea between Grado and Marano in 1986, is to be exhibited. The ship, built at the end of the 2nd or beginning of the 3rd century AD, and about 16m by 5m, was carrying wine and fish sauce in amphorae, and a wooden barrel full of pieces of broken glass (for recycling).

THE COAST

The **Laguna di Grado**—a maze of channels, dunes and *mote* (islands) punctuated by *casoni* (straw and cane huts)—provides a winter home to herons, cormorants, swans, teal and swamp hawks. You can visit the islet of **Barbana** by hiring a private boat in Grado (usually available every hour daily in summer, and at weekends in winter; the journey takes c. 30 minutes and the boatman will wait while you visit the island). The church here, built in 1593 and rebuilt since 1918, contains a venerated statue of the Virgin, and there is an annual procession of boats on the first Sunday in July. Away to the west, on the adjacent Laguna di Marano, is **Lignano Sabbiadoro**, a huge planned tourist resort with some 400 hotels along a sandy spit.

The coastal plain north and west of Aquileia is studded with points of historical and artistic interest, mostly dating from the early Christian era and the High Middle Ages. Officially in the Veneto but an important junction on the road to Pordenone, **Portogruaro** is a medieval town with an interesting urban plan. Its two main streets run parallel on either side of the River Lemene, which is still navigable from here to Caorle on the sea. The cathedral, with a Romanesque campanile, was rebuilt in 1793. The handsome 14th-century Loggia Municipale was enlarged in 1512. The arcaded Via Martiri della Libertà is lined with 14th–15th-century houses. A museum contains finds from the Roman station of Concordia Sagittaria, from which the nearby village of **Concordia** (with a 15th-century cathedral above remains of an earlier church, and a fine 11th-century baptistery) takes its name.

Sesto al Reghena and San Vito al Tagliamento

At **Sesto al Reghena** on the border with the Veneto, you can visit the former Benedictine abbey church of **Santa Maria in Sylvis** (*open daily 8–7.30*), founded in 762 and fortified and surrounded by a moat in the 9th century (the walls were demolished in 1939). It has an unusual plan, preceded by a vestibule and large aisled atrium. To the left of the entrance a little loggia has a fragment of a fresco with courtly scenes (12th century). On the right, steps lead up to the *salone* with a fine wooden ceiling and delightful painted decoration in pastel shades in imitation of curtains with flowers above. The fragment of the head of St Michael is the oldest fresco to have survived in the abbey (12th century).

The vestibule has frescoes of *Heaven* and (very ruined) *Hell*, traditionally attributed to Antonio da Firenze. The little refectory, on the right, has more fresco fragments. The large atrium has sculptured fragments, a detached lunette of *St Benedict*, and an unusual scene of three figures on horseback and three coffins, thought to date from 1316.

The church has a remarkable fresco cycle in the presbytery (including scenes from the *Life of St Benedict*) dating from the early 14th century by the *bottega* of Giotto. The crypt, rebuilt at the beginning of the 20th century, contains the splendid reliquary urn of St Anastasia, adapted in the late Middle Ages from an 8th-century abbot's throne. Also here is a late 13th-century sculpted diptych of the *Annunciation* (with a view of the fortified abbey in the background) and a stone 15th-century *Pietà*. On the lawn outside you can see the foundations of the first Lombard early-Christian church.

San Vito al Tagliamento is an interesting little town with a pleasant long piazza in front of its duomo and tall campanile. The cathedral contains some important works by Pomponio Amalteo. Also in the piazza are Palazzo Fancello, with a painted façade and, next to it, the 15th-century Palazzo Rota (the town hall) with a fine garden (a public park). At the end of the piazza the Torre Raimonda hosts the town library and museum (*on the top floor; open Mon–Fri 10–12 & 3–6.30*). It contains prehistoric and Roman finds from the area, as well as Renaissance ceramics and 15th-century frescoes. There is also a small museum of farm life (*Palazzo Altan, Via Altan 47, open Mon–Sat 9– 12.30, Thur 3–5*), part of the Museo Provinciale della Vita Contadina.

PORDENONE

Several kilometres northwest of San Vito, in the midst of verdant farmland, Pordenone (*map on p. 372*) is a very pleasant provincial capital with a delightful long corso. Modern buildings, some of them by the prominent 20th-century architect Gino Valle, have been successfully integrated into the town. The River Noncello was once navigable down to the Adriatic, and Pordenone was for centuries important as a port. Cotton factories were established here in 1840, and it is still the industrial centre of Friuli. The town is best known as the birthplace of the painter Giovanni Antonio de' Sacchis (c. 1483–1539), called Il Pordenone (*see below*).

Pordenone (c. 1483–1539)

According to Vasari, Pordenone taught himself to paint. Certainly his early works are fairly unsophisticated. As he matured, he learned to paint in the Venetian style, with all that that implies in terms of colour and dreamy romanticism. His manner shows a particular closeness to that of Giorgione and Titian. When he left northern Italy in the late 1520s, however, he fell under the spell of Michelangelo, and his style altered forever, becoming much less spatial, much more sculptural, with highly mannered gesture and with an unsettling, barely suppressed violence. His writhing figures seem to invade the viewer's space and intimidate him/her. There is also something nostalgic and almost Gothic in his love of fancy dress and posing figures, and something faintly Germanic in his dwelling on the more tortured and gruesome aspects of martyrdom. All in all, Pordenone is a fascinating hybrid of Gothic and German elements forced through the Michelangelo mangle.

EXPLORING PORDENONE

The long, undulating Corso Vittorio Emanuele begins in the central Piazza Cavour and winds through the old centre. It is lined on either side by arcades and has interesting houses from all periods. Beyond some 13th- and 14th-century palaces is the Neoclassical façade of the former theatre. A side road leads to the Chiesa del Cristo (or Santa Maria degli Angeli), with two fine 16th-century portals, one by Pilacorte. Back in the corso the monumental Palazzo Gregoris (no. 44), has masques in the Venetian style. No. 52 has faded frescoes attributed to Pordenone, and no. 45, the former Palazzo dei Capitani, has good fresco decoration (also on its side façade in Via Mercato). Palazzo Montereale-Mantica (no. 56) has a fine interior with Baroque stuccoes (recently restored).

Via Castello and Via della Motta lead to Palazzo Mantica, with a fresco attributed to Pordenone. In Piazza della Motta is the **Museo Civico delle Scienze** (*open Mon–Fri 9.30–12.30 & 3–6*), with an unusual collection, arranged on three floors, some of it in old-fashioned showcases. Opposite, the former church of **San Francesco**, with damaged 15th-century frescoes, is used for exhibitions. Also in the piazza are the 18th-century civic library (with the Lion of St Mark over the door) and the 13th-century castle (now a prison).

At Corso Vittorio Emanuele 51 is Palazzo Ricchieri, which houses the **Museo Civico d'Arte** (*open Tues–Fri 9.30–12.30 & 3–6*). The palace dates from the 15th century and has fine painted wooden ceilings and some remains of mural paintings. The collection consists mainly of 16th–18th-century works by regional artists including Pordenone and Luca Giordano. It also contains a 15th-century seated wooden *Madonna* attributed to Andrea Bellunello, a wooden crucifix by the circle of Donatello, and an altar frontal in gilded and painted wood of c. 1508.

The corso ends in front of the delightful Palazzo Comunale, which has a projecting clock tower in a Venetian Renaissance style (16th-century) at odds with its 13th-century Emilian Gothic core. Beyond is Piazza San Marco with pretty houses, some with frescoes. The **cathedral** has a Romanesque campanile and good west portal by Pilacorte (1511). In the light interior are altarpieces by Pordenone (*Madonna della Misericordia*, 1515), Marcello Fogolino and Pomponio Amalteo. The **Museo Diocesano d'Arte Sacra** (Via Revedole 1. *Open Tues 9–1, Sat 9–12.30*) displays sculpture, painting and liturgical objects documenting the history of Christianity between the Livenza and the Tagliamento from the 4th century to the present day.

At the other end of the corso, beyond Piazza Cavour, is Corso Garibaldi, with two grand palaces in the Venetian style facing each other. A side road leads to the 16th-century church of **San Giorgio**, with one of the more eccentric bell towers in Italy—a giant Tuscan column (1852).

AROUND PORDENONE

Spilimbergo, in the lovely countryside northeast of Pordenone, has a pleasant, spacious green. Along one side is the flank of its large cathedral, whose organ (1515) has doors painted by Pordenone, and the presbytery is covered with 14th-century frescoes attributed to the school of Vitale da Bologna. At the end of the piazza is the entrance (across the dry moat, now a garden) to the castle. Built in the 12th century and reconstructed after a fire in 1511, the fortress encloses a pleasant medley of 16th–18th-century palaces, notably one with restored frescoes on its façade attributed to Bellunello. There is a fine view of the Tagliamento valley, and you can visit the mosaic school (one of four in Italy) by appointment (*T: 0427 2155*).

North of Spilimbergo are the village churches of **Vacile**, with apse frescoes by Pordenone; **Lestans**, with frescoes by Pomponio Amalteo; and **Valeriano**, where two churches side by side (recently restored) both have frescoes by Pordenone.

South of Spilimbergo, **Provesano** has a church with lovely frescoes in the sanctuary by Giovanni Francesco da Tolmezzo, and a stoup and font by Pilacorte. Further south is **Valvasone**, where the cathedral has a splendid organ (recitals in September) dating from 1532 and restored in 1974, with painted doors begun by Pordenone in 1538 and completed by Pomponio Amalteo. Nearby, the church of San Pietro has a tiny Venetian 17th-century organ and frescoes by Pietro da Vicenza. The castle, which encloses an 18th-century theatre, is in very poor condition. A medieval pageant is held here in September.

Just to the west of Pordenone is the old town of **Porcia**, which has an interesting old centre. From **Sacile**, further west, there is a pretty branch railway line which leads northeast and crosses the Tagliamento to **Gemona** (*see p. 514*).

PRACTICAL INFORMATION

GETTING AROUND

• **By rail:** There is a direct rail service from Venice to Pordenone, continuing on to Udine; fast Intercity trains make the Venice–Pordenone run in c. 1hr. Branch lines run from Pordenone to Portogruaro, and via Sacile to Gemona. Buses meet trains at Cervignano for Aquileia and Grado.

• **By bus:** Bus services run from Gorizia to Aquileia and from Pordenone to points throughout the province (information from ATAP, T: 0434 522 526, and APT Gorizia, T: 0481 593 511).

INFORMATION OFFICES

Aquileia Piazza Capitolo 4, T: 0431 919 491, www.aquileiaturismo.info
Grado Viale Dante Alighieri 72, T: 0431 877 111, www.gradoturismo.info
Pordenone Corso Vittorio Emanuele 38, T: 0434 21912.

HOTELS

Bannia di Fiume Veneto (*map p. 372*)
€€ **L'Ultimo Mulino**. Small (7 rooms) and quaint, occupying an ancient mill. Via Molino 45, T: 0434 957911, www.ultimomulino.com
Rivarotta di Pasiano (*map p. 372*)
€€ **Villa Luppis**. Charming hotel in a former Benedictine monastery with park and pool. Via San Martino 34, T: 0434 626969, www.villaluppis.it
Pordenone
€€ **Ark**. Simple, comfortable, centrally located. Via Mazzini 43, T: 0434 27901, F: 0434 522353.

€€ **Villa Ottoboni**. Elegant and refined, occupying a 16th-century villa and the adjacent building. Piazzetta Ottoboni 2, T: 0434 21967, F: 0434 208148.
Portobuffolè (*map p. 372*)
€€ **Villa Giustinian**. An 18th-century Venetian villa with gardens. Via Giustiniani 11, T: 0422 850244, www.villagiustinian.it

YOUTH HOSTELS

Aquileia
€ **Domus Augusta**, Via Roma 25, T: 0431 91024 or 348 741 2893, info@ostelloaquileia.it
San Vito al Tagliamento
€ **Europa**, Via P. Amalteo 39, T: 0434 876898, ostelloeuropa@tin.it

RESTAURANTS

Andreis (Ponte Molassa, *map p. 372*)
€ **La Molassa**. Old-fashioned *osteria* offering fresh local ingredients and great wines. Closed Tues and Nov–Easter. T: 0427 76147.
Aquileia
€ **La Colombara**. Restaurant specialising in seafood, accompanied by regional and Italian wines. Closed Mon and Jan. Località la Colombara (on the road to Grado), T: 0431 91513.
Cavasso Nuovo (*map p. 372*)
€€ **Ai Cacciatori**. Good regional food, wines and views. Closed Mon evening and Tues (except in summer). Via Diaz 4, T: 0427 777800.
Grado
€€€ **Adriatico**. Traditional recipes.

Closed Thur in winter. Campiello della Torre 2, T: 0431 85555.

€€ **Tavernetta all'Androna**. Traditional dishes prepared with an innovative twist. Closed Tues and Dec–Feb. Calle Porta Piccola 4, T: 0431 80950.

Pordenone

€€ **La Vecia Osteria del Moro**. Centrally located, in a renovated 14th-century convent, and renowned throughout the region for its excellent traditional fare (try the s'ciosi, snails). Closed Sun (and Sat in summer), Jan and Aug. Via Castello 2, T: 0434 28658.

Cordenòns (map p. 372)

€ **Al Curtif**. In an old farmhouse, around a stone court (curtif in dialect). Closed Mon evening, Tues and Aug. Via del Cristo 3, T: 0434 931038.

San Quirino (map p. 372)

€€ **La Primula**. Traditional restaurant (with rooms) known for its delicious regional dishes, especially pork. Closed Sun evening, Mon, Jan and July. Via San Rocco 47, T: 0434 91005.

Spilimbergo

€€ **La Torre**. Traditional restaurant serving good local specialities. In the castle. Closed Sun evening and Mon. T: 0427 50555.

€ **Da Afro**. Friendly, old-fashioned osteria. Closed Tues and Jan. Via Umberto I 14, T: 0427 2264.

LOCAL SPECIALITIES

The most distinctive local products are Grave del Friuli wines and Pordenone knives. Mosaics are made at Spilimbergo. There is a market in Pordenone (Piazza della Motta) Wed and Sat.

FESTIVALS & EVENTS

Pordenone Festa della Città, patron saint's day celebration, 25 April. Estate in Città, theatre, music and cinema, summer. Giostra del Castello, 15th-century tournament in costume, Sept. Le Giornate del Cinema Muto, annual silent-film festival, Oct. Incontriamoci a Pordenone, music and theatre in streets and squares, Oct. Natale Pordenonese con Presepe Subacqueo—an underwater Christmas crèche, 24 Dec.

Polcenigo (map p. 372). Sagra dei Sést, annual basket fair, Sept.

Roveredo in Piano (map p. 372). Gioco dei Pindoi, re-enactment of a medieval game played with stones, last Sun in Aug.

Sacile (map p. 372). Sagra dei Osei, annual game fair held on 16 Aug since 1274.

Sesto al Reghena Estate Musicale, music and theatre in a medieval abbey, summer. Presepe Vivente, over 100 players form a living Christmas crèche, 24 and 26 Dec.

Spilimbergo Spilimbergo Fotografia, international photography show, Sept.

Valvasone Concerti di Musica Antica, organ music concerts in the cathedral, Sept.

Carnival celebrations and patron saints' feast days with processions and festivities throughout the area. Cantine Aperte, presentation and tasting of new wines on estates throughout the region, May. Folkfest, international ethnic music festival throughout the region, July. Estate a Teatro, theatre in towns around Pordenone, summer.

LIGURIA

Stretching between the French frontier and the borders of Tuscany, the region of Liguria comprises the narrow strip of land lying between the Mediterranean and the Maritime Alps and the Apennines. It is territory that has always been easier of access by sea than by land, and the Ligurians are noted seafarers. Traditionally they have been influenced more by immigrations from overseas than by invasions from the interior. Traces of Punic and Greek connections are evident, and Genoa was an important Roman seaport.

GENOA

Genoa is built on an unlikely site: the irregular seaward slopes of an amphitheatre of hills. Today it is an important container port, but at the height of its power it ruled the destinies of the entire seaboard. It preserves many relics of its ancient, honourable history, including the numerous palaces and magnificent art collections of its great maritime families (many still in private hands). The town is famous as the birthplace of Christopher Columbus. To celebrate the 500th anniversary of his discovery of America (1992), new buildings went up, but the facelift was only partially successful. Genoa suffered from chaotic town planning after the Second World War (witness the raised motorway running between the old town and the port), and an attempt by Renzo Piano to revitalise the old port area has only been partially successful.

Nevertheless, the old city, clustered round the old port, is still a most interesting district, with its tall houses in steep, narrow alleys or *carugi*, and quaint old-fashioned shops. There are long-term plans to restore the area.

Impressions of Genoa

Genoa is the crookedest and most incoherent of cities; tossed about on the sides and crests of a dozen hills, it is seamed with gullies and ravines that bristle with those innumerable palaces for which we have heard from our earliest years that the place is celebrated. (...) Down about the basements, in the little, dim, close alleys, the people are for ever moving to and fro, or standing in their cavernous doorways or their dusky, crowded shops, calling, chattering, laughing, scrambling, living their lives in the conversational Italian fashion.

Henry James, 'Italy Revisited', 1877, in Portraits of Places, 1883

The dock-front of Genoa is marvellous. Such heat and colours and dirt & noise and loud wicked alleys with all the washing of the world hanging from the high windows.

Dylan Thomas, letter to his parents, 5 May 1947

HISTORY OF GENOA

The position of Genoa, at the northernmost point of the Tyrrhenian Sea and protected by mountains, has given it a lasting maritime importance. The original Ligurian inhabitants established early contact with the first known navigators of the Mediterranean, the Phoenicians and Greeks, and there was a trading-post here in the 6th century BC. In the 3rd century BC Genoa allied itself with Rome against the Carthaginians, and when the town was destroyed by the Carthaginians in 205 BC, it was rebuilt under the Roman praetor Cassius.

Roman connections were not entirely severed until the arrival of the Lombards in 641. In the succeeding centuries the sailors of Genoa withstood the attacks of Saracen pirates and captured their strongholds of Corsica and Sardinia. Sardinia was taken with the help of Pisa, and its occupation led to two centuries of war, which ended in the final defeat of the Pisans at Meloria (1284). With this success began the building of Genoa's great colonial empire, which extended as far as the Crimea, Syria and North Africa.

Power in the Genoese Republic was in the hands of the *podestà* and the *capitani del popolo*, with intervals of submission to Emperor Henry VII (1311–13) and to Robert of Anjou, King of Naples (1318–35). In 1340 came the election of the first doge, Simone Boccanegra. Petrarch, on a visit in 1358, described the city as '*la superba*' (the proud), a name used by numerous subsequent travellers to Genoa. Chaucer was sent to Genoa in 1372–73 by Edward III to arrange a commercial treaty with the maritime republic. Its territorial ambitions led to collisions with Venice, however; the subsequent war ended in the defeat of the Genoese at Chioggia (1380). Continual strife between the Genoese patrician families (Doria, Spinola and Fieschi) made the city an easy victim to the rising military powers, and it had a succession of foreign rulers in the 15th century. In 1528 Andrea Doria (c. 1466–1560), the greatest of the Genoese naval leaders, formulated a constitution for Genoa that freed the city from foreign rule, though it established despotic government at home and was followed (1547–48) by the insurrections of Fieschi and Cibo.

The growing might of the Ottoman Empire, the transfer of trade with America to Atlantic ports, and the maritime hegemony of Spain, brought about the rapid decline of Genoa in the 17th century, and in 1684 Louis XIV entered the town after a bombardment. In 1768 the Genoese sold their rights to their last remaining colony, Corsica, to France. Napoleon entered Genoa in 1796, and formed the Ligurian Republic in 1802. This soon became a French province, but in 1815, after Napoleon's fall, Genoa was joined to Piedmont by the Treaty of Vienna. It went on to become a stronghold of the Risorgimento, with Giuseppe Mazzini (born in Genoa) as the leading spirit. Garibaldi led his expedition against Sicily from here in 1860.

EXPLORING GENOA

Piazza de Ferrari and the Palazzo Ducale

Map 11.

NB: *Museum cards are on sale at participating museums, the bookshop of the Musei di Strada Nuova, the Palazzo Ducale, the Aquarium, main railway stations in Liguria, the Club Eurostar lounge at Genoa-Brignole station and main AMT ticket offices.*

Piazza de Ferrari, where numerous main roads converge, is at the centre of the city. Behind the Garibaldi monument is the **Teatro Carlo Felice**, rebuilt on a huge scale by Aldo Rossi in 1987–91. Only the Neoclassical pronaos of the old theatre survives; the rest was destroyed by fire. The new building includes a massive rectangular tower. In front of this is the Neoclassical **Accademia Ligustica di Belle Arti** (1827–31), a surviving building by the same architect as the Teatro (Carlo Barabino). A gallery on the first floor of this famous art school (*open Tues–Sun 3–7*) contains paintings by Ligurian artists of the 14th–19th centuries.

The **Palazzo Ducale** (*open Tues–Sun 9–9*) is a magnificent large building of various periods surrounding Piazza Matteotti. The left wing, Palazzo di Alberto Fieschi, was the seat of the *capitano del popolo* in 1272, and from 1294 the meeting place of the *comune*. It became the residence of the doges from 1340 onwards, and Andrea Vannone carried out radical modifications c. 1591–1620, adding the attractive spacious vestibule with a light courtyard at either end. The palace was reconstructed by Simone Cantoni in 1778–83 and given a Neoclassical façade. On the upper floors are the Salone del Maggior Consiglio and the doges' chapel, frescoed by Giovanni Battista Carlone. The palace is now a cultural centre.

On the southeast side of the square is the Baroque church of **Sant' Ambrogio o del Gesù**, built 1589–1606 by Giuseppe Valeriani. The sumptuous, colourful interior has frescoes by Giovanni Carlone and altarpieces by Guido Reni and Rubens.

The cathedral

Map 11.

In Via San Lorenzo is the flank of the **cathedral of San Lorenzo**, a Romanesque-Gothic building consecrated (unfinished) in 1118 and modified in the 13th–14th centuries and during the Renaissance. On the south side are Roman sarcophagi, a 15th-century Grimaldi family tomb, and the Romanesque portal of San Gottardo. The façade (restored in the 20th century) has doorways in the French Gothic style. The campanile on the south side was completed in 1522; the north one is unfinished, with a loggetta of 1447. On the north side are the 12th-century portal of San Giovanni and many more classical sarcophagi.

The interior is distinguished by its dark Corinthian columns. The proportions were altered when the nave roof was raised in 1550 and the cupola, by Galeazzo Alessi, added in 1567. The pulpit dates from 1526. The lunette over the west door has early 14th-century frescoes. In the south aisle, beside a British naval shell that damaged the church without exploding in 1941, is a marble relief of the *Crucifixion* of 1443. The

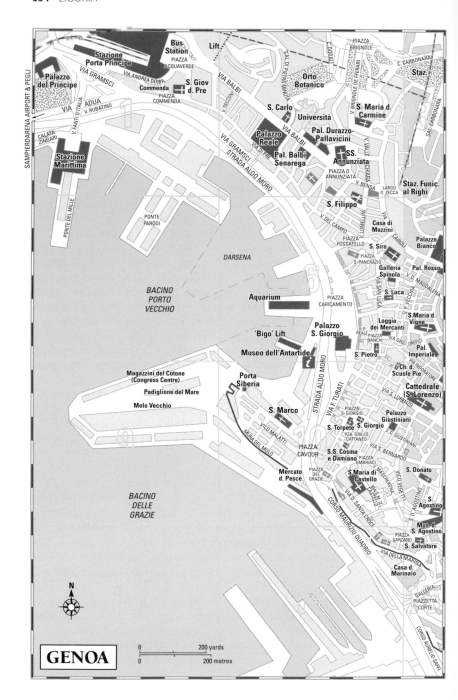

SAMPIERDARENA AIRPORT & PEGLI

Stazione
Porta Principe

Bus
Station
PIAZZA
ACQUAVERDE

Lift

PIAZZA
BRIGNOLE

C. CARBONARA

Staz.

Palazzo
del Principe

VIA GRAMSCI

VIA ANDREA DORIA

VIA ADUA
V. RUBATINO

Commenda
PIAZZA
COMMENDA

S. Giov
d. Pre

VIA BALBI

V. TACCONI

Orto
Botanico

V. BRIGNOLE DE FERRARI

SAL. CARBONARA

SAL. DI PIETRA MINUTA

VIA FANTI D'ITALIA

S. Carlo

Università

VIA BALBI

S. Maria d.
Carmine

CALATA
ZINGARI

Palazzo
Reale

VIA DI PRE

Pal. Durazzo-
Pallavicini

V. VALLE

Stazione
Marittima

VIA GRAMSCI

STRADA ALDO MORO

Pal. Balbi
Senarega

SS.
Annunziata

V. CHIARA

PIAZZA D.
ANNUNZIATA

V. BENSA

LARGO
D. ZECCA

Staz. Funic.
al Righi

PONTE DEL MILLE

PONTE
PARODI

S. Filippo

V. DEL CAMPO

LOMELLINI

VIA CAIROLI

Staz. Funic.
al Righi

Casa di
Mazzini

DARSENA

PIAZZA
FOSSATELLO

PIAZZA
S. PANCRAZIO

S. Siro

Palazzo
Bianco

BACINO
PORTO
VECCHIO

Galleria
Spinola

VIA SAN LUCA

Pal. Rosso

V. O. MADDALENA

Aquarium

PIAZZA
CARICAMENTO

S. Luca

S.Maria d.
Vigne

'Bigo' Lift

Palazzo
S. Giorgio

Loggia
dei Mercanti

V. P.
REALE

PIAZZA
BANCHI

VIA DEGLI OREFICI

Pal.
Imperiale

Museo dell'Antartide

S. Pietro

Ch. d.
Scuole Pie

VIA INDORATORE

Magazzini del Cotone
(Congress Centre)

Porta
Siberia

STRADA ALDO MORO

Cattedrale
(S. Lorenzo)

VIA S. LORENZO

Padiglione del Mare

Molo Vecchio

S. Marco

VICO MALATTI

VIA E. TURATI

PIAZZA
S. GIORGIO

S. Giorgio

Palazzo
Giustiniani

MURA DEL MOLO

S. Torpete

PZA. GRILLO
CATTANEO

VIA S. BERNARDO

V. D. GIUSTINIANI

PIAZZA
CAVOUR

S.S. Cosma
e Damiano

PIAZZA
EMBRIACI

S. Donato

Mercato
d. Pesce

PIAZZA
DEL
GRAZIE

S.Maria di
Castello

VICO V. DI
MASCHERONA

VICO VEGETTI

BACINO
DELLE
GRAZIE

CORSO MAURIZIO QUADRIO

VIA D. SANTA CROCE

VIA D. CASTELLO

S.
Agostino

S. D. GIUSTINI

Mus. d.
S. Agostino

PIAZZA
SARZANO

S. Salvatore

VIA DELLA MARINA

Casa d.
Marinaio

N

GALLERIA
PIAZZETTA
CORTE

CORSO AURELIO SAFFI

GENOA

| 0 | | 200 yards |
| 0 | | 200 metres |

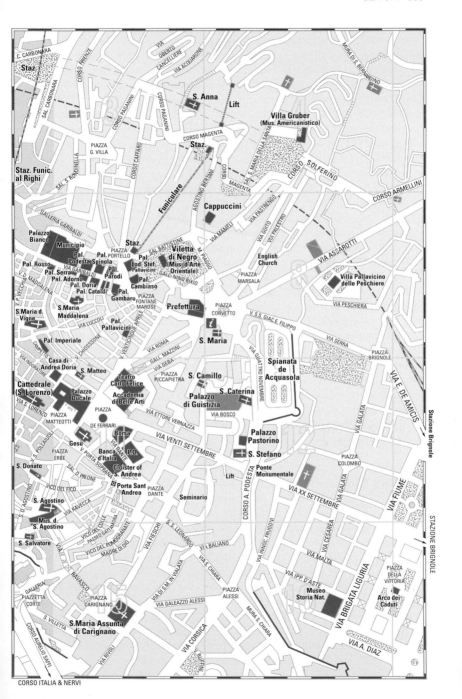

chapel to the right of the high altar holds a painting by Federico Barocci. The stalls in the apse date from 1514–64. In the chapel to the left of the high altar are wall and ceiling paintings by Luca Cambiaso (*see p. 540*) and Giovanni Battista Castello.

The great chapel of St John the Baptist was designed by Domenico and Elia Gaggini (1451–65), with a richly decorated front. It contains statues by Matteo Civitali and Andrea Sansovino (1504), a baldacchino of 1532, and a 13th-century French shrine for the relics of St John the Baptist. In the adjoining chapel is the tomb of Giorgio Fieschi (d. 1461) by Giovanni Gaggini. The treasury contains ancient glass, copes, the Byzantine *Zaccaria Cross* and precious reliquaries in vaults.

Between Palazzo Ducale and the cathedral is Via Reggio, which skirts the left wing of Palazzo Ducale and the Torre del Popolo (1307), known as the Grimaldina. At no. 12 is the cloister of San Lorenzo (c. 1180).

Piazza San Matteo, reached along Salita allo Arcivescovato, was created in the 12th century when it was surrounded by the mansions and church of the Doria family, with striped black-and-white façades. **San Matteo**, founded in 1125 but rebuilt by the Doria in 1278, has a striped black-and-white Gothic façade with inscriptions recounting the glorious deeds of the Dorias.

The interior was transformed in 1543–47 for Andrea Doria by Giovanni Angelo Montorsoli. The sanctuary is an interesting sculptural work by Montorsoli (with the help of Silvio Cosini). The nave was decorated with stuccoes and frescoes by Giovanni Battista Castello (Il Bergamasco) and Luca Cambiaso. The crypt and staircase, decorated with marbles and stuccoes, were designed by Montorsoli for the tomb of Andrea Doria. An archway on the left of the church leads to the cloister (1308–10) by Magister Marcus Venetus.

Opposite the church is the Casa di Lamba Doria (no. 15), built in the 13th century with a portico. The **Casa di Andrea Doria** (no. 17) was built for Lazzaro Doria in 1468 and presented to the famous admiral (*see box*) by his native city in 1528. No. 14 is the Casa di Branca Doria, with a charming relief over the portal.

Andrea Doria (c. 1466–1560)
Doria began his career as a mercenary general in the service of Francis I of France. Following a disagreement, he switched allegiances and fought for the Habsburgs instead, reaching an understanding with the Holy Roman Emperor Charles V that however much territory he won for the empire, the independence of Genoa would remain secure. In 1528 he became virtual ruler of Genoa, though he was careful not to dissolve the city state's ancient oligarchical councils and senate. He was also admiral of the Genoa fleet, and went to Spain's aid against the Ottoman Turks. A gifted seaman, Doria has gone down in history as the man who discovered how to sail against the wind. His portrait by Bronzino (Brera, Milan) shows him in the guise of Neptune, self-assured and semi-naked, a sturdy trident standing in for what the drapery barely conceals.

The old port

Map 6.

Piazza Caricamento faces the Porto Vecchio, Genoa's old harbour. Here is the Gothic **Palazzo di San Giorgio** (restored in 1992), begun c. 1260 and extended towards the sea in 1570. The façade facing the harbour was frescoed by Lazzaro Tavarone in 1606–08. Once the palace of the *capitani del popolo*, it became in 1408 the seat of the famous Banco di San Giorgio, which was largely responsible for the prosperity of the city from the mid-15th century onwards. Here citizens could lend money for compound interest, and the idea of cheques was introduced. It is now occupied by the Harbour Board.

Across the road and under the *sopraelevata* (or Strada Aldo Moro), an ugly raised motorway (1965) that distributes traffic from the western suburbs to the city, is the **Molo Vecchio** (Map 9). The quay was begun in 1257 by the Cistercian friars Oliverio and Filippo; the imposing Porta Siberia, designed by Galeazzo Alessi, dates from 1553. The area was redesigned by Renzo Piano in 1992: he converted the old cotton warehouses into a congress centre, and created an open-air space on the quay for spectacles and fairs, next to the Bigo, an unusual metal structure that serves as a 'crane' for a lift from which there is a panoramic view (*open daily 10–dusk*). In this area are two new museums: the **Museo Nazionale dell'Antartide** (*open June–Sept Tues–Sun 10.30–6.30; Oct–May Tues–Fri 9.45–5.30, Sat, Sun and holidays 10–6*) documenting Italian scientific expeditions to Antarctica and giving visitors an experience of conditions there; and the **Padiglione del Mare e della Navigazione** (*open June–Sept daily 10.30–8; Oct–May Tues–Fri 10.30–5.30, weekends and holidays 10.30–6*), a maritime museum with models and reconstructions of ships, documenting life at sea at various historical periods.

The **Aquarium** (*open Tues–Wed and Fri 9.30–7; Thur and Sat–Sun 9.30–8.30; last entry 90mins before closing*), also designed by Piano in 1992, is the largest in Europe (much visited by school parties), with 50 huge tanks that can be viewed both from an underwater level and from above. The natural habitat of the Red Sea and the Caribbean coral reef have been reconstructed; and you can admire some 20,000 creatures, including dolphins, seals and sharks, and tropical fish.

Galleria Spinola and its neighbourhood

Map 7.

Just behind Palazzo San Giorgio is **Piazza Banchi**, which was were the money-changers had their tables (*banchi*) until the end of the 18th century. The Loggia dei Mercanti was designed by Vannone in 1589–95. It was turned into an exchange—the first of its kind in Italy—in the 19th century. From here Via San Luca leads north. This was the main street of the city from the Middle Ages to the 18th century, when it was the principal place of residence of the great Genoese families. It is now full of shops and offices. The little church of **San Luca**, to the right, rebuilt in 1626, is a fine example of Genoese Baroque architecture, with an interior frescoed by Domenico Piola. It contains sculptures by Filippo Parodi and an altarpiece by Giovanni Benedetto Castiglione (*see p. 540*).

Beyond, Vico Pellicceria leads right to Piazza Pellicceria, with Spinola family town-houses. No. 1 is now the **Galleria Nazionale di Palazzo Spinola** (*Map 7; open Tues–Sat 8.30–7.30, Sun and holidays 1–8, last entry 1 hour before closing*). This 16th-century mansion became the property of the Spinola in the early 18th century when the collection of paintings was formed. It is a particularly interesting example of a patrician Genoese residence that preserves more or less intact its 17th–18th-century decorations, as well as its furniture and paintings.

The Collections

The first two floors have been restored as far as possible to their original state. The third floor is occupied by the Galleria Nazionale della Liguria, with restored works from churches, and an important porcelain collection.

First-floor: The Salone has a vault frescoed by Lazzaro Tavarone c. 1615, and bronzes by Ferdinando Tacca. The Primo Salotto contains works by Stefano Magnasco, Giovanni Battista Gaulli (Il Baciccio), and Giovanni Battista Carlone. The Secondo Salotto contains a *Portrait of Ansaldo Pallavicino* by van Dyck, another of him with his father by Domenico Fiasella (who also painted him as doge: this portrait is in the dining room), and a *Portrait of a Lady* by Bernardo Strozzi.

Second floor: This was decorated for Maddalena Doria (wife of Nicolò Spinola) in 1734. The Salone has another ceiling fresco by Tavarone, completed in the 18th century by Giovanni Battista Natali, who also painted the walls as a setting for paintings by Domenico Piola, Gregorio de Ferrari, Luca Giordano and Bernardo Strozzi. The Primo Salotto still has its 18th-century decorations and furniture. The Secondo Salotto displays paintings by Guido Reni, Luca Cambiaso, Valerio Castello and Bernardo Strozzi. The *Four Evangelists* are by van Dyck. The Terzo Salotto has works by Carlo Maratta, Bernardo Castello, Giulio Cesare Procaccini and Francesco Vanni. The *Virgin in Prayer* is by Joos van Cleve, who stayed in Genoa in 1515–20 and again in 1525–28. The charming Galleria degli Specchi (1736) was probably designed by Lorenzo de Ferrari, who painted the vault fresco. The Quinto Salotto has a *Portrait of Paolo Spinola* by Angelica Kauffmann, and 18th-century furniture.

Third floor: Highlights of the Galleria Nazionale della Liguria's collections include an *Ecce Homo* by Antonello da Messina, an equestrian portrait of *Gio Carlo Doria* by Rubens, a *Portrait of a Lady with a Child* by van Dyck, a statue of Justice, part of the funerary monument of Margaret of Brabant by Giovanni Pisano, a *Portrait of Scipione Clausone* by Tintoretto, and bronzes by Giambologna. The two small female portraits by Mignard are in exquisite 17th-century frames (one by Filippo Parodi).

Top floor: This has a fine display of European and Asian porcelain that belonged to the Spinola, and a collection of antique textiles. A spiral staircase leads up from here to a little terrace with a delightful view of the city.

SOME PATRICIAN PALACES

'These great edifices,' wrote Henry James, 'with their mottled and faded complexions, lift their big ornamental cornices to a tremendous height in the air, where, in a certain indescribably forlorn and desolate fashion, overtopping each other, they seem to reflect the twinkle and glitter of the warm Mediterranean.'

Palazzo Bianco

Via Garibaldi 11. Open Tues–Fri 9–7, Sat–Sun 10–7, www.museopalazzobianco.it

Built for the Grimaldi c. 1565 and enlarged after 1711 by Giacomo Viano for Maria Durazzo, widow of Giovanni Francesco Brignole Sale, the palace was presented to the municipality in 1884 by Maria Brignole Sale. It contains part of her collection, together with later acquisitions, with some particularly beautiful Flemish and Dutch paintings. Highlights include a number of works by Luca Cambiaso (*Madonna and Child with St Mary Magdalene, Christ at the Column, St Jerome, Madonna della Candella*). The masterpieces of the collection are Hans Memling's *Christ Blessing*; Jan Provost's (*Annunciation*), and Gerard David's *Madonna della Pappa*, c. 1510. Antony van Dyck's *Christ and the Coin* shows the artist's stylistic debt to Titian. There is also Rubens' celebrated *Venus and Mars*, painted in Antwerp between 1632 and 1635, and Caravaggio's splendid *Ecce Homo*, in which a highly symbolic use of light underscores the purity and meekness of Christ.

Palazzo Rosso

Via Garibaldi 18. Open Tues–Fri 9–7, Sat–Sun 10–7, www.museopalazzorosso.it

Almost opposite Palazzo Bianco, this magnificent building of 1671–77 was erected for Ridolfo and Gio Francesco Brignole Sale. Like Palazzo Bianco it was bequeathed to the city (in 1874) by Maria Brignole Sale. The collection includes fine portraits of the Brignole family by van Dyck. There are also works by Dürer, Guercino and Lodovico Carracci. The Genoese School (Bernardo Strozzi, Giovanni Benedetto Castiglione) is well represented.

Palazzo Doria Tursi (the town hall)

Via Garibaldi 9. Open Mon–Thur 9–12 & 1–4, Fri 9–12 & 1–3.

Flanked by raised gardens, the palace was begun in 1568 for Nicolò Grimaldi, and the loggias were added in 1597 around the magnificent courtyard. It contains the Guarneri violin (1742), which belonged to Genoa-born Nicolò Paganini (1784–1840), as well as three letters from Columbus.

Palazzo Balbi-Durazzo

Via Garibaldi 10. Open Mon–Tues 8.15–1.45, Wed–Sun 8.15–7.15.

Designed c. 1650 for the Balbi family, it was remodelled in 1705 for the Durazzo by Carlo Fontana. From 1842 to 1922 it was the royal seat in Genoa, and it contains some sumptuous 18th-century rooms. There is also a *Crucifixion* by van Dyck, and works by Luca Giordano and Bernardo Strozzi.

GENOESE ART

The greatest name of the 16th century is Luca Cambiaso (1527–85), a precocious talent who frescoed the Palazzo Doria (now the Prefettura) aged only 17. The geometric forms he uses in his drawings almost foreshadow Cubism. Cambiaso's influence carried over into Lazzaro Tavarone and Bernardo Castello, though their derivative Mannerist style lacks true originality. Genoa's most fruitful time was her Seicento. The city has always been receptive to foreign ideas, and interestingly it was influence from outside Italy that inspired the art of this period. Through its close commercial links with the Netherlands, the city acquired many Dutch and Flemish paintings; Rubens and van Dyck were in Genoa in the early 17th century; other influence came from the Urbino-born Federico Barocci, and from Caravaggio. The greatest native artist of the age is Giovanni Benedetto Castiglione (c. 1610–65, known as Grechetto), who is said to have invented the monotype. He was much influence by the Netherlandish painters, and was in turn much admired by Tiepolo. Bernardo Strozzi (1581–1644) took monastic vows as a young man, but cast aside his habit and went on to leave his artistic mark on the city. Domenico Piola (1628–1708) was a fresco artist of some genius. Also important is Domenico Fiasella. Though not a notably great artist, he was much sought-after in his day, and extremely. prolific. He, like so many of his contemporaries, was a confirmed Caravaggist.

The architecture of medieval Genoa is characterised by the black-and-white striped façades of the older churches, and the earliest sculpture came from the workshops of the Pisano family and the Comacini. Galeazzo Alessi, the Perugian architect, worked here during the Renaissance, and the Gaggini family of sculptors were active in the 16th–17th centuries.

The old town

Map 10–11.

Some charming portals survive in this district, in white marble or black slate, often bearing reliefs of St George, patron of the city. There are also numerous Baroque tabernacles with religious images on the streets. Via Canneto il Lungo is a typical long street of the old town, with food shops and some handsome doorways.

Santa Maria di Castello is a Romanesque church with 15th-century Gothic additions. It occupies the site of the Roman castrum and preserves some Roman columns. Inside, on the west wall, is a late-15th-century fresco by Lorenzo Fasolo; in the south aisle, altarpieces by Aurelio Lomi, Pier Francesco Sacchi and Bernardo Castello. Next to the new altar is a wooden crucifix (c. 1100, the *Black Christ*); in the sanctuary, a marble group of the *Assumption of the Virgin* by Antonio Domenico Parodi; and in the chapel to the left of the sanctuary, *St Rosa of Lima* by Domenico Piola. The baptistery contains a 15th-century polyptych, some ruined 15th-century frescoes and a Roman sarcophagus. The sacristy has a beautifully carved portal (inner face) by Giovanni Gaggini and Leonardo Riccomanni (1452).

The Dominican convent (1445–1513) has pretty frescoes in the loggia of the second cloister, possibly by Iustus de Alemania, the German painter who signed and dated (1451) the *Annunciation* on the wall. In the upper loggia (view of the port), with Roman and medieval capitals, is a tabernacle of the *Trinity* by Domenico Gaggini, and a detached fresco in monochrome of the *Vision of St Dominic*, attributed to Braccesco. The old library has a polyptych of the *Annunciation* by Giovanni Mazone (1470; one of only two works known by this local artist). The museum (*open Mon–Sat 9–12 & 3.30–6, Sun and holidays 9–12 & 3.30–6.30*) contains liturgical items, sculptures, paintings (*Coronation of the Virgin*, a painting showing Flemish influence, signed and dated 1513 by Ludovico Brea), miniatures and a reconstructed monastic cell.

Piazza San Giorgio, an important market square in the Middle Ages, has two attractive, domed and centrally planned churches: San Giorgio, documented as early as 964 and reconstructed in 1695, and San Torpete, rebuilt with an elliptical cupola after 1730.

The church of **San Donato**, probably founded in the early 12th century, has a splendid polygonal campanile and a fine doorway. In the beautiful basilican interior are a late-14th-century painting by Nicolò da Voltri and a triptych of the *Adoration of the Magi* by Joos van Cleve.

The Stradone Sant'Agostino leads up past a building of the faculty of architecture of the university to Piazza Sarzano, once a centre of the old city, but partly derelict since the war. Here is the pink building (1977–84) of the **Museo di Architettura e Scultura Ligure di Sant'Agostino** (Map 15; *open Tues–Fri 9–7, Sat, Sun and holidays 10–5*), housing the city's collection of architectural fragments, sculptures and detached frescoes. Highlights of the collection include, on the first floor, fragments of the funerary monument of Margaret of Brabant (d. 1311), by Giovanni Pisano (whose *Madonna* graces the Scrovegni Chapel in Padua); and on the second floor, 15th-century black slate architraves with reliefs of *St John the Baptist* and *St George*. There are also carved masks by Taddeo Carlone; detached frescoes by Luca Cambiaso; 16th-century sculptures; paintings by Domenico Piola; and sculptures by Pierre Puget and Antonio Canova, as well as 15th-century English alabaster carvings. The 13th-century Gothic church of Sant'Agostino, with a graceful campanile and spire, has been restored for use as an auditorium.

The northern waterfront

Map 1.

Via Balbi ends in **Piazza Acquaverde**, with a monument (1862) to Columbus in front of Principe Railway Station, an impressive building of 1854. Downhill to the left is the church of **San Giovanni di Prè**, founded in 1180, with a severe interior (much restored); the church has been turned round and a false apse created at the west end, the entrance being in the original apse. An upper and lower church adjoin the Commenda, the Commendery of the Knights Hospitaller, built at the same time as a convent and hospice for crusaders. On Piazza Commenda is the fine five-spired campanile and flank of the church (with Gothic windows), next to the beautiful triple loggia of the Commenda, altered in the Renaissance (restored in 1992).

A fence separates the main quay of the harbour from the wharves and landing stages. On the point is the **Lanterna**, a medieval lighthouse restored in 1543; nearby is the skyscraper housing Genoa's World Trade Centre.

Near the maritime station, at Via Adua 6, **Palazzo del Principe** has been opened to the public (*Tues–Sun 10–5*) after renovation. Two buildings here were acquired by Andrea Doria in 1521 and were made into one by Domenico Caranca (1529); Montorsoli may have added the loggia (1543–47), facing the garden. Charles V and Napoleon were entertained here in 1533 and 1805 respectively, and the composer Verdi wintered here from 1877. Still owned by the Doria Pamphili family, the palace contains frescoes by Perin del Vaga and stuccoes by Luzio Romano and Guglielmo della Porta in the vestibule and on the stairs, as well as portraits of Andrea Doria (by Sebastiano del Piombo) and Giannettino Doria (attributed to Bronzino).

From San Giovanni di Prè, the long and dilapidated Via di Prè (Map 2) leads back towards the centre parallel to the sea.

AROUND GENOA

The **Staglieno cemetery** (*open daily 8–5*) was laid out, with extensive gardens, in 1844–51 and has intriguing 19th-century funerary sculpture. The conspicuous colossal statue of Faith is by Santo Varni, and near the upper gallery, in a clump of trees, is the simple tomb of Mazzini, surrounded by memorials to members of Garibaldi's 'Thousand' (*see next page*). To the left of the Pantheon and the main enclosure—on the third terrace, planted with oak trees—is the Protestant temple and cemetery: Constance Mary Lloyd, the wife of Oscar Wilde, is buried here. From the viale a long staircase ascends to the English cemetery designed by Gino Coppedè in 1902. This includes the British military cemetery from both world wars.

A single-track railway line (29km) built in 1929 winds up the Val Bisagno, the Valpolcevera and the Valle Scrivi from Piazza Manin, to end at Casella. It has splendid views.

Pegli, now at the western limit of the city, was once a popular weekend resort of the Genoese. It still has a few fine villas backed by pine woods. The Villa Doria, a 16th-century mansion with a pleasant public park (and containing frescoes by Lazzaro Tavarone), houses the **Museo Navale** (*open Tues–Sat 9–1*). This illustrates the history of the great Genoese maritime republic and includes a portrait of Columbus attributed to Ridolfo Ghirlandaio. The splendid, luxuriant garden of **Villa Durazzo-Pallavicini** (*open Apr–Sept Tues–Sun 9–7; Nov–March 10–5*), created in the 1840s, includes a partly underground lake and a 'Chinese' temple. The villa of 1837 houses the Museo di Archeologia Ligure (*open Tues–Fri 9–7, Sat–Sun 10–7*), notable for prehistoric finds from Ligurian cave-dwellings, and pre-Roman necropolis finds from the city of Genoa.

East of the city

The eastern districts of the city include **Albaro**, which has numerous villas. From Piazza Vittoria, Corso Buenos Aires leads east to Piazza Tommaseo, where steps mount to Via Pozzo, rising below the Villa Saluzzo Bombrini, known as Villa Paradiso, with its beautiful garden. Built by Andrea Vannone in the 16th century, it is one of the best preserved villas in the district. Via Pozzo ends at Via Albaro, with Villa Saluzzo Mongiordino (no. 1), where Byron lived in 1822. Further on to the left, the Faculty of Engineering of the university occupies the splendid Villa Giustiniani Cambiaso (1548, to a design by Galeazzo Alessi), with another garden. The little church of San Giuliano d'Albaro, built in 1240, was enlarged in the 15th century. In Via San Nazaro, the Villa Bagnerello (plaque) was where Dickens lived in 1844 before moving into Genoa: 'I was set down in a rank, dull, weedy courtyard, attached to a kind of pink jail; and was told I lived there'.

A short way east is the tiny old fishing port of **Boccadasse**, well preserved, still with its old gas lamp standards. It has good fish restaurants and a popular ice-cream shop. Above it is a mock medieval castle by Gino Coppedè.

Further east is **Quarto**, where a monument marks the starting-point of Garibaldi and the 'Thousand' (*I Mille*) on their expedition to Sicily (5 May 1860). The expedition was the first major campaign in the five-year war that united the many city-states of Italy under the rule of a single king, Vittorio Emanuele of Savoy. In Villa Spinola, where Garibaldi stayed while planning the expedition with his friend Candido Augusto Vecchi, is a small Garibaldi Museum (*open daily except Wed 9–6*).

Nervi, 11km east of the centre of Genoa, is now included in its municipal limits. It became the earliest winter resort on the Riviera di Levante in 1863. The Passeggiata Anita Garibaldi extends for nearly 2km between the railway and the rock-bound shore. The Parco Municipale incorporates the gardens of Villa Gropallo, Villa Serra and Villa Grimaldi. In Villa Serra is a gallery of modern art (*closed at the time of writing; T: 010 557 2057*). Villa Grimaldi is home to the Frugone collection of 19th- and 20th-century art (*open Tues–Fri 9–7, Sat–Sun 10–7*). Further east is the charming park of the Villa Luxoro (*open Tues–Fri 9–1, Sat 10–1*), with a small museum of furniture, lace, paintings, etc.

PRACTICAL INFORMATION

GETTING AROUND

• **Airport bus** (Volabus): Leaves every half hour from Brignole Station (Piazza Verdi), with stops in Piazza de' Ferrari (Map 11) and at Principe Station (Piazza Acquaverde). Buses also connect Brignole Station with Milan (Malpensa) and Nice.

• **By rail:** The main rail line from Rome to Paris follows the Tyrrhenian coast to Genoa, then continues via Turin. Fast Eurostar trains link Rome to Genoa in c. 4hrs 15mins; Intercity in c. 5hrs. Both stop at La Spezia and often at Sarzana, Sestri Levante, Chiavari and Rapallo.

Genoa also has frequent connections to Turin (1hr 30mins), Milan (1hr 30mins) and Pisa (1hr 40mins). There is also one daily Interregionale to and from Bologna (4hrs 50mins).

Genoa has two main railway stations: Porta Principe (Map 1) is the more central, but nearly all trains stop also at Brignole. Commuter trains also stop at Voltri and Nervi.

• **By sea:** The main quay for passenger and car ferries is Ponte Colombo, next to the Stazione Marittima at Ponte Andrea Doria and Ponte dei Mille (Map 5). Regular car ferries to Sardinia, Sicily and Tunis. Stazione Marittima, T: 010 256 682. Ferries to/from Sardinia: Tirrenia, T: 010 26981; Grimaldi, T: 010 55091; Tris, T: 010 576411. To/from Sicily: Grimaldi, 010 55091. To/from Corsica: Moby Lines, T: 010 252755; Tris, T: 010 576411. Tunis: Cemar, T: 010 589595. Organised trips round Genoa harbour by motor boat (c. 1hr) depart from the Stazione Marittima (Ponte dei Mille, Calata Zingari; Map 1). Information from Cooperativa

Battellieri (T: 010 265712), and Alimar (T: 010 255975).

• **Genoa city transport:** A ticket valid for one day on any line can be purchased at the AMT offices at Via Montaldo 1, Piazza della Vittoria 88r, Via D'Annunzio 8 and Via Reti 15. Single-journey tickets valid for 90mins on buses and trains in the metropolitan area can be purchased at newsstands and tobacconists.

• **Funicular railways:**
  F: Fargo della Zecca (Map 6)—Righi Via San Nicolò.
  H Piazza Portello (Map 7)—Corso Magenta.

• **Rack railway:**
  G Via del Lagaccio, near Piazza Principe (Map 1)—Granarolo. Lifts.
  L Via XX Settembre—Corso Podestà (Ponte Monumentale; Map 12).
  M Corso Magenta—Via Crocco.
  N Piazza Portello—Spianata di Castelletto.

• **Taxis:** Radiotaxi, T: 010 5966; Cooperativa Taxisti Genovesi, T: 010 594690; Cooperative Auto Pubbliche, T: 010 522 0573.

INFORMATION OFFICES

At Principe Station (T: 010 246 2633), the airport (T: 010 601 5247), in Palazzina Santa Maria, near the aquarium (T: 010 248711), and at the Stazione Marittima, Terminal Crociere (seasonal, T: 010 246 3686); www.apt.genova.it

HOTELS

Genoa
€€€ **Bristol Palace**. 19th-century ambience, in the centre of the city. Via XX

Settembre 35, T: 010 592541,
www.hotelbristolpalace.com
€€€ **City**. Centrally located, modern
and comfortable. Via San Sebastiano 6, T:
010 5545.
€€ **Agnello d'Oro**. A warm, simple,
family-run place. Via Monachette 6, T:
010 246 2084, www.hotelagnellodoro.it
€€ **Alexander**. Near Porta Principe station, with good views over the harbour.
Via Bersaglieri d'Italia 19, T: 010 261371,
www.hotelalexander-genova.it
Pegli
€€ **Torre Cambiaso**. Calm and quiet, in
a lovely park with pool. Via Scarpanto 49,
T: 010 665055.

RESTAURANTS

Genoa
€€ **Bruxaboschi**. Family run trattoria,
specialising in traditional recipes. Closed
Sun evening, Mon, Aug and Dec–Jan. Via
F. Mignone 8, S.Desiderio, T: 010
3450302.
€€ **Ferrando**. Good Ligurian fare and
great views, with garden seating in sum-
mer. Closed Sun evening, Mon, Wed
evening, Jan and Aug. Via Carli 110, T:
010 751925.
€€ **Gran Gotto**. Excellent seafood and
an interesting wine list. Closed midday
Sat, Sun, holidays and Aug. Viale Brigate
Bisagno 69r, T: 010 583644.
€€ **La Berlocca**. Regional dishes with
special focus on vegetables and seafood.
Famous pastas. Closed Mon, Sat–Sun
midday and July–Aug. Via dei Macelli di
Soziglia 45r, T: 010 2474162.
€€ **La Bitta nella Pergola**. Known for
its excellent fish dishes. Closed Sun
evening, Mon, Jan and Aug. Via Casaregis
52r, T: 010 588543.

€€ **Ostaia da Ü Santu**. Nice trattoria
specialising in traditional Ligurian recipes.
Closed Sun evening Mon–Tue and Dec
25–Jan 31. Via Santuario delle Grazie 33,
Località Voltri, T: 010 6130476.
€€ **Rina**. Family run trattoria with good
seafood dishes; closed Mon and Aug. Via
Mura delle Grazie 3r, T: 010 2466475.
€€ **Santa Chiara**. Personal interpretations of traditional regional dishes and
summer seating on a seafront terrace.
Closed Sun, Dec–Jan and Aug. Via Capo
Santa Chiara 69r, Località Boccadasse, T:
010 377 0081.
€€ **Antica Osteria del Bai**. An outstanding seafood restaurant worth the
7km drive from Genoa; closed Mon, Jan
and Aug. Via Quarto 12, Località Quarto
dei Mille, T: 010 387478.

LOCAL SPECIALITIES

Genoa is the home of focaccia, the delicious soft, low white bread that goes well
with just about anything. You can buy
focaccia in most bakeries and grocery
shops—plain (have it sliced open and
stuffed with cold meats, cheeses, sun-
dried tomatoes, olive spread, etc. for a
truly memorable sandwich) or topped
with cheese, onions or potatoes. Equally
good but less well known is *farinata*, a
type of pizza made with chick-pea flour,
extra virgin olive oil, water and salt. A
popular food from Nice to Pisa, in Genoa
it is sold in modest snack bars called
farinotti. These include **Sa Pesta**, 16 Via
dei Giustiniani; **Sciamadda**, 19 Via
Ravecca; and **Spano**, 35 Via Santa Zita.
For a good Ligurian wine to drink with
your focaccia or *farinata*, try **Vinoteca
Sola**, Piazza Colombo 13r.

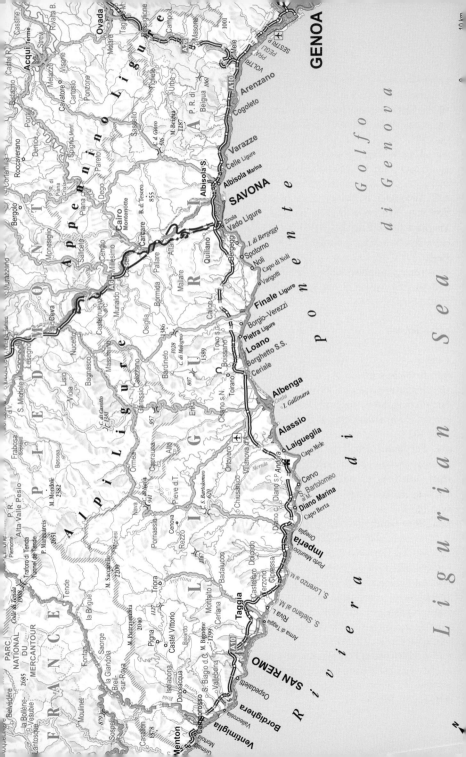

THE RIVIERA DI PONENTE

The coast west of Genoa has a mild climate and luxuriant vegetation with palms, bougainvillaea and exotic plants. It has been important for its cut flower industry (especially roses and carnations) since the early 20th century, and is now usually known as the Riviera dei Fiori. Though chaotic new building has ruined much of the coast close to Genoa, the interesting town of Albenga is still well preserved.

West to Savona

Albisola Superiore, the first town of any importance west of Genoa, was the birthplace of Pope Julius II (Giuliano della Rovere, 1443–1513), the warrior pope and nemesis of Cesare Borgia, caricatured by Erasmus for his love of things martial. It was he who signed the warrant permitting Henry VIII to marry his brother's widow Catherine of Aragon. He was a generous patron of Michelangelo, Bramante and Raphael. Albisola has been famous since the 16th century for its ceramics, examples of which are displayed in a museum in Villa Faraggiana.

Savona was a maritime power and rival of Genoa up until the 16th century. Its old district, overlooking the inner harbour, is surrounded by the regular streets of the new town. Traditionally its industries were iron founding and shipbreaking. Today it has a thermo-electric plant. In the main arcaded Via Paleocapa is the 16th-century church of San Giovanni Battista, with 18th-century paintings. The theatre (1850–53) is named after the native lyric poet Gabriello Chiabrera (1553–1638), known as the Italian Ronsard. Near a terrace of pretty Art Nouveau houses overlooking the harbour is the 14th-century Torre Pancaldo, named after Leon Pancaldo of Savona, Magellan's Genoese pilot.

Via Pia, with stone doorways, leads into the old town. The cathedral was built in 1589–1605 (façade of 1886). It contains an altarpiece by Albertino Piazza, a Romanesque font, and choir stalls of 1500. A little diocesan museum contains works by Ludovico Brea and the Master of Hoogstraten, and the 17th-century oratory of Santa Maria di Castello holds a polyptych by Vincenzo Foppa and Lodovico Brea (1490). Facing the cathedral is Palazzo Della Rovere, begun for Julius II by Giuliano da Sangallo, but never finished.

On the right of the cathedral is the Cappella Sistina, erected by Sixtus IV in memory of his parents and given a harmonious Baroque interior in 1764. It contains a fine marble tomb, with figures of the two della Rovere popes, Sixtus IV and Julius II. In Piazza del Mercato are two 12th-century towers. The small Pinacoteca Civica (*open Mon, Wed and Fri 8.30–1; Tues and Thur 2–7, Sat 8.30–1 & 3.30–6.30, Sun 3.30–6.30*) contains works by Donato de Bardi, Vincenzo Foppa and Giovanni Battista Carlone, and hosts a biennial ceramics exhibition (odd years).

The Fortezza del Priamar, on a hill on the southern seafront by the public gardens, was erected by the Genoese in 1542. The Risorgimento rebel Mazzini (*see p. 19*) was imprisoned here in 1830–31.

West from Savona

On the coast road west of Savona is **Zinola**, with a British military cemetery containing 104 graves, mostly from the wreck of the *Transylvania*, torpedoed off Savona in 1917. Beyond the headland of Bergeggi, with its islet offshore, is **Spotorno** with a fine sandy beach. D.H. Lawrence wrote *Lady Chatterley's Lover* here in 1926.

Noli, an important port in the Middle Ages, preserves its walls and three tall towers of brick, as well as some old houses and an 11th-century church.

The old village of **Finalborgo**, 2km inland from Finale Marina, has a church with a fine octagonal campanile (13th century). It contains a 16th-century tomb of the del Carretto family, whose ruined castle is nearby. In the cloister of Santa Caterina is the Museo Archeologico del Finale (*open summer Tues–Sun 10–12 & 4–7; winter 9–12 & 2.30–5*) with finds from the many local limestone caves in which prehistoric remains have been discovered. On the old Roman road further inland are about a dozen Roman bridges (1st century AD), five of them intact.

Loano, an old seaside town with palm groves, has a town hall in the Palazzo Doria (1578), which contains a 3rd-century mosaic pavement. Via Cavour 32 was the birthplace of Rosa Raimondi, Garibaldi's mother. Inland is the Grotta di Toirano, a remarkable stalactite cavern, with the only footprints of Mousterian man (probably Neanderthal) so far discovered, and a museum of local prehistory.

Albenga

Albenga was the Roman port of Albium Ingaunum, but is now over a kilometre from the sea, as the course of the Centa River was altered in the 13th century. It still has most of its medieval walls (on foundations of the 1st century BC) and three 17th-century gates; also about a dozen 12th–14th-century brick tower-houses, mostly well restored. The town has expanded towards the sea since the 19th century.

The cathedral, on late-4th- or early-5th-century foundations, with an elegant campanile of 1391, was reconstructed in its medieval form in 1967. The 5th-century **baptistery**, ten-sided without and octagonal within, preserves a fine Byzantine mosaic of the 5th or 6th century in its principal apse, and 8th-century transennae. The Palazzo Vecchio del Comune (1387 and 1421), incorporating a tall tower of c. 1300, houses the **Civico Museo Ingauno** (*open summer Tues–Sun 10–12.30 & 2.30–6; winter 9.30–12 & 3.30–7.30*) with prehistoric, Roman and medieval remains.

The charming **Piazzetta dei Leoni** has three Renaissance lions brought from Rome in 1608. The former bishop's palace has external frescoes (15th century). The little diocesan museum inside contains finds from the cathedral and paintings by Guido Reni and Domenico Piola. Via Bernardo Ricci (the Roman decumanus) crosses Via delle Medaglie (the cardo maximus) at the 13th-century Loggia dei Quattro Canti.

In Piazza San Michele is the **Museo Navale Romano** (*open summer Tues–Sun 9.30–12.30 & 3.30–7.30; winter 10–12.30 & 2.30–6*), containing more than 100 wine amphorae and marine fittings salvaged since 1950 from a Roman vessel sunk offshore in 100–90 BC. This is the largest Roman transport ship ever found in the Mediterranean; it was carrying more than 10,000 amphorae of wine (700 of which were recovered) from Campania to southern France and Spain. Attached to the museum is an important centre for underwater archaeology. In a fine 18th-century hall there is a collection of Albisola pharmacy jars. You can see scanty remains of the Roman city along the River Centa.

Alassio to Imperia

Alassio, a popular coastal resort, has an exceptionally mild winter climate and an excellent sandy beach. It is at the head of a wide, beautiful bay, facing almost due east. It was well known to the English by the end of the 19th century—they built the church of St John here—and is famed for the luxuriance of its gardens. While wintering here in 1904 Elgar composed his overture *In the South (Alassio)*. Carlo Levi, the writer and painter, spent much time in Alassio, and a collection of his paintings is to be exhibited in the town.

Offshore is the **Isola Gallinara**, or Gallinaria (boat trips from the *porto turistico* or from Loano). Little remains of the once powerful Benedictine monastery founded here in the 8th century, which at one time owned most of the Riviera di Ponente. St Martin of Tours took refuge from his Arian persecutors here in 356–60. The island is now privately owned; it has been a protected area since 1989, with lovely vegetation and grottoes, and interesting birdlife.

A short way west of Alassio is **Laigueglia**, a resort with an 18th-century church by Gian Domenico Baguti. Inland is Andora Castle, the finest medieval building on the Riviera del Ponente. Circular walls enclose a ruined castle and a late 13th-century church. A medieval bridge crosses the Merula.

Continuing westward, you come to **Cervo**, a very well-preserved medieval *borgo*, with a rich Baroque church by Giovanni Battista Marvaldi (1686). **Diano Marina**, an olive-growing town, with a sandy beach, is a summer and winter resort.

Imperia was created in 1923 by the fusion of Porto Maurizio, Oneglia and adjoining villages. Oneglia is at the mouth of the Impero torrent, from which the province takes its name. It is an important centre of the olive-oil trade, and has a large pasta factory on the seafront. Grock (Adrien Wettach), the great Swiss clown, died in the eclectic Villa Grock in 1959. There is a maritime museum, the Museo Navale Internazionale del Ponente Ligure, in Piazza Duomo (*open summer Wed and Sat 9pm–11pm; winter 3.30–7*), and an olive oil museum, the Museo dell'Olivo, Via Garessio 13 (*open Mon–Sat 9–12 & 3–6.30*).

San Remo and Taggia

San Remo is the largest summer and winter resort on the Italian Riviera, visited since the mid-19th century for its superb climate. Its villas and gardens lie in an amphitheatre in a wide bay, although the sea is separated from the town by the old railway line. Edward Lear (1812–88) spent his last years at San Remo, and built the Villa Emily (now Villa Verde) and Villa Tennyson (both named after Tennyson's wife). He died at the latter and was buried in San Remo. Alfred Nobel (1833–96) also died here, and it was here, in 1878, that Tchaikovsky finished his Fourth Symphony and *Eugene*

Onegin. The empress of Russia, Maria Alexandrovna, consort of Alexander II, lived here, surrounded after 1874 by a large Russian colony. The town is famous for its annual festivals, especially the International Song Contest.

Via Roma and the parallel Via Matteotti are the main streets of the modern town. In the latter, at no. 143, is the early-16th-century Palazzo Borea d'Olmo, which houses a small museum with an archaeological collection and Pinacoteca (*open Tues–Sat 9–12 & 3–6*). To the southwest, surrounded by gardens, in an Art Nouveau building (1904–06) by Eugenio Ferret, is the Casinò Municipale (*always open*), with celebrated gaming rooms.

The Corso dell'Imperatrice, lined with magnificent palm trees, leads past the Russian church (San Basilio) to the Parco Marsaglia, in which there is a monument to Garibaldi by Leonardo Bistolfi (1908).

Along the shore in the other direction, Via Nino Bixio leads to the Genoese fort of Santa Tecla (1755) and the mole of the old harbour. Corso Trento e Trieste continues along the waterfront, past the harbour for private boats, to the public gardens. The old district of La Pigna has quaint narrow streets. The duomo here is a 13th-century building enlarged in the 17th century.

Nearby **Taggia** is an interesting old village in a pretty position. The 15th-century Gothic church of San Domenico contains works by Ludovico Brea; the convent houses a small museum (*open Mon–Sat 9–12 & 3–6*) displaying paintings, sculpture, manuscripts, miniatures and prints ranging in date from the 14th to the 18th centuries. In the old walled town is a palace attributed to Bernini and the parish church, perhaps designed by him. A 16th-century bridge (on Romanesque foundations) of 16 arches crosses the Argentina.

The road to France

At the head of the pretty Valle Argentina is **Triora**, with remains of its fortifications, a painting by the Sienese artist Taddeo di Bartolo in the Collegiata, and a museum of witches and witchcraft (*open Mon–Fri 3–6.30, Sun and holidays 10–12 & 3–6.30*).

Ospedaletti, on a sheltered bay, is a horticultural centre, and has fine palms and eucalyptus trees.

Bordighera is another winter resort with a mild climate. It became known in Britain after 1855, when Giovanni Ruffini's *Doctor Antonio*, set in the town, was translated, and became a best-seller. By the end of the 19th century a large English colony had been established here. In Via Romana is the villa where Queen Margherita of Savoy (widow of Umberto I) died in 1926. It faces the Museo Bicknell, a local natural history and archaeology museum (*open Mon–Fri 9.30–1 & 1.30–4.45*), founded by the Englishman Clarence Bicknell in 1888. The International Library, at Via Romana 30, was also founded by Bicknell.

Ventimiglia is divided by the Roia into an old medieval town on a hill to the west and a new town on the coastal plain between the railway and the Via Aurelia. At the east end of the latter is the site of the Roman Albintimilium where Agricola spent his boyhood. Since its decline in the 13th century, Ventimiglia has had all the characteristics of a frontier town. In the old town is the 11th–12th-century cathedral with a portal of 1222; its apse adjoins the 11th-century baptistery. In San Michele (*open Sun only 10.30–12*), rebuilt c. 1100, the stoups are made up from Roman milestones. The Forte dell'Annunziata houses an archaeological museum (*open Tues–Sat 9–12.30 & 3–5, Sun and holidays 10–12.30*), founded in 1900 by Sir Thomas Hanbury (*see below*). It contains finds from the Roman *municipium*.

The lower town expanded after 1872 when it became an important station on the railway line to France. The excavations (begun in 1876) of the Roman town, which include a theatre of the 2nd century AD, and baths, are now isolated by modern buildings and the railway; you can see them from a viaduct on the Aurelia.

A road runs west to **La Mortola**, where the upper road (right) leads to a wooded cape with the Giardino Hanbury (*open June–Oct daily 9.30–7; Nov–Feb 10–5; March–Apr 9.30–6*), a remarkable botanic garden founded in 1867 by Sir Thomas Hanbury and his brother Daniel, a botanist. The splendid garden was famous in the late 19th century. It was acquired by the Italian State from the Hanbury family in 1960, and since 1983 has been run by Genoa University, which is now trying to rescue it from the grave state of abandon in which it was left after 1979. Hanbury collected exotic plants from all over the world—particularly from Asia and Africa. There are also woods of umbrella pines and cypresses, carob trees and palms, as well as medicinal plants, citrus fruits, etc. A section of the Roman Via Aurelia was exposed here by Hanbury, and a plaque recalls famous travellers who passed along this route (including Dante, Machiavelli and Pius VII).

On the beach below the frontier village of **Grimaldi**, at the Balzi Rossi, are several caves where relics of Palaeolithic man, dating as far back as 240,000 years ago, were discovered in 1892. Some of these are exhibited in the Museo Nazionale Preistorico (*open Tues–Sun 8.30–7.30*), founded here in 1898, again by Sir Thomas Hanbury. Ponte San Luigi is on the French frontier.

In the flowery Val Nervia, inland from Ventimiglia, is the pretty village of **Dolceacqua** beneath its splendid castle, first built in the 10th–11th centuries and transformed in the 15th and 16th by the patrician Genoese Doria family. It is now empty, though there are plans to turn it into an events centre. Below the village is a single-arched 15th-century bridge. **Pigna** is another pretty village (with late 15th-century works by Giovanni Canavesio); built on an interesting plan, it stands in a picturesque position opposite the fortified village of Castel Vittorio.

PRACTICAL INFORMATION

GETTING AROUND

• **By bus:** There are local bus services between the main towns; for information and schedules contact Riviera Trasporti, T: 0184 502030.

• **By rail:** The main rail line from Italy to southern France runs the length of the Riviera di Ponente; from Genoa to Nice takes c. 3hrs. The French TGV runs as far as Menton, making it possible to reach the area from Paris in c. 8hrs. Genoa enjoys frequent connections to Turin (1hr 30mins), Milan (1hr 30mins) and Pisa (1hr 40mins). There is also one daily Interregionale to and from Bologna (4hrs 50mins). Slow trains serve Savona from Turin and Alessandria (connection to Milan); and there is a scenic mountain railway from Cuneo to Ventimiglia (1hr 50mins).

INFORMATION OFFICES

Alassio Via Mazzini 62, T: 0182 647027, www.inforiviera.it
Albenga Via Martiri della Libertà 1, T: 0182 558740, www.inforiviera.it
San Remo Largo Nuovoloni 1, T: 0184 59059, www.rivieradeifiori.org
Informagiovani: Piazza Colombo, T: 0184 505002.
Savona Corso Italia 157r, T: 019 840 2321, www.inforiviera.it
Ventimiglia Via Cavour 61, T: 0184 351183, www.rivieradeifiori.org.

HOTELS

Many places are open only from spring to early autumn. The latter are marked

in the text; those without a specific mention of season are open all year round.

Alassio
€€ **Dei Fiori**. Warm and friendly, in a renovated townhouse. Viale Marconi 78, T: 0182 640519/640296/646376, www.hoteldeifiori-alassio.it
€€ **Grand Hotel Diana**. By the sea, with a lovely garden terrace. Closed Nov–Jan. Via Garibaldi 110, T: 0182 642701, www.dianagh.it
€€ **Regina**. A comfortable place on the seafront promenade. Closed Nov–Mar. Viale Hanbury 220, T: 0182 640215, F: 0182 660092

Cenova
€ **Negro**. In the hills above Alassio, a calm, quiet place with 12 rooms. Via Canada 10, T: 0183 34089, www.cenova.it/Albergo.htm

Finale Ligure
€€ **Punta Est**. An 18th-century villa in a shady park overlooking the sea. Closed Nov–Apr. Via Aurelia 1, T: 019 600612, www.puntaest.com

San Remo
€€€ **Royal**. A fine hotel with lush gardens, heated pool, and outside dining in fair weather; closed Nov–Dec. Corso Imperatrice 80, T: 0184 5391, www.royalhotelsanremo.com

YOUTH HOSTELS

Finale Ligure
€ **Castello Vuillermin**, Via G. Caviglia 46, T: 019 690515, hostelfinaleligure@libero.it
Savona
€ **Villa De Franceschini**, Via alla Strà

29, T: 019 263222,
concaverdehostel@iol.it

RESTAURANTS

Alassio

€€€ **Il Palma**. Delicious interpretations of traditional Ligurian recipes, in a historic building in the heart of town. Closed Wed and Dec–Feb. Via Cavour 5, T: 0182 640314.

Albisola Marina

€€ **Da Mario**. Traditional fish restaurant, with outside seating in summer. Closed Wed and Sept. Corso Bigliati 70, T: 019 481640.

Albisola Superiore

€€ **Au Fundegu**. Family-run restaurant situated in a beautiful historic building, specialising in traditional recipes. Closed Thur. Via Spotorno 87, T: 019 480341.

€ **Trattoria del Molino**. Country trattoria with good local food and outstanding views. Closed Tues. Piazza Cairoli 2, Località Ellera, T: 019 49043.

Arma di Taggia

€€ **La Conchiglia**. Outstanding regional cuisine, especially fish. Closed Wed (open Wed evening in July–Aug), June and Nov–Dec. Lungomare 33, T: 0184 43169.

Bergeggi

€€€ **Claudio**. Superior traditional restaurant (with rooms) on a clifftop above the sea. Closed Mon, midday Tues and Jan. Via XXV Aprile 37, T: 019 859750.

Bordighera

€€ **Carletto**. A truly outstanding fish restaurant. Closed Wed, June–July and Nov–Dec. Via Vittorio Emanuele 339, T: 0184 261725.

€€ **Il Tempo Ritrovato**. Refined restaurant that offers a limited but daily changing menu and carefully prepared regional and innovative recipes. Closed Sun. Via Vittorio Emanuele 144, T: 0184 261207.

€ **La Via Romana**. Excellent traditional fish restaurant. Closed Wed and midday Thur. Via Romana 57, T: 0184 266681.

€ **Magiargè**. Simple *osteria* offering delicious local cooking and good wines. Closed Thur. Piazza Giacomo Viale, T: 0184 262946.

Borgo Verezzi

€€ **Da Casetta**. A warm family-run place in a historic building, serving regional specialities. Closed midday (except Sun and holidays), Tues and Nov. Piazza San Pietro 12, T: 019 610166.

€€ **D.O.C.** Delicious Ligurian food in an elegant villa setting. Closed Mon (midday only in summer). Via Vittorio Veneto 1, T: 019 611477.

Imperia

€€ **Lanterna Blu**. Truly outstanding seafood and excellent French and Italian wines, by the harbour. Closed Wed, Oct and Dec. Via Scarincio 32, Località Porto Marizio, Borgo Marina, T: 0183 650178.

Mele (near Voltri)

€€ **Osteria dell'Acquasanta**. *Osteria* offering traditional dishes from Liguria and northern Italy and good wines. Closed Mon. Via Acquasanta 281, Località Acquasanta, T: 010 638035.

San Remo

€€€ **Da Giannino**. One of the region's best restaurants, serving delicious local specialities, especially fish. Closed Sun evening, Mon and Oct.

Lungomare Trento e Trieste 23, T: 0184 504014.

€€€ **Paolo e Barbara**. Outstanding Ligurian cuisine with a personal twist. Closed Wed and midday Thur, Dec–Jan and June–July. Via Roma 47, T: 0184 531653.

€€ **Il Bagatto**. Restaurant serving personal interpretations of traditional recipes. Closed Sun and June–July. Via Matteotti 145, T: 0184 531925.

€€ **La Pignese**. Traditional trattoria, serving good local dishes. Closed Mon and June. Piazza Sardi 7, T: 0184 501929.

€€ **Osteria del Marinaio**. Good seafood and other local specialities. Closed Mon and Oct–Dec. Via Gaudio 28, T: 0184 501919.

Savona

€€ **A Spurcacciuna**. Restaurant of the Hotel Mare, offering especially good seafood. Closed Wed and Dec–Jan. Via Nizza 89r, T: 019 264065.

€€ **Molo Vecchio**. Elegant restaurant with outdoor dining on the sea, offers regional and creative recipes and an excellent wine selection. Closed Tues. Via Baglietto 8r, T: 019 854219.

€ **Bosco delle Ninfe**. An old-fashioned *osteria* known for good seafood. Closed Mon. Via Ranco 10, T: 019 823976.

Vallecrosia

€€ **Giappun**. Excellent seafood served with flair. Closed Wed, July and Nov. Via Maonaira 7, T: 0184 250560.

Varigotti

€€ **Muraglia-Conchiglia d'Oro**. Outstanding fish and other regional dishes. Closed Wed (and Tues, Oct–Mar), Jan–Feb. Via Aurelia 133, T: 019 698015.

Ventimiglia

€€€ **Baia Beniamin**. Exquisite seafood restaurant (with rooms), on a luxuriant little bay. Closed Sun evening and Mon (Mon only in summer), Apr and Nov. Corso Europa 63, Località Grimaldi Inferiore, T: 0184 38002.

€€€ **Balzi Rossi**. A very fine regional restaurant with outside seating in summer and beautiful views of sea and coast. Closed Mon, midday Tues (and midday Sun in summer), March and Nov–Dec. Ponte San Ludovico 11, T: 0184 38132.

MARKETS

Alassio *Collezionismo d'Antiquariato*, antiques, days vary.

Albenga *Mercato dell'Antiquaritato e del Curioso*, antiques and curiosities, mid-July and mid-Aug.

Arma di Taggia *Collezionismo Sotto i Portici*, collectables, third Sat of the month.

Dolceacqua *Mercatino Biologico, dell'Articianato e dell'Antiquariato*, mixing antiques, crafts and organic foods, last Sun of the month.

Finale Ligure *Mercato dell'Antiquariato*, antiques, first Sat and Sun of the month.

Savona *Mercato dell'Antiquariato*, antiques, first Sat and Sun of the month.

Ventimiglia *Mercatino Brocante*, crafts, antiques and flowers, first three Sats and last Sun of the month.

FESTIVALS & EVENTS

Cervo International Chamber Music Festival, Aug.

Imperia *Rally delle Palme*, car race, Apr; *Infiorata del Corpus Domini*, Corpus Christi flower festival (also at Diano Marina and Cervo), June; *Raduno di Vele d'Epoca*, biennial antique sailing boat show, in even years, Sept.

San Remo *Concorso Internazionale di Arte Floreale Città di San Remo*, international flower show, and *San Remoinfiore*, flower display along the Corso, Jan. *San Remo Rally Storico 'Coppa dei Fiori'*, antique car rally, Apr. International San Remo Yacht Meeting, May; *Festival internazionale del Film e del Video Musicale*, film and music video festival, *Regata della Giraglia*, regatta, June; *Campionato Mondiale dei Fuochi d'Artificio*, world fireworks championship, July; *San Remo Imagine Jazz-San Remo Blues*, jazz-blues festival, July–Aug. *Rally San Remo-Rally d'Italia*, car races, Sept.

Taggia *La Luna e i Suoi Raggi*, street-theatre festival, July–Aug. *Festa di Primavera*, concerts, art and flower shows throughout the Riviera dei Fiori, March.

THE RIVIERA DI LEVANTE

The coastal strip east of Genoa is known as the Riviera di Levante. Although the beauty of the landscape, with olive groves and luxuriant gardens, has been threatened by indiscriminate new building, its character is as tenacious as that of its inhabitants. The best-preserved part is the lovely peninsula of Portofino. Further to the east and south are the Cinque Terre, five tiny villages huddled on a dramatic, rocky coast. At the eastern tip of Liguria lies the Gulf of La Spezia, ringed with lovely villages.

PORTOFINO & ITS PENINSULA

The delightful Penisola di Portofino is of great botanic interest for its characteristic Mediterranean *macchia* (scrub forest) mixed with thick vegetation more typical of central Europe. A scenic road (one of several on the peninsula) skirts its eastern shore to **Portofino**, a romantic fishing village with pretty houses, now an exclusive resort in a beautiful position, partly on a small wooded headland, and partly in a little bay which has offered a safe anchorage to boats since Roman times. Portofino was much visited by the English in the 19th century. It is now the haunt of wealthy yachtsmen and well-heeled Italians, many of whom own villas here. High above the village, towards the **Punta del Capo**, is the little church of San Giorgio, which is reputed to contain the relics of St George, brought by Crusaders from the Holy Land. In front of the church is the 16th-century Castello Brown, reconstructed in the 18th century; (*open Tues–Sun 10 7, closed Jan*).

Camogli, on the west side of the peninsula, is a picturesque little fishing port descending steeply to a rocky shore. It was famous for its merchant ships in the days of sail, its fleet having played a prominent part in the naval battles of Napoleon, of Louis-Philippe, and in the Crimea. It is interesting for its architecture, with unusually tall houses lining the seafront. The Dragonara castle has an aquarium (*open 10–12, 3–7; winter Fri–Sun only*). The Museo Marinaro (*open Mon, Thur–Fri 9–12, Wed, Sat–Sun also 3–6 or 4–7*) has models of ships, ex-votos, navigational instruments, etc.

A pretty walk leads south from Camogli to San Rocco, the Romanesque church of San Nicolò, and (1 hour 15mins) **Punta Chiappa**, a fishing hamlet, where the view is remarkable for the ever-changing colours of the sea. A rough-hewn altar on the point reproduces in mosaic a graffito found at San Nicolò.

Golfo di Tigullio

On the east side of the peninsula, on the broad bay between Portofino and Sestri Levante known as the Golfo di Tigullio, is **Santa Margherita Ligure**, a fishing village that became a seaside resort at the turn of the 20th century. It is still one of the most popular resorts of the Riviera. The lovely park of the 16th-century Villa Durazzo is open daily in summer. In the church of the Cappuccini is a fine 13th-century statue of the *Madonna Enthroned*.

A sheltered beach (Monterosso al Mare) on the Riviera di Levante.

On the road south to Portofino is the former 14th-century monastery of La Cervara, where Francis I of France was held prisoner after the Battle of Pavia (1525, *see p. 151*), and where Gregory XI rested on the return of the papacy from Avignon to Rome (1377).

The pretty road from Santa Margherita to Rapallo passes **San Michele di Pagana**, where the church contains a fine *Crucifixion* by van Dyck. Nearby, in a large garden, is the Villa Spinola, where the Treaty of Rapallo was signed in 1920 between Italy and the new Kingdom of Serbs, Croats and Slovenes, agreeing the independence of Fiume (now Rijeka, Croatia). Italy also undertook to renounce all other claims to Dalmatian territory. The church of San Lorenzo della Costa has a triptych by Quentin Metsys (1499).

Rapallo, in a sheltered position at the head of its gulf, was much visited by the English in the 19th and 20th centuries. It is the best known holiday resort on the Riviera di Levante and is popular both in summer and winter. The lovely surroundings, which used to be the main attraction of Rapallo, were spoilt by new buildings in the 1960s and 1970s, and the mole of the new port has blocked the view out to sea. In the town are the Collegiate church (1606), and the restored castle in the harbour (open for exhibitions). In the 19th century Villa Tigullio, surrounded by a public park, is a museum illustrating the local handicraft of lace-making. The Villino Chiaro, on the coast road, was from 1910 the home of writer Max Beerbohm (1872–1956). Ezra Pound also spent much time in Rapallo after 1959. A winding road ascends inland through woods to the sanctuary of Montallegro, where the 16th-century church contains frescoes by Genoese artist Nicolò Barabino and a Byzantine painting.

PORTOFINO WALKS

Delightful walks can be taken in the Portofino area. The local visitor information office hands out free maps, and trails are generally clearly marked and well maintained. The quickest and easiest walk takes you from Portofino over the hill of San Giorgio to the Punta del Capo (15mins), with a lighthouse and a small café serving refreshments (including home-made ice-cream) in summer. Another easy walk of c. 1 hour takes you to Santa Margherita, passing the tiny sandy bay of Paraggi, at the mouth of a wooded glen. A bridlepath involving some stiff climbs leads in an hour and a half to Portofino Vetta, in a large park beneath Monte di Portofino (610m). From the summit there is a wonderful view, and there are beautiful short walks throughout the area.

A very popular walk (1 hour 30mins–2 hours; moderately strenuous) leads via Case del Prato to San Fruttuoso di Capodimonte, a picturesque little hamlet on the sea in a rocky inlet of a lovely bay surrounded by wooded hills. It can only be reached by boat (from Camogli, Portofino, Santa Margherita Ligure and Rapallo) or on foot. Its Benedictine abbey (*open May–Sept Tues–Sun 10–6; Oct and March–Apr 10–4; Dec–Feb weekends only 10–4; closed Nov*) was founded here beside an abundant spring, and was of great importance in the 11th and 12th centuries. It was reconstructed by one of the great Genoese families, the Doria, in the 13th century, but deserted by the monks in 1467. It survived under Doria patronage until 1885, after which the buildings were taken over by fishermen and severely damaged by the sea in 1915. They were donated by the Doria Pamphili family to the FAI (Italian environment foundation) in 1983.

The abbey and church are supported on large vaulted arches. The upper cloister was built in the 12th century and restored in the 16th (it includes Roman and medieval capitals). The lower cloister and church, with an unusual dome, date in part from the 10th century. The 13th-century crypt contains Doria tombs in white marble and grey stone. The grey square Torre Doria was erected on the point in 1561 as a defence against pirates. A bronze statue of Christ, by Guido Galletti (1954), stands offshore, eight fathoms down, as protector of all those who work beneath the sea.

Chiavari and Sestri Levante

Chiavari is a shipbuilding town with an arcaded old main street and a sandy beach and port for small boats at the mouth of the Entella. Here Garibaldi, on his arrival in exile from the south, was arrested on 6 September 1849 'in the most polite and friendly manner possible', since his forebears came from the town. Chiavari was also the family home of two other prominent figures of the Risorgimento, Nino Bixio and Giuseppe Mazzini. A large necropolis dating from the 8th–7th centuries BC has been excavated here; the finds are exhibited in the little archaeological museum in the

17th–18th-century Palazzo Rocca. On the second floor of the palace are 16th–17th-century paintings, representative of the Genoese school, including the Torreglia collection.

Inland, on Monte Caucaso, is **Monteghirfo**, an isolated hamlet amid chestnut woods with a local ethnographic museum; and in the Sturla Valley is **Terrarossa**, popularly thought to be the home of Columbus's grandparents. In a side valley (reached from Borzonasca) is the lovely **abbey of Borzone**, with a church of c. 1244.

Lavagna, a resort separated from Chiavari by the Entella bridge, has a long sandy beach and is famous for its slate quarries. A pretty road leads up the valley to the early Gothic Basilica dei Fieschi, founded by Innocent IV (Sinibaldo Fieschi, d.1254), who was born in Lavagna.

Sestri Levante, in a delightful position at the base of the peninsula of Isola (once an island), is a summer resort, spoilt since the 1950s by new buildings. From Piazza Matteotti, with the 17th-century parish church, a street ascends past the restored Romanesque church of San Nicolò to the Grand Hotel dei Castelli, rebuilt with antique materials (1925) on Genoese foundations, with a magnificent park, at the end of the peninsula. Marconi carried out his first experiments in short-wave radio transmission from the Torretta here. The Galleria Rizzi has a modest collection of local paintings (*open Apr–Oct Sun 10.30–1; May–Sept Wed 4–7; June–Sept 9.30pm–11.30pm*).

THE CINQUE TERRE

The Cinque Terre are five delightful little medieval villages—Riomaggiore, Manarola, Corniglia, Vernazza and Monterosso al Mare—on a beautiful unspoilt stretch of rocky coast. These were remote fishing hamlets accessible only by sea before the advent in 1874 of the railway, which tunnels through the high cliffs between the railway stations. The Cinque Terre are now famous, having remained relatively isolated and been largely preserved from new building, as no coastal road has ever been built here; by car they can only be reached along winding, steep inland roads.

The approach from Sestri is made via **Bonassola**, a village in beautiful surroundings. A sea grotto here has been turned into a marine study centre. **Levanto**, on the coast to the south, once a secluded bathing resort in a little bay, has been developed for tourism. It has lovely gardens, and a good sandy beach, and preserves remains of its old walls along with a 13th–15th-century church.

A steep, winding inland road (or an equally steep and winding coastal trail) leads from here to **Monterosso al Mare**, the northernmost and largest of the Cinque Terre. It has a good church of 1300 and, higher up, the church of San Francesco with a *Crucifixion* attributed to van Dyck. One of Italy's greatest modern poets, the Genoa-born Eugenio Montale (1896–1981), spent much of his youth at Monterosso. It now has some incongruous new buildings, and the sandy beach is crowded in summer.

Vernazza is a charming port, interesting for its architecture—the cylindrical tower is one of Italy's oldest lighthouses (torches were burned at the top). It also has a Gothic church (on two levels) and pleasant cafés on the harbour. **Corniglia**, the highest of the five villages, lies above the sea, surrounded by orchards and vineyards (it has been known for its excellent wine since Roman times). It has a Gothic church. **Manarola** has an equally spectacular position with splendid views.

Riomaggiore, connected to La Spezia by road, has an interesting layout on the steep cliffside. The fishermen have to pull their boats up on shore (and further up into the streets in rough weather). The village came under the control of the Genoese Republic in 1276. The 14th-century parish church contains a 15th-century triptych and a painting by Domenico Fiasella. The 19th-century post-Impressionist landscape painter Telemaco Signorini often stayed here.

In the Val di Vara, inland from the Cinque Terre, is **Varese Ligure** with a 15th-century castle of the Fieschi (well restored). A steep road leads up from here to the spectacular Passo di Cento Croci (1053m) on the border with Emilia Romagna.

Beyond Riomaggiore, if you're walking, you join the lofty Cinque Terre high trail, which in three hours of challenging hiking takes you across the wild, rocky peninsula of Portovenere. Excursion boats from the Cinque Terre follow the same route, affording truly memorable views of the sea and coast.

Vernazza.

Portovenere harbourfront.

PORTOVENERE & THE GULF OF LA SPEZIA

Portovenere, the ancient Portus Veneris, a dependency of Genoa since 1113, is a charming fortified village built on the sloping shore of the Bocchette, the narrow strait (114m wide) separating the Isola Palmaria from the mainland. On a rocky promontory at the southern end of the village, the restored 6th- and 13th-century church of San Pietro commands a splendid view of Palmaria and the lofty cliffs of the Cinque Terre. The **Grotto Arpaia,** formerly beneath it, collapsed in 1932. It was known as Byron's Cave, for it was from here that the poet started his swim across the gulf to San Terenzo to visit Shelley at Casa Magni, in 1822 (*see below*).

In the upper part of the village is the beautiful 12th-century church of San Lorenzo, above which (steep climb) towers the 16th-century castello (*open daily 10–12 & 2–6; winter 3–5*). Below the church, steps descend to the characteristic 'Calata Doria', where tall houses rise from the sea.

The rugged island of **Palmaria**, with numerous caves, can be visited by boat (daily service) from Portovenere. The island has been purchased by a developer and is in danger of being turned into a tourist resort. On the northern point is the old Torre della Scuola, built by the Genoese in 1606 and blown up by the English fleet in 1800. The island is noted for the gold-veined black *portoro* marble.

On the opposite (northern) shore of the gulf is the Bay of Lerici, with the fishing village of San Terenzo. On a small cape is Casa Magni, the 'white house with arches', the last home of Shelley (1822).

SHELLEY'S LAST DAYS

In 1822 the Shelleys moved to a new home on the bay of Lerici. Mary Shelley wrote: 'I am convinced that the few months we passed there were the happiest he had ever known. He was never better than when I last saw him, full of spirits and joy, embark for Leghorn, that he might there welcome Leigh Hunt to Italy'. Shelley's plan was to set up a periodical, with Hunt as editor and himself and Byron as contributors. It was to be entitled *The Liberal*, and would challenge the more conservative views of *Blackwoods* and *The Quarterly Review*. But nothing was to come of the plan. On that fatal voyage to Livorno, on 8 July 1822, Shelley and his friend Lieutenant Williams were caught in a storm. Their little boat, a schooner custom-built in Genoa, sank like a stone. The two bodies were recovered on the beach near Viareggio, where they were cremated in the presence of Byron and Leigh Hunt.

Lerici is a resort with a splendid 13th–16th-century castle (*opened by appointment with the custodian; T: 0187 965108*). Tuscan coaches were embarked here by felucca for Genoa before the modern Via Aurelia was built.

A coast road, roughly paralleled by a beautiful walking trail, runs on above the charming little bay of **Fiascherino** (where D.H. Lawrence lived in 1913–14), to **Tellaro**, a medieval village that rises sheer from the sea—and that has suffered damage due to the instability of the rocks here. A higher by-road from Lerici continues around the wooded peninsula up to **Montemarcello**, a pretty village of red and pink houses surrounded by olives, with fine views of Tellaro and of the Gulf of La Spezia. A path leads to Punta Corno with a bird's-eye view of the coast.

La Spezia

La Spezia, at the head of its fine gulf, has been one of the chief naval ports of Italy since a naval arsenal was built here in 1861. Laid out in the late 19th century, the town forms a rectilinear L round a prominent hill.

The Castello San Giorgio hosts the Museo Civico (*open daily except Tues, 9.30–12.30 & 5–8*) with an archaeological section that contains interesting Ligurian statue-stelae from a Lunigiana cult of the Bronze and Iron Age, found on the bed of the River Magra, and Roman remains from Luni. Santa Maria Assunta, the cathedral until 1975, was founded in 1271 but later rebuilt. It contains a large coloured terracotta by Andrea della Robbia. At the seaward end of Corso Cavour are fine public gardens. The Naval Arsenal, the most important in Italy, was built by Domenico Chiodo in 1861–69. Next door is the Museo Tecnico Navale (*open summer Mon–Sat 8.30–1.15 & 4.15–9.45, Sun 8.30–1.15; winter Mon–Sat 8.30–6, Sun 10.15–3.45*), where models and relics collected since 1571 illustrate the marine history of Savoy and Italy. The Castello di San Giorgio dates from the 13th century. The Museo Amedeo Lia (*open Tues–Sun 10–6*), opened in

1996, contains an important collection (made since the 1940s) of 13th–15th-century paintings (Coppo di Marcovaldo, Pietro Lorenzetti, Bernardo Daddi, Sassetta, Giovanni Bellini), as well as later works, decorative arts, illuminated manuscripts, small bronzes.

Sarzana and the Lunigiana

The last Ligurian city before Tuscany, **Sarzana** is an ancient fortified town, once of great strategic importance as the southeastern outpost of the Genoese Republic. The *cittadella*, a rectangular fort with six circular bastions, was rebuilt for Lorenzo de'Medici in 1487 by Francesco di Giovanni (Il Francione). For years used as a prison, it is now empty and awaiting restoration. On the main Via Mazzini is the cathedral (the see of the Bishop of Luni was transferred here in 1204). It contains a panel painting of the *Crucifixion*, signed and dated 1138 by a certain Guglielmus, and 15th-century marble reliefs by Leonardo Riccomanni of Pietrasanta. Some of the paintings are by Domenico Fiasella, who was born here in 1589. Nearby is Sant'Andrea, the oldest monument in the town, probably dating from the 11th century. The 16th-century portal has pagan caryatids. The church of San Francesco, north of the town, contains the tomb by Giovanni di Balduccio of Guarnerio degli Antelminelli, son of Castruccio Castracani, who died as a child in 1322. Castracani was a great *condottiere*, who served a number of emperors in the Ghibelline cause. His romanticised and embellished biography was written by Machiavelli. On a hill to the east is the Fortezza di Sarzanello, known as the Fortezza of Castruccio Castracani, restored by the Florentines in 1493 to designs by Il Francione and Luca del Caprina.

Ameglia, with picturesque houses dominated by a 10th-century castle, overlooks the yacht basin at Bocca di Magra. The old port of Luni and a necropolis have been excavated here. A road leads back across the river to the site of the important Roman colony of **Luni**. It was founded in 177 BC beside the sea on the site of a prehistoric settlement famous for its statue-stelae, displayed in La Spezia and in the museum of Pontremoli. Of great commercial and strategic importance in the 2nd century AD, Luni was well known for its marble. A bishopric by the 5th century and still thriving in the Middle Ages, it was important enough to lend its name to the whole district, the Lunigiana. By the 13th century, partly because of the flooding of the river Magra, and malaria, the town had disappeared. Its lost greatness is mentioned by Dante in *Il Paradiso*, where he talks of Luni having 'passed away'. The walled city has a typical Roman plan, with remains of the forum and capitolium (150 BC) dedicated to Jupiter, Juno and Minerva, as well as traces of two houses and another large temple. The Museo Archeologico Nazionale (*open daily 9–7*), in the centre of the excavated area, contains finds from here and the surrounding territory (Ortonovo, Ameglia, etc.), including marble sculptures, bronzes and mosaics. An honorific inscription is dedicated to M. Acilius Glabrio, who defeated Antiochus III at Thermopylae in 191 BC. To he east, outside the walls, is the amphitheatre dating from the 2nd century AD.

A road leads inland from Luni to the pretty old village of **Castelnuovo Magra**. In the church are a painting of the *Crucifixion* attributed to van Dyck and a large *Calvary* by Brueghel the Younger. The 13th-century Malaspina castle has associations with Dante.

PRACTICAL INFORMATION

GETTING AROUND

• **By rail:** The main rail line from Rome to Paris follows the Tyrrhenian coast to Genoa. Fast Eurostar trains cover the 500km from Rome to Genoa (Brignole Station) in c. 4hrs 15mins; Intercities in c. 5hrs. Both stop in Liguria at La Spezia and often at Sarzana, Sestri Levante, Chiavari and Rapallo. There is one Intercity daily from Florence to Genoa, stopping at Sarzana (1hr 40mins), La Spezia (1hr 50mins), Sestri Levante (2hrs 20mins), Chiavari (2hrs 30mins) and Rapallo (2hrs 40mins). Commuter trains run up and down the coast at frequent (c. 30mins) intervals throughout the day. Local trains run between Sestri Levante and La Spezia at c. hourly intervals, with stops at Monterosso al Mare, Vernazza, Corniglia, Manarola and Riomaggiore (the Cinque Terre). Village-to-village journey time is c. 10mins.

• **By boat:** In summer from Rapallo and Santa Margherita Ligure every 30mins for Portofino and San Fruttuoso. In winter, 3 or 4 services daily. Information from Servizio Marittimo del Tigullio (T: 0185 284670). Regular services also from Camogli every hour in summer to San Fruttuoso; from La Spezia and Lerici in the Gulf of La Spezia, and (June–Sep) from Monterosso al Mare for the Cinque Terre. Information from Navigazione Golfo dei Poeti (T: 0187 732987, www.navigazionegolfodeipoeti.it).

• **By bus:** There are local bus services between the main towns on the Riviera.

INFORMATION OFFICES

La Spezia Viale Mazzini 47, T: 0187 770900, www.aptcinqueterre.sp.it
Portofino Via Roma 35, T: 0185 269024, www.apttigullio.liguria.it
Portovenere Piazza Bastreri 7, T: 0187 790691, www.portovenere.it
Rapallo Lungomare Vittorio Veneto 7, T: 0185 230346, www.apttigullio.liguria.it

HOTELS

Places open only from spring to autumn are marked in the text; those without a mention of season are open year-round.

Ameglia
€ **Garden**. Small (10 rooms) and secluded, on the sea at the mouth of the River Magra. Via Fabricotti 162, Località Bocca di Magra, T: 0187 65086, F: 0187 65613.
€ **Il Gabbiano**. Small (10 rooms) and comfortable, with good views and outside restaurant seating in summer. Closed Oct–May. Via della Pace 2, Località Montemarcello, T: 0187 600066.

Camogli
€€ **Cenobio dei Dogi**. An elegant old place with terraced park overlooking the sea. Via Cuneo 34, T: 0185 7241, www.cenobio.it

Chiavari
€ **Mignon**. Small and pleasant, not far from the waterfront. Closed Nov. Via Salietti 7, T: 0185 324977, www.hotelmignonchiavari.it

La Spezia
€€ **Firenze e Continentale**. Provincial

elegance in an early-20th-century townhouse. Closed Dec. Via Paleocapa 7, T: 0187 713210/713200, www.hotelfirenzecontinentale.it

Lerici

€€ **Doria Park**. Quiet and restful, with good sea views. Closed Dec–Jan. Via Doria 2, T: 0187 967124, F: 0187 966459.

€€ **Europa**. High up in the hills, surrounded by trees, with good views of the gulf. Via Carpanini 1, T: 0187 967800, www.europahotel.it

€€ **Il Nido**. In the olive groves 4km outside town. Closed Nov–Mar. Via Fiascherino 75, Località Fiascherino, T: 0187 969263/ 964593/967286, www.hotelnido.com

€ **Byron**. A simple place on the sea, with great views. Via Carpanini 1, T: 0187 967104, F: 0187 967409.

Levanto

€€ **Stella Maris**. Small (8 rooms) and cosy, near the waterfront. Closed Nov. Via Marconi 4, T: 0187 808258, www.hotelstellamaris.it

Manarola

€ **Ca' d'Andrean**. 10 rooms in a renovated oil- and wine-press. Closed Nov. Via Discovolo 101, T: 0187 920040, www.cadandrean.it

Monterosso al Mare

€€ **Palme**. Modern and comfortable, with a small garden. Closed Nov–March. Via IV Novembre 18, T: 0187 829013/829037, www.hotelpalme.it

Portofino

€€€ **Splendido**. One of the top European luxury hotels, above the town with magnificent views in all directions. Closed Jan–March. Salita Baratta 16, T: 0185 269551, www.splendido.orient-express.com

€€ **Nazionale**. Quiet elegance, excellent location. Closed Dec–Feb. Via Roma 8, T: 0185 269575, www.nazionaleportofino.com

€€ **Piccolo**. A cosy little place with pleasant garden and good sea views. Closed Nov. Via Duca degli Abruzzi 31, T: 0185 269015, F: 0185 269621.

Portovenere

€€ **Paradiso**. A pleasant family-run establishment, with comfortable rooms and good views of the gulf. Via Garibaldi 34, T: 0187 790612, www.paradisohotel.net

Rapallo

€€ **Astoria**. A tastefully renovated Art Nouveau villa on the sea. Closed Dec–Jan. Via Gramsci 4, T: 0185 273533, www.astoriarapallo.it

€€ **Grand Hotel Bristol**. An Art Nouveau villa in a shady park, with roof-garden restaurant and views of the gulf. Closed Jan–Feb. Via Aurelia Orientale 369, T: 0185 273313, F: 0185 55800.

€€ **Riviera**. An Art Nouveau villa, by the park, with sea views. Closed Nov–Dec. Piazza IV Novembre 2, T: 0185 50248, www.hotel-riviera.it

Riomaggiore

€ **Due Gemelli**. Small (13 rooms) and secluded (amid the vineyards and pine woods by the sea, 9km from the town), with good views. Località Campi, T: 0187 731320, www.duegemelli.it

Santa Margherita Ligure

€€€ **Grand Hotel Miramare**. An old-fashioned Riviera hotel, on the sea with park and pool. Lungomare Milite Ignoto 30, T: 0185 287013, www.grandhotelmiramare.it

€€€ **Imperial Palace**. A place from another century, with park and pool by the sea. Closed Dec–Feb. Via Pagana 19, T: 0185 288991, F: 0185 284223.

€€ **Continental**. Elegant and refined, in a palm-and pine-shaded garden by the sea. Via Pagana 8, T: 0185 286512, www.hotel-continental.it

€ **Fasce**. Small and cosy. Closed Jan–Feb. Via Bozzo 3, T: 0185 286435, www.hotelfasce.it

Sestri Levante

€€ **Due Mari**. A renovated patrician villa with garden Closed Nov–Dec. Vico del Coro 18, T: 0185 42695, F: 0185 42698.

€€ **Grand Hotel dei Castelli**. A Gothic-revival castle in a shady park. Closed Oct -Apr. Via alla Penisola 26, T: 0185 485780, www.hoteldeicastelli.com

€€ **Grand Hotel Villa Balbi**. Occupying a luxurious 17th-century villa and outbuildings, with large park and heated pool. Closed Nov–March. Viale Rimembranza 1, T: 0185 42941, www.villabalbi.it

€€ **Miramare**. Calm and comfortable, with a garden on the bay. Via Cappellini 9, T: 0185 480855, www.miramaresestrilevante.com

€€ **Vis a Vis**. On a headland amid olive groves, with good views over the town and sea. Closed Dec. Via della Chiusa 28, T: 0185 42661/480801, www.hotelvisavis.it

€ **Sereno**. A small (10 rooms), quiet, family-run establishment. Via Val di Canepa 96, T: 0185 43302/3, www.hotelsereno.com

Chiavari

€ **Camping Al Mare**, Via Preli 30, T: 0185 304633, F: 0185 304633.

Ameglia

€€ **Dai Pironcelli**. Simple trattoria with good local food and excellent wines. Open evenings only (all day Sun), closed June and Nov. Via delle Mura 45, Località Montemarcello, T: 0187 601252.

€€ **Locanda delle Tamerici**. Restaurant (with rooms) serving truly outstanding seafood, with outside seating in summer. Closed Tues and midday Wed (except in summer). Via Litoranea 106, Località Fiumaretta, T: 0187 64262.

€€ **Paracucchi-Locanda dell'Angelo**. Restaurant (with rooms) offering innovative fish dishes. Closed Mon (except in summer) and Jan. Via XXV Aprile, Località Ca' di Sgabello, T: 0187 64391.

Castelnuovo Magra

€€ **Armanda**. Family run trattoria offering traditional home cooking. Closed Wed, June 15–30. Piazza Garibaldi 6, T: 0187 674410.

€€ **Trattoria Armanda**. Historic trattoria, a paragon of traditional Ligurian Levante cooking. Closed Thur, late June–early July, Dec 24–Jan 6. Piazza Garibaldi 6, T: 0187 674410.

Chiavari

€€€ **Ca' Peo**. Restaurant (with rooms) offering outstanding Ligurian mountain and seafood dishes. Closed Mon and midday Tues. Via dei Caduti (Strada Panoramica) 80, Località Leivi, T: 0185 319696.

€€ **Enoteca Piccolo Ristorante**. Family-run restaurant, creative regional cooking. Closed Tues, Aug 1–15. Via Bontà 22, T: 0185 306498.

€€ **Lord Nelson**. A well-known seafood restaurant (with rooms). Closed

Wed (except in Aug) and Nov–Dec. Corso Valparaiso 27, T: 0185 302595.

La Spezia

€ **Al Negrao**. Traditional trattoria offering simple regional dishes. Closed Mon, Dec–Jan and Sept. Via Genova 430, T: 0187 701564.

€€ **Parodi**. Good traditional restaurant specialising in fish. Closed Sun. Viale Amendola 212, T: 0187 715777.

€€ **Quinto Chilometro**. Romantic restaurant in an historic building, creative cooking, specialising in meats and mushrooms. Closed Wed and July. Via Montalbano 1, T: 0187 700130.

Lerici

€€ **Barcaccia**. Elegant restaurant with open-air space, specialising in creative fish recipes. Closed Thur, Mon,Wed, Fri midday, Feb and Nov. Piazza Garibaldi 8, T: 0187 967721.

€€ **Conchiglia**. Good traditional seafood restaurant, with outside seating in fair weather. Closed Wed (except in summer), Nov and Feb. Piazza del Molo 3, T: 0187 967334.

€€ **Due Corone**. Romantic restaurant on the Lungomare, offers traditional regional recipes. Closed Tues (in winter), Jan–Feb. Via Mazzini 13, T: 0187 967417.

€€ **Frantoio**. Elegant and warm restaurant in an old oil press, regional cooking. Closed Mon and July. Via Cavour 21, T: 0187 964174.

€€ **Miranda**. Elegant hotel restaurant offering seafood and innovative recipes. Closed Mon and Jan–Feb. Via Fiascherino 92, Località Tellaro, T: 0187 968130.

Levanto

€€ **Hostaria da Franco**. Trattoria offering creative interpretations of traditional regional recipes and outside seating in summer. Closed Mon (except in summer) and Nov. Via Olivi 8, T: 0187 808647.

Portofino

€€€ **Da Puny**. Traditional seafood restaurant, with good views of the town and its bay. Closed Thur and Dec–Feb. Piazza Martiri dell'Olivetta 5–7, T: 0185 269037.

€€ **Strainer**. Restaurant on the sea, specialising in fish dishes. Closed Wed and Nov. Molo Umberto I 19, T: 0185 269189.

Portovenere

€€ **Da Iseo**. Simple seafood restaurant with outside seating in summer. Closed Wed and Dec–Jan. Calata Doria 9, T: 0187 900610.

€€ **La Marina-Da Antonio**. Traditional trattoria specialising in fish. Closed Thur and March. Piazza Marina 6, T: 0187 790686.

€€ **Locanda Lorena**. Romantic restaurant on the sea, traditional fish recipes. Closed Wed, Jan–March. Via Cavour 4, Isola Palmaria, T: 0187 792370.

€€ **Taverna del Corsaro**. Excellent fish and good wine list. Closed Tues and Nov–Dec. Calata Doria 102, T: 0187 790622.

Rapallo

€€ **Da Monique**. A traditional restaurant with good seafood and nice views. Closed Tues and Jan–Feb. Lungomare Vittorio Veneto 6, T: 0185 50541.

€€ **Ü Gianco**. Creative interpretations of traditional Ligurian recipes, in a scenic location. Closed midday (except weekends), Wed evening, Jan–Feb, June–July, Sept–Dec. Via San Massimo 78, Località San Massimo, T: 0185 261212.

Recco

€€ **Da Vittorio**. Traditional trattoria (with rooms) serving hearty regional dishes. Closed Thur and Nov–Dec. Via Roma 160, T: 0185 74029.

€€ **Manuelina**. Traditional restaurant with excellent regional fare, garden and pool. Closed Wed and Jan. Via Roma 278, T: 0185 74128.

Santa Margherita Ligure

€€ **Cesarina**. Traditional trattoria specialising in fish. Closed Tues, Nov and March. Via Mamell 2c, T: 0185 286059.

€€ **Faro**. Family-run restaurant, creative fish cooking. Closed Tue, Nov. Via Maragliano 24, T: 0185 286867.

€€€ **Stalla dei Frati**. Elegant fish restaurant with a wonderful view and garden. Closed Mon, Nov Via Giovanni Pino 27, Frazione Nozarego, T: 0185 289447.

Sarzana

€€ **La Compagnia dei Balenieri**. Good trattoria specialising in regional recipes. Closed midday (except Sun), Mon. Via Rossi 28, T: 0187 603537.

€ **Il Cantinone**. Simple trattoria in an ancient wine cellar in the heart of the old town. Closed Mon, March and Sept. Via Fiasella 59, T: 0187 627952.

Sestri Levante

€€ **El Pescador**. Delicious seafood on the harbour. Closed Tues and Dec–March. Via Queirolo 1, T: 0185 42888.

€€ **Fiammenghilla dei Fieschi**. Truly outstanding regional cuisine. Closed midday (except Sun and holidays), Mon, Jan–Feb and Nov. Via Pestella 6, Località Trigoso, T: 0185 481041.

Tellaro

€€ **Miranda**. A simple but excellent restaurant (with rooms), in a quiet village on a headland. Closed Jan–Feb. Via Fiascherino 92, T: 0187 968130.

Vernazza

€€ **Gianni Franzi**. Creative interpretations of traditional Ligurian recipes. Closed Wed (except in summer) and Jan–March. Piazza Marconi 5, T: 0187 812228.

WINE BARS

Castelnuovo Magra

€ **Mulino del Cibus**. Wine bar serving good hot and cold meals. Open evenings only; closed Mon. Via Canale 46, Località Canale, T: 0187 676102.

La Spezia

€ **Cabaret Voltaire**. Popular and with recherché little snacks. Closed midday. Via Napoli 92, T: 347 4607587.

€ **Nettare e Ambrosia**. Wine bar serving good hot and cold dishes. Closed Sun and Aug. Via Fazio 85, T: 0187 737252.

Sestri Levante

€ **Bottega del Vino**. Wine bar with good *bruschette*, cheeses etc. Open evenings only, closed Thur. Via Nazionale 530, T: 0185 43349.

FESTIVALS & EVENTS

Camogli Blessing of the Fish, second Sun in May, and Stella Maris procession of boats to the Punta della Chiappa, first Sun in Aug.

La Spezia *Grande Estate Spezina* music festival, summer.

Sarzana National Antiques Show, Aug.

EMILIA ROMAGNA

Emilia Romagna, as the name of a district, dates only from the Risorgimento (c. 1860), but its use is derived from the Via Emilia, the great Roman road built in 187 BC, by M. Aemilius Lepidus, as a military thoroughfare from which to guard the newly conquered lands of Cisalpine Gaul. Emilia is the north and western part of the region, occupying the area between the middle and lower Po, the Apennines and the Adriatic. Bologna is the chief town. The eastern and southern part of the region is Romagna. All the principal towns, except Ferrara and Ravenna, lie along the line of the Via Emilia at the foot of the Apennines. The climate here is subject to extremes, and the summers are often unpleasantly hot.

Ravenna (*see p. 653*) was the capital of the western Roman Empire from 402, after the fall of Rome, until it was taken by Odoacer who, like his successor Theodoric, made it the capital of a short-lived Gothic Empire. It was conquered by the Byzantines in 540 and was governed by exarchs of the Eastern Empire for two centuries. In 757 Romagna came into possession of the popes, who maintained at least a nominal suzerainty here until 1860; in the 13th–15th centuries, however, the effective rule of the da Polenta clan gave Ravenna a pre-eminent position in the world of learning.

The history of Emilia is a confusing one, with Romagna following quite a separate course. It was invaded in the 5th–8th centuries by the Goths, Lombards and Franks. In the early Middle Ages Guelphs and Ghibellines struggled for power in the region, and Piacenza and Parma came under the influence of Milan. The dominion of the Este family at Ferrara in the 13th century extended over Modena and Reggio, while the Pepoli and Bentivoglio at Bologna, the Ordelaffi at Forlì, and the Malatesta at Rimini held temporary sway before the 16th century. Papal power was later firmly established in Romagna and at Ferrara and Bologna, whereas the Farnese family, descended from the son of Pope Paul III, made Modena the capital of a new duchy and the centre of a court of some pretensions. The ex-empress Marie Louise (wife of Napoleon) became Duchess of Parma, with Piacenza and Lucca, in Tuscany, also subject to her rule; the rest of Emilia went to Austria, as successor of the Este dynasty, and Romagna remained papal land. In 1860 Emilia and Romagna were united with Piedmont. Emilia, and Romagna especially, played an important part in the Second World War: the Romagnole partisans were particularly active in 1945.

BOLOGNA

Bologna, the capital of Emilia, is one of the oldest cities in Italy, and the seat of a famous university. The old town, built almost exclusively of red brick, has attractive porticoes along almost every street. Often unjustly left out of tourist itineraries, it is in fact one of the finest cities in northern Italy, with its own important Bolognese school of painting.

HISTORY OF BOLOGNA

Felsina, an important Etruscan city on the site of Bologna, was overrun by the Gauls in the 4th century BC. They named their settlement Bononia, and the name was retained by the Romans when they conquered the plain of the Po in 225–191 BC. After the fall of the Western Empire, Bologna became subject to the exarchs of Ravenna and later formed part of the Lombard and Frankish dominions. It was recognised as an independent commune by Emperor Henry V in 1116; its university first became prominent at about this time. One of the foremost cities of the Lombard League (1167), Bologna reached the height of its power after the peace of Constance (1183) and sided with the Guelphs. Taddeo Pepoli founded a lordship here c. 1337, which was held in turn by the Visconti, the Pepoli and the Bentivoglio, under the last of whom (Giovanni II Bentivoglio; 1463–1506) Bologna attained fame and prosperity. Pope Julius II reconquered the city in 1506, and for three centuries Bologna was incorporated into the Papal States, except for a brief interval (1796–1814) when it was part of Napoleon's Cisalpine Republic. In 1814 Bologna was occupied by the British, in support of the Austrians against Napoleon. Unsuccessful insurrections broke out in 1831 and 1848, and the town was held by an Austrian garrison from 1849 until the formation of the Kingdom of Italy in 1860. For months, Bologna was the focal point of German resistance in the Second World War, but its artistic treasures escaped damage.

Around Piazza Maggiore

Map 11.

In the centre of the city is the large, peaceful Piazza Maggiore, known simply as *la piazza* to the Bolognese. It is adjoined by Piazza Nettuno, and both are surrounded by splendid public buildings. **Palazzo del Podestà** was begun at the beginning of the 13th century, but remodelled in 1484. At the centre of the building is the tall tower (Arengo) of 1212: two passageways run beneath it, and in the vault are statues of the patron saints of the city by Alfonso Lombardi (1525).

Fronting Via dell'Archiginnasio is the handsome long façade of **Palazzo dei Banchi** (1412, remodelled by Vignola 1565–68), once occupied by moneylenders. At street level are the Portico del Pavaglione and two tall arches that give access to side streets. You can see the dome of Santa Maria della Vita and the top of the Torre degli Asinelli above the roof of the palace. On the other side of the great church is **Palazzo dei Notai**, the old College of Notaries, part of which was begun in 1381 and the rest completed by Bartolomeo Fieravanti (1422–40).

San Petronio

Although the immense church of San Petronio was never the cathedral, it is the most important religious building in Bologna and one of the most remarkable brick buildings in existence. Begun in 1390 to designs by a little-known architect, Antonio di Vincenzo, it is dedicated to St Petronius, bishop of Bologna 431–50 and patron saint of the city. Medieval houses were demolished so that the huge church could be erected here, at the political centre of the city, as a symbol of civic pride and independence. The church was designed to be twice this size; its construction went on until the mid-17th century, when the nave-vault was completed.

The immense, incomplete brick façade has a beautiful pink-and-white marble lower storey with three canopied doorways on which exquisite reliefs illustrate biblical history from the Creation to the time of the Apostles. The central doorway is famous for its sculptures, by Jacopo della Quercia. They are his masterpiece, begun in 1425 and left unfinished at his death in 1438. On the pilasters are ten bas-reliefs, mostly by assistants, illustrating the story of Genesis, and a frieze of half-figures of prophets. The architrave bears five scenes of the childhood of Christ. In the lunette are statues, also by Jacopo, of the *Madonna and Child with St Petronius* (St Ambrose was added in 1510). The archivolt above them is decorated with panels of prophets (1510–11); the central figure is by Amico Aspertini.

The interior

The great white and pink **nave**, 41m high, is lit by round windows and is separated from the aisles by ten massive compound piers. Because of its orientation (north to south), the church is unusually light. The splendid Gothic vaulting dates from 1648; it is a masterpiece by Girolamo Rainaldi, who adapted the 16th-century designs of Terribilia and Carlo Cremona. The side chapels are closed by beautiful screens, many of them in marble dating from the late 15th century, others in ironwork. The four 11th -12th-century crosses placed outside the chapels once marked the limits of the late medieval city. The church is home to many fine works of art, and is one of the best places in the city to gain an appreciation of Bolognese art at its height.

The first chapel in the **south aisle** has a German *Madonna della Pace* of 1394, framed by a painting by Giacomo Francia (son of Francesco). The stained glass in the fourth chapel is by Jacob of Ulm (1466). Jacob died in Bologna and is buried in the church of San Domenico (*see p. 580*). In the fifth chapel is a *Pietà* (1519) by Amico Aspertini, and in the sixth chapel is Lorenzo Costa's *St Jerome*. In the ninth chapel is a statue of St Anthony of Padua and monochrome frescoes by Girolamo da Treviso (1526). Girolamo worked at the court of Henry VIII of England from 1538, and died on the battlefield in France (where he had gone in the capacity of military engineer). The design of the stained glass here is attributed to Pellegrino Tibaldi. The screen of the tenth chapel is particularly beautiful; it dates from c. 1460. The altarpiece is by Bartolomeo Passarotti. Beneath the organ, opposite the eleventh chapel, is a *Lamentation* group by Vincenzo Onofri (1480).

Charles V was crowned emperor at the **high altar** in 1530 by Pope Clement VII. The artist chosen to design the triumphal arch for Charles and the Pope's entry into Bologna was Amico Aspertini.

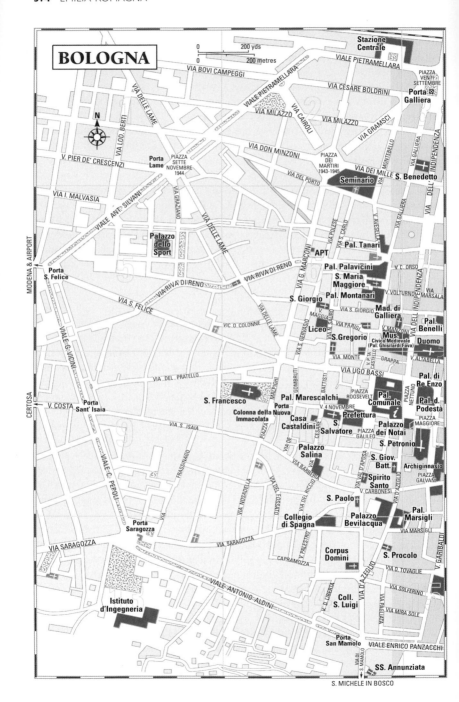

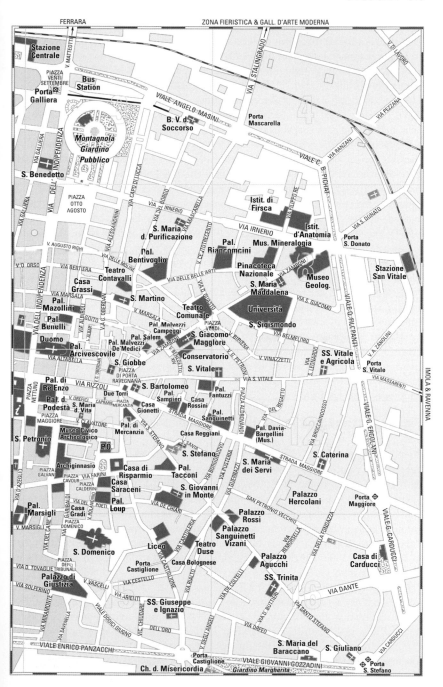

At the east end of the **north aisle** is a small museum (*open 10–12.30 & 2.30–5.30 except Sun morning*). It contains numerous drawings for the completion of the façade of the church, submitted right up to 1933 (including works by Baldassare Peruzzi, Domenico Tibaldi—brother of Pellegrino—and Palladio). In the eleventh chapel are two large painted organ panels by Amico Aspertini. The ninth chapel has a *St Michael* by Denys Calvaert (1582). The Barbazzi monument, with a bust by Vincenzo Onofri, is from 1479. The eighth chapel has a painting of *St Roch* by Parmigianino. In front of the monument of Bishop Cesare Nacci, by Vincenzo Onofri (1479), begins the meridian line, nearly 67m long, traced in 1655 by the astronomer Gian Domenico Cassini. It has since been several times adjusted; a hole in the roof admits the sun's ray. The seventh chapel has a particularly fine screen attributed to Pagno di Lapo. The altarpiece is by Lorenzo Costa (1492). The sixth chapel has an *Assumption* by Scarsellino (c. 1600), who worked with the Carracci, and a statue of Cardinal Giacomo Lercaro by Giacomo Manzù (1954). The fifth chapel was decorated in 1487–97. The altarpiece is a late-15th-century Ferrarese work, and the paintings are by Francesco Francia and Lorenzo Costa. Between this chapel and the next is a fine late-14th-century statue of St Petronius in gilded wood.

The fourth chapel, the beautiful Cappella Bolognini, has a fine marble balustrade. The gilded polychrome wood Gothic altarpiece was painted by Jacopo di Paolo in 1410. The remarkable frescoes are by Giovanni da Modena. The second chapel is a Baroque work by Alfonso Torreggiani (1743–50) with a fine grille and the tomb of Benedict XIV. Outside the chapel are frescoes by Lippo di Dalmasio and a *Madonna* attributed to Giovanni da Modena, who also executed the allegorical frescoes in the first chapel. Above the right door on the inside façade are *Adam and Eve*, attributed to the Ferrarese sculptor Alfonso Lombardi.

Piazza Nettuno and Palazzo d'Accursio

Map 11.

Piazza Nettuno takes its name from the Neptune Fountain, decorated with a splendid figure of Neptune and other bronze sculptures by Giambologna (1566). Fronting both Piazza Nettuno and Piazza Maggiore is the long façade of the huge **Palazzo Comunale** (Map 10), which incorporates Palazzo d'Accursio and is made up of several buildings of different dates, modified and restored over the centuries. The entrance gateway is by Galeazzo Alessi (c. 1555), and the bronze statue above it is of Pope Gregory XIII, the reformer of the calendar, who was born Ugo Buoncompagni in Bologna in 1502. To the left, under a canopy, is a Madonna in terracotta by Niccolò dell'Arca (1478).

Palazzo d'Accursio, to the left, was acquired by the *comune* in 1287 from Francesco d'Accursio on his return from the court of King Edward I of England. The loggia was used as a public granary. Taddeo Pepoli began to unite various palaces on this site as a town hall in 1336, and in 1425–28 the military engineer Fieravante Fieravanti rebuilt the palace to the right of the main entrance. The whole edifice was fortified in the 16th century and used by the papal legates as their residence.

Giambologna's Neptune in Piazza Nettuno.

From the courtyard the grand staircase, a ramp ascribed to Bramante, leads up to the first floor, where the Chamber of Hercules contains a colossal terracotta statue by Alfonso Lombardi and a *Madonna* by Francesco Francia (1505). On the second floor the Sala Farnese has a good view of the piazza. Here is the entrance to the **Collezioni Comunali d'Arte** (*open Tues–Sat 9–5.30, Sun 10–6.30*), a collection of paintings and furniture in a wing of the Palazzo d'Accursio, that was used by the Cardinal legates of the city from 1506 up to the 19th century. The long gallery was decorated in the 17th century by the papal legate Pietro Vidoni. The 18th- and early-19th-century period décor of the Sale Rusconi (rooms 11–16) is largely the product of the paintings and furniture left to the museum by the Rusconi family. The collection includes works by Carlo Francesco Nuvolone, Artemisia Gentileschi (*Portrait of a Condottiero*), Donato Creti (mostly painted in 1710–20), Francesco Francia (*Crucifixion*), Amico Aspertini, Lodovico Carracci, Giuseppe Maria Crespi, Francesco Hayez (*Ruth*) and Pelagio Pelagi.

The **Museo Morandi** (*open Tues–Sun 10–6*) contains the most representative collection of Giorgio Morandi's works in existence, donated to the city by his family. There are also works of art owned by the painter and a reconstruction of his studio.

Also in Piazza Nettuno is the battlemented **Palazzo di Re Enzo**, built in 1246, which was the prison of Enzo (1225–72), King of Sardinia and illegitimate son of Emperor Frederick II, from his capture at Fossalta in 1249 until his death in 1272.

BOLOGNESE ART & ARCHITECTURE

The predominant material in the architecture of Bologna has always been brick, for both structural and decorative purposes, and the late-Gothic buildings of the 14th century show the height attained by local skill in brick designing. Sculptors who left important works in the city include Nicola Pisano, Jacopo della Quercia and Giambologna. Art in the early 14th century was dominated by the expressive love of ornament of Giovanni da Modena. The wealthy court of the Bentivoglio attracted Lorenzo Costa from Ferrara (c. 1490). Francesco Francia, a goldsmith by training, formed a partnership with Costa and can be said to have founded the Bolognese school of painting. One of its greatest pupils was Amico Aspertini (c. 1470–1552), described by Vasari as eccentric and semi-insane. Certainly a prodigy, his frescoes and altarpieces depart entirely from the gentle restraint of Francia his master, and display a quick-witted, extemporised style that foreshadows Mannerism. At the end of the 16th century the Bolognese school entered an important revival period with the Carracci and Bartolomeo Passarotti, master of the genre scene, who probably trained under Annibale Carracci. The Flemish-born artist Denys Calvaert was also active in Bologna (he died in the city in 1619). Though not a great painter in his own right, his influence was important: Francesco Albani and Guido Reni both trained in his academy (Albani also studied under Lodovico Carracci). Another artist to feel the Carracci's influence was Guercino (1591–1666), who dominated Bolognese painting for a quarter of a century with his exuberant brushwork and dramatic colour and light effects.

The Museo Civico Archeologico and the Archiginnasio

Map 11.

Via dell'Archiginnasio skirts the east flank of San Petronio. Beneath the marble-paved Portico del Pavaglione, with elegant uniform shopfronts, the windows enclosed in tall wooden frames, is the entrance to the **Museo Civico Archeologico** (*open Tues–Sat 9–6.30, Sun and holidays 10–6.30*), especially notable for its Etruscan material and Egyptian section. Highlights include a seated statuette of King Neferhotep I (18th century BC); heads of Pharaohs Thutmosis III (1479–26 BC), Amenhotep III (1390–53 BC) and Apries (589–570 BC); a group of Amenhotep and his wife Merit (late 18th or early 19th Dynasty, 1319–1279 BC); a large statue of the dignitary Uahibra (Amasis Kingdom, 570–526 BC). A lateral wing has exhibits related to writing and the cult of the dead.

On the ground floor, the entrance hall and courtyard contain a Roman lapidarium. Here are Roman tombstones from the city and its province, dating between the 1st century BC and the 2nd century AD; a statue of the emperor Nero wearing a sumptuous breastplate (1st century AD), found on the site of the Roman theatre; two Etruscan sandstone monuments, decorated with palm leaves and winged sphinxes, dating from the late 7th century BC and milestones from the Via Emilia. A large hall on the right side of the courtyard houses the *gipsoteca*, with casts made at the end of the 19th century of famous Greek and Roman masterpieces.

On the first floor is a vast collection of Villanovan and Etruscan finds from the burial-grounds of Felsina, the Umbro-Etruscan predecessor of Bologna. The long gallery, decorated in the 19th century with copies of Etruscan painted tombs, contains tomb-furniture illustrating the development of the Umbrian (9th–6th century BC) and Etruscan (6th–mid-4th century BC) civilisations. The Umbrian tombs contain urns with scratched, painted and (later) stamped geometric decoration, whereas the Etruscan tombs bear reliefs in sandstone and contain fine Attic vases (the so-called 'Etruscan' ware) and various objects of daily use in bronze, bone, etc. In case 20 is a beautiful bronze situla (6th century BC), with exquisite reliefs of a ceremonial procession.

Greek works of art are also held here, including a head of Minerva, said to be a copy of the *Athene Lemnia* of Phidias, and the *Cup of Codrus*, a fine red-figured Attic vase.

In the narrow road to the left of the museum, next to the indoor market, is the church of **Santa Maria della Vita**, rebuilt in 1687–90 with a cupola. It contains a dramatic evocation of grief, the terracotta *Lamentation over the Dead Christ*, a superb work by Niccolo dell'Arca, thought to date from 1463.

Further along the Portico del Pavaglione is the **Archiginnasio**, built by Antonio Morandi in 1562–65 for the university, which had its seat here until 1800. The upper floor is shown by the doorman on request (*open Mon–Sat 9–1*). The wooden anatomical theatre was built in 1637 by Antonio Levanti. By the 14th century the university had acquired notoriety as the first school where the dissection of the human body was practised. The baldacchino over the Reader's Chair is supported by two remarkable anatomical figures by Ercole Lelli (1734). In the Aula Magna, Rossini's *Stabat Mater* was given its first performance under the direction of Donizetti. From here you can see the long series of school rooms, now part of the Biblioteca Comunale, with c. 700,000 volumes and 12,000 manuscripts. A monument commemorating the physicist Luigi Galvani (1737–98; *see p. 586*) stands in front of the building.

San Domenico

Map 15.

The church of San Domenico was dedicated by Innocent IV in 1251 to St Dominic, founder of the order of Preaching Friars, who died here in 1221 two years after establishing the convent on this site. It is still one of the principal Dominican convents in Italy, with about 40 monks. The church was remodelled by Carlo Francesco Dotti (1728–31).

The **Chapel of St Dominic** was rebuilt in 1597–1605 (and restored in the 19th century). Here you can see the saint's monumental sarcophagus, a masterpiece of sculpture. It was carved with scenes from the saint's life in high relief in 1267 to a design by Nicola Pisano, mostly by his pupils, including Fra Guglielmo and Arnolfo di Cambio. The lid of the sarcophagus is decorated with statuettes and festoons by Niccolò dell'Arca, who took his name from this tomb ('*arca*' in Italian). Niccolò died in 1492. Three years later, the 20-year-old Michelangelo—who was staying for a year with Gianfrancesco Aldovrandi—carved three statuettes: the right-hand angel bearing a candelabrum (the other is by Niccolò dell'Arca), St Petronius holding a model of Bologna, and (behind) St Proculus (with a cloak over his left shoulder). Girolamo Corbellini carved the last statue (St John the Baptist) in 1539. The sculpted scenes in relief below the sarcophagus and between the two kneeling angels are by Alfonso Lombardi (1532). The altar beneath dates from the 18th century. Behind the tomb in a niche is a reliquary by Jacopo Roseto da Bologna (1383) holding the saint's skull. In the apse of the chapel is the *Glory of St Dominic*, by Guido Reni.

In the **south transept** is a painting by Guercino of *St Thomas Aquinas*. Here marquetry doors by Fra Damiano Zambelli (1538) lead into the sacristy. The little museum (*open 9–12, 3.30–6 except Sun and holidays*) contains a bust of *St Dominic* (1474), a very fine work in polychrome terracotta by Niccolò dell'Arca; paintings and frescoes by Lippo di Dalmasio, Lodovico Carracci and Bernardino Luini; intarsia panels by Fra Damiano; and books of anthems. The **choir** has stalls (1541–51) in marquetry also by Fra Damiano. The painting of the *Magi* is by Bartolomeo Cesi. A marquetry door opposite the sacristy (usually unlocked) leads into the charming **Cloister of the Dead**, its fourth side closed by the exterior of the apse and cupola of the chapel of San Domenico. This is where foreigners who died in Bologna were buried, including students and professors from the university. A simple tomb slab opposite the apse of the Chapel of St Dominic marks the burial place of people from the British Isles. Off the Chiostro Maggiore is **St Dominic's cell** (normally shown on request by a monk), with relics of the saint and a 13th-century painting of him.

The little chapel to the right of the choir (light on the right) contains a *Marriage of St Catherine* signed by Filippino Lippi (1501). In the **north transept**, an inscription of 1731 marks the tomb of King Enzo (*see p. 577*). The adjoining chapel holds a 14th-century wall monument (altered in the 16th century) to Taddeo Pepoli and a painted crucifix signed by Giunta Pisano. In the Chapel of the Relics at the end of the transept is the tomb of Beato Giacomo da Ulma (Jacob of Ulm), the painter on glass, who died in Bologna in 1491. In the **north aisle**, the chapel opposite that of St Dominic has an altarpiece incorporating small paintings of the *Mysteries of the Rosary* by Lodovico Carracci, Bartolomeo Cesi, Denys Calvaert, Guido Reni and Francesco Albani. There is a legend that the Virgin gave a rosary to St Dominic as protection against Albigensianism, and for much of the Middle Ages Confraternities of the Rosary were under Dominican control. On the second altar is *St Raimondo* by Lodovico Carracci.

The Due Torri area

Map 11.
Piazza di Porta Ravegnana is dominated by the famous **Due Torri**, two leaning towers, now isolated by traffic, one of which is exceptionally tall. At one time some 180 such towers existed in the city. Wealthy Bolognese merchants built them as symbols of their prestige, each vying to be taller than the other. Medieval Bologna must have been a veritable forest of brick. The **Torre degli Asinelli**, thought to have been built

The Torre degli Asinelli, almost 100m tall, with the Torre Garisenda behind it.

by the Asinelli family or by the *comune* (1109–19), is 97.5m high and leans 1.23m out of the perpendicular. The masonry at the base was added in 1488. A flight of 500 steps takes you up to the top (*open daily 9–5 or 6*).

The **Torre Garisenda**, built by the Garisendi family at the same time as the other, was left unfinished owing to the subsidence of the soil and was shortened for safety in 1351–60. It is now only 48m high and leans 3.22m out of the perpendicular; but it was higher when Dante wrote the descriptive verses about the 'tilted tower', with clouds scudding past its top, making it appear to be falling (*Inferno*, xxxi, 136). The lines are inscribed at the base of the tower.

Beside the Due Torri is the church of **San Bartolomeo**, where the rich decoration of the portico (1515), by Formigine (the architect Andrea Marchesi, from Modena), has been worn away (although it was restored in 1993). The ornate interior, with small domes over the side aisles, is largely the work of Giovanni Battista Natali (1653–84). In the fourth chapel of the south aisle is an *Annunciation* by Francesco Albani (1632). The tondo of the *Madonna* in the north transept is by Guido Reni.

The narrow Via dell'Inferno, which leads out of the piazza, is on the site of the ghetto of Bologna (the synagogue was at no. 16). The **Jewish Museum**, at Via Valdonica 1 (*open Sun–Thur 10–6, Fri 10–4*) documents the history of Jewish life in Bologna and Emilia Romagna from the Middle Ages to the present day.

Adjoining Piazza di Porta Ravegnana is Piazza Mercanzia with the **Palazzo della Mercanzia**, arguably the best-preserved example of ornamented Italian Gothic architecture in the city. It was built in 1382–84 from the plans of Antonio di Vincenzo (architect of San Petronio) and Lorenzo da Bagnomarino.

In Via de' Pepoli (right) is the 17th-century **Palazzo Pepoli-Campogrande** (with frescoes by Donato Creti and Giuseppe Maria Crespi), which houses some 18th-century paintings from the Pinacoteca (*open Sat 1–7, Sun 9–7*).

Impressions of Bologna

Among a revengeful people who seek satisfaction with the stiletto—these dark arcades afford the best opportunities at night to lie in wait and wreak their vengeance on an unsuspecting adversary.

Washington Irving, Journal, 24 April 1805

Wordsworth... has been all day very uncomfortable—annoyed by the length of the streets.

Henry Crabb Robinson, Diary, 7 June 1837

First thing at Bologna tried Bologna sausage on the principle that at Rome you go first to St Peter's.

Herman Melville, Journal of a Visit to Europe and the Levant, 30 March 1857.

Santo Stefano

Map 11.

At the east end of an attractive piazza, in a peaceful corner of the town, stands the monastic complex of **Santo Stefano**, an ancient, picturesque group of buildings mentioned as early as 887 and dedicated as a whole to St Stephen the Martyr. Three churches face the piazza: Santi Vitale e Agricola, the oldest ecclesiastical building in the city, San Sepolcro, and the Crocifisso, with a 12th-century pulpit on its front.

The Crocifisso, restored in 1924, has a painted crucifix by Simone dei Crocifissi (c. 1380) hanging in the raised chöir. The crypt has some 11th-century details and a jumble of capitals. The 18th-century *Pietà* is the work of Angelo Piò, and the Aldovrandi tomb dates from 1438.

On the left is the entrance to the polygonal church of San Sepolcro, perhaps founded as a baptistery in the 5th century but dating in its present form from the 11th century. It has a brick cupola and interesting architectural details. The imagined imitation of the Holy Sepulchre at Jerusalem is partly hidden by the Romanesque pulpit and a stair and altar placed against it in the 19th century. In the centre, behind a grille, is the tomb of St Petronius.

To the left again is the church of **Santi Vitale e Agricola**, a venerable building perhaps of the 5th century, with massive columns and capitals, incorporating many fragments of Roman buildings. The three apses (rebuilt in the 8th and 11th centuries) are lit by tiny alabaster windows. The altars in the side apses are 8th- or 9th-century Frankish sarcophagi enclosing the relics of St Vitalis and St Agricola, martyred in Bologna under the emperor Diocletian.

From San Sepolcro is the entrance to the **Cortile di Pilato** (12th century); in the middle of this open court is Pilate's Bowl (8th century) bearing an obscure inscription relating to the Lombard kings Luitprand and Ilprand. From here you can see the beautifully patterned brickwork of the exterior of San Sepolcro. On a pillar in a little window is a delightful cockerel sculpted in the 14th century.

Off the court is the **church of the Martyrium**, with a façade reconstructed in 1911. The chapel has good capitals and remains of 14th–15th-century frescoes. In the left chapel (light) is a charming group of wooden statues of the *Adoration of the Magi* painted by Simone dei Crocifissi (c. 1370). The chapel of San Giuliano, also off the courtyard, has 14th-century frescoes. A door from the court leads into the cloister, which has two beautiful colonnades, the lower one dating from the 11th century, and the upper from the 12th century, with fine capitals. Here you can see the Romanesque campanile.

There is a small museum off the cloister (*open daily 9–12 & 3.30–6.15*), in poor condition. It includes more works by Jacopo di Paolo, Michele di Matteo, Simone dei Crocifissi and Gothic and late Gothic works by Jacopo di Paolo, Michele di Matteo and Lippo di Dalmasio.

TERRACOTTA IN BOLOGNA

Emilia Romagna has few good stone quarries, but it is blessed with wonderful clays. Hence all the brick rather than stone architecture in the region, and hence, too, the pre-eminence of Faenza for ceramics. Whether Emilian terracotta sculpture would have developed as highly without what had gone before in Florence with Desiderio da Settignano, Sansovino and others is perhaps debatable; but certainly the area has a grand tradition in churches and on public buildings of terracotta figures and groups (much of it polychrome). And, of course, with terracotta an artist can be much bolder with gesture and movement than is ever possible with stone. Possibly the finest example of the genre is Niccolò dell'Arca's *Lamentation* in Santa Maria della Vita: six free-standing figures grouped in moving, almost Baroque, poses around the dead body of Christ—a wonderfully dramatic piece. Other masters working in Bologna include Vincenzo Onofri (fl. 1479–1506) and Sperandio da Mantova (c. 1425–1506).

San Giovanni in Monte

Map 11.

Across Via Santo Stefano and Via Farini, on a little hill, stands the church of **San** Giovanni in Monte. Of ancient foundation, in its present form it is a 13th-century Gothic building with extensive 15th-century additions. The façade has a great portal of 1474, and above it an eagle in painted terracotta by Niccolò dell'Arca.

In the pleasant interior the columns are partly decorated with frescoes by Giacomo and Giulio Francia. The stained-glass tondo on the west wall is by the Cabrini, to a design by Lorenzo Costa or Francesco del Cossa (1481). The Romanesque cross on an inverted Roman pillar capital bears a figure of Christ in fig wood attributed to Alfonso Lombardi. In the south aisle are altarpieces by Girolamo da Treviso, Lippo di Dalmasio (fresco) and Lorenzo Costa (*Enthroned Madonna with Saints*, 1497).

The *Madonna in Glory* on the east wall is another fine work by Lorenzo Costa, and the crucifix is by native 14th-century artist Jacopino da Bologna. The north transept is a good architectural work of 1514 built for the blessed Elena Duglioli Dall'Oglio (1472–1520), who is buried here. She also commissioned the famous St Cecilia altarpiece for the chapel from Raphael: now in the pinacoteca, it is substituted here by a poor copy still enclosed in the original frame by Formigine. In the north aisle are works by Francesco Gessi, Luigi Crespi and (second chapel) Guercino.

The Strada Maggiore and Piazza dei Servi

Map 11–12.

The Strada Maggiore is an attractive old street running southeast on the line of the Via Emilia, where a series of characteristic Bolognese mansions of all periods from the 13th–19th centuries, some of them restored, can be seen. Casa Gelmi (no. 26) was built for the composer Gioacchino Rossini in 1827. Rossini studied at the Conservatorio here.

Beyond opens Piazza dei Servi, with its porticoes. Here at no. 44 is Palazzo Davia-Bargellini, built in 1638, with two atlantes flanking the gateway. The fine staircase dates from 1730. The palace contains the **Museo Civico d'Arte Industriale e Galleria Davia-Bargellini** (*open Tues–Sat 9–2; Sun and holidays 9–1*), founded in 1924 and still preserving the character of its original arrangement. It includes domestic artefacts, wrought-iron work, ceramics, an 18th-century puppet theatre, a dolls' house, woodcarvings, Emilian furniture, and paintings by Vitale da Bologna, Bartolomeo Vivarini, Giuseppe Maria Crespi, Bartolomeo Passarotti (portraits of the Bargellini family) and Prospero Fontana. There is also a good collection of terracottas by Giuseppe Maria Mazza and Angelo Piò.

The four porticoes of **Piazza dei Servi**, built in a consistent style at various periods from the 14th century to 1855, are a continuation of the wide arcades in the Strada Maggiore alongside the church of Santa Maria dei Servi. Begun in 1346 and enlarged after 1386, this is one of the most attractive Gothic buildings in Bologna.

The interior of the church is very dark. The fourth south chapel has a painting, by Denys Calvaert, of *Paradise* (1602). On the left pillar outside the sixth chapel is a fresco fragment attributed to Lippo di Dalmasio. Outside the door into the sacristy are frescoes by Vitale da Bologna that survive from the 14th-century church. In the ambulatory are a polyptych by Lippo di Dalmasio (in very poor condition), and a delightful high relief in terracotta by Vincenzo Onofri. The chapel to the left of the east chapel preserves Cimabue's *Enthroned Madonna* (light) and a 15th-century fresco by Pietro di Giovanni Lianori. On the choir wall is the Grati monument by Vincenzo Onofri.

In Via Guerrazzi, to the south, is (no. 13) the Accademia Filarmonica, founded in 1666, to which Mozart was elected in 1770 at the age of 14. At Viale Carducci 5, on the right beyond Porta Maggiore, is the **Casa di Carducci** and **Museo del**

Risorgimento (*open Tues, Wed and Fri–Sun 9–5*), where the poet Giosuè Carducci (*see p. 31*) lived from 1890 to 1907.

Piazza Aldovrandi, with chestnut trees and a street market, leads north to Via San Vitale. Here on the left, beyond an old city gate (11th–12th-century), is the church of **Santi Vitale e Agricola**, rebuilt in 1824, except for its 12th-century crypt. It is dedicated to two saints martyred under Diocletian in the arena, thought to have been in this area. Inside are frescoes attributed to Giacomo Francia and Bagnacavallo (*see p. 665*).

San Giacomo Maggiore and its neighbourhood

Map 7.

On Via Zamboni, facing Piazza Rossini, is **Palazzo Magnani** by Domenico Tibaldi (1577–87). The Salone (*open to visitors when not in use*) has a beautiful frescoed frieze of the *Founding of Rome* by the Carracci (1588–91). You can also view paintings by Tintoretto, Lodovico Carracci, Simone Cantarini, Domenico Induno, Giuseppe Maria Crespi and Guercino.

The Romanesque church of **San Giacomo Maggiore**, was begun in 1267 (restored in 1915). Its aisleless nave is surmounted by a bold vault of unusually wide span. The chapels are crowned by a mid-18th-century terracotta frieze of statues and urns. On the south side are altarpieces by Bartolomeo Passarotti (1565), Innocenzo da Imola (in a frame by Formigine) and Lodovico Carracci. The eleventh chapel was designed by Pellegrino Tibaldi, who also painted the frescoes.

The ambulatory has a large painted crucifix by Jacopo di Paolo (c. 1420), on the left wall. The damaged frescoes of the *Life of St Mary of Egypt* are by Cristoforo da Bologna. In the third chapel are a polyptych by Jacopo di Paolo and a crucifix signed by Simone dei Crocifissi (1370). On the choir wall is the funerary monument of a philosopher and a doctor, both called Nicolò Fava, by a follower of Jacopo della Quercia.

The Cappella Bentivoglio (light switch on the floor), at the end of the north aisle, was founded in 1445 by Annibale Bentivoglio and enlarged for Giovanni II, probably by Pagno di Lapo Portigiani. Its altarpiece is by Francesco Francia (c. 1488). The frescoes from the Apocalypse, of the *Triumph of Death* and of the *Enthroned Madonna* with charming portraits of Giovanni II Bentivoglio and his family, are all by Lorenzo Costa.

Opposite the chapel is the tomb of Anton Galeazzo Bentivoglio, father of Annibale, one of the last works of Jacopo della Quercia (1435; with the help of assistants). The *Madonna in Glory* in the last chapel is by Bartolomeo Cesi.

The **Oratory of Santa Cecilia** (entered from no. 15 under the side portico of the church) has interesting frescoes by Francesco Francia, Lorenzo Costa and their pupils, including Amico Aspertini. They were painted in 1504–06 by order of Giovanni II Bentivoglio. The altarpiece is also by Francia.

Along the side of the church a delightful vaulted portico of 1477–81 connects Piazza Rossini with Piazza Verdi. Here is the best view of the fine brick campanile (1472). The Teatro Comunale, by Antonio Bibiena (1756; façade 1933), occupies the site of the great palace of the Bentivoglio, which was destroyed in a riot in 1507 and left in ruins until 1763 (the Bolognese called it *Il Guasto*—the Ruin).

The university

Map 8.

The university of Bologna is the oldest in Italy, founded in the second half of the 11th century and already famous just a century later. Since 1803 its headquarters have been in Palazzo Poggi (Via Zamboni no. 33), built by Pellegrino Tibaldi (1549), and containing his frescoes of the story of Ulysses. The university library (Via Zamboni 35) has a fine 18th-century reading-room. Here Cardinal Mezzofanti (1774–1849), who spoke 50 languages and was called by Byron 'the universal interpreter', was librarian, and his own library is added to the collection. You can visit the Museo Storico dello Studio, and numerous other scientific collections belonging to the university, by appointment. The Torre dell'Osservatorio dates from 1725.

THE UNIVERSITY OF BOLOGNA

Irnerius, the celebrated jurist and founder of the School of Glossators, taught here between 1070 and 1100. He revived the study of the Roman system of jurisprudence, which his disciples spread over Europe—in 1144 Vacarius went to England, perhaps summoned by Thomas Becket. His *Liber pauperum* became the core law text book at Oxford University. In return, many Englishmen and Scotsmen served as rectors at Bologna. Here Petrarch was taught, and Copernicus embarked on his studies of astronomy. In 1789 the university became renowned for the discoveries of Luigi Galvani. His experiments in applying an electric charge to severed frogs' legs and making them twitch in response was in fact the foundation stone of electro-technology and neuroscience. The term galvanism is derived from his name. Bologna is also remarkable for the number of its female professors, among them the learned Novella d'Andrea (14th century), Laura Bassi (1711–88), mathematician, scientist and mother of 12, and Clotilde Tambroni, professor of Greek 1794–1817.

Today the university is known particularly for its School of Medicine and for its Division of Art, Music and Drama (DAMS). Umberto Eco, author of *The Name of the Rose*, teaches semiotics here.

The Pinacoteca Nazionale

Map 8. *Open Tues–Sun 9–6.30.*

The **Accademia di Belle Arti** occupies an old Jesuit college with a handsome courtyard in Via delle Belle Arti. In this building is the Pinacoteca Nazionale, one of the most important collections of paintings in northern Italy. The gallery is especially important for its pictures of the Bolognese school, but also has paintings by artists who worked in Bologna (including Giotto, Raphael and Perugino).

NB: The paintings are arranged by period and school. The rooms are unnumbered but are numbered in the description below and on the floor plan.

PINACOTECA NAZIONALE

4: Three galleries around the cloister display works by the 14th-century Bolognese school, including Vitale da Bologna (*St George and the Dragon*), Jacopino da Bologna, Giovanni da Modena and Simone dei Crocifissi.

5: Works by Giotto and Lorenzo Monaco.

7–10: The 15th-century Bolognese school is represented by Michele di Matteo and Vitale da Bologna (detached frescoes and *sinopie*).

11: The Long Gallery has the most important works of the 15th–16th centuries. In the first section the Venetian school is represented by Antonio and Bartolomeo Vivarini, Cima da Conegliano (*Madonna*) and Marco Zoppo. Beyond is the Ferrarese school, with Francesco del Cossa (*Enthroned Madonna*), Ercole de' Roberti (*St Michael Archangel*), Lorenzo Costa and Marco Palmezzano. Painters of the Bolognese school include Francesco Francia (*Felicini Altarpiece*) and Amico Aspertini. At the far end is Raphael's famous *Ecstasy of St Cecilia* (reproduced on the cover of this guide). Also here are works by Perugino, Giulio Romano and Parmigianino (*Madonna and Saints*). Works by the 16th-century Emilian mannerists include Bartolomeo Passarotti, Camillo Procaccini and

Pellegrino Tibaldi. There are also works by 15th–16th-century foreign schools, including El Greco. The fragment from a *Crucifixion* is by Titian.

12: This gallery contains fine works by Guido Reni, including the large *Pietà dei Mendicanti*, with a model of Bologna.

13: Large works by Annibale, Lodovico and Agostino Carracci, including the *Madonna Bargellini* by Lodovico and the *Last Communion of St Jerome* by Agostino.

14: Works by Giorgio Vasari and Federico Barocci.

15: Bolognese 17th–18th-century paintings, including Francesco Albani.

16–19: Works by Guercino, Domenichino, Francesco Albani, Giuseppe Maria Crespi, the Gandolfi and Donato Creti.

20: Here are displayed seven huge altarpieces by Domenichino, Guercino, Francesco Albani, Lodovico Carracci and Carlo Cignani.

The Basilica of San Martino and the duomo
Map 7.

Founded in 1217, the basilica was remodelled in the mid-15th century, and the façade was rebuilt in 1879.

Inside, on the south side, are altarpieces by Girolamo da Carpi and Amico Aspertini, and a fragment by Vitale da Bologna. The pretty organ in the sanctuary, by Giovanni Cipri, dates from 1556. On the north side, beside the sacristy door, are fresco fragments by Simone dei Crocifissi. The altarpieces are by Lorenzo Costa, Lodovico Carracci and Bartolomeo Cesi. The first chapel, built in 1506, contains paintings by Francesco Francia and Amico Aspertini. The statue of the Madonna is attributed to Jacopo della Quercia. Here also is a fresco fragment of the *Nativity*, recently uncovered and attributed to Paolo Uccello (very difficult to see).

From here to the duomo, go west along Via Marsala, and then turn left down Via dell'Indipendenza, a busy main street, opened in 1888. Probably founded before the 10th century, the **duomo** was rebuilt several times after 1605 and is now essentially a 17th-century Baroque building with an elaborate west front by Alfonso Torreggiani (18th century). The choir is the work of Domenico Tibaldi (1575). The crypt, campanile and two delightful red marble lions survive from the Romanesque building.

Inside, the second chapel of the south aisle preserves the skull of St Anne, presented in 1435 by Henry VI of England to Nicolò Albergati. Above the inner arch of the choir is an *Annunciation*, frescoed by Lodovico Carracci. A 12th-century *Crucifixion* group carved in cedar wood surmounts the high altar.

The area behind the cathedral is an interesting survival of medieval Bologna, with many old houses and remains of the towers erected by patrician families.

Parmigianino: *Madonna and Child with St Margaret and Other Saints* (1529–30). Pinacoteca Nazionale.

The Museo Medievale
Map 6. Open Mon–Sat 9–5.30, Sun and holidays 10–6.
On Via Manzoni, beneath a raised portico, is the entrance to Palazzo Ghisilardi-Fava, begun in 1483. This is home to the **Museo Civico Medievale e del Rinascimento**, a beautifully arranged museum of medieval and Renaissance sculpture and applied art.

Ground Floor
Rooms 1 and 2: Exhibits illustrate the origins of the collections in the 17th and 18th centuries.
Room 4 (on the other side of the courtyard, which has 16th-century Jewish tombstones): 14th-century tombs by the dalle Masegne. The second courtyard (on Via Porta di Castello) has a medieval lapidary collection.
Rooms 5 and 6: Medieval metalwork and ivories, including a bronze 13th-century Mosen ewer in the shape of a horse and rider. Room 5 has remains of the Roman imperial palace in the first city walls, destroyed in 1116.
Room 7: The room is dominated by the over-life-size bronze and beaten-copper statue of Pope Boniface VIII by Manno Bandini (1301), formerly on the façade of Palazzo Pubblico. The 14th-century cope is one of the finest works ever produced in *opus anglicanum* (English medieval embroidery). It includes scenes showing the martyrdom of St Thomas Becket.

Lower Ground Floor
Room 9: Contains a statuette of St Peter Martyr by Giovanni di Balduccio.
Room 10: Has remains of a Roman building on this site, and charming 14th-century tombs of university lecturers.
Room 11: The red-marble tomb slab of Bartolomeo da Vernazza (d. 1348).
Room 12: Triptych of the *Madonna and Child with Saints*, carved in bas-relief by Jacopo della Quercia and assistants, and a terracotta *Madonna* in high relief, also by Jacopo. The interesting recumbent image of a saint in stuccoed and painted wood is by Antonio Federighi.
Room 13: 15th-century floor tombs and the tomb of Pietro Canonici (d. 1502), attributed to Vincenzo Onofri.

First Floor
Room 15: A major collection of bronzes, which include the model for the Neptune Fountain by Giambologna, the first version of the famous *Mercury* by the same artist, *St Michael and the Devil*, by Alessandro Algardi, and a bronze bust of Gregory XV by Gian Lorenzo Bernini.
Room 16: A fine display of illuminated choir books (13th–16th centuries).
Rooms 17–20: The collection of applied arts. Among the more notable items are a ceremonial sword and sheath given to Lodovico Bentivoglio by Pope Nicholas V (Room 17); a collection of European armour (Room 18); an ivory parade saddle (German, 15th century) in Room 19; and Turkish armour and bronzes from the 13th–15th centuries (Room 20).
Rooms 21–22: Northern European ivories, and Venetian and German glass, including a rare blue glass cup with a gilt enamelled frieze, perhaps from the Barovier workshop in Murano (mid-15th century), and two vessels probably made for the wedding of Giovanni Bentivoglio and Ginevra Sforza in 1464.

West of the centre

Via Manzoni enters Via Galliera (Map 6), the main north–south artery of the city before Via dell'Indipendenza was built. It has been called the Grand Canal of Bologna, from the splendour of its palazzi. A short way to the right is Palazzo Montanari (1725), next to the church of Santa Maria Maggiore, with 16th-century statues of Mary Magdalen and St Roch attributed to Giovanni Zacchi. In the other direction Via Porta di Castello ascends through an archway across Via Monte Grappa into the busy Via Ugo Bassi. Straight across, a road skirts the interesting exterior of the huge Palazzo Comunale into Piazza Roosevelt. In Via IV Novembre (no. 7) is the birthplace of Guglielmo Marconi. Opposite is the huge Classical exterior of the flank of **San Salvatore**. The church contains the tomb of Guercino and works by Lippo di Dalmasio, Girolamo da Treviso, Girolamo da Carpi, Vitale da Bologna and Garofalo.

In Via Val d'Aposa is the charming façade of **Spirito Santo** (Map 10), a gem of ter-racotta ornament, in very good condition. The **Collegio di Spagna** (Map 14; *open only by special permission)* was founded in 1365 for Spanish students. It is the last sur-vivor of the many colleges, resembling those at Oxford and Cambridge, which exist-ed in Bologna in the Middle Ages. It still has a high scholastic reputation. Ignatius Loyola and Cervantes are among its famous students.

Via Urbana follows the delightful garden wall of the college (you can see part of the external painted decoration on the building from here), back to Via Tagliapietre. Here on the right is the church of **Corpus Domini** (Map 14) built in 1478–80, with a ter-racotta portal by Sperandio. In a 17th-century chapel (opened by a closed order of nuns) are preserved the relics of St Catherine de'Vigri (d. 1463), an erudite ascetic of Bologna, greatly venerated.

Nearby, at Via d'Azeglio 54, is **San Procolo**, a church of ancient foundation, with a Romanesque façade. In the choir is an interesting Roman sarcophagus, probably dec-orated in the late 15th century. **Palazzo Bevilacqua** (Map 10) is a good example of the imported Tuscan style of 1474–82, with a splendid courtyard. The Council of Trent held two sessions in this building in 1547, having moved from Trento to Bologna to escape an epidemic.

San Francesco

Map 10.

The Porta Nuova, one of the old city gates, leads into the long Piazza Malpighi beside the Colonna dell'Immacolata, with a copper statue designed by Guido Reni. Here is San Francesco, in many ways the most attractive church in Bologna. The churchyard holds the tombs of the glossators Accursio (d. 1260), Odofredo (d. 1265) and Rolandino de'Romanzi (d. 1284). The glossators were commentators on the law, who had their own school, founded at Bologna University. Their commentaries sowed the seeds of modern civil law.

The church is in a more or less French Gothic style, begun in 1236, completed early in 1263, but considerably altered since. The façade (c. 1250) has two carved 8th-cen-tury *plutei* and 13th–14h-century majolica plaques in the pitch of the roof. The smaller of the two towers was completed in 1261; the larger and finer, the work of Antonio di Vincenzo (1397–c. 1402), is surrounded by decorative terracotta. Inside are the terracotta tomb of Pope Alexander V, completed by Sperandio in 1482, in the north aisle; and the Fieschi tomb (1492) in the south aisle. The choir has a marble reredos by Jacobello and Pier Paolo dalle Masegne (1388–92). On the sanctuary walls are frescoes by Francesco da Rimini, and a crucifix attributed to Pietro Lianori hangs in the east chapel of the ambulatory.

At Via dei Gombruti 23 (off Via Portanuova) the 'Old Pretender', son of King James II of England and Mary of Modena, stayed during several visits to Bologna.

The outskirts of Bologna

In the southern part of the town are the pleasant **Giardini Margherita** (Map 16), laid out in 1875. The church of **Santa Maria della Misericordia** (Map 15), enlarged in the 15th century, has stained-glass windows by Francesco Francia. The little church of the **Madonna del Baraccano** (Map 16) has a good fresco by Francesco Cossa. Further south, reached by Via Murri, at Via Toscana 19, is the Villa Aldovrandi, with an 18th-century theatre (*open on the first and third Thur of each month at 3*).

On a hill to the southwest (bus 30) stands the former Olivetan convent of **San Michele in Bosco** (beyond Map 14), with a splendid view of Bologna. Here, on 1 May 1860, Camillo Cavour and Vittorio Emanuele II met to approve the sailing of the 'Thousand' to Sicily (*see p. 543*). The church, rebuilt since 1437 and completed in the early 16th century, has a façade ascribed to Baldassare Peruzzi (1523). In the cloister are the remains of an important fresco cycle by Lodovico Carracci, Guido Reni and others. The primitive church of **San Vittore**, on the next hill to the south (at Via San Mamolo 40), dates from the 11th and 12th centuries, though it was altered in 1864.

The sanctuary of the **Madonna di San Luca** (*marked on the map on p. 570*) is a famous viewpoint, reached by bus 20 from Via Indipendenza to the public park of **Villa Spada** in Via Saragozza (Map 13) at the foot of the hill of San Luca. From here a minibus (roughly every 30mins) ascends the hill. The church is connected with Porta Saragozza (Map 13), just over 3km away, by a portico of 666 arches (1674–1793). Where the portico begins the ascent of the hill is the **Arco del Meloncello**, by Carlo Francesco Dotti (1718). The sanctuary, built by Dotti in 1725–49, contains a *Noli me Tangere* by Guercino, and paintings by Calvaert.

Outside Porta Sant'Isaia (Map 9) are the huge sports stadium, built in 1926, and the **Certosa** (bus 14), founded in 1334, suppressed in 1797, and consecrated in 1801 as the public cemetery of Bologna. It was much admired by Byron. The 14th–16th-century church contains marquetry stalls (1539) and frescoes by Bartolomeo Cesi. The tomb of the poet Carducci lies near a statue of Murat, by Vincenzo Vela (1865). The Etruscan necropolis of Felsina was discovered in the precincts of the Certosa in 1869.

Around Bologna

The Pistoia road, which leads south from Bologna, passes **Pontecchio Marconi**. This is the resting place of Bologna-born Guglielmo Marconi (1874–1937), whose first experiments in the transmission of signals by Hertzian waves were made at his father's Villa Griffone above the town. Marconi's mausoleum was designed by the prominent early Modernist architect Marcello Piacentini. In the park is a relic of the boat *Elettra* from which, while at anchor in the port of Genoa in 1930, Marconi lit up the lights of Sydney.

At **Marzabotto**, in the park of Villa Aria, are remains of an Etruscan city, thought to be Misa (6th–4th centuries BC). Excavations have revealed traces of houses, temples and two necropoli (*site open daily 8–7*); the Museo Nazionale Etrusco houses the finds (*open daily 9–1 & 3–6.30*).

The road continues south to **Porretta Terme**, a little spa on the Reno, with warm springs of sulphurous and alkaline waters, beyond which it enters Tuscany.

PRACTICAL INFORMATION

GETTING AROUND

• **By air:** Airport buses: no. 91 to and from the station at 41mins past the hour; Aerobus every 15mins to and from the airport in 20mins; stops in Via Ugo Bassi and Via dell'Indipendenza, at the station and at the trade-fair ground.

• **By rail:** Bologna is Italy's most important rail junction. The main north–south line closely follows the Via Emilia from Milan to Bologna; fast Eurostar trains make the journey in 1hr 40mins nonstop. Intercities are slower, stopping at Piacenza, Parma, Reggio Emilia and/or Modena. Eurostars and Intercities will also take you to Bologna from Florence (1hr), Ancona (2hrs, stopping at Rimini, Forlì and/or Faenza), Venice (via Padua, 1hr 50mins) and Verona (1hr 20mins). Commuter trains (Regionali and Interregionali) serve Ravenna and other centres in the region.

• **By car:** The centre of the city is closed to traffic (except for those with special permits) every day including holidays 7–8, and cars are controlled electronically. Access is allowed to hotels by arrangement with the hotel. The large free car park outside the historic centre in Via Tanari has a minibus service every 15mins to the station (from there Piazza Maggiore is reached by buses 25 and 30). Car parks in the historic centre (with hourly tariff and limited space) include Piazza Roosevelt and Piazza 8 Agosto (closed Fri–Sat). A map of car parks is published by the *comune*.

• **By bus:** Nos 25, 30, 37 or 90 from the railway station to Via Ugo Bassi (for Piazza Maggiore). Bus 30 continues to San Michele in Bosco. Bus 29 from Via Ugo Bassi for San Mamolo; and bus 14 for the Certosa. Bus 20 from Via Indipendenza to Villa Spada (and from there minibuses every 30mins to the Madonna di San Luca).

The bus station at Piazza XX Settembre (Map 3, T: 051 242150) has excellent services to nearly all places of interest in the region, as well as long-distance and international services.

• **By taxi:** Radio Taxi, T: 051 372727, 051 534141.

INFORMATION OFFICES

Bologna Piazza Maggiore 1e, T: 051

246541, www.emiliaromagnaturismo.it, and at the station (T: 051 246541) and airport (International Arrivals, T: 051 647 2036).

HOTELS

Bologna

The city has numerous hotels of all categories, but they are often all full when big trade fairs are being held (especially in spring and autumn).There is a scheme called *Bologna non solo week-end* which offers good rates at certain hotels at weekends, and in the summer.

€€€ **Al Cappello Rosso**. In business since the 14th century. Via de' Fusari 9, T: 051 261891, F: 051 227179, www.alcappellorosso.it

€€€ **Baglioni**. Elegant and refined, with a good restaurant. Via dell'Indipendenza 8, T: 051 225445, F: 051 234840, www.baglionihotels.com

€€ **Corona d'Oro** 1890. Central and comfortable. Closed July–Aug. Via Oberdan 12, T: 051 236456, F: 051 262679.

€€ **Orologio**. In an ancient building with views over Piazza Maggiore. Via IV Novembre 10, T: 051 231253, F: 051 260552, orologio.hotel-bologna.net

€€ **Re Enzo**. Comfortable and centrally located. Via Santa Croce 26, T: 051 523322, F: 051 554035, www.hotelreenzo.it

€€ **Touring**. Calm, cosy and friendly, with great views from the rooftop terrace. Via de' Mattuiani 1/2, T: 051 584305, F: 051 334763, www.hoteltouring.it

€€ **Tre Vecchi**. A classic place to stay in Bologna, conveniently located between the station and Piazza Maggiore.

Via dell'Indipendenza 47, T: 051 231991, F: 051 224143.

Loiano

€€ **Palazzo Loup**. Small, quiet and restful, an 18th-century villa with gardens in a picturesque part of the Apennines; closed Dec–Feb. Via Santa Margherita 21, Località Scanello, T: 051 654 4040, F: 051 654 4040.

YOUTH HOSTELS

Bologna

€ **Due Torri–San Sisto 2**, Via Viadagola 5, T: 051 501810, F: 051 501810.

€ **San Sisto**, Via Viadagola 14, T: 051 501810, F: 051 501810.

RESTAURANTS

Bologna

€€€ **Al Ghisello**. Garden restaurant with outstanding Emilian fare. Closed Mon and Aug. Via Crocioni 7a, T: 051 614 6874.

€€€ **Al Pappagallo**. Good ambience and great food in the heart of the old city. Closed Sun. Piazza della Mercanzia 3c, T: 051 232807.

€€€ **Franco Rossi**. Innovative cooking, interesting selection of cheeses, oils and wines. Closed Sun and July. Via Goito 3, T: 051 238818.

€€€ **Rodrigo**. Another famous fish restaurant, with excellent desserts; closed Sun. Via della Zecca 2h, T: 051 220445.

€€ **Bitone**. Traditional Emilian recipes prepared with a personal twist. Closed Mon–Tues and Aug. Via Emilia Levante 111, T: 051 546110.

€€ **Cantina Bentivoglio**. Great selections of wines, good food, cold and cooked. Closed Aug. Via Mascarella 4b, T: 051 265416.

€€ Da Sandro al Navile. Good food and great wines from Emilia and other regions. Closed Sun, Dec–Jan and Aug. Via del Sostegno 15, T: 051 634 3100.

€€ Diana. Delicious regional food and wines—a favourite of the Bolognese. Closed Mon, Jan and Aug. Via Indipendenza 24, T: 051 231302.

€€ Godot. Good selection of wines, creative and traditional food. Closed Sun and Aug. Via Cartoleria 12, T: 051 226315.

€€ Le Maschere. Famous for fish. Closed Sun and Aug. Via Zappoli 5b, T: 051 261035.

€€ Nuovo Notai. Traditional regional cuisine, in a historic building. Closed Sun. Via De Pignatari 1, T: 051 228691.

€€ Pernice e Gallina. Dishes from the regional tradition, specialising in game; great selection of cheeses, desserts and wines. Closed Sun–Mon midday and Aug. Via dell'Abbadia 4, T: 051 269922.

€€ Torre de' Galluzzi. Creative cuisine, especially fish, in a medieval tower. Closed midday Sat June–Sept, Sun, Jan and Aug. Corte de' Galluzzi 5a, T: 051 267638.

€ Gigina. Trattoria specialising in high quality Emilian food, good selection of wines. Closed Sat and Aug. Via Stendhal 1b, T: 051 322132.

€ Paradisono. Good trattoria specialising in frogs and other Bolognese delicacies. Closed Tues (except in summer). Via Coriolano Vighi 33, T: 051 566401.

€ Riff-Raff. Large selection of wines from southern Europe and the world, coupled with special southern foods. Closed Mon and Aug. Via del Pratello 3c, T: 051 222888.

Loiano

€€ Palazzo Loup. Hotel restaurant, specialising in regional cooking and grilled meats, good wine selection. Closed Dec 23–Jan 31. Via Santa Margherita 21, T: 051 6544040.

€ Benvenuti. Family-run restaurant serving local dishes. Closed Mon, Feb, June and Oct. Via Roma 13, T: 051 654102.

WINE BARS

€ Bottega del Vino Olindo Faccioli. Wine bar offering good cold dishes and a limited selection of hot dishes. Open evenings only, closed Sun. Via Altabella 15b, T: 051 223171.

€ Cantina Bentivoglio. A good wine bar; open evenings only, closed Mon. Via Mascarella 4b, T: 051 265416.

€ Divinis. Great selection of wines, matched by interesting selections of cheeses and cold meats. Closed Sun and Aug. Via Battibecco 4c, T: 051 2961502.

€ Osteria del Sole. Wine bar that serves light snacks. Vicolo Ranocchi 1.

CAFÉS & PASTRY SHOPS

Casa Dolciaria Giuseppe Majani. A historic confectioner. Via Carbonesi 5.
Gelateria delle Moline. For Bologna's best ice-cream. Via delle Moline 13d.
Pasticceria Impero. For coffee and pastries. Via Indipendenza 39.

SPECIALITY FOOD SHOPS

Antica Drogheria Calzolari. A good selection of Bolognese food and wines. Via Petroni 9.
Boutique del Formaggio. For local and

Italian cheeses. Viale Oriani 16 (near Santo Stefano).

ENTERTAINMENT

Bologna probably has more theatres per square metre than any other Italian city. There are opera, ballet and concert programmes at the Teatro Comunale, late Oct–May, as well as numerous other classical music series. Examples include *I Concerti di Musica Insieme*, Oct–March; *Balletti d'Autunno*, ballet, Oct–March; *Concerti d'Organo ai Servi*, organ concerts at Santa Maria dei Servi, Oct–May; *Il Sabato all'Accademia Filarmonica*, chamber music, Jan–Dec; *I Concerti del Circolo della Musica*, Oct–March; *I Concerti dell'Associazione Giovanile Musicale*, Oct–March; *Concerti d'Organo all'Antoniano*, Oct; *Immagini e Suoni nel Tempo*, concerts at the Pinacoteca Nazionale, Jan–May; *Conoscere la Musica*, spring concerts offered by the Conservatory, Feb–Apr; Bologna Festival: *I Grandi Interpreti*, Apr–June; *Organi Antichi*, organ concerts on antique instruments, Apr–Dec; *La Camera della Musica*, concerts in the Cappella Farnese, May; *Concerti di Villa Mazzacorati*, Oct–Apr and summer; *Concerti Capire la Musica*, autumn–winter; *Festival di Santo Stefano*, June.

Non-classical series include *Suoni nel Mondo*, ethnic music series, autumn–winter; *Rassegna Jazz alla Cantina Bentivoglio*, Oct–June; *Rassegna Jazz al Chet Baker*, Oct–June; *Concerti Jazz all'Osteria dell'Orsa*, autumn–spring; *Concerti Rock, blues & soul* at Ruvido Club, autumn–spring.

The *Bologna dei Musei* museum card, available in 1-day and 3-day versions, gives free or reduced admission to museums throughout the city. Available at participating museums.

SHOPPING

The things to buy in Bologna are eatables: *tortellini, raviole, mortadella, passatelli,* etc. Markets are held on Fri and Sat in Piazza 8 Agosto (Map 7). Daily food markets in Via Ugo Bassi and Via Pescherie Vecchie. *Mostra Mercato dell'Antiquariato di Santo Stefano*, antiques market, second Sat and Sun of the month, except Jan, July and Aug. *Celò Celò Mamanca* collectables market, Thur except July–Aug, Via Valdonica and Piazza San Martino. *Decomela Art*, crafts fair, second weekend of the month (except July–Aug).

FESTIVALS & EVENTS

Festivals include *Bologna Est*, with concerts, theatre, etc., July–Sept; and Porretta Soul Festival, at Porretta Terme, July. Open-air cinema at sites around the city in summer.
San Petronio, the patron saint, is celebrated on 4 Oct with a fair in Via Altabella; other religious festivals include San Giuseppe, March; San Luca and Santa Rita, May; Sant'Antonio, June; Santa Lucia, Nov–Dec.
Special sports events include the famous Mille Miglia antique car race, May.

MODENA & REGGIO EMILIA

M odena and Reggio Emilia are two ideal microcities: they combine small-town scale with big-city amenities such as symphony orchestras and opera. Each year they turn up in the list of Italy's most pleasant urban environments.

NB: This section is covered by the map on p. 570.

MODENA

The prosperous provincial capital of Modena, with the ancient Via Emilia slicing through the city centre, has figured prominently in Italian history. It has a beautiful Romanesque cathedral, and a number of churches with expressive 16th-century works by the local sculptor Antonio Begarelli. The Galleria Estense has a fine collection of paintings formed by the Este family in the early 16th century. The name of Modena is also associated with the Maserati motor works, and especially with the Ferrari works, founded by Enzo Ferrari (1898–1989) outside the town at Maranello.

HISTORY OF MODENA

The Roman colony of Mutina, established in the 2nd century BC on a site already inhabited by Gauls and Etruscans, diminished in importance under the Roman Empire. The present city dates its prosperity from the time of Countess Matilda of Tuscany (d. 1115), who supported the Guelphs and the Pope's authority. After her death Modena became a free city and, in rivalry with Bologna, inclined more to the Ghibelline faction. In 1288 the Este family gained control of the city, and the duchy of Modena was created for Borso d'Este in 1452. Mary of Modena (1658–1718), Catholic queen of James II of England and mother of the Old Pretender, was the daughter of Alfonso IV d'Este. Este rule lasted until 1796, when Napoleon took the town and added it to his Cisalpine Republic. The duchy was reconstituted in 1814–59 through an alliance of the Este with the house of Austria: first under Francesco IV, grandson of Ercole III and of Empress Maria Theresa, and ultimately under his son Francesco V, a despotic and unpopular ruler who retained his position only thanks to Austrian troops. Modena joined the Kingdom of Italy in 1859.

The duomo

The splendid Romanesque duomo was begun in 1099 on the site of two earlier churches built over the tomb of St Geminianus (d. 397), patron saint of the town. The Como architect Lanfranco worked together with sculptor Wiligelmus, who here produced some remarkable Romanesque sculptures. The work was continued by Campionese artists (from the region of Campione d'Italia on Lago di Lugano) in the 12th–14th centuries.

On the façade, the west portal is a superb work by Wiligelmus (the two lions are restored Roman works). On the left of the door is the foundation stone of the church, to which was added a dedication to Wiligelmus. Across the front of the façade are four bas-reliefs with stories from Genesis, also by Wiligelmus (1100; they were formerly all aligned, but two were moved up when the side doors were added). Above the loggia, with finely carved capitals by the school of Wiligelmus and Campionese artists, is a large rose window by Anselmo da Campione (1200).

On the south side, which flanks the Piazza Grande, are more beautifully carved capitals by Wiligelmus and his school. The first door is the Porta dei Principi, also by Wiligelmus, with six very fine bas-reliefs of the *Life of St Geminianus*. The lion on the right is a copy made in 1948 after damage to the porch. Above to the right is a very damaged bas-relief of *Jacob and the Angel*. The Porta Regia is by the Campionese school (1209–31). In the last arch on the south side are four reliefs describing the *Life of St Geminianus* by Agostino di Duccio (1442). The exterior of the apse is also very fine, and there is another inscription here of the early 13th century, recording the foundation of the church by Lanfranco. On the north side, the Porta della Pescheria has delightful carvings by the school of Wiligelmus on the archivolt, showing an assault on a castle.

The beautiful interior is of pale red brick with a red-marble floor. The Romanesque arcades have alternate slender columns and composite piers that support an early-15th-century vault. The capitals are by Wiligelmus and his school. The two stoups are carved out of Roman capitals. In the south aisle, the Cappella Bellincini has frescoes by Cristoforo da Lendinara and his school dating from c. 1475, with the *Last Judgement* and a frescoed triptych inside a terracotta arch. The small terracotta *Adoration of the Shepherds* (1527) is a beautiful work by Antonio Begarelli, a sculptor who learned his craft in the family workshop. In the north aisle, the wooden statue of St Geminianus probably dates from the 14th century. The elaborately carved terracotta ancona is attributed to Michele da Firenze, and the detached fresco of the *Madonna della Piazza* to Cristoforo da Modena (late 14th century). The pulpit is by Enrico da Campione (1322). The second altarpiece is by Dosso Dossi. On the stairs is a wall monument to Claudio Rangoni (d. 1537) to a design by Giulio Romano.

The rood-screen, supported by lions and crouching figures, forms the approach to the raised choir. The coloured sculptures are splendid works by Anselmo da Campione (1200–25). They represent the *Evangelists* (on the pulpit), and *Scenes of the Passion*. Above hangs a wooden crucifix in high relief (1200).

In the choir, a screen of slender, red-marble coupled columns in two tiers by Campionese artists surrounds the beautiful altar table. In the apse is a restored statue in bronze and copper of *St Geminianus* by Geminiano Paruolo (1376). The inlaid stalls

Modena's duomo, from Piazza Grande.

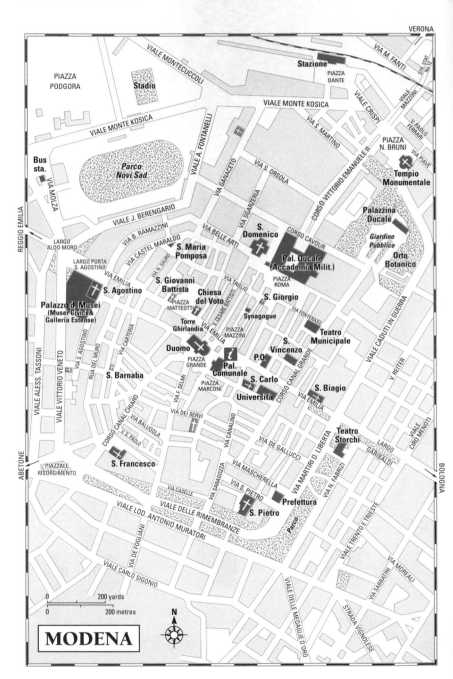

are the masterpiece of the brothers Cristoforo and Lorenzo da Lendinara. In the left apse is a polyptych by Serafino Serafini. The four inlaid portraits of the *Evangelists* are by Cristoforo da Lendinara, and there is more inlaid work by Lendinara in the sacristy. The Lendinara brothers were famed for their illusionistic intarsia pictures.

In the crypt (with remarkable capitals, some attributed to Wiligelmus) are the tomb of St Geminianus and an expressive group of five terracotta statues known as the *Madonna della Pappa*, by Guido Mazzoni (1480). The tiny organ here by Domenico Traeri dates from 1719.

Around Piazza Grande

The north side of the duomo is connected by two Gothic arches to the **Torre Ghirlandina**, the beautiful detached campanile of the cathedral, 86m high and slightly inclined. It was begun at the same time as the cathedral, the octagonal storey being added in 1319; the spire was rebuilt in the 16th century. The interior can be visited on Sun and holidays (*open Apr–Oct Sun 10.1 & 3 7, closed Aug*). Nearby is the **Museo Lapidario** (*open summer Wed–Sun 10–12.30 & 4–7; winter Tues–Sun 9.30–12.30 & 3.30–6.30*), containing sculpture from the cathedral.

In Piazza Grande is the **Palazzo Comunale**, with an arcaded ground floor and a clock tower. The building was first erected in the 12th century, but dates in its present form from a reconstruction of 1624. The Sala del Fuoco has fine frescoes (1546) by Niccolò dell'Abate.

Piazza Grande, viewed from the duomo.

From Piazza della Torre beside the Torre Ghirlandina, the Via Emilia runs west through the centre of the town past the domed **Chiesa del Voto**, built in 1634 (with 17th-century works by Francesco Stringa and Lodovico Lana) and the church of San Giovanni Battista. On the other side of the Via Emilia is the church of **Sant'Agostino**, with a sumptuous interior designed by Giovanni Giacomo Monti in 1664. The *Deposition* here (1524–26), with stucco figures bearing traces of colour, is the master-piece of Antonio Begarelli. The detached 14th-century fresco of the *Madonna and Child* is by Tommaso da Modena.

Galleria Estense

Open Tues–Sun 8.30–7.30.
Situated on the top floor of the huge Palazzo dei Musei (built in 1771 as a poorhouse), the Galleria Estense is a fine collection of pictures put together by the Este family in the early 16th century, notable especially for its works by the 15th–17th-century Emilian schools. The most important part of the collection was dispersed during the Napoleonic era, and ended up in Dresden. The rooms are not numbered, but the collection is displayed in roughly chronological order (although the paintings are often moved around). The room numbers given below correspond to the plan of the gallery on display.

Atrium: Cases containing a sampling of the Este collections are displayed here, notably Egyptian and Italic antiquities and bronzes by L'Antico (including the Gonzaga vase).

Long Gallery: Divided into nine small rooms, this gives a broad representation of Northern Italian painting from the 14th–16th centuries.

Room I: 14th–15th-century works including paintings by Tommaso da Modena and Barnaba da Modena.

Rooms II–III: Representative works by, among others, Cristoforo Lendinara, Bartoloemo Bonascia and Francesco Bianchi Ferrari.

Room IV: Terracotta statues by 16th-century Emilian artists.

Room V: Works by Francesco Botticini (*Adoration of the Child*), Giuliano Bugiardini and Andrea del Sarto (*Madonna and Child with St Elisabeth and St John*).

Room VI: Flemish works by Albrecht Bouts and *Madonnas* by Joos van Cleve and Mabuse.

Room VII–VIII: *Deposition* by Cima da Conegliano and works by Vincenzo Catena, Giovanni Cariani, Francesco Maineri and Filippo Mazzola (father of Parmigianino).

Room IX–X: The *Madonna Campori* by Correggio, and works by Lelio Orsi. There is also a beautiful 16th-century portable writing desk.

Room XI: Works by the Ferrara school, including Girolamo da Carpi and Dosso Dossi. Also here is the Estense harp, beautifully decorated at the end of the 16th century.

Room XII: The 'Wunderkamera', with an assembly of exotic and extravagant items from the Este collections.

Room XIII: 16th-century Emilian paintings, including works by Garofalo (d. 1559), who helped establish the

High Renaissance style (with Raphael as his model) in this region of Italy.

Room XIV: 16th–18th-century portraits, notably the *Portrait of Francesco I* by Velázquez.

Rooms XV–XVI: A collection of medals including some by Caradosso, Pisanello, Moderno, Bonacolsi and Giovan Cristoforo Romano. The marble head of a veiled lady is by François Duquesnoy. There is also a carving by Grinling Gibbons.

Rooms 1–4: The last four large rooms hold 16th–17th-century works. Room 1 has works by the Venetian school, including Tintoretto (notably the octagons with scenes from Ovid's *Metamorphoses* for the villa of Vittore Pisani), Il Padovanino, Veronese (*Saints*), Palma il Giovane, Pietro Liberi and Jacopo Bassano. Rooms 2 and 3: Emilian school: Guercino (*Martyrdom of St Peter*), Guido Reni, Lodovico Carracci, Prospero Fontana (*Holy Family*), Scarsellino, Pier Francesco Cittadini (still lifes) and Carlo Cignani (*Flora*). A marble bust of *Francesco I d'Este*, founder of the collection, by Gian Lorenzo Bernini (1652), stands near the entrance to this room. Room 4: 17th-century works by Camillo and Giulio Cesare Procaccini, Pomarancio, Il Cerano, Rosa da Tivoli, Salvator Rosa, Daniele Crespi and Charles le Brun; and 12 panels from the ceiling of Palazzo dei Diamanti in Ferrara by the Carracci and others.

Museo d'Arte Medievale e Moderna and the Museo Archeologico Etnologico
Open Tues–Sat 9–12 & 3–6, Sun and holidays 10–1 & 3–7.
Both collections are housed on the floor below the Galleria Estense. The medieval and 'modern' holdings include the terracotta *Madonna di Piazza* commissioned from Begarelli in 1523 for the façade of the Palazzo Comunale; reliquary crosses; musical instruments including a harpischord by Pietro Termanini (1741) and flutes made by Thomas Stanesby (1692–1754) in London; scientific instruments including the microscope of Giovanni Battista Amici; ceramics; and arms. Room 8 preserves its furnishings of 1886, when it was opened to display the Gandini collection of ancient fabrics, textiles and embroidered silks (with about 2,000 fragments dating from the 11th to the 19th centuries).

The large hall (10) displays the archaeological holdings, arranged chronologically from the Palaeolithic era onwards. There is an important section devoted to Mutina, Roman Modena. The ethnological material is arranged in rooms 11, 12 and 13, with exhibits from New Guinea, pre-Columbian Peru, Asia, South America and Africa. The last room (14) displays the Matteo Campori (1857–1933) collection of paintings with 17th- and 18th-century works, and a collection of cameos.

Also on the first floor is the city archive and the **Biblioteca Estense** (*open daily except Sun and holidays 9–1*), with illuminated manuscripts, notably the Bible of Borso d'Este, illuminated by Taddeo Crivelli and Franco Russi; a 14th-century edition of Dante; and the missal of Renée of France, by Jean Bourdichon (16th century). Renée was the wife of Ercole II of Modena, and was noted for her Calvinist sympathies.

Palazzo Ducale and environs

Via Sauro leads north from the Via Emilia to Santa Maria Pomposa, where Lodovico Antonio Muratori (1672–1750), provost of the church from 1716 and an eminent historian (nicknamed the 'Father of Italian History'), is buried. He lived and died in the adjacent house, now a museum (*open Mon–Fri 5.30pm–7.30pm*), which preserves his autograph works and other mementoes. Via Cesare Battisti leads north from Piazza Grande to the church of **San Domenico**, rebuilt in 1708–31. In the baptistery is a colossal terracotta statuary group by Begarelli, thought to represent *Christ in the House of Martha*.

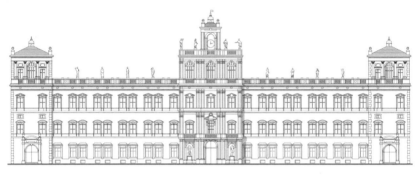

PALAZZO DUCALE

The huge Palazzo Ducale, now the Italian Military Academy, was begun in 1634 by the Roman architect Bartolomeo Avanzini for Francesco I, on the site of the old Este castle. The interior (*open for guided visits Sun, except holidays, 10 & 11 by reservation; T: 059 206660*) has a fine courtyard and a monumental 17th-century staircase. In the state apartments, with portraits and frescoes by Francesco Stringa, the Salone d'Onore has a ceiling fresco by Marcoantonio Franceschini, and the Salottino d'Oro has elaborate decorations dating from 1751. There is a museum illustrating the history of the academy, founded in 1669.

Behind the palace (entered from Corso Cavour) are pleasant public gardens laid out in 1602. The Palazzina dei Giardini, a garden pavilion begun in 1634 by Gaspare Vigarani (and altered in the 18th century), is used for exhibitions by the Galleria Civica. It adjoins the botanical gardens (opened on request at the Istituto Botanico of the university) founded by Francesco III in 1758. Beyond the other end of the gardens is the huge Tempio Monumentale, a war memorial built in an eclectic style by Achille Casanova and Domenico Barbanti in 1929.

From Piazza Roma, in front of Palazzo Ducale, a narrow street leads south past the Baroque church of **San Giorgio**, by Gaspare Vigarani, to Piazza Mazzini and the synagogue, built in 1869–73 (*open by appointment; T: 059 223978*), which adjoins the Via Emilia.

Elsewhere in town

In the southern part of the town, reached from the duomo by the arcaded Corso Canal Chiaro, is the church of **San Francesco** (1244; altered in the 19th century), which contains a terracotta *Descent from the Cross* (1530–31), by Begarelli. To the east is the Baroque church of **San Bartolomeo**, with paintings by Giuseppe Maria Crespi and others. Further east the 15th-century church of **San Pietro**, with an ornamented brick front, contains sculptures by Antonio Begarelli, an organ with 16th-century paintings, and a good painting by Francesco Bianchi Ferrari. Beyond the church is a pleasant park with a war memorial of 1926 and the Teatro Storchi (1886), Modena's important prose theatre. Further west, near the Via Emilia, is the university, founded c. 1178, in a building of 1773. North of Via Emilia rises the 17th-century church of **San Vincenzo**, with Estense tombs and paintings by Matteo Rosselli and Guercino.

AROUND MODENA

Carpi

The most interesting place in the province of Modena is the town of Carpi, with an attractive centre and some fine palaces, now surrounded by extensive industrial suburbs. From 1327 to 1525 it was a lordship of the Pio family, famous as patrons of the arts, who after 1450 were called Pio di Savoia. The huge piazza, laid out in the 15th–16th centuries, with a lovely portico, is particularly handsome.

Here the Pio Castle houses the **Museo Civico** (*closed at the time of writing; T: 059 649977*), founded in 1914, which contains some fine works in *scagliola*, a material made from selenite, which is used to imitate marble and *pietre dure* (the town was famous in the 17th–18th centuries for its production of *scagliola* works). There is also a museum that commemorates the victims deported to Nazi concentration camps in Germany in the Second World War (*open Jan–June and Sept–Dec, Thur, Sat–Sun and holidays 10–12.30 & 3.30–7; July–Aug 10–12.30 & 4–8*). The largest Nazi internment camp set up in Italy in 1944 was at **Fossoli**, 5km outside Carpi; it is described at the beginning of *Se Questo è un'Uomo* (*If This is a Man*) by Primo Levi, who was deported from here to Auschwitz in 1944. He survived to write about the ordeal.

Beneath the portico in the piazza is a 19th-century pharmacy. The **duomo**, begun in 1514, contains terracottas and sculptures by Antonio Begarelli. The Teatro Comunale (with a fine interior) dates from 1857–61. The Portico del Grano dates from the end of the 15th century.

Behind the castle is the *pieve* of **Santa Maria in Castello** (known as La Sagra), with its tall campanile. The 12th-century church was greatly reduced in size in 1514. It contains the sarcophagus of Manfredo Pio (1351), a marble ambone attributed to Niccolò (12th century) and two frescoed chapels of the early 15th century.

On Corso Manfredo Fanti is the late 17th-century church of **Sant'Ignazio**, which contains a fine high altar in *scagliola* (1696) and a large 17th-century painting by Bonaventura Lamberti. To the south is the church of **San Nicolò**, built on a central plan in 1494. It also contains fine *scagliola* altars. Further south are the Rococo church of the **Crocifisso** (with a *Madonna* by Begarelli) and **San Francesco**, with the tomb of Marco Pio attributed to the school of Jacopo della Quercia, and a fresco of the *Enthroned Madonna* attributed to Giovanni da Modena. Via Giulio Rovighi is on the site of the ghetto, where the Jewish community was forced to live between 1719 and 1796. The synagogue at no. 57 was in use until 1922.

North and east of Modena

Nonantola, with two 14th-century towers, is famous for its abbey, founded in 752 and rebuilt in brick in the 13th century (*open Mon–Sat 7am–8pm, Sun 7–12.30 & 3–8*). The portal has reliefs by the school of Wiligelmus (1121). The church contains the tombs of Popes St Sylvester and Adrian III. In the refectory are fresco fragments dating from the early 12th century. **Mirandola** was a principality of the Pico family, the most famous member of which was Giovanni Pico (1463–94, known as Pico della Mirandola), the humanist and scholar noted for his learning, a famous figure of the Italian Renaissance. There are family tombs in the church of San Francesco and scanty remains of the Pico ducal palace in the main piazza.

South of Modena

South of Modena on the Panaro is **Vignola**, a fruit-growing centre, famous for its cherries. It was the birthplace of the architect Jacopo Barozzi, called Il Vignola (1507–73). He became the most important successor to Michelangelo in Rome. The fine castle (*open Tues–Sat 9–12 & 2.30–6, summer 3.30–7; Sun and holidays 10–12 & 2.30–6, summer 3.30–7*) was built by Uguccione Contrari between 1401 and 1435. The chapel has very interesting late-Gothic frescoes by an unknown artist.

At **Maranello**, next to the Ferrari works, a museum, the Galleria Ferrari (*open daily 9.30–6*), preserves mementoes of Enzo Ferrari, vintage cars, etc.

At **Sassuolo** is the Palazzo Ducale, rebuilt for the Este in 1634, with an interesting park. This gem of Baroque architecture is by Bartolomeo Avanzini, who also built the Palazzo Ducale in Modena, it contains decorations by Jean Boulanger (and by Angelo Michele Colonna and Agostino Mitelli in the *salone*). It is open for special exhibitions.

On the road to Abetone (the principal ski resort of Tuscany) across the Apennines is Pavullo nel Frignano, the 19th-century residence of the Dukes of Modena (now home to a small gallery of contemporary art, with works by local artists).

REGGIO EMILIA

Reggio Emilia (or Reggio nell'Emilia) is the large, flourishing centre of an important agricultural area. Excellent Parmesan cheese (*Parmigiano-Reggiano* or *Grana*) is produced here. It was the Roman Regium Lepidi and is still divided in two by the Via Emilia: the southern part of the town retains a medieval pattern, whereas broad streets and open squares predominate to the north. The most settled period of Reggio's turbulent history was under the Este domination (1409–1796).

In the centre of the Via Emilia is the little Piazza del Monte. Here is the altered 14th-century **Palazzo del Capitano del Popolo**, part of which is the Palazzo dell'Albergo Posta, transformed in the 16th-century into a hospice and restored in an eclectic style in 1910. It adjoins the central Piazza Prampolini. The Romanesque **cathedral** has an unfinished façade added in 1555 by Prospero Sogari, who also carved the statues of Adam and Eve above the central door. The unusual tower bears a group of the *Madonna and Donors*, in copper, by Bartolomeo Spani (1522), who also carved the tomb of Valerio Malaguzzi, uncle of Ariosto, in the interior. The tomb of Bishop Rangone and the marble ciborium are also by Sogari.

It was here, in the Palazzo Comunale, that the green, white and red tricolour was proclaimed the national flag of Italy in 1797. The **Sala del Tricolore** has a small museum (*open Tues–Sat 9.30–12.30; Sun 9.30–12.30 & 3–5*). A passageway leads into the piazza in front of the church of **San Prospero**, guarded by six red marble lions. Rebuilt in 1514–27, it has a choir frescoed by Camillo Procaccini and fine inlaid stalls.

PARMIGIANO-REGGIANO CHEESE

Parmigiano-Reggiano comes from a strictly defined area: both the cheese and the milk from which it is made are produced only in the provinces of Parma, Reggio Emilia, Modena and Mantua, by a consortium of 600 small dairies. The cows graze in open pastures or are fed locally grown fodder, and all-natural fermenting agents are used to give the cheese its particular flavour and texture.

Today as eight centuries ago, the process is the same: milk, fire, rennet, and the skill and knowledge of cheese masters are the basic ingredients. The giant truckles are aged naturally for at least a year (usually two years or more), all the while being brushed and turned, and inspected daily to check that they match up to strict consortium standards.

Parmigiano-Reggiano is a DOP (*Designazione d'Origine Protetta*) product, which means it meets special EU quality standards. If buying a truckle (or, more likely, part of one), you should look for ID markings on the rind: the words PARMIGIANO-REGGIANO, the identification number of the dairy, the month and year of production, the acronym DOP in pin-dot stencil, and the fire-marked oval brand of the Consorzio Tutela. If you're buying a pre-packaged slice, the oval brand will appear on the wrapper.

Real Parmigiano-Reggiano is straw-coloured, and the colour is always uniform throughout the cheese. Inside, the cheese forms long, thin flakes radiating from, or converging towards, the centre. The internal mass tends to be soft, minutely granulated, and dotted with barely visible holes. Although these traits remain constant, it is still possible to detect differences between individual cheeses. As is the case with any hand-made product, each truckle has a touch of individuality.

On the other side of the Via Emilia is the huge Piazza Martiri del 7 Luglio, with the **Musei Civici** (*open Mon–Sat 9–12, Sat also 3–7, Sun and holidays 10–1 & 3–7*). Here the collections still have their charming, old-fashioned displays. The Collezione Spallanzani, founded in 1772 and bought by the city in 1799, is a delightful natural history collection (including fossils). Upstairs are the Galleria Fontanesi, founded in 1893, with pictures by Emilian painters from the 15th to the 19th centuries, and the Museo Chierici, with archaeological material (including Etruscan finds), arranged for study purposes. The numismatic collection has examples from the Reggio mint. The prehistoric finds from the locality include a 5th-century treasure (with a fine gold fibula).

Across the garden, with a harrowing bronze monument (1958) to Italian Resistance heroes, is the elegant Teatro Municipale (1852–57), with a high theatrical reputation. Behind the theatre are extensive public gardens in which a Roman family tomb of c. 50 AD has been placed. In Piazza della Vittoria, beside the Teatro Ariosto, designed in 1741 by Antonio Cugini (and rebuilt after a fire in 1851), is the Gothic-revival spire of the **Galleria Parmeggiani**, with a fine 16th-century Hispano-Moresque doorway brought from Valencia. The eclectic collections include medieval metalwork and 14th–16th-century paintings of the Flemish and Spanish schools, including the *Redeemer* by El Greco.

Off the south side of the Via Emilia (reached from the broad Corso Garibaldi) is the splendid Baroque church of the **Madonna della Ghiara** (1597–1619), with a well-preserved interior (restored in 1996), its vaults and domes beautifully decorated with frescoes and stuccoes by early-17th-century Emilian artists including Alessandro Tiarini, Lionello Spada and Camillo Gavasseti. An altarpiece by Guercino has been removed for restoration. A museum (*open Sun 3.30–6.30*) displays the cathedral treasury.

Around Reggio Emilia

Correggio was the birthplace of the painter Antonio Allegri (1489–1534), nicknamed Correggio (*see p. 618*), whose house is in Borgovecchio. The Palazzo dei Principi, begun in 1507, contains a small museum with 16th-century Flemish tapestries and a tempera *Head of Christ* by Mantegna. The 18th-century Teatro Asioli has been restored. San Quirino (1516–87) has an interesting interior.

Novellara has a castle (now the town hall) of the Gonzaga, dating in part from the 14th century. It contains a small museum with detached frescoes of the 13th–16th centuries and a remarkable series of ceramic jars made for a pharmacy in the 15th–16th centuries.

Gualtieri has the vast Piazza Bentivoglio as its main square (with a garden in the centre). It was begun in 1580 by Giovanni Battista Aleotti. Palazzo Bentivoglio, also by Aleotti, has 17th-century frescoes in the Salone dei Giganti.

Guastalla was once the capital of a duchy of the Gonzagas. In the square is a statue of the mercenary captain Ferrante Gonzaga (d. 1457), by Leone Leoni. The Basilica della Pieve is an interesting Romanesque church.

Brescello (*marked on the map on p. 238*) is a town of Roman origins. In the central piazza is a copy of a statue of Hercules by Jacopo Sansovino (the original is kept in the Museo Comunale). Sir Anthony Panizzi (1797–1879), librarian of the British

Museum, was born in the town. The church of Santa Maria Maggiore (1830–37) was used as the setting of the film of *Don Camillo* (based on the book written in 1950 by Giovanni Guareschi), and there is a little museum with mementoes of the film.

ACETO BALSAMICO TRADIZIONALE DI MODENA

The traditional balsamic vinegar of Modena is made exclusively in Modena province. The best vinegar is obtained from crushed Trebbiano and Lambrusco grape-must that is heated and reduced over an open flame, naturally fermented, then aged in wooden casks. The ageing process darkens and concentrates the liquid so that the finished product is rich and glossy, smooth and syrupy, with a complex, penetrating bouquet and an agreeable, balanced acidity. Its inimitable flavour, a delicate balance between sweet and sour, comes out entirely in the ageing: despite what one might think, no aromatic substances are added at any time. Production follows simple yet precise steps that must be followed with care and in the proper order. Nevertheless, each master vinegar-maker brings a personal touch to his or her own small output. These secrets are passed down, usually by word of mouth, from generation to generation, giving a distinct personality to each brand of balsamic vinegar.

PRACTICAL INFORMATION

GETTING AROUND

• **By air:** Bologna's Guglielmo Marconi Airport is 36km from Modena and 61km from Reggio Emilia. It handles daily flights to and from domestic and international destinations.

• **By rail:** Italy's main north–south line closely follows the Via Emilia from Milan to Bologna. Some Eurostar and most Intercity trains stop at Reggio Emilia (1hr 20mins from Milan, 40mins from Bologna) and/or Modena (1hr 30mins from Milan, 30mins from Bologna). You can reach both cities without changing trains from Rome/Florence and from Bari/Ancona. Commuter trains (Regionali and Interregionali) connect Modena with

Mantua and Verona, and Reggio Emilia with Guastalla and Sassuolo.

Modena has two railway stations: Piazza Dante for all main line services; Piazza Manzoni for local trains to Fiorano and Sassuolo.

• **By car:** Free parking outside Modena centre at Parco Novi Sad, Viale Vittorio Veneto, Viale Berengario, Viale Fontanelli and Viale Sigonio. Pay parking in Piazza Roma. In Reggio Emilia, free parking on Via Cecati; pay parking along Via Nacchi and in the former Caserma Zucchi near the bus station.

• **By bus:**

Modena Trolleybus 7 from the station to the museums and Via Emilia (for the duomo). ATCM also run services to

localities in the province from the bus station in Via Molza.
Reggio Emilia Minibus A from the station to Piazza del Monte. Bus station for the province (service operated by Azienda Consorziale Trasporti, T: 0522 431667) in the former Caserma Zucchi, Viale Allegri 9.

INFORMATION OFFICES

Modena Via Scudari 12, T: 059 206660, www.comune.modena.it/ infoturismo
Reggio Emilia Piazza Prampolini 5c, T: 0522 451152, www.emiliaromagnaturismo.it

HOTELS

Modena
€€ **Canalgrande**. Elegant and refined, in an 18th-century palace with luxuriant garden and excellent restaurant. Corso Canal Grande 6, T: 059 217160, www.canalgrandehotel.it
€ **Centrale**. A recently renovated, simple place in the historic city centre. Via Rismondo 55, T: 059 218808, www.hotelcentrale.com
€ **Libertà**. Central, in an ancient townhouse. Via Blasia 10, T: 059 222365, F: 059 222502, www.hotelliberta.it
Reggio Emilia
€€ **Delle Notarie**. A classic provincial hotel with a good restaurant. Closed Aug. Via Palazzolo 5, T: 0522 453500, F: 0522 453737.
€€ **Posta**. Pleasant and comfortable, in the heart of town. Piazza Del Monte 2, T: 0522 432944, www.hotelposta.re.it
Albinea
€ **Viganò**. A simple, comfortable, fami-

ly-run place with a pleasant garden 15km south of Reggio. Via Garibaldi 17, T: 0522 347292, F: 0522 347293.

YOUTH HOSTELS

Correggio
€ **La Rocchetta**, Corso Cavour 19, T: 0522 632361, F: 0522 632361, ostello_correggio@hotmail.com
Guastalla
€ **Quadrio Michelotti**, Via Lido Po 11, T: 0522 839228, F: 0522 839228.
Modena
€ **San Filippo Neri**, Via Santa Orsola 48/52, T: 059 234598, F: 059 234598, hostelmodena@hotmail.com
€ **Tricolore**, Via dell'Abadessa 8, T: 0522 454795.
Reggio Emilia
€ **Basilica della Ghiara**, Via Guasco, T: 0522 452323, F: 0522 454795.

RESTAURANTS

Modena
€€€ **Fini**. The best place in town for traditional Modenese cuisine and fine wines. Closed Mon–Tues, Dec and July–Aug. Rua Frati Minori 54, T: 059 223314.
€€€ **Hostaria Giusti**. Specialising in traditional and old recipes, good cheeses, selection of wines and spirits. Closed Sun–Mon and holidays, Aug and Dec. Via Farini 75, T: 059 222533.
€€ **Bianca**. Good, upmarket trattoria. Closed midday Sat, Sun, Dec and Aug. Via Spaccini 24, T: 059 311524.
€€ **Borso d'Este**. Creative interpretations of regional dishes. Closed midday Sat, Sun and Aug. Piazza Roma 5, T: 059 214114.

€€ **Francescana**. Elegant trattoria specialising in traditional recipes, good selection of wines. Closed Sat midday–Sun and first week of Jan and Aug. Via Stella 22, T: 059 210118.

€€ **Oreste**. Delicious Modenese specialities. Closed Sun evening, Wed and July. Piazza Roma 31, T: 059 243324.

€€ **Stallo del Pomodoro**. Good wine selection, regional food. Closed Sat midday, Sun and 25 Dec–6 Jan. Largo Hannover 63, T: 059 214664.

€€ **Vinicio**. Personal interpretations of traditional recipes, with garden seating in summer. Closed Sun–Mon, Dec–Jan and Aug. Via Emilia Est 1526, Località Fossalta, T: 059 280313.

Reggio Emilia

€€ **Caffè Arti e Mestieri**. Restaurant offering creative variations on traditional recipes. Closed Sun–Mon, Dec and Aug. Via Emilia San Pietro 16, T: 0522 451300.

€€ **Cinque Pini-Da Pelati**. The best in town, serving regional cuisine with a personal twist. Closed Tues evening, Wed and Aug. Via Martiri di Cervarolo 46, T: 0522 553663.

Carpi

€ **Teresa Baldini**. Traditional *osteria* serving wholesome local dishes. Closed evenings, Thur and Aug.

Cavriago (*see map p. 612*)

€€ **Picci**. Elegant restaurant that offers regional food and an excellent selection of wines. Closed Sun evening–Mon and Jan, Aug. Via XX Settembre 4, T: 0522 371801.

Nonantola

€€ **Osteria di Rubbiara**. Traditional *osteria* offering good Modenese cuisine, especially fresh pasta. Closed Tues, Thur, Sun evening, Aug and Dec. Via Risaia 2, Località Rubbiara, T: 059 549019.

Rubiera

€€ **Da Arnaldo-Clinica Gastronomica**. Hotel restaurant serving excellent local fare. Closed Sun, midday Mon, Christmas, Easter and Aug. Piazza XXIV Maggio 3, T: 0522 626124.

Soliera

€€ **Lancellotti**. Restaurant (with rooms) offering delicious seasonal delicacies. Closed Sun–Mon, Dec–Jan and Aug. Via Grandi 120, T: 059 567406.

FESTIVALS & MARKETS

Modena San Geminiano (patron saint), 31 Jan with a fair. Carnival celebrations on the Thur preceding Shrove Tuesday. Pavarotti & Friends, benefit concert, June (Pavarotti was born in Modena); International Military Band Festival, July.

Reggio Emilia Market on Tues and Fri in Piazza Prampolini and Piazza San Prospero; Jazz Festival, April; San Prospero (patron saint), 24 Nov.

PARMA & PIACENZA

Perhaps because of their nearness to the foggy Po, Parma and Piacenza have a slightly melancholy air—but the atmosphere is not unpleasant. Indeed, many residents—and visitors—see it as a virtue. Parma is famous for its architecture and its paintings by Correggio—and of course for its ham and its Parmesan cheese; Piacenza for its churches; and the whole area for its scrumptious cuisine.

PARMA

Parma is the second city of Emilia. It has some very fine works of art and important buildings, all grouped close together in the centre of the city. There is a beautiful baptistery; and delightful frescoed domes by Correggio (who arrived in the city around 1520) grace the Camera di San Paolo, the cathedral and the church of San Giovanni Evangelista. The huge Palazzo della Pilotta is now restored so that the splendid Farnese theatre can be visited as well as the Galleria Nazionale, with a large collection of paintings of the highest interest—including masterpieces by Correggio and fine examples of the later Emilian schools. Parma is a gastronomic centre, famous for Parmesan cheese and Parma ham, and Italians from as far afield as Florence or Milan have been known to drive here for a Sunday lunch.

HISTORY OF PARMA

There was a Roman station here, on the Via Emilia. In the 12th–14th centuries the town had a republican constitution, but from c. 1335 onwards it was ruled by a succession of ducal families: the Visconti, Terzi, Este and Sforza. In 1531 it became a papal dominion and in 1545 Paul III passed it over, along with Piacenza, to his illegitimate son Pier Luigi Farnese, who was given the title of duke. The house of Farnese, and their heirs, the Spanish house of Bourbon-Parma, held the duchy until 1801. In 1815 the Congress of Vienna assigned Parma to the ex-empress Marie Louise, daughter of Franz I of Austria and wife of Napoleon, but in 1859 the widow of her son Charles III was obliged to hand it over to the King of Italy.

Piazza duomo and the baptistery

The peaceful, cobbled Piazza Duomo is dominated by the pink-and-white **baptistery**, a splendid octagonal building in red Verona marble. Its extremely interesting design shows the influence of French Gothic architecture and of ancient Roman buildings. It was begun in 1196 by Benedetto Antelami, and is the most famous work of this influential architect. His first known work is his *Descent from the Cross* in the cathedral (*see*

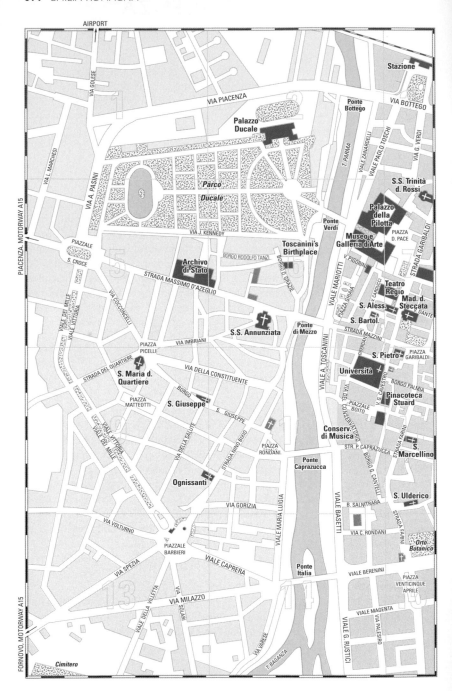

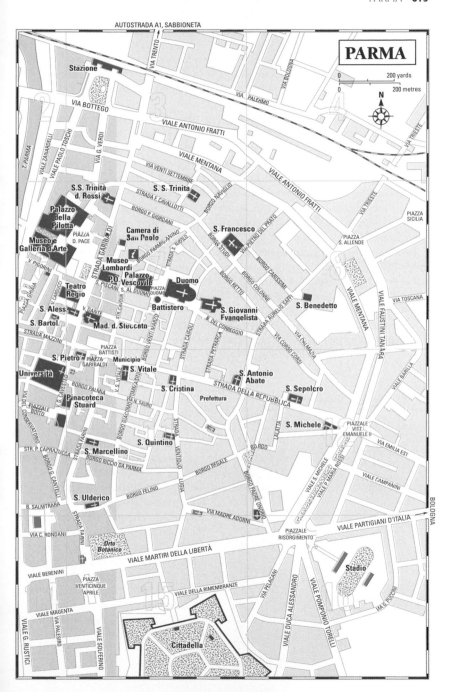

AUTOSTRADA A1, SABBIONETA

PARMA

0 ————— 200 yards
0 ————— 200 metres

N

VIA TRENTO
VIA BOLOGNA
VIA PALERMO
VIA TRIESTE

Stazione

VIA BOTTEGO

VIALE ZANARDELLI
VIALE P. PAOLO TOSCHI
VIA G. VERDI

VIALE ANTONIO FRATTI

VIALE MENTANA

VIA VENTI SETTEMBRE

VIALE ANTONIO FRATTI

S.S. Trinità
d. Rossi

S. S. Trinità

STRADA F. CAVALLOTTI
BORGO SAVIGLIO
VIA TRIESTE

PIAZZA
SICILIA

BORGO P. GIORDANI

Palazzo
della
Pilotta

PIAZZA
D. PACE

Camera di
San Paolo

STRADA GARIBALDI
BORGO PARMIGIANINO
BORGO S. NICOLÒ

S. Francesco

VIA PIETRO DEL PRATO
BORGO STUDI

PIAZZA
S. ALLENDE

Museo e
Galleria d'Arte

V. PIGORINI

Museo
Lombardi

Palazzo
Vescovile

P.O.

S. PISCANI
V. AL DUOMO

Duomo

PIAZZA
DUOMO

BORGO RETTO
BORGO COLONNE
BORGO CARISSIMI

Teatro
Regio

V. CARDUCCI

Battistero

S. Giovanni
Evangelista

S. Benedetto

VIALE MENTANA
VIA FAUSTINI TANARA
VIA TOSCANA

S. Aless.

V. DANTE

S. Bartol.

Mad. d. Steccato

STR. CAVOUR

B. DEL CORREGGIO

STRADA AL DUOMO

STRADA AURELIO SAFFI
VIA DALMAZIA

STRADA MAZZINI

BORGO VENTI MARZO

STRADA PETRARCA

VIA C. CORSO CORSI

PIAZZA
BATTISTI

S. Pietro

PIAZZA
GARIBALDI

Municipio

S. Vitale

Università

BORGO PALMIA

V. G. CAVESTRO

Pinacoteca
Stuard

STRADA CAIROLI

S. Cristina

S. Antonio
Abate

STRADA DELLA REPUBBLICA

S. Sepolcro

VIALE BARILLA

PIAZZALE
BOITO

VIA DEL CONSERVATORIO

BORGO GIACOMO TOMMASINI

V.S. VITALE

STRADA FARINI

S. N. SAURO

Prefettura

STRADA
VENTIDUO

S. Michele

PIAZZALE
VITT.
EMANUELE II

VIA EMILIA EST

STR. P. CAPRAZUCCA

BORGO G. CANTELLI

S. Marcellino

BORGO RICCIO DA PARMA

S. Quintino

BORGO REGALE

LUGIA

BORGO PADRE ONORIO

VIALE S. MICHELE
VIALE P. MARIA ROSSI

VIALE CAMPANINI

S. Ulderico

BORGO FELINO

B. SALNITRARA

STRADA FARINI

VIA MADRE ADORNI

PIAZZALE
RISORGIMENTO

VIALE PARTIGIANI D'ITALIA

BOLOGNA

VIA C. RONDANI

Orto
Botanico

VIALE MARTIRI DELLA LIBERTÀ

Stadio

VIA PELACANI
VIALE DUCA ALESSANDRO
VIALE POMPONIO TORELLI
VIA G. PUCCINI

VIALE BERENINI

PIAZZA
VENTICINQUE
APRILE

VIALE DELLA RIMEMBRANZE

VIALE MAGENTA
VIA PALEGIRO
VIA SOLFERINO

Cittadella

VIALE G. RUSTICI

p. 618). The church of Sant'Andrea at Vercelli, where the arrival of Gothic forms can clearly be seen, is also his (*see p. 80*). The baptistery was completed after 1216 by Campionese masters (Campionese being a term used to describe masons, sculptors and architects from the Campione d'Italia region who were active in Italy and Switzerland up until the end of the 14th century).

The exterior has three doorways bearing splendid carvings by Antelami. The lunette over the north door shows the *Madonna, Adoration of the Magi* and *Dream of Joseph*. In the architrave beneath are the *Baptism of Christ, Banquet of Herod* and *Beheading of the Baptist*. The genealogical trees of Jacob and the Virgin adorn the door jambs. The west door depicts the *Last Judgement* in the lunette and architrave, and the south door illustrates the *Legend of Barlaam and Josaphat*. Between the doors are blind arches with Classical columns, and a frieze of 79 small panels carved with stylised reliefs, fantastic animals, etc., which almost girdles the edifice. Four delicate galleries, with small columns, encircle the building's upper storeys.

The interior, on a different design from the exterior, is covered by a beautiful dome. It has more splendid carvings by Antelami, including the fine capitals surmounting the tall columns on either side of the niches. Above is another series of columns in front of two galleries. There are coloured reliefs of the *Flight into Egypt, David* and the *Presentation in the Temple* over the doors and altar; between them are angels and the *Annunciation* figures, in the apses of the niches. Fourteen figures of the *Months*, winter and spring (some with reliefs of the signs of the zodiac below) have been set in the lower gallery. The red-porphyry altar is carved with the figures of John the Baptist, a priest and a Levite. In the

centre is a font, and against the wall a stoup supported by a lion, also carved by Antelami. Six statues, formerly in niches on the exterior, are displayed around the walls.

The cupola has lovely tempera paintings of 1260–70, in a Byzantine style, with the *Story of Abraham, Life of St John the Baptist, Christ and the Prophets*, and the *Apostles* and the *Symbols of the Evangelists*. The painted decoration of the lunettes below dates from the same period. The lower part of the walls has 14th-century votive frescoes, including two attributed to Buffalmacco—an interesting claim. Buffalmacco is mentioned by Boccaccio as a celebrity artist, but no works have been attributed to him with any certainty.

PARMA: THE BAPTISTERY

Parma's Romanesque duomo.

The duomo

This splendid 11th-century church was modified by Antelami in the 12th century. The projecting pink-and-white porch, supported by two huge lions, has reliefs of the months added around the arch in 1281. The doors themselves date from 1494. The campanile was built in 1284–94.

Inside, the Romanesque structure is still clearly visible, although it was entirely covered in later centuries by frescoes in the vault, nave, aisles and west end. Notice also the finely carved 12th-century capital—also Romanesque. High up on the inner façade is a fresco of the *Ascension* painted by Lattanzio Gambara (1573). Gambara was a tailor's son taken under Giulio Campi's wing in Cremona and given an artist's training. These frescoes are one of his finest achievements, painted with the help of fellow Cremonese Bernardino Gatti. More frescoes by Gambara, showing the *Life of Christ*, can be seen above the matroneum in the nave. The vault is frescoed by a pupil and follower of Parmigianino, Girolamo Mazzola Bedoli (1557). The statue of the Archangel Raphael (formerly on the campanile) dates from c. 1294.

In the cupola (light in the south transept) is the celebrated *Assumption* by Correggio (1526–30), one of the most remarkable dome frescoes in existence. The spandrels hold the four patron saints of Parma. The colossal figures of the Apostles appear above, in a crowd behind a balustrade between the round windows. Christ descends from a golden Heaven to greet His mother, surrounded by angels and clouds. It is said that when Titian saw the dome he commented that if it were to be turned upside down and filled with gold, Correggio would still not receive the recompense he deserved for such a masterpiece.

The south aisle has ceiling frescoes by Alessandro Mazzola (son of Girolamo). In the last chapel is a *Crucifixion with Saints* by Bernardino Gatti. The south transept preserves a relief (from the pulpit) of the *Descent from the Cross* by Antelami, his earliest known work, signed and dated 1178.

A sarcophagus carved by Campionese sculptors serves as high altar. The choir (difficult to see) and apse have frescoes by Girolamo Mazzola Bedoli. The beautiful stalls are signed by Cristoforo da Lendinara, and the bishop's throne is by Antelami. The crypt has good capitals and two fragments of Roman pavement. The last chapel in the north aisle was entirely frescoed in the 15th century.

Opposite the duomo is the **Palazzo Vescovile**, first built in the 11th century, with a well-restored façade that shows successive additions of 1175 and 1234. The courtyard dates from the 16th century. Just out of the piazza you can see a red palace on the site (plaque) of the birthplace of the medieval chronicler Frate Salimbene (1221–c. 1290). The 16th-century seminary, with a double blind arcade, and the early 20th-century doorway of a pharmacy, can be seen on the south side of the duomo.

Correggio (c. 1490–1534)
Born Antonio Allegri in a small town near Modena (*see p. 570*), Correggio was most active in Parma, and is especially known for his decoration of the abbess's apartments in San Paolo, which takes as its central subject Diana, goddess of chastity. Scholars believe he may have studied Mantegna's work in Mantua: certainly there are similarities of style, notably the use of the *sotto in sù* (literally 'upwards from under') technique, which creates the illusion of movement and suspension in space by a daring use of foreshortening. This is seen to particular effect in his dome of the *Assumption* in Parma's duomo (*see above*).

San Giovanni Evangelista

Behind the duomo, facing its pretty apse, is the church of San Giovanni Evangelista, built over an earlier church in 1498–1510, with a façade of 1604–07. Its dome holds another splendid fresco by Correggio (1521), the *Vision of St John at Patmos* (light in the north transept), showing Christ surrounded by the apostles appearing to St John at his death. In the spandrels are the *Church Fathers*, and over the sacristy door in the north transept is a lunette fresco of the *Young St John Writing*, also by Correggio. The walls of the nave have a beautiful frieze by Francesco Maria Rondani (on cartoons by Correggio) of *Prophets and Sibyls*. The vault is frescoed by Michelangelo Anselmi.

The entrance arches of the first, second and fourth north chapels have lovely frescoes by Parmigianino: the first chapel has a font made out of a Roman urn, and delightful frescoed putti; the fourth chapel has an altarpiece by Girolamo Mazzola Bedoli. The frieze in the transepts dates from the late 15th or early 16th century.

Statues by Antonio Begarelli adorn the south transept. The *Crowning of the Virgin* in the main apse is a copy made in 1587 by Cesare Aretusi of a larger work, formerly here, by Correggio. On the high altar is a *Transfiguration* by Girolamo Mazzola Bedoli. The stalls date from 1513–38. In the sixth chapel in the north aisle is *Christ Carrying the Cross* by Michelangelo Anselmi.

A door at the side of the façade of the church gives entrance to the Benedictine monastery (used by 20 monks; *open daily 6.30–12 & 3.30–6.30*) with three lovely cloisters, a chapter house and a library (*open on Sun and holidays only*).

The **Spezeria di San Giovanni** (entrance at Borgo Pipa 1; *open Tues–Sun 9–1.45*), the monks' ancient pharmacy, was founded in 1298 and in use up to 1881. It preserves its 16th-century furnishings. You can also see 17th-century vases, mortars, pharmaceutical publications, etc.

From Piazza Duomo, Strada al Duomo leads to Strada Cavour, the main shopping street. This leads left to Piazza Garibaldi with the 17th-century Municipio and Palazzo del Governatore, and a number of cafés.

The Camera di San Paolo

In the other direction, the Strada Cavour ends at a war memorial tower. Just to the left, approached by an avenue of japonica trees, is the entrance to the **Camera di San Paolo** (*open Tues–Sun 8.30–1.45*), part of the private apartment of Abbess Giovanna

Palazzo del Governatore in Piazza Garibaldi.

Piacenza in the former Benedictine convent of San Paolo. Beyond several rooms with paintings by Alessandro Araldi, is the little room with celebrated frescoes by Correggio, commissioned by the abbess in 1518 or 1519 (the artist's first commission in Parma). The Gothic umbrella vault is decorated with a dome of thick foliage supported by wickerwork (canes cover the ribs of the vault). The abbess' coat of arms appears in the centre, surrounded by drapes off which hang festoons of fruit. Through 16 oculi in the arbour you can see groups of putti at play, against the open sky. The monochrome lunettes below have painted trompe-l'oeil statues and reliefs of mythological subjects, and below is a frieze of rams' heads with veils stretched between in which are hung plates and pewterware (which may signify that the room was used as a refectory). Over the fireplace is Diana returning from the hunt, also by Correggio.

The significance of these remarkable Humanistic frescoes, in which the artist uses a careful play of light, is uncertain: the abbess was a particularly cultivated lady who lived in the convent for 17 years and was unsuccessful in her attempt to prevent it from becoming a closed community in 1524. The frescoes remained unknown to the outside world until the 18th century, which probably accounts for their excellent state of preservation.

The room next door has another vault adorned with grotesques by Alessandro Araldi, painted four years earlier.

Strada Pisacane continues Strada al Duomo to Strada Garibaldi, which runs through one side of the huge, untidy Piazza della Pilotta. At Strada Garibaldi 15 is the **Museo Glauco Lombardi** (closed at the time of writing) with a collection relating to Empress Marie Louise, the daughter of Emperor Franz I of Austria, married to Napoleon in 1809 in order to broker a peace. Just to the left is the **Teatro Regio** (*open Mon–Sat 10.30–12*), which opened in 1829 with Bellini's *Zaira*. It is one of the most famous opera houses in Italy. The conductor Arturo Toscanini (1867–1957), who was born in Parma, played in the orchestra.

The Madonna della Steccata and Palazzo della Pilotta

Also in Via Garibaldi is the church of the **Madonna della Steccata**, built in 1521–39 on a Greek-cross plan by Bernardino and Giovanni Francesco Zaccagni. The fine exterior includes an elegant dome surrounded by a balustrade, and 18th-century statues on the roof.

The interior has superb frescoes by the Parma school, all carried out between 1530 and 1570, though not by Parmigianino (*see box overleaf*). On the barrel vault between the dome and apse are six tempera figures of the *Virgins*, Parmigianino's last work. The fresco of the *Assunta* in the dome is by Bernardino Gatti (inspired by Correggio). The side apses and arches are frescoed by Girolamo Mazzola Bedoli. The *Crowning of the Virgin* in the apse is by Michelangelo Anselmi (to a design by Giulio Romano). The organ doors are early works by Parmigianino. The tomb of Field-Marshal Count Neipperg (1775–1829), second husband of Marie Louise, is by Lorenzo Bartolini (1840).

On the other side of Strada Garibaldi, on the bank of the river, is **Palazzo della Pilotta**, a gloomy, rambling palace built for the Farnese family c. 1583–1622, but left unfinished; it was badly bombed, and half of it was demolished in the Second World War. It contains the Museo Archeologico Nazionale (*open Tues–Sun 8.30–7.30*), Teatro Farnese and Galleria Nazionale (*open Tues–Sun 8.30–2; admission with separate tickets*). The entrance is under the portico towards the river (*see below*).

The Museo Archeologico Nazionale is interesting chiefly for its finds from Veleia. They include a fine group of Roman statues, the *tabula alimentaria* (the largest Roman bronze inscription known) and the bronze head of a boy (1st century BC).

On the lower floor are palae-olithic finds from the region

Leonardo da Vinci: *La Scapiliutu* (c. 1508).

around Parma; material from the pile-dwellings of Parma and the lake-villages of its territory; and Roman inscriptions, bronzes, amphorae and mosaic pavements.

Teatro Farnese and Galleria Nazionale

The huge **Teatro Farnese** was built in 1617–18 in wood and stucco by Giovanni Battista Aleotti for Rannuccio I, Duke of Parma. It has a U-shaped cavea that could seat 3,000 spectators. Above are two tiers of loggias, with arches modelled on Palladio's theatre at Vicenza, although the stage in this theatre had movable scenery. Used only nine times after its inauguration in 1628 (when it was flooded for a mock sea-battle), it fell into ruin in the 18th century and was almost entirely destroyed by a bomb in the Second World War. It has been beautifully reconstructed. Most of the painted decoration (including the ceiling fresco) has been lost, although two painted triumphal arches survive at the sides, with stucco equestrian statues of Alessandro and Ottavio Farnese.

From the stage of the theatre you enter the **Galleria Nazionale**, founded by Philip of Bourbon-Parma in 1752. A walkway leads into the Romanesque section, with 10th–11th-century wooden doors from San Bertoldo, and three capitals carved by Benedetto Antelami. Beyond are exhibited early Tuscan works (Agnolo Gaddi, Nicolò di Pietro Gerini, Spinello Aretino, Fra Angelico); inlaid stalls by Bernardino da Lendinara; and local 15th-century works (*St Peter Martyr* and *Stories from his Life*, by the circle of Agnolo and Bartolomeo degli Erri). Beyond paintings by Francesco Francia and Cima da Conegliano (*Madonna and Child with Saints*) is an exquisite *Head* *of a Girl* (*La Scapiliata*) by Leonardo da Vinci (c. 1508), owned by the Gonzaga in 1531. The two marble bas-reliefs are by Giovanni Antonio Amadeo.

Beyond a corridor with tiles made in Faenza in 1482 is a room with 16th-century Emilian works by Cristoforo Caselli, Filippo Mazzola, Garofalo and Dosso Dossi. Stairs lead up to another room with 16th-century Emilian works (Michelangelo Anselmi), and works by Giulio Romano, Holbein (*Portrait of Erasmus*), Sebastiano del Piombo and Bronzino. On the balcony above are interesting works by Girolamo Mazzola Bedoli and El Greco, and large works by the Carracci. The room below displays works by Guercino and Gian Lorenzo Bernini (two marble busts of Rannuccio II). At the end: portraits by Frans Pourbus the Younger; a *Portrait of Isabella Clara Eugenia* and *Madonna and Child*, both by van Dyck; Flemish landscapes; and works by Canaletto and Bernardo Bellotto.

A walkway, with early maps and prints of Parma and 19th-century views of the city, leads back to the Teatro Farnese. Beneath the cavea is the entrance to the last section of the gallery, displayed in the small rooms of the Rocchetta, with the masterpieces of Correggio and Parmigianino. The works by Correggio include several frescoes and the *Madonna della Scodella* (his finest work, c. 1525–30), *Madonna and Child, with St Jerome, an Angel, and Mary Magdalene* (1527–28), *Deposition* (1524), and the *Martyrdom of Four Saints*. Parmigianino is represented by a superb figure known as the *Turkish Slave*, his self-portrait, and a fine collection of drawings.

In an oval room nearby are two colossal basalt statues dating from the 2nd century AD from the Orti Farnesiani on the Palatine in Rome, and a large Neoclassical hall exhibits 18th- and 19th-century works including portraits by Zoffany and Jean Marc Nattier, and a seated statue of Marie Louise by Canova. The last room has smaller 18th-century works (Zoffany, Maria Callani and Vigée-Lebrun).

Parmigianino (1503–40)
Born into the Mazzola family of Parma artists, Parmigianino first made his name with some frescoes for San Giovanni Evangelista (*see p. 618*). Vasari says that as a young man he appeared more angelic than human. Later in life Vasari accuses him of allowing himself to go to seed and neglecting to trim his beard. When Parmigianino failed to complete a cycle of frescoes for Santa Maria della Steccata, he was imprisoned for breach of contract. Nevertheless, the ordeal doesn't seem to have broken his spirit or his style. A refined and sophisticated artist, Parmigianino perfected the stretched and elongated lineaments of the human form which were to become such a hallmark of Mannerism.

Across the river

On the other side of the Parma River, across Ponte Verdi, is the entrance to the **Parco Ducale**. Created in 1560 as the private park of Palazzo Ducale, these pleasant public gardens (worth a visit for their fine chestnut, beech and plane trees) are usually crowded with people. There is a second entrance on Viale Pasini. **Palazzo Ducale** (*open Mon–Sat 9.30–12*) was built as a summer residence for Ottavio Farnese in 1564; it has a wing furnished in the French Neoclassical style.

A pretty road leads south from Ponte Verdi towards Borgo Rodolfo Tanzi. The house at no. 3 in this street is the simple birthplace of Toscanini, now a small museum with mementoes of the conductor (*open Tues–Sun 10–1 & 3–6*). The nearby church of the **Annunziata** is an impressive Baroque building (1566); the graceful **Ospedale della Misericordia**, begun c. 1214 and enlarged in the 16th century, houses the state archives, with the archives of the duchy.

The southern quarters

In the southern part of the town, on the east bank of the river, the **University of Parma** occupies a 16th-century building ascribed to Galeazzo Alessi and Vignola. Nearby, at Via Cavestro 14, is the **Pinacoteca Stuard** (*open Wed–Mon 9–6.30*) with 14th–19th-century paintings (including works by Paolo di Giovanni Fei, Bernardo Daddi, Paolo Uccello, Lanfranco and Guercino). The church of **Sant'Antonio Abate**, in Strada della Repubblica to the east, was begun by Francesco Bibiena in 1712 and finished in 1766.

The **Museo Cinese ed Etnografico** (*open Mon–Fri 9–12 & 3.30–7, Sat 9–12*), in Via San Martino on the southern outskirts of the town, has a small collection of Asian art. In the Villetta Cemetery, further south, the embalmed body of Paganini rests beneath a classical canopy.

AROUND PARMA

Fidenza and Salsomaggiore

Fidenza is the most important town in the province of Parma. Known as Borgo San Donnino from the 9th century to 1927, it occupies the site of the Roman Fidentia Iulia, where St Domninus was martyred by the Emperor Maximian in 291. It was on the Via Francigena, the pilgrim route from Britain and France to Rome, and there are several carvings of pilgrims on the façade of its cathedral.

The **cathedral**, built during the 13th century, has a façade with particularly interesting Romanesque sculptures by Antelami and his school. On the left tower are two reliefs, one showing *Herod Enthroned*, and the other the *Three Kings on Horseback*. In the tympanum of the left door are *Pope Adrian II and St Domninus*, with *Charlemagne* on the left and a *Miracle of St Domninus* on the right. The arch is carved with figures of animals. The column on the right has a capital ingeniously carved with a scene of *Daniel in the Lions' Den*. On either side of the central door are fine statues of David and Ezekiel, both by Antelami. The doorway has beautifully carved capitals and a relief of the *Martyrdom of St Domninus* in the architrave, with *Prophets, Apostles* and *Christ* in the lunette. On the right of the door is a relief showing an angel leading a group of poor pilgrims towards Rome. The right door is crowned by the figure of a pilgrim, and beneath in the tympanum is St Domninus. The lunette is carved with figures of animals. On the right tower is another frieze showing a group of pilgrims. In the beautiful interior, on the first right pillar (above the capital) is the figure of Christ with a relief of a *Battle of Angels* below, both by Antelami. The fourth south chapel (1513) has good terracotta decorations and frescoes. The stoup by the school of Antelami includes the figure of Pope Alexander II. In the last chapel on this side is a wooden statue of the Madonna and Child of 1626, and remains of very early frescoes. In the raised choir, high up between the apse vaults, are good sculptures, including a figure of *Christ as Judge* by Antelami and a fresco of the *Last Judgement* dating from the 13th century. The crypt has interesting capitals, including one of *Daniel in the Lions' Den*. Here is displayed a seated statue of the Madonna and Child by Antelami (damaged in 1914) and the Arca of St Domninus with carved scenes of his life (1488). Nearer the altar is a 3rd-century Roman sarcophagus.

Just off the piazza is the medieval Porta San Donnino. The restored town hall and the theatre, dating from 1812, face the main Piazza Garibaldi. At the end of Via Berenini, Palazzo delle Orsoline hosts the **Museo del Risorgimento**, entered from the street on the left, at no. 2 (*open summer Tues, Thur 4–6, Wed, Fri and Sat 10–12; winter Tues–Sat 10–12*), with an interesting collection relating to the period from 1802–1946. The huge Jesuit college and church dates from the end of the 17th century.

Salt was extracted from the waters of **Salsomaggiore Terme** from the Roman era until the mid-19th century. After 1839 Salsomaggiore became one of the most famous spas in Italy; its saline waters are used even today to treat rheumatic, arthritic and post-inflammatory disorders. The Grand Hotel des Thermes (now a congress centre) was opened in 1901 and bought in 1910 by Cesare Ritz. It contains Art Nouveau works by Galileo Chini, who also decorated the spa building opened in 1923. There are still several Art Nouveau and Art Deco buildings in the town.

Verdi's home ground

At **Roncole Verdi**, north of Fidenza, is the simple birthplace of the composer Giuseppe Verdi (1813–1901), author of *Aida*, *Nabucco* and many other famous operas. His house is *open Apr–Sept Tues–Sun 9.30–12.30 & 3–7; Oct–March Tues–Sun 9.30–12.30 & 2.30–5.30*. **Busseto**, a charming small town, was the lordship of the Pallavicini in the 10th–16th centuries. It has many buildings decorated with terracotta in the Cremonese style. The battlemented castle contains the town hall and the little Teatro Verdi (1868), and the Villa Pallavicino (attributed to Vignola) houses the civic museum (*closed at the time of writing; T: 0524 931711*) with mementoes of Verdi. At **Sant'Agata di Villanova sull'Arda** is the Villa Verdi, built by Verdi in 1849 as a summer residence. The house here is *open Tues–Sun 9–12 & 2.30 or 3–7*; it contains relics and a bust by Vincenzo Gemito.

Parma Province is rich in feudal strongholds. **Fontanellato** has a moated 13th-century castle of the Sanvitale family (*open for guided tours Apr–Oct daily 9.30–11.30 & 3–6; Nov–March Tues–Sun 9.30–11.30 & 3–5*). It contains a little room with delightful frescoes by Parmigianino (1524), as well as 16th–18th-century furnishings, ceramics, etc. The Rocca Meli Lupi at **Soragna** has 16th-century works of art (*open for guided tours daily 9–11 & 2 or 3–4.30 or 6*). The synagogue has a Jewish museum (*open on Sun and holidays 10–12.30 & 3–6, Tues–Fri 10–12 & 3–5*). Nearer the Po are the fortresses of the Rossi family at **Roccabianca** and **San Secondo Parmense** (*open Apr–Sept for guided visits, Mon–Sat at 10, 11, 3, 4, 5, 6; Oct–March Tues–Sun at 10, 11, 2, 3, 4, 5*), with frescoes by the Campi.

The Certosa and the east

On the eastern outskirts of Parma is the **Certosa di Parma** (*open Mon–Fri 9–12 & 2–4, Sat 8–12, Sun and holidays 8–10*), from which Stendhal's famous novel *La Chartreuse de Parme* takes its name. First built in 1282, the Carthusian monastery has been enlarged and remodelled several times over the centuries. The present church contains frescoes by Sebastiano Galeotti, Francesco Natali and others.

Montechiarugolo has a good castle of 1406 (*guided visit Sat–Sun and holidays 3–6*), and Montecchio Emilia preserves parts of the old ramparts. **Torrechiara** has the finest castle (*open Tues–Fri 8.30–4, Sat–Sun 9–5*) in the province, built for Pier Maria Rossi (1448–60), with its 'golden room' frescoed by Benedetto Bembo (c. 1463). Other rooms are decorated by Cesare Baglione and his followers.

Mamiano lies near the Parma River south of Parma. The village itself is not very interesting, but the nearby **Villa Mamiano**, surrounded by a beautiful park, is well worth the drive down. It was the residence of the connoisseur, musicologist and art historian Luigi Magnani (d. 1984). His collections are now held by the Fondazione Magnani Rocca, and there is a remarkable private museum here (*open March–Nov Tues–Sun 10–6*). The paintings include works by Dürer (*Madonna and Child*); Carpaccio (*Pietà*); Filippo Lippi (*Madonna and Child*); Gentile da Fabriano (*St Francis Receiving the Stigmata*); van Dyck (*Equestrian Portrait of Giovanni Paolo Balbi*); Titian (*Madonna and Child with St Catherine, St Dominic and a Donor*, c. 1512/14); and Goya (allegorical family portrait of the *Infante Luis de Bourbon*, a conversation piece of 1789). There is also a splendid modern collection, with works by Monet, Renoir, Cézanne and Giorgio Morandi.

The ruined castle of **Canossa** (*open summer Tues–Sun 9–12.30 & 3–7; winter 9–3*) was the home of Countess Matilda of Tuscany, who was responsible for the submission of Emperor Henry IV to Pope Gregory VII in 1077. Only the foundations of the castle of that time remain; the ruins above ground date from the 13th century and later.

PIACENZA

Piacenza, situated at the strategic point where the Via Emilia touches the Po, possesses a beautiful cathedral and several fine churches, as well as some interesting museums. Its name (the French for which is *Plaisance*) is derived from the Latin *Placentia*.

HISTORY OF PIACENZA

An important centre of trade since Roman times, Piacenza has an uncanny way of popping up almost at random in European history. The peace negotiations ratified at Constance (1183) between Frederick Barbarossa and the Lombard League were conducted in the church of Sant'Antonino here. In 1545 Pope Paul III created the dukedom of Parma and Piacenza for his illegitimate son Pier Luigi Farnese; the pope's grandson, Alessandro Farnese (1545–92), was governor of the Low Countries from 1578 until his death. Piacenza was the first city to join Piedmont by plebiscite in 1848.

EXPLORING PIACENZA

The town centre

The centre of the old city is **Piazza Cavalli**, named after its pair of bronze equestrian statues of Duke Alessandro (1625) and his son and successor, Ranuccio Farnese (1620). The city commissioned these fine works from Francesco Mochi, who also designed the pediments. Palazzo del Comune is a fine Gothic building begun in 1280, built of brick, marble and terracotta.

Via XX Settembre leads out of the square, past **San Francesco**, a church begun in 1278 with a transitional façade. The fine Gothic interior has a pretty apse with an ambulatory.

The **cathedral**, an imposing Lombard Romanesque church (1122–1240), stands at the end of the street. The beautiful polychrome façade, in sandstone and red Verona marble, has been restored. The left porch and door are attributed to the school of Wiligelmus. The central door was heavily restored at the end of the 19th century; the original elements include the archivolt with signs of the zodiac, the two telamones (supporting male figures), and capitals above. The lions were replaced in the 16th century. The right door is by Master Niccolò. It has finely carved panels of the *Life of Christ*, including three unusual scenes of the *Temptations in the Desert*.

From the piazza on the south side you can see the exterior of the drum and the 14th-century campanile, crowned by a gilded angel, a weather vane placed here in the early 14th century by Pietro Vago. Beyond the *chiostri del duomo* you can glimpse the exterior (from the Strada della Prevostura) of the early 12th-century apse, a carved window with four figures, and pretty loggias above.

Massive cylindrical pillars divide the nave and aisled transepts. Set into the pillars are little square reliefs by local sculptors (c. 1170) showing the work of the guilds that paid for the erection of each column. Above the arches are 12th-century figures of *Saints and the Madonna* (left) and *Prophets* (right). At the west end are two capitals attributed to Nicolò, one with the story of *Saul and David*, and one showing the *Stoning of St Stephen*. On the west wall are paintings by Camillo Procaccini and Lodovico Carracci. Three votive frescoes of the *Madonna*, dating from the 14th–15th century, adorn a nave pillar.

The architecture of the transepts is particularly fine, and there are interesting remains of frescoes here (early 12th-century and c. 1390). The frescoes in the vault of the central octagon were begun by the great Lombard artist Morazzone, but he completed just two sections before his death. The frescoes in the rest of the vault (and the lunettes below) were completed by Guercino. A lunette over the entrance to the sacristy has a Giottesque *Madonna*. The two ambones are 19th-century reconstructions.

In the raised choir the high altar has a sculpted gilded reredos (late 15th century), behind which are good stalls of 1471. The two large 18th-century Neoclassical paintings are by the local painter Gaspare Landi. The apse fresco and those in the sanctuary vaults are by Camillo Procaccini and Lodovico Carracci.

Unloved?

A brown, decayed, old town, Piacenza is. A deserted, solitary, grass-grown place, with ruined ramparts; half-filled-up trenches, which afford a frowzy pasturage to the lean kine which wander about them: and streets of stern houses, moodily frowning at the other houses over the way. The sleepiest and shabbiest of soldiery go wandering about, with the double curse of laziness and poverty, uncouthly wrinkling their misfitting regimentals; the dirtiest of children play with their impromptu toys (pigs and mud) in the feeblest of gutters; and the gauntest of dogs trot in and out of the dullest of archways, in perpetual search of something to eat which they never seem to find.

Charles Dickens, Pictures from Italy, 1846

The north and west

Via Chiapponi leads to the church of Sant'Antonino, rebuilt in the 11th century with an octagonal lantern tower, which dates in part from the 10th century, supported inside on a group of massive pillars. The huge north porch was added in 1350.

Nearby is the Teatro Municipale (1803–10) with a little museum (ring for admission at Via Verdi 41). At Via San Siro 13 is the **Galleria Ricci-Oddi**, with a representative collection of Italian 19th–20th-century painting (*closed at the time of writing; T: 0523 320742*). The collection was begun in 1902 by Giuseppe Ricci-Oddi (1868–1937) and donated by him to the city in 1924. The charming building, with excellent natural lighting, was built expressly for the collection.

Via Sant'Antonino is prolonged by the busy Corso Garibaldi. In this street are (right) the 12th-century front of **Sant'Ilario**, with a relief of *Christ and the Apostles* on the architrave, and (at the end of the street) **Santa Brigida**, also 12th century. A little to the left is **San Giovanni in Canale**, a 13th- and 16th-century church, well restored. Nearby in Via Taverna, at the Collegio Morigi, is a **Museo di Storia Naturale** (*open Mon–Sat except holidays 8.30–12.30, Thur also 3–5.30*), with small natural history collections from the province of Piacenza and the Po river basin.

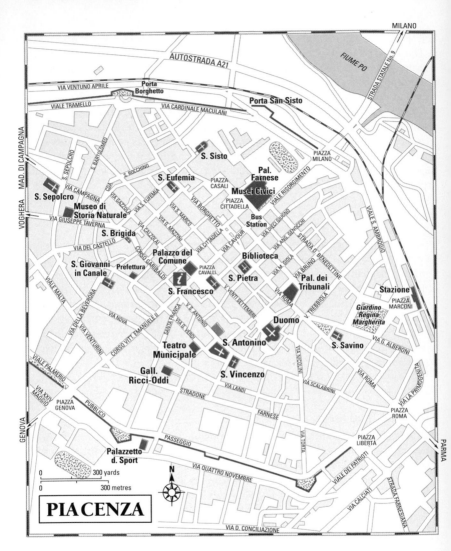

MILANO

AUTOSTRADA A21

FIUME PO

STRADA STATALE No. 9

VIA VENTUNO APRILE

Porta
Borghetto

VIALE TRAMELLO

VIA CARDINALE MACULANI

Porta San Sisto

PIAZZA
MILANO

S. Sisto

Pal.
Farnese

Musei Civici

PIAZZA
CASALI

S. Eufemia

PIAZZA
CITTADELLA

VIA RISORGIMENTO

VIALE S. AMBROGIO

MAD. DI CAMPAGNA

VIA SEPOLCRO

S. BARTOLOMEO

S. ROCCHINO

VIA CAMPAGNA

S. Sepolcro

Museo di
Storia Naturale

VIA GIUSEPPE TAVERNA

VIA CALZOLAI

VIA S. EUFEMIA

VIA GAZZOLA

VIA S. MARCO

VIA G. MAZZINI

VIA BORGHETTO

VIA CITTADELLA

VOGHERA

S. Brigida

VIA DEL CASTELLO

Palazzo del
Comune

PIAZZA
CAVALLI

VIA CAVOUR

Biblioteca

VIA DIECI GIUGNO

Bus
Station

STRADA D. BENEDETTINE

VIA ANG. GENOCCHI

VIA M. GIOIA

S. Giovanni
in Canale

CORSO GARIBALDI

Prefettura

VIALE MALTA

VIA DELLA BEVERORA

VIA NOVA

VIA VENTURINI

CORSO VITT. EMANUELE II

SANTA FRANCA

VIA S. ANTONIO

VIA G. VERDI

S. Francesco

V. VENTI SETTEMBRE

S. Pietra

Pal. dei
Tribunali

VIA BRUNO

VIA ROMA

V. TREBBIOLA

Duomo

Stazione

PIAZZA
MARCONI

Giardino
Regina
Margherita

VIA G. ALBERONI

VIALE PALMERIO

VIA XXV
MAGGIO

PIAZZA
GENOVA

PUBBLICO

GENOVA

Teatro
Municipale

Gall.
Ricci-Oddi

STRADONE

S. Antonino

S. Vincenzo

VIA LANDI

FARNESE

VIA NICOLINI

VIA SCALABRINI

S. Savino

VIA ROMA

VIA LA PRIMOGENITA

PIAZZA
ROMA

Palazzetto
d. Sport

PASSEGGIO

VIA TORTA

PIAZZA
LIBERTA

VIA DEI PATRIOTI

VIA CALCIATI

STRADA FARNESIANA

PARMA

0   300 yards
0   300 metres

N

PIACENZA

VIA QUATTRO NOVEMBRE

VIA D. CONCILIAZIONE

Via Campagna leads northwest from beyond Santa Brigida to (15 minute walk) the church of the **Madonna di Campagna**, a graceful Renaissance building by Alessio Tramello (1528). Tramello is chiefly known for his work in Piacenza. In inspiration he owes much to Alberti and Bramante. This church is built on a Greek-cross plan, with four little domed corner chapels. The central dome, beautifully lit by small windows in a loggia, has frescoes by Pordenone (1528–31). The decoration of the drum and the pendentives was completed by Bernardino Gatti (1543). There are more works by Pordenone in other parts of the church, including a corner chapel with scenes from the *Life of St Catherine*, and another with scenes of the *Nativity*. Other paintings are by Giulio Cesare and Camillo Procaccini, Guercino and Camillo Boccaccino.

Via Sant'Eufemia leads northeast past the church of Sant'Eufemia, with an early 12th-century front (restored); straight ahead is **San Sisto**, another pretty church by Tramello (1511), inspired in part by Alberti's Sant'Andrea in Mantua. It was for this church that Raphael painted his famous *Sistine Madonna*, sold by the convent to the Elector of Saxony in 1754, and now at Dresden. On the north choir pier is the monument to Margaret, Duchess of Parma (1522–86), governor of the Netherlands from 1559 to 1567; the fine stalls date from 1514.

Palazzo Farnese and Collegio Alberoni

Via Borghetto leads back towards the centre. On the left, in Piazza Cittadella, the huge **Palazzo Farnese** houses the Musei Civici (*open Tues, Wed, Thur 8.45–1, Fri–Sat 8.45–1 & 3–6, Sun 9.30–1*). The palace was begun for Duchess Margaret in 1558 by Francesco Paciotto and continued after 1564 by Vignola, but left only half-finished. Vignola was much sought-after by the Farnese. His most famous and influential creation is probably the Jesuit church of Il Gesù in Rome. This palazzo has a grand if plain exterior, divided into three floors by protruding cornices and numerous well-proportioned windows. Adjoining to the left is the smaller 14th-century Rocca Viscontea. In the courtyard you can see the 15th-century loggia of the castle and a huge double loggia with niches of the Palazzo Farnese.

Inside you can view the duke's apartment, decorated with paintings by Sebastiano Ricci illustrating the life of the Farnese Pope Paul III, and by Giovanni Evangelista Draghi recounting the life of Alessandro Farnese, the Duke of Parma who waited in the Netherlands for the Armada.

In the basement, in remarkable vaulted rooms once used as kitchens and storerooms, is a fine collection of 50 carriages dating from the 18th and 19th centuries. Here begins the remarkable spiral staircase designed by Vignola that ascends to the top of the palace. Climb to the second floor for a glimpse of the deconsecrated ducal chapel, built to an octagonal design in 1598.

Underground rooms in a wing of the palace are to exhibit the archaeological section, which includes the celebrated Fegato di Piacenza, an Etruscan divination bronze representing a sheep's liver, marked with the names of Etruscan deities. The pinacoteca, approached through a beautiful iron gate with the Farnese arms at the foot of the stairs, is housed in the duchess's apartments on the second floor. Highlights include 16th-century paintings by Girolamo Mazzola Bedoli and Camillo Boccaccino, and a tondo by Botticelli.

Beyond the southern outskirts of the city, at San Lazzaro Alberoni, is the **Collegio Alberoni**, with an important collection of works of art (*open by appointment; T: 0523 609730*), including *Christ at the Column* by Antonello da Messina; 18 Flemish tapestries; Flemish paintings (Mabuse, Provost, and still lifes); church silver and vestments;

engravings by Piranesi; and scientific instruments. These belonged to Giulio Alberoni (1664–1752), a gardener's son who rose to be a cardinal and the able minister of Philip V of Spain.

AROUND PIACENZA

On the northern border of Piacenza Province, on the Po, is **Monticelli d'Ongina**, with a 15th-century castle frescoed by Bonifacio Bembo, and an ethnographic museum illustrating life on the river (*open Sun and holidays 3–6*).

Cortemaggiore, a 15th-century 'new town' built by the Pallavicini family, has two fine churches; the former Franciscan church has frescoes by Pordenone.

At **Alseno** the abbey of Chiaravalle della Colomba (*open Mon–Sat 8.30–11.30 & 2.30–5.30, Sun and holidays 8.30–12 & 2–6*) has a Romanesque church and a 13th-century Gothic cloister with coupled columns.

In the pretty Arda valley is **Castell' Arquato**, a picturesque hill-town with double gates. In the attractive piazza stand the Palazzo Pretorio of 1293 and the Romanesque Collegiata with a 14th-century cloister, off which is a museum (*open 9–12 & 2.30–5 or 6*) with church silver, sculpture and paintings. The 14th-century Rocca Viscontea can also be visited. The 16th-century Torrione Farnese is in the lower town, near the 13th-century fountain. A geological museum with marine fossils from the area, etc., is housed in the former hospital (16th century). Another museum is dedicated to Luigi Illica, in the librettist's house.

Near Lugagnano Val d'Arda, in pretty countryside, is **Veleia** (*open daily 9–dusk*), the picturesque ruins of a small Roman town which flourished in the 1st century BC, first excavated in the 18th century. There is a small archaeological museum here.

Near **Gazzola**, west of the Trebbia river, is the medieval Castello di Rivalta (*privately owned; open at weekends 9–12 & 3–6.30 or by appointment; T: 0523 978104*), enlarged in the 15th and 18th centuries, which retains its original furnishings and paintings by Pordenone.

Bobbio, in the southwest corner of the province, is noted for its learned monastery founded in 612 by the Irish St Columbanus, who died here in 615. The basilica, a 15th–17th-century building, has a crypt with some traces of the primitive church and the tomb of St Columbanus (1480). The museum (*open Sat 3–4.30, Sun and holidays 11–12 & 3–5*), contains a remarkable Roman ivory bucket with a representation of Orpheus (or David) in high relief (4th century). The heavily-restored cathedral is 12th-century, and beyond, a humpback bridge, possibly Roman, probably 7th-century in part, crosses the River Trebbia.

PRACTICAL INFORMATION

GETTING AROUND

• **By air:** Parma's Giuseppe Verdi Airport has regular flights to Rome and Milan Malpensa, and seasonal flights to Olbia in Sardinia. Bus 11 links the airport to central Parma.

• **By rail:** Italy's main north–south line closely follows the Via Emilia from Milan to Bologna. Some Eurostar and most Intercity trains stop at Parma (50mins from Milan, 1hr 20mins from Bologna) and/or Piacenza (40mins from Milan, 1hr 10mins from Bologna). You can reach both cities without changing trains from Rome/Florence and from Bari/Ancona. Commuter trains (Regionali and Interregionali) connect Modena with Mantua and Verona, and Reggio Emilia with Guastalla and Sassuolo.

• **By bus:** Buses from the bus station in Piazzale della Chiesa (Parma) to the main places in the province, operated by TEP (T: 0521 282657, www.tep.pr.it) and APAM (T: 0376 2301). Country buses (operated by ACAP, T: 0523 337245) from Piazza Cittadella (Piacenza) to places in the province and cities in Emilia.

• **By taxi:** T: 0521 252562.

INFORMATION OFFICES

Parma Via Melloni 1a, T: 0521 218889, www.emiliaromagnaturismo.it
Informagiovani: Via Melloni 1b, T: 0521 218749.
Piacenza Piazza Cavalli 7, T: 0523 329324, www.emiliaromagnaturismo.it
Informagiovani: Via Taverna 37, T: 0523 334013, www.comune.piacenza.it/informagiovani/index.htm

HOTELS

Parma
€€ **Grand Hotel Baglioni**. Modern and fairly refined, with Art Nouveau antiques. Closed Aug. Viale Piacenza 12c, T: 0521 292929, F: 0521 292828.
€€ **Park Hotel Stendhal**. Modern and comfortable, with a good restaurant. Piazzetta Bodoni 3, T: 0521 208057, F: 0521 285655.
€€ **Park Hotel Toscanini**. Overlooking the River Parma, also with a good restaurant. Viale Toscanini 4, T: 0521 289141, F: 0521 283143.
€€ **Torino**. Somewhat simpler than the others, but friendly and centrally located. Closed Jan and Aug. Borgo Mazza 7, T: 0521 281046, F: 0521 230725, www.hotel-torino.it
€€ **Villa Ducale**. A renovated villa with park, 2km north on the road to Mantua. Via del Popolo 35, T: 0521 272727, F: 0521 780756, www.villaducalehotel.com
Piacenza
€€ **Grande Albergo Roma**. The classic place to stay, provincial elegance and a good restaurant with views. Via Cittadella 14, T: 0523 323201, F: 0523 330548, www.grandealbergoroma.it
Quattro Castella
€€ **Casa Matilde**. An aristocratic villa in a shady park in the hills 14km southwest of Reggio. Località Puianello, T: 0522 889006, F: 0522 889006.

YOUTH HOSTEL

Parma
€ **Cittadella**. Parco Cittadella 5, T: 0521 961434.

RESTAURANTS

Parma
€€ **Al Tramezzino**. Represents the culinary tradition of Parma at its best. Closed Mon and July. Via Del Bono 5b, Località San Lazzaro, T: 0521 484196.
€€ **Angiol d'Or**. An excellent taste of tradition. Closed Sun, Dec and Jan. Vicolo Scutellan 1, T: 0521 282632.
€€ **Antichi Sapori**. Traditional trattoria situated a few kilometres from the centre of town, good traditional Parmesan food with a personal twist. Closed Tues and 1–15 Jan, 1–15 Aug. Strada Montanara 318, T: 0521 648165.
€€ **Cocchi**. Restaurant of the Hotel Daniel—a good, conservative place with an interesting wine list. Closed Sat, 24–26 Dec and Aug. Via Gramsci 16a, T: 0521 981990.
€€ **Cortile**. Elegant trattoria specialising in traditional regional cooking. Nice wine selection. Closed Sun and 1–20 Aug. Borgo Paglia 3, T: 0521 285779.
€€ **Da Romeo**. Trattoria with genuine Parmesan food and a good wine list. Closed Thur and 15 Aug–15 Sept. Botteghino (6km from the centre of town), Via Traversetolo 185, T: 0521 641167.
€€ **La Greppia**. The most creative of the restaurants specialising in traditional local cuisine. Closed Mon–Tues and July. Strada Garibaldi 39a, T: 0521 233686.

€€ **Patrizzi**. Probably the best *cucina parmense* in the city centre. Closed 25 Dec, Mon and Sun evenings June–Aug. Strada della Repubblica 71, T: 0521 285952.
€€ **Santa Croce**. Elegant restaurant with garden, dishes from the region and innovative cooking; closed Sat midday-Sun and 1–20 Jan, 10–25 Aug. Via Pasini 20, T: 0521 293529.
€€ **Tramezzino**. Traditional restaurant specialising in regional dishes; interesting selection of wines and spirits. Closed Mon and July. Via Del Bono 5b, Località San Lazzaro, T: 0521 454196.
€€ **Viole**. Creative and seasonal cooking, good desserts and wines selection. Closed Wed–Thur midday and 15 Jan–10 Feb, 13–20 Aug. Località Castelnuovo. Strada Nuova di Castelnuovo 60a, T: 0521 601000,
Piacenza
Fornovo del Taro
€€ **Trattoria di Cafragna-Camorali**. Great country trattoria, serving delicious renditions of local dishes. Closed Sun evening (also midday Sun in July), Dec–Jan and Aug. Località Cafragna, T: 0525 2363.
Bobbio
€€ **San Nicola**. Restaurant offering excellent regional food and wines, in a former convent. Closed Mon evening and Tues. Contrada dell'Ospedale, T: 0523 932355.
Collecchio
€€ **Villa Maria Luigia** Traditional regional food in a villa with garden seating in summer. Closed Wed evening, Thur and Jan. Via Galaverna 28, T: 0521 805489.
Fidenza
€€ **I Gemelli**. An interesting seafood

restaurant. Closed Mon and June–July. Via Gialdi 14, T: 0524 528506.

€ **Astoria**. Good Emilian home cooking. Closed Mon. Via Gandolfi 7, T: 0524 524588.

Noceto

€ **Aquila Romana**. Great food and outstanding value, in a historic building. Closed Mon–Tues and midday July–Aug. Via Gramsci 6, T: 0521 625398.

Roccabianca

€€ **Hostaria da Ivan**. Simple *osteria* popular with locals. Closed Mon–Tues, Jan and Aug. Via Villa 73, Località Fontanelle, T: 0521 870113.

Soragna

€€ **Antica Osteria Ardenga**. Good local *osteria*. Closed Tues–Wed, Jan and July. Via Maestra 6, Località Diolo, T: 0524 599337.

WINE BARS

Parma

€ **Antica Osteria Fontana**. Wine bar with great *salumi* and traditional Parmesan sandwiches. Closed Sun–Mon and July–Aug. Via Farini 24a, T: 0521 286037.

€ **Bottiglia Azzurra**. Charming wine bar serving good food. Closed Sun and midday and July–Aug. Borgo Felino 63, T: 0521 285842.

€ **Ombre Rosse**. Warm wine bar with a wide selection of vintages and good cooking. Closed Sat midday–Sun midday. Vicolo Giandemaria 4, T: 0521 289234.

REGIONAL SPECIALITIES

Italians from all over Emilia Romagna flood this area at weekends for the little antiques markets held in the various towns and villages. Parma is particularly well-known for its gastronomic specialities—notably Parmigiano-Reggiano cheese; Parma ham (*prosciutto di Parma*) and various salamis (*salame di Felino, culatello di Zibello, spalla cotta di San Secondo*); Fragno black truffles; Borgotaro mushrooms; Lambrusco, Malvasia, Fortana, Profumo and Violetta di Parma wines.

EVENTS & FESTIVALS

Parma *Suoni nel Tempo*, classical music concert series at the Galleria Nazionale, Teatro Farnese and Teatro Reggio, Jan–May.

Piacenza *Fiera di Sant'Antonio* and *Fiera di San Giuseppe*, with markets of local food and crafts. Other seasonal markets at Grazzano Visconti, Cortemaggiore, Castell'Arquato and Caorso.

Busseto Monthly guided visit to places of Verdian significance, with music.

Castell'Arquato Medieval market and banquet, May.

Fidenza Classical music and opera season, spring. *La Gostra di Maggio*, theatre festival, May.

Fontanellato Classical music and opera season, winter–spring.

Grazzano Visconti *Il Corteo*, historic pageant, May. *Alla Corte del Re*, music and dance in historic costume, first Sun of every month, Apr–Sept. *Notte di Faba*, medieval market and banquet, July.

Salsomaggiore Gino Gandolfi International Piano Competition, March. Giuseppe Verdi International Choral Festival and Competition, July.

FERRARA & ITS PROVINCE

Ferrara is famed as the residence of the Este dukes, whose court was one of the most illustrious of the Italian Renaissance. The town lies in a fertile plain near the right bank of the Po: today it is an important market for fruit, and is also one of the most pleasing towns in northern Italy, well-administered and with a peaceful atmosphere. Cycling is the main means of getting about. The city is divided into two distinct parts: the southern district retains many attractive cobbled streets and medieval houses, whereas the area to the north, defined by Jacob Burckhardt as the first modern city in Europe, was laid out in the 15th century by Ercole I d'Este.

NB: This chapter is covered by the map on p. 652.

HISTORY OF FERRARA

Originating probably as a refuge of the Veneti in the marshes of the Po, Ferrara first became important under the Exarchate of Ravenna (6th century). The Guelph family of Este, after a decisive defeat of the Ghibellines by Azzo Novello at Cassano in 1259, established the earliest and one of the greatest northern Italian principalities here. Ferrara remained under the sway of the Este dukes until 1598, and their court attracted a great many poets, scholars and artists, while trade and commerce flourished. Nicolò II (1361–88) gave hospitality to Petrarch; Alberto (1388–93) founded the university; Nicolò III (1393–1441) was the patron of Pisanello, and in his city (1438) the eastern emperor John VI Palaeologus met Pope Eugenius IV for the ecumenical council, later transferred to Florence. Lionello (1441–50) inaugurated the age of artistic pre-eminence that Borso (1450–71) continued; Ercole I (1471–1505) laid out the northern district of the city; and Alfonso I (1505–34), husband of Lucrezia Borgia, was the patron of Ariosto and Titian. Ercole II (1534–59) exiled his wife Renée, the daughter of Louis XII of France and the protectress of John Calvin, who lived for a while in Ferrara under the assumed name of Charles Heppeville; Alfonso II (1559–97) was the patron of Tasso and began the reclamation of the marshes.

In 1598 the city was annexed to the States of the Church on the pretext that Cesare d'Este, heir apparent to the duchy in a collateral line, was illegitimate. The Este left the city, and Ferrara soon lost its importance.

The Castello Estense

Map 7. *Open Tues–Sun 9.30–5.30.*

The former palace of the Este dukes, right in the centre of town, is a massive quadrilateral surrounded by a moat (still filled with water) and approached by drawbridges. It was begun in 1385 for Duke Nicolò II by Bartolino da Novara, who incorporated the 13th-century Torre dei Leoni into the northern corner of the fortress and added three more identical towers. It was altered by Girolamo da Carpi in the 16th century and readapted in the 20th century to house the administrative offices of the province.

After an earthquake in 1570 the piano nobile was refurbished to house the state apartments, as well as an antiquarium and a library. The overall plan was commissioned by Alfonso II d'Este (fifth Duke of Este) from Pirro Ligorio, the Neapolitan antiquary and architect who had been working at the Este court since 1568. Ligorio also designed the overall iconographic scheme underlying the painted decoration of the various rooms. The actual execution of the frescoes was entrusted to a group of artists active in Ferrara, including the local Camillo Filippi and his son Sebastiano (Il Bastianino), the Modenese Ludovico Settevecchi and Leonardo da Brescia.

The interior
You enter the castello from the lovely courtyard. The first two rooms on the ground floor display architectural remains from the castle, including reliefs with the Este coat of arms and carved keystones. The itinerary leads down a ramp into the kitchen, or **Sala del Caminetto**. Here are three badly ruined frescoes (1577) by Pirro Ligorio (the only ones to have survived of the hundred that once decorated the courtyard), and a large-scale model of Ferrara after the plan published by Bolzoni. At the end of a corridor, wooden steps lead down to the grim dungeons beneath the **Torre dei Leoni**, where Parisina, wife of Nicolò III, and her lover, Ugo, his illegitimate son, were imprisoned and murdered; the cells were last used for political prisoners in 1943.

An artillery ramp, by which the cannons were taken up to the bastions, leads round the Torre dei Leoni past another prison, and a modern iron staircase continues up to the first floor. Here a loggia opens onto the **Giardino degli Aranci**, a charming little walled hanging garden designed by Girolamo da Carpi for the Este duchesses (with delightful views of the town). The **Camerino del Baccanali** is beautifully frescoed by Camillo Filippi and his sons Cesare and Sebastiano (Il Bastianino). The Chapel of Renée of France was one of the few Calvinist chapels in Italy to survive the Counter-Reformation. The Sala dell'Aurora, Saletta dei Giochi and Salone dei Giochi have delightful ceiling frescoes by the Filippi (in the last two, around the walls, are copies made in 1911 of the frescoes in Palazzo Schifanoia). The tiny **Stanzina delle Duchesse** was entirely decorated with grotesques by the Filippi c. 1555–65.

San Giuliano and the Palazzo Comunale
The chapel of San Giuliano (1405) stands in the piazzetta on the west side of the castle. Off Corso Martiri della Libertà is a monument to the great preacher and reformer Savonarola, born in Ferrara in 1452, and burned at the stake in Florence in 1498. The Palazzo Comunale, built for Azzo Novello (1243), was considerably altered in the late 15th century by Pietro Benvenuti and Biagio Rossetti. The bronze statues of Nicolò III and Borso, on the Classical arch (to a design attributed to Leon Battista Alberti) and column in front, are 20th-century reproductions of the 15th-century originals destroyed in 1796. The arcaded courtyard has a fine staircase by Pietro Benvenuti (1481).

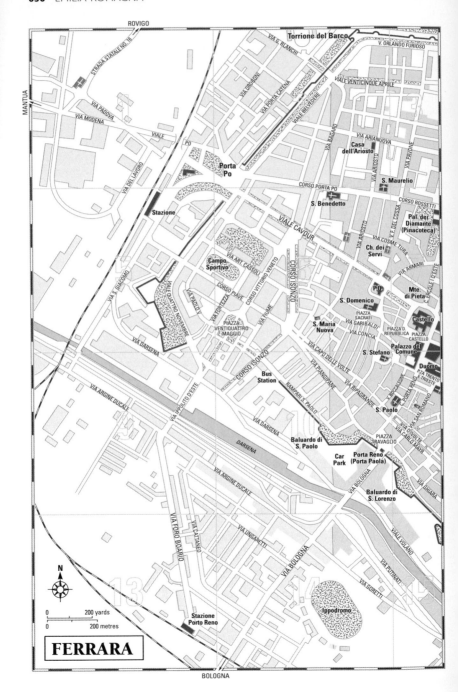

FERRARA

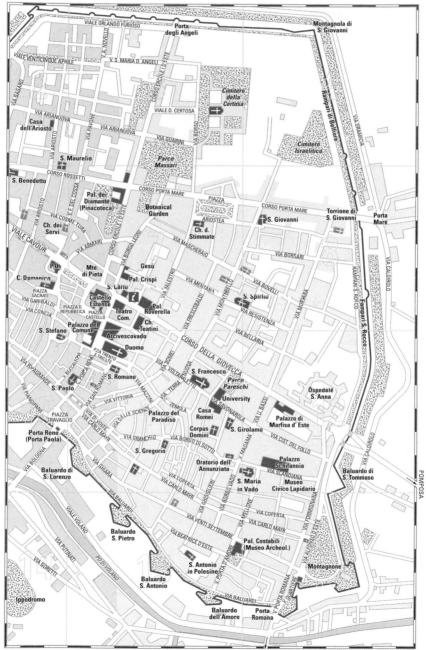

Ferrara cathedral: 13th-century tribune with a statue of the Virgin.

The cathedral

Map 11.

The cathedral, begun in 1135 for Guglielmo II degli Adelardi by the architect and sculptor Master Niccolò, was almost complete by the end of the 13th century. The church was dedicated to the Virgin Mary and to St George, both of whom feature prominently on the façade. Niccolò's reliefs on the central portal include the architrave with scenes of the Life of Christ (*Visitation, Nativity, Adoration of the Magi, Circumcision, Flight into Egypt* and *Baptism of Christ*), and a lunette with *St George Killing the Dragon*. The portal is crowned by an elaborate 13th-century tribune housing a statue of the *Madonna and Child* by Cristoforo da Firenze (1427). Above is an architrave with the *Resurrection from the Graves*, and representations of the blessed and the damned, surmounted by a tympanum with the *Last Judgement*. The lunettes at the sides of the tribune show further scenes of the blessed and damned. The whole was carved by an unknown 13th-century sculptor. To the right of the side door is a statue of Alberto d'Este (1393). The south side is partly obscured by a charming little portico of shops added in 1473. The massive, unfinished campanile, southeast of the church, was built from 1412 to 1596 to a plan attributed to Leon Battista Alberti.

The interior, remodelled in 1712–18, is preceded by a narthex with a 5th-century sarcophagus and the original pilasters from the main portal. On the west wall are two detached frescoes by Garofalo, representing *St Peter* and *St Paul*. The north side has altarpieces by Garofalo (1524) and Francesco Francia. In the transepts are terracotta busts of the *Apostles* by Alfonso Lombardi. The south transept also has a *Martyrdom of St Lawrence* by Guercino (1629) and the altar of the Calvary, composed in 1673 from large 15th-century bronze groups of statuary by Niccolò and Giovanni Baroncelli and Domenico di Paris. Below is the effigy tomb of Bishop Bovelli (d. 1954). A *Last Judgement* by Bastianino (1580–83) adorns the apse.

The **Museo della Cattedrale** (*open Tues–Sun 9–1 & 3–6*) is housed in the church of San Romano, opposite the south side of the cathedral. It contains good Flemish tapestries and illuminated choir books; *St George* and an *Annunciation* by Cosmè Tura (1469), from the doors of the old cathedral organ; the *Madonna of the Pomegranate* and a statuette of St Maurelius, both by Jacopo della Quercia (1408); and charming 12th-century reliefs of the *Months* (September, with the grape harvest, is particularly notable) from the old south doorway.

A one-time ghost town

Fallen into decadence and plagued by malaria, Ferrara had been largely abandoned by the time most Grand Tourists of the 18th and 19th centuries saw it.

My pen was just upon the point of praising its cleanliness ... till I reflected there was nobody to dirty it.

> *Hester Lynch Piozzi, Observations ... in the Course of a Journey, 1789*

You are in a dream, in the heart of a romance; you enjoy the most perfect solitude, that of a city which was once filled with 'the busy hum of men', and of which the tremulous fragments at every step strike the sense, and call up reflection. In short, nothing is to be seen of Ferrara, but the remains, graceful and romantic, of what if was.

> *William Hazlitt, Notes of a Journey through France and Italy, 1826*

More solitary, more depopulated, more deserted, old Ferrara than any city of the solemn brotherhood The grass so grows up in the silent streets, that any one might make hay there, literally, while the sun shines. But the sun shines with diminished cheerfulness in grim Ferrara; and the people are so few who pass and repass through the places, that the flesh of the inhabitants might be grass indeed, and growing in the squares.

> *Charles Dickens, Pictures from Italy, 1846*

Around the old ghetto

The Seminario, at Via Cairoli 32, occupies the 16th-century Palazzo Trotti, which contains two rooms frescoed by Garofalo (1519–20), with remarkable perspectives.

In the piazza south of the cathedral are the Torre dell'Orologio and a department store in an ugly building of 1957 on the site of the 14th-century Palazzo della

Ragione. The pretty, arcaded Via San Romano leads south through an interesting medieval part of the town. The street ends at Porta Reno (or Porta Paolo), built in 1612 to a design by the native architect Giovanni Battista Aleotti. Nearby is the imposing church of **San Paolo**, begun in 1575 by the architect Alberto Schiatti. It contains 16th–17th-century paintings and frescoes by Girolamo da Carpi (*St Jerome*), Bastianino, Scarsellino (fresco in the apse with the *Abduction of Elias*) and Domenico Mona (*Adoration of the Magi, Conversion* and *Martyrdom of St Paul*, all in the presbytery). Along the aisles are some beautiful 18th-century terracotta sculptures by Filippo Bezzi and Francesco Casella.

Before the gate the pretty Via delle Volte, which runs beneath numerous arches, leads left. It crosses Via Scienze, in which (at no. 17) is **Palazzo Paradiso**. The building dates from 1391 and has a façade of 1610 by Giovanni Battista Aleotti. In the **library** (Biblioteca Ariostea, *open Mon–Fri 8–12.30, Sat–Sun 8–12.30 & 3.30–6.30*) are the tomb of the poet Ludovico Ariosto (1474–1533), manuscript pages of Ariosto's epic poem *Orlando Furioso*, and autographs of Ariosto and Tasso. Nearby in Via Mazzini is the synagogue, in the area which was the ghetto of Ferrara from 1627 to 1848, although a large Jewish community from Spain had lived freely in the town during the period of the Este dukes. The **Museo Ebraico di Ferrara** is at Via Mazzini 95 (*open for guided tours Sun–Thur 10, 11, 12*). The itinerary includes three synagogues, a small collection of documents, fabrics and religious objects, and a section devoted to the history of the Jewish community of Ferrara from the 15th century to the Second World War.

You can see well preserved old houses of the 15th-century city and little churches in the narrow lanes lying between Via Scienze and Via Borgo Vado. At Via Gioco del Pallone 31 is the house that belonged to Ariosto's family.

The attractive Via Voltapaletto (Map 11), east of the cathedral, leads past the handsome Palazzo Costabili (no. 11; 17th century), decorated with busts and trophies, to the spacious church of **San Francesco**. The church was partly rebuilt in 1494 by Biagio Rossetti, following the plan devised by Brunelleschi for his church of San Lorenzo in Florence. The frescoes above the arches (*Franciscan Saints*) and on the vault are good Ferrarese works of the 16th century. In the north aisle are a fine fresco of the *Seizure of Christ in the Garden* (1524) by Garofalo and an altarpiece by Scarsellino.

From the Casa Romei to the Oratorio

Map 11.

Via Savonarola continues to the **Casa Romei** at no. 30 (*open Tues–Sun 8.30–7*). The house is one of the best examples of an aristocratic home in 15th-century Ferrara. It was begun around 1440 for the wealthy Giovanni Romei, who served the Este court as a diplomat and (in 1474) married Polissena d'Este. In keeping with Giovanni's will, the house was donated after his death to the Poor Clare nuns of the adjacent convent of Corpus Domini and was used to house pilgrims and other visitors to the city (one of the guests was Lucrezia Borgia). It remained in the nuns' hands until the confiscation of monastic properties under Napoleon.

Off the central courtyard are two rooms with frescoes representing respectively the *Prophets*, with philosophical truths and biblical prophecies written on scrolls, and the *Sibyls* (probably executed after Romei's marriage to Polissena d'Este). The frescoes in the courtyard date from the 16th century. On the upper floor are frescoes by the Filippi (second half of the 16th century) and a noteworthy collection of detached frescoes, mainly of the 14th century, from Ferrarese churches that were either ruined or suppressed.

ART, ARCHITECTURE, LITERATURE & MUSIC

Ferrara had a productive school of painting, much of it overlapping with Bologna, where the court of the Bentivolglio attracted artists of talent and repute. One of the finest Ferrarese masters was Cosmè Tura—a great painter, of whose work all too little survives. With his hard outlines and vigorous modelling, there is a lack of Italian sweetness and sensuality to his work, but its glyptic astringency is difficult to forget. Unjustly treated both by posterity and by his patron, who replaced him with Ercole de' Roberti, Tura died penniless in 1495. Ercole worked both in Ferrara and in Bologna. He partnered another great Ferrarese artist, Francesco del Cossa, on the zodiac frescoes in the Palazzo Schifanoia (*see p. 642*), then followed Cossa to Bologna, until he was appointed court painter at Ferrara. The deceptively crude, spiky naivety of his art masks great sophistication and emotion. Other important names associated with Ferrara include Dosso Dossi and his brother Battista, and Il Garofalo, a follower of Raphael, and high priest of the High Renaissance.

Ferrara was also the birthplace of a great sculptor, Alfonso Lombardi (1497–1537), and of a great architect, Biagio Rossetti (c. 1447–1516). Rossetti's greatest achievement is the 'Addizione', the northern extension of the city, one of the greatest feats of town planning of all time (*see p. 645*). The extraordinary, multi-pinnacled Palazzo dei Diamanti is also his (*see p. 646*). The court of the Este was also noted for its music. The composer Girolamo Frescobaldi (1583–1643) was born in Ferrara. At the end of the 16th century the '*concerto delle donne*' at the Este court had an important influence on the development of the madrigal. Robert Browning wrote several poems about Ferrara, and *My Last Duchess* (written in 1842) probably refers to Alfonso II and his wife. The writer Giorgio Bassani was born in Ferrara in 1916, and his novel *Il Giardino dei Finzi Contini* is set here.

Across Via Savonarola is the seat of the university, founded in 1391. The church of **San Girolamo** (1712) faces the house (no. 19) where Savonarola spent the first 20 years of his life. The church of **Corpus Domini** has a 15th-century façade in Via Campofranco (if closed, enquire at the convent, Via Pergolato 4). After a fire that greatly damaged the interior, the church was refurbished in 1770 by Antonio

Foschini. Most of the lavish painted decoration dates from that period. The capitular room at the back contains several floor tombs of members of the Este family, notably Alfonso I and II d'Este, and of Lucrezia Borgia (wife of Alfonso I; d. 1519) and two of her sons. Via Savonarola ends at the severe Palazzo Saracco.

Via Ugo Bassi, to the left, leads to Corso della Giovecca, where no. 174 is the **Palazzina di Marfisa d'Este** (*open Tues–Sun 9.30–1 & 3–6*). Built in 1559 at the commission of Francesco d'Este for his daughter Marfisa, it was restored in 1938. The ceilings are decorated with grotesques and mythological scenes, by Camillo Filippi and his sons Sebastiano and Cesare, which were extensively restored in the late 19th century. It also houses a good collection of period furniture, a supposed portrait of James I of England, and a damaged bust in profile of Ercole I d'Este, by Sperandio. The Loggia degli Aranci in the garden has a vault painted with trellised vines and birds.

Via Madama, to the right, continues as Via Borgo Vado, where the church of **Santa Maria in Vado**, another work of Rossetti (1495–1518), has a handsome interior covered with 17th- and 18th-century paintings. Nearby, at Via Borgo di Sotto 47, is the **Oratorio dell'Annunziata** (ring for admission at the convent at no. 49). The elegant façade is by the Ferrarese Gian Battista Aleotti (1612). The interior (*open Mon–Sat 9–12 & 3–6*; entered from the convent in Via Borgo di Sotto) is a rectangular room decorated in 1548 with frescoes attributed to Camillo Filippi, Pellegrino Tibaldi and Nicolò Rosselli, and trompe-l'oeil perspectives by Francesco Scala. The paintings were commissioned by the Confraternità della Buona Morte (who assisted the condemned) and represent the *Legend of the True Cross* according to the apocryphal text of Jacopo da Varagine. They are very damaged and in need of restoration. On the altar wall is a 15th-century *Resurrection* with members of the Confraternità, and on the opposite wall an *Assumption* signed by Lamberto Nortense.

Palazzo Schifanoia

Map 12. *Open open Tues–Sun 9–6.*
In Via Scandiana is Palazzo Schifanoia (entrance at no. 27), begun in 1385 and enlarged in 1391, 1458, and in·1469 by Pietro Benvenuti and Biagio Rossetti. Stairs lead up to the **Salone dei Mesi**, decorated for Duke Borso d'Este with delightful frescoes of the Months, one of the most renowned secular fresco cycles of the Renaissance (now in rather poor condition). They were painted by Francesco Cossa with the help of Ercole de' Roberti and other (unidentified) masters of the Ferrarese school.

The frescoes follow a complicated decorative scheme referring to the months of the year in three bands: above are 12 scenes illustrating the triumph of a divinity; the middle band has the sign of the zodiac for that month, flanked by two symbolic figures, and the lower part of the walls are decorated with scenes from the court of Duke Borso. The cycle reads as follows:

West wall: Very ruined scenes illustrating January and February.
East wall (opposite the present entrance): This is the best preserved section, and is known to have been decorated by Francesco Cossa. March:

Triumph of Minerva, showing her on a chariot drawn by two unicorns; the sign of Aries; hawking scenes. April: *Triumph of Venus* (her chariot drawn by swans); Taurus; Duke Borso returning from the hunt and the Palio of St George. May: *Triumph of Apollo*; Gemini; fragments of farming scenes.

North wall: June: *Triumph of Mercury*; Cancer; scenes of the duke in a landscape. July: *Triumph of Zeus*; Leo; the duke receiving visitors, and scenes of women working hemp. August: *Triumph of Ceres*; Virgo. The scenes for September are usually attributed to Ercole de' Roberti: *Triumph of Vulcan*, with Vulcan's forge, and a love scene in bed thought to represent Mars and Rhea Silvia, from whose union Romulus and Remus were born; Libra; Borso receiving Venetian ambassadors.

South wall: The last three months are almost totally obliterated. There is a display of illuminated manuscripts here.

The **Sala degli Stucchi** (1468–70) has a delightful ceiling attributed to Domenico di Paris. The adjoining room has another good ceiling and a display of 14th–15th-century ceramics.

The main staircase leads back downstairs. Halfway down is the entrance to rooms that contain material from the municipal collections of arts and antiquities, including (in the first room) Egyptian works, two Greek red-figure vases and Roman glass. The next three rooms on a mezzanine floor (with remains of painted decoration on the walls) display 15th–16th-century ceramics. On the floor below are exhibited ivories and *Scenes of the Passion* in alabaster, made in Nottingham in the early 15th century; 15th-century intarsia stalls; plaques and medals by Pisanello, Matteo de' Pasti and Sperandio; sculptures including a bust by Guido Mazzoni and two *Madonnas* attributed to Domenico di Paris; 16th-century bronzes (Giovanni Francesco Susini, Giambologna and Duquesnoy), 18th-century marble busts, and a *Portrait of Cicognara* by Canova (1822).

Across the street is the **Lapidario Civico** (*open as Palazzo Schifanoia*), arranged in the 15th-century former church of Santa Libera. The collection of Roman works was formed in 1735 by Marchese Bevilacqua. Among the funerary stelae and sarcophagi are those of Annia Faustina and of the Aurelii (both dating from the 3rd century AD).

Palazzo Costabili

Via Camposabbionario leads to the ruins of the once-imposing church of **Sant'Andrea**, one of the principal churches of Ferrara and former home to many of the frescoes and paintings now exhibited in the pinacoteca (*see p. 646*). Until the 19th century the church also held the remains of the great Ferrarese architect Biagio Rossetti, who was buried here in 1516. After a series of fires and earthquakes the ruined church was deconsecrated in 1867 and turned into a military warehouse. The north wall was destroyed in the 1960s to make way for an ugly concrete secondary school.

Via Camposabbionario ends in Via XX Settembre. Number 152 is the house that Biagio Rossetti designed as his own home. It is now home to **Musarc** (*open daily 10–1*

& 3–6), a museum of architecture that has a permanent collection of Frank Lloyd Wright's plans and drawings for the Solomon R. Guggenheim Museum in New York and mounts three temporary exhibitions per year.

At Via XX Settembre 124 is **Palazzo Costabili**, also called the Palazzo di Lodovico il Moro. It was commissioned in 1495 from Biagio Rossetti by Antonio Costabili, who was the ambassador of the Este at the Sforza court of Lodovico il Moro in Milan (Lodovico married Beatrice d'Este in 1490). The building, one of Rossetti's master-pieces, was left unfinished in 1504. Off the beautiful square courtyard are two rooms decorated by Garofalo and his assistants around 1517. The first has lunettes with *Prophets* and *Sibyls*, and monochrome paintings on the ceiling; the second is painted with the *Story of St Joseph*. Off the portico on the south side of the courtyard is the so-called Aula Costabiliana or Sala del Tesoro with a stunning illusionistic ceiling depict-ing a polygonal dome and balcony with figures (members of the Costabili family) looking out at the viewer. The inspiration is clearly derived from Mantegna's Camera degli Sposi in the Palazzo Ducale at Mantua (*see p. 258*). The three rooms are currently closed to the public.

A beautiful staircase leads up from the courtyard to the **Museo Archeologico Nazionale** (*open Tues–Sun 9–2*), established in 1935 to hold finds from the necro-polis of Spina (*see p. 649*) in the Trebba valley near Comacchio (excavated 1922–35). The collection was enlarged in the 1950s following the discovery of further tombs in the adjacent Pega valley. The tomb artefacts date between the 6th and the 3rd cen-turies BC and are mainly linked to the idea of banquets and symposia intended to accompany the dead to the afterlife. Spina was an extremely rich port that traded extensively with Greece and Etruria. The relation with Greece is witnessed by a con-spicuous number of Hellenic pots of great quality (mainly Attic red-figure vases of the 5th century BC) forming one of the richest collections of its kind in Italy.

The southeastern corner of town

Gardens crown the ramparts of **Montagnone** (Map 16), and a park extends north above the walls built by Alfonso I (1512–18). Paths continue from here for c. 5km around the walls as far as Porta Po, interrupted only at Porta Mare. The walls are described in greater detail below.

Via Porta Romana leads south through the walls and across the Po di Volano canal to the church of **San Giorgio** (beyond Map 16), which was the cathedral of Ferrara in the 7th–12th centuries, then rebuilt in the 15th century and partly renovated in the 18th. The campanile is by Rossetti (1485). Inside are the magnificent tomb of Lorenzo Roverella, physician to Julius II and afterwards Bishop of Ferrara, by Ambrogio da Milano and Antonio Rossellino (1475); and the pavement tomb of Cosmè Tura. From Porta Romana a path takes you along a good stretch of walls built by Alfonso II.

Near Palazzo Costabili, off Via Beatrice d'Este, is the convent of **Sant'Antonio in Polesine** (ring for admission). The monastery was originally established in the late Middle Ages by the Eremitani di Sant'Agostino on what was then an island in the River Po. It subsequently passed to a community of Benedictine nuns founded in

1254 by Beatrice II d'Este, who promoted the reconstruction of the complex. Beatrice died in 1264 and was beatified in 1270; her relics and marble tombstone (from which miraculous water issues) are kept on the side of the cloister flanking the church.

The church is divided into two parts, of which the oldest, to the east, houses the nuns' choir (with beautiful wooden stalls decorated with tarsia work of the late 15th century) and three chapels with frescoes dating from the 14th to the 16th century. The frescoes in the north chapel, executed in the early 14th century, show a strong influence of Giotto and represent the *Lives of Christ and the Virgin*. The iconography of some scenes is unusual: the *Visitation* includes Zacharias, who normally is not shown; the *Nativity* follows a Byzantine prototype with a double representation of Christ, one spiritual and prefiguring his death (hence the tomb), the other temporal and in need of human care (he is being washed by the midwives). The *Flight into Egypt* is absolutely unique in its representation of Jesus on Joseph's shoulder, instead of the Virgin's lap. On the left wall, the *Dormition of the Virgin* again follows a Byzantine scheme with Christ in a mandorla holding the personification of the Virgin's soul.

The cycle continues in the south chapel, with the scenes of the *Garden of Gethsemane, Judas's Betrayal* and the *Mocking of Christ* on the left wall, all belonging to the same school of painters that decorated the left chapel. The representation of Christ ascending the ladder to the Cross, painted in the lunette on the right wall, is highly unusual. Somewhat later in date (mid-14th-century) and belonging to a different school of painters (of Bolognese influence) are the scenes of the *Dance of Salome, Christ in Limbo, Crucifixion, Deposition* and *Entombment*, as well as the *St John the Baptist* and *St John the Evangelist* on either side of the window.

The frescoes in the central chapel date mainly from the 15th century, whereas the vault is decorated with grotesques of the late 16th century. The lunettes on the side walls depict the scallop shell of Santiago de Compostela, as pilgrims travelling to the saint's shrine in Spain along the Via Romea departed from this church. On the walls are representations of the *Virgin Enthroned among Saints, Martyrs and Doctors of the Church*. Particularly interesting are a scene of the *Stoning of St Stephen* on the right wall, and the *Coronation of the Virgin*. The wooden crucifix at the top has been ascribed to the school of Cosmè Tura.

Behind the central chapel is a room decorated with 17th-century paintings inserted in the ceiling, a 16th-century panel with the *Virgin* and the *Mysteries of the Rosary* over the altar, and a fresco of the *Flagellation* attributed to Ercole de' Roberti on the entrance wall. At the other side of the choir is the newer part of the church, with an illusionistic ceiling painted in the 17th century by Francesco Ferrari.

Palazzo dei Diamanti and the Pinacoteca

Map 7.
The area of the city north of the castle and the broad, busy Corso della Giovecca was developed by Ercole I in the early 15th century with wide thoroughfares and fine palaces and gardens. Known as the 'Addizione', it was planned and laid out by Biagio Rossetti.

Corso Giovecca 37 is a fragment of the old **Arcispedale Sant'Anna**, where Tasso was confined as a lunatic in 1579–86; behind is a 15th-century cloister of the former Basilian convent. The fine church of **San Carlo** is by Giovanni Battista Aleotti (1623). In Via Borgo Leoni is the church of the **Gesù**, which contains a *Pietà* in terracotta by Guido Mazzoni (1485). Nearby, at Via De Pisis 24, is the **Museo Civico di Storia Naturale** (*open Tues–Sun 9–6*). On the other side of Corso Giovecca is the church of the Teatini (1653), which contains a *Presentation in the Temple* by Guercino.

Palazzo dei Diamanti

The handsome, cobbled Corso Ercole I d'Este leads north past several palaces and garden walls to **Palazzo dei Diamanti**, begun by Rossetti for Sigismondo d'Este c. 1492 and remodelled around 1565. It takes its name from the diamond emblem of the Este, repeated 12,600 times on its façade (the rustication is cut into diamond-shaped points). The palace contains the **Pinacoteca Nazionale** (*open Tues–Sat 9–2, Sun and holidays 9–1; Thur 9–7*), especially notable for its paintings of the Ferrarese school. The rooms are unnumbered, but the works are all labelled.

The Vendeghini-Baldi Collection: Displayed in a room to the left, the collection includes works by Garofalo, Michele Coltellini, Bartolomeo Vivarini, Andrea Mantegna, Ercole de' Roberti, Jacopo and Giovanni Bellini, and Gentile da Fabriano. Another series of rooms displays works by the Maestro di Figline, Simone dei Crocifissi, Ercole de' Roberti, Giuseppe Mazzuoli, the school of Piero della Francesca, and Cosmè Tura. Early and mid-16th-century painters represented include Gian Francesco Maineri, Michele Coltellini, Domenico Panetti, Bastianino, and Lodovico and Agostino Carracci. The 17th- and 18th-century works include paintings by Scarsellino, Guercino and Pietro Muttoni. **Collezione Sacrati Strozzi:** Works include *Madonna*s by Biagio d'Antonio and Francesco Bianchi Ferrari, two 15th-century muses, *Christ in the Garden* attributed to Battista Dossi, and two interesting 16th-century views of Ferrara.

The Salone d'Onore: This room, with its fine wooden ceiling of 1567–91, holds 13th–14th-century frescoes from the church of San Bartolo and the ruined Sant'Andrea, as well as frescoes by Serafino Serafini (*Apotheosis of St Augustine*) and Garofalo (the *Old and New Testament*, formerly in Palazzo Costabili). Also here are two works of 1565 by Camillo and Sebastiano Filippi. **The Apartment of Cesare and Virginia d'Este:** These rooms beyond the Salone d'Onore preserve their 16th-century decoration. Here are displayed a painting by Vittore Carpaccio and works by 16th-century painters from Ferrara (Ortolano, Mazzolino, Sebastiano Filippi, Scarsellino and Carlo Bononi), with Garofalo and Dosso Dossi especially well represented (notice especially Garofalo's *Massacre of the Innocents* and the huge *Costabili Polyptych* from the church of Sant'Andrea, begun by Garofalo and finished by Dosso Dossi).

The northern districts

Beside Palazzo dei Diamanti, at no. 17, is the **Museo Michelangelo Antonioni** (*open Tues–Sun 9–1 & 3–6*), with a collection documenting the work of the film director, who was born in Ferrara.

Corso Porta Mare leads east from Palazzo dei Diamanti. At no. 2 is the **Orto Botanico** (*open Mon–Sat 9–1, Tues and Thur 9–5, Sat–Sun and holidays 10–1 & 3–6*). Beyond is the Palazzo Bevilacqua Massari, which houses the **Museo d'Arte Moderna e Contemporanea** as well as the **Museo Boldini**, devoted to the Ferrarese painter Giovanni Boldini (1842–1931). Both museums are entered from Via Porta Mare 9 (*open Tues–Sun 9–1 & 3–6*). The palazzo was built in the 16th century. In the late 18th it was given a first-floor enfilade of 14 rooms that follows the model of French royal palaces. Today these richly decorated apartments display Boldini's paintings, from the beginning of his career in Italy to his French period, testifying to his interest in the Impressionists. After his move to Paris in 1870, Boldini became established as a painter of Parisian high society—an accomplishment exemplified by the portraits of the *Comtesse de Rasty* (1878), the *Little Subercaseuse* (1891), *Princess Eulalia of Spain* (1898), and the magnificent *Lady in White* (1890) and *Lady in Pink* (1916). The rest of the first floor houses paintings of the 19th-century Italian school, as well as works of the Ferrarese symbolists Gaetano Previati (1852–1920) and Giuseppe Mentessi (1857–1931). 20th-century Italian art (Achille Funi, Roberto Melli, Mario Pozzati, Filippo de Pisis) is on the ground floor. Four rooms in the west wing accommodate the Malabotta collection of works by another celebrated Ferrarese artist, Filippo de Pisis (1896–1956). The paintings by Giorgio de Chirico and the Metaphysical School are currently not on display.

METAPHYSICAL PAINTING

This term is generally applied to the work of Giorgio de Chirico and Carlo Carrà from 1915 to 1918, and to that of Giorgio Morandi, who came together with Carrà towards the end of the war. De Chirico himself wrote in 1938: 'To be truly immortal a work of art must stand completely outside human limitations; logic and common sense are detrimental to it. Thus it approximates dream and infantile mentality.... One of the stronger sensations left to us by prehistory is that of presage. It will always be with us. It is as if it were an eternal proof of the non-sense of the universe.' Although de Chirico had read Schopenhauer and Nietzsche, the actual metaphysics of the movement are obscure; in practice it involved using objects (often mannequins and statues) as signs, placing them in unusual combinations and architectural perspectives that create an atmosphere of mystery. De Chirico's earlier paintings (before 1915)—particularly those done in Paris, where he knew Picasso, Paul Guillaume and Apollinaire—already possessed these qualities, especially the powerful but mysterious sense of presage. They were intensified in the work he did when he was confined to hospital as a conscript at Ferrara in 1915.

Corso Ercole I d'Este leads north toward the city walls. A detour along Via Arianuova to the left brings you to the **Casa dell'Ariosto**, the house built by the poet Ariosto, who died here in 1533. At the end of Corso Ercole I is the former **Porta degli Angeli**. This was the gate by which the Este left Ferrara in 1598, never to return, and it was closed the following year. The walls were begun in 1451 at the southern limit of the city, and in 1492 Biagio Rossetti was commissioned to build the walls around Ercole I's northern extension. Alfonso I and Alfonso II strengthened the fortifications, and more work was carried out on them by the popes in the 17th and 18th centuries. Their total length is 9.2km, and paths and avenues surmount them for some 8.5km.

Eight semicircular towers survive to the left of Porta degli Angeli; at the northwest angle is the Torrione del Barco. The most interesting and best-preserved stretch of the walls (followed by a picturesque path open to cyclists) is from the Porta degli Angeli to the Porta Mare (Map 8). The view north extends across the former Barco, the ducal hunting reserve, as far as the Po, an area of some 1,200ha, destined to become a park. Inside the walls you can see the orchards that surround the Certosa and the Jewish cemetery; in the distance are the towers of the castle.

AROUND FERRARA

Ferrara has a small province, most of which is to the east of the town in the southern part of the Po Delta, where the Po di Volano reaches the sea in a nature reserve.

The northern Po Delta, which lies in the Veneto, is described on pp. 482–83.

The Po River wetlands

The once marshy country between Ferrara and the sea, where the Po enters the Adriatic, has been the subject of land-reclamation schemes ever since the time of Alfonso II d'Este (16th century). It is a place of wild natural beauty: the dunes in the Po di Goro delta, in particular, are of great interest to naturalists. The **Gran Bosco della Mesola**, one of the last wooded areas in the Po Delta, has been included in the recently-established Parco Regionale del Delta del Po, a nature reserve that you can explore by boat, on Camargue horses or by bike along the marshland banks (*open Sun and holidays, 8–dusk; information: www.parks.it/parco.delta.po.er*). Yellow iris, waterlily and ditchreed offer a natural setting for numerous bird species, and the meanders of the delta host a large colony of European pond turtles. There is also sport fishing for eels, carp and perch. On the Po di Goro is the splendid **Castello di Mesola**, a hunting lodge of Alfonso II, built in 1583 by Antonio Pasi (to a design by Giovanni Battista Aleotti), now used for exhibitions.

The abbey of Pomposa

The isolated Benedictine abbey of Pomposa (*open daily 8.30–7*), at Codigoro, was founded in the 7th–8th century on what was then an island, but was gradually deserted in the 17th century because of malaria. It is still one of the most evocative sites on the delta, marked by its fine campanile, 48m high.

The church dates from the 8th–9th centuries, and was enlarged in the 11th century. It is preceded by an atrium with beautiful Byzantine sculptural decoration. The fine basilican interior, with good capitals and a mosaic floor from the 12th century, is covered with charming 14th-century frescoes representing *Scenes from the Old and New Testament* and the *Apocalypse*. Some of these, including the *Christ in Glory* in the apse, have been attributed to Vitale da Bologna.

The monastic buildings include the chapterhouse and refectory, both with important frescoes of the Bolognese school. There is a small museum above the refectory. Guido d'Arezzo (c. 995–1050), inventor of the modern musical scale, was a monk here. The Palazzo della Ragione (abbot's justice court) is a beautiful 11th-century building, altered in 1396.

Comacchio, Spina and the coast

To the south are fields where rice is cultivated, and the marshes of the Valle Bertuzzi (visited by migratory birds). **Comacchio** is an interesting little town that grew to importance because of its salt-works. It is now important for fishing and curing eels—the huge shoals of eels that make for the sea in Oct–Dec are caught in special traps. The town was continuously attacked by the Venetians and destroyed by them in 1509. The pretty canal-lined streets are crossed by numerous bridges, notably the 17th-century Trepponti, which traverses no fewer than four canals. The Loggia dei Mercanti, duomo and Loggiata dei Cappuccini all date from the 17th century.

In the drained lagoon northwest of Comacchio the burial-ground of the Greco-Etruscan city of **Spina** yielded a vast quantity of vases and other pottery (kept in the archaeological museum in Ferrara). Founded c. 530 BC, it was a port carrying on a lively trade with Greece, but it barely outlasted the 4th century BC. Part of the city itself, laid out on a regular grid plan with numerous canals, was located by aerial survey in 1956, and excavations continue.

The dwindling **Valli di Comacchio** are now more than two-thirds drained, to the detriment of the egrets, herons, stilts, terns and avocets that were once found here in profusion. The area has recently been incorporated in the Parco Regionale del Delta del Po. At **Porto Garibaldi** (formerly Magnavacca) the Austrian navy captured the last 200 'Garibaldini', leaving Garibaldi alone with Anita (his Brazilian wife and companion in arms) and his comrade Leggero. Anita died at Mandriole, on the southern shore of the lake (monument), now in the province of Ravenna near the vast pine woods of San Vitale, which hide the view of the sea.

PRACTICAL INFORMATION

GETTING AROUND

• **By air:** Ferrara lies 45km from Bologna's Guglielmo Marconi Airport, with daily flights to and from domestic and international destinations.

• **By rail:** Ferrara is situated on the main rail line from Padua (50mins north) to Bologna (25mins south). From most other places to the south, east and west the quickest way to get there is via Bologna. Commuter trains connect to Rimini via Ravenna, and to Mantua via Suzzara.

• **By bus:** Buses 1 and 9 go from the station to the castle. Services for the province (including Comacchio) depart from the bus station on Corso Isonzo (Map 6).

• **By bicycle:** Cycles can be hired on Corso Giovecca (next to the information office).

INFORMATION OFFICES

Ferrara Castello Estense, T: 0532 209370, www.ferrarainfo.com, www.emiliaromagnaturismo.it Offices are open in summer at Comacchio and Pomposa.

HOTELS

Ferrara
€€€ **Duchessa Isabella**. A beautiful, luxurious old townhouse with coffered ceilings, Ferrara-school frescoes and a good restaurant. Closed Aug. Via Palestro 70, T: 0532 202121, F: 0532 202638.
€€ **Annunziata**. A friendly, family-run place, quiet and comfortable. Piazza Repubblica 5, T: 0532 201111, F: 0532 203233, www.annunziata.it
€€ **Astra**. Comfortable and well-managed, with antiques here and there. Viale Cavour 55, T: 0532 206088, F: 0532 764377.
€€ **Locanda della Duchessina**. A miniature version of the Duchessa Isabella (5 rooms), under the same management. Closed Aug. Vicolo del Voltino 11, T: 0532 206981.
€€ **Ripagrande**. In a Renaissance townhouse, with garden restaurant seating in summer. Via Ripagrande 21, T: 0532 765250, www.ripagrandehotel.it
€ **Locanda Borgonuovo**. Even smaller than the Locanda della Duchessina (4 rooms), but just as nice. Via Cairoli 29, T: 0532 211100, F: 0532 246328, www.borgonuovo.com/locanda.html

YOUTH HOSTELS

Argenta (Ferrara)
€ **Ostello di Campotto**, Via Cardinala 27, T: 0532 808035, F: 0532 808035, ostellodicampotto@libero.it
Ferrara
€ **Estense**, Corso Biagio Rossetti 24, T: 0532 204227, F: 0532 204227, hostelferrara@hotmail.com

RESTAURANTS

Ferrara
€€ **Antico Giardino**. Restaurant with garden, specialising in regional home dishes, interesting selection of cheeses and wines. Closed Mon. Via Martinelli 28, T: 0532 412587.

€ **La Provvidenza**. A restaurant known for its hearty local fare. Closed Mon and Aug. Corso Ercole I d'Este 92, T: 0532 205187.

€ **Il Bagattino**.Trattoria, simple but good. Closed Mon. Via Correggiari 6, T: 0532 206387.

€€ **L'Oca Giuliva**. Wine bar offering good hot and cold meals. Closed Mon, midday Tues and Jan. Via Boccacanale di Santo Stefano 38, T: 0532 207628.

€€ **Lanzagallo**. 10km from the centre of the city. Good restaurant specialising in *cacciagione* (game) and fish from the nearby rivers and sea. Closed Sun evening (in summer all day long)–Mon and 5 days in July and 15 in January. Via Ravenna 1084, T: 0532 718001.

€€ **Quel Fantastico Giovedì**. Restaurant serving Emilian dishes with an innovative twist. Closed Wed, Jan and July–Aug. Via Castelnuovo 9, T: 0532 760570.

Among Ferrara's many good cafés are **Roverella** and **Europa**, in Corso Giovecca. **Al Brindisi**, at Via Adelardi 11, a wine bar, serves good cold meals. **Perdonati**, at Via San Romano 108, makes traditional Ferrarese breads.

Street markets in Ferrara Mon and Fri; antiques and crafts markets, first weekend of the month (except Aug), in Piazza Municipale and Piazza Savonarola.

The Palio of Ferrara (San Giorgio) is held at the end of May with races (horses, mules, etc.) in Piazza Ariostea; Buskers Festival, street musicians' festival, last week in Aug.

HISTORY OF RAVENNA

Ravenna today stands several kilometres inland, but in ancient times it was situated on a marshy lagoon. Its importance began with the construction, by the emperor Augustus, of the port of Classis, south of the city, as one of the two bases for the Adriatic fleet. Ravenna, linked to the port by a canal, now gained the trappings of a prosperous Roman town. Its greatest period, however, began much later, in 401, when the emperor Honorius moved the imperial court and civil administration here from Milan, where his father Theodosius I had been conducting the military operations of the empire. Though Honorius was much criticised for removing himself from the front line, the move meant that Ravenna became in effect the capital of the western empire, and over the next hundred years was adorned with palaces and churches. It is the latter, with their brilliant array of mosaics, which remain the glory of the city, their importance enhanced because so many of the contemporary rivals in Constantinople were destroyed by iconoclasts in the 8th century.

The last of the western emperors, Romulus Augustulus, was deposed by the German commander Odoacer in 476, and Ravenna became his capital. It was here, in 493, that he was murdered at a banquet by the Ostrogoth Theodoric (see p. 13). Theodoric died in 526. In 527, in a desperate attempt to regain the western empire, the eastern emperor Justinian ordered an invasion of Italy. Ravenna fell to his general Belisarius in 540. In 568 authority in the west was delegated to an exarch, a local ruler who combined civil and military powers but who remained subordinate to Constantinople. The eastern empire's hold on Ravenna was precarious, however, with the main threat coming from the Lombards, to whom it finally fell in 751. Anxious about this intrusion, the Pope called on the Franks to retake the city, and in 757 it became part of the papal territories.

Even though the port of Classis began to silt up, Ravenna emerged as one of the many city communes of northern Italy in the 12th century, and like many of them it passed almost without historical record into a seigniory. In the 13th–14th centuries the city was governed by the da Polenta family, distinguished for their hospitality to Dante. The beautiful Francesca da Rimini was a daughter of that family, married by proxy to the hunchbacked lord of Rimini, Gianciotto Malatesta. Gianciotto's brother Paolo became Francesca's lover; when Gianciotto discovered their secret, he killed them both. Dante turned the story into his *Divine Comedy*.

Ravenna prospered as part of the Venetian Republic in the 15th century, but Venice lost control after its defeat at the battle of Agnadello in 1509. A massacre of Ravenna's citizens followed at the hands of the invading French armies in 1512, and the city then passed by treaty to the Papacy. Now outside the mainstream of Adriatic commerce, it entered a long decline and was transferred, like the rest of papal territory outside Rome, to the new kingdom of Italy in 1861.

ART & ARCHITECTURE IN RAVENNA

With so many of the early mosaics of Constantinople destroyed in the icono-clasm of the 8th century, those of Ravenna have special importance. There are earlier wall mosaics in Italy, for instance in Santa Costanza in Rome, where the iconography of the mid-4th century is as much pagan as Christian. However, by the 5th century the Christian imagery is more developed. The mosaics of Ravenna include scenes from the Old Testament, of the life and miracles of Christ (the earliest known narrative cycle of the life of Christ is that in Sant'Apollinare Nuovo) and the lives of the apostles. The pre-eminence of Christ the Good Shepherd in the oratory of Galla Placidia is another good example. In contrast with contemporary mosaics in Rome (such as those in the church of Santa Maria Maggiore, built by a bishop with no particular allegiance to an emperor), the mosaics of Ravenna show a close link to royal or imperial power. Thus it was that Theodoric was originally represented beside his palace in Sant'Apollinare Nuovo (before he and his attendants were cut out by the agents of Justinian). The emperor Justinian and his empress Theodora are also shown in procession on the walls of San Vitale, in a style which harks back to the pro-cessional reliefs of Augustan Rome. Justinian and Theodora never visited Ravenna, so their prominence must be a mark of respect or allegiance by the builders of the church after the Byzantine conquest of 540. They are shown bringing symbols of the Eucharist to the church, as if to underline the powerful relationship between emperor and orthodox Christianity.

Ravenna is often described as a showcase of Byzantine art, and this is not sim-ply because the design of San Vitale draws directly on a model in Constantinople. It is also because the link that is made between ruler and reli-gion prefigures the theocratic world view of the Byzantine empire. One can go further, too, and note the different emphases in Western and Byzantine Christian art. Western Christianity increasingly stressed the need for redemption through the portrayal of the sufferings of Christ on the cross (in ever more grotesque detail as the centuries progressed). Byzantine art concentrates on the salvation offered by Christ and He, or God the Father, is invariably represented as a pro-tective figure looking down from above. In San Vitale the apse mosaics make explicit reference to the power of the Eucharist to transform. The atmosphere of a Byzantine church is deliberately other-worldly—it is hardly surprising that a contemporary described the dome of Hagia Sophia in Constantinople as if it were suspended from heaven. The chanting, the incense and the shimmering light on the gold of the mosaics are all designed to transcend the material world.

Mosaic of the Empress Theodora (c. 547 AD), in the church of San Vitale.

San Vitale

NB: San Vitale, the Oratory of Galla Placidia and the Museo Nazionale are now all approached through one entrance in Via San Vitale, at the end of Via Fanti. This itinerary may change as restoration of the convent buildings proceeds. There is plenty to see, so you would do well to visit the monuments first and the museum last. The best light in which to see the mosaics is usually between 12 and 1.

A garden in the northwest corner of the city centre surrounds Ravenna's most famous monumental complex: San Vitale, the most precious example of Byzantine art extant in Western Europe. Theodoric allowed orthodox and Arian congregations to worship side by side in Ravenna, and in 521, five years before Theodoric's death, the orthodox bishop Ecclesius, backed by funds from a wealthy banker, Julius Argentarius, put in hand the building of a church to house the relics of San Vitale, martyred by tradition in the 3rd century. Ecclesius knew Constantinople well, and it was the church of Sts Sergius and Bacchus there which seems to have given him the Byzantine model for a centrally planned church, which provided a dramatic contrast to the basilicas of the earlier Ravenna churches. Before the building was finished, however, the eastern emperor Justinian's troops invaded Italy in an attempt to win back the western empire. Ravenna fell in 540 and the as yet unfinished San Vitale was adorned with magnificent mosaics of Justinian and his empress Theodora. San Vitale was eventually finished by the energetic orthodox bishop Maximian in 548.

Tour of the church

The narthex, which stands oblique to the church, was formerly preceded by an atrium. The octagonal building is surrounded by a double gallery and surmounted by an octagonal cupola.

The impressive interior is famous for its decoration in marble and mosaics (always partly under restoration). The remarkable plan comprises two concentric octagons with seven exedrae or niches and an apsidal choir. The eight pillars that support the dome are encased in marble (largely renewed) and are separated by the exedrae with their triple arches. Higher up is the matroneum, or women's gallery, and above all is the dome, built—for lightness—from two rows of terracotta tubes laid horizontally and fitting into one another. The vault paintings are 18th century; the intended mosaic decoration was probably never executed.

The chief glories of the church are in the choir and apse. On the triumphal arch are mosaics of *Christ and the Apostles with St Gervasius and St Protasius*, the sons of the patron saint. On either side are two constructions of antique fragments patched together in the 16th–18th centuries, including four columns from the ancient ciborium (the first on the left is of rare green breccia from Egypt), and a fragment with putti of a Roman frieze known as the Throne of Neptune. Within the arch, on either side, are two columns with lace-work capitals beneath impost blocks bearing the monogram of Julianus. In the lunettes are mosaics: on the right, *Offerings of Abel and of Melchizedech*; in the spandrels, *Isaiah* and the *Life of Moses*; on the left, *Hospitality* and *Sacrifice of Abraham*; at the sides, *Jeremiah* and *Moses on the Mount*. The upper gallery has magnificent capitals and mosaics of the *Evangelists*, and the vault mosaics of *Angels* and the *Paschal Lamb* amid foliage are also very fine. The stucco decoration beneath the arches is beautiful. In the centre is the reconstructed altar, with a translucent alabaster top (usually covered).

The apse has the lower part of its walls covered with marble inlay, a modern reconstruction from traces of the original plan. In the centre of the mosaic, in the semidome, Christ (beardless) appears between two angels who present St Vitalis and Bishop Ecclesius with a model of the church. On the side walls are two fine processional friezes: on the left, Justinian with his train of officials, soldiers and clergy, among whom are Archbishop Maximian and Julianus Argentarius or Belisarius. Here is the ruler as the elect of Christ (Justinian is shown carrying a paten for the Eucharistic bread, and note the *chi-rho* sign on the shield of one of his attendants). On the right is Theodora with her court, and in front of the apsidal arch are Jerusalem, Bethlehem and two angels.

To the right of the apse, beyond an apsidal chamber, is the Sancta Sanctorum (kept locked). Further on is the former entrance to the campanile (originally one of the staircase towers giving access to the matroneum); beneath an adjoining arch are some fine stuccoes. The second staircase tower, still preserving some original work, is on the other side of the narthex; its stairs (now closed) ascend to the matroneum. Some early-Christian sarcophagi are kept in the church.

ABOUT MOSAICS

Mosaics are composed of tesserae, individual cubes of coloured glass, stone, and enamel set in a plaster bed. The pictorial design for a mosaic was sketched onto the wall beforehand. Early mosaic technique had a limited range of tessera colours, which encouraged a rather non-naturalistic pictorial style with attention focused on line and simplified colour definition. Blue was made by adding cobalt; green with copper oxide; and red with copper. Gold and silver were obtained by overlaying the tesserae with a thin layer of glazed metal. In more opulent mosaics, such as those produced under Justinian at Ravenna, mother-of-pearl was also used, as well as white and grey marble. The earliest mosaics at San Marco in Venice (*see p. 402*) date from the 11th century, and in terms of style they cling quite strongly to their Byzantine cousins. Here the tesserae were set into the plaster at different depths and angles, in order to catch as much light as possible and create a brilliant, sparkling glow. In the mid-15th century Venice saw the arrival of Florentine painters who designed mosaics with tesserae laid as smoothly as possible, minimising surface irregularity and eliminating the fantastic light effects. These artists also developed a range of colours that could produce delicate tonal gradations. With these innovations, mosaics lost the stylisation of earlier works and gained a painterly naturalism in the depiction of form, becoming, in essence, 'paintings in stone'.

The Oratory of Galla Placidia

The first great builder in Ravenna was the formidable Galla Placidia, Honorius' half-sister and wife of the emperor Constantius II. She dominated the empire for ten years after his death in 421 (as regent to their son Valentinian III). A small oratory, once believed to be her mausoleum, is the earliest setting for mosaics which survive. You approach it from the north side of San Vitale, along a pathway across a lawn. This small cruciform building (*open as San Vitale*), erected towards the middle of the 5th century, has a plain exterior decorated with blind arcades and pilasters. The interior, lit by alabaster windows, is famous for its magnificent, predominantly blue mosaics, especially interesting for the classic character of the figures and for their excellent state of preservation (although they are restored periodically).

Over the entrance is the *Good Shepherd*; in the opposite lunette, *St Lawrence* with his gridiron; in the side lunettes, *Stags Quenching Their Thirst at the Holy Fount*. The vaults and arches of the longer arm of the cross are decorated to represent rich hangings and festoons of fruit. In the shorter arm are four *Apostles*; the other eight are on the drum of the cupola. The pendentives hold the symbols of the Evangelists. Above all is the Cross in a star-strewn sky. The three empty sarcophagi are no longer considered to have held the remains of Galla Placidia, Constantius and Valentinian III; only one of them is of 5th-century workmanship.

The Museo Nazionale

Open Tues–Sun 8.30–7.30.
Occupying the former Benedictine Monastery of San Vitale, the museum contains an excellent, varied collection of treasures. The monastic collections were taken over by the municipality in 1804, and in 1887 the museum was nationalised. Recent archaeological finds from the territory are kept here.

Mezzanine floor: A splendid collection of coins is beautifully displayed in chronological order from the Roman period onwards. The stairs continue up to a group of rooms that were closed at the time of writing: a hall with a marble statue of Venice by Enrico Pazzi (1884), the first director of the museum, and recent donations; a large room displaying funerary stelae (1st century BC–1st century AD), many of them belonging to sailors, and finds (6th–5th centuries BC) from the necropolis of San Martino in Gattara including a large Greek krater; and a corridor beyond, containing four mosaics decorated with birds.

First floor: A large hall (once part of the monastery dormitory) displays a collection of 16th–17th-century armour. Small rooms off this contain ceramics (Ravenna, Deruta, Faenza, Urbino, Castelli, etc.) and some detached frescoes (including one from San Vitale dating from the 13th century). Beyond is a corridor with a collection of icons of the Cretan-Venetian school, dating from the 14th to the 17th centuries. Beyond this is a room with a large sinopia found beneath the apse mosaic in Sant'Apollinare in Classe. The next room contains marble reliefs from the so-called Palazzo di Teodorico (*see p. 663*). In the rooms that surround the second cloister are 6th-century transennae, including a relief of *Hercules and the Stag*, and the cross from the top of San Vitale. There is also a beautiful collection of ivories, including a relief of *Apollo and Daphne* (530 AD), a 6th-century diptych from Murano, and evangelistary covers. A fine display of medieval fabrics has some precious examples from the tomb of St Julian at Rimini, and the so-called 'Veil of Classis' with embroideries of Veronese bishops of the 8th–9th centuries.

The church of **Santa Maria Maggiore** (525–32, rebuilt 1671), adjoining the complex of San Vitale, preserves Byzantine capitals above Greek marble columns, and a tiny cylindrical campanile (9th–10th century).

The cathedral and the Battistero Neoniano

The cathedral, founded early in the 5th century by Bishop Ursus and often known as the Basilica Ursiana, was almost totally destroyed in 1733. The columns of the central arch of the portico and those on either side of the central door are from the original church. The round campanile, many times restored, dates from the 10th century. In the nave is the 6th-century ambo of St Agnellus, pieced together in 1913. The south transept chapel holds two huge 6th-century sarcophagi. In the ambulatory is a good relief of *St Mark in his Study* (1492, ascribed to Pietro Lombardo). The north transept chapel has an altarpiece and frescoes by Guido Reni and his school.

Adjoining the cathedral is the octagonal **Battistero Neoniano** (or Battistero degli Ortodossi; open *9.30–5.30 or 6.30*), converted from a Roman bath-house, perhaps by Bishop Neon (mid-5th century). The plain exterior is decorated with vertical bands and small arches. The remarkable interior is entirely decorated with mosaics and sculptural details that blend with the architectural forms. The original floor is now more than 3m below the present surface.

Eight corner columns support arches decorated with mosaics of *Prophets*. In the niches and on the wall-spaces arranged alternately beneath the arches are mosaic inscriptions and marble inlaid designs from the original Roman baths. Each arch of the upper arcade encloses three smaller arches; the stucco decoration is very fine. In the dome, built from hollow tubes like that of San Vitale, are mosaics of the *Baptism of Jesus* (the old man with the reed represents the Jordan), the *Apostles*, the *Books of the Gospel* and four thrones, remarkable for their contrasting colours. The font is of the 12th–13th century. In the niches are a Byzantine altar and a pagan marble vase.

The Museo Arcivescovile and Biblioteca Classense

Open Apr–Sept 9.30–7; Oct–Mar 9.30–5.30; Nov, Dec, Jan, Feb 9.30–4.30.
The museum contains some exquisite works and incorporates a little chapel with beautiful early 6th-century mosaics. In the first room are a lapidary collection, with fragments and mosaics from the original cathedral and from San Vitale; the silver Cross of St Agnellus, probably dating from 556–69 and restored in the 11th century and the 16th; a headless 6th-century porphyry statue, thought to be Justinian; and the marble pulpit from Santi Giovanni e Paolo (596). The so-called 'Chasuble of St John Angeloptes' may be a 12th-century work.

On the left is a chapel built by Bishop Peter II (494–519) and preceded by an atrium with a barrel vault covered with a delightful mosaic of birds. The chapel also contains beautiful mosaics in the vault.

In the end room is the famous ivory Throne of Maximian, an Alexandrine work of the 6th century, exquisitely carved with the *Story of Joseph*, the *Life of Christ* and figures of *St John the Baptist* and the *Evangelists*.

The **Biblioteca Classense**, entered from Via Baccarini (*open Sun–Fri 8.30–7*), in a 16th–17th-century building, contains the former monastic library of the monastery of Sant'Apollinare in Classe, founded in 1515 and augmented by Pietro Canneti (1659–1730). The Aula Magna, designed by Giuseppe Antonio Soratini, with stuccoes and a frescoed ceiling and carved bookcases, can be visited on request (*open daily except Sat afternoon and Sun and holidays, 8–7*). The important library, owned by the municipality since 1803, has many prize volumes, including a 10th-century text of Aristophanes, illuminated manuscripts, choir books, works relating to Dante and a collection of Byron's letters. Byron lived in Ravenna in 1819 with the Count and Countess Guiccioli. Palazzo Guiccioli (Via Cavour 54), is where he wrote the end of *Don Juan*, *Marino Faliero*, and other poems.

San Francesco and the Sepolchro di Dante

Across Piazza Caduti from the cathedral, the church of San Francesco, built by Bishop Neon in the 5th century and remodelled in the 10th, was almost entirely rebuilt in 1793. The 10th-century campanile was restored in 1921. The lovely basilican interior has 22 columns of Greek marble. In the north aisle are three sarcophagi (including one with *Christ and the Apostles* dating from the 5th century), and the tombstone of Ostasio da Polenta (1396) in red marble (with his death mask). Beyond the tomb of Luffo Numai, by Tommaso Fiamberti (1509), the 4th-century tomb of St Liberius serves as high altar. Steps beneath it lead down to an opening overlooking the 9th–10th-century crypt, partly flooded. Here you can see the foundations of an earlier church with its restored mosaic pavement. The first chapel on the south side has carved pilasters by Tullio Lombardo (1525).

On the left of San Francesco is the so-called Cappella di Braccioforte (1480, restored in 1920), containing several early-Christian sarcophagi. To the left again, by a little memorial bell-tower (1921) is the **Sepolchro di Dante** (tomb of Dante; *open daily 9–7*). Dante, a victim of internecine squabbles among the Guelph faction, was exiled from his native Florence in 1302. He found refuge first in Verona, and then with the da Polenta family of Ravenna, and spent his last years with them, finishing the *Divine Comedy* under their patronage. He died on the night of 13–14 September 1321. The mausoleum was commissioned from Camillo Morigia by Cardinal Luigi Gonzaga in 1780 to enshrine an older tomb, with a relief by Pietro Lombardo (1483), and an epitaph by Bernardo Canaccio (1357). This in turn covers the antique sarcophagus in which the poet's remains were originally interred in the old portico of San Francesco. The bronze doors by Lodovico Pogliaghi and the coloured marble in the interior were added in 1921.

The **Museo Dantesco**, entered through a restored 15th-century cloister at Via Dante 4 (*open Apr–Sept Tues–Sun 9–12 & 3.30–6; Oct–March 9–12*), first opened in 1921, has mementoes of the poet and material relating to various memorials to him. The room, decorated by artists influenced by the Arts and Crafts movement in England, was intended as a homage to Dante.

Of romance and ruin

Ravenna itself preserves perhaps more of the old Italian manners than any City in Italy—it is out of the way of travellers and armies—and thus they have retained more of their originality. They make love a good deal, and assassinate a little.

Lord Byron, letter to Lady Byron, 20 July 1819

Ravenna, where Robert positively wanted to go to live once, has itself put an end to all those yearnings. The churches are wonderful: holding an atmosphere of purple glory, and if one could just live in them, or in Dante's tomb—well, otherwise, keep me from Ravenna. The very antiquity of the houses is white-washed, and the marshes on all sides send up stenches new and old, till the hot air is sick with them.

Elizabeth Barrett Browning, letter, 1848

We ended in Ravenna and felt the splendour of Rome dying among barbarians in a way that I never felt again until I reached the ruins of the Levant.

Freya Stark, Traveller's Prelude, 1950

From Sant'Agata to the Accademia

The 5th-century basilican church of Sant'Agata Maggiore has a squat round campanile completed in 1560, and sarcophagi on the lawn outside. The basilican interior (if closed, ring at Via Mazzini 46), similar to San Francesco, contains Roman and Byzantine capitals, a very unusual fluted 7th-century pulpit, an early-Christian sarcophagus used as a high altar, and two Renaissance baldachins over the altars.

Via Cerchio, to the south, ends opposite **Santa Maria in Porto**, a church begun in 1553 with a sumptuous façade by Morigia (1780). It contains fine stalls by Mariano (1576–93) and other French craftsmen, and (over the altar in the north transept) a marble Byzantine relief called *La Madonna Greca* (probably 11th century). In the public gardens behind is the early 16th-century Loggetta Lombardesca.

The former monastery of the Canonici Lateranensi, adjoining the church, houses the **Accademia di Belle Arti**. The fine, large **Pinacoteca Comunale** here (*open June–Sept Tues, Wed and Thur 9–1 & 5–8, Fri 9–1 & 5–9, Sat–Sun 9–1; Oct–May Tues, Wed, Thur, Fri 9–1 & 3–6, Sat–Sun 10–6*) is spaciously arranged around a pretty cloister in the well-lit rooms of the convent. It includes works by Lorenzo Monaco, Ludovico Brea, Antonio Vivarini, Gentile Bellini, Luca Longhi, Palma Giovane and Paris Bordone. The beautiful effigy of Guidarello Guidarelli is the work of Tullio Lombardo (1525). Guidarello was a soldier, troop captain to Cesare Borgia. He was killed at Imola in 1501 following a trifling quarrel at a masked ball. Legend says that any girl who kisses the effigy will marry the following year.

San Giovanni Evangelista

At the corner of Viale Farini is Piazza Anita Garibaldi, adorned by a monument to the heroes of the Risorgimento. Here, the 14th-century marble doorway of the church of San Giovanni Evangelista has been reconstructed on a new wall that encloses a little garden in the church precinct. The church was built by Galla Placidia in fulfilment of a vow made in 424 during a storm at sea. It was well restored after most of the façade and the first four bays were destroyed and the notable galleried apse, as well as the aisles, seriously damaged in the Second World War. The 10th–14th-century campanile survives (leaning to the west); two of the bells date from 1208.

In the basilican interior some columns, with their capitals and impost blocks, are original. Mosaics from the 13th-century floor, their naïve designs illustrating episodes from the Fourth Crusade, are displayed round the walls. Fresco fragments of the 14th-century Riminese school can be seen in a chapel off the north aisle. The chapel at the end of the south aisle has a little 8th-century carved altar.

Theodoric's legacy

In Via di Roma is a building known as the Palazzo di Teodorico, really the ruined church of **San Salvatore** (entered from Via Alberoni; *open daily 8.30–7*). Fine mosaics and part of a marble intarsia floor found in 1914 in a palace nearby are exhibited on the walls and on an upper floor, approached by a spiral stair.

Sant'Apollinare Nuovo

Sant'Apollinare Nuovo (*open 9.30–5.30 or 6.30*), to the north of this, is one of the most beautiful basilicas in Ravenna. Theodoric was, like all the Goths, an Arian Christian; in other words he believed that Christ was a later creation of God the Father, a view which had been declared heretical by the emperors the 380s. This church was built by Theodoric in the early 6th century, and in its heyday was at the core of a Gothic quarter of the city which boasted at least six Arian churches, all of which competed in opulence with the well-endowed orthodox churches of the local Roman community. Dedicated originally to Jesus and later to St Martin (the present dedication dates from the 9th century), the church passed from the Arians to the orthodox Christians under Archbishop Agnellus. The triumph of orthodoxy over Arianism is marked by the replacement of the mosaic portraits of Theodoric and his attendants with later decoration.

The floor and the 24 Greek marble columns of the interior were raised in the 16th century. They are surmounted by a panelled ceiling of 1611; the arcades bulge noticeably to the north. Two magnificent bands of mosaics adorn the nave walls: that on the north side represents the port of Classis, with a procession of 22 virgin martyrs preceded by the Magi who offer gifts to the Infant Jesus seated on His mother's lap between four angels. On the south side are Ravenna, showing the façade of Theodoric's palace, and a procession of 26 martyrs approaching Christ enthroned. Above, on either side, are 16 fathers of the Church, or prophets; higher still, 13 scenes from the Life of Christ.

The stucco decoration of the arches is very fine. The ambo in the nave dates from the 6th century. In the apse, reconstructed in 1950 (and being restored), are the recomposed altar, transennae, four porphyry columns, and a marble Roman chair.

The Battistero degli Ariani

The church of **Santo Spirito** (*open Mon–Sat 9.30–12.30 & 3–5 or 6, Sun 12–5*) was converted, like Sant'Apollinare, to the orthodox cult by Agnellus in the mid-6th century. Fourteen columns and an ambo from the original church were retained after a rebuilding in 1543. Beside it is the tiny **Battistero degli Ariani** (now Santa Maria in Cosmedin; *open daily 8.30–7.30*), built by Theodoric in the early 6th century. It contains splendidly preserved mosaics of the *Baptism of Christ* and of the *Apostles* in the dome.

The Mausoleo di Teodorico

At the north end of Via di Roma is Porta Serrata, a gate of 1582. The Circonvallazione alla Rotonda leads east through unattractive suburbs past the rugged bastions of the Venetian Rocca di Brancaleone (which now enclose delightful public gardens). Beyond the railway (a rather unpleasant walk of c. 20 minutes along a busy road), in a clump of trees to the left, is the Mausoleum of Theodoric (*open 8.30–6 or 7*; bus 2 from the station, every 30 minutes).

This remarkable two-storeyed tomb is unique in the history of architecture; its solid structure shows the influence of Syrian buildings as well as Roman models. Begun by the great Ostrogoth himself in c. 520, it was built of hewn Istrian stone without mortar and crowned by an unusual monolithic roof. It was never finished, and for a time, until 1719, it was used as a monastic church (Santa Maria al Faro).

The ten-sided lower storey has a deep recess on every side. The upper floor, which is decorated with unfinished arcading, was approached by two 18th-century staircases, which collapsed in 1921. The monolithic cupola of Istrian limestone from Pula has a diameter of 11m and weighs about 300 tons. The crack, which is clearly visible, was probably the result of a harsh knock received during its installation. It is not known how the monolith was transported here. Inside is a porphyry bath which was used as the royal sarcophagus.

AROUND RAVENNA

Sant'Apollinare in Classe

About 5km south of Ravenna and reached either by rail (Classe station, on the Rimini line), or—better—by road (buses 4 and 45 from Ravenna station) across the Ponte Nuovo (1736) and the site of Classis, is the basilica of Sant'Apollinare in Classe (*open Mon–Sat 8.30–7.30, Sun 1–7*), built for Bishop Ursicinus with funds given by the banker Julianus Argentarius in 535–38 and consecrated by Archbishop Maximian in 549. The narthex which preceded the church has been reconstructed. The magnificent late-10th-century campanile is the tallest and most beautiful of all the towers of Ravenna.

The wide, bare interior has 24 lovely Greek marble-veined columns with square Byzantine bases and beautiful capitals. In the centre of the nave is the altar of Archbishop Maximian, restored in 1753. At the west end of the church are eight columns from the two original ciboria, and a fragment of the original mosaic floor. The aisles hold a series of magnificent sarcophagi, complete with lids, dating from the 5th to the 8th centuries. At the end of the north aisle are a 9th-century ciborium and an interesting altar with a 5th-century relief of *Christ and the Apostles*.

The mosaics of the apse are extremely interesting, though much altered. On the outside arch are five rows of mosaics, replete with early-Christian symbolism, showing figures of saints, palm trees (the Tree of Life), sheep (symbols of the Apostles), and Christ in a roundel with the symbols of the Evangelists. In the apse itself is a Cross on a blue ground with the symbol of the Transfiguration; below is a field of lilies (symbols of light and life) and trees with birds and sheep (representing the blessed in Paradise) and St Apollonius at prayer in the centre. Below this, to the right and left, are two large scenes, with the Sacrifices of Abel, Melchizedech and Abraham, and Constantine IV granting privileges for the church of Ravenna to Archbishop Reparatus in the 7th century. Between the windows are the figures of the four bishops Ursicinus, Ursus, Severus and Ecclesius (6th century). The arches of the windows are also decorated with columns in mosaic.

The **Pineta di Classe** (east of the basilica beyond the railway), whose sylvan grandeur was celebrated in poetry by Dante and Byron, is now sadly diminished Although it has been designated a nature reserve, it is threatened by the industrial development on the outskirts of Ravenna.

Bagnacavallo and Villanova

Bagnacavallo is a small town with a charming theatre (1855) in its central piazza. In Via Garibaldi, next to a 13th-century tower, is the convent of San Giovanni where Allegra, daughter of Byron and Claire Claremont, died in 1821 at the age of five (plaque). Another former convent, Le Cappuccine, the orchard of which is now a pretty public garden, houses a pinacoteca (*open Tues–Sun 10–12 & 3–6 or 4–7*) with paintings by Bartolomeo Ramenghi (1484–1542), called Il Bagnacavallo after his native town, a local ethnographic museum, a library and a natural history museum. The Collegiata and Carmine also have paintings by Bagnacavallo. San Francesco, next to its huge convent, has a small Flemish painting and the tombstone of Tiberio Brandolini. Piazza Nuova is a charming little 18th-century oval cobbled marketplace surrounded by porticoes.

The church of San Pietro in Silvis, just outside the town (ring at the house next door if closed), has a lovely basilican interior of the Ravenna type, probably dating from the early 7th century, with a raised presbytery above the crypt. It has frescoes in the apse by Pietro da Rimini (c. 1323; being restored).

At **Villanova**, on the river Lamone, is an interesting local museum illustrating life on the wetlands in the district, with handicrafts made from the reeds which grow in the marshes.

Lugo

The pleasant little town of Lugo has interesting 18th-century architecture. The Teatro Rossini was begun in 1757–59 by Francesco Petrocchi, and Antonio Bibiena designed the boxes, stage and three backcloths in 1761. It is built entirely of wood (with excellent acoustics), and the stage is the same size as the auditorium, which seats 500. Important opera productions were given here in the 18th century, and concerts are now held in spring. The huge Neoclassical Pavaglione was built at the end of the 18th century on the site of a marketplace in use since 1437; the arcading on one side dates from the early 16th century. Beneath the porticoes are attractive shops with uniform fronts, and a market is held here on Wednesdays. Opera performances took place here in 1598 and again in the 17th century.

The colossal incongruous monument (intended for another site) dedicated to Francesco Baracca, aviator and First World War hero, was inaugurated here in 1936 by Mussolini. The Rocca Estense, the seat of the *comune* (*open daily except Sun and holidays*) dates in its present form from the 15th–16th centuries. In the well-restored courtyard is a 15th-century well-head. Upstairs, the Salotto Rossini has a portrait (1828) of the composer, who lived in the town as a child in 1802–04. The hanging garden is now a public park.

The church of the Carmine preserves an organ by Gaetano Callido (1797) used by Rossini. At Via Baracca 65 is the Museo Francesco Baracca (*open Tues–Sun 10–12 & 4–6*) with mementoes of the pioneer aviator (1888–1918), born in Lugo, including his plane used in the First World War. There was an important Jewish community in the town from the 15th century onwards, and their cemetery survives.

Imola

Southwest of Ravenna, on the Via Emilia, the town of **Imola** stands on the site of the Roman Forum Cornelii, founded by L. Cornelius Sulla in 82 BC. It still preserves the main outlines of its Roman plan. The cathedral was entirely rebuilt in the 18th century. The early-14th-century castle was rebuilt by Gian Galeazzo Sforza, whose daughter Caterina married Girolamo Riario, lord of Imola, and held the fortress after his death until her defeat by Cesare Borgia (1500). It contains a collection of arms and armour. In the small pinacoteca is a painting by Innocenzo Francucci (Innocenzo da Imola; c. 1494–c. 1550). It was here that Cesare Borgia's dashing captain Guidarello Guidarelli (*see p. 662*) was stabbed to death as the result of a personal squabble.

PRACTICAL INFORMATION

GETTING AROUND

• **By rail:** Ravenna is not on a major rail line, but you can get there by commuter train (Diretti or Regionali) from Ferrara (1hr), Bologna (1hr 10mins) or Faenza (30mins).
• **By bus:** Buses **4** and **44** run on weekdays from the station to the basilica of Sant'Apollinare in Classe. Country buses (operated by ATM, T: 0544 689911) run from Piazzale Farini (opposite the train station) to places of interest in the province, including Bagnacavallo and Lugo, and to the resorts on the coast. Faenza is best reached from Ravenna by train.
• **By bicycle:** Cycles can be rented in Ravenna from the Coop San Vitale, Piazza Farini (at the station).

INFORMATION OFFICES

Ravenna Via Salara 8–12, T: 0544 35404, www.turismo.ravenna.it, www.emiliaromagnaturismo.it May–Sept at Viale delle Industria 14, T: 0544 451539 and Via Maggiore 122, T: 0544 482961.
Informagiovani: Via Guido da Polenta 4, T: 0544 36494.
Imola Via Mazzini 14/16, T: 0542 602207, www.emiliaromagnaturismo.it

HOTELS

Ravenna
€€ **Bisanzio**. Central and fairly elegant, with a nice garden. Via Salara 30, T: 0544 217111, www.bisanziohotel.com

€ **Centrale Byron**. Warm and modern, in a well-renovated old townhouse. Via IV Novembre 14, T: 0544 212225, www.hotelbyron.com
Imola
€€ **Molino Rosso**. In a recently renovated mill, with good restaurant. Strada Statale Selice 49, T: 0542 63111, www.molinorosso.it
Lugo
€€ **Ala d'Oro**. In an aristocratic townhouse, with a good restaurant. Corso Matteotti 56, T: 0545 22388, www.aladoro.it
€€ **San Francisco**. Quiet and comfortable. Closed Dec–Jan and Aug. Via Amendola 14, T: 0545 22324.

YOUTH HOSTELS

Bagnacavallo
€ **Antico Convento di San Francesco**, Via Cadorna, T: 0545 60622, info@ostellosanfrancesco.com
Ravenna
€ **Dante**, Via Aurelio Nicolodi 12, T: 0544 421164, hostelravenna@hotmail.com

RESTAURANTS

Ravenna
€ **Ca' de' Vén**. *Osteria* situated in a beautiful old palace, offers good regional food and wines. Closed Mon and 24 Dec–6 Jan. Via Ricci 24, T: 0544 30163.
€€ **Hotel Romea Ponte Nuovo**. Nice hotel restaurant specialising in regional cooking, seafood and grilled meats, excellent wine and spirits selection.

Closed Fri and 28 July– 27 Aug. Via Romea Sud 1, T: 0544 61247.

€€ **La Gardèla**. Good restaurant specialising in regional grilled food, interesting wine selection. Closed Thur, Feb and Aug. Via Ponte Marino 3, T: 0544 217147.

€€ **Marchesini**. Traditional restaurant that offers ancient regional recipes, seafood and international cooking. Closed Sun. Via Mazzini 6, T: 0544 212309.

€€ **Sorriso**. Family-run restaurant, specialising in traditional regional dishes and grilled meats. Closed Tues and one week in Nov. Viale delle Nazioni 12, T: 0544 530462, Località Marina di Ravenna.

€€ **Taverna San Romualdo da Antonio**. Nice restaurant a few kilometers from the centre of town, great wine selection, good regional food. Closed Tues. Via Sant'Alberto 364, T: 0544 483447.

€€ **Tre Spade**. Elegant restaurant in a villa with park and outside seating in summer. Closed Sun evening, Mon and Aug. Via Faentina 136, T: 0544 500522.

Castel Guelfo di Bologna
€€€ **Locanda Solarola**. Restaurant (with rooms) in an ancient farmhouse, offering the best in local cuisine. Well worth the drive. Closed Jan and Aug. Via Santa Croce 5, T: 0542 670102.

Imola
€€€ **San Domenico**. Restaurant widely renowned for its creative interpretations of traditional Emilian recipes. Closed Sun evening (all day Sun June–Aug) and Mon, Jan and July–Aug. Via Sacchi 1, T: 0542 29000.

€€ **Molino Rosso**. Hotel restaurant offering international and traditional dishes, seafood and grilled meats and an excellent wine selection. Strada Statale Selice 49, T: 0542 640300.

€€ **Naldi**. Personal interpretations of traditional Emilian recipes. Closed Sun, Jan and Aug. Via Santerno 13, T: 0542 29581.

€€ **Osteria del Vicolo Nuovo**. Fine trattoria with a good wine list, in the town centre. Closed Sun–Mon, July–Aug. Via Cadronchi 6, T: 0542 32552.

EVENTS & FESTIVALS

Ravenna *Mister Jazz*, jazz festival, April. Ravenna Festival, classical music festival in June–July. *Mosaico di Notte*, international organ music festival in Aug, with concerts every Mon in the basilica of San Vitale. Feast of Sant'Apollinare, 23 July. Medieval market second Sun in Sept.

Imola *Gran Premio San Marino*, Formula 1 auto race, May.

THE TOWNS OF ROMAGNA

The towns of Romagna—the largest of which are Faenza, Forlì, Cesena and Rimini—are very different in atmosphere from their more industrialised neighbours to the north. Here the primary activity is still farming—except at Rimini, which in the mid-to-late-20th century became famous throughout Europe as a meeting-place for young (and not so young) singles. But even here, the atmosphere is mellow and relaxed out of season. The countryside is green and gently rolling, and noteworthy monuments of art and architecture abound.

FAENZA

Faenza, like so many Italian towns, has had a turbulent history. The powerful Manfredi family played a leading part in its affairs from the early 13th century until 1501, though they did not prevent the city from being severely damaged in 1241 by Holy Roman Emperor Frederick of Hohenstaufen, and again sacked in 1376 by the mercenary soldier Sir John Hawkwood, then in the papal service. In 1501 Cesare Borgia took the town and killed the last of the Manfredi, and from 1509 Faenza was included in the States of the Church. Today it comes across as a pleasant old town on the Lamone river, long famous for its manufacture of the glazed and coloured pottery known as majolica or 'faience'. There are still some 60 working potteries in the town. The street names are indicated by faience plaques, and several houses have ceramic decoration. The town, still with its Roman plan, is divided into two by the Via Emilia (Corso Mazzini and Corso Saffi).

EXPLORING FAENZA

The broad Viale Baccarini, which connects the station with the town, leads straight to the **Museo Internazionale delle Ceramiche** (*open Apr–Oct Tues–Sat 9–7, Sun and holidays 9.30–1 & 3–7; Nov–March 9–1.30, Sat–Sun and holidays also 3–6*). The museum holds the best and most extensive collection of Italian majolica in Italy, covering all periods, but with particularly superb examples of 15th–16th-century Faentine ware. It also has pre-Columbian, Minoan, Greek and Etruscan ceramics, and an Oriental and Middle Eastern collection. The 20th-century works include splendid pieces by Picasso and Matisse.

A long hall on the first floor presents the evolution of Faentine ceramics from the early Middle Ages to the Renaissance. The section beyond samples Italian Renaissance ceramics produced in various regions. The finest examples include ceramics from Tuscany (notice the rare Medici porcelain dish shown in a separate vitrine), Umbrian ware from Gubbio and Deruta, and ceramics from Urbino, notably a dish with the *Adoration of the Magi* from the workshop of Guido Durantino, a cup with the *Penitent St Jerome*, and a cup with Venus, lovers and musicians. The next gallery illustrates standard formulas and the inevitable decline of majolica after the foundation of European porcelain manufactures (such as Sèvres and Meissen) in the early 18th century. A ramp leads down to the Modern and contemporary galleries.

A CONNOISSEUR'S GUIDE TO FAIENCE

The so-called archaic ware produced from the mid-13th century to the first half of the 15th has a white tin-glazed body decorated with two colours only (brown and green), which after 1350 were gradually replaced by blue. In the late 14th and early 15th century the so-called Zaffera ware made its appearance, decorated with cobalt blue and manganese brown thickly applied on a white ground to produce a relief effect. In the 15th century, the import of tin glazed wares from the island of Majorca (hence the Italian name for faience, majolica) introduced the lustre technique as well as Islamic decorative motifs. Their combination with the existing Italian tradition gave rise to an Italo-Moresque style which is particularly evident in the blue Zaffera ware that includes yellow and purple details to imitate the lustre effects of Hispanic wares.

Further influences in the 15th century came from Chinese porcelain imported from Venice. The immediate consequence was the development of more delicate shapes (imitating Ming porcelain) and an enriched decorative repertoire, which found expression in a blue monochromy on white ground. The great period of Faentine majolica was 1450–1520, when the most famous of the 40 potteries in the town was that of the brothers Pirotti (the Ca' Pirota). The earliest authenticated specimen of faience, in the Cluny Museum in Paris, is a votive plaque dated 1475, though the technique is documented as early as 1142.

The typically Faentine motif of the curled leaf (or 'Gothic foliage') was developed in the late 15th and early 16th centuries. The first historiated wares made their appearance around the same time, thanks to the crosslinks between potters and painters and to the circulation of illustrated books (after the invention of printing), which made famous paintings and woodcuts available to the *maiolicari* and introduced new themes such as mythology. The discovery of the grotesques of the Domus Aurea in Rome, and the decoration of the Vatican Logge by Raphael, provided further inspiration for subsequent ceramic production.

Monochrome ware was also highly valued from the 16th century onwards. Examples include the beautiful Faenza white, with its characteristic shapes obtained from plaster moulds, and the blue-ground majolica called *smalto berrettino*, decorated with delicate grotesques.

The town centre

The large, impressive Piazza della Libertà, with arcades and a fountain of 1619–21 (by Domenico Paganelli), is the centre of town life. Here is the **cathedral**, begun by

Giuliano da Maiano in 1474, a Renaissance building with an unfinished front. It contains good sculpture including a Bosi monument by the local sculptor Pietro Barilotti (1539), the reliquary urn of St Terenzio with beautiful carvings in very low relief, and the tomb of St Savinus (first bishop of Faenza, early 4th century), with exquisite reliefs by Benedetto da Maiano (1474–76). An altarpiece by Innocenzo da Imola, in the fourth south chapel, represents the *Holy Family with the Infant St John and Sts Peter and Paul.*

On the other side of the Via Emilia is the picturesque arcaded Piazza del Popolo with a clock tower by Domenico Paganelli (reconstructed in 1944), the Palazzo del Podestà (partly of the 12th century) and the *municipio*, once the palace of the Manfredi. The Voltone della Molinella is a shopping arcade with a beautiful frescoed vault and *grottesche* by Marco Marchetti (1566). The Bottega dei Ceramisti Faentini here exhibits and sells ceramics made in the town. In a pleasant cobbled courtyard is the Neoclassical Teatro Comunale Masini. Designed by the local architect Giuseppe Pistocchi (1780–87), it has a charming interior with statues and reliefs by Antonio Trentanove.

Further southwest, reached by Via Cavour, is **Palazzo Milzetti** (*open Mon–Sat 8.45–1.45, Thur also 2.15–4.30, Sun 1.30–6.15*), a fine building also by Giuseppe Pistocchi (1794–1802), with a Neoclassical interior on two floors and its decoration and furnishings intact. Many of the rooms have delightful tempera paintings by Felice Giani. On the piano nobile is an impressive octagonal room designed by Giovanni Antonio Antolini, with stuccoes by Antonio Trentanove. The apartments on the lower floor are decorated with charming ceiling frescoes whose tiny, refined grotesques imitate Pompeiian styles. The oval bathroom, with grotesques on a black background, is particularly beautiful.

Nearby rises the 10th-century campanile of Santa Maria Vecchia. In Borgo Durbecco, beyond the Lamone bridge, is the small Romanesque church of the Commenda, with a remarkable fresco (1533) by Girolamo da Treviso. The next street to the right, beyond the Barriera, leads to a British military cemetery.

BRISIGHELLA

Brisighella is a charming little town in the foothills of the Apennines above Faenza. It lies in a lovely valley beneath three conical hills—one crowned by a clock-tower of 1290 (rebuilt in 1850), another by a 14th-century Manfredi castle with two drum towers (restored by the Venetians in the 16th century). Inside the castle is a local ethnographic museum, the **Museo del Lavoro Contadino** (*open April–Oct Tues–Sun 10–12 & 3.30–7; Oct–March Sat 2.30–4.30, Sun 10–12 & 2.30–4.30*), and the third by a 17th-century sanctuary; all are reached by pretty paths. A delightful medieval pageant is held by candlelight in June and July in the town. Excellent olive oil is produced in the vicinity.

Above the main street runs the Strada degli Asini, a picturesque covered lane with a wooden vault and arches. The **Museo Ugonia** (*open summer Fri–Sun 10–12 & 3.30–7.30; winter Sat 3–6.30, Sun 10–12 & 3–6.30*) contains a very interesting collection, beautifully displayed, of lithographs and watercolours by Giuseppe Ugonia (1880–1944). The church of the **Osservanza** contains fine stuccowork of 1634 and a painting by Marco Palmezzano (d. 1539), a native of Forlì.

Just outside the town is the 16th-century **Villa Spada** (with an 18th-century façade), surrounded by a large garden. A little beyond stands the **Pieve del Tho** (ring for admission at the house on the right). This ancient church, first mentioned in 909, is thought to be on the site of a Roman building. The interior has primitive columns and capitals, on one of which is an inscription mentioning four late Roman emperors. It is thought that Tho may come from *ottavo*, referring to the eighth mile on a Roman road from the Adriatic. You can see Roman remains beneath the church.

FORLÌ & ENVIRONS

An undistinguished provincial capital and agricultural centre, Forlì takes its name from the Roman Forum Livii, a station on the Via Emilia, which bisects the town. Its urban architecture suffered under the influence of Mussolini, born nearby.

In the central piazza is the church of **San Mercuriale** (12th–13th centuries but altered later), dedicated to the first bishop of Forlì. It has a fine contemporary campanile, 76m high, a high relief of the school of Antelami above the west door, and a graceful cloister. In the red-brick interior are paintings by Forlì's famous son, the artist Marco Palmezzano (1460–1539) and the tomb of Barbara Manfredi (d. 1466), wife of Pino II Ordelaffi. Beneath the apse are remains of the 11th century church and the crypt of 1176.

The Palazzo del Municipio, dating from 1459, was altered in 1826. Corso Garibaldi, with some 15th–16th-century mansions, leads to the cathedral, mainly an elaborate reconstruction of 1841, but preserving a huge tempera painting of the *Assumption*, the masterpiece of Carlo Cignani, an artist of the Bolognese school who died in Forlì in 1706. The campanile, in Piazza Ordelaffi, was formerly the watchtower of the Orgogliosi, a rival family to the Ordelaffi, who ruled the town from 1315 to 1500.

At the south end of the town is the **Rocca di Ravaldino** (1472–82; now a prison), where Caterina Sforza was besieged by Cesare Borgia in 1499–1500. Caterina, Countess of Forlì, had refused to allow her son to marry Cesare's sister Lucrezia. In revenge their father, Pope Alexander VI, had given Caterina's lands to Cesare.

A former hospital (1772) in Corso della Repubblica houses the **Pinacoteca Civica** (*open Tues–Sun 9–1.30, Tues and Thur also 3–5.30*), first opened to the public in 1846 and in this location since 1922. It is one of only a few museums in Italy to have preserved its old-fashioned arrangement. The gallery possesses a single work (the *pestapepe*, a druggist's street sign) attributed to the famous local painter Melozzo da Forlì (Melozzo degli Ambrogi; 1438–95), but it contains a fine collection of paintings by his most important follower, Marco Palmezzano (including an *Annunciation*), as well as paintings by Fra Angelico (two tiny panels of the *Nativity* and *Christ in the Garden*), Cavalier di Arpino, Lodovico Carracci, Carlo Cignani, Lorenzo Costa,

Lorenzo di Credi, Bartolomeo Ramenghi and Silvestro Lega. It has sculptures by Bernardo and Antonio Rossellino, and Pier Paolo and Jacobello dalle Masegne.

There is a museum of musical instruments in Palazzo Gaddi. In the church of Santa Maria dei Servi the tomb of Luffo Numai (1502) has good reliefs by Tommaso Fiamberti.

The town of **Predappio** was the birthplace of Benito Mussolini (1883–1945). The village, originally a hamlet called Dovia in the commune of Predappio Alta, received communal rank in 1925, and many new public buildings were erected. In the cemetery are Mussolini's remains, finally interred there in 1957, and those of his wife 'Donna Rachele' (Rachele Guidi), buried there in 1979. Predappio was taken from the Germans by Poles of the Eighth Army in October 1944. There is an Indian and British military cemetery nearby.

CESENA & ENVIRONS

Cesena now lacks distinction, although it enjoyed a period of brilliance under the Malatesta family (1379–1465). The most interesting building is the Biblioteca Malatestiana (*open Mon–Sat 9–12.30 & 3–6 or 4–7; Sun and holidays 10–12.30*). Two Roman silver plates (early 5th-century AD) with banquet scenes in gold and niello, are displayed in the vestibule. A handsome doorway, with a relief of the Malatesta heraldic elephant, leads into the perfectly preserved old library, a beautiful aisled basilica built in 1447–52 by Matteo Nuti for Domenico Malatesta Novello. Some precious old books, in their original presses, are still kept chained to the reading desks. The opaque windows look onto the cloister. Another room contains a display of some of the the 340 valuable manuscripts, including some with 15th-century illuminations, and 48 incunabula, which belong to the library.

Near the 15th-century Palazzo del Ridotto (rebuilt in 1782) is the church of the Suffragio, with a late-Baroque interior and a high altarpiece by Corrado Giaquinto (1752). The **cathedral**, begun in 1385, contains 15th-century sculpture. The theatre was opened in 1846.

The central Piazza del Popolo has a pretty fountain of 1583, opposite which steps lead up to the public gardens surrounding the 15th-century **Rocca Malatestiana** (*open Tues–Sun 9.30–12.30 & 3–7*), which was a prison until 1969 and has been heavily restored. It contains 17th-century tournament armour and a Garibaldi collection. From the battlements are views of the coast, including the tower of Cesenatico, and inland to the Apennines. One of the towers houses a local ethnographic museum.

From Piazza del Popolo, Viale Mazzoni leads round the foot of the castle hill to San Domenico with 17th-century paintings. In Via Aldini is the **Pinacoteca Comunale** with works by Sassoferrato, Antonio Aleotti and Giovanni Battista Piazzetta.

Outside the town is the **Madonna del Monte**, a Benedictine abbey rebuilt in the 15th–16th centuries with a collection of ex-votos and a *Presentation in the Temple* by Bolognese master Francesco Francia. A British military cemetery northeast of Cesena recalls the heavy fighting in this area by the Eighth Army in October 1944.

Cesenatico was the port of Cesena (designed in 1502 by Leonardo da Vinci for Cesare Borgia) from which Garibaldi and his wife Anita set sail on their flight towards Venice in August 1849. It is now the biggest of the seaside resorts here, which stretch for some 30km south to Rimini and Pesaro. Near Gatteo a Mare is the mouth of the Rubicone river, the fateful Rubicon which Caesar crossed in defiance of Pompey in 49 BC. A Roman bridge (c. 186 BC) survives over the river inland at Savignano sul Rubicone.

RIMINI

Rimini was first visited for its bathing beaches in 1843; by the 1950s it was the largest seaside resort on the Adriatic. Its beaches extend along the shore in either direction; some 16 million tourists visit this coast every year (there are 2,800 hotels in the province). The old city, over a kilometre from the sea front, is separated from it by the railway. Although Rimini is a somewhat characterless town, it contains the famous Tempio Malatestiano, one of the most important Renaissance buildings in Italy. It also has a good local museum, and it preserves a splendid Roman arch and bridge.

HISTORY OF RIMINI

Rimini occupies the site of the Umbrian city of Ariminum, which became a Roman colony c. 268 BC and was favoured by Julius Caesar and Augustus. In the 8th century it became a papal possession, and it was contended between the papal and imperial parties in the 12th–13th centuries. Malatesta di Verucchio (1212–1312), Dante's 'old mastiff', was the founder of a powerful dynasty of Guelph overlords, the most famous of whom was Sigismondo (1417–68), a man of violent character but an enthusiastic protector of art and learning. Malatesta's son, Giovanni the Lame, was the husband of the beautiful Francesca da Rimini (d. 1258), whose love for her brother-in-law Paolo inspired one of the tenderest passages in Dante's *Inferno* ('we read no more that day'). Pandolfo (d. 1534) surrendered the town to Venice, but after the battle of Ravenna (1512) it fell again into papal hands. In the Second World War Rimini, bombarded from sea or air nearly 400 times, was the scene of heavy fighting between the Germans and the Eighth Army and was captured by Canadians in September 1944. The film director Federico Fellini was a native of Rimini, and some of his films were inspired by the town.

The town centre

In the centre of the old town is the arcaded Piazza Tre Martiri, with the little **Oratory of St Anthony** on the spot where the saint's mule miraculously knelt in adoration of the Sacrament. Via IV Novembre leads east to the **Tempio Malatestiano** (*open daily 7–12 & 3.30–7*), one of the outstanding monuments of the Italian Renaissance, built

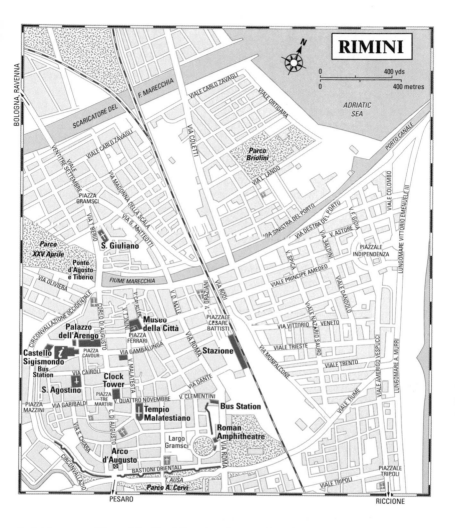

in Istrian stone. The original building (on the site of a 9th-century church) was a late 13th-century Franciscan church, used by the Malatesta family in the 14th century for their family tombs. In 1447–48 Sigismondo Malatesta transformed this into a personal monument, as his own burial place. He commissioned Leon Battista Alberti to redesign it (with the help of Matteo de' Pasti in the interior) and had Agostino di Duccio decorate it with exquisite sculptural reliefs. The decline of Sigismondo's fortunes caused the suspension of the work in 1460, and the Franciscans completed the building. The façade, on a high basement, is inspired by the form of the Roman triumphal arch (and by the nearby Arch of Augustus, a Roman gate). One of the masterpieces of Alberti, it had a lasting effect on 16th- and 17th-century church architecture in Italy. The upper part is incomplete. The two sides have wide arches surmounting the stylobate, beneath which (on the south side) are seven plain Classical sarcophagi containing the ashes of eminent members of Sigismondo's court. Latin and Greek inscriptions record Sigismondo and his victories.

The interior has been beautifully restored. The spacious nave is flanked by a series of deep side chapels connected by remarkably fine sculptural decoration by Agostino di Duccio, and closed by fine balustrades in red-and-white veined marble. The walls are covered with beautiful sculptural details (including the vaults and window frames). On the right of the entrance is the tomb of Sigismondo, whose armorial bearings (the elephant and rose) and initials (SI) recur throughout the church.

In the first chapel on the south side is a seated statue of St Sigismund supported by elephants' heads, and very low reliefs of angels, all elegant works of Agostino di Duccio. In the niches are statues of the Virtues and armour-bearers. The little sacristy (formerly the Chapel of the Relics) preserves its original doors surrounded by marble reliefs including two putti on dolphins. Inside is a damaged fresco (above the door) by Piero della Francesca (1451), representing Sigismondo kneeling before his patron, St Sigismund of Burgundy, and relics found in Sigismondo's tomb. The third chapel has a frieze of putti at play on the entrance arch and (over the altar) *St Michael*, by Agostino. Here is the tomb of Isotta degli Atti, Sigismondo's mistress and later his third wife. The crucifix was painted for the church by Giotto before 1312. The fourth chapel has more superb decoration representing the planetary symbols and signs of the zodiac, also by Agostino.

The fourth chapel on the north side is the masterpiece of Agostino, with reliefs representing the *Arts and Sciences*. The third chapel has particularly charming putti. In the first chapel (of the Ancestors) are figures of prophets and sibyls, a tiny *Pietà* (15th-century, French), above the altar, and the Tomb of the Ancestors, with splendid reliefs by Agostino.

The end chapels and presbytery do not belong to the original Malatesta building: the original design may have incorporated a dome at the east end. It was completed by the Franciscans (and rebuilt in the 18th century and again after the Second World War). The temple has served as the cathedral of Rimini since 1809.

Roman remains and the Corso d'Augusto

Behind the temple and across Largo Gramsci, in a residential area with a children's playground, you can see the fenced-off ruins of the Roman amphitheatre; only two brick arches remain above the foundations.

Corso d'Augusto leads south to the ugly Piazza Giulio Cesare. The **Arco d'Augusto**, a single Roman archway (c. 27 BC; restored) with composite capitals, marked the junction of the Via Emilia with the Via Flaminia here. It was later inserted into the medieval walls. Further up the corso is the **Cinema Folgor**, built in the 1920s and often visited by Fellini as a child. There are plans to turn it into a study centre dedicated to the director. The corso runs through the south end of Piazza Cavour, with a fountain of 1543 incorporating Roman reliefs and a seated 17th-century statue of Paul V. Here are two restored Gothic buildings: the battlemented Palazzo dell'Arengo (1204), now used for exhibitions, and the 14th-century Palazzo del Podestà, now the town hall. At the end is the Neoclassical façade of the theatre, built in 1857 by Poletti, which hides the foyer (used for exhibitions): the theatre itself was bombed in the Second World War and is still in ruins behind.

The northwest

The Castello Sigismondo, which dates from 1446, is the seat of the **Museo delle Culture Extraeuropee**, founded by Delfino Dinz Rialto (1920–79) in 1972 (*open Tues–Fri 8.30–12.30, Sat–Sun and holidays also 5–7*). It contains a remarkable ethnological collection. The first section is dedicated to Oceania, on the lower floor is material from pre-Columbian America, and on the upper floor material from Africa.

In Via Sigismondo the Romanesque church of Sant'Agostino has a fine campanile, damaged 14th-century frescoes by local artists (including Giovanni da Rimini) and a huge painted 14th-century crucifix.

Via Gambalunga leads from Piazza Cavour past the town library to Piazza Ferrari, where excavations of a Roman house are in progress. Beyond the church of the Suffragio, at Via Tonini 1, in the ex-Jesuit college built by Alfonso Torreggiani in 1746–55, is the **Museo della Città** (*open summer Tues–Sat 10–12.30 & 4.30–7.30, Tues 9pm–11pm, Sun and holidays 4.30–7.30; winter Tues–Sat 8.30–12.30 & 5–9, Sun and holidays 4–7*). The two masterpieces of the collection are Giovanni Bellini's *Dead Christ with Four Angels*, commissioned by Sigismondo Pandolfo Malatesta c. 1460, and Domenico Ghirlandaio's *Pala of St Vincent Ferrer*, commissioned by Pandolfo IV, with portraits of the Malatesta family. Also interesting are the works by Riminese artists, including a fine crucifix by Giovanni da Rimini (14th century), and 17th-century works. There are also three works by Guercino and a painting by Guido Reni.

At the far end of the corso is the **Ponte d'Augusto e Tiberio**, a five-arched bridge across the Marecchia begun by Augustus in the last year of his life and finished by Tiberius (21 AD). It is remarkably well-preserved (and used by cars and pedestrians). Its handsome dedicatory inscriptions are still in place in the centre of the bridge. The north arch was rebuilt after the Goths destroyed it in order to cut Narses off from Rome in 552.

Across the river

The church of **San Giuliano**, in the suburb beyond the bridge, contains a fine *Martyrdom of St Julian* painted by Paolo Veronese. The pleasant public Parco XXX Aprile occupies the former bed of the River Marecchia (now channelled to the north).

Viale Principe Amadeo was laid out in the 19th century to connect the old town with the sea. It is lined with pretty Art Nouveau villas with their gardens. By the railway line is the only skyscraper in the city. The sandy beaches along the coast northwest and southeast of Rimini, ruined by uncontrolled new building begun in the 1950s, attract millions of holidaymakers every year from all over Europe. There is a continuous line of resorts, including Riccione, with numerous hotels.

AROUND RIMINI

Santarcangelo di Romagna

Santarcangelo is a pleasant small town. The Sferisterio, below the walls in the lower town, was built for ball games (and is now used for the game of *tamburello*). In Via Cesare Battisti are the fish market of 1829 and the Collegiata, with a Venetian polyptych. Also in this street is an old family-run shop where fabrics are still printed by hand (the wheel dates from the 17th century); all the old books of samples have been preserved.

Uphill, Piazza delle Monache has a local museum of paintings and archaeology in a well-restored 17th-century palace. Also in the piazza is the entrance to a grotto (*opened on request at the information office; T: 0541 624537*), used as a wine cellar since the 16th century. A passageway leads to a remarkable circular underground room with an ambulatory and niches carved in the tufa rock, possibly a pagan temple. There are many other similar grottoes beneath the town.

Further uphill is the picturesque old *borgo*, with three long straight streets of low houses leading from the Gothic-revival clock-tower to the 14th–15th-century *rocca* (still privately owned by the Colonna family), recently restored and opened to the public (*by appointment: T: 0541 620832*). The **Museo Etnografico Usi e Costumi della Gente di Romagna**, in Via Montevecchi (*open Tues–Sat 9–12, Tues, Thur and Sat also 3–6 or 4–7, Sun and holidays 3–6 or 4–7*), has collections documenting popular traditions (symbolism, social life, work, ritual aspects, arts) of southern Romagna.

The Marecchia Valley

In the pleasant, wide Marecchia valley, with hilly outcrops, is Villa Verucchio, with an early medieval Franciscan convent. The church contains a 14th-century Riminese fresco. **Verucchio** is an attractive hill-town from which the Malatesta clan set out to conquer Rimini. Its site, on a low hill where the river Marecchia emerges into the plain, has been of strategic importance since earliest times, and an Etruscan centre flourished here in the 7th century BC. An ancient *pieve* lies at the foot of the hill. From the pretty Parco dei Nove Martiri an old walled mule track leads up to the rocca. A lane descends to the former convent of Sant'Agostino, beautifully restored as the seat of the Museo Civico Archeologico (*open Apr–March Sat 2.30–6.30; Oct–March Sat 2.30–6.30, Sun 10–12.30 & 2.30–6.30*), with finds from an important Etruscan and Villanovan necropolis (9th–7th centuries BC) at the foot of the hill. Particularly beautiful is the amber and gold jewellery. The rocca (*open as the museum*) has a splendid view of the Adriatic coast (Rimini and Cesenatico marked by their two skyscrapers) and inland to the Marche. The Collegiata has a 14th-century Riminese painted cross, and an early-15th-century cross attributed to Nicolò di Pietro in the north transept.

Montebello is a delightful little hamlet with just one street. Steps lead up to the entrance to the Castello dei Guidi di Romagna, still privately owned by the Guidi (*open daily 2.30–6.30 or 7.30; in winter at weekends only*). The old church is now used as a wine bar. There are fine views over the beautiful river valley and the former estate (now a nature reserve), which includes the castle of Saiano (reached by a path) with a church perched on an outcrop of rock. San Marino is also prominent. The courtyard is part-12th century (with a tower built onto the rock), and part-Renaissance.

The interior, interesting for its architecture, has particularly good furniture in the Renaissance wing. A pretty corner room in the medieval part of the castle has an interesting collection of *cassoni* (marriage chests), including three dating from the 13th and 14th centuries, an old oven, and a painted Islamic panel thought to date from the 11th century. The family still owns a private archive dating from 980. There is a small garden inhabited by peacocks inside the walls. The castle was used for a time as German headquarters in the Second World War, and during a battle here 386 Gurkhas (part of the British Eighth Army) lost their lives; their military cemetery is on the San Marino road south of Rimini.

SAN MARINO

The tiny Republic of San Marino (6 sq km; population 23,000) lies a few kilometres south of Rimini, on the border with the Marche. The republic is famous for having preserved its independence for more than 16 centuries. It is said to have been founded c. 300 by Marinus, a pious stonemason from Dalmatia who fled to the mountains to escape Diocletian's second persecution. Most of its territory consists of the peaks and slopes of the limestone Monte Titano (739m).

The capital, **San Marino**, is totally given over to the tourist trade. The three medieval citadels (Rocca, Cesta and Montale) are connected by a splendid walkway that follows the crest of the hill and has fine views of the Adriatic coast. The church of **San Francesco** has a *St Francis* by Guercino and a *Madonna and Child* attributed to Raphael. The legislative power is vested in a Council General of 60, from whom ten (the Congress of State) are chosen as an executive, and 12 as a council that functions as a Court of Appeal; the chiefs of state are two 'regent captains', who hold office for six months (investiture April and October). San Marino has its own mint, postage stamps, police force and an army of about 1,000 men.

PRACTICAL INFORMATION

GETTING AROUND

• **By air:** Rimini's Miramare Airport (c. 6km south of the city) has summer charter flights from all over Europe. There are also flights to and from Forlì.

• **By rail:** Italy's main Adriatic rail line closely follows the Via Emilia from Bologna to Rimini. Most Eurostar and Intercity trains stop at Faenza (30mins from Bologna), Forlì (40mins), Cesena (50mins) and Rimini 1hr 10mins). Commuter trains (Regionali and Interregionali) connect Imola and Faenza with Lugo and Ravenna, Faenza with Florence, and Rimini with Ravenna and Ferrara.

• **By bus:** In Rimini trolley-buses depart from Piazza Tre Martiri to the station and the shore, from where there are frequent services via Bellariva and Miramare to Riccione. Country buses run to destinations throughout the region.

INFORMATION OFFICES

Brisighella Piazza Porta Gabalo 5, T: 0546 81166.

Faenza Piazza del Popolo 1, T: 0546 25231.

Forlì Piazza Morgagni 9, T: 0543 714335; Piazza XC Pacifici 2, T: 43 712435, www.emiliaromagnaturismo.it

Rimini Piazza Malatesta 28, T: 0541 716371; Piazzale Cesare Battisti 1 (stazione), T: 0541 51331. www.emiliaromagnaturismo.it

Branch offices are open in summer at Santarcangelo di Romagna (Via Cesare Battisti 5) and at Verucchio (Piazza Malatesta 15).

HOTELS

Brisighella
€€ **Torre Pratesi**. The nicest place in the area, with just four rooms in a medieval watchtower. Località Cavina, T: 0546 84545, F: 0546 84558.
€ **La Meridiana**. Calm and quiet, with a shady garden on the river. Closed Nov–March. Viale delle Terme 19, T/F: 0546 81590, www.lameridianahotel.it

Faenza
€€ **Vittoria**. Comfortable rooms and a good restaurant, in a 16th-century palace. Corso Garibaldi 23, T: 0546 21508, www.hotel-vittoria.com

Rimini
€€€ **Grand**. A huge Belle Epoque affair, first opened on the seafront in 1908 and truly grand in elegance and service. Parco Fellini 2, T: 0541 56000, www.grandhotelrimini.com
€€ **Duomo**. In a renovated building near the centre of the old town. Via Giordano Bruno 28, T: 0541 24215/56399, www.hotelduomo.com

Riccione
€€€ **Grand Hotel des Bains**. A fine old property that lives up to its name, with three restaurants, two pools and every room a different colour. Viale Gramsci 56, T: 0541 601650, www.grandhoteldesbains.com

RESTAURANTS

Brisighella
€€ **Cantina del Bonsignore**. Very nice restaurant in the basement of a historic building; good selection of regional wines associated with regional and creative

food. Closed Wed and midday (except Sun and holidays), and in Aug and Jan. Via Recuperati 4a, T: 0546 81889.

€€ **Infinito**. Elegant restaurant with garden and terrace, specialising in regional and creative cooking. Closed Mon and midday from Tue to Fri, one week in Jan, 1–14 Oct. Via del Trebbio 12/14, T: 0546 80437.

€ **La Grotta**. Very good regional cuisine at excellent prices. Closed Tues, Jan and July. Via Metelli 1, T: 0546 81829.

€ **Trattoria di Strada Casale**. Good country restaurant outside the village, offering good service, great wine and excellent regional food. Closed Wed and midday (except Sat and Sun), Jan, May and Sept. Via Statale 22, T: 0546 88054.

Castrocaro Terme

€€ **Antica Osteria degli Archi**. Elegant restaurant in an historic building with open-air tables, specialising in regional cooking, seafood and vegetarian dishes. Closed Mon. Piazzetta San Nicolò 2, T: 0543 768281.

€€ **La Frasca**. Restaurant (with rooms) offering excellent interpretations of regional recipes, with garden seating in summer. Viale Matteotti 34, T: 0543 767471.

Cesena

€€ **Casali**. Restaurant of the Hotel Casali, offering good traditional Emilian fare. Closed Fri (June–Sept), Mon (Oct–May) and July–Aug. Via Benedetto Croce 81, T: 0547 27485.

€ **Cerina**. Trattoria specialising in traditional regional dishes. Closed Mon evening, Tues and Aug. Via San Vittore 936, T: 0547 661115.

€€ **Micheletta**. The oldest *osteria* in town: excellent traditional dishes, with organic ingredients. Closed Sun, Jan and Aug. Via Fantaguzzi 26, T: 0547 24691.

Cesenatico

€€€ **Vittorio**. One of the best fish restaurants on the Costa Romagnola. Closed Tues and Dec–Jan. Via Andrea Doria 3, Onda Marina harbour, T: 0547 81173.

€€ **Gallo**. Excellent fish seafood and *alla brace* fish. Closed Wed. Via Baldini 21, T: 0547 81067.

Forlì

€€ **La Casa Rusticale dei Cavalieri Templari**. In an ancient house of the Knights Templar, offering good meat and seafood dishes, interesting desserts and wines. Closed Sun–Mon and Aug and Christmas. Viale Bologna 275, T: 0543 701888.

€€ **Monda**. Family run trattoria, regional dishes and grilled meats. Closed Wed, Thur, Sun and Aug. Via Monda 72, T: 0543 86372.

Rimini

€€ **Lo Squero**. Genuine Emilian dishes, especially fish. Closed Tues (in low season), Nov and Dec. Lungomare Tintori 7, T: 0541 27676.

FESTIVALS & MARKETS

Faenza The *Palio del Niballo*, a Renaissance tournament, takes place in June. At certain periods of the year (usually between June and Oct) a portable kiln (with a wood fire) is set up outside the duomo, and pottery is fired on the spot to be sold for charity.

Rimini *Sagra Musicale Malatestiana*, classical-music festival, dates announced annually; *Adriaticocinema*, film festival in Rimini and other regional sites, May–June. Market around the castle, Wed and Sat.

PRACTICAL INFORMATION

PLANNING YOUR TRIP

When to go

The best time to visit northern Italy is May–June or September–October. The earlier spring and later autumn months are often wet and chilly, with strong northerly winds. The height of the summer is unpleasantly hot, especially in the Po Valley and the larger towns. The upper Alpine valleys are cool in summer, while in the high Alps the winter sports season can extend to midsummer. Seaside resorts are crowded from mid-June to early September; before and after this season many hotels are closed and the beaches are practically deserted.

Maps

The Touring Club Italiano (TCI) publishes several sets of excellent maps, including *Carta Stradale d'Europa: Italia* on a scale of 1:1,000,000; the *Atlante Stradale Touring* (1:800,000); and the *Carta Stradale d'Italia* (1:200,000). The latter is divided into 15 sheets covering the regions of Italy. These are also published as an atlas called the *Atlante Stradale d'Italia*, in three volumes. *Centro* and *Nord* cover the northern mainland. These maps are available from TCI offices and many booksellers.

The Istituto Geografico Militare, Via Cesare Battisti 10, Florence, publishes a map of Italy on a scale of 1:100,000 in 277 sheets and a field survey, partly 1:50,000, partly 1:25,000, which are invaluable for the detailed exploration of the country, especially its more mountainous regions; the coverage is, however, still far from complete at the larger scales and some of the maps are out of date.

Road maps, city maps and custom itineraries (in English) may be found on the web at www.mappy.com and www.viamichelin.com

Health and insurance

EU citizens have the right to health services in Italy if they have an E111 form (available from post offices). Italy has no medical programme covering the US or Canada; visitors are advised to take out insurance before travelling. First aid (*Pronto Soccorso*) is available at all hospitals, railway stations and airports. For emergencies, T: 113 (Polizia di Stato) or 112 (Carabinieri).

Disabled travellers

All new public buildings are obliged to provide facilities for the disabled. Historic buildings are more difficult to convert, and access difficulties still exist. Hotels that cater for the disabled are indicated in tourist board lists. Airports and railway stations provide assistance, and certain trains are equipped to transport wheelchairs. Access to town centres is allowed for cars with disabled drivers or passengers, and special parking places are reserved for them. For further information, contact the tourist board in the city of interest.

ACCOMMODATION

Hotels

A selection of hotels, chosen on the basis of character or location, is given at the end of each chapter. They are classified as expensive (€200 or over), moderate (€100–200) or inexpensive (under €100). It is advisable to book well in advance, especially between May and October; if you cancel the booking with at least 72 hours' notice you can claim back part or all of your deposit. Service charges are included in the rates. By law breakfast is an optional extra, although a lot of hotels will include it in the room price. When booking, always specify if you want breakfast or not. If you are staying in a hotel in a town, it is often more fun to go round the corner to the nearest café for breakfast. Hotels are now obliged (for tax purposes) to issue an official receipt: you can be fined if you leave the premises without one.

Bed and breakfast

B&B accommodation is offered in most areas. Rooms are usually in private homes, and can be booked through a central agency. Contact Caffelletto, Via di Marciola 23, 50020 San Vincenzo a Torri (Firenze) Italy, T: 055 7309145, www.caffelletto.it; BedandBreakfast.com, 1855 Blake Street, Suite 201, Denver, CO 80202, USA, T: 800 462 2632 (from outside the USA, 303 274 2800), www.bedandbreakfast.com, support@bedandbreakfast.com; or Bed & Breakfast in Europe, www.bedandbreakfastineurope.com/italia/en.htm

Residences

A new type of hotel, called a *residenza*, has been introduced into Italy. Residences are normally in a building, or a group of houses of historic interest, often a castle or a monastery. They may have only a few rooms, and sometimes offer self-catering. They are listed separately in tourist agency lists, with their prices.

Farm stays—Agriturismo

The short-term rental of space in villas and farmhouses (*agriturismo*) is an alternative form of accommodation. Terms vary greatly, from bed-and-breakfast to self-contained flats. For travellers with their own transport, or for families, this as an excellent (and usually cheap) way of visiting the Italian countryside. Some farms require a minimum stay. Cultural or recreational activities, such as horse-riding, are sometimes also provided. Information is supplied by local tourist offices. The main organisations dealing with *agriturismo* are:

Agriturist, Corso Vittorio Emanuele 101, 00186 Roma, T: 06 685 2342,
www.agriturist.it, agriturconfagricoltura.it

Terranostra, Via Nazionale 89/A, 00184 Roma, T: 06 482 8862, www.terranostra.it, terranostra@coldiretti.it. Terranostra publishes an annual list of *agriturismo* accommodation under the title Vacanze Natura.

Turismo Verde, Via Caio Mario 27, 00192 Roma, T: 06 3268 7430,
www.turismoverde.it, turismoverde@cia.it

Camping

Camping is well organised throughout Italy. Campsites are listed in the local information offices' publications. Full details of the sites in Italy are published annually by the **Touring Club Italiano**, Corso Italia 10, 20122 Milano (T: 02 8901 1383, www.touringclub.it) in *Campeggi e Villaggi Turistici in Italia*. The **Federazione Italiana Campeggiatori**, (at Via Vittorio Emanuele 11, 50041 Calenzano, Florence, T: 055 882 391, www.federcampeggio.it) publishes an annual guide, *Guida Camping d'Italia*, and maintains an information office and booking service.

Youth Hostels

The **Associazione Italiana Alberghi per la Gioventù** (Italian Youth Hostels Association), Via Cavour 44, 00184 Rome, T: 06 487 1152, www.ostellionline.org, runs many hostels, which are listed in its free annual guide. A membership card of the **AIG** or the **International Youth Hostel Federation** is required. Details from the **Youth Hostels Association**, Trevelyan House, Dimple Road, Matlock, Derbyshire, DE4 3YH, T 0870 770 8868, www.yha.org.uk, and from the **National Offices of American Youth Hostels, Inc.**, at **Hostelling International-USA**, 8401 Colesville Road, Suite 600, Silver Spring, MD 20910, T: 301 495 1240, F: 301 495 6697, www.hiayh.org.

Religious institutions

Religious institutions sometimes offer simple but comfortable accommodation at reasonable prices. For listings of convents, monasteries etc. offering accommodation, contact the *Arcivescovado* of the city of your choice (for Milan, for instance, the address is: Arcivescovado di Milano, Milano, Italia), or the local tourist information office.

GETTING AROUND

By car

The easiest way to tour northern Italy is by car. Regardless of whether you are driving your own car or a hired vehicle, Italian law requires you to carry a valid driving licence. You must also keep a red triangle in the car (you can hire one from ACI for a minimal charge and returned it at the border).

As 80 per cent of goods transported travel by road, lorries pose a constant hazard on, and the degree of congestion in even the smallest towns defies imagination.

Certain customs differ radically from those of Britain or America. Pedestrians have the right of way at zebra crossings, although you're taking your life in your hands if you step into the street without looking. Unless otherwise indicated, cars entering a road from the right are given precedence. Trams and trains always have right of way. If an oncoming driver flashes his headlights, it means he is proceeding and not giving you precedence. In towns, Italian drivers frequently change lanes without warning. They also tend to ignore pedestrian crossings.

Roads in Italy

Italy's motorways (*autostrade*; for information: www.autostrade.it) are indicated by green signs or, near the entrance ramps, by large boards of overhead lights. All are toll-roads. At the entrance to motorways, the two directions are indicated by the name of the most important town (and not by the nearest town), which can be momentarily confusing. Dual-carriageways are called *superstrade* (also indicated by green signs). Italy has an excellent network of secondary highways (*strade statali*, *regionali* or *provinciali*, indicated by blue signs marked SS, SR or SP; on maps simply by a number).

Parking

Many cities have closed their centres to traffic (except for residents). Access is allowed to hotels and for the disabled. It is always advisable to leave your car in a guarded car park, though with a bit of effort it is almost always possible to find a place to park free of charge, away from the town centre. However, to do so overnight is not advisable. Always lock your car when parked, and never leave anything of value inside it.

By rail

Information on rail links is given in individual chapters. The Italian Railways (Trenitalia) run eight categories of train.

ES (Eurostar), high-speed trains running between major Italian cities.

EC (Eurocity), international express trains running between the main Italian and European cities.

EN (Euronotte), overnight international express trains with sleeping car or couchette service.

IC (Intercity), express trains running between major Italian cities.

E (Espressi), long-distance trains, not as fast as the Intercity trains.

IR (Interregionali), intermediate-distance trains making more stops than the Espressi.

R (Regionali), local trains stopping at all stations.

M (Metropolitani), surface or underground commuter trains.

Booking seats

Seats can be booked in advance, as early as two months ahead and as late as three hours before departure, from the station booking office (*usually open daily 7am–10pm*), or at travel agencies representing Trenitalia.

Tickets

Tickets must be bought at the station, from travel agents representing Trenitalia, or on the Internet (www.trenitalia.it) before starting a journey, otherwise a fairly large supplement has to be paid on the train. Most tickets are valid for 60 days after the date of issue. Some trains charge a special supplement; and on others seats must be booked in advance. It is therefore necessary to specify which train you are taking as well as the destination. You must stamp the date of your journey on the ticket in the meters located on or near the station platforms before you get on the train. There are limits on travelling short distances on some trains. Children under four travel free and those between four and twelve pay half price. There are also reductions for families and for groups of as few as two persons.

By bus
Information on regional bus services is given in each individual section.

Cycling and walking
Cycling and walking have become more popular in Italy, and more information is available locally. The local offices of the CAI (Club Alpino Italiano) and the WWF (Worldwide Fund for Nature) provide all the information necessary (*see individual sections*).

Taxis
These are hired from ranks or by telephone; there are no cruising cabs. Before engaging a taxi, it is advisable to make sure it has a meter in working order. Fares vary from city to city but are generally cheaper than London taxis, though considerably more expensive than New York taxis. No tip is expected. Supplements are charged for late-night journeys and for luggage. There is a heavy surcharge when the destination is outside the town limits (ask roughly how much the fare is likely to be).

LANGUAGE

Even a few words of Italian are a great advantage in Italy, where any attempt to speak the language is appreciated. Local dialects vary greatly, but even where dialect is universally used, nearly everybody can speak and understand Italian. Double consonants call for special care as each must be sounded. Consonants are pronounced roughly as in English with the following exceptions:

c and **cc**	before e and i have the sound of **ch** in chess
ch	before e and i has the sound of **k**
g and **gg**	before e and i are always soft, like **j** in jelly
gh	always hard, like **g** in get
gl	nearly always like **lli** in million (there are a few exceptions, for example, *negligere*, where it is pronounced as in English)
gn	like **ny** in lanyard
gu and **qu**	always like **gw** and **kw**
j	like **y** in you
s	voiceless like **s** in six, except when it occurs between two vowels, when it is pronounced like the English **z** or the s in rose
sc	before e and i is pronounced like **sh** in ship
ss	always voiceless
z and **zz**	usually pronounced like **ts**, but occasionally have the sound of **dz** before a long vowel

Customs and etiquette

Attention should be paid to the more formal manners of the Italians. It is customary to open conversation in shops and such places with the courtesy of *buon giorno* (good day) or *buona sera* (good evening). The deprecatory expression *prego* (don't mention it) is everywhere the obligatory and automatic response to *grazie* (thank you). The phrases *per piacere* or *per favore* (please), *permesso* (excuse me), used when pushing past someone (essential on public vehicles), *scusi* (sorry; also, I beg your pardon, when something is not heard), should not be forgotten. A visitor will be wished *Buon appetito!* before beginning a meal, to which he should reply *Grazie, altrettanto*. This pleasant custom may be extended to fellow passengers taking a picnic meal on a train. Shaking hands is an essential part of greeting and leave-taking. In shops and offices a certain amount of self-assertion is taken for granted, since queues are not the general rule and it is incumbent on the inquirer or customer to get him or herself a hearing.

OPENING TIMES

The opening times of museums and monuments are given in the text, though they often change without warning. National museums and monuments are usually open Tues–Sun 9–2 or 7, plus evening hours in summer. Archaeological sites generally open at 9 and close at dusk. Naturally, as opening times are constantly being altered, care should be taken to allow enough time for variations.

Some museums are closed on the main public holidays: 1 January, Easter, 1 May, 15 August and 25 December. Smaller museums have have suspended regular hours altogether and are now open by appointment only. Their telephone numbers are included in the text. Entrance fees vary (from free to €8) according to your age and nationality; British citizens under 18 and over 60 are entitled to free admission to national museums and monuments because of reciprocal arrangements in Britain. During the *Settimana per i Beni Culturali e Ambientali* (Cultural and Environmental Heritage Week), usually held early in December, entrance to national museums is free for all.

Churches open early in the morning (often for 6 o'clock Mass), but are normally closed during the middle of the day (12–3, 4 or 5), although cathedrals and larger churches may be open throughout daylight hours. Smaller churches and oratories are often open only in the early morning, but the key can usually be found by inquiring locally. The sacristan will also show closed chapels and crypts, and a small tip should be given. Some churches now ask that sightseers do not enter during a service, but normally visitors may do so, provided they are silent and do not approach the altar in use. At all times they are expected to cover their legs and arms, and generally dress with decorum. An entrance fee is becoming customary for admission to treasuries, bell-towers and so on. Lights (operated by coins) have been installed in many churches to illuminate frescoes and altarpieces. In Holy Week most of the images are covered and are on no account shown.

Government offices usually work Mon–Sat 8/9–1/2; businesses Mon–Fri 8.30/9–12.30/1 and 2.30/3–6. Shops generally open Mon–Sat 8.30/9–1 and

3.30/4–7.30/8. Shops selling clothes and other goods are usually closed on Monday morning, food shops on Wednesday afternoon, except from mid-June–mid-September, when all shops are closed on Saturday afternoon instead. In resorts during July and August many shops remain open from early morning until late at night.

ADDITIONAL INFORMATION

Banking services

Money can be changed at banks, post offices, travel agencies and some hotels, restaurants and shops, though the rate of exchange can vary considerably. It is easiest to use an ATM machine. In most cities they are open 24hrs a day, and offer the best exchange rates.

Banks are open Mon–Fri 8.30–1.30 & 2.30–3.30. The afternoon one-hour opening varies from bank to bank, and many close early (about 11) the day before a national holiday. Exchange offices are usually open seven days a week at airports and most main railway stations. A limited number of euros can be obtained from conductors on international trains and at certain stations. For small amounts of money, the difference between hotel and bank rates may be negligible, as banks tend to take a fixed commission.

Crime and personal security

Pickpocketing is a widespread problem in towns all over Italy: it is always advisable not to carry valuables, and be particularly careful on public transport. Never wear conspicuous jewellery; women should keep their handbags on the side nearer the wall (never on the street side). Crime should be reported at once to the police or the local *carabinieri* office (found in every town and small village). A statement has to be given in order to get a document confirming loss or damage (essential for insurance claims). Interpreters are provided. For emergencies, T: 113 (Polizia di Stato) or 112 (Carabinieri).

Electric current

The electric current in Italy is AC 220 volts/50 cycles. Electrical appliances with a different current need a transformer. Check the voltage with your hotel before using an appliance. Appliances made in the UK or USA will need an adaptor.

Embassies and consulates

UK	80/A Via Venti Settembre, Rome, T: 06 4890 3777. Open Mon–Fri 9.30–1.30.
US	121 Via Veneto, Rome, T: 06 46741. Open Mon–Fri 8.30–12.
Canada	30 Via Zara, Rome, T: 06 4459 8421. Open Mon–Fri 8.30–12.30 and 1.30–4.
US Consulate	Via Principe Amedeo 2/10, Milan, T: 02 290 351.
Canadian Consulate	Via Vittor Pisani 19, Milan, T: 02 669 7451; night line T: 02 669 4970).

Emergency numbers

Police: T: 113 (Polizia di Stato) or 112 (Carabinieri).
Medical assistance: T: 118.

Pharmacies

Pharmacies (*farmacie*) are usually open Mon–Fri 9–1 & 4–7.30 or 8. A few are open also on Saturdays, Sundays and holidays (listed on the door of every pharmacy). In all towns there is also at least one pharmacy open at night (also shown on the door of every pharmacy).

Photography

There are few restrictions on photography in Italy, but permission is necessary to photograph the interiors of churches and museums and may sometimes be withheld. Care should also be taken before photographing individuals, notably members of the armed forces and the police. Photography is forbidden on railway stations and civil airfields, as well as in frontier zones and near military installations.

Public holidays

Italian national holidays are as follows:

1 January	25 April (Liberation Day)
Easter Sunday and Easter Monday	1 May (Labour Day)
15 August (Assumption)	1 November (All Saints' Day)
8 December (Immaculate Conception)	25 December (Christmas Day)
26 December (St Stephen)	

Each town keeps its patron saint's day as a holiday.

Telephone and postal services

Stamps are sold at tobacconists (*tabacchi*, marked with a large white 'T') and post offices. *Posta ordinaria* is regular post; *posta prioritaria* receives priority handling, including transport by air mail, and is only slightly more expensive. Correspondence can be addressed to you in Italy c/o the post office by adding '*Fermo Posta*' to the name of the locality.

Phonecards are sold at post offices, tobacconists and some newsstands. For all calls in Italy, local and long distance, dial the city code (for instance, 02 for Milan), then the telephone number. For international and intercontinental calls, dial 00 plus the country code, then the city code (for numbers in Britain drop the initial zero), and the telephone number. You can reach an AT&T operator on T: 172 1011, MCI on 172 1022, or Sprint on 172 1877. For directory assistance T: 12 (for numbers in Italy) or 176 (for international numbers). You can receive a wake-up call on your phone by dialling 114 and following the prompts (in Italian).

Tipping

A service charge of 15 to 18 per cent is added to hotel bills. The service charge is already included when all-inclusive prices are quoted, but it is customary to leave an additional tip in any case. As a guideline and depending on the category of your hotel, a tip of €1–2 is suggested for hotel staff except the concierge, who may expect a little more (€2–3).

Restaurants add a service charge of approximately 15% to all bills. It is customary, however, to leave a small tip (5–10%) for good service. In cafés and bars, leave 15% if you were served at a table and 10–20 cents if standing at the counter. At the theatre, opera and concerts, tip ushers 50 cents or more, depending on the price of your seat.

FOOD & DRINK

Restaurants

Italian food is usually good and inexpensive. Generally speaking, the least pretentious *ristorante* (restaurant), *trattoria* (small restaurant) or *osteria* (inn or tavern) provides the best value. A selection of restaurants is given at the end of each chapter. Prices are given as expensive (€80 or more per head) moderate (€30–80) and inexpensive (under €30). Many places are considerably cheaper at midday. It is always a good idea to reserve.

Restaurants are now obliged (for tax purposes) to issue a receipt: you can be fined if you leave the premises without one. Prices on the menu do not include a cover charge (shown separately, usually at the bottom of the page), which is added to the bill. The service charge (*servizio*) is now almost always automatically added at the end of the bill; tipping is therefore not strictly necessary, but a few euro are appreciated. Note that many simpler establishments do not offer a written menu.

Bars and cafés

Bars and cafés are open from early morning to late at night and serve numerous varieties of excellent refreshments that are usually taken standing up. As a rule, you must pay the cashier first, then present your receipt to the barman in order to get served. It is customary to leave a small tip for the barman. If you sit at a table the charge is usually higher, and you will be given waiter service (so don't pay first). However, some simple bars have a few tables that can be used with no extra charge, and it is always best to ask, before ordering, whether there is waiter service or not.

Coffee

Italy is considered to have the best coffee in Europe. *Caffè* or *espresso* (black coffee) can be ordered *alto* or *lungo* (diluted), *corretto* (with a liquor), or *macchiato* (with a dash of hot milk). A *cappuccino* is an *espresso* with more hot milk than a *caffè macchiato* and is generally considered a breakfast drink. A glass of hot milk with a dash of coffee in it, called *latte macchiato* is another early-morning favourite. In summer, many drink *caffè freddo* (iced coffee).

Snacks

Gelato (ice cream) is always best from a *gelateria* where it is made on the spot. *Panini* (sandwiches) are made with a variety of cold meats, fish, cheeses, or vegetables, particularly *melanzane* (aubergines) or *zucchine* (courgettes) fried in vegetable oil; vegetarians may also ask for a simple sandwich of *insalata e pomodoro* (lettuce and tomato). *Pizze* (a popular and cheap food throughout Italy), *arancini* (rice croquettes with cheese or meat inside), and other snacks are served in a *pizzeria*, *rosticceria* and *tavola calda*. A *vinaio* often sells wine by the glass and simple food for very reasonable prices. Sandwiches are made up on request at *pizzicherie* and *alimentari* (grocery shops), and *fornai* (bakeries) often sell individual pizzas, focaccias, *schiacciate* (bread with oil and salt) and cakes.

Pasta

Pasta is an essential part of most meals throughout Italy. A distinction is drawn between *pasta comune* (spaghetti, rigatoni and so on) produced industrially and made of a simple flour and water paste, and *pasta all'uovo* (tortellini, ravioli and so on), made with egg.

Pasta comes in countless forms. An ordinary Italian supermarket usually stocks about 50 different varieties, but some experts estimate that there are more than 600 shapes in all. The differences of shape translate into differences of flavour, even when the pasta is made from the same dough, or by the same manufacturer. The reason for this is that the relation between the surface area and the weight of the pasta varies from one shape to another, causing the sauce to adhere in different ways and to different degrees. Even without a sauce, experts claim to perceive considerable differences in flavour, because the different shapes cook in different ways. Northern Italy is home to *pasta fresca*, usually home-made, from a dough composed of flour, eggs, and just a little water.

A SHORT HISTORY OF PASTA

Whereas the invention of egg pasta is generally credited to the Chinese, the origin of *pastasciutta* (flour-and-water pasta) may well be Italian. The Etruscan Tomb of the Reliefs at Cerveteri, near Rome, has stucco decorations representing pasta-making tools: a board and a rolling-pin for rolling out the dough, knives and even a toothed cutting-wheel for making decorative borders. References to lasagne may be found in Cicero and other Roman writers; the name itself is probably derived from the Latin *lagana* or *lasana*, a cooking pot.

By the end of the Middle Ages pasta was known throughout Italy. The 14th-century *Codice del l'Anonimo Toscano*, preserved in the library of Bologna University, contains several serving suggestions; and in the *Decameron*, Boccaccio describes an imaginary land of grated parmesan cheese inhabited by people whose only pastime is the making of '*maccheroni e raviuoli*'. Of course, tomato sauce was unheard of until the discovery of America: Boccaccio's contemporaries cooked their macaroni and ravioli in chicken broth and dressed it with fresh butter. An early American appreciator of *pastasciutta* was Thomas Jefferson, who in 1787 brought a spaghetti-making machine from Italy to the United States.

Regional cuisine

The cuisine of northern Italy is as varied as its topography. What follows is a brief summary of the kind of local fare you can expect to find as you explore this culturally and historically diverse region.

Valle d'Aosta

In the rugged Valle d'Aosta game, wild herbs, vegetables, nuts and berries, grains and potatoes are the basic ingredients of a simple but tasty culinary tradition. In the Valle d'Aosta proper a Provençal French tradition prevails, but in the Val di Gressoney, where the local population is of Germanic descent, the cuisine is more similar to that of the Alto Adige.

Characteristic dishes are *mocetta* (cured chamois or goat ham); *polenta concia* (cornmeal polenta and *fontina* cheese); *soupe cogneintze* (a soup of rye bread, *fontina* cheese, rice and meat broth, cooked in a clay pot and baked in the oven); *camoscio o capriolo alla valdostana* (usually a leg or fillet of chamois or mountain goat marinated in spiced red wine, browned in its own marinade, sprinkled with grappa and served with fresh or grilled polenta) and *carbonade* (salted and spiced beef sliced thin and cooked in a wine and onion sauce). Desserts include *blanc manger* (a pudding of milk, sugar and vanilla) and *brochat* (a dense cream of milk, wine and sugar eaten with rye bread). *Caffè valdostano* is strong, hot coffee served in a wooden cup with four, six or eight spouts (you'll want to drink it with friends), flavoured with lemon and lots of grappa, and served flambé.

Piedmont

Although other Italians consider the Piedmontese to be quiet, unexpressive, even gruff or crusty, they do not hesitate to acknowledge that Piedmontese cuisine is superb.

Outstanding regional dishes include the appetisers *vitello tonnato* (*vitel tonné* in dialect, made with boiled spiced veal sliced thin and smothered in a sauce of tuna, anchovies and capers) and *cipolle ripiene* (baked onions stuffed with parmesan cheese, egg, butter, spices and, sometimes, braised beef or sausage).

Good first courses are *agnolotti* (ravioli of Provençal origin; *agnolotti grassi* are made with veal and other meats mixed with egg and cheese; *agnolotti magri* with spinach, cream, egg and cheese) and *fonduta* (a hot dip with *fontina* cheese, milk, and egg yolks sprinkled with truffles and white pepper).

Main courses include *bagna cauda* (a hot spicy sauce with garlic and anchovies used as a dip for raw vegetables), *brasato al barolo* (beef marinated in a Barolo wine sauce with lard, carrots and spices, then slowly braised in the marinade together with meat broth and tomatoes) and *volliti misti con salsa verde* (various types of meat stewed together with a green sauce made with herbs).

A very special Piedmontese dessert is *zabaione* (named after San Giovanni Baylon, the patron saint of pastry chefs: egg yolks, Marsala wine and sugar whipped together in a double boiler and served, usually, with dry biscuits).

Turin was the first city in Europe to process cocoa. The most famous expression of this tradition is the *giandujotto*, the famous sweet made from cocoa and hazelnuts, named after the Turin Carnival character Gianduja. In the Langhe you will encounter the white truffle of Alba, and *tajarin*, the only authentically Piedmontese pasta (thin ribbon-like egg noodles, handmade and served with meat dripping, butter and sage).

Lombardy
Lombardy is prime grazing land, and its cuisine is characterised by abundant meat and cheese, and by the use of butter rather than olive oil.

The tastiest appetisers come from the Valtellina. They are *bresaola* (salted, air-dried beef sliced thin and served with olive oil, lemon and pepper); *cicc* (a thin focaccia made with buckwheat polenta and cheese, fried in lard) and *sciatt* (soft, round buckwheat pancakes dressed with cheese and grappa: the word, in dialect, means 'toad').

Good first courses are the ravioli, typical of Bergamo and Brescia, known as *casonei* (made with *salame*, spinach, egg, raisins, *amaretti*, cheese and breadcrumbs, served in a butter and sage sauce); *risotto alla milanese* (rice toasted with butter, onion and beef marrow, then cooked in meat broth with saffron); *pizzoccheri* from the Valtellina (ribbons of buckwheat pasta boiled together with potatoes and vegetables and dressed with a sauce of sautéed garlic, butter and *bitto* cheese); and the Mantuan *tortelli di zucca* (large tortellini filled with amaretti, pumpkin, egg, spiced apples and parmesan cheese, usually served in a butter and cheese sauce).

As a main course, try *costoletta alla milanese* (a breaded veal cutlet fried in butter); *osso buco*, another Milanese dish (sliced veal shin cooked slowly in tomato sauce and *gremolada*, a mixture of lemon zest, rosemary, sage and parsley, usually served with rice); *lavarelli al vino bianco* (lake fish sautéed in butter, parsley and white wine), especially popular around the Lombard lakes; and the signature dish of Pavia, *rane in umido*, frogs cooked in a sauce of tomatoes and leeks.

An interesting local relish (usually served with boiled meats) is *mostarda di Cremona* (a fruit compote made with honey and white wine and seasoned with mustard and other spices).

Good Lombard desserts include the Milanese Christmas cake *panettone*; Bergamasque *polenta dolce* (cornflour cooked with milk, egg yolks, amaretti, butter and cinnamon); and Mantuan *torta sbrisolona* (wheat and cornflour, sugar, egg yolks, chopped almonds, baked until dry then crumbled rather than sliced).

Trentino-Alto Adige
The cuisine of the Trentino is a medley of Venetian, Lombard, and Tyrolean influences. The basic ingredients here are polenta and cheese. The most typical Trentine polenta is made from potatoes; dressed with cream, it is found in traditional dishes such as *smacafam* (baked with lard and sausage). Many dishes are hand-me-downs from the Austro-Hungarian tradition; examples include *canederli*, the Trentine version of *Knödel* (large stuffed bread dumplings), *gulasch*, smoked meat with sauerkraut, and *zelten alla trentina* (bread dough baked with eggs and dried fruit).

In Bolzano, Bressanone, and the Dolomites a marked Germanic bias prevails. Distinctive dishes that can be eaten as a first or as a main course include *Knödel* (*canederli*), *Gertensuppe* (barley soup with chopped speck), *Frittatensuppe* (soup with strips of omelette), *Milzschittensuppe* (served with toast with spleen spread), *Rindgulasch* (beef goulash), *Schmorbraten* (stew), *Gröstl* (boiled diced beef and boiled potatoes, sautéed), various sausages (*Würstel*) and speck. The incomparable sweets of the region include strudel, *Zelten* (Christmas cake of rye bread dough with figs, dates, raisins, pine nuts and walnuts) and *Kastanientorte* (chestnut cake served with cream).

The Veneto

In the area around Venice rice is served in a variety of ways, especially with seafood and vegetables. Classic specialities are *risi e bisi* (risotto with peas) and *risotto nero* (coloured and flavoured with cuttlefish ink). Thick soups are also popular. The best of these is *pasta e fasioi* (pasta and beans), which is eaten lukewarm, having been left to 'set up' for an hour or so before being served—generally in deep plates or, better yet, clay bowls.

Fish and seafood form the basis of Venice's best main courses. Local specialities include *granseola* (lagoon crabs), *sarde in saor* (marinated sardines) and *seppioline nere* (cuttlefish cooked in their own ink). An outstanding seafood dish is the *brodetto di pesce* or *boreto di Grado*—rigorously in *bianco* (without tomatoes), which testifies to its origins in an age before the discovery of America. Cornmeal polenta is another staple, often served with the famous *fegato alla venziana* (calves' liver and onions).

Paduan cuisine is basically Venetian with local variations. Distinctive first courses are rice and tagliatelli *in brodo d'anatra* (duck broth), and *risotto con rovinasassi* (chicken giblets).

Rice is a basic ingredient of the cuisine of Vicenza, too. It was once grown extensively on the low, wet plains at the foot of the Alps. Here you'll find a wide range of *risotti*—with squash, asparagus, hops and quail, flanked by *bigoli* (a local variant of spaghetti) in duck sauce. The best-known local speciality is *baccalà alla vicentina* (salt cod stewed with milk and onions and grilled polenta), followed closely by *bovoloni*, *bovoletti* or *bogoni* (snails in butter, garlic, and parsley), *piccioni torresani allo spiedo* (pigeon on the spit) and *cappone alla canavera* (capon cooked inside an ox bladder).

Many Veronese specialities are also common in other cities of the Veneto. A Veronese speciality is gnocchi in butter or tomato sauce, or topped with the famous *pastizzada de caval* (horsemeat stewed with aromatic herbs). Distinctive main courses include fish from Lago di Garda, including a rare variety of carp, and *boliti misti* with *pearà* (a sauce of breadcrumbs, butter, ox marrow, parmesan cheese, salt and pepper). Among Veronese sweets, the most delectable are certainly the great fluffy cake *pandoro* and the less well-known *natalini* and Easter *brasadella*.

The leading role in Trevisan cuisine is played by *radicchio trevigiano* (the long, narrow heads of Treviso's red lettuce), which is eaten in salads, grilled, fried or in risotto. Other specialities are *risotto al tajo* (made with shrimp and eel) and *risotto alla sbiraglia* (with chicken and chicken stock). Trevisans claim to have invented the rich dessert *tiramisù*.

In the hills and woodlands to the north, around Belluno, Feltre and Asolo, local dishes present a singular combination of alpine and Venetian influences. Characteristic first courses include *casunzei* (ravioli with pumpkin or spinach, ham and cinnamon) and *lasagne da formel* (dressed with a sauce of nuts, raisins, dried figs and poppy seeds). Favourite main courses feature game stewed in a rich sauce (*salmì*).

Friuli-Venezia Giulia

Wave after wave of invasion, war and devastation meant that nutrition was often reduced to the bare essentials in this region: little meat (generally pork), and porridges made of millet, buckwheat and corn with milk, cheese, vegetables and wine were the traditional fare here. The dishes for which the region is best known today developed during the 19th century and have their roots in Bohemian, Austrian, Hungarian, Jewish, Slavic, Greek and Turkish traditions.

Triestine cuisine features a variety of bittersweet specialities, such as *pistum* (bread balls with aromatic herbs and raisins, served in broth), *lasagne al papavero* (lasagne dressed with sugar, butter and poppy seeds), *gnocchi di prugne* (potato gnocchi stuffed with prunes), and *lepre alla boema* (stuffed hare in a sauce of white vinegar and sugar). Old favourites include *iota* (bean soup, common throughout the region), *brovada* (white turnips fermented in the dregs of pressed grapes and served with polenta meal, and the traditional goulash. There is an excellent choice of fish, including *sardoni in savor* (marinated sardines) and *granseola alla triestina* (the spiky scarlet spider-crabs of the Adriatic, dressed with oil and lemon and served in their shells).

Rice is a major ingredient of the cuisine of Udine and its environs. The most typical main courses are *boliti* (boiled meats) served with marinated vegetables; stews with rich sauces accompanied by abundant polenta; and last but not least, goulash and tripe. Winter lettuces are sautéed with lard or bacon and vinegar. The lightly salted *prosciuto di San Daniele* is considered the best in Italy.

Liguria

Liguria huddles by its sea like a lone individual cut off from the 'family' of Italian regions by steep, rugged mountains. In some areas the mountains plunge directly into the sea and have had to be terraced to permit the cultivation of the olive and vine; in other areas the small alluvial basins of mountain torrents are intensely planted with orchards and vegetable gardens. In both cases the farmer's life is a hard one (not by chance, young people are rapidly abandoning the countryside for the city). Even the fishing, in the shallow waters of the Mar Ligure, is meagre.

The end result is that Ligurian cooking is *povera*, 'poor' in terms of ingredients, but rich in imagination. The region's two great contributions to Italian cuisine are *focaccia*, the low, soft, salty bread that can be used as a support for just about anything, and *torta salata*, the 'savoury pie' that can be filled with anything and everything. Also distinctive is *pesto*, the famous sauce made from fresh basil, garlic, pine nuts and ewe's cheese and served with trofie, trenette or other pastas.

Good things to try in Liguria are *torta pasqualina*, traditionally made for Easter but now available throughout the spring: a flaky pastry stuffed with beet greens, milk curd, parmesan and eggs), *cappon magro* (a Genoese treat made with a large fish and several oysters or shellfish, various vegetables, and a rich sauce of anchovies, garlic, pine nuts, capers, hard-boiled egg yolk, olives, parsley, oil and vinegar), *corzetti* (a small butterfly pasta usually dressed with butter, sweet marjoram and pine nuts, but also with the rich, spicy meat sauce *tòcco*), *buridda di seppie* (sliced cuttlefish cooked with olive oil, tomatoes, spices and fresh peas), *coniglio in umido* (rabbit browned in olive oil and butter, then stewed with garlic, rosemary, onion, white wine, black olives and pine nuts), *vitello all'uccelleto* (diced veal browned in olive oil and butter, with bay, white wine and sliced artichokes in season).

Emilia Romagna
Emilia Romagna stands on the border between the 'land of butter' and the 'land of olive oil'—between the European tradition of the north and the Mediterranean culture of the south. Ostensibly one region, in reality Emilia Romagna is two entities with very different characters, histories and traditions. There is an 'inland' part—Emilia—comprising the five provinces of Bologna, Modena, Reggio Emilia, Parma and Piacenza, and an Adriatic seaboard—Romagna—with the provinces of Ferrara, Ravenna, Forlì and Rimini.

Emiliani and *romagnoli* are different by temperament. The former are easygoing and fun-loving; the latter hot-tempered and resolute. These character differences reappear at the table. Emilian cuisine, which glides along softly and persuasively on flavours tempered in the amalgam of delicious butter and delicate sauces, becomes increasingly sharp and aggressive as one crosses the invisible border of Romagna.

A cross-cultural sampling of appetisers might include *belecott* (boiled ground pork spiced with cinnamon, cloves and nutmeg, from the area around Ravenna), *erbazzone or scarpazzone* (a simple country dish popular throughout the region, made with boiled spinach sautéed with spiced lard, mixed with parmesan cheese and egg, then baked in a crust) and the famous *piada* or *piadina* of Romagna (which bears a tell-tale resemblance to the unleavened breads of Greece and the Middle East: made with flour, water and lard, it is often stuffed to make a fold-round sandwich).

First courses not to be missed include *anolini di parma* (fresh egg pasta stuffed with braised beef sauce, breadcrumbs, parmesan cheese, egg and other ingredients, usually served in broth), *brodetto alla romagnola* (a rich fish-and-tomato soup), *lasagne alla bolognese* (the classic dish of oven-baked pasta squares, meat sauce, white sauce and parmesan cheese) *and pasticcio alla ferrarese* (a sumptuous legacy of the Este court: macaroni or other short pasta in a pie crust with meat sauce, white sauce and mushrooms).

Characteristic sweets are *buricchi* (an invention of the Emilian Jewish community: little square pastries filled with almonds and sugar), *erbazzone dolce* (an interesting twist on the classic *erbazzone* described above: the beet greens are mixed with ricotta cheese, sugar, almonds and other ingredients) and *torta nera* (a rich Modenese cake made with almonds, sugar, butter, chunks of chocolate, cocoa, eggs, coffee and sometimes rum).

Wine
Most Italian wines take their names from the geographical area in which they are produced, the blend of grapes of which they are made, and the estate on which the grapes were grown. The best come in numbered bottles and are marked DOC (*di origine con-*

trollata). This is Italy's *appellation controlée*, which specifies maximum yields per vine, geographical boundaries within which grapes must be grown, permitted grape varieties and production techniques. Superior even to DOC is the DOCG (*di origine controllata e garantita*), where the denomination is also guaranteed. DOCG wines from northern Italy include Barolo and Barbaresco from Piedmont and Franciacorta from Lombardy. This is not to say that DOCG wines are automatically superior to any other. The plethora of regulation inevitably runs the risk of sclerosis, and winemakers wanting to experiment with alternative grape varieties or vinification techniques found themselves barred from the DOC or DOCG classifications, and had to label their vintages IGT (*vino da tavola con indicazione geografica tipica*). IGT denotes a *vin de pays*, a wine of special regional character. This does not necessarily mean that an IGT wine is of lesser quality than a DOC. Indeed, in some cases it may be particularly interesting. Simple *vino da tavola* is table wine. It can be excellent, but the quality is not guaranteed.

Valle d'Aosta

Vineyards in the Valle d'Aosta are necessarily small, stolen from the mountainside. But winemaking is heavily subsidised, which has enabled people to maintain and modernise methods and facilities, and to devote new energies to the making of high-quality wines in small quantities.

A single DOC (Valle d'Aosta/Vallée d'Aoste) covers the whole region, embracing a variety of single varietal wines, plus *coupages* (blends) called simply *Bianco, Rosso, Rosato* and *Novello*. A particularly good geographical sub-appellation is Chambave, which is vinified as Moscato, Moscato Passito, and Rosso (a blend of Petit Rouge, Dolcetto, Gamby and Pinot Nero grapes), while the autoctonous Blanc de Morgex grape is used in the delicious Valle d'Aosta Blanc de Morgex and La Salle.

ORDERING WINES

Red wines are *vini rossi* on the wine list; white wines, *vini bianchi*; rosés, *chiaretti* or *rosati*. Dry wines are *secchi*; sweet wines, *amabili* or *dolci*. *Vino novello* is new wine. *Moscato* and *passito* is wine made from grapes that have been left on the vine or dried before pressing.

When ordering, remember also that many DOC wines come in versions labelled *spumante, liquoroso, recioto* and *amarone*. Spumante is the Italian equivalent of champagne and uses some of the same methods to obtain its foamy (*spumante*) effervescence. It is much bubblier than sparkling whites such as Prosecco, which is popular both before meals and as a light dinner wine. *Liquoroso* means 'liqueur-like' and usually refers to dessert wines. The term *recioto* is applied to wines made from grapes that have been dried like raisins; *amarone* is the dry, mellow version of *recioto*.

1997 and 1998 are two of the best Italian vintages of the 20th century.

Piedmont

Piedmont is one of the finest wine-growing areas in Italy. The region counts 49 DOC and DOCG wines, and one district—Asti—is second only to the Chianti in terms of quantity of wine produced.

Dolcetto is a dry, single varietal red. Grown throughout Piedmont, it low in acid and high in tannin, which accounts for its bittersweet mixture of softness and astringency. The most famous is Dolcetto d'Alba, from the Langa Albese, mainly in the province of Cuneo. **Freisa** is another single varietal wine, available in *secco* and *amabile* versions. It has delicate raspberry and rose scents and a fresh flavour. The best comes from Asti and from Chieri. **Grignolino** is the signature wine of Asti and the Monferrato. Difficult to make, it has a light, ruby-red colour matched with a surprisingly tannic, tart, grassy flavour.

As many as 12 Piedmontese DOC wines, including Barbaresco, Roero and Barolo, are made from the **Nebbiolo** grape. **Barolo** is possibly Italy's best red wine, grown in a small area south of Alba. It is tannic and strong (minimum 13 per cent alcohol), and wonderfully rich and fragrant; it can age up to 15 years and is *riserva* after five.

Barbera is a single varietal wine made from grapes grown on the hills around Alba, Asti and in the Monferrato. Light and tart when young, this high-acid variety can mellow with ageing to become much rounder and more harmonious. Barbera's popularity in the past as a low-priced table wine has tarnished its reputation, which is now improved thanks to new growing and vinification techniques. Barbera del Monferrato, made with a small percentage of Freisa, Grignolino and/or Dolcetto grapes, can be lightly sparkling.

Cortese is a single varietal white wine grown in three areas: Alto Monferrato, Gavi and Colli Tortonesi. Sometimes made with small percentages of other non-aromatic whites, it is perfect with appetisers, delicate pasta and rice dishes, and soups. It is Piedmont's oldest and most familiar dry white wine. **Gavi**, probably the most famous Piedmontese white, is the best expression of the Cortese grape. It is produced in a small area between Gavi and Novi Ligure, and is good with fish and seafood.

Lombardy

Lombardy has one DOCG and 15 DOC wines. The DOCG, **Franciacorta**, is the most famous and important (as well as the most expensive). It is particularly known for its Chardonnays, Pinot Noirs and *metodo classico* sparkling wines.

Probably the most interesting Lombard wines are the **Valtellina** reds, made from Nebbiolo, here called Chiavennasca, by small boutique growers. The DOCs Valtellina and Valtellina Superiore are divided into four sub-appellations: Grumello, Inferno, Sassella and Valgella, all delicious with red and white meat. Late-pressed (forced) grapes make the rich, strong (16 per cent alcohol) and very special **Sfurzat**. The spectacular vineyards of the Valtellina cling like moss to the rocks of this steep Alpine valley, in terraces at altitudes as high as 800m.

Alto Aldige

The indication Trentino precedes the name in almost all the DOC wines from the vineyards in this province; in addition to Trentino Bianco and Trentino Rosso there are single-variety red, whites, and three desert wines, Moscato Giallo (also *liquoroso*), Moscato Rosa (also *liquoroso*) and Vin Santo. The denomination Valdadige (white, red, rosé, Pinot Grigio and Schiava) refers to a territory that also includes parts of the provinces of Bolzano and Verona.

Because the Alto Adige is bilingual, its wine labels are in Italian and German. The DOC wines, whose area of production embraces the entire province of Bolzano-Alto Adige, carry the designation Alto Adige after the name (in German, the term Südtiroler precedes the name). The whites produced in the Valle dell'Isarco bear the denomination Valle Isarco (or Bressanone, in German Eisacktaler).

From hills around Bolzano come the two reds Colli di Bolzano (Bozner Leiten) and Santa Maddalena. The light red Lago di Caldaro (Kalterersee) comes from the vineyards on the lake of the same name. Terlano (Terlaner) is a white wine produced east of Bolzano. The denomination Valdadige or Etschtaler covers territory which extends into the provinces of Trento and Verona.

The Veneto

The shores of Lake Garda, the Soave district, the Valpolicella and a corner of the Valdadige produce Veronese DOC wines. From Garda come the red Bardolino, Bardolino Chiaretto and Bardolino Classico, and the Bianco di Custoza and Lugana whites. Soave makes an excellent dry white, while the Valpolicella region makes Valpolicella and Valpantena reds. Bardolino, Soave and Valpolicella Classico are made from grapes grown in the oldest vineyards.

The DOC wines of Vicenza come from Gambellara, from the Colli Berici and from the Breganzese. Gambellara is always white, whereas the Colli Berici and Breganzese areas produce both whites and reds.

Three different regional denominations precede the names of Trevisan DOC wines: Conegliano Valdobbiadene, Montello e Colli Asolani and Piave. The first is limited to Prosecco white (Prosecco di Valdobbiadene and Prosecco di Conegliano). Montello e Colli Asolani makes Cabernet and Merlot reds as well as Prosecco white. The Piave growing area, shared with the province of Venice, produces Cabernet, Merlot, Pinot Nero and Raboso reds, in addition to Pinot Bianco, Pinot Grigio, Tocai and Verduzzo whites.

The best Paduan wines are the Colli Euganei Bianco and Rosso, the Cabernet and Merlot reds and the Moscato, Pinot Bianco and Tocai Italico whites.

Friuli-Venezia Giulia

The best wines of the Trieste area include the three DOC wines that carry the name of the Carso, the plateau behind the city: they are the white Malvasia del Carso and the reds Rosso del Carso and Terrano del Carso.

The DOC wines of Udine come from three distinct growing districts, indicated on the labels respectively as Grave del Friuli, Aquileia e Latisana and Colli Orientali del Friuli. Common to these denominations are Cabernet and Merlot reds, a pleasant rosé (*rosato*), and the Pinot Bianco, Pinot Grigio, Chardonnay, Verduzzo Friulano, Sauvignon, Traminer Aromatico and Tocai Friulano whites.

Liguria

The lie of the land in Liguria—a strip of steep hills hinged between sea and mountains—makes all farming, and especially grape-growing, difficult. So, one understands why winemaking is a dying art here, and why Ligurian wines are made in such small quantities that they rarely make it out of the region.

The growing districts are located at the two ends of the region: the Riviera di Levante produces the legendary Cinque Terre and Sciacchetrà whites, the Colli di Luni white and red, and the Colline di Levanto and Golfo del Tigullio red, white and rosé. The Riviera di Ponente is best known for **Rossese di Dolceacqua**, undoubtedly the finest Ligurian wine. It takes its name from a small village in the Valle Nervina but is made throughout Imperia Province and around Ventimiglia. It is a light, straightforward red, with a soft, aromatic flavour. It is made in very small quantities.

Emilia Romagna

Emilia Romagna is traditionally considered the homeland of sparkling wines, where quantity triumphs over quality. This judgement is not altogether fair, for the vast and varied market offers, if not great wines, excellent quality/price ratios. The only DOCG is Albana di Romagna, a white made in the provinces of Ravenna, Forlì and Bologna. It is vinified *secco*, *amabile*, *dolce* and *passito*. Albana secco is dry and somewhat tannic, warm and harmonic, good with fish, soups and egg dishes. Albana amabile has a characteristic fragrant nose and is good with cakes and fruit.

The DOC Colli Bolognesi, which also appears on labels as Monte San Pietro or Castelli Medioevali, covers seven or eight kinds of grape, and is often subdivided by territory.

The best-known wine of Emilia is Lambrusco, a fresh, fruity, dry or sparkling red best with heavy meat sauces and pork dishes.

GLOSSARY OF ART TERMS

Aedicule, originally a shrine; used to describe the frame of a door, window or other aperture, usually with columns or pilasters bearing a lintel

Ambo (pl. *ambones*), pulpit in a Christian basilica; two pulpits on opposite sides of a church from which the gospel and epistle were read

Amphora, antique vase, usually of large dimensions, for oil and other liquids

Ancona, retable or large altarpiece (painted or sculpted) in an architectural frame

Arca, wooden chest with a lid, for sacred or secular use. Also, monumental sarcophagus in stone, used by Christians and pagans

Architrave, lowest part of the entablature, resting on the columns

Archivolt, moulded frame carried round an arch

Atlantes (or Telamones), male figures used as supporting columns

Atrium, forecourt, usually of a Byzantine church or a classical Roman house

Attic, topmost storey of a Classical building, hiding the spring of the roof

Badia, *abbazia*, abbey

Baldacchino, canopy supported by columns, usually over an altar

Basilica originally a Roman building used for public administration; in Christian architecture, an aisled church with a clerestory and apse, and no transepts

Borgo, a suburb; street leading away from the centre of a town

Bottega, the studio of an artist; the pupils who worked under his direction

Bozzetto, sketch, often used to describe a small model for a piece of sculpture

Broletto, name often given to the town halls of northern Italy

Bucchero, Etruscan black terracotta ware

Campanile, bell-tower, often detached from the building to which it belongs

Camposanto, cemetery

Canopic vase, Egyptian or Etruscan vase enclosing the entrails of the dead

Cantoria, singing-gallery in a church

Capital, the top of a column

Capitolium, a temple of Jupiter, Juno and Minerva

Cardo, the main street of a Roman town, at right-angles to the decumanus

Caryatid, female figure used as a supporting column

Cassone, a decorated chest, usually a dower chest

Cavea, the part of a theatre or amphitheatre occupied by the rows of seats

Cella, sanctuary of a temple, usually in the centre of the building

Cenacolo, scene of the Last Supper, often in the refectory of a convent

Chiaroscuro, distribution of light and shade, apart from colour in a painting; rarely used as a synonym for grisaille

Ciborium, casket or tabernacle containing the Host

Cipollino, onion-marble; a greyish marble with streaks of white or green

Cippus, sepulchral monument in the form of an altar; a stone marking a grave or boundary

Cryptoporticus, a semi-underground covered portico used in Roman architecture for the construction of terraces or as a covered market

Decumanus, the main street of a Roman town running parallel to its longer axis

Diptych, painting or ivory tablet in two sections

Dossal, an altarpiece

Duomo, cathedral

Entablature, the continuous horizontal element above the capital (consisting of architrave, frieze and cornice) of a Classical building

Etruscan, of, relating to, or characteristic of Etruria, an ancient country in central Italy, its inhabitants, or their language

Exedra, semicircular recess in a Byzantine church

Ex-voto, tablet or small painting expressing gratitude to a saint; a votive offering

Forum, open space in a town serving as a market or meeting-place

Fresco, (in Italian, *affresco*), painting executed on wet plaster. On the wall beneath is sketched the sinopia, and the cartoon is transferred onto the fresh plaster (*intonaco*) before the fresco is begun, either by pricking the outline with small holes over which a powder is dusted, or by means of a stylus, which leaves an incised line. In recent years many frescoes have been detached from the walls on which they were executed.

Gonfalon, banner of a medieval guild or commune

Graffiti, design on a wall made with an iron tool on a prepared surface, the design showing in white. Also used loosely to describe scratched designs or words on walls

Greek cross, cross with the arms of equal length

Grisaille, painting in tones of grey

Grotesque, painted or stucco decoration in the style of the ancient Romans (found during the Renaissance in Nero's Golden House in Rome, then underground, hence the name, from 'grotto'). The delicate ornamental decoration usually includes patterns of flowers, sphinxes, birds, human figures etc, against a light ground

Herm (pl. *hermae*), quadrangular pillar decreasing in girth towards the ground, surmounted by a bust

Hexastyle, having six columns

Historiated, adorned with figurative painting or sculpture, usually comprising a narrative

Hypogeum, subterranean excavation for the internment of the dead (usually Etruscan)

Iconostasis, a screen or partition, covered with icons, that divides the public part of a church from that reserved for the clergy

Impost block, a block with splayed sides placed above a capital

Intarsia, inlay of wood, marble, or metal

Intrados, underside or soffit of an arch

Krater, antique mixing-bowl, conical in shape with rounded base

Latin cross, cross with a long vertical arm

Lavabo, hand basin usually outside a refectory or sacristy

Loggia, covered, arcaded or colonnaded gallery or balcony, usually at ground or first-floor level

Lunette, semicircular space in a vault or ceiling, often decorated with a painting or relief

Mandorla, tapered, almond-shaped aura around a holy figure (usually Christ or the Virgin)

Matroneum, gallery reserved for women in early Christian churches

Metope, panel between two triglyphs on the frieze of a Doric temple

Narthex, vestibule of a Christian basilica

Niello, black substance used in an engraved design

Nymphaeum, a sort of summer house in the gardens of baths, palaces, etc., originally a temple of the Nymphs, decorated with statues of those goddesses, and often containing a fountain

Oculus, round window or aperture

Ottonian, 10th- and 11th-century art from the Holy Roman Empire

Pala, large altarpiece

Palaeochristian, from the earliest Christian times up to the 6th century

Palazzo, any dignified and important building

Paliotto, a vestment, hanging, or covering of any material that covers the front part of a Christian altar

Pantocrator, the Almighty

Pediment, gable above the portico of a classical building

Pendentive, concave spandrel beneath a dome

Peristyle, court or garden surrounded by a columned portico

Pietà, group (usually featuring the Virgin) mourning the dead Christ

Pietre dure, hard or semi-precious stones, often used in the form of mosaics to decorate cabinets, table tops etc.

Pieve, parish church

Pinacoteca, an art gallery specialising in the exhibition of painting

Pluteus, a low wall that encloses the space between column bases in a row of columns

Podium, a continuous base or plinth supporting columns, and the lowest row of seats in the cavea of a theatre or amphitheatre

Polyptych, painting or tablet in more than three sections

Predella, small painting or panel, usually in sections, attached below a large altarpiece

Presepio, literally, crib or manger. A group of statuary of which the central subject is the infant Jesus in the manger

Pronaos, porch in front of the cella of a temple

Prostyle, edifice with free-standing columns, as in a portico

Pulvin, cushion stone between the capital and the impost block

Putto, figure of a child sculpted or painted, usually nude

Reredos, decorated screen behind an altar

Rocca, citadel above a town

Rood screen, a screen below the crucifix dividing the nave from the chancel

Scagiola, a material made from selenite, used to imitate marble or *pietre dure*

Scuola, (pl. *scuole*), Venetian lay confraternity, dedicated to charitable works

Sinopia, large sketch for a fresco made on the rough wall in a red earth pigment called sinopia, because it originally came from Sinope on the Black Sea

Soffit, underside or intrados of an arch

Spandrel, the triangular space on either side of an arch

Squinch, small arch thrown across an angle as support block for a circular dome above a square space

Stele, upright stone bearing a monumental inscription

Stemma, coat of arms or heraldic device

Stoup, vessel for holy water, usually near the entrance door of a church

Stylobate, basement of a columned temple or other building

Telamones, see *Atlantes*

Tempietto a small temple

Tessera, a small cube of marble, glass or brick, used in mosaic work

Tetrastyle, having four columns

Thermae, originally simply baths, later elaborate buildings fitted with libraries, assembly rooms, gymnasia, circuses, etc.

Tondo, round painting or bas-relief

Trabeation, a construction system whereby verticals (eg columns) support horizontals (eg lintels) rather than arches or vaults

Transenna, open grille or screen, usually of marble, in an early Christian church separating nave and chancel

Triglyph, blocks with vertical grooves on either side of a metope on the frieze of a Doric temple

Triptych, painting in three sections

Trompe l'oeil, literally, a deception of the eye. Used to describe illusionist decoration, painted architectural perspectives, etc.

Tympanum, the face of a pediment within the frame made by the upper and lower cornices; also, the space within an arch and above a lintel or a subordinate arch

Villa, country-house with its garden

INDEX

Explanatory or more detailed references (where there are many), or references to places where an artist's work is best represented, are given in bold. Numbers in italics are picture references. Dates are given for all artists, architects and sculptors.

Editor-in-chief: Annabel Barber
Consulting editors: Charles Freeman, Nigel McGilchrist, Judy Tither

Historical introduction: Charles Freeman. Charles Freeman is a freelance academic historian
with a long-standing interest in Italy and the Mediterranean. His *Egypt, Greece and Rome,
Civilizations of the Ancient Mediterranean* (second edition, Oxford University Press, 2004)
is widely used as an introductory textbook to the ancient world. His most recent book,
The Horses of St.Mark's (Little Brown, 2004), is a study of the famous horses through their history
from Constantinople and Venice. He leads study tours of Italy for the Historical Association
and has recently been elected a Fellow of the Royal Society of Arts.

Contributor (wine sections): Joseph Kling

Design: Anikó Kuzmich, Regina Rácz
Regional maps: Dimap Bt.
City maps: The Mapping Company
Repro Studio: Timp Kft.
Architectural elevations: Michael Mansell RIBA & Gabriella Juhász
Floor plans: Imre Bába
With special thanks to Hannah Henry, Richard Robinson

Photography:
Photo editor: Hadley Kincade
Imre Baric: pp: 392, 407, 409. Paul Blanchard: pp. 276, 293, 302, 303, 307, 436, 493.
Balázs Glódi: pp. 230, 315. Bill Hocker: pp. 50, 474, 558, 561, 581. Monica Larner: pp. 69, 70,
79, 81, 92, 184, 191, 211, 242, 281, 330, 365, 530, 562, 601. Phil Robinson: pp. 101, 204, 240,
260, 334, 344, 350, 399, 443, 577, 599, 617, 619, 638. Archivio Fotografico Pinacoteca Nazionale
di Bologna: front cover & p. 589. © Biblioteca Ambrosiana (Auth. No. INT 38/04): p. 128.
Bridgeman Art Library/Alinari p. 461. The Bridgeman Art Library, London
(www.bridgeman.co.uk): pp. 385, 655. Giraudon/Bridgeman Art Library p. 655. Courtesy of the
Civici Musei e Gallerie di Storia e Arte, Udine: pp. 509, 510. Courtesy of the Italian
Ministry of Culture: pp. 111, 115, 259, 417, 419, 422. Courtesy of the Museo del Castelvecchio,
Verona (© Umberto Tomba): pp. 3, 343, 340. Courtesy of the Museo Civico Ala Ponzone,
Pinacoteca, Cremona: p. 245. Courtesy of the Villa Manin: p. 504

Printed in Hungary by Dürer Nyomda Kft, Gyula.

ISBN 1–905131–01–1